P9-CRP-419

FROM THE KITCHEN OF

THE MARTHA STEWART LIVING COOKBOOK

The New Classics

THE MARTHA STEWART LIVING COOKBOOK

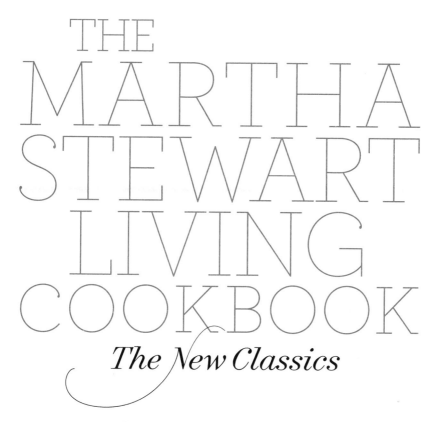

The New Classics

By the Editors of Martha Stewart Living

CLARKSON POTTER • PUBLISHERS • NEW YORK

PUBLISHED IN THE UNITED STATES BY CLARKSON POTTER/PUBLISHERS,
AN IMPRINT OF THE CROWN PUBLISHING GROUP, A DIVISION OF RANDOM HOUSE, INC., NEW YORK.
WWW.CROWNPUBLISHING.COM
WWW.CLARKSONPOTTER.COM

WWW.MARTHASTEWART.COM

CLARKSON N. POTTER IS A TRADEMARK AND POTTER AND COLOPHON
ARE REGISTERED TRADEMARKS OF RANDOM HOUSE, INC.

ALL OF THE RECIPES AND PHOTOGRAPHS IN THIS BOOK HAVE BEEN PREVIOUSLY PUBLISHED
IN SLIGHTLY DIFFERENT FORM IN *MARTHA STEWART LIVING* MAGAZINE.

LIBRARY OF CONGRESS CATALOGING-IN-PUBLICATION DATA
THE MARTHA STEWART LIVING COOKBOOK: THE NEW CLASSICS / THE EDITORS OF MARTHA STEWART LIVING—1ST ED.
INCLUDES INDEX.
1. COOKERY.   I. MARTHA STEWART LIVING.   II. TITLE.
TX714.M34633   2007
641.5—DC22   2007006088

ISBN 978-0-307-39383-8

PRINTED IN THE UNITED STATES OF AMERICA

DESIGN BY AMBER BLAKESLEY, MARY JANE CALLISTER, AND MATT PAPA

10 9 8 7 6 5 4 3 2 1

FIRST EDITION

contents

acknowledgments

THE RECIPES IN THIS book represent the creativity and hard work of many people, over many years. A special thank you to our very talented editorial director of food and entertaining, Lucinda Scala Quinn, who leads the team that creates the recipes in *Martha Stewart Living*, as well as to food editor Jennifer Aaronson and deputy food editor Sarah Carey, who offered careful guidance throughout the creation of this book. Thank you also to the many other food editors, recipe testers, and kitchen assistants who have worked in the *Martha Stewart Living* test kitchens since 2001, among them Christine Albano, Sara Backhouse, John Barricelli, Tara Bench, Shira Bocar, Frances Boswell, Stephana Bottom, Monita Buchwald, Samantha Connell, Carolyn Coppersmith, Kristine Croker Fiordalis, Stephanie Fletcher, Yolanda Florez, Amy Gropp Forbes, Allison Hedges, Aida Ibarra, Heidi Johannsen, Carmen Juarez, Shelly Kaldunski, Anna Kovel, Judith Lockhart, Rachael Macchiesi, Denise Mickelsen, Claire Perez, Melissa Perry, Elizabeth Pilar, Gertrude Porter, Lori Powell, Darlene Schrack, Nicole Slaven, Susan Spungen, Susan Sugarman, Susan Testa, Laura Trace, Brittany Williams, and Avery Wittkamp.

Their food always looks as delicious as it tastes, as you can see in the photographs in this book. For creating those images, thank you to the brilliant photographers (see their names on page 672) as well as *Martha Stewart Living* design director James Dunlinson and deputy creative director Ayesha Patel and their teams of art directors and stylists. Thanks also to our photo department, including Heloise Goodman, Andrea Bakacs, Joni Noe, and Alison Vanek Devine.

Producing this book required the dedication of special projects editor in chief Amy Conway, executive editor Ellen Morrissey, and assistant managing editor Robb Riedel. Heartfelt thanks to Evelyn Battaglia, who brought expertise and enthusiasm to every stage of the project and whose considerable talents are reflected throughout the book. Under the direction of art director William van Roden, associate art director Amber Blakesley created the book's elegant, modern cover, and worked with Mary Jane Callister on an overall design that is fresh but timeless. Thank you, too, to Denise Clappi, Lori Key, Matt Papa, and Emily Burns for their help with so many details.

As always, our executive team of Gael Towey, Lauren Podlach Stanich, Margaret Roach, and Eric A. Pike lent valuable support to the project. And thanks to our colleagues at Clarkson Potter: Jenny Frost, Lauren Shakely, Doris Cooper, Jane Treuhaft, Amy Boorstein, Mark McCauslin, and Derek Gullino.

introduction

The *Martha Stewart Living* test kitchens are always exciting and inspiring. There, on the ninth floor of the Starrett-Lehigh building in Manhattan, you will find a big team of talented cooks busy at the stoves and the work stations, mixing, stirring, measuring, chopping, kneading, sautéing, tasting, and fine-tuning. Right next door in our photo studios, more food is being prepared and "styled" for the photographs being taken. And just down the hall, editors are at their computers writing recipes or debating the best way to phrase a step.

This big, bustling operation evolved from a very small start, back in 1990. But the most important things have not changed: I and all of our food editors have always shared a dedication to quality, a passion for the very best ingredients, a thirst for knowledge (and desire to share what we learn), and a sincere appreciation of the ever-changing world of food and cooking. Our food department creates many hundreds of recipes every year; this book contains more than 1,200 of our favorites culled from *Martha Stewart Living* since 2001. I hope you'll try many of them and use them again and again, as I do. And because an avid cook can never have too many fine recipes, I recommend you look at *The Martha Stewart Living Cookbook: The Original Classics* as well. It contains more than 1,100 recipes published between 1990 and 2000. The two books together make a wonderfully comprehensive set; this one even includes an index for both volumes. You could start on page one of either book, cook every recipe, and never get bored! *Martha Stewart*

pantry

ANCHOVIES These tiny salt-cured fish are a staple of the cuisines of France, Spain, and Italy, where they are used to impart depth of flavor to sauces, such as salsa verde and bagna cauda, as well as to many meat, poultry, and vegetable dishes. When possible, buy anchovies that are salt-packed and sold in jars rather than those packed in oil and sold in tins. To tame their saltiness, rinse anchovies briefly under cold running water before using. Avoid overcooking, or cooking in oil that is too hot, as they will fry and harden instead of dissolving; mashing them first helps them blend quickly. Keep unopened tins at room temperature; once opened, transfer the fillets to an airtight container, cover with oil, and refrigerate for up to a month. Salt-packed anchovies have a much longer shelf life, and will keep for up to a year at room temperature (even after opening).

BEANS Black beans, cannellini beans, and chickpeas are versatile—add them to salads or combine them with rice or pasta for hearty side dishes or meatless main courses. Before using, rinse canned beans under cold running water and allow them to drain thoroughly. Once opened, transfer beans to an airtight container and refrigerate for up to a week.

CANNED MILK (EVAPORATED MILK AND SWEETENED CONDENSED MILK) Both products are made by removing about half the water from fresh milk, but sweetened condensed milk has sugar added while evaporated milk does not. They are not interchangeable. Evaporated milk lends creaminess to sauces and desserts; it can be mixed with an equal amount of water and used in place of fresh milk in a pinch. Sweetened condensed milk has a very sweet, distinctive flavor, and is used in pies, candies, and other desserts; it is the only milk used in dulce de leche, a creamy Spanish sauce with a caramel flavor, and one of three milks in Pastel Tres Leches, a classic Mexican cake. Canned milk can be kept in the pantry for months; once opened, the milk should be refrigerated in an airtight container and used within several days.

CANNED TOMATOES You can find tomatoes in many forms (diced, crushed, seasoned, and so on), but whole tomatoes (in juice, not puree) are the most versatile. The tomatoes will break down over long, slow cooking, making them ideal for stews, braises, and meat sauces. They can also be cut with kitchen scissors or crushed with your hands for use in quick-cooking sauces and dishes or pureed for a smooth consistency (instead of using canned tomato sauce).

CANNED TUNA Oil-packed tuna from Italy, particularly Sicily, has the best flavor. The cans will keep, unopened, for up to a year; after opening, transfer the tuna to a tightly sealed container and use within a few days.

CAPERS Capers are the salt-processed, unopened flower buds of a trailing shrub that thrives in the arid climate along the shores of the Mediterranean. Tangy and pungent, with a slight astringency, capers are an essential ingredient in many well-known dishes such as caponata, pasta puttanesca, and salad Niçoise, as well as classic sauces such as rémoulade. Nonpareils, the tiniest capers, are the most expensive but have the most delicate flavor. Capers are either packed in brine or salt; since they are rinsed and drained before using, the salt-packed type actually have a less salty taste. Capers keep indefinitely in unopened jars. Once opened, they are best used within a year; refrigerate brine-packed capers and keep salt-packed capers at room temperature (in a well-sealed jar).

CHUTNEYS Chutneys, a broad category of relishes with roots in India, often have a chunky texture and can be made with chiles, herbs, spices, fruits, and vegetables (mango is the most widely known, but tomato, cranberry, and others are also common). Pair them with grilled meats or cheeses, add to chicken salad, or blend with mayonnaise for a flavorful sandwich spread. Chutneys should be refrigerated and used within a few months after opening.

COCONUT MILK Canned coconut milk, made from coconut meat that is steeped in boiling water and then strained to form a creamy liquid, is widely used in Eastern and Caribbean cooking. It should not be confused with coconut cream, which is made the same way but with less water, or with sweetened cream of coconut, generally used to make blended cocktails. Before opening, shake the can to mix the coconut milk thoroughly. Unopened cans will keep for up to eighteen months; transfer the contents of opened cans to an airtight container and refrigerate for up to a week.

COUSCOUS A staple of North African cuisine, couscous is a tiny pasta made from hard-wheat flour (durum) or precooked semolina. The larger pearls of Israeli couscous are lightly oven-dried, giving them a faintly golden color and toasted flavor (it is often labeled "toasted"). The large pearls also have a more toothsome texture. Keep couscous in the original container until opened, then store it in an airtight container for up to a year.

DIJON MUSTARD Dijon is a general term for a French-style mustard, which is prized for its clean, sharp flavor. It's made from brown or black mustard seeds, white wine, must (unfermented grape juice), and seasonings. It can be used on sandwiches and in sauces, vinaigrettes, and other salad dressings.

DRIED HERBS AND SPICES Most spices will lose their potency after about a year, but their flavor will deteriorate faster if stored improperly. Keep them in airtight containers, away from heat or direct sunlight; label them with the date of purchase so you'll know when it's time to replenish. For the freshest flavor, buy whole spices when possible and then grind just what you need in a spice or coffee grinder (or with a mortar and pestle).

DRIED PASTA Stock an assortment of shapes for different sauces, such as spaghetti, bucatini, and perciatelli for tomato sauces; linguine for clam sauce; capellini for light, delicate sauces (or no sauce at all); penne, rigatoni, and pappardelle for meaty ragus; and fusilli, farfalle, and fettucine for cream sauces. Whole-wheat pastas offer more nutritional benefits (and a slightly chewier texture). Dried pasta can be stored in its original package until opened, then transferred to airtight containers; for best results, use within a year.

GRAINS Except as noted, the following items can be stored in the pantry for up to one year; transfer to airtight containers after opening.

barley Of the various types of barley available, pearl barley is the easiest to find and to use. It comes in three sizes: coarse, medium, and fine. Barley adds substance and flavor to soups (beef barley is a classic), stews, pilafs, and other side dishes. Its earthy flavor pairs well with mushrooms, and is enhanced by a brief toasting before cooking in water or broth.

cornmeal Cornmeal is made from dried corn kernels that are steel-ground, a process by which the hull and germ of the kernel are removed. Cornmeal is typically white or yellow, depending on the variety of corn used; the taste is virtually the same. It is sold in three varieties: fine (also known as corn flour), medium (the most common), and coarse. Fine and medium cornmeal are used frequently in baking; coarse cornmeal is used to make polenta. Stone-ground cornmeal, a coarser relative of cornmeal, is water-ground; this process results in the meal retaining some of the hull and germ, giving foods a deeper flavor and rougher texture. Store stone-ground cornmeal in the freezer for up to a year.

lentils These tiny, round legumes grow in small pods. When ripe, the pods are picked, dried, and smashed to release the seeds, which are then dried further and left whole or split. The most common form is brown, but they are also available in green (also called French, or *lentilles de Puy*) as well as red, black, and yellow (used primarily in Indian cooking). Because they lose moisture over time, older lentils will take longer to cook than fresher ones. Before using, sort through lentils to remove any shriveled ones and small stones and twigs, and then rinse well.

oats Rolled oats, also called old-fashioned oats, are whole oats that have been steamed and flattened to make them more tender; they cook in about 15 minutes. Quick-cooking oats have been cut into smaller pieces before steaming and then rolled even thinner; they cook in about 5 minutes. It is generally acceptable to substitute one for the other in most recipes, but never substitute instant oatmeal. Steel-cut oats or Irish oatmeal, which are not rolled, take longer to cook, but have a pleasantly chewy texture.

HOISIN SAUCE Although ingredients vary by brand, this thick, dark brown sauce is generally made with soybeans, chiles, and spices. It is widely used in Chinese cooking as a condiment as well as in marinades, glazes, sauces, and other dishes. Bottled hoisin will keep almost indefinitely in the refrigerator.

NUTS AND DRIED FRUIT These staples can be used in a wide array of dishes and cooking, both sweet and savory, so stock at least a few of the following: walnut and pecan halves, almonds (whole and sliced), hazelnuts, raisins (dark and golden), currants, dates, apricots, and figs. Nuts can turn rancid easily, so store them in the freezer for up to six months. Dried fruit can be kept at room temperature for up to a year; keep them well sealed to preserve freshness and prevent stickiness.

OILS Store vegetable oils in their original bottles, in a cool, dark place, for up to six months. Nut oils should be refrigerated and used within three months. There are three types to keep in your pantry:

neutral-tasting oils These flavorless oils are good to use when you don't want to affect the taste of a dish. They also have high smoke points (the temperature at which the oil will cause foods to burn), making them ideal for sautéing, frying, and other high-temperature cooking. Good choices include canola oil, corn oil, peanut oil, and vegetable oil.

nut and seed oils Flavorful nut oils, such as walnut and hazelnut, are generally not used in cooking, but as condiments. Drizzle them onto salads, vegetables, and rice and pasta dishes. There are two basic types of sesame oil to look for: regular (light-colored) and toasted (dark). Regular sesame oil, which has a mild nutty taste and a high smoke point, is the most versatile and is more commonly used in cooking, especially frying. Toasted sesame oil has a richer, more assertive flavor; it is used sparingly in marinades and salad dressings, and can be drizzled over cooked dishes just before serving. It can also be combined with a neutral vegetable oil for stir-frying.

olive oils These oils can be used to impart flavor as well as for cooking. Extra-virgin olive oil is perfect for lower-temperature sautéing, for salads and marinades, and for drizzling over pasta and rice dishes. Light and extra-light olive oils have been cut with vegetable oils so they are light in flavor but not in fat. Grapeseed oil is a good alternative to olive oil; with its mildly nutty flavor, it can be used in salad dressings and marinades, while its high smoke point makes it perfect for all types of cooking.

ORZO Orzo means "barley" in Italian, but it's actually a type of pasta. It looks like rice and makes a fine substitute as a side or in salads and soups. Toasting orzo before cooking will give it a deeper flavor.

PANTRY VEGETABLES These essential ingredients are part of any well-stocked kitchen, and are sturdy enough to keep in a cupboard or other cool, dark, dry spot, but not the refrigerator. Garlic, onions, shallots, and potatoes will generally keep for about a month. Dried mushrooms, such as porcini or shiitake, can be kept in a well-sealed container for several months.

PEPPERCORNS There are three basic types of peppercorns: black, white, and green. The black kind is picked when the berry is slightly underripe, then dried until black and shriveled; it has a slightly hot flavor. The green type is also picked when underripe

and then either preserved in brine or sold dried; it is tart, slightly fruity, and especially good in chutneys and mustards. The white variety is a fully ripened berry that has had its skin removed before being dried; it is slightly milder tasting than black pepper and is often used instead of black pepper to preserve the appearance of a light-colored dish. The pink peppercorn is not a peppercorn at all, but a dried berry from the Baies rose plant; it is mild and slightly sweet. Peppercorns are available whole, cracked, or ground. For the freshest flavor, buy them whole and then grind just what you need at a time. Like all spices, peppercorns should be stored in tightly sealed containers, away from heat or light.

RICE It helps to keep a variety of rices in your pantry at all times, as they make an easy side dish and are used in many types of cooking across the world. Keep rice in its original packaging until opening, then store it in an airtight container at room temperature. Martha likes to write cooking instructions for each and affix them to the lid of the container for handy reference (for example, "combine 1 cup water, ½ cup rice, and ½ teaspoon salt; cook 25 minutes"). For best results, use within a year.

arborio rice: When properly prepared, this short-grain Italian rice develops a creamy texture and a chewy center and has an exceptional ability to absorb flavors, making it ideal for risotto. Carnaroli is similar in starch content.

basmati rice: With its slender long grains, basmati is prized for its delicate nutty aroma. It is an essential element of Indian cooking.

brown rice (medium- to long-grain) is the entire grain of rice with only the inedible husk removed. The nutritious, high-fiber bran coating gives it its light tan color. When cooked, brown rice has a strong, nutty flavor and chewy texture. Medium-grain brown rice is starchier than the long-grain variety.

jasmine rice: This long-grain rice has the aroma of basmati but the softer, starchier texture of medium-grain rice. It is ideal for serving with Thai curries.

sushi rice: Japanese sushi rice is a short-grained, glutinous white rice that becomes moist, firm, and sticky when cooked. If you can't find Japanese sushi rice, substitute short-grained white rice (called pearl).

white rice (medium- to long-grain), which has been stripped of the husk and bran, has a mild flavor and firm texture, making it a versatile vehicle for carrying the flavor of other ingredients. Medium-grain is a little stickier than the long-grain variety. Converted white rice, which is made by soaking, pressure-steaming, and then drying unhulled grains, takes slightly longer to cook than unconverted white rice; it also has a pale tan color. Instant or quick white rice has been fully or partially cooked before being de-hydrated and packaged; this should not be substi-tuted in recipes.

white rice (short-grain, or pearl): The fat, almost round grains of short-grain white rice have a higher starch content than medium- and long-grain rice. They become moist and viscous when cooked, caus-ing the grains to stick together. Also called glutinous rice (even though it is gluten-free), this variety is most often used in Asian cooking.

wild rice is actually the seed of a grass found in the Great Lakes region of the United States. It is har-vested by hand and it has a nutty flavor and chewy texture, making it particularly good in rice salads and stuffings. Although wild rice can take up to an hour to cook, it is important to watch it carefully toward the end; overcooking produces starchy results.

SALT The two most common types are kosher (coarse) salt and table (iodized) salt. Kosher salt is a good choice for cooking (and brining) and for use at the table. Since coarse salt does not contain any ad-ditives or iodine, it has a cleaner flavor and is not as strong or sharply acidic as table salt; it also dissolves quickly in cold water. When seasoning foods, the larger grain of coarse salt make it easier to control the amount you use (and the saltiness of the dish). In most recipes, these salts can generally be used in-terchangeably, without altering amounts, though you may prefer to use table salt for baking.

   If you want to add a more distinctive accent to dishes, consider one of the many types of sea salts. Fleur de sel, one of the rarest and most prized of sea salts, comes from the Brittany region of France; it has a mild salty taste and is best used as a condiment, sprinkled over salads, egg dishes, fish, and other foods at the table. Gray salt also hails from Brittany, and has a stronger saltiness. Maldon, an English sea salt, consists of small white crystalline flakes that can easily be crushed with your fingers and added to dishes as they cook or once they are at the table. Sun-dried sea salts also come from Sicily and Maine; they are perfect for garnishing the rims of cocktail glasses.

SOY SAUCE Soy sauce is traditionally made by fer-menting whole boiled soybeans with wheat or bar-ley. Varieties can range from dark to light in color

and thick to thin in texture. Light soy sauce is gen-erally saltier and thinner than dark and is used when the flavor of the sauce is desired but the color is not. Dark soy sauce is less salty and provides a richer fla-vor and hue to a dish, due to the addition of caramel color. Tamari, a similar sauce, is brewed from whole soybeans but contains no wheat; it has a more pro-nounced flavor and is often used to season long-cooking dishes such as soups and stews. Both types are very versatile and can be used in marinades and dressings and as a table condiment. Soy sauce will keep indefinitely in a cool pantry.

SUN-DRIED TOMATOES Sun-dried tomatoes are available dry-packed or oil-packed. Dry ones need to be softened by soaking in water or another liquid be-fore using, while oil-packed tomatoes can be used right out of the jar and often have a more consistently chewy texture (the oil can be used to flavor sauces and salad dressings). Use sun-dried tomatoes throughout the year to make sandwiches, pizza, sal-ads, and pasta dishes. The dry-packed tomatoes will keep almost indefinitely in a well-sealed bag; oil-packed tomatoes should be refrigerated after open-ing and used within a month or so.

TOMATO PASTE Tomato paste is highly concentrated and generally used as a thickener and flavor en-hancer in soups, stews, and tomato-based sauces. A little paste goes a long way; many recipes often call for just one or two tablespoons. The rest should be transferred to an airtight container and can be re-frigerated for several weeks. Or it can be frozen for up to six months: Drop 1 tablespoon of tomato paste into each section of an ice-cube tray and freeze until solid, then pop frozen cubes into a resealable plastic bag and return to the freezer until ready to use.

VINEGARS Because they add brightness to every-thing from salad dressings to sauces, vinegars are pantry essentials. Experiment with different types; those made with wine and sherry are the most ver-satile. For the longest shelf life (up to a year), store bottles in a cool spot, away from direct sunlight.

balsamic vinegar is made from the boiled-down must of white grapes. With its sweetness and intense flavor, balsamic should be used sparingly. It is deli-cious in vinaigrettes (often in combination with other vinegars) or drizzled over strawberries. When used in cooking, add balsamic vinegar only at the end or just before serving to retain its flavor.

cider vinegar is derived from fermented apple cider. Mild-tasting and slightly sweet, it is what gives coleslaws and sauerkraut their familiar tang. You can also use it instead of lemon juice to enhance the flavor of apples in pies and other desserts.

red-wine and white-wine vinegars are made from fermented wines. They are most frequently used in salad dressings and marinades and as last-minute additions to sauces and stews.

rice-wine vinegar, made from fermented rice wine, is much milder and faintly sweeter than other wine-based vinegars. Look for unseasoned rice-wine vinegar (seasoned vinegars are clearly labeled as such).

sherry vinegar, produced in Spain from fermented fino sherry, is prized for its concentrated, balanced flavor. It is essential in gazpacho and wonderful in vinaigrettes, but it can also be used sparingly in cooking to give dishes depth of flavor.

WORCESTERSHIRE SAUCE This dark, piquant sauce is usually made from garlic, soy sauce, tamarind, onions, molasses, anchovies, vinegar, and seasonings. It can be used at the table or to flavor meats, marinades, soups, and salad dressings. There is also a light-colored version for use with fish and poultry. It will keep almost indefinitely in a cool spot.

BAKING NEEDS

BAKING POWDER Baking powder combines the leavening action of baking soda with a premixed acidic agent. When mixed with water or other liquid, baking powder releases carbon dioxide gas bubbles that cause a bread or cake to rise. Before buying, check the date on the bottom of the canister; it loses its potency over time, and usually needs to be replaced after one year. To test if your baking powder is still active, mix 1 teaspoon powder with ⅓ cup hot water; it should bubble instantly.

BAKING SODA Baking soda is another type of leavener. When used with an acidic ingredient, such as buttermilk or yogurt, baking soda produces gas bubbles, causing bread or cakes to rise. It should be mixed with the other dry ingredients before a liquid is added, as baking soda reacts immediately when moistened. Keep it in a cool spot and check the expiration date on the bottom of the box. It's also good as a household cleaner, and an open box in the refrigerator will help eliminate any odors (buy one specifically for this purpose; do not use it in recipes).

CHOCOLATE Keeping chocolate bars and chips on hand is a must for spur-of-the-moment desserts. Semisweet is the most commonly called for, but some people prefer the taste of bittersweet. Unsweetened chocolate is used in some recipes and cannot be swapped for the others. If you prefer a richer flavor, explore the higher-quality brands such as Callebaut and Scharffen Berger. Unopened packages should be stored in a cool, dry, dark spot for up to a year; once they've been opened, wrap the packages in plastic or foil, or place in a resealable plastic bag. Don't worry if a grayish-white bloom develops on the chocolate; it doesn't affect the flavor and can be scraped off.

COCOA POWDER Cocoa powder is unsweetened chocolate with most of the cocoa butter removed. Dutch-processed cocoa, which is treated with alkali, a mineral salt that helps to neutralize cocoa's natural acidity, is richer, darker, and less bitter than regular unsweetened cocoa; it is also more powdery and does not dissolve readily in cold milk. Although the two types can often be used interchangeably, it's a good idea to use what is called for in a recipe.

CORN SYRUP Because corn syrup prevents crystallization, it's an important ingredient in some candies, jams, jellies, frostings, and glazes. It is also used in pie fillings, including pecan. There are two types to choose from: light corn syrup, which has been stripped of all color and cloudiness and has a purer flavor, and dark corn syrup, with added caramel flavor and coloring. Store syrup at room temperature in its original container for up to a year.

CORNSTARCH Dense, powdery cornstarch comes from the endosperm, or white heart, of the corn kernel. It is commonly used instead of flour as a thickening agent for pie fillings and custards; it is also added to gravies, soups, and savory sauces (especially in Chinese cooking). Because it tends to form lumps, cornstarch should be blended with a small amount of cold or room-temperature liquid to form a slurry, or paste, before being stirred into a hot mixture. Keep in a cool spot, tightly sealed, and use within a year.

CREAM OF TARTAR This powder is tartaric acid derived from fermented grapes. It increases the stability and volume of whipped egg whites in meringues or angel food cake. It is also used to give some candy and frostings a creamier consistency. Cream of tartar will keep for a year or longer in a cool spot.

FLOUR Different flours have different amounts of protein, which will affect the way each behaves in a recipe: The protein in flour forms an elastic network that helps contain the gases that make doughs and batters rise as they bake. It is only necessary to sift flour if a recipe specifically calls for it, but you may want to run a whisk through it before measuring to break up any clumps. Store in airtight containers at room temperature for up to a year; choose containers with wide mouths for easy scooping.

all-purpose flour is made from a blend of high-protein hard wheat and low-protein soft wheat; use it to make piecrusts, cookies, pancakes, waffles, and biscuits. Look for the unbleached variety.

bread flour, with its high protein content, is appropriate for making yeast breads and popovers.

cake, or pastry, flour is a fine-textured, low-protein flour best used for cakes, pastries, and quick breads, where a tender crumb is desired. Most recipes call for cake flour that is not self-rising (meaning baking powder and salt have been added), so be sure to check the label before buying.

wheat flour: Unlike white flour, wheat flour contains the bran and germ of the wheat berry. It has higher fiber, nutritional, and fat content than white flour. Many recipes call for a combination of white and wheat flour for improved flavor and texture, as using all wheat flour can give very chewy results.

GELATIN There are two forms of gelatin: granulated, which is easiest to find, and sheet (or leaf), available at gourmet and baking supply shops. Granulated gelatin must always be softened first by soaking in cold water for several minutes; sheet gelatin must be soaked a bit longer, but it is preferred by many professional bakers for the creamier texture it develops. Four sheets of gelatin equals one package of powdered. Check for expiration dates on packets of powdered gelatin; sheet gelatin will keep for about ten months at room temperature. Besides making jelled desserts, gelatin can be used to stabilize mousses, whipped creams, and dessert sauces.

MOLASSES Molasses is made from the juice extracted from cane sugar during the refining process; the juice is boiled, then sugar crystals are removed from the resulting liquid, leaving behind the thick syrup that is molasses. Light molasses is made by boiling the juice once; for dark molasses, it's boiled twice. The light version has a subtle sweetness and is most often used for pancakes and waffles. Dark molasses, which is less sweet and has a deeper taste, is preferred for baking. Both light and dark are sold in two forms: sulfured (which has been processed with sulfur as a preservative and is sweeter and thicker) and unsulfured, often preferred for its sharper, more pronounced taste. If a recipe calls for unsulfured molasses, you can use sulfured, but the outcome might be slightly different; adding a bit less sugar might help balance the flavor. Blackstrap molasses, created by boiling sugarcane juice three times, is very dense and bitter tasting and should not be substituted for other types of molasses. Stored in a cool, dark place, molasses will keep for up to a year.

SUGAR Besides sweetness, sugar adds tenderness to doughs, stability to meringues, and a golden-brown hue to the surface of almost any baked good. Humidity can make sugars lumpy, so keep them in well-sealed containers in a cool, dry spot. Double-wrap brown sugars to keep them moist.

brown sugar, a combination of granulated sugar and molasses, has a softer texture, darker color, and distinctive flavor. Light brown sugar has a more delicate taste than dark; they can usually be used interchangeably. If your brown sugar has hardened, there are a couple of ways to soften it. To use it right away, place a half pound in a microwaveable bowl, drape with a damp paper towel, and cover with plastic wrap; heat at ten-second intervals, just until it becomes soft, then break apart the lumps with a fork. If you have more time, place an apple or bread slice in the bag overnight (no longer), which will return the sugar to its optimal consistency.

confectioners' sugar, also called powdered sugar, is made by grinding granulated sugar to a fine powder, then sifting and adding a small amount of cornstarch to prevent caking. It dissolves easily in icings and candies, and can be dusted over finished desserts.

granulated sugar has a fine grain that makes it perfect as a table sweetener and cooking ingredient.

superfine sugar has finer crystals than granulated sugar (though not as fine as confectioners'), and is often used to make meringues or fine-textured cakes, such as angel food. Because it dissolves quickly, superfine is good for sweetening cold drinks.

turbinado sugar is made by steaming raw sugar to remove impurities. The caramel-colored coarse crystals are slightly crunchy and have a mild molasses flavor. Sprinkle it on cereal or stir it into hot drinks.

VANILLA BEANS AND EXTRACT The thin black fruit of an orchid, vanilla beans are actually pods that are picked when green, then cured and fermented. To preserve the flavor and aroma of vanilla beans, store them carefully: Wrap tightly in plastic, then put them in an airtight container and keep in a cool, dark place for six months to a year. Vanilla extract is made by steeping chopped vanilla pods in alcohol and water and then aging the strained liquid. Always buy extract that is labeled "pure" (imitation vanilla offers little flavor and a bitter aftertaste); Mexican and Tahitian extracts are worth the extra cost. Tightly sealed, vanilla extract will last indefinitely at room temperature.

VEGETABLE SHORTENING Shortening is made by hydrogenating vegetable oils to make them solid. It is virtually flavorless and used for making tender piecrusts and other baked goods. Store shortening at room temperature for up to a year.

REFRIGERATED GOODS

BACON Besides being delicious on its own, bacon lends incomparable flavor to many dishes, such as chowders and other soups, baked beans and collard greens, and savory custards and tarts. There are many types; look for bacon that is free of nitrates and other artificial ingredients. Thick-sliced bacon, along with its melted fat, provides not only flavor but also a hot dressing for wilting spinach or other greens. The subtler flavor of Canadian bacon (which is also lower in fat and calories than American-style bacon), is an essential component of eggs Benedict. Pancetta, a traditional Italian bacon, is cured but not smoked; it is highly flavorful and slightly salty, and a small amount is all it takes to flavor pasta sauces and other dishes. All bacon can be tightly wrapped and kept for up to three weeks in the refrigerator or three months in the freezer.

BUTTER Unsalted butter has the purest flavor. It is ideal for all types of cooking, especially baking. European-style butters are also good for baking, especially pastries and shortbread, as well as for spreading at the table. They have a higher percentage of butterfat (typically 83 percent compared to 80 percent) and a richer, more distinctive taste.

CHEESE Of all the many types of cheese available, the following are among the more versatile. Of course, it's also nice to keep a supply of favorites, such as Cheddar and Muenster, for making grilled cheese or for quickly putting together an appetizer to share with unexpected guests.

fontina cheese is a cow's milk cheese with a mildly sweet, nutty, buttery flavor. Smooth and shot through with tiny holes, fontina is a very good melting cheese and is excellent on pizza and in hot sandwiches.

goat cheese Made from goat's milk, this soft and creamy cheese is usually sold in logs or disks; French goat cheeses are often called chèvre. Goat cheese is particularly good in egg dishes, salads, sandwiches, and savory tarts, as well as paired with fresh fruit as a light snack or dessert. Aged goat cheeses are more pungent and often have a rind; they are harder in texture and not generally a good substitute for fresh in recipes (but they are delicious as a snacking cheese). Keep fresh goat cheese, loosely wrapped, in the least cold part of the refrigerator. It should not be frozen, but you may want to pop it in the freezer for five or ten minutes to make it easier to slice.

gruyère is another wonderful melting cheese, and is traditionally used in making croque-monsieurs.

parmesan This popular cheese is a hard, dry cheese made from skimmed or partially skimmed cow's milk. The finest of the many kinds of Parmesan is Parmigiano-Reggiano (the name should be printed on the perimeter of the rind), produced in the Emilia-Romagna region of Italy. Known for its sumptuous flavor, this cheese can appear at any point of the meal, from hors d'oeuvres to dessert. A good alternative is Pecorino Romano. For the best flavor, buy wedges of cheese (instead of already grated) and grate just before using or serving. To keep Parmesan, wrap it in parchment paper and then plastic, and store it on the bottom shelf (or in the cheese bin) of the refrigerator.

EGGS Eggs come in many sizes; large is the most common and the size most often used in our recipes. Shell color has nothing to do with flavor or nutritional value, but is determined by the breed of the hen. When buying eggs, check to make sure the eggs are clean and free of cracks, and look on the carton for an expiration date. To store, refrigerate eggs in their original carton; it will help protect the delicate, porous shells from cracking and absorbing odors. Eggs are freshest within a week of purchase, but will keep longer (up to a month).

FRESH HERBS Fresh herbs have a singular ability to brighten any dish. To store, wrap them in damp paper towels, then place in a resealable plastic bag; keep them in the refrigerator's vegetable bin. Leafy herbs, such as basil, will keep for up to a week; sturdier herbs such as thyme and rosemary will keep a bit longer. Wash leafy herbs as soon as you bring them home, before storing.

FRESH GINGER Fresh ginger adds brightness to many dishes, making vegetables taste fresher and giving bite to seafood. The fine sharpness cuts through rich sauces and meats, such as duck or pork, and is a key note in many chutneys, curries, and pickling brines. When buying ginger, look for roots that are hard and seem swollen. The skin should be smooth; wrinkling is a sign of age. Unpeeled ginger keeps for up to three weeks when wrapped in a paper towel or placed in a paper bag, and then refrigerated in an airtight container. Freezing can preserve the flavor and makes it easier to grate.

LEMONS AND LIMES A squeeze of lemon or lime juice makes fish, vegetables, fruit salad, and many other foods taste better. The juice and zest are also flavorful components of many dishes and baked goods. Keep fruit in a plastic bag in the fruit or vegetable bin of the refrigerator for up to two weeks.

MILK Although you can sometimes substitute one type of milk for another, it's best to use what is called for in a recipe. Whole milk, for instance, will produce a much creamier texture than skim. However, if a recipe calls for heavy cream and you don't have any, whole milk can often be used instead. Keep buttermilk on hand for making salad dressings, biscuits, pancakes, and some cakes and quick breads. You can make your own buttermilk in a pinch: add a tablespoon of white vinegar or lemon juice for each cup of regular milk called for, and let sit for ten minutes before using in a recipe.

OLIVES Olives can be used in salads, sandwiches, pasta dishes, pizza toppings, and more. Purplish kalamata are meaty and tangy (and easy to pit); other common varieties include Niçoise, Gaeta, and picholine, which have a slightly salty, nutty flavor and are ideal as appetizers. When possible, buy olives in bulk instead of in jars or cans. They will keep for several months, as long as they are submerged in oil or brine, and stored in a sealed container.

SPECIALTY ITEMS

ASIAN FISH SAUCE This dark brown sauce is made from fermented fish (often anchovies) and has a pungent aroma and a subtle, salty taste. It is a popular condiment in Southeast Asia, particularly Thailand (where it's known as nam pla) and Vietnam (nuoc nam). Nam pla is also added during cooking, often with soy sauce, tamarind, or other seasonings. Opened bottles should be refrigerated, where they will keep almost indefinitely.

ASIAN NOODLES Here are the most common types of Asian noodles; as with Italian pasta, it is a good idea to have a few types on hand at all times for making soups, salads, and other dishes. Unopened, they can be kept in their original packages almost indefinitely. Once opened, store in a tightly sealed bag or container and use within a year.

cellophane noodles, also known as bean threads or glass noodles, are made from processed mung beans. They are opaque in their dried form, but once they have been soaked in hot water, they become clear and gelatinous. These noodles are generally prized for their texture, since they have very little flavor. Capellini or vermicelli can often be substituted.

chinese egg noodles, made from wheat flour and whole eggs or egg whites, come in various widths. They are usually sold in small tangled nests that are meant to be dropped into hot soups (without prior cooking). Fresh egg noodles can also be found in the refrigerated section of many supermarkets.

rice noodles, also known as rice-stick noodles and rice vermicelli (slightly thinner strands), are made from rice flour. There are two shapes: round and flat. The extra-thin rice vermicelli are also known as mi fen (Chinese), bun (Vietnamese), and sen mee (Thai). They are usually soaked to soften in hot water before eating. Rice sticks are the flat version. Medium-size sticks are called pho. The slightly wider Thai version is called jantaboon.

soba noodles, made from buckwheat flour, have a nutty flavor and are rich in fiber and protein. These noodles are extremely versatile, and can be served hot or cold in soups, salads, and stir-fries.

somen noodles, the most prized of all Japanese noodles, have a delicate flavor and texture. They are made from wheat flour and a little oil and are always packaged in small bundles. The difference between somen and other Japanese noodles is the way they are made: Somen are made by pulling; other noodles are made by rolling and cutting.

udon These thick, white, slippery Japanese noodles are made from wheat or corn flour. Udon may be round, square, or flat. Their neutral flavor makes them the ideal addition to robust flavored soups and sauces. Udon can be found in both fresh and dried forms at Asian markets.

ASIAN WRAPPERS

dumpling wrappers Most supermarkets carry at least one or two types of frozen dumpling wrappers, usually wonton or shao mai skins. You can find more of a variety of fresh and frozen wrappers at Asian markets; if you have access to one, buy an assortment of wrappers and store them, well wrapped, in the freezer, where they'll keep for up to six months. Fresh wrappers will last for up to a month in the refrigerator; frozen ones defrost fully in about an hour. Paper-thin yet durable spring-roll skins are sold only frozen and can be thawed and frozen repeatedly without any deterioration in quality. When making dumplings, fill one at a time and keep the remaining wrappers covered with a damp paper towel so they do not dry out. Once formed, dumplings can be steamed, boiled, or fried. Besides their traditional use in making Asian-style dumplings, some wrappers (especially wonton) are a convenient substitute for fresh pasta when making ravioli and other filled shapes.

rice-paper wrappers: These round or triangular wrappers are made from a mixture of rice flour, water, and salt, which is machine-rolled paper thin, then dried in the sun on bamboo mats, the weave of which gives them their unique texture and pattern. They are brittle, so moisten them with water before using and keep them covered with a damp paper towel while you work. These wrappers can be used uncooked, as when making summer rolls. They are also sturdy enough for steaming or deep-frying.

BUCKWHEAT FLOUR Buckwheat flour is the ground seeds of the buckwheat plant, which is not a grain but actually an herb. Because it is rather dense, buckwheat flour is generally combined with another flour in a three-to-one ratio to achieve an appealing texture without sacrificing its deep, pleasantly sour flavor. Perhaps the most familiar food made with buckwheat is blini; soba noodles are another. Store the flour in an airtight container at room temperature for up to a year.

BULGUR WHEAT Popular in Middle Eastern dishes, such as tabbouleh, bulgur wheat is steamed, dried, and crushed wheat kernels. It has a tender, chewy texture and comes in coarse, medium, and fine grinds. Store in a cool, dark spot for up to a year.

CAVIAR Caviar is the roe, or egg mass, of sturgeon, the best of which is generally considered to come from female sturgeon caught in the Caspian Sea. Three species of sturgeon swim in this sea: beluga, the largest; midsize osetra; and sevruga, the smallest. Beluga roe varies in color from pale to dark gray and is the most delicately flavored caviar: subtle, buttery, and creamy. Though smaller than beluga, osetra eggs have a more assertive taste: nutty and voluptuous. Their color ranges from gold (very rare) to dark brown. Sevruga eggs are tiny, nearly black, and sweet—almost fruity. The general rule for serving caviar is to purchase one to two ounces per guest and buy the best you can afford. Beluga is the priciest, sevruga the least expensive. Serve the caviar in its tin on a bed of ice. Store in the coldest part of the refrigerator for up to two weeks. Once opened, a tin should not be resealed.

CHILE OIL Used extensively in Chinese cooking, chile oil is made by steeping dried red chiles in flavorless vegetable oil. Chile oil will keep almost indefinitely when stored in a cool, dark place.

CHILE PASTE Made of a pungent mixture of ground chiles, oil, salt, and sometimes garlic, chile paste is used in cooking as well as at the table. The flavor is intensely concentrated and ranges from mild to very hot, depending on the types of chiles included. Heat it along with the oil when making stir-fries, or serve it as an accompaniment to grilled or roasted meat or fish. It should keep indefinitely in the refrigerator.

CHILE PEPPERS, DRIED Because the drying process concentrates their heat, dried chiles are hotter than fresh. They vary in size, which generally indicates how hot they are: The larger the chile, the milder it will be. Larger chiles can be chopped and sprinkled into sauces for subtle heat. Smaller chiles should be used sparingly and prepared with caution; handle the seeds carefully, since they harbor much of the heat. (If you prefer, wear gloves when working with them.) Look for dried chiles that are shiny, pliable, and evenly colored. Keep them in a tightly sealed container at room temperature; they are best used within a year of purchase.

CHIPOTLE CHILES Chipotle chiles are smoked jalapeños with a complex flavor that is hot, smoky, and sweet. They're typically sold canned, packed in adobo—a spicy, vinegary, tomato-based sauce. Both the chiles and the sauce are used in a wide variety of dishes. Once opened, transfer the contents to an airtight container and refrigerate, for up to several months. Also look for dried chipotles, which can be used in similar ways to other dried chiles (above), and chipotle powder, both sold at Mexican groceries and many supermarkets.

COCONUT Packaged coconut is available in several forms. Sweetened shredded coconut and unsweetened flaked coconut are primarily used in making desserts. Dessicated coconut, which is dried, shredded, and unsweetened, is a fine substitute for fresh; it is commonly called for in Thai and Indian cooking. Be careful about substituting sweetened for the unsweetened varieties, as you may need to adjust the amount of sugar or other ingredients. Unopened packages can be kept for up to six months; opened bags should be refrigerated (tightly sealed) and used within a month. If flaked or shredded coconut becomes too dry, soak it in milk for thirty minutes, then drain well and pat dry.

FILÉ POWDER Made from the dried leaves of the sassafras tree, filé powder is an earthy seasoning used in Creole cooking. Use it for thickening gumbos, but be sure to add it at the end of cooking to avoid a gluey consistency. Keep it with other spices in your kitchen, preferably in a cool, dark place.

FIVE-SPICE POWDER Composed of an equal mixture of cinnamon, cloves, fennel seed, star anise, and Szechuan peppercorns, five-spice powder imparts a fragrant, sweet, and spicy flavor to dishes.

GALANGAL This Indian root has a strong, spicy taste similar to ginger, and is usually combined with ginger and lemongrass in Thai and Southeast Asian cooking. The whole root form is generally found only at Asian markets; grate it or, for more subtle flavor, steep it in hot soups and sauces (and then discard). The powdered form is more readily available, and will last for six months when kept in a tightly sealed container in a cool, dark spot.

GARAM MASALA A blend of cumin, pepper, cardamom, cinnamon, and other spices gives garam masala a spicy heat. It is a staple of northern Indian cooking, where it adds depth of flavor to curries and other traditional dishes. It should be added near the end of cooking time, and stored in a cool, dark place.

HARISSA PASTE This peppery North African relish is a mix of dried red chiles, garlic, tomato puree, olive oil, salt, and ground cumin, coriander, and caraway seeds. It is commonly added to couscous, stews, sauces, and marinades, either during cooking or at the table; because it is so fiery, start with a little and then add more to taste. Imported from Tunisia, harissa is sold in tubes in specialty-food stores. Once opened, refrigerate for up to a year.

HERBES DE PROVENCE This classic blend of dried herbs, frequently used in southern French cooking, typically includes thyme, basil, fennel, savory, sage, rosemary, tarragon, and lavender, although other herbs can be found in some versions. You can make your own (using equal parts of the herbs) or buy it in the spice section of most supermarkets. Keep it on hand for seasoning sauces, soups, and a variety of other dishes; it is especially delicious with roasted chicken, rack of lamb, and vegetables.

KAFFIR LIME LEAVES These lime leaves have a citrus aroma and flavor and are primarily used in Thai cooking. Frozen lime leaves are a good substitute for fresh; dried leaves are much less flavorful, so use up to twice as many as a recipe calls for if substituting for fresh (but don't chop them; use them like bay leaves and discard before serving). If you can't find lime leaves, substitute 1 teaspoon of grated lime or lemon zest for each leaf.

LEMONGRASS Lemongrass is an herb that grows in long stalks; it has a citrusy flavor and fragrance and is a staple of Southeast Asian cooking. Use only the lower, fleshy portion for cooking, as the flavor is more highly concentrated there than in the flattened blades. First, remove any dry or tough outer layers; then, if you like, bruise the stalks with the back of a knife to help release the flavor. The stalks can be used whole or cut into slices; they can also be dried and either ground into a powder (one teaspoon of dried lemongrass is as potent as one fresh stalk) or reconstituted by soaking in water for two hours. Keep the stalks, tightly wrapped in paper towels, for up to three weeks in the refrigerator. Or seal them in plastic storage bags and freeze for several months.

MIRIN This slightly syrupy, sweet rice wine is highly prized in Japanese cuisine for its ability to add a delicate sweetness to foods and to impart depth of flavor; it is commonly added to sushi rice. Made from fermented, glutinous rice, mirin is generally used only for cooking, although some finer varieties can be sipped. Mirin is sold in most supermarkets, where it is sometimes labeled "rice wine." It will keep indefinitely in a cool pantry.

PANKO Made from wheat flour and honey, these large and flaky Japanese breadcrumbs are most commonly used to coat foods before deep-frying. They create a wonderful crispy texture and maintain it long after frying. Store panko in an airtight container at room temperature for up to a year.

PEPITAS Pepitas, which are pumpkin seeds, are very popular in Mexican cooking; they are sold raw or roasted at many health-food stores and supermarkets. Peptitas can be sprinkled on salads or on a variety of dishes as a garnish, or ground into a paste and stirred into soups and sauces (where they will also act as a thickener). Like all seeds, pepitas should be stored in an airtight container in the refrigerator or freezer and used within several months.

QUINOA There are more than 1,800 varieties of this protein-rich grain in a range of hues; the quinoa (pronounced keen-wah) most readily available in the grocery store is generally the color of toasted nuts. The tiny, bead-shaped grains are cooked like rice but require only half the cooking time and can be used in place of rice in many dishes. Quinoa will keep in the cupboard in a well-sealed container for up to a year.

STAR ANISE This small eight-pointed fruit pod looks like a star and tastes like licorice (or anise seed). It is used to flavor custards, dessert sauces, and sorbets and many savory dishes, including stews and braised meats. Use a clean coffee grinder (or spice mill) to grind star anise to a powder, or break off points from the pod, bundle in cheesecloth, and add to the cooking liquid as foods simmer or braise.

SESAME SEEDS Sesame seeds are available in many colors, but white, tan, and black are the most common. Tan and black seeds are similar in flavor, while the white seeds are more delicate; toasting the seeds intensifies their nutty taste. They have a slightly sweet flavor that enhances bread, pastry, cookies, and other baked goods as well as many savory preparations. Sesame seeds have a high oil content and tend to turn rancid rather quickly; store them in the refrigerator in an airtight container for up to six months, or in the freezer for up to a year.

TAHINI This thick, creamy paste, made from ground and toasted sesame seeds, is a staple in Middle Eastern cooking, where it's used to make hummus and baba ghanoush as well as halvah. Much like natural peanut butter, tahini separates as it sits. To reincorporate the oil, transfer the contents to a large bowl and stir vigorously. Return the unused portion to the original container, and store in the refrigerator for up to three months.

TAMARIND The tamarind is the fruit of a tall evergreen tree native to Africa. Intensely tart, tamarind is essential in Indian cooking, and is an important ingredient in many curry dishes and chutneys (as well as Worcestershire sauce). Try adding it to a marinade, grilling glaze, or any number of richly flavored meat dishes. It is sold in powder, paste, or bottled forms. Powdered tamarind must be dissolved in hot water before use; the other types can be used straight from the container. Store the powder as you would other spices; the paste and bottled forms are more perishable, so check the label for expiration dates. If you cannot find tamarind, substitute lemon juice with a touch of brown sugar for a similar flavor.

TURMERIC Turmeric is the root of a tropical plant related to ginger, and is primarily grown in India and the Caribbean. Because it has a biting, pungent flavor, turmeric is more commonly used for its bright yellow-orange color. Powdered turmeric is widely available; store in a cool, dark place for no more than a year.

WASABI Also known as Japanese horseradish, wasabi is the root of a perennial Asian plant. It has a distinctively sharp flavor and is used as a condiment, often with sushi. Wasabi is available fresh, powdered, or as a paste; the powdered form is easiest to find and keeps indefinitely in a cool, dry place. Powdered wasabi can be reconstituted with water to make a paste. Mix the paste with soy sauce when making a dipping sauce for sushi and dumplings, or with mayonnaise for a spicy sandwich spread.

equipment

SMALL APPLIANCES

BLENDER Even if you reserve it for a few purposes—making smoothies and pureeing soups, for instance—a blender should be powerful (at least 500 watts). Besides being the best tool for giving sauces a velvety consistency, a blender is essential for making margaritas and other blended cocktails. An immersion (or stick) blender is a convenient alternative to a standard blender, especially for pureeing soups and sauces; you use this wand-style tool by inserting it right into the pot.

COFFEE/SPICE GRINDERS Whenever possible, we recommend using freshly ground spices for their superior flavor. Although you can buy a hand-cranked spice grinder (similar to a pepper mill), an electric coffee grinder is a nice alternative. The steel blades can grind whole spices into fine powder in just a few seconds. Buy two: one to use for spices, the other for coffee beans. It's a good idea to clean the bowl after each use; process a few tablespoons of uncooked rice grains or small bits of bread for several seconds.

ELECTRIC JUICER Nothing can chop, shred, and spin the pulp of fruits and vegetables to extract every bit of juice the way an electric juicer can. If you like to make your own vegetable and fruit juices, either to drink or to use in cooking, this tool is a good (and not particularly substantial) investment, especially given the cost of juices purchased from a store.

FOOD PROCESSOR A food processor is an enormous help with many common, time-consuming tasks, including chopping, slicing, and shredding vegetables and other ingredients; grinding nuts; and making purees and breadcrumbs. It also offers an efficient way to mix dough for pastry and bread. Processors range in size, but one with a 7-cup bowl will suffice for most home cooks. Most come equipped with a multipurpose blade and two disks for shredding and slicing. Special dough blades are also available.

ICE CREAM MACHINE There are many versions available in a range of sizes and prices; the compact ones (with a 1.5-quart capacity) have a metal canister that can handily tuck into your freezer (allowing you to make ice cream on the spur of the moment). Choose among old-fashioned hand-cranked machines or the newer electronic ones that allow you to prepare a batch of ice cream, frozen yogurt, gelato, or sorbet in about thirty minutes.

MINI FOOD PROCESSOR (MINI CHOPPER OR MINI PREP) Some kitchen chores, such as chopping nuts and mincing herbs, do not require the power or heft of the standard-size processor. A 3-cup version is the perfect size for making small batches of sauces, spreads, pesto, and dips.

MIXERS A sturdy standing mixer with paddle, whisk, and dough-hook attachments is a must for the avid baker. You can use it to mix cake batters and cookie dough, whip buttercream and other frostings, and even blend and knead bread dough. A hand mixer is a convenient alternative for some easy tasks, like whipping cream or egg whites.

POTS AND PANS

Every kitchen should have these essential items: a 10-inch skillet, a 2-quart saucepan, a 4-quart saucepan, and a large (8-quart) stockpot. A roasting pan is also necessary for cooking meats, poultry, fish, and vegetables; look for a pan with a fitted rack. A nonstick 10-inch skillet is perfect for making omelets, a covered sauté pan for braising meat. Always look for thick, heavy pans, as they tend to be durable and the best distributors of heat. Those made of aluminum (preferably anodized to make them harder) or stainless steel are good options for everyday use.

As your needs expand, you may want to add some of the following pieces.

DOUBLE BOILER A double boiler, essentially two pans in one, provides gentle, indirect heat: The bottom pan holds simmering water, which becomes the heat source for the top pan. (You can improvise by setting an appropriately sized heatproof mixing bowl over a pot of simmering water.) Do not allow the water to touch the bottom of the top pot (or bowl), or the mixture may scorch. A double boiler is often preferred when melting chocolate or preparing custards and delicate cream sauces.

DUTCH OVEN The shape and design of this heavy pot is ideal for long, slow cooking methods, such as braising. The thick bottom and sides evenly distribute heat and prevent hot spots; a tight-fitting lid traps in moisture. A 5- to 6-quart Dutch oven is best for braising meats and vegetables as well as making stews, casseroles, and pot roasts. Dutch ovens are ovenproof, so you can start by browning meat and other ingredients on the stove, then cover and transfer to the oven for even cooking.

GRILL PAN Since they are used on top of the stove, these pans are a practical substitute for an outdoor grill. During cooking, the raised ridges give foods the characteristic grill marks (preheat the pan until very hot); they also allow the fat to drip below the food as it cooks. If you buy a cast-iron pan, be sure to season it before the first use; after that, avoid washing with soap, as it will remove the seasoned finish.

WOK Originally from China, the wok is designed to cook food rapidly, its round-bottomed shape evenly spreading heat across its surface. Besides being especially suited for stir-frying, the wok can be used for steaming, deep-frying, and making stews.

TOOLS AND GADGETS

CITRUS REAMER Using an old-fashioned wooden reamer is a great way to quickly juice lemons and limes. The ridged, teardrop-shaped head is about the size of an egg and has a pointed tip that penetrates the fruit. To extract the most juice possible, roll the fruit on a work surface to soften it before halving, and then twist the reamer back and forth into the flesh, over a bowl. Strain the juice before using.

COLANDER A colander is invaluable for draining pasta and vegetables. Most are footed, so they can stand in the sink, and have handles for easy transport. They come in many sizes, and are made of plastic, stainless steel, or porcelain ceramic.

CUTTING BOARDS Whether you prefer plastic or wood boards, you may want to consider buying at least two to avoid cross-contamination: use one for raw meat and another for produce. It's also helpful to have one large and one small board. To keep boards from slipping as you work, place a damp paper towel underneath.

FOOD MILL Although you can use a food processor or blender to puree food, a food mill gives you greater control over the texture. Most models have three interchangeable disks, each perforated with fine, medium, or coarse holes for making purees of different thickness. Food mills also strain out seeds, skins, and other fibrous bits, so they are especially helpful for making applesauce as well as the smoothest sauces and soups. Fitted with the coarse disk, the food mill will produce mashed potatoes that are wonderfully fluffy.

GRATERS

box grater A box grater is versatile and convenient. Use it for grating cheese, citrus zest, raw fruits and vegetables, and whole nutmeg. Three sides offer different-size holes for grating; the slicing blades on the fourth side create thin, uniform pieces.

citrus zester This tool is designed to remove only the flavorful outer zest from citrus fruit in long, thin strips, leaving the bitter white pith behind. Use it to make colorful garnishes from carrots, cucumbers, beets, and other vegetables, too.

rasp-style grater The tiny, razorlike holes of this ruler-shaped grater (Microplane is one brand) make quick, efficient work of removing the outer zest of whole fruit; the unique design creates the finest, fluffiest zest. This tool can also be used to grate chocolate, whole nutmeg, and hard cheeses.

KNIVES If properly cared for, good knives will last a lifetime. Before buying one, try it out; a knife should feel like an extension of your hand, the blade and the handle balanced. Look for knives made of carbon or stainless steel. Always wash and dry knives by hand, and store them carefully, preferably in a drawer tray with slits that isolate each blade, or in a felt-lined drawer that is wide enough to accommodate the width of each knife. Be sure to use a steel regularly to hone the blade's edges, and a stone every few months to sharpen it. Although it seems there is a knife for every job, a basic set of the following five knives (plus kitchen shears) are really all you need.

boning knife The narrow blade of a 5- to 6-inch boning knife can reach between meat and bones, allowing you to easily trim off fat, tendons, and cartilage. A stiff blade is good for boning cuts of beef; a flexible one is better for poultry.

chef's knife The broad, substantial blade with a curved bottom is specially designed to be rocked back and forth. Although often considered an all-purpose knife, it is ideally suited for chopping and slicing firm vegetables and mincing (or cutting into fine julienne) delicate herbs without bruising. Use the flat side of the blade to smash garlic cloves (for easy peeling), to crush herbs, or to crack peppercorns and other whole spices. Chef's knives are available with either an 8- or 10-inch blade; choose the one you are comfortable working with.

kitchen shears Use shears when a knife won't do, such as for snipping herbs, trimming vegetables, and cutting through the twine of a trussed bird.

paring knife With a 3-inch or shorter blade, this knife is flexible enough to handle small jobs, such as trimming, coring, and peeling.

serrated knife Also called a bread knife, a serrated knife has a scalloped blade (or serrated edge) that can cut through foods that are hard and crisp on the outside and tender inside (such as bread). Using a sawing motion allows you to cut soft fruits and vegetables, such as peaches and tomatoes, as well as cakes and delicate pastries, which might otherwise be crushed or torn by the pressure of a slicing knife. This is also the knife to use for chopping bar chocolate. Be sure to buy a knife with at least an 8-inch blade, or longer if you like larger loaves of bread.

slicing knife Marked by its long, flexible blade, a slicing knife is perfectly designed for carving roasts, evenly slicing meat and poultry, and filleting fish.

MANDOLINE This tool makes it possible to quickly and easily slice vegetables and potatoes paper thin; it can also be adjusted to create julienne or waffle-patterned pieces. If you do a lot of slicing, you may want to invest in a high-quality stainless-steel French model. Otherwise, look for the plastic Japanese mandoline (such as the Benriner), which is significantly smaller and less expensive, making it convenient for the home kitchen.

MEASURING CUPS AND SPOONS These are basics that each kitchen needs: a glass measuring cup for liquids (or a few in different sizes); a nesting set of cups for dry measures; and a nesting set of spoons. Stainless steel is a good choice for nesting cups and spoons, as it is long lasting and easy to clean.

MEAT MALLET (OR MEAT POUNDER) The waffled side is used for tenderizing beef; the flat side, for pounding and flattening cuts of meat and poultry, such as when making medallions or paillards.

MELON BALLER This simple tool can do more than scoop a melon into uniform balls. Use it to seed a halved cucumber or core a halved apple or pear; when making hors d'oeuvres, use it to hollow out cherry tomatoes or form soft cheese into little orbs.

MIXING BOWLS A set of wide stainless-steel nesting bowls will be able to handle almost any task in the kitchen. Those with a generous width are helpful for prepping, folding, and whipping. Get at least five different sizes so you can do more than one job at a time.

PIZZA PEEL This shovel-like flat wooden board with tapered edges and a long handle is used to slip pizza in and out of a hot oven and onto a pizza stone. When the peel is lightly dusted with semolina or cornmeal, the pizza may be formed directly on it.

PIZZA STONE Essentially a heavy round or square slab of stone, this simple piece of equipment can dramatically improve the quality of home-baked breads and pizza crusts. When bread is placed directly on the stone, heat is distributed evenly, from the bottom; this is essential for heating the dough quickly and encouraging a light, airy loaf. The porous texture helps absorb excess moisture, creating very crisp crusts. To use the stone, set it on the lowest shelf, then preheat the oven with the stone in place. Pizza stones vary in size, so be sure to measure the width and depth of your oven rack before purchasing one.

PIZZA WHEEL Besides being the perfect tool for slicing through pizza and flatbreads, a pizza wheel can be used to cut pie or pastry dough into strips or other shapes and to trim the edges of rolled-out pie or cookie dough. It is also great for cutting homemade pasta dough to make ravioli.

SIEVES Sieves are available in fine, medium, and coarse mesh, as well as in several sizes, so you may want to buy an assortment. Use a fine-meshed sieve for sifting dry ingredients and dusting cakes and other sweets with cocoa or confectioners' sugar; use others for straining soups or sauces.

SPATULAS Silicone spatulas are great for folding cake batters or transferring them from bowl to baking pan. They are heatproof up to 800° F., won't pick up or impart flavors from other foods, and are safe to use on nonstick pots and pans. A set of three (1-, 2-, and 3-inch) silicone spatulas is ideal. Metal spatulas are useful for other purposes: Choose at least one thin, flexible spatula for flipping pancakes or patties and removing cookies from baking sheets; a long, wide spatula is ideal for lifting fish out of a pan or for transferring a cake to and from a turntable or stand. Offset spatulas, which have angled handles for easy maneuvering, are good for icing cakes and spreading batters in pans.

STEAMERS Collapsible metal baskets are fine for steaming a batch of vegetables. The larger, 10-inch baskets will allow vegetables enough room to cook evenly, without becoming soggy.

Because they can be stacked, Chinese bamboo steamers are terrific for steaming different types of food at one time. Before using, soak a new bamboo steamer for at least 20 minutes in cool water to rid it of its bamboo odor. To prevent the food from sticking to the bamboo during cooking, line the basket with lettuce leaves or a ceramic plate.

THERMOMETERS

candy This is an indispensable tool for making candy, syrup, jams, and jellies. Choose a model that is easy to read, with an adjustable clip on the back for use with pans of different depths. Since it measures temperatures up to 400°F, a candy thermometer can generally be used for deep frying (when the oil needs to be maintained at 350°F), but we recommend buying a separate one for each purpose.

meat A meat thermometer allows you to determine whether a roast is ready to come out of the oven, without having to cut into the meat and lose precious juices. There are several models: some are inserted into the meat before it goes into the oven; others, called instant-read or rapid-response thermometers, are inserted near the end of cooking time (resulting in fewer juices being lost).

TONGS Kitchen tongs enable you to grasp foods that might otherwise slip off a spatula or spoon. They are ideal for turning meat and chicken when browning or roasting, lifting vegetables out of boiling water, and for cooking on the grill.

VEGETABLE PEELER A U-shaped (or harp-shaped) peeler has a wide blade that can tackle even thick-skinned produce, such as butternut squash and fresh ginger. Besides peeling fruit (even citrus) and vegetables, use it to shave cheese, cut zucchini and cucumbers into ribbons, and make chocolate curls.

WHISKS These multitasking tools handle myriad tasks, including beating egg whites, making roux, and stirring together dry ingredients when preparing batters and dough. The most versatile whisk measures from 3 to 3½ inches across at the widest point and is more elongated than a balloon whisk. A small whisk (8 inches long and about 1½ inches at its widest point) is handy for mixing glazes, marinades, and vinaigrettes; a flat whisk (12 inches long) reaches into the corners of pans to keep custards and puddings from scorching during cooking.

WOODEN SPOONS Though they come in many sizes and shapes, you really need just two wooden spoons. They should have long handles for stirring all the way to the bottom of deep pots. Reserve one for savory, the other for sweet. You might also want to buy two flat wooden spoons for scraping across the bottom of pans when cooking custards and thick sauces; those with angled edges will reach into the corners.

BAKING EQUIPMENT

BAKING SHEETS There are two basic types of baking sheets: rimmed baking sheets (also called jelly-roll pans or sheet pans) and baking sheets that are either flat or have a raised lip (also called cookie sheets). For both types, look for ones made of heavy-duty aluminum; they won't warp and buckle over time and will ensure even cooking. Large ones can be more efficient than smaller sheets, but make sure they are at least two inches smaller than the inside of your oven to allow proper air circulation. There's no need to buy sheets with nonstick coating; line them with parchment paper or a baking mat such as Silpat instead. Use rimmed baking sheets for items such as nuts, which can easily roll off when sliding the pan in and out of the oven, or for food that releases juices. Flat baking sheets allow cookies to brown more evenly. If you like cookies that are crisp, avoid insulated sheets.

BENCH SCRAPER If you are a frequent baker, you will reach for this tool again and again. When rolling out pie dough, run the flat edge under the edges of the dough prevent sticking. When kneading bread dough, use it to loosen the bits of dough from the surface. Use the scraper to neatly divide mounds of dough in half, such as when making pâte brisée, or into uniform triangles, as when making scones.

BOWL SCRAPER With its rounded edge, this inexpensive plastic tool is designed to scrape dough and batter from mixing bowls when transferring them to a work surface or baking pan.

BUNDT PAN The edges of this ring-shaped pan make distinguished pound cakes and coffee cakes. Choose one made of professional-grade aluminum.

CAKE PANS It's a good idea to have a variety of shapes and sizes on hand. A standard 9-inch (2-inch deep) round cake pan is compatible with most recipes for layer cakes (buy two); there are also "professional" cake pans that are 3 inches deep. An 8- or 9-inch square pan will handle brownies and other bar cookies, as well as some cakes. A 13 × 9-inch pan is a must for sheet cakes (and can also accommodate lasagna and other savory dishes).

MUFFIN TINS If you enjoy baking muffins and cupcakes, you'll want to have a combination of sizes: two or three standard 12-cup pans, two jumbo pans, and two mini muffin pans.

NONSTICK BAKING MATS Made of rubberized silicone, these mats (Silpat is a common brand) are great for baking items such as cookies or meringues that might stick to an unlined cookie sheet. They are well worth the initial cost, since, unlike parchment paper, they are extremely long lasting, and can be used over and over. Silicone mats can withstand extremely high oven temperatures and are easy to clean. Don't put the mats in the dishwasher; wipe them with a sponge and dry them flat so they retain their shape.

OFFSET SPATULA The handle of this spatula is set at an angle so your hand is raised away from the work surface, making for more even spreading of frostings and batters, and easier flipping of crêpes and blini. An offset spatula with a 4-inch blade is a good multipurpose size; smaller ones are better for more delicate jobs, such as decorating cupcakes and cookies.

PARCHMENT PAPER Naturally nonstick, parchment is ideal for lining baking sheets and pans. The baked goods will be easy to remove and the pans easy to clean. Roll a small piece of parchment into a cone, snip the pointed tip, and you have a disposable piping bag for royal icing and melted chocolate.

PASTRY BAG Pastry bags range in size from 8 to 24 inches long. Smaller ones are perfect for decorating cakes and cookies, larger ones for piping dough and batters, as when making puffs or gougeres. The 16-inch bag is a good multipurpose length. Look for reusable vinyl-coated cotton bags, which shouldn't absorb odors and are easy to clean.

PASTRY BRUSHES Two basic pastry brushes, one with nylon bristles, the other with natural, are essential. Durable nylon bristles are best for brushing melted butter on muffin tins and other baking pans; they are also great for brushing glazes and sauces onto meats and vegetables. Natural bristles are softer than nylon; use them to apply glazes to pies, cakes, and tarts. Though not essential, a third brush, reserved and labeled as a "dry brush," is very helpful for sweeping away excess flour from dough when rolling it out as well as excess crumbs from cakes before frosting.

PASTRY TIPS Pastry tips allow you to create decorative toppings on everything from hors d'oeuvres to birthday cakes and holiday cookies. They can be purchased individually or in sets; the sets provide a variety of options as well as a convenient storage case. Most sets also come with a plastic coupler, which has two parts: a piece that fits inside the pastry bag (where the tip usually goes) and a ring that screws on the outside, allowing you to lock the pastry tip in place. The coupler allows you to use the same pastry bag to pipe different decorations.

PIE DISHES Because metals can react with some acidic fruits, your best bet is to buy glass or ceramic pie dishes. A 9-inch pan is the most commonly called for, but 8- or 10-inch ones are versatile options. If you bake frequently, consider buying a deep-dish pan.

RAMEKINS Traditionally used for baking pots de crème and crème brûlées, these small ovenproof dishes also enable you to make individual-size cakes, custards, soufflés, puddings, and frozen mousses. They can help you organize your ingredients as you get started, too; for example, measure spices into one dish, lemon zest into another.

ROLLING PINS There are two types of pins: one with handles on both ends, called a baker's pin, and one without, called a French pin. When choosing a baker's pin, look for one that rotates around an axis attached to the handles (rather than handles that are stationary); those with ball bearings inside roll particularly smoothly. Most baker's pins are made of wood; marble is also a good choice for rolling out pastry dough, since it stays cool. French pins, constructed of solid wood, are lighter and longer than baker's pins. They allow you to distribute pressure evenly, and to roll out large pieces of dough.

ROTATING CAKE STAND A turntable is essential for decorating cakes. It elevates the cake, making it easier to reach and more comfortable to work on. It also allows the cake to rotate as you work, making it easier to apply frosting and pipe decorations.

SOUFFLÉ DISH A 2-quart dish made of porcelain, with straight, ridged sides and a flat bottom, will work for most soufflé recipes. It can also be used for baking casseroles and other savory dishes.

SPRINGFORM PAN Cheesecakes and other dense, moist cakes (such as tortes) call for this type of pan, which features a spring-loaded clamp allowing the side of the pan to be removed when the cake is ready to be unmolded. Invest in a heavy-duty nonreactive pan with a protruding lip, which keeps thin batter from leaking through. (If you are setting the pan in a water bath during cooking, wrap the bottom and side with heavy-duty aluminum foil to prevent water from seeping into the pan.) Because of its removable sides, a springform pan can also double as a tart pan.

TART AND TARTLET PANS These pans have removable bottoms and come in a wide range of sizes; some have fluted edges, others straight. The smaller pans are ideal for hors d'oeuvres as well as individual tarts. Flan rings, essentially bottomless tartlet pans that are set on a baking sheet, can often be used instead.

menus

SIMPLE BUFFET BRUNCH
SERVES 6

yogurt parfaits with blueberries and lemon · 585

granola with flaxseed · 588

wilted baby spinach with crispy shallots · 356

bread pudding with ham, leeks, and cheese · 585

currant scones · 565

PASSOVER SEDER
SERVES 10

matzo ball soup with duck meatballs · 121

apple charoset · 341

brisket with dried fruits · 251

roasted fennel with thyme · 351

mashed potatoes with olive oil · 384

pecan torte · 489

almond macaroons · 540

EASTER LUNCH
SERVES 8 TO 10

caviar and chopped eggs on biscuits · 96

garden and snap pea soup with vidalia
onions · 110

roasted whole leg of lamb with
fresh herb rub · 262

fresh mint jelly · 628

three grain pilaf · 241

flageolet · 344

grilled ramps with asparagus · 369

brandy snaps · 554

blackberry tartlets · 478

CELEBRATING SPRING
SERVES 8

goat cheese and pistachio-stuffed dates · 75

watercress and green bean salad (doubled) · 153

popovers with wild mushroom sauce · 81

citrus-roasted salmon with spring
pea sauce · 310

almond custard cake with
strawberry-rhubarb sauce · 492

MOTHER'S DAY BRUNCH
SERVES 12

mini corn cakes with goat cheese
and pepper jelly · 69

chilled fennel and leek soup · 110

arugula risotto · 244

seared shrimp with lemon and garlic · 315

lemon semifreddo cake · 433

peach tea punch · 608

CINCO DE MAYO PARTY
SERVES 6 TO 8

tortilla chips with classic Mexican
guacamole (doubled) · 621

mango and tomato salsa · 616

chile-cheese tamales · 73

Mexican fiesta soup with roasted tomatillo
and cilantro pesto (doubled) · 111

pastel de tres leches · 511

limeade · 606

white-wine sangria · 612

SPRING

MEZZE PARTY
SERVES 6 TO 8

To complete the menu, buy assorted olives and serve with lavash and pita breads, plus dried fruit for dessert, such as figs and dates, and candy, such as nougat and candied orange peel.

crisped haloumi cheese · 88

dressed feta cheese · 88

eggplant caviar · 629

hummus dip · 92

toasted couscous tabbouleh · 247

lamb kofta with yogurt mint sauce · 67

tomatoes à la greque · 89

rose water sherbet · 427

BACKYARD PICNIC
SERVES 6

buttermilk vichyssoise with watercress · 127

ham and cheese tartines · 206

niçoise tartines with peperonata · 207

roasted cherry tomato tartines · 207

mixed baby lettuces with anchovy vinaigrette · 156

haricots verts with mustard vinaigrette · 357

strawberry tartlets · 464

WEEKEND ITALIAN DINNER FOR FRIENDS
SERVES 6

marinated olives with oregano and fennel seeds · 84

potato foccacia · 573

cioppino · 116

romaine salad with prosciutto crisps · 157

chocolate-espresso mascarpone puddings · 438

VEGETARIAN SPRING SUPPER
SERVES 8

green salad with toasted walnuts, walnut oil, and green beans · 149

grilled mushroom burgers with white bean puree (doubled) · 201

fingerling potato salad with sugar snap peas · 170

rhubarb and strawberry ice cream · 418

lemon poppyseed cookies · 538

AFTERNOON TEA
SERVES 12

dried apricot and sage scones (doubled) · 565

cucumber and smoked salmon "sandwiches" · 98

almond-crusted curry chicken salad tea sandwiches · 101

mozzarella, prosciutto, and pesto butter tea sandwiches · 102

smoked duck and chutney butter tea sandwiches · 103

walnut shortbread · 544

lemon-blueberry petits fours · 547

SUMMER

SUMMER

ASIAN HORS D'OEUVRES PARTY
SERVES 10 TO 12

spicy seared scallops canapés · 66

vietnamese summer rolls with sweet and sour
dipping sauce · 82

pork and mango rolls · 96

asian mini crab cakes · 85

lettuce bundles with spicy peanut noodles
(doubled) · 99

korean barbecued ribs with pickled greens · 254

VEGETARIAN SUMMER HARVEST BUFFET
SERVES 6

fresh green tart · 213

orecchiette with green tomatoes, caramelized
onions, and corn · 226

farro salad with thinly sliced zucchini, pine nuts,
and lemon zest · 245

multicolored pepper and bean salad with
ricotta salata and herbs · 175

cherry sherbet in tuile bowls · 432

FISH TACO PARTY
SERVES 6 TO 8

Set out the items buffet style, accompanied by
traditional garnishes, including corn tortillas,
cabbage, avocados, jalapeños, radishes,
and sour cream.

grilled mahimahi · 317

beer-battered cod · 317

roasted tomato and chipotle salsa · 635

cucumber relish · 629

spicy pineapple and mint salsa · 625

green rice · 240

saucy black beans · 348

watermelon-tequila refreshers · 610

key lime bars · 541

watermelon ice · 422

LAKESIDE PICNIC
SERVES 6

sparkling fresh lemonade · 607

warm cheese and glazed pecan dip
(halved) · 636

grilled bread with chimichurri · 82

barbecued baby-back ribs · 272

farmstand raw vegetable salad · 157

florence's potato salad · 391

rhubarb-berry crumbles · 403

KABOB PARTY
SERVES 8

barbecued chicken kabobs with potatoes
and summer squash · 285

shrimp kabobs with lemon wedges
and cilantro · 320

curried lamb kabobs with cherry tomatoes
and red onions · 265

brine-cured pork kabobs with jalapeños
and pineapple · 269

tomato and corn tabbouleh salad · 176

lemon aïoli · 628

grilled bread with chimichurri · 82

coconut ice milk · 427

TUSCAN SUPPER
SERVES 6 TO 8

classic garlic bruschetta · 85

spaghetti with garden vegetables · 220

trout with rosemary and white beans · 306

grilled sausage with arugula pesto · 268

mixed mushroom salad · 167

zuppa inglese with chocolate sauce · 447

AUTUMN

THANKSGIVING WITH ITALIAN FLAVORS
SERVES 12

polenta squares with prosciutto · 80

mushroom and celery salad with
parmesan cheese · 152

perfect roasted turkey
(without the stuffing) · 290

chestnut and sausage stuffing · 379

mashed squash and potatoes with amaretti · 384

braised escarole with currants · 370

savory cranberry jelly · 621

chocolate-almond-marsala cookies · 537

cranberry tart with crème fraîche
whipped cream · 457

pumpkin and ricotta crostata · 459

PACKABLE FALL FEAST
SERVES 6

roasted cauliflower and manchego
hand pies · 100

pear and autumn-vegetable soup · 143

pan-fried potato and fontina frittata · 600

roasted chicken salad with
sour cream dressing · 184

mini pear and blueberry spice cakes · 499

apple pie–spiced cider · 614

AUTUMN HARVEST DINNER
SERVES 10 TO 12

bruschetta with roasted peppers and
herbed ricotta · 85

molasses-glazed grilled pork loin
with roasted plums · 266

chopped beet salad with feta and pecans · 161

autumn greens with apples, radishes,
and cheddar frico · 146

roasted root vegetables with sage
and garlic · 354

concord grape sorbet · 423

ELEGANT SIT-DOWN DINNER FOR TEN
SERVES 10

portofino cocktails · 610

thyme crackers with artisanal cheeses
and apricot mustard · 627

roasted olives · 95

herbed tomato soup · 119

beef tenderloin with mushrooms
and thyme · 257

roasted brussels sprouts with almonds
and honey · 359

mashed potatoes and celery root · 390

organic lettuces with fig vinaigrette · 150

port-caramel chocolate tartlets · 455

honey-roasted salted figs · 416

AUTUMN

PASTA DINNER FOR FOUR
SERVES 4

broccoflower and toasted country bread
with bagna cauda · 68
beet and mâche salad with
aged goat cheese · 154
pasta with scallops, garlic,
grape tomatoes, and parsley · 219
baked pears with vanilla mascarpone · 395

FALL SOUP PARTY
SERVES 8 TO 10

sesame crunch sticks · 91
clam and corn chowder · 132
roasted vegetable soup · 132
mushroom and wild rice soup · 133
ice-cream sandwiches with
molasses-ginger cookies · 430

VEGETARIAN DINNER
SERVES 6 TO 8

cauliflower soup with
toasted pumpkinseeds · 125
butternut squash ravioli with
fried sage leaves (doubled) · 230
buttermilk-leek galette · 213
roasted parsnip, celery heart, and apple salad
with hazelnut vinaigrette · 150
pear stracciatella ice cream with
chocolate syrup · 426
chocolate sandwich cookies · 552

AUTUMN PIE PARTY
SERVES 10

For this potluck-style party, assign a pie
to each of your guests.

pumpkin-pecan pie · 472
buttermilk pie · 464
pear-fig-walnut pie · 458
apple pie with cheddar crust · 460
crisp coconut and chocolate pie · 472
shoofly pie · 456
plum galette · 473
peanut butter tart · 479
apple pie–spiced cider · 614

STEAKHOUSE DINNER
SERVES 4

iceberg lettuce with blue cheese dressing
and toasted almonds · 156
grilled marinated strip steak with scallions · 253
the best onion rings · 364
spinach soufflé · 367
sour cream–thyme rolls · 563
sunken chocolate cakes with
coffee ice cream · 513

WINTER

A CHILI BUFFET
SERVES 10

chili con carne · 112

smoky pinto beans · 364

crisp romaine salad · 150

chunky peanut, chocolate, and
cinnamon cookies · 550

ALL-DAY OPEN HOUSE
SERVES 8 TO 10

honeydew fizzes · 611

cheese balls three ways · 74

maple-glazed smoked vermont ham · 267

black-eyed pea and jalapeño salad
(doubled) · 171

collard greens with bacon · 351

brown sugar cornbread · 561

julia dunlinson's potato griddle scones · 573

cornmeal biscotti with dates and almonds · 540

FESTIVE HOLIDAY COCKTAIL PARTY
SERVES 8 TO 10

chicken liver pâté · 73

fruits de mer platter · 76

ham and gruyère thumbprints · 84

asian mini crab cakes · 85

parmesan-dusted meatballs · 95

smoky cashews · 106

mini chicken b'steeyas · 86

palmiers · 527

cranberry, tangerine, and pomegranate
champagne punch · 609

grapefruit sparkler · 610

NEW YEAR'S EVE DINNER
SERVES 6 TO 8

spicy seared scallop canapés · 66

chicken liver pâté · 73

red and golden beet cheese tart · 212

roasted duck breasts with wild mushroom
stuffing and red wine sauce · 299

tarragon green beans · 349

glazed baby turnips and cipollini onions · 345

mixed green salad with date-walnut
vinaigrette · 155

blood-orange pavlovas with grand marnier · 394

cream cheese–walnut cookies · 537

VALENTINE'S DINNER
SERVES 2

roasted carrot soup · 124

haricots verts with mustard vinaigrette · 357

crimson couscous · 245

spice-crusted leg of lamb with herb oil · 259

baked pears with vanilla mascarpone · 395

SUNDAY NIGHT SUPPER
SERVES 6

arugula and radicchio with
parmesan shavings · 154

buttermilk-onion pull-apart rolls · 562

pancetta-wrapped pork roast · 267

quick pear chutney · 625

cauliflower puree · 361

prune tart · 466

white-wine sangria PAGE 612

asian mini crab cakes PAGE 85

spicy seared scallop canapés PAGE 66

ed red lentil soup with crispy fried ginger PAGE 131

soba noodles with tofu, avocado, and snow peas PAGE 218

chilled asian chicken soup PAGE 116

asian pear salad PAGE 156

spicy chicken salad in lettuce cups PAGE 182

thai beef salad PAGE 180

red and golden beet cheese tart PAGE 212

(opposite) scallion tart PAGE 87

lighter chicken potpie PAGE 214

(opposite) shrimp with kale and white beans baked in parchment PAGE 309

spicy squash pasta PAGE 237 · *(opposite) gratinéed macaroni and cheese with tomatoes* PAGE 227

rice noodles with chinese broccoli and
shiitake mushrooms PAGE 228

(opposite) korean barbecued ribs
with pickled greens PAGE 254

46

spice-cured turkey PAGE 296

starters

....

asparagus timbale

SERVES 6 TO 8

You will need a metal brioche pan that measures 8 inches across the top and 3½ inches at the base. Be sure to fit the plastic wrap into the curves, smoothing it as much as possible before filling.

- 1 teaspoon coarse salt, plus more for cooking water
- 10 ounces medium asparagus, tough ends trimmed
- ½ cup defrosted frozen spinach (about 4 ounces)
- 1 tablespoon unsalted butter
- ½ cup chopped onion
- 1 small garlic clove, chopped
- 5 large eggs
- ⅛ teaspoon freshly ground pepper
- ¼ teaspoon freshly ground nutmeg
- 1 cup heavy cream
- ½ cup mâche or field greens (optional)

1. Preheat the oven to 325° F. Line a 9 × 13-inch baking pan with a kitchen towel. Line the brioche pan with plastic wrap.

2. Prepare an ice bath; set aside. Bring a medium pot of water to boil, and add salt. Add the asparagus, and cook just until tender and bright green, 1 to 2 minutes. Using a slotted spoon, transfer the asparagus to the ice bath. Drain, and set aside. Add the spinach to the boiling water, and cook 4 minutes. Transfer to a colander to drain; set aside.

3. In a small skillet, melt the butter over medium-low heat. Add the chopped onion and garlic; sauté, stirring frequently, until the onion is softened and just starting to color, 6 to 8 minutes. Remove from heat.

4. Bring a large pot of water to a boil. Cut the asparagus spears in half crosswise. Slice the bottom ends in half lengthwise, and then cut them crosswise into thin half-moons; set aside. In the bowl of a food processor fitted with the metal blade, combine the asparagus tops, reserved spinach, and onion mixture. Process until very smooth, about 5 minutes, stopping to scrape down the sides as necessary. Transfer to a large bowl. Add the eggs, salt, pepper, and nutmeg; whisk to combine. Set aside.

5. In a small saucepan over medium heat, heat the cream until bubbles form around the edges and it starts to steam, about 2 minutes. Remove from heat. Whisking constantly, slowly add the cream to the egg mixture. Stir in the reserved sliced asparagus. Pour the custard into the lined brioche pan, and place it in the lined baking pan. Carefully pour the hot water into the baking pan until it reaches halfway up the sides of the brioche pan.

6. Bake until the center is firm when gently touched with your finger, about 65 minutes. Transfer the brioche pan to a wire rack; let cool 5 minutes. Carefully invert the pan onto a serving platter, and gently lift the pan to remove. Slice into wedges; serve garnished with greens, if desired.

spicy seared scallop canapés

MAKES 48

- 6 tablespoons all-purpose flour
- 1½ teaspoons cayenne pepper, or more to taste
- 1 tablespoon ground cumin
- 1 tablespoon ground coriander
- 1½ teaspoons coarse salt
- ¾ teaspoon ground cardamom
- 24 sea scallops (about 1½ pounds), halved
- 1 12-inch-long daikon radish, peeled and cut into 48 ¼-inch-thick rounds
- 5 romaine lettuce leaves, very thinly sliced
  Olive oil cooking spray

1. Combine the flour, cayenne pepper, cumin, coriander, salt, and cardamom in a small bowl. Dip each halved scallop into the flour mixture to coat.

2. Place the daikon rounds on a serving platter. Top each with shredded lettuce; set aside.

3. Heat a medium nonstick skillet over medium heat. Coat with olive oil spray, add the coated scallops, and sear until light golden brown and cooked through, about 1 minute per side. Transfer each seared scallop half to a daikon round. Serve warm or at room temperature.

FIT TO EAT RECIPE PER HALF-SCALLOP: 20 CALORIES, 0 G FAT, 5 MG CHOLESTEROL, 2 G CARBOHYDRATE, 59 MG SODIUM, 3 G PROTEIN, 0 G FIBER

grilled quesadillas

SERVES 12

These quesadillas, filled with mango chutney and cheese, can be assembled ahead of time and wrapped in plastic until ready to grill.

- ¾ cup Major Grey's chutney
- 12 6-inch flour tortillas
- 1½ cups sharp Cheddar cheese, grated on the large holes of a box grater
- ¾ cup sour cream, for garnish
  Tomatillo Salsa (recipe follows)

Preheat the grill. Using a spatula, spread 2 tablespoons of the chutney evenly over 6 tortillas. On each, sprinkle ¼ cup cheese over the chutney; top with the remaining tortillas. Grill until the cheese is melted and the tortillas are slightly golden, about 2 minutes on each side. Using a sharp knife or scissors, cut each tortilla into 6 wedges. Serve with sour cream and salsa.

tomatillo salsa

MAKES 3 CUPS

- 1½ pounds tomatillos, husks removed
- 1 jalapeño pepper
- 1 small yellow onion, finely chopped
- 2 tablespoons red-wine vinegar
- ¼ cup chopped fresh cilantro
  Coarse salt and freshly ground pepper

Preheat the grill. Roast the tomatillos and jalapeño until soft and slightly charred, about 10 minutes. Set aside to cool. Remove the charred skin from the jalapeño. Halve the jalapeño lengthwise; remove the seeds. Chop finely, and set aside. Chop the tomatillos. Place them in a bowl, and add the jalapeño, onion, vinegar, and cilantro. Season with salt and pepper.

lamb kofta

SERVES 6 TO 8

Kofta can be prepared up to 30 minutes before serving; place the patties on a baking sheet, cover with aluminum foil, and keep warm in a 250°F oven.

- 1 pound ground lamb
- 4 teaspoons Spice Mixture (recipe follows)
- 1 teaspoon paprika
- ¼ teaspoon ground cinnamon
- 1 large egg
- ½ onion, grated on the large holes of a box grater (½ cup)
- 1 garlic clove, minced
- ⅓ cup pine nuts, toasted and chopped
- ⅓ cup finely chopped fresh flat-leaf parsley
- 1 teaspoon coarse salt
- 1 tablespoon olive oil
  Yogurt Mint Sauce, for serving (recipe follows)

1. In a large bowl, combine all the ingredients except the oil and yogurt sauce. Mix thoroughly with your hands or a wooden spoon. Form the mixture into 1½-inch balls, and flatten the balls into ovals or football shapes, about ¼ inch thick.

2. In a large nonstick skillet, heat ½ tablespoon of the oil over medium-high heat. Add half the lamb patties. Cook until the first side is golden brown, about 3 minutes; flip the patties, and cook 2 minutes more. Transfer to a paper-towel-lined plate.

3. Wipe the skillet with a paper towel; heat the remaining ½ tablespoon oil. Repeat the process with the remaining lamb patties. Serve warm or at room temperature with yogurt sauce on the side.

spice mixture

MAKES ¼ CUP

- 4½ teaspoons ground coriander
- 4 teaspoons ground cumin
- 1½ teaspoons ground nutmeg
- 1 teaspoon ground cinnamon
- ½ teaspoon ground cloves
- ½ teaspoon cayenne pepper

Mix the spices together in a small bowl or container. Store, tightly sealed, at room temperature up to 3 months.

yogurt mint sauce

MAKES 1 CUP

- 8 ounces plain whole-milk yogurt, preferably Greek-style
- 3 tablespoons finely chopped fresh mint
- 1½ teaspoons fresh lemon juice
- 1 small garlic clove, minced

Combine all ingredients in a small bowl, and stir well to combine. Sauce can be made up to 1 day ahead; store in an airtight container in the refrigerator. Serve chilled or at room temperature.

avocado with grapefruit and sweet-onion salsa

SERVES 4

Cut the avocados just before serving to keep them from discoloring.

- 2 pink grapefruits
- ¼ cup finely chopped sweet onion
- 2 tablespoons chopped fresh cilantro
  Coarse salt
- 2 avocados, cut in half, pitted and peeled

1. Cut off both ends of the grapefruits, and remove the peel, pith, and outer membranes, following the curve of the fruit with a paring knife. Working over a bowl to catch the juices, use the knife to carefully slice between the sections and membranes of each grapefruit to remove the segments. Slice each grapefruit segment into small pieces, and set aside.

2. Place the onion in a small bowl. Squeeze the remaining juice from the grapefruit membranes over the onions, and let stand 20 minutes to soften. Pour off and discard the juice. Add the grapefruit segments and cilantro. Add enough reserved grapefruit juice to moisten. Season with salt. To serve, place 3 to 4 tablespoons salsa on each of the avocado halves.

broccoflower and toasted country bread with bagna cauda

SERVES 4

- 1 head broccoflower, leaves and tough stems discarded
  Coarse salt
- 1 loaf country bread, sliced 1 inch thick
  Bagna Cauda (recipe follows)

1. Preheat the oven to 450° F. Prepare an ice bath; set aside. Fill a stockpot with 1 inch water, and bring to a boil. Place the broccoflower in a steamer insert; sprinkle with salt. Cover tightly, and steam until just tender when pierced with a paring knife, about 10 minutes. Transfer to the ice bath; drain, and pat dry.

2. Arrange the slices of bread on a baking sheet; toast until the edges are brown, 10 to 12 minutes. Turn; toast until the edges of the other side are brown, about 3 minutes. Serve with bagna cauda and broccoflower.

bagna cauda

MAKES ABOUT 1¼ CUPS

Allow this robust dip to mellow overnight in the refrigerator. Before serving, bring it to room temperature, or reheat it gently in a saucepan.

- 2 tablespoons unsalted butter
- 3 large garlic cloves, roughly chopped
- ½ 3-ounce tin anchovy fillets, drained and roughly chopped
- ⅓ cup olive oil
- 1 tablespoon milk

1. Melt the butter in a small sauté pan over medium-low heat. Add the garlic, and cook until softened but not browned, 1 to 2 minutes. Add the anchovies and oil, and reduce heat to low. Cook, stirring occasionally, until the mixture is softened and lightly browned, about 20 minutes. Remove from heat; let cool slightly.

2. Transfer the mixture to the jar of a blender, and add the milk; puree until thick and smooth, about 2 minutes. Transfer to an airtight container, and store in the refrigerator until ready to serve, preferably overnight and up to 4 days.

mini corn cakes with goat cheese and pepper jelly

MAKES 42

An old-fashioned cast-iron skillet with shallow round indentations is ideal for making uniform corn cakes. Since these pans can be rather hard to find, you can use a regular cast-iron skillet and achieve equally lovely results. Pepper jelly adds a bit of sweetness and subtle heat. Look for it at farmer's markets and in gourmet shops.

1½ cups all-purpose flour
¼   cup sugar
½   cup yellow cornmeal
1   tablespoon baking powder
½   teaspoon salt
1¼ cups milk
2   large eggs, room temperature
⅓   cup vegetable oil, plus more for the pan
3   tablespoons unsalted butter, melted
1   15¼-ounce can corn kernels, drained
8   ounces fresh goat cheese, thinly sliced
1   cup pepper jelly

1. Whisk together the flour, sugar, cornmeal, baking powder, and salt in a medium bowl. In a small bowl, whisk together the milk, eggs, oil, and butter until smooth and combined. Add the milk mixture to the flour mixture, and stir just until the batter is combined; fold in corn kernels.

2. Heat a cast-iron skillet over medium heat, and rub it with enough oil to coat the surface. Drop batter by the tablespoon to make 2-inch cakes. Cook until undersides are golden brown, 45 to 60 seconds; turn over, and continue cooking until other sides are browned and cakes are heated through, about 1 minute. To serve, top each cake with a slice of goat cheese and a dollop of pepper jelly.

marinated goat cheese with oregano

SERVES 4 TO 6

5   goat cheese buttons
¼   cup oregano flowers and leaves
1   garlic clove, peeled
1   teaspoon whole black peppercorns
1   cup extra-virgin olive oil

Combine the goat cheese, oregano, garlic, and peppercorns in a jar. Add the olive oil. Store, refrigerated, up to 5 days.

tropical fruit and crab salsa

MAKES 4½ CUPS

You can serve this chunky salsa in seashells as an hors d'oeuvre with cocktails, but it would also be ideal as a dip for Fried Plantain Chips (recipe follows).

1   small onion, cut into ¼-inch dice
1   ripe mango, peeled, pitted, and sliced into ¼-inch dice
1   ripe papaya, peeled, seeded, and cut into ¼-inch dice
¼   pineapple, peeled, cored, and cut into ¼-inch dice
1   jalapeño pepper, seeds and ribs removed, cut into ¼-inch dice
¼   cup fresh lime juice
¼   cup fresh cilantro leaves, chopped
½   pound jumbo lump crabmeat, picked over and rinsed
    Coarse salt
    Freshly ground black pepper

Combine the onion, mango, papaya, pineapple, jalapeño, lime juice, and cilantro in a large bowl. Toss well to combine. Add the crabmeat, and toss gently. Season with salt and pepper. Serve immediately.

fried plantain chips

SERVES 4 TO 6

Select plantains that are firm and green.

- 8 cups vegetable oil
- 4 ripe plantains, peeled and sliced lengthwise

  Coarse salt

In a large, heavy-bottomed saucepan, heat the oil over medium-high heat until it is hot but not smoking, about 350° F on a deep-fry thermometer. Working in batches, fry the plantain slices until they are golden and crisp, 4 to 5 minutes. Transfer to a paper-towel–lined baking sheet; sprinkle with salt while still hot. Serve immediately.

warm red lentil dal with pita chips

SERVES 6

Serve this dal as a dip with pita chips or as a side dish with grilled meats or fish.

- ½ pound red lentils (about 1¼ cups), picked over and rinsed
- 1 14½-ounce can low-sodium chicken broth, or homemade, skimmed of fat
- 1 cup water
- ½ teaspoon turmeric
- 2 tablespoons unsalted butter
- 4 garlic cloves, minced
- 1¼ teaspoons cumin seeds
- ½ teaspoon crushed red pepper flakes
- 1 large tomato, seeded and finely diced
- ¼ cup fresh mint, finely chopped
- ½ teaspoon coarse salt

1. In a medium saucepan, combine the lentils, broth, water, and turmeric. Bring to a boil, reduce heat, and simmer, stirring occasionally, until the lentils are tender, about 20 minutes.

2. Meanwhile, melt the butter in a small saucepan; add the garlic, cumin seeds, and crushed red pepper. Cook, stirring, until fragrant, about 3 minutes.

3. Remove the lentils from heat, and stir in the garlic mixture, diced tomato, mint, and salt. Serve warm.

FIT TO EAT RECIPE PER SERVING: 189 CALORIES, 5 G FAT, 11 MG CHOLESTEROL, 25 G CARBOHYDRATE, 291 MG SODIUM, 12 G PROTEIN, 3 G FIBER

baked oysters with spinach and champagne beurre blanc

MAKES 24

- 2 to 3 cups rock or coarse salt
- 2 dozen oysters, shucked, liquor and bottom shells reserved separately
- 1 cup heavy cream
- 1 cup dry champagne or sparkling wine
- 3 large shallots, minced (about ½ cup)
- ¼ cup white-wine vinegar
- 2½ sticks (1¼ cups) cold unsalted butter, cut into pieces

  Coarse salt and freshly ground white pepper
- 1 pound fresh or 2 10-ounce packages frozen spinach, thawed

  Snipped fresh chives, for garnish

1. Pour the salt into a rimmed baking sheet. Nestle the oyster shells in the salt; set aside.

2. Bring the cream to a boil. Reduce to a simmer; cook until reduced by half. Remove from heat.

3. Meanwhile, place the champagne, shallots, and vinegar in another small saucepan. Bring to a simmer, and cook until the liquid is almost evaporated. Add the reduced cream, and cook for 1 minute.

4. Remove pan from heat, and whisk in butter, 1 piece at a time, adding each piece before the previous one melts completely. (The sauce should not get hot enough to liquefy.) Add ½ cup oyster liquor; season with salt and pepper. Keep warm.

5. If using fresh spinach, rinse it thoroughly several times, and place in a saucepan with just the water that clings to the leaves. Cover the pan, and cook the spinach until bright green and just tender, about 2 minutes. Drain well, and roughly chop. (Squeeze excess moisture from thawed frozen spinach.)

6. Preheat the broiler with the rack set 5 inches from the heat source. Divide the spinach equally among the shells. Top with the shucked oysters. Spoon on enough sauce to cover the oysters, about 1 tablespoon per shell. Place under the broiler until the sauce bubbles and the edges of the oysters start to curl, about 1 minute. Garnish with chives, and serve.

moules poulette (broiled mussels with mushrooms, lemon, and cream)

MAKES ABOUT 36

2 cups dry white wine

2 pounds large mussels, scrubbed and debearded

2 tablespoons unsalted butter

1 tablespoon all-purpose flour

1 cup thinly sliced mushrooms, such as shiitake or oyster (3 ounces)

½ cup heavy cream

Juice of 1 lemon (about 2 tablespoons)

1 teaspoon coarse salt

¼ teaspoon freshly ground pepper

½ cup grated Gruyère cheese (1 ounce)

1. Bring the wine to a simmer in a large skillet over high heat. Add the mussels, and cook, stirring frequently, until they have opened, up to about 5 minutes. Transfer the mussels as they open to a bowl to cool. Strain the cooking liquid through a fine-mesh strainer into a measuring cup, reserving 1 cup liquid and discarding any grit.

2. Discard any mussels that did not open or that have broken shells. Open each mussel, discarding the empty half-shell. Loosen each mussel from its shell, and arrange the mussels on an ovenproof platter or rimmed baking sheet. Cover with plastic wrap; refrigerate while making the sauce.

3. Mash 1 tablespoon butter with the flour until smooth; set aside. Melt the remaining tablespoon butter in a small saucepan over medium heat. Add the mushrooms, and cook until tender, about 4 minutes. Add the reserved mussel liquid, and bring to a boil. Whisk in the butter-and-flour mixture. Whisk in the cream, lemon juice, salt, and pepper. Simmer

until reduced by two-thirds and thickened. Remove the pan from the heat, and keep warm.

4. Heat the broiler. Position the rack 3 to 4 inches from the heat. Remove the mussels from the refrigerator, and spoon sauce over each one until well coated. Sprinkle with grated cheese, and place under the broiler until golden brown, 3 to 4 minutes. Serve immediately.

shrimp summer rolls

MAKES 8

1 pound (about 30) small shrimp, peeled and deveined

8 9-inch-round rice papers

8 large red-leaf lettuce leaves, cut in half lengthwise

1 medium carrot, peeled, cut in matchsticks

1 small daikon radish, peeled, cut into matchsticks

1 red bell pepper, seeds and membranes removed, cut in matchsticks

1 bunch fresh chives, ends trimmed

¼ cup packed mint leaves

Soy Dipping Sauce (recipe follows)

1. Bring a large pot of water to a boil. Reduce to a simmer. Add the cleaned shrimp; poach until pink and cooked through, about 2 minutes. Slice the cooked shrimp in half lengthwise. Set aside.

2. Fill a pan (large enough to hold the rice paper) with hot water. Dampen a clean kitchen towel with water; spread it out on a clean surface. Dip 1 sheet rice paper in the hot water for 5 seconds; transfer to the dampened towel, and smooth out (the wrapper will still feel hard, but it will soften as it sits).

3. Place 4 shrimp halves in a row, cut side up, 2 inches from the bottom edge. Place 2 pieces of lettuce over the shrimp. Top with more shrimp halves, some carrots, daikon, pepper, chives, and mint.

4. Fold the bottom edge of the rice paper over the filling. Continue to roll tightly so the shrimp halves are enclosed but still showing through the rice paper.

5. Place the finished roll on a plate; cover with a damp paper towel. Continue until all the ingredients are used. Serve with dipping sauce.

soy dipping sauce
MAKES ABOUT 1 CUP

- ½ cup soy sauce
- ½ cup rice-wine vinegar
- 2 tablespoons thinly sliced scallions

Combine all ingredients, and serve.

chicken and corn empanadas
MAKES 24

- ¼ cup olive oil
- 1½ cups finely chopped white onion
- 1 teaspoon crushed red pepper flakes
- 1 teaspoon dried oregano, preferably Mexican
  Coarse salt
- ½ cup finely chopped red bell peppers
- ½ cup finely chopped green bell peppers
- 5 small ears corn, kernels removed (about 1½ cups)
- 1 pound boneless, skinless chicken thigh meat, cut into ¼-inch pieces
- 2 tablespoons dry white wine
- 6 ounces Monterey Jack cheese, shredded
  Empanada Dough (recipe follows), chilled
- 1 large egg, lightly beaten with 1 tablespoon water

1. Heat the olive oil in a large skillet over medium heat. Add the onion, red pepper flakes, and oregano. Sauté, stirring occasionally, until lightly browned, about 4 minutes. Season with the salt. Cook for 1 minute. Add the red and green peppers and corn. Cook until the peppers soften and any liquid has evaporated, about 3 minutes.

2. To the same pan, add the chicken and wine, and season with salt. Cook until the chicken is just cooked through and almost all of the liquid has evaporated, about 3 minutes. Refrigerate the filling

until chilled; stir in the cheese. The filling may be prepared and refrigerated, covered, for up to 2 days.

3. Fill a small bowl with cold water. Roll out the dough to a thickness of ⅛ inch. Using a 5-inch-diameter plate as a template, cut out 24 circles. Spoon about ¼ cup chilled filling into the center of a circle, leaving a ½-inch border. Brush the border with cold water. Fold the dough over, stretching it slightly, to form a half-moon shape. Beginning at one end, press the edges together to seal, while trying to remove any air pockets. Press again to ensure the empanadas are well sealed. Using a fork or your fingers, crimp the edges to form a decorative edge. Repeat with the remaining circles and filling.

4. Brush the empanadas with egg wash, and refrigerate at least 30 minutes (but no longer than 1 day). Once filled, the empanadas may be frozen and baked later, without defrosting, in a preheated 350°F oven for 30 to 40 minutes.

5. Preheat the oven to 400°F. Line two baking sheets with parchment paper. Arrange the empanadas on the baking sheets. Bake until puffed and browned and the filling is bubbling inside, 15 to 20 minutes. Serve immediately.

empanada dough
MAKES ENOUGH DOUGH FOR 24 EMPANADAS

- 4 cups all-purpose flour, plus more for kneading
- 2 teaspoons baking powder
- 1 teaspoon coarse salt
- ¾ cup lard
- ¾ cup (1½ sticks) cold unsalted butter, cut into pieces
  Cold water (about ¾ cup)

Combine the flour, baking powder, and salt in a food processor fitted with the steel blade. Add the lard and butter, and pulse until the mixture is the texture of coarse meal. With the processor running, slowly add enough water to form a firm dough. Transfer to a lightly floured work surface, and knead until the dough comes together and becomes smooth. Wrap in plastic wrap, and chill for 1 hour.

chile-cheese tamales

MAKES 16

The tamales can be made through step 4 up to a month in advance and frozen; steam directly from the freezer (cooking time will be longer—follow recipe directions to check for doneness).

- 4 ounces dried corn husks
- 3 cups corn kernels, drained well
- ½ cup (4 ounces) fresh pork lard or solid vegetable shortening
- 2 cups masa harina mixed with 1½ cups hot water, cooled to room temperature
- 2 tablespoons sugar
- 1½ teaspoons coarse salt
- 1½ teaspoons baking powder
- 2 poblano chiles, roasted, seeds and ribs removed, and cut into ¼-inch strips
- 2 cups (8 ounces) grated Monterey Jack cheese

1. Place the husks in a deep saucepan; cover with water. Bring to a boil over high heat. Remove from heat; set a plate over the husks to keep them submerged. Soak 1 hour.

2. Prepare the filling: Place 2 cups corn in the bowl of a food processor; pulse to a medium-coarse puree. Add the lard; pulse five or six times. Add the masa harina, sugar, salt, and baking powder; pulse until combined. Process until the mixture is light, fluffy, and evenly combined, about 1 minute; scrape down the sides of the bowl once or twice.

3. Transfer the mixture to a bowl; stir in the remaining 1 cup corn until combined. Chill the filling until ready to assemble.

4. Remove a large husk from the water; pat dry. Unroll, and tear along the grain to make ¼-inch-wide strips (you need two per tamale). Remove another large piece; pat dry. Place on a work surface, pointed end facing away from you; scoop ¼ cup batter into the middle; spread into a 4-inch square, leaving a 1½-inch border. Place some chile strips down the center; sprinkle with 2 tablespoons cheese. Pick up

the long sides of the husk so the batter encases the filling. Bring the sides together to form a cylinder. Fold the wide end under; tie with a husk strip. Tie the pointed end near batter; fray the exposed husk. Repeat with the remaining husks, batter, poblanos, and cheese.

5. Fill a wok or large skillet with 2 inches water. Line the bottom of a bamboo steamer basket with husks; set the basket in place. Lay the tamales in the steamer over high heat. When steam puffs out, reduce heat to medium. Steam 1 hour 15 minutes; add water to the pan as necessary. Check for doneness by unwrapping a tamale; the mixture should release easily and feel soft. If it sticks, rewrap; steam 15 to 20 minutes more. Remove from heat; let stand 15 minutes; tamales will stay warm about 1 hour.

chicken liver pâté with toast points

MAKES 2 CUPS

- ½ ounce mixed dried wild mushrooms, such as porcini, shiitake, or wood ear
- ⅔ cup boiling water
- 4 tablespoons unsalted butter
- 1 pound fresh chicken livers, tough membranes removed, rinsed and patted dry
- 4 sprigs thyme, leaves roughly chopped
  Coarse salt and freshly ground pepper
- ½ garlic clove, minced
- 1 tablespoon brandy
- 1 slice white bread, crusts removed, cut into cubes
- 1 tablespoon fresh lemon juice
  Toast Points (recipe follows)

1. Place the mushrooms in a bowl; pour the boiling water over. Cover; let steep until soft, about 15 minutes. Strain through a sieve, reserving the liquid. Finely chop the mushrooms.

2. Meanwhile, in a large sauté pan, melt 1 tablespoon of the butter over medium-high heat. Add half the chicken livers and half the thyme; season with salt and pepper. Sauté until the livers are lightly browned on the outside and light pink on the inside, 6 to 7 minutes, adding half the garlic after 5 min-

utes. Remove from heat; stir in ½ tablespoon of the brandy. Transfer the mixture and all juices to a large bowl. Repeat with the remaining livers.

3. Melt 2 tablespoons of the butter in the pan; add the bread cubes and reserved mushroom liquid, scraping up browned bits from the bottom of the pan. Combine with the liver mixture. Working in batches if necessary, transfer the mixture to the bowl of a food processor fitted with the metal blade. Process until smooth, about 3 minutes. Add lemon juice; adjust seasoning. Transfer to a 2-cup dish.

4. Melt the remaining butter in a small saucepan over low heat. Skim off the white foam from the surface; discard. Drizzle the melted butter butter over the pâté; refrigerate, covered, until the butter is set, at least 1 hour and up to 4 days. Bring to room temperature before serving; scrape off the butter, if desired. Serve with toast points.

toast points
SERVES 6

12 slices good-quality white bread, such as brioche, pain de mie, or Pullman

Preheat the oven to 375°F. Slice crusts off bread, and cut each slice into quarters to form four triangles. Place in a single layer on a rimmed baking sheet; toast in oven until bread is golden and beginning to crisp, about 15 minutes, turning once. Transfer to a wire rack; let cool slightly.

cheese balls three ways
MAKES THREE 4-INCH CHEESE BALLS

Make all three flavored balls, or prepare just one or two, adjusting the ingredients accordingly.

base recipe

½ cup (1 stick) unsalted butter, softened

3 packages cream cheese (8 ounces each)

2 tablespoons fresh lemon juice

½ teaspoon Worcestershire sauce

5 dashes hot sauce (such as Tabasco)

½ teaspoon coarse salt

¼ teaspoon freshly ground white pepper

cheddar and cranberry

8 ounces sharp orange Cheddar cheese, finely shredded

2 tablespoons store-bought chutney

¾ cup dried cranberries, finely chopped

Water crackers, for serving

roquefort and walnut

6 ounces Roquefort cheese

1 shallot, minced (about 1 tablespoon)

2 teaspoons brandy (optional)

1 cup toasted walnuts, coarsely chopped

Vegetable chips (such as Terra Chips Sweets and Beets), for serving

goat cheese and scallions

8 ounces goat cheese

2 tablespoons finely chopped scallions

⅓ cup finely chopped fresh curly-leaf parsley

1 English cucumber, cut into ⅛-inch-thick slices, for serving

1. Put the butter, cream cheese, lemon juice, Worcestershire sauce, hot sauce, salt, and pepper into the bowl of an electric mixer fitted with the paddle attachment; mix on medium speed until combined. Divide equally among 3 medium bowls.

2. Stir the Cheddar and chutney with the base mixture in the first bowl. Form into a ball. If not using immediately, refrigerate up to 3 days or freeze up to 1 month. Roll the cheese ball in the cranberries to coat before serving. Serve with crackers.

3. Stir the Roquefort and shallot with the base mixture in the second bowl; add brandy, if desired. Form into a ball. If not using immediately, refrigerate up to 3 days; freeze up to 1 month. Roll in the walnuts to coat before serving. Serve with chips.

4. Stir the goat cheese and scallions with the base mixture in the remaining bowl. Form into a ball. If not using immediately, refrigerate up to 3 days or freeze up to 1 month. Roll in the parsley to coat before serving. Serve with cucumber slices.

lemon-parsley gougères
MAKES 60

6 tablespoons unsalted butter

1 teaspoon coarse salt

¼ teaspoon cayenne pepper

¾ cup all-purpose flour

5 large eggs

Zest of 1 lemon

3 scallions, finely chopped

3 tablespoons finely chopped fresh curly-
leaf parsley

1. Bring 1 cup water and the butter, salt, and cayenne to a boil in a heavy 4-quart saucepan; boil until the butter has melted. Remove from heat; stir in the flour. Return to the burner; cook, stirring, until the mixture comes together and pulls away from the pan, about 2 minutes more.

2. Remove from heat. Using a wooden spoon, beat in 4 of the eggs, 1 at a time, until they are incorporated and smooth. Stir in the lemon zest, scallions, and parsley.

3. Transfer the mixture to a piping bag, and cut a ½-inch opening. Pipe 1-inch rounds onto baking sheets lined with parchment paper. Alternatively, drop rounded teaspoons of batter onto baking sheets lined with parchment. If not using immediately, freeze up to 1 month in airtight containers or resealable plastic bags.

4. Preheat oven to 400°F. Whisk together the remaining egg and 1 teaspoon water in a small bowl; lightly brush on top of each puff. Bake until lightly golden brown, about 20 minutes. Serve immediately.

goat cheese and pistachio-stuffed dates
MAKES 16

You can make the goat cheese filling one day ahead and refrigerate it. These hors d'oeuvres can be assembled several hours before serving. Loosely cover them with plastic wrap, and refrigerate for up to 3 hours. Bring to room temperature before serving.

4 ounces soft goat cheese

3 tablespoons shelled salted pistachios,
toasted and coarsely chopped

1 tablespoon finely chopped fresh chives,
plus more for garnish

Freshly ground pepper

8 plump, soft dried dates (preferably
Medjool), pitted and halved lengthwise

1. Stir together the goat cheese, 2 tablespoons of the pistachios, and the chives in a small bowl until smooth. Season with pepper.

2. Arrange the dates, cut side up, on a platter. Fit a pastry bag with a large round tip, and fill it with the goat cheese mixture. Pipe the mixture onto each date half to cover. (Alternatively, pipe the goat cheese mixture using a resealable plastic bag with 1 inch cut from one corner, or simply spread the mixture on the dates with a butter knife.) Garnish the dates with the remaining tablespoon pistachios and more chives.

fruits de mer platter

SERVES 6 TO 8

Fill a tiered platter with just as much seafood as it can hold comfortably; refrigerate the rest until you are ready to replenish the platter.

for the court bouillon

½ bottle (375 ml) dry white wine
¼ cup coarse salt or sea salt
2 lemons, halved
1 teaspoon paprika
1 teaspoon coriander seeds
1 teaspoon celery seed
3 bay leaves

for the fruits de mer

2 live lobsters (each 1¼ pounds)
6 king crab legs (1¾ pounds total)
2 pounds large shrimp in shells
24 oysters
12 littleneck clams

for serving

   Crushed ice
2 to 4 ounces caviar, such as North American osetra
   Toast Points (page 74)
   Saffron Mayonnaise (recipe follows)
   Classic Cocktail Sauce (recipe follows)
   Mignonette Sauce (recipe follows)
   Lemon wedges

1. Make the court bouillon: Prepare a large ice-water bath. Fill a 3-gallon pot with cold water. Add the wine, salt, lemons, paprika, coriander seeds, celery seed, and bay leaves. Bring to a boil.

2. Cook the seafood: Add the lobsters, head first, to the court bouillon. Cover; return to a boil. Cook 10 minutes. Using tongs, transfer the lobsters to the ice-water bath. Add the crab legs to the court bouillon. Return to a boil; cook 8 minutes. Transfer the lobsters to a plate; immediately add the crab legs to the ice-water bath, adding more ice as needed. Add the shrimp to the court bouillon. Return to a boil; cook until the shrimp are pink and opaque,

about 3 minutes. Add the shrimp to the ice-water bath; let the crab legs and shrimp cool completely. Transfer to a plate.

3. Separate the tails, claws, and knuckles from the lobsters; using kitchen shears or a knife, split the tails lengthwise through the shells, then halve crosswise. Crack the claws and knuckles so the meat can be easily removed (see how-to on page 78). Separate the crab legs at the knuckles. Using kitchen shears, cut away a piece of shell so the meat can be easily removed. Peel and devein the shrimp, leaving the tails intact. Transfer the lobster pieces, crab legs, and shrimp to a rimmed baking sheet; wrap tightly in plastic. Refrigerate until ready to serve, or overnight.

4. Assemble the platter: Just before serving, fill a 3-tiered glass serving stand with crushed ice. Shuck the oysters and clams (see how-to, opposite); set them flat on the bottom tier so the juices do not spill. Arrange the lobsters and shrimp on the middle tier. Put the caviar into a small bowl, and set it in the center of the top tier; arrange the crab legs around the caviar. Serve with toast points, saffron mayonnaise, the cocktail sauce, mignonette sauce, and lemon wedges.

saffron mayonnaise

MAKES ABOUT 1 CUP

You can use store-bought mayonnaise, if you like; skip step 1.

1 large egg
   Pinch of dried mustard
   Coarse salt
½ cup light olive oil
½ cup canola oil
1 tablespoon plus 1 teaspoon fresh lemon juice
¼ teaspoon saffron threads

1. Process the egg, mustard, and ¼ teaspoon salt in a food processor until pale and foamy, about 1½ minutes. Combine the oils; with the machine running, add the oil, drop by drop, through the feed tube until the mixture begins to thicken (about

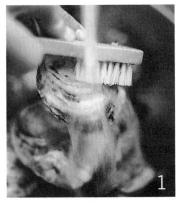

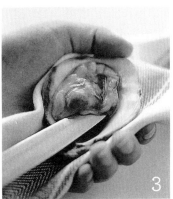

SHUCKING CLAMS AND OYSTERS

The right tools are important: Use a clam knife to shuck clams, and an oyster knife to shuck oysters. Wear work gloves or use a kitchen towel to protect your hands. Open shellfish right before serving, and keep them on ice before and after shucking. Discard any already opened shells.

TO SHUCK OYSTERS (TOP ROW):

1. Wash the oysters with a scrubbing brush.

2. Hold an oyster flat side up; wedge the tip of a knife inside the joint as far as possible. Twist the knife to pry the halves apart.

3. Scrape the meat from the top half; scoop under the oyster to loosen the meat from the bottom.

TO SHUCK CLAMS (BOTTOM ROW):

1. Hold a clam in your palm; wedge the side of the knife between the halves of the shell. Carefully twist the knife to pry the halves apart.

2. Some clams are stubborn—open obstinate shells from the back. Insert the knife at the joint; bang the knife against a hard surface, holding the clam in place with your thumb, until the muscle releases. Turn the clam around, and force the halves apart.

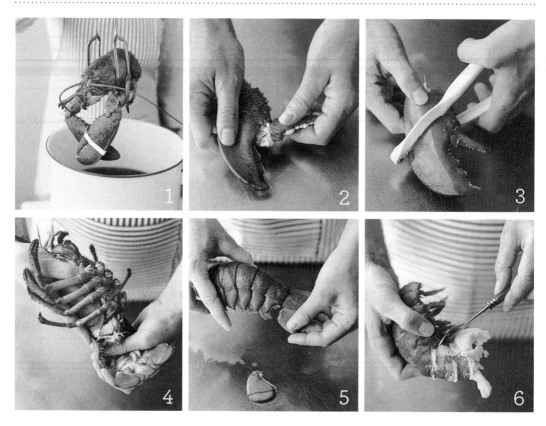

EXTRACTING LOBSTER MEAT

1. Remove the lobster from the pot with tongs; let cool. If you like, snip the tips of the claws and let the liquid drain out. Remove the rubber bands. Twist the claws with their knuckles from the body. Separate the knuckles from the claws. Crack the knuckles open and separate the meat.

2. Grasp the thumb, and bend it back to snap it off.

3. Crack the claw in half; remove the meat.

4. Pull off the legs. Twist the tail from the joint where it meets the body.

5. Pull off the tail fins. Bend the tail backward to crack off the end of the shell.

6. Use your fingers to push the tail meat out the opposite side; remove with a fork.

¼ cup oil; do not stop the machine). Add the remaining oil in a slow, steady stream, processing until incorporated. Gradually add 1 tablespoon of the lemon juice.

2. Grind the saffron with a mortar and pestle. Transfer to a bowl. Add the remaining teaspoon lemon juice; let stand until the liquid turns yellow, 5 minutes. Strain; discard the saffron threads.

3. Put the mayonnaise into a small bowl; drizzle in the saffron liquid, stirring. Season with salt, if desired. Cover; refrigerate until ready to serve, or overnight.

NOTE *The egg in this recipe is not fully cooked. It should not be prepared for pregnant women, babies, young children, the elderly, or anyone whose health is compromised.*

classic cocktail sauce
MAKES ABOUT 1 CUP

If using prepared horseradish, reduce the amount of lemon juice to 1 tablespoon.

- 2 tablespoons grated peeled fresh horseradish (or prepared horseradish)
- 2 tablespoons fresh lemon juice
- ¼ teaspoon coarse salt
- ¾ cup ketchup
- ¼ teaspoon hot sauce (optional)

Stir together the horseradish, lemon juice, and salt in a small bowl. Stir in the ketchup and hot sauce, if desired. Cover; refrigerate until ready to serve, or overnight.

mignonette sauce
MAKES ABOUT 1 CUP

- 1 shallot, finely chopped
- 1½ teaspoons coarsely ground pepper
- ½ cup sherry vinegar
- ½ cup champagne vinegar or white wine vinegar

Stir together the shallot, pepper, and vinegars. Let stand 20 minutes before serving.

thyme-cheddar twists
MAKES 18

- 1 cup milk
- 4 tablespoons sugar
- 2 envelopes active dry yeast (2 scant tablespoons)
- 3 cups all-purpose flour, plus more for dusting
- 1 teaspoon salt
- 8 tablespoons (1 stick) cold unsalted butter, cut into pieces, plus 3 tablespoons unsalted butter, melted
- 3 large egg yolks
  Vegetable oil, for bowl
- 1½ cups coarsely grated sharp white Cheddar cheese (about 4 ounces)
- 2 tablespoons chopped fresh thyme
- 2 teaspoons freshly ground pepper
- 1 large egg beaten with 1 tablespoon water, for egg wash

1. Heat the milk in a small saucepan over medium heat until it registers 110°F on an instant-read thermometer; transfer to a bowl. Stir in 2 tablespoons of the sugar. Sprinkle with yeast; let mixture stand until foamy, about 10 minutes.

2. Process the flour, remaining 2 tablespoons sugar, salt, and butter pieces in a food processor until the mixture resembles coarse meal. Add the milk mixture and the yolks; process until combined. Transfer to a well-oiled bowl; cover with plastic wrap. Refrigerate 4 hours or overnight.

3. Preheat the oven to 375°F. On a lightly floured work surface, roll out the dough to form a 15 × 18-inch rectangle. Brush the surface with melted butter. Sprinkle the dough evenly with cheese, thyme, and pepper.

4. Fold the dough in half horizontally. Roll out to form a 10 × 18-inch rectangle. Cut into 10-inch-long, ½-inch-wide strips.

5. Twist 2 strips around each other; pinch the edges to keep the strips from unraveling. Shape the twist to form a spiral; transfer to a baking sheet lined with parchment paper. Repeat with the remaining strips.

6. Brush the twists with egg wash. Bake until deep golden brown, 20 to 22 minutes.

polenta squares with prosciutto

MAKES 48

Coarse salt

2 cups yellow cornmeal

2 teaspoons extra-virgin olive oil,
   plus more for the pan

6 slices prosciutto, cut into ¼-inch pieces

1 garlic clove, finely chopped

   Freshly ground pepper

6 ounces Taleggio cheese, cut into ½-inch
   cubes (48 pieces)

   Fresh marjoram sprigs, for garnish

1. Bring 7 cups water to a boil in a large saucepan; add 4 teaspoons salt. Whisking constantly, add the cornmeal, a little at a time. Reduce the heat to medium-low; cook, stirring frequently with a wooden spoon, until the polenta pulls away from the sides of the pan and is very thick, about 25 minutes.

2. Heat the oil in a medium skillet over medium-low heat until hot but not smoking. Add the prosciutto and garlic. Cook, stirring, until the prosciutto is slightly crisp, about 5 minutes; stir into the polenta. Season with salt and pepper, if desired.

3. Pour the polenta mixture into a 9 × 13-inch baking pan; smooth with a dampened spatula. Let cool at least 1 hour.

4. If not serving the polenta immediately, cover it with plastic wrap, and refrigerate until ready to use (or overnight).

5. Trim ¼ inch from all sides of the polenta. Cut into 48 squares. Preheat the broiler with the rack 5 inches from the heat. Lightly brush a metal baking pan with oil; heat under the broiler 30 seconds. In batches, broil the squares in the pan, 2 minutes. Place a cheese cube on each square; season with pepper. Broil until the cheese is melted, about 1½ minutes. Garnish with marjoram sprigs.

pita crisps with feta-radish spread

SERVES 4

The thick consistency of Greek yogurt is ideal for this spread. If your grocer doesn't sell it, use another whole-milk yogurt, and drain it for 30 minutes in a fine sieve set over a bowl. You can make the spread one day ahead and refrigerate it (cover with plastic wrap); wait until just before serving to stir in the parsley and radishes.

5 tablespoons extra-virgin olive oil

2 pocket pitas, split open

1 package sheep's-milk feta cheese
   (8 ounces), coarsely chopped

¼ cup plain whole-milk yogurt,
   preferably Greek

2 tablespoons fresh lemon juice

3 tablespoons coarsely chopped fresh
   flat-leaf parsley

4 radishes, quartered and thinly sliced
   (about ½ cup)

1. Preheat the oven to 350° F. Using 2 tablespoons of the oil, brush the insides of the pita rounds. Cut each round into 6 wedges. Arrange the wedges in a single layer on a baking sheet, oiled side up; toast until golden brown and crisp, 7 to 10 minutes.

2. Meanwhile, pulse the feta, yogurt, lemon juice, and remaining 3 tablespoons oil in a food processor just until the mixture is thick and spreadable, about 10 pulses. Transfer to a medium bowl, and stir in the parsley and radishes. Serve with pita crisps.

popovers with wild mushroom sauce

MAKES 12

We used morel mushrooms, a spring variety known for its nutty flavor and pitted flesh, but any wild mushrooms, an assortment, or even cultivated mushrooms will also make a nice sauce. You can prepare the popover batter in advance, and refrigerate it for up to one day. Let it stand at room temperature for 20 minutes before baking. The sauce can also be made one day ahead. Let it cool completely, then refrigerate. Reheat over medium-low heat, adding heavy cream to thin, if necessary. If you have leftovers, keep them in an airtight container for up to one day.

2 cups whole milk

4 large eggs

2 tablespoons unsalted butter, melted, plus
   8 tablespoons (1 stick) unsalted butter

2 cups all-purpose flour

2 teaspoons coarse salt, plus more
   for seasoning

½ cup vegetable oil or vegetable shortening

4 shallots, finely chopped

2 pounds fresh wild mushrooms, such as
   morels, halved, or quartered if large

¾ cup medium-dry sherry

3 cups heavy cream

2 tablespoons finely chopped
   fresh tarragon

   Freshly ground pepper

1. Whisk together the milk, eggs, and melted butter in a medium bowl; set aside. Whisk together the flour and salt in a separate medium bowl. Pour the milk mixture into the flour mixture; whisk until blended. Cover; let the batter stand 1 hour.

2. Preheat the oven to 450°F. Put 2 teaspoons of the oil into each cup of 2 standard 6-cup popover pans or a large (each cup having a 1-cup capacity) 12-cup muffin tin. Place the pans on a rimmed baking sheet. Transfer to the oven; heat the oil in the pans 20 minutes.

3. Pour the batter into the popover cups, filling each two-thirds full. Bake (do not open the oven while popovers cook) 15 minutes. Reduce the oven temperature to 350°F; continue to bake the popovers until well browned and crusty, about 20 minutes more. Invert the popovers to unmold. Transfer to a bowl lined with a clean kitchen towel; cover to keep warm.

4. Meanwhile, heat the remaining 8 tablespoons butter in a large skillet over medium heat. Add the shallots; cook, stirring occasionally, until fragrant, about 2 minutes. Add the mushrooms; cook, stirring occasionally, until golden, about 5 minutes. Add the sherry; cook until the liquid is reduced by half, about 2 minutes. Raise heat to medium-high; add the cream, and bring to a boil, stirring. Reduce heat to low, and simmer 1 minute. Stir in the tarragon, and season with salt and pepper.

5. To serve, place the popovers on plates, and spoon mushroom sauce on top.

prosciutto crostini and fresh figs with gorgonzola

MAKES 20 OF EACH HORS D'OEUVRE

If you can't find lemon thyme, use small, fresh basil leaves instead.

½ baguette

2 tablespoons extra-virgin olive oil

10 ounces Gorgonzola dolce, room
    temperature

¼ pound prosciutto, very thinly sliced and
    torn into bite-size pieces

    Fresh lemon thyme, for garnish

10 fresh figs, halved lengthwise

    Fresh tarragon, for garnish

1. Preheat the broiler. Cut the baguette into 20 slices (each about ¼ inch thick); transfer to a baking sheet. Brush the tops with oil. Broil until golden, 1 to 2 minutes.

2. Let cool, then spoon 1 teaspoon cheese onto each round. Top with prosciutto; garnish with lemon thyme.

3. Spoon about 1 teaspoon cheese onto each fig half; garnish with tarragon.

vietnamese summer rolls

MAKES 12

- 12 8-inch round rice paper wrappers
- 36 large shrimp, boiled until cooked through, peeled, deveined, and halved lengthwise
- 3 ounces thin dried rice stick noodles, prepared per package instructions
- 2 medium carrots, peeled into ribbons
- 4 cups mâche
- 2 cups fresh mint leaves
- 2 cups fresh cilantro leaves
  Sweet and Sour Dipping Sauce (recipe follows)

1. Soak a wrapper in warm water for 30 seconds; immediately lay it flat on a work surface. Lay 6 shrimp halves, cut side up, on the bottom third, leaving a ½-inch border; top with 2 tablespoons each noodles, carrot, mâche, mint, and cilantro.

2. Fold the bottom of the wrapper over the fillings; roll over once, tuck in the sides, and roll. Cut in half; cover with a damp paper towel. Repeat to make remaining rolls. Serve with the dipping sauce.

sweet and sour dipping sauce

MAKES ABOUT ½ CUP

- 1 teaspoon crushed red pepper flakes
- ¼ cup fresh lime juice (about 2 limes)
- 1 tablespoon minced garlic
- 3 tablespoons sugar
- ¼ cup Asian fish sauce (such as nam pla)

Soak the red pepper flakes in the lime juice for 4 minutes. Add the garlic, sugar, and fish sauce; stir until the sugar is dissolved.

grilled bread with chimichurri

SERVES 6

Ciabatta, a long, flat Italian bread, is ideal for this recipe, but you could also use a rustic round loaf; instead of splitting it horizontally, cut 6 1¼-inch-thick slices. You can refrigerate leftover chimichurri in an airtight container for up to 2 days.

- ½ cup plus 2 tablespoons olive oil
- 1 medium onion, thinly sliced
- ½ cup packed fresh flat-leaf parsley leaves
- ½ teaspoon coarse salt
- 2 tablespoons red-wine vinegar
- 2 tablespoons packed fresh cilantro leaves
- 1 tablespoon fresh oregano leaves
- 1 tablespoon fresh lemon juice
- 2 garlic cloves, finely chopped
- ¼ teaspoon freshly ground pepper
- ½ teaspoon ground cumin
- ⅛ teaspoon cayenne pepper
- 1 loaf ciabatta, halved horizontally

1. Heat 1 tablespoon of the oil in a medium skillet over medium heat until hot but not smoking. Add the onion, and stir to coat. Cook, stirring, until softened, 3 to 4 minutes. Reduce heat to low, and continue to cook, stirring occasionally, until golden brown, 7 to 8 minutes more. Let cool.

2. Make the chimichurri: Process the onion, parsley, salt, vinegar, cilantro, oregano, lemon juice, garlic, pepper, cumin, cayenne, and 5 tablespoons of the oil in a food processor until the ingredients are finely chopped and the mixture comes together, about 15 seconds. Set aside.

3. Preheat a grill to medium-high (if using a charcoal grill, the coals are ready when you can hold your hand 5 inches above the grill for just 3 to 4 seconds). Using the remaining ¼ cup oil, brush the cut sides of the bread. Grill, cut side down, without turning, until underside is lightly charred, about 4 minutes. Cut each bread half crosswise into 3 pieces, and spread each piece with chimichurri.

spiked clams and oysters

SERVES 6

Using tequila as a steaming liquid enhances the flavor of the clams and oysters, but it's fine to use water instead. Setting the skillet over a grill gives the dish a touch of smokiness, or you can use your stove turned to medium-high heat.

½ cup tequila

12 littleneck clams (about 1¼ pounds), scrubbed well

12 oysters, such as Malpeque or bluepoint (about 2 pounds), scrubbed well

Chipotle Mayonnaise (recipe follows)

Bloody Mary Sauce (recipe follows)

Lime-Mint Sauce (recipe follows)

1. Preheat a grill to medium-high (if using a charcoal grill, the coals are ready when you can hold your hand 5 inches above the grill for just 3 to 4 seconds). Pour the tequila into a medium cast-iron skillet. Add the clams and oysters; tightly cover the skillet with foil. Transfer the skillet to the grill.

2. Cook the oysters and clams until they open (check frequently after 8 minutes, lifting a corner of the foil with tongs). Using the tongs, transfer the clams and oysters as they open to serving bowls; continue to cook until all the oysters and clams are open, up to 5 minutes more. (Discard any that remain closed.) Serve with chipotle mayonnaise and sauces.

chipotle mayonnaise

MAKES ABOUT 1 CUP

¾ cup mayonnaise

1 tablespoon chipotle chiles in adobo

1 teaspoon fresh lime juice

⅛ teaspoon ground cumin

1 garlic clove

Coarse salt

Process the mayonnaise, chipotles, lime juice, cumin, and garlic in a food processor until smooth. Season with salt. If not serving immediately, refrigerate in an airtight container up to 4 days.

bloody mary sauce

MAKES ABOUT ⅔ CUP

½ pint cherry tomatoes (about 1 cup)

1½ teaspoons Worcestershire sauce

¼ teaspoon hot sauce, such as Tabasco

1½ teaspoons fresh lemon juice

1 small celery stalk, chopped, plus leaves for garnish (optional)

Coarse salt

1½ teaspoons finely grated peeled fresh horseradish, or prepared horseradish to taste

1. Blend the tomatoes, Worcestershire sauce, hot sauce, lemon juice, and celery in a blender until smooth. Transfer the tomato puree to a small saucepan, and season with salt.

2. Cook over medium heat, stirring occasionally, until the puree is reduced slightly, about 8 minutes.

3. Pass the puree through a fine sieve set over a bowl, pressing on the solids to extract the liquid; discard the solids. Stir in the horseradish. (If not serving immediately, refrigerate in an airtight container up to 1 day.) Just before serving, garnish the sauce with celery leaves, if desired.

lime-mint sauce

MAKES 1 CUP

¼ cup fresh lime juice plus 1 tablespoon freshly grated lime zest (2 to 3 limes)

½ cup packed fresh mint leaves

3 tablespoons sugar

3 tablespoons tequila

1. Bring the lime juice, zest, mint, sugar, and ½ cup water to a boil in a small saucepan. Remove from heat; cover, and let steep until completely cooled, 20 to 25 minutes.

2. Pass the lime juice mixture through a fine sieve set over a bowl, pressing on the solids to extract the liquid; discard the solids. (If not serving immediately, refrigerate in an airtight container up to 1 day.) Just before serving, stir in tequila.

oysters with serrano chile, avocado, and cherry tomatoes

SERVES 4

1 dozen fresh oysters, scrubbed, shucked, and left on the half shell

1 serrano chile, very thinly sliced

1 ripe avocado, cut into ¼-inch dice

6 cherry tomatoes, quartered

Arrange the oysters on a bed of crushed ice. Top each with a piece of chile, some avocado, and 2 tomato quarters, and serve.

marinated olives with oregano and fennel seeds

MAKES 3 CUPS

The olives can be prepared three days ahead and refrigerated, covered. Bring to room temperature before serving.

1¼ pounds assorted brine-cured olives (3 cups), such as Alfonso, Gaeta, and Sicilian, rinsed and drained well

3 tablespoons extra-virgin olive oil

1 teaspoon fennel seeds, crushed

2½ tablespoons chopped fresh oregano

1 garlic clove, thinly sliced

Stir together the olives, oil, fennel seeds, oregano, and garlic in a medium bowl. Cover, and let stand at room temperature, stirring occasionally, 1 hour.

ham and gruyère thumbprints

MAKES 36

½ cup (1 stick) unsalted butter, cut into large pieces

½ teaspoon coarse salt

1 cup all-purpose flour

4 large eggs

½ teaspoon freshly ground pepper

½ cup finely chopped or ground Black Forest ham (2 ounces)

1 cup finely shredded Gruyère cheese, plus 36 ½-inch cubes for centers (8 ounces total)

1. Preheat the oven to 400° F. Bring the butter, salt, and 1 cup water to a boil in a large, heavy saucepan over medium heat, stirring occasionally (the butter will melt). Add the flour; stir vigorously until incorporated. Continue to cook, stirring, until the mixture pulls away from the sides and a thin film forms on the bottom of the pan, 1 to 2 minutes. Remove from heat; let cool 5 minutes.

2. Transfer the dough to a large bowl; add the eggs, one at a time, beating with a wooden spoon to incorporate each egg before adding the next, about 2 minutes. Stir in pepper, ham, and shredded cheese.

3. Spoon dough into a pastry bag fitted with a ½-inch star tip. On a baking sheet lined with a Silpat baking mat or parchment paper, pipe 1½-inch-wide rosettes, 1 inch apart. Make a deep indentation in the center of each with your thumb (dampen the thumb to keep it from sticking to the dough). Bake until crisp and golden, 25 to 30 minutes. Transfer thumbprints to a wire rack to cool completely. Press a cheese cube into center of each.

4. Place on clean baking sheets; freeze (uncovered) until firm, about 1 hour. Transfer to an airtight container; freeze until ready to use, up to 6 weeks.

5. To serve, preheat the oven to 425° F. Place the thumbprints on ungreased baking sheets; bake until heated through and cheese is melted, 10 to 14 minutes. Serve warm.

asian mini crab cakes

MAKES ABOUT 24

- 8 ounces jumbo lump crabmeat, picked over and rinsed
- ¼ cup mayonnaise, plus 3 tablespoons for garnish
- 2 scallions, trimmed and finely chopped
- 2 tablespoons soy sauce
- 2 teaspoons wasabi paste
- 1 teaspoon finely grated lime zest
- ½ cup plus 2 tablespoons plain bread crumbs
- ½ cup all-purpose flour
- ½ teaspoon coarse salt
- ½ teaspoon freshly ground pepper
- 2 large eggs
- ¼ cup sesame seeds
- ⅔ cup vegetable oil, plus more if needed
- 1 English cucumber, for garnish
- ½ cup drained pickled ginger, for garnish

1. Flake the crabmeat with a fork in a medium bowl; stir in ¼ cup of the mayonnaise and the scallions, the soy sauce, ½ teaspoon of the wasabi, and the zest. Stir in 2 tablespoons of the bread crumbs. Cover with plastic wrap; chill 1 hour.

2. In a medium bowl, whisk the flour, salt, and pepper; set aside. In a small bowl, beat the eggs with 1 tablespoon water; set aside. In a shallow bowl, stir together the sesame seeds and remaining ½ cup bread crumbs.

3. Form 1 scant tablespoon crab mixture into a ball; dip in the seasoned flour. Flatten into a ¾-inch-high cake about 1¼ inches in diameter. Repeat with the

- -

SIX EASY BRUSCHETTA

CLASSIC GARLIC BRUSCHETTA
Cut a loaf of rustic Italian bread into ½-inch-thick slices (about 24). Lightly char the slices on a grill or under the broiler, and rub with the cut side of 4 halved garlic cloves; drizzle with high-quality extra-virgin olive oil, and sprinkle with coarse salt.

FAVA BEANS WITH ARUGULA PESTO Boil 2 cups shelled fresh fava beans (about 2½ pounds in pods) 2 to 3 minutes; plunge into an ice-water bath. Slip off the skins. Process 1 medium bunch arugula (6 ounces), ¼ cup extra-virgin olive oil, ¼ cup grated Pecorino Romano cheese, 1 tablespoon fresh lemon juice, and ½ teaspoon coarse salt in a food processor until smooth. Toss with the beans; season with freshly ground pepper. Spoon onto 6 to 8 slices classic bruschetta. Top with Pecorino shavings. Drizzle with olive oil.

TOMATO AND BASIL Seed and chop 2 ripe large tomatoes. Stir in 1 tablespoon sugar and 1 teaspoon coarse salt; let stand until the tomatoes release their juices, 30 minutes. Toss with 4 torn fresh basil leaves. Spoon the tomato mixture and juices onto 6 to 8 slices classic bruschetta. Drizzle with olive oil.

POACHED TUNA Heat ½ to ¾ cup extra-virgin olive oil (enough to cover tuna) and 4 lemon slices in a small saucepan over very low heat until warm. Add a generously salted 8-ounce tuna steak. Poach the tuna, turning once, until it is opaque on the outside but still a bit pink in the center, about 15 minutes. Remove the tuna from the pan, reserving the oil; flake the fish with a fork. Pass the poaching oil through a fine sieve into a medium bowl; stir in the flaked tuna and 1 tablespoon each fresh lemon zest and drained and rinsed capers. Season with freshly ground pepper. Spoon onto 8 slices classic bruschetta. Drizzle with some of the poaching oil.

CANNELLINI BEANS WITH HERBS
Canned beans make this a good option year-round. Heat 1 minced garlic clove and 4 minced anchovy fillets in 2 tablespoons extra-virgin olive oil until fragrant, 1 minute. Stir in one 19-ounce can cannellini beans, drained and rinsed, and 1 teaspoon each chopped fresh rosemary, sage, and thyme. Cook until the beans are warm, 3 minutes. Spoon onto 6 to 8 slices classic bruschetta. Drizzle with olive oil.

ROASTED PEPPERS AND HERBED RICOTTA Stir together 1 cup ricotta cheese, ½ teaspoon coarse salt, and 2 tablespoons each extra-virgin olive oil and chopped fresh oregano; season with freshly ground pepper. Spread the ricotta on 8 slices classic bruschetta. Cut 1 roasted red bell pepper into 8 strips. Place 1 strip on each slice. Drizzle with olive oil.

remaining crab mixture. Dip the cakes in the egg mixture, then roll in the bread crumb mixture.

4. Heat the oil in a large skillet over medium heat until hot but not smoking. Add half the crab cakes; cook, turning once, until golden and crisp on both sides, about 1½ minutes. Using a slotted spatula, transfer to paper-towel–lined plates to drain. Repeat with the remaining cakes, adding more oil if needed. Let cool completely.

5. Transfer to a parchment-lined baking sheet. Freeze (uncovered) until firm, about 1 hour. Transfer to an airtight container; freeze up to 6 weeks.

6. To serve, preheat the oven to 425°F. Place the crab cakes on an ungreased baking sheet, and bake until heated through, 10 to 14 minutes.

7. Meanwhile, stir together the remaining 3 tablespoons mayonnaise and 1½ teaspoons wasabi. Using a vegetable peeler, make 24 2 × ¾-inch ribbons from the cucumber. Fold each into thirds.

8. Dot each crab cake with ½ teaspoon wasabi mayonnaise; top with cucumber and ginger.

mini chicken b'steeyas

MAKES 54

- 4 *tablespoons vegetable oil*
- 1 *whole boneless and skinless chicken breast (about 10 ounces), halved*
   Coarse salt and freshly ground pepper
- 1 *onion, finely chopped*
- ½ *teaspoon ground ginger*
- ¼ *teaspoon ground turmeric*
- 1½ *teaspoons ground cinnamon, plus more for dusting*
- ¾ *cup confectioners' sugar, plus more for dusting*
- 2 *large eggs, lightly beaten*
- ¼ *cup golden raisins, finely chopped (optional)*
- ½ *cup whole blanched almonds (2 ounces), toasted*
- 12 *sheets (17 × 12 inches each) frozen phyllo dough, thawed*
- ½ *cup (1 stick) unsalted butter, melted, for brushing*

1. Heat 1 tablespoon of the oil in a medium skillet over medium heat. Season the chicken with salt and pepper on both sides; cook, turning once, until just cooked through, about 10 minutes. Transfer to a plate; let cool, then finely chop. Transfer the chicken and any juices to a large bowl. Set aside.

2. Heat the remaining 3 tablespoons oil in the same skillet over medium heat. Add the onion; cook, stirring occasionally, until softened, about 4 minutes. Add the ginger, turmeric, and ½ teaspoon of the cinnamon; cook, stirring, until fragrant, about 1 minute.

3. Stir ¼ cup of the sugar into the mixture. Add the eggs; cook, stirring, until they are scrambled but still moist. Transfer to the bowl with the chicken. Stir in the raisins, if desired. Season with salt and pepper; let cool.

4. In a food processor, pulse the nuts until finely ground. Transfer to a bowl; stir in the remaining ½ cup sugar and 1 teaspoon cinnamon.

5. On a clean work surface, unfold a sheet of phyllo with a short side facing you; cover the remaining sheets with a damp kitchen towel. Lightly brush with melted butter; sprinkle with about one-sixth of the nut mixture. Lay another phyllo sheet on top; lightly brush with butter. Cut the stack lengthwise and then crosswise into thirds to make 9 equal rectangles.

6. Working with one rectangle at a time, place 1 tablespoon chicken mixture 1 inch from the end of a short side, leaving a ½-inch border on the long sides. Fold ½ inch of the long sides over filling. Starting from the end with the filling, roll into a log. Repeat the process to make 54 logs. Brush with butter, and arrange seam sides down on parchment-lined baking sheets.

7. Freeze (uncovered) until firm, about 1 hour. Transfer to airtight containers, and freeze until ready to use, up to 6 weeks.

8. To serve, preheat oven to 425°F. Place logs on parchment-lined baking sheets; bake, rotating sheets halfway through, until golden brown and crisp, 12 to 15 minutes. Let cool slightly before dusting with sugar and cinnamon. Serve warm.

scallion tarts

MAKES TWO 8-INCH-SQUARE TARTS

Baked tarts can be frozen up to 3 weeks. Without thawing, reheat them in a 350°F oven for about 10 minutes. Instead of large tarts, you can make individual-size tartlets: Cut the pastry into eight 4-inch squares; bake for about 20 minutes.

All-purpose flour, for work surface

1 *standard package (17.3 ounces; 2 sheets) frozen puff pastry, thawed*

8 *bunches scallions (2¼ pounds), trimmed and cut into matchsticks*

1 *garlic clove, minced*

1 *red Thai chile, ribs and seeds removed, minced*

½ *cup walnuts (2 ounces), finely chopped*

½ *cup kalamata olives, pitted and coarsely chopped*

2 *tablespoons extra-virgin olive oil*

Coarse salt and freshly ground pepper

1 *large egg yolk*

½ *cup freshly grated Parmesan cheese (2 ounces)*

1. Preheat the oven to 400°F. On a lightly floured work surface, roll out the pastry sheets just to smooth creases; trim the edges slightly to make even.

2. Place each sheet on a parchment-lined baking sheet. Freeze 20 minutes.

3. Place the scallions, garlic, chile, walnuts, olives, and oil in a medium bowl. Season with salt and pepper; toss. Set aside.

4. In a small bowl, whisk together the egg yolk and 1 teaspoon water. Brush a ½-inch border around the edges of the dough with egg wash. Divide the scallion mixture between the sheets, leaving a ¼-inch border; sprinkle each with cheese.

5. Bake until the crust is golden brown, about 30 minutes. Transfer to a wire rack. Serve warm or at room temperature.

shallot and date empanadas

MAKES 12

Instead of raw shallots, try using the same quantity of roasted shallots. Remove the skins and slice into thirds. Unbaked empanadas can be frozen up to 3 weeks; without thawing, bake in a 375°F oven for about 30 minutes. Baked empanadas can be refrigerated up to 1 day or frozen up to 2 weeks; reheat in a 350°F oven for 15 to 20 minutes.

1¾ *cups all-purpose flour, plus more for work surface*

1½ *teaspoons caraway seeds, coarsely chopped*

1 *teaspoon sugar*

1 *teaspoon table salt*

¾ *cup (1½ sticks) chilled unsalted butter, cut into small pieces*

8 *ounces cream cheese, well chilled*

2 *tablespoons olive oil*

1 *pound shallots, cut lengthwise into sixths*

Coarse salt and freshly ground pepper

6 *dried dates, pitted and quartered*

2 *teaspoons fresh thyme*

1 *large egg yolk*

1 *tablespoon heavy cream*

1. In a food processor, pulse the flour, caraway seeds, sugar, and table salt several times to combine. Add the butter and cream cheese; pulse until the mixture just begins to come together. (Gently squeeze the dough; if it doesn't hold together, add 1 tablespoon cold water.) Turn out the dough onto plastic wrap; flatten into a disk. Wrap, and refrigerate 1 hour.

2. Preheat the oven to 400°F. Line a baking sheet with parchment paper; set aside. Heat the oil in a medium skillet over medium heat. Add the shallots; cook, turning occasionally, until golden, about 10 minutes. Season with coarse salt and pepper; remove the skillet from heat.

3. On a generously floured work surface, roll out the dough to ⅛ inch thick. Using a 4-inch cookie cutter, cut out 12 rounds from the dough. Brush the border of one round with water. Place 2 date quarters in the center of the round, then top with shallots, dividing evenly. Add a pinch of thyme; season with coarse salt and pepper. Bring three sides up and crimp together in the center, enclosing the filling. Pinch the edges to seal. Place on prepared baking sheet. Repeat with the remaining dough and filling. Freeze 15 minutes.

4. In a bowl, beat together the egg yolk and cream. Brush the empanadas with egg wash. Bake until golden brown; about 30 minutes. Transfer to a wire rack. Serve warm or at room temperature.

crisped haloumi cheese

SERVES 6 TO 8

Haloumi is a semihard cheese made from sheep's milk; look for it at Middle Eastern markets.

- 5 teaspoons nonpareil capers, chopped
   Grated zest and juice of 1 lemon
- 1 pound (2 packages) haloumi cheese

1. In a small bowl, mix the capers with the lemon zest and juice; set aside. Slice each block of cheese crosswise into ¼-inch-thick slices.

2. Heat a nonstick skillet over medium heat. Working in batches, arrange the cheese slices in a single layer in the skillet. Cook until golden brown, about 3 minutes per side. Transfer to a serving dish; spoon the caper mixture over the cheese. Serve warm.

dressed feta cheese

SERVES 6 TO 8

We particularly like the flavor and firm texture of Bulgarian feta cheese, which is easy to slice, but other types can also be used.

- 1 pound feta cheese, drained well
- 5 large sprigs fresh dill
- 5 sprigs fresh flat-leaf parsley
- 1 scallion, including green parts
- 1 teaspoon whole pink peppercorns
- 1 teaspoon crushed red pepper flakes
- 2 tablespoons extra-virgin olive oil

1. Cut the feta into ½-inch-thick slices, wiping the knife each time to keep the cheese from crumbling. Arrange on a serving dish.

2. Pick the leaves from the herbs, and chop finely. Slice the scallion into thin rounds. Combine herbs and scallion in a small bowl; stir in peppercorns, red pepper flakes, and 1 tablespoon of the oil. Spoon the herb mixture over the feta. Drizzle with the remaining tablespoon oil, and serve.

mushroom crostini

SERVES 4

- 1 small (or ½ large) baguette
- 2 tablespoons extra-virgin olive oil, plus more for brushing
   Coarse salt and freshly ground pepper
- 1 shallot, thinly sliced into rings
- 8 ounces chanterelles or other wild mushrooms, trimmed and coarsely chopped
- 12 rounds (¼ inch thick) goat cheese, cut from a log (about 6 ounces), room temperature
   Fresh chives, snipped, for garnish

1. Preheat the oven to 375° F. Cut the baguette crosswise into 12 ¼-inch-thick slices; place them on a baking sheet. Brush with oil; season with salt and pepper. Toast in the middle of the oven until golden, 8 to 10 minutes. Set aside to cool.

2. Heat 2 tablespoons oil in a medium skillet over medium heat. Add the shallot; cook, stirring, until soft, about 3 minutes. Add the mushrooms; cook, stirring occasionally, until tender and any juices have evaporated, 7 to 10 minutes. Season with salt and pepper.

3. Place a round of goat cheese on top of each crostini; top with 1 tablespoon mushroom mixture. Sprinkle with chives. Serve warm.

tomatoes à la grecque

SERVES 6 TO 8

This dish can be prepared several hours ahead and served chilled or at room temperature. Peel and slice the cucumbers just before serving.

2 pounds small ripe tomatoes
Coarse salt and freshly ground pepper
¼ cup olive oil
1 garlic clove, minced
¼ cup white-wine vinegar
1 tablespoon fresh lemon juice
½ teaspoon ground coriander
2 cucumbers
1 tablespoon dried oregano, for garnish

1. Slice the tomatoes lengthwise into quarters, through the stem. Place in a medium bowl; season with salt and pepper.

2. Heat the oil in a small saucepan over medium heat. Add the garlic; cook, stirring, until soft but not browned, about 1 minute. Add the vinegar, lemon juice, and coriander. Let simmer 1 minute.

3. Immediately pour the hot vinaigrette over the tomatoes, and let them marinate at room temperature until completely cooled. Alternatively, cover with plastic wrap and refrigerate until ready to serve.

4. Just before serving, peel the cucumbers, leaving on stripes of skin for decoration, if desired. Halve the cucumbers lengthwise; scrape out the seeds with a spoon, and discard. Cut the cucumber into ½-inch semicircles. Garnish the tomatoes with the oregano, and serve the cucumbers in a separate bowl.

crostini with salt cod brandade

SERVES 10

1 pound choice-grade skinless and boneless salt cod
4 garlic cloves, mashed
1 cup heavy cream
½ cup extra-virgin olive oil, plus more for drizzling
1 tablespoon plus 2 teaspoons fresh lemon juice (about 1 lemon)
Coarse salt and freshly ground pepper
1 baguette, sliced on the bias into ¼-inch-thick pieces

1. Rinse the salt cod, and place it in a large reusable plastic container. Submerge the cod in cold water, and place, covered, in the refrigerator. Allow to soak overnight. Drain the cod, and replace the water with fresh cold water. Let soak overnight again.

2. Remove the cod from the soaking liquid, and place it in a large pot. Cover with cold water, and bring to a boil over high heat. Reduce heat to low, and simmer 20 minutes. Drain cod; let cool, and break into large pieces. Transfer to a food processor; add garlic, and process until the mixture is coarsely chopped.

3. In a small saucepan set over medium heat, warm the cream until hot; do not bring to a boil. While processing the cod mixture, slowly add the cream through the feed tube. Add the oil and lemon juice in the same manner; blend until creamy and fluffy. Season with salt and pepper.

4. Heat the broiler with the rack placed in the upper third of the oven. Lay the baguette slices on a baking sheet; drizzle each slice with oil. Season with salt and pepper. Place the baking sheet under the broiler; toast the bread until the edges are lightly browned, about 1 minute. Remove from the oven; let cool. Spread the brandade on the crostini; serve.

stuffed quahogs

MAKES 10

Quahogs are found mainly off the eastern coast of the United States; steamer clams may be used instead.

- 1 baguette, crusts removed and insides cut into ¼-inch dice (about 4 cups)
- ¼ pound chorizo, chopped into ¼-inch dice
- 10 quahogs (about 5 pounds)
- ⅓ cup olive oil
- 10 garlic cloves, chopped (about ¼ cup)
- 2 onions, finely chopped (about 3 cups)
- ½ teaspoon crushed red pepper flakes
- 2 large eggs
- 2 tablespoons finely chopped fresh basil
- 1 tablespoon finely chopped fresh oregano
- 2 tablespoons finely chopped fresh flat-leaf parsley

  Freshly ground black pepper
- 2 tablespoons unsalted butter, cut into small pieces

1. Preheat the oven to 300° F. Place the cubed bread on a rimmed baking sheet. Toast until dry, about 15 minutes. Set aside.

2. In a sauté pan set over medium-high heat, cook the chorizo, stirring occasionally, until the fat is rendered and the chorizo is lightly browned, about 4 minutes. Using a slotted spoon, remove the chorizo from the fat, and transfer it to a paper-towel–lined plate. Blot dry, and set aside.

3. Under running water, scrub the clams clean. Place in a large stockpot, and add ⅔ cup water. Cover the pot, and place over high heat. Steam until all clams have opened, about 10 to 15 minutes. Remove the clams from the pot, discarding any that did not open; strain the broth through a paper-towel–lined fine strainer; set aside.

4. Remove the meat from the shells. Chop into ¼-inch pieces; set aside. Separate the shells into halves; clean them thoroughly by boiling in a large pot of water for 5 minutes. Remove the shells from the pot; let cool.

5. In a large sauté pan set over medium heat, warm the olive oil. Cook the garlic, onions, and red pepper flakes, stirring, until the onions are soft and translucent, about 8 minutes. Let the mixture cool to room temperature.

6. In a large mixing bowl, beat 1 cup reserved clam broth into the eggs. Add the onion mixture, clams, chorizo, and herbs; toss well. Add the bread cubes. Fold together until just mixed. Season with pepper.

7. Heat the grill. Fill each clamshell with stuffing, about ¼ to ⅓ cup filling per shell. Dot the top of each filled shell with butter. Place the quahogs, stuffing side up, on the grill; cook, covered, for 10 minutes. Transfer to a serving plate; serve warm.

bûcheron with cucumbers, basil, and figs

SERVES 6

Bûcheron is a tangy, mild goat cheese. We like to serve it drizzled with a deep, intensely flavored extra-virgin olive oil.

- 1 baguette, halved lengthwise and cut into 3-inch-long pieces
- ½ pound Bûcheron or other soft goat cheese, sliced
- 6 fresh figs, halved, for garnish
- 3 tablespoons extra-virgin olive oil
- 2 cucumbers
- 1 sprig basil, for garnish

1. Preheat the oven to 300° F. Arrange the bread slices on a baking sheet. Toast in the oven, turning once, until golden, about 5 minutes per side. Remove from the oven, and set aside on a serving plate.

2. Arrange the cheese with the figs on serving plates. Allow to come to room temperature. Drizzle the oil over the cheese. Slice the cucumbers into spears, peeling the skins if waxy, and place, as desired, around the cheese. Garnish with basil. Serve with toast on the side.

potato skins with pancetta and mixed herbs

SERVES 10 TO 12

Assembled wedges can be stored in the refrigerator, covered with plastic wrap, until ready to bake, up to 1 day.

- 8 small to medium russet potatoes
- 1 tablespoon olive oil
- ½ pound pancetta, finely chopped
- 4 tablespoons unsalted butter
- 3 tablespoons finely chopped mixed fresh herbs, such as rosemary, sage, and thyme
- 16 ounces white and/or yellow sharp Cheddar cheese, grated (about 2 cups)
- 8 ounces fontina cheese, grated (about 1 cup)

1. Preheat the oven to 400°F. Place the potatoes on a baking sheet, and rub with the oil. Bake until tender when pierced with a paring knife, 55 to 60 minutes. Remove from the oven; let stand until cool enough to handle. Reduce oven temperature to 350°F.

2. Cut each potato in half lengthwise, and use a small spoon to scoop out the insides, leaving about ¼-inch border all around. Reserve the insides for another use. Slice each potato shell in half again lengthwise for a total of 32 wedges.

3. In a medium skillet, cook the pancetta over medium heat, stirring frequently, until just starting to turn brown and crisp, 9 to 10 minutes. Remove from heat; use a slotted spoon to transfer the pancetta to drain on paper towels. Set aside.

4. Melt the butter in a small saucepan. Brush each potato wedge with butter; sprinkle with herb mixture. Cover each wedge with about 1 tablespoon Cheddar cheese. Sprinkle each wedge with ½ teaspoon pancetta and a little more herb mixture. Sprinkle the remaining Cheddar and the fontina cheese over the tops.

5. Bake until the cheese is melted and the potatoes are heated through, 8 to 10 minutes. Remove from the oven; serve hot.

sesame crunch sticks

MAKES ABOUT 54

Serve with Hummus Dip (recipe follows).

- 3 cups all-purpose flour, plus more for work surface
- 2 teaspoons baking powder
- 2 teaspoons salt
- ½ cup (1 stick) chilled unsalted butter
- 1 cup buttermilk
- 1¼ cups sesame seeds, toasted
- 1 large egg
- 1 tablespoon sugar
- 1 tablespoon soy sauce

1. In the bowl of a food processor, pulse the flour, baking powder, and salt until combined. Add the butter; pulse until the mixture resembles coarse meal. Transfer to a medium bowl; stir in the buttermilk and 1 cup of the sesame seeds until the mixture forms a dough. Divide into quarters; wrap in plastic. Chill 20 minutes.

2. Preheat the oven to 350°F. In a small bowl, whisk together the egg, sugar, and soy sauce. Transfer one piece of dough to a lightly floured work surface; roll out into a rectangle about ⅛ inch thick. Use a sharp knife or pizza wheel to cut the rectangle into strips about ⅜ inch wide and 10 inches long. Brush the strips with egg mixture; sprinkle with the remaining ¼ cup sesame seeds.

3. Arrange the strips on a parchment-lined baking sheet. Bake until just golden, 15 to 20 minutes. Transfer to a wire rack to cool. Repeat with remaining dough.

hummus dip

1   can (15½ ounces) chickpeas, drained and
    rinsed

1   large or 2 small garlic cloves, roughly
    chopped

    Pinch of ground cumin

    Pinch of ground nutmeg

5   tablespoons extra-virgin olive oil

2   tablespoons tahini

1   tablespoon water, plus more as needed

3   tablespoons fresh lemon juice (1 lemon)

¾   teaspoon coarse salt

Combine all the ingredients in the bowl of a food
processor; pulse until smooth and creamy, adding
more water if needed. Transfer to a serving dish or
airtight container, and place in the refrigerator, covered, until ready to serve, up to 5 days. Serve chilled
or at room temperature.

bruschetta with fontina and asparagus

SERVES 10

Truffle oil can be found at most gourmet shops.

1   loaf (about ¾ pound) French bread, sliced
    into 10 ¼-inch-thick slices

1   garlic clove, crushed

2   tablespoons olive oil

    Coarse salt

1½ large bunches (1¼ pounds) asparagus,
    tough ends trimmed

8   ounces fontina or Monterey Jack cheese,
    grated on the large holes of a box grater
    (about 2 cups)

2   ounces Parmesan cheese, grated on the
    small holes of a box grater (about ¼ cup)

2   tablespoons truffle oil (optional)

1. Heat the grill or broiler. Grill the bread slices until
golden on both sides. Rub one side of each slice
with garlic; brush lightly with oil.

2. Preheat the oven to 350° F. Bring a large saucepan
of water to a boil over high heat; add salt generously. Add the asparagus, and cook until tender,
about 3 minutes. Drain the asparagus, and set aside.

3. Place the toasted bread on a baking sheet, and
sprinkle the fontina evenly over the slices. Arrange
3 to 4 asparagus spears on top of each. Sprinkle the
Parmesan over the asparagus, dividing evenly.

4. Bake until the cheese has melted, about 10 minutes. Remove from the oven, and drizzle with truffle oil, if using.

chickpea fritters

MAKES ABOUT 20

7   tablespoons extra-virgin olive oil

1   onion, finely diced

2   tablespoons sesame seeds

1   tablespoon ground cumin

    Pinch of cayenne pepper

1   can (15½ ounces) chickpeas, rinsed and
    drained

2   tablespoons fresh lemon juice

1   large egg white

1   teaspoon coarse salt, plus more for
    seasoning

5   tablespoons all-purpose flour

    Tzatziki, for serving (opposite)

1. In a medium sauté pan, heat 3 tablespoons of the
oil over medium heat. Add the onion; cook, stirring,
until soft and translucent, about 3 minutes. Add the
sesame seeds, cumin, and cayenne; cook, stirring,
until the sesame seeds have begun to brown lightly
and the spices are very fragrant, about 2 minutes;
set aside.

2. In a food processor, combine the chickpeas,
lemon juice, egg white, salt, and 1 tablespoon of the
oil. Pulse several times to form a semismooth paste.
Transfer to a large bowl; stir in the onion mixture.
Fold in the flour until just combined. Using your
hands, form the batter into 1¼-inch patties, each
about ⅓ inch thick.

3. In a 12-inch sauté pan, heat 2 tablespoons of the oil over medium-low heat. Cook half the patties, without flattening, until golden brown, about 3 minutes per side. Transfer the patties to a paper-towel–lined plate, and season with salt. Repeat with remaining patties and tablespoon oil. Serve immediately with tzatziki.

zucchini-scallion fritters

MAKES ABOUT 28

- 1 pound (about 2 medium) zucchini, grated on the large holes of a box grater
- 2½ teaspoons coarse salt, plus more for seasoning
- 3 large scallions, thinly sliced
- ¼ cup finely chopped fresh dill
- ½ cup finely chopped fresh mint
- 3 large eggs, lightly beaten
- ½ cup grated Kefalotyri cheese or Pecorino Romano
- 5 tablespoons all-purpose flour
- 3 tablespoons extra-virgin olive oil
  Tzatziki, for serving (recipe follows)

1. In a colander, sprinkle the zucchini with 1¼ teaspoons of the salt; toss to combine, and let stand at room temperature 45 minutes. Transfer the zucchini to a clean kitchen towel; squeeze out any remaining juice.

2. In a large bowl, combine the zucchini, the remaining 1¼ teaspoons salt, and the scallions, dill, mint, eggs, and cheese. Fold in the flour until just combined.

3. Line a large platter or baking sheet with paper towels; set aside. In a large sauté pan, heat 2 tablespoons of the oil over medium-low heat. Using half the batter, drop heaping teaspoons directly into pan to create about 14 1½-inch patties, each about ¼ inch thick. Cook the patties, without flattening, until

golden brown, about 2 minutes per side. Using a slotted spatula, transfer the zucchini fritters to the paper-towel–lined platter, and season with salt. Repeat with the remaining batter and tablespoon oil. Serve immediately with tzatziki.

tzatziki

MAKES 2 CUPS

- 1 English cucumber, cut into 1½ × ⅛-inch matchsticks
- 1½ teaspoons coarse salt, plus more for seasoning
- 1¼ cups Greek yogurt or Strained Yogurt (recipe follows)
- 1 large garlic clove, minced
- 2 tablespoons white-wine vinegar
- 2 tablespoons extra-virgin olive oil
- ¼ cup chopped fresh dill
  Freshly ground pepper

1. In a colander, sprinkle the cucumber with 1½ teaspoons salt; toss to combine. Let stand at room temperature 30 minutes.

2. In a medium bowl, combine the cucumber, yogurt, garlic, vinegar, oil, and dill. Season with salt and pepper.

strained yogurt

MAKES 1½ CUPS

- 32 ounces whole-milk yogurt

Put the yogurt in a cheesecloth-lined sieve placed over a bowl. Cover the bowl; refrigerate at least 4 hours. Discard liquid.

herb fritters

SERVES 4

Crisp herb fritters are an unusual way to savor fresh herbs. Dipped in beer batter, fried lightly in oil, and served with lemon wedges, they make a delightful accompaniment to a glass of wine. If the batter is too thick, thin with a little water; if it is too thin, add a little flour.

- 2 large eggs, separated
- 1½ tablespoons vegetable oil, plus more for frying
- ½ cup beer
- ¾ cup all-purpose flour
- 3 ounces assorted herbs, such as basil, mint, sage, parsley, oregano, tarragon, and chives
- 1 teaspoon coarse salt, plus more for seasoning
- ¼ teaspoon freshly ground pepper
- 1 lemon, cut into wedges

1. Whisk together the yolks, oil, and beer in a bowl. Slowly add the flour, whisking until just combined. Set aside for 20 minutes. Wash and dry the herbs. Whisk the egg whites to soft peaks; fold into the beer batter. Add the salt and pepper.

2. In a heavy-bottomed saucepan, heat 1 inch oil over medium heat until hot but not smoking, about 375° F on a fry thermometer. Dip each herb into the batter, shaking off excess, until lightly coated. Place the herbs in the oil, turning until golden, about 1 minute. Drain on paper towels; season with salt. Serve with lemon wedges.

shrimp and avocado seviche

SERVES 8 TO 10

- 4 limes
- 2 pounds medium shrimp
- ¼ cup fresh lime juice (about 3 limes)
- 6 scallions, trimmed and finely chopped
- 2 to 4 serrano chiles, finely chopped
- ¼ cup cider vinegar
- 2 teaspoons finely chopped fresh thyme
- 1 teaspoon dried oregano, preferably Mexican
- 2 large ripe avocados, peeled, pitted, and diced
- ¼ cup finely chopped fresh cilantro
- 2 teaspoons salt
  Tortilla chips, for serving

1. Fill a large pot with 1 quart water. Cut the 4 limes in half, and squeeze their juice into the pot; add the lime halves. Bring to a boil, then turn off heat; let the mixture steep about 10 minutes. Return to a boil.

2. Add the shrimp to the pot. As soon as the water returns to a rolling boil, pour the shrimp mixture into a colander; discard the cooking liquid and limes. Return the shrimp to the pot; cover, and let stand 15 minutes. Transfer the shrimp to a baking sheet and spread them out; let stand until cool enough to handle.

3. Peel and devein the shrimp, and cut them into thirds. Transfer to a medium bowl; stir in ¼ cup lime juice and the scallions, chiles, vinegar, thyme, and oregano. Let stand at room temperature 1 hour, stirring occasionally.

4. When ready to serve, stir the avocados, cilantro, and salt into shrimp mixture. Serve with tortilla chips.

parmesan-dusted meatballs

SERVES 8 TO 10

⅓ cup plus 3 tablespoons sliced
   almonds, toasted
1½ teaspoons sugar
¾ cup plain bread crumbs
¼ cup milk
½ pound ground beef chuck
½ pound ground pork
1 large egg, lightly beaten
½ cup finely grated Parmesan cheese,
   plus more for garnish
⅓ cup finely chopped fresh flat-leaf parsley
3 tablespoons dried currants
2 teaspoons salt
⅛ teaspoon ground allspice
3 tablespoons olive oil

1. In a food processor, pulse ⅓ cup of the almonds with the sugar until finely ground. Coarsely chop the remaining almonds.

2. In a bowl, mix the bread crumbs and milk. Add the almonds, beef, pork, egg, ½ cup Parmesan, parsley, currants, salt, and allspice. Mix until combined. Form into 1-inch balls.

3. Heat 1½ tablespoons of the olive oil in a heavy 12-inch skillet over medium heat. Add half the meatballs, and sauté until they are cooked through, about 7 minutes. Transfer the meatballs to a platter. Repeat with the remaining oil and meatballs. Garnish with Parmesan, and serve immediately.

watermelon skewers

SERVES 8 TO 10

¼ large seedless watermelon, cut
   into ¾-inch cubes
2 bunches fresh mint, leaves separated
10 ounces ricotta salata, cut
   into ½-inch cubes
   Freshly ground pepper (optional)

1. Arrange the melon cubes on a serving platter. Lay a mint leaf on top of each, then add a cheese cube. Insert skewers through each stack; sprinkle with pepper, if desired.

2. Chill, covered, until ready to serve, up to 3 hours.

blue cheese with crudités

SERVES 6

1 pound radishes (about 16)
1 pound celery (about 8 stalks)
1 wedge blue cheese (5 ounces), such as
   Danish blue, Stilton, or Gorgonzola

Halve the radishes, if desired. Arrange the radishes, celery, and cheese on a platter.

FIT TO EAT RECIPE PER SERVING: 109 CALORIES, 7 G FAT, 18 MG CHOLESTEROL, 7 G CARBOHYDRATE, 428 MG SODIUM, 6 G PROTEIN, 3 G FIBER

roasted olives

MAKES ABOUT 2 CUPS

2 cups assorted brine-cured olives, rinsed
¼ cup extra-virgin olive oil
¼ teaspoon crushed red pepper flakes
   Pinch of freshly ground black pepper
2 bay leaves
3 rosemary sprigs
4 strips orange zest (4 inches each)

Preheat the oven to 400° F. Stir all the ingredients in an 8-inch-square baking dish. Cover with foil; bake until fragrant and heated through, 20 to 30 minutes. Serve warm.

caviar and chopped eggs on biscuits

SERVES 8

- 3 large eggs
- 2 teaspoons Dijon mustard
- 1 tablespoon mayonnaise
  Coarse salt and freshly ground pepper
- 16 whole-wheat digestive biscuits
- 2 50-gram tins of black caviar
  Freshly chopped chives, for garnish

1. Place the eggs in a saucepan with enough cold water to cover by 2 inches. Bring to a boil over medium-high heat, cook for 1 minute, cover, and remove from heat. Let stand for 10 minutes. Drain the eggs, cover with ice, and place under cold running water to stop cooking.

2. Peel the eggs; finely chop. Place in a bowl with the mustard and mayonnaise; stir to combine. Season with salt and pepper.

3. To serve, place 1 rounded teaspoon egg mixture on a digestive biscuit, top with caviar, and garnish with chives.

pork and mango rolls

MAKES 24

- ½ cup fish sauce
- ¼ cup canola oil
- ¼ cup rice wine vinegar
- 1 stalk lemongrass, crushed
- 2 cloves garlic, finely sliced
- ½ inch piece ginger, finely sliced
- 1 green chile pepper, finely sliced
- 2 teaspoons freshly ground black pepper
- 1 pork tenderloin (about 1 pound), silverskin trimmed
- 6 8½-inch rice paper wrappers
- 1 bunch watercress, washed
- ½ mango, peeled and cut into matchsticks
- ½ small jícama, peeled and cut into matchsticks
- 1 cup fresh basil leaves, washed and dried

1. Make the marinade: Combine the fish sauce, canola oil, rice wine vinegar, lemongrass, garlic, ginger, chile pepper, and black pepper in a medium bowl. Transfer to a resealable plastic bag; add the pork, and refrigerate 3 hours or overnight.

2. Preheat the grill or grill pan to medium. Remove the pork from the marinade. Place on the grill; cook, turning as necessary, until a meat thermometer registers 160° F. Remove from the grill; let cool. When cool enough to handle, slice the meat ⅛ inch thick.

3. Dip a rice paper wrapper into a bowl of warm water for 5 seconds; transfer to a clean work surface (the wrapper will still feel hard but will soften as it sits). Lay watercress on the bottom third of the rice paper. Top with some pork, mango, jícama, and basil. Roll (you needn't tuck in ends). Place on a plate; cover with a damp paper towel. Continue filling and rolling rice paper until all the ingredients are used. Trim the ends; halve. Halve each half again on the diagonal to make hors d'oeuvres; serve.

wild mushroom crackers

MAKES ABOUT 7 DOZEN

These crackers use powder made from dried mushrooms ground with a mortar and pestle or in a spice grinder.

- ¼ pound (1 stick) unsalted butter, room temperature
- ½ pound (8 ounces) goat cheese
- 2 cups all-purpose flour, plus more for dusting
- ⅓ cup mushroom powder, from ¾ ounce dried mushrooms
- ¼ teaspoon freshly ground pepper
- ¼ cup milk
  Coarse salt

1. Preheat the oven to 350° F. In the bowl of an electric mixer fitted with the paddle attachment, mix the butter and goat cheese on medium speed until well combined. Add the flour, mushroom powder, and pepper; mix until just combined and crumbly. Scrape down the sides of the bowl, and add the milk. Mix on low speed until the dough comes together; it should be quite stiff.

2. Divide the dough into thirds. Wrap two pieces in plastic wrap; set aside. On a lightly floured work surface, roll out the third piece to ⅛ inch thick. Cut the dough with a 2-inch cookie or biscuit cutter. Arrange the crackers on a baking sheet, and prick each with a fork once or twice. Sprinkle with salt, and bake for 15 to 20 minutes or until they start to brown.

3. Remove from the oven; let cool on a wire rack. Repeat with the remaining dough, rerolling the scraps once. Serve when cool, or store in an airtight container for up to 1 week.

herbed cheese with pears, pine nuts, and honey

SERVES 4

Cheese drizzled with honey is a traditional Mediterranean appetizer; when mixed with fruit and nuts, it makes a tantalizing dessert.

8 ounces part-skim ricotta cheese

3 tablespoons pine nuts

6 ounces fresh goat cheese, room temperature

1 teaspoon fresh thyme leaves, finely chopped

2 teaspoons fresh flat-leaf parsley, finely chopped

½ teaspoon finely grated lemon zest

2 ripe but firm Bartlett pears

2 tablespoons plus 2 teaspoons flavorful honey, such as buckwheat, chestnut, or leatherwood

1. Preheat the oven to 350° F. Place the ricotta in a fine sieve set over a bowl; let the excess liquid drain, about 30 minutes. Meanwhile, spread the nuts in a single layer on a rimmed baking sheet. Toast in the oven until lightly browned, tossing occasionally, about 7 minutes. Transfer to a plate; let cool.

2. In a food processor or medium bowl, mix together the goat cheese and drained ricotta until creamy and thoroughly combined. Stir in the thyme, parsley, and lemon zest; set aside.

3. Slice each pear into 6 wedges. Divide the herbed cheese among 4 serving plates, spooning it into mounds. Arrange 3 pear wedges next to the cheese on each plate. Sprinkle with nuts; drizzle about 2 teaspoons honey over each portion of cheese and pears. Serve immediately.

FIT TO EAT RECIPE PER SERVING: 320 CALORIES, 17 G FAT, 37 MG CHOLESTEROL, 28 G CARBOHYDRATE, 229 MG SODIUM, 16 G PROTEIN, 2 G FIBER

vegetarian pâté

MAKES 3 CUPS

5 large eggs

¼ pound string beans, ends trimmed, cut into 1-inch pieces

1 tablespoon unsalted butter

1 red onion, cut into ¼-inch dice (1 cup)

¾ cup toasted walnuts

1 tablespoon soy sauce

2 tablespoons mayonnaise

1 tablespoon olive oil

2 tablespoons finely chopped chives
Coarse salt and freshly ground pepper
Bread or crackers, for serving

1. Fill a large bowl with ice and water; set aside. Place the eggs in a medium saucepan with enough water to cover by 2 inches. Place over high heat; bring to a boil. Turn off heat; cover. Let stand for 12 minutes. Transfer the eggs to the ice-water bath to stop cooking. When the eggs are cool, peel them under cold running water, cut into quarters, and set aside. Let the cooking water return to a boil; blanch the string beans for 2 to 3 minutes. Transfer to the ice-water bath to stop the cooking.

2. Melt the butter in a medium sauté pan over medium heat. Add the onion; cook until caramelized, 8 to 10 minutes. Remove from heat; cool to room temperature.

3. Combine the eggs, beans, walnuts, soy sauce, mayonnaise, and oil in the bowl of a food processor. Pulse until finely chopped but not pureed. Stir in the sautéed onion and chives; season with salt and pepper. Serve at room temperature with bread or crackers.

batter-fried stuffed
squash blossoms

SERVES 4 TO 6

To stuff the squash blossoms easily, spoon the filling into a pastry bag fitted with a coupler; pipe it directly into each blossom.

- 1   cup ricotta cheese
- 1   cup all-purpose flour
      Coarse salt and freshly ground pepper
- 1   cup plus 2 tablespoons milk
- 3   ounces (about 1 cup) mozzarella cheese, cut into ¼-inch cubes, room temperature
- 1   tablespoon coarsely chopped fresh marjoram
- 2   tablespoons coarsely chopped fresh flat-leaf parsley
- 16 large (about 4 ounces) squash blossoms
- 1   quart light olive oil

1. Place the ricotta cheese in a double layer of cheesecloth. Tie up the ends, and hang over a bowl to drain. Place in the refrigerator for 2 to 3 hours, or overnight.

2. In a medium bowl, whisk together the flour with salt and pepper to taste. Slowly whisk the milk into the flour to make a paste. Continue to add milk slowly, whisking constantly, until the batter is slightly thickened and has a very smooth consistency; set aside.

3. Remove the ricotta from the cheesecloth, and discard the liquid. In another medium bowl, stir together the drained ricotta, mozzarella, marjoram, and parsley, and season with salt and pepper. Gently open the squash-blossom petals, and, using a small spoon or pastry bag, fill a blossom about two-thirds full with the ricotta mixture. Wrap the petals around the mixture to seal. Using your fingers, gently press the blossom to evenly distribute the filling. Repeat, filling all the blossoms.

4. In a small saucepan fitted with a deep-fry thermometer, heat the olive oil over medium-high heat to 375° F. Place the stuffed blossoms in the reserved batter until completely coated. Lift out, and gently drag the blossom against the edge of the bowl to remove excess batter. Carefully slip as many blossoms into the hot oil as will comfortably fit without crowding. Fry the blossoms until golden brown, 2 to 3 minutes. Remove from the oil with a slotted spoon, and transfer to several layers of paper towels to drain. Sprinkle with salt, and serve immediately.

cucumber and smoked
salmon "sandwiches"

SERVES 8 TO 10

- ¼ pound smoked salmon, finely chopped
- 2   tablespoons finely chopped red onion
- 2   teaspoons finely chopped fresh cilantro
- 1   jalapeño pepper, seeded and finely chopped
      Finely grated zest of 1 lime
      Coarse salt and freshly ground pepper
- 1   English cucumber
- ¼ cup crème fraîche, well chilled
- 1   lime, peeled and segmented, each segment cut into 4 pieces

1. Make the tartare: In a small bowl, combine the salmon, onion, cilantro, jalapeño, and zest. Season with salt and pepper.

2. Using a paring knife or vegetable peeler, remove the skin on two opposite sides of the cucumber. Trim the ends, and cut the cucumber crosswise into 48 ¼-inch-thick slices. Place the slices on paper towels to dry.

3. Using a butter knife or a small offset spatula, spread about ½ teaspoon crème fraîche on half of the cucumber slices, and then top with 1 teaspoon tartare. Place the remaining cucumber slices on top, followed by a small dollop of crème fraîche and a piece of lime. Serve immediately, or chill, covered with plastic wrap, up to 1 hour.

lettuce bundles with spicy peanut noodles

SERVES 6 TO 8

This is a great dish to serve at an informal lunch or dinner party. Set out all the ingredients, and let your guests assemble their own bundles. Store-bought roasted duck or chicken can be used; skip step 2.

- ½ cup Spanish peanuts or other peanuts
- 2 boneless whole duck or chicken breasts
- ½ cup plus 3 tablespoons soy sauce
  Canola oil
- 1 large garlic clove
- 1 ¾-inch piece ginger, peeled and cut in half
- 2¼ teaspoons chile paste
- ¼ cup plus 3 tablespoons smooth, good-quality peanut butter
- 3 tablespoons sugar
- ¼ cup plus 1½ teaspoons peanut oil
  Juice of 1 lime
- 4½ tablespoons water, or more if needed
  Coarse salt
- 6 ounces vermicelli or capellini (angel hair) noodles
- 2 ounces garlic chives or scallions, cut into 4-inch lengths
- 1 Japanese or Kirby cucumber, thinly sliced
- 2 heads Boston or other butterhead lettuce, leaves separated

1. Preheat the oven to 350°F. Place the peanuts in a single layer on a rimmed baking sheet; toast until they are golden and aromatic, 5 to 8 minutes. Shake the pan halfway through to ensure the nuts toast evenly. When cool enough to handle, roughly chop the nuts; set aside.

2. Place the duck or chicken breasts in a resealable plastic bag with ½ cup of the soy sauce, and let marinate for 1 hour. Heat a lightly oiled grill or cast-iron skillet over medium-high heat until very hot. Grill the duck or chicken breasts until cooked through, 5 to 7 minutes per side for duck and 4 to 6 minutes per side for chicken. Let cool slightly, and shred with your fingers, or cut into ½-inch-wide strips with a knife.

3. In a food processor, pulse the garlic and ginger until finely chopped. Add the remaining 3 tablespoons soy sauce, the chile paste, peanut butter, sugar, peanut oil, lime juice, and water, and pulse until smooth. (For a thinner sauce, add 1 or 2 more teaspoons water; pulse to combine.) Set aside.

4. Bring a large pot of water to a boil. Salt the water, add the noodles, and cook until al dente, about 8 minutes. Drain in a colander, and rinse with cold water to stop the cooking.

5. Dress the noodles with ½ cup of the peanut sauce, and transfer to a medium serving bowl. If desired, set the bowl into a larger bowl filled with ice to keep the noodles chilled at the table. Arrange the reserved peanuts, remaining sauce, chives, cucumber, and lettuce in serving dishes on the table. Guests can assemble their own rolls by wrapping noodles, a little sauce, and their choice of meat and fillings in a lettuce leaf.

herb-marinated cheese

SERVES 4

Serve this quick appetizer with a hearty brown bread.

  8 ounces Bûcheron or other ripened goat's-milk cheese
  ½ small red onion, thinly sliced into half-moons
  1 teaspoon fresh thyme
  1 teaspoon fresh oregano
     Pinch of crushed red pepper flakes
  ¼ cup extra-virgin olive oil
  1 tablespoon red-wine vinegar
     Coarse salt and freshly ground black pepper
     Sliced whole-grain bread

1. Cut the cheese crosswise into ½-inch slices, and arrange the slices on a serving platter.

2. Sprinkle the cheese slices with onion, herbs, and red pepper flakes. Drizzle with the olive oil and vinegar. Season with salt and pepper.

3. Let sit at room temperature for about 30 minutes. Serve with sliced bread.

roasted cauliflower and manchego hand pies

MAKES 8

  1 small head cauliflower, florets separated and thinly sliced (about 4 cups)
  7 tablespoons extra-virgin olive oil
     Coarse salt and freshly ground pepper
  ⅔ cup hazelnuts, toasted, skins removed
  1 garlic clove
  1 teaspoon finely grated lemon zest
  2 teaspoons finely chopped fresh rosemary
     All-purpose flour, for work surface
     Cheese Short Crust, made with Manchego cheese (page 216)
  5 ounces Manchego cheese, thinly sliced
  1 tablespoon heavy cream
  1 large egg yolk

1. Preheat the oven to 375°F. Toss the cauliflower with 3 tablespoons of the oil in a medium bowl; season with salt and pepper. Spread on a rimmed baking sheet. Roast until golden brown, about 7 minutes. Flip the cauliflower; roast 5 minutes more. Let cool.

2. Put the nuts and garlic in a food processor. With the machine running, slowly add the remaining 4 tablespoons oil until the mixture is finely chopped. Add the lemon zest and 1 teaspoon of the rosemary; season with salt and pepper. Process until combined.

3. Roll out half of the dough on a lightly floured surface to a ¼-inch thickness. Cut out 8 4-inch rounds. Transfer to a rimmed baking sheet lined with parchment. Spread 2 teaspoons hazelnut mixture onto each round, leaving a ¼-inch border. Divide the cauliflower among the rounds. Top with cheese and the remaining teaspoon rosemary, dividing evenly; sprinkle with pepper. Whisk the cream and egg yolk in a small bowl. Brush the edges of the dough with egg wash. Set aside.

4. Roll out the remaining dough on a lightly floured surface to a ¼-inch thickness. Cut out 8 4-inch rounds. Cut out 8 flowers from scraps with a small flower-shaped cookie cutter. Place a dough round on top of each pie; gently press the edges with a fork to seal. Brush the crusts with egg wash; place a flower on each pie. Brush the flowers with egg wash. Refrigerate until cold, about 20 minutes. Bake until the crust is golden brown, 30 to 32 minutes. Serve warm or at room temperature.

almond-crusted curry chicken salad tea sandwiches

MAKES 2 DOZEN

- 1 cup sliced blanched almonds
- 1 whole skinless and boneless chicken breast (about 10 ounces)
- 1 teaspoon coarse salt
- 1 small onion, unpeeled and quartered
- 4 whole black peppercorns
- 5 cups water
- 1½ cups mayonnaise
- 2 teaspoons curry powder
- 2 tablespoons mango chutney
- ¾ teaspoon white-wine vinegar
- 3 tablespoons unsweetened shredded coconut, toasted
- ½ cup (1 stick) unsalted butter, room temperature
- 24 thin slices white bread

1. Preheat the oven to 350° F. Spread the almonds on a baking sheet, and toast until fragrant and golden, 5 to 7 minutes. Transfer to a bowl to cool, and gently crush. Set aside.

2. In a medium saucepan, combine the chicken, salt, onion, peppercorns, and water. Bring to a boil over medium-high heat; reduce heat, and simmer until the chicken is cooked through, about 20 minutes. Transfer the chicken to a plate to cool; reserve the stock for another use.

3. When the chicken is cool enough to handle, shred the meat and chop it into small pieces. Return to the plate; cover, and place in refrigerator until ready to use.

4. In a small bowl, combine the mayonnaise, curry powder, chutney, vinegar, and toasted coconut; stir to combine. Reserve ½ cup curry mayonnaise, and stir the remaining mayonnaise into the chicken. Thinly spread butter on 2 slices bread; cover 1 slice with a thin layer of chicken salad, and top with the other bread slice. Set aside. Repeat with the remaining ingredients.

5. Stack several sandwiches; use a serrated knife to trim the crusts and cut into 2 rectangles. Arrange the sandwiches in a single row on the serving tray; they should rest on one long edge with the short ends standing upright. Spread a dab of reserved curry mayonnaise on the short ends, and gently pat on the almonds. Serve immediately. (Do not cover with damp paper towels, or the almonds will become soft.)

bacon and egg salad tea sandwiches

MAKES 3 DOZEN

- 6 large hard-boiled eggs, peeled and finely chopped
- ½ cup mayonnaise
- 2½ teaspoons Dijon mustard
- ¼ teaspoon cayenne pepper
- 6 slices bacon (about 5 ounces), cooked and coarsely chopped
- ½ teaspoon hot pepper sauce, such as Tabasco

  Coarse salt and freshly ground black pepper
- 5 tablespoons unsalted butter, room temperature
- 18 thin slices white bread
- ¼ cup finely chopped chives

1. Place the chopped eggs in a medium bowl. Add the mayonnaise, mustard, cayenne, and bacon; stir to combine. Add the hot pepper sauce, and season with salt and pepper.

2. Thinly spread butter on 2 slices of bread; cover 1 slice with egg salad, and top with the other slice. Use a serrated knife to trim the crusts and cut into 4 squares. Dip one edge of each square in the chopped chives. Repeat with the remaining ingredients. Cover the sandwiches with damp paper towels until ready to serve.

mozzarella, prosciutto, and pesto butter tea sandwiches

MAKES 2 DOZEN

To make perfectly round sandwiches, cut each of the layers separately with the same biscuit cutter. Ask your butcher to slice the prosciutto more thickly than usual so it can be cut easily without tearing; you will need 1 round for each sandwich.

- 6 tablespoons (¾ stick) unsalted butter, room temperature
- ¾ cup fresh basil, packed (about 2 ounces), rinsed well, and dried
- ½ garlic clove
- 3 tablespoons finely grated Parmesan cheese
- 1 tablespoon pine nuts
- 8 ounces sliced prosciutto
- 1 pound fresh mozzarella cheese
- 2 loaves rustic bread (about 2 pounds), cut into 48 ¼-inch slices

1. Make the pesto butter: Combine the butter, basil, garlic, Parmesan, and pine nuts in the bowl of a food processor fitted with the metal blade; process until blended. Set aside. Lay the prosciutto slices flat on a piece of plastic wrap, and cover with another piece. Place in freezer 10 minutes.

2. Remove the prosciutto from the freezer; use a 2¼-inch round cutter to cut into rounds. Slice the mozzarella ⅛ inch thick, and cut into rounds. Cut the bread using the same cutter, being sure to remove all the crust.

3. Spread a thin layer of pesto butter on 2 bread rounds. Layer 1 round with a round each of mozzarella and prosciutto; top with the other bread round. Repeat with the remaining ingredients. Cover with damp paper towels until ready to serve.

roquefort butter and red pear tea sandwiches

MAKES 2 DOZEN

The red skins of the pears are a colorful accent to these simple tea sandwiches. Use the Roquefort butter in other combinations, such as with watercress or thinly sliced tomato.

- Juice of 1 lemon
- 2 tablespoons water
- 1 red pear, cored and very thinly sliced
- 4 ounces Roquefort cheese, crumbled
- ½ cup (1 stick) unsalted butter, room temperature
- ⅛ teaspoon freshly ground pepper
- 16 thin slices white bread or brioche

1. Combine the lemon juice and the water in a small bowl; immerse the sliced pears until ready to use to prevent discoloration. Blot dry with paper towels before using.

2. In a medium bowl, gently stir the Roquefort into the butter, leaving small bits of cheese. Be careful not to overmix, or the butter will turn blue. Add the pepper.

3. Spread a thin layer of Roquefort butter on 2 slices of bread. Line 1 slice with pears, overlapping slightly, and top with the other bread slice. Use a serrated knife to trim the crusts and cut into 3 rectangles (about 1 × 3 inches). Repeat with the remaining ingredients. Cover with damp paper towels until ready to serve.

smoked duck and chutney butter tea sandwiches

MAKES 2 DOZEN

- 1 cup (2 sticks) unsalted butter, room temperature
- 6 tablespoons peach or apricot chutney
- 24 thin slices black or pumpernickel bread
- 1 pound smoked duck breasts, trimmed of fat, very thinly sliced
- 1 bunch watercress, cleaned and trimmed

1. In the bowl of a food processor fitted with the plastic blade, combine the butter and chutney; pulse until well combined.

2. Thinly spread chutney butter on 2 bread slices. Cover 1 slice with thin layers of duck and watercress; top with the other bread slice. Use a serrated knife to trim the crusts and cut into 2 triangles. Repeat with the remaining ingredients. Cover with damp paper towels until ready to serve.

stuffed marinated hot red cherry peppers

MAKES 14; SERVES 7 AS A FIRST COURSE

- 14 hot red cherry peppers, cored and seeded, tops reserved
- 4 ounces young pecorino or provolone cheese, cut into ¼-inch cubes
- 14 small sprigs fresh marjoram
- ¼ cup extra-virgin olive oil
- 2 tablespoons red-wine vinegar
- 1 garlic clove, minced
- 2 teaspoons coarse salt
- ¼ teaspoon freshly ground black pepper
  Crusty bread, for serving

1. Stuff each pepper with cheese and a sprig of marjoram. Transfer the stuffed peppers and pepper tops to a glass loaf pan.

2. Whisk the oil, vinegar, garlic, salt, and pepper in a small bowl. Pour over the peppers. Let marinate at room temperature 1 hour.

3. Preheat the oven to 400°F. Place the tops on the peppers. Cook until the cheese has melted and the peppers are tender, 12 to 15 minutes. Let cool slightly. Serve with bread.

dijon baby lamb chops

SERVES 6 TO 8

- ½ cup Dijon mustard
- 3 tablespoons packed light-brown sugar
  Coarse salt and freshly ground pepper
- 2 racks baby lamb chops (8 ribs and about 1¼ pounds each), frenched
  Mint sprigs, for garnish
  Red Currant–Mint Dipping Sauce (recipe follows)

1. Stir the mustard, brown sugar, ½ teaspoon salt, and ¼ teaspoon pepper in a bowl. Brush the mixture all over the lamb. Transfer to a large resealable plastic bag; refrigerate for at least 6 hours (up to overnight).

2. Preheat the oven to 450°F. Bring the lamb to room temperature. Transfer to a rimmed baking sheet. Roast until golden brown and an instant-read thermometer inserted into the thickest part registers 125° to 130°F, 15 to 20 minutes. Remove from the oven, and tent with foil. Let rest 10 minutes. Just before serving, cut the lamb racks into individual chops. Garnish with mint sprigs. Serve with dipping sauce.

red currant–mint dipping sauce

MAKES ABOUT 1½ CUPS

- 1½ cups red currant jelly
- 1 tablespoon red-wine vinegar
- 1 cup coarsely chopped mint leaves

Whisk the jelly, vinegar, and 1 tablespoon water in a medium bowl until smooth. Fold in the mint. The sauce can be refrigerated in an airtight container up to 6 hours.

easy pea ravioli with mint

SERVES 4 AS A FIRST COURSE

- 3 tablespoons olive oil
- 1 shallot, finely chopped (about ¼ cup)
- 1 garlic clove, minced
- 2¼ cups shelled fresh or thawed frozen peas
- ¼ cup plus 2 tablespoons dry white wine
  Coarse salt and freshly ground pepper
- 40 wonton wrappers (3½ inches each)
- 1 large egg, lightly beaten
- ¼ cup (½ stick) unsalted butter
- 4 fresh mint leaves, thinly sliced

1. Heat the oil in a medium skillet over medium heat. Add the shallot; cook, stirring occasionally, until translucent, 3 to 4 minutes. Add the garlic; cook until soft, 2 to 3 minutes. Add the peas, wine, 1 cup water, and 1½ teaspoons salt; season with pepper. Simmer until the liquid has almost evaporated and the peas are tender, 12 to 15 minutes. Let cool slightly.

2. Puree the pea mixture in a food processor. Brush the edges of 10 wrappers with egg. Place 1 tablespoon puree in centers. Top with a dry wrapper; seal edges. Trim using a 3-inch round cutter. Repeat with the remaining wrappers and purée.

3. Working in batches, cook the ravioli in salted simmering water until they are soft and rise to the surface, about 2 minutes. Meanwhile, melt the butter in a medium skillet over medium heat; add the ravioli to the skillet, and cook until the butter is frothy and the ravioli is coated, 2 to 3 minutes. Sprinkle with mint. Serve immediately.

radishes with herbed ricotta dip, sweet butter, and fleur de sel

SERVES 12

We used a combination of French breakfast, white icicle, and pink beauty radishes, but you can use any variety you'd like. When the weather is hot, sprinkle radishes with crushed ice before serving to keep them crisp.

- 1 pound low-fat fresh ricotta cheese
- 2 tablespoons finely chopped fresh flat-leaf parsley
- 1 tablespoon finely chopped fresh dill
- 1 tablespoon finely chopped fresh basil
  Coarse salt and freshly ground pepper
- 4 bunches radishes, trimmed if desired
- ¼ cup (½ stick) sweet unsalted butter, softened, for serving
  Fleur de sel, for serving

1. Make the dip: Stir the ricotta, parsley, dill, and basil in a medium bowl. Season with salt and pepper. The dip can be refrigerated in an airtight container up to 2 days.

2. Serve the radishes with bowls of dip, butter, and fleur de sel.

fried anchovies and sage

SERVES 6

- Whole milk, for soaking
- 18 best-quality anchovy fillets
- 36 small to medium, narrow, fresh sage leaves
- 1 to 2 tablespoons instant flour (such as Wondra)
- 1 large egg, lightly beaten
  Extra-virgin olive oil, for frying

1. Put the milk into a shallow dish. Add the anchovy fillets; soak 10 minutes. Drain on paper towels, and pat dry. Cut the fillets to be the same length as the sage leaves. Lay each sage leaf face up on a large cutting board. Place an anchovy fillet on half of the sage leaves; crush with fork tines, being careful not to tear leaves. Sandwich with another leaf, face down. Press with the back of a spoon to seal.

2. Preheat the oven to 200° F. Put the flour into a bowl and the egg into another. Heat ¼ inch oil in a medium skillet over medium-high heat. Coat 6 of the anchovy-sage sandwiches with flour, shaking off any excess, then with egg, allowing excess to drip off. Fry, turning once, until golden, 45 seconds to 1 minute per side. Drain on paper towels. Transfer to the oven to keep warm. Repeat with the remaining anchovies. Serve immediately.

whole-grain bread with cheese and candied shallots
SERVES 8

3 tablespoons extra-virgin olive oil
1 pound shallots, thinly sliced
   Coarse salt
1 tablespoon pure maple syrup
½ teaspoon balsamic vinegar
   Freshly ground pepper
   Soft, mild cheese, such as farmer cheese or goat cheese, for serving
   Sliced whole-grain bread, for serving
   Thyme leaves, for garnish

1. Heat the oil in a medium skillet over medium-high heat. Add the shallots and a pinch of salt. Cook, stirring often, until the shallots have softened and browned, about 20 minutes.

2. Reduce the heat to medium-low, and stir in the maple syrup and vinegar. Cook 2 minutes, then season with salt and pepper. Candied shallots can be refrigerated in an airtight container up to 1 week; bring to room temperature before serving. To serve, spread cheese onto bread slices; top with the candied shallots, and garnish with thyme leaves.

croquettes with serrano ham and manchego cheese
SERVES 8 TO 12 AS A TAPA; MAKES ABOUT 16

2   tablespoons unsalted butter
2   tablespoons olive oil
¼   cup finely chopped onion
    Coarse salt and freshly ground pepper
7   tablespoons all-purpose flour, plus more for shaping
¾   cup whole milk
6   tablespoons finely chopped serrano ham
⅓   cup plus ¼ cup grated Manchego cheese (about 1¾ ounces)
3   large eggs
1½ cups fresh bread crumbs
    Vegetable oil, for frying
    Fresh flat-leaf parsley sprigs, for garnish

1. Heat the butter and oil in a medium saucepan over medium heat until the butter has melted. Add the onion; season with salt and pepper. Cook, stirring occasionally, until the onion is translucent, about 3 minutes. Add the flour; cook, stirring, 1 minute. Whisk in the milk, and cook, whisking, 3 minutes. Whisk in the ham and ⅓ cup cheese. Season with salt and pepper as desired. Spread the mixture onto a baking sheet, and let cool completely. The mixture can be refrigerated in an airtight container up to 2 days.

2. Whisk together the eggs in a shallow dish. Stir together the bread crumbs and remaining ¼ cup cheese in another shallow dish. Scoop tablespoons of the cooled mixture, and shape with floured hands into 2-inch ovals. Working with 1 oval at a time, coat in the beaten egg, then in the bread crumb mixture. Transfer to a parchment-lined baking sheet.

3. Heat 2½ inches oil in a large, heavy stockpot until it registers 375° F on a deep-fry thermometer. Working in batches to avoid crowding, fry the croquettes, flipping once, until dark golden brown, 1 to 2 minutes total. Using a slotted spoon, transfer to paper towels to drain. (Adjust the heat between batches as needed to keep oil at a steady temperature.) Serve warm, garnished with parsley sprigs.

fried herbed almonds

MAKES 2 CUPS

These crunchy thyme-flecked nuts are delicious served with sherry and slices of Manchego cheese.

3   tablespoons extra-virgin olive oil
2   cups whole blanched almonds
2   tablespoons fresh thyme leaves
     Coarse salt and freshly ground pepper

1. Heat the oil in a large skillet over medium heat. Add the almonds, and cook, stirring occasionally, until lightly golden and fragrant, 10 to 12 minutes.

2. Stir in the thyme leaves. Remove from the heat. Season with salt and pepper. Spread out on a rimmed baking sheet, and let cool completely. The almonds can be stored in an airtight container at room temperature up to 2 weeks.

tamari and maple roasted almonds

MAKES 2 CUPS

These tangy glazed nuts go perfectly with a glass of sherry.

10   ounces whole shelled almonds (2 cups)
¼   cup reduced-sodium tamari
3   tablespoons pure maple syrup
      Nonstick cooking spray

1. Preheat the oven to 350° F. Spread the almonds in a single layer on a rimmed baking sheet, and bake until lightly toasted and fragrant, 7 to 8 minutes.

2. In a medium bowl, combine the tamari and maple syrup. Add the almonds, and toss until thoroughly coated. Lightly cover the baking sheet with cooking spray, and spread the almonds evenly on the sheet.

3. Roast in the oven until deep brown, stirring once, 15 to 17 minutes. Immediately transfer to a clean baking sheet and spread out the almonds, separating them so the nuts don't touch. Let cool before serving.

FIT TO EAT RECIPE PER SERVING: 306 CALORIES, 24 G FAT, 0 MG CHOLESTEROL, 17 G CARBOHYDRATE, 401 MG SODIUM, 11 G PROTEIN, 6 G FIBER

smoky cashews

MAKES 2 CUPS

2   cups unsalted cashews (about 9 ounces)
2   tablespoons finely chopped fresh
     rosemary
1   teaspoon smoked hot paprika
2   tablespoons light brown sugar
2   teaspoons coarse salt
1   tablespoon unsalted butter, melted

Preheat the oven to 350° F. Spread the cashews in a single layer on a rimmed baking sheet. Toast in the oven, stirring once or twice, until golden, 10 to 12 minutes. Toss with the remaining ingredients. Serve warm or at room temperature.

soups

AND

stews

....

beef shin and carrot stew

SERVES 6

6 beef shins (10 to 12 ounces each)
  Coarse salt and freshly ground pepper
  All-purpose flour, for dredging
3 sprigs fresh parsley
3 sprigs fresh thyme
7 whole allspice
10 whole black peppercorns
¼ cup plus 2 tablespoons extra-virgin
  olive oil
4 leeks, white and pale-green parts only,
  coarsely chopped and rinsed well
3 celery stalks, cut into ½-inch cubes
4 garlic cloves, crushed
1 can (14.9 ounces) stout, such as Guinness
1½ cups homemade or low-sodium
  store-bought beef stock
1 strip (2 inches long) orange zest
1½ pounds small boiling potatoes, peeled,
  if desired
1 pound Thumbelina carrots, scrubbed
  (or other carrots, peeled and cut into
  1½-inch pieces)
  Coarsely chopped fresh curly-leaf parsley,
  for garnish

1. Preheat the oven to 375° F. Generously season the beef with salt and pepper. Dredge the beef in the flour; shake off excess.

2. Wrap the parsley, thyme, allspice, and peppercorns in cheesecloth, and tie with kitchen twine to form a bouquet garni.

3. Heat 3 tablespoons of the oil in a Dutch oven or large ovenproof saucepan over medium-high heat. Working in batches, brown the beef, 3 to 4 minutes per side, adding more oil (up to 2 tablespoons) as needed. Transfer the beef to a bowl.

4. Add 1 tablespoon oil to the fat in the pot. Stir in the leeks, celery, and garlic; cook, stirring occasionally, until softened, about 7 minutes. Add the stout; cook, scraping up the browned bits from the bottom of the pot.

5. Return the beef to the pot. Add the stock, bouquet garni, zest, and enough water to cover. Season with salt and pepper. Bring to a boil over medium-high heat. Cover the pot; transfer it to the oven. Braise the beef 2 hours.

6. Add the potatoes and carrots. Cover the pot; braise 1 hour more. Discard the bouquet garni. Garnish the stew with parsley.

curried apple soup

SERVES 4

1 tablespoon unsalted butter
2 shallots, minced
2 teaspoons freshly grated ginger
1½ tablespoons curry powder
2 Granny Smith apples, peeled, cored,
  and cut into 1-inch pieces
1 small russet potato, peeled and cut into
  1-inch pieces
1 teaspoon coarse salt, plus more
  for seasoning
3¾ cups homemade or low-sodium canned
  chicken stock
½ cup heavy cream or milk
  Freshly ground pepper
  Sour cream, for garnish

1. Melt the butter in a medium saucepan over medium heat. Add the shallots; cook until soft and translucent, about 2 minutes. Add the ginger and curry powder; cook, stirring, 1 minute. Add the apples, potato, salt, and chicken stock. Bring to a simmer over medium-high heat, and cook until the potato is tender when pierced with a paring knife, about 12 minutes. Remove from heat, and let cool slightly.

2. Use an immersion blender, or transfer mixture to the jar of a blender, working in batches if necessary so as not to fill more than halfway; puree just until smooth (do not overprocess). Return the soup to the pan; stir in the cream, and season with salt and pepper. Place over medium heat until just heated through; do not let the soup boil. Divide among serving bowls, and garnish with sour cream.

elwood's ham chowder

MAKES ABOUT 5 QUARTS

This recipe is courtesy of Donald Barickman; it was created with and named for his father, Elwood.

- 1 tablespoon vegetable oil
- 1 pound Virginia ham, cut into ½-inch pieces
- 2 large onions, cut into ½-inch pieces (about 3 cups)
- 4 garlic cloves, thinly sliced
- 2 bunches collard greens (about 1 pound), stems discarded, washed, and roughly chopped
- 1 28-ounce can whole tomatoes with juice, roughly chopped
- 7 cups homemade or low-sodium canned chicken stock
- 2 cups homemade or low-sodium canned beef stock
- 8 medium red potatoes, cut into ½-inch cubes (about 6 cups)
- 1½ tablespoons chopped fresh thyme leaves
- 1½ tablespoons chopped fresh flat-leaf parsley

Coarse salt and freshly ground pepper

Hot pepper sauce, such as Tabasco (optional)

1. Heat the oil in a large stockpot over medium-low heat. Add the ham, and cook until it starts to release juices, about 2 minutes; do not brown. Add the onions and garlic; cook, stirring occasionally, until soft, about 10 minutes.

2. Working in batches, if necessary, so as not to overcrowd the pot, cook the collard greens, tossing frequently with tongs, until thoroughly wilted. Add the tomatoes and juice, chicken and beef stocks, potatoes, thyme, and parsley. Bring to a boil, and reduce heat to a gentle simmer; cook, stirring and skimming any foam from the surface occasionally, until the potatoes are easily pierced with a paring knife, 30 to 40 minutes. Remove from heat; season with salt, black pepper, and hot pepper sauce, as desired. Serve hot.

miso soup with tofu, spinach, and carrots

SERVES 4

Be sure to purchase firm or extra-firm tofu for this soup, as it will hold up better in hot liquid than softer varieties. Because the flavor and healthful qualities of miso are affected when boiled or with prolonged exposure to high temperatures, it should be added only at the end of cooking. Whisk it with a bit of liquid first so it is quickly and evenly distributed. We used white miso, which is lower in sodium, but you can use darker types for a stronger, more pronounced flavor.

- 3 cups homemade or low-sodium canned vegetable or chicken stock, skimmed of fat
- 2 cups water
- 2 carrots, cut into matchsticks (about 1 cup)
- ⅓ pound spinach, stems removed, cut into 1-inch strips
- 6 ounces extra-firm tofu, cut into ¾-inch cubes
- 2 tablespoons white miso
- 1 scallion, sliced crosswise into 1-inch strips

1. In a medium saucepan, bring the stock and the water to a boil over high heat. Reduce heat to medium-low, and add the carrots. Cook until the carrots are crisp-tender, about 2 minutes.

2. Add the spinach and tofu, and stir to combine. Continue cooking just until the spinach is wilted and the tofu is heated through, about 1 minute more.

3. Meanwhile, place the miso in a small bowl, and stir in ¼ cup cooking liquid until the miso is dissolved. Add the mixture to the saucepan, stirring to combine. Do not let the soup boil once miso has been added.

4. Remove from heat. Ladle the soup into 4 serving bowls. Sprinkle with scallions. Serve immediately.

garden and snap pea soup with vidalia onions

SERVES 8

We like this soup best when served hot, but it is also delightfully refreshing well chilled.

- 2 tablespoons unsalted butter
- 2 medium Vidalia or other sweet onions, roughly chopped

  Coarse salt and freshly ground pepper
- 6 cups homemade or low-sodium store-bought chicken stock, plus more for thinning
- 1¼ pounds sugar snap peas, ends trimmed and string removed (about 1¼ cups)
- 1¾ pounds garden peas, shelled (1¾ cups)
- ½ cup heavy cream

1. Prepare an ice-water bath, and set aside. Melt the butter in a medium saucepan over medium-low heat. Add the onions, and season with salt and pepper. Cook, stirring frequently, until the onions are translucent, about 8 minutes.

2. Add the stock; bring to a boil. Reserve about ¼ cup each snap and garden peas. Add the remaining snap peas to the saucepan, and return the stock to a boil. Add the remaining garden peas; cook until all the peas are tender, about 4 minutes. Transfer the pan to the ice-water bath. Stir until the mixture is cool.

3. Working in batches, transfer the mixture to the jar of a blender; process until it is smooth. Return to the saucepan, and set over medium heat. Stir in the cream, and adjust the consistency with more stock, if needed. Season with salt and pepper.

4. Meanwhile, prepare a small ice-water bath, and bring a small saucepan of water to a boil. Add the reserved snap peas and garden peas. Blanch until they are just tender, 2 to 3 minutes. Using a slotted spoon, transfer the peas to the ice-water bath; drain in a colander. Cut the snap peas into small pieces.

5. To serve, divide the soup among soup bowls, and garnish each serving with blanched mixed peas.

chilled fennel and leek soup

MAKES 4½ QUARTS

This soup must be served very cold, so for best results, prepare it a day ahead and let it chill overnight in the refrigerator.

- 6 medium leeks (about 1¼ pounds), white and light green parts only, thinly sliced
- ½ cup (1 stick) unsalted butter
- 1 large yellow onion, diced
- 1 teaspoon fennel seeds
- ½ teaspoon coarse salt, plus more for seasoning
- ⅛ teaspoon freshly ground pepper, plus more for seasoning
- 2 garlic cloves, minced
- 3 medium fennel bulbs (about 2 pounds), trimmed and roughly chopped
- 8 cups homemade or low-sodium canned chicken stock
- 4 cups cold water
- 2 tablespoons Pernod (optional)

  Chervil sprigs, for garnish

1. Place the leeks in a large bowl of cold water; stir, and let stand 5 minutes to let dirt and sand settle to the bottom. You may need to repeat this several times, changing the water each time. Once they are clean, let drain on paper towels.

2. Melt the butter in a large saucepan over medium-low heat. Add the onion and fennel seeds along with the salt and pepper. Cook, stirring occasionally, until the onion is softened and translucent, about 10 minutes. Add the garlic; cook until fragrant but not brown, about 2 minutes.

3. Add the leeks and fennel to the pan, and cook until the vegetables are tender, about 10 minutes. Add the chicken stock and the water, and bring to a boil; reduce heat, and simmer 20 minutes more.

4. Remove from heat, and let cool slightly. Working in several batches, transfer the soup to the jar of a blender, being careful not to fill more than halfway and to cover the lid with a kitchen towel, as hot liquid expands when blended. Puree until smooth.

Transfer to an airtight container, and place in refrigerator to chill completely, at least 4 hours or overnight.

5. To serve, stir in the Pernod, if using, and season with salt and pepper. Ladle into soup bowls, and garnish with chervil.

mexican fiesta soup with roasted tomatillo and cilantro pesto

SERVES 4

Cilantro's pungent fragrance partners well with fruity tomatillos in a lively pesto. The mixture offsets the spiciness of the cumin and jalapeño in this delectable soup.

- 4   tomatillos, peeled and rinsed
- ⅔ cup fresh cilantro leaves, packed, rinsed well
- 2   garlic cloves, minced
- 2   tablespoons freshly squeezed lime juice
- 1   small white onion, diced
- 1   jalapeño pepper, diced, plus more sliced for garnish (optional)
- ½ teaspoon ground cumin
- 1   28-ounce can whole peeled tomatoes (about 8 tomatoes), drained and crushed
- 3   ears corn, quartered
- 4   cups homemade or low-sodium store-bought chicken stock, skimmed of fat
    Freshly ground pepper
- ½ ripe avocado, pitted, cut into ¼-inch-thick slices
    Nonstick cooking spray

1. Preheat the oven to 375°F. Place the tomatillos on a small rimmed baking sheet. Roast in the oven, turning once midway through, until they are softened and slightly charred, about 25 minutes. Remove from the oven, and let cool slightly. Transfer to the bowl of a food processor; add the cilantro, 1 garlic clove, and lime juice. Process until smooth and combined; set aside.

2. Lightly coat the bottom of a large nonstick saucepan with cooking spray. Add the onion,

remaining garlic clove, and diced jalapeño; cook, stirring occasionally, over medium heat until the onion is softened, about 7 minutes. Add the cumin, tomatoes, corn, and chicken stock. Bring the liquid to a boil; reduce heat, and simmer until the vegetables are tender, 12 to 15 minutes.

3. Remove from heat; stir in 3 tablespoons reserved tomatillo mixture, and season with pepper. Add the sliced avocado. Ladle into serving bowls; garnish with jalapeño slices, if desired. Serve with the remaining tomatillo pesto.

FIT TO EAT RECIPE PER SERVING: 230 CALORIES, 6 G FAT, 3 MG CHOLESTEROL, 41 G CARBOHYDRATE, 717 MG SODIUM, 9 G PROTEIN, 7 G FIBER

pea bisque with shrimp and tarragon

SERVES 6

- ½ pound green split peas, picked over and rinsed
- 2   8-ounce bottles clam juice
- 6   cups water
- 1   medium onion, chopped
- 1   10-ounce box frozen baby peas, thawed
- 1   pound medium shrimp, peeled and halved lengthwise
- 3   garlic cloves, minced
- 1½ tablespoons lemon zest, finely grated
- 1   teaspoon hot paprika
- ¼ teaspoon coarse salt
- 1   tablespoon unsalted butter
- 1   tablespoon fresh lemon juice
- 1   tablespoon fresh tarragon, finely chopped

1. Place the split peas in a large bowl with enough water to cover by 2 inches; let stand for 6 hours or overnight.

2. Drain the split peas, and transfer them to a large stockpot. Add the clam juice, water, and onion; bring to a boil, reduce heat, and simmer, stirring occasionally, until the peas soften, 35 to 40 minutes.

3. Stir in the baby peas, and simmer for 5 minutes. Let the soup cool slightly. Place in the bowl of a food processor, working in batches, if necessary; puree until smooth. Press through a fine sieve into a large saucepan, and keep warm over low heat.

4. In a large bowl, stir together the shrimp, garlic, lemon zest, paprika, and salt. Melt the butter in a nonstick medium skillet over medium-high heat. Add the shrimp, and cook, stirring, until they begin to turn pink and opaque. Add the lemon juice, and stir for 1 minute more. Remove from heat, and stir in the tarragon.

5. Ladle the bisque into 6 shallow soup plates, and place a mound of shrimp in the center of each.

chili con carne
SERVES 12

You can control the heat of this chili by increasing or decreasing the number of chiles; be sure to have good ventilation over the stove when pan-roasting them. If you have two large cast-iron skillets, save time by using both at once. If you like, serve the chili with other traditional garnishes, such as shredded Cheddar and Monterey Jack cheese, sour cream, and chopped cilantro.

> 1 *pound dried pinto beans, soaked according to package directions*
> ¼ *cup plus 3 tablespoons corn oil*
> 3½ *pounds plum tomatoes (about 18)*
> 2½ *pounds medium yellow onions (about 7), stem ends trimmed, quartered lengthwise with skins left on*
> 10 *garlic cloves (skins left on)*
> 4 *mulato chiles*
> 3 *ancho chiles*
> 1 *14½-ounce can low-sodium beef broth*
> 1 *cup water*
> 5 *pounds ground round or ground chuck*
> 1 *tablespoon coarse salt*
> 2 *ounces Mexican chocolate or semisweet chocolate, chopped*
> ½ *teaspoon freshly ground black pepper*
> *Lumpy Guacamole (recipe follows)*

1. Drain and rinse the soaked beans, and place them in a large saucepan with water to cover by 2 inches. Bring to a boil, reduce heat, cover, and simmer gently until the beans are tender, about 1½ hours. (You can prepare the beans 1 or 2 days ahead; let cool, cover, and refrigerate in their liquid.)

2. Heat 2 tablespoons of the oil in a 12-inch cast-iron skillet over medium heat; add the tomatoes, and cook, turning occasionally, until skins begin to char, about 5 minutes. Cover the pan, reduce heat to medium-low, and continue to cook, turning, until the tomatoes have softened, 7 to 8 minutes more. Transfer to a large bowl. When cool enough to handle, peel and core the tomatoes. Place the tomato flesh in a clean bowl, and reserve.

3. While the tomatoes cool, place two-thirds of the onion quarters in the same skillet with 2 tablespoons of the oil. Cover, and cook over medium heat, turning occasionally, until nicely charred and softened, 12 to 15 minutes. Transfer to a bowl to cool. Repeat with the garlic cloves, remaining onion, and another tablespoon oil. When cool enough to handle, peel the garlic and onion, cutting off and discarding roots and peels and adding the flesh to the bowl with the tomato. Transfer the vegetables and any juices to a blender in batches (fill no more than halfway), and puree until nearly smooth. Set aside in a large bowl.

4. Tear the chiles in half, and discard the stems and seeds. In the same skillet over medium heat, toast the chiles in the remaining 2 tablespoons oil, turning with tongs, until smoky, about 3 minutes. Transfer to the blender. Bring the broth and water to a boil, pour over the chiles, and let stand until the chiles are pliable, about 5 minutes. Puree the chiles and broth, and stir into the tomato mixture.

5. In a 7-quart Dutch oven over medium heat, cook one-third of the meat, breaking it up with a spoon and stirring occasionally, until nicely browned, about 8 minutes. While the meat is cooking, brown another third of the meat in the skillet. Then add that batch to the first in the Dutch oven. Stir the tomato mixture into the meat in the Dutch oven. Brown the remaining beef in the same skillet; add to the Dutch oven. Drain the cooked beans; add them to pot with the salt.

6. Bring the chili to a boil, reduce heat, cover, and simmer gently, stirring, until the meat is tender and the sauce is thick, about 1½ hours. Stir in the chocolate; season with pepper. Serve with the guacamole.

lumpy guacamole
MAKES 6 CUPS

This lively guacamole can also be served as a dip with tortilla chips. If you want to make it a day ahead, be sure to press plastic wrap directly on the surface of the guacamole to prevent browning.

- 6   ripe Hass avocados
- ¼   cup fresh lime juice
- ¼   cup fresh lemon juice
- 4   plum tomatoes, finely diced
- 1   medium onion, finely diced
- 1   jalapeño pepper, minced (with seeds, if desired)
- 3   garlic cloves, minced
- 1¼ teaspoons coarse salt
- ½   teaspoon freshly ground pepper, or to taste

Halve the avocados, and remove the pits. Score the flesh into cubes with a small, sharp knife, and scrape them into a bowl. Stir in the lime juice, lemon juice, tomatoes, onion, chile, and garlic. Season with salt and pepper.

winter vegetable chicken stew
SERVES 6

- 12 ounces boneless, skinless chicken thighs (about 4 pieces)
- 1   pound boneless, skinless chicken breast halves (about 3 pieces)
- ½   teaspoon coarse salt, plus more for cooking water
- ⅛   teaspoon freshly ground pepper
- 4   slender carrots, peeled
- 3   large celery ribs
- 2   medium parsnips (6 ounces), peeled

- 4   small onions, peeled and quartered lengthwise, with roots attached
- 3   cups water
- 1   14½-ounce can low-sodium chicken broth, skimmed of fat
- 1   tablespoon fresh rosemary leaves or 1 teaspoon dried
- ½   pound wide egg noodles
- ¼   cup finely chopped fresh flat-leaf parsley
- 1   tablespoon unsalted butter
- 4   garlic cloves, thinly sliced
- 1   bunch (1½ pounds) Swiss chard, coarsely chopped, with stems
- 2   ounces shaved Parmesan cheese

1. Cut the chicken into 1-inch pieces; season with salt and pepper. Heat a 6-quart Dutch oven over medium heat until hot. Add half of the chicken to the pot; cook, turning occasionally, until nicely browned, about 7 minutes. Transfer to a large bowl. Repeat.

2. Meanwhile, cut the carrots, celery, and parsnips into ¾-inch pieces. Place the vegetables, onions, browned chicken, water, broth, and rosemary in the Dutch oven; scrape the browned bits from the bottom. Cover; bring to a simmer over low heat. Cook, stirring occasionally, until the vegetables are barely tender, about 10 minutes.

3. Cook the noodles in a pot of boiling salted water until al dente; drain and return to pot. Stir in parsley, chicken, and any collected juices in the bowl. Cook on low until the chicken is heated through, 1 to 2 minutes. Remove from heat; keep warm.

4. Meanwhile, melt the butter in a large nonstick skillet over medium-high heat. Add the garlic; stir until golden, about 1 minute. Add the chard; cook, turning occasionally, until tender, about 5 minutes. Divide the chard among 6 bowls. Ladle the soup on top; serve with shaved Parmesan cheese.

FIT TO EAT RECIPE PER SERVING: 481 CALORIES, 11 G FAT, 142 MG CHOLESTEROL, 55 G CARBOHYDRATE, 724 MG SODIUM, 41 G PROTEIN, 6 G FIBER

chicken tortilla soup

SERVES 6

Steps 1 and 2 can be done up to 1 day ahead; refrigerate until ready to serve.

- 1¼ *pounds boneless, skinless chicken breast halves (3 to 4 pieces)*
- 2 *cups cilantro stems and sprigs plus 2 tablespoons finely chopped cilantro*
- 2 *14½-ounce cans low-sodium chicken broth, skimmed of fat*
- 3 *cups water*
- 1½ *tablespoons corn oil*
- 4 *plum tomatoes*
- 2 *small onions, halved lengthwise (unpeeled)*
- 4 *garlic cloves (unpeeled)*
- ½ *teaspoon coarse salt*
- 1¼ *cups fresh or frozen corn kernels*
- ¾ *cup rinsed, drained canned chickpeas*
- 5 *fresh corn tortillas (5½-inch diameter), cut in ¼-inch-wide strips*
- ½ *small avocado*
- 2 *tablespoons fresh lime juice*
- 1 *tablespoon minced jalapeño pepper*
- 3 *tablespoons reduced-fat sour cream*

1. In a large saucepan, combine the chicken, 2 cups cilantro, broth, and water. Bring to a boil, reduce heat, and simmer gently until the chicken is just cooked through, about 10 minutes. Transfer the chicken to a plate; let cool. Cut into ½-inch dice. Strain the broth through a fine strainer lined with several layers of cheesecloth; reserve. Wipe out the pot.

2. Heat ½ tablespoon of the oil in a cast-iron skillet over medium-high heat until hot. Add 3 of the tomatoes and the onions and garlic; cover and cook, turning the vegetables occasionally, until the skins are nicely charred, about 10 minutes. Remove from heat. When the vegetables are cool enough to handle, remove the skins, stems, and cores; discard.

Place the tomatoes, onions, and garlic in a blender with ½ cup reserved broth; blend until smooth. Scrape the mixture into the saucepan; cook, stirring, over medium heat until thickened and darker, about 6 minutes. Stir in the remaining broth, ¼ teaspoon salt, corn, chickpeas, and chicken. Remove from heat.

3. Preheat the oven to 375° F. Place the tortilla strips on a rimmed baking sheet; toss with the remaining tablespoon oil and ⅛ teaspoon salt. Bake until golden and crisp, about 12 minutes, turning once or twice. Cool.

4. Finely dice the avocado; gently rinse with cold water. Place in a bowl. Finely dice the remaining tomato, and add to the avocado with the lime juice, jalapeño, chopped cilantro, and remaining ⅛ teaspoon salt. Rewarm the soup; ladle into bowls. Garnish with the avocado mixture, sour cream, and tortilla strips.

braised lamb stew

SERVES 8 TO 10

The stew can be made without dried limes or lime powder; just use the ½ cup lime juice called for as a substitute for the powder.

- 6 *tablespoons extra-virgin olive oil*
- 4 *pounds boneless leg of lamb, cut into 1-inch cubes*
- 4 *medium onions, peeled and thinly sliced (about 1½ pounds)*
- 4 *cloves garlic, thinly sliced*
- 1 *tablespoon coarse salt*
- 2 *teaspoons freshly ground pepper*
- 2 *teaspoons ground turmeric*
- ½ *teaspoon ground saffron, dissolved in 1 tablespoon hot water*
- 6 *whole dried Persian limes, pierced*
- 1 *cup dried kidney beans*

4   cups water
6   cups finely chopped fresh flat-leaf parsley
2   cups finely chopped garlic chives or
    scallions
2   cups finely chopped fresh cilantro
1   teaspoon ground fenugreek
4   tablespoons dried Persian lime powder or
    ½ cup fresh lime juice

1. Heat 4 tablespoons of the olive oil in a medium stockpot over medium heat. Add the lamb, onions, and garlic, and cook, stirring occasionally, until the meat is no longer pink and the onions are softened, about 20 minutes. Add the salt, pepper, turmeric, saffron water, whole dried Persian limes, and kidney beans; cook a few minutes more. Add the water. Bring to a boil, cover, and simmer over low heat, stirring occasionally.

2. Meanwhile, heat a large nonstick skillet over medium-low heat. Add the chopped parsley, chives, cilantro, and fenugreek. Cook, stirring frequently, until they are wilted, about 10 minutes. Add the remaining 2 tablespoons oil, and cook, stirring constantly, until the herbs are very fragrant, about 10 minutes more.

3. Add the sautéed herbs and lime powder to the lamb mixture. Cover; simmer until the meat and beans are tender, about 2½ hours. Uncover the stew, and cook until the beans are very tender and stew has thickened slightly. Adjust the seasoning, if necessary, and serve hot.

cream of belgian endive soup
SERVES 8 TO 10

2   medium leeks, white and light-green parts
    only
8   heads Belgian endive, plus more for
    garnish
2   medium russet potatoes
3   tablespoons unsalted butter
½   cup dry white wine
5   cups homemade or low-sodium canned
    chicken or vegetable stock
1   cup heavy cream
1½ teaspoons coarse salt
¼   teaspoon freshly ground white pepper
    Generous pinch of freshly grated nutmeg

1. Cut the leeks in half lengthwise. Rinse well under cold running water to remove any grit. Thinly slice crosswise; set aside.

2. Cut the endives in half lengthwise, and cut out the cores. Thinly slice crosswise; set aside.

3. Peel the potatoes, and cut into ½-inch pieces. Set aside in a bowl of cold water.

4. Heat the butter in a saucepan over medium heat. Add the leeks; cook until they start to soften, about 3 minutes. Drain the potatoes well; add to the pot along with the sliced endive. Cook until the vegetables begin to soften, about 10 minutes; do not let brown.

5. Add the wine and stock, and bring to a gentle simmer. Cook until the vegetables are very tender, about 1 hour. Cool slightly.

6. Transfer the soup in batches to a blender (fill no more than halfway), or pass it through a food mill. Return the soup to a clean saucepan; stir in the cream. Bring to a simmer; remove from heat. Season with the salt, pepper, and nutmeg. Garnish with the endive.

cioppino

SERVES 6

¼ cup extra-virgin olive oil

1 medium onion, thinly sliced

4 garlic cloves, minced

1 dried bay leaf

2 tablespoons finely chopped fresh oregano

2 tablespoons finely chopped fresh flat-leaf parsley

½ teaspoon crushed red pepper flakes

2 cups dry white wine

2 cups fish stock

½ cup clam juice

1 28-ounce can crushed tomatoes, with juice

1 15-ounce can plum tomatoes, drained, chopped

6 cherrystone clams, scrubbed

6 mussels, scrubbed, debearded

6 sea scallops, muscles removed

8 ounces cod or other white fish, cut into 1-inch pieces

8 ounces cleaned squid, bodies cut into rings

6 large shrimp, peeled, tails intact, deveined

1. Heat the oil in a large pot over medium-high heat. Add the onion, garlic, and bay leaf. Cook until the onion is translucent, about 5 minutes. Add the oregano, parsley, and red pepper flakes. Cook 1 minute. Add the wine, stock, clam juice, and tomatoes. Reduce heat; simmer gently 30 minutes. (You can make the soup to this point up to 2 days ahead, and chill. Reheat; add seafood.)

2. Add the clams; cook, covered, for 10 minutes. Add the mussels; cook, covered, checking often and using tongs to transfer open clams and mussels to a bowl. Discard any that do not open. Add the scallops, cod, squid, and shrimp to the pan; simmer gently until the seafood is cooked through, about 5 minutes. Gently stir in the cooked clams and mussels; ladle into bowls, and serve.

chilled asian chicken soup

MAKES 1 QUART

You can use the mushroom broth from this recipe in other soups and dishes as well; it is particularly good in risottos. For a heartier version, add cooked and drained soba or udon noodles, or serve brown rice on the side. This soup can be prepared through step 2 up to 3 days in advance; for best results, store the broth separately from all other items. Proceed with step 3 the day the soup will be served.

6 cups water

½ cup mixed dried mushrooms, such as porcini, shiitake, oyster, or wood ear

1 whole chicken breast (about 10 ounces)

1 carrot, roughly chopped

1 tablespoon roughly chopped jalapeño pepper

1½ tablespoons roughly chopped fresh ginger

3 garlic cloves, crushed

1 teaspoon whole black peppercorns

1 tablespoon sugar

½ cup firm tofu, cut into ¼-inch dice

Juice of 1 lime (about 3 tablespoons)

1½ tablespoons roughly chopped fresh mint

1½ tablespoons roughly chopped fresh basil

1½ tablespoons roughly chopped fresh cilantro

1 teaspoon soy sauce

1. Bring the water to a boil in a medium saucepan. Remove from heat, and add the mushrooms; let sit until softened, at least 30 minutes. Strain the mushrooms through a cheesecloth-lined sieve to remove any sandy grit; discard the mushrooms.

2. Return the mushroom broth to a clean medium saucepan, and add the chicken, carrot, jalapeño, ginger, garlic, and peppercorns. Bring just to a boil; reduce heat, and simmer over medium heat 20 minutes, or until the broth is reduced to about 4 cups. Strain through a fine sieve back into the saucepan, reserving the broth and discarding everything but the chicken.

3. Remove the chicken meat from the bones, and shred the meat. Return the chicken meat to the mushroom broth; add the sugar, tofu, lime juice, herbs, and soy sauce, and stir to combine. Transfer to a covered container; refrigerate until well chilled, at least 2 hours or overnight before serving.

FIT TO EAT RECIPE PER SERVING: 149 CALORIES, 6 G FAT, 32 MG CHOLESTEROL, 11 G CARBOHYDRATE, 188 MG SODIUM, 14 G PROTEIN, 1 G FIBER

cold curried buttermilk soup with corn and poblano chile

MAKES 1 QUART

This soup can be made up to 1 day ahead and stored, covered, in the refrigerator; stir it again before serving, as it may separate while it sits. Poblano chiles vary in heat from mild to hot; you may need more or less to taste. If you like, garnish each serving with more cooked corn.

- 1 teaspoon vegetable oil
- ½ yellow onion, finely chopped (about 1 cup)
- ½ poblano chile, seeded and finely chopped (about ½ cup)
- 1 large garlic clove, minced
- 1 teaspoon ground coriander
- ½ teaspoon ground cumin
- ⅛ teaspoon ground turmeric
- 2¼ cups corn kernels (about 4 ears)
- 3 cups nonfat buttermilk
- ¾ teaspoon coarse salt

1. Heat the oil in a medium saucepan over medium heat. Add the onion, poblano chile, and garlic; sauté until the onion is soft and translucent and the chile and garlic are tender and fragrant, about 5 minutes.

2. Add the coriander, cumin, and turmeric, and cook until they are toasted and fragrant, about 2 minutes. Add the corn, and sauté until the kernels are lightly browned, about 5 minutes. Remove from heat, and let cool slightly.

3. Transfer 1½ cups of the corn mixture to the bowl of a food processor fitted with the metal blade, and add the buttermilk and salt; puree until the mixture is smooth. Transfer to a large bowl or plastic storage container; stir in the remaining corn mixture.

Cover with plastic wrap, and place in the refrigerator until the soup is well chilled, at least 2 to 3 hours before serving.

FIT TO EAT RECIPE PER SERVING: 177 CALORIES, 4 G FAT, 7 MG CHOLESTEROL, 27 G CARBOHYDRATE, 643 MG SODIUM, 9 G PROTEIN, 5 G FIBER

cucumber coconut soup

SERVES 6

- 2 cups homemade or low-sodium store-bought chicken stock
- 1 whole skinless, boneless chicken breast
- 2 tablespoons extra-virgin olive oil
- 1 onion, finely chopped
- 1 large garlic clove, minced
- 1 jalapeño pepper, seeded and minced
- 2 pounds cucumbers, peeled, seeded, and cut into ½-inch pieces
- 1 13½-ounce can unsweetened coconut milk
- ½ cup lightly packed fresh cilantro leaves
- ¼ cup fresh lime juice
  Coarse salt and freshly ground pepper

1. Bring the chicken stock to a boil in a small saucepan. Add the chicken; return to a simmer, and reduce heat. Cook, covered, until the chicken is cooked through, about 12 minutes. Transfer the chicken to a plate, reserving the stock, and let cool.

2. Heat the olive oil in a medium sauté pan over medium heat. Add the onion; cook until soft and translucent, about 4 minutes. Add the garlic, jalapeño, and cucumbers; cook 1 minute more. Add the reserved chicken stock, and bring to a simmer; cook until the cucumbers are tender, about 5 minutes. Remove from heat; let cool slightly.

3. Working in batches, transfer the cucumber mixture to a blender or food processor, and puree until smooth. Add the coconut milk and cilantro to the last batch, pureeing until cilantro is very finely chopped. Transfer to a large bowl, and cover with plastic wrap; refrigerate until completely cool. Stir in the lime juice, and season with salt and pepper.

4. To serve, shred the chicken into bite-size pieces. Ladle the soup into bowls; top each with chicken, and garnish with some cilantro leaves.

creamy caramelized onion soup

MAKES 8 CUPS; SERVES 6 TO 8

- 6 tablespoons unsalted butter
- 1¼ pounds leeks (3 to 4), white and pale-green parts only, rinsed well and coarsely chopped
- 5 garlic cloves, thinly sliced
- 7 large shallots (about 14 ounces), thinly sliced
- 2 large Vidalia onions (about 20 ounces each), cut into ¼-inch-thick slices
- ¾ cup dry white vermouth
- 4 cups homemade or low-sodium store-bought chicken stock
  Coarse salt
- 1 cup heavy cream

1. Melt 4 tablespoons of the butter in a large saucepan over medium heat. Add the leeks, garlic, shallots, and half of the onions. Cook, stirring occasionally, until the vegetables are very soft and translucent, about 10 minutes. Reduce heat to medium-low, and cook, stirring occasionally, until the vegetables are deep golden brown, about 25 minutes.

2. Add the vermouth, stock, and 1 teaspoon salt. Bring to a boil. Reduce heat to medium-low. Simmer, stirring occasionally, 15 minutes. Let cool. Puree the onion mixture in batches in a blender until smooth, about 3 minutes per batch. Set aside.

3. Meanwhile, melt the remaining 2 tablespoons butter in a medium skillet over medium-low heat. Add the remaining onion. Cook, stirring occasionally, until the onion is very soft and golden brown, about 45 minutes. Cover, and set aside.

4. Return the onion puree to the saucepan. Stir in the cream. Reheat over medium heat, stirring, until heated through but not boiling. Season with salt, if desired. Serve, topped with caramelized onions.

chilled yogurt-spinach soup with shrimp

MAKES 5 CUPS; SERVES 4

- 1½ cucumbers (about 1 pound), peeled, seeded, and cut into 1-inch pieces
- 2 7-ounce containers plain low-fat (2 percent) Greek yogurt
- 1¾ cups low-sodium store-bought chicken broth
- 2 scallions, white and pale-green parts cut crosswise into ½-inch pieces, dark-green parts julienned
  Coarse salt and freshly ground pepper
- 1 tablespoon olive oil
- 2 garlic cloves, minced
- 5 ounces baby spinach
- 1 tablespoon plus 1 teaspoon finely chopped red onion
- 1 tablespoon plus 1 teaspoon fresh lemon juice
- 1 pound rock shrimp, rinsed well

1. Stir together the cucumbers, half the yogurt, ¾ cup of the broth, the pieces of scallions, and 1 teaspoon salt; season with pepper. Heat the oil in a large skillet over medium heat until hot but not smoking. Add the garlic; cook until just golden, about 1 minute. Add the spinach; cook, stirring, until wilted, about 3 minutes. Stir into the yogurt mixture.

2. Working in batches, puree the mixture in a food processor. Transfer to a large bowl, and stir in the remaining yogurt, the onion, and the lemon juice. Refrigerate, covered, until cold, about 1 hour.

3. Meanwhile, put the remaining 1 cup broth, ¾ cup water, and ½ teaspoon salt in a medium saucepan; season with pepper. Bring to a boil. Add the shrimp; cook until pink and cooked through, 2 to 3 minutes. Drain. Refrigerate the shrimp, covered, until cold, about 1 hour. Divide the soup and shrimp among 4 bowls. Garnish with julienned scallions.

zucchini-mint soup

SERVES 4

You can also serve this soup cold or at room temperature. Puree it in batches to prevent overflow (particularly because you do so while it's hot), if needed. You can stir in a small amount of water to thin the soup after pureeing it, if you like.

- 2 tablespoons extra-virgin olive oil
- 1 medium white onion, finely chopped (about 1¼ cups)
- 1 small garlic clove, crushed with the flat side of a large knife
  Coarse salt
- 3 medium zucchini (about 1½ pounds), thinly sliced crosswise
- 1¼ cups homemade or low-sodium store-bought chicken stock
- 2 tablespoons thinly sliced fresh mint leaves

1. Heat the oil in a medium saucepan over medium heat. Add the onion, garlic, and ¾ teaspoon salt. Cook, stirring often, until the onion is translucent, about 2 minutes. Add the zucchini; cook, stirring occasionally, until the skins turn bright green, about 3 minutes. Add the stock and 1 cup water; bring to a boil. Reduce heat to medium-low. Simmer, partially covered, until the zucchini is tender, about 12 minutes. Let cool slightly.

2. Puree the zucchini mixture in a food processor. Return to the pan. Stir in 1 tablespoon of the mint. Season with salt, if desired. Sprinkle with the remaining tablespoon mint. Serve immediately. Keep warm on stove over medium-low heat, if necessary.

herbed tomato soup

MAKES ABOUT 8 CUPS

- ¼ cup plus 2 tablespoons olive oil
- 2 medium onions, coarsely chopped
- 12 large garlic cloves
- 2 celery stalks, coarsely chopped
- ¼ cup chopped fresh flat-leaf parsley
- 2 tablespoons coarsely chopped fresh lovage or celery leaves
- 1 tablespoon plus 1 teaspoon coarse salt
- 6 pounds tomatoes, chopped
- 1 to 1½ cups homemade or low-sodium store-bought chicken stock
- ½ cup thinly sliced fresh basil leaves
  Crostini, for serving (recipe follows)

1. Heat the oil in a large pot over medium heat. Add the onions, garlic, celery, parsley, lovage, and salt. Cook, stirring, until the onions are translucent, about 5 minutes. Stir in the tomatoes and stock; bring to a boil. Reduce heat; simmer until the tomatoes are soft and mixture is slightly reduced, 15 to 20 minutes. Stir in the basil; cook until fragrant, about 5 minutes.

2. Pass the soup through the medium plate of a food mill set over a large bowl; discard the solids. Reheat; serve with crostini.

crostini

MAKES 10

- 10 ⅓-inch-thick slices rustic Italian bread
- 10 tablespoons extra-virgin olive oil
- 1 tablespoon coarse salt

Preheat the oven to 400°F. Arrange the bread in a single layer on a rimmed baking sheet. Brush with the oil; sprinkle with the salt. Bake until the edges are golden, 5 to 8 minutes.

spring vegetable soup with pesto

SERVES 6

1 cup dried navy or white beans, rinsed

1 bay leaf

1 teaspoon fresh thyme, finely chopped

2 medium leeks, diced and rinsed well

2 medium carrots, diced

8 ounces Red Bliss or Yukon Gold potatoes, peeled and cubed

1 pound plum tomatoes, cubed

2 cups low-sodium vegetable broth

2 small garlic cloves

2 cups loosely packed fresh basil leaves

¼ cup finely grated Parmesan cheese

2 tablespoons extra-virgin olive oil

4 ounces green beans, cut into ½-inch pieces

1 small zucchini, cubed

1 cup fresh shelled or thawed frozen peas

1 teaspoon coarse salt

   Freshly ground pepper

1. Cover the beans with 6 cups cold water in a large pot. Bring to a boil; remove from heat. Let stand, covered, 1 hour.

2. Drain the beans; return to the pot. Cover with 3 quarts cold water. Add the bay leaf and thyme; bring to a boil. Reduce heat to medium; simmer, partially covered, until the beans are barely tender, about 2 hours.

3. Add the leeks, carrots, potatoes, tomatoes, broth, and 2 cups water. Simmer, partially covered, until the beans are tender, about 30 minutes to 1 hour.

4. Make the pesto: Finely chop the garlic in a food processor. Add the basil; process. Add the cheese and oil; process until combined.

5. Add the green beans and zucchini to the pot. Cook, uncovered, 20 minutes. Add the peas; cook until soft, 5 to 10 minutes. Season with salt and pepper. Divide among bowls; top each with 1 heaping teaspoon pesto.

vietnamese beef noodle soup with ginger

SERVES 4

The stock must be refrigerated at least 6 hours; make it 1 day ahead.

8 whole star anise

1 whole cinnamon stick

6 whole cloves

1 piece (4 inches) peeled fresh ginger

2 medium onions, halved

4 pounds oxtail, rinsed thoroughly

6 scallions, white and pale-green parts only, cut into 2-inch pieces, plus 4 scallions, thinly sliced on the diagonal

1 teaspoon whole black peppercorns

1 teaspoon coarse salt

8 ounces eye of round or sirloin of beef

8 ounces thin rice noodles (rice sticks)

2 shallots, thinly sliced

¾ cup fresh bean sprouts

¾ cup fresh cilantro sprigs

¾ cup fresh basil leaves

1 lime, quartered

1. Make the stock: Heat the star anise, cinnamon, and cloves in a small, dry skillet over medium-high heat until fragrant, about 2 minutes. Transfer to a 6-quart stockpot.

2. Preheat the broiler. Broil the ginger and onions, flipping once, until blackened, about 5 minutes per side. Transfer to the pot. Add the oxtail, 2-inch scallion pieces, and peppercorns. Add 5 quarts water; bring to a boil. Skim foam. Add the salt. Reduce heat. Simmer, skimming occasionally, 2½ hours.

3. Pour the stock through a large sieve into a large bowl; discard the solids. Let cool 20 minutes. Pour through a cheesecloth-lined sieve into a large bowl. Refrigerate, covered, 6 hours or overnight.

FIT TO EAT RECIPE PER SERVING: 414 CALORIES, 6 G FAT, 24 MG CHOLESTEROL, 63 G CARBOHYDRATE, 312 MG SODIUM, 24 G PROTEIN, 4 G FIBER

4. Make the soup: Chill the beef in the freezer until firm, about 2 hours. Cover the noodles with cold water. Let stand until the noodles are softened, about 30 minutes; drain.

5. Cut the beef in half. Place each half flat side down, and cut the beef against the grain as thinly as possible. Allow the beef to warm to room temperature.

6. Skim the fat from the stock; discard. Transfer the stock to a pot; add the shallots, and bring to a boil. Reduce heat, and simmer until the shallots are soft, about 15 minutes.

7. In a medium pot of boiling water, cook the noodles until just tender, about 10 seconds; drain.

8. Divide the noodles, beef, and sprouts among 4 bowls. Add the simmering stock (it will cook the beef gently). Top with thinly sliced scallions and herbs; serve each bowl with a lime wedge.

matzo ball soup with duck meatballs

SERVES 10

1 fresh duck (about 7 pounds), cut into 8 pieces

   Coarse salt and freshly ground pepper

6 carrots, cut into 2-inch pieces

6 celery stalks, cut into 2-inch pieces

6 medium onions, quartered (do not peel)

6 sprigs fresh flat-leaf parsley and ¼ cup chopped leaves, plus leaves for garnish

6 fresh thyme sprigs and ¼ cup chopped leaves

14 ounces shiitake mushrooms, stemmed

6 large eggs plus 1 large egg white

2 cups matzo meal

1. Preheat the oven to 400° F. Season the duck with salt and pepper. Transfer to a roasting pan. Add the carrots, celery, and onions; season with salt and pepper. Roast the duck and vegetables, turning occasionally, until the duck is browned, about 1½ hours.

2. Transfer the duck and vegetables to a 12-quart stockpot, reserving the fat. Pour the fat through a fine sieve into a bowl; cover and refrigerate. Add 8 quarts cold water and the herb sprigs to the pot. Bring to a boil; continue to boil for 10 minutes. Reduce heat to low; simmer 1½ hours.

3. Pour the stock through a sieve into another large pot; reserve the meat, and discard the vegetables. Season the stock with salt and pepper. Let cool. Skim off any fat, and add to the reserved fat in refrigerator.

4. Remove the meat from the bones; discard the skin and bones. Process the meat, mushrooms, 2 eggs, the egg white, 1 cup matzo meal, the chopped herbs, ¼ cup reserved fat, 1 tablespoon salt, and ½ teaspoon pepper in a food processor until a paste forms. Shape into 60 1¼-inch meatballs. Refrigerate, covered, until ready to use.

5. Melt ¼ cup reserved duck fat in a small saucepan over low heat. Lightly beat the remaining 4 eggs in a bowl. Whisk in the melted fat, ¼ cup water, and 1 teaspoon salt; season with pepper. Stir in the remaining cup matzo meal. Refrigerate, covered, until slightly firm, 30 minutes to 1 hour.

6. Bring the stock to a boil. Scoop out 26 1¼-inch balls of the matzo mixture, and add to the stock. Reduce heat; simmer 10 minutes. Add the meatballs; simmer 10 minutes. Garnish with parsley.

chicken soup with parsley dumplings

SERVES 6

4 boneless, skinless chicken breast halves (about 1¼ pounds total), each cut into 3 pieces

6 boneless, skinless chicken thighs (about 1¼ pounds total)

4 medium carrots (about ¾ pound), cut on the diagonal into ¼-inch rounds

1 medium onion, thinly sliced into half-moons

2 celery stalks, cut into ¼-inch pieces

1 garlic clove, thinly sliced

1 bay leaf

1½ cups homemade or low-sodium store-bought chicken stock

Coarse salt

1 teaspoon coarsely chopped fresh thyme

¼ cup plus 2 tablespoons yellow cornmeal

¾ cup all-purpose flour

1 teaspoon baking powder

2 tablespoons finely chopped shallot

1 tablespoon freshly grated lemon zest

¾ cup finely chopped fresh flat-leaf parsley

2 tablespoons finely grated Parmesan cheese

1½ tablespoons cold unsalted butter, cut into small pieces

½ cup low-fat (1 percent) milk

1. Bring 2 quarts water and the chicken, carrots, onion, celery, garlic, bay leaf, stock, and ⅛ teaspoon salt to a boil in a medium pot; skim froth. Reduce heat to medium-low; gently simmer 20 minutes. Add the thyme.

2. Meanwhile, whisk together the cornmeal, flour, baking powder, ½ teaspoon salt, shallot, zest, parsley, and cheese in a medium bowl. Add the butter, and blend it in with your fingertips until the mixture resembles coarse meal. Add the milk, and stir with a fork just until a dough forms.

3. Roll the dough into 1-inch balls; add all at once to the simmering broth. Cover; simmer, undisturbed, until the dumplings are cooked through, about 20 minutes. Divide the soup among 6 bowls.

beet soup with indian spices

SERVES 6

Buying beets with the greens attached—as required for this recipe—is a sure way to know they're fresh. Beets are often cooked before they're peeled or cut to keep nutrients intact. Here, the prep work is done first without sacrifice: The juices that result make up the nutritious broth and give the soup its deep flavor and color.

5 or 6 medium red beets with greens (about 2½ pounds with greens), stems and greens cut off and reserved

2 teaspoons canola oil

1 medium onion, halved lengthwise and cut into thin half-moons

1 tablespoon minced garlic

1½ teaspoons ground cumin

1 teaspoon ground coriander

Pinch of cayenne pepper, or to taste

⅛ teaspoon freshly ground pepper

3 plum tomatoes, seeded and cut into ¼-inch dice (about 1¼ cups)

¾ teaspoon coarse salt

1¾ cups homemade or low-sodium store-bought chicken stock

⅓ cup plain low-fat yogurt

1. Cut the beet greens into thin strips and the stems into ¼-inch pieces; set both aside. Peel the beets with a vegetable peeler; cut into ¼-inch-thick matchsticks. Set aside.

2. Heat the oil in a large saucepan over medium heat until hot but not smoking. Add the onion; cook, stirring occasionally, until softened and just browned, about 7 minutes. Add the garlic; cook until fragrant, about 1 minute. Add the cumin, coriander, cayenne, and pepper; cook, stirring, until fragrant, about 1 minute.

3. Add the tomatoes and salt; cook, scraping up any browned bits from the bottom of the pan, until the juices are released, about 2 minutes. Add the stock and 4½ cups water (for a thinner consistency, add up to 5 cups water); bring to a boil. Add the beets and stems. Reduce heat; simmer until the beets are tender, about 35 minutes.

4. Add the greens; cook until just tender, about 5 minutes. Divide the soup among 6 bowls; divide the yogurt among the servings.

southwestern corn chowder

SERVES 4 TO 6

- 4 ounces bacon (5 or 6 slices), cut into ½-inch pieces
- 1 medium onion, cut into ½-inch cubes
- 1 large carrot, cut into ½-inch cubes
- 2 celery stalks, cut into ½-inch cubes
- 1 fresh small poblano chile, seeded and cut into ¼-inch dice

  Coarse salt
- ½ teaspoon ground cumin

  Freshly ground pepper

  Pinch of cayenne pepper
- 1 cup dry white wine
- 1 pound Yukon Gold potatoes, peeled and cut into ½-inch cubes
- 5 cups homemade or low-sodium store-bought chicken or vegetable stock
- 3 cups fresh corn kernels (about 6 ears)
- 1 cup heavy cream
- ¼ cup chopped fresh cilantro, plus more for garnish

  Hot sauce, such as Tabasco (optional)

1. Heat a large, dry pot over medium heat. Add the bacon pieces, and cook, stirring occasionally, until crisp, about 5 minutes. Transfer with a spatula or slotted spoon to paper towels to drain.

2. Add the onion to the pot; cook until just softened, about 4 minutes. Add the carrot, celery, and poblano; cook until the vegetables are just tender, about 5 minutes. Stir in 1 teaspoon salt, the cumin, ¼ teaspoon pepper, and the cayenne. Raise heat to high; add the wine. Cook until most liquid has evaporated, 2 to 3 minutes. Add the potatoes and stock; bring to a boil. Reduce heat to medium-low; gently simmer until all the vegetables are tender, about 20 minutes.

3. Stir in the corn and cream; cook until the corn is tender (do not let cream boil), about 5 minutes more. Stir in the ¼ cup cilantro. Season with salt and pepper. Garnish with cilantro and reserved bacon pieces; add hot sauce, if desired.

mushroom soup with poached eggs and parmesan cheese

SERVES 4

- ½ ounce dried mushrooms, such as porcini (about ½ cup)
- 2 cups boiling water
- 1½ tablespoons extra-virgin olive oil
- 1 medium onion, halved and thinly sliced into half-moons
- 3 garlic cloves, minced
- 1 celery stalk, finely chopped (about ½ cup)
- 1 pound cremini or white mushrooms, caps and stems thinly sliced lengthwise (about 6 cups)
- ½ teaspoon coarse salt
- ½ cup dry white wine
- 2 cups homemade or low-sodium store-bought chicken or vegetable stock
- 1 tablespoon finely chopped fresh tarragon, plus 4 sprigs for garnish
- 4 large eggs
- 1 ounce Parmesan cheese, thinly shaved with a vegetable peeler

  Freshly ground pepper

1. Soak the dried mushrooms in boiling water, covered, until soft, about 20 minutes. Lift out the mushrooms; squeeze over the liquid. Finely chop; set aside. Pour the liquid through a fine sieve into a bowl; reserve.

2. Heat the oil in a medium saucepan over medium heat until hot but not smoking. Add the onion, garlic, and celery; cook, stirring occasionally, until soft, about 8 minutes. Add the fresh mushrooms and salt; cook, stirring occasionally, until most of the liquid has evaporated and the mushrooms are soft, about 12 minutes. Raise heat to high. Add the wine, reserved mushrooms and liquid, stock, and 1½ cups water; bring to a simmer. Reduce heat to medium-low; cook 30 minutes. Add the chopped tarragon.

3. Fill another medium saucepan three-quarters full with water; bring to a bare simmer over medium heat. Crack the eggs into the pan; cook until the whites are set but the yolks are slightly runny, 3 to 4 minutes.

4. Divide the soup among 4 bowls. Transfer 1 egg to each bowl; divide the cheese among the eggs. Season each serving with pepper, and garnish with a tarragon sprig.

roasted carrot soup

SERVES 2

You can make this soup through step 2 the day before your dinner; refrigerate, covered, until you're ready to finish.

- 1 small onion
- 1 bunch carrots (about 1 pound), peeled and cut into 2-inch chunks
- 1 small Belgian endive, quartered lengthwise
- 2 tablespoons olive oil
- ¼ teaspoon coarse salt, plus more for seasoning

   Pinch of freshly ground pepper, plus more for seasoning

- 1 bay leaf
- 2 cups homemade or low-sodium store-bought chicken stock, plus more for thinning
- ⅓ cup heavy cream or milk
- ¼ teaspoon grated peeled fresh ginger, or to taste

   Crème fraîche, for garnish (optional)

1. Preheat the oven to 450°F. Cut the onion into 8 wedges (keep the root end intact to hold the layers together). Toss the onion, carrots, endive, oil, salt, and pepper in a medium bowl. Transfer to a rimmed baking sheet, and spread in a single layer. Roast the vegetables, turning occasionally, until the edges are deep golden brown, about 30 minutes.

2. Cut off the root end from the onion. Transfer all vegetables to a large saucepan, and add the bay leaf. Add enough stock to just cover (about 2 cups). Bring to a simmer, and cook until the carrots are very soft, about 30 minutes. Let cool slightly, and discard the bay leaf. Puree the vegetables and stock in a blender until smooth (work in batches, if necessary, to avoid filling blender more than halfway).

3. Transfer the puree to a clean pan; place over low heat. Stir in the cream; add stock to thin the soup to desired consistency. Season with salt and pepper; stir in the ginger. If desired, pipe crème fraîche onto each serving, or place a dollop on top.

broccoli soup with cheddar toasts

SERVES 8

This soup derives its body and rich flavor from pureed broccoli stems and florets.

- 1½ tablespoons extra-virgin olive oil
- 1 medium onion, coarsely chopped
- 2 garlic cloves, coarsely chopped
- 2 bunches broccoli (about 3¼ pounds), stems and florets chopped separately into ½-inch pieces
- 7 cups homemade or low-sodium store-bought chicken stock
- 1 teaspoon coarse salt
- 1 cup skim milk
- ⅛ teaspoon cayenne pepper
- 2 ounces extra-sharp Cheddar cheese, grated or crumbled (about ½ cup)
- 8 thin slices crusty baguette

1. Heat the oil in a large pot over medium heat until hot but not smoking. Add the onion, garlic, and broccoli stems; cover, and cook, stirring occasionally, until the vegetables are soft, about 15 minutes. Add the stock and salt; cover, raise heat to medium-high, and bring to a boil. Add the broccoli florets; reduce heat, and simmer, uncovered, until the florets are just tender, about 10 minutes.

2. Remove the soup from heat, and let cool, about 10 minutes. Fill a blender no more than halfway to puree the soup in batches until smooth. Return the soup to the pot; stir in the milk and cayenne. Cook over medium heat until heated through (do not boil).

3. Heat the broiler. Divide the cheese among the bread slices; toast under the broiler until melted and golden brown, 45 to 60 seconds. Divide the soup among bowls. Top each bowl with a cheese toast, and serve.

cauliflower soup with toasted pumpkinseeds
SERVES 8 TO 10

White pepper is used because of its color, but black pepper will also work.

- 1   fresh or dried bay leaf
- 4   whole cloves
- 1¾   cups homemade or low-sodium store-bought chicken stock
- 1   head cauliflower, trimmed and cut into 1-inch florets
- 1   russet potato, peeled and quartered
- 1   bulb fennel, trimmed and chopped into 2-inch pieces
- 1   large white onion, coarsely chopped
- ½   cup milk
-   Pinch of freshly grated nutmeg
-   Coarse salt and freshly ground white pepper
-   Toasted Pumpkinseeds (recipe follows)
- ¼   cup pumpkinseed oil (optional)

1. Wrap the bay leaf and cloves in cheesecloth; tie with kitchen twine. Place in a large saucepan; add the stock, cauliflower, potato, fennel, onion, and 5½ cups water. Bring to a boil; reduce heat, and simmer until the vegetables are very tender, about 25 minutes. Discard the clove bundle.

2. Working in batches and filling the blender no more than halfway, puree the soup until smooth. Return the soup to the saucepan; stir in the milk. Place over medium heat until just heated through (do not boil). Add the nutmeg, and season with salt and pepper.

3. Sprinkle the soup with pumpkinseeds, and drizzle with pumpkinseed oil, if desired. Serve hot or at room temperature.

toasted pumpkinseeds
MAKES 1 CUP

- 1   cup raw pumpkinseeds or pepitas, hulled
- 1   tablespoon olive oil
-   Coarse salt

Preheat the oven to 375°F. Combine the seeds and oil on a parchment-lined rimmed baking sheet. Season with salt; toss to combine. Spread in a single layer. Toast until crisp, stirring occasionally, about 10 minutes.

four-onion ginger soup with goat cheese toasts
SERVES 6

You will need to make the stock at least 1 day before you make the soup.

- 12   thin slices bacon (about ½ pound)
- 1½   pounds each white, yellow, and red onions, thinly sliced lengthwise
- 1   piece (1 ounce) fresh ginger, peeled and finely julienned (⅓ cup)
- 1½   pounds shallots, thinly sliced
- 2   tablespoons very thinly sliced fresh sage leaves, plus leaves for garnish
- 2   quarts Dark Chicken Stock (recipe follows)
-   Coarse salt and freshly ground pepper
- ½   baguette, halved lengthwise
-   Olive oil, for brushing
- 3   ounces fresh goat cheese

1. In a large high-sided skillet, cook the bacon over medium heat, turning occasionally, until crisp, about 10 minutes. Transfer the bacon to a paper-towel–lined plate to drain. Pour off all but 1½ tablespoons fat; reserve for another use.

2. Add the onions and ginger to the skillet; cook over medium heat, stirring occasionally, 30 minutes. Add the shallots and sage. Continue cooking, stirring occasionally as onions reduce, until they are very soft and caramelized, about 1 hour. (Add a few tablespoons stock or water if the onions start to stick to the skillet.)

3. Preheat the oven to 350° F. Pour the stock into the skillet, and bring it to a boil. Reduce heat to a simmer, and cook 15 minutes more. Season with salt and pepper.

4. Meanwhile, cut each bread half diagonally into 6 ½-inch-thick pieces. Brush with oil; season with salt and pepper. Arrange on a baking sheet, and toast in the oven until golden, about 20 minutes.

5. Spread the toasts with goat cheese; top each with a bacon slice. Divide the soup among 6 bowls; garnish with sage leaves, and serve each with 2 toasts on the side.

dark chicken stock

MAKES 2 QUARTS

- 3 pounds chicken thighs
- 3 pounds chicken wings
- 2 large Spanish onions, quartered
- 1 bunch carrots, trimmed and cut into 2-inch pieces
- 7 stalks celery, cut into 2-inch pieces
- 1 garlic head, halved crosswise
- 2 fresh or dried bay leaves
- 1 tablespoon whole black peppercorns
- ½ bunch fresh flat-leaf parsley

1. Preheat the oven to 450° F. Arrange the chicken pieces in a single layer in a large roasting pan. Roast, turning once halfway through, until skins are golden brown and crisp, about 1½ hours. Add the onions, carrots, celery, and garlic; roast 30 minutes more. Transfer to a large stockpot; set aside.

2. Pour 1 cup water into the roasting pan; bring to a boil over high heat. Deglaze the pan, scraping up the browned bits from the bottom with a wooden spoon; pour the liquid into the pot. Add the bay leaves, peppercorns, parsley, and 3½ quarts water; bring to a boil over high heat, skimming foam from surface. Reduce heat; simmer 3 hours.

3. Remove the solids from the stock; discard. Strain the stock through a fine sieve into a large bowl. Let cool completely. Cover with plastic wrap; refrigerate until the fat has risen to surface. Skim off fat before using.

pureed spinach-potato soup

SERVES 4

- 2 tablespoons unsalted butter
- 1 onion, cut into ½-inch pieces
- 3 garlic cloves, minced
- 1½ pounds (about 5 small) Yukon Gold potatoes, peeled and cut into ½-inch pieces
- ¼ cup dry sherry or white wine
- 1 quart homemade or low-sodium store-bought chicken broth
- 2 bunches (about 1¼ pounds) spinach, tough stems removed, leaves rinsed well and dried

  Coarse salt and freshly ground pepper

1. Melt the butter in a large saucepan over medium heat. Add the onion, garlic, and potatoes; stir to coat. Cook, stirring, 2 minutes.

2. Pour the sherry, broth, and 2 cups water into the pan; stir to combine. Bring to a boil. Reduce heat to medium-low; cover, and simmer until the potatoes are very tender, about 15 minutes.

3. Stir the spinach into the pan, and cook until wilted and bright green, about 3 minutes. Remove from heat. Puree the soup with an immersion blender until smooth. (Alternatively, use a regular blender, working in batches so as not to fill the jar more than halfway. Return the mixture to the saucepan.) Season with salt and pepper, and serve.

stracciatella

SERVES 4 TO 6

- 6 cups homemade or low-sodium store-bought chicken stock
- 4 large eggs, lightly beaten
- 2 tablespoons fresh flat-leaf parsley, roughly chopped, plus more for garnish
- 2 tablespoons freshly grated Parmesan cheese, plus more for garnish

  Coarse salt and freshly ground pepper

1. In a large saucepan, bring the stock to a boil over medium-high heat. Reduce heat to low; keep at a gentle simmer.

2. In a medium bowl, whisk together the eggs and parsley. Using a fork, stir the stock in a quick circular motion, creating a whirlpool; pour in the egg mixture in a steady stream. Sprinkle in the cheese; season with salt and pepper. Ladle into bowls; garnish with parsley and cheese.

buttermilk vichyssoise with watercress

SERVES 6

This chilled soup is traditionally garnished with fresh chives. We added the peppery snap of watercress and the tang of buttermilk to give it bite.

- 3 tablespoons unsalted butter
- 4 leeks, white and light green parts only, halved lengthwise and then thinly sliced into half-moons, washed well and drained
- 3 large white potatoes, peeled and cut into 1-inch pieces
- 4½ cups homemade or low-sodium store-bought chicken stock
- 3 cups cleaned watercress leaves, loosely packed

  Coarse salt and freshly ground white pepper
- 1 cup half-and-half
- 1 cup buttermilk

1. Melt the butter in a stockpot over medium-low heat. Add the leeks, and cook, covered, until tender, about 15 minutes.

2. Add the potatoes, stock, and 2 cups water. Bring to a boil; simmer until the potatoes are tender, about 20 minutes. Cool completely; stir in 2 cups of the watercress.

3. Working in batches, puree the soup in a blender until smooth. Transfer the pureed soup to a large bowl. Season with salt and white pepper. Stir in the half-and-half; chill at least 1 hour. Add the buttermilk just before serving. Adjust seasoning; if necessary, thin the soup with a bit more chicken stock or water to achieve the desired consistency. Garnish with the remaining cup watercress leaves.

french lentil soup

SERVES 8 TO 10

You can easily double this recipe and refrigerate leftovers in airtight containers for up to 3 days. The soup can also be frozen for up to 3 months. We used French lentils, but other types of lentils may also be used.

- 2 tablespoons olive oil
- 1 small onion, finely chopped
- 2 carrots, finely chopped
- 1 stalk celery, finely chopped
- 1 small red bell pepper, seeds and ribs removed, finely chopped
- 1 teaspoon dried oregano
- ½ cup French green lentils, rinsed and drained
- 3 tablespoons bulghur wheat
- 1½ quarts Wild Mushroom Stock (recipe follows)

  Coarse salt and freshly ground black pepper

1. Place a large saucepan over medium heat, and add the oil. Add the onion, and cook until translucent, about 5 minutes, stirring occasionally. Stir in the carrots, celery, bell pepper, and oregano until combined. Stir in the lentils and bulghur wheat.

2. Add the stock to the pot; cover, and simmer over low heat just until the lentils are tender, about 45 minutes. Remove from heat; season with salt and pepper. Serve hot.

wild mushroom stock

MAKES 3 QUARTS

4 cups plus 3½ quarts water
4 ounces dried porcini mushrooms
2 tablespoons unsalted butter
2 tablespoons olive oil
1 large onion, coarsely chopped
2 large carrots, coarsely chopped
2 parsnips, coarsely chopped
2 stalks celery, coarsely chopped
1 bunch (about 1½ pounds) red or green Swiss chard, cut into 1-inch pieces
1 dried bay leaf
  Several sprigs thyme
  Several sprigs flat-leaf parsley

1. Bring 4 cups water to a boil. Place the dried mushrooms in a medium heatproof bowl; pour the boiling water over the mushrooms. Let stand until softened, about 20 minutes. Strain through a fine sieve into another bowl, reserving the liquid and mushrooms separately. Set aside.

2. In a medium stockpot, heat the butter and oil over medium heat. Add the onion, and cook until caramelized, about 20 minutes, stirring occasionally. Add the reserved mushrooms along with the carrots, parsnips, and celery; cook, stirring often, until the vegetables are softened and fragrant, about 20 minutes.

3. Stir the Swiss chard into the vegetable mixture in the pot. Add 3½ quarts cold water, reserved mushroom liquid (being careful to leave behind any sediment), bay leaf, thyme, and parsley. Cover the pot, and bring to a boil; reduce heat, and simmer, uncovered, about 1 hour.

4. Remove the pot from the heat, and strain the mixture through a fine sieve or cheesecloth-lined colander into a large heatproof bowl or saucepan, pressing down on the vegetables with the back of a wooden spoon to extract as much liquid as possible. Discard the solids. Store the stock in airtight containers in the refrigerator up to 3 days or in the freezer up to 6 months.

hearty beef stew

SERVES 10

This recipe uses the shredded meat and tomato pieces left over from making the beef stock (recipe follows). Serve over egg noodles or rice.

  Basic Beef Stock (recipe follows)
1 pound pearl onions, peeled
5 medium carrots, cut into matchsticks
½ small bunch fresh dill, roughly chopped
  Coarse salt and freshly ground pepper
1 10-ounce package frozen green peas, thawed

1. In a stockpot, combine the stock and reserved beef and tomato pieces. Cover; bring to a simmer over medium-high heat. Add the onions, carrots, and dill. Cook, uncovered, until the onions are soft, about 30 minutes. Season with salt and pepper.

2. When ready to serve, add the peas, and cook just until tender and heated through, about 3 minutes. Serve hot.

basic beef stock

MAKES 3½ QUARTS

Reserve the shredded beef and tomato pieces to make Hearty Beef Stew (recipe above). Refrigerate the stock in airtight containers for up to 30 days or freeze for up to 6 months.

6 pounds beef short ribs, trimmed of excess fat
  Coarse salt and freshly ground pepper
3 quarts plus 1 cup water
1 28-ounce can peeled whole tomatoes, roughly chopped, juice reserved
2 dried bay leaves
10 whole black peppercorns
½ small bunch fresh dill, roughly chopped

1. Preheat the oven to 450° F. Arrange the ribs in a large roasting pan; sprinkle generously with salt and pepper. Roast 1½ hours, turning the ribs halfway through.

2. Combine 3 quarts water and the tomatoes and their juice in a stockpot. Bundle the bay leaves, peppercorns, and dill in a small piece of cheesecloth; tie with kitchen twine, and add to the pot.

3. Transfer the roasted ribs to the pot. Pour off and discard the fat from the roasting pan. Pour the remaining cup water into the pan, and place over medium-high heat. Bring to a boil, stirring with a wooden spoon to scrape up any browned bits from the bottom, until the liquid is reduced by half. Transfer the liquid and bits to the stockpot.

4. Cover the pot; bring the mixture to a simmer over high heat, but do not boil. Reduce heat to a gentle simmer, and place a smaller pot lid directly on surface of stock to keep ingredients submerged; cook until the meat is very tender and pulls away from the bone, about 1½ hours. Skim the surface with a spoon as needed.

5. Prepare an ice-water bath. Remove the herb bundle from the pot, squeezing out the liquid into the pot, and discard. Strain the stock through a sieve into a large heatproof bowl set in the ice-water bath. Stir frequently until the stock is room temperature.

6. Transfer the ribs and tomato pieces to another bowl. When cool enough to handle, pull the rib meat from the bones, and shred it with your fingers. Discard the bones. Store the meat and tomato pieces in an airtight container in the refrigerator, up to 3 days.

7. Transfer the cooled stock to airtight containers; refrigerate at least 6 hours or overnight. With a large metal spoon, skim off and discard fat layer that has collected on the top. If storing, leave fat layer intact (it helps seal in flavor).

shredded chicken and soba noodle soup

SERVES 10

Look for soba noodles in the Asian section of your supermarket.

2½	quarts Basic Chicken Stock (recipe follows)
2	whole skinless chicken breasts, halved
	Coarse salt
½	pound soba noodles
1	pound firm or extra-firm tofu, cut into ¼-inch dice
	Freshly ground pepper
2	small carrots, julienned
2	red radishes, trimmed and julienned
½	bunch watercress, tough stems removed, for garnish

1. In a medium stockpot, bring the chicken stock to a simmer over medium heat. Add the chicken breasts; return to a simmer. Reduce heat; simmer until the chicken is cooked through, about 20 minutes. Transfer the chicken to a plate, and set aside until cool enough to handle. Cover, and keep the stock at a low simmer.

2. Meanwhile, bring a medium saucepan of water to a boil over high heat. Add salt, and stir in the soba noodles. Cook until the soba is al dente, according to package instructions. Drain; set aside.

3. Remove the chicken meat from the bones, and shred it into bite-size pieces. Add the tofu to the simmering stock just until heated through. Season with salt and pepper.

4. To serve, ladle the stock and tofu into soup bowls. Add shredded chicken to each bowl, and mound soba noodles in the center. Sprinkle with the carrots and radishes; garnish with watercress.

basic chicken stock

MAKES ABOUT 5 QUARTS

Refrigerate the stock in airtight containers for up to 3 days or freeze for up to 6 months. We added canned broth to fortify the stock's flavor, but you can replace it with water, if you prefer.

3 carrots, cut into thirds

2 stalks celery, cut into thirds

1 bulb fennel, cut into large chunks

3 tablespoons fennel seeds, toasted

1 teaspoon whole black peppercorns

1 whole chicken (4 to 6 pounds)

2 pounds chicken wings, necks, and backs

3 quarts homemade or low-sodium store-bought chicken broth

2 quarts cold water

1. In a large stockpot, combine all the ingredients. Cover, and bring to a boil over medium-high heat; reduce heat to a very gentle simmer. Cook, uncovered, 1 hour, checking occasionally to make sure the liquid is barely bubbling, and skim the surface with a large metal spoon as needed.

2. Transfer the whole chicken to a cutting board. Let cool slightly, and pull the meat from the sides. (Reserve the meat for another use; store in the refrigerator up to 3 days, covered well with plastic wrap.)

3. Return the chicken bones to the pot. Place a smaller pot lid on the surface of the stock to keep the solids submerged. Simmer until the bones fall apart when poked, 2½ to 4 hours. Skim the surface as needed.

4. Prepare a large ice-water bath. Strain the stock through a fine sieve into a large heatproof bowl, discarding the solids. Set the bowl in the ice-water bath, and let the stock cool to room temperature, stirring frequently.

5. Transfer the stock to airtight containers. Refrigerate at least 8 hours or overnight. With a large metal spoon, skim off and discard the fat layer that has collected on the top. If storing, leave the fat layer intact (it helps to seal in flavor).

coconut fish chowder

SERVES 6

1 tablespoon unsalted butter

1 small onion, cut into very thin wedges

2 garlic cloves, finely chopped

4 fresh or frozen kaffir lime leaves

2 cups homemade or frozen fish stock

6 ounces baby potatoes, cut into ½-inch chunks

2 stalks celery, thinly sliced on the bias

¼ pound green beans, stem ends trimmed, cut into 1½-inch lengths

1 1-inch piece fresh ginger, peeled and finely julienned (about 2 tablespoons)

3 cups unsweetened coconut milk

1 pound cod fillets, cut into large chunks
   Coarse salt and freshly ground pepper

½ bunch fresh chives, cut into 1½-inch lengths, for garnish

6 tablespoons freshly grated or desiccated coconut, for garnish

1. Heat the butter in a large saucepan or small stockpot over medium heat. Add the onion, and cook, stirring occasionally, until translucent, 3 to 4 minutes. Add the garlic and lime leaves; cook 1 minute. Add the fish stock, potatoes, celery, green beans, and ginger; bring to a simmer over medium heat. Cook 7 to 9 minutes.

2. Reduce heat to low. Add the coconut milk, and bring almost to a simmer. Add the fish; without stirring, simmer until the fish is opaque and the vegetables are tender, about 5 minutes. Season with salt and pepper. Ladle the soup into bowls; garnish with chives and coconut. Serve immediately.

spiced red lentil soup with crispy fried ginger

SERVES 6

After it has finished cooking, this soup will continue to thicken; thin it with hot chicken stock or water, if desired.

for the red lentil soup

- 1 tablespoon olive oil
- 1 Spanish onion, cut into ½-inch dice
- 4 garlic cloves, minced
- 3 tablespoons minced fresh ginger (3-inch piece)
- 1 teaspoon ground cumin
- ½ teaspoon curry powder
- 2 plum tomatoes, cut into ½-inch dice
- 2 cups red lentils, picked over and rinsed
- 4 cups homemade or low-sodium store-bought chicken stock
- 4 cups water
- 1 dried bay leaf
- 1 teaspoon coarse salt

  Freshly ground pepper
- ½ cup plain low-fat yogurt, for serving

for the crispy fried ginger

- 2 teaspoons canola or peanut oil
- 1 piece (about 5 inches) fresh ginger, peeled and cut into very thin strips (about 2 inches long)

1. In a large, heavy-bottomed pot, heat the oil over medium-high heat. Add the onion, garlic, ginger, cumin, and curry powder; cook, scraping any browned bits from the bottom of pot with a wooden spoon, until the onion is soft and light golden, about 10 minutes. Reduce heat to medium, and add the tomatoes. Cook about 5 minutes.

2. Stir the lentils, chicken stock, water, and bay leaf into the pot; raise heat to medium-high, and bring to a simmer. Reduce heat to low; cook, stirring occasionally, until the lentils are tender, about 30 minutes. Add the salt; season with pepper. Remove from heat. Let stand about 10 minutes.

3. Meanwhile, make the fried ginger: In a medium sauté pan, heat the oil over medium heat. Add the ginger in a single layer; cook, stirring constantly, until the strips begin to turn crisp and deep golden, about 4 minutes. Using a slotted spoon or tongs, transfer to paper towels to drain. Keep warm until ready to serve.

4. Remove the bay leaf from the pot, and discard. Using an immersion or regular blender (working in batches so as not to fill the jar more than halfway), puree the soup until completely smooth. Return the soup to low heat until warmed through. Divide the soup among 6 serving bowls; top each bowl with about 1 tablespoon yogurt. Garnish with fried ginger; serve.

udon noodles with shiitake mushrooms in ginger broth

SERVES 4

This recipe will serve four as a first course or light lunch. To serve the noodles as a meal, add a few cups of diced firm tofu or cooked chicken breast to the simmering broth in step 3.

- 8 ounces Japanese udon or soba noodles
- 2 teaspoons sesame oil
- 2 teaspoons vegetable oil
- 1½ tablespoons minced fresh ginger (1½-inch piece)
- 2 shallots, very thinly sliced
- ¼ pound (about 12) shiitake mushrooms, stemmed, caps wiped clean and quartered
- 2 cups homemade or low-sodium store-bought chicken stock
- 1 teaspoon rice-wine vinegar
- 2 teaspoons low-sodium soy sauce
- 3 cups (about 3 ounces) spinach, tough stems discarded, rinsed well, drained, and cut into 2-inch-wide strips
- 4 scallions, thinly sliced diagonally into 2-inch pieces

1. Bring a large pot of water to a boil. Add the noodles, and cook until al dente, according to package instructions, about 8 minutes. Drain in a colander, toss with the sesame oil, and return to the pot. Keep warm.

2. Meanwhile, in a medium sauté pan, heat the vegetable oil over medium heat. Add the ginger, shallots, and mushrooms; cook, stirring constantly, until the mixture begins to soften and turn golden brown, about 2 minutes.

3. Stir the chicken stock, vinegar, and soy sauce into the pan, and bring to a simmer. Cook until the mushrooms are very tender, about 5 minutes. Add the spinach and scallions, and stir to combine.

4. To serve, divide the noodles among 4 shallow bowls; ladle the soup over the noodles.

clam and corn chowder
SERVES 8 TO 10

 6 *ears corn, shucked*

 2 *Spanish onions*

 1 *large carrot, cut into large pieces*

 3 *stalks celery, cut into large pieces*

 1 *teaspoon whole black peppercorns*

 1 *dried bay leaf*

 4 *sprigs thyme*
    Coarse salt and freshly ground pepper

 1 *cup dry white wine*

 4 *pounds littleneck clams, scrubbed*

 2 *tablespoons unsalted butter*

1¼ *pounds small red potatoes, cut into chunks*

 ¾ *cup heavy cream*

 2 *tablespoons chopped fresh chives*

 1 *tablespoon chopped and seeded jalapeño pepper*

1. Make the stock: Cut the corn kernels from the cobs; set aside. Slice 1 of the onions, unpeeled, into 8 wedges. In a stockpot, combine the cobs, onion wedges, carrot, celery, peppercorns, bay leaf, and thyme. Add 2 quarts water; bring to a boil. Reduce heat to a simmer, and cook 1 hour. Season with salt and pepper. Strain; discard the solids. The stock can be refrigerated up to 1 week.

2. In a large, wide saucepan, bring the wine to a simmer. Add the clams. Cover; steam until the clams open, 5 to 7 minutes. Discard any unopened clams. Drain in a sieve set over a bowl; reserve and chill the liquid. Shuck the clams; halve large ones. Refrigerate, submerged in a bit of reserved liquid.

3. Finely dice the remaining onion. In a large stockpot set over medium heat, melt the butter. Add the diced onion; cook, stirring, until translucent, about 6 minutes. Add the potatoes and reserved corn kernels; cook 3 to 4 minutes.

4. Add 3½ cups reserved stock and 1 cup reserved clam liquid to the pot, leaving behind any sediment. Bring to a boil; reduce to a simmer. Cook until the potatoes are tender, about 25 minutes. Stir in the cream, and remove from heat. Puree 2 cups; return to the pot, and stir. (Cooled chowder can be refrigerated, covered, overnight.)

5. Add the chives, jalapeño, and reserved clams to the pot. Adjust the seasoning; serve.

roasted vegetable soup
SERVES 8 TO 10

 2 *medium eggplants (about 2 pounds)*

 2 *red onions, each cut into 8 wedges*

 2 *tablespoons olive oil*
    Coarse salt and freshly ground black pepper

2½ *pounds ripe plum tomatoes*

 6 *large garlic cloves*

 3 *large red bell peppers (about 2 pounds)*

 1 *quart homemade or low-sodium store-bought chicken stock*

 2 *cups lightly packed fresh basil leaves (about 1 large bunch), plus more for garnish*

 1 *sprig marjoram*

 1 *large piece (3 by 4 inches) Parmesan rind (from a 3-ounce piece), plus grated Parmesan for garnish*

 1 *15-ounce can chickpeas, drained and rinsed*

1. Preheat the oven to 425°F. Prick the eggplants, and place them in a baking pan with the onions; toss with the oil. Season with salt and pepper. Roast in the upper third of the oven, turning once, until the eggplants are soft and the onions browned, about 1¼ hours. Let cool.

2. Meanwhile, season the tomatoes with salt and pepper; place in a baking pan with the garlic. Roast on the lower rack of the oven until the tomatoes are soft and juicy, about 30 minutes. Let cool.

3. Roast the peppers over a gas burner or on a baking sheet under the broiler until blackened, turning as each side chars. Transfer to a bowl; cover with plastic wrap. Let steam 20 minutes. Using paper towels, rub off the skins; remove the stems and seeds.

4. Remove the stems and skins from the eggplants. Coarsely chop the flesh; place in a stockpot. Add the roasted vegetables and any accumulated juices from the baking sheets. Add the stock, 1½ cups basil, marjoram, cheese rind, and chickpeas; bring to a boil over medium-high heat. Reduce heat; simmer, partially covered, until the vegetables are very tender, about 1½ hours.

5. Discard the rind; pass the soup through a food mill, discarding the solids. Thin with water if needed. Finely chop the remaining ½ cup basil; stir into the soup. Season with salt and pepper. Garnish with cheese and basil.

mushroom and wild rice soup

SERVES 8 TO 10

1   ounce dried porcini mushrooms

½   teaspoon coarse salt, plus more for seasoning

½   cup wild rice

1   tablespoon olive oil

1¼ pounds assorted mushrooms, such as button, cremini, shiitake (stems removed), and chanterelle, sliced into bite-size pieces

Freshly ground pepper

1   tablespoon unsalted butter

3   leeks (white and pale-green parts only), quartered lengthwise and thinly sliced

½   cup sherry or Madeira

3   tablespoons soy sauce

6   cups homemade or low-sodium store-bought chicken stock

2   tablespoons heavy cream

1   tablespoon finely chopped fresh flat-leaf parsley

1. In a spice mill or coffee grinder, pulse the porcini to a fine powder. Set aside.

2. In a small saucepan, bring 1 cup water to a boil. Add the salt and wild rice. Cover; reduce heat to medium-low. Cook until tender, 45 to 50 minutes. Drain; set aside.

3. In a large saucepan, heat half the oil over medium-high heat. Add half the mushrooms; season with salt and pepper. Cook until browned and tender, about 7 minutes; transfer to a bowl. Repeat with the remaining oil and mushrooms.

4. Reduce heat to medium-low. Melt the butter; add the leeks. Cook, stirring, until softened, about 5 minutes. Stir in the mushroom powder; cook 1 minute. Add the sherry and soy sauce; cook 1 minute more.

5. Add the stock to the pot; bring to a boil over medium-high heat. Add the mushrooms; return to a boil. Reduce heat to medium; cook 20 minutes. Stir in the wild rice, cream, and parsley; adjust seasoning, and serve.

porcini and white bean stew

SERVES 4

1¾ cups homemade or low-sodium
  store-bought chicken stock

¾ ounce dried porcini mushrooms

1 tablespoon olive oil

1 small onion, thinly sliced

2 garlic cloves, thinly sliced

½ teaspoon coarse salt

¼ teaspoon freshly ground pepper

4 ounces fresh white mushrooms, quartered

3 small tomatoes (about 1 pound),
  coarsely chopped

1 small sprig fresh rosemary, plus
  more for garnish

1 19-ounce can white beans, drained
  and rinsed

1. Bring the stock and ½ cup water to a boil in a small pan. Add the porcini. Let stand until soft, about 20 minutes. Remove the porcini with a slotted spoon; coarsely chop. Set aside. Strain the soaking liquid through cheesecloth; set aside.

2. Heat the oil in a medium pan over medium-high heat. Add the onion, garlic, salt, and pepper. Cook, stirring occasionally, until the onion is translucent, about 3 minutes. Add the white mushrooms; cook, stirring occasionally, until tender, about 5 minutes. Stir in the porcini, tomatoes, rosemary, soaking liquid, and beans. Bring to a boil. Reduce heat to medium; simmer until cooked through, about 15 minutes. Remove the cooked rosemary; discard. Garnish with fresh rosemary sprigs.

FIT TO EAT RECIPE PER SERVING: 251 CALORIES, 5 G FAT, 0 MG CHOLESTEROL, 40 G CARBOHYDRATE, 352 MG SODIUM, 13 G PROTEIN, 8 G FIBER

white bean chili with herbed yogurt cheese

SERVES 6

3 cups dried navy or other white beans

2 small poblano chiles

1 tablespoon unsalted butter

4 cloves garlic, minced

1 onion, cut into ¼-inch dice

1 large carrot, cut into ¼-inch dice

2 stalks celery, cut into ¼-inch dice

1 teaspoon ground cumin

1 teaspoon ground coriander

½ teaspoon paprika

¼ teaspoon cayenne pepper (optional)

30 ounces homemade or low-sodium store-
  bought chicken stock, skimmed of fat

8 cups water

1½ teaspoons coarse salt

¼ teaspoon freshly ground black pepper

4 radishes, grated

  Cilantro sprigs, for garnish

  Herbed Yogurt Cheese (recipe follows)

1. Pick over the dried beans, discarding any stones or broken beans; rinse. Place in a large saucepan, cover with cold water by 2 inches, and bring to a strong boil over high heat. Cover, and remove from heat; let stand 1 hour. Drain the beans; set aside.

2. Meanwhile, place the peppers directly on a gas burner over high heat or on a grill. As they turn black, turn with tongs. (Alternatively, place the peppers on a baking pan; broil in the oven, turning as the peppers become charred.) Transfer the charred peppers to a medium bowl; cover with plastic wrap. Let the peppers rest 15 minutes. Transfer to a work surface (do not rinse). Peel off the blackened skin; discard. Halve the peppers; remove the seeds and ribs and discard. Cut the peppers into ¼-inch pieces; set aside.

3. Heat the butter in a large saucepan over medium heat. Add the garlic, onion, carrot, and celery. Cover; cook, stirring occasionally, until softened and slightly browned, about 15 minutes. Add the cumin, coriander, paprika, and cayenne, if using; stir to combine. Stir in the stock, water, beans, and half the roasted poblano chiles. Cover; cook until the beans are soft, about 1½ hours. Uncover; simmer gently until the beans begin to fall apart, about 30 minutes more. Season with salt and pepper. Serve the chili garnished with the remaining poblano chiles, radish, cilantro, and yogurt cheese, if desired.

FIT TO EAT RECIPE PER CHILI SERVING: 369 CALORIES, 169 MG CALCIUM, 4 G FAT, 6 MG CHOLESTEROL, 572 MG SODIUM, 22 G PROTEIN, 11 G FIBER

herbed yogurt cheese
MAKES ABOUT 1 CUP

1   8-ounce container plain fat-free yogurt
2   teaspoons fresh lime juice
¼   cup chopped fresh cilantro
¼   cup chopped fresh flat-leaf parsley
¼   teaspoon coarse salt
    Pinch of freshly ground pepper

Line a colander or strainer with several thicknesses of cheesecloth; set over a bowl. Add the yogurt; drain for 1 hour. Transfer the yogurt to bowl of food processor; add the lime juice, cilantro, parsley, salt, and pepper. Purée until well combined. Chill until ready to use, up to 1 week.

FIT TO EAT RECIPE PER SERVING: 8 CALORIES, 29 MG CALCIUM, 0 G FAT, 0 MG CHOLESTEROL, 29 MG SODIUM, 1 G PROTEIN, 0 G FIBER

cock-a-leekie
SERVES 6

This traditional Scottish soup is made with chicken stock, leeks, and potatoes. If you make this soup ahead, you may need to add a bit of water or stock when reheating it.

1¼   pounds skinless chicken thighs (on the bone; 4 pieces)
1¼   pounds skinless chicken breast halves (on the bone; 3 pieces)
4   14½-ounce cans low-sodium chicken broth, skimmed of fat
2   cups white wine or water
2   large celery ribs, halved crosswise
1   large carrot, peeled
2   large garlic cloves, peeled
6   leeks, white and light-green parts only, halved lengthwise, thinly sliced crosswise
12   pitted prunes, quartered (⅔ cup packed)
½   cup barley
½   cup finely chopped fresh flat-leaf parsley

1. Heat a 6-quart Dutch oven on medium-high until hot. Add the thighs; cook until browned, turning once, about 8 minutes. Transfer to a bowl. Repeat with the breasts.

2. Add the broth, wine, celery, carrot, and garlic to the Dutch oven. Bring to a boil; scrape any browned bits from the pot. Return the chicken to the pot, reduce heat, and simmer, skimming as necessary, for 1 hour. Transfer the chicken to a plate; let cool. Transfer the vegetables to another plate; reserve.

3. Add the leeks, prunes, and barley to the broth. Bring to a boil, reduce heat, and simmer until thick, about 40 minutes more. Once the chicken has cooled, shred the meat. Finely dice the carrot and celery. Stir the chicken, carrot, celery, and parsley into the soup, heat through, and serve.

FIT TO EAT RECIPE PER SERVING: 416 CALORIES, 5 G FAT, 132 MG CHOLESTEROL, 32 G CARBOHYDRATE, 754 MG SODIUM, 43 G PROTEIN, 5 G FIBER

lamb stew with jerusalem artichokes

SERVES 6

- 3 tablespoons extra-virgin olive oil
- 1½ pounds boneless lamb shoulder, cut into 1½-inch cubes

  Coarse salt and freshly ground black pepper
- 1½ pounds Jerusalem artichokes (about 15 small), peeled, cut into ¾-inch cubes, and reserved in cold water (drain and pat dry before using)
- 2 cups coarsely chopped onion (about 1 large)
- 2 garlic cloves, minced (about 1 tablespoon)
- 1 tablespoon freshly grated ginger (1-inch piece)
- 1 whole cinnamon stick
- 2 whole cloves
- 2 green cardamom pods, lightly crushed
- ½ teaspoon crushed red pepper flakes
- 1 35-ounce can whole peeled plum tomatoes with juice
- 1 cup homemade or low-sodium store-bought chicken stock
- ⅛ teaspoon crumbled saffron threads
- 1 10-ounce jar small caperberries, drained
- ¼ cup finely chopped fresh cilantro

1. Heat 2 tablespoons of the oil in a large, heavy pot over medium-high heat. Season the lamb with salt and black pepper; brown the meat (in batches, if necessary) on all sides, about 8 minutes. Transfer to a bowl.

2. Cook the artichokes in the remaining tablespoon oil in the same pot over medium-high heat, stirring occasionally, until well browned on all sides, about 7 minutes. Using a slotted spoon, transfer the artichokes to a separate bowl.

3. Add the onion, garlic, and ginger to the remaining oil in the pot; sauté over medium-high heat, stirring occasionally, until the onion is translucent, about 4 minutes. Add the cinnamon, cloves, cardamom, and red pepper flakes; cook, stirring constantly, 2 minutes.

4. Stir in the tomatoes and juice, stock, saffron, and 1 teaspoon salt. Using the side of a wooden spoon, break up the tomatoes. Add the reserved lamb; bring the mixture to a boil. Reduce heat to low; cover, and simmer until the meat is tender, about 1 hour.

5. Return the reserved artichokes to the pot. Continue to simmer until the artichokes are tender, about 25 minutes; add the caperberries during the final 5 minutes of cooking. Season with salt and black pepper; stir in the cilantro. Discard the cinnamon, cloves, and cardamom before serving.

cilantro gazpacho

MAKES 2 QUARTS; SERVES 12

Martha served this gazpacho over tomato aspic in a glass as a portable first course, but the gazpacho can also be served on its own.

- 5 pounds ripe tomatoes, seeds removed
- 2½ pounds cucumber, peeled, seeds removed
- 2 red bell peppers, seeds removed
- 1 jalapeño pepper, seeds removed
- 4 scallions, white and light-green parts only
- 1 large garlic clove, peeled
- ½ cup extra-virgin olive oil
- ¾ cup fresh cilantro, roughly chopped

  Juice of 2 limes (5 tablespoons)

  Coarse salt and freshly ground pepper

  Hot pepper sauce

  Tomato Aspic (recipe follows)

  Big Croutons (recipe follows)

1. Roughly chop the tomatoes, cucumber, red and jalapeño peppers, scallions, and garlic. Place in a large bowl; toss with ¼ cup olive oil, ½ cup cilantro, and the lime juice. In a food processor or blender, puree half the vegetables until smooth. With the motor running, slowly add the remaining olive oil to the puree in a steady stream until the mixture emulsifies. Pass the puree through a fine-mesh strainer into a medium bowl, and set aside. Discard the pulp in the strainer.

2. In a food processor or blender, pulse the remaining vegetables in batches, letting them remain chunky. Alternatively, chop the vegetables by hand. Combine the mixture with the reserved puree; mix well. Stir in the remaining cilantro. Season with salt, pepper, and hot pepper sauce to taste.

3. Pour ¼ cup aspic into 12 6-ounce glasses; chill until set, at least 1 hour. Ladle ½ cup gazpacho into each glass, and serve garnished with a big crouton.

tomato aspic
MAKES 3 CUPS

- 4 *pounds ripe tomatoes, seeds removed*
- 1 *jalapeño pepper, seeds removed*
- 1½ *teaspoons coarse salt*
- ½ *cup water*
- 6 *packets powdered gelatin (¼ cup plus 2 teaspoons)*

1. In a food processor or blender, puree the tomatoes and jalapeño until smooth. Line a large bowl with a double layer of cheesecloth. Transfer the puree to the prepared bowl. With kitchen twine, tie the cheesecloth to enclose the tomato puree; tie the bundle to a large wooden spoon. Rest the spoon across the top of a stockpot or deep jar, letting the juices drip into the pot for about 3 hours. Pour the tomato water through a fine chinois or sieve into a bowl. Add salt; stir to combine.

2. Place ½ cup cold water in a small heatproof bowl. Sprinkle the gelatin evenly over the water; set aside 5 minutes to soften. Bring a small saucepan of water to a simmer; place the bowl of gelatin over it. Stir until the gelatin is dissolved; remove the bowl from heat. Stir in some of the tomato water to reduce the temperature, then stir all of the gelatin mixture into the remaining tomato water.

big croutons
MAKES 12

These can be made a day ahead and stored in an airtight container after cooling.

- ¼ *cup extra-virgin olive oil*
- 4 *tablespoons unsalted butter*
- ¼ *cup chopped fresh flat-leaf parsley*
- 1 *baguette, cut into ¼-inch-thick slices*

Combine the olive oil and butter in a small saucepan; heat over medium heat until the butter is melted. Stir in the parsley. Spread over the bread; grill until crisp, 1 to 2 minutes on each side. Alternatively, toast the croutons in a 350° F oven until golden brown, 10 to 15 minutes.

chestnut mushroom soup
SERVES 4 TO 6

For a velvety smooth texture, pass the soup through a fine strainer after the mixture has been processed and before adding the cream.

- 1 *pound fresh chestnuts*
- 6 *ounces cremini mushrooms*
- 2 *ounces shiitake mushrooms, stems removed*
- 2 *tablespoons unsalted butter*
- 1 *tablespoon extra-virgin olive oil*
  Coarse salt and freshly ground pepper
- 1 *small onion, chopped*
- 1 *clove garlic, halved*
- 8 *sprigs fresh thyme, plus leaves for garnish*
- 6 *cups homemade or low-sodium store-bought chicken stock*
- 2 *cups water*
- ½ *cup heavy cream*

1. Preheat the oven to 350° F. Using a chestnut knife or a small paring knife, make an incision about ⅛ inch deep through the shell and into the flesh of each chestnut almost all the way around the circumference. Transfer to a chestnut pan or rimmed baking pan. Roast in the oven until the chestnuts are tender, about 35 minutes. Turn the oven off.

Leaving the pan with the chestnuts in the oven, remove several at a time. Working quickly, place 1 chestnut in a towel, and, holding both, peel the chestnut while still hot. Remove and discard the shells and inner skin; set aside.

2. Roughly chop all but 2 cremini and 2 shiitake mushrooms. Heat 1 tablespoon of the butter with the olive oil in a small stockpot over medium-high heat. Add the chopped mushrooms, and season with salt and pepper. Cook the mushrooms, stirring occasionally, until they start to brown, about 5 minutes. Add the onion, garlic, and thyme sprigs. Reduce heat to medium-low, and cook until the onions are translucent, about 8 minutes. Add all but 4 chestnuts, and cook until golden, about 5 minutes. Add the chicken stock and water, raise heat to high, and bring to a boil. Reduce heat, and simmer until the chestnuts are falling-apart tender, about 1 hour. Remove and discard the thyme sprigs, and let stand about 10 minutes.

3. Let the soup cool slightly. Pass the soup through a sieve, and transfer the solids, reserving the liquid, to a food processor or blender. Puree, in batches, until very smooth. Add the reserved liquid, and process for 1 minute. Adjust the seasoning with salt and pepper, if necessary. Transfer to the stockpot, stir in the cream, and place over low heat until hot.

4. Cut the 4 reserved chestnuts and the 4 reserved mushrooms into ¼-inch-thick slices. Melt the remaining tablespoon butter in a small skillet over medium-high heat. Add the chestnuts and mushrooms, and cook until crisp and golden brown, 3 to 4 minutes. Divide the soup among soup bowls, and garnish with sautéed chestnuts, mushrooms, and thyme leaves.

poached salmon, leek, and fennel soup

SERVES 6

- 3 leeks, white and light-green parts only
- 1 tablespoon extra-virgin olive oil
- 3 carrots, peeled and cut into ¼-inch-thick slices
- 1 small fennel bulb, trimmed and cut into wedges, fronds reserved for garnish
- 2 celery stalks, cut crosswise into ¼-inch slices
- 4 sprigs fresh flat-leaf parsley
- 4 sprigs fresh thyme
- 1 14½-ounce can fat-free vegetable stock
- 2 teaspoons coarse salt
- ½ teaspoon freshly ground pepper
- 1 1-pound salmon fillet, skin removed, cut into 1-inch cubes
- 1 bunch (about 3 ounces) spinach, washed and cut into 1½-inch-wide strips

1. Slice the leeks crosswise into ¼-inch coins. Place in a bowl of cold water; move the leeks with your fingers so the sand falls to the bottom. Lift the leeks from the water with your fingers or a slotted spoon, and drain; set aside.

2. Heat the oil in a saucepan over medium heat. Add the leeks, carrots, fennel, and celery. Cook until softened, about 5 minutes. Add the parsley, thyme, stock, salt, pepper, and 5 cups water. Bring to a boil; reduce to a simmer. Cook 30 minutes. Turn off heat; add the salmon and spinach. Poach until just cooked through, about 3 minutes. Garnish with fennel fronds; serve.

FIT TO EAT RECIPE PER SERVING: 177 CALORIES, 8 G FAT, 42 MG CHOLESTEROL, 10 G CARBOHYDRATE, 202 MG SODIUM, 17 G PROTEIN, 3 G FIBER

summer vegetable pot au feu

SERVES 4

- 2 teaspoons extra-virgin olive oil
- 2 ounces pearl onions, peeled
- 3 garlic cloves, peeled
- ¼ cup dry white wine
- 4 ounces round baby orange and yellow carrots, thinly sliced
- 1 small bay leaf
- 2 sprigs fresh thyme
- 2 sprigs fresh flat-leaf parsley
- ¾ cup homemade or low-sodium store-bought chicken stock
- 4 ounces baby new potatoes
- 9 ounces assorted baby summer squashes, cut in half
- 1 ounce young sugar snap peas, stem ends trimmed
- 1 ounce fresh or frozen lima beans, shelled

1. Heat the oil in a large skillet over medium-high heat. Add the onions and garlic; cook until golden. Add the white wine; cook until most of it has evaporated, about 3 minutes. Add the carrots, bay leaf, thyme, parsley, stock, and ¾ cup water; simmer 5 minutes. Add the potatoes; simmer 7 minutes. Add the squash; cook until just tender, about 5 minutes. Add the peas and lima beans, and cook 2 minutes.

2. Remove the skillet from heat; remove and discard the herb sprigs. Divide the vegetables and broth among 4 shallow bowls, and serve.

chicken stew with carrots, chickpeas, and raisins

SERVES 6

- 1 tablespoon all-purpose flour
- 2 pounds skinless, bone-in chicken thighs
- ½ teaspoon coarse salt
- 1 can (14 ounces) low-sodium chicken broth
- 1 cup drained canned chickpeas, rinsed
- 3 carrots, peeled and coarsely chopped
- ½ cup raisins
- 1 small onion, chopped
- 2 garlic cloves, minced
- 2 tablespoons finely chopped peeled fresh ginger
- 4 to 5 sprigs fresh thyme
- 1 tablespoon Dijon mustard
- 1 teaspoon finely grated lemon zest
- 1 box (5.8 ounces) couscous

1. Preheat the oven to 350°F. Place the flour in an ovenproof bag; shake to coat inside. Place bag in a small roasting pan.

2. Season chicken with the salt, and place in bag. Add broth, chickpeas, carrots, raisins, onion, garlic, ginger, thyme, mustard, and zest to bag; tie bag closed, and shake to combine. Set in pan, and make four ½-inch slits in bag near opening. Bake chicken mixture in bag in the roasting pan until chicken is very tender, 1 hour 30 minutes.

3. While the chicken cooks, prepare the couscous according to package instructions, omitting any fat. Serve chicken and sauce over couscous.

FIT TO EAT RECIPE PER SERVING: 381 CALORIES, 10 G FAT, 76 MG CHOLESTEROL, 46 G CARBOHYDRATE, 473 MG SODIUM, 28 G PROTEIN, 5 G FIBER

spring vegetable stew
with sweet-potato dumplings

SERVES 6

for the dumplings

1 medium sweet potato (about 12 ounces),
 peeled and cut into large chunks

 Coarse salt

1¼ cups all-purpose flour

½ teaspoon baking powder

 Freshly ground pepper

2 large eggs, lightly beaten

2 tablespoons finely chopped fresh
 flat-leaf parsley

for the stew

2 lemons, halved

4 medium artichokes (10 ounces each)

3 tablespoons unsalted butter

10 ounces red pearl onions, blanched and
 peeled

1 rind Parmesan cheese (about 5 inches
 long; or substitute 5-inch piece cheese)

2½ cups homemade or low-sodium store-
 bought vegetable stock (not roasted)

1 teaspoon coarse salt

¼ teaspoon freshly ground pepper

12 orange or yellow baby carrots, peeled, or
 3 medium carrots, peeled, halved
 lengthwise, and cut into 3-inch pieces

2 tablespoons finely chopped fresh
 tarragon

6 ounces asparagus, trimmed and cut into
 3-inch pieces (about 1¼ cups)

1. Make the dumplings: Place the sweet potato in
a saucepan; cover with water by 1 inch. Bring to a
boil; add a large pinch of salt. Reduce the heat; simmer until tender, about 15 minutes. Meanwhile,
whisk the flour, baking powder, 1½ teaspoons salt,
and a pinch of pepper in a bowl; set aside.

2. Drain the sweet potato. Pass it through a ricer
onto a baking sheet. Spread out; let cool 15 minutes.
Transfer to a bowl. Stir in the eggs and parsley. Add
the flour mixture; stir just until a sticky dough forms.

3. Meanwhile, make the stew: Fill a medium bowl
with cold water. Squeeze the juice of 1½ lemons into
the water; add the rinds. Remove and discard the
tough outer leaves from 1 artichoke. Cut off the top
third; peel the stem. Halve the artichoke lengthwise;
remove the fuzzy choke, and discard. Cut into
1-inch-thick wedges, and place in the lemon water.
Repeat with the remaining artichokes.

4. Melt the butter in a medium stockpot over
medium heat. Add the onions; cook, stirring occasionally, 3 minutes. Add the Parmesan rind. Drain
the artichokes; add to pot. Stir in the stock and 4½
cups water; add salt and pepper. Bring to a boil. Add
the carrots. Reduce the heat; simmer, partially covered, 10 minutes. Squeeze the remaining ½ lemon
into pot; stir in tarragon.

5. Using 2 spoons, form 18 dumplings, dropping
into the stew as you work. Cover; cook 7 minutes.
Add the asparagus. Cook, covered, until the
dumplings are cooked through and the vegetables
are tender, about 3 minutes. Remove the rind before serving.

potato soup
with baby artichokes
SERVES 8

You can substitute eight small artichokes for the baby artichokes: Prepare them as directed below, removing all but the tender inner leaves and scooping out the choke. Adjust the cooking time accordingly. Fan leaves of artichoke hearts, and place one in each bowl.

- 2 lemons, halved crosswise
- 24 baby artichokes
- 6 cups homemade or low-sodium store-bought chicken stock
- 4 tablespoons unsalted butter
- 2 small onions, finely chopped
  Coarse salt
  Freshly ground white pepper
- 2 pounds Yukon Gold potatoes, peeled and cut into 1-inch pieces
  Fresh chives, cut into 1-inch pieces, for garnish

1. Fill a large bowl with cold water, and squeeze the juice of 3 lemon halves into the water; add the rinds. Working with 1 artichoke at a time, remove the tough outer leaves (reserve about 8 cups leaves, and discard remaining). Trim the tops so the artichokes are 1 inch long. Peel the stems to remove tough, dark-green parts, and cut the stems flat so that the artichokes can stand upright. Rub the artichokes with juice from the remaining lemon half; place the artichokes in the lemon water. Cover with damp paper towels. The artichokes can be refrigerated in lemon water overnight; cook just before serving.

2. Put the reserved artichoke leaves and the stock into a large stockpot. Bring to a boil over medium-high heat. Reduce heat to medium-low, and simmer for 10 minutes. Pour through a fine sieve into a large bowl, and discard the leaves (you should have about 4 cups liquid). Set aside.

3. Melt the butter in a medium stockpot over medium-high heat. Add the onions, ½ teaspoon salt, and ¼ teaspoon pepper. Cook, stirring occasionally, until the onions are translucent, about 4 minutes. Add the potatoes and reserved artichoke broth. Bring to a boil over medium-high heat. Reduce heat to medium-low. Simmer, partially covered, until the potatoes are tender when pierced with the tip of a knife, 10 to 15 minutes. Let cool slightly.

4. Meanwhile, fill a clean large stockpot with 2 inches of water. Insert a steamer basket, and bring water to a boil. Add the artichoke hearts to steamer basket. Cover, and steam until artichoke hearts are tender but not falling apart, 15 to 20 minutes (begin checking after 15 minutes). Season with salt. Transfer the artichoke hearts to a platter, and cover to keep warm.

5. Working in batches, coarsely purée the soup in a food processor (do not overprocess). Pass through a medium-mesh sieve into another pot. Season with salt and pepper. The soup can be refrigerated in an airtight container overnight; reheat over medium-low heat before serving.

6. Ladle the soup into bowls. Fan leaves of artichoke hearts, if desired; place 3 hearts in each bowl. Garnish soup with chives.

cavolo nero and
cannellini bean soup

SERVES 4

1½ pounds cavolo nero (also called Tuscan
    kale), stemmed and coarsely chopped

2   tablespoons extra-virgin olive oil

⅓   cup finely chopped red onion

3   garlic cloves, thinly sliced

1   dried red chile, crumbled

½   teaspoon fennel seeds

4   cups homemade or low-sodium store-
    bought chicken stock

8   ounces dried cannellini beans, soaked
    according to package instructions

1   medium tomato, seeded and finely
    chopped (about ¾ cup)

¼   teaspoon coarse salt
    Freshly ground pepper

¼   loaf Tuscan bread (about 6 ounces),
    cut into ½-inch-thick slices and toasted

1. Prepare an ice bath; set aside. Bring a large
saucepan of water to a boil. Add the kale; cook until
just tender, 3 to 5 minutes. Drain, reserving ¼ cup
cooking liquid. Plunge the kale into the ice bath.
Drain.

2. Heat the oil in a large saucepan over medium
heat. Add the onion; cook, stirring occasionally, until
tender, about 5 minutes. Add the garlic, chile, and
fennel seeds; cook, stirring occasionally, 2 minutes.

3. Stir in the stock, beans, and tomato. Bring to a
boil. Reduce to a simmer, and cook, stirring occasionally, until beans are tender, 30 to 40 minutes.

4. Add the kale and reserved cooking liquid. Season with salt and pepper. Cook, stirring, until the
kale is tender, about 5 minutes. Divide the bread
and soup among 4 bowls.

FIT TO EAT RECIPE PER SERVING: 290 CALORIES, 7 G FAT,
1 MG CHOLESTEROL, 47 G CARBOHYDRATE, 687 MG SODIUM,
13 G PROTEIN, 4 G FIBER

thai hot-and-sour chicken soup
with wide rice sticks

SERVES 6

Some varieties of noodles suggest soaking them
in boiling water instead of cooking them; check
your package instructions before preparing them.

7   ounces wide rice sticks

6   cups homemade or low-sodium store-
    bought chicken stock

2   lemongrass stalks, bottom 8 inches only,
    trimmed and crushed

16 slices (¼ inch thick each) jarred or
    canned bamboo shoots

1   piece (1½ inches) peeled fresh galangal
    or ginger, thickly sliced

8   fresh or frozen kaffir lime leaves, plus
    more thinly sliced for garnish

3   tablespoons Asian fish sauce
    Juice of 2 limes

1   tablespoon palm or granulated sugar

4   fresh Thai chiles, thinly sliced

2   boneless, skinless chicken breast halves
    (6 ounces each), cut into ½-inch-thick,
    2-inch-long strips

3   ounces snow peas, trimmed

3   ounces oyster mushrooms

½   cup chopped (½-inch pieces) Chinese
    yard-long or green beans

¼   cup chopped garlic chives or scallions,
    plus more for garnish

1. Bring a large pot of water to a boil. Add the noodles; cook according to package instructions, 6 to
8 minutes. Drain; rinse under cold running water.
Set aside.

2. Bring the stock, lemongrass, bamboo shoots,
galangal, and 4 lime leaves to a boil in a large pot.
Reduce the heat; simmer 8 minutes. Stir in half of
the fish sauce, half of the lime juice, half of the sugar,
and half of the chiles; cook 4 minutes.

3. Stir in the chicken, and cook until the chicken is
cooked through, about 3 minutes. Taste, and add
more fish sauce, sugar, or chiles as desired. Discard
the lemongrass and lime leaves. Stir in the snow

peas, mushrooms, beans, chives, and remaining 4 lime leaves. Remove from heat, and stir in remaining lime juice. Divide the soup and noodles among 6 serving bowls; garnish with lime leaves and chives.

japanese salmon ramen with chile-ginger dressing and wheat noodles

SERVES 6

for the salmon

1½ pounds salmon fillet, skinned
    Coarse salt and freshly ground pepper
5   tablespoons store-bought teriyaki marinade
    Vegetable oil, for rubbing

for the dressing

2   tablespoons black or red-wine vinegar
¼   cup sweet chili sauce
6   tablespoons Asian fish sauce
1   piece (2 inches) peeled fresh ginger, finely grated

for serving

1   pound thin wheat noodles or soba noodles
1   tablespoon plus ¼ teaspoon instant dashi stock powder
3   scallions, white parts cut into 1-inch pieces, green parts thinly sliced
1½ cups tatsoi or baby spinach
1   tablespoon toasted sesame seeds

1. Season the salmon with salt and pepper. Transfer to a resealable bag. Add the teriyaki marinade; gently toss to coat. Refrigerate at least 1 hour (up to 4 hours).

2. Make the dressing: Whisk together the vinegar, chili sauce, fish sauce, and ginger in a small bowl; set aside.

3. Bring a large pot of water to a boil. Add the noodles, and cook according to package instructions, 3 to 5 minutes. Drain, and rinse under cold running water to stop the cooking. Set aside.

4. Remove the salmon from the marinade, and rub with oil; reserve marinade. Heat a large nonstick skillet over medium-high heat until hot. Add the salmon; cook, flipping once, until dark brown, about 3 minutes per side for medium-rare. Add about half of the reserved marinade during last minute of cooking, and flip salmon to coat. Transfer to a plate. Let stand 5 minutes. Flake into large chunks.

5. Bring 6 cups water to a boil in a large pot. Stir in the dashi powder and white part of scallion. Reduce to a simmer, and cook 3 minutes. Set aside.

6. To serve, divide the noodles among 6 serving bowls; ladle some dashi broth over noodles. Divide the salmon and tatsoi among bowls. Drizzle with dressing; sprinkle with sesame seeds and green part of scallions. Serve immediately.

pear and autumn-vegetable soup

SERVES 6

2   medium Bartlett pears (8 to 10 ounces each) and 4 small Bartlett pears (about 6 ounces each)
1   sugar pumpkin or butternut squash (about 1 pound), peeled and cut into 2-inch pieces
1   turnip (about 3 ounces), trimmed, peeled, and cut into 1-inch pieces
1   sprig fresh sage
1½ teaspoons coarse salt
¼   cup heavy cream
½   teaspoon freshly ground white pepper

1. Preheat the oven to 200° F. Using a mandoline or a very sharp knife, cut 2 medium pears lengthwise into paper-thin slices. Arrange the slices in a single layer on a rimmed baking sheet. Bake until pears are dry, about 1 hour. Let cool completely on sheet on a wire rack.

2. Meanwhile, peel the remaining 4 pears; halve lengthwise, and core. Place the pears, pumpkin, turnip, sage, and 1 teaspoon salt in a 4-quart stockpot. Cover with water (at least 4 cups). Bring to a boil. Reduce the heat, and simmer until vegetables are tender, about 20 minutes.

3. Pour the mixture through a sieve into a medium bowl, reserving the broth and discarding the sage. Puree the solids in a food processor or blender, adding up to ½ cup reserved broth as needed.

4. Return the puree to the pot. Stir in 3 to 4 cups reserved broth to achieve desired consistency. Bring the soup to a simmer over medium-low heat. Whisk in cream, remaining ½ teaspoon salt, and the pepper. Serve garnished with dried pears.

roasted pumpkin and mushroom soup

SERVES 8

 1 sugar pumpkin (about 2 pounds), cut into 8 wedges (do not remove seeds)

 6 ounces shiitake mushrooms

 4 medium leeks, trimmed and cut crosswise into 1½-inch pieces, rinsed well

 3 tablespoons extra-virgin olive oil

    Coarse salt

12 large sprigs fresh thyme

10 large fresh sage leaves

 6 garlic cloves (do not peel)

 2 shallots, thinly sliced

 6 large sprigs fresh flat-leaf parsley

 1 bay leaf

    Freshly ground pepper

1. Preheat the oven to 375°F. Place 7 pumpkin wedges on a heavy rimmed baking sheet. Peel and seed the remaining wedge, and cut into ½-inch cubes; set the cubes aside and add peel and seeds to baking sheet. Remove the stems from 2 mushrooms; thinly slice the caps, and set the sliced caps aside with reserved pumpkin cubes. Add the stems and remaining mushrooms to the baking sheet. Julienne 2 white pieces of leek, and set aside with the reserved pumpkin and mushroom; set aside remaining leeks.

2. Drizzle the pumpkin and mushrooms on baking sheet with the oil, and sprinkle with ½ teaspoon salt; toss to coat. Add the thyme, sage, and garlic to sheet, and toss to combine; spread out in a single layer. Bake until the pumpkin is lightly browned and garlic is soft, 40 to 45 minutes.

3. Transfer the roasted vegetables to a large stockpot. Place the hot baking sheet on a stove burner over medium heat, and add 1 cup water, scraping browned bits with a wooden spoon. Add the deglazed liquid to pot. Add the leeks, shallots, parsley, bay leaf, and 12 cups water. Bring to a boil. Reduce heat to medium-low; simmer, partially covered, 45 minutes. Uncover, and raise heat to medium. Cook 15 minutes more. Pour through a fine sieve into a medium saucepan; discard solids.

4. Add the reserved julienned leek, pumpkin, and mushrooms to the saucepan, and season with salt. Bring to a simmer over medium heat; cook until the vegetables are tender, about 10 minutes. Season with salt and pepper, and serve.

salads

....

arugula and cannellini salad with olive vinaigrette

SERVES 4

This colorful salad can also be served family style in a large bowl; toss the arugula in the vinaigrette along with the beans and tomatoes, and let everyone help himself. Niçoise olives have an appealing nuttiness that complements the peppery arugula.

½ cup pitted oil-cured olives, such as Niçoise (about 36)

¼ cup water

1 garlic clove

½ cup packed fresh basil leaves

2 teaspoons sherry vinegar

½ teaspoon ground cumin

1 15½-ounce can white beans, rinsed and drained

1½ cups pear, grape, or cherry tomatoes, halved

½ red onion, thinly sliced

1 bunch arugula (about 6 ounces), trimmed and washed

1. Make the vinaigrette: Combine the olives and the water in the bowl of a food processor fitted with the metal blade. Process until the olives are finely chopped. Add the garlic, basil, vinegar, and cumin; process until the mixture is smooth and combined, stopping to scrape the sides of the bowl with a rubber spatula as needed.

2. In a medium bowl, combine the beans, tomatoes, and red onion, and gently toss. Pour the vinaigrette over the bean mixture, and toss well to coat. To serve, divide the arugula leaves among 4 plates, and mound the bean mixture on top.

FIT TO EAT RECIPE PER SERVING: 210 CALORIES, 13 G FAT, 0 MG CHOLESTEROL, 18 G CARBOHYDRATE, 442 MG SODIUM, 5 G PROTEIN, 5 G FIBER

autumn greens with apples, radishes, and cheddar frico

SERVES 10 TO 12

Look for pumpkinseed oil in gourmet shops or health-food stores.

2 tablespoons sherry vinegar

2 teaspoons Dijon mustard
    Coarse salt and freshly ground pepper

¼ cup pumpkinseed oil

6 tablespoons extra-virgin olive oil

2 Granny Smith apples

6 radishes, scrubbed and trimmed

9 cups mixed greens (about ¾ pound), washed and dried
    Cheddar Frico (recipe follows)

1. Make the vinaigrette: In a small bowl, whisk together the vinegar and mustard; season with salt and pepper. Whisking constantly, slowly add the pumpkinseed oil and then the olive oil in a steady stream until thick and emulsified.

2. Slice the apples and radishes on the thinnest setting of a mandoline or with a sharp knife. Place in a serving bowl; add the mixed greens, and toss to combine.

3. Drizzle the vinaigrette over the salad mixture, and toss well to coat evenly. Serve immediately with Cheddar Frico.

cheddar frico

MAKES 26

Frico, or "little trifles" in Italian, are very thin and crisp. When sprinkling the cheese mixture in the skillet, don't worry if there are spaces; the cheese will melt into a lacy whole. In Italy, frico are traditionally made with Montasio cheese, but other cheeses, such as Cheddar, Asiago, and Parmesan, produce excellent results.

10 ounces sharp white Cheddar cheese, grated (about 5 cups)

1 tablespoon all-purpose flour

1. In a medium bowl, toss together the cheese and flour. Heat a large nonstick skillet over medium-low heat. Sprinkle about 1½ tablespoons of the cheese mixture into the skillet to form a 4-inch round.

2. Cook until the cheese is starting to melt and become firm, 1½ to 2 minutes. Using a small offset spatula, turn; continue cooking until it is firm and slightly golden, 15 to 30 seconds more.

3. Immediately drape the frico over a rolling pin, and let cool slightly to set the shape. Repeat with the remaining cheese mixture. If the skillet gets too hot and the frico begin to color too quickly, remove from heat for several minutes before proceeding.

warm goat cheese with wasabi pea crust, peas, and greens
SERVES 6 AS AN APPETIZER

Wasabi peas are a popular cocktail snack. In this recipe, they are ground and used to encrust goat cheese buttons, providing an innovative alternative to bread crumbs. For best results, slice the goat cheese with a piece of thread.

- 2 cups wasabi peas
- 1 12-ounce log firm fresh goat cheese
- ¾ cup extra-virgin olive oil
- ½ tablespoon wasabi paste
- 3 tablespoons rice-wine vinegar
- 1 tablespoon mayonnaise
- Pinch of sugar
- Coarse salt
- 5 ounces sugar snap peas, ends trimmed and string removed (about 1½ cups)
- 5 ounces snow peas, trimmed (about 1½ cups)
- 6 ounces pea shoots

1. Place 1½ cups wasabi peas in the bowl of a food processor fitted with the metal blade. Process until a coarse powder forms; transfer to a large plate.

2. Slice the goat cheese log into 6 1-inch-thick disks. Pour ½ cup olive oil on a small plate. Place the disks, one at a time, in the oil, turning to completely coat. Dredge in the wasabi powder, turning to coat all sides, and shake off excess. Transfer to a baking sheet; cover with plastic wrap. Refrigerate 1 hour.

3. Preheat the oven to 425° F. Prepare an ice-water bath, and set aside. In a small bowl, whisk together the wasabi paste and vinegar. Whisk in the mayonnaise, sugar, and remaining ¼ cup oil until mixture is smooth. Season with salt; set aside.

4. Bring a medium saucepan of water to a boil, and generously add salt. Add the sugar snap and snow peas; blanch until they are tender and bright green, about 2 minutes. Drain in a colander; transfer the peas to the ice-water bath to stop cooking and preserve their color. Drain; pat dry with paper towels.

5. Remove the coated goat cheese disks from the refrigerator. Bake until soft and hot in the center, about 7 minutes. Remove from the oven.

6. Combine the blanched peas, pea shoots, and remaining ½ cup wasabi peas in a large bowl. Season with salt, and drizzle with wasabi paste dressing. Toss well to lightly coat, and divide among 6 salad plates. Place 1 goat cheese disk on each plate, and serve immediately.

garden tomato salad
SERVES 20 TO 25

To prevent bruising, snip the basil with sharp kitchen scissors rather than cutting it with a knife. You may use any combination of tomatoes; cut cherry tomatoes in half.

- 11 pounds (about 33) ripe medium tomatoes, cut into 1-inch pieces
- 2 medium red onions, halved lengthwise and thinly sliced into half-moons
- 1 cup extra-virgin olive oil
- 1 tablespoon coarse salt
- 2 teaspoons freshly ground pepper
- 1 bunch fresh basil leaves, washed well

Combine the tomatoes and onions in a large serving bowl. Drizzle with the olive oil, and sprinkle with the salt and pepper. Cover with plastic wrap; let stand at room temperature at least 1 hour to allow flavors to develop. Snip the basil, and toss it into the salad just before serving.

caesar salad

SERVES 4

2 garlic cloves

⅛ teaspoon coarse salt

¼ pound rustic bread (half a small loaf), crusts removed, cut into ¼-inch cubes

1 anchovy fillet (optional)

1 tablespoon fresh lemon juice

½ teaspoon Worcestershire sauce

¼ teaspoon Dijon mustard

½ teaspoon freshly ground pepper

2 tablespoons extra-virgin olive oil

2 heads romaine lettuce (about 10 ounces each), outer leaves discarded, inner leaves cut into 1-inch-wide strips

½ ounce Parmesan cheese, shaved

1. Preheat the oven to 350° F. In a medium bowl, mash 1 garlic clove with the salt to form a smooth paste. Add the bread cubes, and toss to combine. Spread the cubes in a single layer on a rimmed baking sheet. Bake until crisp and golden brown, about 20 minutes, turning once.

2. Make the vinaigrette: In a small bowl, mince the remaining garlic clove with the anchovy, if using, to form a smooth paste. Whisk in the lemon juice, Worcestershire sauce, mustard, and pepper. Slowly whisk in the oil.

3. In a large serving bowl, toss the lettuce with the vinaigrette and reserved croutons. Serve immediately, garnished with shaved Parmesan.

FIT TO EAT RECIPE PER SERVING: 186 CALORIES, 10 G FAT, 4 MG CHOLESTEROL, 19 G CARBOHYDRATE, 338 MG SODIUM, 7 G PROTEIN, 3 G FIBER

jícama and orange salad with citrus-cumin vinaigrette

SERVES 4

Oranges are an excellent source of vitamin C. For maximum health benefits, cut or juice them just before serving. Vitamins A and C and iron are also provided by baby spinach.

2 oranges

1 jícama (about 1½ pounds), peeled and julienned

3 ounces baby spinach, rinsed

Citrus-Cumin Vinaigrette (recipe follows)

Cut both ends off the oranges, and remove the peel and pith. Slice the fruit crosswise into ¼-inch rounds, and remove seeds. Transfer the slices to a large bowl, and combine with the jícama and spinach. Toss with the vinaigrette, and serve.

FIT TO EAT RECIPE PER SERVING: 144 CALORIES, 4 G FAT, 0 MG CHOLESTEROL, 27 G CARBOHYDRATE, 55 MG SODIUM, 3 G PROTEIN, 7 G FIBER

citrus-cumin vinaigrette

MAKES ¾ CUP

Cumin seeds contain vitamin E as well as flavonoids, both powerful antioxidants.

1 teaspoon cumin seeds

½ cup fresh orange juice

2 tablespoons fresh lemon juice

1 tablespoon extra-virgin olive oil

1 tablespoon honey

2 teaspoons Dijon mustard

Freshly ground pepper

Pinch of coarse salt

1. Toast the cumin seeds in a small skillet over medium-high heat until fragrant, about 2 minutes. Remove from heat; cool slightly. Finely grind in a spice grinder.

2. Blend all the ingredients until smooth. Refrigerate, covered, up to 3 days.

FIT TO EAT RECIPE PER SERVING: 66 CALORIES, 4 G FAT, 0 MG CHOLESTEROL, 9 G CARBOHYDRATE, 34 MG SODIUM, 1 G PROTEIN, 0 G FIBER

spinach salad with fennel and blood oranges

SERVES 4

If fresh is unavailable, look for packages of pre-washed baby spinach. Blood oranges are named for their vivid red-streaked flesh.

3 blood oranges
  Juice of 1 lemon
2 tablespoons sherry vinegar
½ teaspoon coarse salt
  Freshly ground pepper
3 slices bacon
1 bulb fennel, very thinly sliced
16 cremini mushrooms, very thinly sliced
1 red onion, very thinly sliced
6 ounces baby spinach

1. Make the vinaigrette: Using a sharp paring knife, peel 2 oranges, following the curve of the fruit; cut between the membranes to remove whole segments. Place in a small bowl; set aside. Juice the remaining orange into a separate small bowl or large glass measuring cup; whisk in the lemon juice, vinegar, and salt. Season with pepper; set aside.

2. In a small skillet, cook the bacon over medium heat until crisp and browned on both sides, about 4 minutes per side. Transfer to drain on paper towels; let cool, and finely crumble.

3. In a large serving bowl, combine the fennel, mushrooms, onion, and spinach. Add the reserved orange segments and vinaigrette, and toss to combine. Divide among serving plates, and sprinkle each with crumbled bacon.

FIT TO EAT RECIPE PER SERVING: 142 CALORIES, 3 G FAT, 4 MG CHOLESTEROL, 26 G CARBOHYDRATE, 468 MG SODIUM, 7 G PROTEIN, 7 G FIBER

green salad with toasted walnuts, walnut oil, and green beans

SERVES 4

Walnut oil can be found at most gourmet markets. Because it is more delicate than other oils, walnut oil should be refrigerated after it has been opened to keep it from going rancid.

6 ounces green beans, ends trimmed, halved crosswise
¼ teaspoon coarse salt
½ teaspoon plus 1 tablespoon walnut oil
2 ounces walnut halves (about ½ cup), toasted and roughly chopped
½ shallot, minced (about 1 tablespoon)
2 teaspoons white-wine vinegar
4 ounces mixed salad greens
  Freshly ground pepper

1. Bring a medium saucepan of water to a boil. Add the beans, and cook until bright green and crisp-tender, about 2 minutes. Using a slotted spoon or tongs, transfer to a medium serving bowl. Immediately toss with the salt and ½ teaspoon walnut oil. Add the walnuts, and transfer to a plate to cool, reserving the bowl.

2. Make the vinaigrette: In a small bowl, combine the shallot with the vinegar. Whisk in the remaining tablespoon walnut oil.

3. Place the salad greens in the reserved bowl, and add the dressing. Toss well to combine, and season with pepper. Divide among 4 plates, and pile the green beans and walnuts on top. Serve immediately.

FIT TO EAT RECIPE PER SERVING: 141 CALORIES, 6 G FAT, 0 MG CHOLESTEROL, 6 G CARBOHYDRATE, 123 MG SODIUM, 5 G PROTEIN, 3 G FIBER

roasted parsnip, celery heart, and apple salad

SERVES 6

Celery hearts are the tender, pale-green inner stalks in a celery bunch.

1½ pounds parsnips (12 to 16), peeled, trimmed, and halved lengthwise (quartered, if large)

2 tablespoons extra-virgin olive oil

Coarse salt and freshly ground pepper

1 bunch celery hearts, cut diagonally into ⅛-inch-thick slices

½ cup celery leaves

1 green apple, such as Granny Smith, cored, halved, and cut into ⅛-inch-thick wedges

Hazelnut Vinaigrette (recipe follows)

1. Preheat the oven to 375°F. Toss the parsnips with the oil; season with salt and pepper. Spread the parsnips in a single layer on a rimmed baking sheet. Roast until golden brown and tender, about 30 minutes. Let cool slightly on the sheet on a wire rack.

2. Divide the parsnips among 6 serving plates. Put the celery hearts and leaves, apple, and ¼ cup vinaigrette in a nonreactive bowl; season with salt and pepper. Toss well, and arrange on top of the parsnips.

hazelnut vinaigrette

MAKES ABOUT ¾ CUP

⅓ cup hazelnuts (about 1 ounce)

¼ cup extra-virgin olive oil

1 shallot, finely chopped

1 tablespoon plus 1 teaspoon sherry vinegar

2 teaspoons fresh lemon juice

Coarse salt

¼ cup hazelnut oil or light vegetable oil, such as canola

Freshly ground pepper

1. Preheat the oven to 375°F. Spread the hazelnuts in a single layer on a rimmed baking sheet. Toast in the oven until the skins split and the flesh turns deep golden brown, 10 to 12 minutes. While they are still hot, rub the hazelnuts in a clean kitchen towel to remove skins (some will remain). Coarsely chop.

2. Heat the hazelnuts, olive oil, and shallot in a small skillet over medium heat, stirring, until the shallot softens, about 2 minutes. Let cool slightly.

3. Stir together the vinegar, lemon juice, and ¾ teaspoon salt in a medium bowl. Whisking constantly, pour in the hazelnut oil and then the hazelnut mixture in a slow, steady stream; whisk until emulsified. Season with salt and pepper.

crisp romaine salad

SERVES 8

2 heads romaine lettuce, leaves separated

3 carrots, thinly peeled

8 ounces radishes, thinly sliced

1 small red onion, thinly sliced

2 tablespoons extra-virgin olive oil

2 tablespoons red-wine vinegar

1 teaspoon coarse salt

¼ teaspoon freshly ground pepper

Put the lettuce, carrots, radishes, and onion in a salad bowl. Just before serving, lightly drizzle with the oil. Add the vinegar, salt, and pepper, and toss to combine.

organic lettuces with fig vinaigrette

SERVES 10

Reserved poaching liquid from Oven-Poached Figs (recipe follows)

1½ tablespoons red wine vinegar

1 teaspoon balsamic vinegar

2 teaspoons finely chopped shallot

Coarse salt and freshly ground pepper

½ cup extra-virgin olive oil

12 cups salad greens

Oven-Poached Figs (recipe follows), for serving

Soft ripened cheeses (such as Camembert or goat cheese), for serving

1. Cook the reserved poaching liquid in a small saucepan over medium heat until reduced to the consistency of syrup (about 2 tablespoons). Let cool completely.

2. Whisk the reduced liquid, vinegars, and shallot in a small bowl. Season with ½ teaspoon salt and ¼ teaspoon pepper. Slowly whisk in the oil until emulsified. Season with more salt and pepper, if desired. Toss the greens with vinaigrette to taste. Serve immediately with figs and wedges of cheese.

oven-poached figs
MAKES 12

12 fresh figs

¼ cup tawny port

¼ cup full-bodied red wine, such as Pinot Noir

3 tablespoons honey

1 strip orange zest (3 inches), plus ¼ cup fresh orange juice

1 cinnamon stick (3 inches)

1 vanilla bean, seeds scraped

2 whole green cardamom pods, split open

2 whole cloves

½ teaspoon whole black peppercorns

1. Preheat the oven to 325°F. Put the figs in an 8-inch-square ceramic or glass baking dish. Pour the port, wine, honey, and orange juice over the figs. Submerge the remaining ingredients in the liquid around the figs. Cover the dish with foil, and bake 1 hour.

2. Remove the foil; continue to bake 45 minutes more, basting 2 or 3 times with the accumulated juices. Let cool completely, turning the figs occasionally to keep them moist.

3. Transfer the figs to a plate. Pour the liquid through a fine sieve into a bowl; reserve for the fig vinaigrette (recipe above). Discard the solids. The figs can be refrigerated in an airtight container up to 3 days.

white wine–poached scallop and herb salad
SERVES 4 TO 6

The scallops and vegetables can be poached and refrigerated up to 1 day ahead. Avoid using an oaky Chardonnay, which may add bitterness.

2½ cups dry white wine

Coarse salt

1 bay leaf

1 to 2 celery stalks, cut into ¼-inch half-moons (about 1½ cups), plus ¼ cup pale green leaves, very coarsely chopped

1 small fennel bulb, halved lengthwise, core removed, cut crosswise into ¼-inch half-moons (about 1½ cups), plus ¼ cup fronds, very coarsely chopped

20 large sea scallops (about 1 pound), tough muscles removed

2 tablespoons fresh lemon juice, plus wedges for garnish

2 tablespoons extra-virgin olive oil, plus more for drizzling

Freshly ground pepper

½ cup fresh flat-leaf parsley, very coarsely chopped

⅓ cup fresh chives, cut into ¾-inch pieces

1. Bring the wine, a pinch of salt, and the bay leaf, celery, and fennel to a boil in a medium saucepan. Reduce to a simmer; cook until the vegetables are just tender, about 8 minutes. Transfer the vegetables to a medium bowl; discard the bay leaf. Set aside. Add the scallops to the pan; simmer until just cooked through, about 3 minutes. Transfer the scallops to the bowl of vegetables; refrigerate until cold, about 30 minutes. Reserve ¼ cup poaching liquid. Refrigerate until cold, about 20 minutes.

2. Stir the lemon juice into the poaching liquid. Add the oil in a slow, steady stream, whisking until emulsified. Slice the scallops in half horizontally; toss with the dressing and vegetables. Season with salt and pepper. Toss the herbs, celery leaves, and fennel fronds in a small bowl, then divide among 4 serving plates. Top each with scallops and vegetables, dividing evenly. Drizzle with oil and dressing from the bowl. Garnish each salad with a lemon wedge.

asparagus and string bean salad with basil

SERVES 4 TO 6

Coarse salt

8 ounces green beans, trimmed

8 ounces yellow wax beans, trimmed

1 pound asparagus, trimmed

1 small shallot, thinly sliced

¼ cup small fresh basil leaves, plus more for garnish

1 tablespoon plus 1 teaspoon sherry vinegar

¼ cup finely grated Pecorino Romano cheese (¾ ounce)

¼ teaspoon sugar

3 tablespoons extra-virgin olive oil

Freshly ground pepper

1. Prepare an ice-water bath. Bring a large pot of water to a boil; add salt. Cook the green beans and wax beans until crisp-tender, about 1 minute. Using a slotted spoon, transfer the beans to the ice-water bath. Drain; transfer to a large bowl.

2. Cook the asparagus in boiling water until crisp-tender, about 1 minute. Transfer the asparagus to the ice-water bath. Drain; cut into 3-inch pieces. Add to the beans. Add the shallot and basil.

3. Make the vinaigrette: Whisk together the vinegar, cheese, sugar, ¼ teaspoon salt, and the oil in a medium bowl until sugar has dissolved. Season with pepper.

4. Add the vinaigrette to the vegetable mixture; toss. Refrigerate in an airtight container (or store in a chilled cooler) until ready to serve, up to 2 hours. Garnish with basil.

fig, feta, and mint salad

SERVES 4

French feta is creamier, milder, and less salty than the Greek version. Arrange this salad on a platter, and let your guests serve themselves.

1 block (8 ounces) French feta cheese

8 ounces fresh figs, halved lengthwise, if desired

2 to 3 tablespoons extra-virgin olive oil

Coarse salt and freshly ground pepper

½ cup fresh mint leaves

Put the feta on a serving platter. Arrange the figs over and around the feta. Drizzle the figs and cheese with the oil; season with salt and pepper. Sprinkle with the mint.

mushroom and celery salad with parmesan cheese

SERVES 12

12 ounces fresh white or cremini mushrooms, thinly sliced

6 ounces fresh chanterelle, porcini, oyster, or yellow oyster mushrooms, thinly sliced

6 celery stalks

7 tablespoons fresh lemon juice (2 to 3 lemons)

3 tablespoons finely chopped shallot

6 tablespoons extra-virgin olive oil

Coarse salt and freshly ground pepper

8 ounces mixed baby lettuces, such as mâche and mesclun

6 ounces Parmigiano-Reggiano cheese

1. Lay the mushrooms on sheets of paper towel; cover with clean, damp kitchen towels. Thinly slice the celery, and transfer it to a bowl; cover with plastic. Refrigerate.

2. Stir together the lemon juice and shallot. Let stand at least 15 minutes or up to 2 hours. Whisk in the oil until emulsified, and season with salt and pepper. Toss the mushrooms and celery with the dressing; let stand 10 minutes. Divide the lettuce among plates, and top with the mushroom mixture. Shave the cheese with a vegetable peeler over tops.

parsley-leaf salad with pine nuts, olives, and orange dressing

SERVES 6

The raw onions in this recipe become milder the longer they stay in the orange juice and vinegar mixture. For a strong onion flavor, let them soak for about 10 minutes; to make them more mellow, marinate for up to 4 hours.

- ¼ cup pine nuts
- 1 navel orange
- ½ teaspoon sherry vinegar or red wine vinegar
- ¼ medium red onion, very thinly sliced into half-moons

  Pinch of coarse salt
- 1 tablespoon capers, rinsed and drained
- ¼ cup brine-cured black olives such as kalamata or Gaeta, pitted and halved
- 3 cups loosely packed fresh flat-leaf parsley leaves (about 2 medium bunches)

  Freshly ground pepper
- 1 tablespoon extra-virgin olive oil

1. Preheat the oven to 375° F. Spread the pine nuts on a rimmed baking sheet; toast in the oven, shaking once, until golden and fragrant, 10 minutes. Transfer to a plate to cool.

2. With a vegetable peeler, peel 8 long pieces of zest from the orange; cut lengthwise into very thin strips. Halve the orange; squeeze 2 tablespoons juice into a medium bowl (reserve unused portion for another use). Add the vinegar, onion, and salt; let stand 10 minutes. Add the capers, olives, parsley, pine nuts, and zest to bowl. Season with pepper; toss thoroughly with oil. Divide among 6 plates.

FIT TO EAT RECIPE PER SERVING: 82 CALORIES, 6 G FAT, 0 MG CHOLESTEROL, 6 G CARBOHYDRATE, 128 MG SODIUM, 3 G PROTEIN, 2 G FIBER

watercress and green bean salad

SERVES 4

To keep watercress fresh, wrap it in damp paper towels and place it in a resealable plastic bag. Stored this way, it can be refrigerated for up to 4 days. Just before making the salad, "crisp" the watercress by soaking it in a bowl of ice water for a few minutes, then gently pat dry.

- ½ teaspoon coarse salt, plus more for seasoning
- 8 ounces green beans, trimmed and cut into 1-inch pieces
- 2 tablespoons finely chopped shallot
- 2 tablespoons fresh lemon juice

  Freshly ground pepper
- 2 tablespoons extra-virgin olive oil
- 1 Kirby cucumber, peeled, halved lengthwise, and thinly sliced
- 1 bunch watercress, thick stems discarded
- ¼ cup packed mint leaves, large leaves torn in half

1. Prepare an ice-water bath; set aside. Bring a medium pot of water to a boil; add salt. Blanch the green beans until crisp-tender, 4 to 5 minutes. Immediately transfer with a slotted spoon to the ice-water bath to stop the cooking. Drain, and set aside.

2. Whisk together the shallot, lemon juice, and ½ teaspoon salt in a large serving bowl; season with pepper. Whisking constantly, pour in the oil in a slow, steady stream; whisk until emulsified.

3. Add the cucumber and reserved green beans to the bowl; toss to coat. Add the watercress and mint; gently toss. Season with salt and pepper.

beet and mâche salad with aged goat cheese

SERVES 4 TO 6

2 pounds mixed beets, such as red and Chioggia

Orange Vinaigrette (recipe follows)

¼ cup fresh chervil leaves

3 ounces mâche or other tender lettuce

Coarse salt and freshly ground pepper

6 ounces Bûcheron or other aged goat cheese, room temperature, for serving

Crackers, for serving

1. Cover the beets with cold water by 2 inches in a large saucepan. Bring to a boil; reduce heat to medium. Simmer until tender, about 30 minutes. Let cool; peel, and halve (quarter if large). Toss with the vinaigrette. Let stand 30 minutes.

2. Toss together the chervil and mâche. Top with the beets and 2 tablespoons vinaigrette from the the bowl. Season with salt and pepper. Serve with goat cheese and crackers.

orange vinaigrette

MAKES 1⅓ CUPS

1 tablespoon orange zest

¾ cup fresh orange juice

2 tablespoons sherry vinegar

½ teaspoon coarse salt

½ cup extra-virgin olive oil

Freshly ground pepper

Stir together the orange zest, orange juice, vinegar, and salt in a small bowl. Pour in the olive oil in a slow, steady stream, whisking until emulsified. Season with freshly ground pepper.

arugula and radicchio with parmesan shavings

SERVES 6

9 ounces fresh arugula (about 8 cups), stemmed

4 ounces radicchio, halved crosswise and cut into thin strips (about 1½ cups)

8 ounces Parmesan cheese, shaved with a vegetable peeler (½ cup)

1½ tablespoons balsamic vinegar

Coarse salt and freshly ground pepper

3 tablespoons extra-virgin olive oil

1. Put the arugula, radicchio, and Parmesan in a serving bowl, and set aside.

2. Whisk the vinegar with salt and pepper to taste in a medium bowl. Whisking constantly, pour in the oil in a slow, steady stream, and whisk until emulsified. Toss the salad with just enough vinaigrette to coat.

shaved cucumber, fennel, and watermelon salad

SERVES 6

Ricotta salata is a firmer version of fresh ricotta; it is perfect for shaving over salads.

4 cucumbers

1 fennel bulb, trimmed, plus 1 tablespoon chopped fronds

3½ pounds watermelon, cut into 1-inch cubes

2 tablespoons fresh lemon juice

2 tablespoons olive oil

Coarse salt and freshly ground pepper

4 ounces ricotta salata

Using a mandoline, slice the cucumbers lengthwise into paper-thin slices; slice the fennel bulb crosswise into paper-thin slices. Combine the cucumbers and fennel in a large serving bowl. Add the watermelon, fennel fronds, lemon juice, and oil. Season with salt and pepper; toss to combine. Using a vegetable peeler, shave the ricotta salata over the salad, and serve.

mixed green salad
with date-walnut vinaigrette
SERVES 6 TO 8

1 cup walnut halves (about 4 ounces)
5 ounces dates, pitted
1 teaspoon Dijon mustard
½ cup cider vinegar
½ cup extra-virgin olive oil
   Coarse salt and freshly ground pepper
1 head green-leaf lettuce
1 head red Bibb lettuce
3 heads Belgian endive (about 12 ounces)
4 ounces baby spinach

1. Preheat the oven to 350°F. Spread the walnuts in a single layer on a rimmed baking sheet, and toast in the oven until golden and fragrant, 10 to 12 minutes. Let cool.

2. In a food processor, pulse 5 dates and the mustard and vinegar until pureed. With the machine running, slowly pour the oil through the feed tube. Season with salt and pepper.

3. Quarter the remaining dates lengthwise. Into a large bowl, tear the lettuce and endive into bite-size pieces; add the spinach, dates, and walnuts. Drizzle with the vinaigrette, and toss to combine. Serve immediately.

red and green salad
with cranberry vinaigrette
SERVES 8

1 head frisée (about 5 ounces)
1 head red-leaf lettuce (about 10 ounces)
4 ounces baby spinach
½ cup fresh or frozen (thawed) cranberries
1 tablespoon raspberry vinegar
2 teaspoons fresh lime juice
1 teaspoon sugar
½ teaspoon coarse salt
¼ cup extra-virgin olive oil
¾ cup dried cranberries
1½ ounces Manchego cheese

1. Tear the frisée and red-leaf lettuce into bite-size pieces; combine with the spinach in a large bowl. Set aside.

2. In a blender, combine the cranberries, vinegar, lime juice, sugar, salt, and oil; puree until the mixture is smooth.

3. Sprinkle the dried cranberries over the salad greens in a bowl; toss to combine. Divide the salad among serving plates. Using a vegetable peeler to shave thin slices, divide the cheese among individual salads. Serve with cranberry vinaigrette on the side.

FIT TO EAT RECIPE PER SERVING: 140 CALORIES, 9 G FAT, 5 MG CHOLESTEROL, 15 G CARBOHYDRATE, 192 MG SODIUM, 3 G PROTEIN, 2 G FIBER

mixed baby lettuces with anchovy vinaigrette

SERVES 6

- 1 teaspoon Dijon mustard
- 6 anchovy fillets, rinsed and mashed
- 2 tablespoons fresh lemon juice
- ⅓ cup extra-virgin olive oil
- 1 tablespoon finely chopped fresh flat-leaf parsley
  Freshly ground pepper
  Mixed baby lettuces, for serving

In a food processor, combine the mustard, anchovies, and lemon juice. Process until smooth. With the machine running, add the oil in a steady stream until smooth and emulsified. Stir in the parsley; season with pepper. Serve in small bowls, with lettuces on the side for dipping.

iceberg lettuce with blue cheese dressing and toasted almonds

SERVES 4

- 2 ounces whole shelled almonds
- 4½ ounces blue cheese, crumbled
- 1½ tablespoons fresh lemon juice
- ⅓ cup buttermilk
- 1½ tablespoons olive oil
  Freshly ground pepper
- 1 head iceberg lettuce, cut into 4 wedges
- 1 Granny Smith apple, cored and cut into ½-inch cubes

1. Preheat the oven to 350°F. Spread the almonds on a rimmed baking sheet, and bake until lightly toasted, 7 to 8 minutes. Let cool, then coarsely chop.

2. In a medium bowl, whisk together the cheese, lemon juice, buttermilk, and oil until smooth, and season with pepper.

3. Break each lettuce wedge in half. Divide among 4 plates; top with apple cubes. Spoon dressing over each serving. Garnish with almonds, and serve.

FIT TO EAT RECIPE PER SERVING: 290 CALORIES, 22 G FAT, 25 MG CHOLESTEROL, 14 G CARBOHYDRATE, 478 MG SODIUM, 12 G PROTEIN, 5 G FIBER

asian pear salad

SERVES 4

- 4 cups mixed frisée, baby arugula, and other small greens (about 11 ounces)
- 8 dates, pitted and quartered lengthwise
- 8 slices prosciutto (about 4 ounces), sliced into ¼-inch-wide strips
- 8 sprigs mint, leaves picked from stems (about 1 cup)
- 1 Asian pear, cored and sliced into ½-inch wedges
- 2 tablespoons fresh lemon juice (about 1 lemon)
- 2 tablespoons extra-virgin olive oil
  Coarse salt and freshly ground pepper

In a large bowl, toss together the greens, dates, prosciutto, mint, and pear. In a small bowl, whisk together the lemon juice and oil; season with salt and pepper. Pour the mixture over the salad. Toss to combine well, and serve immediately.

hearts of lettuce with russian dressing

SERVES 8 TO 10

- 3 small heads lettuce
- 1½ cups mayonnaise
- ½ cup ketchup or chili sauce
- ½ cup sour cream
- ½ cup finely chopped cornichon or sweet pickle relish
- 2 tablespoons chopped fresh dill
- 4 teaspoons chopped drained capers
- 2 shallots, finely chopped

Cut the lettuce in wedges; arrange in a bowl. Whisk together the remaining ingredients. Pour over the lettuce; serve. The dressing can be stored, refrigerated, up to 1 week.

farmstand raw vegetable salad

SERVES 6

Chioggia beets are pink on the outside and striped on the inside. Because they are not cooked in this recipe, choose tender baby beets. You can use red or golden beets if Chioggia beets are unavailable. After your grill becomes hot, grill the lemon halves, cut side down, until lightly charred. Remove, let cool slightly, and squeeze their warm juice over the vegetables.

- 6 ounces sugar snap peas, sliced diagonally into 1-inch lengths
- 2 Kirby cucumbers, sliced
- 2 ears fresh corn, kernels cut off cobs
- 12 baby Chioggia beets, scrubbed and halved lengthwise
- 1 lemon, halved
- 2 tablespoons extra-virgin olive oil
  Coarse salt and freshly ground pepper

In a large bowl, combine the peas, cucumbers, corn, and beets. Squeeze the lemon juice over the vegetables, and drizzle with the oil. Season with salt and pepper. Toss to combine, and serve at room temperature.

haricots verts and goat cheese salad with almonds

SERVES 6

- 2 ounces whole almonds (about ½ cup)
  Coarse salt
- 1½ pounds haricots verts, ends trimmed
- 1½ teaspoons sherry vinegar
- 1 tablespoon extra-virgin olive oil
  Freshly ground pepper
- 2½ ounces fresh goat cheese, crumbled

1. Preheat the oven to 350° F. Spread the almonds on a rimmed baking sheet, and place in the oven. Toast until they are fragrant and golden, about 10 minutes. Remove from the oven; let cool. Roughly chop; set aside.

2. Meanwhile, bring a stockpot of water to a boil, and add salt and the haricots verts; cook until their color brightens and the beans are crisp-tender, about 4 minutes. Drain, and transfer to a baking sheet; let cool, about 5 minutes.

3. While still warm, toss the beans in a serving bowl with the vinegar and olive oil; season with salt and pepper. Add the goat cheese, and stir to melt slightly and coat the beans. Sprinkle with the almonds, and serve.

romaine salad with prosciutto crisps

SERVES 4

The small inner leaves of romaine lettuce are tender and crisp, perfect for this salad. Use a vegetable peeler to shave the Pecorino Romano.

- 2 tablespoons extra-virgin olive oil, plus more for the pan
- 4 slices prosciutto (about 2 ounces)
- 1 tablespoon balsamic vinegar
- 1 teaspoon fresh thyme leaves, roughly chopped
  Coarse salt and freshly ground pepper
- 6 ounces hearts of romaine, leaves torn in half
- 1 ounce Pecorino Romano shavings

1. Preheat the oven to 400° F. Lightly brush a baking sheet with olive oil, and arrange the prosciutto in a single layer. Place in the oven, and bake until crisp, 5 to 10 minutes. Remove from the oven, and let cool on a wire rack.

2. Combine the olive oil, balsamic vinegar, and thyme; season with salt and pepper, and whisk to combine. Add the romaine and shaved Pecorino Romano, and toss to combine. Serve topped with prosciutto crisps.

green gazpacho salad

SERVES 6

- ½ cup slivered almonds
- 4 ounces baguette or other French bread, cut into ½-inch cubes (1½ cups)
- 1 yellow tomato, seeded, cut into ½-inch dice
- 1 green bell pepper, seeded, cut into ½-inch dice
- 1 cucumber, peeled, seeded, and cut into ½-inch dice
- 2 stalks celery, cut into ½-inch dice
- 1 small red onion, cut into ½-inch dice
- 2 scallions, thinly sliced
- 1 cup (about 6 ounces) green seedless grapes, cut in half
- ¼ cup finely chopped flat-leaf parsley
- 2 tablespoons finely chopped tarragon
- ¼ cup extra-virgin olive oil
- 2 tablespoons sherry or white-wine vinegar
- 1 teaspoon coarse salt
- ¼ teaspoon freshly ground pepper
- 1 head Boston or butter lettuce, torn into bite-size pieces

1. Preheat the oven to 350° F. Place the nuts on a rimmed baking sheet and the bread cubes on a baking sheet; toast until the nuts are aromatic and the bread is dried and barely golden, about 8 to 10 minutes; set aside.

2. In a large bowl, combine the tomato, pepper, cucumber, celery, red onion, scallions, grapes, parsley, tarragon, half the almonds, and the bread cubes. Drizzle with the olive oil and vinegar. Add the salt and pepper. Toss well to combine. Let sit for 30 minutes for flavors to blend. Serve over the lettuce, garnished with the remaining almonds.

wilted brussels sprouts salad with warm apple cider dressing

SERVES 6

- 1 pound Brussels sprouts, trimmed
- 4 ounces spinach (about 3 cups lightly packed leaves), washed, stems removed
- 1 small head radicchio
- 1 garlic clove, finely chopped
- ⅓ cup apple cider vinegar
- 2 tablespoons honey mustard
- 1½ tablespoons sugar
- 1 teaspoon coarse salt
- ¼ teaspoon freshly ground pepper
- ½ cup extra-virgin olive oil
  Goat cheese, for garnish
  Toasted caraway seeds, for garnish

1. Thinly slice the Brussels sprouts crosswise into strips. Repeat with the spinach leaves and radicchio. Place the Brussels sprouts, spinach, and radicchio in a large bowl, and toss to combine; set aside.

2. In a small saucepan, whisk together the garlic, apple cider vinegar, honey mustard, sugar, salt, and pepper over medium heat. Slowly drizzle in the olive oil while whisking constantly. Bring to a simmer, and cook until the mixture thickens slightly, about 3 minutes. Pour over the Brussels sprouts mixture, and toss to combine. Serve the salad warm, garnished with goat cheese and caraway seeds, or store in refrigerator up to 2 days, and serve cold.

classic panzanella

SERVES 6

1 medium red onion (about 6 ounces), peeled and thinly sliced

5 1-inch-thick slices 1- to 4-day-old stale Tuscan-style bread

Coarse salt

2 pounds ripe beefsteak tomatoes, cored and cut into large chunks

4 Kirby cucumbers (about 12 ounces), peeled and sliced

5 tablespoons extra-virgin olive oil

3 tablespoons red-wine vinegar

Freshly ground pepper

1 cup packed fresh basil leaves

1. Cover the onion slices with cold water; let soak about 30 minutes, changing the water three or four times. Drain, and transfer to a large bowl or dish.

Meanwhile, cover the bread with cold water, and let stand until the bread is softened, about 10 minutes.

2. Squeeze the bread to remove as much water as possible. Arrange the bread on a double layer of paper towels; cover with another double layer, and press down to extract any remaining water. Sprinkle the bread with about 1 teaspoon salt. Set aside for 5 minutes.

3. Using your fingers, pluck the bread into bite-size pieces, and transfer to the dish containing the onions. Toss to combine.

4. Prepare the cucumbers and tomatoes. Add to the bowl with the bread mixture.

5. Drizzle the oil and vinegar over the salad; season with salt and pepper.

6. Tear the basil leaves in half; add to the bowl. Gently toss to combine. Set aside in a cool place, 30 to 45 minutes. Toss and serve.

new classic panzanella
SERVES 6

You can intensify the garlic flavor by rubbing an additional clove on one side of the toasted bread before tearing it into chunks.

- 1 *garlic clove, peeled*
- 2 *pounds ripe beefsteak tomatoes, cored and cut into large chunks*
- 1 *medium red onion, peeled and thinly sliced*
- 5 *tablespoons extra-virgin olive oil*
- 3 *tablespoons red-wine vinegar*
  Coarse salt and freshly ground pepper
- 5 *1-inch-thick slices day-old Tuscan-style bread*
- 4 *Kirby cucumbers (about 12 ounces), peeled and sliced*
- 1 *cup packed fresh basil leaves*

1. Place the garlic on a cutting board; hit it with the side of a large knife to break it open a bit. Place the tomatoes, onion, and garlic in a large nonreactive bowl. Drizzle the oil and vinegar over the vegetable mixture; season with salt and pepper. Toss; let stand, covered, in a cool place, about 1 hour.

2. Place the bread on a hot grill or under a heated broiler; toast until both sides are slightly charred, 2 to 3 minutes. Remove from heat, rub lightly with garlic, if desired; tear the bread into bite-size chunks. When ready to serve, add the cucumbers, basil, and bread to the tomatoes.

3. Toss to coat the bread thoroughly with the marinating liquid. Adjust the seasoning with salt and pepper, and remove the garlic clove.

VARIATION[S]: *To either version of this salad, try adding cubed fresh mozzarella or bocconcini, roasted bell peppers, sliced fresh fennel, or capers. Experiment using other in-season vegetables.*

endive and treviso radicchio salad with anchovy dressing
SERVES 4

Soaking the anchovies in red-wine vinegar gives them a wonderful pickled flavor.

- 6 *anchovy fillets*
- ¼ *cup plus 1 tablespoon red-wine vinegar*
- 1 *garlic clove, smashed and peeled*
- ½ *teaspoon coarse salt*
- 3 *tablespoons extra-virgin olive oil*
- ¼ *teaspoon freshly ground pepper*
- 4 *endives, sliced ¼ inch lengthwise*
- 1 *head Treviso radicchio, leaves separated*

1. In a small bowl, submerge the anchovies in ¼ cup red-wine vinegar. Let soak for 30 minutes; drain, and discard the liquid.

2. Place the anchovies and garlic on a cutting board. Sprinkle with salt, and mince into a paste; place in a medium bowl. Whisk in the remaining tablespoon vinegar, the olive oil, and the pepper. Set aside.

3. Arrange the sliced endives and Treviso radicchio leaves on 4 salad plates. Drizzle the anchovy mixture over each. Serve immediately.

hearty bacon and lemon chicory salad
SERVES 4

- 8 *slices bacon*
- 1 *medium red onion, sliced thinly lengthwise*
- 1 *small head chicory, roughly chopped*
- 1 *small head frisée, roughly chopped*
  Juice of 1 lemon
- 3 *tablespoons extra-virgin olive oil*
- 1 *teaspoon coarse salt*
- ½ *teaspoon freshly ground pepper*

1. Place the bacon in a large skillet over medium heat. Cook until it is golden and crisp. Drain on paper towels. Break into 1- to 1½-inch pieces; set aside. Drain all but 1½ tablespoons bacon fat from the pan. Add the onion. Cook over medium heat until soft and golden, about 5 minutes. Remove from heat.

2. Place the chicory, frisée, bacon, and onion in a large bowl. In another bowl, whisk the lemon juice, olive oil, salt, and pepper. Drizzle over the salad, and toss. Serve the salad immediately.

chopped beet salad with feta and pecans

SERVES 12 TO 14

We used several varieties of beets, including Golden Globe and Chioggia, for a colorful salad, but you may use any variety you like.

- ½ cup pecans
- 4 bunches small beets (16 to 20 beets)
- 3 tablespoons cider vinegar
- 3 tablespoons olive oil
- 4 ounces feta cheese, crumbled
- 2 tablespoons freshly chopped flat-leaf parsley, plus sprigs for garnish
  Coarse salt and freshly ground pepper

1. Preheat the oven to 350°F. Place the pecans on a baking sheet, and toast until fragrant, about 10 minutes. Transfer to a bowl to cool. Coarsely chop, and set aside. Raise oven temperature to 450°F.

2. Trim the greens and long roots from the beets. Wrap in 2 to 3 aluminum foil packets, dividing the beets according to size. Place in the oven, and roast until tender, 45 to 60 minutes, depending on the size of the beets. Using paper towels to protect your hands, wipe the skins from the beets. Cut them into wedges, and transfer to a serving bowl.

3. Drizzle the vinegar and olive oil over the beets; toss to coat (beets can be made ahead). When ready to serve, add the feta, parsley, pecans, and salt and pepper to taste; toss to combine. Garnish with the parsley sprigs.

avocado filled with mixed herb and shallot vinaigrette

SERVES 6

- 3 tablespoons champagne vinegar
- 1 tablespoon fresh lemon juice
- 1½ teaspoons Dijon mustard
- 6 tablespoons canola oil
- ½ teaspoon salt
- ⅛ teaspoon freshly ground pepper
- 1 small shallot, finely chopped
- ¼ cup loosely packed fresh herbs, such as dill, chervil, parsley, and tarragon, coarsely chopped
- 3 ripe avocados, such as Hass or bacon

1. Combine the vinegar, lemon juice, and mustard in the jar of a blender. Slowly add the oil in a steady stream, blending until incorporated. Add the salt and pepper. Stir in the chopped shallot and herbs.

2. Slice the avocados lengthwise, rotating the knife around the pit. Twist the two halves of the avocado in opposite directions to separate. Embed the knife in the pit, and twist to separate the pit from the avocado. Fill each avocado half with a spoonful of the vinaigrette, and serve immediately.

....

RIPENING AVOCADOS

When they are perfectly ripe, avocados will yield slightly when pressed. To speed ripening, place avocados in a paper bag with an apple or a banana, and store at room temperature for a few days. To keep them from becoming too soft, store ripened avocados in the refrigerator for up to 2 days.

....

warm leeks vinaigrette

SERVES 6

4 teaspoons sherry vinegar

4 teaspoons Dijon mustard

1 tablespoon honey

1 teaspoon coarse salt

¼ teaspoon freshly ground pepper

4 teaspoons extra-virgin olive oil

3 bunches leeks (about 15 leeks)

1. Whisk together the vinegar, mustard, honey, salt, and pepper in a large bowl. Slowly drizzle in the olive oil, whisking constantly, until well combined; set aside.

2. Trim the leeks to about 6 inches, leaving only the white and light green parts. Trim the roots, and cut the leeks in half lengthwise. Wash well under cold running water to remove any dirt; set aside.

3. Place a metal steamer basket in a large saucepan. Fill with water to the bottom of the basket, and bring to a simmer. Add the leeks, cover, and steam until tender, about 10 minutes. Remove the leeks, and drain on paper towels to remove any water. Place the leeks in the bowl with the vinaigrette, and toss to combine. Serve hot or at room temperature.

FIT TO EAT RECIPE PER SERVING: 121 CALORIES, 4 G FAT, 0 MG CHOLESTEROL, 22 G CARBOHYDRATE, 255 MG SODIUM, 2 G PROTEIN, 3 G FIBER

summer-squash salad with herbs and pecorino fresco

SERVES 6

If you can find it, use Zephyr squash, which is yellow with a pale-green tip. You can also use a mix of young green and yellow squashes.

1 pound small, young summer squashes (about 8), cut into ¼-inch-thick rounds (halved if large)

2 tablespoons fresh oregano or thyme leaves

1 tablespoon extra-virgin olive oil
   Freshly ground pepper

6 ounces pecorino fresco, crumbled (about 1½ cups)

Toss together squashes, herbs, and oil in a large bowl; season with pepper. Add cheese; toss. Let stand at room temperature 15 minutes before serving.

shaved beet and dandelion salad

SERVES 8

2 teaspoons finely chopped shallot

1 teaspoon Dijon mustard

2 anchovy fillets, finely chopped

2 tablespoons sherry vinegar
   Coarse salt and freshly ground pepper

¼ cup plus 2 tablespoons extra-virgin olive oil

1 small red or yellow beet, peeled and shaved into very thin pieces

2 bunches dandelion or arugula, or a combination (about 20 ounces total), trimmed to bottom of leaf, torn if large

In a large bowl, whisk together shallot, mustard, anchovies, and vinegar; season with salt and pepper. Whisk in oil in a slow, steady stream. Add beet and dandelion. Toss to coat.

cucumber, string bean, and olive salad

SERVES 4

To pit the olives, place them on a cutting board, and press firmly with your thumb. The olives will split, and the pits can be easily removed.

   Coarse salt

½ pound string beans

2 cucumbers (1¼ pounds)

¼ pound oil-cured black olives, pitted, torn in half

¼ cup fresh flat-leaf parsley leaves

1 teaspoon Dijon mustard

1 tablespoon red-wine vinegar
   Freshly ground pepper

2 tablespoons extra-virgin olive oil

1. Fill a large bowl with ice and water; set aside. Bring a pot of water to a boil. Salt the water; add the string beans, and cook until bright green and just tender, 3 to 4 minutes. Drain, and transfer to the ice-water bath until cool. Drain, and cut in half lengthwise.

2. Peel the cucumbers, and split them lengthwise. Remove the seeds using a melon baller or a spoon. Cut into ½-inch-thick slices on the diagonal. Combine with string beans, olives, and parsley leaves in a medium serving bowl.

3. Whisk together the mustard, red-wine vinegar, and salt and pepper to taste in a small bowl. Slowly add the olive oil, whisking constantly. Toss with the salad just before serving.

chilled shrimp and chopped tomato salad with crisp garlic croutons

SERVES 8 TO 10

We recommend serving this juicy salad as a first course, either alone or accompanied by mixed greens. We used beefsteak tomatoes, but any fresh, ripe tomatoes would be equally delicious.

- 3 *quarts water*
- 2 *tablespoons coarse salt, plus more for seasoning*
- ¼ *teaspoon whole peppercorns*
- 1 *teaspoon paprika*
- 2 *dried bay leaves*
- 2 *tablespoons fresh lemon juice*
- 2 *pounds large shrimp, peeled and deveined*
- 5 *garlic cloves*
- 2 *red bell peppers, seeds and ribs removed*
- 4 *ripe beefsteak tomatoes (about 1¾ pounds)*
- 1 *medium cucumber, peeled, seeded, and cut into ¼-inch dice*
- 1 *green bell pepper, seeds and ribs removed, cut into ¼-inch dice*
- ½ *small red onion, finely diced (about ¾ cup)*
- 2 *tablespoons roughly chopped fresh marjoram or oregano*

- 2 *tablespoons plus 1 teaspoon red-wine vinegar*
- ½ *cup extra-virgin olive oil, plus more for drizzling, if desired*
- 6 *slices rustic bread, crusts removed, cut into ½-inch cubes (about 2½ cups)*
   Freshly ground black pepper

1. Prepare an ice-water bath; set aside. In a 5-quart stockpot, combine the water with 2 tablespoons salt, the peppercorns, paprika, bay leaves, and lemon juice; bring to a boil. Reduce heat to medium; simmer 5 minutes. Add the shrimp; stir once. Cook until the shrimp are pink and opaque, about 1½ minutes. With a large sieve, transfer the shrimp to the ice bath. Chill thoroughly, at least 2 minutes, and drain in the sieve. Cut each shrimp in half crosswise. Place in a bowl, cover with plastic wrap, and refrigerate until ready to use.

2. In a food processor fitted with the metal blade, chop the garlic. Remove 2 teaspoons; set aside. Quarter 1 red pepper and 1 tomato; add to the remaining garlic in the processor. Pulse until a coarse puree forms. Pour into a large mixing bowl.

3. Cut the remaining red pepper and 3 tomatoes into ¼-inch dice, and add to the bowl along with the cucumber, green pepper, red onion, marjoram, vinegar, and ¼ cup olive oil; stir to combine.

4. Meanwhile, in a large sauté pan, heat 2 tablespoons olive oil over medium heat, and fry half the bread cubes until they just begin to turn crisp and golden brown, about 3 minutes. Add half the reserved chopped garlic and a pinch of salt; cook, stirring frequently, until the garlic is fragrant and the bread cubes are golden brown, about 1 minute more. Transfer to a large plate, and repeat the process with the remaining garlic and bread cubes. Just before serving, toss the shrimp and half the croutons into the salad mixture, season with salt and pepper, and drizzle with more olive oil, if desired. Serve the remaining croutons on the side or on top of each portion.

warm eggplant salad

SERVES 4

12 ounces small round white eggplants,
    sliced ¼ inch thick

    Salt

½   cup extra-virgin olive oil

    Freshly ground pepper

1   small red onion, peeled, thinly sliced

2   ounces French feta cheese, crumbled

⅓   cup oil-cured black olives, pitted,
    quartered lengthwise

2   teaspoons fresh oregano leaves

1. Sprinkle the eggplant slices with salt on both sides. Place in a colander over a bowl, and let stand 1 hour to drain. Discard the liquid, and rinse under cold running water. Place the eggplant slices on several layers of paper towel; press out the water.

2. Transfer the eggplant to a nonreactive surface. Generously brush both sides with oil; sprinkle with pepper. Heat 2 tablespoons oil in a large skillet over medium-high heat. Add slices of eggplant (without crowding); cook until golden brown on both sides, about 6 minutes. Drain on paper towels. Repeat the process with the remaining slices.

3. Place the eggplant, onion, feta, olives, and oregano in a large bowl. Drizzle with the remaining olive oil, and season with salt and pepper, if necessary. Gently toss the mixture to combine, and serve warm or at room temperature.

watercress, pink grapefruit, and walnut salad

SERVES 4

for the dressing

2¼ tablespoons minced ginger

¼   teaspoon minced garlic

1   tablespoon fresh lime juice

1½ teaspoons rice-wine vinegar

¼   teaspoon Asian sesame oil

⅛   teaspoon sugar

3   tablespoons extra-virgin olive oil

for the salad

1   pink grapefruit

8   ounces watercress (about 2 bunches),
    thick stems removed

½   cup walnuts, coarsely chopped

⅛   teaspoon coarse salt

    Freshly ground pepper

1. Make the dressing: Whisk together ginger, garlic, lime juice, vinegar, sesame oil, and sugar in a small bowl. Gradually add olive oil, whisking constantly until fully combined. Set aside.

2. Remove peel and pith from grapefruit. Holding over a medium bowl, carve out flesh between the membranes, letting segments drop into the bowl (you should have about ¾ cup segments). Add watercress. Pour dressing over watercress and grapefruit; toss to coat. Sprinkle with walnuts. Season with salt and pepper.

FIT TO EAT RECIPE PER SERVING: 216 CALORIES, 20 G FAT, 0 MG CHOLESTEROL, 8 G CARBOHYDRATE, 59 MG SODIUM, 4 G PROTEIN, 2 G FIBER

mâche with fennel, carrot, and orange

SERVES 4

Mâche, or lamb's lettuce, is a tender, nutty green. If it's unavailable, try watercress as a delicious substitute.

- 2 tablespoons plus 1 teaspoon fresh lemon juice
- 1 tablespoon champagne vinegar
- ½ teaspoon coarse salt

  Pinch of sugar

  Freshly ground pepper
- ¼ cup extra-virgin olive oil
- ¼ pound baby or halved regular carrots, peeled into ribbons (about 2½ cups)
- ½ medium fennel bulb (about 10 ounces), trimmed, halved lengthwise, and thinly sliced crosswise
- 1 medium shallot, halved lengthwise and thinly sliced
- 3 small oranges, peel and pith removed, carved into segments using a sharp knife (about 1¼ cups)
- 4 cups mâche

1. Make the dressing: Whisk together lemon juice, vinegar, salt, and sugar in a medium bowl; season with pepper. Add oil in a slow, steady stream, whisking constantly until emulsified.

2. Make the salad: Toss carrots and fennel in a bowl with dressing to coat. Let stand until softened, about 15 minutes. Using a slotted spoon, transfer carrot-fennel mixture to a large bowl; discard excess dressing. Add shallot, orange segments, and mâche; toss to combine. Divide salad among 4 serving plates.

SIDE SALADS

white bean salad with carrots and tomatoes

SERVES 4 TO 6

- 1 cup dried white beans, such as navy
- 2 medium carrots, peeled and cut into ¼-inch dice
- 1 small red onion, finely chopped
- 1 cup grape tomatoes, halved lengthwise
- 1 tablespoon finely chopped fresh flat-leaf parsley
- ¼ cup red-wine vinegar
- 1 tablespoon fresh thyme, chopped
- ½ teaspoon sugar
- 3 tablespoons olive oil

  Coarse salt and freshly ground pepper

1. Put the beans into a large bowl; cover with water by 2 inches. Cover with plastic wrap. Let soak at room temperature 6 hours (or overnight). Drain; rinse.

2. Transfer the beans to a medium saucepan; cover with cold water by 1½ inches. Bring to a simmer. Cook, covered, until tender, about 25 minutes. Drain. Rinse with cold water, and let cool completely. Transfer to a bowl; cover with plastic wrap. Refrigerate 15 minutes.

3. Add the carrots, onion, tomatoes, and parsley to beans; toss well. Whisk together the vinegar, thyme, sugar, oil, and ½ teaspoon salt in a bowl until sugar has dissolved; season with pepper. Toss the vinaigrette with the bean mixture. Season with salt and pepper. Refrigerate in an airtight container (or store in a chilled cooler) until ready to serve, up to 4 hours.

roasted carrot and beet salad

SERVES 4

For a complete meal, serve this salad with pita bread, feta cheese, and hummus. If you are on a low-sodium diet, substitute a less salty cheese for the feta.

- 4 medium red beets (about 1 pound without greens), ½ inch of stems left intact
- 2 tablespoons plus 2 teaspoons extra-virgin olive oil
- 1 pound carrots (about 8 medium), cut on the diagonal into 1-inch pieces
- ½ teaspoon coarse salt
- 2 tablespoons fresh lemon juice
- 2 tablespoons coarsely chopped fresh flat-leaf parsley
- 1 tablespoon finely chopped fresh thyme
  Freshly ground pepper

1. Preheat the oven to 375°F. Toss the beets with 1 teaspoon oil on a rimmed baking sheet. Cover the sheet with foil. Roast the beets until tender, 45 to 55 minutes. Let cool. Trim and peel the beets; cut into ½-inch cubes.

2. Meanwhile, toss the carrots, 1 teaspoon oil, and ¼ teaspoon salt on another rimmed baking sheet. Roast the carrots until browned and tender, about 40 minutes. Let cool to room temperature.

3. Stir the lemon juice, remaining ¼ teaspoon salt, and the parsley and thyme in a small bowl. Whisk in the remaining 2 tablespoons oil until emulsified. Season with pepper. Toss the beets and carrots with the dressing in a medium bowl. The salad can be refrigerated in an airtight container up to 3 days.

FIT TO EAT RECIPE PER SERVING: 405 CALORIES, 22 G FAT, 25 MG CHOLESTEROL, 44 G CARBOHYDRATE, 892 MG SODIUM, 12 G PROTEIN, 10 G FIBER

three-bean salad with honey-mustard vinaigrette

SERVES 4

- Juice of 2 limes
- 1½ tablespoons finely chopped fresh tarragon leaves
- 1½ tablespoons finely chopped fresh chives
- 1 tablespoon honey
- 1½ teaspoons Dijon mustard
- ¼ teaspoon coarse salt
- ¼ pound haricots verts or green beans, trimmed and cut into thirds
- 1 cup canned kidney beans, drained and rinsed
- 1 cup canned cannellini beans, drained and rinsed
- 1 ounce mâche or watercress, trimmed, rinsed, and spun dry
  Freshly ground pepper

1. Make the vinaigrette: In a small bowl, whisk together the lime juice, tarragon, chives, honey, mustard, and salt until combined. Set aside.

2. Prepare an ice-water bath; set aside. Bring a medium saucepan of water to a boil. Add the haricots verts or green beans; simmer until bright green but still crisp, about 2 minutes. Using a slotted spoon, transfer the haricots verts to the ice bath, and let cool completely. Drain in a colander, and pat dry with paper towels. Place in a large serving bowl. Add the kidney beans and cannellini, and drizzle with vinaigrette. Toss to coat. Gently toss in the mâche or watercress; season with pepper. Serve.

FIT TO EAT RECIPE PER SERVING: 105 CALORIES, 0 G FAT, 0 MG CHOLESTEROL, 21 G CARBOHYDRATE, 164 MG SODIUM, 6 G PROTEIN, 6 G FIBER

corn-mango salad

SERVES 6 TO 8

- 6 cups fresh corn kernels (from 6 cooked ears of corn)
- 1 large mango, peeled and cut into ¼-inch dice (2 cups)
- 10 scallions, white and pale-green parts only, cut into very thin matchsticks
- ¼ cup thinly sliced fresh red chile (1 to 2 chiles)
- 1 cup fresh lime juice (about 7 limes)
- 1¼ teaspoons coarse salt

Toss the corn, mango, scallions, chile, lime juice, and salt in a large bowl. Refrigerate, covered, 30 minutes, or up to 2 days. Serve cold or at room temperature.

mixed mushroom salad

SERVES 6 TO 8

- ¼ cup fresh lemon juice (about 2 lemons)
- 1 tablespoon coarsely chopped fresh oregano
- 1 tablespoon coarsely chopped fresh flat-leaf parsley
- 1 tablespoon coarsely chopped fresh marjoram
- 1 teaspoon coarse salt
  Freshly ground pepper
- ¾ cup extra-virgin olive oil, plus more for drizzling
- 6 cups thinly sliced mixed fresh mushrooms, such as cremini, shiitake, oyster, and button (about 1 pound)
- 2 bunches arugula (about 1 pound)
- ½ small head radicchio (about 8 ounces), thinly sliced
- 3 ounces Parmesan cheese, shaved with a vegetable peeler into 1-inch-thick strips

1. In a large bowl, whisk together the lemon juice, herbs, salt, and ½ teaspoon pepper. Whisk in the oil. Reserve 1 tablespoon dressing; set aside. Add the mushrooms to the remaining dressing, and toss to combine. Set aside.

2. Toss together the arugula, radicchio, and reserved dressing. Arrange on a large platter. Top with the mushroom mixture. Sprinkle with the Parmesan cheese, and drizzle with oil. Season with pepper.

cucumber salad with radish and dill

SERVES 4 TO 6

This salad tastes best up to 1 hour after making it. To make ahead store the salad components separately (up to 3 hours), and toss before serving.

- 1 English cucumber or 3 Kirby cucumbers, halved lengthwise, seeded, and thinly sliced
- 4 large radishes (about 6 ounces), thinly sliced
  Zest of 1 lemon, plus 2 tablespoons fresh lemon juice (1 lemon total)
- 6 ounces feta cheese, coarsely crumbled (about 1½ cups)
- 2 tablespoons white-wine vinegar
- 1 tablespoon finely chopped fresh dill, plus more, torn, for garnish
- ½ teaspoon sugar
- 1 garlic clove, crushed with the flat side of a large knife
  Coarse salt and freshly ground pepper
- ¼ cup plus 1 tablespoon olive oil

1. Put the cucumber, radishes, and lemon zest in a medium bowl. Add the cheese.

2. Make the vinaigrette: Whisk together the lemon juice, vinegar, dill, sugar, and garlic in another medium bowl; season with salt and pepper. Whisk until the sugar has dissolved. Whisk in the oil in a slow, steady stream until emulsified.

3. Add the vinaigrette to the cucumber mixture; toss well. Garnish with the dill. Discard the garlic clove before serving. Refrigerate the salad in an airtight container up to 1 hour.

quinoa and apple salad with curry dressing

SERVES 4

¼ cup raw whole almonds

1 cup white quinoa

1 teaspoon honey

1 tablespoon finely chopped shallot

1 teaspoon curry powder

¼ teaspoon coarse salt

2 tablespoons fresh lemon juice

Freshly ground pepper

2 tablespoons extra-virgin olive oil

2 tablespoons dried currants

1 small McIntosh apple, cut into ⅛-inch-thick wedges

¼ cup loosely packed fresh mint leaves, coarsely chopped, plus more for garnish

1. Preheat the oven to 375°F. Spread the almonds on a rimmed baking sheet; toast in the oven until lightly toasted and fragrant, about 7 minutes. Let cool; coarsely chop the nuts.

2. Rinse the quinoa thoroughly in a fine sieve; drain. Bring 2 cups water to a boil in a medium saucepan. Add the quinoa; return to a boil. Stir the quinoa, cover, and reduce heat. Simmer until the quinoa is tender but still chewy, about 15 minutes. Fluff the quinoa with a fork; let cool.

3. Whisk together the honey, shallot, curry powder, salt, and lemon juice in a large bowl. Season with pepper. Whisking constantly, pour in the oil in a slow, steady stream; whisk until the dressing is emulsified. Add the quinoa, currants, apple, mint, and nuts; toss well. Garnish with mint.

FIT TO EAT RECIPE PER SERVING: 304 CALORIES, 14 G FAT, 0 MG CHOLESTEROL, 38 G CARBOHYDRATE, 154 MG SODIUM, 8 G PROTEIN, 5 G FIBER

QUINOA

Although only recently becoming popular in the United States, quinoa (pronounced KEEN-wah) has been grown and enjoyed in South America for centuries. There are plenty of good reasons to incorporate quinoa into your own diet. For one thing, it is incredibly healthful. Quinoa is an excellent source of protein that provides all the essential amino acids usually found only in animal proteins; it also offers iron, calcium, B vitamins, and vitamin E. Preparing quinoa is quick and easy. It takes less time to cook than long-grain rice, and is almost as versatile in its uses.

Quinoa, which is actually the seed of the quinoa plant, is available in white and red varieties. Both are equally nutritious, but the red seeds have a slightly nuttier flavor (and are a bit harder to find). The seeds are tiny, but the kernels become light and fluffy during cooking, expanding to four times their original size. You will notice a curled wisp emerging from each tiny kernel as you cook. This is the external germ, a healthful and crunchy part of the seed. Soups, salads, pilafs, stuffings, and baked goods are all excellent ways to use quinoa, which is delicious hot or cold.

classic creamy coleslaw

SERVES 6 TO 8

1 tablespoon Dijon mustard

1 tablespoon cider vinegar

1 tablespoon fresh lemon juice

1 tablespoon sugar

1 teaspoon coarse salt

½ cup mayonnaise

¼ cup sour cream

1 small green cabbage (about 1¾ pounds), finely shredded

2 medium carrots, cut into ⅛-inch-thick matchsticks or coarsely grated

½ small onion, coarsely grated (optional)

1. Whisk together the mustard, vinegar, lemon juice, sugar, salt, mayonnaise, and sour cream in a small bowl. Refrigerate the dressing, covered, until ready to use, or up to 2 days.

2. Put the cabbage, carrots, and onion (if desired) in a large bowl. Pour in the dressing, and toss thoroughly. Refrigerate, covered, until the slaw begins to soften, 1 to 2 hours. If not using immediately, refrigerate, covered, up to 2 days. Just before serving, toss the coleslaw again.

italian potato salad
SERVES 10

8   large eggs
3   pounds small red potatoes
    Coarse salt
2   to 3 tablespoons muscatel wine vinegar or white balsamic vinegar
1   cup loosely packed fresh flat-leaf parsley leaves, coarsely chopped
1   medium red onion, coarsely chopped (about ¾ cup)
¼   cup best-quality extra-virgin olive oil
    Freshly ground pepper

1. Prepare an ice-water bath; set aside. Cover the eggs with water in a medium saucepan; bring to a full boil. After 1 minute, cover; turn off heat. Let stand 8 minutes. Rinse; transfer to ice-water bath.

2. Cover the potatoes with water by 1 inch in a large saucepan. Bring to a boil; add salt. Simmer until just tender, about 15 minutes (do not overcook). Drain the potatoes; let cool slightly. Halve lengthwise.

3. Transfer the potatoes to a medium bowl. Add vinegar to taste; gently toss. Stir in the parsley and onion. Gently tossing, pour in the oil in a slow, steady stream; toss until incorporated. Season with salt and pepper.

4. Just before serving, peel and quarter the eggs, and arrange them on top of the salad.

red and green cabbage slaw with bacon
SERVES 6 TO 8

This slaw can be made up to 1 day ahead and refrigerated. Refrigerate the cooked bacon separately, wrapped in paper towels, in a resealable plastic bag; reheat it on a baking sheet in a 325°F oven until it's warm and crisp.

½   medium red cabbage (about 1 pound), finely shredded
¼   medium green cabbage (about ½ pound), finely shredded
½   pound smoked bacon (about 8 strips), cut into ¼-inch pieces
1   teaspoon caraway seeds (optional)
3   tablespoons olive oil
1   garlic clove, minced
¼   cup plus 3 tablespoons cider vinegar
2   teaspoons sugar
2½ teaspoons coarse salt
    Freshly ground pepper
1   Granny Smith apple (optional)

1. Toss the cabbages together in a large bowl; set aside. Cook the bacon in a medium skillet over medium heat, stirring occasionally, until crisp, about 5 minutes. Transfer with a slotted spoon to paper towels to drain; set aside. Pour off all but about 1 tablespoon fat from the skillet.

2. Add the caraway seeds to the skillet, if desired; cook over medium heat, shaking the skillet often, until the seeds begin to pop, about 1 minute. Add the oil and garlic; cook, stirring, 10 seconds (do not let the garlic brown). Remove from heat; pour in the vinegar. Add the sugar and salt; stir until dissolved. Pour the dressing over the cabbage. Season with pepper. Toss thoroughly. Let stand at least 1 hour, or refrigerate, covered, overnight.

3. Just before serving, cut the apple into ¼-inch-thick wedges or matchsticks. Add to the dressed cabbage along with the bacon, and toss again.

fingerling potato salad with sugar snap peas

SERVES 4 TO 6

1½ pounds fingerling or other small potatoes,
    cut into ½-inch-thick rounds

    Coarse salt

8   ounces sugar snap peas, plus more,
    split, for garnish (optional)

½   small red onion, thinly sliced

    Creamy Tarragon Vinaigrette (recipe
    follows)

    Freshly ground pepper

    Fresh tarragon and tarragon flowers,
    for garnish (optional)

1. Cover the potatoes with cold water by 2 inches in a medium saucepan. Bring to a boil; add 3 tablespoons salt. Reduce heat to medium-high; simmer the potatoes until tender, about 8 minutes. Transfer to paper towels to drain.

2. Bring another medium saucepan of water to a boil; add 2 tablespoons salt. Blanch the snap peas until just tender, 1 to 2 minutes. Let cool in an ice-water bath. Drain, and pat dry.

3. Toss the potatoes, snap peas, onion, and vinaigrette in a bowl. Season with salt and pepper. Garnish with the split snap peas, tarragon, and tarragon flowers, if desired.

creamy tarragon vinaigrette

MAKES ABOUT 1 CUP

2   teaspoons tarragon vinegar

¾   teaspoon Dijon mustard

    coarse salt and freshly ground pepper

½   cup extra-virgin olive oil

½   cup sour cream

2   tablespoons finely chopped fresh
    tarragon

Stir together vinegar and mustard; season with salt and pepper. Pour in olive oil in a slow, steady stream, whisking until emulsified. Stir in sour cream and tarragon.

wheatberry salad

SERVES 8

Wheatberries are a nutty grain often used in salads and breads. Look for hard red winter wheatberries—summer wheatberries become too soft after they're cooked.

2   cups hard red winter wheatberries (about
    13 ounces)

2   tablespoons plus ½ cup extra-virgin
    olive oil

1   cup diced red onion (1 small onion)

½   cup balsamic vinegar

½   cup sliced scallions, cut diagonally into
    ¼-inch slices (about 6 scallions)

1   small red bell pepper, seeded and cut
    into ¼-inch dice (1 cup)

1   small yellow bell pepper, seeded and
    cut into ¼-inch dice (1 cup)

1   cup diced carrots (2 carrots)

½   teaspoon salt

½   teaspoon freshly ground black pepper

1. Bring a medium saucepan of water to a boil. Add the wheatberries; cook until tender, 30 to 40 minutes. Drain; set aside.

2. Heat 2 tablespoons olive oil in a large sauté pan over low heat. Cook the onion until translucent, stirring occasionally, about 10 minutes. Remove the pan from heat; add remaining ½ cup olive oil and balsamic vinegar.

3. In a large bowl, combine the wheatberries, onion mixture, scallions, peppers, carrots, salt, and pepper. Allow to sit for at least 1 hour at room temperature so the wheatberries absorb the flavors. Serve at room temperature.

black-eyed pea and jalapeño salad

SERVES 4

Piquant jalapeño chiles complement the earthy flavor of black-eyed peas in this fiber-rich side salad; they also add crunch, along with the diced red onion.

- 2 cans (15 ounces each) black-eyed peas, drained, rinsed, and excess water shaken out
- 2 fresh jalapeño peppers, seeds and ribs discarded, flesh cut into ¼-inch dice
- 1 small red onion, cut into ¼-inch dice
- ¾ cup sprouts, such as sunflower or alfalfa
- ¼ cup extra-virgin olive oil
- 2 tablespoons red-wine vinegar

  Coarse salt and freshly ground black pepper

Put the black-eyed peas, jalapeños, onion, and sprouts in a large bowl. Add the oil and vinegar, and toss well. Season with salt and pepper.

vidalia onion slaw

SERVES 10 TO 12

- 2 tablespoons plus 1½ teaspoons coarse salt
- 4 Vidalia or other sweet onions, cut into ¼-inch dice
- 1½ cups mayonnaise
- ¼ cup apple cider vinegar
- 1 tablespoon sugar
- 1 teaspoon ground celery seed
- ½ teaspoon freshly ground pepper

1. Prepare a large ice-water bath; set aside. Bring a stockpot of water to a boil; add 2 tablespoons salt and the onions; simmer until the onions are translucent but still crisp, about 4 minutes. Transfer to the ice bath to cool. Drain; pat dry with paper towels.

2. Transfer to a large bowl, and mix with the mayonnaise, vinegar, sugar, celery seed, remaining 1½ teaspoons salt, and pepper. Serve, or store, covered with plastic wrap, in the refrigerator up to 2 days.

crunchy jícama, apple, and carrot slaw with creamy orange dressing

SERVES 8

- 1 cup mayonnaise
- ½ cup sour cream
- ¼ cup fresh orange juice
- 2 tablespoons cider vinegar
- 1 tablespoon minced fresh basil

  Coarse salt and freshly ground pepper
- 2 Granny Smith apples
- 1 jícama (about 1 pound), peeled
- 2 carrots
- ½ small head green cabbage, finely shredded

1. In a small bowl, whisk together the mayonnaise, sour cream, orange juice, vinegar, and basil; season with salt and pepper. Refrigerate, covered, until ready to use.

2. Slice the apples, jícama, and carrots on the thinnest setting of a mandoline or with a sharp knife; then cut the slices into julienne, about 2 inches long.

3. In a large bowl, toss the julienned apples, jícama, carrots, and cabbage with the mayonnaise mixture. Cover with plastic wrap, and refrigerate until ready to serve.

beet, cabbage, and carrot slaw with caraway seeds

SERVES 6

1   teaspoon caraway seeds

2   tablespoons fresh lemon juice

1   tablespoon white or yellow miso paste

1   small shallot, halved lengthwise and thinly sliced into half-moons

2   tablespoons extra-virgin olive oil
    Freshly ground pepper

2½ cups julienned or grated beets (about 2)

2   cups finely shredded red cabbage (¼ medium)

1½ cups julienned or grated carrots (about 3)

1. Make the dressing: In a small bowl, combine the caraway, lemon juice, miso, and shallot. Slowly whisk in the oil until emulsified. Season with pepper. Set aside.

2. In a large bowl, combine the beets, cabbage, and carrots. Drizzle dressing over the vegetables, and toss until combined. Serve chilled or at room temperature.

FIT TO EAT RECIPE PER SERVING: 79 CALORIES, 5 G FAT, 0 MG CHOLESTEROL, 8 G CARBOHYDRATE, 172 MG SODIUM, 2 G PROTEIN, 3 G FIBER

broccoli and white bean salad

SERVES 4

1   large bunch broccoli (about 1 pound)
    Coarse salt

1   can (15½ ounces) cannellini beans, drained and rinsed

½   small red onion, halved and thinly sliced into half-moons

1   tablespoon freshly squeezed lemon juice, plus 1 tablespoon finely grated lemon zest (about 1 lemon)

2   tablespoons extra-virgin olive oil

¼   teaspoon crushed red pepper flakes
    Freshly ground black pepper

¾   cup shaved Pecorino Romano or Parmesan cheese (about 2 ounces)

1. Cut the tops off each head of broccoli, and trim into 1-inch florets; set aside. Peel each stem to remove the tough outer layer. Slice the peeled stems on the bias into ¼-inch pieces; set aside.

2. Prepare an ice-water bath; set aside. Bring a large pot of water to a boil. Add a generous amount of salt and the broccoli florets. Cook over high heat until the florets are tender when pierced with the tip of a paring knife, about 4 minutes. Using a slotted spoon, transfer to the ice bath. Add the stems to the boiling water; cook until tender when pierced with the tip of a paring knife, about 3 minutes. Transfer to the ice bath. Let the florets and stems cool completely, and drain.

3. In a large mixing bowl, combine the broccoli, beans, onion, lemon juice and zest, oil, and red pepper flakes. Stir to combine; season with salt and pepper. Top with cheese; serve immediately.

warm bean, snap pea, and tomato salad

SERVES 4

Cannellini are white Italian kidney beans. Try substituting cranberry, pinto, or other dried beans in this salad. To save time, use canned beans in place of dried.

- 4 ounces wax beans, trimmed and cut into 1-inch pieces (about 1 cup)
- 4 ounces sugar snap peas, trimmed and cut in half (about 1 cup)
- 1 tablespoon extra-virgin olive oil
- 4 scallions, sliced into ¼-inch rounds
- 3 garlic cloves, minced
- 1½ cups cooked cannellini beans, drained
- 2 beefsteak tomatoes, cut into ½-inch dice, juice and seeds reserved
- ½ teaspoon coarse salt
  Freshly ground black pepper
- 1 cup loosely packed fresh basil leaves

1. Prepare an ice-water bath; set aside. Bring a medium pot of water to a boil over high heat. Add the wax beans, and cook until crisp-tender and bright, about 2½ minutes. Remove the beans with a slotted spoon, and immediately plunge into the ice bath. Drain, and set aside. Repeat with the snap peas, blanching them about 1 minute.

2. Heat the oil in a large sauté pan over medium heat. Add the scallions and garlic; cook, stirring occasionally, until soft but not browned, about 3 minutes. Add the cannellini beans, and cook until just heated through, about 2 minutes more.

3. Transfer the mixture to a large bowl. Add the wax beans, snap peas, tomatoes and reserved juice and seeds, and salt. Season with pepper. Using a sharp knife, cut the basil into very thin strips; add to the bean mixture. Toss to combine; serve warm.

FIT TO EAT RECIPE PER SERVING: 177 CALORIES, 4 G FAT, 0 MG CHOLESTEROL, 28 G CARBOHYDRATE, 255 MG SODIUM, 9 G PROTEIN, 11 G FIBER

corn and couscous salad

SERVES 4

- 1 teaspoon curry powder
- 2 teaspoons grainy mustard
- 1 tablespoon white-wine or sherry vinegar
  Coarse salt and freshly ground pepper
- 4 tablespoons extra-virgin olive oil
- ¾ cup couscous
- 1 Vidalia or other sweet onion, diced
- 3 garlic cloves, minced
- 1 red chile, minced (optional)
- 3 cups fresh corn kernels (about 4 cobs)
- ¼ cup finely chopped fresh cilantro

1. In a medium bowl, whisk together the curry powder, mustard, and vinegar. Season with salt and pepper. While whisking, slowly drizzle in 3 tablespoons oil; whisk until emulsified. Set aside.

2. Place the couscous in a large bowl. Bring 1 cup water to a boil; pour over the couscous; stir to combine. Cover with a plate; let steam until the water is absorbed, about 5 minutes. Fluff with a fork; set aside.

3. Heat the remaining tablespoon oil in a large skillet over medium heat. Add the onion, and cook, stirring, until softened, about 4 minutes. Stir in the garlic and chile; cook, stirring, until softened, about 2 minutes. Add the corn, and cook until bright yellow and just tender, about 2 minutes. Stir the corn mixture into the couscous. Add the curry vinaigrette and cilantro; toss to combine. Serve warm or at room temperature.

lentils with tarragon, shallots, and beets

SERVES 8 TO 10

To prevent the lentils from becoming too soft as they cool, spread them on a baking sheet.

3½ pounds beets, trimmed

2 tablespoons plus ¼ cup extra-virgin olive oil

3½ teaspoons coarse salt, plus more for seasoning

¼ cup water, plus more for cooking lentils

1 pound French green lentils, picked over

2 garlic cloves

2 dried bay leaves

1 shallot, minced

1 teaspoon Dijon mustard

2 tablespoons plus 1 teaspoon balsamic vinegar

1 tablespoon chopped fresh tarragon
    Freshly ground pepper

1. Preheat the oven to 350°F. In a medium bowl, toss the beets with 2 tablespoons oil and 1½ teaspoons salt. Arrange on a rimmed baking sheet; pour ¼ cup water into the pan. Cover with foil; roast until the beets are easily pierced with the tip of a knife, 45 to 60 minutes. Remove from the oven; let cool. Peel and cut into ½-inch cubes.

2. Meanwhile, combine the lentils, garlic, and bay leaves in a 6-quart saucepan; add enough cold water to cover by about 3 inches. Bring to a boil over medium-high heat. Reduce heat to medium-low; simmer, stirring occasionally, until the lentils are tender but not mushy, 10 to 20 minutes. Stir in the remaining 2 teaspoons salt, and cook about 5 minutes more. Drain in a colander; let cool.

3. In a small bowl, combine the shallot, mustard, and vinegar; let stand 15 minutes. Slowly whisk in the remaining ¼ cup oil in a steady stream.

4. Transfer the lentils to a large serving bowl. Add the vinaigrette and the tarragon; toss well to combine. Toss in the beets. Season with salt and pepper. Serve, or cover and refrigerate up to 4 hours; bring to room temperature before serving.

french potato salad with white wine and celery leaves

SERVES 6

2½ pounds Yukon Gold potatoes
    Coarse salt

3 tablespoons roughly chopped shallots

2 tablespoons white wine

2 tablespoons white-wine vinegar
    Freshly ground pepper

3 tablespoons extra-virgin olive oil

⅓ cup loosely packed celery leaves from inner stalks, torn in half

1. Place the potatoes in a stockpot, and add enough cold water to cover by 4 inches. Bring to a boil over high heat, and add salt; reduce heat, and cook until the potatoes are easily pierced with a fork, about 20 minutes. Drain; let cool slightly. Peel the potatoes, and cut into quarters or eighths.

2. Meanwhile, in a large serving bowl, combine the shallots with the wine and vinegar. While still warm, add the potatoes to the bowl; season with salt and pepper. Drizzle in the oil; toss to coat. Sprinkle with the celery leaves, and serve immediately.

multicolored pepper and bean salad with ricotta salata and herbs

SERVES 10 TO 12

You can prepare the vegetables up to 2 hours before serving and keep them covered in the refrigerator. If desired, include some poblano or other chiles along with the peppers. You can substitute feta cheese for the ricotta salata.

Coarse salt
½ pound green beans, ends trimmed
½ pound yellow wax beans, ends trimmed
3 shallots, peeled and thinly sliced into half-moons (about ¾ cup)
¼ cup capers, rinsed and drained (optional)
3 tablespoons sherry vinegar
5 tablespoons extra-virgin olive oil
3 pounds assorted bell peppers, quartered, seeds and ribs removed
Freshly ground black pepper
½ cup loosely packed fresh basil leaves
½ cup loosely packed fresh mint leaves
6 to 7 ounces fresh ricotta salata cheese

1. Prepare a large ice-water bath; set aside. Fill a stockpot with water; bring to a boil, and add a generous amount of salt. Add the green beans and wax beans to the boiling water, and cook just until they are crisp-tender and their color brightens, 3 to 4 minutes. Transfer the beans to the ice bath to stop the cooking and to preserve the color. Drain, and pat dry with paper towels. Slice the larger beans in half lengthwise. Set aside in a large bowl.

2. Make the vinaigrette: In a small bowl, combine the shallots, capers (if using), vinegar, and a pinch of salt; let stand 15 minutes. Whisking constantly, slowly add the olive oil.

3. Meanwhile, slice the peppers as thinly as possible using a sharp knife or mandoline. Add to the bowl with the beans. Drizzle with the vinaigrette, and toss to combine; season with salt and black pepper. Just before serving, tear the basil and mint leaves into small pieces, and crumble the ricotta salata. Stir the herbs and cheese into the salad.

orzo salad with roasted carrots and dill

SERVES 8 TO 10

3 pounds carrots (about 4 bunches)
4 garlic cloves, unpeeled
¼ cup extra-virgin olive oil
Coarse salt
1 pound orzo
Grated zest and juice of 2 lemons
4 scallions, white and light-green parts, roughly chopped
½ cup loosely packed fresh dill, roughly chopped
Freshly ground pepper

1. Preheat the oven to 450° F with a rack in the lower shelf. Cut the carrots diagonally into 2-inch pieces. On a rimmed baking sheet, toss the carrots and garlic with 2 tablespoons oil and a pinch of salt. Roast until the carrots are tender and browned, about 15 minutes. Transfer the sheet to a wire rack to cool. Squeeze the garlic cloves from their skins; mince to form a coarse paste. Set aside.

2. Bring a large saucepan of water to a boil; add salt. Stir in the orzo; cook until al dente, according to package instructions, about 7 minutes. Drain; while still hot, transfer the orzo to a large bowl, and toss with the remaining 2 tablespoons oil. Let cool slightly, and add the roasted carrots.

3. Meanwhile, in a small bowl, mix together the lemon zest, lemon juice, scallions, and roasted garlic. Add the dill, and pour the mixture over the orzo mixture. Stir to combine; season with salt and pepper. Serve, or store, covered with plastic wrap, in the refrigerator up to 1 day; bring to room temperature before serving.

spicy asian slaw

SERVES 6 TO 8

for the dressing

- 1 cup mayonnaise
- 2 tablespoons toasted sesame oil
- 2 tablespoons mirin or rice wine vinegar
- ¼ cup chili sauce
- 3 tablespoons fresh lime juice
- 1 tablespoon grated ginger
- 1 teaspoon coarse salt
- ¼ teaspoon freshly ground pepper
- 2 teaspoons sesame seeds

for the slaw

- ½ small head red cabbage (about 1 pound)
- ½ head napa cabbage (about 1 pound)
- 1 turnip, peeled (about 9 ounces)
- 1 small daikon, peeled (about 8 ounces)
- 1 large carrot, peeled
- 4 scallions, thinly sliced on the diagonal
- 1 red bell pepper, seeded and thinly sliced
- ¼ cup finely chopped fresh mint leaves
- ¼ cup finely chopped fresh cilantro

1. Make the dressing: In a medium bowl, whisk together the mayonnaise, sesame oil, vinegar, chili sauce, lime juice, ginger, salt, pepper, and sesame seeds; set the dressing aside.

2. Make the slaw: Core the red and napa cabbages, quarter, and slice very thinly. Transfer to a large bowl. Fill the bowl with cold water to cover the cabbage. Swish the cabbage around with your hands so any dirt settles to the bottom of the bowl. Lift the cabbage, and transfer to a colander to drain. Place in a large bowl; set aside.

3. Using the large holes of a box grater, grate the turnip, daikon, and carrot. Add to the bowl of cabbage along with the scallions, red bell pepper, mint, and cilantro. Add the reserved dressing, and toss to combine. Cover with plastic wrap, and let sit at least 2 hours in the refrigerator, but preferably overnight. Serve chilled. The slaw will keep in refrigerator for up to 4 days.

tomato and corn tabbouleh salad

SERVES 8

- 1 cup bulghur wheat
- 3 cups boiling water
- 6 ears corn
- ½ cup extra-virgin olive oil
- 2 teaspoons coarse salt, or to taste
- ¼ teaspoon freshly ground pepper, or to taste
- 2 garlic cloves, or to taste, minced
  Juice of 4 limes
- 4 large ripe tomatoes, diced
- ½ cup loosely packed fresh mint, finely chopped
- ½ cup loosely packed fresh flat-leaf parsley, finely chopped
- ¼ cup fresh chives, cut into small pieces

1. In a bowl, cover the bulghur with the boiling water. Let stand 45 minutes. Drain well; return to a bowl. Set aside.

2. Place the corn on a cutting board, and, using a sharp knife, carefully cut the kernels from the cob, taking care the corn does not roll as you work. Heat 2 tablespoons olive oil in a large sauté pan over medium heat. Add one-third of the corn, season with salt and pepper, and cook, stirring, until the corn is caramelized and golden, about 7 minutes. One minute before the corn is done, add one-third of the minced garlic, and mix with the corn. Transfer the corn to a baking pan to cool. When the corn is finished, deglaze the pan with a little lime juice; stir, using a wooden spoon, to loosen any browned bits on the bottom of the pan. Add to the corn. Repeat with the remaining corn 2 more times. Set aside for the corn to cool.

3. Combine the bulghur with the remaining 2 tablespoons oil, tomatoes, remaining lime juice, mint, parsley, and chives. Add the corn; mix well. Chill 30 minutes before serving. Adjust the seasoning with salt and pepper.

celery root rémoulade
(celeri rémoulade)

SERVES 6

Traditional rémoulade is made with mayonnaise. We have lightened this traditional side dish with a lemony yogurt dressing.

- 1 medium celery root, about 12 ounces
- 1 Granny Smith apple
  Juice of 1 lemon, about 2 tablespoons
- ½ cup nonfat plain yogurt
- 2 tablespoons heavy cream
- 4 teaspoons Dijon mustard
- 1 teaspoon coarse salt
- ¼ teaspoon freshly ground pepper

1. Peel the celery root; core the apple. Grate both on the large holes of a box grater. Place in a medium bowl, and toss with the lemon juice.

2. In another bowl, whisk together the yogurt, cream, Dijon, salt, and pepper. Add to the grated celery root and apple, and toss to combine. Refrigerate until ready to serve.

FIT TO EAT RECIPE PER SERVING: 61 CALORIES, 2 G FAT, 7 MG CHOLESTEROL, 9 G CARBOHYDRATE, 454 MG SODIUM, 2 G PROTEIN, 3 G FIBER

green papaya salad

SERVES 8

If you can't find Vietnamese coriander, you can use fresh cilantro.

for the dressing

- 1 fresh red Thai chile, finely chopped
- 2 tablespoons Asian fish sauce
- 2 tablespoons sugar
  Juice of 1 lime

for the salad

- 2 pounds green (unripe) papaya, peeled and seeded
- 12 sprigs fresh Vietnamese coriander, leaves and stems separated and stems coarsely chopped, plus 1 sprig for garnish

1. Make the dressing: Stir together chile, fish sauce, sugar, lime juice, and 3 tablespoons water in a medium bowl.

2. Make the salad: Thickly shred papaya with a mandoline or box grater. Transfer to a large bowl. Stir in coriander leaves and chopped stems. To serve, drizzle salad with dressing, and toss to combine. Garnish with a sprig of coriander.

radicchio-cabbage slaw
with honey

SERVES 4

- 3 tablespoons honey
- 3 tablespoons sherry vinegar
- 1 teaspoon coarse salt
- ⅓ cup extra-virgin olive oil
  Freshly ground pepper
- 1 medium head napa cabbage (about 1 pound), halved lengthwise, then cut crosswise into ¼-inch-thick strips
- 2 small heads radicchio (about 8 ounces), halved lengthwise, then cut crosswise into ¼-inch-thick strips

1. Whisk together honey, vinegar, and salt in a small bowl. Add oil in a slow, steady stream, whisking until well blended. Season with pepper.

2. Toss together cabbage and radicchio in a large bowl. Add dressing; toss to combine. Cover, and refrigerate at least 5 minutes. Just before serving, toss again. The slaw can be refrigerated in an airtight container up to 1 day.

asian steak salad
with spicy vinaigrette

SERVES 4

In this nutritious salad, papaya, red bell pepper, and cabbage provide vitamins A and C, while carrots contribute large amounts of beta carotene. Cilantro and mint supply flavonoids, and peanuts add vitamin E and selenium, all potent antioxidants.

for the marinade

Juice and grated zest of 1 lime

1   tablespoon grated fresh ginger

1   garlic clove, minced

1   scallion, white and light-green parts only, sliced into ¼-inch rounds

for the salad

12   ounces flank steak

Freshly ground black pepper

1   red bell pepper, stem and seeds removed, julienned

2   carrots, peeled and julienned

1   head napa cabbage, tough outer leaves removed, julienned

1   papaya, peeled, seeds removed, cut into 2-inch pieces

¼   cup fresh cilantro leaves, packed

¼   cup fresh mint leaves, packed

1   cup bean sprouts (optional)

Spicy Vinaigrette (recipe follows)

2   tablespoons chopped toasted peanuts, for garnish

1. Prepare the marinade: Place the lime juice, zest, ginger, garlic, and scallion in a small bowl, and whisk to combine. Place the steak in a shallow dish; cover with the marinade, turning to completely coat. Transfer to the refrigerator, and marinate 1 hour.

2. Remove the steak from the refrigerator 30 minutes before cooking; let sit at room temperature. Heat a grill or grill pan over medium-high heat. Remove the steak from the marinade, and season with black pepper. Sear the steak until browned on the outside and cooked to desired doneness inside, 5 to 6 minutes on each side for medium-rare. Transfer to a cutting board; let cool slightly, and thinly slice on the bias.

3. In a large bowl, combine the red bell pepper, carrots, cabbage, papaya, cilantro, mint, and bean sprouts, if using. Drizzle with the vinaigrette, and toss well to combine. Arrange the vegetables and steak on 4 serving plates. Garnish each serving with 1½ teaspoons chopped peanuts.

FIT TO EAT RECIPE PER SERVING: 323 CALORIES, 19 G FAT, 44 MG CHOLESTEROL, 20 G CARBOHYDRATE, 245 MG SODIUM, 21 G PROTEIN, 5 G FIBER

spicy vinaigrette

MAKES ½ CUP

Sesame oil is a good source of vitamin E.

Juice and grated zest of 2 limes

2   tablespoons sesame oil

2   tablespoons water

2   tablespoons rice-wine vinegar

1½   tablespoons grated fresh ginger

1   garlic clove, minced

1   teaspoon crumbled dried chile pepper or red pepper flakes

¼   teaspoon coarse salt

Combine all the ingredients in a small bowl, and whisk to combine.

FIT TO EAT RECIPE PER SERVING: 68 CALORIES, 7 G FAT, 0 MG CHOLESTEROL, 2 G CARBOHYDRATE, 121 MG SODIUM, 0 G PROTEIN, 0 G FIBER

chicken salad with mango and mint on flatbread

SERVES 6

¼ cup fresh lime juice (2 to 3 limes)

¼ cup fresh lemon juice (about 2 lemons)

3 tablespoons canola oil

2 tablespoons soy sauce

1 tablespoon honey

12 mint leaves, roughly chopped

1 piece (1 inch) peeled fresh ginger, finely grated

2 whole boneless, skinless chicken breasts
Coarse salt

6 ounces sugar snap peas, trimmed

4 cups arugula, trimmed (about 4½ ounces)

4 ounces pea shoots
Freshly ground pepper

1 small mango, peeled, pitted, and cut into matchsticks

1 small jícama, peeled and cut into matchsticks

6 soft lavash (or other soft flatbread)

1. Make the dressing: Blend the lime juice, lemon juice, oil, soy sauce, honey, mint, and ginger in a blender until smooth. Set aside.

2. Put the chicken in a medium stockpot, and cover with water by 1 inch. Bring to a boil. Reduce heat. Simmer the chicken until cooked through, 10 to 12 minutes.

3. Transfer the chicken to a bowl. Let cool slightly. Shred the chicken with your fingers; transfer to a bowl. Reserve 2 tablespoons dressing; add the remaining dressing to the chicken. Toss well.

4. Prepare an ice-water bath. Bring a medium saucepan of water to a boil; add salt. Cook the sugar snap peas until crisp-tender, about 30 seconds. Transfer to the ice-water bath to stop the cooking. Drain.

5. Put the sugar snap peas, arugula, and pea shoots into a medium bowl. Add remaining 2 tablespoons dressing; toss. Season with salt and pepper.

6. Add the mango and jícama to the chicken; toss well. Season with salt and pepper.

7. Arrange the arugula mixture over each lavash, dividing evenly. Top with the chicken salad. Roll up the lavash to enclose the filling. Cut in half diagonally, and serve.

shrimp salad with peas and chervil vinaigrette

SERVES 4 TO 6

You can use tarragon in place of chervil.

3 tablespoons fresh chervil leaves, coarsely chopped, plus more for garnish

1 garlic clove, finely grated
Finely grated zest of 1 lemon, plus 3 tablespoons fresh lemon juice (1 lemon total)

3 tablespoons extra-virgin olive oil

¼ teaspoon coarse salt
Freshly ground pepper

18 medium shrimp, peeled and deveined, tails left intact

1 cup frozen petit peas, thawed

8 ounces snow peas, trimmed and cut lengthwise diagonally into thin strips

1. Preheat the broiler. Make the vinaigrette: Whisk together the chervil, garlic, lemon zest, lemon juice, oil, and salt in a small bowl; season with pepper.

2. Toss the shrimp with 1 tablespoon vinaigrette. Place the shrimp on a rimmed baking sheet lined with foil; broil until cooked through, 3 to 4 minutes. Let cool completely. Refrigerate in an airtight container until ready to use, up to 2 hours.

3. Combine the peas, snow peas, shrimp, and remaining vinaigrette; toss. Refrigerate in an airtight container (or store in a chilled cooler) until ready to serve, up to 3 hours. Toss before serving.

minestrone salad

SERVES 4

- 1 teaspoon coarse salt, plus more for seasoning
- 8 ounces gemelli or other pasta, such as penne or rotini
- 4 tablespoons extra-virgin olive oil
- 1 small onion, cut into ¼-inch dice
- 2 garlic cloves, minced
- 1 carrot, peeled and cut into ½-inch dice
- 1 zucchini (about 6 ounces), cut into ½-inch dice
- 4 ounces green beans, cut into 1-inch pieces
- 1¼ cups corn kernels, cut from 1 ear, or frozen
    Freshly ground pepper
- 2 tablespoons balsamic vinegar
- 1 15-ounce can cannellini beans, rinsed and drained
- 1 pound assorted tomatoes, roughly chopped

1. Bring a medium saucepan of water to a boil. Add 1 teaspoon salt to the boiling water. Add the gemelli, and cook until al dente, 8 to 10 minutes. Drain, and rinse under cold water; set aside.

2. Heat 2 tablespoons olive oil in a large skillet over medium heat. Add the onion and garlic, and cook until they begin to soften, about 2 minutes. Add the carrot, and cook until it softens, about 4 minutes. Add the zucchini, green beans, and corn. Cook until the vegetables are tender, stirring occasionally, 10 to 15 minutes more. Season with salt and pepper. Transfer to a medium bowl to cool. Stir in the remaining 2 tablespoons olive oil, vinegar, beans, tomatoes, and reserved pasta. Season to taste with more salt and pepper, if desired. Serve chilled or at room temperature.

thai beef salad

SERVES 6

- 6 tablespoons fresh lime juice (about 3 limes)
- 2½ tablespoons Thai fish sauce (nam pla)
- 1 fresh Thai or serrano chile, seeded and finely chopped (about 1 tablespoon)
- 1 teaspoon sugar
- 2 teaspoons finely chopped fresh cilantro
- 2 teaspoons finely chopped fresh mint
- 4 scallions, white and pale-green parts only, thinly sliced on the diagonal
- 3 shallots, thinly sliced into rings
- 3 Kirby cucumbers, peeled, halved lengthwise, and cut into ¼-inch-thick half-moons
- 12 ounces baby arugula (about 5 cups)
- 2 tablespoons olive oil
- 1 boneless sirloin steak (1½ pounds)
- ½ teaspoon coarse salt
    Freshly ground pepper
- ½ cup unsalted peanuts, coarsely chopped (about 2½ ounces)

1. Preheat the oven to 400° F. Make the dressing: Whisk together the lime juice, fish sauce, chile, and sugar in a small bowl until the sugar is dissolved. Stir in the cilantro and mint. Set aside. Toss together the scallions, shallots, cucumbers, and arugula in a large bowl; set aside.

2. Heat the oil in a large ovenproof skillet over high heat until hot but not smoking. Sprinkle the steak all over with salt; season with pepper. Brown the steak, turning once, about 2 minutes per side. Transfer the skillet to the oven; cook the steak to desired doneness, about 6 minutes for medium-rare.

3. Transfer the steak to a cutting board, and let stand at least 5 minutes. Cut the steak across the grain into ¼-inch-thick slices.

4. Add the steak to the salad. Drizzle with dressing, and toss. Sprinkle with peanuts.

FIT TO EAT RECIPE PER SERVING: 382 CALORIES, 26 G FAT, 63 MG CHOLESTEROL, 12 G CARBOHYDRATE, 712 MG SODIUM, 26 G PROTEIN, 3 G FIBER

niçoise salad

SERVES 6

1 pound red fingerling or other small
  potatoes
  Coarse salt
  Garlic Vinaigrette (recipe follows)
  Freshly ground pepper

4 large eggs

½ pound green beans, halved crosswise

1 head Boston lettuce

1 red or green bell pepper, cut into ¼-inch-
  thick rings

½ pound cherry tomatoes, halved

½ English cucumber, peeled and sliced

½ fennel bulb, trimmed, halved lengthwise,
  and very thinly sliced

2 cans (6 ounces each) tuna, preferably
  Italian oil-packed, flaked

¾ cup Niçoise or oil-cured black olives

1 scallion, chopped

2 tablespoons coarsely chopped fresh flat-
  leaf parsley

1 tablespoon drained capers (optional)

1. Bring the potatoes to a boil in a large saucepan of water. Add salt; reduce heat, and simmer until tender, 10 to 15 minutes. Drain; let cool slightly.

2. Cut the potatoes into bite-size pieces; peel any loose skins. Dress with enough vinaigrette to coat lightly (reserve remainder). Season with salt and pepper. Set aside.

3. Prepare an ice-water bath; set aside. Cover the eggs with water in a small saucepan; bring to a full boil. After 1 minute, cover and turn off heat. Let stand 6 minutes. Rinse; transfer to the ice-water bath.

4. Prepare another ice-water bath; set aside. Bring a medium saucepan of water to a boil; add salt. Blanch the green beans until crisp-tender, 1 to 2 minutes. Drain; rinse with cold water. Let stand in the ice-water bath until cool. Drain; pat dry.

5. Peel the eggs, and halve lengthwise. Arrange the lettuce and then the potatoes, green beans, bell pepper, tomatoes, cucumber, fennel, tuna, eggs, and olives on a platter.

6. Sprinkle with scallion and parsley, and with capers if desired. Drizzle with vinaigrette, and serve with the remainder.

garlic vinaigrette

MAKES ABOUT 1 CUP

1 garlic clove, lightly crushed with the flat
  side of a knife

1 tablespoon Dijon mustard

2 tablespoons red-wine vinegar

2 tablespoons fresh lemon juice
  Coarse salt and freshly ground pepper

¾ cup olive oil

Put the garlic, mustard, vinegar, and lemon juice in a small bowl; season with salt and pepper; whisk until blended. Whisking constantly, pour in the oil in a slow, steady stream until emulsified. Let stand at least 30 minutes; discard the garlic.

red romaine salad with walnuts and eggs

SERVES 4 TO 6

6 large eggs

1 head red-leaf romaine, torn into pieces

1 cup walnut halves, toasted
  Basic Vinaigrette (page 628)
  Coarse salt and freshly ground pepper

1. Put the eggs in a medium saucepan of water; bring to a boil. After 2 minutes, cover; turn off heat. Let stand 6 minutes. Let cool in an ice-water bath.

2. Drizzle the lettuce and walnuts in a bowl with 5 tablespoons vinaigrette (or to taste); toss. Peel the eggs; halve. Serve on top of the salad. Season with salt and pepper.

spicy chicken salad in lettuce cups

SERVES 4 TO 6

Ground, toasted rice adds crunch and a slight nuttiness to this salad. Thai basil, available at gourmet and farmers' markets, has a licorice flavor, but you can use regular basil instead.

- 1 tablespoon jasmine rice or another long-grain rice
  Coarse salt
- 1 pound ground chicken
  Lime-Chile Dressing (recipe follows)
- ¼ cup chopped fresh Thai basil, plus more for garnish
- ¼ cup chopped fresh cilantro, plus more for garnish
  Freshly ground pepper
- 1 head Boston lettuce, leaves separated
- 1 carrot, peeled and cut into matchsticks
- ½ daikon radish, peeled and cut into matchsticks
- 3 tablespoons salted, roasted peanuts, chopped

1. Toast the rice in a dry nonstick skillet over medium-high heat until deep golden, 1 to 2 minutes. Coarsely grind with a mortar and pestle or in a food processor.

2. Bring a medium pot of water to a boil; add 1 tablespoon salt. Boil the chicken, separating it into pieces with a spoon, until cooked through, 3 to 4 minutes.

3. Transfer the chicken to a medium bowl with a slotted spoon; reserve ¼ cup cooking liquid. Add the dressing, rice, herbs, and cooking liquid; toss. Season with salt and pepper.

4. For each serving, put about ¼ cup chicken in a lettuce leaf. Garnish with carrot, daikon, basil, cilantro, and nuts.

lime-chile dressing

MAKES ABOUT ½ CUP

- 5 tablespoons fresh lime juice
- 3 tablespoons Asian fish sauce
- 2 tablespoons rice-wine vinegar
- 1 tablespoon sugar
- 2 fresh red hot chiles, finely chopped
- 2 garlic cloves, minced
- 2 shallots, thinly sliced
- 2 tablespoons finely chopped fresh cilantro

Stir together all ingredients except the cilantro, and let stand at least 15 minutes (and up to a day in the refrigerator). When ready to serve, stir in the cilantro.

rice salad with rock shrimp and asparagus

SERVES 4

Rock shrimp are small and a bit sweet. You can also use small regular shrimp.

- Coarse salt
- 1 bunch asparagus (about 1 pound), trimmed
- 1 cup jasmine rice
- 1½ teaspoons toasted sesame chile oil
- 2 teaspoons olive oil
- 1 pound rock shrimp, peeled
- 2 tablespoons plus 1 teaspoon fresh lemon juice
  Freshly ground pepper
- ½ cup sliced almonds, toasted
- 1 tablespoon freshly grated lemon zest

1. Prepare an ice-water bath; set aside. Bring a medium pot of water to a boil; add a large pinch of salt. Blanch the asparagus until bright green and tender, about 3 minutes. Immediately transfer with tongs to the ice-water bath to stop the cooking. Drain well; pat dry. Cut the spears on the diagonal into thin pieces; set aside.

2. Bring the rice and 1½ cups water to a boil in a medium saucepan. Cover, and reduce heat to medium-low. Simmer until the liquid is absorbed and the rice is tender, about 10 minutes; set aside.

3. Heat the sesame and olive oils in a large skillet over medium-high heat until hot but not smoking. Add the shrimp; stir to coat. Stir in the lemon juice, and season with salt and pepper; cook until the shrimp are pink and cooked through, about 3 minutes. Stir the shrimp, rice, asparagus, and almonds in a large bowl. Garnish with lemon zest.

smoked mackerel, cucumber, and potato salad with mustard dressing

SERVES 4

Although fresh mackerel can be hard to find, smoked mackerel is often sold in the refrigerated section of supermarkets; it is also available from mail-order sources. We used the peppered variety, but any type will do.

- ¾ pound small waxy potatoes, such as fingerling or new potatoes
- 1 small shallot, very thinly sliced
- 4 teaspoons white-wine vinegar
- 2 teaspoons Dijon mustard
- 4 teaspoons olive oil
- 2 tablespoons roughly chopped fresh dill
- ½ cucumber, peeled, halved lengthwise, and sliced into ½-inch half-moons

  Freshly ground pepper
- 12 ounces smoked mackerel, broken into bite-size pieces

  Handful of tender salad greens, such as arugula, watercress, or tatsoi

1. Place the potatoes in a small saucepan, and cover with cold water. Bring to a boil; reduce heat, and simmer until tender when pierced with a fork, about 12 minutes. Drain in a colander; let cool slightly. Slip off the skins; discard. Cut the potatoes into halves or quarters, if desired.

2. Meanwhile, make the dressing: In a medium bowl, combine the shallot, vinegar, and mustard. Whisk in the oil until emulsified. Sprinkle the dill into the bowl.

3. Add the cucumber and cooked potatoes to the dressing in the bowl; season with pepper. Toss to coat evenly. Divide the salad among 4 plates; arrange the mackerel on each. Serve, garnished with greens.

FIT TO EAT RECIPE PER SERVING: 234 CALORIES, 15 G FAT, 15 MG CHOLESTEROL, 7 G CARBOHYDRATE, 800 MG SODIUM, 20 G PROTEIN, 3 G FIBER

frisée with lardons and poached eggs

SERVES 4 AS AN APPETIZER

- 2 tablespoons distilled white vinegar
- 4 large eggs
- 1 large head frisée (about 5 ounces), washed and spun dry
- 6 ounces (about 4 slices) thick-cut bacon, cut into ¼-inch-thick strips
- 3 tablespoons finely chopped shallot
- ¼ cup red-wine vinegar

  Coarse salt and freshly ground pepper

1. Bring a large, deep skillet of water to a boil. Reduce to a simmer; add the white vinegar. Fill a saucepan with warm water; set aside. Break an egg into a small bowl; holding the bowl just over the vinegar water, gently slide the egg into the water. Repeat with the remaining eggs. Poach about 2 minutes (longer for firm yolks). Use a slotted spoon to transfer the eggs to the pan of warm water.

2. Place the frisée in a large bowl; set aside. Cook the bacon, stirring occasionally, in a medium sauté pan over medium-high heat until golden brown, about 3 minutes. Add the shallot; cook 1 minute. Add the red-wine vinegar; bring to a boil, swirling to combine. Pour over the frisée. Season with salt and pepper; toss to coat evenly.

3. Divide among 4 plates. Drain the eggs, and top each salad with one. Sprinkle the eggs with salt and pepper. Serve immediately.

roasted chicken salad

SERVES 6

Use a store-bought roasted chicken to save time. To take this salad on a picnic, pack it in an air-tight container and keep it fresh in a cooler.

- 1 cup pecan halves (about 3 ounces), broken in half lengthwise
- 1 whole roasted chicken (about 3 pounds), skin removed
- 8 scallions, white and light-green parts only, trimmed and thinly sliced
- 2 stalks celery, strings removed and thinly sliced
- 8 ounces lady apples (about 4), or Fuji apples (about 2 medium), cored and sliced into bite-size pieces
- 5 tablespoons golden or dark raisins
- 1 tablespoon coarsely chopped fresh oregano leaves
  Coarse salt and freshly ground pepper
  Sour Cream Dressing (recipe follows)

1. Preheat the oven to 350°F. Spread the pecans in a single layer on a rimmed baking sheet. Toast in the oven until fragrant, stirring occasionally, about 10 minutes. Remove pecans from the pan, and let cool completely.

2. Pull the chicken from the bone; discard the bones, and cut the meat into ¾-inch pieces. Transfer to a medium bowl; add the scallions, celery, apples, raisins, and oregano. Season with salt and pepper. Add the dressing; toss to combine. Chill, covered, until ready to serve.

sour cream dressing

MAKES ABOUT 1 CUP

- ½ cup mayonnaise
- 2 tablespoons sour cream
- ¼ cup cider vinegar
  Coarse salt and freshly ground pepper

In a small bowl, whisk together the mayonnaise, sour cream, and vinegar; season with salt and pepper. Refrigerate, covered, until ready to use, up to 4 days.

salmon and golden beet salad with crisp bacon

SERVES 4

- 8 small golden beets (about 10 ounces)
- 3 tablespoons extra-virgin olive oil
- ¼ teaspoon coarse salt
- 4 slices turkey bacon (about 2¼ ounces), sliced crosswise into thin strips
- ½ lemon, sliced into 4 rounds
- 4 salmon fillets (6 ounces each)
- 1 shallot, finely chopped
- 1½ tablespoons white-wine vinegar
- 1 pound baby spinach
  Freshly ground pepper

1. Preheat the oven to 350°F. On a piece of aluminum foil, toss the beets with 1 tablespoon oil and the salt; wrap the beets in foil to make a packet. Cook until the beets are easily pierced with a fork, about 35 minutes. Let cool; peel the beets, and slice them into ¼-inch-thick rounds.

2. Cook the bacon on another baking sheet until crisp, about 10 minutes. Transfer to a paper-towel–lined plate; let drain.

3. Place the lemon slices and 6 cups water in a large saucepan; bring to a boil. Reduce heat; add the salmon, and cook at a bare simmer until flaky, about 12 minutes. Transfer the fish to a plate; let cool.

4. Make the dressing: In a small bowl, whisk together the shallot, vinegar, and remaining 2 tablespoons oil until emulsified.

5. Place the spinach and beets in a bowl. Add the dressing and some bacon; season with pepper. Toss to combine. Divide among plates; top each with a salmon fillet. Garnish with the remaining bacon.

FIT TO EAT RECIPE PER SERVING: 465 CALORIES, 26 G FAT, 122 MG CHOLESTEROL, 12 G CARBOHYDRATE, 537 MG SODIUM, 46 G PROTEIN, 5 G FIBER

chicken and shredded cabbage salad with noodles and peanut sauce

SERVES 12

The broth left over from poaching chicken breasts makes a delicious soup base. Refrigerate it in an airtight container up to 3 days or freeze up to 2 weeks; bring to a boil before using.

- 3 quarts water
- 2 stalks celery, cut in half lengthwise
- 1 2-inch piece fresh ginger, thinly sliced
- 2 garlic cloves
- 8 sprigs cilantro, including stems, roughly chopped (about ¾ cup), plus ½ cup loosely packed leaves for garnish
- 2 tablespoons toasted sesame oil
-    Coarse salt
- 3 boneless, skinless chicken breasts (about 3 pounds)
- 1 pound somen or vermicelli noodles
- ½ head green cabbage
- 1 bunch carrots, peeled (about 6 carrots)
- 2 serrano or jalapeño peppers, seeds and ribs removed
- ½ cup loosely packed fresh mint leaves, chopped
- 1 cup Peanut Sauce (recipe follows)
- ½ cup roasted unsalted peanuts

1. In a large saucepan, combine the water with the celery, ginger, garlic, chopped cilantro, 1 tablespoon sesame oil, and a pinch of salt; bring to a boil over high heat. Add the chicken breasts, and reduce heat to medium. Simmer until the chicken is cooked through, about 12 minutes. Remove from heat, and let stand until the chicken is cool enough to handle, about 10 minutes. Transfer the chicken to a cutting board, and cut it into ¼-inch strips, or shred as finely as possible with your fingers. Place in a medium bowl, and set aside.

2. Bring a large pot of water to a boil; add salt. Cook the noodles until they are al dente, according to package instructions, about 3 minutes. Transfer to a colander, let drain, and rinse under cold water until they are cool. Place in a medium bowl, and toss with the remaining tablespoon sesame oil; set aside.

3. Cut the cabbage in half, and remove the core. Slice the cabbage and carrots as thinly as possible with a mandoline or sharp knife. Place in a large bowl. Cut the serrano chiles into very thin strips, and add to the bowl along with the shredded chicken and mint. Just before serving, pour the peanut sauce over the mixture, and toss to coat. Place the noodles on a large serving platter, and pile the chicken mixture on top. Sprinkle with peanuts and cilantro leaves.

peanut sauce

MAKES 2½ CUPS

This recipe makes more than you will need for the salad; serve extra sauce on the side so guests can help themselves. Unused sauce can be stored, covered, in the refrigerator up to 4 days.

- 1 5-inch piece fresh ginger, minced or grated (about 3 tablespoons)
- 2 shallots, minced (about ⅓ cup)
- ¼ cup Asian fish sauce
- ½ cup low-sodium soy sauce
- ¾ cup fresh lime juice
- 1 cup smooth peanut butter
- ¼ cup toasted sesame oil

In a large bowl, combine the ginger, shallots, fish sauce, soy sauce, and lime juice. Whisk in the peanut butter; whisk in the sesame oil.

cucumber, corn, and crab salad

SERVES 4 TO 6

We serve this salad on whole-grain toast as an open-face sandwich, but it is also delicious mounded on a bed of crisp salad greens.

1½ cucumbers, peeled, seeded, and cut into ¼-inch dice
    Coarse salt
1 pound jumbo lump crabmeat, picked over and rinsed
2 ears corn, kernels cut from cobs
½ small red onion, finely diced
1 avocado, peeled, pitted, and cut into ¼-inch dice
    Cucumber Vinaigrette (recipe follows)
    Freshly ground pepper

1. Sprinkle the cucumber lightly with salt, and place in a fine sieve set over a medium bowl. Cover with plastic wrap, and place in the refrigerator 30 minutes. Rinse and drain well; discard the liquid.

2. Combine the crabmeat, corn, onion, avocado, cucumber, and ½ cup cucumber vinaigrette in a large bowl, and stir to combine. Season with salt and pepper. Store in an airtight container in the refrigerator until ready to serve.

cucumber vinaigrette

MAKES ABOUT 1 CUP

½ cucumber, peeled and seeded
2 tablespoons sherry vinegar
2 tablespoons Dijon mustard
1 tablespoon chopped fresh tarragon
½ cup grapeseed oil
    Coarse salt and freshly ground pepper

Place the cucumber, vinegar, mustard, and tarragon in a food processor, and process until smooth. With the machine running, drizzle in the grapeseed oil; process until emulsified. Season with salt and pepper. Refrigerate, covered, up to 2 days.

arugula salad with french lentils, smoked chicken, and roasted peppers

SERVES 6

The lentils can be made up to a day in advance and the salad assembled at the last minute. Poached or grilled chicken breast would produce equally appetizing results.

½ pound French green lentils, picked over and rinsed
1 14½-ounce can low-sodium chicken broth, or homemade, skimmed of fat
1 cup water
4 sprigs thyme, plus ½ tablespoon fresh thyme leaves
2 red bell peppers
2½ tablespoons extra-virgin olive oil
1 tablespoon red-wine vinegar
1 tablespoon balsamic vinegar
½ teaspoon coarse salt, plus more for seasoning
6 ounces baby arugula (about 6 cups)
6 ounces smoked skinless, boneless chicken breast, cut into matchsticks
    Freshly ground pepper

1. In a medium saucepan, combine the lentils, broth, water, and thyme sprigs. Bring to a boil, reduce heat to medium-low, and simmer, uncovered, until the lentils are tender, about 20 minutes. Drain and set aside in a bowl to cool.

2. While the lentils are cooking, roast the red peppers over a gas flame or under the broiler, turning occasionally, until blackened. Place in a heatproof bowl, cover with plastic wrap, and let stand until cool. Peel and seed the peppers, and cut into ½-inch slices. Place the strips in a small saucepan with 1 ½ tablespoon oil; cover, and cook gently over low heat, stirring occasionally, until meltingly tender, about 10 minutes. Set aside, and let cool.

3. In a large bowl, whisk together the vinegars, salt, thyme leaves, and remaining 2 tablespoons oil until blended. Add half of the dressing to the lentils, and toss to coat. Add the arugula, chicken, and cooled pepper strips to the remaining dressing, and toss.

Season both salads with salt and pepper. Arrange the lentils into mounds on each of 6 salad plates, form a well in the center of each, and fill with the arugula mixture.

FIT TO EAT RECIPE PER SERVING: 250 CALORIES, 9 G FAT, 15 MG CHOLESTEROL, 26 G CARBOHYDRATE, 560 MG SODIUM, 17 G PROTEIN, 3 G FIBER

taco salad

SERVES 6

To reduce the fat, we eliminated the cheese and toasted the corn tortillas in the oven rather than frying them in oil.

- 2 *ears corn, husks and silk removed*
- 3 *corn tortillas, cut into 16 wedges each*
- ¾ *cup nonfat plain yogurt*
- 2 *limes*
- ⅓ *cup fresh cilantro leaves*
- 1½ *tablespoons finely chopped and seeded jalapeño pepper*
- ½ *teaspoon coarse salt*
- 1 *pound ground turkey*
- 1 *teaspoon chili powder*
- 1 *teaspoon ground cumin*
- ½ *pound iceberg lettuce, torn into 2-inch pieces (about 3 cups)*
- 1 *cup canned black beans, drained and rinsed*
- 2 *plum tomatoes, cut into ½-inch-thick wedges (about 1 cup)*
- ½ *red onion, peeled and cut into ¼-inch-thick wedges (about 1 cup)*
- 1 *small mango, peeled, seeded, and cut into ¼-inch-thick wedges (1½ cups)*

1. Bring a large saucepan of water to a boil over high heat. Add the corn, and reduce heat to medium; simmer until the kernels are tender, 5 to 10 minutes. Transfer the corn to a plate; let cool. Slice the kernels off the cobs; place in a small bowl, and set aside (you should have about 1¼ cups).

2. Preheat the oven to 350° F. Spread the tortilla wedges in a single layer on a rimmed baking sheet; bake until crisp, turning once, about 10 minutes. Remove from the oven; let cool, and set aside.

3. Make the dressing: In a medium bowl, whisk together the yogurt, juice from 1 lime, cilantro, jalapeño, and salt. Set aside.

4. In a medium nonstick skillet, brown the turkey over medium heat, stirring frequently, until no longer pink, about 7 minutes. Stir in the chili powder, cumin, and juice from remaining lime.

5. Transfer the mixture to a large serving bowl. Add the lettuce, beans, tomatoes, onion, mango, and reserved corn and tortillas. Toss to combine well. Drizzle with yogurt dressing; serve immediately.

FIT TO EAT RECIPE PER SERVING: 233 CALORIES, 2 G FAT, 37 MG CHOLESTEROL, 32 G CARBOHYDRATE, 207 MG SODIUM, 25 G PROTEIN, 6 G FIBER

southwestern cobb salad

SERVES 6 TO 8 AS A MAIN DISH

- ¼ *cup freshly squeezed lime juice, plus juice of 2 limes*
- ¼ *cup plus 2 tablespoons extra-virgin olive oil*
- ¼ *cup soy sauce*
- 1 *teaspoon ground cumin*
- 1 *teaspoon crushed red pepper flakes*
- 4 *boneless, skinless chicken breast halves*
- 4 *large eggs*
- ½ *pound thick-sliced bacon*
- 1 *yellow bell pepper*
- 1 *poblano chile*
- 1 *tomato, seeded and cut in ½-inch pieces*
- ½ *cup roughly chopped pitted black olives (2½ ounces)*
- 1 *sweet onion, cut into ¼-inch pieces*
  Coarse salt and freshly ground black pepper
- 2 *ripe but firm Hass avocados, peeled and cut into ½-inch pieces*
- ½ *cup chopped fresh cilantro*
- ⅛ *teaspoon cayenne pepper (optional)*
- 1 *15-ounce can black beans, rinsed and drained*
- 1 *small head romaine lettuce, torn in 1-inch pieces*
  Green Goddess Dressing (recipe follows)

1. Combine the ¼ cup lime juice, ¼ cup oil, soy sauce, ½ teaspoon cumin, and red pepper flakes in a small bowl. Place the chicken breasts in a large resealable plastic bag. Pour the marinade into the bag, and refrigerate at least 1 hour or overnight.

2. Heat a grill or grill pan over medium-high heat. Lift the chicken from the bag, allowing the excess marinade to drain off. Cook until grill marks appear and the chicken is cooked through, about 5 minutes per side. Cool the chicken completely, and cut into ½-inch pieces; set aside.

3. Place the eggs in a saucepan with cold water to cover. Bring to a boil. Cover; remove from heat. Let sit 11 minutes. Drain; rinse under cold running water until cooled. Peel and roughly chop the eggs.

4. Heat a skillet over medium heat. Cook the bacon until crisp, and drain on paper towels. Crumble when cool; set aside.

5. Place the yellow and poblano peppers directly on the trivet of a gas burner over high heat or on the grill or grill pan used for the chicken. Turn the peppers with tongs as they char. (Alternatively, place the peppers on a baking pan; broil in the oven, turning as each side becomes charred.) Transfer to a large bowl; cover immediately with plastic wrap. Let the peppers sweat until cool enough to handle. Peel off the blackened skin and discard. Remove the seeds; chop the yellow pepper into ½-inch pieces and the poblano into ¼-inch pieces; set aside separately.

6. In a bowl, combine the yellow pepper, tomato, olives, and half the chopped onion. Sprinkle with salt and pepper; set aside. In another bowl, combine the poblano with the avocados, ¼ cup cilantro, juice of 2 limes, cayenne pepper (if using), and remaining ½ teaspoon cumin; season with salt and pepper; set aside.

7. Combine the black beans with the remaining ¼ cup cilantro and chopped onion. Drizzle with the remaining 2 tablespoons olive oil, and season with salt and pepper; set aside.

8. Arrange the romaine on a platter. Arrange the chicken, eggs, bacon, tomato, avocado, and bean mixture in sections across the romaine. Drizzle with dressing; serve.

green goddess dressing
MAKES 1½ CUPS

Let dressing sit overnight to meld flavors.

- ½ cup mayonnaise
- ½ cup sour cream
- 2 tablespoons buttermilk
- 1 tablespoon white-wine vinegar
- 1 teaspoon Worcestershire sauce
- 1 bunch chives, coarsely chopped (½ cup)
- 2 green onions, coarsely chopped
- 2 tablespoons chopped fresh cilantro
- 2 tablespoons chopped fresh flat-leaf parsley
- 1 teaspoon sugar
- 1 teaspoon coarse salt
- ½ teaspoon freshly ground black pepper
  Pinch of cayenne pepper (optional)

Combine all the ingredients in a blender or food processor; process until smooth. Refrigerate in an airtight container up to 3 days.

fennel crab salad on beefsteak tomatoes
SERVES 6 TO 8

- 1½ pounds beefsteak tomatoes (about 2), preferably orange or yellow
- 10 ounces baby fennel bulbs (about 3 or 4)
- 1 tablespoon freshly squeezed lemon juice
- ½ pound jumbo lump crabmeat
- 5 ounces purslane or watercress
- 2 tablespoons olive oil
  Coarse salt and freshly ground pepper

Cut the tomatoes into ½-inch slices; set aside. Remove the outer peel from the fennel if necessary. Using a mandoline, thinly shave the fennel, and toss with the lemon juice; set aside. Remove any shells from the crabmeat, and set aside. Arrange the purslane on a serving dish, and top with the tomatoes, shaved fennel, and crabmeat. Lightly drizzle each tomato with olive oil, and sprinkle with salt and pepper; serve immediately.

lobster salad with grapefruit, avocado, and hearts of palm

SERVES 8 AS AN APPETIZER

4 1¼-pound lobsters

2 ruby red or pink grapefruits

1 tablespoon finely minced shallots

1¼ teaspoons Dijon mustard

2 tablespoons white-wine vinegar

1 tablespoon freshly chopped lemon basil or regular basil, plus leaves for garnish

Coarse salt and freshly ground pepper

¼ cup extra-virgin olive oil

2 avocados, peeled and pitted

4 hearts of palm, cut into ½-inch-thick rounds

1 large head Boston lettuce (8 ounces)

1. Fill a large bowl with ice and water; set aside. Bring a stockpot of water to a boil. Boil the lobsters for 10 minutes; transfer to the ice bath until cool. Break off the claws and tails; use the bodies to make a stock, or discard. Split the tail lengthwise with a sharp knife; remove the meat. Slice the tail into bite-size pieces. Remove the claws from the shells, keeping them whole if possible. Chill the lobster meat.

2. Cut the ends off the grapefruit; remove the peel, pith, and outer membranes. Lift the sections away from the membranes, and reserve. Squeeze ½ cup juice from the membranes into a bowl for dressing.

3. Place the shallots, mustard, vinegar, grapefruit juice, and lemon basil in a bowl; season with salt and pepper. Whisk to combine. Gradually whisk in the olive oil; adjust seasoning.

4. Cut the avocados into ½-inch-thick wedges; coat with a little grapefruit juice to prevent discoloration. Add the lobster, grapefruit, and hearts of palm. Line 8 dishes with 1 lettuce leaf each. Tear the remaining lettuce into bite-size pieces; add to the lobster mixture. Drizzle with dressing; toss. Fill the lettuce leaves with salad; garnish with lemon basil.

chopped lemongrass chicken salad

SERVES 8

4 whole boneless, skinless chicken breasts (4 pounds)

Lemongrass Marinade (recipe follows)

2 teaspoons coarse salt, plus more for seasoning and cooking water

½ teaspoon freshly ground pepper, plus more for seasoning

1 pound sugar snap peas, strings removed

2 shallots, roughly chopped

1 1-inch-piece peeled fresh ginger, roughly chopped

½ cup freshly squeezed lime juice

¾ cup fresh mint leaves

¾ cup fresh cilantro leaves

6 tablespoons canola oil

1 head romaine lettuce, chopped into pieces

2 mangoes, peeled, pitted, and cut into ½-inch dice

3 red bell peppers, cored, seeded, and cut into 1-inch-long matchsticks

1 fennel bulb, trimmed, cored, and cut into ¼-inch dice

6 scallions, white and pale-green parts only, thinly sliced

1. Place the chicken between sheets of plastic wrap; pound to ½-inch thickness. Place in a plastic or glass dish; coat with marinade. Cover; chill 4 hours or overnight.

2. Heat the grill or broiler. Season the chicken with salt and pepper; grill until golden brown and cooked through, 4 to 5 minutes per side. Set aside to cool.

3. Fill a large bowl with ice and water; set aside. Bring a large saucepot of water to a boil; add salt. Add the snap peas; cook until bright green and still crisp, about 2 minutes. Transfer to the ice bath to cool. Drain; cut into ¾-inch pieces.

4. Place the shallots and ginger in a food processor; process until very finely chopped. Add the lime juice, ½ cup mint, ½ cup cilantro, the salt, and pepper; process until herbs are finely chopped. Slowly add oil through feed tube with motor running.

5. Layer the romaine, mangoes, chicken, red pepper, fennel, snap peas, and scallions in a large bowl. Top with the remaining mint and cilantro. Serve with dressing on the side, or add dressing to the bowl.

lemongrass marinade
MAKES 1⅔ CUPS

This marinade may be made in advance and kept in the refrigerator for 2 days.

- 4   stalks lemongrass, tough outer leaves removed, cut into pieces
- 1   1-inch piece peeled fresh ginger, roughly chopped
- 4   garlic cloves
- 2   shallots, peeled and roughly chopped
- 2   tablespoons brown sugar
- ½   cup mirin
- 2   tablespoons Asian fish sauce
- 6   tablespoons canola oil

Add the lemongrass, ginger, garlic, and shallots through the feed tube of a food processor with motor running. Process until very finely chopped. Add the sugar, mirin, and fish sauce; process until pureed, scraping the sides as needed. With the motor running, slowly add the oil; process until incorporated.

warm butter-poached lobster salad with tarragon-citrus dressing
SERVES 2

- Coarse salt
- 2   tablespoons distilled white vinegar
- 1   live lobster (about 1¼ pounds)
- 1   tangelo, tangerine, or orange (7 ounces), plus 1 cup juice, strained
- ½   cup (1 stick) cold unsalted butter, cut into small pieces
- 1   sprig fresh tarragon, plus 10 leaves
- ¼   teaspoon freshly ground white pepper
- 4   leaves Bibb lettuce

1. Bring a large pot of water to a boil; add 2 tablespoons salt and the vinegar. Plunge lobster head first into water; cook 3 minutes (meat will not be fully cooked). Transfer lobster to a cutting board.

2. Using a kitchen towel to protect your hands, twist off tail and claws; discard body. Twist fan off end of tail, and push meat out of shell. Alternatively, use kitchen shears to cut up length of tail, and pull shell away from meat. Cut tail meat in half lengthwise, and transfer to a plate lined with paper towels; set aside. Separate claws from knuckles; twist and pull off pincers, being careful to keep meat intact. With back of knife, crack knuckle end of claw to loosen shell. Gently remove whole piece of meat; set aside with tail. Using your finger or the handle of a spoon, push knuckle meat out of shell. Wipe any white residue off meat. Meat can be refrigerated in an airtight container up to 2 hours ahead; bring to room temperature before poaching.

3. Remove peel and pith from tangelo using a sharp knife. Working over a bowl, carve out flesh between membranes, allowing segments to drop into bowl. Squeeze juice from membranes into bowl. Transfer juice in bowl to a separate bowl; reserve juice for dressing.

4. Put ⅓ cup juice into a small saucepan; bring to a boil. Reduce heat to low, and whisk in butter, 1 piece at a time, until smooth. Add a pinch of salt and the tarragon sprig. Submerge lobster meat in the butter sauce. Poach until opaque and cooked through, 2½ to 3 minutes.

5. Whisk 3 tablespoons warm poaching liquid into 2 tablespoons reserved juice in bowl; whisk in pepper and ½ teaspoon salt. Add lobster to dressing; toss gently to coat. Just before serving, add tangelo segments and tarragon leaves; toss gently to combine. Season with salt.

6. Arrange 2 lettuce leaves on each serving plate. Place lobster and tangelo segments on top. Spoon dressing over top.

basque salad

SERVES 4 TO 6

for the salad

- 1 pound small Yukon Gold potatoes
- 1 cup dry sherry
- ½ teaspoon saffron threads
- 1 tablespoon extra-virgin olive oil
- 1 fillet wild striped bass (1 pound), skin on
  Coarse salt and freshly ground pepper
- 3 ounces dried chorizo sausage, cut into
  ¼-inch-thick slices
- 4 shallots, thinly sliced into rings
- 6 littleneck clams, scrubbed well
- 12 mussels (about 8 ounces), scrubbed well
  and debearded
- 2 tablespoons fresh lemon juice
- 2 pounds medium tomatoes, cut into
  ¼-inch-thick slices

for the dressing

- 1 tablespoon fresh lemon juice
- 2 tablespoons finely chopped fresh flat-leaf
  parsley
- 2 tablespoons finely chopped fresh basil
- 2 tablespoons extra-virgin olive oil

for serving

- Saffron Aïoli (recipe follows)
- 1 baguette, torn into large pieces and
  lightly toasted

1. Cover the potatoes with cold water in a medium saucepan. Bring to a boil. Reduce to a simmer. Cook until potatoes are tender when pierced with a sharp knife, about 15 minutes. Drain; let cool completely.

2. Preheat the oven to 475° F. Heat sherry in a small saucepan over medium-low heat until warm, 2 to 5 minutes. Add saffron, and stir until it has dissolved. Set aside.

3. Heat oil in a cast-iron skillet in oven 5 minutes. Season fish with salt and pepper; set aside. Remove skillet from oven, and add fish, skin side down. Drizzle with the sherry mixture. Add sausage and shal-

lots. Roast 10 minutes. Remove from oven; brush fish with pan juices. Add clams and mussels. Roast until fish is cooked through and clams and mussels have opened, about 10 minutes (discard any shellfish that remain closed). Transfer skillet to a wire rack. Drizzle with lemon juice. Let cool 15 minutes.

4. Arrange tomato slices on a platter. Cut cooled potatoes into ¼-inch-thick rounds; arrange over tomatoes. Top with seafood mixture; reserve 2 tablespoons pan juices.

5. Make the dressing: Whisk reserved pan juices, lemon juice, parsley, and basil in a medium bowl. Gradually add oil, whisking until emulsified.

6. Drizzle salad with dressing. Serve with saffron aïoli and toasted baguette.

saffron aïoli

MAKES ABOUT 1 CUP

- 2 large egg yolks
- 1 garlic clove
- ½ teaspoon saffron threads
  Coarse salt and freshly ground pepper
- ¾ cup plus 2 tablespoons extra-virgin
  olive oil
- 2½ teaspoons fresh lemon juice

Put egg yolks, garlic, and saffron into a food processor; season with salt and pepper. Process until smooth. With processor running, gradually add oil, drop by drop at first, then in a slow, steady stream, until a thick mayonnaise forms. Mix in lemon juice. Transfer to a small dish. Serve at room temperature; do not leave unrefrigerated longer than 1 hour. Aïoli can be refrigerated, covered, up to 2 days.

NOTE *The egg yolks in this recipe are not fully cooked. It should not be prepared for pregnant women, babies, young children, the elderly, or anyone whose health is compromised.*

french country salad

SERVES 4

for the dressing

- 1 tablespoon champagne vinegar
- 1 tablespoon grainy Dijon mustard
  Coarse salt and freshly ground pepper
- 3 to 4 tablespoons extra-virgin olive oil
- ½ cup walnut halves, toasted and finely chopped

for the salad

- 8 cipollini onions (about 4 ounces), peeled and halved if desired
- ½ cup balsamic vinegar
  Coarse salt and freshly ground pepper
- 2 tablespoons unsalted butter
- 1 medium apple (preferably Golden Delicious), cored and cut into ½-inch-thick slices
- 8 slices French cooked ham or boiled ham
- 1 head Bibb or Boston lettuce, leaves separated
- 3 ounces Gruyère cheese, thinly sliced
- 8 slices rustic bread, for serving

1. Make the dressing: Whisk champagne vinegar, mustard, and ½ teaspoon salt in a medium bowl. Gradually add oil, whisking until emulsified. Stir in walnuts. Season with pepper. Set aside.

2. Stir onions, balsamic vinegar, and ½ teaspoon salt in a skillet; season with pepper. Bring to a boil. Reduce to a simmer. Cook, stirring occasionally, until onions have absorbed most of the liquid, 8 to 10 minutes. Drain. Let onions cool.

3. Melt butter in a medium skillet over medium-high heat. Add apple; cook, flipping once, until just beginning to brown and soften, 1 to 3 minutes per side. Remove from heat; set aside.

4. To serve, arrange 2 slices of ham on each of 4 plates. Toss lettuce with dressing; divide among plates. Arrange cheese and apple slices on top, evenly dividing among plates. Garnish each plate with 2 onions. Serve with bread.

white bean salad with spicy roasted tomatoes and broccoli

SERVES 4

The ingredients can be prepared the day before and refrigerated.

- 2 bunches broccoli, trimmed, florets and stems cut into 1-inch pieces (4 cups)
- 3 large garlic cloves, thinly sliced
- 5 teaspoons extra-virgin olive oil
- ½ teaspoon coarse salt
- 1 pound large cherry tomatoes, halved (about 3 cups)
- 1 tablespoon coarsely chopped fresh oregano
- ¼ teaspoon crushed red pepper flakes
- 1½ teaspoons Dijon mustard
- 1 tablespoon red-wine vinegar
- 1 teaspoon fresh lemon juice
  Freshly ground pepper
- 2 cups drained jarred or canned large white beans, such as large lima beans or gigande beans
- 2 ounces baby spinach (about 2 cups)

1. Preheat the oven to 375°F. Toss together broccoli, half the garlic, 2 teaspoons oil, and ¼ teaspoon salt, and arrange on a rimmed baking sheet. Roast until broccoli is just tender, 15 to 20 minutes. Transfer to a plate; let cool completely.

2. Toss together tomatoes, remaining garlic, the oregano, red pepper flakes, remaining ¼ teaspoon salt, and 1 teaspoon oil. Arrange on baking sheet. Roast until tomatoes have softened and skins begin to wrinkle, 15 to 20 minutes. Transfer to a plate; let cool completely.

3. Whisk mustard, vinegar, and lemon juice in a small bowl. Whisk in remaining 2 teaspoons oil; season with pepper.

4. Just before serving, toss together beans, broccoli, tomatoes, spinach, and dressing. The salad can be refrigerated in an airtight container up to 8 hours.

FIT TO EAT RECIPE PER SERVING: 253 CALORIES, 1 G SATURATED FAT, 5 G UNSATURATED FAT, 0 MG CHOLESTEROL, 38 G CARBOHYDRATE, 700 MG SODIUM, 14 G PROTEIN, 14 G FIBER

sandwiches
AND
savory pies

....

asian salad wraps

MAKES 18

To julienne the vegetables, cut them into thin matchstick-size pieces using a sharp knife or a mandoline. Refrigerate them in an airtight container until ready to use, up to 3 hours.

- ¼ cup plus 3 tablespoons hoisin sauce
- ¼ cup fresh lime juice
- 3 tablespoons soy sauce
- 3 tablespoons toasted sesame seeds
- 2 tablespoons mild Asian chile oil
- 1 tablespoon Asian fish sauce
- 1 tablespoon packed light-brown sugar
- 4 ounces thin, dried rice stick noodles
- 2 tablespoons fresh cilantro leaves, coarsely chopped
- 18 round rice-paper wrappers (6 inches in diameter)
- 1 head green-leaf lettuce, leaves separated, inner stalks of leaves cut out
- ½ small red bell pepper, julienned
- ½ small yellow bell pepper, julienned
- 1 small jícama (about 12 ounces), peeled and julienned
- 2 medium carrots, peeled and julienned
- 1 package (3½ ounces) enoki mushrooms
- 3½ ounces pea shoots (about 2 cups), trimmed
- 18 fresh chives

1. Whisk together the hoisin sauce, lime juice, soy sauce, toasted sesame seeds, Asian chile oil, fish sauce, and brown sugar in a medium bowl.

2. Cook the noodles according to package instructions; drain. Combine the noodles, hoisin mixture, and cilantro in a large bowl; toss. Let stand at room temperature, tossing occasionally, 15 minutes.

3. Soak 1 rice-paper wrapper in a bowl of hot water until softened, 30 seconds to 1½ minutes. Lay the wrapper flat on a paper towel or a piece of parchment paper. Cover with another paper towel or piece of parchment paper. Repeat with 2 more wrappers. Lay the wrappers flat on a clean work surface.

4. Place 1 lettuce leaf (or part of a leaf) on top of 1 wrapper so the top edge of the leaf extends over the top edge of the wrapper. Top with a mix of bell peppers, jícama, carrots, mushrooms, and pea shoots. Place a small amount of the marinated noodles on top of the vegetables.

5. Fold the bottom two-thirds of the wrapper up over the filling. Fold 1 side over the filling and roll up tightly, being careful not to tear the wrapper. Gently tie a chive around the middle of the wrap to hold it together. Transfer to a large platter; cover with a damp paper towel. Repeat with the remaining wrappers and filling, working 3 at a time.

6. Refrigerate in an airtight container (or store in a chilled cooler) up to 2 hours until ready to serve.

herbed egg salad in pitas

SERVES 4

- 12 hard-cooked eggs, peeled, cut into ¼-inch dice
- ½ cup mayonnaise
- 2 teaspoons finely chopped fresh dill
- 2 teaspoons finely chopped fresh tarragon leaves
- 1 teaspoon finely chopped fresh chives
- 2 scallions, white parts only, finely chopped
  Zest of 1 lemon
- 2 teaspoons drained capers, rinsed
  Coarse salt and freshly ground pepper
- 4 pita breads

1. Gently stir together the eggs, mayonnaise, dill, tarragon, chives, scallions, lemon zest, and capers in a medium bowl using a rubber spatula. Season with salt and pepper.

2. Cut 1 inch from the top of each pita to open the pocket. Fill each with egg salad, dividing evenly. Refrigerate in an airtight container until ready to serve, up to 4 hours.

shrimp and chive rolls
MAKES 12

- 2 pounds (about 60) small shrimp, peeled and deveined
- 4 ounces rice vermicelli
- ¼ cup fresh lime juice (2 limes)
- 2 tablespoons sesame oil
- ¼ teaspoon coarse salt
- 12 8½-inch rice-paper wrappers
- ½ seedless cucumber, cut into matchsticks
- ½ pound (about 2 cups) bean sprouts
- 1 bunch fresh chives, ends trimmed
- 1 head Boston lettuce, washed
- 1 bunch fresh mint
- 1 bunch fresh cilantro

1. Bring a large pot of water to a boil. Reduce to a simmer. Add the cleaned shrimp; poach until pink and cooked through, about 2 minutes. Slice 12 cooked shrimp in half lengthwise. Set aside.

2. Bring a medium pot of water to a boil. Cook the vermicelli until softened, about 2 minutes. Remove from heat; drain. Transfer to a bowl. Add the lime juice, sesame oil, and salt; toss. Set aside.

3. Dip a rice-paper wrapper into a bowl of warm water for 5 seconds; transfer to a clean work surface (the wrapper will still feel hard but will soften as it sits). Lay ¼ cup vermicelli on the bottom third of the rice paper; top with about 4 uncut shrimp and some cucumber and bean sprouts. Roll halfway, tucking in the ends. Place the chives and 2 shrimp halves on the roll; continue to roll so the chives and shrimp are enclosed but still showing through the rice paper.

4. Place the finished roll on a plate; cover with a damp paper towel. Continue filling and rolling rice papers until all ingredients are used. Serve with lettuce, mint, and cilantro on the side.

fried egg–topped sandwiches
MAKES 4

- 8 slices good-quality white bread
- 4 ounces fontina, Gruyère, or mozzarella cheese, thinly sliced
- 2 tablespoons fresh oregano, roughly chopped, plus more for garnish
  Coarse salt and freshly ground pepper
- 2 tablespoons milk
- 6 large eggs
- 4 tablespoons extra-virgin olive oil

1. Cut the bread into 8 rounds with a 3¾-inch cookie cutter. Top half with a few slices of cheese; sprinkle with oregano, salt, and pepper. Top with the remaining bread rounds; press gently to adhere.

2. In a small bowl, whisk together the milk and 2 eggs. Heat 2 tablespoons oil in a large nonstick skillet over medium heat. Dip the sandwiches, one at a time, into the egg mixture, letting the excess drip back into the bowl; transfer to the skillet. Cook until golden and the cheese has melted, about 2 minutes per side. Transfer to serving plates.

3. Wipe the skillet with a paper towel. Heat the remaining 2 tablespoons oil. Crack the remaining 4 eggs into the skillet, one at a time. Fry until the whites are just set, about 2 minutes. Carefully place an egg on each sandwich. Season with salt and pepper; garnish with oregano, and serve.

croque monsieur

MAKES 4

2 tablespoons unsalted butter, plus more for
  spreading, room temperature
2 tablespoons all-purpose flour
1 cup milk
½ teaspoon coarse salt
  Pinch of freshly ground nutmeg
  Pinch of cayenne pepper
  Pinch of freshly ground black pepper
8 slices rustic French or firm white
  sandwich bread
¼ cup Dijon or whole-grain mustard
½ pound cooked ham, thinly sliced
⅓ pound Gruyère cheese, thinly sliced, plus
  1 cup freshly grated (about 2 ounces)

1. Melt the butter in a small saucepan over medium heat until just starting to bubble. Add the flour, and cook, whisking constantly, until smooth but not browned, about 3 minutes.

2. Whisking constantly, slowly add the milk; continue cooking while whisking until mixture has thickened, about 3 minutes more. Remove from heat, and add salt, nutmeg, cayenne, and black pepper. Transfer to a bowl; place plastic wrap directly on surface of sauce, and set aside.

3. Heat the broiler. Heat a griddle or large cast-iron skillet over medium-low heat. Smear one side of bread slices with mustard. Top 4 slices with a layer each of ham and cheese; cover with the remaining 4 bread slices, pressing gently to adhere. Generously butter the outer sides, spreading all the way to the edges.

4. Place the sandwiches on the griddle or in the skillet. Cook until the bread is golden brown and cheese has melted, 3 to 4 minutes a side. Transfer to a work surface; divide béchamel sauce evenly over tops, spreading to edges; sprinkle with grated cheese.

5. Transfer to the broiler, and cook until the cheese topping is melted and golden, 2 to 3 minutes. Serve immediately.

fried catfish sandwiches

MAKES 12

  Vegetable oil, for frying
4 cups yellow cornmeal
1 teaspoon crushed red pepper flakes
2 tablespoons coarse salt
2 teaspoons freshly ground pepper
1 teaspoon garlic powder
12 catfish fillets (about 8 ounces each), cut
  in half crosswise
24 slices white bread
  Mayonnaise, for serving (optional)
  Pickle relish, for serving (optional)
1 Vidalia or other sweet onion, sliced into
  ¼-inch rounds

1. Fill a deep, heavy-bottomed skillet with about 2½ inches oil. Place over medium heat until the oil registers 365° F on a deep-fry thermometer. Meanwhile, combine the cornmeal, red pepper flakes, 1 tablespoon salt, 1 teaspoon pepper, and garlic powder in a shallow bowl or large plate.

2. Season the catfish fillets on both sides with the remaining tablespoon salt and teaspoon pepper. Dredge the fillets in the cornmeal mixture, turning to coat both sides. Working in batches so as not to overcrowd the pan, carefully submerge the fillets in the oil, and fry until the crust is crisp and golden and the fish is cooked through, about 3 minutes. Transfer to a large plate.

3. To serve, spread the bread slices with mayonnaise and relish, as desired. Place the catfish fillets on half the slices, and top each with a few onion slices and one of the remaining slices of bread.

blackened salmon sandwiches

MAKES 4

The spice rub can be stored in an airtight plastic container for up to 1 month.

- 1 teaspoon cumin seed
- 1 teaspoon fennel seed
- 1 teaspoon dried oregano
- 1 teaspoon dried thyme
- 2 teaspoons paprika
- ½ teaspoon ground cayenne pepper
- 2 teaspoons coarse salt
- ½ teaspoon freshly ground black pepper
- 2 tablespoons prepared horseradish
- ¼ cup plain low-fat yogurt
- 1 tablespoon honey
- 4 4-ounce salmon fillets, skin removed
- 4 slices crusty bread
- 1 bunch arugula, stems trimmed
- ½ small red onion, thinly sliced crosswise

1. Place the cumin seed, fennel seed, oregano, and thyme in a spice grinder. Pulse until finely chopped but not powdery. Transfer to a small bowl; stir in the paprika, cayenne pepper, 1½ teaspoons salt, and ¼ teaspoon black pepper; set aside.

2. In another small bowl, whisk together the horseradish, yogurt, honey, remaining ½ teaspoon salt, and ¼ teaspoon pepper; set aside.

3. Heat a heavy skillet over medium-high heat. Coat each fillet with 2 teaspoons spice blend; pat with your fingers. Place the fillets in the hot skillet. Cook until well browned, about 5 minutes. Flip the fillets; cook through, about 5 minutes more. Transfer to a plate; set aside.

4. To assemble, spread the bread with the horseradish mixture. Top with arugula and onion. Flake the salmon into chunks; place on the sandwiches. Drizzle with the remaining horseradish mixture; serve immediately.

FIT TO EAT RECIPE PER SERVING: 261 CALORIES, 8 G FAT, 63 MG CHOLESTEROL, 21 G CARBOHYDRATE, 772 MG SODIUM, 26 G PROTEIN, 1 G FIBER

lobster rolls

MAKES 8

Top-split buns are the time-honored choice for lobster rolls, but side-split buns can be used instead. Some people like only mayonnaise or melted butter on their lobster meat, but we love the added flavor that fresh herbs provide.

- 1½ pounds cooked, shelled lobster meat (about 4 1½-pound lobsters), chopped into ½-inch pieces
- 2 tablespoons mayonnaise
- ½ teaspoon finely chopped fresh chives (optional)
- ½ teaspoon finely chopped fresh tarragon or chervil (optional)
- 1 teaspoon fresh lemon juice (or to taste)
  Coarse or sea salt
  Freshly ground pepper
- 8 top-split hot dog buns
- 1½ tablespoons unsalted butter, melted, for rolls

1. Stir together the lobster and mayonnaise. Stir in the chives and tarragon (if desired) and the lemon juice; season with salt and pepper. Refrigerate, covered, while preparing rolls, or up to 2 hours.

2. Heat a large, heavy skillet or griddle over medium heat until hot. Lightly brush the outside of the buns with butter; transfer to the skillet. Cook, turning once, until buns are golden brown, about 1½ minutes per side.

3. Spoon about ½ cup lobster mixture into each bun. Serve immediately.

lobster clubs

MAKES 4

Remade as a club, the lobster roll trades its usual bun for brioche and takes on the customary bacon, lettuce, and tomato.

 1 pound cooked lobster meat, sliced into 1-inch pieces
 ½ cup plus 2 tablespoons mayonnaise, plus more for spreading
 3 tablespoons chopped fresh tarragon
 3 tablespoons chopped fresh parsley
 5 teaspoons fresh lemon juice
   Pinch of cayenne pepper
   Coarse salt and freshly ground pepper
 8 slices brioche, toasted
 4 leaves Boston lettuce
 8 slices bacon, cooked
 8 slices tomato

1. In a bowl, toss together the lobster, mayonnaise, herbs, lemon juice, and cayenne; season with salt and pepper.

2. Spread additional mayonnaise on the toasted brioche; top each of 4 slices with a lettuce leaf, some lobster mixture. 2 slices bacon, and 2 slices tomato. Top with remaining toast.

fried green tomato clubs

MAKES 4

 4 slices bacon
 ¾ cup stone-ground yellow cornmeal
 1 teaspoon salt
 1 teaspoon freshly ground pepper
   Pinch of cayenne pepper
   Pinch of sugar
 2 green tomatoes, thinly sliced
 4 biscuits or English muffins, split and toasted
   Mayonnaise, for serving
   Pickled Red Onions (recipe follows)
 4 slices sharp Cheddar cheese
   Hot sauce, for serving (optional)

1. Cook the bacon in a skillet until crisp; drain on paper towels and reserve the drippings in the pan.

2. In a shallow dish, mix together the cornmeal, salt, pepper, cayenne, and sugar. Add the tomatoes, and toss to coat.

3. Heat the reserved drippings over medium heat; add the tomatoes, and fry until golden, about 2 minutes per side.

4. Spread the mayonnaise over the cut sides of the biscuits; fill each with 1 to 2 slices fried tomatoes, 1 slice each bacon and cheese, and pickled onions. Sprinkle with hot sauce, if desired.

pickled red onions

MAKES 2 CUPS

You'll need to make these onions at least 1 week in advance.

 4 red onions, cut into ¼-inch-thick slices
 1½ teaspoons coarse salt
 1½ cups cider vinegar
 ¾ cup sugar
 7 whole black peppercorns
 3 whole allspice
 2 whole cloves
 1 whole cinnamon stick
 1 bay leaf
 1 small dried red chile

1. Put the onions in a colander set in a large bowl. Toss with the salt; refrigerate 1 hour. Rinse the onions under cold water; drain.

2. Bring the vinegar, sugar, spices, bay leaf, and chile to a boil in a medium saucepan, stirring constantly. Let cool completely.

3. Add the onions to the vinegar mixture in the pan; bring to a boil. Immediately transfer the onions to an airtight container using a slotted spoon. Let the vinegar mixture cool completely; pour over the onions. Refrigerate at least 1 week before serving (onions will keep 2 weeks more).

lemongrass pork burgers

MAKES 6

Thai chiles are small, fresh red or green chiles, and are very hot. For a milder flavor, remove the seeds. You can substitute 1 fresh serrano chile. The flavors of Southeast Asia were the inspiration for these lean burgers, which are wrapped, Vietnamese-style, in lettuce.

- 3 shallots, thinly sliced
- 1½ stalks fresh lemongrass, bottom 6 inches only, finely chopped (6 tablespoons)
- 1 piece (2 inches) peeled fresh ginger, coarsely chopped
- 1 pound ground pork
- 1½ teaspoons coarse salt
- ½ teaspoon freshly ground pepper
  Vegetable oil, for brushing
- ¼ cup plus 2 tablespoons fresh lime juice (about 3 limes)
- ¼ cup Asian fish sauce
- 3 to 6 fresh Thai chiles (depending on desired heat), thinly sliced crosswise
- 2 heads Boston lettuce (6 medium cup-shaped leaves reserved, remaining leaves shredded crosswise)
- ½ cup fresh cilantro leaves
- ¼ cup fresh mint leaves
  Cucumber wedges, for serving (optional)

1. Process 2 shallots, the lemongrass, and the ginger in a food processor until finely ground. Transfer the shallot mixture to a medium bowl. Using your hands, gently combine the shallot mixture, pork, salt, and pepper (do not overwork the meat). Shape into 6 patties. Refrigerate, covered, until cold, about 1 hour (or overnight).

2. Preheat the grill to medium-high (if using a charcoal grill, coals are ready when you can hold your hand 5 inches above grill for just 3 to 4 seconds). Brush the grill and the burgers with oil. Grill the burgers, flipping once, until cooked through, about 5 minutes per side.

3. Make the salad: Stir together the remaining shallot, lime juice, fish sauce, and chiles in a small bowl. Toss together the shredded lettuce, cilantro, and mint in a medium bowl. Add the dressing; toss.

4. To serve, top each burger with some of the salad, then wrap in a Boston lettuce leaf.

grilled hamburgers with goat cheese

MAKES 6

If your grill is large enough, you can cook everything at once. Give the hamburgers about a 2-minute head start so everything is ready to come off the grill at the same time.

- 3 pounds lean ground chuck
- 1 tablespoon each finely chopped fresh thyme, oregano, rosemary, and flat-leaf parsley
  Coarse salt and freshly ground pepper
- 3 large tomatoes, thickly sliced
- 2 large onions, thickly sliced
- 2 tablespoons extra-virgin olive oil
- 5 ounces fresh goat cheese, sliced into 6 equal portions
- 1 head romaine lettuce, chopped
- 1 head red or white endive, thinly sliced crosswise

1. Heat the grill to medium. In a large bowl, place the ground chuck and herbs. Season with salt and pepper. Using your hands, mix the ingredients together until combined. Form into 6 patties; set aside.

2. Brush the tomato and onion slices with oil, and season with salt and pepper. Grill the tomato and onion slices until slightly charred on both sides (onion should be tender), 4 to 6 minutes for tomatoes and 6 to 8 minutes for onions. Remove from the grill, and keep warm.

3. Grill the hamburger patties, 3 to 5 minutes per side for medium-rare. When they have reached desired doneness, place cheese on top of each patty. Grill until the cheese is slightly melted.

4. To serve, stack slices of onion and tomato on a serving platter with romaine and endive. Place the hamburgers on top.

roasted garlic turkey burgers

MAKES 4

1¼ pounds ground dark-meat turkey

1¼ cups coarsely grated aged provolone cheese (about 5 ounces)

¼ cup Roasted Garlic (recipe follows)

2½ teaspoons finely chopped fresh sage

Coarse salt and freshly ground pepper

Vegetable oil, for brushing

4 small ciabatta rolls, split

1 tablespoon olive oil, plus more for brushing rolls

Juice of ½ lemon

1 small bunch watercress, trimmed

¾ cup Grilled Tomato Sauce (recipe follows)

1. Using your hands, gently combine the turkey, cheese, roasted garlic, sage, and ½ teaspoon each salt and pepper in a medium bowl (do not overwork the meat). Shape into 4 patties (about 5 inches in diameter). Refrigerate, covered, until cold, about 1 hour (or overnight).

2. Preheat the grill to medium-high (if using a charcoal grill, coals are ready when you can hold your hand 5 inches above grill for just 3 to 4 seconds). Brush the grill and the burgers with vegetable oil. Grill, flipping once, until cooked through, 3 to 4 minutes per side. Toast the rolls, cut sides down, on grill; brush the cut sides with olive oil.

3. Whisk the lemon juice and 1 tablespoon olive oil in a medium bowl; season with salt and pepper. Add the watercress; toss.

4. Spread grilled tomato sauce on the bottom half of each roll. Top each with a burger, one-quarter of the watercress salad, and the top half of the roll.

roasted garlic

MAKES ABOUT ½ CUP

Use half of this recipe in the burgers and half for the grilled tomato sauce.

4 large garlic bulbs, tops cut off to expose cloves

1 tablespoon olive oil

Preheat the oven to 400° F. Place the garlic, cut sides up, on a large piece of foil. Drizzle with the oil; wrap in foil. Bake until softened, about 1 hour and 15 minutes. Let cool, then squeeze the pulp from the skins into a small bowl.

grilled tomato sauce

MAKES ABOUT 1⅓ CUPS

2 tablespoons olive oil, plus more for brushing

2 large beefsteak tomatoes, halved crosswise

Coarse salt and freshly ground pepper

¼ cup Roasted Garlic (recipe above)

1. Preheat the grill to high (if using a charcoal grill, coals are ready when you can hold your hand 5 inches above grill for just 1 to 2 seconds). Brush the grill and the tomatoes with oil. Season the tomatoes with salt and pepper.

2. Grill the tomatoes until softened and slightly charred, 3 to 4 minutes per side. Let stand until cool enough to handle. Peel the tomatoes; discard skins.

3. Put the tomatoes, garlic, and oil in a bowl; mash with a fork. Season with salt and pepper. The sauce can be refrigerated in an airtight container for up to 3 days.

shrimp and cod burgers

MAKES 4

12 ounces medium shrimp, peeled, deveined, and cut into chunks

8 ounces cod, cut into chunks

¾ cup fine fresh bread crumbs

¼ cup drained capers, rinsed

2 medium scallions, thinly sliced

3 tablespoons chopped fresh flat-leaf parsley

¼ cup fresh lemon juice (1 to 2 lemons)

1¼ teaspoons coarse salt

¾ teaspoon freshly ground pepper

Vegetable oil, for brushing

4 hamburger buns

Red leaf lettuce, for serving

Tarragon Tartar Sauce, for serving (optional; recipe follows)

Lemon wedges, for serving

1. Process half of the shrimp in a food processor until a paste forms. Add the cod, remaining shrimp, and the bread crumbs, capers, scallions, parsley, lemon juice, salt, and pepper. Pulse until just combined (do not overprocess).

2. Using dampened hands, shape into 4 patties. Refrigerate, covered, until cold and firm, about 1½ hours (or overnight).

3. Preheat the grill to medium-high (if using a charcoal grill, coals are ready when you can hold your hand above grill for just 3 to 4 seconds). Brush the grill and the burgers with oil. Grill, flipping once, until cooked through, about 3 minutes per side. Toast the buns on the grill during the last minute of cooking, if desired. Serve the burgers on the buns; top with lettuce. Serve with tartar sauce, if desired, and the lemon wedges.

tarragon tartar sauce

MAKES 1¼ CUPS

1 cup mayonnaise

3 tablespoons sweet relish

1 tablespoon fresh lemon juice

3 tablespoons drained capers, rinsed

1 tablespoon chopped fresh tarragon

1 teaspoon coarse salt

⅛ teaspoon freshly ground pepper

Stir together the mayonnaise, relish, lemon juice, capers, tarragon, salt, and pepper in a medium bowl. The sauce can be refrigerated in an airtight container up to 1 week.

grilled mushroom burgers with white bean puree

MAKES 4

We topped these burgers with smoked Cheddar cheese, but you can use another type of cheese, or omit it entirely. To clean the mushroom caps, wipe them with a damp paper towel; do not rinse or soak them because they will remain soggy even after cooking.

2 large garlic cloves, minced

2 tablespoons chopped fresh thyme

1 cup cooked or canned cannellini beans, drained and rinsed

2 tablespoons extra-virgin olive oil

Freshly ground pepper

8 large portobello mushroom caps (about 1 pound), stems trimmed

4 teaspoons balsamic vinegar

2 large red onions (about 1 pound), peeled and cut into thin rings

Olive oil cooking spray, for onions

4 whole-grain hamburger buns

2 ounces smoked Cheddar cheese, thinly sliced into 4 equal portions

½ small bunch arugula (about 2½ ounces), rinsed well and dried

1. Heat a grill or grill pan over medium heat. Make the bean puree: In a food processor, combine one-quarter of the garlic (about ½ teaspoon), 1 tablespoon thyme, the cannellini beans, and 1 teaspoon oil; process to form a smooth and spreadable paste. If the mixture is too thick, add 1 teaspoon water. Season with pepper, and pulse to combine. Set aside.

2. Combine the remaining garlic, tablespoon thyme, and oil on a plate or in a baking pan. Place the mushroom caps in the garlic mixture, and turn to coat. Season with pepper; drizzle with vinegar.

3. Place the onion slices on a plate, and lightly coat each side with cooking spray. Grill the onions until lightly charred on the first side, about 3 minutes. Flip the onions, and continue grilling until tender and charred on the other side, about 3 minutes more. Transfer to a clean plate; keep warm.

4. Place the mushrooms on the grill, stem side up, working in batches if necessary. Grill until browned on the first side and juices have begun to collect in the centers, about 5 minutes. Flip the mushrooms, and continue cooking until the stem side of each cap is browned and center is tender, about 4 minutes more.

5. Split the hamburger buns in half, and place cut side down on the grill; cook until warm and toasted. Transfer to a work surface. Spread ¼ cup bean puree on the bottom half of each bun, and top with 2 grilled mushroom caps. Layer each with sliced cheese, grilled onions, and a small handful of arugula. Top each with matching roll halves, and serve.

grilled chicken and escarole sandwiches with white-bean spread

MAKES 4

You can make the white-bean spread ahead of time; store it in an airtight container in the refrigerator until ready to use, up to three days. The chicken will need to marinate for at least two hours before being grilled.

1   teaspoon finely chopped fresh oregano

1   teaspoon red-wine vinegar

3   tablespoons extra-virgin olive oil

1   whole boneless, skinless chicken breast (about 12 ounces), split and pounded to ½ inch thick

1   tablespoon minced garlic

1   cup drained jarred or canned white beans (reserve ¼ cup liquid)

1   teaspoon finely chopped fresh rosemary

¾   teaspoon coarse salt
    Freshly ground pepper
    Vegetable oil cooking spray

8   slices multigrain bread

4   small radishes, thinly sliced

1   cup thinly sliced escarole

1. Whisk together the oregano, vinegar, and 1 tablespoon oil. Brush marinade onto both sides of chicken. Transfer chicken to a nonreactive dish; cover, and refrigerate at least 2 hours or overnight.

2. Put remaining 2 tablespoons oil and the garlic into a large skillet. Cook over medium heat, stirring occasionally, until garlic has softened, about 2 minutes. Add beans and reserved liquid, and rosemary. Cook, mashing beans with the back of a wooden spoon, 5 minutes. Add ¼ teaspoon salt; season with pepper. Transfer to a small bowl. Cover; set aside.

3. Heat a large grill pan over medium-high heat. Coat with cooking spray. Add chicken. Grill, turning once, until cooked through, 3 to 4 minutes per side. Season with remaining ½ teaspoon salt. Transfer to a plate; let cool slightly. Cut chicken into ¼-inch-thick slices; set aside.

4. Toast the bread. Spread each slice with white-bean spread, dividing evenly. Top 4 slices with the chicken, radishes, and escarole, and then the remaining bread.

FIT TO EAT RECIPE PER SERVING: 409 CALORIES, 13 G FAT, 49 MG CHOLESTEROL, 43 G CARBOHYDRATE, 541 MG SODIUM, 29 G PROTEIN, 6 G FIBER

roasted eggplant, zucchini, and chickpea wraps

MAKES 4

- 1 tablespoon balsamic vinegar
- 1½ teaspoons fresh lemon juice
- 3 tablespoons extra-virgin olive oil
- 1 tablespoon coarsely chopped fresh thyme leaves
- 1 tablespoon coarsely chopped fresh oregano leaves
  Vegetable oil cooking spray
- 1 large eggplant, cut into 1-inch cubes
- 1 medium zucchini, cut into 1-inch cubes
- 1 small onion, peeled, root end left intact, halved lengthwise, cut into 8 wedges
- 1 cup drained canned chickpeas, rinsed
- 6 ounces cherry tomatoes (about 11 tomatoes), halved (quartered if large)
- ½ teaspoon coarse salt
  Freshly ground pepper
- 4 ounces fresh part-skim mozzarella, thinly sliced
- 4 whole-wheat lavash pieces or whole-wheat wraps (2 ounces and 8 inches each)

1. Preheat the oven to 400°F. Whisk together the vinegar, lemon juice, 1 tablespoon oil, and 1 teaspoon each thyme and oregano in a small bowl; set vinaigrette aside.

2. Lightly coat a large rimmed baking sheet with cooking spray. Toss eggplant, zucchini, onion, and remaining 2 teaspoons each thyme and oregano in a large bowl. Spread in a single layer on prepared baking sheet. Drizzle with remaining 2 tablespoons oil. Roast, tossing occasionally, until golden, 30 to 35 minutes. Let cool slightly.

3. Transfer vegetable mixture to a large bowl. Add chickpeas, tomatoes, and salt; season with pepper. Drizzle with vinaigrette; toss to coat. Arrange mozzarella in center of lavash pieces or wraps. Top each with 1¼ cups vegetable salad. Roll up; cut in half.

FIT TO EAT RECIPE PER SERVING: 371 CALORIES, 18 G FAT, 20 MG CHOLESTEROL, 34 G CARBOHYDRATE, 622 MG SODIUM, 19 G PROTEIN, 9 G FIBER

steak sandwiches

MAKES 4

- 1 tablespoon whole black peppercorns
- 1 tablespoon whole white peppercorns
- 1 tablespoon whole coriander seeds
- 1 teaspoon brown mustard seeds
- 1 New York strip steak (about 1 pound; ¾ to 1¼ inches thick)
- 4 garlic cloves
- ½ cup plus 2 tablespoons plus 1 teaspoon extra-virgin olive oil
- 1 Vidalia onion, halved and cut into ¼-inch-thick slices
  Coarse salt
- 4 ciabatta rolls, halved
- ½ teaspoon fresh lemon juice
- 1 ounce baby arugula

1. Coarsely grind together the spices in a spice grinder, then rub steak all over with spice mixture. Refrigerate 30 minutes.

2. Blend garlic and ½ cup oil in a blender until combined. Set garlic oil aside.

3. Heat 2 tablespoons olive oil in a medium skillet over medium heat. Add onion, and cook, stirring occasionally, until caramelized, about 25 minutes.

4. Bring steak to room temperature. Preheat grill to medium (if using a charcoal grill, coals are ready when you can hold your hand 5 inches above grill for just 5 or 6 seconds). Season steak with salt. Grill, flipping once, until medium-rare, about 8 minutes per side. Let rest 10 minutes.

5. Brush cut sides of rolls with garlic oil to taste. Grill rolls, cut sides down, until slightly charred around edges.

6. Whisk remaining teaspoon olive oil, the lemon juice, and a pinch of salt in a small bowl. Add arugula; toss to combine.

7. Thinly slice steak at an angle. Divide steak, onion, and arugula among rolls.

smoked salmon croque madames

MAKES 4

- 5 tablespoons unsalted butter, softened
- 1 tablespoon all-purpose flour
- ⅔ cup whole milk
  Coarse salt and freshly ground pepper
- 8 slices white Pullman bread or thinly sliced sandwich bread
- 2 tablespoons Dijon mustard
- 5 ounces smoked salmon
- ¼ cup small dill sprigs, plus more for garnish
- 2 cups grated Comté cheese
- 4 large eggs

1. Make the béchamel sauce: Melt 1 tablespoon butter in a wide medium saucepan over medium-high heat. Whisk in flour; cook, whisking, 30 seconds. Gradually whisk in milk; cook, whisking, until mixture comes to a boil and has thickened, about 2 minutes. Remove from heat. Season with salt and pepper.

2. Using remaining 4 tablespoons butter, butter 1 side of each piece of bread. Set aside 4 slices. Spread unbuttered sides of remaining 4 slices with mustard; top with salmon. Scatter dill over salmon. Top each with ¼ cup cheese. Sandwich with remaining bread, buttered side up.

3. Preheat broiler. Heat a large nonstick skillet over medium-low heat. Add sandwiches; cook, turning once, until golden brown, about 2 minutes per side. Spread 2 tablespoons reserved béchamel sauce on top of each sandwich; sprinkle each with ¼ cup remaining cheese. Broil until cheese is bubbling and golden brown.

4. Meanwhile, heat a large nonstick skillet over medium heat. Crack eggs into skillet. Cover, and cook until whites are set but yolks are still soft, about 2 minutes. Season with salt and pepper. Place 1 egg on top of each sandwich, and serve.

roast beef sandwiches

MAKES 6

To make slicing easier and more precise, make the beef a day ahead and refrigerate it overnight.

- 2 tablespoons olive oil
- 1 tablespoon unsalted butter
- 1½ pounds beef eye of round
- 1½ teaspoons coarse salt
- ½ teaspoon freshly ground pepper
- 3 firm, ripe avocados
- 2 medium tomatoes, cut into ¼-inch-thick slices
  Lettuce and radicchio, for serving
- 12 slices rustic bread (½ inch thick each)
  Horseradish Cream (recipe follows)

1. Preheat the oven to 425°F. Heat a large ovenproof skillet over medium-high heat until warm. Add oil and butter; heat until oil is hot and butter has melted.

2. Season beef with salt and pepper; place in skillet. Cook until beef is well browned on all sides, about 5 minutes.

3. Transfer skillet to oven. Bake until an instant-read thermometer registers 130°F for medium-rare, 18 to 22 minutes. Transfer beef to a cutting board; let rest at least 20 minutes before slicing.

4. Slice beef very thinly crosswise. Peel and pit avocados; cut into ½-inch-thick slices. Arrange tomatoes, lettuce, radicchio, avocados, and beef over half the bread. Spread horseradish cream onto each remaining bread slice, and place on top of sandwich, spread side down.

horseradish cream

MAKES ABOUT 1 CUP

- 8 ounces cream cheese, room temperature
- ¼ cup prepared horseradish, or to taste
- ½ teaspoon coarse salt
- ¼ teaspoon freshly ground pepper

Stir together all ingredients in a small bowl until smooth. Spread can be refrigerated, covered, up to 1 week. Bring to room temperature before using.

oyster po'boys

MAKES 4

- ½ cup (1 stick) unsalted butter
- 2 tablespoons minced garlic
- 4 ciabatta rolls, split
- ⅔ cup whole-wheat flour
- ½ cup powdered milk
- ½ teaspoon cayenne pepper
- 1½ teaspoons coarse salt
- 2 tablespoons finely chopped fresh flat-leaf parsley
- 2 tablespoons finely chopped fresh chives
  Freshly ground pepper
- 32 shucked fresh large oysters, drained
  Vegetable oil, for frying
- 2 ounces arugula
- 4 anchovy fillets, rinsed
- 8 lemon segments

1. Preheat the oven to 400°F. Melt butter in a saucepan with garlic. Puree in a food processor; set aside. Remove some of the bread from inside rolls. Place rolls on a baking sheet, cut sides up; set aside.

2. Whisk flour, powdered milk, cayenne, salt, and herbs in a bowl; season with pepper. Dredge oysters in mixture. Heat 1 inch oil in a large skillet over medium-high heat. Meanwhile, spoon 2 teaspoons garlic butter over each roll. Bake until golden brown, about 5 minutes.

3. Fry oysters in batches until golden brown, 30 to 45 seconds per side. Transfer to paper towels. To serve, fill the rolls with the oysters, arugula, anchovies, and lemon.

cheddar sandwiches with quick pickles and honey-mustard spread

MAKES 4

Tangy homemade pickles and onions bring intense flavor and satisfying heft to these sandwiches. However, you can omit step 1 and use jarred pickles; just do keep in mind that these may increase your sodium intake.

- 1 large Vidalia onion, thinly sliced
- 1 medium English cucumber, thinly sliced
- 1 cup cider vinegar
- ¼ cup honey (preferably raw or cream honey)
- 2 bay leaves
- 1½ teaspoons finely chopped peeled fresh ginger
- 1¼ teaspoons brown mustard seeds
- ½ teaspoon coarse salt
- 2 teaspoons grainy mustard
- 4 small whole-wheat rolls, halved
- 4 ounces sharp white Cheddar cheese, thinly sliced

1. Put onion and cucumber into a heatproof non-reactive medium bowl; set aside. Bring vinegar, 2 tablespoons honey, bay leaves, ginger, mustard seeds, salt, and ½ cup water to a boil in a medium saucepan. Reduce heat, and simmer, stirring occasionally, 5 minutes. Pour over onion and cucumber. Cover loosely, and let cool completely, stirring occasionally to submerge vegetables. The pickled vegetables can be refrigerated in an airtight container up to 2 weeks.

2. Stir together remaining 2 tablespoons honey and the mustard; spread on bottom of rolls. Divide cheese among rolls; top each with ⅓ cup drained pickled vegetables and top half of roll. The sandwiches can be stored, wrapped in parchment, in a cool place up to 4 hours.

FIT TO EAT RECIPE PER SERVING: 343 CALORIES, 7 G SATURATED FAT, 1 G UNSATURATED FAT, 30 MG CHOLESTEROL, 46 G CARBOHYDRATE, 664 MG SODIUM, 11 G PROTEIN, 5 G FIBER

chicken wraps with mango, basil, and mint

MAKES 4

The chicken and the mango dressing can be made a day ahead and refrigerated separately.

for the chicken

1 garlic clove
½ shallot
¼ cup loosely packed fresh basil leaves
1 teaspoon extra-virgin olive oil
½ teaspoon coarse salt
¼ teaspoon ground cinnamon
  Freshly ground pepper
2 boneless, skinless chicken breast halves (about 12 ounces total)

for the dressing

½ shallot
½ mango, peeled and cut into 2-inch pieces
2 teaspoons fresh lime juice
  Pinch of cayenne pepper

for assembling

4 lavash breads (3½ ounces each)
½ mango, peeled and cut into ½-inch-thick spears
8 fresh basil leaves
8 fresh mint leaves

1. Preheat the oven to 375°F. Make the chicken: Finely chop garlic and shallot in a food processor. Add basil and oil, and process until mixture forms a coarse paste. Stir in salt and cinnamon, and season with pepper. Make a few shallow ½-inch slits on both sides of chicken; rub all over with the basil mixture. Place on a rimmed baking sheet. Bake chicken until cooked through, 12 to 15 minutes. Let cool completely, then shred chicken into small pieces; set aside.

2. Make the dressing: Finely chop shallot in the clean bowl of the food processor. Add mango, and process until smooth. Add the lime juice and cayenne, and process until combined.

3. Assemble wraps: Spread about ¼ cup mango dressing in center of each lavash. Top with chicken, mango, and herbs. Roll up diagonally to form a cone. Wraps can be refrigerated, wrapped in parchment and plastic, up to 4 hours.

FIT TO EAT RECIPE PER SERVING: 350 CALORIES, 4 G SATURATED FAT, 8 G UNSATURATED FAT, 54 MG CHOLESTEROL, 29 G CARBOHYDRATE, 457 MG SODIUM, 26 G PROTEIN, 1 G FIBER

ham and cheese tartines

MAKES 6

This recipe works equally well with other cheeses: Try a mild fontina or Comté in place of the Gruyère.

½ pound Gruyère cheese, grated on the large holes of a box grater (about 2 cups)
½ pound cream cheese
2 teaspoons fresh thyme leaves
  Coarse salt and freshly ground pepper
6 slices (½ inch thick) sourdough bread, cut from an oval loaf
4 ounces cooked ham, cut into 12 slices
3 to 4 red radishes, very thinly sliced

1. Preheat the oven to 400°F. In a food processor, pulse half the Gruyère cheese and all the cream cheese until smooth, about 30 seconds. Transfer the mixture to a small mixing bowl. Fold in the thyme, and season with salt and pepper. Set aside.

2. Place the bread on a baking sheet, and toast in the middle of oven, flipping halfway through, until golden brown on both sides, about 12 minutes.

3. Spread the reserved cheese mixture on each slice of toast, dividing evenly, and sprinkle with the remaining Gruyère. Place 2 slices of ham on each toast. Arrange the radishes on top, and serve.

niçoise tartines
with peperonata

MAKES 6

Peperonata is an Italian mixture of stewed sweet peppers, tomatoes, onions, and garlic. In this dish, the peperonata is combined with classic Provençal ingredients to make a flavorful topping for toast.

- 2 tablespoons extra-virgin olive oil
- 1 large onion, thinly sliced
- 3 garlic cloves
- 3 red bell peppers, ribs and seeds removed, julienned
  Pinch of hot paprika, plus more to taste
  Coarse salt and freshly ground black pepper
- 6 slices (½ inch thick) sourdough bread, cut from an oval loaf
- 2 large eggs
- 1 can (about 6 ounces) tuna packed in oil (preferably Italian), drained
  Fleur de sel, or sea salt (optional)
- 3 teaspoons capers, drained and rinsed
- 1 lemon, for garnish

1. Preheat the oven to 400°F. Heat the oil in a large nonstick sauté pan. Add the onion and garlic; sauté, stirring frequently, over medium heat until lightly browned, about 8 minutes. Add the bell peppers and paprika; continue cooking until the peppers are soft and juicy, about 30 minutes. Season with salt and black pepper.

2. Meanwhile, place the bread on a baking sheet; toast in the middle of the oven, flipping halfway through, until the bread is golden brown on both sides, about 12 minutes.

3. Prepare an ice-water bath; set aside. Place the eggs in a medium saucepan; add enough water to cover by about 1 inch. Bring to a full boil; cook 1 minute. Turn off heat; cover, and let stand 12 minutes. Transfer the eggs to the ice bath until cool. Peel the eggs; slice each about ¼ inch thick.

4. Spread the red pepper mixture over slices of toast; top with tuna, dividing evenly. Place a few slices of egg on top of the tuna. Season with fleur de sel or sea salt, if using, and black pepper. Garnish with capers, and zest the lemon over the top just before serving.

roasted cherry tomato tartines

MAKES 6

- 1 pint mixed cherry tomatoes
- 4 to 6 garlic cloves (unpeeled)
- 2 tablespoons extra-virgin olive oil
- 2 or 3 sprigs fresh thyme or rosemary
  Coarse salt and freshly ground pepper
- 6 slices (½ inch thick) sourdough bread, cut from an oval loaf
- 7 ounces (about ¾ cup) tapenade
- 8 ounces mild goat cheese
- 1 cup fresh basil leaves, for garnish

1. Preheat the oven to 450°F. In a medium bowl, toss the tomatoes with the garlic, oil, and herbs; season with salt and pepper.

2. Transfer the tomato mixture to a large (10-inch) cast-iron skillet, spreading it in an even layer. Roast in the oven, stirring occasionally, until the tomatoes are soft and slightly blackened, 25 to 30 minutes. Remove from heat. Let cool completely.

3. Reduce the oven heat to 400°F. Toast the bread on a baking sheet in the middle of the oven, flipping halfway through, until golden brown on both sides, about 12 minutes.

4. Spread 1 to 2 tablespoons tapenade over each toast. Divide the goat cheese evenly among the toasts; spoon some of the tomatoes and their juices on top. Garnish with basil leaves, and serve.

classic panino

MAKES 1

- 1 ciabatta roll
- 2 teaspoons extra-virgin olive oil
- ¼ teaspoon coarse salt
- ¼ teaspoon freshly ground pepper
- 2¼ ounces sliced fresh buffalo mozzarella
- ¾ ounce shaved Parmesan cheese
- 1 ounce thinly sliced prosciutto
- 8 fresh basil leaves
  Olive oil, for the pan

1. Halve the ciabatta roll. Drizzle the cut sides with the extra-virgin olive oil; sprinkle with salt and pepper. Layer the mozzarella, Parmesan, prosciutto, and basil on the bottom half. Top with the other half.

2. Heat a grill pan over medium heat until almost smoking. Lightly brush the pan with olive oil. Grill the panino until browned and crisp on the bottom, 3 to 4 minutes. Flip with a spatula; grill until browned on the other side. Serve hot.

. . . .

OTHER PANINI IDEAS

These grilled Italian sandwiches can be filled with other ingredients, some traditional, others more novel. Before starting, lightly brush cut or inner sides of the bread with olive oil, and season with salt and pepper. Then follow the recipe for the Classic Panino.

1. Fontina cheese, fresh buffalo mozzarella, rosemary, and toasted walnuts on a baguette.

2. Sardines, Parmesan cheese, shaved fennel, red onion, and lemon juice on rustic bread.

3. Hot sopressata, Taleggio cheese, and paper-thin lemon slices on ciabatta.

4. Goat cheese, black olives, and radicchio on rustic bread.

5. Bacon, Gorgonzola dolce, and baby spinach on a baguette.

. . . .

grilled margherita pizzas

MAKES SIX 9-INCH PIZZAS

Pizza Dough (recipe follows)
Extra-virgin olive oil
Pizza Sauce (recipe follows)
- 1 pound fresh mozzarella, thinly sliced
  Coarse salt and freshly ground pepper
  Basil leaves, for garnish

1. Heat a grill until medium-hot. Generously brush one side of the pizza dough with oil; grill, oiled side down, until the underside is golden brown and the top begins to bubble, 3 to 5 minutes. Quickly brush the top with oil; flip the crust. Top with thin layers of sauce and cheese. Grill until the cheese is just melted, the sauce is hot, and the crust is cooked through, 3 to 5 minutes more.

2. Slide the pizza with a large spatula onto a cutting board. Season with salt and pepper. Arrange basil on top. Repeat to make more pizzas.

pizza dough

MAKES ENOUGH FOR SIX 9-INCH PIZZAS

The dough is easiest to handle when it's well chilled—keep it in the refrigerator until right before it hits the grill. Depending on the size of your grill, you can make more than one pizza at a time. (Instead of making six pizzas, another option is to make four large ones; cut the dough into quarters before rolling it out.) If you don't own a grill, you can make the pizzas on a grill pan.

- 2 cups warm water (about 110° F)
- ½ teaspoon sugar
- 2 envelopes active dry yeast (2 scant tablespoons)
- 3 tablespoons extra-virgin olive oil, plus more for the bowl
- 6 to 7 cups all-purpose flour, plus more for dusting
- 1 tablespoon salt

1. Stir the warm water, sugar, and yeast in a small bowl until the yeast is dissolved. Let stand until foamy, about 5 minutes. Brush a large bowl with oil, and set aside.

2. Stir together 6 cups flour and the salt in a large bowl. Pour in the yeast mixture and the oil; stir mixture until all of the flour is incorporated. Continue to stir until a stiff dough forms. Turn out the dough onto a lightly floured surface, and knead with floured hands, dusting with as little flour as possible if dough seems sticky, just until the ball becomes smooth, 2 to 3 minutes. Reshape the dough into a ball. (Alternatively, put 6 cups flour, the salt, yeast mixture, and oil in the bowl of an electric mixer fitted with the paddle attachment. Mix on medium speed until the dough is smooth and slightly sticky to the touch, 2 to 3 minutes. If the dough seems too sticky, add up to 1 cup flour, 2 tablespoons at a time, mixing after each addition. Knead 4 or 5 turns to form a ball.)

3. Place the dough in the oiled bowl, smooth side up. Tightly cover with plastic wrap, and let rise in a warm, draft-free spot until doubled in bulk, about 40 minutes.

4. Remove the plastic wrap; punch down the dough. Fold the dough back onto itself 4 or 5 times; leave the smooth side up. Cover with plastic wrap; let rise again until doubled in bulk, 30 to 40 minutes.

5. Punch down the dough, and transfer it to a clean work surface. Cut the dough with a bench scraper or knife into sixths. Knead each piece 4 or 5 turns to form a ball. Cover all but one with plastic wrap.

6. On a lightly floured work surface, flatten the dough ball into a disk. Loosely cover with plastic wrap; let rest 5 minutes. Using a rolling pin or your fingertips, flatten and push the dough evenly out from the center to form a 9-inch circle (or a 7 × 11-inch rectangle or rough oval).

7. Line a baking sheet with parchment paper, and sprinkle with flour. Place the dough on top. Cover with another sheet of parchment, and sprinkle with flour. Roll out and stack the remaining dough balls.

8. Wrap the baking sheet with plastic wrap; refrigerate the pizza dough until ready to use, up to 1 day, or freeze up to 1 month (thaw in the refrigerator before using).

cornmeal pizza dough
MAKES ENOUGH FOR SIX 9-INCH PIZZAS

Follow the recipe for Pizza Dough (recipe above), reducing the all-purpose flour to 5 cups. Stir in 1 cup yellow cornmeal with the flour. Dust with or mix in additional all-purpose flour as directed.

pizza sauce
MAKES ABOUT 4 CUPS;
MAKES ENOUGH FOR SIX 9-INCH PIZZAS

2 cans (28 ounces each) whole peeled plum tomatoes
¼ cup olive oil
3 sprigs oregano
4 teaspoons coarse salt
¼ teaspoon freshly ground pepper

1. Crush the tomatoes with your hands in a large bowl. Heat the oil in a large skillet over medium heat until hot but not smoking. Add the crushed tomatoes, oregano, salt, and pepper, and reduce heat to medium-low. Cook, stirring occasionally, until thickened, 40 to 50 minutes.

2. Pass the sauce through a food mill into a bowl; discard the solids. (Alternatively, process sauce in a food processor until smooth.) If not using immediately, refrigerate the sauce in an airtight container up to 1 week, or freeze up to 1 month.

grilled pizzas with leeks, asparagus, and mushrooms

MAKES SIX 9-INCH PIZZAS

2   tablespoons extra-virgin olive oil, plus more for brushing

2   medium leeks, halved lengthwise, cut into thin half-moons, and rinsed well

8   ounces shiitake mushrooms, stemmed and cut into ¼-inch-thick slices

8   ounces thin asparagus, trimmed and cut into 1½-inch pieces

¼   cup dry white wine

1   tablespoon finely chopped fresh thyme, plus more for garnish

    Coarse salt and freshly ground pepper

    Pizza Dough (page 208)

4   ounces Taleggio or other soft cheese (such as Camembert or Brie), sliced

    Truffle oil, for drizzling (optional)

1. Heat the olive oil in a large skillet over medium heat until hot but not smoking. Add the leeks; cook, stirring, until beginning to soften, about 5 minutes. Add the mushrooms; cook until tender and juices have evaporated, about 4 minutes. Add the asparagus and wine; cook until the asparagus is bright green and the wine has evaporated, about 2 minutes. Stir in the thyme; season with salt and pepper. Set aside.

2. Heat a grill until medium-hot. Generously brush one side of the pizza dough with olive oil; grill, oiled side down, until the underside is golden brown and the top begins to bubble, 3 to 5 minutes. Quickly brush the top with olive oil; flip the crust. Top with a thin layer of cheese and some of the asparagus mixture. Grill until the cheese is just melted, the topping is hot, and the crust is cooked through, 3 to 5 minutes more.

3. Slide the pizza with a large spatula onto a cutting board. Season with salt and pepper. Sprinkle with more thyme and with a small amount of truffle oil, if desired. Repeat to make more pizzas.

grilled pizzas with plums, prosciutto, goat cheese, and arugula

MAKES SIX 9-INCH PIZZAS

    Cornmeal Pizza Dough (page 209)

    Extra-virgin olive oil

8   ounces soft goat cheese, crumbled

4   ounces prosciutto, cut into thin strips

2   large plums or apricots, pitted and cut into thin wedges

2   bunches arugula, trimmed

    Coarse salt and freshly ground pepper

1. Heat a grill until medium-hot. Generously brush one side of the pizza dough with oil; grill, oiled side down, until the underside is golden brown and the top begins to bubble, 3 to 5 minutes. Quickly brush the top with oil; flip the crust. Top with some of the cheese, prosciutto, and plums. Grill until the toppings are hot and the crust is cooked through, 3 to 5 minutes more.

2. Slide the pizza with a large spatula onto a cutting board. Drizzle the arugula with oil in a large bowl, and toss. Drizzle the pizza with oil; top with some of the arugula (or serve it on the side). Season with salt and pepper. Repeat to make more pizzas.

grilled pizzas with tomato, avocado, and pepper jack cheese

MAKES SIX 9-INCH PIZZAS

½   medium red onion, finely chopped

1   pint cherry or grape tomatoes, quartered

2   avocados, preferably Hass, pitted and coarsely chopped

2   tablespoons extra-virgin olive oil, plus more for brushing

⅓   cup fresh lime juice (about 3 limes), plus lime wedges for serving (optional)

    Coarse salt and freshly ground pepper

    Cornmeal Pizza Dough (page 209)

4   ounces coarsely grated pepper Jack cheese (about 1⅓ cups)

    Sour cream, for garnish (optional)

1. Toss the onion, tomatoes, and avocados with oil and lime juice in a medium bowl. Season with salt and pepper; set aside.

2. Heat a grill until medium-hot. Generously brush one side of the pizza dough with oil; grill, oiled side down, until the underside is golden brown and the top begins to bubble, 3 to 5 minutes. Quickly brush the top with oil; flip the crust. Top with a layer of cheese. Grill until melted and the crust is cooked through, 3 to 5 minutes more.

3. Slide the pizza with a large spatula onto a cutting board. Season with salt and pepper. Top with avocado mixture. Dot with sour cream and serve with limes, if desired. Repeat to make more pizzas.

grilled quattro formaggi pizzas

MAKES SIX 9-INCH PIZZAS

This Italian classic typically showcases four cheeses ("quattro formaggi") with different characteristics. For our rendition, we topped the crust with fontina (semifirm), mozzarella (soft and fresh), Gorgonzola (blue-veined), and Pecorino Romano (hard and aged).

Pizza Dough (page 208)
Extra-virgin olive oil
4 *ounces coarsely grated fontina cheese (about 1⅓ cups)*
1 *pound fresh mozzarella, thinly sliced*
4 *ounces Gorgonzola cheese, crumbled (about 1 cup)*
4 *ounces Pecorino Romano, thinly shaved*
Coarse salt and freshly ground pepper

1. Heat a grill until medium-hot. Generously brush one side of the pizza dough with oil; grill, oiled side down, until the underside is golden brown and the top begins to bubble, 3 to 5 minutes. Quickly brush the top with oil; flip the crust. Top with a thin layer of all four cheeses. Grill until just melted and the crust is cooked through, 3 to 5 minutes more.

2. Slide the pizza with a large spatula onto a cutting board. Season with salt and pepper. Repeat to make more pizzas.

summer squash lattice tart

SERVES 6

All-purpose flour, for work surface
½ *recipe Martha's Perfect Pâte Brisée (page 647)*
2 *medium green zucchini (about 10 ounces)*
2 *medium yellow squash (about 10 ounces)*
2 *tablespoons unsalted butter*
2 *large leeks (about 12 ounces), white part only, cut into ⅓-inch dice*
Salt and freshly ground pepper
½ *cup grated Gruyère cheese (1 ounce)*
1 *large whole egg*
1 *large egg yolk*
¼ *cup heavy cream*
Olive oil, for brushing

1. Preheat the oven to 375° F. Have ready a 4½ × 14-inch bottomless rectangular tart form or one with a removable bottom on a parchment-lined baking sheet. On a lightly floured surface, roll the dough into a 7 × 16-inch rectangle. Fit the dough into the mold, and trim the sides flush with the top of the mold. Transfer the shell to the freezer to chill for 20 minutes.

2. Remove the shell from the freezer, prick the bottom with a fork, and line with parchment paper cut to fit. Fill with dried beans or metal pie weights. Bake until the crust is just beginning to brown, about 15 minutes. Remove from the oven, and remove the beans or weights. Return the crust to the oven, and bake until golden brown, about 10 minutes more. Remove from the oven, and set aside on a wire rack.

3. Using a mandoline or vegetable peeler, very thinly slice 1 green zucchini and 1 yellow squash lengthwise. Place the slices in a colander in a single layer, and sprinkle lightly with salt. Place the colander in a bowl; let drain for 30 minutes.

4. Cut the remaining zucchini and squash into ⅓-inch dice. Melt the butter in a large skillet over high heat. Add the leeks and squash, and season with salt and pepper. Cook until golden brown but still firm, about 8 minutes. Evenly distribute the cooked vegetables in the crust. Sprinkle the Gruyère on top.

5. Place the salted squash slices in between double layers of paper towels. Gently press down to remove as much liquid as possible. Alternating squash colors, weave a lattice pattern over the top of the cheese and vegetables, covering the entire surface. Trim or tuck in the ends to fit.

6. In a medium bowl, whisk together the egg, egg yolk, and cream, and season with salt and pepper. Lift the edges of the lattice in several places, and pour in the egg mixture. Using a pastry brush, coat the lattice with olive oil. Bake, loosely covered with aluminum foil, until the custard is set, 30 to 35 minutes. Remove the lattice tart from the oven, and place on a wire rack to cool slightly before serving.

red and golden beet cheese tart

MAKES ONE 9 × 13-INCH TART

　　 All-purpose flour, for dusting
1½ 　disks Martha's Perfect Pâte Brisée (page 647)
1½ 　pounds (without greens) red, golden, and Chioggia beets
　2 　tablespoons extra-virgin olive oil, plus more for drizzling
　　 Coarse salt
　1 　pound soft goat cheese, room temperature
　4 　ounces fresh ricotta cheese (scant ½ cup)
　2 　teaspoons finely chopped fresh thyme, plus about 1 teaspoon whole leaves
　　 Freshly ground pepper
½ 　cup grated fontina cheese

1. Preheat the oven to 375°F. On a lightly floured surface, place 1½ disks pâte brisée next to each other; roll out to ⅛ inch thick. Press firmly into a 9 × 13-inch rimmed baking sheet, leaving a 1-inch overhang on all sides. Tuck the edges of dough under to create a double thickness; press firmly against the pan. Prick the dough with a fork. Refrigerate 30 minutes.

2. Line the shell with parchment or foil; fill with pie weights or dried beans. Bake until golden brown, about 30 minutes. Transfer to a wire rack. Remove the weights and parchment. Let the shell cool completely. (Leave oven on.)

3. Trim all but ½ inch of stems from the beets; rinse. Toss with the oil and 1 teaspoon salt. Transfer to a rimmed baking sheet; cover tightly with foil. Roast until the beets are tender, 45 to 60 minutes. When cool enough to handle, peel the beets with a paring knife. Cut into thin rounds.

4. Raise oven temperature to 425°F. Stir together the goat cheese, ricotta, and chopped thyme until well combined; season with pepper. Spread the mixture over the tart shell, filling all the way to edges.

5. Arrange the beets over the cheese mixture, overlapping the slices slightly and alternating colors. Lightly season with salt. Sprinkle the fontina and whole thyme leaves on top. Lightly drizzle with oil, and then season with pepper. Bake until golden brown, about 25 minutes. Serve warm.

pasta, prosciutto, and potato pie

SERVES 6

1¾ 　pounds russet potatoes (3 to 4 medium)
　2 　tablespoons unsalted butter, softened
　2 　scallions, white and light-green parts, finely chopped
　　 Coarse salt and freshly ground pepper
　1 　cup whole milk
　1 　cup heavy cream
　1 　small dried red chile, crumbled
　4 　large eggs
　4 　large egg yolks
¼ 　cup sour cream
1½ 　cups grated Parmesan cheese
¼ 　teaspoon freshly grated nutmeg
　2 　tablespoons extra-virgin olive oil
　1 　shallot, finely chopped
½ 　large bunch Swiss chard (14 ounces), stemmed and coarsely chopped
¾ 　pound penne, cooked according to package instructions
¼ 　pound prosciutto, thinly sliced into ¼-inch strips
　3 　tablespoons fresh oregano, coarsely chopped

1. Preheat the oven to 375° F. Bake the potatoes on a rimmed baking sheet until tender, about 45 minutes. Let cool slightly. Peel the potatoes; discard the skin. Mash with a potato masher. Stir the potatoes, butter, and scallions in a medium bowl; season with salt and pepper. Press the potato mixture evenly into the bottom of a 9-inch springform pan. Bake until light golden, 25 to 30 minutes. Let cool on a wire rack.

2. Bring the milk and cream to a boil in a medium saucepan over medium-high heat, stirring occasionally. Remove from heat; stir in the chile. Whisk in the eggs, egg yolks, sour cream, Parmesan, and nutmeg. Season with salt and pepper; set aside.

3. Heat the oil in a large skillet over medium heat. Add the shallot; cook, stirring occasionally, until light golden, about 2 minutes. Add the chard; cook, stirring occasionally, until wilted, 3 to 4 minutes. Season with salt and pepper.

4. Stir the pasta, Parmesan mixture, chard mixture, prosciutto, and oregano in a large bowl. Spread over the crust. Bake until golden brown and set, about 45 minutes. Let cool slightly before serving.

buttermilk-leek galette

MAKES ONE 9-INCH TART

All-purpose flour, for work surface

- *1 sheet frozen puff pastry from a standard package (17.3 ounces), thawed*
- *2 tablespoons unsalted butter*
- *5 leeks, white and pale-green parts only, washed well, and cut crosswise into ½-inch-thick pieces*
- *¼ cup nonfat buttermilk*
- *2 teaspoons Dijon mustard*
- *Coarse salt and freshly ground pepper*
- *5 ounces fresh goat cheese, crumbled*
- *1 large egg yolk*
- *1 tablespoon heavy cream or water*

1. Line a baking sheet with parchment paper, and set a 9-inch tart ring (about 2 inches deep) on top; set aside. On a lightly floured work surface, roll out the puff pastry to about ⅛ inch thick. Using a sharp paring knife, trim the dough to a 13-inch round, and lay it over tart ring. Fit into the ring, and fold in the edges against the inside of the ring, pressing gently to seal. Refrigerate 20 minutes.

2. Preheat the oven to 400° F. In a large nonstick skillet set over medium heat, melt the butter. Add the leeks; cook, stirring, until soft, about 7 minutes. Add the buttermilk and mustard, and cook until slightly thickened, about 2 minutes. Season with salt and pepper. Remove from heat; set aside.

3. To assemble the tart, layer the goat cheese and the leek mixture on the chilled pastry, ending with goat cheese. In a small bowl, beat together the egg yolk and cream. Brush the pastry with egg wash, and bake until golden, about 35 minutes. Serve warm.

fresh green tart

MAKES ONE 13½ × 4-INCH TART

You can substitute any variety of ripe tomato for the heirlooms called for here.

- *Almond Tart Dough (recipe follows)*
- *2 teaspoons sherry vinegar*
- *1 teaspoon extra-virgin olive oil*
- *1 green bell pepper, ribs and seeds removed, diced*
- *1 English cucumber, peeled, halved, and seeds removed, cut crosswise into ¼-inch-thick half-moons*
- *2 small green heirloom tomatoes, quartered*
- *2 scallions, white and pale-green parts only, cut diagonally into ⅛-inch pieces*
- *Coarse salt and freshly ground black pepper*
- *Almond-Arugula Pesto (recipe follows)*
- *¼ cup fresh chervil, for garnish*
- *Toasted whole almonds, for garnish*

1. Preheat the oven to 375° F. Press the tart dough into a 13½ × 4-inch rectangular tart pan with a removable bottom. Using a fork, lightly prick all over the bottom of the dough. Refrigerate 20 minutes.

2. Remove the tart shell from the refrigerator. Line with parchment paper; fill with pie weights or dried beans. Bake until the edges start to brown, about 15 minutes. Remove the parchment and weights; continue baking until the crust is golden, 8 to 10 minutes more. Transfer to a wire rack, and let cool completely.

3. In a medium bowl, whisk together the vinegar and oil. Add the bell pepper, cucumber, tomato, and scallions; toss together. Season with salt and black pepper.

4. Spread the pesto evenly over the bottom of the tart shell. Arrange the vegetable mixture on top. Garnish with chervil and almonds.

almond tart dough

MAKES ENOUGH FOR ONE
13 1/2 × 4-INCH TART

- 1 cup all-purpose flour
- 3 tablespoons whole almonds, toasted
- 2 tablespoons sesame seeds, toasted
- 1¼ teaspoons salt
- ¼ teaspoon ground coriander
- ¼ teaspoon ground cumin
- 6 tablespoons chilled unsalted butter, cut into small pieces
- 1 large egg yolk
- 2 tablespoons ice water

1. In a food processor, pulse the flour, almonds, sesame seeds, salt, and spices. Add the butter and process until the mixture resembles coarse meal. With the machine running, add the egg yolk and ice water through the feed tube in a slow, steady stream. Process until the dough just comes together (do not overprocess).

2. Turn out the dough onto a clean work surface. Flatten into a disk. Wrap in plastic; chill at least 1 hour or overnight.

almond-arugula pesto

MAKES ENOUGH FOR ONE
13 1/2 × 4-INCH TART

- ¼ cup whole almonds, toasted
- ¾ cup arugula, rinsed well
- ¼ cup fresh flat-leaf parsley leaves
- 1 tablespoon crème fraîche
- 3 tablespoons extra-virgin olive oil
- 2 teaspoons fresh lemon juice
- 1 garlic clove
   Coarse salt and freshly ground pepper

In a food processor, pulse all the ingredients except salt and pepper until smooth. Season with salt and pepper. The pesto can be refrigerated in an airtight container for up to 2 days.

lighter chicken potpie

SERVES 6

- 1 tablespoon unsalted butter, plus ¼ cup melted butter
- 2 medium shallots, thinly sliced
- 1 garlic clove, minced
   Coarse salt and freshly ground pepper
- 1½ cups reserved stock from Poached Chicken (recipe follows)
- 2 tablespoons all-purpose flour
- 4 medium carrots, cut on the diagonal into ¼-inch-thick slices
- 3 medium celery stalks, cut on the diagonal into ¼-inch-thick slices
   Poached Chicken (recipe follows)
- 3 tablespoons coarsely chopped fresh flat-leaf parsley, plus about ½ cup leaves for crust and sprigs for garnish
- ½ teaspoon finely chopped fresh tarragon
- ½ cup slightly thawed frozen peas
- 6 sheets phyllo dough, thawed if frozen
   Flaked sea salt, for sprinkling (optional)

1. Preheat the oven to 425° F. Melt 1 tablespoon butter in a medium saucepan over medium heat. Add shallots, garlic, ½ teaspoon salt, and ¼ teaspoon pepper. Cook, stirring occasionally, until shallots are translucent, about 3 minutes. Stir in 1 cup stock.

Whisk remaining ½ cup stock into the flour in a small bowl. Whisk into shallot mixture. Bring to a boil, whisking constantly. Reduce to a simmer. Cook 5 minutes, whisking occasionally.

2. Add carrots and celery. Bring to a boil. Stir in chicken. Return to a boil. Remove from heat. Stir in chopped parsley and tarragon. Let cool. Stir in peas. Transfer to a 2-quart (8 ½ × 12-inch) baking dish.

3. Brush 1 sheet of phyllo with melted butter. Sprinkle with parsley. Repeat with remaining phyllo, parsley, and butter; do not sprinkle parsley on final layer. (Keep unbuttered phyllo covered with plastic wrap and a damp kitchen towel.) Drape the crust over the cooled filling; tuck in the edges. Cut four 4-inch slits in the crust for vents. Sprinkle with sea salt, if desired.

4. Bake until crust is golden brown and juices are bubbling, about 30 minutes. Remove from oven, and recut vents. Serve immediately in shallow bowls.

poached chicken

MAKES ENOUGH FOR 1 POTPIE

1 whole chicken (about 4 pounds), cut into 8 pieces

2 celery stalks, cut into 4-inch pieces

2 medium carrots, peeled and cut into 4-inch pieces

1 medium onion, quartered

6 sprigs fresh flat-leaf parsley

3 sprigs fresh thyme

¼ teaspoon whole black peppercorns

2 cans (14 ounces each) low-sodium store-bought chicken broth

1 teaspoon coarse salt

1. Place chicken in a large stockpot. Add remaining ingredients and enough water to cover chicken. Bring to a boil over high heat. Skim off any foam and discard. Reduce heat to low; simmer until chicken has just cooked through, about 25 minutes.

2. Transfer chicken to a plate, and let cool slightly. Pour stock through a fine sieve into a bowl; discard solids. Set aside 1 ½ cups stock for potpie; reserve remaining stock for another use. Remove meat from skin and bones, and tear into bite-size pieces. (You should have about 4 cups.) Refrigerate, covered, until ready to use, up to 2 days.

alsatian potato pie

SERVES 6

3 Yukon Gold potatoes (about 1½ pounds), peeled and cut into ¼-inch-thick rounds

Coarse salt

1 cup heavy cream

5 garlic cloves, crushed with the flat side of a large knife

½ teaspoon freshly grated nutmeg

Freshly ground pepper

2 tablespoons unsalted butter

1 medium leek, white and light-green parts only, halved lengthwise, thinly sliced crosswise, and washed well

¼ cup chopped fresh flat-leaf parsley

1 large egg yolk

1 package (14 ounces) frozen puff pastry (such as Dufour), thawed

All-purpose flour, for work surface

1½ cups grated Comté or Gruyère cheese

1. Cover the potatoes with water in a medium saucepan. Bring to a boil over high heat. Add a pinch of salt; cook until just tender, 13 to 15 minutes. Drain. Let cool.

2. Bring ¾ cup plus 3 tablespoons cream, the garlic, and the nutmeg to a boil in a small saucepan over medium-high heat. Cook until reduced by half. Season with salt and pepper; set aside.

3. Melt the butter in a skillet over medium heat. Add the leek; cook, stirring occasionally, until softened, about 5 minutes. Remove from heat. Stir in the parsley; season with salt and pepper. Set aside.

4. Preheat the oven to 400°F. Whisk the egg yolk and remaining tablespoon cream in a small bowl; set aside. Divide the puff pastry on a lightly floured surface into 2 6 × 13-inch rectangles. Set 1 rectangle on a baking sheet lined with parchment paper. Add half of the potatoes, leaving a ½-inch border all around and overlapping the potatoes slightly. Top with half of the leek mixture and ¾ cup cheese; season with salt and pepper. Repeat the layering with the remaining potatoes, leeks, and cheese.

5. Brush the edges of the dough with egg wash. Cover with the remaining dough rectangle; gently press edges with a fork to seal. Cut 2-inch slits lengthwise in the center of the crust, 2 inches apart. Brush with egg wash. Refrigerate until cold, about 30 minutes.

6. Bake the pie until golden brown and puffy, about 35 minutes. Remove from the oven. Pour the cream mixture into the pie vents with a funnel. Bake 10 minutes more. Let stand 15 minutes before serving.

cherry tomato, bocconcini, and zucchini pie
SERVES 4 TO 6

2 tablespoons extra-virgin olive oil

1 shallot, finely chopped (about ¼ cup)

1 small zucchini (7½ ounces), halved lengthwise and cut crosswise into ½-inch-thick half-moons

1½ pounds cherry tomatoes, plus cherry tomatoes on the vine for garnish

½ cup grated Parmesan cheese

4 ounces bocconcini

3 tablespoons fresh basil, chopped

1 teaspoon finely grated lemon zest

¼ cup plus 2 tablespoons all-purpose flour, plus more for work surface

1 tablespoon sugar

Coarse salt and freshly ground pepper

Cheese Short Crust, made with Parmesan cheese (recipe follows)

1 tablespoon heavy cream

1 large egg yolk

1. Heat 1 tablespoon oil in a medium skillet over medium heat. Add the shallot; cook, stirring occasionally, until softened, about 3 minutes. Add the zucchini; cook, stirring occasionally, until it is light golden and the liquid has been released, about 5 minutes. Transfer to a large bowl; set aside.

2. Halve one-third of the tomatoes. Stir the halved and whole tomatoes, cheeses, basil, lemon zest, flour, and sugar into the shallot-zucchini mixture. Season with salt and pepper. Set aside.

3. Roll out the dough on a lightly floured surface to a 13-inch circle, about ¼ inch thick. Make 7 3-inch-long cuts around the edge of the dough, evenly spaced. Trim to make 7 rounded flaps. Transfer to a 10-inch pie plate. Drizzle the crust with the remaining tablespoon oil. Spread with the filling. Fold in the flaps of crust, slightly overlapping. Put the tomatoes on the vine in the center. Refrigerate until cold, about 20 minutes.

4. Preheat the oven to 375° F. Whisk the cream and egg yolk in a small bowl. Brush the crust with egg wash. Bake the pie on a rimmed baking sheet until the crust is golden brown and the juices are bubbling, about 45 minutes.

cheese short crust
MAKES ENOUGH FOR ONE 10-INCH PIE

2¼ cups all-purpose flour

½ cup grated Manchego or Parmesan cheese

Pinch of sugar

1 teaspoon coarse salt

¾ cup (1½ sticks) cold unsalted butter cut into pieces

1 egg yolk

¼ to ½ cup ice water

Pulse the flour, cheese, sugar, salt, and butter in a food processor until the mixture resembles coarse meal. Add the egg yolk; pulse to combine. With the processor running, drizzle in ¼ cup water until the dough just comes together. (If the dough is still crumbly, add up to ¼ cup more water, 1 tablespoon at a time.) Do not process for more than 20 seconds. Wrap the dough in plastic. Refrigerate until cold, about 30 minutes.

pasta, rice,
AND
grains

....

soba noodles with vegetables and mint

SERVES 4

Coarse salt

8 ounces sugar snap peas, trimmed, strings removed

12 ounces soba noodles

1 tablespoon plus 1 teaspoon toasted sesame oil

1 tablespoon plus 1 teaspoon peanut oil

2 medium carrots (about ½ pound), peeled and shaved into thin strips using a vegetable peeler

1 teaspoon minced peeled fresh ginger

4 scallions, thinly sliced crosswise

1 tablespoon tamari soy sauce

¼ cup coarsely chopped fresh mint

Freshly ground pepper

1. Prepare an ice-water bath; set aside. Bring a large (8-quart) pot of water to a boil; add salt. Add the peas; cook until bright green and crisp-tender, about 2 minutes. Using a slotted spoon, immediately transfer the peas to the ice-water bath to stop the cooking; drain.

2. Return the water to a boil; cook the noodles according to package instructions. Drain. Rinse the noodles with cold water; drain.

3. Transfer the noodles to a large bowl. Add the oils; toss to combine. Add the reserved peas and the carrots, ginger, scallions, tamari soy sauce, and mint; season with pepper. Toss to combine. Serve at room temperature.

soba noodles with tofu, avocado, and snow peas

SERVES 4

1 2-inch piece fresh ginger, peeled and sliced into very thin strips

1 serrano or jalapeño pepper, seeded and sliced into very thin strips

¼ cup sugar

3 tablespoons fresh lime juice (about 3 limes)

2 tablespoons low-sodium soy sauce

1 package (14 ounces) extra-firm tofu, cut into ¾-inch cubes and patted dry

1 package (about 8 ounces) soba noodles

4 ounces snow peas, thinly sliced

1 teaspoon vegetable oil

1 English cucumber, peeled, halved crosswise, then sliced lengthwise into thin strips

10 to 12 chives, cut into 1-inch pieces

1 ripe avocado, pitted, peeled, and sliced

2 tablespoons sesame seeds

1. In a small saucepan, bring the ginger, chile, sugar, and ⅓ cup water to a boil. Reduce heat to low; cook until ginger and chile are soft, about 5 minutes. Use a slotted spoon to transfer the ginger and chile to a bowl; set aside. Reserve syrup.

2. Make the dressing: In a shallow bowl, whisk together the lime juice, soy sauce, and 2 teaspoons reserved syrup. Add the tofu; toss to coat. Set aside.

3. In a pot of boiling water, cook the noodles according to package instructions. Drain; transfer to a large bowl. Add the peas; drizzle with the oil and 1 tablespoon dressing. Toss to coat; let cool.

4. To serve, add the cucumber, chives, tofu, and dressing to the bowl; toss to combine. Divide among plates; top with the avocado and reserved ginger and chile. Sprinkle with sesame seeds.

FIT TO EAT RECIPE PER SERVING: 547 CALORIES, 20 G FAT, 0 MG CHOLESTEROL, 75 G CARBOHYDRATE, 822 MG SODIUM, 28 G PROTEIN, 7 G FIBER

pasta with scallops, garlic, grape tomatoes, and parsley

SERVES 4

Coarse salt

1 pound linguine or spaghetti

5 tablespoons olive oil

4 garlic cloves, thinly sliced

½ teaspoon crushed red pepper flakes

1 pound bay or sea scallops, tough muscles removed

1 pint container ripe grape tomatoes

Freshly ground black pepper

2 tablespoons chopped fresh flat-leaf parsley, plus more for garnish

1 tablespoon unsalted butter

1. Bring a large pot of water to a boil, and add salt generously. Add the pasta; cook until al dente according to package instructions. Drain in a colander, reserving ¼ cup cooking water.

2. Heat the oil in a large sauté pan over medium-high heat. Add the garlic and red pepper flakes; toast until lightly golden and fragrant, about 1 minute. Transfer the garlic to a small bowl; set aside.

3. Add the scallops to the pan (if using sea scallops, cut in half); sauté until opaque, about 2 minutes. Add the tomatoes, and cook, stirring frequently, until the skins begin to split, 2 to 3 minutes; crush a few with the back of the spoon. Season with salt and pepper. Remove from heat.

4. Add the pasta, parsley, reserved cooking water, and butter; toss to combine. Divide among bowls, and serve immediately; garnish with reserved garlic and parsley.

spinach linguine with walnut-arugula pesto

SERVES 6

The pesto can be made up to 1 hour before serving without losing its freshness; store it at room temperature.

2 small garlic cloves

3 ounces walnut pieces (about ¾ cup), toasted and cooled

4 ounces arugula, trimmed and roughly chopped

½ teaspoon coarse salt

1 ounce Parmesan cheese, finely grated (about ⅓ cup)

1 pound spinach linguine

1 tablespoon extra-virgin olive oil

Freshly ground pepper

1. In the bowl of a food processor fitted with the metal blade, pulse the garlic until very finely chopped. Add the walnut pieces and arugula; process until a coarse paste forms, about 5 seconds. Transfer to a serving bowl. Stir in the salt and Parmesan cheese, and set aside.

2. Bring a large pot of water to a boil. Add the linguine, and cook until al dente according to package instructions, about 8 minutes. Drain in a colander, and immediately add to the bowl with the walnut-arugula mixture. Drizzle with the oil, and season with pepper. Toss thoroughly until coated evenly. Serve immediately.

FIT TO EAT RECIPE PER SERVING: 415 CALORIES, 13 G FAT, 4 MG CHOLESTEROL, 59 G CARBOHYDRATE, 826 MG SODIUM, 16 G PROTEIN, 9 G FIBER

spaghetti with garden vegetables

SERVES 6 TO 8

- 3 tablespoons extra-virgin olive oil
- 2 large carrots, peeled and finely chopped
- 1 small red onion, finely chopped
- 2 large celery stalks, peeled and finely chopped
- 2 garlic cloves, crushed with the flat side of a large knife
- 1 cup torn fresh basil leaves
- 1 teaspoon crushed red pepper flakes

   Coarse salt
- ½ cup dry white wine
- 2 small yellow summer squash, halved lengthwise and cut into ¼-inch-thick half-moons
- 2 small zucchini, halved lengthwise and cut into ¼-inch-thick half-moons
- 2 small eggplants, cut into ½-inch cubes
- 3 medium tomatoes, coarsely chopped
- 2 teaspoons chopped fresh marjoram

   Freshly ground pepper
- 1 pound spaghetti or bucatini

   Freshly grated Parmesan cheese, for serving

1. Stir together the oil, carrots, onion, celery, and garlic in a large saucepan. Cook over medium-low heat 2 minutes. Add ½ cup basil, the red pepper flakes, and 1 teaspoon salt. Cover. Cook, stirring often, until the vegetables are caramelized, about 15 minutes.

2. Add the wine to the saucepan. Raise heat to medium. Cook until the wine has almost completely reduced, about 5 minutes. Add the yellow squash, zucchini, and eggplants. Cook 5 minutes. Add the tomatoes. Cover. Cook until the vegetables are tender, 10 to 12 minutes. Add the marjoram and ½ teaspoon salt; season with pepper.

3. Bring a large pot of water to a boil; add salt. Add the pasta; cook until al dente. Drain. Transfer to a large bowl. Add the vegetable mixture and remaining ½ cup basil to the pasta. Toss to combine. Serve with Parmesan cheese.

spaghetti with clams

SERVES 4

   Coarse salt
- 1 pound spaghetti
- 2 tablespoons olive oil
- 2 garlic cloves, minced
- 1 small dried chile, crumbled, or pinch of red pepper flakes
- 1½ pounds littleneck clams, scrubbed
- 1 cup dry white wine
- 2 tablespoons coarsely chopped fresh flat-leaf parsley, plus whole leaves for garnish

   Juice of 1 lemon
- 3 tablespoons unsalted butter

   Freshly ground black pepper

1. Bring a large pot of water to a boil; salt generously. Add the spaghetti, and cook until slightly underdone, about 7 minutes. Drain the pasta, reserving 1 cup of the cooking liquid. Set aside.

2. Meanwhile, heat the oil in a large skillet over medium heat. Add the garlic and chile; cook until the garlic is golden, about 2 minutes. Add the clams and white wine, and raise heat to high. Bring to a boil; cover, and cook, shaking occasionally, 2 to 3 minutes, until the clams open. Stir in the parsley. Transfer to a bowl; set aside.

3. Return the skillet to medium-high heat. Add the reserved pasta water and lemon juice; reduce until slightly thickened, about 2 minutes. Remove from heat; whisk in the butter. Add the clam mixture and spaghetti. Cook over medium-low heat until heated through, 2 to 3 minutes. Season with salt and pepper; garnish with parsley.

spaghetti alla carbonara

SERVES 4 TO 6

Coarse salt

1 pound spaghetti

4 ounces pancetta, coarsely chopped

2 tablespoons extra-virgin olive oil

3 garlic cloves, minced

4 large eggs

½ cup freshly grated Parmesan cheese

¼ cup freshly grated Pecorino Romano cheese

Freshly ground pepper

1. Bring a large pot of water to a boil; add salt. Add the pasta; cook until al dente. Drain. While the pasta cooks, cook the pancetta in a large skillet over medium-high heat, stirring occasionally, until golden brown, 6 to 7 minutes. Using a slotted spoon, transfer the pancetta to a bowl.

2. Reduce heat to medium-low. Add the oil to skillet; heat until hot but not smoking. Add the garlic; cook until golden, about 3 minutes. Lightly beat the eggs in a large serving bowl; set aside. Add the pasta to skillet; toss. Transfer to the eggs. Add the cheese and pancetta; toss. Season with pepper.

NOTE *The eggs in this dish are not fully cooked; it should not be prepared for pregnant women, babies, young children, the elderly, or anyone whose health is compromised.*

ravioli stuffed with fava beans, ricotta, and mint with brown butter sauce

MAKES ABOUT 3½ DOZEN; SERVES 6 TO 8

You can substitute fresh or frozen peas for the fava beans. Drain the ricotta in a sieve set over a bowl for about 10 minutes to remove excess liquid. Try to find the denser buffalo ricotta for this recipe. If you use regular ricotta, the filling won't be as thick.

3 cups shelled fresh fava beans (3 pounds in pods)

10 ounces ricotta cheese (preferably buffalo ricotta), drained in a sieve

½ cup finely grated Parmesan cheese, plus more for sprinkling

⅓ cup finely chopped fresh mint

1 tablespoon fresh lemon juice

Coarse salt

Fresh Pasta Dough (recipe follows)

All-purpose flour, for dusting

Yellow cornmeal, for dusting

1 stick (8 tablespoons) unsalted butter

Freshly ground pepper

1. Bring a large pot of water to a boil; add the beans. Cook until tender, 6 to 7 minutes. Transfer to an ice-water bath; let cool 1 minute. Drain; squeeze the beans from the skins. Transfer 2 cups of the beans to a food processor. Add the cheeses, mint, lemon juice, and ¾ teaspoon salt. Process until smooth. Refrigerate the filling at least 1 hour (up to 2 days).

2. Divide the dough into 4 pieces. Dust 1 piece of dough with flour (cover the remaining pieces with plastic wrap). Set the rollers of a pasta maker to the widest setting; roll the dough through. Fold the dough into thirds; pass through again, narrow side first. Repeat until smooth, 3 or 4 more times. Run the dough through progressively narrower settings, using additional flour as needed, until very thin (at least 5 inches wide). Cut the sheet crosswise into manageable pieces.

3. Dust 2 rimmed baking sheets with cornmeal; set aside. Place 1 piece of pasta sheet on a lightly floured work surface (keep the unused pieces covered). Space heaping tablespoons of filling 3 inches apart on lower half of sheet.

4. Using a wet pastry brush, moisten the pasta around each mound of filling. Fold the top half of the sheet over the filling to meet the edge; press around the mounds to eliminate air and to seal.

5. Cut the pasta into 2½- to 3-inch squares using a pizza wheel. Brush away excess flour. Place the ravioli on cornmeal-dusted baking sheets. Roll out the remaining pasta dough, and repeat. (If serving that day, cover the ravioli with plastic wrap, and refrigerate on baking sheets until ready to use. If making ahead, freeze on baking sheets until firm, about 1 hour, and then transfer to an airtight container; freeze until ready to use, up to 1 month.)

6. Bring a large pot of water to a boil; add salt. Add half the ravioli; gently stir once. Cook at a gentle boil until the ravioli are just tender, 3 to 5 minutes. Transfer to a colander using a slotted spoon; drain. Cover to keep warm. Repeat with remaining ravioli.

7. Meanwhile, melt 4 tablespoons butter in a large skillet over medium heat. Reduce heat to low; cook the butter until lightly browned, 3 to 4 minutes. Add half the ravioli to the skillet; toss to coat. Using a slotted spoon, transfer the ravioli to a platter; cover to keep warm. Repeat with the remaining ravioli.

8. Cook the remaining 4 tablespoons butter until lightly browned as above. Add the reserved cup beans; cook over low heat until warm, about 20 seconds. Transfer the ravioli to serving plates. Spoon the beans and butter over ravioli. Sprinkle with cheese; season with salt and pepper.

fresh pasta dough
MAKES 1 POUND

- 2 cups all-purpose flour, plus more for dusting
- 4 large eggs

1. Mound the flour on a clean work surface; make a well in the center. Crack the eggs into the well; beat lightly with a fork. Gradually bring small amounts of flour into the well, incorporating it into the eggs using the fork. When most of flour has been incorporated, fold in the remaining flour using a bench scraper.

2. On a clean work surface lightly dusted with flour, knead the dough until smooth and elastic, about 10 minutes. Wrap in plastic; let stand at room temperature 1½ hours (or refrigerate overnight) before rolling out. The dough can be frozen in an airtight container up to 1 month.

spicy whole-wheat linguine with red peppers
SERVES 6

- 1 pound whole-wheat linguine
- ½ cup extra-virgin olive oil
- 1 teaspoon crushed red pepper flakes
- 4 garlic cloves, minced
- 4 medium red bell peppers, cut lengthwise into ¼-inch-thick strips
- 1 teaspoon coarse salt

1. Bring 6 quarts water to a boil in a large pot. Add the pasta; cook according to package instructions until al dente.

2. Meanwhile, heat the oil, red pepper flakes, and garlic in a medium saucepan over medium heat, stirring occasionally, until the oil is hot but not smoking, about 2 minutes. Add the bell pepper strips, and cook until very soft, about 20 minutes.

3. Drain the pasta well. Rinse with warm water; shake out excess. Return the pasta to the pot. Stir salt into the bell pepper mixture; add to the pasta, and toss well to coat.

FIT TO EAT RECIPE PER SERVING: 447 CALORIES, 19 G FAT, 0 MG CHOLESTEROL, 63 G CARBOHYDRATE, 396 MG SODIUM, 12 G PROTEIN, 11 G FIBER

penne with basil and caciocavallo

SERVES 4

If you have trouble finding caciocavallo cheese, you can substitute grated Parmigiano-Reggiano.

- *3 cups loosely packed fresh basil leaves, torn, plus more for garnish*
- *2 garlic cloves, peeled, crushed with the flat side of a large knife*
- *¼ cup extra-virgin olive oil, plus more for drizzling*
- *Coarse salt*
- *1 pound penne*
- *2 cups grated caciocavallo cheese, plus more for sprinkling and serving*
- *2½ teaspoons cracked black pepper*

1. Stir together the basil, garlic, and oil in a serving bowl; let stand 30 minutes. Bring a large pot of water to a boil; add salt. Add the pasta; cook until al dente. Reserve ½ cup cooking liquid; drain the pasta.

2. Add the hot pasta, cheese, pepper, and reserved cooking liquid to the basil mixture; toss well. Sprinkle with cheese, and drizzle with oil; garnish with basil. Serve with more cheese.

trofie with pesto, green beans, and potatoes

SERVES 4 TO 6

- *12 ounces fingerling or small new potatoes, cut into ½-inch-thick rounds or pieces*
- *Coarse salt*
- *1 pound trofie (or fusilli or penne)*
- *4 ounces green beans, trimmed and halved crosswise*
- *Pesto (recipe follows)*
- *Freshly ground pepper*
- *Freshly grated Parmesan cheese, for serving*

1. Cover the potatoes with cold water by 2 inches in a medium saucepan. Bring to a boil; add salt. Reduce heat to medium; simmer the potatoes until tender, about 10 minutes. Drain.

2. Bring one large pot and one medium pot of water to a boil; add salt to both. Add the pasta to the large pot; cook until al dente. Add the green beans to the medium pot; cook until tender, 5 to 6 minutes. Drain the pasta and green beans.

3. Heat the pesto in a large skillet over medium heat until warm. Stir in the potatoes, pasta, and green beans; cook until heated through. Season with salt and pepper. Serve with cheese.

pesto

MAKES ABOUT 1¼ CUPS

- *3 cups loosely packed fresh basil leaves*
- *2 tablespoons pine nuts, toasted*
- *1 garlic clove*
- *½ teaspoon coarse salt*
- *¾ cup plus 2 tablespoons extra-virgin olive oil*
- *2 tablespoons freshly grated Parmesan cheese*
- *Freshly ground pepper*

Process the basil, pine nuts, garlic, and salt in a food processor until combined. With the processor running, add the oil in a slow, steady stream; process until smooth. Stir in the cheese. Season the pesto with pepper. The pesto can be refrigerated, covered by a thin layer of olive oil in an airtight container, up to 1 week.

baked gnocchi with cheese

SERVES 4 TO 6

1 cup heavy cream

6 ounces fontina or Taleggio cheese, grated (about 1½ cups)

Pinch of freshly grated nutmeg

¼ teaspoon freshly ground pepper

Unsalted butter, for baking dish

1 tablespoon coarse salt

Basic Potato Gnocchi (recipe follows)

1. Heat the cream in a small saucepan over medium heat until just simmering. Add two-thirds of the cheese; stir until melted. Stir in the nutmeg and the pepper. Remove from heat; cover to keep warm.

2. Preheat the oven to 400°F. Butter an 8-inch-square baking dish; set aside. Bring a large pot of water to a boil; add the salt. Add half the gnocchi; when they rise to the top (after about 2 minutes), continue to cook until tender, about 15 seconds more. Transfer the gnocchi with a slotted spoon to the buttered dish. Repeat the process with the remaining gnocchi.

3. Pour the cheese sauce over the gnocchi, and gently toss. Sprinkle the remaining cheese on top. Bake the gnocchi until golden brown, about 25 minutes.

basic potato gnocchi

SERVES 4 TO 6

You can use this recipe to make spinach gnocchi: Thaw 1 10-ounce package frozen spinach, very finely chop the leaves, and squeeze out the moisture. Add it to the potatoes in the bowl, and sprinkle with an additional 2 tablespoons flour. Formed gnocchi can be refrigerated on a floured baking sheet, uncovered, up to 12 hours.

2 cups all-purpose flour, plus more for dusting

2 pounds Yukon Gold or russet potatoes

1 tablespoon plus 2½ teaspoons coarse salt

2 large eggs

¼ teaspoon freshly ground pepper

1. Lightly flour a baking sheet; set aside. Put the potatoes in a large saucepan, and cover with cold water by 2 inches. Bring to a boil; add 1 tablespoon salt. Reduce to a simmer; cook until the potatoes are very tender, about 25 minutes.

2. Drain the potatoes. When they are cool enough to handle, peel them, then pass them through a ricer or food mill into a medium bowl. Sprinkle with the flour, and add the eggs. Sprinkle with the remaining 2½ teaspoons salt and the pepper. Stir mixture with a fork to combine well.

3. Turn out the dough onto a lightly floured surface; gently knead until it is soft and smooth, about 3 minutes. Divide the dough into 4 to 6 pieces. Roll each piece into a long rope about ¾ inch thick. Cut the ropes crosswise into 1-inch gnocchi.

4. Roll a cut side of each dumpling against the tines of a fork with your thumb (forming ridges on one side and an indentation on the other). Set aside on the floured baking sheet until ready to cook.

spinach gnocchi with tomato sauce

SERVES 4 TO 6

1 tablespoon extra-virgin olive oil

1 small onion, finely chopped

3 garlic cloves, minced

¼ cup dry white wine

1 can (28 ounces) whole plum tomatoes with juice, coarsely chopped

1 can (14½ ounces) tomato sauce

2 sprigs basil

¼ teaspoon crushed red pepper flakes

1 tablespoon coarse salt, plus more for seasoning

Freshly ground pepper

Basic Potato Gnocchi, made with spinach (recipe above)

Thinly shaved Parmesan cheese, for serving

1. Heat the oil in a large saucepan over medium heat until hot but not smoking. Add the onion and garlic; cook, stirring occasionally, until onion is translucent, 5 to 7 minutes. Add the wine; cook until

GNOCCHI 101

Although there are several kinds of gnocchi (Italian for "dumplings"), the most basic (and versatile) are made from potatoes, with flour added to balance the moisture content and just enough egg to bind the mixture. Properly prepared gnocchi are light and airy in the center, with a surface that is gently resistant and supple.

The trick to perfect gnocchi lies in getting just the right amount of flour in the dough: If the dumplings are too wet, they'll fall apart and dissolve when slipped into the water to cook; too much flour, and they'll be dense and inelegant. Here are a few helpful tips: Always wait until after boiling the potatoes to peel them; this way, they will not absorb as much water during cooking. The cooked potatoes should be fed through a ricer or a food mill; a food processor will turn the potatoes into a gluey mess. As for which potatoes to choose, Yukon Gold has a desirably rich flavor, but dry, starchy potatoes, such as russets, will yield the lightest dumplings.

Although the process itself is relatively simple, making your own gnocchi will take some practice and patience until you perfect your technique and gain an understanding of just how much flour your dough needs. Nevertheless, even a less than perfect gnocchi is still delicious.

1. Pass the cooked potatoes through a ricer or food mill; a ricer will yield a finer texture.

2. Gently knead the dough, adding a small amount of flour if the dough is too sticky. Don't overwork the dough, or the dumplings will be dense, not pillowy.

3. A bench scraper is handy for dividing the dough.

4. Use your fingertips to form each piece into a rope.

5. Roll each dumpling over the tines of a fork to create grooves to trap the sauce.

6. Use a slotted spoon to remove the gnocchi from the boiling water; they aren't sturdy enough to be poured into a colander.

most of the liquid has evaporated. Add the tomatoes and juice, tomato sauce, basil, and red pepper flakes. Reduce heat to medium-low; simmer until slightly thick, about 30 minutes. Season with salt and pepper. Remove from heat; cover to keep warm.

2. Bring a large pot of water to a boil; add the salt. Add half the gnocchi; when they rise to the top (after about 2 minutes), continue to cook until tender, about 15 seconds more. Transfer the gnocchi with a slotted spoon to the pan with sauce. Repeat the process with the remaining gnocchi.

3. Reheat the gnocchi over low heat; gently toss. Serve with cheese shavings.

gnocchi with mushrooms and gorgonzola sauce
SERVES 4 TO 6

- 3 tablespoons extra-virgin olive oil, plus more for brushing
- 1 tablespoon coarse salt, plus more for seasoning
  Basic Potato Gnocchi (page 224)
- 1 cup heavy cream
- 1 cup homemade or low-sodium store-bought chicken stock
- 4 ounces Gorgonzola cheese
  Pinch of freshly grated nutmeg
  Pinch of cayenne pepper
  Freshly ground pepper
- 12 ounces assorted mushrooms, such as chanterelle, cremini, and portobello, stemmed and coarsely chopped

1. Lightly brush a rimmed baking sheet with oil; set aside. Bring a large pot of water to a boil; add the salt. Add half the gnocchi; when they rise to the top (after about 2 minutes), continue to cook until tender, about 15 seconds more. Transfer the gnocchi with a slotted spoon to the oiled baking sheet. Repeat the process with the remaining gnocchi.

2. Bring the cream and stock to a boil in a large saucepan over medium-high heat. Reduce heat, and let the mixture simmer until slightly thickened and reduced by one-third, about 10 minutes. Add the

cheese; stir until melted. Stir in the nutmeg and cayenne. Season with salt and pepper. Remove from heat; cover to keep warm.

3. Heat the oil in a large skillet over medium heat until hot but not smoking. Add the mushrooms, and cook, stirring occasionally, until they are tender and any released liquid has evaporated, about 4 minutes. Add the gnocchi; cook, stirring occasionally, until heated through. Pour the Gorgonzola sauce over the gnocchi; gently toss.

orecchiette with green tomatoes, caramelized onions, and corn
SERVES 6 TO 8

- 2 tablespoons unsalted butter
- 1 large Vidalia or other sweet onion, cut into ¼-inch-thick slices
- 2 pounds green tomatoes (about 6 medium), coarsely chopped
- 3 tablespoons sugar
- 1 cup fresh corn kernels (about 2 ears)
  Coarse salt and freshly ground pepper
- 1 tablespoon chopped fresh thyme
- 1 pound orecchiette or other short, dried pasta, cooked according to package instructions

1. In a large skillet over medium heat, melt the butter. Add the onion, and cook, stirring, until it begins to soften, about 6 minutes. Add the tomatoes, and sprinkle the sugar over the mixture. Cook, stirring, until the tomatoes are tender and golden brown, about 20 minutes.

2. Add the corn; season with salt and pepper. Cook, stirring, until the corn is tender and just starting to brown, about 4 minutes. Stir in the thyme.

3. Add the vegetable mixture to the cooked pasta, and stir until combined. Serve immediately.

rigatoni with sausage and broccoli rabe

SERVES 4 TO 6

- 7 garlic cloves (3 quartered and 4 crushed)
- ¼ cup plus 3 tablespoons extra-virgin olive oil

  Coarse salt
- 1 medium bunch broccoli rabe (about 1 pound), trimmed
- ½ cup sun-dried tomatoes in olive oil, drained
- 1 small dried red chile, crumbled, or ¼ teaspoon crushed red pepper flakes
- 1 pound sweet Italian sausages with fennel, cut into ½-inch-thick pieces
- 12 plum tomatoes, seeded and cut into 4 wedges (or 4 cups canned whole plum tomatoes, drained and seeded, cut into 4 wedges)
- 1 pound rigatoni, cooked

  Freshly ground pepper

1. Preheat the oven to 350°F. Place the quartered garlic in the center of a square of foil lined with parchment paper. Fold up the edges of the foil to form sides. Drizzle the garlic with 3 tablespoons oil, and season with salt. Fold the foil up over the garlic to seal, forming a pouch. Transfer to a baking sheet. Roast the garlic until soft and golden brown, about 20 minutes.

2. Bring a large pot of water to a boil; add salt. Add the broccoli rabe, and cook until bright green, 1 to 2 minutes. Drain. Cut crosswise into 1-inch pieces; set aside. Puree the sun-dried tomatoes in a blender. Transfer to a small bowl; set aside.

3. Cook the remaining ¼ cup oil and the crushed garlic, the chile, and a pinch of salt in a large skillet over medium heat until fragrant, 1 to 2 minutes. Add the sausage; cook, stirring often, until browned, about 10 minutes.

4. Stir in the broccoli rabe, sun-dried-tomato puree, and plum tomatoes. Cook until the liquid has reduced, 10 to 12 minutes more.

5. Toss the cooked pasta with roasted garlic. Stir the pasta mixture into the sauce in the skillet. Season with salt and pepper.

gratinéed macaroni and cheese with tomatoes

SERVES 6 TO 8

You can use six 2-cup gratin dishes to make individual servings. The baking time will be a bit shorter; cook until bubbling and golden.

- 7 tablespoons unsalted butter, plus more for dish
- 1¼ cups small pieces torn baguette or other crusty bread
- 1 tablespoon chopped fresh thyme

  Coarse salt and freshly ground pepper
- 1 pound elbow macaroni or other short, tubular pasta
- 1 quart milk
- 5 tablespoons all-purpose flour

  Pinch of freshly grated nutmeg
- 4 cups grated sharp white Cheddar cheese (about 1 pound)
- 1 pound red and yellow tomatoes in all sizes, cut into 1-inch pieces if large or halved if small (cherry, grape, or pear)

1. Preheat the oven to 375°F. Butter a 9 × 13-inch baking dish or a 3-quart casserole dish; set aside. Melt 2 tablespoons butter, and pour over the bread in a medium bowl; toss. Add 1 teaspoon thyme, ½ teaspoon salt, and ¼ teaspoon pepper; toss.

2. Bring a large pot of water to a boil; add salt. Cook the pasta until just beginning to soften, 2 to 3 minutes (it will not be fully cooked). Drain and rinse.

3. Warm the milk in a saucepan over medium heat. Heat the remaining 5 tablespoons butter in a high-sided skillet (or a pot) over medium until foaming. Add the flour; whisk 1 minute. Slowly whisk in the warm milk. Cook, whisking, until bubbling and thickened, 8 to 10 minutes. Remove from heat.

4. Add 2 teaspoons salt, ½ teaspoon pepper, the remaining 2 teaspoons thyme, the nutmeg, and cheese to pan; stir until the cheese is melted.

5. Stir the pasta and tomatoes into the cheese sauce. Pour into the buttered dish; sprinkle with the bread topping. Bake until bubbling and golden, about 30 minutes. Let cool slightly before serving.

whole-wheat pasta with lentils, spinach, and leeks

SERVES 4

If you like, grate some Parmesan cheese over the tossed pasta just before serving, or offer grated cheese on the side.

- 2 cups (14 ounces) French green lentils
- 2 garlic cloves
- 1 dried bay leaf
- 1 pound small whole-wheat chiocciole or other small tubular pasta
- 2 tablespoons extra-virgin olive oil
- 4 leeks (about 1¾ pounds), white and light-green parts only, sliced into ⅛-inch rounds, washed well and drained
- 1 teaspoon chopped fresh thyme
- 1½ teaspoons coarse salt
    Freshly ground black pepper
- 8 ounces baby spinach, washed

1. In a medium saucepan, combine the lentils, 1 garlic clove, and the bay leaf. Add enough cold water to cover by 2 inches. Bring to a boil over medium-high heat. Reduce heat to medium-low, and simmer until the lentils are tender, 20 to 25 minutes. Drain, and discard the garlic clove and bay leaf; set the lentils aside.

2. Bring a large pot of water to a boil. Add the pasta; cook until al dente, according to package instructions, about 7 minutes. Drain the pasta, reserving 1 cup cooking liquid. Place the pasta in a large bowl.

3. Meanwhile, mince the remaining garlic clove. In a large sauté pan, heat the oil over medium heat. Add the minced garlic, leeks, and thyme; cook, stirring occasionally, until the leeks are soft but not browned, about 5 minutes. Add the cooked lentils and salt; season with pepper.

4. Add the spinach and reserved cooking liquid to the pan; toss to wilt the spinach, about 2 minutes. Pour the mixture over the pasta, tossing to combine. Serve immediately.

FIT TO EAT RECIPE PER SERVING: 638 CALORIES, 9 G FAT, 0 MG CHOLESTEROL, 120 G CARBOHYDRATE, 793 MG SODIUM, 29 G PROTEIN, 11 G FIBER

rice noodles with chinese broccoli and shiitake mushrooms

SERVES 4

Similar greens—such as yow choy, also known as choy sum (which looks almost identical to bok choy but bears small yellow flowers), broccolini, or even regular broccoli—will work well in this dish if you can't find Chinese broccoli. You can buy wide rice noodles at Asian grocery stores, or use the narrow rice noodles (often labeled "pad thai noodles") that many supermarkets carry.

- 8 ounces wide (about ⅜ inch) or other rice noodles
- 12 ounces Chinese broccoli (also called gai lan), cut into 2-inch pieces
- 3 tablespoons low-sodium tamari soy sauce
- 1 tablespoon plus 1 teaspoon Thai fish sauce (also called nam pla)
- 1 tablespoon plus 1 teaspoon rice wine vinegar (not seasoned)
- 1 teaspoon sugar
- ¾ cup homemade or low-sodium store-bought chicken stock
- 1 tablespoon canola oil
- 1 tablespoon minced peeled fresh ginger, or more to taste
- 2 garlic cloves, minced
- 8 shiitake mushrooms, stemmed, caps quartered
- 2 teaspoons cornstarch mixed with 2 tablespoons cold water
- 4 scallions, white and pale-green parts only, cut on the diagonal into 1-inch pieces
- 2 teaspoons toasted sesame oil
    Crushed red pepper flakes, for sprinkling (optional)
    Sesame seeds, for sprinkling (optional)
    Coarse salt, for sprinkling (optional)

1. Cover the noodles with very hot water in a large bowl, and let soak 30 minutes. Drain the noodles, and set aside.

2. Meanwhile, bring a large pot of water to a boil. Add the broccoli; cook until crisp-tender, about 1 minute. Drain; set aside.

3. Stir together the tamari, fish sauce, vinegar, sugar, and stock in a small bowl; set aside. Heat the canola oil in a large nonstick skillet or a wok over medium heat until hot but not smoking. Add the ginger, garlic, and mushroom caps; cook, stirring, until the mushrooms are soft, about 2 minutes.

4. Add the tamari mixture to the skillet; bring to a simmer over high heat. Stir in the cornstarch mixture, and simmer 2 minutes. Add the reserved noodles and broccoli, along with the scallions, and toss to coat. Drizzle with the sesame oil, and toss again. Serve with red pepper flakes, sesame seeds, and salt for sprinkling, if desired.

pasta with fennel, sardines, and pine nuts

SERVES 4

- 1 pound penne, trenette, or other short pasta
- 2 tablespoons extra-virgin olive oil
- ¼ cup pine nuts
- 1 onion, finely chopped
- 2 fennel bulbs, trimmed and thinly sliced, plus ¼ cup green fronds
- 4 garlic cloves, finely chopped
- 1 teaspoon coarse salt
  Freshly ground pepper
- 2 cans (3.75 ounces each) sardines packed in olive oil
  Grated zest and juice of 1 lemon, plus 1 lemon for serving

1. Bring a large pot of water to a boil. Cook the pasta until al dente, according to package instructions, about 8 minutes.

2. Meanwhile, combine the oil and pine nuts in a large sauté pan. Cook over medium heat, stirring occasionally, until the nuts are lightly toasted, 3 to 4 minutes.

3. Add the onion, sliced fennel, garlic, and salt to pan; season with pepper. Cook, stirring occasionally, until the onion is soft and light golden, 9 to 10 minutes. Add the sardines; stir in the lemon zest and juice. Chop the reserved fennel fronds; stir into the mixture.

4. Drain the pasta, reserving about ¼ cup cooking liquid. Add the pasta to the mixture in the pan along with enough cooking water to coat; toss to combine. Divide among 4 serving plates; grate lemon zest over each. Serve immediately.

FIT TO EAT RECIPE PER SERVING: 571 CALORIES, 17 G FAT, 20 MG CHOLESTEROL, 73 G CARBOHYDRATE, 548 MG SODIUM, 28 G PROTEIN, 13 G FIBER

pasta verde

SERVES 4

- 2 tablespoons grainy mustard
- 2 tablespoons white wine or sherry vinegar
- ¼ cup plus 2 tablespoons extra-virgin olive oil
  Coarse salt and freshly ground pepper
- 1 pound gemelli or other short pasta
- 1 sweet onion, halved lengthwise, then cut crosswise ¼ inch thick
- 2 small zucchini, halved lengthwise, then cut crosswise ¼ inch thick
- 8 ounces snap peas, tough strings removed
- 3 ounces baby spinach (or 1 bunch regular spinach, stems trimmed and leaves coarsely chopped)
- 1 small bunch scallions, thinly sliced (about ½ cup)
- ¼ cup packed fresh basil leaves, cut into very thin strips

1. In a medium bowl, whisk together the mustard and vinegar. While whisking, slowly drizzle in ¼ cup oil until emulsified. Season with salt and pepper. Set aside. Cook the pasta in a large pot of boiling salted water until al dente, according to package instructions, about 8 minutes. Drain; return to pot. Set aside.

2. Meanwhile, heat the remaining 2 tablespoons oil in a large skillet over medium heat. Add the onion; cook until just softened, about 4 minutes. Add the zucchini; cook, stirring, until tender, about 4 minutes. Add the snap peas and spinach; cook, stirring, until bright green, about 2 minutes. Remove from heat; stir in the scallions and basil. Add to the pasta along with the vinaigrette; toss. Serve warm or at room temperature.

broccoli with orecchiette

SERVES 4

Broccoli, a cruciferous vegetable, contains signifi-
cant amounts of vitamins A and C, as well as calcium, iron, and riboflavin.

- 8 ounces orecchiette (ear-shaped pasta)
- 1 tablespoon extra-virgin olive oil
- 2 garlic cloves, minced
- 1 bunch (about 1½ pounds) broccoli,
  stalks peeled and trimmed, stalks and
  florets roughly chopped
- 1 teaspoon coarse salt
  Freshly ground black pepper
- 2 tablespoons freshly grated Pecorino
  Romano cheese

1. Bring a large stockpot of water to a boil. Add the
pasta, and cook until al dente, stirring occasionally
to keep the pasta from sticking, about 8 minutes.
Transfer to a colander to drain, reserving ½ cup
cooking liquid. Set the pasta aside.

2. Heat 1 teaspoon olive oil in a large skillet over
medium heat. Add the garlic; sauté until golden,
stirring to avoid burning, about 2 minutes. Add the
broccoli and reserved cooking liquid; cook, stirring,
until the broccoli is tender and bright green, about
3 minutes. Add the salt, and season with pepper.
Remove from heat.

3. Add the reserved pasta to the pan, and toss well
to coat. Transfer to 4 serving bowls; drizzle each
with ½ teaspoon olive oil, and garnish each serving
with 1½ teaspoons grated cheese.

FIT TO EAT RECIPE PER SERVING: 284 CALORIES, 5 G FAT,
4 MG CHOLESTEROL, 49 G CARBOHYDRATE, 801 MG SODIUM,
12 G PROTEIN, 5 G FIBER

butternut squash ravioli with fried sage leaves

MAKES ABOUT 24 RAVIOLI; SERVES 4

- 1¾ cups Roasted Squash Puree, made with
  butternut squash (recipe follows)
- 6 tablespoons unsalted butter
- ½ cup chopped shallots (about 3)
- 1½ tablespoons chopped fresh sage, plus 24
  whole sage leaves for garnish
  Coarse salt and freshly ground pepper
  Pinch of ground nutmeg
- ½ cup semolina, for dusting
  Fresh Pasta Dough (page 222)
  All-purpose flour, for dusting
- ¼ cup olive oil
- ¼ cup freshly grated Parmesan cheese,
  for garnish (2 ounces)

1. In a small saucepan, cook the squash puree over
medium heat, stirring frequently, until it stops releasing moisture and is reduced to 1¼ cups, 10 to
12 minutes. Transfer to a small bowl to cool.

2. In a small saucepan, melt 2 tablespoons butter
over medium heat. Add the shallots; cook, stirring,
until soft and beginning to brown, 3 to 5 minutes.
Add the chopped sage; cook, stirring, 1 minute
more. Remove from heat; combine with the squash.
Season with salt and pepper; stir in the nutmeg. Let
cool completely.

3. Generously dust 2 baking sheets with semolina;
set aside. Divide the pasta dough into 4 pieces;
cover the unused pieces with plastic wrap to keep
them from drying out. Dust a piece of dough lightly
with flour. Using a pasta maker, roll the dough
through the widest opening. Fold the dough into
thirds, and pass it through machine again, layered
side first. Repeat process three or four more times,
until the dough is smooth. Continue running the
dough through the remaining settings, using additional flour sparingly, until the pasta sheet is very
thin. The dough should be at least 5 inches wide.

4. Place the dough on a lightly floured surface;
halve crosswise. Cover half with plastic wrap. On
the other half, place scant tablespoons of squash
filling 1 inch apart in 2 rows. Using a pastry brush

dipped in water, lightly moisten the pasta around each mound of filling. Top with the remaining half-sheet of pasta; press around the mounds to eliminate the air inside and to seal. Cut the pasta into 2½-inch squares. Brush away excess flour. Place the ravioli on the prepared baking sheets. Repeat with the remaining dough and filling.

5. In a small saucepan, heat the oil over medium-high heat. Drop a few sage leaves at a time into the hot oil, and fry until the oil around the leaves stops bubbling but before the leaves brown, about 5 seconds. Using a slotted spoon, transfer to a paper-towel–lined plate; set aside.

6. Bring a large stockpot of water to a boil. Add salt and the ravioli. Gently stir once, and cook at a gentle boil until the ravioli have floated to the top and are just tender, 3 to 5 minutes. Using a slotted spoon, divide evenly among 4 plates.

7. In a small saucepan, melt the remaining 4 table-spoons butter over medium heat, and cook until lightly browned and aroma is nutty, 6 to 8 minutes. Drizzle over the ravioli, and garnish with cheese and fried sage leaves. Serve immediately.

roasted squash puree
MAKES ABOUT 2¼ CUPS

3 pounds squash, such as butternut, orange Hokkaido, or buttercup, halved and seeded

Canola oil, for baking sheet

1. Preheat the oven to 400°F. Place the squash halves, skin side up, on an oiled rimmed baking sheet. Bake until fork tender, about 1¼ hours. Remove from the oven. Turn over; let stand until cool enough to handle.

2. Scoop the flesh into a food processor, and discard the skin. Puree until smooth. Refrigerate the squash puree in an airtight container up to 4 days, or store in the freezer up to 1 month.

pasta with peas, crab, and basil
SERVES 6 TO 8

Pappardelle are long, flat, wide noodles; fettuccine or linguine work just as well. We recommend chopping the peas slightly before cooking them; otherwise, they have a tendency to roll off the pasta when you eat.

Coarse salt

1 pound pappardelle

4 tablespoons unsalted butter

2 shallots, minced

2 pounds garden peas, shelled and roughly chopped (2 cups)

Freshly ground pepper

1 pound lump crabmeat, rinsed and picked over

1 cup heavy cream

¼ cup loosely packed fresh basil leaves, roughly chopped, plus more for garnish

1. Bring a large saucepan of water to a boil, and generously add salt. Stir in the pasta; cook according to package instructions until it is al dente. Transfer to a colander, and let drain.

2. Meanwhile, melt the butter in a large sauté pan over medium heat. Add the shallots, and cook until they are translucent and fragrant, about 2 minutes. Add the peas, and season with salt and pepper; cook until the peas are tender and bright green, 4 to 5 minutes. Add the crab, and continue cooking, stirring constantly, until it is heated through, about 1 minute more. Add the pasta, and stir to combine.

3. Stir in the cream and basil, and cook until the mixture is just heated through. Remove from heat; season with salt and pepper. Divide among serving plates, and garnish with basil. Serve immediately.

linguine with
two-olive tapenade
SERVES 4

The tapenade can also be served as a dip for crudités or a zesty sauce for grilled fish. For best results, choose olives with distinctive flavors, such as those suggested below.

½ pound linguine
⅓ cup pitted brine-cured olives, such as kalamata (about 16)
⅓ cup pitted ripe green olives, such as Picholine (about 18)
   Finely grated zest of 1 lemon
2 garlic cloves
2 tablespoons plus ⅓ cup roughly chopped fresh flat-leaf parsley, plus whole sprigs for garnish
½ teaspoon freshly ground black pepper
¼ teaspoon crushed red pepper flakes
1 6-ounce can tuna packed in water, drained
1½ cups cherry tomatoes, quartered

1. Bring a large pot of water to a boil. Add the linguine; cook according to package instructions, stirring occasionally, until it is al dente. Remove from heat, and transfer the linguine to a colander; let drain, reserving ¼ cup cooking water.

2. Make the tapenade: In the bowl of a food processor fitted with the metal blade, combine the olives, lemon zest, garlic, 2 tablespoons parsley, black pepper, and red pepper flakes. Process until the mixture is finely chopped and combined.

3. Transfer the linguine to a large serving bowl, and toss with the reserved cooking water. Add the tapenade, tuna, tomatoes, and remaining ⅓ cup chopped parsley; toss well to coat. Serve immediately, garnished with parsley sprigs.

FIT TO EAT RECIPE PER SERVING: 365 CALORIES, 9 G FAT, 13 MG CHOLESTEROL, 51 G CARBOHYDRATE, 912 MG SODIUM, 19 G PROTEIN, 5 G FIBER

oyster mushroom
and chard ravioli
SERVES 6

1¾ cups homemade or low-sodium store-bought chicken stock
½ ounce dried oyster mushrooms
1 small bunch ruby chard (8 ounces)
1 sprig fresh thyme
2 teaspoons olive oil
1 ounce thinly sliced prosciutto
1 small onion, finely chopped
2 tablespoons grated Parmesan cheese
36 wonton wrappers, thawed if frozen
   Pinch of coarse salt

1. Bring the stock and ½ cup water to a simmer in a small saucepan. Add the mushrooms. Let stand until soft, about 20 minutes. Remove the mushrooms with a slotted spoon, and transfer to a work surface; coarsely chop. Set aside. Pour the soaking liquid through a fine sieve into a medium bowl; discard the solids. Return the soaking liquid to the pan; set aside.

2. Separate the leaves from the stems of the chard; reserve the stems. Coarsely chop the leaves. (You should have about 4 cups leaves.) Set aside. Cut the stems into ¼-inch dice. Add the stems and thyme to the soaking liquid in the pan, and bring to a simmer. Remove from heat; let stand 10 minutes. Pour through a fine sieve into a medium bowl. Reserve ¼ cup simmered chard stems for garnish; discard the remaining solids. Cover the broth, and set aside.

3. Heat the oil in a large skillet over medium heat. Add the prosciutto; cook, stirring occasionally, until crisp, about 5 minutes. Transfer to a plate. Add the onion to the skillet; cook, stirring occasionally, until translucent, about 3 minutes. Stir in the mushrooms and chard leaves. Cook, stirring occasionally, until the chard is wilted, about 5 minutes. Transfer to a medium bowl; let cool completely. Coarsely chop the prosciutto; stir into the chard mixture. Add the Parmesan, and stir to combine.

4. Working with a few wrappers at a time, put 1 heaping tablespoon mixture onto the center of each wrapper. Brush the edges with water. Top each filled wrapper with another wrapper. Press the edges and centers to seal. (Uncooked ravioli can be frozen in a single layer on a baking sheet and then stored in a resealable plastic bag up to 1 month.)

5. Bring a large pot of water to a boil. Add salt. Add the ravioli in batches; cook until they rise to the top and are heated through, about 3 minutes. Carefully transfer 3 ravioli to each serving bowl; cover. Repeat with remaining ravioli.

6. Bring the broth to a simmer. Spoon ¼ cup broth into each bowl; garnish with reserved chard stems.

FIT TO EAT RECIPE PER SERVING: 194 CALORIES, 4 G FAT, 10 MG CHOLESTEROL, 32 G CARBOHYDRATE, 666 MG SODIUM, 8 G PROTEIN, 2 G FIBER

pastitsio

SERVES 10 TO 12

for the meat sauce

- 2   tablespoons extra-virgin olive oil
- 2   white onions, cut into ¼-inch dice
- 2   pounds ground lamb
- 2   teaspoons coarse salt
- 2   teaspoons ground cinnamon
- ½   teaspoon freshly ground pepper
- ¼   teaspoon ground nutmeg
- ½   cup red wine
- 1   6-ounce can tomato paste
- 2   bay leaves

for the béchamel

- 6   tablespoons unsalted butter
- 9   tablespoons all-purpose flour (½ cup plus 1 tablespoon)
- 2   teaspoons baking powder
- 3   cups milk
- 1   cup freshly grated Parmesan cheese
- 2   teaspoons coarse salt
- ¼   teaspoon freshly ground black pepper
- ¼   teaspoon ground nutmeg
     Pinch of cayenne pepper

to assemble

     Butter for the baking dish
- 1   1-pound box curly elbow macaroni, uncooked

1. To make the sauce, heat the olive oil in a large skillet with sides over medium heat. Add the onions, and cook until they begin to soften, about 3 minutes. Add the lamb, salt, cinnamon, pepper, and nutmeg. Cook, breaking into pieces, until the lamb is no longer pink. Add the wine, and cook until the liquid is almost evaporated. Stir in the tomato paste, bay leaves, and 2 cups water. Cover, and let simmer 30 minutes, skimming the fat occasionally. Remove from heat, and set aside, covered.

2. For the béchamel, melt the butter in a large saucepan over medium heat. When the butter is bubbling, add the flour and baking powder. Cook, stirring constantly with a wire whisk, for 1 minute. While whisking, slowly pour in the milk. Continue cooking, whisking constantly, until the mixture bubbles and becomes thick. Remove the pan from heat, and stir in the Parmesan, salt, black pepper, nutmeg, and cayenne pepper. Set aside, covered, until ready to assemble.

3. Preheat the oven to 375° F. Butter a 9 × 13-inch glass or other ovenproof baking dish; set aside. Bring a large saucepan of water to a boil. Add the pasta; cook 2 to 3 minutes less than manufacturer's instructions, until very al dente. Transfer to a colander; drain well. Stir the noodles into the meat mixture. Pour the meat and pasta mixture into the prepared pan. Spread béchamel over the mixture, and bake until the top is set and golden brown, 30 to 40 minutes. Let sit 10 minutes before serving.

....

BÉCHAMEL BASICS

This classic French sauce is used in many dishes, including soufflés, croque monsieurs, and even macaroni and cheese. When making béchamel sauce, cook the roux (butter and flour mixture) long enough to avoid a floury taste, but don't let it brown. Whisking constantly while adding flour then milk prevents lumps from forming.

....

baked mushroom linguine

SERVES 10 TO 12

- 4 ounces dried mushrooms (such as porcini or chanterelle)
- 2 sprigs fresh rosemary
- 2 sprigs fresh thyme, plus 2 teaspoons finely chopped
- 7 tablespoons unsalted butter
- 5 tablespoons all-purpose flour
- 1½ cups heavy cream
- 1 onion, diced
- 1 pound button mushrooms, stems removed, quartered
- 1 pound shiitake mushrooms, stems removed, sliced
- 2½ teaspoons coarse salt
- ½ teaspoon freshly ground pepper
- 1 pound linguine, uncooked
- ½ cup grated Romano cheese

1. Place the dried mushrooms in a bowl, and pour 4 cups boiling water over them. Let sit 30 minutes to allow flavors to infuse. Wrap the rosemary and thyme sprigs in cheesecloth, and tie with kitchen string; set aside. Lift out the mushrooms with a slotted spoon, and place in another bowl. Press the mushrooms to release any retained stock, and pour the liquid back into the bowl; set the mushrooms aside. Strain the mushroom liquid through a fine-mesh sieve lined with a paper towel. You should have about 4 cups mushroom stock; set aside.

2. Melt 5 tablespoons butter in a large saucepan over medium heat. When bubbling, add the flour. Cook, stirring, until the mixture begins to brown, about 3 minutes. While whisking, slowly pour in the mushroom stock. Continue cooking, whisking constantly, until the mixture bubbles and becomes thick. Stir in the cream and reserved herb bundle. Reduce to a gentle simmer, and cook 30 minutes, stirring occasionally, to allow flavors to infuse.

3. Meanwhile, heat the remaining 2 tablespoons butter in a large skillet over medium heat. Add the onion, and cook until it begins to soften, about 3

minutes. Add the button mushrooms, cook until they release their juices, and make room in the pan. Add the remaining mushrooms, and cook until all are tender, about 5 minutes. Add the mushroom sauce to the skillet, and stir to combine. Season with the salt and pepper, and set aside.

4. Preheat the oven to 375° F. Bring a large pot of water to a boil. Add the pasta; cook 2 to 3 minutes less than manufacturer's instructions, until very al dente. Transfer the noodles to a colander, and rinse with cold water to stop the cooking. Stir the noodles into the mushroom mixture. Sprinkle with grated cheese, and bake until browned on top and mixture is bubbling, about 30 minutes. Transfer the dish to a wire rack to cool 5 minutes before serving.

orzo with peas and mint

SERVES 4

- 1 cup orzo (Greek pasta)
- 2 tablespoons unsalted butter
- 1 shallot, minced (about 2 tablespoons)
  Zest of 1 lemon
- 1 pound fresh peas, shelled, or 2 cups frozen peas
  Coarse salt and freshly ground pepper
- 2 tablespoons freshly chopped mint

1. Cook the orzo according to package directions. Melt the butter in a medium saucepan over medium heat. Add the shallot and lemon zest, and sauté until translucent.

2. Add the peas, and cook until bright green and tender, adding a little water if the shallots brown before peas are tender.

3. Add the cooked orzo, season with salt and pepper, and toss to combine. Remove from heat, and stir in the mint.

traditional lasagne bolognese

SERVES 10 TO 12

This lasagne was designed for a deep-dish baking pan. You can use a standard 9 × 13-inch baking pan, but you will have excess sauce; the sauce can be frozen and used over pasta another time. The lasagne can be assembled up to 1 day ahead and left to cool completely. Cover, unbaked, and refrigerate up to 1 day in advance, or freeze, unbaked, up to 3 weeks in advance. Defrost overnight in the refrigerator; bake as directed below.

Bolognese Sauce (recipe follows)
1 3-pound container ricotta cheese
3 large egg yolks
1 cup (about 3 ounces) grated Parmesan cheese
1 tablespoon plus 1½ teaspoons coarse salt
¼ teaspoon freshly ground black pepper
¼ teaspoon ground nutmeg
   Pinch of cayenne pepper
2 tablespoons extra-virgin olive oil
1 1-pound box uncooked lasagne noodles
1 pound fresh mozzarella, sliced into ¼-inch rounds

1. Bring the sauce to room temperature. In a large bowl, whisk the ricotta, egg yolks, Parmesan, 1½ teaspoons salt, black pepper, nutmeg, and cayenne pepper. Chill the filling until ready to assemble the lasagne.

2. Preheat the oven to 400° F. Butter an 11 × 14 × 3-inch lasagne baking pan. Bring a large pot of water to a boil. Add the olive oil and the remaining tablespoon salt. One at a time, add the lasagne noodles; cook until al dente, 2 to 3 minutes less than the manufacturer's instructions. Remove the noodles with tongs; drain in a colander.

3. Spread about 3 cups sauce on the bottom of the baking dish. Place a single layer of lasagne noodles over the sauce, overlapping them slightly. Spread about 2 cups sauce over the noodles and about half of the ricotta filling mixture over the sauce.

4. Top with a layer of lasagne noodles, again slightly overlapping them. Repeat with more sauce and the remaining ricotta filling mixture. Top with a final layer of lasagne noodles. Spread a layer of sauce over the noodles, and finish with a layer of sliced mozzarella rounds.

5. Bake until the sauce is bubbling and the cheese is melted, at least 1 hour. Cover with aluminum foil if the cheese starts to brown too early. Let the lasagne stand 10 to 15 minutes before serving.

bolognese sauce

MAKES ABOUT 3 QUARTS

3   tablespoons unsalted butter
3   tablespoons extra-virgin olive oil
2   onions, cut into ¼-inch dice
3   stalks celery, cut into ¼-inch dice
3   carrots, peeled and cut into ¼-inch dice
2   pounds ground sirloin
2   pounds ground veal
1   quart whole milk
2   cups red wine
3½ cups homemade or low-sodium store-bought beef broth
1   cup tomato paste
1½ teaspoons coarse salt
¾   teaspoon freshly ground pepper

1. Heat the butter and olive oil in a large cast-iron or enamel pot over medium heat.

2. Add the onions, and cook until they begin to soften, about 5 minutes. Add the celery and carrots, and cook until the vegetables are tender, 8 to 10 minutes. Add the ground sirloin and veal, and cook, stirring occasionally, until the meat is no longer pink. Add the milk, and cook at a gentle simmer, skimming fat from surface, until the liquid has reduced by half, about 50 minutes.

3. Add the wine, and simmer until liquid is reduced by half again, about 40 minutes.

4. Add the beef stock, tomato paste, salt, and pepper; simmer gently until the sauce thickens, 40 to 45 minutes. If using for lasagne, set aside to cool slightly before assembling.

fettuccine with brussels sprout leaves, brown butter, and toasted walnuts

SERVES 6

To remove individual Brussels sprout leaves, cut the stem out of each sprout and gently ease apart all the leaves.

- 1 teaspoon coarse salt, plus more for cooking water
- 16 ounces fettuccine
- ½ cup (1 stick) plus 3 tablespoons unsalted butter
- 2 ounces walnuts
- 1 medium red onion, sliced into thin wedges
- 2 garlic cloves, minced
- 1 pound Brussels sprouts, leaves separated
- ¼ teaspoon freshly ground pepper
- ½ teaspoon finely chopped fresh sage
- ¼ teaspoon finely chopped fresh thyme
  Freshly grated Parmesan cheese, for serving

1. Preheat the oven to 350° F. Bring a large saucepan of water to a boil; add salt. Add the pasta, and cook until al dente, 8 to 10 minutes. Drain, transfer to a medium bowl, and toss with 1 tablespoon butter. Cover, and keep warm while proceeding.

2. Spread the walnuts on a baking sheet, place in the oven, and toast until fragrant, about 10 minutes. When cool enough to handle, chop coarsely; set aside. Place ½ cup butter in a small saucepan over medium-high heat. Cook until the butter begins to brown and is very fragrant, about 8 minutes. Strain, discarding the solids, into a glass measuring cup or a small bowl, and set aside.

3. Heat the remaining 2 tablespoons butter in a large skillet over medium heat. Add the onion and garlic, and cook until they start to soften, about 2 minutes. Add the sprout leaves, sprinkle with salt, pepper, and herbs, and continue cooking until the leaves are bright green and tender and the onions are translucent, 3 to 5 minutes. Add the pasta to the skillet, and drizzle with the brown butter. Toss to combine, and cook until warmed through, season-ing with salt and pepper if needed. Transfer to a serving dish, and garnish with walnuts and Parmesan cheese. Serve immediately.

angel-hair pasta with sautéed oysters and chorizo

SERVES 4

- 3 tablespoons extra-virgin olive oil
- 4 ounces dried, hot chorizo sausage, thinly sliced into rounds
- ¼ cup (½ stick) unsalted butter
- 2 tablespoons all-purpose flour
- ½ teaspoon paprika
- ¼ teaspoon freshly ground white pepper
  Pinch of cayenne pepper
  Coarse salt
- 2 tablespoons sherry
- 1¼ cups heavy cream
- 2 dozen shucked fresh oysters, plus ⅔ cup strained oyster liquor
- 8 ounces angel-hair pasta
- ¼ teaspoon finely grated orange zest

1. Bring a large pot of water to a boil. Meanwhile, heat oil in a large saucepan over medium-high heat. Add chorizo. Cook, stirring, until crisp, about 3 min-utes. Transfer to a plate lined with paper towels, and let drain. Wipe out pan.

2. Melt butter in the pan over medium heat. Add flour, spices, and 1 teaspoon salt. Cook, whisking constantly, 3 minutes (do not brown). Add sherry, and cook, whisking, 1 minute. Whisk in cream and oyster liquor. Bring to a simmer, and whisk until thick, about 3 minutes.

3. Add salt to boiling water; add pasta, and cook until al dente. Drain. Add oysters to sauce; gently poach until just cooked through, 1 to 2 minutes. Add pasta; toss. Divide among plates. Top with chorizo; sprinkle with orange zest.

herbed spaetzle

SERVES 4

- 1 cup whole milk
- 8 sprigs fresh thyme, plus 1 tablespoon thyme leaves
- ¼ cup packed fresh flat-leaf parsley
- 3 large eggs
- 1½ cups all-purpose flour
  Coarse salt and freshly ground pepper
- 3 tablespoons unsalted butter

1. Bring milk and 4 thyme sprigs to a boil in a small saucepan. Remove from heat. Discard thyme. Transfer milk to a blender; add parsley, thyme leaves, and eggs. Blend until combined.

2. Whisk flour and 1½ teaspoons salt in a medium bowl. Gradually whisk in milk mixture until smooth.

3. Bring a medium saucepan of salted water to a boil. Working with about ¼ cup batter at a time, press batter through ¼-inch holes of a colander or spaetzle maker into boiling water. Cook until spaetzle float to top, 1 to 2 minutes. Using a slotted spoon, transfer to an ice-water bath. Drain.

4. Melt butter in a medium nonstick skillet over medium-high heat. Add half of the spaetzle; cook, stirring occasionally, until golden, about 6 minutes. Transfer to a bowl. Repeat. Season with salt and pepper. Garnish with remaining thyme.

spicy squash pasta

SERVES 4 TO 6

- 2 pounds autumn squash, such as sugar pumpkin, calabaza, or butternut
- ¼ cup extra-virgin olive oil, plus more for drizzling
  Coarse salt and freshly ground pepper
- 2 small garlic cloves, minced
- ½ teaspoon crushed red pepper flakes
- 1 teaspoon finely chopped fresh thyme
- 1 teaspoon thinly sliced fresh sage
- 1 teaspoon finely chopped fresh rosemary
- 1 pound perciatelli or bucatini
- 3 tablespoons coarsely chopped fresh flat-leaf parsley, plus leaves for garnish
- ¾ cup fresh ricotta cheese
  Freshly grated Parmesan cheese

1. Preheat the oven to 400° F. If using pumpkin or calabaza, cut into wedges; if using butternut squash, cut in half. Remove seeds; reserve for another use. Drizzle with oil; season with salt and pepper. Place squash, cut side up, on a rimmed baking sheet lined with parchment paper. Bake 10 minutes. Flip squash; bake until very tender, 40 to 50 minutes more. Let cool slightly, about 10 minutes. Scoop flesh into a medium bowl; discard skins.

2. Heat 2 tablespoons oil in a medium skillet over medium heat. Add garlic, a large pinch of salt, red pepper flakes, and ¾ teaspoon each thyme, sage, and rosemary. Cook, stirring, until garlic is golden and fragrant, about 5 minutes. Add squash; cook, stirring and mashing with a spoon, until heated through.

3. Meanwhile, bring a large pot of water to a boil. Add a pinch of salt. Add pasta; cook until al dente. Drain well.

4. Heat remaining oil in a large skillet over medium heat. Add cooked pasta, parsley, and remaining thyme, sage, and rosemary. Season with salt. Toss to combine; cook until heated through.

5. Divide pasta evenly among serving bowls. Top with squash mixture and ricotta, dividing evenly. Garnish with parsley; drizzle with oil. Serve with Parmesan.

cold sesame noodles

 1 *package (10½ ounces) dried udon noodles*
 1 *baby bok choy*
 ¼ *cup smooth peanut butter*
 5 *tablespoons toasted sesame oil*
 3 *tablespoons soy sauce*
 ¼ *cup rice wine vinegar (not seasoned)*
 1 *large garlic clove, minced*
 2 *teaspoons sugar*
 ½ *teaspoon crushed red pepper flakes*
    Sesame seeds, for garnish

1. Bring a large pot of water to a boil; cook the noodles according to package directions. Drain; let cool completely.

2. Bring 3 cups water to a boil in a medium saucepan; boil the bok choy 30 seconds. Drain; rinse well. Let cool; coarsely chop.

3. Whisk together the peanut butter, oil, soy sauce, vinegar, garlic, sugar, and red pepper flakes. Put the sauce, noodles, and bok choy into a bowl; toss well. Sprinkle with seeds. Refrigerate in an airtight container until ready to serve, up to 2 days.

baked saffron rice

SERVES 8 TO 10

 3 *cups basmati rice*
5½ *cups water*
 1 *tablespoon coarse salt*
 4 *tablespoons extra-virgin olive oil*
 ¼ *teaspoon ground saffron, dissolved in 2 tablespoons hot water*

1. Rinse the rice well; drain in a colander. Place in a deep nonstick pot or rice cooker with water and salt. Bring to a boil over high heat; reduce to a simmer. Cook until all the liquid is absorbed, 15 to 20 minutes.

2. Drizzle the oil over the top of the rice; stir gently with a wooden spoon. Gently press the rice into an even layer. Reduce heat to medium-low. Place a clean dish towel over the top of the pot; cover firmly,

wrapping the sides of the towel around the top of the lid to prevent steam from escaping. Cook over medium-low heat for 50 to 60 minutes. Gently pull the rice away from the side of the pan with a spatula—there should be a nice golden crust.

3. Remove from heat, remove the lid, and drizzle saffron water over the rice. Cover immediately, and allow to cool 5 minutes.

4. Remove the lid; invert carefully onto a serving plate. Serve warm, cut in wedges.

jamaican rice and beans

SERVES 8

This island staple is also known as "Jamaican coat of arms." Some people add chiles to make it spicy, but we like it mild and slightly sweet to complement the heat of jerk chicken. For this dish, there's no need to soak the kidney beans before cooking.

 ¾ *cup dried red kidney beans, rinsed and drained*
 2 *large garlic cloves, crushed with the flat side of a large knife*
1¼ *cups unsweetened coconut milk*
2½ *cups long-grain rice*
 3 *scallions, finely chopped*
1½ *teaspoons finely chopped fresh thyme*
    Coarse salt and freshly ground pepper

1. Bring the beans, garlic, coconut milk, and 2 cups water to a boil in a medium saucepan. Reduce heat to low. Cover, and cook until the beans are tender but not mushy, 1 hour and 50 minutes to 2 hours.

2. Stir in 2½ cups water and the rice, scallions, thyme, and 1 tablespoon salt; season with pepper. Bring to a boil. Stir once, then reduce heat to low. Cook, covered, without stirring, until all the liquid has been absorbed, about 20 minutes. Let stand, covered, 15 minutes. Fluff the mixture with a fork, and season with salt and pepper.

yellow rice pilaf

SERVES 4

Coarse salt

1½ cups long-grain rice

2 tablespoons extra-virgin olive oil

1 onion, cut into ½-inch dice

1 carrot, cut into ¼-inch dice

1 cup frozen peas, thawed and drained

1 teaspoon ground turmeric

½ teaspoon ground cumin

¼ teaspoon ground paprika

Freshly ground pepper

1. Fill a medium saucepan with water, and bring to a boil; add salt and the rice. Cook until the rice is just tender, 15 to 20 minutes. Drain, and transfer the rice to a serving bowl.

2. Meanwhile, heat the oil in a large skillet over medium-high heat. Add the onion, and cook, stirring, until it begins to soften, about 4 minutes. Add the carrot; cook, stirring, until the vegetables are tender, about 5 minutes. Stir in the peas, turmeric, cumin, and paprika; cook until heated through. Transfer the mixture to the bowl with the rice, and stir to combine. Season with salt and pepper. Serve warm or at room temperature.

PERFECT RICE

Cooking rice on the stove is easy, as long as you keep these tips in mind: To trap the steam, leave the lid on as much as possible while cooking; let the rice sit afterward to absorb the water completely; and always fluff it with a fork just before serving.

It also helps to have a basic understanding about the different types of rice. Most rice is classified as either white or brown; the color is determined by the way that the grain is processed. White rice is stripped of its husk, bran, and germ. Brown rice has the bran and germ intact, and takes longer to cook. In general, the shorter the grain, the more starch it contains. Some types of rice, especially Asian varieties such as basmati and jasmine, benefit from rinsing to remove the excess starch and any impurities. American enriched rices, however, have been coated with vitamins, and rinsing will only serve to wash those away. If you do rinse the rice (either under running water or by submerging it in cold water and

then draining it), reduce the amount of water you cook with by ¼ cup.

Finally, although many recipes call for cooking 1 cup rice with 2 cups water, try reducing the water to 1½ cups; this ratio produces lighter, fluffier results.

To cook rice on the stove:

1. Bring the water to a boil in an uncovered pan over medium-high heat; add a pinch of salt and the rice, then stir once and return to a boil. As soon as it boils, reduce the heat to low; cover, and set the timer to 15 minutes for white rice and 30 for brown.

2. Leave the lid on throughout the cooking process; if you lift it, return it quickly. Toward the end of the cooking time, check the rice. You'll know it's done when there are craters in the surface that aren't full of water.

3. Let the rice sit before serving, covered but removed from heat, 5 to 10 minutes for white and 15 for brown. Fluff with a fork before serving.

If you cook rice often, you may want to invest in a rice cooker. These handy machines are nearly foolproof if you follow the manufacturer's instructions. (Note: If your machine was made in Asia, the instructions may assume the rice has been rinsed and therefore underestimate the amount of water needed; if you don't rinse, use the 1½ cups water to 1 cup rice ratio). Rice cookers will also hold cooked rice at the perfect temperature for hours. Here is the basic process:

1. Put the rice in the cooker and add a pinch of salt and the water; secure the top and press the start button. The machine will automatically adjust the cooking time for white or brown rice.

2. When the cooker stops, the rice is ready to eat; there is no need to let the rice sit before serving. When dishing out the rice, use a wooden or plastic spoon to avoid scratching the nonstick canister.

thai fried rice

SERVES 1

This recipe is a good way to use any leftover rice you might have; it can easily be doubled.

- 2 tablespoons peanut oil
- 4 to 8 garlic cloves, very finely chopped (more if not using optional ingredients)
- 1 to 2 ounces thinly sliced boneless pork (optional)
- 2 cups cold cooked rice (preferably Thai jasmine)
- 1 cup torn Asian greens (such as cabbage, bok choy, or mustard greens)
- 2 teaspoons Thai fish sauce, or to taste

for garnish and accompaniments
- ¼ cup fresh cilantro leaves
- 6 thin cucumber slices
- 1 small scallion, trimmed (optional)
- 2 lime wedges
- ¼ cup Thai Fish Sauce with Hot Chiles (recipe follows)

1. Heat a large, heavy wok over high heat. When it is hot, add the oil, and heat until very hot. Add the garlic, and stir-fry until just golden, about 20 seconds. Add the pork, if using, and cook, stirring constantly, until all the pork has changed color completely, about 1 minute.

2. Add the rice, breaking it up with wet fingers as you toss it into the wok. With a spatula, keep moving the rice around the wok. Keep scooping and tossing it. Occasionally press the rice against the wok with the back of a spatula, and soon it will become more manageable; good fried rice has a faint seared-in-the-wok taste. Cook for about 30 seconds. Add the greens, and then the fish sauce, and stir-fry for 30 seconds to 1 minute.

3. Turn out onto a dinner plate, and garnish with the coriander, cucumber slices, scallion, if using, and lime wedges. Squeeze the lime onto the rice as you eat it, along with the chile sauce. The salty, hot taste of the sauce brings out the full flavor of the rice.

thai fish sauce with hot chiles

MAKES ABOUT 1 CUP

- ½ cup Thai bird chiles, stems removed
- 1 cup Thai fish sauce

1. In the bowl of a food processor fitted with the metal blade, pulse the chiles to chop them finely (stop before they become mushy). Or, wearing rubber gloves to protect your hands, use a cleaver or a sharp knife to mince the chiles on a cutting board.

2. Transfer the minced chiles (with their seeds) to a glass or plastic container, and add the fish sauce. Cover, and store in refrigerator. The sauce will keep indefinitely, losing the chiles' heat over time; top with extra chiles or fish sauce. Serve in small individual condiment bowls.

green rice

SERVES 6 TO 8

- 2 tablespoons vegetable or olive oil
- 1 white onion, cut into ¼-inch dice
- 2 garlic cloves, minced
- 1½ cups long-grain rice
- 2½ cups homemade or low-sodium store-bought chicken or vegetable stock, or water
- ½ cup finely chopped fresh cilantro
- 1 poblano chile, seeded and finely chopped
  Coarse salt and freshly ground pepper

1. Heat the oil in a large saucepan over medium heat. Add the onion; cook until it is soft and translucent, about 8 minutes. Add the garlic; cook 2 minutes. Add the rice, and stir to coat. Add the stock, and bring to a boil; reduce heat to a simmer. Cover, and cook until the rice is tender, about 15 minutes.

2. Turn off heat; let stand, covered, until the liquid is absorbed, 5 to 10 minutes. Fluff with a fork; stir in the cilantro and poblano. Season with salt and pepper. Serve hot.

coconut almond rice

SERVES 6

We serve this creamy rice dish with grilled skewered shrimp and a spicy lime dipping sauce.

- *1 stalk fresh lemongrass, outer leaves peeled, 3-inch-long piece cut from root end and sliced in half lengthwise*
- *2 cups unsweetened coconut milk*
- *1 cup water*
- *2 to 4 fresh or frozen kaffir lime leaves*
- *2 teaspoons coarse salt*
- *1½ cups long-grain rice*
- *¼ cup slivered almonds, toasted*
- *½ cup lightly packed fresh cilantro leaves, coarsely chopped, plus several sprigs for garnish*
- *Freshly ground pepper*

1. In a medium saucepan, combine the lemongrass, 1¾ cups coconut milk and the water, kaffir lime leaves, and salt. Heat over medium-high heat until the milk just begins to simmer. Stir in the rice, and reduce heat to a simmer. Cover; cook until the rice is tender, 20 to 25 minutes.

2. Stir in the nuts, cilantro, and remaining ¼ cup coconut milk; season with pepper. Discard the lemongrass. Serve immediately, garnished with cilantro sprigs.

three-grain pilaf

SERVES 8

- *2 tablespoons unsalted butter*
- *1 small onion, finely chopped*
- *1½ cups jasmine rice, rinsed*
- *½ cup red rice, rinsed*
- *1 cup quinoa, rinsed*
- *¾ teaspoon coarse salt*

Melt butter in a medium saucepan over medium heat. Add onion; cook, stirring occasionally, until onion is soft and pale gold, 8 to 10 minutes. Stir in 4 cups water, the grains, and salt. Raise heat to high; bring to a boil. Reduce heat to low, and stir. Cover, and cook until grains are tender, 20 to 25 minutes. Remove from heat, and let stand, covered, 10 minutes. Fluff with a fork, and serve.

lemon risotto with asparagus and peas

SERVES 4 AS A MAIN COURSE
OR 6 AS AN APPETIZER

If you would prefer a simple lemon risotto, omit the asparagus and peas.

- *6 cups homemade or low-sodium store-bought chicken stock*
- *4 tablespoons unsalted butter*
- *1 small onion, finely chopped*
- *1 cup Arborio rice*
- *½ cup dry white wine*
- *6 thin asparagus spears, trimmed and cut into 1-inch lengths*
- *1 cup thawed frozen peas*
- *1 teaspoon finely grated lemon zest, plus 2 tablespoons fresh lemon juice*
- *1 cup chopped fresh flat-leaf parsley*
- *½ cup finely grated Parmigiano-Reggiano cheese, plus more for serving*
- *Coarse salt and freshly ground pepper*

1. Bring the stock to a boil in a medium saucepan; turn off heat.

2. Melt 2 tablespoons butter over medium heat in another medium saucepan. Add the onion; cook, stirring constantly, until translucent, 6 to 7 minutes. Add the rice; cook, stirring constantly, until the edges of the grains are translucent, 2 to 3 minutes. Raise heat to medium-high. Add the wine; cook, stirring constantly, until the wine has completely evaporated.

3. Add ½ cup stock; cook, stirring constantly, until the stock has been completely absorbed and a wooden spoon drawn through the rice leaves a trail in its wake. Continue adding about 4 more cups stock, ½ cup at a time, waiting for each addition to be absorbed before adding the next. (It should take about 13 minutes.)

4. Stir in the asparagus. Add ½ to 1 cup more stock, in same manner as described above. About 1 minute before the risotto is done, stir in the peas. The risotto is done when the liquid looks creamy and the grains are cooked but still slightly firm in centers. (The total cooking time will be 16 to 20 minutes.)

5. Remove from heat; stir in ½ cup stock. (You may have stock left over.) Stir in the zest, juice, remaining 2 tablespoons butter, parsley, and cheese. Season with salt and pepper. Serve with more cheese.

....

MAKING RISOTTO WITH BROWN RICE OR FARRO

The key here is presoaking the grains: Cover 1 cup brown rice or farro with cold water by 2 to 3 inches in a medium saucepan. Bring to a boil; boil 1 minute. Turn off heat; let stand 1 hour. Drain. Follow Lemon Risotto with Asparagus and Peas (page 241). Cooking time will be about 22 minutes, so add the asparagus after 18 minutes.

....

yellow pepper risotto with shrimp and zucchini

SERVES 8 TO 10 AS A MAIN DISH; 10 TO 12 AS A STARTER

This recipe was developed by Christopher Israel, formerly the chef and a co-owner at one of Bruce Carey's restaurants.

- 4 *yellow bell peppers*
- 6 *tablespoons olive oil*
- 2 *pounds medium shrimp, peeled and deveined, tails intact, shells rinsed and reserved*
- 1 *teaspoon coarse salt, plus more for seasoning*

   Freshly ground black pepper, for seasoning
- 10 *tablespoons unsalted butter*
- 2 *large zucchini, chopped into ¼-inch pieces*
- 3 *quarts homemade or low-sodium store-bought chicken stock*
- 6 *shallots, minced*
- 2 *cups Arborio or Carnaroli rice*
- 1 *cup dry white wine*
- ½ *cup loosely packed fresh basil, finely chopped, plus more for garnish (optional)*

1. Place the bell peppers directly on a gas-stove burner over high heat, turning with tongs as soon as each side is blistered and blackened. (Alternatively, roast the peppers under the broiler.) Transfer to a bowl; cover with plastic wrap. Let stand until cool enough to handle. Peel the peppers, discarding the skins; cut in half, and discard the seeds and ribs. Transfer the peppers to the bowl of a food processor fitted with the metal blade. Puree until smooth; set aside.

2. Heat 2 tablespoons oil in a large skillet over medium heat. In a large bowl, toss the shrimp with ¾ teaspoon salt, and season with black pepper. Arrange one-third of the shrimp in a single layer in skillet. Cook until they are opaque and cooked through, 3 to 4 minutes, turning once. Transfer to a plate; repeat with the remaining oil and shrimp, wiping out the skillet with paper towels between batches, as needed. Set aside, and cover loosely with foil to keep warm.

3. In the same skillet, melt 2 tablespoons butter over medium heat. Add the zucchini and remaining ¼ teaspoon salt, and season with pepper. Cook until the zucchini is just tender and bright green, 3 to 4 minutes. Remove from heat; set aside.

4. Place the stock in a large saucepan over medium heat. Add the shrimp shells, and bring to a boil. Remove from heat, and strain through a fine sieve, discarding the shells. Return the stock to the pan, and bring back to a boil; keep at a low simmer.

5. Meanwhile, melt 6 tablespoons butter in a large heavy-bottomed saucepan over medium heat. Add the shallots, and cook, stirring constantly, until they are soft and translucent, about 4 minutes. Add the rice; cook, stirring constantly, until the grains are glossy and make a sound like glass beads clicking, 3 to 4 minutes.

6. Add the wine to the rice mixture. Cook, stirring constantly, until the wine is completely absorbed by the rice.

7. Using a ladle, add about ¾ cup hot stock to the rice along with a few tablespoons reserved pepper puree. Stir constantly with a wooden spoon at moderate speed until the mixture is just thick enough to leave a clear wake behind the spoon; be careful not to stir too vigorously, or the mixture may become gluey.

8. Continue adding hot stock, ¾ cup at a time, along with some puree, stirring constantly, until the rice is mostly translucent but still opaque in the center, a total of 18 to 25 minutes. You may not need to use all of the stock and can add smaller amounts as you go along. The final mixture should be thick enough to suspend the rice in liquid that is the consistency of heavy cream.

9. Remove from heat, and stir in the reserved shrimp and zucchini, remaining 2 tablespoons butter, and the basil. Season with salt and black pepper, and garnish with basil, if desired. Serve immediately.

risotto with peas, marjoram, and asiago
SERVES 4

Perfect risotto is easy to make; the keys are to be sure the stock is fully incorporated after each addition and to avoid overcooking the rice. If you prefer, you may use Parmesan instead of Asiago cheese in this recipe.

- 6 to 8 cups homemade or low-sodium store-bought chicken stock
- 3 tablespoons extra-virgin olive oil
- 2 shallots, minced
- 1 cup Arborio or Carnaroli rice
- ½ cup dry white wine
- 1½ pounds garden peas, shelled (1½ cups)
- 3 tablespoons unsalted butter
- 1 cup grated Asiago cheese (about 4 ounces)
- 1 tablespoon coarsely chopped fresh marjoram leaves, plus several sprigs for garnish

  Coarse salt and freshly ground pepper

1. Bring the stock to a boil in a medium saucepan over medium heat; reduce heat, and keep at a low simmer.

2. Meanwhile, heat the oil in a large, heavy-bottomed saucepan over medium heat. Add the shallots, and cook, stirring frequently, until they are softened and translucent, about 4 minutes. Add the rice; cook, stirring frequently, until it is thoroughly coated and slightly fragrant, 3 to 4 minutes. Add the wine, and cook, stirring constantly, until it is completely absorbed.

3. Using a ladle, add ¾ cup hot stock to the rice mixture; stir constantly with a wooden spoon until it is thick enough to leave a clear wake.

4. Continue adding stock, ¾ cup at time, stirring constantly after each addition, until the rice is mostly translucent but still opaque in the center and the liquid is the consistency of heavy cream, a total of 18 to 20 minutes; the mixture will continue to thicken slightly when removed from heat. About 12 minutes into cooking, stir in the peas. Watch carefully, adding smaller amounts of liquid if necessary to make sure it does not overcook. The rice should be al dente but no longer crunchy, and the peas tender and bright green.

5. Remove from heat. Stir in the butter, cheese, and chopped marjoram; season with salt and pepper. Serve garnished with marjoram sprigs.

arugula risotto

SERVES 12

Because this recipe makes a large quantity of risotto, be sure to use a wide, shallow saucepan or skillet to let the rice cook evenly.

    3   to 3½ quarts (12 to 14 cups) homemade
        or low-sodium canned (6 14½-ounce cans)
        chicken stock
    ¼   cup extra-virgin olive oil
    8   shallots, minced
    3   cups Arborio or Carnaroli rice
  1½   cups dry white wine
    ½   cup (1 stick) unsalted butter
  1½   cups freshly grated Parmigiano-Reggiano
        cheese, plus more for serving
    ¼   cup plus 2 tablespoons Arugula Puree
        (recipe follows)
        Coarse salt and freshly ground pepper
        Arugula flowers, for garnish (optional)

1. Bring the chicken stock to a simmer in a large stockpot over medium heat; cover, and keep at a steady simmer until ready to use. At the same time, heat the oil in a large, heavy-bottomed saucepan over medium heat. Add the shallots to the oil; cook, stirring occasionally, until the shallots are softened and translucent, about 10 minutes. Add the rice, and cook, stirring constantly, until the rice is thoroughly coated and makes a clicking noise, 3 to 4 minutes. Add the wine; cook, stirring constantly, until the wine is completely absorbed.

2. Using a ladle, add about 1½ cups hot stock to the rice; cook, stirring constantly with a wooden spoon, until most of the liquid has been absorbed and the mixture is just thick enough to leave a clear trail behind the spoon. Add another ¾ cup hot stock to rice; cook, stirring constantly, until most of liquid is absorbed.

3. Continue adding stock, ¾ cup at a time, stirring constantly after each addition, until the rice is mostly translucent but still opaque in the center, and the liquid is the consistency of heavy cream, 20 to 25 minutes. The rice should be al dente but no longer crunchy. Watch carefully, and gradually reduce the amount of added liquid to make sure the mixture does not overcook; it will continue to thicken after it is removed from heat.

4. Remove from heat. Stir in the butter, cheese, and arugula puree; season with salt and pepper. To serve, mound risotto in the center of shallow serving bowls, and sprinkle with additional cheese. Garnish with arugula flowers, if desired.

arugula puree

MAKES ½ CUP

This verdant puree can be tossed with pasta or drizzled over boiled potatoes just like pesto. It can be stored in an airtight container for up to 5 days in the refrigerator.

  2¾   teaspoons coarse salt
    1   bunch arugula (about 3½ ounces),
        stems removed
    ⅓   cup extra-virgin olive oil
    ⅛   teaspoon freshly ground pepper

1. Prepare an ice-water bath; set aside. Bring a medium saucepan of water to a boil, and add 2½ teaspoons salt and the arugula. As soon as the water returns to a boil, remove from heat. Using a slotted spoon, transfer the arugula to the ice bath to stop the cooking. Working in batches, remove the arugula from the ice bath and place on paper towels to drain, squeezing out as much excess water as possible.

2. Transfer the arugula to the jar of a blender. Add the oil, remaining ¼ teaspoon salt, and the pepper; puree until smooth and thickened with a small amount of unincorporated oil on the surface. Before using, stir gently to combine.

farro salad with thinly sliced zucchini, pine nuts, and lemon zest

SERVES 8 TO 10

Farro is a type of hulled wheat that has been cultivated in Italy for centuries. Look for it at gourmet shops and health-food stores, where it is also sold as spelt. Other grains, such as barley or bulgur wheat, can also be used; cook them according to package instructions.

- ¾ pound farro
- Coarse salt
- 1 small shallot, minced
- Grated zest and juice of 1½ lemons
- 3 tablespoons extra-virgin olive oil
- ½ cup pine nuts
- 1 pound zucchini, ends trimmed
- ½ cup loosely packed fresh flat-leaf parsley leaves, roughly chopped
- Freshly ground pepper
- 4 ounces Parmigiano-Reggiano cheese

1. Place the farro in a large saucepan, and add enough cold water to cover by about 3 inches. Bring to a boil over high heat; add salt, and stir once. Reduce heat to medium, and simmer until the farro is al dente, according to package instructions, 10 to 12 minutes. Drain, and let cool.

2. In a small bowl, combine the shallot with the lemon juice and salt; let stand 15 minutes. Meanwhile, in a small sauté pan, heat the oil over medium heat, and add the pine nuts. Cook, stirring, until they are lightly toasted, about 5 minutes. Remove from heat, and add the lemon zest.

3. Using a mandoline or sharp knife, slice the zucchini crosswise as thinly as possible; place in a large bowl. Add the farro, pine nut mixture, and parsley; stir to combine. Stir in shallot mixture; season with salt and pepper. Transfer to a large serving bowl.

4. Using a vegetable peeler, shave half the cheese over the salad; toss to combine. The salad can be stored up 6 hours in refrigerator, covered with plastic wrap. Just before serving, shave the remaining cheese on top.

crimson couscous

SERVES 2

To make this recipe in advance, dice the beet and prepare as directed in step 1, and refrigerate it in the liquid, covered, up to 1 day.

- ½ cup peeled, diced (¼ inch) beet (about 1 medium beet)
- ½ teaspoon coarse salt, plus more for seasoning
- ½ tablespoon unsalted butter
- ⅛ teaspoon ground coriander
- ⅛ teaspoon ground cumin
- ½ cup couscous
- ¼ cup dried apricots, cut into ¼-inch dice
- 2 tablespoons dried currants
- 1 teaspoon finely grated orange zest
- 2 tablespoons fresh orange juice
- Freshly ground pepper

1. Bring ¾ cup water, the diced beet, and the salt to a boil in a medium saucepan. Reduce heat; simmer the beet, covered, until tender, about 15 minutes. Reserve ½ cup cooking liquid; drain the beet. (If you have less than ½ cup liquid, add water to fill.)

2. Return the beet and liquid to the pan. Add the butter, coriander, and cumin; bring to a boil. Stir in the couscous; cover, and remove from heat. Let stand until liquid is absorbed, about 5 minutes.

3. Fluff the couscous with a fork. Stir in the apricots, currants, zest, and orange juice. Season with salt and pepper.

barley pilaf with pearl onions

SERVES 8

You can substitute frozen pearl onions for fresh, if you like, and skip step 1.

- 10 ounces white pearl onions (about 2 cups)
- 1 tablespoon chicken fat, margarine, or unsalted butter
- 2 cups pearl barley
- 1 quart homemade or low-sodium store-bought chicken stock, plus more if needed
  Coarse salt and freshly ground pepper

1. Bring a large saucepan of water to a boil. Add the onions, and blanch until the skins loosen, about 1 minute. Drain the onions in a colander, and rinse with cold water. Peel the onions, and set aside.

2. Heat the fat in a large saucepan over medium-low heat until hot but not smoking. Add the barley; cook, stirring frequently, until the barley is browned and fragrant, about 15 to 20 minutes.

3. Add the stock and reserved onions. Bring to a boil, then reduce to a simmer. Season with salt and pepper. Cover, and cook the barley until it is tender but chewy and all the liquid has been absorbed, about 40 minutes; if all the liquid is absorbed and the barley is still not done, add a few tablespoons stock or water, and continue cooking. Serve hot.

mixed-grain pilaf

SERVES 12

- 3 tablespoons extra-virgin olive oil
- 2 tablespoons unsalted butter
- 1 large onion, finely chopped (1½ cups)
- 2 garlic cloves, minced
- 4 cups thinly sliced white mushrooms (about ¾ pound)
- ¾ cup thinly sliced cremini mushrooms (about 2 ounces)
- 2 cups pearl barley
- 1 cup hard wheat berries
- 1 cup wild rice
- ½ cup millet
- 7 cups homemade or low-sodium store-bought chicken stock
  Coarse salt and freshly ground pepper

1. Preheat oven to 350° F. Heat oil and butter in a large ovenproof Dutch oven over medium heat. Add onion and garlic; cook, stirring occasionally, until softened, 6 to 8 minutes. Add mushrooms. Raise heat to medium-high, and cook, stirring occasionally, until mushrooms are softened, about 5 minutes. Stir in all of the grains. Cook, stirring often, 12 minutes. Stir in stock; bring to a boil.

2. Cover, and transfer to oven. Bake until grains are tender, 40 to 50 minutes (check after 40 minutes, but don't remove lid before then). Season with salt and pepper. Serve immediately.

toasted couscous tabbouleh

SERVES 4

Toasting couscous in the pan before adding water imparts a nuttiness that complements the distinctive flavors of mint and parsley.

- 1 medium red onion, peeled and cut into ¼-inch dice
- 2 cups water, plus more for soaking
  Nonstick cooking spray
- 8 ounces Israeli couscous
- 1½ teaspoons coarse salt
- ¼ cup roughly chopped fresh flat-leaf parsley
- ¼ cup roughly chopped fresh mint leaves
- 2 teaspoons extra-virgin olive oil
- 2 teaspoons fresh lemon juice
  Lemon wedges, for garnish

1. Place the red onion in a small bowl, and cover with water. Let soak 30 minutes; transfer to paper towels, and drain.

2. Lightly coat a medium saucepan with cooking spray, and place over medium heat. Add the couscous; cook, stirring constantly, 1 minute. Add the water, and bring to a boil. Add 1 teaspoon salt; cook until all the water has been absorbed and the couscous is al dente, about 8 minutes. Remove from heat; let cool completely.

3. In a large bowl, combine the couscous, reserved red onion, parsley, mint, oil, and lemon juice; toss to combine. Season with remaining ½ teaspoon salt. Serve, garnished with lemon wedges.

FIT TO EAT RECIPE PER SERVING: 253 CALORIES, 3 G FAT, 0 MG CHOLESTEROL, 48 G CARBOHYDRATE, 718 MG SODIUM, 8 G PROTEIN, 4 G FIBER

wheatberries with vegetables

SERVES 8 TO 10 AS A SIDE DISH

This is an excellent accompaniment to meat or fish; it can also be served as an entrée.

- 1 cup wheatberries
- 1 quart water
- 1 small head broccoli (about 15 ounces), trimmed and cut into florets
- 2 teaspoons olive oil
- 1 medium yellow onion, peeled and diced
- 2 garlic cloves, peeled and minced
- 1 28-ounce can tomatoes, chopped
- ¼ cup chopped fresh oregano
- 1 large yellow zucchini, quartered lengthwise and cut into ¼-inch slices
- ½ small eggplant, cut into ½-inch pieces
- ½ teaspoon coarse salt
- ¼ teaspoon freshly ground pepper

1. Place the wheatberries in a small stockpot over high heat. Add the water. Cover; bring to a boil. Reduce heat to low. Simmer until tender, at least 40 minutes. Drain; set aside.

2. Fill a large bowl with ice and water; set aside. Bring a medium pot of water to a boil. Add the broccoli, and blanch until bright green, 1 to 2 minutes. Drain, and transfer to the ice bath, and set aside.

3. Heat the olive oil in a large skillet over medium-low heat. Add the onion and garlic, and cook, stirring frequently, until translucent, about 10 minutes. Raise heat to medium, and add the tomatoes, oregano, zucchini, eggplant, salt, and pepper; cook, stirring occasionally, until the vegetables have softened, about 15 minutes. Add the broccoli and wheatberries, and continue to cook until the broccoli and wheatberries are heated through, about 3 minutes more. Serve.

FIT TO EAT RECIPE PER SERVING: 64 CALORIES, 2 G FAT, 0 MG CHOLESTEROL, 39 G CARBOHYDRATE, 260 MG SODIUM, 8 G PROTEIN, 9 G FIBER

meat

....

BEEF

daube de boeuf provençal

SERVES 6

You can make this stew 1 day ahead to allow its flavors to mellow and mingle.

    4   sprigs fresh thyme
    1   dried bay leaf
    3   whole cloves
    1   teaspoon whole black peppercorns
    3   strips orange zest (2 to 3 inches each),
        plus 2 tablespoons fresh orange juice
    1   medium onion, coarsely chopped
        (about 1 cup)
    2   garlic cloves, crushed with the flat side
        of a large knife
    1   celery stalk, cut crosswise into ½-inch
        pieces (about ½ cup)
    3   medium carrots, cut crosswise into 1-inch
        pieces (about 1¼ cups)
    1   bottle (750 ml) rich red wine, such as
        Côtes de Provence, Côtes du Rhône,
        Syrah, or Shiraz
    4   pounds beef chuck roast, cut into
        1½-inch cubes
    ¼   cup extra-virgin olive oil
    1   tablespoon tomato paste
    ½   cup homemade or low-sodium store-
        bought beef or chicken stock
    ½   cup Niçoise olives, pitted and rinsed
        Coarse salt

1. Make a bouquet garni: Put the thyme, bay leaf, cloves, peppercorns, and zest on a piece of cheese-cloth; tie into a bundle. Combine the onion, garlic, celery, carrots, bouquet garni, and wine in a large nonreactive bowl. Add the beef, and toss to coat. Cover, and marinate in the refrigerator 12 to 24 hours, stirring occasionally.

2. Preheat the oven to 300°F. Remove the beef from the wine mixture; pat dry with paper towels. Set aside. Transfer the wine mixture to a heavy pot, and bring to a boil. Reduce heat, and simmer 5 minutes. Set aside.

3. Heat 2 tablespoons oil in a large skillet over medium-high heat. Cook half of the beef, turning, until deeply browned, about 2 minutes per side. Transfer to a plate. Repeat with the remaining oil and beef.

4. Stir the tomato paste into the stock; add to the skillet, scraping up browned bits with a wooden spoon. Add to the wine mixture. Stir in the olives and beef. Season with salt. Bring to a simmer over medium-high heat.

5. Cover the daube; transfer to the oven. Cook 2 hours. Reduce oven temperature to 275°F if the daube starts to boil. After 2 hours, stir in the orange juice. Cook until the beef is very tender, about 30 minutes more.

grilled rib chops with mojo sauce

SERVES 6

Serve this dish with a platter of mixed garden tomatoes drizzled with olive oil and sprinkled with coarse salt.

    1¼ teaspoons whole cumin seeds
    ¼   cup minced garlic (about 6 cloves)
    1   fresh serrano chile, seeded and minced
        (about 1 tablespoon plus 1 teaspoon)
        Coarse salt
    ½   cup olive oil
    3   tablespoons fresh orange juice, plus
        2 tablespoons finely grated orange zest
        (about 2 oranges)
    3   tablespoons fresh lime juice (2 to 3 limes)
    2   tablespoons fresh lemon juice
    ¾   cup chopped fresh flat-leaf parsley
        Freshly ground pepper
    6   beef rib chop steaks (each about
        12 ounces and 1 inch thick)

1. Make the mojo sauce: Toast the cumin seeds in a dry small skillet over high heat, swirling the pan occasionally, until fragrant, about 1 minute. Grind the cumin seeds, garlic, chile, and 1½ teaspoons salt with a mortar and pestle until the mixture forms a coarse paste. Transfer to a small bowl.

2. Heat the oil in a small saucepan over medium heat. Pour over the chile mixture. Let cool completely. Stir in the juices, orange zest, and parsley; season with pepper. The sauce can be refrigerated, covered, until ready to use, up to 2 days (bring to room temperature before serving).

3. Heat the grill to medium (if using a charcoal grill, the coals are ready when you can hold your hand 5 inches above grill for 5 to 6 seconds). Season the rib chops with salt and pepper. Grill, turning once, until cooked to desired doneness, 3 to 5 minutes per side for medium-rare. Serve with the mojo sauce.

brisket with dried fruits

SERVES 10

- 3 tablespoons extra-virgin olive oil
- 5 pounds beef brisket
    Coarse salt and freshly ground pepper
- 4 medium onions, halved and thinly sliced
- 4 garlic cloves, thinly sliced
- 1 can (28 ounces) whole peeled plum tomatoes, coarsely chopped, with juice
- 2¾ cups homemade or low-sodium store-bought beef stock
- ⅓ cup cider vinegar
- 1 bag (14½ ounces) prepared sauerkraut, drained
- 1 cup pitted prunes
- 1 cup dried Black Mission figs
- 1 cup dried apricots
- 1 cup pitted dates

1. Preheat the oven to 400°F. Heat the oil in a large roasting pan over high heat. Season the beef with salt and pepper. Brown the beef in the pan all over, about 4 minutes per side. Transfer to a platter. Add the onions and garlic to the pan; reduce heat to medium. Cook, stirring, until the onions just turn golden, about 5 minutes. Add the tomatoes and juice, the stock, and the vinegar; bring to a boil.

2. Return the meat to the pan; cover with foil. Cook in the oven until fork tender, about 1½ hours. Turn the meat; add the sauerkraut and dried fruits. Cover; cook until the meat is very tender and the sauce is reduced, about 1½ hours. Let stand 30 minutes. Slice the meat against the grain. Serve with sauce.

roast beef with horseradish sauce

SERVES 4

After the beef finishes cooking, let it stand at room temperature for at least 10 minutes before carving. Keep in mind it will continue to cook after it has been removed from the oven.

- 1 top or bottom round beef roast (about 2 pounds), tied
    Coarse salt and freshly ground pepper
- 2 tablespoons vegetable oil
- 6 small onions, halved lengthwise
- 1 cup sour cream
- ¼ cup grated peeled fresh horseradish (or prepared horseradish)
- 1 tablespoon fresh lemon juice

1. Preheat the oven to 375°F. Sprinkle the beef with ½ teaspoon salt, and season with pepper. Heat the oil in a large ovenproof sauté pan over high heat until hot but not smoking. Add the beef; brown on all sides, about 5 minutes total. Remove the pan from heat.

2. Place the onion halves in the pan, cut sides down. Transfer the pan to the oven. Cook the beef and onions until an instant-read thermometer inserted into the center of the beef registers 140°F (for medium-rare), 35 to 40 minutes. Transfer the beef to a wire rack set over a rimmed baking sheet, and let stand 10 minutes before carving. Reserve the onions.

3. Stir together the sour cream, horseradish, lemon juice, ¼ teaspoon salt, and pepper to taste in a small bowl. Serve the beef with the horseradish sauce and roasted onions.

knockwurst with braised cabbage and apples

SERVES 6

4 tablespoons unsalted butter

2 medium onions, thinly sliced

3 pounds green cabbage (about 1 head), cored and thinly sliced

1 large, tart green apple, such as Granny Smith, peeled, cored, and chopped

1 cup apple cider

⅓ cup cider vinegar

2 tablespoons packed light-brown sugar

1 tablespoon coarse salt

1 teaspoon freshly ground pepper

9 knockwurst (about 2 pounds)

Whole-grain mustard, for serving

1. Melt the butter in a large, heavy-bottomed pot over medium-low heat. Add the onions; cook, stirring occasionally, until very soft and golden brown, about 18 minutes.

2. Stir in the cabbage, apple, cider, vinegar, sugar, salt, and pepper. Cover; cook, stirring occasionally, until the cabbage is very soft, about 1 hour.

3. Tuck the sausages into the cabbage; cover the pot. Cook until heated through, about 20 minutes. Serve with mustard.

seared sirloin steak with olive relish

SERVES 4

1 tablespoon honey

3 tablespoons sherry vinegar

Coarse salt and freshly ground pepper

¼ cup olive oil, preferably Spanish, plus more for the skillet

½ red onion, finely chopped (about ½ cup)

1 tablespoon minced garlic (2 medium cloves)

⅓ cup brine-cured pitted green olives, such as Picholine, cut into ¼-inch-thick rounds

1 navel orange, peel and pith cut off, flesh cut into ½-inch cubes

¼ cup coarsely chopped fresh flat-leaf parsley, plus sprigs for garnish

1 boneless sirloin steak (1½ pounds and 1 inch thick)

MEAT TEMPERATURES

Meat temperature guidelines recommended by the USDA are designed to protect consumers from the pathogens that cause food-borne diseases. Because these pathogens can cause serious health complications (or even worse in very rare cases), it is necessary to adhere to them strictly when preparing food for children, pregnant women, the elderly, and people with weakened immune systems. When cooking meat for healthy adults, however, many chefs feel comfortable diverging from the USDA guidelines, cooking most cuts—except ground meat—between 5 and 20 degrees lower, which should produce juicier, more flavorful results. Poultry is an exception to the rule of lowering temperatures; the USDA's recently revised recommendation for cooking poultry at 165 degrees is also endorsed by most professional chefs. Ground meat must also be cooked through, to the USDA's guidelines.

To ensure accurate temperatures, you will need to calibrate your thermometer often. To do this, stand the device in ice water or boiling water; if it does not read 32 or 212 degrees, respectively, adjust it. If it cannot be calibrated properly, make sure to note the difference when you cook. Always insert the thermometer into the densest portion of the meat, avoiding bones, as they are hotter than the rest of the cut and may yield a false reading. For whole poultry, turn the bird so its neck cavity faces you, and insert the thermometer through the thigh, near the socket. For all types of meat, remember to allow for resting time. After it's out of the oven, the internal temperature of meat will continue to rise as much as 5 to 10 degrees, depending on the size of the cut. Finally, remember to let meat stand at room temperature before serving or carving; this allows all of the juices, which concentrate in the center during cooking, to redistribute. Smaller cuts should rest for 5 minutes; medium 15 to 20, and large cuts, 30 minutes.

1. Whisk together the honey and vinegar in a medium bowl; season with salt and pepper. Whisking constantly, pour in the oil in a slow, steady stream; whisk until emulsified. Stir in the onion, garlic, olives, orange, and parsley; set aside.

2. Season the steak all over with 1 teaspoon salt and ½ teaspoon pepper. Coat a 12-inch seasoned cast-iron skillet with a thin layer of oil; heat over medium-high heat until very hot. Sear the steak, turning once, 6 to 8 minutes per side for medium-rare. Transfer to a plate, and tent with foil; let stand 10 minutes before slicing.

3. To serve, cut the steak against the grain into ¼-inch-thick slices, and arrange on a platter. Spoon the relish on top; garnish with parsley sprigs.

sauerbraten

SERVES 10 TO 12

You can refrigerate the sauerbraten, covered, for up to 2 days. (In fact, the flavors develop nicely when the dish is made ahead of time.)

- 1 bottom round of beef (4 to 5 pounds)
  Coarse salt and freshly ground pepper
- 4 tablespoons vegetable oil
- 4 garlic cloves, coarsely chopped
- 2 large onions, cut into thin slices
- 2 dried bay leaves
- ¼ cup tomato paste
- ¼ cup ketchup
- 1 cup red-wine vinegar
- 2 cups dry red wine, such as Burgundy
- ¼ cup sour cream

1. Season the beef with salt and pepper. Tie kitchen twine around the beef at 2-inch intervals and once from end to end. Heat 2 tablespoons oil in a large (8-quart), heavy-bottomed pot over medium heat until hot but not smoking. Brown the meat all over, including the ends, about 3 minutes per side; transfer to a plate. Keep the pot on the stove, and reduce heat to medium-low.

2. Add the remaining 2 tablespoons oil and the garlic and onions to the pot. Cook, stirring often, until the onions are softened, 5 to 7 minutes. Add the bay leaves, tomato paste, ketchup, vinegar, and wine. Raise the heat to medium-high; bring the mixture to a boil.

3. Return the beef to the pot; add 2 cups water. Cover the pot with a tight-fitting lid. Reduce heat to medium-low; simmer 2 hours. Turn the beef; continue to simmer until tender, 1½ to 2 hours more. Let cool slightly.

4. Transfer the beef to a cutting board. Remove the twine; let the beef stand 15 minutes. Skim the fat from the sauce. Bring the sauce to a simmer over medium heat; cook until the liquid is reduced by one-quarter, about 7 minutes. Season with salt and pepper. Remove from heat; whisk in the sour cream.

5. Cut the beef across the grain into ¼-inch-thick slices. Return the slices to the pot to immerse in sauce, then transfer to a large serving platter. Ladle more sauce on top.

grilled marinated
strip steak with scallions

SERVES 4

- 4 boneless strip steaks (about 10 ounces each)
- 1 bunch scallions
- ¼ cup Worcestershire sauce
- ¼ cup soy sauce
- 1 teaspoon dry mustard
- 1 teaspoon freshly ground pepper
- ½ teaspoon ground cumin
  Grated zest of 1 lemon
  Coarse salt

1. Place the steaks in a large, shallow nonreactive dish. Slice 3 scallions into thin rounds, and combine with the remaining ingredients except the salt in a small bowl; whisk to combine. Pour the marinade over the steaks; cover with plastic wrap, and set aside at room temperature 40 minutes, turning the steaks once.

2. Heat a grill or grill pan. Remove the steaks from the marinade, letting the excess drip off, and pat dry with paper towels. Season both sides generously with salt. Grill until they are well browned on the outside and cooked to desired doneness, or about 6 minutes on each side, for medium-rare. Transfer to a large serving platter; cover with foil, and let rest 10 minutes. Grill the remaining scallions, about 1 minute on each side, and serve with the steaks.

korean barbecued ribs with pickled greens

SERVES 4 TO 6

Both the ribs and the greens need to marinate overnight, so plan accordingly.

2½ pounds flanken-style short ribs, cut ½ inch thick

for the marinade

- 4 garlic cloves, minced
- 3 scallions, white and pale-green parts only, very finely chopped
- ¼ cup packed dark-brown sugar
- 2 tablespoons granulated sugar
   Pinch of coarse salt
- ¼ cup fresh lime juice (2 to 3 limes)
- ½ cup soy sauce
- ⅓ cup mirin
- 2 tablespoons toasted sesame oil
- 3 tablespoons sesame seeds, toasted
- 1 teaspoon Asian chili sauce or ½ teaspoon crushed red pepper flakes (optional)

for the pickled greens

- 1 pound Taiwan bok choy or napa cabbage, cut into ½-inch strips (8 cups)
- 1 bunch scallions, white and pale-green parts only, cut into ½-inch pieces
- 3 garlic cloves, halved lengthwise
- 2 small dried hot red chiles or a pinch of crushed red pepper flakes (optional)
- 2 teaspoons toasted sesame oil

- 1 piece peeled fresh ginger (about 1 inch), cut into thin matchsticks
- ¼ cup rice-wine vinegar (not seasoned)
- ¼ cup mirin
- 1 teaspoon coarse salt
   Vegetable oil, for brushing

1. Cut each short rib crosswise into 3 pieces, cutting between the bones. Soak the ribs in a large bowl of ice-water for at least 20 minutes, or up to 2 hours.

2. Make the marinade: Stir together the marinade ingredients in a medium bowl until the sugar is dissolved. Drain the ribs; pat dry. Put the ribs and marinade in a 9 × 13-inch glass baking dish; turn each rib to coat. Cover, and refrigerate overnight.

3. Make the pickled greens: Put the greens and scallions in a medium bowl, and set aside. Cook the garlic and chiles in the sesame oil in a small saucepan over medium heat until the garlic is pale golden, 2 to 3 minutes. Add the ginger, and cook, stirring, until fragrant, about 2 minutes.

4. Remove from heat; stir in the vinegar, mirin, and salt. Immediately pour the contents of the pan over the greens, and toss to coat. Let cool to room temperature. Cover with plastic wrap; refrigerate overnight.

5. Preheat the broiler, with the rack about 6 inches from the heat source. Line a rimmed baking sheet with foil, and very lightly brush with vegetable oil. Lift the ribs from the marinade, and arrange in a single layer on sheet (discard marinade).

6. Broil the ribs (checking often) until well browned on top, about 5 minutes. Turn; continue to cook until well browned on other side, about 4 minutes more. Serve with chilled pickled greens.

beef paillards
with arugula and capers

SERVES 6

2¼ pounds beef tenderloin, cut
      into 12 3-ounce steaks
      Basic Marinade (page 647)
1   small red onion, cut in paper-thin rounds
3   tablespoons red-wine vinegar
      Coarse salt
6   ounces baby arugula or chopped arugula
2   ribs celery, very thinly sliced on the bias
1   tablespoon fresh lemon juice
1   tablespoon extra-virgin olive oil
      Freshly ground pepper
¼   cup capers, drained

1. Cut open two sides of a resealable plastic bag. Place 1 steak in the bag; pound to ¼-inch thickness with a meat pounder. Transfer to a nonmetal container. Repeat with the remaining steaks. Add the marinade. Chill 2 hours.

2. Place the onion in a bowl with the red-wine vinegar and salt to taste; toss to combine.

3. Heat a grill or grill pan. Place the arugula, celery, lemon juice, and olive oil in a medium bowl; toss to combine. Season with salt and pepper. Remove the meat from the marinade; season with salt and pepper. Grill for 1 minute on each side, until browned. To serve, place 2 pieces of beef on each plate; sprinkle with capers. Top with arugula salad and pickled onions, dividing evenly.

filet mignon with
herb-and-cheese potatoes

SERVES 2

3   tablespoons unsalted butter, softened
3   tablespoons chopped fresh cilantro
⅓   teaspoon minced garlic
⅓   cup finely grated cotija cheese
⅛   teaspoon cayenne pepper (or to taste)
1   tablespoon extra-virgin olive oil
2   russet potatoes (about 9 ounces each),
      peeled and cut lengthwise into ⅛-inch-
      thick slices and again into ⅛-inch-wide
      strips, set aside in a bowl of cold water
2   pieces filet mignon (7 ounces and 1½
      inches thick each), room temperature
      Coarse salt and freshly ground pepper
1   teaspoon vegetable oil

1. Preheat the oven to 375° F. Stir together butter, 1 tablespoon cilantro, and ½ teaspoon garlic in a small bowl. Cover; refrigerate until ready to use. Stir together remaining 2 tablespoons cilantro and ½ teaspoon garlic, the cheese, and cayenne in a medium bowl; set aside.

2. Brush a rimmed baking sheet with the olive oil; set aside. Drain potatoes; pat dry. Add to bowl with cheese mixture; toss to coat. Arrange potatoes in a single layer on prepared baking sheet. Bake 20 minutes; turn potatoes, and cook until golden, about 20 minutes more.

3. Meanwhile, season both sides of beef with salt and pepper. Heat a medium skillet over high heat. Brush both sides of beef with vegetable oil; place in skillet. Reduce heat to medium-high. Cook beef 7 minutes; turn, and cook until medium-rare, 7 to 8 minutes more. Top each with cilantro butter; serve with potatoes.

hanger steak with shallots

SERVES 4

½ cup extra-virgin olive oil

¼ cup sherry vinegar

2 garlic cloves, crushed

4 teaspoons Dijon mustard, plus more
for serving

1 tablespoon Worcestershire sauce

1½ pounds hanger steak

5 medium shallots, halved or quartered
Coarse salt and freshly ground pepper

1. Whisk together ¼ cup oil, the vinegar, garlic, mustard, and Worcestershire sauce in a large glass dish. Place steak in dish; turn to coat with marinade. Let steak marinate, turning once, 20 minutes.

2. Heat 2 tablespoons oil in a large skillet over medium-high heat. Add shallots; cook, stirring often, until just golden, 2 to 3 minutes. Reduce heat to medium-low. Season with salt. Cook, adding ¼ cup water in batches as needed to keep shallots from sticking, until tender and caramelized, 15 to 18 minutes. Transfer shallots to a plate.

3. Wipe out skillet. Heat 2 tablespoons oil over medium-high heat. Remove steak from marinade; pat dry. Season with salt and pepper. Cook steak, turning once, until an instant-read thermometer registers 140°F (for medium-rare), 10 to 12 minutes per side. Tent with foil; let stand at room temperature 10 minutes. Season with pepper.

4. Meanwhile, wipe out skillet; reheat shallots over medium heat. Thinly slice steak. Serve with shallots and mustard.

porterhouse with jalapeño butter

SERVES 2

Filet mignon can be prepared this way as well: Sear two 8-ounce steaks over direct heat for 3 minutes per side; grill over indirect heat until medium-rare, 5 to 6 minutes more per side.

½ cup (1 stick) unsalted butter, softened

1 fresh jalapeño pepper, seeded and
finely chopped

1 garlic clove, minced

1 porterhouse steak (2½ pounds, 1½ inches
thick), room temperature
Coarse salt and freshly ground pepper

1. Preheat a grill to medium-high (if you are using a charcoal grill, coals are ready when you can hold your hand 5 inches above grill for just 3 to 4 seconds). Stir butter, jalapeño, and garlic in a bowl; set aside.

2. Season both sides of steak with salt and pepper. Grill over hotter part of grill, covered, flipping once, until browned, 3 to 4 minutes per side. Slide to cooler part of grill; grill, covered, flipping once, until medium-rare, 7 to 8 minutes more per side. Remove from grill, and let rest 10 minutes. Serve with jalapeño butter.

grilled knockwurst

SERVES 4 TO 6

Grilled knockwurst goes well with yellow or Dijon mustard and soft pretzels. The knockwurst will char quickly on the grill; be sure to turn it frequently.

6 knockwurst
Mushrooms and Garlic Grilled in
a Packet (recipe follows), for serving

Preheat a grill to medium (if you are using a charcoal grill, coals are ready when you can hold your hand 5 inches above grill for just 5 to 6 seconds). Grill knockwurst, turning frequently, until marked by grill and heated through, about 5 minutes. Cut each knockwurst on the diagonal into ½-inch slices. Serve with grilled mushrooms and garlic.

mushrooms and garlic grilled in a packet

SERVES 4 TO 6

Serve this packet hot off the grill, but be cautious when opening it.

- 12 ounces cremini mushrooms, halved if large
- 6 garlic cloves, peeled
- ¼ cup coarsely chopped fresh flat-leaf parsley
- 1 tablespoon finely chopped fresh thyme
- 3 tablespoons extra-virgin olive oil
  Coarse salt and freshly ground pepper

1. Preheat a grill to medium (if you are using a charcoal grill, coals are ready when you can hold your hand 5 inches above grill for just 5 to 6 seconds). Cut a piece of heavy-duty foil and a piece of parchment to 12 × 18 inches. Place foil on a work surface; lay parchment on top. Toss the mushrooms, garlic, parsley, thyme, and oil in a medium bowl; season with salt and pepper. Mound the mushroom mixture in the center of the parchment paper, allowing a 3-inch border all around.

2. Hold the long sides of parchment and foil; bring together, and fold twice, creasing to seal firmly. Fold short ends twice, creasing to seal firmly.

3. Grill packet until you hear mushrooms and liquid sizzling, 10 to 15 minutes. Flip packet, and grill until mushrooms are soft, about 15 minutes more. (Press lightly to test tenderness, or unfold center of packet to check, but be careful of steam escaping.) Remove packet; let stand 5 minutes before serving.

beef tenderloin with mushrooms and thyme

SERVES 10 TO 12

- 1 beef tenderloin (4 to 5 pounds), tied
  Coarse salt and freshly ground pepper
- ¼ cup extra-virgin olive oil
- 8 ounces shiitake mushrooms
- 1 bunch fresh thyme sprigs
  Shallot-Brandy Sauce (recipe follows)

1. Preheat the oven to 425° F. Season beef with salt and pepper. Heat 2 tablespoons oil in a large skillet over medium-high heat. Add beef, and brown on all sides.

2. Toss mushrooms with remaining 2 tablespoons oil in a bowl; season with salt and pepper. Add mushrooms and 3 thyme sprigs to skillet; place in oven. Cook until beef registers 125° F for medium-rare, 18 to 20 minutes. Let stand 20 minutes. Serve warm or at room temperature with mushrooms and shallot-brandy sauce. Garnish with thyme.

shallot-brandy sauce

MAKES ABOUT 2 CUPS

- 3 tablespoons unsalted butter
- 2 tablespoons extra-virgin olive oil
- 1 cup finely chopped shallots
- 1 tablespoon minced garlic
- ¾ cup brandy
- 4 cups homemade or low-sodium store-bought beef stock
- 1 cup heavy cream
- ¼ cup coarsely chopped fresh thyme
  Coarse salt and freshly ground pepper

Heat butter and oil in a large skillet over medium heat. Add shallots and garlic; cook, stirring often, until soft, about 5 minutes. Remove from heat; add brandy. Bring to a boil. Cook until reduced by half. Whisk in stock and cream, and cook until thickened, about 10 minutes. Stir in thyme; season with salt and pepper.

short ribs with root vegetables

SERVES 8

This recipe is inspired by ones that use flanken, a cut of beef from the chuck end of short ribs. In Jewish custom, the meat is boiled and served with horseradish. Our version uses braised boneless ribs and pairs them with earthy vegetables.

- 6 pounds boneless beef short ribs, trimmed
  Coarse salt and freshly ground pepper
- ¼ cup olive oil
- 3 large onions (9 ounces each), halved lengthwise and cut crosswise into ¼-inch slices
- 6 garlic cloves, finely chopped
- ⅓ cup packed dark-brown sugar
- 2½ cups apple cider
- 1½ cups low-sodium store-bought chicken stock
- 1 tablespoon fresh thyme leaves
- 1 tablespoon finely chopped fresh rosemary
- ⅓ cup finely chopped fresh flat-leaf parsley, plus more for garnish
- 1 pound parsnips, peeled and cut into ½-inch slices
- 1¾ pounds carrots, peeled and cut on the diagonal into 1-inch pieces
- 1½ pounds Yukon Gold potatoes, peeled and cut into 1-inch pieces

1. Preheat the oven to 325° F. Place a wire rack over a rimmed baking sheet; set aside. Season beef with salt and pepper. Heat oil in a 9-quart Dutch oven over high heat until hot but not smoking. Working in batches, cook the beef, flipping once, until browned, 2 to 3 minutes per side. Transfer beef to the wire rack. Reduce heat to medium-low.

2. Add onions to pot; cook, stirring occasionally, until translucent, about 10 minutes. Raise heat to medium. Add garlic; cook 3 minutes, stirring occasionally. Stir in brown sugar, cider, stock, and ½ cup water. Add thyme, rosemary, and parsley. Return beef to pot. Bring to a boil. Remove from heat.

3. Cover; transfer to oven. Cook until almost fork-tender, about 1½ hours.

4. Remove pot from oven. Stir in parsnips, carrots, and potatoes. Return to oven; cook until fork tender, 1 hour 10 minutes more. Gently transfer beef and vegetables to a baking sheet or a plate.

5. Skim fat from cooking liquid. Simmer over medium heat until reduced by about half, about 7 minutes. Return beef and vegetables to pot. Season with salt and pepper; toss gently. Transfer to serving platter. Sprinkle with parsley.

LAMB

spice-crusted rack of lamb

SERVES 2

Rack of lamb is truly a special-occasion treat. Usually, you need to order it through a butcher, at the supermarket or in a butcher shop. Ask him to french the bones. He will know what you're talking about, and you will sound as if you do, too. This means removing excess meat and fat from the bones, which looks nice and makes the chops dainty and neat to eat. It is really important to let the meat rest for 10 minutes before serving (it will finish cooking and reabsorb juices). This time also lets you pull together the final elements of the meal.

- 1 rack of lamb (8 ribs, about 1¼ pounds), frenched
  Coarse salt and freshly ground pepper
- ¼ cup yellow mustard seeds
- 2 teaspoons fennel seeds
- 1 tablespoon olive oil
  Herb Oil (recipe follows), for serving

1. Preheat the oven to 375°F. Cut the rack into 2 4-rib pieces, and season the meat generously with salt and pepper.

2. Toast the mustard and fennel seeds in a large seasoned cast-iron (or ovenproof) skillet over medium heat, stirring constantly, until fragrant, 1 to 2 minutes. Transfer to a plate to cool slightly.

3. Heat the oil in the skillet until hot but not smoking. Place 1 piece of lamb in the skillet, bone side down, and brown all over, 1 to 2 minutes per side. Transfer to a plate; repeat with the remaining piece of lamb. Roll the meat in spices to coat (do not coat the cut sides on either end).

4. Return the meat to the skillet; transfer to the oven. Roast the meat until an instant-read thermometer inserted into the center (avoiding the bones) registers 135°F, for medium-rare, 18 to 24 minutes.

5. Remove the meat from the skillet, and let stand at least 10 minutes. Cut the meat into individual or double chops, and cross the bones, if desired. Serve with herb oil.

herb oil

MAKES ABOUT 1 CUP

A tasty herb oil is a nice alternative to a heavy or complicated sauce. It's quick and easy to make, and it looks and tastes great. Herb oil can be refrigerated up to 2 days before using; bring to room temperature before serving.

- 1 cup mint leaves
- ½ cup flat-leaf parsley leaves
- ½ cup extra-virgin olive oil
- ¼ teaspoon coarse salt

1. Bring a small saucepan of water to a boil. Prepare an ice-water bath. Add the mint and parsley to the boiling water; cook 30 seconds. Drain, and plunge the herbs into ice-water bath immediately.

2. Wrap the herbs in a paper towel; squeeze out as much liquid as possible. Puree the herbs with the oil in a blender until well blended, about 3 minutes. Stir in the salt.

braised lamb shanks
with tomato and fennel

SERVES 4

Serve with Polenta (page 377).

    4   1½-pound lamb shanks, trimmed
        Coarse salt and freshly ground pepper
    ½   cup all-purpose flour
    4   tablespoons extra-virgin olive oil
    2   tablespoons unsalted butter
    2   medium onions, sliced ¼ inch thick
    1   large leek, white and light-green
        parts only, washed well, sliced into ¼-inch
        half-moons
    4   garlic cloves, thinly sliced
    1   cup dry red wine
    2   cups homemade or low-sodium store-
        bought chicken stock
    1   28-ounce can peeled whole plum
        tomatoes, drained
    2   tablespoons tomato paste
    1   tablespoon fresh thyme leaves
    2   dried bay leaves
    2   medium fennel bulbs, sliced ¼ inch thick

1. Preheat the oven to 375°F. Season the lamb all over with salt and pepper. Place the flour in a shallow bowl. Dredge the lamb in the flour, turning to coat evenly; shake off excess. Heat the oil and butter in an 8-quart Dutch oven or skillet over medium heat. Working in two batches, cook until the shanks are well browned, about 5 minutes per side. Transfer the shanks to a large plate; drain off all but 2 tablespoons fat from the skillet.

2. Place the skillet over medium heat; add the onions and leek, and sauté until they are lightly browned, about 6 minutes. Add the garlic; cook 4 minutes more. Add the red wine; deglaze the pan by scraping up any browned bits with a wooden spoon. Return the shanks to the skillet, and add the chicken stock, tomatoes, tomato paste, thyme, and bay leaves. Bring to a boil; cover, and place in oven. Braise 2 hours; add the fennel, and cook 30 minutes.

3. Using a slotted spatula, transfer the shanks and vegetables to a large bowl. Cover; set aside. Using a ladle, skim the fat from the surface of the cooking liquid; cook over medium heat until the liquid is thickened, 5 to 7 minutes. Return the shanks and vegetables to the pan; cook until heated through. Remove from heat, and season with salt and pepper.

....

LEG OF LAMB 101

The term leg of lamb *generally refers to the hind leg and hip of the animal. This cut can be pricy. Though the cost may make some home cooks wary, they needn't be intimidated: Leg of lamb is very straightforward to prepare. Furthermore, a few leg cuts are actually quite a bargain—for example, the foreleg, or shoulder, has more connective tissue and is fantastic in stews.*

Generally, the meat of the upper portion of the leg is more tender than that of the lower section and does well with dry heat methods, such as roasting, grilling, and sautéing. Meat from the relatively inexpensive shank (the leg below the knee joint) is full of connective tissue. Slow cooking at gentle heat in moist conditions, such as braising or stewing, breaks this tissue down into soft gelatin, making the meat meltingly tender and enriching the pot liquor. A butcher should be able to quickly butterfly a leg for you, removing its bones to leave a slab of meat that is ideal for broiling or grilling, or stuffing and rolling, then roasting.

When buying lamb, look for meat that is firm and bright, pink to light red in color, with smooth, white fat rather than yellow. The cut surface of the bones should be red and moist. Avoid meat that is darker, slightly purplish, strong-smelling, or with bones that are white and dry (signs of an older animal). Most American lamb is largely grain-fed, making it slightly more tender and milder tasting than grass-fed imported lamb.

....

mint and pistachio stuffed leg of lamb

SERVES 6 TO 8

Large cuts of meat are often stuffed after being boned. Here, fresh mint, pistachios, and lemon juice bring Middle Eastern flavors to lamb.

- 2 cups fresh mint leaves
- 2 cups fresh flat-leaf parsley leaves
- 1 cup unsalted roasted pistachio nuts
- 2 garlic cloves
- 1½ tablespoons fresh lemon juice
- ½ cup plus 1 tablespoon extra-virgin olive oil
- Coarse salt and freshly ground pepper
- 1 6- to 7-pound leg of lamb, trimmed of excess fat and butterflied (about 2 inches thick)
- 1 cup homemade or low-sodium store-bought chicken stock

1. Preheat the oven to 350°F. Place the mint, parsley, pistachios, garlic, and lemon juice in the bowl of a food processor fitted with the metal blade. Pulse to combine. With the machine running, add ½ cup olive oil through the feed tube; process until smooth. Season with salt and pepper.

2. Lay the lamb flat on a clean work surface. Spread the mint mixture evenly over the lamb, leaving a 1-inch border all around. Starting at the narrow end, roll the lamb into a tight log; tie well with kitchen twine, being sure to secure both ends.

3. Heat the remaining tablespoon olive oil in a cast-iron skillet over medium heat. Place the lamb in the pan, and cook until browned on all sides, 7 to 10 minutes. Place in the oven; roast until a meat thermometer registers 140°F when inserted in the center, about 1 hour 10 minutes. Transfer the lamb to a platter or cutting board, and let rest 15 minutes.

4. Meanwhile, make the pan sauce: Pour off the fat from the skillet. Add the stock, and deglaze the pan by scraping up any browned bits with a wooden spoon. Simmer until the liquid is slightly thickened, about 5 minutes. Remove from heat, and serve with the stuffed lamb.

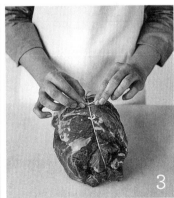

STUFFING THE LAMB

1. After pureeing the ingredients, slather the stuffing onto the butterflied leg, leaving a ½-inch border all around.

2. Starting at one short end, roll up the lamb securely to completely enclose the stuffing.

3. Tie the lamb lengthwise with kitchen twine to keep it from opening during cooking.

roasted whole leg of lamb with fresh herb rub

SERVES 8

1 6- to 7-pound leg of lamb, trimmed
   Coarse salt and freshly ground pepper

2 garlic cloves, thinly sliced

2 tablespoons plus 2 teaspoons Dijon
   mustard

2 tablespoons chopped fresh thyme,
   plus 1 bunch for pan and garnish

1 tablespoon chopped fresh rosemary,
   plus 1 bunch for pan and garnish

2 tablespoons extra-virgin olive oil

2 onions, peeled and quartered

4 carrots, peeled

4 stalks celery

6 new potatoes, halved if large

2 tablespoons all-purpose flour

2 tablespoons unsalted butter, softened

½ cup dry red wine

1 cup homemade or low-sodium store-
   bought beef stock

1. Preheat the oven to 500°F. Season the lamb with salt and pepper. Make 1-inch slits all over; place a sliver of garlic in each. Rub 2 tablespoons mustard over the lamb; coat evenly with the thyme and rosemary, patting gently.

2. Rub the oil over the bottom of a roasting pan; cover with herb bunches. Place the lamb on top. Roast 20 minutes; reduce heat to 375°F. Add the onions, carrots, celery, and potatoes; season with salt and pepper. Roast until a meat thermometer inserted near center, avoiding bone, reads 140°F, about 70 minutes. Transfer the lamb and vegetables to a platter; let rest 20 minutes.

3. Meanwhile, make the sauce: Knead the flour and butter together. Pour off the fat; place the pan over medium heat. Add the wine; reduce by half. Add the remaining mustard and stock. Stir; reduce slightly. Strain into a saucepan; simmer. Add the butter mixture in small pieces, whisking constantly. Remove from heat; season with salt and pepper. Garnish with herbs.

spice-rubbed lamb chops

SERVES 2

1 teaspoon dried thyme

½ teaspoon ground cumin

½ teaspoon ground coriander

¼ teaspoon paprika

½ teaspoon coarse salt
   Freshly ground pepper

2 lamb rib chops (about 5½ ounces each)

2 teaspoons extra-virgin olive oil

1 ounce arugula (about 2 cups)

1. Stir together the thyme, cumin, coriander, paprika, and salt in a small bowl; season with pepper. Put the lamb chops on a plate; rub each side with spice mixture. Let stand at least 10 minutes, or up to 1 hour.

2. Heat 1 teaspoon oil in a medium heavy skillet over medium-high heat until very hot. Add the chops. Reduce heat to medium. Cook the chops, flipping halfway through, until deeply browned, about 10 minutes total for medium-rare. Transfer each chop to a serving plate. Divide the arugula between the plates; drizzle with the remaining teaspoon oil.

FIT TO EAT RECIPE PER SERVING: 175 CALORIES, 12 G FAT, 48 MG CHOLESTEROL, 1 G CARBOHYDRATE, 330 MG SODIUM, 15 G PROTEIN, 1 G FIBER

northern indian
lamb meatballs

SERVES 4

2 small garlic cloves
1 piece (1 inch) peeled fresh ginger, sliced
2 tablespoons vegetable oil
1 large onion, finely chopped
½ teaspoon ground turmeric
¾ teaspoon cayenne pepper
2 tablespoons plus 1 teaspoon ground
   coriander
1 can (8 ounces) plain tomato sauce
1 dried bay leaf
   Coarse salt
12 ounces ground lamb
1 cup fine fresh bread crumbs
⅓ cup finely chopped fresh cilantro
1 large egg
6 prunes, quartered
½ teaspoon garam masala
   Pickled vegetables, for serving
   Indian flatbread, for serving

1. Process the garlic, ginger, and 1½ teaspoons water in a food processor until a chunky paste forms; set aside.

2. Heat the oil in a medium saucepan over medium heat until hot but not smoking. Add the onion; cook, stirring, until translucent, about 3 minutes. Set aside one-quarter of the onion in a large bowl.

3. Add 1 tablespoon garlic paste, ½ cup water, the turmeric, ½ teaspoon cayenne, and 2 tablespoons coriander to the onion in the skillet. Cook 3 minutes, stirring. Add the tomato sauce, 1½ cups water, and the bay leaf. Season with salt. Bring to a boil. Reduce heat to medium-low; simmer.

4. Mix the reserved onion, lamb, bread crumbs, cilantro, egg, 1 teaspoon each garlic paste and salt, and remaining teaspoon coriander and ¼ teaspoon cayenne. Divide into 24 pieces; roll into balls. Stuff each meatball with a prune quarter; roll to enclose.

5. Add the meatballs to the simmering sauce (add water if the meatballs are not covered by the sauce). Cook until the sauce has thickened, about 40 minutes. Stir in the garam masala.

grilled lamb chops
with lemon yogurt sauce

SERVES 4

Low-fat plain yogurt can be used instead.

1 cup whole-milk plain yogurt
1 tablespoon fresh lemon juice
⅛ teaspoon paprika
⅛ teaspoon ground cumin
8 rib lamb chops
1½ teaspoons coarse salt
½ teaspoon freshly ground pepper
   Mint sprigs for garnish (optional)

1. Make the yogurt sauce: Combine the yogurt, lemon juice, paprika, and cumin in a small bowl, and set aside in the refrigerator.

2. Make the chops: Heat the grill to medium. Sprinkle the chops with salt and pepper, and grill until cooked through, 5 to 6 minutes per side. Serve with the yogurt sauce and mint sprigs, if desired.

individual lamb pies

SERVES 4

- 3 tablespoons vegetable oil
- 1 pound lamb stew meat, cut into 1½-inch cubes
- Coarse salt and freshly ground pepper
- 1 medium onion, finely chopped
- 2 celery stalks, cut into ¼-inch dice
- 4 ounces white button mushrooms, cut into ¼-inch pieces
- 1 piece (1 inch) peeled fresh ginger, minced (about 1 tablespoon)
- 1 tablespoon fresh thyme, coarsely chopped
- Pinch of ground cloves
- 1 cup homemade or low-sodium store-bought lamb or beef stock
- ½ cup dry red wine
- 4 ounces pitted prunes, halved
- Short Pastry Crust (recipe follows)
- All-purpose flour, for work surface
- 1 tablespoon heavy cream
- 1 large egg yolk

1. Heat 2 tablespoons oil in a medium heavy pot over medium-high heat. Season the lamb with salt and pepper. Cook the lamb until browned on all sides, about 8 minutes. Transfer to a medium bowl. Add the remaining tablespoon oil to the pot. Add the onion, celery, and mushrooms; cook, stirring occasionally, until the vegetables are softened, about 6 minutes. Stir in the ginger, thyme, cloves, lamb, stock, wine, and ½ cup water. Bring to a simmer; cover, and reduce heat to medium-low. Gently simmer until the lamb is tender, about 2½ hours. Stir in the prunes. Season with salt and pepper. Let cool completely.

2. Divide the dough in half. Wrap half in plastic; refrigerate until ready to use. Roll out other dough half on a lightly floured surface to a ¼-inch thickness. Cut out 4 6-inch rounds. Transfer 1 round to each of 4 5-inch pie plates. Divide the stew among the pies. Roll out the remaining dough to a ¼-inch

thickness. Cut out 4 7-inch rounds. Randomly punch out circles from the rounds with a ½-inch round pastry tip (such as Ateco #806). Cover each pie with a round. Tuck the edges under; press gently to seal. Refrigerate until cold, about 30 minutes.

3. Preheat the oven to 400° F. Whisk the cream and egg yolk in a small bowl. Brush the crusts with egg wash. Bake the pies on a rimmed baking sheet until crusts are golden brown and juices are bubbling, about 30 minutes. Transfer to a wire rack to cool slightly, about 15 minutes.

short pastry crust

MAKES ENOUGH FOR
FOUR 5-INCH DOUBLE-CRUST PIES OR
ONE 13 × 4½-INCH DOUBLE-CRUST PIE

- 2½ cups all-purpose flour
- 1 teaspoon salt
- 6 tablespoons cold unsalted butter
- 2 tablespoons cold vegetable shortening
- ¼ to ½ cup ice water

Pulse the flour, salt, butter, and shortening in a food processor until the mixture resembles coarse meal. With the processor running, drizzle in ¼ cup water until the dough just comes together. (If the dough is still crumbly, add up to ¼ cup more ice water, 1 tablespoon at a time.) Do not process for more than 20 seconds. Divide the dough in half; wrap each in plastic. Refrigerate until cold, about 30 minutes.

curried lamb kabobs with cherry tomatoes and red onions

MAKES 8

1 garlic clove, minced

½ teaspoon turmeric

1 teaspoon ground coriander

1 teaspoon ground cumin

½ teaspoon dried oregano

6 tablespoons extra-virgin olive oil

1 tablespoon fresh lemon juice

¼ cup loosely packed mint leaves, chopped

2 pounds lamb shoulder, cut into 1-inch cubes

1 pound cherry tomatoes, mixed colors

4 small red onions, cut into 8 wedges

1½ tablespoons coarse salt

2 teaspoons freshly ground pepper

1. Whisk together the garlic, turmeric, coriander, cumin, oregano, 4 tablespoons olive oil, lemon juice, and mint in a small bowl. Add the lamb. Toss to coat; refrigerate, covered, for at least 2 hours or overnight.

2. Thread 4 cubes of lamb, alternating with tomatoes and onion, on each of 8 skewers. Brush with some of the remaining olive oil. Season with salt and pepper.

3. Arrange the skewers, off direct heat, on a medium-hot grill. Grill, rotating the skewers and brushing with olive oil as necessary to prevent sticking, until the lamb is cooked through but pink inside, about 8 minutes, depending on the heat of the grill. The vegetables should be soft.

PORK

pork chops with herb stuffing

SERVES 4

1 cup cubed (⅜ inch) rustic bread without crusts

1 tablespoon unsalted butter

¼ cup olive oil

½ cup finely chopped onion

¾ cup finely chopped celery

¼ cup plus 1 tablespoon mixed chopped parsley and thyme

2¼ teaspoons ground coriander

½ cup plus 3 tablespoons chicken stock

Coarse salt and freshly ground pepper

4 bone-in pork chops (9 ounces each), cut horizontally to the bone

2 garlic cloves, minced

¼ cup dry sherry

1. Preheat the oven to 350° F. Toast the bread cubes on a baking sheet until golden, about 7 minutes. Heat the butter and 1 tablespoon oil in a 12-inch ovenproof skillet over medium heat. Cook the onion, stirring, until soft, about 3 minutes. Add the celery; cook 1 minute. Transfer to a bowl. Reserve the skillet. Toss the bread, herbs, ¼ teaspoon coriander, and 3 tablespoons stock with the onion mixture. Season with salt and pepper.

2. Stuff the chops. Using a fork, mix and mash the garlic, 2 teaspoons coriander, ½ teaspoon salt, and 1 tablespoon oil; rub onto the pork. Heat 2 tablespoons oil in the skillet over medium-high heat. Cook the pork until golden brown, 2 to 3 minutes; flip, and transfer the skillet to the oven. Cook until the pork registers 155° F, about 15 minutes. Transfer to a plate; cover.

3. Add the sherry and ½ cup stock to the skillet. Cook over medium-high heat, stirring, until reduced by half. Serve with pork.

molasses-glazed grilled pork loin

SERVES 8 TO 10

Leave a cool spot on the grill for cooking the roasts after they are glazed; turn them frequently to avoid burning.

- 1   12-ounce jar unsulphured molasses
- ¼   cup grainy mustard
- 2   teaspoons dry mustard
     Coarse salt and freshly ground pepper
- 2   boneless pork loin roasts (3 to 4 pounds each)

1. Heat a charcoal or gas grill. In a small bowl, whisk together the molasses, grainy mustard, and dry mustard, and season with salt and pepper. Set aside.

2. Tie each pork loin with kitchen twine in four to five places to form a nice, round shape. Season liberally with salt and pepper. Sear until well browned on all sides, 15 to 20 minutes total.

3. Brush with the glaze, and cook, turning and basting frequently, 5 minutes. Move to the cooler part of the grill, and close the lid. Continue cooking, basting and turning occasionally, until an instant-read thermometer registers 160°F, 30 to 40 minutes.

4. Transfer the pork to a serving platter, and let rest 10 minutes before carving.

roasted pork shoulder with sage and coriander

SERVES 10

- 2   tablespoons whole black peppercorns
- 2   tablespoons coriander seeds
- 4   garlic cloves, thinly sliced
- 2   large shallots, thinly sliced
- 2   tablespoons chopped fresh sage
     Coarse salt
- ¼   cup extra-virgin olive oil
- 1   boneless pork shoulder (about 6 pounds), trimmed

1. Toast the peppercorns and coriander seeds in a small sauté pan over medium-low heat until fragrant, about 5 minutes. Let cool completely. Transfer to a food processor. Add the garlic, shallots, sage, and 1 tablespoon salt, and grind to a chunky paste. With the processor running, slowly add the oil; mix until well combined.

2. Untie the pork, if tied. Rub the pork with the spice mixture. Put it in a resealable plastic bag, and expel air; seal the bag. Marinate in the refrigerator, turning occasionally, overnight or up to 3 days. Let stand at room temperature 1 to 2 hours before cooking.

3. Preheat the oven to 450°F. Roll the pork, and tie it into a compact log with kitchen twine. Transfer to a small roasting or medium baking pan. Roast 20 minutes. Reduce oven temperature to 350°F; continue to cook until an instant-read thermometer inserted into the thickest part registers 150°F, about 2 hours 15 minutes. Transfer to a warmed platter, cover with foil, and let rest 10 to 15 minutes before slicing.

maple-glazed smoked vermont ham

SERVES 15 TO 20

One to two hours before baking, remove the ham from the refrigerator and let it come to room temperature.

- 1 smoked bone-in ham (10 to 12 pounds), room temperature
- ½ cup apricot jam
- 2 tablespoons Dijon mustard
- ¾ cup pure maple syrup
- 2 tablespoons dark rum
- 1 garlic clove, minced
  Fresh bay leaves, for garnish (optional)
  Kumquats, for garnish (optional)

1. Preheat the oven to 350°F. Fit a large roasting pan with a rack; place the ham on the rack. Cover tightly with foil. Bake, rotating the pan halfway through, 4 hours.

2. Meanwhile, make the glaze: In a small saucepan, heat the jam until liquefied. Strain through a fine sieve into a small bowl; discard the solids. Stir in the mustard, maple syrup, rum, and garlic.

3. After 4 hours, remove the ham from the oven, and brush with the glaze. Continue baking the ham, glazing every 15 minutes, until an instant-read thermometer inserted into thickest part of the ham (avoiding bone) registers 140°F, about 1 hour more.

4. Remove from the oven, and transfer to a carving board or platter. Garnish the ham with bay leaves and kumquats, if desired. Slice thinly around the bone, and serve hot or at room temperature.

pancetta-wrapped pork roast

SERVES 4

- 1 pork loin (1½ pounds)
  Coarse salt and freshly ground pepper
- 1 tablespoon extra-virgin olive oil
- 2 tablespoons finely chopped fresh rosemary, plus several sprigs
- ¼ pound pancetta (Italian bacon) or bacon, thinly sliced
- 8 to 10 cipollini or small white onions, unpeeled
- 1 teaspoon unsalted butter, softened
- 1 teaspoon all-purpose flour
- 1 cup chicken stock, preferably homemade

1. Preheat the oven to 375°F. Season the pork with salt and pepper. Heat the oil in a large cast-iron skillet over medium heat. Sear the pork on all sides until browned, about 10 minutes. Remove from heat.

2. Rub the pork with the chopped rosemary; wrap with the pancetta, overlapping strips slightly. Lay a rosemary sprig on top; tie the pork with kitchen twine. Scatter onions and rosemary sprigs around the pork. Roast in the oven, basting occasionally with cooking juices, until the internal temperature is 145°F on a meat thermometer, 35 to 40 minutes. Remove from the oven. Transfer the pork and onions to a platter; cover with foil.

3. Make the pan sauce: In a small bowl, combine the butter and flour. Pour off the fat from the skillet; place over medium heat. Add the stock, scraping bottom of skillet to loosen browned bits. Bring to a boil; reduce the liquid slightly, about 2 minutes. Whisk in the butter mixture; cook until thickened. Season with salt and pepper. Serve hot with the pork and onions.

five-spice pork tenderloin

SERVES 6

Five-spice powder is a pungent seasoning mix used widely in Chinese cooking. It is made of equal parts ground cloves, cinnamon, fennel seed, star anise, and Szechuan peppercorns. For a recipe, see page 650.

¼ cup Chinese five-spice powder

2 teaspoons coarse salt

1 pork tenderloin (about 1¾ pounds)

3 tablespoons canola oil

1. Preheat the oven to 400° F. Combine the spice powder and salt on a plate; generously coat the pork tenderloins. Heat a large ovenproof skillet over medium-high heat, and pour in the oil. Add the tenderloins; brown well on all sides, about 4 minutes per side.

2. Transfer to the oven, and roast until the meat is cooked through, about 15 minutes or until a meat thermometer inserted in the center registers 160° F. Remove from the oven; let rest 5 minutes before slicing. Serve.

grilled sausage with arugula pesto

SERVES 4

Save extra pesto to use on other grilled meats or fish. It will last up to 1 week in the refrigerator.

1 bunch (about 4 ounces) arugula, stems trimmed, washed

4 cloves garlic, peeled and smashed

1 cup freshly grated Parmesan cheese

1½ teaspoons coarse salt

½ teaspoon freshly ground pepper

½ cup extra-virgin olive oil

8 assorted Italian pork sausages, both hot and sweet varieties (about 1 pound)

1. Make the pesto: Place the arugula and garlic in the bowl of a food processor. Pulse until finely chopped, scraping down the sides if necessary. Add the cheese, salt, pepper, and olive oil, and puree until smooth and well combined.

2. Heat a grill to medium-high. Prick the sausages with a fork to allow excess fat to drip. Grill until cooked through, about 4 minutes per side. Serve the pesto over the grilled sausages.

boneless pork chops with apple chutney

SERVES 4

4 tablespoons olive oil

2 teaspoons coarse salt, plus more for seasoning

1 teaspoon freshly ground black pepper, plus more for seasoning

4 boneless center-cut pork chops, cut ¾ inch thick (1¼ pounds)

1 large onion, cut into ½-inch dice

4 green apples (such as Granny Smith), peeled, cored, and cut into ½-inch dice

½ cup cider vinegar

½ cup golden raisins

1 teaspoon ground ginger

¼ teaspoon dry mustard

Pinch of cayenne pepper

1. Preheat the oven to 400° F. Heat 2 tablespoons olive oil in an ovenproof skillet over medium heat. Sprinkle salt and pepper on both sides of the pork chops; add to the skillet. Sauté until golden brown, about 2 minutes; flip. Cook 2 minutes more; place the pan in the oven. Roast until the meat is cooked through and registers 155° F on an instant-read thermometer, about 5 minutes. Transfer to a platter.

2. Meanwhile, in a large saucepan, heat the remaining 2 tablespoons olive oil over medium heat; add the onion. Sauté over medium heat until translucent and beginning to brown, about 6 minutes. Add the apples; sauté 4 minutes more. Add the vinegar, raisins, ginger, mustard, and cayenne. Stir well to combine; cover. Continue cooking, stirring occasionally, until the apples are very tender but still holding their shape, about 3 minutes. Season with salt and pepper; serve over the pork chops.

brine-cured pork kabobs with jalapeños and pineapple

MAKES 8

Brine-curing the pork makes it soft, tender, and juicy. The pork is cut into small pieces, so it only needs to be cured for 4 hours.

- 6 cups cold water
- ¼ cup sugar
- 3 tablespoons coarse salt, plus more for seasoning
- 2 bay leaves
- 1 tablespoon whole black peppercorns
- 1 tablespoon allspice berries
- 3 cloves garlic, chopped
- 1¾ pounds pork loin, cut into 1½-inch cubes
- ½ pineapple, peeled, cored, and cut into 1-inch chunks
- 16 medium jalapeño or other hot peppers, cut in half lengthwise
  Spicy Molasses Glaze (recipe follows)
- 1 teaspoon freshly ground black pepper
- 2 tablespoons extra-virgin olive oil

1. Combine the water, sugar, salt, bay leaves, peppercorns, allspice, and garlic in a nonreactive bowl. Add the pork, cover, and refrigerate for at least 4 hours or overnight. Drain, and set aside.

2. Thread 4 cubes of pork, alternating with pineapple chunks and pepper halves, onto 8 skewers. Brush with glaze, and season with salt and pepper.

3. Arrange the skewers, off direct heat, on a hot grill. Grill, rotating the skewers and brushing with remaining glaze and olive oil to prevent sticking as necessary, until the pork is cooked through but juicy in the center, about 12 minutes, depending on the heat of the grill. The pineapples and peppers should be soft and charred.

spicy molasses glaze

MAKES ABOUT 1 CUP

Brush on fish, chicken, and burgers.

- 2 tablespoons molasses
- 3 cloves garlic, minced
- 2 serrano chiles or jalapeño peppers, minced
- 1 piece (1 inch) fresh ginger, peeled and grated
- ½ teaspoon crushed red pepper flakes
- ¾ cup extra-virgin olive oil
- ½ tablespoon coarse salt
  Pinch of freshly ground black pepper

Whisk the molasses, garlic, chiles, ginger, red pepper flakes, and oil in a small bowl. Season with salt and pepper. Keep sealed at room temperature up to 1 week.

chipotle-marinated pork tenderloin with black bean salsa

SERVES 4

Make the chile-lime marinade the day before, and let the pork marinate overnight before cooking.

for the pork

- 1 canned chipotle chile in adobo sauce
- 3 garlic cloves
- ½ cup coarsely chopped white onion
- 2 tablespoons fresh lime juice
- 1 teaspoon sherry vinegar
- 1 teaspoon dried Mexican oregano
- 1 pound pork tenderloin, trimmed of fat

for the salsa

- 1 can (19 ounces) black beans, drained and rinsed
- 1 cup grape tomatoes, quartered
- ¼ cup finely chopped white onion
- ¼ cup finely chopped fresh cilantro
- 3 tablespoons fresh lime juice
- 2 teaspoons minced canned chipotle chile in adobo sauce
- ½ teaspoon ground cumin

1. Make the pork marinade: Process chile, garlic, onion, lime juice, vinegar, and oregano in a blender until smooth. Rub marinade all over the pork. Transfer pork to a dish, and cover with plastic wrap. Refrigerate overnight.

2. Preheat the oven to 350°F. Heat a grill pan over high heat. Grill pork until seared on all sides, about 2 minutes per side. Transfer pan to the oven; cook until an instant read thermometer inserted into center of meat registers 145°F, 20 to 25 minutes. Let pork stand at room temperature 5 to 10 minutes before slicing.

3. Meanwhile, make the salsa: Stir together the black beans, tomatoes, onion, cilantro, lime juice, chile, and cumin in a small bowl. Serve with the pork.

FIT TO EAT RECIPE PER SERVING: 308 CALORIES, 8 G FAT, 75 MG CHOLESTEROL, 27 G CARBOHYDRATE, 572 MG SODIUM, 31 G PROTEIN, 9 G FIBER

choucroute garni
SERVES 8

1   teaspoon whole coriander seeds

1   teaspoon whole juniper berries

4   whole cloves

½   teaspoon whole black peppercorns

½   teaspoon whole caraway seeds

2   dried bay leaves

6   garlic cloves, crushed

3   tablespoons vegetable oil

2   medium onions, thinly sliced

½   teaspoon coarse salt

1   pound double-smoked bacon, cut into
     1-inch-thick slices

½   pound fresh bacon or salt pork (in 1 piece)

1¼ pounds smoked pork butt, sliced
     crosswise into 1-inch-thick pieces

4   pounds fresh sauerkraut, rinsed
     and drained

1   bottle (750 ml) dry Riesling

8   medium red or Yukon Gold potatoes,
     or a combination (about 1½ pounds total),
     peeled if desired

8   small carrots, peeled

3   coarse-textured smoked pork sausages,
     such as Hungarian kielbasa, bauerwurst,
     or smoked bratwurst (12 ounces total)

3   fine-textured pork-and-beef sausages,
     such as knockwurst or frankfurters
     (12 ounces total)

3   mild-spiced fine-textured white veal-
     and-pork sausages, such as weisswurst
     or bockwurst (12 ounces total)

     Fresh parsley sprigs, for garnish

     Variety of mustards, for serving

1. Make a spice bundle: Place spices, bay leaves, and garlic on a square of cheesecloth; tie into a bundle with kitchen twine.

2. Heat oil in a very large Dutch oven over medium heat. Add onions and salt. Cook, stirring occasionally, until onions are translucent, about 5 minutes. Add bacon, pork butt, and spice bundle. Cover with sauerkraut. Add wine and enough water to come 1 inch below sauerkraut. Bring to a boil. Reduce heat to medium-low; cover, and simmer 45 minutes.

3. Add potatoes and carrots. Cover; cook until almost tender, about 20 minutes.

4. Using a skewer or the tip of a paring knife, poke a few holes into each sausage to prevent them from bursting. Place kielbasa in a dry skillet over medium heat. Cook, turning often, until browned, about 8 minutes. Put all sausages into the Dutch oven. Cover; cook until heated through, about 15 minutes.

5. Using a slotted spoon, transfer sausages and vegetables to a plate. Drain sauerkraut, and arrange on a serving platter. Arrange sausages and vegetables on top. Garnish with parsley; serve with mustards.

crispy pork-stuffed anaheim chiles

SERVES 4 TO 6

4 pounds boneless pork shoulder, trimmed and cut in 2-inch pieces

1 tablespoon coarse salt

12 large Anaheim chiles

12 ounces Monterey Jack cheese, grated (about 3½ cups)

   Quick Purple Tomatillo Sauce (recipe follows)

   Fresh cilantro sprigs, for garnish

   Flour tortillas, warmed, for serving

1. Place pork in a large, heavy pot. Sprinkle with salt. Add water to cover. Bring to a boil. Reduce to a simmer. Cook, stirring occasionally, until pork is brown, about 1½ hours (when water has evaporated, pork will brown in its fat). Set aside.

2. Preheat the oven to 375°F. Place chiles directly over the flame of a gas-stove burner on high heat. Roast, turning with tongs, until blackened all over. (Alternatively, broil chiles on a baking sheet, turning, until skin has charred.) Transfer chiles to a large bowl, and cover immediately with plastic wrap. Set aside to steam, about 15 minutes. Peel chiles; discard skins. With stems intact, slit each chile lengthwise; carefully remove seeds and veins. Place, slit side up, on a baking sheet.

3. Spread 2 tablespoons cheese in bottom of each chile, then fill with ⅓ cup pork. Sprinkle chiles with the remaining 2 cups cheese. Spoon 1 tablespoon tomatillo sauce over top of each chile. Bake 15 minutes. Garnish with cilantro; serve with tortillas and remaining tomatillo sauce.

quick purple tomatillo sauce

MAKES ABOUT 2 CUPS

10 small purple or green tomatillos (about 10 ounces total), husked and washed

½ small onion, coarsely chopped

2 jalapeño peppers, coarsely chopped

6 sprigs fresh cilantro, leaves only

1½ teaspoons coarse salt

1. Put the tomatillos in a medium saucepan; cover with water by 1 inch. Bring to a boil, then reduce to a simmer. Cook 4 minutes. Drain, reserving ½ cup cooking liquid.

2. Process tomatillos, onion, jalapeños, cilantro, salt, and ¼ cup liquid in a blender until a slightly chunky sauce forms, adding more liquid as needed. Refrigerate in an airtight container up to 3 days.

sautéed pork cutlets

SERVES 4

8 pork cutlets (3 ounces each)

1 teaspoon coarse salt

½ teaspoon freshly ground pepper

2 to 4 tablespoons extra-virgin olive oil

   Juice of 1 lemon, plus lemon wedges for serving

2 tablespoons finely grated Parmesan cheese, plus Parmesan curls shaved with a vegetable peeler for garnish (about 1 ounce total)

   Fresh flat-leaf parsley for garnish

   Grainy mustard for serving

1. Place pork cutlets between two sheets of parchment paper; using a meat mallet or a small, heavy skillet, pound to ⅛ inch thick. Season both sides of pork with salt and pepper.

2. Heat 2 tablespoons oil in a large saucepan over medium-high heat. Working in two batches, add pork to pan, and cook, flipping once, until golden brown, 1½ to 2 minutes per side. (If pan becomes dry, add more oil.) Transfer to a platter.

3. Drizzle lemon juice over pork, and sprinkle with grated Parmesan. Garnish with Parmesan curls and parsley. Serve with lemon wedges and mustard.

barbecued baby-back ribs

SERVES 12

You can cook the ribs a day ahead and store them, wrapped in plastic, in the refrigerator; bring them to room temperature before grilling.

6 racks baby-back ribs
4 celery stalks, coarsely chopped
2 medium carrots, coarsely chopped
1 large onion, coarsely chopped
1 garlic clove, halved
 Coarse salt and freshly ground pepper
2 recipes Pierre's Barbecue Sauce
 (recipe follows)

1. Divide ribs between 2 large pots. Cover with cold water. Bring to a boil. Reduce to a simmer, and cook 3 minutes, skimming any foam that rises to the surface. Drain; rinse under cold water. Cover ribs with cold water again.

2. Divide celery, carrots, onion, and garlic between pots; add 1 tablespoon salt to each pot. Bring to a boil. Reduce to a simmer, and cook until ribs are tender, about 1 hour. Drain; discard vegetables.

3. Preheat a grill to medium (if you are using a charcoal grill, coals are ready when you can hold your hand 5 inches above grill for just 5 to 6 seconds). Season ribs generously with salt and pepper; brush with barbecue sauce. Grill, turning frequently and brushing with sauce occasionally, until heated through and marked by grill, about 15 minutes. Cut into servings of about 3 ribs each; brush with more sauce. Serve immediately.

pierre's barbecue sauce

MAKES 2½ TO 3 CUPS

This sauce was created by chef Pierre Schaedelin.

2 red bell peppers
½ cup olive oil
4 large onions, coarsely chopped
3 garlic cloves, crushed
¼ teaspoon ground coriander
½ teaspoon ground chili powder
½ teaspoon cayenne pepper
⅔ cup packed dark-brown sugar
5½ pounds tomatoes, cut into chunks
 Coarse salt and freshly ground pepper
⅓ cup white wine vinegar
¼ cup Dijon mustard
2 tablespoons honey
4 teaspoons Worcestershire sauce
1 tablespoon soy sauce

1. Place the peppers directly over the flame of a gas-stove burner on high heat or on a grill. Roast peppers, turning with tongs, until blackened all over. (Alternatively, broil peppers on a baking sheet, turning as each side becomes charred.) Transfer to a large bowl, and cover immediately with plastic wrap. Set aside to steam 15 minutes. Peel peppers; discard skin. Remove stems, seeds, and ribs; cut each pepper into pieces. Set aside.

2. Heat oil in a large pot over medium-high heat. Add onions, garlic, and roasted peppers; cook, stirring occasionally, until onions are dark golden brown on the edges, 8 to 10 minutes. Stir in coriander, chili powder, and cayenne pepper; cook 30 seconds. Add sugar; cook, stirring occasionally, 2 minutes. Add tomatoes, 2 teaspoons salt, and ½ teaspoon pepper; cook, stirring occasionally, until tomatoes have broken down and are very soft, about 20 minutes.

3. Stir in the vinegar, mustard, honey, Worcestershire sauce, and soy sauce. Pour through a coarse sieve into a medium bowl, pressing out liquid with a spoon; discard solids. Return to stove, and bring to a boil. Reduce to a vigorous simmer, and cook, stirring occasionally, until reduced slightly and thickened, 15 to 20 minutes. Taste, and adjust for seasoning. The sauce can be refrigerated in an airtight container up to 3 days.

poultry

....

breaded chicken cutlets with sage

SERVES 4

To fry the sage leaves for garnish, place them in hot oil until they start to curl, about 3 seconds; remove with a slotted spoon.

- 2 pounds boneless, skinless chicken cutlets (8 to 10 pieces), pounded about ¼ inch thick, if needed

  Coarse salt and freshly ground pepper
- 1½ cups buttermilk
- ½ teaspoon hot sauce, such as Tabasco
- 2 cups plain dried bread crumbs (about 8 ounces)
- ⅓ cup finely chopped fresh sage, plus fried leaves for garnish

  Vegetable oil, for frying

1. Preheat the oven to 200°F. Season the chicken with salt and pepper. Stir the buttermilk, hot sauce, 1½ teaspoons salt, and ¼ teaspoon pepper in a medium bowl. Add the chicken; turn to coat well. Let marinate for about 15 minutes. Stir the bread crumbs and sage in another bowl; set aside.

2. Heat about 1 inch oil in a large skillet until it reaches 365°F on a deep-fry thermometer. Working with 1 cutlet at a time, transfer the chicken from the buttermilk mixture to the bread crumb mixture, coating both sides completely. Gently place in the hot oil. Cook, turning halfway through with tongs, until crisp and dark golden, about 5 minutes. Transfer to a rack or paper towels to drain. Transfer to a baking sheet, and put in the oven to keep warm. Remove any bits of coating from the skillet with a slotted spoon, and discard before adding more chicken. Repeat with the remaining chicken. Garnish with the fried leaves.

roasted herbed chicken with vermouth pan sauce

SERVES 4

Roasting the garlic in its skin mellows and sweetens its flavor; to remove the cloves, squeeze them with your fingers or press on the cloves with a butter knife.

- 1 whole chicken, rinsed, patted dry, and cut into 8 pieces

  Coarse salt and freshly ground pepper
- 3 tablespoons extra-virgin olive oil
- 1½ teaspoons finely chopped fresh tarragon
- 1 tablespoon finely chopped fresh thyme
- 1½ teaspoons finely chopped fresh flat-leaf parsley
- 8 garlic cloves, unpeeled
- ½ cup dry vermouth
- ¼ cup homemade or low-sodium store-bought chicken stock

1. Preheat the oven to 400°F, with the rack in the center. Put the chicken in a large bowl; season with salt and pepper. Add the oil, tarragon, thyme, and parsley, and toss to coat. Transfer the chicken and herbs to a 15½ × 13-inch roasting pan; do not crowd. Scatter the garlic in the pan. Cook until the chicken skin is golden and crisp and the juices run clear when the thigh is pierced with a sharp knife, 45 to 50 minutes.

2. Transfer the chicken and garlic to a serving dish, and cover loosely with aluminum foil; set aside. Skim the fat from the pan with a spoon, and discard. Set the roasting pan over medium-high heat on stove. Add the vermouth, and cook, scraping up browned bits with a wooden spoon, until reduced by about half, about 4 minutes. Stir in the stock. Bring to a simmer; continue to cook until reduced by about half, about 2 minutes more. Pour through a fine sieve into a medium bowl, and discard the solids. Skim the fat with a spoon, and discard. Serve the sauce alongside the chicken and garlic.

chicken holy basil

SERVES 4 TO 6

10 garlic cloves, minced

6 fresh Thai chiles, thinly sliced crosswise

¼ cup plus 2 tablespoons vegetable oil

2 pounds boneless, skinless chicken breasts, cut into 1-inch pieces

1 tablespoon plus 1 teaspoon Asian fish sauce

2 teaspoons soy sauce

4½ teaspoons sugar
    Freshly ground pepper

3 cups loosely packed fresh holy basil leaves, plus more for garnish
    Sticky or steamed jasmine rice, for serving

1. Mash together the garlic and chiles using a mortar and pestle or the flat side of a large knife. Heat the oil in a wok or large skillet over medium-high heat. Add the garlic mixture. Cook, stirring, until the garlic is just golden, about 20 seconds.

2. Add the chicken; cook, stirring often, until the chicken is cooked through, about 4 minutes. Stir in the fish sauce, soy sauce, sugar, and 1½ teaspoons pepper. Add the basil; cook, stirring constantly, 1 minute. Season with more pepper, if desired. Serve over rice. Garnish with basil.

broiled yogurt-ginger chicken breasts

SERVES 4

For a side dish, try basmati rice cooked with a pinch of saffron.

1 container (32 ounces) plain yogurt

1 piece (5 inches) peeled fresh ginger, grated (about ¼ cup)

½ teaspoon ground cumin

½ teaspoon cayenne pepper
    Coarse salt

4 boneless, skinless chicken breast halves (about 8 ounces each)

1 small red onion, thinly sliced

1 cucumber, peeled, seeded, and chopped

3 sprigs fresh cilantro, stems removed
    Juice of 1 lime

1. Stir together the yogurt, ginger, cumin, ¼ teaspoon cayenne, and ½ teaspoon salt in a 9 × 13-inch baking dish.

2. Starting on one long side, cut each chicken piece almost in half horizontally (stop about ½ inch before reaching opposite side). Open each piece like a book.

3. Add the chicken to the marinade in the dish; turn to coat. Cover with plastic wrap. Refrigerate at least 1 hour or up to 8 hours.

4. Preheat the broiler. Toss together the red onion, cucumber, cilantro, lime juice, remaining ¼ teaspoon cayenne (or to taste), and a pinch of salt in a small bowl.

5. Transfer the chicken to a broiler pan. Discard the marinade. Broil the chicken, rotating the pan once, until cooked through, about 10 minutes. Top with the cucumber mixture.

baked crisp parmesan-romano chicken

SERVES 4

Serve this dish with arugula, tomatoes, blanched green beans, and crumbled Parmesan cheese tossed with extra-virgin olive oil and vinegar.

¼ cup extra-virgin olive oil, plus more for the baking sheet

¼ cup plus 1 tablespoon red-wine vinegar

½ teaspoon coarse salt

¼ teaspoon crushed red pepper flakes

½ teaspoon dried oregano

1 garlic clove, minced

1 whole chicken (3½ to 4 pounds), rinsed well, patted dry, and cut into 8 pieces

1 cup fresh bread crumbs

¼ cup freshly grated Parmesan cheese

¼ cup freshly grated Pecorino Romano cheese

2 tablespoons finely chopped fresh flat-leaf parsley

¼ teaspoon freshly ground pepper

1. Preheat the oven to 400°F. Whisk together the oil, vinegar, salt, red pepper flakes, oregano, and garlic in a 9 × 13-inch baking dish. Add the chicken to the marinade in the dish, turning each piece to coat. Cover with plastic wrap, and refrigerate at least 1 hour or up to 8 hours.

2. Stir together the bread crumbs, cheeses, parsley, and pepper in a medium bowl. Line a rimmed baking sheet with parchment paper. Oil the parchment.

3. Dredge each chicken piece in the bread crumb mixture to coat; shake off excess. Transfer to the prepared baking sheet.

4. Bake the chicken until the bread crumbs are golden and the chicken is cooked through, 45 to 50 minutes. Using a spatula, loosen the chicken from the sheet before serving.

lemon-tarragon roast chicken with vegetables

SERVES 4 TO 6

Red onions, cut at an angle, form a V-shaped roasting rack for the chicken.

- 1 whole chicken (3½ to 4 pounds), rinsed, trimmed of excess fat, and patted dry
- 1 garlic bulb, halved horizontally
- 2 sprigs fresh tarragon, plus 1 tablespoon chopped tarragon leaves
- 3 tablespoons unsalted butter, softened
- 1 shallot, finely chopped
  Coarse salt and freshly ground pepper
- 2 lemons (1 halved, 1 thinly sliced)
- 5 red onions (2 large and 3 small), peeled
- 4 long, thin carrots, peeled (halved or quartered lengthwise if large)
- 3 stalks celery
- 6 small red potatoes, halved (or 3 russet potatoes, cut into thirds)
- ½ cup dry white wine
- ½ cup homemade or low-sodium store-bought chicken stock

1. Preheat the oven to 400°F. Rub the chicken inside and out with 1 garlic half. Place both garlic halves and the tarragon sprigs in the cavity. Stir together the butter, shallot, chopped tarragon, ½ teaspoon salt, and ¼ teaspoon pepper. Loosen the skin near the cavity with your hands; spread the butter mixture under the skin all over the flesh.

2. Squeeze juice from the lemon halves over the chicken; place in cavity. Season the bird with 1 teaspoon salt and ½ teaspoon pepper.

3. Halve the large onions horizontally at an angle. Arrange in the middle of a 9 × 13-inch roasting pan to form a square. Position halves so the slanted ends of each pair face each other, inward, and almost touch. Place the chicken, breast side up, on the onion rack.

4. Quarter the small onions; arrange with the carrots, celery, and potatoes around bird. Tuck the lemon slices between the wings and breast and the legs and breast. Pour the wine and stock over the vegetables.

5. Roast the chicken and vegetables, basting 2 or 3 times with the pan juices, until an instant-read thermometer inserted into the thickest part of chicken thigh registers 165°F and juices run clear, 1 to 1½ hours.

6. Remove the pan from the oven, and let the chicken stand 10 minutes. Carve the chicken. Arrange the chicken and roasted vegetables (including rack onions) on a platter. Spoon the pan juices over the meat.

mini chicken potpies
with herb dough

MAKES 8 4-INCH PIES

1   whole chicken (4 pounds), rinsed
    and patted dry

4   cups homemade or low-sodium
    store-bought chicken stock

1   large onion, halved

2   bay leaves

½   teaspoon whole black peppercorns

3   sprigs fresh thyme, plus 2 tablespoons
    thyme leaves

1   celery stalk, cut crosswise into thirds

5   tablespoons unsalted butter

9   ounces medium red potatoes,
    cut into ½-inch chunks

12 white, red, or yellow pearl onions
    (halved lengthwise if large)

1   medium leek, white and pale green
    parts only, cut into ¼-inch-thick rounds
    and rinsed well

2   medium carrots, peeled and cut
    into ¼-inch-thick rounds

6   ounces white mushrooms, halved
    lengthwise (quartered if large)

¼   cup plus 1 tablespoon all-purpose flour,
    plus more for dusting

1   cup milk

2   tablespoons coarsely chopped fresh
    flat-leaf parsley

    Finely grated zest of 1 lemon

2   teaspoons coarse salt

½   teaspoon freshly ground pepper

    Martha's Perfect Pâte Brisée (page 647)

2   tablespoons mixed fresh herb leaves,
    such as flat-leaf parsley, sage, chives,
    thyme, dill, rosemary, and oregano

1   large egg

1. Put the chicken, stock, large onion, bay leaves, peppercorns, thyme sprigs, and celery in a large (8-quart) pot. Add just enough water to cover the chicken. Cover the pot; bring the mixture to a boil. Uncover; reduce heat. Simmer 1 hour.

2. Transfer the chicken to a cutting board (reserve the stock in the pot). Remove the skin from the chicken; discard. Cut the meat from the bones; discard the bones. Using a fork, shred the meat into bite-size pieces; set aside.

3. Pour the stock through a fine sieve into a large bowl; discard the solids. Set aside 2 cups stock. (Reserve the remaining stock for another use. Cooled stock can be frozen in an airtight container up to 4 months; thaw in the refrigerator.)

4. Melt the butter in a large skillet over medium-high heat. Add the potatoes and pearl onions. Cook, stirring occasionally, until the potatoes begin to turn golden, about 5 minutes. Add the leek, carrots, and mushrooms; cook, stirring occasionally, until softened, about 5 minutes more. Add the flour; cook, stirring, 1 minute.

5. Stir in the reserved 2 cups stock and the milk. Bring to a simmer; cook, stirring constantly, until thick and bubbling, 2 to 3 minutes. Stir in the chicken, parsley, thyme leaves, zest, salt, and pepper.

6. Divide the chicken mixture evenly among 8 4 × 2-inch ramekins. Let cool slightly.

7. Preheat the oven to 375°F. Roll out the pâte brisée on a lightly floured surface to ¼ inch thick. Arrange the mixed herbs on top; roll out the dough with a lightly floured pin to ⅛ inch thick, gently pressing herbs.

8. Using a fluted (or plain) round dough cutter (4½ inches in diameter), cut out 8 rounds from the dough. Lightly beat the egg with 1 tablespoon water. Brush the top edges of the ramekins with egg wash. Place a dough round over each ramekin; gently press to seal. Chill in the freezer until the dough is firm, about 10 minutes.

9. Brush the dough with egg wash. Cut 4 slits in top of each dough round for steam vents. Bake until the crust is golden brown and the filling is bubbling, 35 to 40 minutes.

southern indian chicken curry with mustard seeds

SERVES 4

This dish was inspired by one of cookbook author Madhur Jaffrey's lamb curries.

¼ cup vegetable oil

6 whole dried red hot chiles, each broken into 3 or 4 pieces

2 teaspoons brown or yellow mustard seeds

1 whole cinnamon stick (3 inches)

½ teaspoon urad dal or yellow split peas

1¼ cups very thinly sliced shallots (about 4)

10 garlic cloves, very thinly sliced

10 fresh curry leaves (optional)

2 teaspoons grated peeled fresh ginger

1¼ cups chopped plum tomatoes (about 3)

1¼ pounds boneless, skinless chicken thighs, cut into 1-inch pieces

¼ teaspoon ground turmeric

   Coarse salt

   Raita, for serving

   Pooris, for serving (optional)

1. Heat the oil in a large Dutch oven over medium-high heat until hot but not smoking. Add the chiles, mustard seeds, cinnamon, and urad dal; cook, shaking the pot, until the seeds pop, about 45 seconds. Add the shallots, garlic, and curry leaves; cook, stirring, until the shallots are golden, about 4 minutes. Add the ginger; cook, stirring, 1 minute. Add the tomatoes; cook, stirring, 2 minutes.

2. Add the chicken; sprinkle with the turmeric and 1½ teaspoons salt. Cook, stirring occasionally, about 4 minutes. Stir in 2 cups water. Bring to a boil. Cover; reduce heat to medium-low. Simmer until the chicken is very tender, about 30 minutes.

3. Uncover. Bring to a boil over medium-high heat. Boil until the sauce coats the meat, about 10 minutes. Season with salt. Serve with raita and pooris, if desired.

chicken scaloppine with arugula, lemon, and parmesan

SERVES 4

To prevent the arugula from wilting, let the chicken cool slightly before serving.

4 boneless, skinless chicken breast halves (about 6 ounces each)

½ teaspoon coarse salt

   Freshly ground pepper

   Olive oil cooking spray

4 teaspoons fresh lemon juice

2 tablespoons extra-virgin olive oil

8 ounces arugula (about 1 bunch)

1 ounce Parmesan cheese, such as Parmigiano-Reggiano

4 lemon wedges

1. One at a time, place the chicken breast halves on a cutting board between 2 sheets of plastic wrap. Pound with the flat side of a meat mallet or the bottom of a small, heavy skillet until ¼ inch thick. Sprinkle each piece all over with ⅛ teaspoon salt; season with pepper.

2. Coat a 12-inch nonstick skillet with cooking spray, and heat over medium heat until hot but not smoking. Put 2 chicken breast halves, smooth sides down, in the pan; they should lie flat without touching. Cook 4 minutes; turn, and cook until no longer pink in the center, 2 to 3 minutes more. Wipe the skillet clean; repeat with the remaining chicken.

3. Whisk together the lemon juice and 4 teaspoons oil in a large bowl. Add the arugula; toss to coat. Divide among 4 plates. Top with a chicken breast half, and drizzle each with ½ teaspoon oil. With a vegetable peeler, shave the cheese over the plates, dividing it evenly. Serve with lemon wedges.

FIT TO EAT RECIPE PER SERVING: 295 CALORIES, 11 G FAT, 103 MG CHOLESTEROL, 6 G CARBOHYDRATE, 480 MG SODIUM, 44 G PROTEIN, 2 G FIBER

rolled chicken breasts with almond-mint pesto and zucchini

SERVES 4

- 1 ounce whole blanched almonds (about ¼ cup)
- 1 medium shallot, coarsely chopped
- 1¼ cups loosely packed fresh mint leaves
- ½ cup finely grated pecorino cheese (about 1 ounce)
- 1 tablespoon plus 2 teaspoons extra-virgin olive oil
- 4 boneless, skinless chicken breast halves (about 6 ounces each)
  Coarse salt and freshly ground pepper
  Olive oil cooking spray
- 3 medium zucchini (about 6 ounces each), cut into 3 × ½-inch strips
- 2 garlic cloves, smashed
- 1 tablespoon red-wine vinegar

1. Toast the almonds in a skillet over medium heat, tossing frequently, until golden and fragrant, about 6 minutes. Let cool completely. Process the almonds and shallot in a food processor until a coarse paste forms. Add 1 cup mint; pulse a few times until coarsely chopped. Add the cheese and oil; pulse a few times until combined. Transfer to a small bowl.

2. One at a time, place the chicken breast halves on a cutting board between 2 sheets of plastic wrap. Pound with the flat side of a meat mallet or the bottom of a small, heavy skillet until ⅛ to ¼ inch thick. Sprinkle each piece all over with ⅛ teaspoon salt; season with pepper.

3. Put the breast halves on a cutting board, smooth side down, and spread evenly with pesto. Roll up the chicken, starting with the pointed tip of each piece. Secure with 2 toothpicks, pushing them in sideways at an angle; set aside.

4. Coat a 12-inch nonstick skillet with cooking spray, and heat over medium-high heat until hot but not smoking. Add the zucchini and garlic; season with ⅛ teaspoon salt. Cook, stirring occasionally, until the zucchini just turns golden brown, about 5 minutes. Reduce heat to medium, and cook, tossing occasionally, 5 minutes. Stir in the vinegar; season with pepper. Transfer the zucchini to a medium bowl, and cover with foil.

5. Wipe the skillet clean. Coat with cooking spray; heat over medium heat until hot but not smoking. Add the rolled chicken, and cook, turning to brown all sides, about 5 minutes. Reduce heat to medium-low, and continue cooking until the chicken is no longer pink in the center, 20 to 25 minutes. Let rest 5 minutes, and cut each roll into 5 pieces. Toss the reserved zucchini with ¼ cup mint. Divide the zucchini and chicken among 4 plates.

FIT TO EAT RECIPE PER SERVING: 339 CALORIES, 13 G FAT, 103 MG CHOLESTEROL, 9 G CARBOHYDRATE, 532 MG SODIUM, 45 G PROTEIN, 3 G FIBER

baked buttermilk chicken

SERVES 4

- Olive oil cooking spray
- 4 chicken drumsticks (about 1 pound), skins removed
- 2 whole boneless, skinless chicken breasts (about 1¾ pounds), halved
- 2½ cups low-fat buttermilk
- 4 cups cornflakes, finely crushed
- ¾ teaspoon Old Bay seasoning
- ½ teaspoon dried thyme
- ½ teaspoon dried basil
- ¼ teaspoon cayenne pepper
  Lemon wedges, for garnish (optional)
  Flat-leaf parsley sprig, for garnish (optional)

1. Preheat the oven to 400° F. Generously coat a rimmed baking sheet with cooking spray; set aside. Rinse the chicken, and pat dry. Transfer to a medium bowl. Pour the buttermilk over the chicken. Cover, and let marinate 1 hour in refrigerator.

2. Toss the cornflakes, Old Bay, thyme, basil, and cayenne in a large bowl. Remove 1 piece of chicken at a time from the buttermilk, letting excess drip back into the bowl; dredge in the cornflake mixture.

3. Transfer the pieces to the baking sheet; lightly coat each with cooking spray. Bake, turning the pieces once, until crisp and cooked through, about 40 minutes. Transfer to a platter; garnish with lemon wedges and parsley, if desired.

FIT TO EAT RECIPE PER SERVING: 362 CALORIES, 5 G FAT, 119 MG CHOLESTEROL, 32 G CARBOHYDRATE, 586 MG SODIUM, 46 G PROTEIN, 1 G FIBER

barbecued chicken

SERVES 8

4 whole chickens (about 3 pounds each)
1¼ quarts Barbecue Sauce (recipe follows)

1. Rinse the chickens inside and out under cold water, and pat dry. Truss the legs with kitchen twine, and set aside.

2. Heat a charcoal or gas grill. If using a charcoal grill, arrange the hot coals around the inside edge of grill. Arrange the chickens, breast sides up, in a row across the center. If using a gas grill, cook the chickens over medium heat until brown on all sides, rotating every 5 to 7 minutes; cover the grill as needed to maintain heat.

3. Baste the chickens with barbecue sauce. Continue cooking, basting frequently, until an instant-read thermometer registers 170°F in the breast and 180°F in the thickest part of the thigh (avoiding bone), about 1 hour. If the chickens brown too quickly before they are cooked through, transfer to baking pans and finish in a 350°F oven.

barbecue sauce

MAKES 2½ QUARTS

This recipe makes enough sauce for 8 chickens. Refrigerate leftover sauce for up to 2 weeks.

3 tablespoons canola oil
2 large onions, finely chopped
6 garlic cloves, minced
2 cans (28 ounces each) crushed tomatoes
2½ cups cider vinegar
2 cups firmly packed dark-brown sugar
1 cup honey
3 tablespoons chili powder
2 tablespoons soy sauce
2 tablespoons hot dry mustard
2 tablespoons paprika
1 tablespoon coarse salt

Heat the oil in a large, heavy-bottomed saucepan over medium heat. Add the onions and garlic; cook until golden brown, about 15 minutes. Add the remaining ingredients; bring to a boil. Reduce heat; simmer uncovered, stirring occasionally, until the sauce thickens, about 2 hours.

chicken and dumplings

SERVES 6

If you want to make the dish in advance, prepare the chicken and sauce through step 2. Let cool completely, then cover and refrigerate overnight. Rewarm gently before proceeding.

for the chicken

1 pound boneless, skinless chicken thighs (5 to 6)
1 pound boneless, skinless chicken breast halves (about 3 pieces)
½ teaspoon fine sea salt, plus more for the cooking water
⅛ teaspoon freshly ground pepper
1 tablespoon unsalted butter
1 large onion, finely chopped
1 14½-ounce can low-sodium chicken broth, skimmed of fat
1½ teaspoons finely chopped fresh thyme
2 tablespoons cornstarch
2 tablespoons all-purpose flour
2 cups low-fat milk
3 carrots, peeled and diagonally sliced ¼ inch thick
½ pound green beans, trimmed and cut into 1-inch pieces

for the dumplings

1 cup all-purpose flour
½ cup yellow cornmeal
2 teaspoons baking powder
¼ teaspoon fine sea salt
2 tablespoons cold unsalted butter, cut in bits
¾ cup low-fat milk

1. Sprinkle the chicken with salt and pepper. Heat a 6-quart Dutch oven over medium; add the thighs. Cook, turning once, until nicely browned on both sides and cooked through, 8 to 10 minutes. Transfer to a platter. Repeat with the breasts; cut the breasts crosswise into thirds.

2. Add the butter to the pot; when melted, add the onion, cover, and cook, stirring occasionally, until softened, about 6 minutes. Stir in the broth and thyme; bring to a boil. Combine the cornstarch and flour in a bowl. Gradually whisk in the milk, and whisk the milk mixture into the broth. Boil, whisking, until thickened, about 5 minutes. Remove from heat; return the chicken to the pot.

3. Bring a saucepan of water to a boil; add salt. Add the carrots and green beans; cook until crisp-tender, about 5 minutes. Drain in a colander, rinsing with cold water to stop the cooking. Stir into the chicken mixture in the pot.

4. Prepare the dumpling dough: In a medium bowl, whisk together the flour, cornmeal, baking powder, and salt. Add the butter; cut into the dry mixture with your fingers until mealy. Pour in the milk; stir with a fork until the dough comes together. Return the chicken mixture to a simmer, and drop the dough by tablespoons on the surface of the stew. Cover; cook for 15 minutes without lifting the lid. (The dumplings will puff up.) Serve.

FIT TO EAT RECIPE PER SERVING: 442 CALORIES, 12 G FAT, 126 MG CHOLESTEROL, 42 G CARBOHYDRATE, 810 MG SODIUM, 40 G PROTEIN, 4 G FIBER

grilled soy-lime chicken breasts
SERVES 4

¼ cup fresh lime juice (about 2 limes)

¼ cup soy sauce

¼ cup extra-virgin olive oil

4 boneless, skinless chicken breasts

1 head Boston lettuce, washed, leaves separated

1 bunch fresh mint

1 bunch fresh cilantro

1. Whisk together the lime juice, soy sauce, and oil in a bowl. Place the chicken breasts on a work surface between 2 layers of waxed paper or plastic wrap. Using the smooth side of a meat pounder, pound the chicken breasts until all the pieces are an even ½-inch thickness.

2. Place the chicken breasts in a resealable plastic bag or glass baking dish. Pour the marinade into the bag or over the chicken in a dish. Refrigerate at least 3 hours or overnight.

3. Heat a grill or grill pan over medium heat. Remove the chicken from the marinade, letting excess drip off. Grill the chicken until cooked through, about 3 minutes per side. Shred or slice the chicken, and serve with lettuce leaves and herbs on the side.

crisp mustard-glazed chicken breasts
SERVES 4

4 boneless chicken breasts, skin on

2 tablespoons olive oil, plus more for the breasts

   Coarse salt and freshly ground pepper

4 tablespoons unsalted butter, softened

2½ tablespoons Dijon mustard

¾ cup coarse bread crumbs

2 tablespoons chopped fresh thyme, plus more for garnish

¾ cup homemade or low-sodium store-bought chicken stock

½ cup heavy cream

1. Preheat the oven to 375°F. Rub the chicken breasts lightly with the olive oil, and season with salt and pepper.

2. Combine 2 tablespoons butter with the mustard; reserve 2 teaspoons for the sauce. Melt the remaining 2 tablespoons butter; mix with the bread crumbs and thyme, and season with salt and pepper.

3. In a large ovenproof skillet, heat oil over medium-high heat. Sear the chicken, skin side down, until crispy, about 5 minutes. Remove from heat. Smear with the mustard mixture, and sprinkle with the bread crumbs. Turn skin side up; apply the mustard mixture and bread crumbs.

4. Transfer the skillet to the oven, and roast until the chicken is cooked through and the top is golden brown, 15 to 20 minutes.

5. Transfer the chicken to a serving platter. Add the stock and cream to the skillet over medium heat, and stir with a wooden spoon until creamy and reduced to ¾ cup, about 3 minutes. Remove from heat, and stir in the reserved mustard mixture. Strain through a fine sieve, and serve with the chicken. Garnish with thyme.

chicken cassoulet with crisp bread crumb topping

SERVES 6

    5 garlic cloves, minced
    1 tablespoon chopped fresh rosemary
 1½ teaspoons chopped fresh thyme
    2 tablespoons balsamic vinegar
    6 boneless, skinless chicken thighs,
       trimmed of fat
    1 pound dried cannellini beans, soaked
       overnight in cold water
    3 carrots, cut into ½-inch pieces
    2 stalks celery, cut into ¼-inch pieces
    1 onion, cut into ¼-inch pieces
    1 dried bay leaf
    2 tablespoons finely chopped fresh sage
    1 teaspoon coarse salt
  ½ teaspoon extra-virgin olive oil
    1 cup fresh bread crumbs

1. Marinate the chicken: In a bowl large enough to hold the chicken thighs, combine 2 garlic cloves, the rosemary, ½ teaspoon thyme, and the vinegar. Add the chicken; toss to coat. Cover; refrigerate 1 to 2 hours.

2. Preheat the oven to 375°F, with the rack in the upper third. Drain the beans, and place them in a large stockpot with the carrots, celery, onion, remaining 3 garlic cloves, bay leaf, sage, and remaining teaspoon thyme. Fill with enough cold water to cover by about 4 inches; bring to a simmer over medium-high heat. Reduce heat to medium-low; cook, stirring occasionally, until the beans are tender, 1½ to 2 hours.

3. Transfer the bean mixture to a colander set over a bowl, reserving the cooking liquid; let cool slightly. Puree half the mixture in the bowl of a food processor fitted with the metal blade. With the motor running, pour in about 1 cup reserved cooking liquid until thick and smooth. Return to the pot with the remaining bean mixture. Add the salt; stir to combine.

4. Brush an 8 × 8 × 2½-inch baking dish with the oil. Remove the chicken from the marinade, and arrange it in a single layer in the prepared dish. Bake until the chicken is cooked through, about 15 minutes.

5. Remove the dish from the oven; pour the bean mixture over the chicken, and sprinkle evenly with the bread crumbs. Set the dish on a baking sheet; return to the oven, and bake until the bread crumbs are golden brown and the beans are bubbling, about 30 minutes. Remove from the oven; serve hot.

FIT TO EAT RECIPE PER SERVING: 446 CALORIES, 5 G FAT, 54 MG CHOLESTEROL, 68 G CARBOHYDRATE, 524 MG SODIUM, 34 G PROTEIN, 18 G FIBER

herb-stuffed chicken breasts

SERVES 4

    1 tablespoon extra-virgin olive oil
    4 leeks, white and light-green parts, washed
       well and sliced into ¼-inch rounds
    1 tablespoon finely chopped fresh rosemary
    1 tablespoon plus 1 teaspoon fresh
       thyme leaves
    1 teaspoon coarse salt
    1 teaspoon freshly ground pepper
    2 whole boneless, skinless chicken
       breasts (about 1⅓ pounds), halved
    2 slices whole-wheat bread
    4 teaspoons Dijon mustard
    1 cup homemade or low-sodium store-
       bought chicken stock, skimmed of fat

1. Preheat the oven to 350°F. In a large ovenproof skillet, heat 1 teaspoon oil over medium heat. Add the leeks, and cook 4 minutes. Add 2 teaspoons each rosemary and thyme; cook 1 minute more. Season with ¼ teaspoon salt and ½ teaspoon pepper. Transfer to a medium bowl; let cool.

2. Using a sharp knife, carve a pocket in the center of each chicken breast by inserting the tip into the thickest part and cutting an opening (leaving about 1 inch uncut on each side), being careful not to cut all the way through the breast. Place 2 tablespoons leek mixture in each pocket. Heat 1 teaspoon oil in a large skillet over medium-high heat.

Add the chicken breasts, and sauté until golden, about 3 minutes on each side. Remove from heat, and transfer to a clean work surface.

3. Place the bread in the bowl of a food processor fitted with the metal blade, and process until fine crumbs form. Transfer the bread crumbs to a bowl. Add the remaining teaspoon rosemary and 1 teaspoon thyme. Season with the remaining ¾ teaspoon salt and ½ teaspoon pepper. Spread 1 teaspoon mustard over one side of each chicken breast, and cover with about 3 tablespoons herbed bread crumbs, pressing gently to adhere. Drizzle the remaining teaspoon oil over all.

4. Place the skillet in the oven; roast the chicken until it is golden and cooked through, about 15 minutes. Remove from the oven; transfer the chicken to a serving dish, and cover with foil while you make the sauce. Place the skillet over medium heat, and add the chicken stock; deglaze the pan, stirring to loosen any browned bits with a wooden spoon. Continue cooking until the stock is reduced by half, about 3 minutes. Remove from heat; add the remaining teaspoon thyme. Serve with the chicken.

FIT TO EAT RECIPE PER SERVING: 296 CALORIES, 7 G FAT, 86 MG CHOLESTEROL, 20 G CARBOHYDRATE, 807 MG SODIUM, 37 G PROTEIN, 2 G FIBER

braised chicken with olives, carrots, and chickpeas

SERVES 4

Serve this stewlike chicken dish over couscous or mashed potatoes, or with a crusty baguette to soak up the flavorful broth. We used Cerignola olives from southern Italy; they are large and firm enough to hold up to slow cooking methods like braising.

- 1 tablespoon olive oil
- 4 whole chicken legs, skinned and cut into thighs and drumsticks (about 2½ pounds)
- 1 medium yellow onion, cut into ½-inch dice
- 3 carrots, cut into ½-inch dice
- 2 garlic cloves, minced
- 1 1½-inch piece fresh ginger, finely chopped (about 2 tablespoons)
- 1 cup low-sodium store-bought chicken broth
- 1 cup water
- 1 cup dry white wine
- 4 sprigs thyme
- ⅓ cup raisins
- ½ cup pitted and roughly chopped large green olives, such as Cerignola (about 6)
- ¾ cup canned chickpeas, rinsed and drained

1. Preheat the oven to 350° F. In a large ovenproof skillet or Dutch oven, heat the olive oil over medium heat. Place the chicken pieces in the skillet, being careful not to overcrowd the pan. Sauté until the chicken is nicely crisped and browned on both sides, about 5 minutes per side. Transfer the chicken to a large plate, and set aside.

2. Reduce heat to medium-low; to the same skillet, add the onion, carrots, garlic, and ginger. Sauté, stirring frequently, until the onion is soft and translucent, about 5 minutes. Add the chicken broth, the water, and wine; bring to a boil, and deglaze the pan by scraping up any browned bits from the bottom with a wooden spoon. Return the chicken to the skillet, and add the thyme. Bring the liquid back to a boil; cover, and transfer to the oven. Braise 45 minutes.

3. Remove the skillet from the oven, and stir in the raisins, olives, and chickpeas. Return to the oven; continue braising, uncovered, 20 minutes more. Remove from oven; discard the thyme. Serve hot.

FIT TO EAT RECIPE PER SERVING: 406 CALORIES, 14 G FAT, 139 MG CHOLESTEROL, 26 G CARBOHYDRATE, 868 MG SODIUM, 36 G PROTEIN, 5 G FIBER

poached chicken with hot english mustard
SERVES 4

This recipe yields excess chicken stock. The excess can be kept in plastic containers and frozen for several months.

- 2 carrots, peeled and cut in half
- 1 stalk celery, cut in half
- 2 onions, cut in half
- 3 stems fresh flat-leaf parsley
- 10 whole black peppercorns
- 1 4-pound whole chicken, rinsed and patted dry
- Coarse salt
- 4 slices French bread, about ⅓ inch thick
- 1 tablespoon extra-virgin olive oil
- 1 small bunch watercress
- ¼ cup hot English mustard, or to taste

1. Place the carrots, celery, onions, parsley, and peppercorns in a stockpot. Add the chicken. Fill the pot with enough cold water to cover the chicken by 1 inch.

2. Set over medium-high heat, and bring the water to a boil. Reduce heat, and allow to simmer, skimming off any foam that rises to the surface, for 1 hour.

3. Remove the chicken from the stock; set aside. Strain the stock through a very fine sieve or chinois. Discard the solids. Transfer the stock to a metal bowl. Set the bowl in another bowl, full of ice water. Let stand until the stock is completely chilled, replacing the ice if necessary, and fat can be skimmed off the surface of the stock.

4. Meanwhile, when the chicken is cool enough to handle, remove the skin and discard. Carefully pull the meat off the bones (it should fall away quite easily), keeping it in large chunks when possible.

5. Return 5 cups stock to the stockpot or a large saucepan. Bring to a boil; adjust the seasoning with salt. Reduce heat to a simmer; simmer until stock has become very flavorful and reduced by 1 cup, about 15 minutes. Add the pieces of chicken; cook just until heated through, about 5 minutes.

6. Toast the bread until golden, and brush with the olive oil. Serve the chicken in a wide bowl with a ladle of hot broth. Add a handful of watercress to each bowl. Place a spoonful of mustard on toast, sprinkle with salt, and serve on the side.

grilled chicken paillards with endive and radicchio
SERVES 6

- 3 whole boneless, skinless chicken breasts, split (about 2 pounds)
  Basic Marinade (page 647)
- 3 heads Belgian endive, halved lengthwise
- 2 large heads radicchio, each cut in 6 wedges
- 2 tablespoons extra-virgin olive oil
  Coarse salt and freshly ground pepper
- 3 lemons, cut in half crosswise
  Rosemary sprigs, for garnish
  Thyme sprigs, for garnish

1. Cut open two sides of a resealable plastic bag. Place 1 chicken breast half in the bag; pound to ¼-inch thickness using a meat pounder. Transfer to a nonmetal container. Repeat with the remaining chicken. Add the marinade. Chill for 2 hours.

2. Brush the endive and radicchio with the olive oil; sprinkle with salt and pepper; set aside. Brush the cut sides of the lemons with olive oil.

3. Heat a grill or grill pan. Remove the chicken from the marinade; grill until browned and cooked through, 2 to 3 minutes on each side. Transfer to a serving platter.

4. Grill the endive, radicchio, and lemons until nicely browned, about 3 minutes; turn as needed. Serve on the platter with the chicken, garnished with rosemary and thyme.

barbecued chicken kabobs with potatoes and summer squash

MAKES 8

The potatoes must be parboiled so they will be done at the same time as the chicken.

1½   *chicken breasts (3 halves), cut into 1-inch cubes*

2   *cups Barbecue Sauce (page 280), or good-quality store-bought*

1   *cup water*

1½   *tablespoons coarse salt*

1¼   *pounds new or baby fingerling potatoes*

¾   *pound green or yellow summer squash (about 2), cut into 1-inch pieces*

2   *tablespoons olive oil*

1   *teaspoon freshly ground pepper*

1. Place the chicken in a large bowl. Add the barbecue sauce; toss. Cover, and refrigerate for at least 30 minutes or overnight.

2. Place the water in a large saucepan. Add 1 tablespoon salt and the potatoes. Bring to a boil over high heat. Reduce heat; simmer until the potatoes are almost tender when pierced with a knife, about 10 minutes. Do not overcook. Drain; halve. Set aside.

3. Thread 4 cubes of chicken, alternating with potatoes and squash, on each of 8 skewers. Gently brush the vegetables with some oil. Season with the remaining ½ tablespoon salt and the pepper.

4. Arrange the skewers, off direct heat, on a medium-hot grill. Grill, rotating the skewers and brushing with olive oil as necessary to prevent sticking, until cooked through, about 12 minutes depending on the heat of the grill. The vegetables should be soft and slightly charred.

chicken enchiladas

SERVES 6 TO 8

These can be made up to 1 day ahead or frozen up to 1 month ahead. Bring to room temperature before baking.

1   *whole chicken (3 to 4 pounds)*

2   *quarts homemade or low-sodium store-bought chicken stock*

2   *tablespoons extra-virgin olive oil*

1   *onion, halved, cut into ¼-inch slices*

2   *green or red bell peppers, seeded and cut into ¼-inch strips*

  Enchilada Sauce (recipe follows)

12   *6-inch corn tortillas*

2   *cups grated Monterey Jack cheese (about 6 ounces)*

2   *cups grated sharp Cheddar cheese (about 6 ounces)*

  Sour cream (optional)

1. Place the chicken in a large pot, and pour the chicken stock over it. Add enough water to cover if necessary. Bring to a boil, reduce to a simmer, and cook until the chicken is cooked through and very tender, about 1 hour. Transfer to a bowl to cool, and reserve the stock to use for the enchilada sauce, if desired. When the chicken is cool enough to handle, remove the meat from the bones, and shred; set aside.

2. Heat the olive oil in a large skillet over medium heat. Add the onion, and cook until the slices start to soften, about 5 minutes. Add the peppers, and cook until tender, about 7 minutes. Transfer to a bowl, and set aside.

3. When ready to assemble, preheat the oven to 350°F. Place the enchilada sauce in a medium saucepan over medium heat. When hot, dip the tortillas into the sauce, one at a time, to soften, and place side by side on 2 baking sheets. Divide the shredded chicken and pepper mixture among the tortillas. Place the cheeses in a bowl, and toss to combine. Top each tortilla with 2 tablespoons grated cheese. Roll up the tortillas, and place snugly, seam side down, in a 9 × 13-inch ovenproof baking dish. Top them with the remaining enchilada sauce and with the remaining grated cheese. Bake until the enchiladas are heated through and the cheese is melted, about 30 minutes. Serve with sour cream, if desired.

enchilada sauce

MAKES 4 CUPS

To tone down the sauce for little mouths, omit some of the chiles.

- 5 long fresh red chiles
- 1 cup homemade or low-sodium store-bought chicken stock
- 2 cups water
- 4 large tomatoes
- 1 small poblano chile
- ¼ cup extra-virgin olive oil
- 1 white onion, cut into ½-inch dice
- 2 scallions, chopped
- 3 garlic cloves, minced
- ½ cup tomato paste
- 1 teaspoon ground cumin
- 1 teaspoon fresh oregano, chopped
- ½ teaspoon coarse salt

1. Cut the chiles in half lengthwise; remove and discard the seeds and ribs. Set aside. In a small saucepan, bring the chicken stock and the water to a simmer. Add the chiles; simmer until tender, about 15 minutes. Set aside. Fill a medium saucepan with water; bring to a boil. Fill a large bowl with ice and water; set aside. Cut an X in the tomato bottoms; add to the boiling water one at a time. Simmer until the skin begins to peel. Transfer the tomatoes to the ice bath immediately; cool. When cool, peel and discard skins; chop, and set aside.

2. Place the poblano pepper directly on the trivet of a gas stove over high heat. Turn the pepper with tongs as each side blackens. (You may also place the pepper on a baking pan and broil in the oven, turning as each side becomes charred.) Transfer to a bowl, cover with plastic wrap, and let steam for

about 15 minutes. Peel off the blackened skin; discard. Cut the pepper in half; discard the seeds. Roughly chop the pepper, and set aside along with any juices that have collected in the bowl.

3. Heat the olive oil in a large high-sided skillet over medium heat. Add the onion, scallions, and garlic; sauté until translucent, about 10 minutes. Add the tomatoes, tomato paste, red chiles and liquid, poblanos and liquid, cumin, oregano, and salt. Stir to combine. Simmer gently for 15 minutes. Transfer to the jar of a blender or a food processor; puree until smooth. Return to the pan; keep hot if assembling enchiladas, or refrigerate up to 4 days.

normandy-style chicken and leeks with crème fraîche

SERVES 4

Hard cider has been fermented, so it contains alcohol. It is a traditional ingredient in Normandy, France, but you can substitute dry white wine.

- 1 whole chicken (about 4 pounds), cut into 8 pieces (each breast half cut in half crosswise), rinsed well and patted dry

  Coarse salt and freshly ground pepper
- 1 tablespoon unsalted butter
- 2 teaspoons olive oil
- 4 small leeks (about 1 pound), white and pale-green parts only, cut crosswise into 3-inch pieces, rinsed well
- 1 cup good-quality hard apple cider
- 1 tablespoon coarsely chopped fresh thyme leaves
- ½ cup Crème Fraîche (recipe follows; or use store-bought)
- 1 tablespoon finely chopped fresh flat-leaf parsley

1. Season chicken with salt and pepper. Melt butter with the oil in a large enameled cast-iron Dutch oven over medium-high heat until just bubbling. Add half the chicken pieces, skin sides down; cook, turning once, until golden, 2 to 3 minutes per side. Transfer chicken pieces to a plate; set aside. Repeat with remaining chicken pieces; add to plate. Remove pot from heat; let cool slightly.

2. Return pot to medium-low heat, and add leeks. Cook, stirring frequently, until leeks begin to soften and are pale golden, about 3 minutes. Add hard cider and thyme. Move leeks to edges of pot, and add all the chicken pieces to pot, skin sides down. Arrange leeks over chicken. Cover, and cook 15 minutes (if liquid is bubbling rapidly, reduce heat to low). Turn chicken pieces, and cook until breasts are cooked through, about 5 minutes more.

3. Transfer chicken breasts to a plate, and cover to keep warm. Adjust leeks so they are submerged in liquid. Cook, uncovered, until the remaining chicken pieces are tender and cooked through, about 10 minutes.

4. Using a slotted spoon, transfer all of the chicken to a warm serving platter. Remove leeks from pot, and arrange the leeks around chicken. Cover with foil, and set aside. Return pot to medium heat. Cook, uncovered, until liquid has reduced by about half (to a scant ⅔ cup), 8 to 10 minutes. Reduce heat to medium-low. Whisk in the crème fraîche and parsley. Ladle pan sauce over chicken and leeks. Serve immediately.

crème fraîche

MAKES ABOUT 2 CUPS

Leftover crème fraîche makes a delicious accompaniment to fruit desserts.

- 2 cups heavy cream
- 2 tablespoons low-fat buttermilk

Stir together cream and buttermilk in a medium bowl. Let stand at room temperature, partially covered, until thick, about 12 hours. Stir; cover, and refrigerate until ready to use, up to 2 weeks.

lemon-thyme chicken paillards

SERVES 6

- 6 boneless, skinless chicken breast halves (about 3 pounds total)
- 6 garlic cloves, halved lengthwise
- 3 lemons, 2 halved crosswise, 1 cut into wedges
- 6 sprigs fresh thyme
  Coarse salt and freshly ground pepper
- 1 tablespoon extra-virgin olive oil
  Arugula Salad (recipe follows)

1. Lay a chicken breast on parchment paper. Starting on 1 long side, cut horizontally into breast but not completely through. Open cut breast like a book. Top with another sheet of parchment. Flatten to an even thickness, about ⅓ inch thick. Repeat with remaining breasts.

2. Rub both sides of each breast with garlic; transfer chicken and garlic to a large resealable plastic bag. Squeeze 2 lemon halves over chicken; add rinds to bag. Thinly slice remaining lemon halves crosswise. Top each breast with a lemon slice and thyme sprig; season with pepper. Drizzle chicken with oil. Marinate in the refrigerator, flipping occasionally, at least 2 hours (up to overnight).

3. Preheat a grill or grill pan to high. Discard marinade, lemon, and thyme. Season chicken with salt and pepper. Grill, flipping once, until cooked through, 2 minutes per side. Serve chicken warm, at room temperature, or cold. Top each breast with salad, dividing evenly; serve with lemon wedges.

arugula salad

SERVES 6

- 1 tablespoon fresh lemon juice
- ¼ teaspoon coarse salt
  Pinch of freshly ground pepper
- 2 tablespoons extra-virgin olive oil
- 2 bunches baby arugula (about 6 cups)
- 1 head radicchio, torn into pieces (about 3 cups)
- 2 cups mâche (about 1 ounce) or 2 endives, leaves separated
- 1 cup grape tomatoes, thinly sliced

1. Whisk lemon juice, salt, and pepper in a small bowl. Gradually add oil, whisking constantly until emulsified

2. To serve, toss arugula, radicchio, mâche, and tomatoes in a large, chilled bowl with just enough dressing to lightly coat.

barbecued chicken wings

SERVES 12

You can bake the chicken wings a day ahead and store them, covered, in the refrigerator; bring them to room temperature before grilling.

24 whole chicken wings
 3 tablespoons olive oil
    Coarse salt and freshly ground pepper
    Pierre's Barbecue Sauce (page 272)

1. Preheat the oven to 400° F. Divide wings between 2 rimmed baking sheets. Drizzle each sheet with 4½ teaspoons oil. Season each with ½ teaspoon salt and a pinch of pepper; toss to combine. Bake until cooked through, about 30 minutes.

2. Preheat a grill to medium-high (if you are using a charcoal grill, coals are ready when you can hold your hand 5 inches above grill for just 3 to 4 seconds). Brush wings with barbecue sauce. Grill, turning and brushing with sauce occasionally, until heated through and marked by grill, 6 to 7 minutes. Serve immediately.

curried chicken with toasted almonds

SERVES 8

14 boneless, skinless chicken thighs (about 3¾ pounds), cut into 1-inch pieces
    Coarse salt
 3 tablespoons plus 2 teaspoons extra-virgin olive oil
 2 tablespoons plus 2 teaspoons curry powder
 1 teaspoon cumin seeds
 1 bay leaf
 1 small cinnamon stick
 2 large garlic cloves, minced
 2 tablespoons finely chopped peeled fresh ginger
 1 small yellow onion, finely chopped
1¼ cups heavy cream
 2 cups homemade or low-sodium store-bought chicken or vegetable stock
 2 Granny Smith apples, cored, quartered
 ½ teaspoon finely grated lime zest, plus 2 tablespoons and 2 teaspoons fresh lime juice (from about 2 limes)
 ¼ cup finely chopped fresh mint, plus sprigs for garnish
    Three-Grain Pilaf (recipe follows)
 ½ cup sliced blanched almonds, toasted

1. Season chicken with salt. Heat 3 tablespoons oil in a Dutch oven over medium-high heat. Brown chicken in batches (so as not to crowd pot), turning once, 2 to 3 minutes per side. Transfer cooked chicken to a plate as you work.

2. Reduce heat to low. Heat remaining 2 teaspoons oil in pot. Add spices, bay leaf, cinnamon stick, garlic, ginger, and onion. Cook, stirring often, until fragrant, about 5 minutes. Add chicken and juices, and stir to coat with spice mixture.

3. Raise heat to medium. Stir in cream, scraping bottom with a wooden spoon. Bring to a simmer. Add stock; return to a simmer. Reduce heat to low. Cook, partially covered, until chicken is tender, 30 to 35 minutes. Season with salt.

4. Just before serving, grate apples into a bowl using the large holes of a box grater. Stir in zest, lime juice, and mint.

5. Spoon curried chicken mixture over pilaf in bowls. Top with about 2 tablespoons apple-mint mixture. Sprinkle with almonds; garnish with mint sprigs.

three-grain pilaf
SERVES 8

- 2 tablespoons unsalted butter
- 1 small onion, finely chopped
- 1½ cups jasmine rice, rinsed
- ½ cup red rice, rinsed
- 1 cup quinoa, rinsed
- ¾ teaspoon coarse salt

Melt butter in a medium saucepan over medium heat. Add onion; cook, stirring occasionally, until onion is soft and pale gold, 8 to 10 minutes. Stir in 4 cups water, the grains, and salt. Raise heat to high; bring to a boil. Reduce heat to low, and stir. Cover, and cook until grains are tender, 20 to 25 minutes. Remove from heat, and let stand, covered, 10 minutes. Fluff with a fork, and serve.

roasted quartered chicken and shallots
SERVES 4

If you can't find precut chicken quarters, ask your butcher to quarter a 5-pound chicken and remove the backbone.

- 1 tablespoon unsalted butter, softened
- 4 pounds chicken quarters, skin on
  Coarse salt and freshly ground pepper
- 4 large shallots, peeled and halved lengthwise

1. Preheat the oven to 450°F. Lightly brush a rimmed baking sheet and the chicken pieces with butter. Lay chicken, skin side up, on sheet; season with 2 teaspoons salt and the pepper.

2. Roast chicken 20 minutes. Remove from oven. Carefully arrange shallots, cut side down, around chicken; season shallots with salt and pepper. Re-turn to oven. Continue roasting, basting chicken occasionally with pan juices, until an instant-read thermometer inserted into thickest part of the thigh (avoiding bone) registers 165°F and shallots are tender and caramelized, about 20 minutes more. Transfer to a platter; loosely tent with foil. Let stand 10 minutes before serving.

moroccan b'steeya
SERVES 6 TO 8

Season the chicken a day ahead so it has time to absorb the flavors.

- 1 whole roaster chicken (about 4 pounds), cut into 8 pieces
  Coarse salt
- 1 medium onion, finely chopped
- 3 garlic cloves, minced
- ⅛ teaspoon crumbled saffron
- ½ teaspoon ground ginger
- 1½ teaspoons ground cinnamon, plus more for sprinkling
- 1 cup coarsely chopped fresh flat-leaf parsley
- ½ cup coarsely chopped fresh cilantro
- ¼ cup unsalted butter, plus ½ cup melted (1½ sticks total)
- 6 large eggs, lightly beaten
- 1 tablespoon fresh lemon juice
  Freshly ground pepper
- 1¾ cups blanched whole almonds, toasted and coarsely chopped
- 3 tablespoons confectioners' sugar, plus more for sprinkling
- ¼ cup orange-flower water
- 1 package (17 ounces) store-bought phyllo dough

1. Put the chicken and ⅓ cup salt in a medium bowl; toss to coat. Refrigerate 1 hour. Rinse the chicken with cold water; pat dry. Mix the chicken, onion, garlic, saffron, ginger, 1 teaspoon cinnamon, ½ cup parsley, and ¼ cup cilantro in a large bowl; cover, and refrigerate overnight.

2. Transfer the chicken mixture to a medium heavy pot. Add enough water to cover (about 4 cups). Bring to a boil; reduce heat to medium. Add ¼ cup butter; cover, and simmer until chicken is falling off the bone, 1 to 1½ hours, adding water to cover if necessary. Transfer the chicken to a plate; let cool. Reserve the poaching liquid. Remove the meat from the bones and shred; discard the skin and bones. Set the chicken aside.

3. Bring the reserved poaching liquid to a boil over high heat; cook until reduced to ¾ cup. Reduce heat to medium-high. Slowly add the eggs; whisk constantly until the mixture is almost set, 4 to 6 minutes. Stir in the remaining ½ cup parsley, ¼ cup cilantro, and the lemon juice. Season with salt and pepper; set aside.

4. Stir together the almonds, sugar, and remaining ½ teaspoon cinnamon in a small bowl; set aside.

5. Preheat the oven to 375° F. Brush a 13-inch paella or pizza pan with 2 tablespoons melted butter. Stir together the remaining melted butter and the orange-flower water in a small bowl. Assemble the b'steeya: Brush a sheet of phyllo with butter mixture. Put it in the pan, leaving a 4-inch overhang. Repeat, buttering and adding 7 more sheets of phyllo, overlapping the layers and fanning out around the pan. (Keep unbuttered phyllo covered with plastic wrap and a damp kitchen towel.)

6. Arrange the chicken mixture evenly over the dough. Pour in the egg mixture. Top with 5 layers phyllo brushed with butter mixture. Sprinkle evenly with almond mixture. Fold up the edges of the phyllo to enclose. Top with 5 layers phyllo brushed with butter mixture; tuck the edges inside the pan. Slightly crinkle 2 unbuttered layers phyllo over top. Bake until golden brown, 35 to 40 minutes. Sprinkle with sugar and cinnamon.

perfect roast turkey

SERVES 12 TO 14

We brined our turkey for 24 hours, so leave plenty of time for this recipe. If you don't brine yours, skip steps 1 and 2. The USDA recommends cooking the turkey until the thickest part of the thigh registers 180° F. For a moister bird, we cooked ours to 165° F; it continues to cook outside the oven as it rests.

- 3 *cups coarse salt, plus more for seasoning*
- 5 *cups sugar*
- 2 *medium onions, coarsely chopped*
- 2 *medium leeks, white and pale-green parts only, rinsed and coarsely chopped*
- 2 *carrots, peeled and coarsely chopped*
- 2 *celery stalks, coarsely chopped*
- 2 *dried bay leaves*
- 3 *sprigs fresh thyme*
- 3 *sprigs fresh flat-leaf parsley*
- 2 *teaspoons whole black peppercorns, plus freshly ground pepper*
- 1 *fresh whole turkey (18 to 20 pounds), rinsed and patted dry, giblets and neck reserved for Gravy (recipe follows)*
- ½ *cup (1 stick) unsalted butter, melted, plus ¼ cup unsalted butter, softened*
- 1½ *cups dry white wine, such as Sauvignon Blanc*
  Chestnut Stuffing (recipe follows)
  Crab apples, fresh rosemary sprigs, and fresh sage, for garnish (optional)

1. Put the salt, sugar, onions, leeks, carrots, celery, bay leaves, thyme, parsley, peppercorns, and 10 cups water in a large stockpot. Bring to a boil, stirring until the salt and sugar have dissolved. Remove from heat; let the brine cool completely.

2. Add the turkey, breast first, to the brine. Cover; refrigerate 24 hours. Remove from the brine; pat dry with paper towels. Let stand at room temperature 2 hours.

3. Preheat the oven to 425°F, with a rack in the lowest position. Stir together the melted butter and wine in a medium bowl. Fold a very large piece of cheesecloth into quarters so it is large enough to cover the breast and halfway down the sides of the turkey. Immerse the cloth in the butter mixture; let soak while you prepare the turkey.

4. Place the turkey, breast side up, on a rack set in a roasting pan. Fold the wing tips under the turkey. Sprinkle 1 teaspoon each salt and pepper inside the turkey. Loosely fill the body and neck cavities with stuffing. Tie the legs together with kitchen twine. Fold the neck flap under; secure with toothpicks. Rub the turkey all over with softened butter; season with salt and pepper.

5. Remove the cheesecloth from the butter mixture, squeezing gently into a bowl. Reserve the butter mixture for brushing. Lay the cheesecloth over the turkey. Place the turkey, legs first, in the oven. Roast 30 minutes. Brush the cheesecloth and exposed turkey with butter mixture. Reduce temperature to 350°F. Roast, brushing every 30 minutes, 2½ hours more; cover with foil if browning too quickly. If making gravy, add the giblets and neck to the pan 1½ hours after reducing the temperature; roast 30 minutes, and reserve.

6. Discard the cheesecloth; rotate the pan. Baste the turkey with the pan juices. Roast, rotating the pan halfway through, until the skin is golden brown and an instant-read thermometer inserted into the thickest part of the thigh registers 180°F and stuffing reaches 165°F, about 1 hour. Transfer to a platter. Set the pan with drippings aside for gravy. Let the turkey stand at room temperature at least 30 minutes. Garnish, if desired.

gravy

MAKES ABOUT 4 CUPS

Add the giblets and neck to the pan with the turkey 1½ hours after the oven temperature is reduced to 350°F in step 5 (recipe above).

> *Giblets and neck from turkey*
> 5 *whole black peppercorns*
> 3 *sprigs fresh thyme*
> 3 *sprigs fresh flat-leaf parsley*
> 1 *sprig fresh rosemary*
> 1 *fresh or dried bay leaf*
> 3 *tablespoons unsalted butter*
> 2 *celery stalks, coarsely chopped*
> 1 *small carrot, coarsely chopped*
> 1 *leek, white and pale-green parts only, rinsed and coarsely chopped*
> 1 *medium onion, coarsely chopped*
> ¾ *cup dry white wine or turkey stock*
> 3 *tablespoons all-purpose flour*
> *Coarse salt and freshly ground pepper*

1. Trim the fat and membranes from the giblets. Rinse the giblets; pat dry. Add the giblets and neck to the pan with the turkey. Roast until browned, about 30 minutes. Set aside.

2. Make a bouquet garni: Tie the peppercorns, thyme, parsley, rosemary, and bay leaf in a square of cheesecloth. Set aside.

3. Make the stock: Melt the butter in a medium saucepan over medium-high heat. Add the vegetables. Cook, stirring, until beginning to brown, 7 to 10 minutes.

4. Reduce heat to medium; add the giblets, neck, bouquet garni, and 1 quart water. Cover, and bring to boil. Reduce heat to medium-low, and cook, uncovered, until reduced to about 3 cups, 50 to 60 minutes. Pour the mixture through a fine sieve into a clean medium saucepan. Keep the stock warm over medium-low heat. Roughly chop the giblets; shred the meat from the neck with a fork. Set aside. Discard the other solids.

5. Transfer the turkey to a large platter. Reserve 3 tablespoons drippings from pan. Pour the remain-

STUFFING 101

1. If using white bread, cut it into ¼- to ½-inch-thick slices, and set out overnight to dry. Break into ¼-inch cubes. (If using cornbread, break ½-inch-thick slices into 1-inch pieces.)

2. If desired, sauté sausage, pork, or beef until cooked through, and remove from the skillet with a slotted spoon.

3. Sauté chopped vegetables in the rendered fat from the meat (or in butter or olive oil) until they are just softened.

4. Combine the cooked meat (or cured meat such as ham), with the vegetables, fruit, nuts, and bread; toss to combine. Add herbs and seasoning, and toss again.

5. Add liquid; taste and adjust seasoning (if using eggs or raw oysters, adjust seasoning first, then decrease any other liquid and add 3 beaten eggs). Toss just until combined; overmixing yields a gummy texture.

6. Stuff the turkey just before roasting it.

ing drippings into a gravy separator; let stand until separated, about 10 minutes. Discard the fat.

6. Deglaze the roasting pan: Place the roasting pan over 2 burners. Add the wine; bring to a boil, stirring with a wooden spoon to loosen any browned bits on the bottom of the pan. Reserve the deglazed liquid.

7. Make the gravy: Put the reserved 3 tablespoons pan drippings from the turkey in a medium saucepan; cook over medium heat until hot. Add the flour, whisking vigorously to combine. Cook, whisking constantly, until fragrant and deep golden brown, about 9 minutes. Whisking vigorously, slowly add the hot stock. Bring to a boil. Reduce heat to a gentle simmer.

8. Stir in the reserved deglazed liquid and separated pan juices. Add the giblets and neck meat. Season with salt and pepper. Simmer, stirring occasionally, until the gravy has thickened to the consistency of heavy cream, about 20 minutes. Pour through a fine sieve into a saucepan; discard the solids. Keep the gravy warm over low heat. Season with salt and pepper.

chestnut stuffing
SERVES 10 TO 12

You will need to dry the bread cubes overnight; transfer them to resealable plastic bags until you're ready to make the stuffing, up to 1 day more.

- 2 loaves good-quality white bread, cut into ¾-inch cubes (about 20 cups)
- 1½ pounds (4 cups) fresh chestnuts, scored with an X
- ¾ cup (1½ sticks) unsalted butter
- 4 small onions, peeled and cut into ¼-inch dice (about 3 cups)
- 1 bunch celery, cut into ¼-inch dice (about 4 cups)
- 3 tablespoons finely chopped fresh sage
- 5 cups homemade or low-sodium store-bought chicken stock
- 1 tablespoon coarse salt
- 3 cups coarsely chopped fresh flat-leaf parsley
  Freshly ground pepper

1. Spread the bread cubes in single layers on baking sheets. Set aside to dry out at room temperature, uncovered, overnight.

2. Bring a medium saucepan of water to a boil. Add the chestnuts; cook until soft, about 20 minutes. Drain; let cool slightly. Peel and quarter the chestnuts; set aside. Peeled chestnuts can be refrigerated in an airtight container 2 to 3 days.

3. Melt the butter in a large skillet over medium heat. Add the onions and celery; cook, stirring, until the onions are translucent, about 10 minutes. Add the sage; cook 3 minutes. Stir in ½ cup stock; cook until reduced by half, about 5 minutes.

4. Transfer the onion mixture to a large bowl. Add the remaining 4½ cups stock, the chestnuts, bread, salt, and parsley; season with pepper. Toss to combine. If not stuffing turkey, transfer to a buttered 17 × 12-inch baking dish. Cover; bake at 350°F for 25 minutes. Uncover; bake until hot and golden brown, 30 minutes more.

thanksgiving leftovers shepherd's pie
SERVES 4 TO 6

To bake individual pies, use 6 10-ounce ramekins, and reduce cooking time to 20 to 30 minutes.

- 3 cups cooked stuffing
- 1 cup cranberry sauce, plus more for topping (optional)
- 1 pound sliced cooked turkey
- 10 ounces glazed carrots (or another leftover vegetable)
- 4 to 6 tablespoons gravy
- 3 to 4 cups mashed potatoes

1. Preheat the oven to 350°F. In a 9- to 10-inch pie plate, mound the stuffing on the bottom; layer with the cranberry sauce, turkey, and carrots. Drizzle with the gravy; spread the potatoes over the surface to the sides of the dish. Top with more cranberry sauce, if desired.

2. Place the pie on a baking sheet, and bake until heated through and the potatoes are golden, 35 to 40 minutes. Let cool slightly.

turkey meatloaf

SERVES 6

- 4 slices white bread, crusts trimmed, torn into pieces
- 8 small sage leaves
- 1½ pounds ground lean turkey
- 1 large yellow onion, cut into eighths
- 1 stalk celery, cut into 2-inch pieces
- ½ teaspoon dried thyme
- 1 large whole egg, lightly beaten
- 2 tablespoons tomato paste
- 4 teaspoons Dijon mustard
- 1¼ teaspoons Worcestershire sauce
- ¾ teaspoon coarse salt
  Freshly ground black pepper
- 1 large egg white
  Cheater's Gravy, (recipe follows)
  Garlic Mashed Potatoes, (recipe follows)

1. Preheat the oven to 400°F, with the rack in the center. Place the bread and sage leaves in the bowl of a food processor; pulse to form fine crumbs. Transfer to a medium bowl, and add the ground turkey.

2. Place the onion and celery in the bowl of the food processor; pulse until finely chopped. Add to the turkey mixture, using your hands to combine. Add the thyme, whole egg, 1 tablespoon tomato paste, mustard, 1 teaspoon Worcestershire, and salt; season with pepper. Combine well. Place in a 9 × 5 × 2½-inch nonstick loaf pan.

3. In a small bowl, combine the egg white with the remaining tablespoon tomato paste and ¼ teaspoon Worcestershire, whisking with a fork until smooth. Spoon the mixture over the meatloaf; spread evenly.

4. Transfer the pan to the oven; place a baking sheet on the lower rack to catch the drippings. Cook until a meat thermometer inserted in the center of the meatloaf registers 180°F, about 1¼ hours. Remove from the oven; let rest 15 minutes, covered with foil.

5. To serve, cut the meatloaf into 12 slices, and divide evenly among 6 serving plates. Serve immediately with hot gravy and mashed potatoes.

FIT TO EAT RECIPE PER SERVING: 200 CALORIES, 3 G FAT, 86 MG CHOLESTEROL, 13 G CARBOHYDRATE, 451 MG SODIUM, 31 G PROTEIN, 1 G FIBER

cheater's gravy

MAKES ABOUT 1 CUP; SERVES 6

We serve this flavorful gravy over meatloaf and mashed potatoes, but it is equally good with other classic comfort foods, such as ham and biscuits.

- 1 cup homemade or low-sodium store-bought chicken stock, skimmed of fat
- 1 teaspoon cornstarch
- 1 tablespoon cold water
- 1 tablespoon chopped fresh flat-leaf parsley

1. In a small saucepan, bring the chicken stock to a boil over high heat. Reduce heat to medium, and simmer until the stock is reduced by half, about 10 minutes.

2. Meanwhile, in a small bowl, whisk together the cornstarch and the water with a fork until smooth; whisk into the simmering stock. Raise heat; return to a full boil. Boil 30 seconds. Remove from heat, and stir in the parsley. Serve.

FIT TO EAT RECIPE PER SERVING: 5 CALORIES, 0 G FAT, 0 MG CHOLESTEROL, 1 G CARBOHYDRATE, 80 MG SODIUM, 0 G PROTEIN, 0 G FIBER

garlic mashed potatoes

SERVES 6

Garlic gives the dish a mellow flavor.

- 1 pound red potatoes, peeled and cut into eighths
- 1 pound russet potatoes, peeled and cut into 1½-inch pieces
- 5 garlic cloves
- ¾ cup nonfat milk
- 2 tablespoons unsalted butter
- ¾ teaspoon coarse salt
  Freshly ground pepper

1. In a medium saucepan, combine the potatoes and whole garlic; add enough cold water to cover by about 2 inches. Bring to a boil over high heat. Reduce heat to a simmer, and cook until the potatoes are easily pierced with a fork, about 15 minutes. Drain the potatoes, and set aside in a warm place.

2. Meanwhile, in the same saucepan, combine the milk, butter, and salt; season with pepper. Heat over low until the butter has melted and the milk is warm to the touch. Pass the potatoes and garlic through a ricer or food mill into saucepan; stir gently to combine. Serve immediately.

FIT TO EAT RECIPE PER SERVING: 178 CALORIES, 4 G FAT, 11 MG CHOLESTEROL, 33 G CARBOHYDRATE, 259 MG SODIUM, 4 G PROTEIN, 3 G FIBER

moussaka

SERVES 6

Moussaka may be assembled 1 day in advance and refrigerated; bake for an additional 15 to 20 minutes, or until the center is hot.

- 2 cups plain nonfat yogurt
- 1 pound ground turkey
- 1 yellow onion, cut into ¼-inch dice
- 1 garlic clove, minced
- 1 teaspoon ground cinnamon
- 1 teaspoon coarse salt, plus more for eggplant
- ¼ teaspoon ground nutmeg
- ¼ teaspoon freshly ground pepper
- 1 28-ounce can whole peeled tomatoes, coarsely chopped
- ¼ cup tomato paste
- ¼ cup chopped fresh oregano
- ½ cup chopped fresh flat-leaf parsley
- 2 medium eggplants (about 2 pounds) Olive oil cooking spray
- ¼ cup (1 ounce) grated Parmesan cheese
- 1 large egg plus 1 large egg white

1. Drain the yogurt in a cheesecloth-lined sieve until thickened, 2 hours or overnight.

2. Heat the turkey in a medium saucepan over medium; cook until browned, about 6 minutes. Using a slotted spoon, transfer to a medium bowl. Add the onion, garlic, cinnamon, salt, nutmeg, and pepper to the saucepan; cook until the onion is translucent, about 10 minutes. Return the turkey to the saucepan; add the tomatoes, tomato paste, and oregano. Bring to a boil; reduce heat, and simmer until the sauce has thickened, about 1 hour. Remove from heat; stir in the chopped parsley. Set aside.

3. Heat the broiler. While the sauce cooks, cut the eggplants into ¼-inch slices. Sprinkle with salt on both sides. Place in a colander over a bowl; let stand 1 hour to drain. Discard the liquid; rinse each slice under cold running water to remove all salt and juice. Place the slices on several layers of paper towels; press out water. Lay the dry slices on a clean baking sheet; coat with olive oil spray; broil until browned, about 2 minutes. Turn; coat with olive oil spray; broil until browned, about 2 minutes more. Repeat until all the eggplant slices have been broiled; set the cooked eggplant aside.

4. Place the drained yogurt in a small bowl. Add the Parmesan and eggs. Whisk together briskly with a fork; set aside.

5. Preheat the oven to 400° F. Assemble the moussaka: Place a layer of eggplant on the bottom of an 8 × 8-inch baking pan. Cover with half the turkey sauce. Place another eggplant layer, then the remaining turkey sauce. Add a final eggplant layer; cover with reserved yogurt mixture. Bake until the mixture is bubbling and the top starts to brown, about 30 minutes. Transfer to a heatproof surface; let sit until the moussaka cools slightly and firms, about 10 minutes. Cut into squares; serve.

FIT TO EAT RECIPE PER SERVING: 266 CALORIES, 9 G FAT, 102 MG CHOLESTEROL, 23 G CARBOHYDRATE, 510 MG SODIUM, 25 G PROTEIN, 3 G FIBER

spice-cured turkey

SERVES 12 TO 14

It may seem like a bit of trouble to brine the turkey, but it is well worth it: This is the best turkey we've ever tasted. If you don't have a stockpot large enough to hold the turkey, you can use a new plastic tub instead. It is helpful to have an extra refrigerator to brine the turkey, as it takes up a lot of space.

for the brine

- 4 cups coarse salt
- 5 cups sugar
- 2 carrots, peeled and cut into 1-inch pieces
- 2 stalks celery, cut into 1-inch pieces
- 2 onions, cut into 1-inch pieces
- 2 leeks, cut into 1-inch pieces and cleaned of all sand
- 3 bay leaves
- 1 head of garlic, cut in half crosswise
- 2 tablespoons whole black peppercorns
- 1 tablespoon ground cumin
- 2 teaspoons crushed red pepper flakes
- 1 teaspoon cloves
- 2 teaspoons whole allspice
- 8 cups water

for the turkey and gravy

- 1 18 to 20-pound organic turkey

  Apple-Chestnut Stuffing (recipe follows)

  Spice Butter, softened (recipe follows)
- ½ cup apple cider
- 3 tablespoons all-purpose flour
- 3 cups homemade or low-sodium store-bought chicken stock

1. In a large stockpot, combine the salt, sugar, carrots, celery, onions, leeks, bay leaves, garlic, peppercorns, cumin, red pepper flakes, cloves, and allspice. Add the water, and bring to a boil. Remove from heat. The brine must cool completely before the turkey is soaked in it: It can be made 1 day ahead or chilled over an ice bath.

2. Rinse the turkey under cold water; pat dry. Place in a stockpot, breast side down. Add the brine and enough water to cover. Cover the stockpot, and refrigerate overnight. Remove the turkey from the brine; drain.

3. Preheat the oven to 425° F. Fill the cavities with stuffing, being careful not to pack too tightly. Secure the skin over the neck cavity with toothpicks or skewers, and tie the legs together with kitchen twine. Rub the turkey generously with spice butter, and place on a rack in a roasting pan.

4. Place in the oven, and roast 30 minutes. Baste, rotate the pan, and reduce oven temperature to 350° F. Continue basting every 30 to 45 minutes, until the temperature taken in the thickest part of the thigh registers 180° F, 3½ to 4 hours. Once the turkey is well browned, cover with foil, in sections, if necessary to prevent overbrowning. Remove the foil for last 30 to 60 minutes, to crisp the skin. Allow the turkey to rest 30 minutes before carving. While the turkey is resting, remove the stuffing.

5. To make the gravy, pour the liquid from the roasting pan into a gravy skimmer; set aside. Place the roasting pan on the stove over medium-high heat; deglaze with ½ cup apple cider, using a wooden spoon to scrape up bits stuck to the pan. Set aside.

6. In a small saucepan, combine 3 tablespoons reserved fat from the pan and the flour; cook 3 to 4 minutes, until browned. Add the reserved apple-cider mixture along with the stock and any separated juices from the pan. Cook over medium heat until thickened. Serve with the turkey.

apple-chestnut stuffing

SERVES 12 TO 14

To save time, you can complete the first three steps and chop onion and celery the day before. If you use shelled chestnuts, chop, then proceed with step 2.

- 2 cups chestnuts (12 ounces in the shells, 8 ounces shelled)
- 1 loaf rustic Italian or French bread (about 1 pound)
- 2 cups prunes, coarsely chopped (12 ounces)
- 1 cup apple cider

3   tablespoons unsalted butter, plus more for baking dish

1   large red onion, finely chopped

2   celery stalks, cut into ¼-inch dice

2   green apples, cored, cut into ¼-inch dice

2   large eggs, lightly beaten

½   cup heavy cream

3   tablespoons finely chopped fresh sage
    Coarse salt and freshly ground pepper

1. Preheat the oven to 350° F. Using a chestnut knife or a small paring knife, make an incision about ⅛ inch deep through the shell and into the flesh of the chestnut almost all the way around the circumference of the nut. Transfer to a chestnut pan or rimmed baking pan. Roast in the oven until the chestnuts are tender, about 35 minutes. Turn the oven off. Leaving the pan with the chestnuts in the oven, remove several at a time. Working quickly, place 1 chestnut in a towel, and, holding both, peel the chestnut while still hot. Remove and discard the shells and inner skin; coarsely chop, and set aside.

2. Remove crusts from the bread, and set aside. Cut the bread into 1-inch cubes. Place in a single layer on two baking sheets, and toast in the oven until dry, 5 to 7 minutes. Set aside to cool. Place the reserved crusts in the bowl of a food processor, and pulse until coarse crumbs are formed.

3. Place the prunes and apple cider in a small saucepan, and bring to a boil over medium-high heat. Reduce to a simmer, and cook until all liquid has been absorbed, 20 to 25 minutes. Set aside.

4. Melt the butter in a large skillet over medium heat, and add the chestnuts, red onion, half the celery, and half the apples. Cook until onion is translucent, about 7 minutes. Set aside to cool.

5. In a large bowl, combine the bread cubes and crumbs, prune mixture, chestnut mixture, remaining celery, apples, eggs, heavy cream, and sage. Stir to combine. The juices from the brine will season the stuffing; stir before serving.

6. The stuffing can be baked in turkey until its temperature reaches 165° F. Excess stuffing can be seasoned with salt and pepper and baked in a buttered baking dish, covered, at 350° F for 30 minutes and then uncovered for an additional 10 minutes.

spice butter
MAKES 1 CUP

1   cup (2 sticks) unsalted butter, softened

2   teaspoons coarse salt

1   teaspoon freshly ground black pepper

1   teaspoon dried thyme

1   teaspoon ground cumin

1   teaspoon garlic powder

1   teaspoon crushed red pepper flakes

¼   teaspoon ground allspice

¼   teaspoon ground cloves

¼   teaspoon ground nutmeg

Combine the butter, salt, pepper, thyme, cumin, garlic powder, pepper flakes, allspice, cloves, and nutmeg in a bowl. Beat on medium speed with an electric mixer or by hand until thoroughly combined. Refrigerate until ready to use, for up to 4 days.

tuscan roast turkey breast
SERVES 10 TO 12

¼   cup extra-virgin olive oil

¼   cup fresh flat-leaf parsley, coarsely chopped

3   tablespoons coarsely chopped fresh rosemary, plus 1 teaspoon finely chopped, plus 5 sprigs for roasting

2   tablespoons coarsely chopped fresh sage, plus 5 sprigs for roasting

2   tablespoons finely grated orange zest

1   tablespoon fennel seeds, coarsely chopped

1   dried chile, crumbled

1   garlic clove, minced

1   turkey breast (about 7 pounds), deboned, trimmed, and butterflied
    Coarse salt and freshly ground pepper

8   ounces pancetta or bacon, thinly sliced

1   cup black seedless grapes (optional)

½   cup dry white wine

2   cups homemade or low-sodium store-bought turkey or chicken stock
    Farro, Orange, and Pine Nut Dressing, for serving (page 377)

1. Stir 3 tablespoons oil, parsley, coarsely chopped rosemary, chopped sage, zest, fennel seeds, chile, and garlic in a bowl. Rub all over turkey, and season with salt and pepper. Place in a shallow, nonreactive baking pan; cover. Refrigerate at least 4 hours (or overnight).

2. Preheat the oven to 375° F. Let turkey stand at room temperature 30 minutes. Put herb sprigs into pan. Roll up turkey. Cover evenly with pancetta, and tie with kitchen twine; return to pan. Drizzle with remaining tablespoon oil; season with pepper. Roast until an instant-read thermometer inserted into the thickest part of the turkey registers 160° F, about 1½ hours. Add grapes to pan if desired during last 20 minutes. Transfer turkey to a cutting board; let rest 20 minutes.

3. Transfer pan juices to a bowl, and reserve for another use. Heat pan on top of stove over medium heat. Add wine, and cook, stirring, until reduced by half. Stir in stock, and bring to a boil. Reduce heat, and simmer until slightly thickened. Stir in finely chopped rosemary, and season with salt and pepper.

4. Slice turkey; transfer to a platter. Serve with herbed pan sauce and dressing.

grilled chile-citrus turkey breast

SERVES 8

For indirect cooking on a charcoal grill, rake hot coals onto opposite sides before grilling; place a foil pan in the center to catch drippings. Set the turkey on the grates over the pan; grill, covered but with the vents partially opened.

- 12 dried cascabel chiles (about 2 ounces) or 5 ancho chiles (dried poblanos)
  - Juice of 2 oranges
  - Juice of 1 lime
- 5 garlic cloves
- 1 small white onion, chopped
- 1 teaspoon coarse salt
- 1 bone-in turkey breast (4 to 6 pounds)
- 24 corn tortillas (6 inches each), warmed for serving

1. Toast chiles in a dry skillet over medium heat, turning occasionally, until slightly softened and pliable, about 5 minutes. Remove seeds and ribs. Place chiles in a small bowl, and cover with boiling water. Let stand 15 minutes.

2. Using a slotted spoon, transfer chiles to a blender. Add orange and lime juices, garlic, onion, and salt; blend until smooth. Transfer ¾ cup sauce to a bowl and refrigerate, covered.

3. Rub turkey with remaining cup sauce. Transfer to a plate, and cover with plastic wrap. Marinate in refrigerator at least 2 hours (up to 12 hours).

4. Preheat grill to medium (if you are using a charcoal grill, coals are ready when you can hold your hand 5 inches above grill for just 5 to 6 seconds). Remove turkey from refrigerator; let stand at room temperature 30 minutes.

5. Grill, covered, over indirect heat until an instant-read thermometer inserted into thickest part of breast registers 165° F, 1 to 1½ hours. (Alternatively, roast in a 400° F oven for about 1 hour 20 minutes.) Transfer to a cutting board; let stand 15 minutes before slicing. Serve with warm tortillas and reserved sauce.

....

HOW TO WARM TORTILLAS

Heat one tortilla on the trivet of a gas stove over medium heat, flipping once, until the tortilla is toasted, about 40 seconds per side. (If you have space on the grill, you can warm the tortillas there.) Transfer to a clean kitchen towel, and loosely wrap (it will steam and become pliable). Repeat the process with the remaining tortillas, stacking them in the towel. If necessary, reheat the tortillas before serving: Wrap the stack in foil, and place in a 200° F oven.

....

roasted duck breasts with wild mushroom stuffing and red wine sauce

SERVES 6 TO 8

The USDA recommends cooking duck breasts until they register 170°F. For a moister breast, we cooked ours to 125°F; after it rests, the duck will be cooked to medium-rare. Chicken is also delicious in this recipe: Substitute four 12-ounce boneless skin-on chicken breast halves for the duck. In step 3, don't score the breasts. To cook, heat 2 teaspoons oil in a large skillet over medium heat; cook until golden brown, about 10 minutes. Flip the chicken, and transfer to the oven. Cook until the chicken reaches 175°F, about 25 minutes. For the sauce, substitute dry white wine for the red wine.

for the stuffing

- 2 loaves day-old rustic white bread, crusts removed, cut into 1-inch cubes (about 12 cups)
- ¼ cup plus 3 tablespoons extra-virgin olive oil
- 2 tablespoons unsalted butter, plus more for baking dish
- 2 leeks, white and pale-green parts only, cut into ¼-inch dice, rinsed well
- ½ pound celery root, peeled and cut into ¼-inch dice
- 2 garlic cloves, minced
- 12 ounces assorted wild and cultivated mushrooms (such as black trumpet, hedgehog, oyster, chanterelle, cremini, and button mushrooms), thinly sliced
- 2 tablespoons finely chopped fresh thyme
  Coarse salt and freshly ground pepper
- 1¼ cups homemade or low-sodium store-bought chicken stock

for the duck

- 4 duck breast halves (each about 14 ounces), cold
  Coarse salt and freshly ground pepper

for the sauce

- ½ cup dry red wine
- 2 tablespoons port (optional)
- ½ cup homemade or low-sodium store-bought chicken stock
  Coarse salt and freshly ground pepper
- 2 tablespoons cold unsalted butter, cut into ½-inch pieces

1. Make the stuffing: Preheat the oven to 350°F. Bake the bread cubes in a single layer on a rimmed baking sheet until just golden, about 25 minutes. Let cool completely. Pulse in a food processor (in batches, if needed) until coarse crumbs form, about 15 seconds; transfer to a bowl. Add ¼ cup oil; toss well. Spread the bread crumb mixture on the baking sheet, and bake, stirring occasionally, until deep golden brown, about 15 minutes. Transfer to a large mixing bowl.

2. Heat the remaining 3 tablespoons oil and 2 tablespoons butter in a large skillet over medium-low heat until the butter has melted. Add the leeks, celery root, and garlic; cook, stirring occasionally, until the leeks are soft, about 15 minutes. Raise heat to medium. Stir in the mushrooms and thyme; season with salt and pepper. Cook, stirring occasionally, until the mushrooms are soft, about 10 minutes. Remove from heat. Stir the vegetable mixture into the bread crumb mixture; let cool completely.

3. Prepare the duck: Place the duck breasts, skin sides up, on a cutting board. Using a sharp knife, score lines, ½ inch apart, in a cross-hatch pattern into the fat; cut almost all the way through, but do not cut into the flesh. Season both sides with salt and pepper. Cut 6 14-inch pieces of kitchen twine. Lay 3 pieces of twine about 2 inches apart on a cutting board. Place 1 duck breast half, skin side down, crosswise over the twine. Place about ½ cup stuffing on top of the duck. Top with another breast half, skin side up. Tie together tightly with the twine. Repeat with the remaining breasts. Stuffed duck can be refrigerated, covered, overnight. Bring to room temperature before cooking.

4. Bake the remaining stuffing: Preheat the oven to 375°F. Butter an 8-inch-square baking dish; set aside. Stir together the remaining stuffing and 1¼ cups stock in a large bowl. Transfer to the prepared dish. Bake until the top is crisp and pale golden brown but the center is still moist, about 30 minutes.

5. Meanwhile, cook the duck: Heat a large skillet over medium heat. Add the duck breasts to the skillet. Cook, turning once, until golden brown, 5 to 7 minutes per side. Transfer the breasts to a plate; pour the fat from the skillet into a heatproof container. Return the breasts to the skillet, and place it in the oven. Cook until an instant-read thermometer inserted into the thickest part of the meat registers 125°F for rare, 25 to 30 minutes. Transfer to a plate; let rest in a warm place, loosely covered with foil, 15 minutes. Pour the fat from the skillet.

6. Make the sauce: Lightly wipe out the skillet, and place it over medium-high heat. Add the wine; cook until reduced by half, about 5 minutes. Add the port, if desired, and the stock. Simmer until reduced by half, about 5 minutes. Add the accumulated juices from the duck to the skillet. Season with salt and pepper; whisk in the butter. Pour the sauce through a fine sieve into a gravy boat. To serve, slice the duck, and drizzle with sauce, with baked stuffing on the side.

chinese duck with shiitake mushrooms and wide rice sticks

SERVES 4

You can purchase a whole roast duck at your local Chinese restaurant. Some varieties of noodles suggest soaking them in boiling water instead of cooking them; check your package instructions before preparing them.

 1 *whole Chinese roast duck*
 4 *whole star anise*
 1 *cinnamon stick (about 4 inches)*
 1 *piece (3 inches) peeled fresh ginger, sliced*
 6 *large scallions, cut into 1-inch pieces*
4½ *teaspoons small dried shrimp (optional)*
4½ *teaspoons Asian fish sauce*
1½ *teaspoons sugar*
 8 *fresh shiitake mushrooms, stemmed, caps sliced if large, left whole if small*
 2 *cups mung bean sprouts*
 4 *heads baby bok choy*
10½ *ounces wide rice sticks*

1. Make the broth: Remove meat with skin from duck; keep legs intact. Cut meat into large chunks; remove excess fat, and discard. Set aside. Remove fat from bones; cut bones into large pieces. Put 6 cups water, the bones, star anise, cinnamon stick, ginger, about two-thirds of the scallions, dried shrimp, fish sauce, and sugar into a large pot. Bring to a simmer; skim foam from the surface. Cook, covered, 45 minutes. Pour through a fine sieve into another large pot; discard solids. Let broth stand 10 minutes; skim fat from the surface. Return to a simmer.

2. Add mushrooms to broth, and cook until they are tender, about 5 minutes. Add duck meat and remaining scallions; cook until duck is heated through. Reduce heat to low, and cover.

3. Bring a large pot of water to a boil. Add sprouts; cook until slightly softened, about 2 minutes. Using a slotted spoon, transfer to a plate. Add bok choy to pot, and cook until bright green and tender, about 5 minutes. Transfer to a plate.

4. Bring a large pot of water to a boil. Add noodles; cook according to package instructions, 6 to 8 minutes. Drain; rinse under cold running water. Set aside.

5. Using a slotted spoon, remove duck meat; divide among 4 serving bowls. Divide noodles, sprouts, and bok choy among bowls. Ladle broth into bowls, dividing evenly. Serve immediately.

roasted cornish hens with pomegranate-molasses glaze

SERVES 4

Pomegranate molasses is sold in many ethnic markets and health-food stores.

⅓ *cup pomegranate molasses*

⅓ *cup extra-virgin olive oil*

¼ *teaspoon freshly ground pepper*

2 *Cornish hens (each 1 to 1½ pounds), rinsed and patted dry*

2 *onions, 1 thinly sliced and the other cut into 8 wedges*

4 *garlic cloves, smashed*

   Cooking spray, for the roasting rack

1 *lemon, cut into 8 wedges*

2 *tablespoons unsalted butter, melted*

   Coarse salt and freshly ground pepper

1. In a small bowl, whisk together the pomegranate molasses, oil, and pepper. Place each hen in a large resealable plastic bag. Divide the marinade evenly between the bags; add the sliced onion and garlic. Seal the bags; turn to coat. Refrigerate at least 4 hours or overnight, turning occasionally.

2. Preheat the oven to 350° F, with the rack in the lower third. Line a shallow roasting pan or rimmed baking sheet with a roasting rack, and coat the rack with spray; set aside.

3. Remove the hens from the plastic bags, letting excess marinade drip off. Place the hens on the rack, breast side up, and tuck the wing tips under the body. Fill each cavity with 4 onion and 4 lemon wedges; tie the legs with kitchen twine. Brush with butter; sprinkle with salt and pepper.

4. Transfer to the oven, and roast until the hens are golden and cooked through, about 1½ hours, rotating the pan every half-hour. If the skin starts to get too dark, cover loosely with foil. Remove from the oven; serve warm.

cornish hens with lemon and herbs

SERVES 4

For more-generous portions, cook one hen per person. If you do, use two roasting pans, and double the other ingredients.

2 *Cornish hens (about 1¾ pounds each), room temperature, rinsed well and patted dry*

1 *bunch fresh thyme (about ½ ounce), plus more for garnish*

2 *lemons, halved, plus wedges for serving*

¼ *cup loosely packed fresh flat-leaf parsley leaves*

3 *tablespoons unsalted butter*

   Coarse salt and freshly ground pepper

1. Preheat the oven to 450° F. Place hens in a roasting pan, breast sides up. Place 2 thyme sprigs and 1 lemon half in cavity of each hen. Loosen skin from breast, and place remaining thyme and the parsley underneath. Squeeze remaining lemon halves over hens. Rub butter all over hens. Season generously with salt and pepper.

2. Roast hens, rotating pan halfway through, until skin turns golden brown and an instant-read thermometer inserted into the thickest part of the thigh registers 180° F, 45 to 50 minutes. Let stand 10 minutes. Cut hens in half lengthwise. Garnish with thyme sprigs, and serve with lemon wedges.

fish

AND

shellfish

· ·

provençal seafood pie

SERVES 4 TO 6

- 2 tablespoons extra-virgin olive oil
- ¼ cup (½ stick) unsalted butter
- 1 leek, white and pale-green parts only, washed well and finely chopped
- 1 fennel bulb, cut into ¼-inch slices
- 2 garlic cloves, minced
- ¾ cup all-purpose flour, plus more for work surface
- 2 cups Fumet (recipe follows) or store-bought fish stock
- 3 canned whole peeled plum tomatoes, crushed
- 1 lobster tail, shelled and cut into 1-inch pieces, shell reserved for Fumet (recipe follows)
- 6 ounces large shrimp, peeled and deveined, shells reserved for Fumet (recipe follows)
- 6 ounces scallops, tough muscles removed, halved
- 6 ounces striped bass fillet, skinned and cut into 1½-inch pieces
- 6 ounces halibut fillet, skinned and cut into 1½-inch pieces
  Coarse salt and freshly ground pepper
- 3 tablespoons chopped fresh flat-leaf parsley
- 1 package (14 ounces) frozen puff pastry (such as Dufour), thawed
- 1 tablespoon heavy cream
- 1 large egg yolk
  Aïoli (recipe follows), for serving

1. Heat the oil and butter in a medium saucepan over medium-high heat. Add the leek, fennel, and garlic; cook, stirring, until the vegetables are softened, about 6 minutes. Add the flour; cook, stirring, 6 to 7 minutes. Whisk in the stock. Bring to a boil. Stir in the tomatoes. Reduce heat to medium-low. Add the lobster, shrimp, scallops, bass, and halibut; cook 5 minutes. Season with salt and pepper. Stir in the parsley. Let cool.

2. Preheat the oven to 400° F. Roll out the dough on a lightly floured surface to a 10-inch square, about ¼ inch thick. Cut out a small vent in the center.

Transfer the stew to an 8-inch-square baking dish. Cover with the dough, allowing excess to overhang. Transfer to the freezer until cold, 20 minutes.

3. Whisk the cream and egg yolk in a small bowl. Brush the crust with the egg wash. Bake the pie on a rimmed baking sheet until crust is golden brown and puffy, 35 to 40 minutes. Serve with aïoli.

fumet

MAKES ABOUT 3 CUPS

- 1 tablespoon extra-virgin olive oil
- 1 medium onion, coarsely chopped
- 1 leek, white and pale-green parts only, washed well and coarsely chopped
  Coarsely chopped fronds from 1 fennel bulb
- 2 garlic cloves
  Reserved lobster shell from Provençal Seafood Pie (recipe above)
  Reserved shrimp shells from Provençal Seafood Pie (recipe above)
- 4 sprigs fresh flat-leaf parsley
- 1 bay leaf
- ½ cup dry white wine
- 1 bottle (8 ounces) clam juice
- 3 canned whole peeled plum tomatoes, crushed
- ¼ teaspoon saffron threads, crumbled
  Pinch of cayenne pepper
  Coarse salt

1. Heat the oil in a medium saucepan over medium-high heat. Add the onion, leek, fennel fronds, and garlic; cook, stirring occasionally, until the vegetables are softened, about 6 minutes. Add the lobster shells and shrimp shells, parsley, and bay leaf; cook, stirring occasionally, 2 minutes. Stir in the wine, clam juice, tomatoes, and 1½ cups water. Reduce heat to medium low; simmer, stirring occasionally, 20 minutes.

2. Pour the stock through a fine sieve into a medium bowl; discard the solids. Add the saffron and cayenne. Season with salt. The fumet can be stored in the freezer up to 3 months.

aïoli

MAKES ABOUT 1 CUP

2 large egg yolks

3 small garlic cloves

Coarse salt

½ teaspoon Dijon mustard

½ cup olive oil

½ cup plus 2 tablespoons extra-virgin olive oil

Process the egg yolks, garlic, a pinch of salt, and mustard in a food processor until smooth. With the processor running, slowly add the oils, drop by drop at first and then in a slow, steady stream, until emulsified. Season with salt.

NOTE: *The eggs in this dish are not fully cooked; it should not be prepared for pregnant women, babies, young children, the elderly, or anyone whose health is compromised.*

black pepper mussels

SERVES 2

Liana DiMeglio of Liana's Trattoria in Fairfield, Connecticut, brought this recipe from Naples, Italy, years ago.

1½ pounds mussels (about 50 small), scrubbed and debearded

2 teaspoons freshly ground pepper

Extra-virgin olive oil, for drizzling

Lemon wedges, for serving

1. Put the mussels and ¼ cup water in a large skillet. Season with 1 teaspoon pepper. Cover, and cook over high heat, stirring once, until the mussels open, 2 to 3 minutes. Discard unopened shells.

2. Transfer the mussels to a serving bowl. Season with the remaining pepper, drizzle with olive oil, and serve with lemon wedges.

TIPS FOR SKINNING FILLETS

● *With the tail end (the narrow end) of the fillet facing you, place a very sharp slicing knife between the flesh and the skin at a 15-degree angle; cut against the skin.*

● *Keep the angle of the knife steady, or you might cut through the skin.*

● *After skinning about 1 inch, take the opportunity to get a firmer grip on the skin. (If it's still slippery, hold it with a paper towel.)*

tuna steaks with mint sauce

SERVES 6

You can use any firm-fleshed fish for this recipe. Scattering salt in the skillet prevents the fish from sticking without adding fat, and also seasons it. This dish is delicious at any temperature.

2 garlic cloves

1½ cups loosely packed fresh mint leaves

1 cup loosely packed fresh flat-leaf parsley

3 tablespoons fresh lemon juice

1 tablespoon red-wine vinegar

¼ to ⅓ cup extra-virgin olive oil

Coarse salt

6 tuna steaks (½ inch thick), cut from the narrow end of the loin

1. Coarsely chop the garlic. Scatter the mint and parsley over the garlic, and continue to chop until the mixture is minced together. Transfer to a small bowl; stir in the lemon juice and vinegar. Stir in the oil to form a slightly thick paste; set aside.

2. Heat a large skillet over high heat; generously scatter salt in the bottom. Add the fish to the skillet. Cook, turning once, until the fish is opaque and just cooked through, 2 to 3 minutes per side.

3. Transfer the fish to a serving platter; spoon mint sauce on top. Serve with more sauce on the side.

mussels in parsley vinaigrette

SERVES 4 TO 8

½ cup plus 3 tablespoons extra-virgin
   olive oil

½ cup thinly sliced shallots, plus
   1 tablespoon finely chopped
   (about 3 total)

½ cup dry white wine

3 pounds mussels (about 100 small),
   scrubbed and debearded

1 teaspoon Dijon mustard

3 tablespoons rice-wine vinegar
   Coarse salt and freshly ground pepper

3 tablespoons finely chopped fresh flat-leaf
   parsley, plus leaves for garnish
   Lettuce leaves, for serving (optional)

1. Heat 2 tablespoons oil in a large pot over medium heat. Add the sliced shallots; cook, stirring, until translucent, about 3 minutes. Add the wine; bring to a boil. Add the mussels; cover and cook, stirring once, until the mussels open, about 3 minutes. Discard unopened shells.

2. Remove the mussels with a slotted spoon; discard the cooking liquid. Chill the mussels in a bowl in the refrigerator, about 1 hour.

3. Whisk together the mustard, chopped shallots, and vinegar; season with salt and pepper. Pour in the remaining ½ cup plus 1 tablespoon oil in a slow, steady stream, whisking until emulsified. Whisk in the parsley. The vinaigrette can be stored in the refrigerator up to 3 days.

4. Toss the chilled mussels with ½ cup vinaigrette. If desired, serve on the half-shell on a bed of lettuce. Garnish with parsley. Drizzle with more vinaigrette, if desired.

trout with rosemary and white beans (trota al rosmarino con fagioli)

SERVES 8

You can serve this dish hot, cold, or at room temperature. Cook the fish in batches if your oven is small. Dried beans work best, but you can substitute 6 cups of drained, rinsed canned beans; begin with step 3.

1 pound dried cannellini beans

14 garlic cloves, 4 peeled and 10 peeled and
   crushed with the flat side of a large knife
   Coarse salt

1 medium tomato, coarsely chopped

½ medium red onion, thinly sliced

2 sprigs fresh sage

1 cup extra-virgin olive oil, plus more
   for the baking sheets
   Freshly ground pepper

8 whole trout (1 pound each), cleaned
   and deboned, heads and tails left on

16 sprigs fresh rosemary
   Juice of 2 lemons, plus 2 more lemons,
   cut into wedges, for serving

¾ cup dry white wine

1. Rinse the beans. Transfer to a large bowl; cover with water by 2 inches. Cover loosely with plastic wrap. Let the beans soak at room temperature 7 hours or refrigerate overnight.

2. Drain the beans. Transfer to a large stockpot. Add 12 cups cold water and 2 crushed garlic cloves. Bring to a boil. Reduce heat to medium-low. Simmer until tender, 40 to 45 minutes. Drain. Season with salt. Transfer to a large bowl.

3. Preheat the oven to 375° F. Add 2 crushed garlic cloves, the tomato, onion, sage, and ¼ cup oil to the bowl with beans. Season with salt and pepper. Toss to combine. Transfer to a 9 × 13-inch baking dish. Bake 15 minutes.

4. Meanwhile, open each fish like a book, and place them on oiled baking sheets, skin sides down. Season with salt and pepper. Rub the flesh with the 4 peeled whole garlic cloves; discard the garlic. Roll each rosemary sprig in oil from the baking sheets;

place 2 sprigs on top of each fish. Drizzle the fish with remaining ¾ cup oil. Arrange the remaining 6 crushed garlic cloves around fish.

5. Remove beans from oven; toss. Bake until slightly golden, about 10 minutes.

6. Bake the fish until the flesh is opaque, about 10 minutes. Remove from the oven; pour the lemon juice and wine over the fish. Bake 2 minutes more. Serve the fish with the beans and lemon wedges.

grilled prawns with pistou
SERVES 4

You can substitute 1 pound large shrimp with shells for the prawns.

- ¼ cup whole raw almonds
- 2 cups loosely packed fresh basil leaves
- 1 cup loosely packed fresh flat-leaf parsley
- 12 anchovy fillets, rinsed
- 2 garlic cloves, peeled
- ¼ cup plus 2 tablespoons extra-virgin olive oil
- Zest of 1 lemon, plus lemon wedges, for serving
- Coarse salt and freshly ground pepper
- 12 prawns, shells and heads intact

1. Preheat the oven to 350° F. Toast the almonds on a rimmed baking sheet in oven, stirring occasionally, until fragrant and golden brown, about 10 minutes. Let cool completely; coarsely chop.

2. Process the almonds, basil, parsley, anchovies, and garlic in a food processor until combined. Add the oil in a slow, steady stream, and process until smooth. Transfer to a large bowl. Stir in the lemon zest; season with salt and pepper. Reserve ¼ cup pistou for dipping.

3. Heat a grill to medium-high (if using a charcoal grill, coals are ready when you can hold your hand 5 inches above grate for just 3 to 4 seconds). Toss the prawns with the remaining pistou. Grill, turning once, until cooked through, about 2½ minutes per side; season with salt and pepper. Serve with the lemon wedges and reserved pistou for dipping.

clams with lemongrass and chiles
SERVES 6 TO 8

This dish is also delicious with mussels. Decrease the amount of chiles if you like it less spicy.

- Coarse salt
- 4 dozen small clams, such as littleneck, rinsed well (about 5 pounds)
- 2 stalks fresh lemongrass, hard outer leaves removed and reserved, bottom 4 inches of stalks thinly sliced crosswise
- 2 tablespoons vegetable oil
- 2 shallots, thinly sliced (about ½ cup)
- 3 garlic cloves, minced
- 2 small fresh green chiles, such as jalapeño, serrano, or Thai chiles, thinly sliced crosswise
- 3 small fresh red chiles, such as cherry peppers or Holland chiles, thinly sliced crosswise
- ½ cup lime juice, plus lime wedges, for garnish (5 limes total)
- ¼ cup Asian fish sauce
- 1 cup loosely packed fresh cilantro leaves, coarsely chopped

1. Dissolve 2 tablespoons salt in a large bowl of cold water. Add the clams. Let soak at room temperature 15 minutes. Drain.

2. Scrub the clams under cold running water. Transfer to a large bowl of fresh cold water. Repeat, scrubbing the clams and rinsing in fresh water until you no longer see any grit. Drain. Refrigerate, uncovered, until ready to use, up to 8 hours.

3. Put the reserved lemongrass leaves in a large pot with ½ inch of water. Bring to a boil. Add the clams. Steam, covered, until the clams open, 6 to 7 minutes. Drain. Discard any unopened clams and the leaves.

4. Add the oil, sliced lemongrass, the shallots, garlic, and chiles. Cook over medium-high heat, stirring constantly, until the lemongrass and shallots turn golden, about 2 minutes. Remove from heat. Add the clams to the pot, and gently stir to coat.

5. Stir together the lime juice and fish sauce; pour over the clams. Transfer the clams to a serving bowl; sprinkle with cilantro. Garnish with lime wedges.

seared salmon with savoy cabbage and lentils

SERVES 4

- 1 cup French green lentils
- 2 medium carrots, peeled and cut into ¼-inch dice (about ¾ cup)
- 2 garlic cloves
- 1 bay leaf
  Coarse salt and freshly ground pepper
- ¼ cup extra-virgin olive oil
- 4 slices thick-cut bacon, cut into ½-inch pieces
- 3 tablespoons unsalted butter
- 1 medium leek, white and pale-green parts only, cut into ½-inch-thick rounds, rinsed well
- 1 small Savoy cabbage (about 1 pound), cored and cut into 1-inch-thick wedges
- 3 tablespoons Dijon mustard
- 4 salmon fillets (at least 2½ inches wide and about 7 ounces each), with skin
- ¼ cup chopped fresh flat-leaf parsley
- ½ lemon

1. Put the lentils, carrots, garlic, and bay leaf in a medium saucepan; cover with cold water by 4 inches. Bring to a boil. Reduce heat; simmer, stirring occasionally, until the lentils are tender, about 15 minutes. Drain; return the mixture to the pan. Add 1 teaspoon salt; season with pepper. Stir in 1 tablespoon oil; cover to keep warm.

2. Cook the bacon in a medium skillet over medium-high heat, stirring occasionally, until crisp. Drain on paper towels. Reserve the fat; wipe the skillet clean. Add the bacon to the lentil mixture.

3. Melt the butter in a medium saucepan over medium-low heat; add the leek. Cook, stirring, until softened, about 8 minutes. Stir in the cabbage and a pinch of salt. Add ¼ cup water. Cover; cook over medium heat, stirring occasionally, until the cabbage is just tender, 4 to 5 minutes. Season with salt and pepper. Cover to keep warm.

4. Stir together the mustard and 1 tablespoon oil in a shallow dish. Season the fillets with salt and pepper. Place the fillets in the dish to coat the skins with the mustard mixture.

5. Add 1 tablespoon reserved bacon fat to the reserved skillet; heat over medium-high heat. In batches, if necessary (allow 1 inch between fillets), cook the fillets, skin sides down, until the skins are browned and very crisp, about 4 minutes. Flip; cook 3 minutes more (for medium-rare).

6. Add the remaining 2 tablespoons oil to the lentil mixture; stir in the parsley. Divide the lentils and salmon among serving plates. Squeeze the lemon over the cabbage; divide among plates.

striped bass with cherry tomatoes and olives

SERVES 4

- ¼ cup extra-virgin olive oil
- 4 garlic cloves, thinly sliced
- 1 pound cherry tomatoes
- ½ cup Gaeta or kalamata olives, pitted and halved
- 3 tablespoons capers, drained
- 2 teaspoons finely chopped fresh oregano
  Coarse salt and freshly ground pepper
- 4 fillets (8 ounces each) striped bass, skinned

1. Preheat the oven to 400° F. Heat 2 tablespoons oil in a medium skillet over medium heat until hot but not smoking. Add the garlic; cook, stirring, until just golden, about 30 seconds. Add the tomatoes; cook until the skins begin to split, 2 to 3 minutes. Stir in the olives, capers, and oregano; cook 30 seconds more. Season with salt and pepper.

2. Coat both sides of the fish with the remaining 2 tablespoons oil; season with salt and pepper. Transfer to a medium roasting pan, skinned side down. Spoon the tomato mixture over the fish. Cook until opaque, 10 to 15 minutes. Serve topped with sauce from the pan.

salmon, spinach, and potatoes baked in parchment

SERVES 2

1 tablespoon unsalted butter, softened

1 tablespoon salt-packed capers,
   rinsed well and coarsely chopped

1 tablespoon coarsely chopped fresh
   flat-leaf parsley

1 garlic clove, finely chopped

1 large russet potato (about 1 pound),
   cut into ⅛-inch-thick slices

   Coarse salt and freshly ground pepper

2 shallots, thinly sliced

3 ounces baby spinach (about 1 cup)

2 salmon fillets (6 ounces and 1½ inches
   thick each), skinned

1 lemon, thinly sliced

1. Preheat the oven to 400° F. Place a rimmed baking sheet in the oven to heat. Cut 2 pieces of parchment paper, each measuring 12 × 17 inches.

2. Stir together the butter, capers, parsley, and garlic in a small bowl; set aside.

3. Divide the potato slices between the parchment rectangles, layering them in stacks to form a bed (slightly larger than the salmon fillet) to one side of crease. Season with salt and pepper.

4. Top each bed of potatoes with one-quarter of the shallots, followed by half the spinach. Place the salmon fillets on top of the spinach. Divide the remaining shallots evenly between the packets. Top each salmon fillet with 2 lemon slices (reserve the remaining slices for garnish). Dot with caper butter; season with salt and pepper.

5. Fold the parchment paper over ingredients at the crease. Starting with one end of the paper and keeping the edges together, make small overlapping pleats the length of the paper, creasing tightly as you go and shaping the edge into an arc. The packet should resemble a half-moon.

6. Carefully transfer the packets to the preheated baking sheet. Bake until the packets have puffed, 15 to 18 minutes. Transfer the packets to plates. Serve immediately, opening the packets at the table. Garnish with the remaining lemon slices.

shrimp with kale and white beans baked in parchment

SERVES 6

This recipe, without the shrimp (and with vegetable stock), makes a nice vegetarian main dish; serve it with grated Parmesan cheese.

1 carrot, peeled and cut into ¼-inch-thick
   rounds (cut into half-moons, if large)

1 celery stalk, thinly sliced (about ¾ cup)

½ medium red onion, finely chopped
   (about ½ cup)

1 can (15 ounces) white beans, such as
   cannellini or navy, drained and rinsed

¾ teaspoon finely chopped fresh rosemary
   or ½ teaspoon dried

2 tablespoons fresh lemon juice

3 tablespoons olive oil

1 teaspoon coarse salt

   Freshly ground pepper

1 small bunch kale (about 12 ounces),
   stems and center ribs discarded, leaves
   thinly sliced crosswise

18 medium shrimp (about 8 ounces),
    peeled and deveined

¾ cup homemade or low-sodium store-
   bought chicken stock

1. Preheat the oven to 400° F. Cut 6 pieces of parchment paper to measure 12 × 13 inches each. Stir together the carrots, celery, onion, beans, rosemary, lemon juice, oil, and salt in a large bowl; season with pepper. Add the kale and shrimp; toss well.

2. Lay the parchment rectangles on a work surface. Divide the shrimp mixture evenly among them, mounding in the center of each. Working with one piece at a time, gather the paper around the filling to form a bundle; loosely tie with kitchen twine (18-inch piece), leaving a small opening. Pour 2 tablespoons stock into the opening of each bundle; tie the twine in a bow tightly to seal.

3. Transfer the bundles to a rimmed baking sheet. Bake 20 minutes; shrimp should be cooked through. Transfer the packets to bowls. Serve immediately, opening the packets at the table.

citrus-roasted salmon with spring pea sauce

SERVES 8

1 side of salmon (about 3 pounds),
   trimmed of fat and excess skin, small pin
   bones removed with tweezers

  Freshly grated zest of 1 orange, plus 2
  oranges, cut into ¼-inch-thick rounds

  Freshly grated zest of 1 lemon, plus 2
  lemons, cut into ¼-inch-thick rounds

  Freshly grated zest of 1 lime

2 teaspoons coarse salt

2 teaspoons sugar

1½ teaspoons freshly ground white pepper

1 teaspoon coriander seeds, crushed

2 tablespoons extra-virgin olive oil

  Spring Pea Sauce (recipe follows)

  Pea shoots or watercress, for garnish

1. Place the salmon, skin side down, in a nonreactive baking dish (glass or ceramic) large enough for it to lie flat.

2. Stir together the zests, salt, sugar, pepper, and coriander in a small bowl. Rub the spice blend all over the salmon. Wrap the salmon in plastic wrap. Refrigerate 2 hours.

3. Preheat the oven to 400° F. Wipe the spice blend from the salmon with paper towels. Let the fish stand at room temperature 20 minutes.

4. Arrange half of the orange and lemon slices in a single layer in a large roasting pan; place the salmon, skin side down, on top. Rub oil all over salmon. Roast until cooked through, about 17 minutes.

5. Cut the salmon crosswise into 8 pieces. Divide the pea sauce among serving plates. Place a piece of salmon on each plate, and garnish with pea shoots and the remaining orange and lemon slices.

spring pea sauce

MAKES ¾ CUP

You can make this sauce with thawed frozen peas instead of fresh, in which case they don't need to be blanched. The sauce can be made up to 1 day ahead and refrigerated in an airtight container. Reheat over medium-low heat, adding water to thin, if necessary.

  Coarse salt

1⅓ cups shelled fresh peas

1 cup loosely packed watercress (1 ounce)

4 teaspoons cold unsalted butter

1. Prepare an ice-water bath; set aside. Bring a medium pot of water to a boil; add salt. Blanch the peas and watercress until bright green, about 45 seconds. Immediately transfer with a slotted spoon to the ice-water bath to stop the cooking.

2. Drain the peas and watercress, then puree in a blender until smooth, adding 4 to 5 tablespoons water to thin (mixture should be just thick enough to coat the back of a spoon). Pass the puree through a fine sieve into a small saucepan. Place over low heat, and whisk in the butter, 1 teaspoon at a time; whisk until emulsified. Season the sauce with salt.

chinese-style steamed sea bass with vegetables

SERVES 2

1 whole sea bass (2 pounds), cleaned
  Coarse salt and freshly ground pepper

4 thin slices peeled fresh ginger,
  plus 2 teaspoons grated ginger

3 garlic cloves, thinly sliced

10 sprigs cilantro, plus 1 tablespoon
  coarsely chopped for garnish

3½ tablespoons toasted sesame oil

1½ pounds baby bok choy, white stems
  cut crosswise into ¾-inch-thick pieces
  and leaves discarded

10 small shiitake mushrooms, stemmed
  and sliced ¼ inch thick

7 scallions, thinly sliced on the diagonal

2½ tablespoons soy sauce

2½ tablespoons rice-wine vinegar

1 tablespoon mirin (Japanese sweet rice
  wine) or packed brown sugar

1. Rinse the fish thoroughly under cold running water; remove any debris from the cavity with a spoon; pat dry. Season the cavity with salt and pepper; stuff with the ginger slices, 4 slices garlic, and the cilantro sprigs. Rub the fish with 1½ tablespoons sesame oil. Season with salt and pepper.

2. Put the bok choy, mushrooms, two-thirds of the scallions, the remaining garlic, the grated ginger, and ¼ teaspoon salt in a medium bowl. Season with pepper, and toss.

3. Transfer half of the bok choy mixture to a 9 × 13-inch baking pan; place the fish on top. Top with the remaining bok choy mixture. Whisk together the soy sauce, vinegar, mirin, and ¼ teaspoon salt; drizzle over the fish. Tightly cover the pan with foil.

4. Pour water to a depth of ¼ inch in another 9 × 13-inch baking pan; bring to a boil on top of the stove. Reduce heat; let simmer. Set the pan with the fish on top; steam until cooked through, 16 to 20 minutes. Transfer to a platter; garnish with the remaining scallions and chopped cilantro. Drizzle with the remaining 2 tablespoons sesame oil.

DEBONING A WHOLE FISH

1. Cut between the head and body until the knife touches the backbone; repeat on tail end. Insert the knife at the tail end; cut

from the backbone to the cavity. With the knife resting against the backbone, continue to cut up to the head.

2. Insert two wide spatulas underneath the flesh of the fish, on top of the backbone, and lift.

3. Lift the tail; remove the backbone, leaving the two fillets.

malaysian shrimp curry

SERVES 4 TO 6

- 2 teaspoons whole coriander seeds
- 1 teaspoon whole cumin seeds
- 8 whole black peppercorns
- 1 tablespoon paprika
- 1 teaspoon cayenne pepper
- ¼ teaspoon ground turmeric
- 1 piece (2 inches) peeled fresh ginger, sliced
- 6 garlic cloves, sliced
- 2 tablespoons vegetable oil
- 1 medium onion, very finely chopped
- 1 can (14 ounces) unsweetened coconut milk
- 1¼ teaspoons coarse salt
- 1½ teaspoons tamarind concentrate (or lemon juice)
- 1½ pounds large shrimp, peeled and deveined, tails left intact
- ½ cup fresh Thai or regular basil leaves
- 6 cups cooked basmati rice, for serving

1. Finely grind the coriander, cumin, and peppercorns in a coffee or spice grinder; transfer to a bowl. Stir in the paprika, cayenne, and turmeric. Process the ginger, garlic, and ¼ cup water in a food processor until smooth; stir into the spices.

2. Heat the oil in a large Dutch oven over medium-high heat until hot but not smoking. Add the onion; cook, stirring often, until translucent, about 5 minutes. Add the spice paste; cook, stirring, 2 minutes. Add 1¼ cups water; bring to a simmer.

3. Reduce heat to medium-low. Cover; simmer 10 minutes. Uncover. Stir in the coconut milk, salt, and tamarind. Simmer until thickened, about 30 minutes.

4. Stir in the shrimp and basil, and simmer, stirring occasionally, until the shrimp are cooked through, about 8 minutes. Serve immediately over rice.

poached cod with parsley sauce

SERVES 4

This main dish is delicious served with boiled potatoes or rice.

- 2 tablespoons unsalted butter
- 2 tablespoons all-purpose flour
- ½ cup whole milk
- ½ cup homemade or store-bought fish or vegetable stock
  Coarse salt
- ¾ cup finely chopped fresh flat-leaf parsley, plus 4 sprigs, for garnish
- 2 tablespoons finely chopped fresh chives
- 1 strip lemon peel (3 inches)
- ¼ cup plus 2 teaspoons fresh lemon juice (about 2 lemons)
- 4 cod fillets (5 ounces each), skinned

1. Melt the butter over medium heat in a small saucepan. Add the flour; whisk until a paste forms. Reduce heat to low; cook, whisking, 2 minutes. Whisking constantly, pour in the milk in a slow, steady stream; whisk until incorporated. Whisk in the stock. Add ½ teaspoon salt, and cook, whisking occasionally, 10 minutes. Remove from heat; let stand 10 minutes to thicken slightly. Stir in the parsley and chives.

2. Meanwhile, bring 1½ quarts water, the lemon peel, ¼ cup lemon juice, and ½ teaspoon salt to a boil in a medium sauté pan or other wide straight-sided pan. Place the fillets in the liquid (do not crowd). Return to a boil, then immediately turn off the heat. Let stand until just cooked through, about 10 minutes.

3. Reheat the sauce over medium-low heat, if necessary, and add the remaining 2 teaspoons lemon juice. Gently lift the fillets from the liquid with a slotted spatula; place 1 fillet on each of 4 plates. Spoon one-quarter of the sauce over each serving, and garnish with a parsley sprig.

FIT TO EAT RECIPE PER SERVING: 214 CALORIES, 8 G FAT, 72 MG CHOLESTEROL, 7 G CARBOHYDRATE, 713 MG SODIUM, 28 G PROTEIN, 1 G FIBER

poached salmon steaks with creamy dill sauce

SERVES 4

½ cup fresh lemon juice (2 juiced halves reserved)

Coarse salt

1½ teaspoons whole black peppercorns

4 salmon steaks (each ¾ inch thick)

1 small fennel bulb, trimmed and sliced

1 small onion, thinly sliced

½ cup finely chopped fresh dill, plus 8 sprigs, plus more sprigs for garnish

8 sprigs flat-leaf parsley

½ cup mayonnaise

½ cup sour cream

¾ cup snipped fresh chives

Freshly ground pepper

1. Bring 6 quarts water, 6 tablespoons lemon juice, the lemon halves, 1 tablespoon salt, and the peppercorns to a boil in a large, wide pot. Reduce heat; let simmer.

2. Season 2 salmon steaks with salt. Place one-quarter each of the fennel and onion and 2 sprigs each dill and parsley on a long sheet of parchment; top with salted steaks, one-quarter each fennel and onion, and 2 sprigs each dill and parsley. Fold the parchment to make a packet. Repeat the process to make another packet.

3. With kitchen twine, tie one packet to a wire rack; place in the pot. Cover; poach until cooked through, about 10 minutes.

4. Use tongs and a spatula to transfer the rack to a rimmed baking sheet. Carefully open the packet. Remove skin and any brown fat; discard. Transfer the fish to a platter, discarding the vegetables; cover. Cook the other packet. Reserve 1 tablespoon cooking liquid.

5. Whisk the mayonnaise, sour cream, 2 tablespoons lemon juice, and cooking liquid in a bowl. Stir in the chopped dill and chives; season with salt and pepper. Garnish the salmon with dill sprigs; serve with sauce.

roasted wild striped bass

SERVES 4

2 bulbs fennel, with stalks and fronds

1 cup dry white wine

1¾ pounds wild striped bass fillets (each 1 to 1½ inches thick)

1 tablespoon extra-virgin olive oil

Coarse salt and freshly ground pepper

1. Preheat the oven to 450°F. Remove the stalks from the fennel bulbs; reserve the bulbs for another use. Remove the feathery fronds from the stalks, and reserve for garnish. Using a sharp knife, halve the stalks lengthwise. Arrange the stalks in the bottom of a 9 × 13-inch baking dish; pour the wine over the stalks. Lay the fish fillets on top; drizzle with oil, and season with salt and pepper.

2. Cover the pan tightly with foil. Roast until the fish is just cooked through and opaque throughout, 20 to 25 minutes. Divide the fish among serving plates, discarding the fennel stalks. Garnish with reserved fronds.

....

BUYING FRESH FISH

Steaks and fillets: These should smell fresh and have plump, moist flesh that is not discolored. Avoid any with flesh that appears dry and has sections that are separating.

Whole fish: Look for gills (just under the head) that are bright red, without any brown spots; eyes that are full and clean, not a discolored white or gray; and skin that is shiny, not dull. The flesh should be firm, and the odor should not be fishy.

....

grilled tuna with cherry tomato salad and herbed bulgur

SERVES 4

- 1 cup bulgur wheat
- 1½ teaspoons coarse salt
- ¼ cup loosely packed inner celery leaves, roughly chopped
- ¼ cup loosely packed fresh mint leaves, roughly chopped
- ¼ cup loosely packed fresh cilantro leaves, roughly chopped
- ¼ teaspoon ground coriander
- ½ pint cherry tomatoes, sliced in half
- 2 scallions, thinly sliced into rounds
- 2 teaspoons extra-virgin olive oil, plus more for the grill
- 3 tablespoons fresh lemon juice
  Freshly ground pepper
- 4 tuna steaks (each 6 ounces and about 1 inch thick)

1. Bring 2 cups water to a boil. Place the bulgur in a large heatproof bowl; cover with the boiling water. Add ¼ teaspoon salt; stir just to combine, and cover tightly with plastic wrap. Let steam until tender but still slightly chewy, 22 to 25 minutes. If all the water has not been absorbed, drain the bulgur in a sieve, then return it to the dried bowl. Let cool. Using a fork, stir in the celery leaves, mint, cilantro, and coriander.

2. Make the cherry tomato salad: In a medium bowl, toss the tomatoes and scallions with the oil, lemon juice, and ¼ teaspoon salt. Season with pepper. Set aside.

3. Heat a lightly oiled grill or grill pan over medium-high heat. Sprinkle both sides of each tuna steak with about ¼ teaspoon salt; season evenly with pepper. Cook until the first side is seared with grill marks, 3 to 4 minutes. Flip the tuna, and cook 3 minutes more for medium-rare. Serve with herbed bulgur on the side and cherry tomato salad spooned on top.

FIT TO EAT RECIPE PER SERVING: 340 CALORIES, 5 G FAT, 77 MG CHOLESTEROL, 31 G CARBOHYDRATE, 781 MG SODIUM, 45 G PROTEIN, 7 G FIBER

slow-roasted salmon with caper and herb relish

SERVES 4

- 4 skinless salmon fillets (6 ounces each)
- 1¼ teaspoons coarse salt
  Freshly ground pepper
- 1 small shallot, finely chopped
- 2 tablespoons capers, drained and rinsed
  Grated zest and juice of 1 lemon, preferably organic
- 1 tablespoon extra-virgin olive oil
- 1 cup loosely packed fresh flat-leaf parsley, roughly chopped
- ⅔ cup chopped mixed fresh herbs, such as tarragon, chervil, dill, and mint
- 1 bunch pencil-thin asparagus, tough ends snapped off

1. Preheat the oven to 250° F, with the rack in the upper third. Place the salmon on a parchment-lined baking sheet. Sprinkle both sides of each fillet with ¼ teaspoon salt; season evenly with pepper. Bake until opaque but still bright pink in the middle, 25 to 30 minutes. Remove from oven.

2. Meanwhile, make the relish: In a small bowl, stir together the shallot, capers, lemon zest and juice, and remaining ¼ teaspoon salt; season with pepper. Add the oil, parsley, and mixed herbs; toss.

3. Place the asparagus in a steamer basket set over a pot of simmering water; steam until the spears are crisp-tender and bright green, 3 to 4 minutes. Divide the asparagus among serving plates. Place a salmon fillet on each plate next to the asparagus, and spoon relish on top of the fish.

FIT TO EAT RECIPE PER SERVING: 360 CALORIES, 22 G FAT, 112 MG CHOLESTEROL, 5 G CARBOHYDRATE, 206 MG SODIUM, 36 G PROTEIN, 2 G FIBER

sole rolls with spinach and lemon slices

SERVES 4

1 teaspoon olive oil

1 shallot, minced

¾ pound spinach, stems removed

Pinch of coarse salt

Freshly ground pepper

1 large lemon, washed

1 tablespoon finely chopped almonds

1 tablespoon mixed finely chopped fresh herbs, such as chervil, parsley, chives, and tarragon

4 fillets (4 ounces each) gray sole, lemon sole, or flounder

¼ cup dry white wine

1. Preheat the oven to 375°F, with the rack in the center. In a large sauté pan, heat the oil over low heat. Add the shallot; cook, stirring frequently, until soft, about 2 minutes. Raise heat to medium; add spinach and salt, and season with pepper. Cook, tossing frequently, until wilted and bright green, about 2 minutes. Transfer to a colander, pressing down to remove liquid. Chop finely; squeeze out remaining liquid. Divide the spinach into 4 equal parts.

2. Slice the lemon in half crosswise; grate the zest of half, and combine with the almonds and herbs in a small bowl; set aside. Slice the other lemon half very thinly into rounds.

3. Lay the fillets flat on a work surface, prettiest side down; place 1 part spinach at the narrow end of each. Roll the fish into a cylinder, enclosing the spinach. Place in a gratin dish, with lemon rounds in between. Pour the wine into the dish. Sprinkle one-quarter of the almond mixture on top of each roll; cover with parchment and then aluminum foil. Bake until the fish is opaque and cooked through, 15 to 20 minutes. Serve immediately.

FIT TO EAT RECIPE PER SERVING: 152 CALORIES, 5 G FAT, 57 MG CHOLESTEROL, 4 G CARBOHYDRATE, 236 MG SODIUM, 22 G PROTEIN, 3 G FIBER

seared shrimp with lemon and garlic

SERVES 12

This versatile dish is equally delicious served piping hot or at room temperature.

4 lemons

4 pounds large shrimp, peeled, deveined, and rinsed

3 garlic cloves, minced

½ cup extra-virgin olive oil

1½ teaspoons coarse salt

¼ teaspoon freshly ground pepper

1. Finely grate the zest of 3 lemons. Juice all 4 lemons; strain the juice, and set aside. Place the shrimp in a large bowl; add the lemon zest, garlic, and ¼ cup olive oil; toss well to coat evenly. Season with salt and pepper.

2. Heat a large sauté pan over medium heat. Add 1 tablespoon olive oil, and heat until the oil is hot but not smoking. Working in batches, arrange a single layer of shrimp in the pan, being careful not to crowd them. Cook until the underside is golden brown, 45 to 60 seconds. Turn over, and continue cooking until the other side is golden brown and the shrimp are cooked through, about 1 minute. Transfer to a large serving platter. Deglaze the pan with 1½ tablespoons reserved lemon juice, stirring up any browned bits with a wooden spoon, and pour the pan sauce over the shrimp. Cover loosely with foil while repeating the process with the remaining batches, adding 1 tablespoon oil each time.

pan-fried scallops on caramelized fennel

SERVES 4

2 pounds fennel bulbs (about 2 medium)
1 garlic clove, finely chopped
2 shallots, finely chopped
2 dried bay leaves
  Zest of 1 orange
½ teaspoon ground cardamom
8 tablespoons olive oil
1 tablespoon coarse salt
  Pinch of freshly ground white pepper
2 teaspoons light-brown sugar
1 14½-ounce can low-sodium chicken broth, or homemade
1 sprig thyme
¾ cup water
8 large scallops (about 14 ounces), muscles removed
⅓ cup fresh flat-leaf parsley, packed
2 tablespoons fresh lemon juice
2 tablespoons toasted pine nuts, for garnish
  Shaved truffle, for garnish (optional)

1. Preheat the oven to 325° F. Trim the feathery tops from the fennel bulbs, and discard. Trim the stem pieces and outer leaves from the bulbs; clean, and reserve 2 cups (about 8 ounces) of these trimmings for the puree. Slice each bulb through the root into 4 ½-inch-thick strips.

2. In a small roasting pan, combine the garlic, 1 shallot, 1 bay leaf, orange zest, ¼ teaspoon cardamom, 3 tablespoons olive oil, ½ teaspoon salt, white pepper, 1 teaspoon brown sugar, and the chicken broth. Add the fennel slices, and gently toss to coat with the mixture. Cover the roasting pan with foil, and cook in the oven until the fennel is tender and most of the liquid has evaporated, about 45 minutes. Remove the fennel from the pan, and transfer to a plate to cool.

3. Coarsely chop the fennel trimmings. In a medium saucepan, heat 1 tablespoon olive oil over medium-high heat. Add the trimmings, the remaining shal-

lot, ¼ teaspoon cardamom, bay leaf, and thyme. Cook, stirring occasionally, until the trimmings soften, about 4 minutes.

4. Add the water, ½ teaspoon salt, and ½ teaspoon brown sugar; bring to a boil. Reduce heat; cover the pan, and simmer until the trimmings are soft when pierced with a fork, about 20 minutes. Remove the bay leaf and thyme; transfer the mixture to the bowl of a food processor. Puree, adding 2 tablespoons oil through the feed tube with the motor running. Set aside.

5. In a large nonstick skillet over medium-high heat, sauté the reserved fennel slices until golden brown, 2 to 3 minutes on each side. Remove from the pan, and set aside. In the same pan, heat the remaining 2 tablespoons olive oil. Add the scallops, and sprinkle with 1 teaspoon salt; sauté until brown on the first side, about 4 minutes. Turn, sprinkle with the remaining teaspoon salt, and add the parsley. Sauté until the other side is brown, about 2 minutes. Remove from heat; add the lemon juice to the pan. Toss the scallops and parsley in the pan juices.

6. To serve, place 2 ¼-cup dollops of fennel puree on each plate; top each dollop with a fennel slice and a scallop. Garnish with wilted parsley leaves, toasted pine nuts, and shaved truffle, if desired.

lighter fish and chips

SERVES 4

2 large russet potatoes (about 1 pound), scrubbed
2 tablespoons extra-virgin olive oil
½ teaspoon coarse salt
½ teaspoon freshly ground pepper
4 6-ounce Chilean sea bass or cod fillets (about 1 inch thick), skin removed
½ cup low-fat buttermilk
½ cup yellow cornmeal
¼ teaspoon paprika
  Lemon wedges, for serving
  Malt vinegar, for serving

1. Preheat the oven to 450° F, with racks in the upper and lower thirds of oven. Cut the potatoes lengthwise into ¼-inch-thick strips. Rinse well in a large bowl of cold water, and pat dry with a kitchen towel. Transfer to a large baking sheet. Drizzle with 1 tablespoon oil, and sprinkle with ¼ teaspoon each salt and pepper; toss well. Arrange strips in an even layer on the sheet. Bake on the lower rack until golden and crisp, about 30 minutes.

2. Meanwhile, place the fish fillets in a large bowl. Add the buttermilk, and gently turn the fish to coat. In another shallow bowl, combine the cornmeal, paprika, and remaining ¼ teaspoon salt and pepper. Add the fillets to the cornmeal one at a time, turning to completely coat. Transfer to a plate while repeating with the remaining fillets.

3. Heat a 12-inch cast-iron skillet over medium-high heat. Add the remaining tablespoon of oil; swirl to coat. Add the fillets, being careful not to overcrowd them. Cook until nicely crusted, about 1 minute; turn over with a spatula. Place the skillet in the top third of the oven, and cook until the fish is still firm but beginning to flake when pressed in the center, about 8 minutes. To serve, divide fish and potatoes among plates; offer lemon wedges and malt vinegar on the side.

FIT TO EAT RECIPE PER SERVING: 366 CALORIES, 11 G FAT, 72 MG CHOLESTEROL, 30 G CARBOHYDRATE, 506 MG SODIUM, 36 G PROTEIN, 2 G FIBER

beer-battered cod

SERVES 6 TO 8

Fried fish is the traditional filling of Baja tacos. They are simply garnished with shredded cabbage, pico de gallo, and sour cream.

- 2   large eggs
- 1   cup beer
- 1½ teaspoons coarse salt
- ½   teaspoon freshly ground black pepper
- 1   cup all-purpose flour
     Pinch of cayenne pepper
     Vegetable oil, for frying
- 1½ pounds cod fillets, cut crosswise into ½-inch-thick strips

1. Whisk together the eggs, beer, ½ teaspoon salt, and ¼ teaspoon black pepper in a medium bowl; set aside. In a separate medium bowl, whisk together the flour, remaining teaspoon salt and ¼ teaspoon black pepper, and cayenne; add to the egg mixture. Whisk until the batter is well combined; let rest 15 minutes.

2. Meanwhile, heat oil in a large cast-iron or heavy skillet until a deep-fry thermometer registers 375° F.

3. Dip the fish strips one at a time into the batter, letting excess drip off. Working in batches, drop carefully into hot oil; fry until the fish is golden and crisp and cooked through, about 4 minutes. Remove with a slotted spoon; drain on paper towels. Serve immediately.

grilled mahimahi

SERVES 6 TO 8

You can use other types of firm, white-fleshed fish, or even shrimp or chicken.

- 3   tablespoons extra-virgin olive oil
- 3   tablespoons fresh lime juice
- 3   garlic cloves, smashed
- ½   teaspoon cumin seeds
- ¼   teaspoon freshly ground pepper
- 2   to 3 sprigs thyme, oregano, or other herbs
- 1½ pounds mahimahi fillets

1. Make the marinade: Combine the olive oil, lime juice, garlic, cumin seeds, pepper, and herbs in a large resealable plastic bag or airtight plastic container. Shake well to combine.

2. Add the fish, and shake gently to coat well with the marinade. Refrigerate at least 1 hour and up to 4 hours.

3. Heat a grill or grill pan. Remove the fish from the marinade, letting excess drip off; grill until browned on the outside and cooked through, about 4 minutes per side, turning once. Serve hot or at room temperature.

halibut with mushrooms

SERVES 10

¼ cup olive oil

4 tablespoons unsalted butter

4 large leeks, white and light-green parts only, cut into thin matchsticks, well washed, and dried (about 10 cups)

4 shallots, thinly sliced into rings (1 cup)

8 medium garlic cloves, thinly sliced
  Coarse salt and freshly ground pepper

10 halibut fillets (each 6 ounces, 1 inch thick; preferably square cuts), skinned

2 pounds oyster mushrooms, halved if large
  Chive Oil, for drizzling (recipe follows)
  Beet Salad, for serving (recipe follows)

1. Preheat the oven to 400° F. Heat 2 tablespoons oil and the butter in a large skillet over medium heat. Add the leeks, shallots, garlic, and ⅛ teaspoon each salt and pepper. Cook, stirring, until the leeks and shallots are translucent, about 3 minutes. Spread into 2 9 × 13-inch baking dishes, dividing evenly. Top with the fish; season with salt and pepper. Set aside.

2. Heat 1 tablespoon oil in the same skillet over medium heat. Add half of the mushrooms and ½ teaspoon salt. Raise heat to medium-high; cook, stirring, until tender, 3 to 5 minutes. Scatter the mushrooms over the fish. Repeat with the remaining oil and mushrooms and ½ teaspoon salt.

3. Bake until the fish is cooked through, 18 to 20 minutes. Transfer to plates. Drizzle with chive oil. Serve with beet salad.

chive oil

MAKES ABOUT ¾ CUP

2 large bunches chives (about 2½ ounces), cut into 1-inch lengths

1 cup extra-virgin olive oil

1. Cook the chives in a small pot of boiling water until bright green, about 10 seconds. Drain; run under cold water. Pat dry.

2. Put the chives in a blender. With the machine running, add the oil in a slow stream; puree. Let stand 1 hour. Strain through a damp cheesecloth-lined sieve; discard the solids.

beet salad

SERVES 10

8 small golden beets and 8 small red beets, stems trimmed to 1 inch

¾ cup extra-virgin olive oil
  Coarse salt and freshly ground pepper

4 tablespoons balsamic vinegar

1. Preheat the oven to 400° F. Drizzle the beets with ¼ cup oil on a rimmed baking sheet; season with salt and pepper. Cover with foil. Bake until tender, about 65 minutes.

2. Let cool. Rub off the skins with paper towels; discard the skins. Cut into wedges. Put the golden and red beets into separate bowls.

3. Whisk the vinegar and remaining oil in a small bowl; season with salt and pepper.

4. Drizzle the beets in the bowls with dressing. Season with salt and pepper, if desired. Toss together just before serving.

barbecued salmon fillets

SERVES 6

- 2 teaspoons canola oil
- 1 onion, roughly chopped
- 2 garlic cloves, smashed
- 1 carrot, peeled and roughly chopped
- 1 celery stalk, roughly chopped
- 2 tomatoes, seeded and roughly chopped
- 2 tablespoons tomato paste
- 2 tablespoons unsulfured molasses
- 2 tablespoons honey
- 2 tablespoons brown sugar
- 2 teaspoons dry mustard
- 1 teaspoon ground cumin
- 1½ teaspoons coarse salt
- ½ teaspoon freshly ground black pepper
  Pinch of cayenne pepper, or to taste
- 6 5-ounce salmon steaks or fillets
  Spiced Pilaf (recipe follows)

1. Heat the oil in a saucepan over medium heat. Add the onion, garlic, carrot, and celery. Cook the vegetables until softened, 5 to 7 minutes. Add the tomatoes; cook the vegetables until very tender, about 10 minutes more. Add the tomato paste, molasses, honey, sugar, mustard, cumin, 1 teaspoon salt, ¼ teaspoon black pepper, cayenne pepper, and 2 cups water; stir to combine. Simmer gently until thickened, about 30 minutes. Transfer to a food processor or blender; puree until smooth. Refrigerate until ready to serve.

2. Heat a grill or grill pan. Season the fish with the remaining ½ teaspoon salt and ¼ teaspoon pepper. Brush generously with sauce. Grill until the fish is cooked through, 2 to 3 minutes per side. When the fish is done, remove and discard the skin. Serve over pilaf drizzled with sauce.

FIT TO EAT RECIPE PER SERVING: 300 CALORIES, 11 G FAT, 78 MG CHOLESTEROL, 21 G CARBOHYDRATE, 363 MG SODIUM, 29 G PROTEIN, 2 G FIBER

spiced pilaf

SERVES 6

- 2 teaspoons canola oil
- 1 red onion, cut into ¼-inch dice
- 2 small carrots, peeled, cut into ¼-inch dice
- 1 stalk celery, cut into ¼-inch slices
- ¼ cup dry white wine
- 1½ cups brown rice
- 1 teaspoon coarse salt
- ¼ teaspoon freshly ground pepper
- ½ teaspoon paprika
- ¼ teaspoon turmeric
- ½ teaspoon ground cumin

1. Heat the oil in a medium skillet over medium heat. Add the onion, carrots, and celery. Cook until tender, 3 to 4 minutes. Add the wine, and cook until most of the liquid has evaporated, about 2 minutes. Transfer to a medium bowl, and set aside to cool.

2. Meanwhile, bring a medium saucepan of water to a boil. Stir in the rice, and cook until tender, 25 to 30 minutes. Drain, and add to the bowl of vegetables. Season with salt, pepper, paprika, turmeric, and cumin. Serve with grilled salmon.

FIT TO EAT RECIPE PER SERVING: 213 CALORIES, 3 G FAT, 0 MG CHOLESTEROL, 40 G CARBOHYDRATE, 203 MG SODIUM, 6 G PROTEIN, 3 G FIBER

baked flounder
with onion and lemon

SERVES 4

Be careful when transferring the fish from the baking dish to the plate—flounder is a fragile fish that falls apart easily.

- 2   lemons, sliced into ¼-inch-thick rounds
- 2   medium onions, peeled and sliced into very thin rounds (8 ounces each)
- 4   tablespoons unsalted butter
- 1   cup dry white wine
- 1   teaspoon freshly chopped thyme, plus several sprigs more
     Salt and freshly ground pepper
- 4   6-ounce flounder fillets

1. Heat the oven to 400° F. Arrange the lemons and onions in a 9 × 13-inch Pyrex baking dish. Dot with the butter; add the wine and ¼ cup cold water. Sprinkle with the chopped thyme; season with salt and pepper. Bake until the onions are soft and translucent, about 40 minutes.

2. Remove the baking dish from the oven. Arrange the fish fillets over the lemons and onions. Season the fillets with salt and pepper. Scatter the fresh thyme sprigs over the fish. Baste the fish with a little cooking liquid. Bake until the fish is just opaque and cooked through, 16 to 18 minutes. Do not overcook. Serve with the cooked onions and lemons.

shrimp kabobs with
lemon wedges and cilantro

MAKES 8

- ½   cup loosely packed cilantro leaves, chopped
- ½   cup extra-virgin olive oil
- 2   pounds large shrimp (about 32)
- 4   lemons, each cut into 8 wedges
- 1   teaspoon coarse salt
- ¼   teaspoon freshly ground pepper

1. Combine the cilantro and olive oil in a large bowl. Set aside. Peel the shrimp to the first knuckle; devein. Rinse; pat dry. Place in the bowl with the cilantro-oil mixture, and coat.

2. Thread 4 shrimp, alternating with lemon wedges, on 8 skewers. Gently brush with a little olive oil remaining in the bowl. Season with salt and pepper.

3. Arrange the skewers, off direct heat, on a medium-hot grill. Grill, rotating the skewers and brushing with olive oil as necessary to prevent sticking, until cooked through, about 6 minutes, depending on the heat of the grill. Lemons should be soft and slightly charred.

. . . .

To keep bamboo skewers from burning, soak them in warm water for at least 30 minutes before using. Cooking times may be a bit shorter for metal skewers, which conduct heat.

. . . .

tuna kabobs with marinated baby artichokes

MAKES 8

The baby artichokes are cooked in advance, so they only need to be grilled for a short time.

- 3 tablespoons Dijon mustard
- 1 tablespoon fresh lemon juice
- ½ teaspoon crushed red pepper flakes
- 8 tablespoons extra-virgin olive oil
- 1 garlic clove, minced
- 1½ pounds tuna loin, cut into 1½-inch cubes
  Marinated Baby Artichokes (recipe follows)
- 1 tablespoon coarse salt
- ½ teaspoon freshly ground black pepper

1. Whisk together the mustard, lemon juice, red pepper flakes, 6 tablespoons olive oil, and garlic in a large bowl. Add the tuna, and toss to coat.

2. Thread 4 cubes of tuna, alternating with artichokes, on each of 8 skewers. Gently brush with some of the remaining olive oil. Season with salt and pepper.

3. Arrange the skewers, off direct heat, on a medium-hot grill. Grill, rotating the skewers and brushing with olive oil as necessary to prevent sticking, until the tuna is brown and charred on the outside and warm but still rare in the middle, about 5 minutes, depending on the heat of the grill. The artichokes should be tender and slightly charred.

marinated baby artichokes

MAKES 2 CUPS

These make a wonderful addition to any summer salad or antipasto. They can also be served as a side dish for roasted or grilled lamb.

- 2 lemons
- 1½ pounds baby artichokes
- 1 head garlic, cut in half
- 2 tablespoons whole black peppercorns
- 2 tablespoons coarse salt
- ¼ cup extra-virgin olive oil
- 1 small bunch fresh thyme
  Pinch of freshly ground black pepper

1. Fill a large bowl with cold water; juice 2 lemons into the water. Set aside. Trim the spiky tops, tough stems, and outer leaves from the artichokes; halve lengthwise. Scrape any pink choke out from the center, leaving the artichoke half intact. Transfer cut artichokes to acidulated water immediately.

2. Drain the artichokes. Fill a large saucepan with water. Add the artichokes, garlic halves, peppercorns, 1½ tablespoons salt, 2 tablespoons olive oil, and thyme to saucepan. Set over high heat; bring to a boil. Reduce heat; simmer, using a few layers of cheesecloth or a plate to keep the artichokes submerged, until tender when pierced with a sharp knife, about 5 minutes.

3. Remove from the heat, and drain. Reserve the artichoke halves, some of the garlic, and a few sprigs of thyme. Place in a bowl, and drizzle with the remaining 2 tablespoons olive oil. Season with the remaining 1½ teaspoons salt and pepper. Keep refrigerated, up to 5 days, until needed.

scallop kabobs
with beets and prosciutto

MAKES 8

If baby beets are not available, use large beets cut into 1-inch chunks.

1½ *pounds baby beets, scrubbed,
      tops trimmed*
  2 *pounds sea scallops, muscle removed*
  ¼ *pound prosciutto, thinly sliced*
  4 *sprigs fresh mint*
  2 *lemons*
  2 *tablespoons extra-virgin olive oil*
  1 *tablespoon coarse salt*
  1 *teaspoon freshly ground pepper*

1. Fill a large saucepan with cold water. Add the beets; bring to a boil. Reduce heat to a simmer; cook until the beets are fork tender, about 15 minutes. Remove from heat. Let cool slightly; rub away the skins with a paper towel. Cut the beets in half, and set aside.

2. Rinse the scallops; pat dry. Wrap the scallops in prosciutto, tucking a leaf or two of mint between prosciutto and scallop. Thread 4 scallops, alternating with beets, on each of 8 skewers. Squeeze the juice of 1 lemon over the skewers. Brush gently with some olive oil, and season with salt and pepper.

3. Arrange the skewers, off direct heat, on a medium-hot grill. Grill, rotating the skewers and brushing with oil as needed to prevent sticking, until cooked through, about 5 minutes, depending on the heat of the grill. The beets should be soft and slightly charred. Remove from the grill; squeeze the remaining lemon over the skewers.

indian-spiced halibut
with yogurt

SERVES 6

If you cannot find fenugreek seed, this curry is equally satisfying when ground fenugreek is substituted; add with the other ground spices.

  2 *tomatoes*
     Curry Powder (recipe follows)
  1 *teaspoon whole fenugreek seed*
  2 *teaspoons coarse salt*
  2 *teaspoons ground mustard*
  ¼ *teaspoon ground cardamom*
     Pinch of ground cloves
  4 *garlic cloves, minced*
  1 *tablespoon freshly grated ginger*
  1 *tablespoon dark-brown sugar*
  1 *tablespoon water*
  4 *teaspoons unsalted butter*
  1 *large onion, thinly sliced*
  1 *14½-ounce can low-sodium vegetable
      stock*
  1 *green chile, finely chopped*
1½ *pounds halibut fillets (or other firm-
      fleshed white-fish fillets, such as cod),
      cut into 6 pieces*
  1 *cup plain nonfat yogurt*

1. Bring a saucepan of water to a boil. Fill a bowl with ice and water. Cut an X in bottom of each tomato; plunge into the boiling water. Cook until the skin starts to peel back, about 30 seconds. Plunge into the ice bath to stop the cooking. When cool, peel off and discard the skins. Cut the tomatoes in half; squeeze out the seeds. Chop; set aside.

2. In a food processor, pulse to combine the curry powder, fenugreek, salt, mustard, cardamom, and cloves. Add the garlic, ginger, brown sugar, and water. Puree until a smooth paste forms; set aside.

3. Heat the butter in a large saucepan over medium heat. Stir in the curry paste; cook until fragrant, about 1 minute. Add the onion and half the stock; cook until the onion starts to soften, about 3 minutes. Add the chile and remaining stock. Bring to boil. Reduce to a gentle simmer, add the fish and tomatoes, and cook until the fish is opaque in the center, 6 to 8 minutes. Remove from heat; stir in the yogurt just before serving.

FIT TO EAT RECIPE PER SERVING: 234 CALORIES, 6 G FAT, 44 MG CHOLESTEROL, 16 G CARBOHYDRATE, 595 MG SODIUM, 27 G PROTEIN, 2 G FIBER

curry powder
MAKES ABOUT 2 TABLESPOONS

- 2 teaspoons coriander seed
- 2 teaspoons cumin seed
- ½ teaspoon cayenne pepper
- ¾ teaspoon ground turmeric
- ¼ teaspoon ground cinnamon

Heat a skillet over medium-high heat. Add the coriander and cumin. Toast the seeds, tossing constantly, until fragrant. Transfer to a spice grinder. Add the cayenne, turmeric, and cinnamon. Pulse to combine. Use immediately.

FIT TO EAT RECIPE PER RECIPE: 36 CALORIES, 2 G FAT, 0 G PROTEIN, 0 G FIBER

steamed striped bass and shiitakes with edamame
SERVES 2

This recipe can be doubled easily. Use a larger steamer, about ten inches in diameter, to cook all four portions at once in the same basket.

- 1¼ teaspoons finely grated peeled fresh ginger
- ¼ teaspoon finely grated orange zest, plus 2 tablespoons fresh orange juice
- ¼ teaspoon ground coriander
- 2 teaspoons toasted sesame oil, plus more for baskets
- 1 tablespoon soy sauce
- 2 teaspoons rice wine (mirin) or sherry
- 2 scallions, finely chopped (about ½ cup) Freshly ground pepper
- 2 fillets striped bass, red snapper, or bluefish (each 4 to 5 ounces, at least ¾ inch thick), skinned
- 6 shiitake mushrooms, stemmed, caps scored with an X
- ¾ pound edamame in shells (soybeans) Sea or coarse salt

1. Stir ginger, orange zest and juice, coriander, oil, soy sauce, wine, and scallions in a medium bowl. Season with pepper. Add fish and mushrooms; turn to coat completely. Marinate 10 minutes.

2. Fill 2 woks or large pots with about 1 inch of water. Bring to a boil. Brush the bottom baskets of two 6-inch, 2-tiered round bamboo steamers with oil. Place 1 fillet and 3 mushrooms in a single layer in each bottom basket; place half the edamame in each top. Cover baskets; carefully set into boiling water. Steam until fish is just cooked through, 10 to 14 minutes, checking occasionally to make sure the water doesn't completely evaporate. Sprinkle the edamame with salt. Serve in baskets.

thai green shrimp curry

SERVES 6

- 3 large fresh green chiles, stems removed, roughly chopped, plus thinly sliced green chiles for garnish (optional)
- 2 tablespoons Lemongrass Paste (recipe follows)
- 3 tablespoons chopped fresh cilantro
- 1 tablespoon coriander seed
- 1 teaspoon cumin seed
- 1 teaspoon coarse salt
- 1 lime
- 8 ounces dried rice noodles
- 4 teaspoons vegetable oil
- 1 red onion, cut into 1-inch pieces
- 1 red bell pepper, seeded, cut into 1-inch pieces
- 2 tablespoons cornstarch
- 2¾ cups cold water
- 1 small (or ½ large) pineapple, peeled, cored, and cut in 1-inch pieces
- 1 3½-ounce package enoki mushrooms
- ¼ cup low-fat canned coconut milk
- 12 jumbo shrimp, peeled, tails intact, deveined

1. Place the chopped chiles, lemongrass paste, cilantro, coriander and cumin seed, and salt in a food processor. Zest the lime; add. Puree until smooth, adding water 1 tablespoon at a time if necessary; set aside. Bring a pan of water to a boil. Add the noodles; cook until just tender, about 5 minutes. Drain; set aside in a bowl of cold water.

2. Heat the oil in a large nonstick skillet over medium heat. Add the lemongrass mixture, and cook until fragrant, about 1 minute. Add the onion; cook until just softened, 6 to 8 minutes. Add the bell pepper; cook until just tender, about 3 minutes. Combine the cornstarch with the water; add to the pan. Add the pineapple, mushrooms, and coconut milk; simmer. Add the shrimp; cook until pink and opaque. Squeeze the juice from the lime; stir into mixture. Serve garnished with sliced chiles, if desired.

FIT TO EAT RECIPE PER SERVING: 277 CALORIES, 6 G FAT, 43 MG CHOLESTEROL, 50 G CARBOHYDRATE, 239 MG SODIUM, 7 G PROTEIN, 2 G FIBER

lemongrass paste

MAKES 1 CUP

Look for fresh lemongrass in Asian markets and some supermarkets.

- 2 teaspoons extra-virgin olive oil
- 6 shallots, finely chopped
- 1 tablespoon freshly grated ginger
- 3 garlic cloves, minced
- 1 stalk lemongrass, pounded, cut in ½-inch pieces (1 tablespoon dried)
- ¼ cup water

Heat the oil in a medium saucepan over medium-low heat. Add the shallots, ginger, garlic, lemongrass, and water. Cover; cook until very tender, 8 to 10 minutes. Uncover; cook until the liquid has evaporated, about 1 minute more. Transfer to a food processor; puree to form a smooth paste. Refrigerate, covered, up to 2 days.

FIT TO EAT RECIPE PER RECIPE: 137 CALORIES, 9 G FAT, 0 MG CHOLESTEROL, 13 G CARBOHYDRATE, 11 MG SODIUM, 2 G PROTEIN, 0 G FIBER

halibut and cockles
in herb broth

SERVES 4

⅓ ounce dried porcini mushrooms

¼ cup fresh basil leaves, plus 3 tablespoons finely chopped

¼ cup coarsely chopped fresh chives, plus 3 tablespoons finely chopped

¼ cup fresh tarragon leaves, plus 3 tablespoons finely chopped

¼ cup fresh flat-leaf parsley, plus 3 tablespoons finely chopped

⅓ cup extra-virgin olive oil

   Coarse salt

3 cups fish stock

1 pound cockles or clams, scrubbed

4 Pacific halibut, striped bass, or Pacific cod fillets (about 1½ pounds total), skinned, bones removed

   Freshly ground pepper

1. Cover mushrooms with boiling water. Let stand until softened, about 3 minutes. Drain, and finely chop; set aside.

2. Put ¼ cup of each of the herbs into a food processor; set aside. Stir together remaining 3 tablespoons of each of the herbs, the mushrooms, oil, and ½ teaspoon salt in a medium bowl; set aside.

3. Bring stock to a boil in a medium pot. Reduce heat to medium-low; add cockles. Cover; cook until cockles open, about 2 minutes. Discard any that do not open. Using a slotted spoon, transfer cockles to a bowl, and cover. (Keep heat on).

4. Season both sides of fish with salt and pepper. Add to stock. Cover; cook, carefully turning once, until center is opaque, 2 to 3 minutes per side. Using a slotted spatula, transfer fish to a plate, and cover.

5. Bring stock to a boil. Pour half the stock into a food processor with herbs; purée (be very careful with hot liquid). Add to remaining stock; pour through a fine sieve into a medium bowl, pressing on herbs; discard herbs. Divide fish and cockles among bowls. Ladle broth into bowls; top fish with reserved herb mixture.

grilled bacon-wrapped
whitefish

SERVES 12

   Olive oil, for brushing

2 whole Great Lakes whitefish or striped bass (about 3 pounds each), cleaned

   Coarse salt and freshly ground pepper

4 lemons (3 cut into ¼-inch-thick rounds; 1 cut into 1-inch pieces, for serving)

1 bunch fresh thyme, plus sprigs for garnish

20 strips bacon (about 1 pound)

1. Preheat a grill to high (if using a charcoal grill, the coals are ready when you can hold your hand 5 inches above grill for just 2 seconds). Brush 2 large fish-grilling baskets with oil. Using a sharp knife, make diagonal slits (in serving-size portions) along both sides of fish. Season both sides with salt and pepper. Reserve 6 to 8 lemon rounds and a few sprigs of thyme; place remaining lemon rounds and thyme inside fish cavities.

2. On a large cutting board, lay 2 bacon slices end to end, slightly overlapping; repeat with 6 more slices, laying pairs parallel to one another, 1 inch apart. Center 1 bacon slice at top and bottom, 1 inch apart from and parallel to overlapping slices. Lay fish over bacon, placing head and tail on single slices. Wrap fish in bacon, and secure with toothpicks. Tuck a few reserved thyme sprigs under bacon. Place fish in basket. Repeat with remaining fish, bacon, and thyme.

3. Grill fish, covered, turning once, until opaque throughout, about 10 minutes per side. Transfer to a platter. Grill reserved lemon rounds until lightly charred. Garnish fish with thyme, grilled lemon slices, and lemon pieces.

spicy mussels and chorizo

SERVES 4

- 3 tablespoons extra-virgin olive oil
- 1 large shallot, minced
- 2 garlic cloves, thinly sliced
- ¼ teaspoon crushed red pepper flakes
- 2 cups dry white wine
- 3 cups canned crushed tomatoes with juice
- 4 ounces dried, hot chorizo, cut on the diagonal into ¼-inch slices
- 1 teaspoon coarse salt
  Freshly ground pepper
- 2 pounds mussels, scrubbed and debearded
- ⅓ cup coarsely chopped fresh flat-leaf parsley

1. Heat oil in a large, heavy stockpot over medium heat. Add shallot; cook, stirring occasionally, until soft, about 3 minutes. Add garlic and red pepper flakes; cook, stirring occasionally, 3 minutes. Add wine; bring to a boil. Add tomatoes and chorizo. Reduce heat, and simmer, stirring occasionally, 15 minutes. Season with salt and pepper.

2. Add mussels. Cover, and continue to cook, shaking pot occasionally, until mussels open, about 10 minutes (discard any unopened ones). Add parsley; toss. Serve immediately.

meatless main dishes

....

sesame-marinated tofu with vegetables

SERVES 4

You can substitute Chinese broccoli with broccolini or dark, leafy greens such as kale, turnip, or mustard greens. Before marinating the tofu, press it as described in step 1 to remove excess moisture.

for the tofu

16	ounces extra-firm tofu
1	teaspoon Dijon mustard
3 to 4	teaspoons toasted sesame seeds
1	teaspoon black sesame seeds (optional)
1	garlic clove, minced
3	tablespoons low-sodium tamari soy sauce

for the stir-fried vegetables

3½	teaspoons canola oil
1	tablespoon freshly minced ginger
2	garlic cloves, minced
12	shiitake mushrooms (about 4 ounces), stems removed, quartered
1	red bell pepper, ribs and seeds removed, sliced into ¼-inch strips
12	ounces Chinese broccoli (2 small bunches), cut crosswise into 2-inch pieces
4	scallions, sliced crosswise into 2-inch pieces
2	teaspoons low-sodium tamari soy sauce
½	teaspoon toasted sesame oil
	Freshly ground black pepper

1. Press the tofu: Slice the tofu into 1-inch slabs, and place in a single layer on a baking sheet lined with cheesecloth or paper towels. Cover with another layer of cheesecloth or paper towels, and place another baking sheet or plate on top. Weight evenly with canned goods or other heavy items. Let stand about 30 minutes. Drain off the liquid, and pat the tofu dry with paper towels.

2. In a large shallow dish, combine the mustard, sesame seeds, garlic, and soy sauce. Place the tofu in the dish, and turn once to coat evenly with the marinade. Let marinate at least 20 minutes at room temperature while preparing the ingredients for the stir-fry.

3. Heat a 12-inch nonstick sauté pan or a wok over medium-high heat, and add 1½ teaspoons canola oil to the pan, swirling to coat. Add the tofu; cook until lightly browned on each side, about 1½ minutes per side. Transfer the tofu to a platter; cover loosely with aluminum foil to keep warm.

4. In the same pan or wok, heat the remaining 2 teaspoons canola oil. Add the ginger and garlic; cook, stirring constantly, until aromatic, about 30 seconds. Add the mushrooms, red pepper, Chinese broccoli, and scallions; cook, stirring constantly, until the vegetables are crisp-tender and bright, about 7 minutes. Add the soy sauce and sesame oil, and stir to combine. Season with pepper, and serve immediately, spooned over the tofu.

FIT TO EAT RECIPE PER SERVING: 191 CALORIES, 10 G FAT, 0 MG CHOLESTEROL, 13 G CARBOHYDRATE, 655 MG SODIUM, 14 G PROTEIN, 5 G FIBER

broiled black pepper tofu

SERVES 4

Grocery stores often carry several kinds of tofu, so be sure to buy the firm variety for this dish. Pressing the tofu removes excess water and allows it to soak up the peppery marinade.

1½	blocks firm tofu (from 2 14-ounce packages)
2	tablespoons tamari soy sauce
1	tablespoon toasted sesame oil
¾	teaspoon freshly ground pepper
	Soy-Lemon Dipping Sauce (recipe follows)

1. Cut the tofu crosswise into 6 slices (about ¾ inch thick each). Cut each slice diagonally into 2 triangles. Line a rimmed baking sheet with a double layer of paper towels. Place the tofu on top, and cover with another double layer of paper towels.

Place another baking sheet or a large plate on top. Weight with heavy objects (such as large cans of food); let stand 20 minutes.

2. Preheat the broiler, with a rack 6 inches from the heat. Stir together the tamari soy sauce, oil, and pepper in a 9 × 13-inch baking dish. Pat the tofu dry with paper towels; transfer to the baking dish. Turn to coat both sides with the marinade. Broil, flipping once, until golden brown, about 4 minutes per side. Serve with dipping sauce.

soy-lemon dipping sauce
MAKES ½ CUP

Tamari soy sauce is similar to regular soy sauce but is slightly thicker and has a richer flavor. It is available at most grocery stores. Besides being the perfect condiment for the tofu, this sauce makes a nice addition to the soba noodles—just drizzle a little bit on top.

- 2 tablespoons minced peeled fresh ginger
- ¼ cup tamari soy sauce
- ½ teaspoon freshly grated lemon zest, plus 1 tablespoon plus 2 teaspoons fresh lemon juice (1 lemon total)
- 1 teaspoon toasted sesame oil

Whisk together ginger, tamari soy sauce, lemon zest, lemon juice, and sesame oil in a small bowl. Set aside at room temperature until ready to serve. Just before serving, stir well.

ABOUT TOFU

Tofu comes in two types: silken, also known as Japanese, and regular, or Chinese. Both are available in soft, firm, and extra-firm consistencies, and both can be found in most grocery stores in the refrigerated section. (You may have to look in the Asian foods section for silken.)

The difference between types of tofu lies in their texture; what separates soft, firm, and extra-firm are their levels of moisture, with soft containing the most water, and extra-firm the least. Regular tofu has a firmer texture than silken, regardless of water content. For soups and sauces, soft tofu works best, while firm or extra-firm are better for grilling and frying and should hold their shape no matter what dish you cook them in.

Silken tofu is smooth, creamy, and custard-like; it works well in pureed dishes, such as salad dressings, smoothies, and puddings. Keep in mind that silken tofu is always softer than regular. An extra-firm silken tofu is still creamier than the soft variety of regular tofu.

Regular tofu also requires pressing before frying or roasting in order to remove some of the liquid and allow the tofu to better absorb flavors. To do this, cut the tofu into the desired shape and size. Line a baking sheet with paper towels, and place the cut tofu on top. Cover the tofu with another layer of paper towels, followed by a second baking sheet. Weight the top of the baking sheet with a heavy skillet or canned goods, and let sit, pressing out excess liquid, 20 to 30 minutes.

When storing tofu, be sure to submerge it in cool water. Keep it in a well-sealed container in the refrigerator, up to 3 days, changing the water every day.

thai green curry with tofu and vegetables

SERVES 2 TO 4

- 2 tablespoons vegetable oil
- 4 garlic cloves, minced
- 3 tablespoons Green Curry Paste (recipe follows)
- 8 ounces green beans or Chinese long beans, trimmed and cut diagonally into 1½-inch pieces
- 1 pound zucchini (about 2 medium), cut into ½ × 2-inch sticks
- ¾ cup homemade or low-sodium store-bought vegetable stock
- ¼ cup canned unsweetened coconut milk
- 3 fresh or frozen kaffir lime leaves
- 2 tablespoons Asian fish sauce
- 1 teaspoon palm or granulated sugar
- 1 tablespoon fresh lime juice
- 1 package (14 ounces) extra-firm tofu, drained and cut into ¾-inch cubes
- 4 cups cooked jasmine or basmati rice, for serving

   Fresh purple, Thai, or regular basil leaves; fresh bean sprouts; and lime wedges, for garnish

1. Heat the oil in a large sauté pan over medium until hot but not smoking. Cook the garlic, stirring, until just starting to brown, 1 to 2 minutes. Add the curry paste; cook, stirring, until fragrant, about 1 minute. Add the green beans and zucchini; cook, stirring, until starting to soften, about 5 minutes.

2. Stir in the stock, coconut milk, and lime leaves. Bring to a simmer; cook, stirring occasionally, until the liquid is slightly thickened, about 6 minutes. Stir in the fish sauce, sugar, and lime juice. Simmer 1 minute.

3. Stir in the tofu, and reduce heat to medium-low. Cover, and cook until the vegetables are tender and the tofu is heated through, about 4 minutes. Serve immediately over rice, garnished with basil, bean sprouts, and lime wedges.

green curry paste

MAKES 1½ CUPS

- 2 cups coarsely chopped fresh cilantro (leaves and stems)
- 2 fresh lemongrass stalks, bottom 4 inches only, thinly sliced
- ⅓ cup fresh Thai or regular basil leaves
- 5 scallions, white and pale-green parts only, chopped
- ⅓ cup fresh lime juice (about 2 limes)
- 2 fresh green Thai chiles, chopped
- 1 tablespoon plus 1 teaspoon finely grated peeled fresh ginger
- 2 garlic cloves, chopped
- 2 fresh or frozen kaffir lime leaves (optional)
- 1 teaspoon coarse salt

Blend all the ingredients in a blender until smooth. The paste can be refrigerated, in an air-tight container, up to 3 days, or frozen up to 3 weeks.

cheese soufflé

SERVES 6

- 4 tablespoons unsalted butter, plus more, melted, for the dish
- 1 cup finely grated Parmesan cheese, plus more for dusting
- 1 large shallot, finely chopped
- 6 tablespoons all-purpose flour
- 1½ cups milk
- 2 tablespoons chopped fresh rosemary
- 2 tablespoons chopped fresh thyme

   Generous pinch of freshly grated nutmeg

   Pinch of cayenne pepper
- 1 cup grated Gruyère cheese

   Coarse salt and freshly ground pepper
- 6 large egg yolks plus 8 large egg whites, room temperature

   Pinch of cream of tartar (if not using a copper bowl)

1. Preheat the oven to 400°F, with a rack in the middle. Brush the outer lip of a 2-quart soufflé dish with melted butter. Tie a sheet of parchment around the dish with kitchen twine so it extends 3 inches above the rim. Brush the inside of both the dish and the collar with melted butter. Dust with Parmesan cheese; tap out excess. Chill the dish in the freezer 15 minutes.

2. Heat the butter in a medium saucepan over medium heat. Add the shallot; cook until soft, 3 to 4 minutes. Add the flour; cook, whisking, 3 minutes. Whisk in the milk, herbs, and spices. Bring to a boil. Reduce heat to low; whisk until thick, about 4 minutes. Add the cheeses; whisk until melted. Season with 1 teaspoon salt and pepper to taste. Pour into a bowl; stir in the yolks.

3. Using a balloon whisk, beat the whites and a pinch of salt in a copper bowl to stiff peaks. (Or beat with an electric mixer in a stainless-steel bowl with cream of tartar.)

4. Spoon one-third of the whites onto the base. Fold them in: Cut through the center of the mixture with a large rubber spatula; gently turn the spatula over. Rotate the bowl a quarter-turn; continue folding in the whites and turning the bowl until mostly combined. Fold in the remaining whites, one-third at a time.

5. Pour the mixture into the prepared dish. Bake 15 minutes. Reduce temperature to 375°F; bake until set, 16 to 18 minutes. Remove the collar, and serve immediately.

orange hokkaido squash soufflés

SERVES 4

If you can't find this squash, use butternut.

- 4 tablespoons unsalted butter, plus more for the ramekins
- 4 tablespoons all-purpose flour, plus more for the ramekins
- 1¼ cups half-and-half
- 3 sprigs thyme
- 1 dried bay leaf
- 2 shallots, coarsely chopped
- 1 cup Roasted Squash Puree, made with orange Hokkaido squash (page 444)
- 4 large egg yolks
- ¾ teaspoon finely chopped fresh marjoram
  Coarse salt and freshly ground pepper
- 4 ounces Gruyère cheese, grated on the large holes of a box grater
- 6 large egg whites

1. Preheat the oven to 375°F. Butter 4 12-ounce ramekins, and line the bottoms and sides with parchment paper. Dust with flour; tap out excess.

2. In a small saucepan, bring the half-and-half, thyme, and bay leaf to a simmer. Remove from heat; let stand, covered, 10 minutes. Strain through a fine sieve into a small bowl. Cover, and keep warm.

3. In a medium saucepan, melt the butter over medium heat. Add the shallots; cook, stirring, until softened, about 3 minutes. Add the flour, and cook, stirring, 3 minutes more. Whisking, add the hot half-and-half in a slow stream; cook, whisking, until the mixture has thickened, about 2 minutes.

4. Place the mixture in the bowl of an electric mixer fitted with the paddle attachment. Beat in the squash puree, then the egg yolks and marjoram. Season with salt and pepper, and fold in the cheese.

5. In the clean bowl of an electric mixer fitted with the whisk attachment, beat the egg whites with a pinch of salt just until stiff peaks form. Gently fold into the squash mixture in 3 additions. Spoon the batter into the ramekins. Bake until the soufflés stop rising and a cake tester inserted gently in the centers comes out clean, 30 to 35 minutes. Serve.

ricotta cheese torta

MAKES 1 7-INCH TORTA; SERVES 4

This delicate torta makes a lovely luncheon dish. Served with our Warm Bean, Snap Pea, and Tomato Salad (page 173), it is perfect for a springtime supper. To drain the ricotta cheese, place it in a fine sieve lined with cheesecloth, and set the sieve over a deep bowl; let stand at least 1 hour at room temperature.

> Vegetable oil cooking spray
>
> 2 to 3 tablespoons fine bread crumbs, preferably homemade
>
> 3 large eggs
>
> ¼ cup chopped fresh flat-leaf parsley
>
> 1 tablespoon chopped fresh marjoram
>
> 1 tablespoon chopped fresh mint
>
> 2 teaspoons finely grated lemon zest
>
> 2 pounds part-skim ricotta, drained
>
> ¾ teaspoon coarse salt
>
> Freshly ground pepper

1. Preheat the oven to 400° F, with a rack in the center. Lightly coat a 7-inch round springform pan with cooking spray. Sprinkle with the bread crumbs, coating evenly.

2. In a medium bowl, whisk together the eggs, parsley, marjoram, mint, and zest. Add the ricotta and salt; season with pepper. Stir to combine. Pour into the prepared pan.

3. Bake until the top is deep golden brown and firm to the touch, about 1 hour.

4. Place the pan on a plate to catch the juices. Let stand until the torta pulls away from the sides, about 10 minutes. Remove from the pan; serve warm or at room temperature.

FIT TO EAT RECIPE PER SERVING: 369 CALORIES, 21 G FAT, 211 MG CHOLESTEROL, 14 G CARBOHYDRATE, 697 MG SODIUM, 30 G PROTEIN, 0 G FIBER

vegetable biryani

SERVES 6

> ½ teaspoon saffron, crumbled
>
> ¼ cup nonfat milk
>
> 1½ cups basmati rice, soaked in cold water 10 minutes and drained
>
> 3 tablespoons canola oil
>
> 2 large onions, thinly sliced
>
> 1½ teaspoons whole cumin seeds
>
> ¾ teaspoon ground cardamom
>
> 1 cinnamon stick, broken into 4 pieces
>
> ½ teaspoon ground cloves
>
> 1 tablespoon minced fresh ginger
>
> 2 garlic cloves, minced
>
> 3 plum tomatoes (about ½ pound), peeled, seeded, and chopped
>
> 6 ounces green beans, cut into thirds (about 1½ cups)
>
> ½ head cauliflower, cut into florets (about 2 cups)
>
> 2 carrots, cut into ½-inch pieces (about ¾ cup)
>
> 1 cup cooked or canned chickpeas, drained and rinsed
>
> 1½ teaspoons coarse salt
>
> 1 cup fresh or frozen peas
>
> 2 ounces (about ½ cup) cashews

1. Preheat the oven to 350° F. Combine the saffron and milk in a small bowl; set aside. Place the rice in a medium saucepan with 1½ cups cold water. Bring to a boil over high heat, stir once, then reduce heat to low. Cover and simmer until the rice has absorbed all the water, about 20 minutes.

2. Meanwhile, heat 2 tablespoons oil in a large sauté pan over medium-high heat. Add the onions; cook, stirring, until golden brown and slightly crisp, about 10 minutes. Remove half the onions from the pan, and reserve. Add the remaining tablespoon oil along with the spices, ginger, garlic, and tomatoes. Cook, stirring, until fragrant, about 2 minutes.

3. Pour 1 cup water into the pan; bring to a simmer over medium-low heat. Add the green beans, cauliflower, carrots, chickpeas, and salt; reduce heat to a simmer, and cover the pan. Cook until the vegetables are crisp-tender, about 10 minutes. Add the peas, and cook until bright green, about 2 minutes. Remove the pan from the heat.

4. Place one-third of the rice in a 3½-quart heavy-bottomed casserole or baking dish with a tight-fitting lid. Drizzle half the saffron milk over the rice. Using a slotted spoon, transfer half the vegetable mixture to the casserole, leaving the liquid behind. Place another third of the rice on top; drizzle with the remaining saffron milk. Repeat with the remaining vegetables and rice. Spread the reserved onions over the top; sprinkle with cashews.

5. Cover, and bake until the casserole is heated through and aromatic, about 30 minutes. Remove from the oven; let cool slightly before serving.

FIT TO EAT RECIPE PER SERVING: 430 CALORIES, 14 G FAT, 0 MG CHOLESTEROL, 67 G CARBOHYDRATE, 516 MG SODIUM, 12 G PROTEIN, 8 G FIBER

layered eggplant and polenta casserole

SERVES 6

Look for precooked polenta logs in the refrigerated section of your grocery store. If using fresh plum tomatoes, peel them by scoring an X in the bottom with a paring knife and plunging them into boiling water for several seconds; transfer to an ice-water bath, and let cool. Slip off and discard the peels and seeds.

2   tablespoons extra-virgin olive oil

1   yellow onion, cut into ¼-inch pieces

4   garlic cloves, minced

2   pounds fresh or canned plum tomatoes, peeled and chopped

¼   teaspoon coarse salt

1   tablespoon balsamic vinegar

1   tablespoon roughly chopped fresh oregano

¾   cup loosely packed basil leaves, roughly chopped

Freshly ground pepper

1¼   pounds medium eggplant, sliced into ¼-inch rounds

1   16-ounce log precooked polenta, sliced into ¼-inch rounds

1. Preheat the oven to 400°F, with a rack in the upper third. In a medium saucepan, heat 1 tablespoon oil over medium heat. Add the onion and garlic, and cook, stirring, until soft and lightly golden, about 8 minutes. Add the tomatoes and salt, and cook, stirring occasionally, until the sauce has thickened, about 30 minutes. Stir in the vinegar, oregano, and basil; season with pepper. Remove the sauce from the heat.

2. Meanwhile, heat a large cast-iron skillet or grill pan over medium heat. Lightly brush the eggplant slices with the remaining tablespoon oil. Working in batches, lay the slices in skillet in a single layer; cook until browned and beginning to soften, 2 to 3 minutes per side. Transfer to a plate.

3. Spoon about ½ cup tomato sauce into a 9-inch-square baking dish, spreading to coat evenly. Arrange the eggplant slices snugly in a single layer. Spoon about 1 cup tomato sauce over the eggplant, and arrange the polenta rounds in slightly overlapping slices on top. Repeat with the sauce and another layer of eggplant. Finish by dotting with the remaining tomato sauce.

4. Cover with foil; bake until bubbling and juicy, about 30 minutes. Remove the foil; continue baking until the sauce is lightly caramelized and the eggplant is tender, about 15 minutes more. Remove from oven; let cool slightly, and serve.

FIT TO EAT RECIPE PER SERVING: 156 CALORIES, 3 G FAT, 0 MG CHOLESTEROL, 30 G CARBOHYDRATE, 343 MG SODIUM, 5 G PROTEIN, 7 G FIBER

curried eggs

SERVES 5

- 4 teaspoons vegetable oil
- 1 shallot, minced
- 1 garlic clove, crushed
- 2 tablespoons grated fresh ginger
- 1 can (28 ounces) chopped tomatoes with juice
- 2 small green chiles, such as jalapeño or serrano, finely chopped, plus more for garnish
- 2 teaspoons ground turmeric
- ½ teaspoon ground cumin
- 3 sprigs cilantro, finely chopped, plus more sprigs for garnish
  Coarse salt and freshly ground pepper
- 5 large eggs

1. Heat the oil in a large skillet over medium heat. Add the shallot, garlic, and ginger; cook until soft, 5 to 7 minutes. Add the tomatoes and their juice, and the chiles, turmeric, cumin, and chopped cilantro. Season with salt and pepper. Cook, stirring occasionally, until the tomatoes are soft and the sauce has thickened, about 15 minutes.

2. Break 1 egg into a small bowl; slide onto the tomato sauce. Repeat with the remaining eggs, arranging them around skillet. Cover, and cook until the egg whites are just set, 4 to 5 minutes. Remove from heat. Season with salt and pepper, and garnish with chiles and cilantro. Serve hot.

sautéed tofu with bitter greens

SERVES 4 TO 6

- 1 1-pound block extra-firm tofu
- 3 tablespoons low-sodium soy sauce
- 2 tablespoons toasted sesame oil
- ½ teaspoon chili paste or Tabasco sauce (optional)
- 3 tablespoons fresh lime juice
- 1 tablespoon grated fresh ginger
- 6 garlic cloves, thinly sliced
- 2 pounds bitter greens, such as collard, mustard, baby bok choy, or dandelion, washed, trimmed, and torn into pieces
- 1 teaspoon sesame seeds, lightly toasted
- ¼ teaspoon crushed red pepper flakes

1. Cut the tofu in half lengthwise, then cut each piece across into 6 slices. Place the tofu on a paper-towel–lined plate. Cover with more paper towels; place another plate on top. Weight with a few soup cans. Chill 30 minutes so towels absorb excess water.

2. In a medium bowl, combine the soy sauce, sesame oil, chili paste or Tabasco sauce, if using, lime juice, ginger, and garlic. Set aside. Transfer the tofu to a medium bowl; toss with half the marinade; let sit for 30 minutes.

3. Heat a nonstick skillet over medium heat. Working in batches, arrange the tofu in a single layer in the pan. Cook until golden brown, about 2 minutes per side. Transfer to a platter; repeat with the remaining tofu. Gradually add the greens to the skillet with the remaining marinade. Cook, tossing occasionally, until the greens are wilted and most of the liquid has evaporated, 5 to 8 minutes. Transfer to the platter with the tofu. Sprinkle with sesame seeds and red pepper flakes; serve.

FIT TO EAT RECIPE PER SERVING: 223 CALORIES, 271 MG CALCIUM, 11 G FAT, 0 MG CHOLESTEROL, 412 MG SODIUM, 15 G PROTEIN, 1 G FIBER

marinated tofu with cold peanut noodles

SERVES 8

Drain the noodles well before coating with sauce.

- 1 tablespoon coarse salt
- 1 8-ounce package soba or other thin wheat noodles
  Coconut Peanut Sauce (recipe follows)
- ¼ cup soy sauce
- ¼ cup mirin
- 2 tablespoons grated fresh ginger
- 2 12.3-ounce packages firm silken tofu
- 12 radishes, sliced paper thin
- 8 ounces jícama, peeled, cut into 1-inch-long matchsticks
- 1 3½-ounce package pea shoots or sprouts

1. Bring a large pot of water to a boil, and add salt. Add the soba noodles; cook until al dente, 4 to 5 minutes. Drain into a large colander; rinse with cold water until completely cool. Drain well. Transfer the noodles to a large bowl; add the peanut sauce to coat.

2. Combine the soy sauce, mirin, and ginger in a bowl. Cut the tofu into 8 pieces; place one on each plate. Drizzle with soy mixture. Divide the noodles among the plates; top with radishes, jícama, and pea shoots.

coconut peanut sauce

MAKES ABOUT ½ CUP

- ¼ cup coconut milk, well shaken
- 2 tablespoons peanut butter
- 1 tablespoon soy sauce
- 1 tablespoon mirin
- 1 (½ inch) piece fresh ginger, peeled, roughly chopped
- 1½ teaspoons brown sugar

Place the coconut milk, peanut butter, soy sauce, mirin, ginger, and sugar in a small food processor or blender; blend until smooth. Serve with the noodles, or store in an airtight container in the refrigerator for up to 5 days.

brown rice with tofu, dried mushrooms, and baby spinach

SERVES 6

- 1½ cups short-grain brown rice
- ½ ounce sliced dried shiitake mushrooms
- 8 ounces extra-firm tofu, drained and cut into ¾-inch cubes
- 1 tablespoon finely chopped peeled fresh ginger
- 4 garlic cloves, minced
- 1 dried red chile, crumbled
- ¼ teaspoon coarse salt
- 3 ounces baby spinach (about 4½ cups)
- ½ cup finely chopped scallions (about 6), white and pale-green parts only
- ¼ cup loosely packed fresh cilantro, finely chopped
- 2 tablespoons plus 1 teaspoon low-sodium soy sauce
- 1½ tablespoons rice-wine vinegar
- 1 teaspoon toasted sesame oil

1. Stir together rice, 3 cups water, the mushrooms, tofu, ginger, garlic, chile, and salt in the bowl of a rice cooker. Cover with lid, and cook until machine switches to the warm setting (about 45 minutes). Let rice stand 15 minutes to finish steaming.

2. Stir in spinach. Cover, and let steam 1 minute with machine still on warm. Stir in scallions, cilantro, soy sauce, vinegar, and sesame oil. Serve immediately.

FIT TO EAT RECIPE PER SERVING: 222 CALORIES, 3 G FAT, 0 MG CHOLESTEROL, 42 G CARBOHYDRATE, 305 MG SODIUM, 8 G PROTEIN, 3 G FIBER

stuffed swiss chard

SERVES 4 TO 6

- 3 large bunches Swiss chard
   Coarse salt
- 3 tablespoons unsalted butter
- 2 tablespoons extra-virgin olive oil
- 2 small leeks, white and pale-green parts only, trimmed, finely chopped, and well washed
- 6 medium scallions, white and pale-green parts only, thinly sliced crosswise
   Freshly ground pepper
- 6 tablespoons pine nuts, toasted
- 3 cups cooked short-grain brown rice
- 1¼ cups finely grated aged provolone
- 6 tablespoons fresh ricotta cheese
- ¾ cup fresh bread crumbs
   Fresh Tomato Sauce (recipe follows)

1. Preheat the oven to 400° F. Choose 12 large chard leaves (each should be about 10 inches long and 5 inches wide) or 24 smaller leaves; set aside. Coarsely chop enough of the remaining leaves to make 4½ cups; reserve remaining leaves for another use. Bring a large pot of water to a boil; add a pinch of salt. Blanch whole leaves, 1 at a time, until tender and bright green, about 5 seconds. Lay flat on a baking sheet lined with paper towels to drain.

2. Melt butter with oil in a medium skillet over medium heat. Add leeks, scallions, 2 teaspoons salt, and ¼ teaspoon pepper. Cook, stirring occasionally, until translucent, about 3 minutes. Add chopped chard, and cook, stirring occasionally, until chard has wilted, about 3 minutes more. Transfer to a medium bowl, and add pine nuts; let stand until cool. Stir in rice, cheeses, and bread crumbs. Season with salt and pepper.

3. Place a blanched leaf facedown on a work surface. Cut out thickest part of stalk, about one-third of the way up leaf; slightly overlap the cut ends. If using smaller leaves, overlap 2 leaves so they are about 10 × 5 inches. Spoon 1 cup filling about one-third of the way up leaf. Fold bottom of leaf over mixture. Fold in sides. Roll to enclose filling completely, creating a 3 × 2-inch bundle. Repeat with remaining leaves and filling.

4. Transfer to a 9 × 13-inch baking dish. Tent with foil. Bake until heated through, about 15 minutes. Spoon warm sauce onto plates; serve 2 or 3 bundles per plate.

fresh tomato sauce

MAKES ABOUT 2½ CUPS

- 3 tablespoons extra-virgin olive oil
- 3 garlic cloves, minced
- 2 pounds ripe tomatoes, coarsely chopped
- 2 teaspoons coarse salt
- ¼ teaspoon freshly ground pepper

1. Heat oil in a medium, straight-sided skillet over medium heat. Add garlic, and cook until fragrant, about 30 seconds. Stir in tomatoes, salt, and pepper. Cook, stirring occasionally, until tomatoes are soft, about 10 minutes.

2. Remove from heat, and let stand 10 minutes. Pass through the medium disk of a food mill. The sauce can be refrigerated in an airtight container up to 3 days. Reheat before serving.

tortilla casserole (budin azteca)

SERVES 8 TO 10

- 4 fresh poblano chiles
- 18 corn tortillas (6 inches each), halved
- 7 tablespoons vegetable oil
- 10 ounces spinach, tough stems removed
  Coarse salt
- 1 small onion, thinly sliced
- 4 garlic cloves, minced
- 2 cans (15 ounces each) black beans, drained
- 1 cup Mexican crema or sour cream, plus more for serving
- 2¼ cups Tomatillo Salsa (recipe follows), plus more for serving
- 1½ cups (8 ounces) grated queso fresco or Monterey Jack cheese, or a combination

1. Place chiles directly over the flame of a gas-stove burner on high heat. Roast chiles, turning with tongs, until blackened all over. (Alternatively, broil chiles on a baking sheet, turning, until skin has charred.) Transfer to a bowl, and cover immediately with plastic wrap. Set aside to steam, about 15 minutes. Peel chiles; discard skins. Remove stems, seeds, and ribs; cut chiles into 1 × ½-inch strips. Transfer to a nonreactive bowl.

2. Preheat the oven to 425°F. Brush tortilla halves on both sides with 3 tablespoons oil. Arrange on baking sheets. Bake, rotating sheets halfway through, until tortillas begin to bubble (before becoming crunchy), 5 to 7 minutes. Set aside. Reduce oven temperature to 350°F.

3. Heat a large skillet over medium heat. Wash spinach, and drain but do not dry. Add spinach to skillet. Cover, and cook until spinach has wilted, about 2 minutes. Season with ¼ teaspoon salt. Transfer to a cutting board; let cool slightly. Squeeze out liquid. Coarsely chop, and set aside.

4. Heat 2 tablespoons oil in a medium skillet over medium heat. Add onion and ½ teaspoon salt; cook, stirring occasionally, until translucent, about 3 minutes. Stir in chiles; cook until heated through, about 1 minute. Transfer to a bowl.

5. Heat remaining 2 tablespoons oil in same skillet. Add garlic, and cook, stirring, 30 seconds. Add beans and ½ teaspoon salt; cook, mashing slightly with the back of a wooden spoon, 2 minutes. Transfer to a bowl; set aside.

6. Line bottom of a 10¼-inch-round, 2½- to 3-inch-deep baking dish with 12 tortilla halves, overlapping slightly. Layer with chile mixture, half the bean mixture, and half the crema. Spread ¾ cup salsa over top. Sprinkle with ½ cup cheese. Repeat for second layer, using spinach instead of the chiles. Top with remaining tortillas, ¾ cup salsa, and ½ cup cheese.

7. Bake until heated through, 45 minutes to 1 hour; cover with foil for last 15 minutes if browning too quickly or becoming too dry. Let stand 15 minutes before serving. Serve with more salsa and crema.

tomatillo salsa

MAKES ABOUT 5 CUPS

- 2 tablespoons vegetable oil
- 1 small onion, finely chopped (about ¾ cup)
- 3 garlic cloves, coarsely chopped
- 2¼ pounds tomatillos, husked and washed
- 1 fresh serrano chile, stemmed and seeded for less heat if desired
- 2 tablespoons coarsely chopped fresh cilantro
- ½ teaspoon coarse salt

1. Heat oil in a medium saucepan over medium heat. Add onion and garlic; cook, stirring occasionally, 1 minute. Stir in tomatillos, 1 cup water, and the chile. Bring to a boil. Reduce to a simmer. Cover, and cook, stirring occasionally, until tomatillos have softened, about 15 minutes. Drain, reserving ¾ cup cooking liquid. Let cool slightly.

2. Working in batches, purée tomatillo mixture in a food processor with reserved cooking liquid. Add cilantro and salt; pulse to combine. The salsa can be refrigerated in an airtight container up to 3 days.

zucchini stuffed with chickpeas and israeli couscous

SERVES 6

- 6 *small zucchini (6 to 7 inches long; 6 ounces each), halved lengthwise*
   Coarse salt
- 2 *tablespoons unsalted butter*
- 1 *tablespoon extra-virgin olive oil*
- 1 *shallot, very thinly sliced into rings*
- 2 *teaspoons minced peeled fresh ginger*
- 1 *medium fresh jalapeño pepper, seeded and finely chopped*
- ½ *teaspoon ground cumin*
- ½ *teaspoon ground coriander*
   Pinch of ground cinnamon
   Pinch of saffron
- ¾ *cup cooked dried or canned chickpeas*
- ¾ *cup Israeli couscous*
- 2 *tablespoons finely chopped fresh flat-leaf parsley, plus sprigs for serving*
- 1 *tablespoon finely chopped fresh cilantro, plus sprigs for serving*
   Lemon wedges, for serving

1. Preheat the oven to 400°F. Set a wire rack on a rimmed baking sheet. Pour 1 cup water onto sheet; set aside. Using a small spoon, scoop out pulp from center of each zucchini, leaving a ¼-inch-thick shell. Transfer pulp to a kitchen towel, and squeeze out excess liquid. Coarsely chop pulp; set aside. Sprinkle zucchini shells with 1 teaspoon salt. Place shells, cut side down, on paper towels to drain.

2. Melt butter with oil in a medium saucepan over medium-high heat. Add shallot, ginger, and jalapeño. Cook, stirring, 1 minute. Stir in 1½ teaspoons salt, the cumin, coriander, cinnamon, and saffron. Cook until fragrant, about 30 seconds. Add zucchini pulp and chickpeas; cook, stirring occasionally, 2 minutes.

3. Stir in 1 cup water. Bring to a boil. Add couscous, and return to a boil. Reduce to a simmer. Cover, and cook, stirring occasionally, until liquid has absorbed and couscous is tender, about 9 minutes. Remove from heat, and let stand, covered, 5 minutes. Stir in parsley and cilantro. Season with salt, if desired.

4. Wipe zucchini shells to remove any liquid. Lightly season with salt. Mound about ¼ cup filling into each zucchini shell. Transfer to prepared rack. Cover with foil, and bake until zucchini are tender and filling is heated through, 20 to 25 minutes. Serve with parsley, cilantro, and lemon.

tortilla española

SERVES 8 TO 12 AS HORS D'OEUVRES, 4 TO 6 AS A MAIN COURSE

- 1 *cup extra-virgin olive oil*
- 3 *medium russet potatoes (about 1¾ pounds total), peeled and cut into ⅛-inch-thick slices*
- 1 *medium onion, halved lengthwise and cut into ⅛-inch-thick slices*
   Coarse salt and freshly ground pepper
- 7 *large eggs*

1. Heat oil in a 10-inch nonstick slope-sided skillet or omelet pan over medium heat. Toss together potatoes, onion, and 1 teaspoon salt in a medium bowl. Add to warm oil; cover, and cook, stirring occasionally, until potatoes are tender, about 12 minutes (do not let the onion brown). Pour into a sieve set over a medium bowl; set oil aside.

2. Lightly beat eggs in a medium bowl with 1 teaspoon salt and ¼ teaspoon pepper. Add potato mixture, and let stand, stirring occasionally, 10 minutes.

3. Heat 2 teaspoons reserved oil in clean skillet over medium heat. Add egg-and-potato mixture; cook, pulling cooked egg away from sides with a rubber spatula to let raw egg flow underneath, until bottom is set and just pale golden (and top is almost set), 5 to 7 minutes. Place a plate, upside down, over skillet (use a plate with a diameter larger than the skillet); invert tortilla onto the plate.

4. Add 1 teaspoon reserved oil to skillet; swirl to coat. Slide tortilla, uncooked side down, back into skillet. If any potatoes slip out from bottom, tuck them back in. Cook, pressing down on tortilla with spatula and tucking in edges to shape sides, until completely cooked through, 4 to 6 minutes more. Slide onto a cutting board. Let cool slightly. Serve warm or at room temperature, cut into wedges.

side dishes

....

lighter mashed potatoes

SERVES 8

16 ounces small-curd low-fat cottage cheese

2 pounds small red potatoes, halved if large
   Coarse salt

¼ teaspoon freshly ground white pepper

2 tablespoons finely chopped fresh chives,
   plus stems for garnish

2 tablespoons unsalted butter, softened

2 tablespoons skim milk

1. Purée half of the cottage cheese in a blender; set aside. Cover potatoes with water by 1 inch in a medium saucepan. Add a large pinch of salt. Bring to a boil. Reduce to a simmer, and cook until tender, about 15 minutes. Drain.

2. Transfer potatoes to a large bowl. Add cottage cheese, pepper, chives, butter, and milk. Season with salt. Mash to desired consistency. Serve garnished with chives.

sautéed brussels sprouts with raisins

SERVES 4

Brussels sprouts are members of the cabbage family. They are in season from late August through March.

1 tablespoon extra-virgin olive oil

10 ounces Brussels sprouts (about 25), stems
   trimmed, and thinly sliced

2 carrots, cut into ¼-inch pieces

¼ cup golden raisins

1 cup homemade or low-sodium store-
   bought chicken broth
   Coarse salt and freshly ground pepper

Heat the oil in a large skillet over medium heat. Add the Brussels sprouts and carrots; sauté until the sprouts start to turn golden brown, about 3 minutes. Add the raisins and chicken broth; continue cooking, stirring occasionally, until the sprouts are tender when pierced with a paring knife, about 12

minutes. If the skillet becomes too dry before the sprouts are tender, add up to 3 tablespoons water, and continue cooking. Remove from heat, and season with salt and pepper. Serve hot.

home fries

SERVES 6

We used small potatoes for this recipe. If your potatoes are larger, adjust the cooking time.

2½ pounds small Yukon Gold potatoes
   Coarse salt

¾ pound thick-sliced bacon, cut into ½-inch
   pieces

1 small red bell pepper, cut into ½-inch dice

1 small yellow bell pepper, cut into
   ½-inch dice

1 red onion (about 10 ounces), cut into
   ½-inch dice

1 tablespoon fresh thyme leaves

2 tablespoons roughly chopped fresh flat-
   leaf parsley
   Freshly ground black pepper

1. Place the potatoes in a medium saucepan. Cover with water; bring to a boil over high heat. Salt the water. Reduce heat to medium-high; cook until the potatoes have softened but are still slightly firm, 12 to 15 minutes. Drain in a colander. When cool enough to handle, peel the potatoes; cut into 1-inch pieces. Set aside.

2. Cook the bacon in a large skillet set over medium heat until all the fat has been rendered and the bacon is crisp and brown, about 15 minutes. Remove the bacon with a slotted spoon; set aside on a paper towel to drain. Pour off all but 2 tablespoons of the bacon fat. Add the reserved potatoes; cook over medium heat, stirring occasionally, until golden on all sides, about 10 minutes. Add the reserved bacon, peppers, onion, and thyme; cook until the vegetables have softened, 5 to 7 minutes. Stir in the parsley, and season with salt and pepper. Remove from heat, and serve.

mashed plantains

SERVES 4

You will need sweet, fully ripened plantains (plátanos maduros, in Spanish) for this Cuban-inspired side dish. They are soft, with peels that are mostly brown or black, and are available in Latin-American markets and many grocery stores.

- 2 fully ripe plantains, peeled and halved lengthwise
- ½ teaspoon coarse salt
  Pinch of cayenne pepper, or more to taste
- 1 tablespoon olive oil
  Juice of ½ lime

1. Preheat the oven to 375°F. Sprinkle the plantains with salt and cayenne; drizzle with the oil to coat. Arrange, cut sides down, on a rimmed baking sheet. Roast until the cut sides of the plantains begin to caramelize, about 20 minutes. Turn the plantains; roast 10 minutes more.

2. Mash the hot plantains on the baking sheet with a potato masher until somewhat smooth (some large chunks should remain). Transfer to a serving bowl, and drizzle with the lime juice.

apple charoset

MAKE ABOUT 3½ CUPS

- 2 Granny Smith apples, peeled, cored, and quartered
- 2 Gala apples, peeled, cored, and quartered
- 1 cup chopped walnuts, toasted
- 1 teaspoon ground cinnamon
- 1 tablespoon plus 1 teaspoon honey
- ¼ cup kosher sweet red wine

Chop the apples in a food processor. Stir with the remaining ingredients in a bowl. The charoset can be refrigerated, covered, up to 4 hours.

southern green beans

SERVES 8 TO 10

- 1 large or 2 small ham hocks
- 1 large onion, cut into quarters
- 1 small dried red chile (optional)
- 8 cups water
- 1 tablespoon sugar
- 2 pounds green beans, ends trimmed
  Coarse salt and freshly ground black pepper

1. Place the ham, onion, and dried pepper, if using, in a medium saucepan; add the water. Bring to a boil over medium-high heat, and reduce to a gentle simmer; cover, and cook 2 hours.

2. Using a slotted spoon or spatula, transfer the ham and onion to a plate, and set aside; discard the dried pepper. Return the liquid to a boil over medium-high heat; cook, stirring occasionally, until the liquid is reduced to 2 cups, about 45 minutes.

3. Meanwhile, shred any meat from the ham hock with a fork, and return it to the saucepan. Add the sugar, stirring until dissolved. Reduce heat to medium; add the green beans, and simmer, stirring occasionally, until the beans are cooked through and most of the liquid has evaporated, about 8 minutes. Remove from heat, and season with salt and black pepper. Transfer to a serving dish. Serve hot.

butternut squash with brown butter

SERVES 4

The easiest way to peel butternut squash is with a vegetable peeler; the harp-shaped variety works particularly well.

- 2 tablespoons unsalted butter
- 1 butternut squash (about 1¾ pounds), peeled, seeded, and cut into ¾-inch cubes
- ½ cup homemade or low-sodium store-bought chicken broth
- ¼ cup water
- 1 tablespoon dark-brown sugar
  Coarse salt and freshly ground pepper

1. Heat the butter in a large skillet over medium-high heat until golden brown. Add the squash; sauté, stirring occasionally, until golden brown and tender when pierced with a fork, about 16 minutes.

2. Add the chicken broth, water, and brown sugar; cook until the liquid has evaporated and the squash is nicely caramelized, about 6 minutes. Remove from heat, and season with salt and pepper. Serve.

church street squash

SERVES 8 TO 10

This savory dish is named for one of the streets in historical Charleston, South Carolina. Crookneck squash is a summer squash that is available year-round in certain regions. You can substitute zucchini or even a winter squash, such as butternut or acorn, depending on what's in season in your area.

- 3 tablespoons unsalted butter
- 2 pounds yellow crookneck squash, cut into ½-inch pieces
- 1 large onion, finely chopped
- ¾ cup freshly grated Cheddar cheese (3 ounces)
- 1 cup sour cream
- 1 teaspoon coarse salt
- ½ teaspoon freshly ground pepper
- 1 large egg, lightly beaten
- ½ teaspoon paprika

1. Preheat the oven to 350°F. Melt 2 tablespoons butter in a large skillet. Add the squash, and cook over medium-low heat until tender. Transfer to a medium bowl, and mash lightly with a fork.

2. Melt the remaining tablespoon butter in the same skillet. Add the onion, and sauté until tender. Add to the bowl with the squash. Stir in the cheese, sour cream, salt, pepper, and egg.

3. Transfer to a 2-quart baking dish, and sprinkle evenly with the paprika. Bake until golden and bubbling, 30 to 35 minutes. Remove from the oven. Serve hot.

scalloped mushrooms

SERVES 8 TO 10

We used frozen pearl onions, but you could use fresh instead. To peel, place them in boiling water for 1 minute, and then let them cool slightly before slipping off their papery skins.

- 9 tablespoons unsalted butter
- 1 1-pound bag frozen pearl onions, thawed and drained
- 3 pounds assorted mushrooms, such as button, cremini, or shiitake, trimmed and cut in half (large ones quartered)
- ¾ cup heavy cream
- 1 cup freshly grated Parmesan cheese (4 ounces)
- 1 teaspoon coarse salt
- ¼ teaspoon freshly ground pepper
- 1 cup plain coarse bread crumbs, preferably homemade

1. Preheat the oven to 350°F. Heat 1 tablespoon butter in a large cast-iron or ovenproof skillet over medium-high heat. Add the onions, and cook until soft and just starting to brown, about 5 minutes. Transfer to a large mixing bowl.

2. Working in 4 batches, melt 2 tablespoons butter in the same skillet; add one-quarter of the mushrooms, tossing to coat evenly with butter. Cook until the mushrooms have released their juices and most of the juices have evaporated, about 5 minutes. Transfer to the bowl with the onions. Repeat the process with the remaining butter and mushrooms.

3. Add the heavy cream, ½ cup Parmesan, salt, and pepper to the bowl; stir until combined. Return the mixture to the skillet, or transfer it to a large baking dish. Sprinkle the bread crumbs and remaining ½ cup Parmesan over the top.

4. Bake until bubbling and nicely golden on top, about 25 minutes. Remove from the oven. Serve hot.

edamame succotash

SERVES 6

If you can't find fresh edamame (soybeans), frozen works just as well. Look for them in the freezer section of your grocery store.

- 1 pound butternut squash, peeled, seeded, and cut into ½-inch pieces (about 3 cups)
- 2 ounces green beans, sliced on the bias into 1-inch pieces
- 2 teaspoons extra-virgin olive oil
- 1 small onion, finely chopped
- 1 garlic clove, minced
- ½ cup homemade or low-sodium store-bought chicken stock, skimmed of fat
- 1 cup fresh or frozen corn kernels
- 1 cup fresh or frozen shelled edamame
- 1 teaspoon roughly chopped fresh thyme
  Pinch of coarse salt
  Freshly ground pepper
- 1 tablespoon roughly chopped fresh flat-leaf parsley

1. In a steamer basket set over a pan of simmering water, steam the squash until just tender enough to be easily pierced with a sharp knife, about 7 minutes. Transfer to a plate; set aside. Add the green beans to the basket; steam until crisp-tender, about 3 minutes. Remove from heat; set aside.

2. In a 10-inch sauté pan, heat the oil over medium heat. Add the onion and garlic; cook, stirring occasionally, until soft and lightly golden, about 3 minutes. Add the chicken stock, and bring to a simmer. Add the corn and edamame; cook, stirring occasionally, until brightly colored and crisp-tender, about 3 minutes.

3. Add the thyme with the steamed squash and green beans; cook until heated through, about 3 minutes, stirring to combine. Season with salt and pepper, and sprinkle with the parsley. Serve immediately.

creamed fresh corn

SERVES 4

- 2 tablespoons olive oil
- 1 jalapeño pepper, seeded and diced
- 8 ears fresh corn, husks and silk removed, kernels cut from cobs
- ¼ cup heavy cream
- 1¼ cups milk
- ¾ teaspoon coarse salt
- ¼ teaspoon freshly ground pepper

1. Heat the oil in a large sauté pan over medium heat. Add the jalapeño, and cook 1 minute. Add the corn; cook, stirring, until the kernels are tender but not browned, about 5 minutes. Remove from heat.

2. Transfer 1½ cups cooked corn to a food processor; add the cream and milk. Process until the mixture is very smooth, about 3 minutes. Pass the mixture through a fine sieve into a medium bowl, pressing down on the solids to extract as much liquid as possible.

3. Return the strained liquid to the sauté pan, and stir to combine with the remaining corn mixture. Cook over medium heat until the liquid just comes to a simmer. Remove from heat, and season with salt and pepper. Serve hot.

quick braised artichokes

SERVES 4

If you like, snip the prickly points of the leaves with scissors before you cook the artichokes. The tender leaves and hearts are delicious dipped in Aïoli (page 305).

- 2 large artichokes
- 1 lemon, halved
- 6 sprigs thyme
- 1 garlic clove, smashed
- 2 dried bay leaves
- ½ teaspoon coriander seeds (optional)
- 2 teaspoons coarse salt
- 1 tablespoon extra-virgin olive oil

1. Cut each artichoke lengthwise into quarters through the stem. Using a spoon, remove the fuzzy choke from the heart of each quarter, and immediately squeeze the juice from one of the lemon halves over all artichokes to prevent them from discoloring.

2. Place all the ingredients, including the remaining lemon half, in a large saucepan; fill with enough cold water to cover the artichokes. Cover the pan, and bring the water to a simmer over high heat. Reduce heat to medium-low; cook just until the artichoke hearts can be pierced with a fork but are not too soft, 10 to 15 minutes. Remove from heat, and let the artichokes sit in the cooking liquid until ready to serve, up to 10 minutes. Transfer carefully to serving plates with a slotted spoon, allowing excess liquid to drain off.

flageolet

MAKES 2 CUPS

Flageolet, pale green kidney beans, are prevalent in French cooking. Their delicate flavor is well suited for simple preparations and is particularly good with lamb.

- 1½ cups dried flageolet beans, sorted and rinsed well
- 8 cups water, plus more for soaking
- 1 sprig rosemary
- 1 dried bay leaf
- 4 tablespoons extra-virgin olive oil
  Coarse salt and freshly ground pepper

1. Place the beans in a large stockpot. Cover with cold water by 2 inches; let soak overnight in the refrigerator.

2. Transfer the beans to a colander to drain. Return to the stockpot; cover with 8 cups water. Add the rosemary and bay leaf. Bring to a boil; reduce heat, and simmer, covered, until the beans are tender, about 1 hour 10 minutes. Transfer to a serving bowl; discard the herbs. Gently toss with the oil, and season with salt and pepper. Serve.

swiss chard with olives

SERVES 4

Don't worry if your pan seems overcrowded with the chard; it will quickly wilt and lose most of its volume as it cooks. Cooking the stems a bit longer than the leaves will ensure they become perfectly tender. If you prefer, seed the jalapeño pepper before using.

- 2 small bunches (about 1¼ pounds) Swiss chard, trimmed and washed
- 1 teaspoon olive oil
- 1 small yellow onion, sliced ¼ inch thick
- 2 garlic cloves, thinly sliced
- 1 jalapeño pepper, finely chopped
- ⅓ cup pitted and roughly chopped brine-cured olives, such as kalamata (about 16)
- ½ cup water

1. Separate the leaves from the stems of the Swiss chard. Roughly chop the leaves, and set aside. Cut the stems into 1-inch pieces.

2. In a large skillet or Dutch oven, heat the olive oil over medium heat. Add the onion, garlic, and jalapeño, and sauté until the onion is translucent, about 6 minutes. Add the Swiss chard stems, olives, and the water; cover, and cook 3 minutes. Stir in the Swiss chard leaves; cover, and continue cooking until both stems and leaves are tender, about 4 minutes. Serve immediately.

FIT TO EAT RECIPE PER SERVING: 101 CALORIES, 5 G FAT, 0 MG CHOLESTEROL, 13 G CARBOHYDRATE, 568 MG SODIUM, 3 G PROTEIN, 2 G FIBER

sugar snap peas with toasted almonds

SERVES 4

½ cup whole almonds (2½ ounces)

3 tablespoons unsalted butter

1 pound fresh sugar snap peas, ends trimmed

3 tablespoons fresh lemon juice (1 lemon)

½ teaspoon coarse salt

¼ teaspoon freshly ground pepper

1. Preheat the oven to 400° F. Spread the almonds on a baking sheet; place in the oven. Toast until the almonds are golden and fragrant, 8 to 10 minutes. Remove from the oven; let cool completely. Transfer half the almonds to a cutting board, and chop coarsely. Place the remaining half in the bowl of a food processor fitted with the metal blade; process until the almonds are finely chopped, 15 to 20 seconds. Add the coarsely chopped almonds, and stir to combine.

2. Melt the butter in a large skillet over medium heat. Add the peas, lemon juice, salt, and pepper; stir until all the ingredients are well combined and heated through, about 2 minutes. Sprinkle with the almonds, and toss to coat. Transfer to a serving bowl, and serve.

braised sweet onions

SERVES 4

2 sweet onions (medium)

3 tablespoons olive oil

½ teaspoon coarse salt

⅛ teaspoon freshly ground pepper

1 cup homemade or low-sodium store-bought chicken stock

3 sprigs thyme

3 sprigs rosemary

1. Preheat the oven to 350° F. Peel the onions, trim the root end, and cut each in half; cut each half into 3 wedges. Heat the olive oil in a 10-inch cast-iron skillet over medium heat. Add the onion wedges, and season with salt and pepper; sauté until golden brown, about 5 minutes on each side.

2. Add the chicken stock, thyme, and rosemary; transfer the pan to the oven. Cook, basting the onions periodically with the cooking liquid, until the onions are tender and the stock has reduced and thickened, 55 to 60 minutes. Remove from the oven, and serve.

glazed baby turnips and cipollini onions

SERVES 6 TO 8

To peel cipollini onions, immerse in boiling water for a few minutes, then remove with a slotted spoon. Allow to cool slightly; slip off the skins.

1 tablespoon unsalted butter

1 teaspoon sugar

Coarse salt and freshly ground pepper

3 to 3½ pounds (about 8 or 9 bunches) baby turnips, peeled and trimmed

3 8-ounce bags cipollini onions, peeled and trimmed

½ cup water

Fresh herbs, for garnish

1. Melt the butter in a large saucepan over medium-low heat. Add the sugar; season with salt and pepper. Cook until the butter starts to color, about 1 minute. Add the turnips and onions, swirling the

pan to evenly coat. Add the water; cover, and cook until almost all the water has evaporated and the vegetables are glazed, about 20 minutes.

2. Remove the cover; continue cooking until the liquid has evaporated and the vegetables are caramelized, 3 to 5 minutes. Season with salt and pepper. Transfer to a large serving platter, and garnish with fresh herbs.

white asparagus with hollandaise sauce

SERVES 6 TO 8

White asparagus spears are generally thicker than their green counterparts, so be sure to trim the tough ends of the stalk and cook until they are perfectly crisp-tender.

- *6 quarts water*
- *3 tablespoons coarse salt*
- *3 to 4 bunches (3 to 4 pounds) white asparagus, peeled and tough ends of stalks trimmed by 1 inch*
- *Hollandaise Sauce (recipe follows)*

Bring the water to a boil in a large stockpot, and add the salt. Place the asparagus spears in the water; cook just until tender, about 5 minutes. Gently transfer to a colander to drain, being careful not to damage the tips. Blot dry with paper towels, and arrange on a large serving platter. Serve warm with hollandaise sauce.

hollandaise sauce

MAKES 3 CUPS

Clarifying the butter is an easy and helpful way to achieve perfect hollandaise sauce.

- *2 cups (4 sticks) unsalted butter*
- *6 large egg yolks*
- *⅓ cup dry white wine*
- *2 tablespoons water*
- *2 teaspoons fresh lemon juice*
- *Coarse salt*
- *Cayenne pepper (optional)*

1. Clarify the butter: Slowly melt the butter in a small saucepan over medium heat, and skim off surface foam. Pour the clear layer of butter into a large glass measuring cup, leaving behind the milky residue, which can be discarded. Let the butter cool until it is lukewarm.

2. Meanwhile, place the egg yolks and wine in a heatproof bowl set over a pan of simmering water. Whisk vigorously until the mixture is very pale and the whisk leaves a trail, 3 to 4 minutes. Remove from heat; continue whisking until the mixture is the same temperature as the butter, about 30 seconds.

3. Whisking constantly, add the butter to the egg mixture, 1 drop at a time at first and gradually increasing to a steady stream. When fully incorporated, stir in the water and lemon juice, and season with salt and cayenne pepper, if desired. Serve immediately, or keep warm over a pan of simmering water removed from heat.

sautéed chicory

SERVES 4

This is a quick and delicious side dish for any season, as chicory is available year-round. Radicchio, a red-leaf chicory, adds a contrasting bitter note as well as a splash of color.

- *2 tablespoons extra-virgin olive oil*
- *2 anchovy fillets, coarsely chopped (optional)*
- *1 head radicchio (about 10 ounces), trimmed and sliced into ½-inch pieces*
- *1 bunch chicory (about 1½ pounds), trimmed and roughly chopped*
- *Coarse salt and freshly ground pepper*
- *Balsamic vinegar, for drizzling*

Heat the olive oil in a large skillet over medium-high heat. Add the anchovies, and cook 1 minute. Add the radicchio and chicory; sauté until slightly wilted, 1 to 2 minutes. Season with salt and pepper. Transfer to a serving platter, and drizzle with balsamic vinegar.

fricassee of wild mushrooms

SERVES 4

14 ounces chanterelle mushrooms, tough
    ends of stems removed

5 tablespoons unsalted butter

1 garlic clove, minced

1 medium shallot, finely chopped

7 ounces blue foot or oyster mushrooms,
   tough ends of stems removed

1 teaspoon coarse salt

½ teaspoon freshly ground pepper

1 teaspoon fresh lemon juice

⅓ cup dry white wine

2 ounces black trumpet mushrooms

6 tablespoons roughly chopped fresh
   flat-leaf parsley

3 tablespoons finely chopped fresh chives

3 tablespoons chopped fresh chervil

1. Rinse the chanterelles quickly with cold water (do not soak) in a colander, and dry thoroughly on paper towels. Wipe the other mushrooms with a damp paper towel, or if necessary, rinse with cold water and dry well on paper towels.

2. In a large sauté pan, melt 3 tablespoons butter over medium heat. Add the garlic and shallot; cook until the shallot begins to soften, about 1 minute. Add blue foot mushrooms; cook, stirring often, until the mushrooms wilt, about 4 minutes. Season with salt, pepper, and lemon juice.

3. Add the white wine, and cook until fully evaporated, 1 to 2 minutes. Add the black trumpet mushrooms, parsley, chives, chervil, and remaining 2 tablespoons butter; cook until the mushrooms wilt, 1 to 2 minutes. Serve immediately.

winter greens and bacon

SERVES 4

Any combination of kale, chard, and mustard or collard greens works well.

4 slices thick-cut bacon, cut
   into ½-inch strips

1 pound kale, ribs removed, leaves
   torn into 2-inch pieces

1 bunch Swiss chard, ribs removed,
   leaves torn into 2-inch pieces

¾ cup water

2 teaspoons apple cider vinegar
   Coarse salt and freshly ground pepper

1. In a large skillet over medium heat, cook the bacon until browned, about 5 minutes. Remove with a slotted spoon, and set aside. Pour off all but 2 tablespoons rendered fat.

2. Add the greens and water to the pan, and bring to a boil. Cover, reduce heat, and simmer until the greens are wilted and almost all the water has evaporated, about 8 minutes.

3. Remove the greens from the heat. Stir in the vinegar, and season with salt and pepper. Toss in the bacon. Serve warm.

carrot, parsnip, and pea gratin

SERVES 6

   Unsalted butter, for baking dish

5 large carrots, cut into 1-inch pieces

5 large parsnips, cut into 1-inch pieces

10 ounces frozen peas, thawed

10 ounces frozen pearl onions, thawed

1 cup heavy cream
   Coarse salt and freshly ground pepper

Preheat the oven to 375° F. Butter a 2-quart gratin or baking dish. Place the carrots, parsnips, peas, and onions in a medium bowl. Pour in the cream; season well with salt and pepper. Toss until well combined. Pour into the baking dish; bake, stirring halfway through, until bubbly and golden brown, 40 to 50 minutes. Serve immediately.

roasted baby artichokes, asparagus, and fennel with olives

SERVES 6

1 *bunch (12 ounces) asparagus*

2 *medium fennel bulbs*

8 *baby artichokes*

1 *lemon, cut in half*

1½ *cups large green olives, such as Cerignola*

¼ *cup extra-virgin olive oil*

2 *tablespoons fresh lemon juice*

1 *teaspoon coarse salt*

¼ *teaspoon freshly ground pepper*

1. Preheat the oven to 375° F. Trim the ends of the asparagus; cut the stalks into 3-inch lengths. Place in a large bowl; set aside. Trim the leaves from the fennel; cut the bulbs in half and into thin wedges. Add to the bowl with the asparagus.

2. Remove and discard any tough outer leaves from the artichokes. Cut into quarters; remove and discard the purple chokes. Rub the artichokes all over with cut lemon to prevent browning; add to the bowl with the asparagus. Add the olives, olive oil, lemon juice, salt, and pepper; toss to combine well.

3. Transfer to a roasting pan. Roast until the vegetables are tender and just starting to brown, about 30 minutes. Serve hot or at room temperature.

provençal roasted tomatoes

SERVES 8 TO 10

These tomatoes hold up well for up to 2 days when stored in the refrigerator; serve as a sandwich filling or pasta topping.

12 *plum tomatoes (about 3 pounds)*

3 *garlic cloves, minced*

2 *tablespoons finely chopped fresh thyme*

2 *tablespoons finely chopped fresh flat-leaf parsley*

   Coarse salt and freshly ground pepper

¼ *cup extra-virgin olive oil*

1. Preheat the oven to 350° F. Fit a wire rack into a rimmed baking sheet. Slice each tomato lengthwise into 4 ½-inch slices. Place on the wire rack.

2. In a small bowl, mix the garlic, thyme, and parsley; season with salt and pepper. Divide evenly among the tomato slices, spooning about ½ teaspoon on each. Drizzle the olive oil over the tomatoes. Roast until the herb mixture is lightly browned and the tomato skins are wrinkled, about 1 hour. Transfer the baking sheet to a wire rack to cool. Serve.

saucy black beans

SERVES 6 TO 8

1 *12-ounce package dried black beans, picked over*

3 *tablespoons vegetable oil*

1 *large white onion, diced*

8 *cups cold water*

   Peel of 1 orange, pith removed (optional)

1 *jalapeño pepper, sliced in half lengthwise and seeded (optional)*

   Coarse salt and freshly ground black pepper

   Hot pepper sauce, such as Tabasco (optional)

1. Place the beans in a large bowl or stockpot; cover with cold water by 2 inches. Let stand at room temperature 4 hours or overnight. Drain, and rinse the beans with cold water; set aside.

2. Heat the oil in a large saucepan over medium heat. Add the onion, and cook until it is soft and translucent but not browned, about 8 minutes. Add the beans and the cold water, along with the orange peel and jalapeño, if desired. Bring to a boil, and reduce heat to a gentle simmer; cover, and cook, stirring occasionally, until the beans are tender and most of the liquid has evaporated, creating a sauce-like consistency, about 2 hours. Most of the liquid should have evaporated.

3. Remove from heat; remove the orange peel and jalapeño, if using. Season with salt, black pepper, and hot pepper sauce, if desired. Serve hot or at room temperature.

brussels sprouts with lemon and walnuts

SERVES 8

2 pounds Brussels sprouts, stem ends trimmed and scored with an X

3 tablespoons unsalted butter

1 garlic clove, minced

Coarse salt and freshly ground pepper

2 teaspoons fresh lemon juice

½ cup walnuts, toasted, coarsely chopped

1. Bring a large pot of water to a boil; insert a steamer rack. Add the Brussels sprouts; steam until bright green and just tender, about 7 minutes. Transfer to a plate.

2. Melt the butter in a large skillet over medium heat. Add the garlic; cook, stirring, until soft, about 2 minutes. Stir in the Brussels sprouts; cook until warmed through, about 2 minutes. Season with salt and pepper. Stir in the lemon juice and walnuts.

tarragon green beans

SERVES 8

3 tablespoons unsalted butter

1 large shallot, finely chopped (½ cup)

2 pounds green beans, trimmed

½ cup dry white wine

2 tablespoons coarsely chopped fresh tarragon, plus sprigs for garnish

Coarse salt and freshly ground pepper

1. Melt the butter in a large, high-sided skillet over medium heat. Add the shallot; cook, stirring constantly, until soft and translucent, 2 to 3 minutes. Add the beans, and gently toss to coat with the shallot mixture. Cook, stirring occasionally, 2 minutes.

2. Add the wine. Raise heat to medium-high; cook, stirring often, 12 minutes. Reduce heat to medium, and cook until the beans are tender, 3 to 5 minutes more. Stir in the tarragon, and season with salt and pepper. Garnish with tarragon sprigs.

sautéed red cabbage with raisins

SERVES 4

2 tablespoons extra-virgin olive oil

1 small red cabbage (about 1¾ pounds), halved, cored, and thinly sliced crosswise

2 small shallots, quartered and separated into layers (about 4 ounces)

2 teaspoons coarse salt

2 tablespoons fresh lemon juice

2½ teaspoons cider vinegar

Freshly ground pepper

⅓ cup raisins

Heat the oil in a large nonstick sauté pan over medium-high heat until hot but not smoking. Add the cabbage and shallots, and cook, stirring occasionally, until the cabbage has softened slightly, about 15 minutes. Stir in the salt, lemon juice, and vinegar. Season with pepper. Cook until the cabbage has wilted and the shallots have softened, 10 to 12 minutes more. Stir in the raisins; serve.

braised cabbage

SERVES 4

Leeks should be cleaned thoroughly. After slicing, place the pieces in a large bowl of cold water. Let stand about 10 minutes, then remove them with a slotted spoon.

2 cans (14½ ounces each) low-sodium chicken broth

1 teaspoon coarse salt

10 whole black peppercorns

1 bay leaf

1 small green cabbage (about 2 pounds), cut into 8 wedges

1 small leek, white and pale-green parts only, halved lengthwise and cut crosswise into ½-inch-thick pieces

Bring the broth, salt, peppercorns, and bay leaf to a boil in a medium pot over medium-high heat. Add the cabbage and leek. Cover; reduce heat to medium. Simmer until the cabbage is tender, 12 to 15 minutes. Transfer the cabbage and some of the broth to a serving platter.

glazed carrots with whole spices and rosemary

SERVES 4 TO 6

- 2 pounds thin, tender carrots in assorted colors, with greens (or regular carrots, halved lengthwise)

  Coarse salt
- 3 tablespoons packed light-brown sugar
- 1 tablespoon plus 1 teaspoon white-wine vinegar
- 2 tablespoons honey
- 1 teaspoon whole pink peppercorns
- 2 tablespoons extra-virgin olive oil, plus more (optional) for drizzling
- 2 sprigs fresh rosemary
- 1 whole star anise

1. Peel and trim the carrots, leaving 1½ inches of the greens intact. Bring a large pot of water to a boil; add 1 tablespoon salt. Add the carrots; cook until bright and just tender, 3 to 4 minutes. Immediately plunge into an ice-water bath. Drain.

2. Preheat the oven to 375°F. Whisk together the sugar, vinegar, honey, and peppercorns.

3. Heat the oil in a large ovenproof skillet over medium-high heat. Add the carrots, rosemary, and star anise; cook, stirring, until the carrots are tender, about 5 minutes. Stir in the honey mixture. Season with salt. Bring to a boil over medium-high heat, turning the carrots to coat.

4. Transfer the skillet to the oven. Roast the carrots until slightly caramelized, 20 to 25 minutes. Drizzle with oil, if desired.

celery root puree

SERVES 4 AS A SIDE DISH

- 1 tablespoon vegetable oil
- 2 medium shallots, finely chopped

  Coarse salt and freshly ground white pepper
- 1 large celery root (about 2 pounds), peeled and cut into 1-inch chunks
- 2 cups milk
- 1 bay leaf
- 2 garlic cloves, crushed

  Pinch of ground nutmeg

1. Heat the oil in a medium, heavy-bottomed pot over medium heat. Add the shallots; season with salt and pepper. Cook, stirring, until translucent, about 5 minutes.

2. Add the celery root, milk, 2 cups water, bay leaf, garlic, and nutmeg. Season with salt and pepper. Bring to a boil. Reduce heat; simmer until the celery root is very tender, about 15 minutes. Let cool.

3. Discard the bay leaf. Transfer the solids to a blender using a slotted spoon. Add ¼ cup cooking liquid. Blend until smooth (add more cooking liquid, if needed). Season with salt and pepper.

sautéed peas and scallions

SERVES 4

Cooking peas only briefly—in a little bit of butter—lets them retain their flavor, color, and texture.

- 2 tablespoons unsalted butter
- 3 cups shelled fresh peas or thawed frozen peas
- 3 scallions, white and pale-green parts only, thinly sliced diagonally

  Coarse salt and freshly ground pepper

Melt the butter in a medium skillet over medium-high heat. Add the peas and scallions. Cook, stirring, until heated through, about 3 minutes. Season with salt and pepper.

roasted fennel with thyme

SERVES 6 TO 8

- 4 large fennel bulbs, trimmed and cut into 8 wedges each
- ¼ cup extra-virgin olive oil
- 3 sprigs fresh thyme, leaves removed and stems discarded, plus 3 whole sprigs

  Coarse salt
- ¼ teaspoon freshly ground pepper

  Juice of 1 lemon

Preheat the oven to 400° F. Toss together the fennel, oil, thyme leaves and sprigs, ½ teaspoon salt, and the pepper in a large bowl. Spread the fennel mixture into a single layer on a rimmed baking sheet. Roast the fennel, turning occasionally, until browned, 50 to 60 minutes. Drizzle with the lemon juice; season with salt.

collard greens with bacon

SERVES 8

- 2 bunches collard greens, stemmed
- 3 tablespoons vegetable oil
- ½ red onion, sliced
- 3 slices bacon, cut crosswise into ¼-inch strips
- 2 tablespoons cider vinegar
- 1 cup homemade or low-sodium store-bought chicken stock

1. Working in batches, stack the greens; cut crosswise into 2-inch-thick strips. Gather the strips; cut crosswise into 2-inch pieces. Transfer to a large bowl of cold water; swish to remove grit. Transfer the greens to a colander using a slotted spoon; let drain. Repeat until the greens are free of grit.

2. Heat the oil in a very large skillet over medium-high heat. Add the onion and bacon; cook until the onion is translucent, about 4 minutes. Add the greens; cook, stirring, until the greens begin to wilt and are reduced in volume.

3. Raise heat to high; add the vinegar. Cook, scraping up brown bits from the bottom of the skillet, until the vinegar has evaporated, about 1 minute.

4. Add the stock; reduce heat. Simmer, covered, until the greens are just tender, 12 to 14 minutes. If making ahead, refrigerate, covered; reheat over low.

baked stuffed red peppers with cherry tomatoes, feta, and thyme

SERVES 4

Filled with tangy feta and a handful of sweet tiny tomatoes, red bell peppers take on a Mediterranean twist. You can also try other varieties of small tomatoes such as grape, currant, or even yellow pear in the filling.

- 2 small red bell peppers (5 to 6 ounces each), halved lengthwise through stem, seeds and ribs removed
- 1 heaping cup cherry tomatoes (about 6 ounces)
- 1½ ounces feta cheese (preferably goat's milk), crumbled
- 1 teaspoon coarsely chopped fresh thyme
- 8 basil leaves, torn into pieces

  Freshly ground pepper
- 1 tablespoon extra-virgin olive oil

1. Preheat the oven to 400° F, with the rack in the top third. Place the bell pepper halves, cut sides up, in a baking dish. Toss together the tomatoes, feta, thyme, and basil in a medium bowl; season with black pepper. Fill each pepper with tomato and feta mixture, dividing evenly. Drizzle each with oil.

2. Bake the stuffed peppers, covered with aluminum foil, until they begin to soften, about 30 minutes. Remove the foil; continue to bake until the tomatoes begin to burst and the cheese turns light brown, 13 to 15 minutes more. Remove the stuffed peppers from the oven, and serve warm.

neapolitan green beans

SERVES 6

 1 *pound green beans, trimmed*
 2 *garlic cloves, thinly sliced*
 ¼ *teaspoon crushed red pepper flakes*
 1 *teaspoon coarse salt*
 1 *medium tomato, cored and torn*
    into pieces
 2 *to 3 tablespoons extra-virgin olive oil*
 1 *large sprig fresh basil*

1. Rinse and drain the green beans; place in a medium saucepan while still slightly wet. Add the garlic, red pepper flakes, salt, tomato, and oil. Cover; cook over medium-low heat, stirring occasionally, until the beans are soft, about 15 minutes.

2. Add the basil sprig; cook, uncovered, stirring constantly, until most of the juices have evaporated, about 5 minutes. Transfer the mixture to a serving bowl. Discard the basil sprig before serving.

broccoli with olives

SERVES 10

 4 *bunches broccoli (about 3 pounds),*
    cut into medium florets
 ½ *cup extra-virgin olive oil*
 1 *teaspoon coarse salt*
 ½ *teaspoon freshly ground pepper*
 1 *cup pitted and slivered kalamata olives*

1. Prepare an ice-water bath; set aside. Put the broccoli in a steamer basket over boiling water, cover, and steam until just tender, about 7 minutes. Briefly plunge into the ice-water bath. Drain; pat dry.

2. Heat ¼ cup oil in a wide sauté pan over medium heat. Add half of the broccoli, ½ teaspoon salt, and ¼ teaspoon pepper; cook, stirring, until golden brown, about 5 minutes. Stir in half of the olives. Cook until heated through. Transfer to a serving dish; cover. Repeat with the remaining oil, broccoli, salt, pepper, and olives. Combine batches. Serve immediately.

maple-glazed parsnips and carrots

SERVES 4 TO 6

 1¼ *pounds parsnips (about 6), peeled,*
     halved lengthwise
 ¾   *pound thin carrots (about 12), peeled,*
     greens trimmed but not removed
 4   *slices bacon, each cut into 4 pieces*
 10 *sprigs fresh thyme*
 ¼   *cup pure maple syrup*
     Coarse salt and freshly ground pepper

Preheat the oven to 450° F, with the rack in the lower third. Place the parsnips, carrots, bacon, and thyme in a single layer on a rimmed baking sheet. Drizzle with the syrup; season with salt and pepper. Toss well to combine. Bake until the bottoms of the vegetables begin to caramelize and turn dark brown, about 20 minutes. Remove from the oven, and toss the vegetables carefully. Return to the oven, and bake until all sides are well browned, about 25 minutes more. Discard the bacon and thyme. Serve immediately.

creamed spinach and pearl onions

SERVES 4

 1¼ *pounds spinach, tough stems discarded,*
     leaves rinsed well (do not pat dry)
 10 *ounces white pearl onions (2½ cups)*
  5 *tablespoons unsalted butter*
  2 *tablespoons all-purpose flour*
 1¼ *cups milk*
  ¾ *cup chopped slab bacon (3 ounces)*
  ½ *cup heavy cream*
     Coarse salt and freshly ground pepper
     Pinch of freshly grated nutmeg
  2 *teaspoons fresh lemon juice*

1. Heat a large pot over high heat until hot. Cook the spinach (with water still clinging to the leaves) in the pot, covered, until beginning to wilt, about 1 minute. Stir, and cook, covered, 1 minute more. Uncover; stir the spinach until completely wilted.

2. Transfer the spinach to a colander; rinse under cold water. Squeeze dry in a clean kitchen towel. Finely chop; set aside.

3. Bring a medium saucepan of water to a boil. Add the onions; cook until the skins soften, about 3 minutes. Remove the onions with a slotted spoon (reserve the water in the pot); rinse. Trim the root ends, and remove the skins. Halve the onions, if large. Return the onions to the cooking water. Cook until tender, about 10 minutes. Drain, and rinse.

4. Melt 4 tablespoons butter in a medium saucepan over medium heat. Add the flour, and whisk until smooth. Whisking constantly, pour in the milk in a slow, steady stream. Boil, whisking constantly, 1 minute. Remove from heat.

5. Melt the remaining tablespoon butter in a large saucepan over medium heat. Add the bacon; cook, stirring occasionally, until well browned, about 6 minutes. Stir in the onions and spinach. Stir in the cream and reserved milk mixture. Add 1 teaspoon salt, ¼ teaspoon pepper, and nutmeg. Cook, stirring, until heated through and thick, about 10 minutes (do not boil). Stir in the lemon juice. Season with salt and pepper.

baked creamed salsify

SERVES 4 TO 6

¼ cup plus 1 teaspoon fresh lemon juice (about 2 lemons)

2 pounds salsify
   Coarse salt

1½ tablespoons unsalted butter

½ cup heavy cream
   Pinch of freshly grated nutmeg
   Freshly ground pepper

¼ cup fresh bread crumbs, lightly toasted

¼ cup freshly grated Parmesan cheese

1. Preheat the oven to 425°F, with the rack in the highest position. Fill a large bowl two-thirds full with cold water; add ¼ cup lemon juice. Trim the salsify, and peel with a vegetable peeler, transferring the salsify to lemon water as you work. Cut the salsify into 2-inch lengths; return to bowl. Drain.

2. Cover the salsify with cold water by 2 inches in a medium saucepan; add ½ teaspoon salt. Bring to a boil. Reduce heat to medium-high. Cook until tender but not mushy, 10 to 15 minutes; drain.

3. Melt the butter in a medium saucepan over medium heat. Stir in the salsify. Stir in the cream and remaining teaspoon lemon juice. Bring to a bare simmer; remove from heat. Add the nutmeg, and season with salt and pepper. Pour the salsify mixture into an 8-inch-square baking dish or 8-cup gratin dish. Sprinkle with the bread crumbs and cheese. Bake until golden brown, about 20 minutes.

roasted radishes with capers and anchovies

SERVES 4

12 ounces radishes (about 12), halved if large

2 teaspoons capers, rinsed and chopped

6 anchovy fillets, finely chopped

1 garlic clove, minced

2 tablespoons extra-virgin olive oil
   Coarse salt and freshly ground pepper

½ lemon, for serving

Preheat the oven to 375°F, with a rack in the upper third. In a small roasting pan, toss together the radishes, capers, anchovies, garlic, and oil; season with salt and pepper. Spread out the mixture evenly. Roast, stirring once, until the radishes are shriveled and fragrant, 30 to 35 minutes. Serve warm with lemon.

roasted root vegetables with sage and garlic

SERVES 4 TO 6

8 ounces rutabagas, peeled and cut into ½-inch cubes or half-moons

8 ounces turnips, peeled and cut into ½-inch cubes or half-moons

8 ounces carrots, peeled and cut into ½-inch cubes or rounds

8 ounces parsnips, peeled and cut into ½-inch cubes or rounds

8 fresh sage leaves

4 garlic cloves (do not peel)

Coarse salt and freshly ground pepper

4½ teaspoons olive oil

Preheat the oven to 375°F. Toss together all the ingredients; spread out in a roasting pan. Roast, stirring occasionally, until golden brown and tender, 50 to 60 minutes.

haricots verts with pecans and lemon

SERVES 4

Coarse salt

1 pound haricots verts or thin green beans, trimmed

½ cup pecans

3 tablespoons sherry vinegar

1 teaspoon sugar

Freshly ground pepper

¼ cup olive oil

1 teaspoon freshly grated lemon zest

1. Preheat the oven to 425°F. Bring a large pot of water to a boil; add salt and the haricots verts. Cook the beans until bright green and crisp-tender, 3 to 4 minutes; drain. Transfer to a serving dish.

2. Meanwhile, spread the pecans in a single layer on a rimmed baking sheet; toast in the oven until fragrant, about 5 minutes. Coarsely chop the nuts when they are cool enough to handle.

3. Whisk the vinegar, sugar, and ¼ teaspoon salt in a small bowl; season with pepper. Whisking constantly, pour in the oil in a slow, steady stream; whisk until emulsified. Just before serving, gently toss the beans with the vinaigrette and chopped nuts; sprinkle with the zest. Serve warm.

cauliflower, prosciutto, and goat cheese gratin

SERVES 6 TO 8

Unsalted butter, for the baking dish

2 small heads cauliflower (about 3 pounds total), cut into 1-inch florets

12 ounces soft goat cheese, crumbled

¼ cup fresh orange juice (1 orange)

¼ cup homemade or low-sodium store-bought chicken stock, or water

2 teaspoons chopped fresh thyme

2 tablespoons all-purpose flour

Coarse salt and freshly ground pepper

3 ounces thinly sliced prosciutto (about 5 slices), coarsely chopped

1. Preheat the oven to 375°F. Butter a 2-quart casserole or an 8-inch-square baking dish; set aside. Bring a large pot of water to a boil. Add the cauliflower; cook until just tender, 4 to 5 minutes. Drain.

2. Whisk together 8 ounces goat cheese and the orange juice, stock, thyme, flour, 1½ teaspoons salt, and ½ teaspoon pepper until smooth. Toss in the cauliflower and prosciutto. Spoon into the buttered dish. Top with the remaining 4 ounces goat cheese.

3. Cover with foil; bake 30 minutes. Remove the foil; bake until bubbling and just golden, about 30 minutes more. Let cool slightly before serving.

individual portobello
mushroom gratins

MAKES 6

2 tablespoons olive oil, plus more for
  the baking sheet

6 portobello mushrooms, stems removed
  and reserved

¼ cup finely grated Parmesan cheese
  (1 ounce)

¼ cup plain dry bread crumbs

3 tablespoons finely chopped fresh flat-
  leaf parsley

3 tablespoons chopped fresh chives

2 shallots, thinly sliced

1 pound white or cremini mushrooms, sliced

½ cup dry white wine

½ cup heavy cream

1 teaspoon coarse salt

¼ teaspoon freshly ground pepper

1. Preheat the oven to 350°F. Lightly oil a rimmed baking sheet. Arrange the portobello caps, gill sides down, on the sheet. Bake until tender, 20 to 25 minutes. Transfer to a plate to cool. Preheat the broiler.

2. Stir together the cheese, bread crumbs, 1 tablespoon parsley, 1 tablespoon chives, and 1 tablespoon oil; set aside.

3. Chop the portobello stems into ½-inch pieces. Heat the remaining tablespoon oil in a large skillet over medium heat until hot but not smoking. Add the shallots; cook, stirring, until softened, about 2 minutes. Add the sliced mushrooms and chopped stems; cook, stirring occasionally, until tender, 6 to 7 minutes. Add the wine; cook until most of the liquid has evaporated, about 2 minutes. Stir in the cream, remaining 2 tablespoons each parsley and chives, and the salt and pepper. Remove from heat.

4. Arrange the portobello caps, gill sides up, on a clean baking sheet. Divide the mushroom mixture and then the crumb mixture among the caps. Broil until bubbling and golden brown, about 2 minutes.

beet and cucumber relish
with grilled asparagus

SERVES 4

If you use beets of different sizes, keep in mind that their cooking times may vary. Take each out of the oven as it's ready (knife-tender).

2 medium red beets (about ½ pound
  without greens), tails and about 1 inch
  of stems left intact

1 cup diced (¼-inch pieces) peeled
  English cucumber

1 teaspoon finely chopped shallot

2 teaspoons balsamic vinegar

2 teaspoons extra-virgin olive oil
  Coarse salt

1 bunch asparagus, trimmed and peeled

½ cup loosely packed fresh basil leaves

1. Preheat the oven to 400°F. Wrap each beet in foil. Roast until tender when pierced with the tip of a knife, 45 minutes to 1 hour. When cool enough to handle, trim the beets and rub off the skins with paper towels, or peel with a paring knife.

2. Cut the beets into ¼-inch dice, and transfer to a medium bowl. Stir in the cucumber, shallot, vinegar, 1 teaspoon oil, and ¼ teaspoon salt. Refrigerate until ready to use, up to 2 hours.

3. Preheat a grill or grill pan until hot. Toss the asparagus with the remaining teaspoon oil and ½ teaspoon salt in a large bowl. Grill the asparagus, turning once, until tender, 4 to 8 minutes (depending on the thickness of the spears).

4. Arrange the asparagus on a platter, and let cool completely. Finely chop the basil, and stir into the beet relish. Using a slotted spoon, spoon the beet relish over the asparagus.

wilted baby spinach with crispy shallots

SERVES 6

Baby spinach is easy to find—either loose at farmers' markets or prewashed and bagged at supermarkets. If possible, get the curly-leaf (crinkled) type, as it doesn't shrink as much during cooking as the flat-leaf variety does.

> Vegetable or light olive oil, for frying
>
> All-purpose flour, for dredging
>
> Coarse salt and freshly ground pepper
>
> 1 large shallot, cut crosswise into rings and separated (about ⅓ cup)
>
> 2 tablespoons extra-virgin olive oil
>
> 1 pound baby spinach

1. Heat ½ inch vegetable oil in a small skillet over medium heat. Meanwhile, put the flour in a bowl, and season with salt and pepper. Dredge the shallot rings in the flour all at once. When the oil is hot (a shallot ring will sizzle on contact), fry the rings in batches, shaking off excess flour before transferring them to the skillet. Fry until golden brown and crisp, 1 to 3 minutes. Transfer the shallot rings with tongs or a slotted spoon to paper towels to drain.

2. Heat the extra-virgin olive oil in a Dutch oven or shallow stockpot over medium heat until hot but not smoking. Add the spinach (if it doesn't fit all at once, wait to add more until some of it cooks down, or cook in two batches). Season with salt and pepper. Cover; cook, uncovering occasionally to toss, until the spinach is wilted, 2 to 3 minutes.

3. Transfer the spinach to a serving bowl with tongs or a slotted spoon, leaving any excess liquid in pot. Sprinkle with the shallot rings; serve immediately.

tomatoes with oregano and lime

SERVES 4

This recipe calls for lime juice—rather than lemon juice or vinegar—to brighten the sweet flavor of summer tomatoes. We used heirloom varieties for their exceptional taste and vivid colors, but you can use any kind or size—from the farmers' market or your own backyard—as long as they are ripe.

> 1¼ pounds assorted ripe tomatoes in all sizes, cut into wedges if large or halved if small
>
> Coarse salt and freshly ground pepper
>
> 3 tablespoons extra-virgin olive oil
>
> Juice of 1 lime (about 2 tablespoons)
>
> 2 tablespoons coarsely chopped fresh oregano

Arrange the tomatoes on a serving platter; season with salt and pepper. Drizzle with the oil and lime juice; sprinkle with the oregano.

ratatouille

SERVES 6

Ratatouille is very versatile. It works equally well as a main course or side dish, and can be served hot, cold, or at room temperature. You can refrigerate it, covered, up to 3 days.

> 1 large eggplant (about 1½ pounds), cut into 1-inch cubes
>
> 4 medium zucchini, cut into 1-inch cubes
>
> ½ cup plus 2 tablespoons extra-virgin olive oil
>
> 2 tablespoons coarsely chopped fresh thyme
>
> Coarse salt and freshly ground pepper
>
> 6 pounds vine-ripened tomatoes (about 10)
>
> 2 bell peppers, 1 red and 1 yellow
>
> 4 garlic cloves, finely chopped
>
> 2 medium onions, halved and cut into half-moons
>
> ½ cup coarsely chopped fresh basil
>
> ½ cup coarsely chopped fresh flat-leaf parsley

1. Preheat the oven to 400° F. Toss together the eggplant, zucchini, ½ cup oil, 1 tablespoon thyme, 1 teaspoon salt, and ½ teaspoon pepper on a large rimmed baking sheet. Roast, tossing occasionally, until the vegetables are golden, about 1 hour.

2. Meanwhile, bring a large pot of water to a boil. Prepare an ice-water bath, and set aside. Cut a small, shallow X in the stem end of each tomato; blanch the tomatoes until the skins begin to loosen, about 30 seconds. Immediately transfer with a slotted spoon to the ice-water bath.

3. Drain the tomatoes. Remove the skins; cut the tomatoes into quarters, discarding the seeds.

4. Place one bell pepper at a time on the trivet of a gas stove burner on high heat; roast, turning occasionally with tongs, until black all over. (Or, broil the peppers in a baking pan, turning them occasionally.) Transfer to a large bowl, and cover with plastic wrap. Let them steam in the bowl until cool enough to handle, about 10 minutes.

5. Remove the skins from the peppers. Discard the tops and seeds. Cut the peppers lengthwise into ½-inch-thick strips.

6. When the eggplant and zucchini are done roasting, heat the remaining 2 tablespoons oil in a large, deep skillet over medium-high heat until hot but not smoking. Add the garlic and onions; cook until soft, about 4 minutes. Add the tomatoes and peppers; cook until the tomatoes are soft, about 7 minutes. Add the eggplant and zucchini, ¼ cup basil, and the remaining tablespoon thyme. Season with salt and pepper.

7. Reduce heat to medium-low; simmer, stirring occasionally, until the vegetables are very soft, about 30 minutes. Stir in the parsley and remaining ¼ cup basil. Cook until heated through, about 1 minute more.

RATATOUILLE TIPS

Ratatouille, a summery vegetable stew, features many of the ingredients—onions, eggplant, bell peppers, zucchini, and, of course, tomatoes and garlic—essential for so many other Provençal specialties. The stew lends itself to interpretation, but these few rules will guarantee superior results:

● *Oven roasting: The eggplant and zucchini should be roasted in the oven before being stewed with the other ingredients (rather than just stewed, as called for in some recipes), to prevent sogginess and concentrate sweetness.*

● *Flame roasting: Charring the bell pepper over a gas stove's flame (or under the broiler) imparts a smoky flavor.*

● *Blanching and peeling: When cooking with fresh tomatoes, it's always a good idea to first remove their skin and seeds, as they affect the texture of the finished dish.*

● *Stewing: Simmering all the ingredients together allows their flavors to meld. For the liveliest taste, reserve some herbs and stir them in at the last minute.*

haricots verts with mustard vinaigrette
SERVES 2

I like to serve these chilled haricots verts with lamb—their crunch and acidity cut the richness of the meat. Blanched haricots verts can be refrigerated, in a resealable plastic bag, up to 1 day. Refrigerate the vinaigrette separately, up to 1 day; bring to room temperature before serving.

Coarse salt

½ pound haricots verts or other thin green beans, trimmed

½ teaspoon finely chopped shallot

1½ teaspoons red-wine vinegar

Freshly ground pepper

½ teaspoon grainy or smooth Dijon mustard

1½ tablespoons extra-virgin olive oil

1. Bring a large saucepan of water to a boil. Prepare an ice-water bath. Add salt to the boiling water, then add the haricots verts; cook just until the beans are bright green all over, 1 to 2 minutes.

2. Drain the beans; rinse immediately with cold water. Transfer to the ice-water bath. When chilled completely, drain; pat dry.

3. Put the shallot and vinegar in a small bowl; season with salt and pepper. Let stand 15 minutes. Whisk in the mustard. Whisking constantly, pour in the oil in a slow, steady stream until emulsified. Set aside until ready to dress the beans; whisk before using.

baby bok choy
with ginger and garlic
SERVES 4 TO 6

2   *pounds baby bok choy (8 to 10), halved lengthwise and soaked in cold water to remove any dirt*

2   *teaspoons minced peeled fresh ginger*

2   *garlic cloves, thinly sliced*

1   *tablespoon plus 1 teaspoon toasted sesame oil*

¼   *cup tamari soy sauce*

2   *tablespoons oyster sauce*

1. Bring a large pot of water to a boil. Add the bok choy (in two batches, if necessary), and cook until tender, 5 to 7 minutes. Drain in a colander; let stand at least 5 minutes. Transfer to a serving dish.

2. Meanwhile, cook the ginger and garlic in oil in a small saucepan over medium-low heat, stirring, until soft, about 8 minutes. Add the tamari and oyster sauce; cook, stirring, until heated through, about 30 seconds more. Pour the sauce over the bok choy; toss to coat.

braised endive
in mustard vinaigrette
SERVES 4

1   *tablespoon unsalted butter*

1½   *pounds Belgian endive (about 6 heads)*

3   *cups homemade or low-sodium store-bought chicken stock*

1½   *tablespoons grainy mustard*

2   *tablespoons red-wine vinegar*

    Coarse salt and freshly ground pepper

¼   *cup extra-virgin olive oil*

1   *tablespoon finely chopped fresh flat-leaf parsley, for garnish*

1. In a large skillet, melt the butter over medium heat. Add the endive, and cook, turning occasionally, until browned on all sides, about 5 minutes. Pour the stock into the skillet; bring to a boil, and cover. Reduce heat to medium-low, and simmer, turning the endive occasionally, until just tender, about 20 minutes.

2. Using a slotted spoon, transfer the endive to a paper-towel–lined plate; discard the stock. Pat the endive dry, and set aside.

3. Make the dressing: In a small bowl, whisk together the mustard and vinegar. Season with salt and pepper. Whisking constantly, pour in the oil in a slow, steady stream; whisk until emulsified. Gently toss each endive in the dressing, coating well. Garnish with the parsley, and serve at room temperature; set any extra dressing on the side.

jerusalem artichoke
and chestnut gratin
SERVES 6 TO 8

1   *pound Jerusalem artichokes (about 10 small), peeled, sliced ¼ inch thick, and reserved in cold water (drain and pat dry before using)*

3   *cups milk*

8   *ounces crème fraîche*

2   *tablespoons fresh lemon juice*

1   *cup grated Gruyère cheese (4 ounces)*

1 tablespoon minced fresh thyme

1½ teaspoons coarse salt

¼ teaspoon freshly ground pepper

½ pound Yukon Gold potatoes, peeled and sliced ¼ inch thick

5 ounces shallots (about 4), thinly sliced

5 ounces jarred or vacuum-packed peeled chestnuts, halved lengthwise

4 slices white bread, trimmed of crusts, lightly toasted and torn into small pieces

1. Preheat the oven to 450° F. In a large saucepan, bring the artichokes and milk just to a boil. Reduce heat; simmer until artichokes are crisp-tender, about 10 minutes. Drain in a colander set over a bowl; reserve ¾ cup milk.

2. In a large bowl, whisk the reserved milk with the crème fraîche, lemon juice, ¼ cup cheese, thyme, salt, and pepper. Add the artichokes, potatoes, shallots, and chestnuts; stir to combine.

3. Pour the mixture into a 1½-quart gratin dish; cover tightly with foil. Bake on a baking sheet until the artichokes are tender when pierced, about 1 hour. Remove the foil; sprinkle the top of the gratin with the bread pieces and remaining ¾ cup cheese. Continue baking, uncovered, until golden brown, 8 to 10 minutes more. Serve warm.

roasted brussels sprouts with almonds and honey
SERVES 8 TO 10

3 pounds Brussels sprouts, trimmed and halved

½ cup (1 stick) unsalted butter, melted

1 cup slivered almonds (4 ounces)

Coarse salt and freshly ground pepper

3 tablespoons honey

3 tablespoons fresh lemon juice (about 1 lemon)

1. Preheat the oven to 400° F. Place the sprouts, butter, and almonds on a rimmed baking sheet. Season with salt and pepper; toss to combine. Roast, stirring, until sprouts are golden brown and tender, 35 to 40 minutes.

2. Transfer to a serving bowl; immediately dress with the honey and lemon juice, and season with salt and pepper. Serve warm or at room temperature.

roasted curried cauliflower
SERVES 4

An Indian-inspired spice blend adds a warm hue and gives this vegetable dish an exotic taste.

1½ tablespoons extra-virgin olive oil

1 teaspoon mustard seeds

1 teaspoon cumin seeds

¾ teaspoon curry powder

¾ teaspoon coarse salt

1 large head cauliflower (about 2 pounds), cut into large florets

Nonstick olive oil cooking spray

1. Preheat the oven to 375° F. Coat a rimmed baking sheet with cooking spray. In a large bowl, stir together the oil, mustard seeds, cumin seeds, curry powder, and salt. Add the cauliflower, tossing to coat thoroughly with the spice mixture.

2. Arrange the cauliflower in a single layer on the prepared sheet. Roast until the florets are browned on bottom and tender when pierced with the tip of a paring knife, about 35 minutes. Serve hot.

turnip hash with broccoli rabe
SERVES 4

½ pound plum tomatoes

½ pound medium turnips, peeled and cut into ½-inch dice

½ pound parsnips, peeled and cut into ½-inch dice

½ pound Yukon Gold potatoes, peeled and cut into ½-inch dice

1 bunch broccoli rabe, cut into ½-inch pieces (about 6½ cups)

1½ tablespoons extra-virgin olive oil

1 medium onion, coarsely chopped

4 garlic cloves, smashed

¾ teaspoon coarse salt

¼ teaspoon crushed red pepper flakes

1 teaspoon coarsely chopped fresh thyme

1. Bring a large pot of water to a boil. Prepare an ice-water bath; set aside. Score an X on the bottom of each tomato with a paring knife. Add the tomatoes to the pot. Boil until the skins are loosened, about 30 seconds; remove the tomatoes with a slotted spoon (keeping the water at a boil), and immediately plunge them into the ice bath. Drain, peel, and seed the tomatoes, then coarsely chop the flesh.

2. Add the turnips to the pot; boil until just tender when pierced with a fork, 3 to 5 minutes. Using a slotted spoon, transfer the turnips to a colander to drain. Repeat the process with the parsnips and then the potatoes. Add the broccoli rabe to the pot, and boil until bright green and crisp-tender, about 1 minute. Drain in a colander; set aside.

3. Heat the oil in a large, heavy skillet over medium heat until hot but not smoking. Add the onion, garlic, salt, red pepper flakes, thyme, and reserved turnips, parsnips, and potatoes; spread evenly to cover bottom of skillet. Cook, without stirring, until the vegetables begin to brown, about 15 minutes.

4. Add the reserved tomatoes and broccoli rabe. Stir once; cook until the vegetables are very tender and browned, about 25 minutes. Serve hot.

tuscan kale with caramelized onions and red-wine vinegar

SERVES 4

Tuscan kale, also known as cavolo nero, dinosaur kale, and lacinato kale, is sweeter and more tender than regular kale, which can be used instead but may require more cooking time.

- 1 tablespoon extra-virgin olive oil
- 1 large red onion, halved and thinly sliced into half-moons
- 1 large garlic clove, thinly sliced
- ¾ teaspoon coarse salt
- 2 tablespoons red-wine vinegar
- 1 pound Tuscan kale, middle stems removed, leaves cut into 1½-inch pieces

1. Combine the oil, onion, garlic, and ¼ teaspoon salt in a large sauté pan; cook over medium heat, stirring occasionally, until the onion is lightly browned, about 5 minutes. Reduce heat to medium-low; cook until the onion is soft, about 10 minutes.

2. Add the vinegar to the pan, and raise heat to medium-high. Add the kale, ¼ cup water, and remaining ½ teaspoon salt; cook, stirring, until the kale begins to soften, about 3 minutes. As the pan becomes dry, add another ¼ cup water, and cook until the kale is tender, about 3 minutes more. Serve immediately.

leeks with mustard vinaigrette

SERVES 4

- 6 leeks (about 2½ pounds), roots and all but 1 inch of green tops trimmed, halved lengthwise and washed well
- 2 tablespoons Dijon mustard
- 2 tablespoons red-wine vinegar
- 2 garlic cloves, minced
- 1 tablespoon minced fresh basil
- ¼ cup extra-virgin olive oil
- ¼ teaspoon coarse salt
- ⅛ teaspoon freshly ground pepper

1. Bring a large pot of water to a boil. With kitchen twine, tie the leeks into 2 bundles, with the green tops at the same ends. Add the bundles to the boiling water. Reduce heat, and simmer until the leeks are tender, about 15 minutes. Remove the leeks; rinse under cold water. Drain well, and gently pat dry with paper towels. Set aside.

2. Make the vinaigrette: In a large bowl, whisk together the mustard, vinegar, garlic, and basil. Slowly whisk in the oil in a fine stream. Whisk in the salt and pepper.

3. Gently toss the leeks in the bowl with the vinaigrette, coating well. Serve chilled or at room temperature.

roasted acorn squash
with pomegranate glaze
SERVES 6

Use a citrus reamer, juicer, or press to extract the pomegranate juice.

- 2 cups fresh pomegranate juice (about 7 pomegranates), plus seeds from ½ pomegranate for garnish
- ¼ cup sugar
- 5 whole allspice
- 5 whole black peppercorns
- 1 dried bay leaf
- 1 whole cinnamon stick
- Unsalted butter, melted, for brushing, plus more at room temperature for the pan
- 3 acorn squash, sliced into 1-inch-thick rings, seeds removed
- Coarse salt

1. Preheat the oven to 450°F. In a small saucepan, combine the juice, sugar, allspice, peppercorns, bay leaf, and cinnamon. Simmer until reduced to a syrup. Drain through a fine sieve into a small bowl, and discard the spices.

2. Line a baking sheet with parchment paper. Butter the parchment. Lay the squash rings on top of the parchment; brush the tops with melted butter, and season with salt.

3. Roast the squash until tender when pierced with a paring knife and the undersides are well browned, about 30 minutes. Turn the squash over, and brush the tops with pomegranate glaze. Continue cooking 5 minutes more. Remove from the oven; brush the squash again with glaze. Transfer to a serving platter; serve immediately, garnished with pomegranate seeds.

cauliflower puree
SERVES 4

For a garnish, sauté a few sliced cauliflower florets in a bit of butter until tender and lightly golden.

- 1 head (1¾ pounds) cauliflower, stem and tough stalks trimmed, florets roughly chopped
- 1 cup water or chicken stock, preferably homemade
- 2 to 3 tablespoons sour cream
- 1 tablespoon unsalted butter, softened
- Coarse salt and freshly ground pepper

1. Combine the cauliflower and water or stock in a medium saucepan, and bring to a boil over high heat. Reduce heat to a simmer, and cook until the cauliflower is very tender, about 10 minutes.

2. Using a slotted spoon, transfer the cauliflower to the bowl of a food processor. Process until smooth, adding 1 to 2 tablespoons cooking liquid, 15 to 20 seconds. Add the sour cream and butter, and process 5 to 10 seconds more. Season with salt and pepper. Serve hot.

mexican-style corn
SERVES 8

Set out the sour cream, cheese, and corn, and let each person fix his own.

- 1 cup sour cream or crème fraîche
- ⅛ teaspoon paprika
- 2 cups grated dry, aged cheese, such as Jack or Asiago
- 8 ears corn on the cob

1. Heat a grill to medium-high. Place sour cream in a small bowl and sprinkle with paprika; set aside. Place cheese in a small bowl; set aside. Grill corn until tender, about 15 minutes, turning frequently.

2. Remove from the grill; when cool enough to handle, pull back the husks and remove the silk. Brush the corn with sour cream, and roll in cheese.

asparagus and shiitake stir-fry

SERVES 4

To clean the mushrooms, simply wipe the caps with a damp paper towel; do not rinse, as they will become soggy. Toast the sesame seeds in a dry skillet over medium heat until golden.

- 1 tablespoon dark sesame oil
- 1 bunch medium or thick asparagus, tough ends trimmed, stalks sliced into 1½-inch lengths
- 8 ounces fresh shiitake mushrooms, trimmed and sliced into ½-inch-thick pieces
- 1 tablespoon sesame seeds, toasted
  Coarse salt and freshly ground pepper

Heat the oil in a large skillet or wok over medium-high heat. Add the asparagus and mushrooms, and sauté just until tender, about 5 minutes. Remove from heat. Sprinkle with the toasted sesame seeds, and season with salt and pepper. Serve hot.

fried green tomato wedges

SERVES 4 TO 6 AS AN APPETIZER

- 2 cups yellow cornmeal
- 4 teaspoons coarse salt, plus more for seasoning
- 1 teaspoon freshly ground black pepper
- ½ teaspoon cayenne pepper
- 2 cups buttermilk
- 2 large eggs
- 2 tablespoons fresh lime juice (about 2 limes)
  Canola oil, for frying
- 3 large green tomatoes, cut into 1-inch-thick wedges
  Basil-Lime Mayonnaise (recipe follows)

1. In a medium shallow bowl, combine the cornmeal, salt, black pepper, and cayenne pepper; set aside. In another shallow bowl, whisk together the buttermilk, eggs, and lime juice (the mixture may appear curdled); set aside.

2. In a large cast-iron or heavy skillet, pour oil to a depth of ½ inch; heat until a deep-fry thermometer measures 375° F. Meanwhile, working in batches, dip the tomatoes in the buttermilk mixture, then in the cornmeal mixture. Set aside on a large plate; repeat with the remaining tomatoes.

3. Fry the tomatoes, working in batches, until golden brown, about 1 minute on each side. Drain on a paper-towel–lined plate. Season with salt while hot. Serve warm with basil-lime mayonnaise.

basil-lime mayonnaise

MAKES 1 ¼ CUPS

- 1 large egg
- ½ teaspoon coarse salt
- ¼ teaspoon freshly ground pepper
- 1 cup canola oil
- 2 teaspoons fresh lime juice
- ¼ cup finely sliced fresh basil leaves

1. In a food processor, pulse the egg with the salt and pepper until foamy and pale, about 1½ minutes. With the machine running, add the oil through the feed tube, 1 drop at a time, until the mixture starts to thicken (do not stop the machine at this point, or the mayonnaise may not come together). Add the remaining oil in a slow, steady stream.

2. When all the oil has been incorporated, slowly add the lime juice, mixing until combined. Add the basil; pulse until combined. Let chill before serving. Fresh mayonnaise can be refrigerated in an airtight container up to 5 days.

NOTE Raw eggs should not be used in food prepared for pregnant women, babies, young children, the elderly, or anyone whose health is compromised.

sautéed okra and tomatoes

SERVES 4

The secret to cooking okra to a crisp-tender texture is a very hot skillet.

- 1 tablespoon whole mustard seeds
- ½ teaspoon whole cumin seeds
- ½ teaspoon ground coriander
- 2 tablespoons extra-virgin olive oil
- 1 small red onion, cut into ½-inch-thick wedges
- 1 pound fresh okra, stems and ends trimmed
- 3 medium tomatoes, seeded and cut into ½-inch-thick wedges

  Coarse salt and freshly ground pepper

1. In a small bowl, combine the mustard seeds, cumin seeds, and coriander; set aside. Heat the oil in a large skillet set over medium heat. Add the onion, and cook, stirring, until soft, about 3 minutes.

2. Raise heat to medium-high; add the spice mixture, okra, and ½ cup water. Cook, stirring, until the okra is bright green and just tender, about 6 minutes, adding more water if the skillet becomes too dry.

3. Add the tomato wedges, and cook until just heated through, about 1 minute. Season with salt and pepper. Serve immediately.

fried yuca with lemon

SERVES 8

Yuca is a starchy root with tough, brown skin, crisp, white flesh, and a mild flavor. It is also known as cassava.

- 5 pounds yuca (about 6 yuca), peeled

  Peanut or canola oil, for frying
- 4 garlic cloves

  Coarse salt

  Lemon wedges, for serving

1. Cut the yuca crosswise into 2-inch pieces. Cut each piece into ¼- to ½-inch-thick strips. Cut out the tough core from the inner edge of each piece; discard the core. Transfer the yuca to a large saucepan. Cover with water by 2 inches. Bring to a boil. Cook until just soft and translucent, about 5 minutes. Drain, and pat dry.

2. Heat 5 inches oil in a 4-quart heavy-bottomed saucepan over medium-high heat until it registers 360°F on a deep-fry thermometer. Fry the garlic until golden, about 1 minute. Discard the garlic. Working in batches of several strips, fry the yuca, turning once, until golden brown, about 4 minutes. Transfer to paper towels using a slotted spoon; let drain. Sprinkle with salt. Serve with lemon wedges.

aunt sara's cheese grits

SERVES 8 TO 10

- ¾ cup (1½ sticks) unsalted butter, plus more for the baking dish
- 3 cups water
- 1½ cups quick-cooking grits
- 1 pound sharp Cheddar cheese, grated
- 1 teaspoon coarse salt
- ½ teaspoon freshly ground pepper
- ½ teaspoon garlic powder
- ½ teaspoon hot pepper sauce, such as Tabasco (optional)
- 3 large eggs, lightly beaten

1. Preheat the oven to 325°F. Butter an 8-inch-square baking dish. Bring the water to a boil in a medium saucepan, and stir in the grits. Reduce heat. Cover; simmer 2 minutes, stirring occasionally.

2. Add the cheese, butter, salt, pepper, garlic powder, and hot pepper sauce, if using. Stir until the cheese has completely melted, and stir in the eggs until well combined.

3. Pour mixture into the prepared pan. Bake until creamy inside and golden on the top, about 1 hour. Let cool slightly on a wire rack before serving.

smoky pinto beans

SERVES 6 TO 8

- 1 pound dried pinto beans, picked over
- ½ white onion, plus more, finely chopped, for garnish
- 2 garlic cloves, crushed
- 2 dried avocado leaves
- 1 teaspoon dried epazote
- 3 fresh cilantro sprigs
  Coarse salt and freshly ground pepper
- 2 plum tomatoes, seeded and chopped
- 2 ounces cotija cheese, crumbled
  Lime wedges, for serving

1. Cover the beans with cold water by 2 inches in a bowl; refrigerate 8 hours.

2. Drain the beans; transfer to a small stockpot. Add the onion, garlic, avocado leaves, epazote, and cilantro; cover with cold water by 2 inches. Bring to a boil; add 1 tablespoon salt. Reduce heat to medium-low; simmer, adding water as needed to cover the beans, until the beans are tender and the liquid is soupy, 2 to 2½ hours. Discard the avocado leaves. Season with salt and pepper. Garnish with onion, tomatoes, and cheese. Serve with lime wedges.

creamy polenta with bacon and sage

SERVES 4

Water or stock can be substituted for any or all of the milk, but milk makes a creamier polenta.

- 2 ounces thickly sliced bacon, cut into ½-inch pieces
- 1 teaspoon chopped fresh sage leaves, plus more whole leaves for garnish
- 4 cups milk
- ¾ cup plus 2 tablespoons quick-cooking polenta
- 3 tablespoons unsalted butter
- ½ teaspoon coarse salt, or more to taste
- ¼ teaspoon freshly ground pepper, or more to taste
- 2 tablespoons extra-virgin olive oil (optional)

1. Place a medium saucepan over low heat. Add the bacon, and cook until crisp and golden, about 8 minutes. Remove the bacon from the saucepan; transfer to a paper-towel–lined plate. Set aside.

2. Add the chopped sage to the saucepan, and cook in the bacon fat until fragrant, about 30 seconds. Add the milk, and bring to a boil.

3. Add the polenta in a steady stream, whisking constantly until it is smooth and creamy, about 6 minutes. Whisk in the butter, and season with the salt and pepper. Transfer to a serving bowl, and crumble the reserved bacon on top. Heat the olive oil in a small sauté pan over medium heat. Add the whole sage leaves, and fry until crisp, about 30 seconds. Remove from the skillet; scatter over the polenta. Serve immediately.

the best onion rings

SERVES 4 TO 6

After cooking the onion rings, keep them warm in a 200°F oven while you finish the remaining batches.

- 1 cup plus 2 tablespoons all-purpose flour
- 1 teaspoon ground cumin
  Pinch of cayenne pepper
- 1 teaspoon coarse salt, plus more for seasoning
- ¾ cup buttermilk
- ¾ cup beer
- 1 large egg
- 4 cups peanut oil
- 2 large white onions (about 2 pounds), sliced crosswise ½ inch thick and separated into rings

1. Combine the flour, cumin, cayenne, and 1 teaspoon salt in a medium bowl. Slowly whisk in the buttermilk, beer, and egg until smooth. Let the batter stand 15 minutes.

2. In a large saucepan, heat the oil over medium-high heat until a deep-fry thermometer registers 375°F. Working in batches, dip the onion slices in the batter, turning to coat. Gently drop the slices into the hot oil. Cook, turning the rings once, until golden brown, about 2 minutes. (Adjust heat between batches as necessary to keep oil at a steady temperature.)

3. Use a slotted spoon to transfer the rings to a paper-towel–lined baking sheet to drain. Season immediately with salt.

black beans with poblano
SERVES 4

2 tablespoons extra-virgin olive oil

2 shallots, thinly sliced

1 poblano chile, seeded and chopped

2 cans (15 ounces each) black beans, rinsed and drained

2 tablespoons fresh lime juice

½ teaspoon ground cumin

Pinch of cayenne pepper

Coarse salt and freshly ground black pepper

Lime wedges, for serving

Heat the oil in a medium skillet over medium heat. Add the shallots and the chile; cook, stirring frequently, until tender, about 5 minutes. Transfer to a large bowl; add the beans, lime juice, cumin, and cayenne pepper. Toss well to combine. Season with salt and black pepper. Serve warm or at room temperature, with lime wedges on the side.

roasted squash wedges
SERVES 4

We used acorn squash for this recipe, but other types, such as butternut or pumpkin, work as well.

2 acorn squash

2 tablespoons butter, melted

2 tablespoons honey

1 teaspoon ground cinnamon

Pinch of ground nutmeg

½ teaspoon coarse salt

¼ teaspoon freshly ground pepper

1. Heat the oven to 400°F. Cut the squash in half through the stem end, and remove the seeds. Cut each half into 3 wedges, 1½ to 2 inches thick. Place the wedges in a large roasting pan.

2. Toss with the butter, honey, cinnamon, nutmeg, salt, and pepper. Roast the squash, tossing occasionally, until tender and golden brown, 35 to 45 minutes.

three-variety squash tian
SERVES 6

For the best flavor, use freshly made bread crumbs for this dish because they have a much fluffier texture. Place as many slices of white bread as will comfortably fit in the bowl of your food processor, and pulse the bread until crumbly. Any leftover bread crumbs can be placed in a resealable plastic bag and frozen for future use.

1¼ pounds assorted squash, such as Costata Romanesco, patty pan, yellow, green, and black, sliced ⅛ inch thick

2 medium ripe tomatoes (1 pound), sliced ⅛ inch thick

3 tablespoons olive oil

5 tablespoons homemade or low-sodium store-bought chicken stock

Coarse salt and freshly ground pepper

2 tablespoons fresh thyme leaves, plus sprigs for garnish

1 cup fresh bread crumbs

2 tablespoons unsalted butter, melted

1. Heat the oven to 350°F. In a 10-inch round gratin dish, arrange the squash slices and tomatoes in an overlapping pattern to fill the dish. Brush the vegetables with olive oil; drizzle the remaining oil on top. Drizzle the chicken stock on top. Sprinkle with salt and pepper and 1 tablespoon thyme leaves.

2. In a medium bowl, combine the bread crumbs, butter, and remaining thyme, and season with salt and pepper. Arrange the bread-crumb mixture on top of the vegetables.

3. Bake until the vegetables are tender and the bread crumbs are golden, about 50 minutes. Remove from the oven. Serve garnished with thyme sprigs.

steamed artichokes with grainy mustard and bacon dressing

SERVES 4

The grainy mustard and bacon dressing is best when made and served immediately. The artichokes, however, can be prepared in advance.

- 4 large artichokes
  Juice of 4 lemons
- 1 teaspoon coarse salt, plus more for seasoning
- 1 teaspoon whole black peppercorns
- 1 large sprig fresh thyme
- 2 garlic cloves
- 2 tablespoons extra-virgin olive oil, plus more for the cooking liquid
- 6 strips thick bacon, cut into ¼-inch pieces
- 2 shallots, finely chopped
- 2 carrots, finely diced
- 1 stalk celery, finely diced
- 2½ tablespoons grainy mustard, plus more to taste
  Freshly ground black pepper

1. Fill a bowl with ice and water; set aside. Trim the artichokes; snap off the tough outer leaves. Cut in half, and cut off the top quarter of each artichoke. Snip the remaining leaf tips with scissors. Trim the bottom of the stem; using a vegetable peeler, peel off the tough outer skin. Spread the leaves to gain easier access to the choke; scoop out the choke with a melon baller. Squeeze some lemon juice onto the heart; squeeze more lemon juice into the ice bath; add lemon halves and artichokes while preparing the rest.

2. Fill a saucepan large enough to accommodate all the artichokes with 2 inches of water. Add salt, peppercorns, thyme, garlic, and 2 tablespoons olive oil; bring to a simmer. Add the artichokes, stem end up; cover the saucepan. Steam until tender, about 25 minutes. The leaves should pull off easily; the heart should feel tender when pierced. Drain well. Cool to room temperature.

3. Meanwhile, cook the bacon in a large sauté pan over medium-low heat until brown and crisp, and the fat is rendered. Using a slotted spoon, remove the bacon from the sauté pan, and set aside.

4. Depending on the amount of bacon fat in the sauté pan, add enough olive oil to make a total of ⅓ cup fat and oil. Add the shallots, carrots, and celery, and cook until the vegetables are soft and fragrant, about 4 minutes. Stir in the grainy mustard, and season with salt and pepper. Return the bacon to the sauté pan. Arrange the artichokes on a serving platter. Spoon the hot mixture into the cavity of each artichoke.

miso-glazed eggplant

SERVES 6

The eggplant can also be served as an hors d'oeuvre, cut into bite-size pieces.

- 5 tablespoons white miso
- 3 tablespoons sake
- 2 tablespoons sugar
- 2 tablespoons peanut or grapeseed oil
- 6 Japanese eggplants (1½ pounds), sliced in half lengthwise
  Zest of 1 lemon, finely grated

1. To prepare the miso paste, combine the miso, sake, and sugar in a small saucepan. Warm over low heat, stirring until the sugar has dissolved. Set aside.

2. Line a baking sheet with a paper towel; set aside. Heat the oil in a large skillet over high heat until almost smoking. Place the eggplant halves, cut side up, in the skillet. Cook for 5 minutes, turn over, and continue cooking for 1 to 2 minutes more, or until golden brown and very soft. Remove the eggplant halves from the skillet, and transfer to the prepared baking sheet.

3. Using an offset spatula, spread 2 teaspoons reserved miso paste evenly over each eggplant half. Garnish with lemon zest. Serve warm. Cut the eggplant halves into pieces if serving as an hors d'oeuvre.

spinach soufflé

SERVES 6

Serve this soufflé immediately in the dish, or let cool and unmold for a denser version.

Cooking spray

3 tablespoons bread crumbs

10 ounces spinach, well washed, tough stems removed

4 teaspoons unsalted butter

3 tablespoons all-purpose flour

1½ cups skim milk

½ teaspoon salt

¼ teaspoon freshly ground pepper

2 whole large eggs, separated

1 cup freshly grated Parmesan cheese (2 ounces)

2 large egg whites

Pinch of cream of tartar

1. Preheat the oven to 400° F. Position the rack in the center of the oven. Coat a 2-quart soufflé dish or 6 individual 8-ounce dishes with cooking spray. Coat with bread crumbs. Tap out excess; set aside.

2. Fill a bowl with ice and water; set aside. Place a steamer basket in a large saucepan; fill with 1 inch water. Bring to a boil, and add the spinach. Cover, and steam until wilted, about 3 minutes. Drain, and plunge into the ice bath to stop the cooking. Let cool, and squeeze out excess water. Place the spinach in the bowl of a food processor; pulse until finely chopped; set aside. You should have about 1 cup.

3. Melt the butter in a small saucepan over medium heat. Whisk in the flour, and cook, stirring constantly, for 3 minutes. Gradually whisk in the milk, and bring just to a simmer. Cook, stirring constantly, until slightly thickened, about 3 minutes. Stir in salt and pepper. Remove from heat, and set aside.

PERFECT SOUFFLÉS

THE BASICS

A soufflé consists of whipped egg whites, which give the dish its characteristic light and airy texture, and a creamy, flavorful base, often thickened with egg yolks. Served right out of the oven, its crisp crust gives way to a soft interior.

KEYS TO SUCCESS

Before whipping the egg whites, be sure your bowl and whisk are clean and dry; just a drop of grease, yolk, or water will prevent the whites from expanding properly. Above all else, don't open the oven door until the end of the baking time, as a fluctuation in temperature, as well as a slammed oven door, can cause a soufflé to fall.

EQUIPMENT

• Copper bowl: Preferred by many chefs for beating egg whites by hand. A chemical reaction between the copper

and the egg whites produces a fluffy, stable foam; beating by hand means that overbeating is unlikely. Just before using copper, clean it with salt and lemon juice or vinegar, then rinse with cold water and dry thoroughly. If you don't have a copper bowl, use a stainless-steel one and an electric mixer; add a pinch of cream of tartar to mimic the chemical reaction that occurs with copper.

• Balloon whisk: Incorporates more air than narrower whisks, making it easier to beat whites to stiff peaks.

• Soufflé dish: Has straight sides that enable the soufflé to climb.

• Large rubber spatula: Allows you to fold in whites with a minimum of strokes.

• Parchment paper and kitchen twine: Needed to form a collar that will support the soufflé as it rises.

• Oven thermometer: Baking a soufflé requires precise temperatures; if you're unsure about your oven, check its accuracy with an oven thermometer.

OVERWHIPPED WHITES

You've taken your whites too far if they lose their glossiness and become clumpy. If you have, then your soufflé won't rise properly. But all is not lost: Add another egg white, whip until the consistency is smooth again, and continue with the recipe.

SERVING SOUFFLÉS

Here's the classic technique: Holding a fork and spoon back to back, pierce the center of the soufflé and part the utensils to let the steam escape. Using the fork and spoon as tongs, portion out the soufflé, making sure everyone gets a little of the browned crust and soft middle.

4. In a large bowl, whisk 2 egg yolks until blended. Whisk in a little white sauce to temper the eggs, then add the remaining sauce, whisking until combined. Add the cooked spinach and grated cheese.

5. Place the 4 egg whites and cream of tartar in the bowl of an electric mixer fitted with the whisk attachment. Beat on low until soft peaks begin to form. Increase speed to high; beat until stiff peaks form and the egg whites are smooth.

6. Using a rubber spatula, transfer one-third of the egg whites to the spinach mixture; gently fold in until blended. Add the spinach mixture to the remaining egg whites; gently fold in until just combined. Pour into the prepared dish or dishes.

7. Place the soufflé in the oven; reduce heat to 375° F. Bake until puffed and golden, 20 to 30 minutes. Serve immediately.

FIT TO EAT RECIPE PER SERVING: 149 CALORIES, 7 G FAT, 85 MG CHOLESTEROL, 11 G CARBOHYDRATE, 488 MG SODIUM, 11 G PROTEIN, 2 G FIBER

eggplant fritters

SERVES 4

1   large eggplant (about 2½ pounds)
¼   cup olive oil
1   small garlic clove, minced
2   tablespoons roughly chopped fresh flat-leaf parsley
½   cup fresh or dry bread crumbs
1   tablespoon grated Parmesan cheese
1   large egg, lightly beaten
¼   teaspoon ground cumin
¼   teaspoon ground coriander
¾   teaspoon coarse salt
¼   teaspoon freshly ground pepper
2   tablespoons canola oil
1   head frisée, washed and dried
1   tablespoon balsamic vinegar

1. Preheat the oven to 425° F. Cut the eggplant in half; place on a rimmed baking sheet. Drizzle with 2 tablespoons olive oil. Place in the oven; cook until tender, about 40 minutes. When cool enough to handle, scoop the flesh into a strainer to drain.

2. Transfer the drained eggplant to a bowl; add the garlic, parsley, bread crumbs, Parmesan, egg, cumin, coriander, salt, and pepper; stir to combine. Form the mixture into 2-inch patties.

3. Heat the canola oil in a large skillet over medium heat. Add the patties, and cook until golden brown, about 2 minutes per side. Drain on paper towels. Place the frisée on a serving platter; drizzle with the remaining 2 tablespoons olive oil and balsamic vinegar. Top with the fritters.

stewed baby artichokes with fava beans

SERVES 6

Frozen lima beans may be substituted for fava beans; start with the second step.

1½   pounds fava beans, shelled
4   cups water
3   tablespoons fresh lemon juice, plus a lemon half for rubbing the cut artichokes
2¼   pounds (about 24) baby artichokes
2   teaspoons olive oil
1   shallot, peeled and finely chopped
3   cloves garlic, peeled and lightly crushed
1   teaspoon salt
¼   teaspoon freshly ground black pepper
¼   teaspoon crushed red pepper flakes
4   sprigs fresh thyme
4   sprigs fresh flat-leaf parsley

1. Fill a large bowl with ice and water; set aside. Bring a medium pot of water to a boil. Add the fava beans; blanch 30 seconds. Remove from water; place in the ice bath until cool. Peel the outer skin from the beans; set aside.

2. Place 4 cups water in a large bowl; add the lemon juice; set aside. Remove the tough outer leaves from the artichokes; cut 1 inch from the tip of each artichoke. Trim and peel the stem of each; rub all over with the lemon half. Place in the lemon water.

3. Heat the olive oil in a saucepan over medium heat. Add the shallot, garlic, salt, black pepper, and red pepper flakes; cook, stirring frequently, until the shallot is lightly browned, about 2 minutes. Add the artichokes, 1 cup lemon water, thyme, and parsley; bring to a simmer. Reduce heat to medium low, and cover; simmer until the artichokes are tender, about 14 minutes.

4. Add the fava beans. Cook until the beans are tender, about 3 minutes more. Serve hot or at room temperature.

FIT TO EAT RECIPE PER SERVING: 197 CALORIES, 3 G FAT, 0 MG CHOLESTEROL, 39 G CARBOHYDRATE, 544 MG SODIUM, 15 G PROTEIN, 9 G FIBER

corn on the cob with lime and melted butter
SERVES 4

Ears of corn, cut into small pieces, make a perfect summer side dish. Plan on one ear per person.

4   ears corn, husked

4   tablespoons unsalted butter, melted
    Coarse salt and freshly ground pepper

2   limes, cut into wedges

1. Bring a large pot of water to a boil. Using a sharp knife, cut each ear of corn into 3 or 4 pieces, each about 1½ inches long. Add the corn to the boiling water, and cook just until the corn is tender, 3 to 4 minutes; this should not take much longer than the time required for the water to return to a boil.

2. Drain the corn. Toss with the melted butter, and season with salt and pepper. Serve with lime wedges to squeeze directly onto corn.

grilled ramps with asparagus
SERVES 4 TO 6 AS A SIDE DISH

Quickly grill ramps to make the most of their wild, earthy flavor.

1   bunch (about 20) ramps

1   bunch thin asparagus

3   tablespoons extra-virgin olive oil
    Coarse salt and freshly ground pepper

1. Heat a grill or grill pan on medium-high heat. Trim and discard the root hairs from the ramps. Trim the tough ends from the asparagus.

2. Place the ramps and asparagus on a baking sheet or in a shallow baking dish. Drizzle with the olive oil, and toss to coat evenly. Season with salt and pepper, and toss to combine.

3. Arrange the ramps and asparagus on the hot grill in a single layer. Grill until hot and grill marks appear, about 1 minute per side. Transfer to a platter, and serve hot or at room temperature.

cauliflower with hazelnut brown butter
SERVES 12 TO 14

1   cup hazelnuts (filberts)

3   small or 2 large heads cauliflower
     (about 3½ pounds)
     Coarse salt

10   tablespoons (1¼ sticks) unsalted butter

2   tablespoons fresh lemon juice

2   tablespoons finely chopped chives

1. Preheat the oven to 350° F. Place the hazelnuts on a baking sheet; toast until fragrant, about 10 minutes. Transfer the nuts to a kitchen towel; rub off the loosened papery skins. Coarsely chop the nuts; set aside.

2. Trim the stems of the cauliflower so they sit flat, keeping the head intact. Bring several inches of water to a boil in a large steamer or in a pot fitted with a rack; add salt to taste. Steam the cauliflower until just tender, about 10 minutes. Transfer to a serving platter.

3. Combine the butter and hazelnuts in a small saucepan. Cook over medium heat until the butter turns brown, 3 to 4 minutes. Remove from heat, and add the lemon juice and chives. Season to taste with salt. Whisk to combine. Pour over the cauliflower, and serve immediately.

pan-fried fennel

SERVES 4

For best results, use a heavy-bottomed sauté pan.

- 2 medium fennel bulbs
- 1 cup all-purpose flour, for dredging
- 1½ cups fresh bread crumbs, for dredging
- 2 teaspoons coarse salt, plus more for seasoning
- ¾ teaspoon freshly ground pepper, plus more for seasoning
- 3 large eggs
- 1½ cups vegetable oil, just enough to yield about ¼ inch in the pan
- 2 lemons, cut into wedges

1. Remove the tops and fronds from the fennel bulbs. Slice each bulb in half widthwise. Cut each half into slices about ⅛ inch thick.

2. Pour the flour into a medium bowl and the bread crumbs into another. Season with the salt and pepper. Crack the eggs into a third bowl; whisk until frothy. Season with salt and pepper. Dredge the fennel lightly in the flour, then in the egg, and then in the bread crumbs, shaking off excess after each step.

3. Heat the oil in a large sauté pan over medium heat. Check to make sure the oil is hot enough by tossing a pinch of flour into the pan. If the flour sizzles, the oil is ready.

4. Fry the fennel slices until golden brown on each side, about 30 seconds per side, working in batches so as not to crowd the pan. Drain on paper towels; season with salt. Serve hot with lemon wedges.

braised escarole with currants

SERVES 6

- 1 tablespoon extra-virgin olive oil
- ½ teaspoon crushed red pepper flakes
- 4 garlic cloves, thinly sliced
- 1 ounce slivered almonds (about ⅓ cup)
- 4 anchovy fillets, rinsed (optional)
- ¼ cup dry sherry
- ½ cup homemade or low-sodium store-bought chicken stock, skimmed of fat
- 1 tablespoon dark-brown sugar
- 2 bunches (2½ pounds) escarole, cleaned, drained, and torn into 2-inch pieces
- ¼ cup currants

1. Heat the oil in a large, high-sided skillet over medium-low heat. Add the red pepper flakes; stir until fragrant, about 1 minute. Add the garlic and almonds; cook until light golden, about 3 minutes. Add the anchovies; stir until mashed and well combined with oil mixture. Add the sherry; cook until most of the liquid has evaporated. Add the stock and sugar; stir until the sugar has dissolved.

2. Add the escarole in batches, tossing and adding more as it wilts until all has been added to the pan. Cover; cook over low heat, stirring occasionally, until wilted.

3. Add the currants, and cook until the escarole is tender, about 10 minutes more. Serve.

FIT TO EAT RECIPE PER SERVING: 112 CALORIES, 5 G FAT, 0 MG CHOLESTEROL, 11 G CARBOHYDRATE, 175 MG SODIUM, 4 G PROTEIN, 6 G FIBER

sautéed spinach with pecans and goat cheese

SERVES 6

- 2 tablespoons extra-virgin olive oil
- 1 medium red onion (about 8 ounces), halved and thinly sliced
- 1¼ pounds baby spinach
- 2 tablespoons sherry vinegar
- ½ cup coarsely chopped pecans
- ¼ cup soft goat cheese (about 2 ounces), crumbled

1. Heat oil in a large skillet over medium heat until hot but not smoking. Add onion; cook, stirring occasionally, until onion has softened, about 5 minutes. Add spinach; cook, tossing, until spinach has started to wilt, about 2 minutes. Transfer to a serving platter.

2. Add vinegar to skillet, and heat 5 seconds. Drizzle over spinach and onion. Sprinkle with pecans and goat cheese. Gently toss. Serve immediately.

FIT TO EAT RECIPE PER SERVING: 195 CALORIES, 14 G FAT, 4 MG CHOLESTEROL, 16 G CARBOHYDRATE, 216 MG SODIUM, 5 G PROTEIN, 6 G FIBER

mustard greens and peas
SERVES 8

¼ cup unsalted butter

1 medium yellow onion (about 5 ounces), thinly sliced

2 garlic cloves, sliced

2 bunches mustard greens (about 2 pounds), trimmed and cut crosswise into 2-inch strips

½ cup homemade or low-sodium store-bought chicken stock

   Coarse salt and freshly ground pepper

10 ounces partially thawed frozen or fresh shelled peas (1¾ cups)

1. Melt butter in a large saucepan over medium heat. Add onion and garlic; cook, stirring occasionally, until translucent, about 2 minutes. Stir in greens and stock; season with salt and pepper. Cover; cook, stirring occasionally, until greens are wilted but not completely cooked, about 8 minutes.

2. Stir in peas. (If you are using fresh peas, cook them 2 minutes in salted boiling water before adding to greens.) Cover, and cook, stirring occasionally, until peas are tender and bright green, about 5 minutes. Transfer to a serving dish with a slotted spoon. Serve immediately.

spicy chickpeas with fresh green chiles
SERVES 4 TO 6

¼ cup vegetable oil

2 onions (about 7 ounces each), 1 chopped, 1 thinly sliced for garnish

½ teaspoon ground cumin

½ teaspoon ground allspice

½ teaspoon ground cinnamon

1 teaspoon ground coriander

⅛ teaspoon cayenne pepper

¾ teaspoon coarse salt

2 garlic cloves, minced

1 piece (1 inch) peeled fresh ginger, chopped (about 1 tablespoon)

2 tablespoons tomato paste

1 can (15 ounces) chickpeas, drained and rinsed

2 to 4 fresh green chiles (such as Pinocchio's Nose or jalapeño), 1 seeded and finely chopped, remaining seeded and thinly sliced lengthwise for garnish

1 ripe tomato, halved and thinly sliced, for garnish

3 large pitas or naan (Indian bread), for serving

8 ounces plain yogurt, for serving

   Lime wedges, for serving

1. Heat oil in a medium skillet over medium heat. Add onion and cumin. Cook, stirring occasionally, until onion is light brown, about 5 minutes. Stir in allspice, cinnamon, coriander, cayenne pepper, and salt; cook 1 minute.

2. Add garlic, ginger, and tomato paste to skillet. Cook about 4 minutes to dry out mixture. Stir in chickpeas and ¼ cup water. Cover; cook until water evaporates and chickpeas are slightly softened, 5 to 8 minutes. Stir in chopped chile.

3. Transfer to a serving platter, garnish with slices of tomato, onion, and chile. Serve with bread, yogurt, and lime wedges.

wilted dandelion greens with sweet onion

SERVES 4

2   tablespoons extra-virgin olive oil

1½ cups thinly sliced Vidalia onion

⅛   teaspoon sugar

1   garlic clove, sliced

1   tablespoon sherry vinegar

3   bunches dandelion greens, stemmed (about 7 ounces)

⅛   teaspoon coarse salt

    Freshly ground pepper

1. Heat oil in a medium skillet over medium heat. Add onion and sugar; cook, stirring occasionally, until onion is golden and has caramelized, about 15 minutes. Add garlic; cook, stirring occasionally, 2 minutes. Add vinegar; cook until vinegar is warm, about 1 minute.

2. Add dandelion greens, and toss to combine. Cook until greens have just wilted, about 1 minute. Season with salt and pepper. Serve immediately.

FIT TO EAT RECIPE PER SERVING: 107 CALORIES, 7 G FAT, 0 MG CHOLESTEROL, 10 G CARBOHYDRATE, 81 MG SODIUM, 2 G PROTEIN, 2 G FIBER

roasted cauliflower and capers

SERVES 8

2   large heads cauliflower (about 4 pounds total), cut into florets

⅓   cup salt-packed capers, rinsed

6   tablespoons extra-virgin olive oil, plus more for serving

    Coarse salt

1   tablespoon coarsely chopped or very small whole fresh marjoram leaves

Preheat the oven to 400° F. Divide cauliflower and capers between 2 rimmed baking sheets. Drizzle each with 3 tablespoons oil; toss to combine. Season with salt. Spread mixture in a single layer. Roast, stirring occasionally, until cauliflower is golden brown and tender, 30 to 40 minutes. Add marjoram; toss to combine. Serve warm or at room temperature, drizzled with oil.

lemony baked onions

SERVES 12

6   medium yellow onions (6 to 8 ounces each), trimmed and halved crosswise, plus 1 small yellow onion, finely chopped (about ¾ cup)

    Coarse salt

½   cup (1 stick) unsalted butter

3½ cups fresh bread crumbs (from about 9 slices white bread)

6   tablespoons fresh lemon juice

1. Preheat the oven to 400° F. Arrange the onion halves in a large, nonreactive baking dish; season with salt. Add ¾ cup water to the dish. Cover the dish with foil. Bake the onions until tender, 40 to 45 minutes.

2. Meanwhile, melt butter in a large skillet over medium heat. Add chopped onion. Cook, stirring, until softened, about 4 minutes. Stir in the bread crumbs. Cook, stirring occasionally, until bread crumbs are golden, about 3 minutes. Add lemon juice; season with salt.

3. Top the onions with the bread-crumb mixture, dividing evenly. Return to the oven, and bake until the topping is crisp and golden brown, 20 to 25 minutes more.

sautéed zucchini and celery

SERVES 12

Use a mandoline or a very sharp knife to cut the celery and zucchini.

¼   cup extra-virgin olive oil, plus more for drizzling

2   medium white onions, thinly sliced

6   medium celery stalks, peeled and cut lengthwise into ⅛-inch-thick slices

2   teaspoons coarse salt

6   medium zucchini, trimmed and cut lengthwise into ⅛-inch-thick slices

    Freshly ground pepper

1. Heat oil in a large skillet over medium-high heat. Add onions, celery, and salt. Cover; cook, stirring occasionally, until onion is translucent, about 5 minutes. Add ½ cup water; cover, and cook until celery is tender, about 5 minutes.

2. Stir in zucchini. Season with pepper. Cook, stirring once or twice, until zucchini is very tender, 5 to 6 minutes. Using a slotted spoon, transfer vegetables to a serving platter, and drizzle with oil. Serve warm or at room temperature.

caramelized turnips and shallots

SERVES 12

1¾ pounds white turnips, peeled and cut into 2½ × 1½-inch pieces

1¾ pounds golden turnips or rutabagas, peeled, cut into 2½ × 1½-inch pieces

10 shallots (about 10 ounces), peeled, root end intact

2 tablespoons plus 2 teaspoons extra-virgin olive oil

Coarse salt and freshly ground pepper

¾ cup red-wine vinegar

2 bay leaves

6 sprigs fresh thyme

¼ cup packed light-brown sugar

3 tablespoons unsalted butter

1. Preheat the oven to 400°F. Put turnips, shallots, and oil on a rimmed baking sheet. Season with salt and pepper; toss. Spread in a single layer. Roast until tender and golden brown, about 35 minutes.

2. Put vinegar, bay leaves, and thyme in a small saucepan. Bring to a simmer; cook until reduced by about half, about 10 minutes. Add sugar and ½ teaspoon salt; stir to dissolve. Add butter, and cook over medium heat until reduced to a syrupy glaze, about 10 minutes. Discard thyme. Pour over roasted vegetables; toss to coat. Serve immediately.

cauliflower gratin with endive

SERVES 8

¼ cup (½ stick) unsalted butter, plus more for dish

2 heads Belgian endive, cut lengthwise into sixths

1 cup fregola Sarda (semolina pasta) or Israeli (large pearl) couscous

2 large heads cauliflower (about 2 pounds), cut into florets

¼ cup all-purpose flour

3 cups milk

2 tablespoons finely chopped fresh marjoram or oregano

1 teaspoon coarse salt

¼ teaspoon freshly ground black pepper

⅛ teaspoon cayenne pepper

3 cups finely grated Gruyère cheese (about 10 ounces)

¼ cup fresh bread crumbs

¼ cup coarsely grated Parmesan cheese (about 2 ounces)

1. Preheat the oven to 400°F, with rack in lower third. Butter a 1½-quart, deep, wide ovenproof dish. Put endive in bottom of dish. Arrange pasta or couscous over endive. Top with cauliflower.

2. Melt butter in a medium saucepan over medium heat. Whisk in flour. Reduce heat to medium-low. Cook, stirring, 2 minutes. Whisk in milk; cook, whisking, until mixture thickens, about 4 minutes. Remove from heat. Whisk in marjoram, salt, black pepper, and cayenne. Whisk in Gruyère until smooth. Pour over cauliflower. Sprinkle with bread crumbs. Set dish on a baking sheet.

3. Bake 30 minutes. Sprinkle with Parmesan. Reduce temperature to 350°F; bake until cauliflower is tender, about 40 minutes. (If browning too quickly, tent with foil.) Transfer to a wire rack; let cool 10 minutes before serving.

green bean casserole with fried shallots

SERVES 8

- 6 tablespoons unsalted butter, plus more for dish
- 1 medium onion (about 6 ounces), cut into ¼-inch dice
- 1 red bell pepper, ribs and seeds removed, flesh cut into ½-inch dice
- 1 pound button mushrooms, trimmed and quartered
- 2 teaspoons coarse salt
- ½ teaspoon freshly ground black pepper
- 1½ pounds green beans, trimmed and cut into 2-inch pieces
- 6 tablespoons all-purpose flour
- 2 cups whole milk
-    Pinch of cayenne pepper
-    Pinch of grated nutmeg
- 1 cup finely grated Parmesan cheese
- ¼ cup fresh bread crumbs
- ¼ cup canola oil
- 4 shallots, cut crosswise into ¼-inch-thick rings

1. Melt 2 tablespoons butter in a large skillet over medium heat. Add onion, and cook, stirring occasionally, until beginning to soften, about 4 minutes. Add bell pepper and mushrooms, and cook, stirring occasionally, until softened and most of the liquid has evaporated, 8 to 10 minutes. Season with 1 teaspoon salt and ¼ teaspoon black pepper. Remove from heat. Let cool completely.

2. Bring a medium saucepan of water to a boil. Add beans; cook until bright green and just tender, 4 to 5 minutes. Drain, and plunge into an ice-water bath to stop cooking. Drain beans, and dry. Toss with mushroom mixture; set aside.

3. Melt the remaining 4 tablespoons butter in a medium saucepan over medium heat. Add ¼ cup flour; whisk constantly until mixture begins to turn golden, about 2 minutes. Pour in milk; continue whisking until mixture thickens, 4 to 6 minutes. Stir in cayenne, nutmeg, and remaining teaspoon salt and ¼ teaspoon black pepper. Remove from heat; let cool completely, stirring occasionally. Pour over bean mixture, and toss.

4. Butter a 13 × 9-inch baking dish. Spread half of the bean mixture into dish. Sprinkle with half of the Parmesan, and then top with remaining bean mixture. Combine remaining Parmesan and bread crumbs; sprinkle over top. Cover with foil, and refrigerate until ready to serve (up to 1 day); bring to room temperature before heating.

5. Heat oil in a medium skillet over medium-high heat. Toss shallots with remaining 2 tablespoons flour. Fry shallots in 2 batches, turning frequently, until golden brown, about 3 minutes. Using a slotted spoon, transfer shallots to paper towels to drain; let cool completely. The shallots can be stored in an airtight container at room temperature up to 1 day.

6. Preheat the broiler, with rack about 8 inches from heat. Cook casserole, covered, until mixture is bubbling and heated through, about 10 minutes. Uncover, and cook until top is golden brown, about 30 seconds. Remove from oven. Sprinkle with fried shallots. Serve immediately.

delicata squash with hot pepper glaze

SERVES 8

- ¼ cup hot pepper jelly
- 3 tablespoons extra-virgin olive oil
- 1 garlic clove, minced
- 4 medium delicata squashes (about 3 pounds total), cut lengthwise into 1-inch-thick wedges, seeds discarded
- 2 teaspoons coarse salt
-    Freshly ground pepper

1. Preheat the oven to 375° F. Stir jelly, oil, and garlic in a small bowl. Place squashes in a large bowl; add jelly mixture and salt. Season with pepper; toss.

2. Divide squash between 2 rimmed baking sheets. Roast until tender and bottoms are golden brown, 30 to 35 minutes. Serve immediately.

pan-roasted balsamic onions

SERVES 8 TO 10

- 10 ounces white pearl onions
- 10 ounces red pearl onions
- 10 ounces cipollini
- 5 tablespoons extra-virgin olive oil
  Coarse salt and freshly ground pepper
- 2¼ pounds leeks, white and pale-green parts only, halved lengthwise and rinsed well
- 1 cup homemade or low-sodium store-bought chicken stock
- ¼ cup balsamic vinegar
- 2 tablespoons unsalted butter
- ½ teaspoon fresh thyme leaves

1. Bring a medium saucepan of water to a boil. Add onions and cipollini, and boil 1 minute. Drain. Let stand until cool enough to handle. Peel, leaving root and stem ends intact. Transfer to a large bowl. Add 2 tablespoons oil, 1 teaspoon salt, and ¼ teaspoon pepper; toss.

2. Toss leeks in a bowl with 1 tablespoon oil and ½ teaspoon salt. Heat 1 tablespoon oil in a large skillet over medium-high heat. Add leeks; cook, stirring occasionally, until slightly tender and lightly browned, about 5 minutes. Transfer to a plate.

3. Add remaining tablespoon oil and the onion mixture to skillet. Cook, stirring occasionally, until browned, 5 to 7 minutes.

4. Reduce heat to medium-low. Add stock, vinegar, and leeks; cover, and cook, stirring occasionally, until onions are tender, about 30 minutes. Uncover; add butter. Raise heat to high. Cook, shaking skillet occasionally, until liquid reduces to a glaze and coats onions, 4 to 5 minutes.

5. Transfer to a serving dish. Sprinkle with thyme, and season with salt and pepper. Serve immediately, or refrigerate in an airtight container up to 1 day; reheat in a 300°F oven to serve.

braised apples with saffron and cider

SERVES 10 TO 12

This recipe can be made a day ahead and refrigerated; reheat before serving.

- ¼ cup (½ stick) unsalted butter
- 1 large shallot, thinly sliced into rings
- 6 apples (about 2 pounds), such as Gala or Winesap, quartered and seeded
- ¼ teaspoon saffron threads, crumbled
- 1½ cups homemade or low-sodium store-bought chicken stock
- 1½ cups apple cider
- ¼ cup dry sherry
- 3 tablespoons dried currants
  Coarse salt and freshly ground pepper

1. Melt butter in a large saucepan over medium heat. Add shallot, and cook, stirring often, until soft, about 4 minutes. Add apples, and turn to coat. Stir in saffron, stock, cider, sherry, and currants, and season with salt. Bring to a boil. Reduce heat to low, and cover. Simmer, stirring occasionally, until apples are tender, 12 to 15 minutes.

2. Using a slotted spoon, transfer apples to a bowl. Raise heat to medium-high, and cook sauce until reduced by half, about 10 minutes more. Season with pepper. Pour sauce over apples. Serve warm or at room temperature.

leek and gruyère bread pudding

SERVES 10 TO 12

This recipe can be made a day ahead and refrigerated; reheat before serving.

- 3 tablespoons unsalted butter, plus more for baking dish
- 1 bunch leeks (4 or 5), white and pale-green parts only, thinly sliced crosswise, rinsed well
- 2 garlic cloves, crushed
- ⅓ cup dry white wine
- 3 cups heavy cream
- 2 cups whole milk
- ½ teaspoon freshly grated nutmeg
  Pinch of cayenne pepper
- 2 teaspoons coarse salt
- ¼ teaspoon freshly ground pepper
- 5 large eggs plus 2 large egg yolks, lightly beaten
- 1 loaf day-old brioche (about 1 pound), crusts removed, cut into ¾-inch slices and then halved crosswise
- 2 cups grated Gruyère cheese
- 1 cup grated Parmesan cheese

1. Preheat the oven to 350°F. Butter a 10-inch (10-cup) round baking dish. Melt butter in a medium saucepan over medium heat. Add leeks and garlic; cook, stirring frequently, until soft, about 10 minutes. Add wine, and bring to a boil. Cook until wine is reduced by half. Transfer half of the leek mixture to a bowl, and reserve.

2. Whisk cream, milk, nutmeg, cayenne, salt, and pepper into leek mixture in pan; bring to a simmer. Add ½ cup hot cream-leek mixture to eggs and yolks in a medium bowl, whisking. Whisk in another cup cream-leek mixture; return egg-leek mixture to pan. Cook, whisking, until thickened, 4 to 5 minutes.

3. Arrange 8 or 9 pieces of bread in prepared dish. Pour 2 cups egg-leek mixture over bread. Sprinkle half the reserved leeks and half the cheeses over bread. Let stand 10 minutes. Arrange remaining bread in a slightly overlapping circle on top, and then add remaining egg-leek mixture. Sprinkle with remaining leeks and cheeses. Let stand 10 minutes.

4. Cover dish loosely with foil, and place in a small roasting pan. Add enough hot water to reach halfway up sides of dish. Bake until golden brown and set, about 55 minutes. Remove foil, and bake until deep golden brown, about 20 minutes more. Let cool in dish on a wire rack. Serve warm or at room temperature.

brown-sugar-spiced red cabbage

SERVES 10 TO 12

This recipe can be made a day ahead and refrigerated; reheat before serving.

- ¼ cup bacon drippings or unsalted butter
- 1 head red cabbage, very thinly sliced
- 1 red onion, halved lengthwise and thinly sliced
- ½ cup cider vinegar
- ½ cup port
- ¼ cup packed light-brown sugar
- ½ cinnamon stick
- 1 fresh bay leaf
  Coarse salt and freshly ground pepper

1. Heat drippings in a large stockpot over medium heat. Add cabbage and onion; cook, stirring occasionally, until tender, about 10 minutes.

2. Add vinegar, port, sugar, cinnamon, and bay leaf; bring to a boil. Reduce heat; cover, and simmer, stirring occasionally, until cabbage is soft, about 1 hour. Season with salt and pepper.

farro, orange, and pine nut dressing

SERVES 10 TO 12

You can make the dressing through step 2 a day ahead; refrigerate in an airtight container. Just before serving, stir in oranges, pine nuts, and parsley.

- 1 tablespoon unsalted butter
- 1 tablespoon extra-virgin olive oil
- 2 shallots, finely chopped (about ½ cup)
- 2 celery stalks, finely chopped
- ¼ cup plus 2 tablespoons coarsely chopped fresh flat-leaf parsley
- 1 tablespoon plus 1 teaspoon finely chopped fresh sage
- 2 teaspoons fennel seeds, coarsely chopped
- 1 dried chile, crumbled
- 2 cups farro
- 3½ cups homemade or low-sodium store-bought turkey or chicken stock
- ½ cup dry white wine
  Coarse salt and freshly ground pepper
- 2 navel oranges, peel and pith removed, flesh cut into segments
- ¼ cup pine nuts, toasted

1. Melt butter with the oil in a medium saucepan over medium heat. Add shallots and celery, and cook, stirring often, until soft, about 3 minutes. Add 2 tablespoons parsley, the sage, fennel seeds, and chile, and cook 1 minute.

2. Stir in farro, stock, and wine, and bring to a boil. Season with 1 teaspoon salt. Reduce heat to low; cover, and cook until farro is tender and has absorbed the liquid, about 30 minutes.

3. When ready to serve, stir in orange segments, pine nuts, and remaining ¼ cup parsley. Season with salt and pepper.

matchstick fries

SERVES 4

Using a mandoline to slice the potatoes is quick and easy. You can do so up to four hours ahead; to prevent browning, place matchsticks in a bowl of cold water in the refrigerator until ready to use, then pat them dry with paper towels.

- Vegetable oil cooking spray
- 2 medium russet potatoes (about 1½ pounds), cut into matchsticks
- 3 tablespoons olive oil
  Coarse salt and freshly ground pepper

1. Preheat the oven to 425°F. Coat 2 baking sheets with cooking spray; set aside. Toss together potatoes, oil, and 1 teaspoon salt in a bowl. Arrange potatoes in a single layer on prepared baking sheets.

2. Bake, turning potatoes with a metal spatula 2 or 3 times and rotating sheets halfway through, until potatoes are crisp and edges turn golden brown, 18 to 20 minutes. Arrange potatoes on a large piece of parchment paper; let cool 5 minutes. Season with salt and pepper.

polenta

MAKES 2¼ CUPS

We served the polenta with Braised Lamb Shanks with Tomato and Fennel (page 260), but it is equally delicious with chicken, veal, or pork, or as part of a vegetarian meal with a salad.

- 4 cups cold water
- 1 teaspoon coarse salt
- 1 cup polenta
- 2 tablespoons unsalted butter

Bring the water to a boil in a medium saucepan; add the salt. Stirring constantly, slowly add the polenta, letting the grains pass through your fingers in a steady stream. Reduce heat; simmer, stirring constantly, until the polenta is tender but not mushy, 30 to 35 minutes. Remove from heat, and stir in the butter. Serve hot.

polenta wedges

SERVES 8

You can make the polenta through step 1 ahead of time; let cool, then cover and refrigerate.

- 3 cups nonfat milk
- 3 tablespoons finely chopped fresh chives
- 2 garlic cloves, peeled and minced
- ½ teaspoon coarse salt
- ¼ teaspoon paprika
- ¾ cup quick-cooking polenta
- 2 ounces Parmesan cheese, grated
- 1 tablespoon unsalted butter
  Olive oil cooking spray

1. Combine the milk, chives, garlic, salt, and paprika in a medium saucepan, and bring to a boil over high heat. While whisking, slowly sprinkle in the polenta. Reduce heat to medium-low; cook, stirring occasionally with a wooden spoon, until the polenta has thickened, 5 to 8 minutes. Add the Parmesan and butter; stir until combined. Spread the polenta evenly in an 8½-inch springform pan; let rest until completely set, about 45 minutes at room temperature.

2. Preheat the broiler. Remove the outer ring from the springform pan. Cut the polenta into 8 wedges. Coat wedges with olive oil spray, and place on a rack in the oven several inches underneath the broiler. Broil the polenta until golden brown on top and heated through, about 8 minutes. Serve.

israeli couscous and fall vegetable stuffing

SERVES 8 TO 10; MAKES ABOUT 8 CUPS (ENOUGH FOR ONE 18-POUND TURKEY)

- 1 small acorn squash (about 1½ pounds), halved and seeded
- ¼ cup extra-virgin olive oil
  Coarse salt and freshly ground pepper
- 2 small turnips, peeled and cut into ½-inch cubes
- 1 celery root, peeled and cut into ½-inch cubes
- 2 tablespoons unsalted butter
- ¾ cup finely chopped shallots
- ½ teaspoon ground coriander
- ¼ teaspoon ground cumin
- ¼ teaspoon hot smoked paprika
- 10 ounces Israeli couscous (about 2 cups)
- 1¾ cups homemade or low-sodium store-bought chicken stock
- 1 fresh bay leaf
- 2 tablespoons chopped fresh thyme
- ½ cup golden raisins
- ½ cup sliced almonds with skins, toasted
- ¼ cup chopped fresh flat-leaf parsley

1. Preheat the oven to 375° F. Drizzle the squash with 1 tablespoon oil; season with salt and pepper. Place, cut sides down, on a rimmed baking sheet; roast 10 minutes.

2. Meanwhile, toss the turnips and celery root with 2 tablespoons oil; season with salt and pepper. Place on the baking sheet with the squash. Continue roasting, stirring once or twice, until the vegetables are tender and golden brown, about 30 minutes.

3. Meanwhile, heat the butter and remaining tablespoon oil in a medium saucepan over medium heat until the butter is melted. Add the shallots; cook until softened, about 3 minutes. Stir in the coriander, cumin, and paprika; cook until fragrant, about 1 minute.

4. Stir in the couscous, stock, bay leaf, 1 tablespoon thyme, and 1 teaspoon salt. Bring to a boil. Cover; reduce heat to low. Cook until the couscous is tender but al dente and the liquid is absorbed, about 6 minutes. Remove from heat. Let stand, covered, 2 minutes. Fluff with a fork.

5. Peel the squash; cut the flesh into ½-inch cubes. Stir together the couscous, vegetables, raisins, almonds, parsley, and remaining tablespoon thyme; season with salt and pepper. Serve, or immediately pack loosely in the turkey cavity, and cook until an instant-read thermometer inserted into the center of the stuffing registers 165° F.

chestnut and sausage stuffing

SERVES 12; MAKES ABOUT 10 CUPS
(ENOUGH FOR ONE 16- TO 18-POUND TURKEY)

- 1 loaf day-old rustic Italian bread (about 1 pound), trimmed of crust and cut into ¾-inch cubes (about 8 cups)
- 1 pound fresh chestnuts
- 1 pound sweet Italian sausage
- 1 tablespoon extra-virgin olive oil
- 2 medium onions, finely chopped
- 4 celery stalks, finely chopped
- 4 garlic cloves, finely chopped
- ½ cup dry white wine
- ½ cup homemade or low-sodium store-bought chicken stock
- 1 tablespoon chopped fresh thyme
- 2 tablespoons chopped fresh sage
- 2 tablespoons chopped fresh flat-leaf parsley
- 2 teaspoons coarse salt
  Freshly ground pepper
- 2 large eggs, lightly beaten
  Unsalted butter, for baking dish

1. Let the bread cubes stand on a baking sheet at room temperature 3 hours to dry.

STUFFING 101

Improvise, using the following formula, to come up with your own stuffing recipes.

BASIC INGREDIENTS

- 1 1-pound loaf bread (or 1½ pounds cornbread), preferably 1 day old
- 4 cups (2 pounds) chopped vegetables (for cooking)
- 1 cup fresh herbs, such as parsley, sage, and thyme
- 2 cups or less liquid (or 3 eggs or butter)
- 1 pound meat
  Butter and/or olive oil
- 4 cups or less fruit, nuts, and more
- 3 tablespoons seasoning

VARIATIONS

Most stuffings have the same foundation: bread. Beyond that, combine complementary flavors, such as citrus rind and fruit juice, or those that contrast, like pecans and dried cherries. Use a variety of colors and textures, too. For best results, include plenty of vegetables, herbs, and spices.

VEGETABLES

These add nuance to the flavor of stuffing and can change its texture, depending on how they are cut and whether they are cooked before being added. Fennel gives a note of sweet anise; mushrooms yield earthy flavor and a meaty texture. Suggestions: onions, celery, carrots, fennel, mushrooms, and leeks.

HERBS AND SPICES

As you season, taste frequently, and adjust accordingly to get a result you like. Used sparingly, dry mustard and cinnamon are good choices. Cayenne pepper and cumin add heat, whereas paprika and turmeric provide color. Suggestions: cumin and fennel seeds, fresh herbs, dried savory and thyme, bay leaf, turmeric and paprika, and cinnamon sticks.

FRUIT, NUTS, AND MORE

Try fresh apples, pears, or oranges; or dried fruit, such as apricots, raisins, or cranberries. Pine nuts, walnuts, and hazelnuts add heft, as do reconstituted dried mushrooms.

Parmesan cheese imparts richness and bite. Suggestions: nuts, dried mushrooms, fresh fruit, dried fruit, and cheese.

BINDERS

The most important ingredient of stuffing may be the binder, for it keeps all the other elements in place. For a fluffy texture, use eggs. Less conventional possibilities include fruit juice (such as apple or orange) and alcohol (wine or liqueur). Suggestions: fruit juice, red or white wine, stock, maple syrup, eggs, and butter.

STUFFING TIPS

- Use ½ to ¾ cup stuffing for each pound of turkey.
- Don't pack the stuffing tightly; it expands as it cooks.
- Use a thermometer to ensure the stuffing reaches 165° F.
- Remove the stuffing as soon as the turkey comes out of the oven.
- Bake any extra stuffing in a buttered covered baking dish at 375° F until it is heated through and the top is golden, 30 to 40 minutes.

2. Lay each chestnut flat on a work surface, and cut an X in the pointed tip of the shell with a paring or chestnut knife. Bring a medium pot of water to a boil. Boil the chestnuts 2 minutes; remove the pot from the heat. Remove the chestnuts with a slotted spoon; peel away the shells. Quarter the nutmeat; transfer to a large bowl. Add the bread.

3. Preheat the oven to 350° F. Split the sausages; scrape the meat into a large sauté pan set over medium heat; crumble with a fork. Cook, stirring occasionally, until cooked through, about 7 minutes. Add the oil; swirl the pan. Add the onions, celery, and garlic. Reduce heat to medium-low. Cook, stirring occasionally, until the vegetables are soft, 15 to 17 minutes. Add to the bread mixture.

4. Add the wine to the pan. Scraping up any brown bits from bottom with a wooden spoon, cook over medium heat until the wine is reduced by half. Add to the bread mixture.

5. Add the stock to the bread mixture; toss. Add the thyme, sage, and parsley. Add the salt, and season with pepper. Stir in the eggs.

6. To bake the stuffing: Place the stuffing in a buttered 9 × 13-inch baking dish; cover with foil. Bake 30 minutes; remove the foil. Bake until golden brown, about 25 minutes. To cook in a turkey: Stuff as directed (page 379). Place remaining 5 cups stuffing in a buttered 8-inch-square baking dish; bake as directed above.

wild rice and corn stuffing

SERVES 8; MAKES ABOUT 7 CUPS
(ENOUGH FOR ONE 18-POUND TURKEY)

- 2 cups wild rice
  Coarse salt
- 2 tablespoons corn or vegetable oil
- 2 small red onions, cut into thin rounds
- 3 garlic cloves, minced (1 tablespoon)
- 2 fresh serrano or jalapeño chiles, thinly sliced
- 1 cup frozen corn kernels, thawed
- ¼ teaspoon freshly ground pepper
- 2 tablespoons fresh lime juice

1. Bring 5 cups water to a boil in a medium saucepan; add the rice and 1 tablespoon salt. Cover; reduce heat. Cook the rice until al dente, 35 to 40 minutes (not all the water will be absorbed). Drain well.

2. Heat the oil in a large skillet over medium-high heat until hot but not smoking. Add the onions and garlic; cook, stirring, until soft, about 2 minutes. Add the chiles; cook 30 seconds.

3. Stir the onion mixture, corn, pepper, and lime juice into the rice; season with salt. Serve, or immediately pack loosely in a turkey cavity, and cook until an instant-read thermometer inserted into the center of the stuffing registers 165° F.

savory twice-baked sweet potatoes

SERVES 6

For a less formal but equally appealing presentation, you can spoon rather than pipe the filling into the shells.

- 3 medium sweet potatoes (1½ to 2 pounds), scrubbed well
- 4 ounces smoked bacon, sliced
- 2 tablespoons dark-brown sugar
- 3 tablespoons unsalted butter, softened
- 2 small shallots, finely minced
- 1 teaspoon minced fresh rosemary, plus more for garnish
- 1 large egg
- 2 tablespoons heavy cream
- 2 ounces Gruyère cheese, finely grated, plus more for garnish
  Coarse salt and freshly ground pepper

1. Preheat the oven to 400° F. Place the sweet potatoes on a parchment-lined baking sheet; bake until tender when pierced with a paring knife, about 45 minutes. Remove from the oven; let cool slightly.

2. Line a rimmed baking sheet with foil; fit with a wire rack. Arrange the bacon strips on the rack, and sprinkle with the brown sugar. Cook until well glazed and crisp, 12 to 15 minutes. Remove from the oven; let cool slightly, and roughly chop. Set aside.

3. Melt 1 tablespoon butter in a small skillet over medium heat. Add the shallots; sauté until soft and fragrant, about 2 minutes. Add the rosemary, and cook 1 minute more. Remove from heat, and set aside.

4. Slice each potato in half lengthwise. Carefully scoop out the flesh, leaving about a ¼-inch border all around the potato halves; set the halves aside on a baking sheet.

5. Place the flesh in the bowl of an electric mixer fitted with the paddle attachment. Add the remaining 2 tablespoons butter and the reserved shallot mixture, egg, cream, and Gruyère. Mix well until combined. Season with salt and pepper.

6. Transfer the mixture to a pastry bag fitted with a star tip; pipe into the reserved halves. Bake until golden, about 20 minutes. Remove from the oven. To serve, garnish with the Gruyère, rosemary, and reserved bacon.

spicy sweet potatoes with lime
SERVES 6

4 medium sweet potatoes (about 2½ pounds), scrubbed well

2 tablespoons extra-virgin olive oil

2 teaspoons ground cumin

1 teaspoon hot paprika

1 teaspoon ground ginger

   Coarse salt and freshly ground white pepper

   Lime wedges, for serving

   Yogurt Dipping Sauce, for serving (recipe follows)

1. Preheat the oven to 400°F. Heat a baking sheet in the oven until hot, about 15 minutes. Meanwhile, slice the sweet potatoes in half lengthwise; slice each half into 3 wedges. Place in a medium bowl, and toss with the oil, cumin, paprika, and ginger. Season with salt and pepper.

2. When the baking sheet is hot, remove from the oven. Arrange the sweet potatoes in a single layer on the sheet. Return to the oven; cook until the potatoes are crisp and golden on the bottom, about 15 minutes. Turn, and continue cooking until golden all over, about 15 minutes more.

3. Remove from the oven; season with salt and pepper. Serve with limes and sauce.

yogurt dipping sauce
MAKES ABOUT 1 CUP

1 cup plain yogurt

3 tablespoons roughly chopped fresh cilantro

2 tablespoons chopped toasted walnuts

1 tablespoon fresh lime juice

½ teaspoon ground cumin

   Coarse salt

Combine all the ingredients in a small bowl. Cover with plastic wrap, and refrigerate until ready to serve, up to 1 day.

potato, zucchini, and tomato gratin
SERVES 4

5 teaspoons extra-virgin olive oil

2 garlic cloves, minced

1 pound Yukon Gold potatoes, peeled

1 medium zucchini (about 8 ounces)

2 vine-ripened or other ripe tomatoes (¾ pound), sliced into ¼-inch rounds

¼ teaspoon coarse salt
Freshly ground pepper

1 teaspoon finely chopped fresh thyme

2 ounces finely grated Cantal or Cheddar cheese

1. Preheat the oven to 375°F, with the rack in the upper third. Coat a 9 × 13-inch gratin dish with 1 teaspoon oil, and sprinkle with the garlic. Using a mandoline or a very sharp knife, slice the potatoes and zucchini as thinly as possible into rounds. Arrange the potatoes, zucchini, and tomatoes in overlapping layers around the prepared dish, and sprinkle with the salt and pepper. Drizzle with the remaining 4 teaspoons oil, and sprinkle with the thyme and cheese.

2. Cover with foil; bake until the potatoes are tender, 35 to 45 minutes. Remove the foil; continue baking until the top is golden brown, about 25 minutes more. Remove from the oven, and serve immediately.

FIT TO EAT RECIPE PER SERVING: 175 CALORIES, 11 G FAT, 15 MG CHOLESTEROL, 14 G CARBOHYDRATE, 255 MG SODIUM, 8 G PROTEIN, 5 G FIBER

baby red potatoes with cilantro
SERVES 20 TO 25

Because the potatoes are cooked and served whole, be sure to select those that are similar in size to ensure they cook evenly.

10 pounds small red new potatoes
Coarse salt

1 cup extra-virgin olive oil
Freshly ground pepper

2 cups loosely packed fresh cilantro leaves

1. Place the unpeeled potatoes in a large saucepan, and cover with cold water. Bring the water to a boil over high heat, and add salt. Reduce heat to a simmer, and cook until the potatoes are tender when pierced with a fork, 15 to 20 minutes. Transfer to a colander, and drain.

2. Place the potatoes in a large serving bowl. Drizzle with the olive oil, and season with salt and pepper. Toss in the cilantro leaves just before serving.

mashed potatoes and peas
SERVES 6

2 pounds medium russet and/or Yukon Gold potatoes

1 tablespoon coarse salt, plus more for seasoning

5 tablespoons unsalted butter

1½ pounds garden peas, shelled (1½ cups)

1 cup milk
Freshly ground pepper

1. Peel and cut the potatoes crosswise into 1½-inch-thick slices. Place the slices in a medium saucepan, and cover with cold water. Bring to a boil over medium heat; add 1 tablespoon salt. Reduce to a low simmer, and cook until the potatoes are tender when pierced with a knife, about 15 minutes. Transfer to a colander; let drain.

2. Meanwhile, melt 1 tablespoon butter in a small sauté pan over medium-low heat. Add the peas, and cook until they are tender and bright green, 4 to 5 minutes. Transfer to the jar of a blender, and add the milk; blend until the mixture is smooth and combined.

3. While still hot, pass the potatoes through a ricer or food mill into a large heatproof bowl. Stir with a wooden spoon until they are smooth, about 1 minute. Using a whisk, incorporate the remaining 4 tablespoons butter. Whisking constantly, add the pureed pea mixture, and season with salt and pepper. Serve immediately, or keep warm over a pan of simmering water.

baked potato slices

SERVES 4

A Japanese or French mandoline is great for slicing vegetables uniformly—anywhere from very thin to thick—and takes much less time than slicing by hand with a knife.

- 1½ pounds Yukon Gold potatoes, peeled, very thinly sliced
- 2 tablespoons olive oil, plus more for pan
- 2 teaspoons fresh thyme leaves
  Coarse salt and freshly ground pepper

1. Preheat the oven to 400°F, and place the rack in the middle of the oven. In a medium bowl, combine the potatoes, olive oil, and thyme. Season with salt and pepper, and toss until well coated.

2. Generously brush a large rimmed baking sheet with olive oil, and overlap the potato slices just slightly. Bake until the potatoes are golden brown and crisp in places, about 30 minutes.

pommes frîtes

SERVES 8 TO 10

Make sure to use at least a 5-quart saucepan so the oil won't bubble over.

- 8 russet potatoes
- 2 to 3 quarts vegetable oil
- 1 tablespoon coarse salt

1. Peel the potatoes, if desired; cut into ½-inch-thick matchsticks. Place in a bowl of cold water to soak for 10 minutes.

2. Heat the oil in a large saucepan (at least 5 quarts) to 325°F. Remove the potatoes from water; dry very well with paper towels. Working in batches, blanch potatoes 2 minutes (they will not take on any color). Drain well; cool completely on pans lined with paper towels.

3. Raise the heat of the oil to 375°F. Preheat the oven to 250°F. Working in batches, fry potatoes until golden, about 3 minutes. Drain well; place on a rimmed baking sheet. Sprinkle with salt; keep warm in the oven while frying the remaining potatoes. Serve immediately.

roasted fingerling potatoes with seasoned salt

SERVES 4

A copper gratin dish or cast-iron skillet is ideal for roasting potatoes, but a rimmed baking sheet works equally well. To ensure the potatoes cook evenly, slice larger ones in half lengthwise and leave smaller ones whole.

- 2 teaspoons coarse salt
- ¼ teaspoon freshly ground pepper
- ¼ teaspoon finely chopped fresh thyme
- ¼ teaspoon finely chopped fresh rosemary
- 1½ pounds fingerling potatoes, scrubbed
- 1 tablespoon extra-virgin olive oil

1. Preheat the oven to 400°F. Heat a large ovenproof gratin dish or skillet in the oven 15 minutes. Combine the salt, pepper, thyme, and rosemary in a small bowl.

2. Toss the potatoes in a medium bowl with the olive oil. Sprinkle generously with the seasoned salt mixture, and arrange the potatoes in a single layer in the preheated pan. Roast until they are golden on the outside and tender when pierced with a sharp knife, 25 to 30 minutes. Remove from the oven, and serve hot with additional seasoned salt on the side.

oven-roasted new potatoes

SERVES 10

- 3 pounds mixed small new potatoes, unpeeled
- ¼ cup extra-virgin olive oil
- 1½ teaspoons coarse salt
- ¼ teaspoon freshly ground pepper

Preheat the oven to 350°F. Toss the potatoes with the oil, salt, and pepper in a large bowl until well coated. Transfer to a 9 × 13-inch metal baking dish and spread in a single layer. Roast, stirring occasionally, until tender, about 1 hour 15 minutes.

baked potato chips

SERVES 4

Vegetable oil cooking spray

2 *pounds russet potatoes, cut into ¼-inch-thick slices*

3 *tablespoons olive oil*

Pinch of cayenne pepper

Coarse salt and freshly ground pepper

1. Preheat the oven to 400° F. Lightly coat 2 rimmed baking sheets with cooking spray; set aside. Put the potatoes, oil, and cayenne in a large bowl; season with salt and black pepper. Toss to combine.

2. Arrange the potato slices on the prepared baking sheets, spacing them ¼ inch apart. Bake, rotating the sheets halfway through, until the potatoes are crisp and golden brown, about 30 minutes. Spread the potatoes on parchment paper; let dry 5 minutes. Sprinkle with salt, if desired.

mashed potatoes with olive oil

SERVES 10

3½ *pounds small Yukon Gold potatoes*

Coarse salt and freshly ground pepper

½ *cup extra-virgin olive oil, plus more for serving*

Cover the potatoes with cold water in a large pot; add salt. Bring to a boil. Cook until tender when pierced with a fork, about 10 minutes; drain. Mash with a potato masher. Stir in the oil; season with salt and pepper. Drizzle with oil, and serve immediately.

mashed squash and potatoes with amaretti

SERVES 12

2 *pounds russet potatoes, peeled and cut into 1-inch cubes (about 6 cups)*

Coarse salt and freshly ground pepper

3 *pounds buttercup squash (about 1 small), peeled, seeded, and cut into 1-inch cubes (about 8 cups)*

6 *tablespoons unsalted butter, plus more for the baking dish*

½ *cup heavy cream*

¼ *teaspoon freshly ground nutmeg*

½ *cup finely grated Parmigiano-Reggiano cheese*

10 *amaretti (Italian almond cookies), crushed into fine crumbs (about ¾ cup)*

1. Cover the potatoes with cold water in a medium saucepan. Bring to a boil; add salt. Reduce heat to medium-high; cook the potatoes until soft, about 25 minutes. In another medium saucepan, cover the squash with cold water. Bring to a boil; add salt. Reduce heat to medium-high; cook until soft, 15 to 20 minutes. Drain the potatoes and squash thoroughly.

2. Force the potatoes through a ricer into a bowl. In a separate bowl, mash the squash with a potato masher; stir in the potatoes.

3. Bring 4 tablespoons butter and the cream to a simmer in a small saucepan over medium heat. Add ½ teaspoon salt and the nutmeg. Season with pepper. Stir the cream mixture and ⅓ cup cheese into the potato mixture. Season with salt and pepper, if desired. Spoon into a buttered 10-inch round baking dish.

4. Preheat the oven to 350° F. Sprinkle the mixture with the crushed cookies and remaining cheese. Dot the topping with the remaining 2 tablespoons butter. Bake until the topping is just browned, 20 to 30 minutes.

classic potato gratin

SERVES 6 TO 8

Unsalted butter, for the baking dish
1 cup heavy cream
Coarse salt and freshly ground pepper
Pinch of freshly grated nutmeg
2 pounds Yukon Gold potatoes, peeled and thinly sliced into rounds
2 cups coarsely grated Gruyère cheese (about 6 ounces)

1. Preheat the oven to 350° F. Butter a 9-inch-square baking dish, and set aside.

2. Whisk together the cream, 1 teaspoon salt, ¼ teaspoon pepper, and the nutmeg in a small bowl, and set aside. Toss the potatoes, 1 teaspoon salt, and ¼ teaspoon pepper in a large bowl.

3. Arrange one-third of the potatoes in the buttered dish, overlapping the slices. Sprinkle with one-third of the cheese. Repeat two more times with the remaining potatoes and cheese (end with a cheese layer). Pour the reserved cream mixture over the top layer. Gently shake the dish back and forth to distribute evenly.

4. Cover with foil; bake 30 minutes. Remove the foil; bake until bubbling and well browned, about 30 minutes more. Let cool slightly before serving.

roasted yam halves

SERVES 4

Halving the yams before roasting greatly reduces the cooking time and allows them to develop a nice golden crust.

2 yams or sweet potatoes (about 2 pounds)
2 tablespoons extra-virgin olive oil
1 tablespoon finely chopped fresh thyme
Coarse salt and freshly ground pepper

Preheat the oven to 400° F. Halve the yams, and place, cut side up, in a shallow baking dish just large enough to hold them in a single layer. Drizzle with the oil, and sprinkle with the thyme. Season with salt and pepper. Bake until golden brown and very tender, 35 to 45 minutes.

southwestern sweet potato gratin

SERVES 8 TO 10

Chihuahua, Cotija, and Mexican crema give the dish authentic flavor, but Monterey Jack, French feta, and sour cream are good substitutes.

Unsalted butter, for baking dish
4 large sweet potatoes (about 4 pounds), peeled and thinly sliced into rounds
Coarse salt and freshly ground pepper
1½ cups grated Chihuahua or Monterey Jack cheese (6 ounces)
1½ cups Cotija or French feta cheese, crumbled (6 ounces)
1 small onion, thinly sliced
1 teaspoon finely chopped canned chipotle chile in adobo (optional)
¼ cup plus 2 tablespoons homemade or low-sodium store-bought chicken stock, or water
¼ cup finely chopped fresh cilantro leaves
1 cup crushed tortilla chips
Lime wedges, for garnish
Mexican crema or sour cream, for garnish (optional)

1. Preheat the oven to 350° F. Butter a 9 × 13-inch baking dish; set aside. Toss the potatoes with 1½ teaspoons salt and ¼ teaspoon pepper. Arrange half of the potatoes in the buttered dish, overlapping the slices. Sprinkle with half of each cheese. Top with onion.

2. Stir the chipotle (if desired) into the stock; drizzle over the onion. Sprinkle with half the cilantro. Top with the remaining potatoes; sprinkle with the remaining cheeses and cilantro. Scatter the chips on top.

3. Cover with foil; bake 30 minutes. Remove the foil; bake until very tender and top is well browned, about 30 minutes more. Let cool slightly before serving. Serve with limes, and with crema, if desired.

skillet sweet potatoes with wild mushrooms

SERVES 8 TO 10

- 1 ounce dried wild mushrooms, such as porcini (about 1 cup)
- 1 cup boiling water
- 2 tablespoons brandy
- 6 tablespoons unsalted butter, melted
   Olive oil, for the skillet
- 6 sweet potatoes (about 5 pounds), peeled and cut into ⅛-inch-thick rounds
   Coarse salt and freshly ground pepper

1. Place the dried mushrooms in a small bowl; cover with boiling water. Let soak, stirring occasionally, until soft, about 30 minutes. Remove the mushrooms; reserve ⅓ cup soaking liquid. Using paper towels, squeeze out excess water from the mushrooms; roughly chop, and set aside.

2. Preheat the oven to 400°F, with the rack in the center. In a small bowl, whisk the brandy, 5 tablespoons butter, and reserved mushroom liquid. Rub a 9-inch seasoned cast-iron skillet with oil. Arrange one-quarter of the potatoes in a single layer on the bottom, overlapping slightly. Scatter one-third of the mushrooms over the potatoes, then drizzle with one-quarter of the brandy mixture. Season with salt and pepper. Repeat the layering two more times; top with the remaining potatoes and liquid; season with salt.

3. Cover the skillet tightly with foil. Bake until the potatoes are just fork-tender, about 35 minutes. Remove the foil, and brush the top with the remaining tablespoon butter. Continue baking until the potatoes are golden brown and tender, 25 to 30 minutes more. Let stand 10 minutes before serving.

lemon and caper mashed potatoes

SERVES 4

To keep mashed potatoes warm for up to 2 hours, place them in a heatproof bowl over a pot filled with 3 inches of barely simmering water; cover to seal in the steam.

- 2 pounds Yukon Gold potatoes, peeled and quartered
   Coarse salt and freshly ground pepper
- 6 tablespoons unsalted butter
- ¾ cup milk
- 2 teaspoons fresh lemon juice, plus 2 teaspoons finely grated lemon zest
- 3 tablespoons capers, drained and coarsely chopped
- ¼ cup coarsely chopped fresh flat-leaf parsley

1. Place the potatoes in a large saucepan, and fill with enough water to cover the potatoes by 1 inch. Bring to a boil over high heat. Add a generous amount of salt; reduce heat to a simmer. Cook until the potatoes are tender when pierced with a paring knife, about 15 minutes. Drain; using a potato masher or potato ricer, mash the potatoes.

2. Meanwhile, in a medium saucepan over medium heat, combine 5 tablespoons butter and the milk, lemon juice, zest, and capers. Heat until the butter is melted and the mixture is warm to the touch.

3. Fold the milk mixture and the parsley into the mashed potatoes, and season with salt and pepper. Dot with the remaining tablespoon butter just before serving.

roasted baby potatoes
with romesco sauce
SERVES 4

Romesco sauce, from the Catalonian region of
Spain, is traditionally served with shellfish. We
serve our version with roasted potatoes. It's even
better the next day, when the flavors have had a
chance to blend: Refrigerate it overnight in a covered container, and bring to room temperature
before serving.

  3 ounces whole blanched almonds
  2 red bell peppers
  1 small garlic clove
  1 teaspoon coarse salt
  ⅛ teaspoon smoked hot paprika
  ¼ cup loosely packed mint leaves
  1 teaspoon sherry vinegar or
     red wine vinegar
  1½ tablespoons extra-virgin olive oil
  1 pound small red and yellow potatoes

1. Preheat the oven to 350° F. Spread the almonds
in a single layer on a rimmed baking sheet; toast in
the oven until lightly golden and fragrant, 7 to 8
minutes. Remove from the oven; cool 15 minutes.

2. Meanwhile, roast the red peppers over a gas
burner until blistered and charred, turning as each
section blackens. (Alternatively, roast the peppers
on a baking sheet under the broiler.) Transfer to a
large bowl, and cover tightly with plastic wrap; let
steam about 15 minutes. Using paper towels, peel
off the blackened skins; remove and discard the
stems and seeds.

3. Raise the oven temperature to 375° F. In a food
processor, combine the almonds, garlic, roasted red
peppers, ¾ teaspoon salt, paprika, mint, and vinegar. Process to a coarse paste, about 1 minute. With
the machine running, add 1 tablespoon oil in a slow,
steady stream until the sauce is smooth. Transfer
the sauce to a small bowl, and set aside.

4. Place the potatoes on a rimmed baking sheet,
and toss with the remaining ½ tablespoon oil and
¼ teaspoon salt. Roast in the oven until the skins
are slightly crisp and the potatoes are tender, shaking the pan once to turn the potatoes, 20 to 30 minutes. Serve hot, with the sauce on the side.

colcannon
SERVES 4

This traditional Irish potato dish can be assembled up to 2 hours ahead and then browned just
before serving.

  1½ pounds russet potatoes
  1   savoy cabbage, trimmed, pale-green
      leaves finely shredded (4 cups)
  1   leek, pale-green and white parts only,
      cut into ½-inch dice
  1   cup milk
  4   tablespoons unsalted butter
  ¼   teaspoon freshly grated nutmeg
      Coarse salt

1. Preheat the broiler. Peel and quarter the potatoes,
and place in a medium saucepan; add enough cold
water to cover. Bring to a boil over high heat; reduce heat to a simmer, and cook until tender when
pierced with a fork, about 15 minutes. Drain the potatoes and return them to the saucepan. Mash them
with a potato masher, or pass them through a ricer;
cover the pan to keep warm.

2. Meanwhile, in another saucepan, combine the
cabbage, leek, milk, 2 tablespoons butter, and nutmeg; season with salt. Cover, and cook over medium
heat, stirring occasionally, until the cabbage and
leek are soft but not browned, about 15 minutes. Stir
into the potatoes.

3. Spread the mixture in an 8-inch-square baking
dish. Make a small well in the center, and place
under the broiler until lightly browned on top, about
5 minutes.

4. Remove from the broiler. Place the remaining 2
tablespoons butter in the well. Serve immediately,
spooning melted butter from the well onto each
serving, if desired.

rösti potatoes

SERVES 6

3½ pounds (about 10) Yukon Gold potatoes,
     peeled and placed in cold water

     Coarse salt and freshly ground pepper

¼ cup clarified butter

1. Preheat the oven to 400° F. Shred the potatoes on the large holes of a box grater. Wrap the potatoes in a clean kitchen towel; squeeze out the liquid. Place in a medium bowl; toss with salt and pepper.

2. Heat half the butter in a 9- or 10-inch ovenproof nonstick sauté pan over medium-low heat. Spread the potatoes in the pan evenly; press down with a spatula to flatten the cake. Cook until the bottom is golden and turning crisp, about 18 minutes.

3. Remove the pan from the heat. Invert the cake onto a plate; slide back into the pan. Return to heat, and spoon the remaining butter around the edges of the pan. Cook until the other side begins to get crisp, about 10 minutes, shaking the pan several times to loosen the cake.

4. Transfer to the oven until cooked through and tender in the center, about 12 minutes. Cut into wedges, and serve.

gratin dauphinoise

SERVES 4 TO 6

2 tablespoons unsalted butter,
    room temperature, plus more for
    the baking dish

3 pounds (8 to 10 small) Yukon Gold
    potatoes

1 large garlic clove, minced

1¼ cups milk

1 cup heavy cream

1½ teaspoons coarse salt

¼ teaspoon freshly grated nutmeg

1 dried bay leaf

    Freshly ground pepper

3 ounces Gruyère cheese, finely grated
    (about 1 cup)

1. Preheat the oven to 400° F, with the rack in the center. Generously butter a 9 × 12-inch glass baking dish. Peel the potatoes, and slice into ⅛-inch-thick rounds. Place the slices in a bowl of cold water as you go to prevent discoloration.

2. In a medium saucepan, combine the garlic, milk, heavy cream, salt, nutmeg, and bay leaf. Bring just to a simmer over medium heat, and pour into the prepared baking dish. Discard the bay leaf.

3. Drain the potatoes in a colander, and transfer to the baking dish. Using a large spoon, toss the potatoes with the milk mixture, pressing down gently to distribute the potato slices evenly. Season with pepper. Dot with butter, distributing evenly over the entire surface; sprinkle with the cheese.

4. Place in the oven; bake until the potatoes can be pierced with a fork and the top is brown, 45 to 50 minutes. Serve immediately.

parsleyed potatoes

SERVES 4

2 *pounds small red potatoes, such as red creamer or Red Bliss*

2 *teaspoons coarse salt*

2 *tablespoons unsalted butter*

2 *tablespoons roughly chopped fresh flat-leaf parsley*

   Freshly ground pepper

1. Using a vegetable peeler or paring knife, peel the middle of each potato, if desired.

2. Place the potatoes and salt in a large saucepan, and cover with cold water. Bring to a boil over high heat; reduce heat to medium-low. Cook until a fork inserted into the center of the potatoes meets only slight resistance, about 20 minutes.

3. Drain the potatoes in a colander; return to the warm saucepan. Toss with the butter and parsley, and season with pepper. Transfer to a serving dish; serve immediately.

grilled herbed potatoes and shallots

SERVES 6

When put directly on the grill, potatoes will burn before they are cooked through. Parboiling potatoes and wrapping them in a foil packet with seasonings allows for perfectly grilled potatoes with lots of golden, flavorful bits. See page 619 for more spice-mix suggestions.

2½ *pounds small new potatoes*

    Coarse salt

 4 *tablespoons extra-virgin olive oil*

 8 *shallots, halved*

12 *sprigs oregano*

    Freshly ground pepper

1. Place the potatoes in a large saucepan, and fill with enough cold water to cover them by 2 inches. Bring to a boil over high heat, and add salt. Reduce heat; simmer until the potatoes are slightly tender when pierced with a fork (but not cooked through), about 10 minutes. Drain; let stand until cool enough to handle. Cut each potato in half.

2. Heat a grill to high. Overlap 2 pieces of foil, each about 3 feet long, to form a cross. Place the potatoes in one layer in the center of the cross. Drizzle the potatoes with 2 tablespoons oil; add the shallots and oregano; season with salt and pepper. Fold the foil, enclosing the potatoes, and seal the edges by crimping.

3. Place the foil packet on the grill, and cook, shaking the packet occasionally with tongs, until the potatoes are cooked through and golden brown, about 20 minutes, depending on the heat of the grill. Remove the packet from the grill, carefully, watching for any steam and hot oil that might escape. Transfer the potatoes to a serving bowl. Drizzle with the remaining 2 tablespoons oil, and adjust the seasoning as desired.

pink potato salad

SERVES 6

Use small red or white potatoes if fingerling potatoes are unavailable.

- 2 cups plain nonfat yogurt
- 1½ pounds fingerling potatoes
- 1 seedless cucumber, cut into ¼-inch-thick half-moons
- 4 ounces (about 1 cup) kalamata olives, pitted and cut in half
- 1 small red onion, sliced into thin half-moons
- ¼ cup picked fresh chervil leaves
- 3 tablespoons red-wine vinegar
- ½ teaspoon ground cinnamon
- ½ teaspoon ground nutmeg
- ½ teaspoon coarse salt
- ¼ teaspoon paprika

1. Drain the yogurt in a cheesecloth-lined sieve for 30 minutes. Place the potatoes in a medium pot, and cover with cold water; bring to a boil over high heat. Boil until tender, about 20 minutes. Remove from heat. Drain; run under cold water to stop the cooking. Set aside until completely cool.

2. Cut the potatoes into 1-inch pieces; place in a bowl. Add the cucumber, olives, onion, and chervil; set aside.

3. Place the drained yogurt (about 1½ cups) in a bowl. Add the red-wine vinegar, cinnamon, nutmeg, salt, and paprika; stir until well combined. Pour over the potato mixture; stir until the potatoes are well coated. Transfer to a serving bowl.

sautéed potatoes

SERVES 4

For crisp browned potatoes, avoid crowding the pan when sauteéing.

- 1½ pounds (about 4) russet potatoes
- 2 tablespoons olive oil
  Coarse salt and freshly ground pepper
- 1 tablespoon unsalted butter
- 2 tablespoons chopped fresh chives

1. Peel the potatoes, and place them in cold water to inhibit discoloration. Remove, and cut into ¾-inch cubes.

2. Heat half the oil in a large sauté pan over medium heat. Pat the potatoes dry; add half to the pan. Season with salt and pepper. Cook, tossing frequently, until the potatoes are golden, 12 to 15 minutes. Add half the butter; as it melts, toss to coat the potatoes.

3. Transfer to a serving plate; keep in a warm place while you repeat with the remaining oil, potatoes, and butter. When ready to serve, toss the potatoes with the chives.

mashed potatoes and celery root

SERVES 12 TO 14

If you prefer a completely smooth texture, you may pass the potatoes and celery root through a food mill or ricer after they have been cooked.

- 4 pounds Yukon Gold potatoes
- 1 pound celery root
- 1 cup heavy cream
- 6 tablespoons unsalted butter
- 1 tablespoon coarse salt
- ¼ teaspoon freshly ground pepper

1. Peel the potatoes, and cut into 1-inch pieces. Peel the celery root using a paring knife, following the shape of the root. Cut into ½-inch pieces. Place the potatoes and celery root in a small stockpot with enough water to cover, and bring to a boil over high heat. Reduce to a simmer, and cook until tender, about 10 minutes. Drain, return to the pot; place over low heat to dry out.

2. Combine the cream, butter, salt, and pepper in a small saucepan, and place over medium heat until the butter is melted and the mixture comes to a simmer. Pour over the potato mixture, and combine, using a potato masher, until fluffy and smooth.

florence's potato salad

SERVES 8

If making this in advance, wait to add the cucumber until just before serving.

- 2 pounds russet potatoes, scrubbed
  Coarse salt and freshly ground pepper
- 3 hard-boiled large eggs, peeled and cut into ½-inch dice
- 1 stalk celery, finely chopped
- 1 red onion, finely chopped
- 1 cucumber, peeled, seeded, and cut into ¼-inch dice
- ¼ cup coarsely chopped flat-leaf parsley
- 3 tablespoons cider vinegar
- 6 tablespoon mayonnaise

1. Place the potatoes in a medium saucepan; cover with water. Bring to a boil over high heat; add salt. Reduce heat to medium; simmer until tender, about 20 minutes. Drain in a colander. When cool enough to handle, peel and cut into ½-inch pieces. Transfer to a medium bowl. Add the eggs, celery, onion, cucumber, and parsley.

2. In a small bowl, whisk the vinegar and mayonnaise; season with salt and pepper. Pour the dressing over the vegetables; stir gently to combine. Adjust the seasoning with salt and pepper. Serve at room temperature.

baked sweet potatoes with caramelized onions and shaved parmesan

SERVES 6

- 6 medium sweet potatoes (8 ounces each)
- 1 tablespoon unsalted butter
- 4 large yellow onions, cut in half, then into ½-inch-thick half-moons
- 3 tablespoons sugar
- 1 teaspoon coarse salt
- ¼ teaspoon freshly ground pepper
- 2 tablespoons balsamic vinegar
- 1½ ounces freshly shaved Parmesan cheese (about ½ cup)

1. Preheat the oven to 450° F. Place the potatoes on a baking sheet; bake until tender, about 45 minutes. Meanwhile, melt the butter in a large nonstick skillet over medium-low heat. Add the onions; cook until soft, about 15 minutes. Sprinkle with the sugar, salt, and pepper; toss to coat. Continue to cook, stirring occasionally, until the onions are very soft and caramelized, about 1 hour more, adding water 1 tablespoon at a time if the pan dries. Stir in the vinegar. Set aside; keep warm.

2. When the potatoes are tender, split them open, and top with the caramelized onions and shaved Parmesan. Serve warm.

fruit desserts

crêpes suzette

MAKES ABOUT 14; SERVES ABOUT 6

Beer, traditionally found in this dish, ferments the batter and adds flavor.

for the batter

- 2 cups milk
- 1 teaspoon sugar
- 5 tablespoons unsalted butter, melted
- 3 large eggs
- 1 tablespoon vegetable oil
- 1¾ cups all-purpose flour
- ½ teaspoon salt
- ½ cup beer (not dark)

for the filling

- 1½ sticks (12 tablespoons) unsalted butter, softened
- 3 tablespoons sugar
- 4 teaspoons Grand Marnier or other orange-flavored liqueur
- Finely grated zest of 1 orange

for the sauce

- 2 cups orange juice
- ¼ cup sugar
- 1 tablespoon cornstarch
- 3 tablespoons Grand Marnier or other orange-flavored liqueur
- 2 tablespoons cold unsalted butter, cut into small pieces

for the garnish

- 2 oranges, peel and pith removed, flesh cut into segments
- Confectioners' sugar, for dusting

1. Make the batter: Whisk together the milk, sugar, butter, eggs, and oil. Sift together the flour and salt. Whisk the milk mixture into the flour mixture. Pour the batter through a fine sieve into a large bowl. Whisk in the beer. Refrigerate, covered, 6 hours (or overnight).

2. Let the batter stand at room temperature 15 minutes. Heat a crepe pan or a 12-inch nonstick skillet over medium heat. Pour ¼ cup batter into the pan,

swirling to cover the bottom. Cook, flipping once, until golden, about 2 minutes per side. Repeat.

3. Make the filling: Stir together the butter, sugar, liqueur, and zest. Spread 2 teaspoons over 1 crêpe. Roll up; place on a baking sheet, seam side down. Repeat until all the crêpes have been rolled.

4. Make the sauce: Bring the juice and sugar to a simmer in a saucepan over medium heat; skim the foam. Whisk together the cornstarch and 1 tablespoon water; add to the pan. Whisk in the liqueur. Cook until thickened, about 5 minutes. Remove from heat; whisk in the butter, 1 piece at a time.

5. Preheat the oven to 350° F. Cover the crepes with foil; heat in the oven 10 minutes. Transfer to plates. Top with sauce and oranges. Dust with confectioners' sugar.

blood-orange pavlovas with grand marnier

MAKES 12

- 6 blood oranges, peel and pith removed
- 7 tablespoons Grand Marnier or other orange-flavored liqueur
- 4 large eggs, separated
- 1¼ cups sugar
- ⅛ teaspoon salt, plus a pinch
- 1 teaspoon distilled white vinegar
- 1 teaspoon pure vanilla extract
- ¼ cup orange juice
- ½ cup heavy cream

1. Preheat the oven to 225° F. Cut the oranges into segments. Toss with 3 tablespoons liqueur; refrigerate until ready to use.

2. Make the meringue: Put the egg whites, 1 cup sugar, and a pinch of salt in the heatproof bowl of an electric mixer. Set over a pan of simmering water; whisk constantly until the sugar is melted and the mixture is hot.

3. Using the whisk attachment, beat the egg white mixture on medium speed until soft peaks form. Raise speed to high; beat until cool, and stiff, glossy peaks form. Beat in the vinegar and vanilla.

4. Using a rubber spatula, mound the meringue into 12 3-inch-wide rounds on parchment-paper–lined baking sheets. Swirl the edges and make a well in the center of each meringue. Bake until crisp and just set in the center, 40 to 50 minutes. Let cool on the sheet on a wire rack. When the meringues are cool enough to handle, peel off the parchment. Let cool completely.

5. Make the custard: Stir together the yolks, orange juice, remaining ¼ cup each sugar and liqueur, and ⅛ teaspoon salt in a large heatproof bowl set over a pan of simmering water; whisk until thickened and a spoon leaves a wake, about 4 minutes. Pass the mixture through a fine sieve into a bowl. Refrigerate until cold, about 1 hour.

6. Beat the cream to soft peaks; fold into the custard. Refrigerate until ready to serve, up to 4 hours (rewhisk before using).

7. Just before serving, mound custard in each meringue. Top the custard mounds with orange segments and their juices.

baked pears with vanilla mascarpone
SERVES 4

Bosc pears must be very ripe; Anjou, which are juicier, can be slightly firm. Avoid enamel baking dishes, as they cause the syrup to burn.

- 4 Anjou or Bosc pears
- 1 tablespoon unsalted butter, softened
- 2 tablespoons sugar
- 1 cup red wine
- 4 sprigs thyme (optional)
   Vanilla Mascarpone (recipe follows)
   Store-bought biscotti

1. Preheat the oven to 425° F. Slice off the bottom of each pear just enough so it will stand upright. Using a melon baller or small spoon, remove the seeds from the bottom. Peel the upper half, leaving the stem intact; pat dry with a paper towel. Rub butter over the peeled part of each pear; stand the pears in a small baking dish (about 7 × 11 inches). Sprinkle with the sugar.

2. Pour the wine into the baking dish; add the thyme sprigs, if using. Bake until the pears are soft when pierced with a paring knife and well browned, about 45 minutes; using a small spoon, baste the pears occasionally with the wine, adding a bit of water as needed to prevent the liquid from evaporating. Remove from the oven.

3. Spoon some of the pan juices into each serving dish, and place a pear on top. Serve with a dollop of mascarpone and several biscotti on the side.

vanilla mascarpone
MAKES ABOUT 1 CUP

For the creamiest results, allow the mascarpone to stand at room temperature for 15 minutes before serving.

- ½ vanilla bean, split and scraped
- 8 ounces mascarpone cheese
- 2 tablespoons confectioners' sugar

Combine all the ingredients in a small bowl, and stir together with a wooden spoon.

watermelon and raspberry salad
SERVES 4

Easy to prepare, this vibrant pink fruit salad can be served on its own or spooned over a scoop of vanilla ice cream or your favorite sorbet.

- 1 4½-pound piece watermelon, peeled, seeded, and cut into 1-inch cubes (about 4 cups)
- 1 pint fresh raspberries
   Juice of 1 lemon
- ¼ cup sugar
   Vanilla ice cream, for serving (optional)

Place the watermelon in a large bowl, and add the raspberries, lemon juice, and sugar; toss to combine. Let stand at least 30 minutes, tossing occasionally, until all the sugar is dissolved. Serve chilled or at room temperature with vanilla ice cream, if desired.

pear pavlova

SERVES 6

for the pears

1 750-ml bottle dry red wine, such as Cabernet or Zinfandel

3 cups water

1 cup sugar

1 teaspoon whole black peppercorns

3 dried bay leaves

2 cinnamon sticks

3 to 6 ripe Bosc pears

for the meringue base

4 large egg whites
   Pinch of salt

¾ cup packed light-brown sugar

¼ cup superfine sugar

1 teaspoon distilled white vinegar

1 teaspoon pure vanilla extract

for the topping

1 cup heavy cream

2 tablespoons superfine sugar

1. Poach the pears: Combine the wine, water, sugar, peppercorns, bay leaves, and cinnamon sticks in a large saucepan. Bring to a boil, and stir until the sugar has dissolved. Reduce the heat to a gentle simmer.

2. Carefully peel the pears, leaving the stems intact. Place in the pan; cover, and cook, rotating occasionally, until the bases of the pears are easily pierced with a paring knife, 20 to 25 minutes, depending on the ripeness of the fruit. Meanwhile, prepare an ice-water bath.

3. Using a large slotted spoon, carefully transfer the pears to a large metal bowl set in the ice bath. Pour the poaching liquid through a fine sieve into the bowl with the pears; let cool completely. Cover with plastic wrap; refrigerate overnight to let the pears absorb the poaching liquid.

4. Preheat the oven to 300°F, with the rack in the center. Line a baking sheet with parchment paper. Using an overturned bowl or cake pan as a guide, trace an 8-inch circle on the parchment; turn the parchment over, marked side down.

5. Make the meringue base: Place the egg whites, salt, and light brown sugar in the bowl of an electric mixer fitted with the whisk attachment. Beat on low speed until well combined and no lumps of sugar remain. Increase speed to medium; beat until soft peaks form, about 9 minutes. With the mixer running, gradually add the superfine sugar. Continue beating until the peaks are stiff and glossy, about 2 minutes. Beat in the vinegar and vanilla.

6. Using a rubber spatula, spread the meringue into the marked 8-inch circle on the baking sheet; form peaks around the edge and a well in the center.

7. Bake the meringue until crisp around the edge and just set in the center, about 1¼ hours. Transfer the baking sheet to a wire rack until the meringue is cool enough to handle. Carefully peel off the parchment; cool meringue completely on the rack.

8. Make the topping: In a small bowl, whip the heavy cream and sugar until stiff peaks form. Cover with plastic wrap; refrigerate until ready to use.

9. Slice the pears in half lengthwise; remove the seeds and stems with a spoon or melon baller, and discard. Cut the pears into ¾-inch pieces, and place in a bowl; cover with plastic wrap, and set aside.

10. Bring 3 cups poaching liquid to a boil in a medium saucepan; reduce heat, and simmer until syrupy and reduced to about 1 cup, 20 to 25 minutes. Meanwhile, prepare another ice-water bath. Pour the syrup into a clean bowl set in the ice bath; stir frequently until cool and thickened.

11. To assemble, carefully place the meringue on a serving platter. Spoon the whipped cream on top, and then add the pears. Serve, sliced into wedges and drizzled with syrup.

LEFTOVER EGG YOLKS

When recipes such as meringues call for egg whites only, don't toss out the yolks. Instead, keep them for recipes that need only the thick and fatty yolk to make them complete. Egg yolks are the key ingredient for fruit curds and custard, for example; yolks serve as thickening and binding agents in both of these creamy dishes. Or use the yolks to make spaghetti carbonara, or a rich hollandaise sauce to serve with eggs Benedict or over fish and vegetables. You could also combine the yolks with vegetable oil, lemon juice or vinegar, and seasonings for a simple homemade mayonnaise. Unlike commercial mayonnaise, this kind lasts only 3 to 4 days when refrigerated in an airtight container, so plan to use it within that time.

If you don't want to use the yolks right away, they can be saved for later. Yolks can be stored in an airtight container and refrigerated for up to 3 days or frozen for up to 4 months. When refrigerating, cover the yolks with a little water to keep them from drying out, and remember to drain the water before use. To prevent them from becoming gelatinous when frozen, add either ⅛ teaspoon salt or 1½ teaspoons sugar (use salt if you plan to use the yolks in savory dishes and sugar for making desserts) to each ¼ cup yolks (about 4). Beat the yolks lightly before mixing in the salt or sugar. Label the container with the date and number of yolks. You will need 1 tablespoon thawed yolk for each large yolk called for in a recipe.

fresh raspberry gelatin and whipped cream

SERVES 4

¾ cup sugar

¾ cup water

½ bunch fresh mint, leaves removed from stems, rinsed well (about ½ cup)

½ cup white grape juice

1 tablespoon fresh lime juice

1½ teaspoons unflavored gelatin (½ envelope)

1 6-ounce container fresh raspberries, rinsed

½ cup heavy cream

1 tablespoon confectioners' sugar

1. Place a medium saucepan over high heat. Add the sugar, water, and mint, and bring to a boil. Reduce heat to medium; simmer 2 minutes, swirling the pan to dissolve the sugar. Strain the mixture through a fine-mesh sieve into a small bowl; discard the mint.

2. Combine the grape juice, lime juice, and gelatin in a medium heatproof bowl set over a pan of simmering water, and stir until the gelatin is dissolved. Remove the bowl from the heat; add the mint syrup and berries, stirring with a wooden spoon to break some berries into pieces. Divide the mixture among 4 6-ounce ramekins. Cover with plastic; refrigerate until firm, at least 4 hours and up to 2 days.

3. Just before serving, place the heavy cream in the bowl of an electric mixer fitted with the whisk attachment; beat on medium speed until soft peaks form, 3 to 4 minutes. Add the confectioners' sugar, and continue beating until soft peaks return, 1 to 2 minutes. To serve, spoon a dollop of whipped cream onto each serving.

thyme-roasted figs over brioche pain perdu

SERVES 6

12 ripe figs (about 12 ounces)
2 to 3 tablespoons thyme-flower honey
4 sprigs thyme, plus more for garnish
¼ cup water, plus more as needed
6 large eggs
¾ cup heavy cream
1 teaspoon ground cinnamon
6 slices (¾ inch) day-old brioche
1½ tablespoons unsalted butter
½ cup crème fraîche
2 tablespoons thyme flowers, for garnish

1. Preheat the oven to 300°F. Combine the figs, honey, thyme, and water in a small ovenproof skillet. Bring to a simmer over medium-high heat. Transfer to the oven; cook until the figs have softened, about 40 minutes, basting occasionally with the cooking liquid. Remove the pan from the heat, and set aside.

2. Combine the eggs, cream, and cinnamon in a medium bowl; whisk to combine. Dip the brioche in the egg mixture, and set aside. Heat the butter in a large nonstick skillet over medium heat. Cook the brioche until golden, about 1 minute on each side. Transfer to a serving platter. Spoon the roasted figs and cooking liquid over the brioche. Top with crème fraîche, and garnish with fresh thyme sprigs and flowers.

melon and berries steeped in red wine, sauternes, basil, and mint

SERVES 4

The steeping liquid needs to chill for at least 4 hours, so plan accordingly.

1 tablespoon roughly chopped basil (about 6 large leaves)
1½ tablespoons coarsely chopped fresh mint (about 12 large leaves), plus whole sprigs for garnish
1 cup Sauternes or other dessert wine
½ cup Cabernet Sauvignon or other red wine
4 tablespoons sugar
1 vanilla bean, split lengthwise
½ Charentais or other melon such as cantaloupe, honeydew, or Crenshaw, scooped into 12 balls
8 ounces strawberries, stems removed and quartered
¼ cup blackberries
6 ounces raspberries (½-pint container)
½ cup chilled rosé champagne
   Fresh currants, for garnish (optional)

1. Prepare an ice-water bath; set aside. Tie the basil and mint in a small square of cheesecloth. In a small saucepan, combine the Sauternes, red wine, sugar, vanilla bean, and mint-basil bundle. Bring the mixture to a boil, stirring to dissolve the sugar. Remove from heat; transfer to the ice bath. Chill until lukewarm. Add the melon, strawberries, and blackberries; transfer to a large bowl. Cover; place in the refrigerator for 4 to 6 hours.

2. To serve, remove the vanilla bean. Stir in the raspberries. Transfer the mixture to 4 bowls. Drizzle about 2 tablespoons champagne over each, and garnish with currants, if desired, and mint.

lemon and cherry trifle

MAKES 6 INDIVIDUAL TRIFLES

2 cups heavy cream

2 recipes Lemon Curd (page 656)

　Poached Cherries (recipe follows)

30 vanilla wafers

　Candied Lemon Zest (recipe follows)

6 fresh cherries, for garnish

In the bowl of an electric mixer fitted with the whisk attachment, beat the cream until soft peaks form. Layer the lemon curd, cherries, wafers, zest, and whipped cream in tall glasses. Cover with plastic wrap; chill in the refrigerator up to 2 hours. Serve; garnish each with a fresh cherry.

poached cherries

MAKES ENOUGH FOR 6 SMALL TRIFLES

2 pounds red or yellow fresh cherries, pitted (5 to 6 cups)

½ cup sugar

1 tablespoon kirsch (optional)

2 tablespoons fresh lemon juice

1. Bring all the ingredients to a simmer in a medium saucepan over medium-low heat; cook, stirring occasionally, until the cherries are tender, about 15 minutes. Transfer the cherries to a large bowl.

2. Continue cooking the remaining mixture in the pan over medium heat until it is slightly thickened, about 3 minutes. Pour over the cherries; let cool. Store in an airtight container in the refrigerator for up to 1 day.

candied lemon zest

MAKES ABOUT ½ CUP

3 lemons

1 cup sugar

½ cup water

Zest the lemons with a vegetable peeler into long strips. Remove the pith; cut the strips into fine julienne. Bring the sugar and water to a boil in a small saucepan, stirring to dissolve the sugar. Add the zest; boil 5 minutes. Cover, and remove from heat; let cool. Strain off the syrup before using. The zest can be stored in an airtight container in the refrigerator up to 2 weeks.

baked apricots with almond topping

SERVES 4

4½ teaspoons unsalted butter, softened, plus more for the dish

¼ cup whole almonds, skin on

3 tablespoons packed light-brown sugar

6 apricots, peeled, halved, and pitted

1. Preheat the oven to 400° F. Butter a 9-inch-square baking dish. Process the almonds and brown sugar in a food processor until the almonds are finely chopped. Add the butter; process until just combined.

2. Place the apricot halves, cut sides up, in the buttered baking dish. Cover the top of each apricot half with almond mixture. Bake until the apricots are soft and the almond mixture is deep golden brown, 15 to 20 minutes. Transfer 3 apricot halves to each serving plate. Serve warm.

grilled peaches
with chilled sabayon

SERVES 4

Sabayon is the French term for zabaglione, a frothy Italian concoction that can be served warm as a sauce or chilled as a creamy dessert on its own. We added a bit of peach-flavored liqueur to enhance the flavor of the fruit, but the sabayon is just as delicious without.

- 5 large egg yolks
- ⅓ cup plus 1 tablespoon sugar
- ⅓ cup champagne or sparkling wine
- 2 tablespoons peach liqueur (optional)
- ¾ cup heavy cream, chilled
- 2 peaches, halved and pitted
- 2 tablespoons unsalted butter, melted
- 2 tablespoons light brown sugar

1. Heat a grill or grill pan. Prepare an ice-water bath; set aside. Make the sabayon: Combine the yolks, sugar, champagne, and liqueur, if using, in a large metal bowl set over a large pan of simmering water. Whisk until the mixture is very thick and has expanded in volume, about 7 minutes. Place the bowl in the ice bath; let cool completely.

2. Place the cream in a large bowl, and beat until stiff peaks form. Fold the whipped cream into the egg yolk mixture. Cover with plastic wrap, and place in the refrigerator at least 20 minutes.

3. Line a grill or pan with heavy-duty foil. Brush the peaches with butter; sprinkle with brown sugar. Grill, cut side down, until the peaches are tender and the sugar is caramelized, 6 to 7 minutes. Divide the sabayon among 4 dishes, and top each with a peach half. Serve.

pineapple floats

MAKES 8

In place of fresh pineapple, you can drain two 8-ounce cans crushed pineapple, roast it, and skip making the syrup.

- 1 pineapple (about 4 pounds), top trimmed
- 1 cup granulated sugar
- 1 vanilla bean, halved lengthwise
- 3 tablespoons packed dark-brown sugar
- 3 tablespoons dark rum
- 1 quart best-quality vanilla ice cream
- 1 liter club soda

1. Preheat the oven to 425° F. Peel the pineapple using a sharp knife, reserving the peels as you work. Cut the flesh lengthwise into quarters; cut out and reserve the core. Transfer the peels and core pieces to a large pot; reserve the flesh.

2. Add 5 cups water to the pot; bring to a boil. Add the granulated sugar and vanilla bean; cook about 30 minutes, mashing the peels occasionally with the back of a spoon to extract juice. Meanwhile, cut the pineapple into ½-inch cubes; transfer to a rimmed baking sheet. Sprinkle with the brown sugar and rum. Cook until just golden, about 20 minutes. Transfer to a bowl; let cool completely. Cover; refrigerate up to 2 days.

3. Pour the pineapple peel mixture from the pot through a sieve into a large bowl; discard the solids. Return the liquid to the pot, and bring to a boil. Cook until reduced to ½ cup, about 4 minutes. Refrigerate the syrup, covered, until ready to serve, up to 2 days.

4. Divide the pineapple evenly among 8 serving glasses. Top with 2 teaspoons syrup and 2 scoops ice cream. Fill with club soda. Drizzle with remaining syrup.

asian pears with star anise baked in parchment

SERVES 4

This recipe is versatile. You can use any firm-flesh pears or apples—or a combination; just be sure the size of the fruits you use is uniform. You can also try another dry whole spice (such as cinnamon or cloves) in place of the star anise.

- 1 lemon
- 2 Asian pears
- 4 whole star anise
- ¼ cup honey
- ¼ cup dry vermouth, dry white wine, cider, or water

1. Preheat the oven to 350° F. Cut 4 pieces of parchment paper to measure 12 inches square each. Juice the lemon into a small bowl. Halve each pear horizontally. Dip the cut sides of the pears in the lemon juice (to prevent browning). Using a melon baller, remove the core from each half.

2. Place 1 star anise in the cored center of each pear half. Drizzle 1 tablespoon honey over each star anise.

3. Place 1 pear half, cut side up, on each piece of paper. Working with one at a time, hold a pear half in paper in the palm of your hand; gather the edges of the paper around the fruit with your free hand. Transfer to a rimmed baking sheet.

4. Pour 1 tablespoon vermouth into each pear half in parchment. Twist the paper tightly around the top of each fruit to seal. Bake 45 minutes; the pears should be tender. Transfer the packets to shallow bowls. Serve immediately, opening the packets at the table.

plum-nectarine buckle

SERVES 8 TO 10

- 6 tablespoons unsalted butter, melted
- 1½ cups all-purpose flour
- 1 cup plus 2 tablespoons sugar
- 1½ teaspoons baking powder
- ⅛ teaspoon ground allspice
  Salt
- 1 large egg
- ⅔ cup whole milk
- 1 teaspoon pure vanilla extract
- ¾ pound plums, halved, pitted, and cut into ½-inch-thick wedges (2 cups)
- ¾ pound nectarines, halved, pitted, and cut into ½-inch-thick wedges (2 cups)
- 1 tablespoon fresh lemon juice
  Crumble Topping (page 403)

1. Preheat the oven to 350° F. Brush a 9-inch-square cake pan or 10-inch cast-iron skillet with 2 tablespoons butter; set aside. Whisk together the flour, ¾ cup sugar, and the baking powder, allspice, and ¾ teaspoon salt in a medium bowl; set aside.

2. Whisk together the egg, milk, vanilla, and remaining 4 tablespoons butter in another medium bowl. Add the egg mixture to the flour mixture; stir to combine. Spread the batter evenly into the buttered pan.

3. Toss the plums, nectarines, lemon juice, remaining ¼ cup plus 2 tablespoons sugar, and a pinch of salt in a large bowl. Spread the fruit mixture evenly over the batter. Sprinkle with the topping. Bake until a cake tester inserted into the center comes out with moist crumbs, about 1 hour and 15 minutes. Let cool in the pan on a wire rack 1 hour before serving.

sour cherry–pistachio crisp

SERVES 8

1¾ pounds pitted fresh or frozen sour
    cherries

½ cup chopped unsalted pistachios

½ cup plus 2 tablespoons all-purpose flour

⅓ cup old-fashioned rolled oats

¼ teaspoon baking powder

    Salt

6 tablespoons unsalted butter, softened

3 tablespoons packed light-brown sugar

¾ cup granulated sugar

2 teaspoons cornstarch

    Pinch of ground cinnamon

1. Preheat the oven to 375° F. If using frozen cherries, spread them in a single layer on a rimmed baking sheet. Let stand at room temperature until cherries have thawed almost completely but still hold their shape, about 30 minutes. Drain off any accumulated liquid.

2. Whisk together the pistachios, flour, oats, baking powder, and ¼ teaspoon salt in a medium bowl; set aside. Put the butter, brown sugar, and ¼ cup granulated sugar in the bowl of an electric mixer fitted with the paddle attachment; mix on medium speed until creamy.

3. Stir the pistachio mixture into the butter mixture until just combined. Work the mixture through your fingers until it forms coarse crumbs ranging in size from small peas to gumballs; set the topping aside.

4. Stir together the cherries, remaining ½ cup granulated sugar, the cornstarch, cinnamon, and a pinch of salt in a medium bowl. Transfer the cherry mixture to an 8-inch-square baking dish. Sprinkle the topping evenly over the cherry mixture. Bake until the topping turns golden and the juices are bubbling, 50 minutes to 1 hour. Let cool on a wire rack 1 hour before serving.

PITTING CHERRIES

To pit a cherry and keep the stem intact, reach for a clean paperclip. Unfold the clip at its center; depending on the size of the cherry, insert either the large or the small end of the paper clip through the bottom of the cherry. Loosen the pit and pull it out.

apricot-almond cobbler

SERVES 8

½ cup whole raw almonds

1 cup all-purpose flour

1 cup plus 2 tablespoons sugar

1½ teaspoons baking powder

    Salt

    Pinch of freshly grated nutmeg

6 tablespoons unsalted butter, melted

½ cup whole milk, room temperature

1 large egg, room temperature

2 tablespoons almond-flavored liqueur,
    such as amaretto

1½ pounds apricots, halved lengthwise,
    pitted, and cut into ¾-inch-thick wedges

1 tablespoon fresh lemon juice

1. Preheat the oven to 375° F. Toast the almonds on a rimmed baking sheet in the oven, stirring occasionally, until fragrant and golden brown, about 10 minutes. Let cool completely. Finely grind the almonds in a food processor; transfer to a medium bowl. Whisk in the flour, ¾ cup sugar, the baking powder, ¾ teaspoon salt, and the nutmeg; set aside.

2. Brush a 10-inch cast-iron skillet with 2 tablespoons butter. Whisk together the remaining 4 tablespoons butter, milk, egg, and liqueur in a medium bowl. Stir the butter mixture into the flour mixture; spread evenly into the skillet.

3. Stir the apricots, remaining ¼ cup plus 2 tablespoons sugar, a pinch of salt, and the lemon juice in a medium bowl; spread evenly over the batter. Bake until a tester inserted into center comes out with moist crumbs, 50 to 60 minutes. Let cool in the skillet on a wire rack 1 hour before serving.

rhubarb-berry crumbles

SERVES 6

- 1½ pounds rhubarb, cut crosswise into ¼-inch-thick slices, leaves discarded
- 2 cups raspberries or sliced strawberries, or a combination
- 1¼ cups sugar
- 2 tablespoons instant tapioca
- ½ teaspoon finely grated orange zest, plus 2 tablespoons fresh orange juice
- Pinch of salt
- Crumble Topping (recipe follows)
- Vanilla yogurt, for serving (optional)

1. Preheat the oven to 375°F. Stir together the rhubarb, berries, sugar, tapioca, orange zest, orange juice, and salt in a bowl. Let stand 15 minutes, stirring occasionally.

2. Divide the rhubarb mixture among 6 small ceramic baking dishes (1 cup capacity and 5½ inches in diameter). Transfer the baking dishes to a rimmed baking sheet lined with parchment paper. Sprinkle with the topping, dividing evenly.

3. Bake until the topping turns golden and the juices are bubbling, 30 to 35 minutes. Let cool on the sheet on a wire rack 30 minutes. Serve with yogurt, if desired.

crumble topping

MAKES ABOUT 1¾ CUPS

- 6 tablespoons unsalted butter, softened
- ¼ cup packed light-brown sugar
- ¼ teaspoon finely grated orange zest (for Rhubarb-Berry Crumbles; optional)
- 1 cup all-purpose flour
- Pinch of salt

Put the butter, brown sugar, and orange zest, if desired, in the bowl of an electric mixer fitted with the paddle attachment. Mix on medium speed until creamy. Stir in the flour and salt. Work the mixture through your fingers until it forms coarse crumbs ranging in size from peas to gumballs.

mixed-berry grunt

SERVES 8

- 1 cup sugar
- ¼ teaspoon plus a pinch of ground cinnamon
- ¾ cup all-purpose flour
- ¾ teaspoon baking powder
- Salt
- ¼ teaspoon ground ginger
- ⅓ cup whole milk, room temperature
- 2 tablespoons unsalted butter, melted
- 4 cups raspberries (about 1½ pints)
- 3 cups blackberries (about 1½ pints)
- 2 tablespoons fresh lemon juice
- Heavy cream, for drizzling

1. Stir together 2 tablespoons sugar and ¼ teaspoon cinnamon in a small bowl; set aside. Whisk together the flour, 2 tablespoons sugar, the baking powder, a pinch of salt, and the ginger in a medium bowl. Stir together the milk and butter in a small bowl. Stir the milk-butter mixture into the flour mixture. Set the batter aside.

2. Gently fold together the raspberries, blackberries, lemon juice, remaining ¾ cup sugar, a pinch of salt, the remaining pinch of cinnamon, and 2 tablespoons water in a large bowl. Transfer mixture to a large, straight-sided skillet. Cover; bring to a boil over medium-high heat, stirring occasionally.

3. Drop 8 large dollops of batter on top of the berry mixture using 2 spoons, spacing them evenly. Sprinkle the dumplings with the cinnamon-sugar mixture. Cover; reduce heat to medium. Cook until the dumplings are cooked through and the juices are bubbling, about 15 minutes. Serve warm, drizzled with cream.

apple-raisin pandowdy

SERVES 8

- 3 pounds mixed apples, such as Rome Beauty, Empire, and Cortland, peeled, cored, and cut into ½-inch-thick wedges
- 1 cup golden raisins
- ¼ cup plus 2 tablespoons packed dark brown sugar
- 2 tablespoons all-purpose flour, plus more for the work surface
- 1 tablespoon fresh lemon juice

  Pinch of ground cardamom

  Pinch of ground allspice

  Pinch of salt
- 2 tablespoons unsalted butter, cut into small pieces

  Toasted Pecan Dough (recipe follows)

  Heavy cream, for brushing

  Sanding sugar, for sprinkling

1. Preheat the oven to 375°F. Toss together the apples, raisins, brown sugar, flour, lemon juice, cardamom, allspice, and salt in a large bowl. Transfer to a 9-inch deep-dish pie plate. Dot the top with butter; set aside.

2. Transfer the dough to a lightly floured work surface. Roll out to an 11-inch round about ⅛ inch thick. Carefully place the dough on top of the apple mixture. Fold the edge under itself, crimping if desired. Chill in the freezer until firm, about 15 minutes.

3. Brush the dough with cream, and sprinkle with sanding sugar. Bake until the crust is set and beginning to brown, about 45 minutes. Remove from the oven; gently push some of the crust into the filling using a spoon. Bake until the crust is golden brown and crisp and the juices are bubbling, 25 to 35 minutes more. If the crust is browning too quickly, cover loosely with foil. Let cool on a wire rack 1 hour before serving.

toasted pecan dough

MAKES ENOUGH FOR 1 PANDOWDY

- ¼ cup pecans
- 1 cup all-purpose flour
- 1 teaspoon sugar
- ½ teaspoon salt
- ½ cup (1 stick) cold unsalted butter, cut into small pieces
- 3 to 4 tablespoons ice water

1. Preheat the oven to 350°F. Toast the pecans on a rimmed baking sheet in the oven, stirring occasionally, until fragrant and golden brown, about 10 minutes. Let cool completely. Coarsely grind the pecans in a food processor. Add the flour, sugar, and salt; process until combined.

2. Add the butter; process until the mixture resembles coarse meal, about 10 seconds. With the processor running, add the ice water in a slow, steady stream just until the dough comes together.

3. Turn out the dough onto a piece of plastic wrap. Shape into a disk; wrap in plastic. Refrigerate at least 1 hour or up to 1 day before using.

lemon crêpes

MAKES ABOUT 18; SERVES 6

The crêpes can be made 1 day ahead and refrigerated, wrapped in plastic wrap. To reheat, wrap them in foil and warm in a 200°F oven.

- 6 tablespoons unsalted butter, cut into small pieces, plus about 1 tablespoon, melted, for the pan
- ¾ cup plus 2 tablespoons all-purpose flour
- ¼ cup sugar
- ¼ teaspoon salt
- 1¼ cups milk (not skim)
- ¼ teaspoon pure vanilla extract
- 3 large eggs

  Lemon-Caramel Sauce (recipe follows)

  Candied Lemon Slices (recipe follows)

1. Bring 2 tablespoons water to a boil in a small saucepan. Reduce heat; add 6 tablespoons butter, a little at a time, whisking until the butter is completely melted.

2. Whisk together the flour, sugar, and salt in a medium bowl. In a separate bowl, whisk together the milk, vanilla, and eggs. Gradually add the milk mixture to the flour mixture, whisking until smooth. Whisk in the butter mixture. Pour the batter through a fine sieve into a bowl; discard lumps. Transfer the batter to an airtight container; refrigerate at least 2 hours (or overnight).

3. Preheat the oven to 200° F. Lightly coat a 6- to 7-inch crêpe pan or nonstick skillet with melted butter. Heat over medium heat until just starting to smoke. Remove the pan from the heat; pour 2 to 3 tablespoons batter (depending on size of pan) in the center. Swirl to cover the bottom. Reduce heat to medium-low; return the pan to the heat. Cook until the edges of the crêpe turn golden and the center is dry, about 45 seconds. Flip the crêpe; cook until the underside is brown in spots, about 45 seconds more.

4. Slide the crêpe onto an ovenproof plate; cover with foil, and transfer to the oven. Repeat the process with the remaining batter, coating the pan with more butter as needed.

5. Fold each crêpe into quarters to form a triangle. To serve, arrange 3 crêpes on each plate; drizzle with lemon-caramel sauce and garnish with candied lemon slices.

lemon-caramel sauce
MAKES ABOUT 1 1/4 CUPS

The sauce can be refrigerated in an airtight container for up to 3 days. Warm over gentle heat just before serving.

- 1 cup sugar
- 3 tablespoons fresh lemon juice
- 1 tablespoon limoncello (Italian lemon-flavored liqueur; optional)
- 2 tablespoons unsalted butter, cut into small pieces

1. Heat the sugar and 1/4 cup water in a medium heavy-bottomed saucepan over medium-high heat, stirring occasionally, until the sugar has dissolved and the syrup is clear. Continue to cook, without stirring, until the syrup comes to a boil, occasionally washing down the sides of the pan with a wet pastry brush to prevent crystals from forming. Let the syrup boil, gently swirling the pan occasionally, until dark amber.

2. Remove from heat; whisk in the lemon juice, liqueur (if desired), butter, and 2 tablespoons water. (The caramel will steam and spatter.) Serve warm.

candied lemon slices
MAKES 1 DOZEN

The lemon slices can be stored in an airtight container at room temperature up to 1 day.

- 1 large lemon
- 1 cup sugar

1. Prepare an ice-water bath; set aside. Using a mandoline or sharp knife, cut the lemon into 12 paper-thin slices; discard the seeds and ends of the rind.

2. Bring a medium saucepan of water to a rolling boil. Remove from the heat, and add the lemon slices; stir until softened, about 1 minute. Drain, and immediately plunge the slices into the ice-water bath. Drain.

3. Bring the sugar and 1 cup water to a boil in a medium skillet, swirling to dissolve the sugar. When the liquid is clear and bubbling, reduce heat to medium-low. Add the lemon slices, arranging them in one layer with tongs. Simmer (do not let boil) until the rinds are translucent, about 1 hour.

4. Transfer to a baking sheet lined with parchment. Let stand until ready to serve.

late summer fruits in rosé

SERVES 6

If you cannot find pluots, a plum-apricot hybrid, you can substitute more plums.

    3   plums
    3   pluots
    ½   bottle dry rosé (about 2 cups)
    ½   cup sugar
    ½   pint blackberries (about 1 cup)
    ½   pint raspberries (about 1⅓ cups)

1. Prepare an ice-water bath. Score an X on the bottom of each plum. Bring a medium saucepan of water to a simmer. Add the plums; cook until the skins begin to loosen at the X, about 1 minute (less if the fruit is very ripe). Transfer to the ice-water bath to cool. Remove the skins; discard. Halve each plum to remove the pit; cut each half into wedges. Repeat the process with the pluots.

2. Whisk the wine, sugar, and 1 cup cold water in a large bowl until the sugar has dissolved. Stir in the plums, pluots, and berries. Refrigerate 1 hour. Divide the mixture among 6 bowls, and serve.

vanilla-bean baked apples

MAKES 4

    4   thick-skinned, mildly sweet apples,
        such as Rome Beauty
    3   tablespoons packed dark-brown sugar
    2   tablespoons unsalted butter, softened
    2   tablespoons finely chopped toasted
        pecans, plus more for sprinkling
    ½   large vanilla bean, halved lengthwise,
        seeds scraped and reserved
    ⅛   teaspoon salt

1. Preheat the oven to 375°F. Using a cylindrical apple corer, core the apples three-quarters of the way down. Fit snugly in an ovenproof skillet or a loaf pan.

2. Stir together the sugar, butter, nuts, vanilla seeds, and salt in a small bowl. Divide the sugar mixture among the apples (about 2 teaspoons each). Sprinkle with nuts. Bake until the apples are soft, about 1 hour. Serve warm with pan syrup spooned on top.

orange-lime mousse

SERVES 4

Homemade citrus curd—a mixture of eggs, sugar, butter, and orange and lime juices—adds tangy flavor to this mousse.

    4   large egg yolks, plus 1 large whole egg
    ¾   cup plus 2 tablespoons sugar
    ¼   cup fresh orange juice
    ¼   cup fresh lime juice (2 to 3 limes)
    6   tablespoons unsalted butter
    1   cup heavy cream, chilled
    1   teaspoon ground cinnamon
    1   lime, halved lengthwise and thinly
        sliced into half-moons
    1   navel orange, halved lengthwise and
        thinly sliced into half-moons

1. Make the citrus curd. Prepare an ice-water bath; set aside. Cook the egg yolks, egg, ¾ cup sugar, and juices in a medium saucepan over medium heat, whisking constantly (be sure to reach the sides and bottom of the pan) until thickened, 5 to 7 minutes. Remove from heat.

2. Whisk in the butter, 1 tablespoon at a time. Set the pan in the ice-water bath; whisk until cool, about 5 minutes. Pass the curd through a sieve into a medium bowl. Press plastic wrap directly onto the surface to prevent a skin from forming. Refrigerate until set, 30 to 45 minutes. Whisk the cream and 2 tablespoons sugar until stiff peaks form; refrigerate.

3. Whisk one-third of the whipped cream into the curd. Gently fold in the remaining whipped cream. Divide among serving bowls; refrigerate until ready to serve. Dust with cinnamon; garnish with citrus.

individual fruit crisps with cinnamon-vanilla ice cream

SERVES 6

This recipe makes 3 peach and 3 cherry crisps. The ice cream is made by mixing cinnamon into store-bought vanilla ice cream and refreezing it. We call for fresh cherries, but frozen ones will work just as well; you'll need to adjust amounts in step 3: Reduce the brown sugar to ⅓ cup and increase the cornstarch to 2 tablespoons.

- 2 pints vanilla ice cream, softened slightly
- 1½ teaspoons ground cinnamon
- 3 large peaches (about 1¼ pounds)
- 2 tablespoons fresh lemon juice
- 1 cup packed dark-brown sugar
- ½ teaspoon ground ginger
- 2 tablespoons cornstarch
- 3 cups sour cherries (about 14 ounces), pitted
- ½ cup yellow cornmeal
- 1 cup all-purpose flour
- ½ teaspoon baking powder
  Pinch of salt
- ¼ cup granulated sugar
- 8 tablespoons (1 stick) unsalted butter, cut into pieces
- ½ cup sliced blanched almonds (1½ ounces), toasted

1. Make the cinnamon-vanilla ice cream: Cover the bottom of an 8-inch-square baking dish with one-third of the ice cream; smooth into an even layer. Sprinkle with ½ teaspoon cinnamon. Repeat to make 2 more ice-cream layers, sprinkling each with ½ teaspoon cinnamon. Cover with plastic wrap, and freeze until ready to use, at least 45 minutes.

2. Preheat the oven to 350°F. Bring a medium saucepan of water to a boil. Cut a small, shallow X in the bottom of each peach. Blanch the peaches until the skins begin to loosen, about 30 seconds; drain. Peel and pit the peaches, and then cut into ¼-inch-thick wedges. Transfer to a bowl; toss with 1 tablespoon lemon juice, ¼ cup brown sugar, the ginger, and 1 tablespoon cornstarch. Set aside.

3. Put the cherries in a bowl; toss with ½ cup brown sugar and the remaining tablespoon lemon juice and cornstarch.

4. Whisk together the cornmeal, flour, baking powder, salt, the remaining ¼ cup brown sugar, and the granulated sugar in a medium bowl. Blend in the butter with a pastry blender or two knives until it resembles coarse meal. Stir in the almonds. Squeeze to form a crumbly topping.

5. Fill 6 mini foil pie plates (each 4½ inches in diameter and 1¼ inches high) with fruit, 3 with cherry mixture and 3 with peach mixture. Transfer to rimmed baking sheets; divide the topping among the fruit pies. Bake until the juices are bubbling, about 30 minutes. Let the crisps cool slightly; serve warm with scoops of cinnamon-vanilla ice cream.

mango-pineapple buckle

SERVES 4

- 1 stick (½ cup) unsalted butter, room temperature, plus more for the baking dish
- 1 small or ½ medium pineapple (about 1¾ pounds), peeled, cored, and cut into ½-inch pieces
- 2 ripe mangoes, peeled and cut into ½-inch pieces
- 2 tablespoons dark-brown sugar
- ¾ cup plus 2 tablespoons all-purpose flour
- 1 teaspoon ground cinnamon
- ½ teaspoon salt
- ¼ teaspoon baking soda
- ½ cup granulated sugar
- 1 teaspoon pure vanilla extract
- 2 large eggs

1. Preheat the oven to 350°F. Butter a 2-quart baking dish. Toss the pineapple, mangoes, and brown sugar together in a bowl. In a separate bowl, whisk together the flour, cinnamon, salt, and baking soda.

2. Beat the butter and granulated sugar in a mixing bowl until fluffy, about 2 minutes. Beat in the vanilla. Add the eggs, one at a time, beating well after each. Add the flour mixture; beat until just combined. Measure out 1 cup fruit mixture; fold the rest into the batter.

3. Spread the batter into the prepared baking dish; sprinkle the reserved fruit over the top. Bake until golden on top and a cake tester inserted in the center comes out clean, 45 to 50 minutes. Serve warm.

mango-papaya salad with mint

MAKES 5 SERVINGS

1   *mango, cut into ½-inch cubes*
1   *papaya, cut into ½-inch cubes*
1   *tablespoon honey*
1   *tablespoon chopped fresh mint*

Stir together all the ingredients. Refrigerate, covered, until ready to serve, up to 2 days.

melon balls with moscato

SERVES 6

2   *honeydew melons (6 pounds each), halved and seeded*
2   *tablespoons small tarragon leaves*
1½ *cups chilled Moscato or other sweet sparkling wine*

With a melon baller, scoop out enough melon to measure 6 cups. Divide the melon among 6 dessert bowls. Sprinkle with tarragon, and pour ¼ cup Moscato over each serving. Serve immediately.

lemon, blackberry, and meringue parfait

SERVES 6

    Swiss Meringue (page 657)
1   *cup crème fraîche*
    Lemon Curd (page 656)
1   *cup ripe blackberries*
1   *cup chilled heavy cream, whipped*

1. Preheat the oven to 200° F, with racks in the upper and lower thirds. Line 2 large rimmed baking sheets with parchment paper. Fit a pastry bag with an Ateco #22 star tip; fill with meringue. Pipe 12 to 16 long swirly shapes onto one of the prepared sheets. Gently spread the remaining meringue ¾ inch thick onto the other.

2. Bake 20 minutes. Reduce the oven heat to 175° F; continue baking until the meringue is dry but still white, 35 minutes more, rotating the sheets halfway through. Transfer to a wire rack to cool completely. Set aside the swirls; crumble the meringue sheet.

3. Meanwhile, in a small bowl, combine the crème fraîche and 1 cup lemon curd; refrigerate.

4. To assemble the parfaits, layer the crème fraîche mixture, crumbled meringue, and blackberries in serving glasses. Spoon some of the remaining ½ cup lemon curd into each glass. Top with whipped cream; garnish with meringue swirls. Serve immediately.

apricot-cherry bake

SERVES 8 TO 10

    Unsalted butter, at room temperature, for the baking dish
3   *pounds small ripe apricots (20 to 24), sliced into sixths*
½   *pound cherries, pitted (about 1¼ cups)*
⅓   *cup all-purpose flour, plus more for the work surface*
1   *cup plus 4 teaspoons sugar*
½   *recipe Martha's Perfect Pâte Brisée (page 647)*

1. Preheat the oven to 400° F. Butter a 2-quart baking dish; set aside. In a large bowl, toss the fruit with the flour and 1 cup sugar. Place in the prepared baking dish.

2. On a lightly floured work surface, roll out the pâte brisée into a 12-inch round. Cut into 4 3-inch strips; then cut the strips crosswise into 3- or 4-inch pieces. Place over fruit mixture in a patchlike pattern. Refrigerate dough about 30 minutes.

3. Lightly brush the dough with water, and sprinkle with remaining 4 teaspoons sugar. Transfer to oven; bake until crust is golden brown and the juices are bubbling, 50 to 60 minutes. Transfer to a wire rack, and let cool before serving.

poached pears with ginger

SERVES 4

These pears may be refrigerated in their cooking liquid overnight.

- 1 cup dry white wine
- 2 tablespoons port or full-bodied red wine
- 3 cups water
- ¼ cup honey
- 1 piece (¾ inch) fresh ginger, peeled and cut crosswise into 6 slices
- 1 vanilla bean, split in half lengthwise and scraped
- 4 ripe, firm Bartlett or Comice pears

1. Bring all the ingredients except the pears to a simmer over medium-high heat in a large saucepan. Reduce heat to medium-low; cook 5 minutes.

2. Meanwhile, peel the pears and cut them in half lengthwise. Use a small spoon or melon baller to scoop out the core and seeds from each half, leaving the stems intact. Trim the fibrous strip from the center with a paring knife. Gently lower the pears into the pot. If they are not completely covered by liquid, lay a piece of parchment paper directly on the pears.

3. Cook until a paring knife slides easily into the pears, meeting slight resistance, 15 to 20 minutes. Remove from heat; let cool in liquid 30 minutes. Use a slotted spoon to transfer the pears to a large bowl; cover with parchment paper. Cook the liquid over medium heat until syrupy, about 15 minutes; discard the vanilla pod and ginger. Let cool. Serve 2 pear halves in each bowl; spoon the syrup over the pears.

FIT TO EAT RECIPE PER SERVING: 235 CALORIES, 1 G FAT, 0 MG CHOLESTEROL, 50 G CARBOHYDRATE, 10 MG SODIUM, 1 G PROTEIN, 5 G FIBER

red currant fool

SERVES 4 TO 6

- 4 tablespoons (¼ cup) unsalted butter
- 3½ cups fresh red currants (about 18 ounces), stems removed
- ¾ cup sugar
- 1½ cups heavy cream

1. Melt the butter in a large skillet set over medium heat, and stir in the currants and sugar. Cover, and reduce heat to low. Cook, stirring occasionally, until the sugar has dissolved and the currants have softened, about 5 minutes.

2. Remove the skillet from the heat, and lightly crush the fruit with the back of a wooden spoon. Don't mash to a puree; some texture should remain. Transfer the mixture to a bowl, and cool completely in the refrigerator before proceeding.

3. In a small bowl, whisk the cream until it holds soft peaks. Set aside ½ cup fruit mixture. Gently fold the whipped cream into the remaining fruit mixture, leaving it marbled. Serve immediately in individual bowls, garnished with a spoonful of the reserved fruit mixture.

southern-style individual peach cobblers

MAKES FOUR 6-INCH COBBLERS

To make one 10-inch cake, melt 2 teaspoons butter in the skillet before adding the batter, and bake for 35 minutes.

- 2 pounds firm, ripe peaches (about 4), pitted and cut into 8 wedges each
- 1 cup sugar
- 1 teaspoon ground cinnamon
- 1½ cups all-purpose flour
- 2 teaspoons baking powder
- ½ teaspoon salt
- 4 tablespoons unsalted butter, melted, plus 4 teaspoons
- ½ cup milk
- 1 large egg

1. Preheat the oven to 400°F. In a large bowl, toss the peaches with ¼ cup sugar and ½ teaspoon cinnamon; set aside. In a medium bowl, whisk together the flour, baking powder, salt, remaining ¾ cup sugar, and remaining ½ teaspoon cinnamon. In another bowl, whisk 4 tablespoons melted butter with the milk and egg. Whisk the butter mixture into the flour mixture.

2. Melt 1 teaspoon butter in a 6-inch ovenproof skillet over medium heat. Once the skillet is hot, remove from heat. Pour one-quarter of the batter into the skillet. Spread the batter evenly over the bottom. Spoon one-quarter of the peach mixture over the batter. Repeat with three more skillets. Transfer to the oven, and bake until the cobblers are set, 25 to 30 minutes. Remove from the oven; let cool slightly. Serve warm in the skillets.

warm nectarine turnovers

MAKES ABOUT 18

If at any point the dough gets too soft to work with or begins to shrink, refrigerate for 15 minutes before proceeding.

- 2 cups all-purpose flour, plus more for the work surface
- 1 teaspoon baking powder
- ½ teaspoon salt
- ½ cup (1 stick) chilled unsalted butter, cut into small pieces
- ½ cup ice water
- 1¾ pounds large, ripe nectarines (about 4)
- ¼ cup granulated sugar
- ¼ cup honey
- 2 to 3 cups vegetable oil, for frying
  Confectioners' sugar, for dusting

1. Sift the flour, baking powder, and salt into a large bowl. Using your fingertips, work the butter into the flour mixture until it resembles coarse meal. Pour in the ice water; toss lightly, gathering the dough into a ball. Dust the dough with a little flour, and flatten it into a disk. Seal the disk in plastic wrap, and refrigerate at least 1 hour or overnight.

2. Halve the nectarines lengthwise, and discard the pits. Leaving the skins on (to give the filling a pretty rose color), chop the fruit into ½-inch chunks.

3. In a large, heavy skillet, place the nectarines, granulated sugar, and honey, and fold together. Bring to a boil over high heat; reduce heat to medium-low. Simmer, stirring, until the mixture is thick enough to hold its shape in a spoon, about 25 minutes. Transfer the filling to a bowl; let cool.

4. On a lightly floured work surface, roll out the dough as thinly as possible (about 1⁄16 inch thick). With a 4-inch fluted cutter, cut the dough into as many rounds as possible. Gather the scraps into a ball, and roll out the dough as before. Again, cut out as many rounds as possible.

5. Place about 1 tablespoon filling on the lower third of each round. Moisten the edges of the rounds lightly with cold water. Fold the rounds in half over the filling, and press the edges together tightly. Seal the edges with fork tines dipped in flour.

6. Preheat the oven to the lowest setting. Line a shallow baking dish with paper towels, and place in the heated oven. In a large, heavy skillet, add enough oil to reach 1 inch up the sides, and place over medium-high heat. When the oil registers 350° F on a deep-fry thermometer, cook the turnovers, turning them occasionally with tongs or a slotted spoon, until they are crisp and golden, about 4 minutes total.

7. Transfer the cooked turnovers to the lined dish in the oven to drain. Keep warm until all the turnovers are cooked. Dust the warm turnovers with confectioners' sugar just before serving.

berry brown betty

SERVES 4

- 3 cups fresh raspberries (red and golden, if available)
- 1½ teaspoons fresh lemon juice
- 5 tablespoons unsalted butter, melted
- 1 tablespoon granulated sugar
- 2 cups fresh brioche bread crumbs (about 6 ounces)
- ⅓ cup packed light-brown sugar
- 2 tablespoons all-purpose flour
  Pinch of freshly grated nutmeg
  Sweetened whipped cream, for serving

1. Preheat the oven to 375° F. In a medium bowl, mix all but ¼ cup berries with the lemon juice, and set aside to macerate. Brush 4 6-ounce ramekins with 1 tablespoon butter; coat the inside of each with granulated sugar, and set aside.

2. In a small bowl, combine the bread crumbs with the remaining 4 tablespoons butter, and set aside. Sprinkle the brown sugar, flour, and nutmeg over the raspberries, and gently toss to combine. Divide one-third of the bread crumbs evenly among the ramekins. Top with half the berries, and then with another third of the bread crumbs. Repeat with the remaining berries and bread crumbs. Gently press down on the layers.

3. Bake until the crumbs are golden and the berry juices are bubbling, about 20 minutes. Remove from the oven, and let cool 5 minutes.

4. Invert the ramekins onto serving plates. Remove the ramekins, and top each dessert with whipped cream; garnish with reserved berries.

blackberry-peach trifle

SERVES 6 TO 8

  Unsalted butter, room temperature, for the baking dish
- 1 cup all-purpose flour, plus more for the baking dish
- 1 pound ripe yellow peaches (about 3)
- 1 pound ripe white peaches (about 3)
- 1 pound fresh blackberries (about 3 heaping cups)
- ¾ cup plus 2 tablespoons sugar
- 3 cups heavy cream
- 2 large eggs
- 1 teaspoon pure vanilla extract
- 1¼ teaspoons baking powder
- ¼ teaspoon salt

1. Preheat the oven to 350° F, with the rack in the center. Butter and flour a 9 × 13-inch baking dish; set aside. Prepare an ice-water bath in a large bowl; set aside. Fill a large saucepan two-thirds full with water; bring to a simmer over medium-high heat. Score the bottom of each peach. Gently put the peaches in the simmering water. Using a slotted spoon, remove the peaches from the water when the skin easily peels away from the flesh, 1 to 2 minutes. Plunge into the ice bath until cool enough to handle; peel immediately.

2. Cut each peach into 8 slices. Cut one-third of the slices in half crosswise (makes about 1½ cups), and set aside. Place the remaining slices in a medium covered bowl, and set aside. In another medium bowl, combine the blackberries and 2 tablespoons sugar. Set aside to macerate, stirring occasionally.

3. In a small bowl, whip 1 cup cream until stiff peaks form; set aside for the batter. Whip the remaining 2 cups cream, and refrigerate.

4. In the bowl of an electric mixer fitted with the paddle attachment, lightly beat the eggs. Add the remaining ¾ cup sugar, and beat until the mixture is pale and thick, about 3 minutes. Stir in the vanilla. Into a small bowl, sift together the flour, baking powder, and salt. Gradually stir the flour mixture into the egg mixture. Gently fold the reserved whipped cream into the batter in 3 additions. Pour the batter into the prepared dish; spread evenly.

5. Scatter the reserved peach pieces and one-third of the blackberries over the batter. Bake until the cake is golden and a cake tester inserted in the center comes out clean, about 35 minutes. Transfer to a wire rack, and let cool completely.

6. To assemble: Cut the cake into 6 pieces. Place 3 pieces in the bottom of a straight-sided glass serving bowl or compote. Spoon half the fruit (and berry juice) over the cake. Spoon half of the refrigerated whipped cream over the fruit. Repeat with the remaining cake, fruit, and cream. Drizzle the remaining berry juice over the trifle.

tropical fruit salad
SERVES 8

  1 *pineapple (about 5 pounds), peeled, cored, and cut crosswise into thin slices*

  1 *papaya (about 1 pound), peeled, halved lengthwise, seeded, and cut crosswise into thin slices*

  1 *star fruit, cut crosswise into thin slices*

  2 *tablespoons sugar*

  ½ *cup fresh lime juice, plus 3 tablespoons grated lime zest strips, for garnish (4 to 6 limes total)*

  Light rum (optional)

Arrange the pineapple on a large platter. Top with a layer each of papaya and star fruit. Sprinkle the fruit with sugar, lime juice, and rum, if desired. Garnish with lime zest.

macerated berry and crème fraîche parfait
SERVES 4

The rich, tangy crème fraîche and a bit of vinegar cut the sweetness of the berries. You can use vanilla ice cream in place of the crème fraîche.

  12 *ounces assorted berries, such as strawberries, blueberries, raspberries, and blackberries*

  2 *tablespoons superfine sugar*

  2 *tablespoons balsamic vinegar*

  1 *8-ounce container crème fraîche*

  Amaretti biscuits

1. Combine the berries in a medium bowl. Sprinkle with the sugar and vinegar. Let sit, stirring occasionally, until the berries soften and start to release juices, about 30 minutes.

2. Layer the berries with the crème fraîche in parfait glasses. Serve immediately or refrigerate up to 3 hours. Just before serving, sprinkle with crumbled amaretti biscuits.

caramelized pineapple with vanilla ice cream
SERVES 6

This dessert relies on the same browning and deglazing techniques used for savory dishes. Many fruits benefit from a quick sauté, and their natural sugars—brought to the surface as juices evaporate—aid in the caramelization process. If you prefer not to use rum, you can substitute more pineapple juice.

  ½ *cup dark rum*

  ½ *cup pineapple juice*

  4 *tablespoons unsalted butter*

  1 *ripe pineapple, peeled, sliced into ½-inch-thick rounds, cored*

  ½ *cup sugar*

  Vanilla ice cream, for serving

1. Combine the rum and pineapple juice in a glass measuring cup. Heat 2 tablespoons butter in a large skillet over medium-high heat until foaming. Add half of the pineapple slices, and cook until well browned on both sides, 5 to 8 minutes. Transfer to a baking pan.

2. Sprinkle the pan with ¼ cup sugar; cook until the sugar caramelizes to a golden brown, 1 to 2 minutes.

3. Turn the heat off or hold the skillet away from the heat, and carefully add ½ cup rum mixture.

4. Turn the heat on or return the pan to the heat, and stir with a wooden spoon, scraping loose any caramelized bits on the bottom of the skillet. Simmer the sauce until reduced and slightly thickened, about 3 minutes. Pour through a fine sieve into a bowl, and set aside. Wash the skillet, and repeat. Cut the pineapple slices, and serve over ice cream drizzled with warm sauce.

classic rhubarb fool with farm-fresh cream

SERVES 6 TO 8

1 *pound red rhubarb (about 9 stalks), leaves discarded, stalks cut into ½-inch pieces (about 4 cups)*

1 *cup sugar*

3 *cups heavy cream*

1. Put rhubarb, sugar, and 2 tablespoons water into a medium saucepan. Cover, and bring to a simmer over medium-high heat. Reduce heat to medium-low. Stir once; cook, uncovered, until rhubarb has completely softened, about 8 minutes. Cool slightly.

2. Transfer rhubarb mixture to a food processor, and purée until smooth. Transfer to a small bowl. Refrigerate rhubarb purée until cool, about 30 minutes.

3. Beat cream with an electric mixer or by hand until soft peaks form. Gently fold rhubarb purée into the whipped cream in 2 batches, leaving some streaks remaining. Spoon into glasses.

sour cherry charlottes

MAKES 6

3½ *cups frozen sour cherries (about 1 pound)*

1 *cup sugar*

3 *tablespoons cornstarch*

24 *slices (about 1 loaf) very thin white sandwich bread, crusts removed*

¾ *cup (1½ sticks) unsalted butter, melted*
Sour Cherry Compote (recipe follows)

1. Toss together cherries, sugar, and cornstarch in a medium bowl. Set aside; let cherries thaw slightly, about 35 minutes.

2. Preheat the oven to 350° F. Using a pastry brush, generously brush one side of each slice of bread with the butter. Reserve 6 slices; cut remaining slices in half to form 36 rectangles. Line sides and bottom of each cup of a jumbo (6-cup) muffin tin with 6 rectangles, overlapping bread and placing buttered side against tin.

3. Toss cherry mixture to combine. Spoon into bread-lined cups. Top each with a reserved bread square, buttered side down; press firmly onto cherries.

4. Bake charlottes until tops and sides are golden and crisp, 35 to 40 minutes. Transfer tin to a wire rack; let stand until charlottes have cooled slightly and are just firm, 15 to 20 minutes. Using an offset spatula or knife, loosen sides of charlottes from tin, and unmold; invert onto serving plates. Serve warm, with warm sour cherry compote on the side.

sour cherry compote

MAKES ABOUT 2 CUPS

3 *cups frozen sour cherries (a little less than 1 pound)*

1 *cup sugar*

2 *tablespoons balsamic vinegar*

Put cherries, sugar, and vinegar into a small saucepan. Cook over medium heat, stirring occasionally, until cherries have burst and mixture begins to thicken, about 10 minutes. Serve warm.

chilled cantaloupe soup
with tarragon syrup

SERVES 6

for the soup

1   large ripe cantaloupe (about 4 pounds),
    seeds and rind removed, cut into chunks,
    plus thin wedges for garnish

¼   cup sour cream

2   tablespoons honey, or to taste

4   teaspoons fresh lemon juice

    Pinch of coarse salt

for the syrup

¾   cup sugar

4   sprigs tarragon, plus more for garnish

1   teaspoon fresh lemon juice

1. Make the soup: Working in 2 batches, purée cantaloupe, sour cream, honey, lemon juice, and salt in
a blender until smooth. Press through a fine sieve
into a bowl. Refrigerate until cold, about 1 hour.

2. Make the syrup: Bring sugar and ¾ cup water to
a boil in a saucepan, stirring until sugar has dissolved. Boil until syrup has reduced to ⅔ cup, about
7 minutes. Remove from heat; add tarragon. Transfer to a bowl; refrigerate until cold, 1 hour.

3. Purée syrup, tarragon, and lemon juice in a
blender until smooth. Refrigerate until ready to use;
stir just before serving.

4. Divide soup among bowls. Drizzle with tarragon
syrup; garnish with cantaloupe wedges and tarragon sprigs.

FIT TO EAT RECIPE PER SERVING: 173 CALORIES, 2 G FAT,
7 MG CHOLESTEROL, 40 G CARBOHYDRATE, 44 MG SODIUM,
1 G PROTEIN, 1 G FIBER

peach-raspberry clafouti

SERVES 6 TO 8

¼   cup (½ stick) unsalted butter, melted,
    plus more for dish

1½ cups Lillet Blanc or white wine

1¼ cups sugar

1   vanilla bean, halved lengthwise,
    seeds scraped and reserved

2   pounds firm, ripe peaches (5 to 7),
    halved and pitted

6   ounces fresh raspberries

4   large eggs

¼   teaspoon salt

6   tablespoons all-purpose flour

1   cup whole milk

1   teaspoon pure vanilla extract

½   teaspoon finely grated orange zest

1. Butter a 12-inch round baking dish; set aside.
Bring Lillet, 1½ cups water, ¾ cup sugar, and the
vanilla bean and seeds to a boil in a large, wide
saucepan over high heat, stirring until sugar has
dissolved. Add peaches, cut side down, and cover
with a round of parchment paper, placing it directly
on top of peaches. Reduce heat to medium. Simmer
until peaches are very tender, about 15 minutes. Remove from heat; let stand 30 minutes.

2. Preheat the oven to 325° F. Using a slotted spoon,
transfer peaches, cut side up, to prepared dish; reserve ¼ cup poaching liquid (discard the vanilla
bean). Arrange raspberries among peaches.

3. Whisk eggs, remaining ½ cup sugar, and the salt
in a medium bowl. Gradually whisk in flour. Whisk
in milk, melted butter, vanilla extract, orange zest,
and reserved poaching liquid. Pour around fruit.

4. Bake until edges are puffed and golden, 40 to
45 minutes. Let cool on a wire rack 20 minutes before serving. The clafouti can be refrigerated, covered, up to 1 day.

sour cherry clafouti

SERVES 6

- 3 cups pitted fresh sour cherries (canned or frozen may be used)
- 3 tablespoons Cognac
  Unsalted butter, for pie plate
- ½ cup sugar
- ¾ cup whole milk
- ¼ cup heavy cream
- 3 large eggs
- 1 teaspoon pure vanilla extract
  Pinch of salt
- ⅔ cup all-purpose flour

1. Preheat the oven to 350° F. Stir together cherries and Cognac; set aside.

2. Butter a 9-inch glass pie plate or a fluted porcelain tart dish. Dust with 1 teaspoon sugar; set aside.

3. Blend milk, cream, eggs, remaining sugar, the vanilla, salt, and flour in a blender on high speed 1 minute, scraping down sides halfway through.

4. Pour ½ cup batter into prepared pie plate. Arrange the cherries evenly over batter; drizzle with the Cognac. Pour remaining batter over cherries.

5. Bake clafouti until top is puffed and golden brown and batter is set, 45 to 60 minutes. Serve warm.

nectarine shortcakes

MAKES 8

- ½ pound nectarines (about 4), cut into ½-inch pieces
- 1 tablespoon fresh lemon juice
- ¼ cup plus 2 teaspoons granulated sugar
- 2 cups all-purpose flour, plus more for work surface
- 1 tablespoon baking powder
- ½ teaspoon coarse salt
- 6 tablespoons cold unsalted butter, cut into small pieces
- 1 cup heavy cream, plus more for brushing
  Fine sanding sugar, for sprinkling

1. Preheat oven to 400° F. Combine nectarines, lemon juice, and 2 teaspoons granulated sugar. Let stand 15 minutes.

2. Whisk together the flour, baking powder, salt, and remaining ¼ cup granulated sugar in a large bowl. Using a pastry blender, cut in the butter until mixture forms small pieces. Stir in the cream. Fold in nectarine mixture.

3. Turn out dough onto a lightly floured surface. Pat into an 8½-inch round. Using a 2½-inch cutter, cut out 8 rounds, and transfer to a parchment-lined baking sheet. Brush with cream; sprinkle with sanding sugar. Bake until golden brown, 20 to 25 minutes. Let cool on a wire rack. Any remaining shortcakes can be stored in an airtight container up to 1 day.

roasted peaches with nougat

SERVES 4

Serve these easy-to-prepare peaches with scoops of ice cream, and drizzle with pan juices.

- 2 tablespoons unsalted butter
- 2 tablespoons packed light-brown sugar
- 4 ripe white peaches, halved lengthwise and pitted
- 3 tablespoons honey
- 4 to 6 ounces chewy almond nougat, coarsely chopped

1. Preheat the oven to 400°F, with rack in upper third. Melt butter in a large ovenproof skillet or sauté pan over medium heat until foaming. Reduce heat to low; add sugar, stirring until it has dissolved. Add peaches, cut side down, and cook until they start to caramelize, 3 to 4 minutes. Flip, and drizzle with honey.

2. Raise heat to medium-high. Bring pan juices to a boil. Remove from heat.

3. Divide nougat pieces among peaches, arranging them in the center of each half. Spoon pan juices over the tops.

4. Roast in oven until nougat melts and peaches turn golden brown and are tender when pierced with a fork, 10 to 12 minutes. Serve immediately.

honey-roasted salted figs

SERVES 6 TO 8

- ¼ cup extra-virgin olive oil, plus more for baking sheet
- ¼ cup honey
- 10 ounces dried Turkish figs
- 10 ounces dried Black Mission figs
- ½ teaspoon coarse salt
- 2 small bunches assorted grapes, such as red and champagne

1. Preheat the oven to 400°F. Lightly brush a rimmed baking sheet with oil. Whisk oil and honey in a large bowl. Add figs; toss to coat. Arrange in a single layer on prepared sheet. Sprinkle with salt.

2. Roast in the oven until fragrant and caramelized, 12 to 15 minutes. Immediately loosen figs from sheet with a metal spatula. Let figs cool slightly, loosening again after 5 minutes. Transfer to a platter; serve with grapes.

frozen desserts

apricot sherbet

SERVES 8

Serve this sherbet with Almond Meringue Wafers (recipe follows).

- 1½ pounds very ripe small apricots (about 12)
- 1 cup sugar
- ¼ cup light corn syrup
- ¼ cup fresh lemon juice (1 to 2 lemons)
- 1½ cups nonfat buttermilk
- 1 cup milk

1. Quarter the apricots, and remove the pits. Place the apricot quarters in a food processor, and puree until smooth, about 1 minute. Transfer to a medium bowl, and add the sugar, corn syrup, and lemon juice. Whisk to combine. Cover the bowl with plastic wrap, and macerate about 1 hour in the refrigerator.

2. Pass the apricot mixture through a fine sieve into a medium bowl; discard the solids. Whisk in the buttermilk and milk. Cover with plastic wrap, and refrigerate until chilled, about 3 hours.

3. Freeze the mixture in an ice-cream maker according to the manufacturer's instructions. Transfer to an airtight container; freeze up to 4 days.

almond meringue wafers

MAKES 2 DOZEN

- 4¼ ounces sliced almonds (about 1¼ cups)
- ¾ cup sugar
- ¼ cup all-purpose flour
- 3 large egg whites, at room temperature
- ¼ teaspoon salt
- 1 teaspoon pure vanilla extract

1. Preheat the oven to 350°F. Line 2 baking sheets with parchment paper; set aside.

2. In a food processor, pulse about 1 cup almonds with ½ cup sugar until the almonds are finely ground. Add the flour, and pulse until combined. Transfer to a bowl.

3. In the bowl of an electric mixer, whisk the egg whites, salt, vanilla, and remaining ¼ cup sugar until soft and shiny peaks form. Gently fold into the dry ingredients until just blended.

4. Drop the batter by the tablespoon, about 1½ inches apart, onto prepared baking sheets. Arrange 3 sliced almonds on top of each cookie.

5. Bake the cookies until the edges are lightly browned, about 14 minutes. Let the cookies cool slightly on baking sheets before transferring to wire racks. Let cool completely before serving. The cookies can be stored in an airtight container at room temperature up to 1 week.

rhubarb and strawberry ice cream

MAKES 1 QUART

Unlike many ice cream recipes, this one does not contain eggs.

- 1 pound trimmed rhubarb, cut into ½-inch pieces (about 3½ cups)
- ¾ cup plus 2 tablespoons sugar
- 2 tablespoons water
- 8 ounces ripe strawberries
- 1 cup heavy cream
- ½ cup milk
- 2 tablespoons kirsch

1. Place the rhubarb, ½ cup sugar, and the water in a saucepan over medium heat. Bring to a boil; reduce heat to medium-low; let simmer, stirring frequently, until rhubarb is very tender and beginning to fall apart, about 12 minutes. Remove from heat; transfer to a bowl; set aside.

2. Place the strawberries in the bowl of a food processor; puree. Strain through a fine sieve or chinois into a bowl; set aside.

3. Scald the cream and milk in a saucepan over medium heat. Do not let boil. Remove from heat, add the remaining 6 tablespoons sugar, and stir until the sugar is dissolved. Allow the mixture to cool to room temperature.

4. In a medium bowl, combine the cooked rhubarb, strawberry puree, cream mixture, and kirsch. Cover with plastic wrap, and chill at least 2 hours or overnight. Freeze in an ice-cream maker according to the manufacturer's instructions.

frozen lemon mousse
SERVES 8

This mousse can be made up to 3 days before serving. Ring molds may be purchased at specialty cookware stores. You can also use an 8-inch springform pan.

    8 to 10 lemons
    2 cups sugar
    8 large egg yolks, plus 2 whole eggs
    1 cup unsalted butter (2 sticks), cut
       into pieces
    1½ cups plus 2 tablespoons heavy cream,
       chilled
       Candied Lemon Zest (recipe follows)
    1 8-ounce container crème fraîche

1. Prepare an ice-water bath in a large bowl. Juice 1 lemon; reserve the juice. Juice the additional lemons to yield 1 cup. Make the lemon curd: Place 1 cup lemon juice and the sugar, egg yolks, whole eggs, and butter in saucepan; whisk to combine. Cook over medium heat, whisking constantly, until it begins to boil, about 10 minutes.

2. Strain the curd through a fine-mesh strainer into a bowl set in the ice bath. Stir periodically until cool; remove from the ice bath. Place plastic wrap directly on the surface of the curd; refrigerate at least 1 hour and up to 3 days.

3. Place 1½ cups chilled heavy cream in large mixing bowl; whisk until soft peaks form. Reserve ½ cup lemon curd for sauce; add the remaining lemon curd to the whipped cream. Fold gently until well combined.

4. Place 8 ring molds, 3 inches in diameter and 2¼ inches high, on a baking sheet lined with parchment. Divide the mousse among the molds, filling each with about ¾ cup. Place in the freezer on the sheet until firm, at least 4 hours.

5. Drain the candied lemon zest; reserve the syrup. Whisk ⅓ cup syrup, reserved ½ cup lemon curd, and juice of 1 lemon in a small bowl. Place the frozen mousse on plates; let warm 4 to 5 minutes before removing the molds. Meanwhile, whisk the crème fraîche and remaining 2 tablespoons cream in a medium bowl until soft peaks form. Remove the molds, spoon lemon sauce around the mousse; top with crème fraîche. Garnish with candied zest; serve.

candied lemon zest
GARNISHES 8 SERVINGS

Use the juice of these lemons for the mousse, and use some of the syrup for lemon sauce. Make this recipe a day before the mousse.

    4 lemons, well scrubbed
    2 cups sugar
    1 cup cool water

1. Remove the zest from the lemons with a vegetable peeler, keeping the pieces long. Remove the white pith using a paring knife. Cut into a fine julienne using a very sharp knife. Place the julienned zest in a small bowl; cover with boiling water. Let stand 30 minutes; drain.

2. Bring the sugar and the cool water to a boil in a small saucepan over medium-high heat. When the sugar is completely dissolved, add the julienned zest, reduce heat to medium low, and cook 10 minutes. Remove from heat, cover, and let stand overnight. Store the zest in the syrup in an airtight container in the refrigerator for up to 2 weeks.

malt ball bombe

MAKES 6 BALLS

Each ball, made in two half-moon metal molds, can easily serve two people.

> 3 *pints chocolate ice cream*
> 1¼ *cups vanilla ice cream*
> 3½ *tablespoons malted milk powder*
> 1 *pound semisweet chocolate, chopped*

1. Chill 12 metal half-moon molds (½-cup capacity) in the freezer. Beat the chocolate ice cream in the bowl of an electric mixer fitted with the paddle attachment until soft but still holding its shape, 1 to 2 minutes; work in batches if necessary. Wearing rubber gloves, remove the molds one at a time from the freezer; fill them with chocolate ice cream, pushing down on the ice cream to prevent air pockets. Make the top even and smooth; return the filled molds immediately to freezer. Let the chocolate ice cream become firm, but not too hard to spoon out, about 1 hour. Remove the molds from the freezer one at a time; use a 1-ounce ice cream scoop or round tablespoon to scoop out ice cream from the center, leaving ½-inch border around the edges. Return the molds immediately to freezer.

2. Soften the vanilla ice cream as above. Add the malted milk powder, and stir just to combine. Remove the molds from the freezer, and fill each center with malted vanilla ice cream, smoothing the top with an offset spatula. Return to the freezer, and chill until firm, 1 hour more.

3. Working with 2 molds at a time, remove from the freezer; dip in warm water for a few seconds. Use your finger to gently slide the ice cream out of the molds. Match two halves, flat sides together; wrap in plastic wrap. Gently press the halves together; return to freezer. Repeat with the remaining molds. Let the balls harden, about 1 hour.

4. Melt the chocolate in the top of a double boiler or a heatproof bowl over a pot of barely simmering water. When melted, remove from heat; stir the chocolate occasionally to let it cool, 8 to 10 minutes. Place a wire rack over a rimmed baking sheet; set aside. Remove 1 malt ball at a time from the freezer; dip in the melted chocolate. Using a spoon or small offset spatula, very quickly turn to coat the ball and lift it out of the chocolate. Place on a wire rack, and let excess chocolate drip off (chocolate will adhere to wire rack if allowed to sit too long). Gently transfer the malt ball bombe to a waxed-paper–lined tray; return to the freezer before the chocolate is completely set. Repeat the process with the remaining balls. If not serving immediately, wrap each ball in plastic wrap after it is completely frozen. Serve on plates with forks.

banana split bombe

SERVES 10 TO 12

Each of this bombe's layers must freeze solid before the next is added. Don't rush the freezing time, or the layers will run together.

> *Cooking spray*
> 2 *pints chocolate ice cream*
> 3 *medium bananas (about 1¼ pounds)*
> 2 *teaspoons milk*
> ½ *cup sugar*
> ½ *teaspoon pure vanilla extract*
> *Hot Fudge Sauce (recipe follows), room temperature*
> 1 *pint vanilla ice cream*
> 1 *cup walnuts, coarsely chopped*
> 2 *tablespoons cold water*

1. Place a circle of parchment in the bottom of an 8 × 3-inch springform pan. Lightly coat the bottom of the pan with cooking spray to adhere the parchment; set aside. Put in freezer for 30 minutes.

2. Beat 1½ pints chocolate ice cream in the bowl of an electric mixer fitted with the paddle attachment until soft but still holding its shape, 1 to 2 minutes. Using a small offset spatula or a spoon, spread the ice cream evenly on the bottom and up the sides of the springform pan. Work quickly, or the ice cream will not stay on the sides very long. If the ice cream starts to fall, return the ice cream–lined pan to the freezer for 10 minutes, and then finish lining. Transfer the ice cream–lined pan to the freezer until hardened, about 45 minutes.

3. In the bowl of a food processor combine 2 bananas, milk, ¼ cup sugar, and vanilla. Process 30 seconds or until smooth, and add the remaining banana. Pulse until there are only small pieces of banana, about the size of peas. Transfer the mixture to a bowl, and set aside.

4. Remove the pan from the freezer, and spread half, about ¾ cup, of the banana mixture into the bottom of the chocolate ice cream–lined pan. Return to the freezer until hardened, about 2 hours. Cover the remaining banana mixture with plastic wrap, and refrigerate. When hardened, remove the pan from the freezer; ladle 1 cup room-temperature hot fudge sauce over the banana layer. Return to the freezer until hardened, about 15 minutes. Set aside the remaining fudge sauce to serve with the finished bombe, or store in a plastic container in the refrigerator for up to 1 week.

5. Soften the vanilla ice cream as above. Remove the pan from the freezer, and add 1 cup softened vanilla ice cream, using a small offset spatula or spoon to spread it evenly. Return the pan to the freezer, and let the ice cream harden, about 1 hour. The remaining soft vanilla ice cream can be returned to its container and stored in the freezer; it will soften quickly when you need it again.

6. Preheat the oven to 350°F. Spread the walnuts evenly on a baking pan, and toast them in the oven, about 7 minutes, until fragrant and lightly golden. Remove from the oven, and let cool. In a medium nonstick sauté pan, combine the remaining ¼ cup sugar and the cold water. Stir over medium-high heat until the sugar is dissolved; stop stirring, and let boil. The sugar will begin to caramelize in the pan; you can pick up the pan and slightly swirl the sugar to allow for even caramelizing. Let the caramel turn to a dark golden brown, about 5 minutes, and immediately add the nuts to the pan. Turn off the heat. Using a wooden spoon, stir the nuts in the caramel to coat them evenly. Transfer the nuts directly onto a Silpat baking mat, and spread them into an even layer. Let cool; break into small pieces.

7. Remove the ice cream mold from the freezer, and sprinkle an even layer of nuts over the vanilla layer. Remove the banana mixture from the refrigerator, and spread the remaining ¾ cup over the nuts.

Quickly return the mold to the freezer, and let chill. When the banana layer has hardened, about 2 hours, resoften the remaining cup vanilla ice cream and spread it evenly with small offset spatula or spoon.

8. When the vanilla ice cream has hardened, soften the remaining cup chocolate ice cream; remove the mold from the freezer. Add the final layer of chocolate ice cream, spreading it all the way to the edges and smoothing the top. If the chocolate ice cream extends above the inside rim of the mold, run your finger around the top of the inside of the rim to give a clean edge. Cover with plastic wrap, and place in freezer to chill, about 4 hours, or overnight. When ready to serve, remove the mold from the freezer, and dip it in very hot water for a few seconds. Unlatch the ring, and gently pull away from the bombe. Using a parchment bottom allows the bombe to slide off the pan base. Transfer the bombe to a cutting board. Using a sharp knife, slice the bombe into wedges, and serve with remaining fudge sauce.

hot fudge sauce
MAKES ABOUT 2⅓ CUPS

- 10 ounces bittersweet chocolate, chopped
- 8 tablespoons (1 stick) unsalted butter
- ½ cup plus 2 tablespoons granulated sugar
- ½ cup water
  Pinch of salt
- ½ cup light corn syrup

1. In a medium saucepan over medium-high heat, combine the chocolate, butter, sugar, water, and salt. Stir continuously until melted and combined. Add the corn syrup, and bring the mixture to a boil.

2. Reduce heat, and simmer on low, stirring occasionally, until thickened, about 10 minutes. Remove from heat, and cool to room temperature.

sweet corn ice cream

MAKES 1½ QUARTS

4 ears fresh sweet corn, shucked
2 cups milk
2 cups heavy cream
¾ cup sugar
9 large egg yolks
   Blackberries, for garnish

1. Using a large knife, slice the kernels from the cobs; place in a large saucepan. Cut or break the cobs into thirds; add to the pot with the milk, cream, and ½ cup sugar. Bring the mixture to a boil, stirring; turn off heat. Remove the cobs, and discard. Using an immersion blender or a blender, puree mixture. Infuse for 1 hour by covering the pan with a tight-fitting lid.

2. Uncover, bring to a simmer, and turn off heat. In a small bowl, whisk the egg yolks and remaining ¼ cup sugar. Add 1 cup hot cream to the yolks, stirring constantly so they do not curdle. Add the yolk mixture to the saucepan, stirring. Cook over medium-low heat, stirring constantly, until thick enough to coat the spoon, about 10 minutes.

3. Pass the custard through a coarse sieve, then through a fine sieve or chinois, pressing down on the solids; discard the solids. Let the custard cool. Cover; chill at least 4 hours. Freeze in an ice-cream maker according to the manufacturer's directions. Serve garnished with blackberries.

key lime ice cream

MAKES ABOUT 1½ QUARTS

8 Key limes or 5 regular limes
2 cups milk
6 large egg yolks
¾ cup plus 2 tablespoons sugar
2 cups very cold heavy cream

1. Grate the lime zest; reserve. Squeeze the limes to yield ½ cup juice. Place the zest in a saucepan with the milk. Scald the mixture; cover. Remove from heat. Steep for 30 minutes.

2. Combine the egg yolks and sugar in a bowl; whisk until pale yellow and thick.

3. Fill a large bowl with ice and water; set aside. Return the milk to the stove, and bring to a simmer. Slowly pour the milk mixture into the egg yolk mixture, whisking constantly.

4. Return the mixture to the saucepan; cook over low heat, stirring constantly with a wooden spoon, until the mixture is thick enough to coat the back of a spoon, about 5 minutes.

5. Remove the pan from the heat; stir in the chilled cream to stop the cooking. Pour through a fine-mesh sieve into a bowl set in an ice-water bath; stir occasionally until cooled. Stir the reserved lime juice into the custard. Cover; chill at least 30 minutes or overnight.

6. Pour the custard into an ice-cream maker, following the manufacturer's instructions. Churn until the ice cream is just set, but not hard. Transfer to an airtight container; freeze at least 4 hours and up to 1 week.

watermelon ice

MAKES 5 CUPS

1 4-pound wedge watermelon
½ cup superfine sugar
¼ cup fresh lime juice
2 tablespoons Campari

1. Remove the rind from the watermelon, cut the flesh into 2-inch chunks, and remove the seeds. Arrange in a single layer on a parchment-lined baking sheet or in a resealable plastic bag; place in freezer until frozen, about 1½ hours. (Transfer to airtight freezer bags if not using immediately.)

2. Place the frozen chunks in a food processor; process until smooth. Add the sugar, lime juice, and Campari; process until fully incorporated, about 5 minutes, scraping down as necessary. Freeze in an airtight container, at least 2 hours, until firm. Stir if the juice starts to separate from ice.

cantaloupe granita
SERVES 4

Look for the ripest melon you can find; it should have a sweet fragrance and a firm exterior that yields slightly at the stem end. Granita can be stored in an airtight container in the freezer for up to 2 weeks. We like to serve the granita over wedges of cantaloupe for added melon flavor.

- 1 cantaloupe (about 3 pounds)
- ¼ cup sugar
- 2 tablespoons fresh lemon juice
- 2 tablespoons water

1. Using a sharp knife, cut the melon in half lengthwise. Remove the seeds with a spoon, and discard. Slice off and discard the skin and pale green flesh. Cut the melon into large chunks.

2. Place in the bowl of a food processor fitted with the metal blade, and puree until smooth. Transfer to a nonreactive stainless-steel bowl, and set aside.

3. Combine the sugar, lemon juice, and the water in a small saucepan. Cook over medium heat until the mixture has thickened slightly. Remove from heat; let cool completely.

4. Stir the sugar syrup into the melon puree; place in the freezer, uncovered, until the mixture is chunky, about 1½ hours, whisking every 20 minutes to keep it from becoming too solid. To serve, divide among 4 shallow bowls.

concord grape sorbet
SERVES 10 TO 12

This sorbet gets its intense purple hue from Concord grapes, which have a deep blue-black skin. The longer you process it in the ice-cream maker, the lighter and fluffier your final product will be. Sugar cones are ideal containers for serving the sorbet al fresco.

- 1½ pounds Concord grapes (1-quart container)
- ¼ cup water
- ⅔ cup Simple Syrup (page 660)
- 1½ tablespoons fresh lemon juice

1. Prepare an ice-water bath; set aside. Combine the grapes and the water in a medium saucepan. Cook over medium-high heat until the liquid begins to bubble and the grapes start releasing liquid, about 4 minutes. Reduce heat, and simmer until the juices are dark purple and the grapes begin to break apart, about 3 minutes.

2. Pass the mixture through a food mill and then through a fine sieve into a large bowl set in the ice bath; stir frequently until completely cool. Stir in the simple syrup and lemon juice.

3. Transfer the mixture to an ice-cream maker, and freeze according to manufacturer's instructions. Transfer to an airtight container, and store in the freezer until ready to serve, up to 2 weeks.

coffee ice cream affogato
SERVES 4

The word *affogato* means "drowned" in Italian; affogato al caffè is the name of a popular dessert in which hot espresso is poured over gelato just before it is eaten. The bitterness of the espresso acts as a pleasant counterpoint to the sweet creaminess of the ice cream. Liqueur intensifies the overall flavor. If you prefer, substitute very strong brewed coffee for the espresso.

- 1 pint best-quality coffee ice cream or gelato
- 4 ounces liqueur, such as sambuca, amaretto, or Frangelico (optional)
- 4 demitasse cups freshly brewed espresso

Just before serving, scoop the ice cream into 4 small bowls or large coffee cups. Divide the liqueur among 4 small glasses, if using; serve the liqueur and espresso alongside each bowl, and let each person pour them over the ice cream.

blackberry ice cream

MAKES ABOUT 2 QUARTS

Wild raspberries, huckleberries, or boysenberries can be used in place of blackberries, if you prefer. Drizzle leftover blackberry puree on top for added flavor.

- 4 cups fresh blackberries
- 1⅓ cups sugar
- ½ cup water
- 1 vanilla bean, split lengthwise and scraped
- 2 cups milk
- 6 large egg yolks
- 2 cups heavy cream

1. Combine 3 cups blackberries with 1 cup sugar and the water in a medium nonreactive saucepan. Bring to a boil over medium heat. Reduce heat to a simmer, and cook, stirring constantly, until the sugar dissolves and the berries begin to fall apart, about 4 minutes.

2. Remove from the heat. Pass the berry mixture through a fine sieve into a medium bowl, gently pressing down on the solids with a wooden spoon to release as much liquid as possible. Measure out ½ cup solids, and set aside; discard the remaining solids. Measure out 1¾ cups strained puree, and return it to the saucepan; reserve any remaining puree for serving. (Store reserved puree in an airtight container in the refrigerator until ready to use.)

3. Place the vanilla bean and scrapings in a saucepan, and add the milk. Bring to a gentle boil over medium heat, and remove from heat. Discard the vanilla pod.

4. Prepare an ice-water bath, and set aside. Combine the egg yolks and the remaining ⅓ cup sugar in the bowl of an electric mixer fitted with the whisk attachment. Beat on medium-high speed until the mixture is pale yellow, 3 to 5 minutes.

5. Using a measuring cup or ladle, slowly pour about ½ cup hot milk mixture into the egg yolk mixture, beating constantly on low speed until blended. Continue adding the milk mixture, about ½ cup at a time, beating until thoroughly combined after each addition.

6. Return the mixture to the saucepan. Cook over medium heat, stirring constantly with a wooden spoon, until it is thick enough to coat the back of the spoon and hold a line drawn across the back of the spoon with your finger, 6 to 8 minutes.

7. Remove from heat; add the reserved strained puree, and immediately stir in the cream to stop the cooking. Pour through a fine sieve into a medium bowl set in the ice bath; let cool completely, stirring occasionally. Cover the bowl with plastic wrap, and place in the refrigerator until thoroughly chilled, at least 30 minutes or overnight.

8. Freeze the mixture in an ice-cream maker according to the manufacturer's instructions; it should still be slightly soft. Stir in the reserved ½ cup blackberry solids and remaining 1 cup blackberries; spin a few times in the ice-cream maker to distribute evenly. Transfer the mixture to an airtight container, and place in the freezer until the ice cream is completely set, at least 4 hours and up to 1 week.

mango-lime granita

SERVES 4

Fresh mangoes are loaded with vitamins A and C. Whisking the granita as it freezes ensures that it reaches the proper consistency.

- 3 cups chopped ripe mango (about 3 mangoes)
- 1 cup water
  Juice of 2 limes (about ¼ cup)
- 2 tablespoons sugar

1. Place the chopped mango in the bowl of a food processor fitted with the metal blade, and process until smooth. Transfer to a medium bowl. Add the water, lime juice, and sugar, and stir to dissolve.

2. Pour the mixture into a 9 × 5-inch deep-sided metal pan, and place in the freezer until nearly set, about 3 hours, whisking the mixture every hour. Remove from the freezer, and scrape the surface with the tines of a fork until it is the texture of shaved ice. Return to the freezer until ready to serve. The granita can be stored in an airtight container in the freezer up to 2 weeks.

FIT TO EAT RECIPE PER SERVING: 108 CALORIES, 0 G FAT, 0 MG CHOLESTEROL, 28 G CARBOHYDRATE, 4 MG SODIUM, 1 G PROTEIN, 1 G FIBER

espresso granita
MAKES ABOUT ¾ QUART

You can substitute espresso in this recipe with 2 cups very strong brewed coffee, although the flavor will not be as intense.

- ¼ cup ground espresso
- 2 cups very hot water
- 1 cup Simple Syrup (page 660)

1. Place the espresso in a medium heatproof bowl, and pour the hot water over it. Let stand to extract as much flavor as possible without becoming bitter, about 30 minutes. The brew should be very strong; it will be diluted with the simple syrup.

2. Strain through a fine-mesh sieve into a deep-sided 9 × 12-inch metal baking pan, and discard the espresso grounds. Add the simple syrup, and stir until well combined. Place in the freezer, uncovered, until the mixture is nearly set, at least 4 hours, whisking it every hour.

3. Remove the mixture from the freezer, and scrape the surface with the tines of a fork until it is the texture of shaved ice. (If necessary, the mixture can be frozen overnight without whisking; remove it from freezer in the morning, and let sit at room temperature about 10 minutes to allow it to soften before scraping.) Serve.

frozen chocolate malted
MAKES TWO 1½-CUP SERVINGS

This dessert was inspired by the Frozen Hot Chocolate at Serendipity, a restaurant in New York City.

- 1¼ cups heavy cream
- ¼ cup milk
- 7 tablespoons sugar
- 6 tablespoons cocoa powder
- 1 tablespoon malted milk powder
- 3 cups ice cubes
  Chocolate shavings, for garnish (optional)

1. Whip ½ cup cream, and set aside.

2. Place the milk, remaining ¾ cup cream, sugar, cocoa, and malted milk powder in the jar of a blender, and blend until smooth and frothy.

3. With the motor running, add the ice cubes, a few at a time, until the mixture is thick and smooth. Pour the mixture into tall glasses, and top with the whipped cream and chocolate shavings, if desired.

cherry ice
SERVES 4

- ½ cup dry white wine
- ⅓ cup honey
- 2 tablespoons fresh lemon juice
- 2 cups pitted cherries, fresh or frozen, plus whole ones for garnish

1. In a medium bowl, whisk together the wine, honey, and lemon juice until combined. Set aside.

2. Place the cherries in a food processor; pulse until finely chopped. Transfer to the bowl with the liquid mixture; stir until combined. Pour into a shallow metal pan and place in the freezer. Stir with a fork every 10 minutes until the mixture is slushy and partially solidified, about 35 minutes. Spoon into serving cups; garnish with whole cherries.

chocolate gelato

MAKES 1½ QUARTS

Use the highest-quality chocolate you can find.

3 cups whole milk

1½ cups heavy cream

⅓ cup unsweetened cocoa powder

8 large egg yolks

⅓ cup sugar

6 ounces bittersweet chocolate, finely chopped

1. Prepare an ice-water bath, and set aside. In a large saucepan, bring the milk, cream, and cocoa to a simmer over medium-low heat. Combine the egg yolks and sugar in the bowl of an electric mixer fitted with the whisk attachment, and beat on medium speed until pale yellow and very thick, 3 to 5 minutes.

2. Add half the milk mixture to the yolk mixture, and whisk until blended. Stir the combined mixture back into the remaining milk mixture. Add the chocolate, and cook over low heat, stirring constantly, until the mixture is thick enough to coat the back of a spoon.

3. Pass the mixture through a very fine sieve into a large mixing bowl. Set the bowl in the ice bath, and chill completely. Freeze in an ice-cream maker according to the manufacturer's instructions until the gelato just holds its shape. Transfer to a metal loaf pan, cover with plastic wrap, and freeze until firm, at least 2 hours.

pear stracciatella ice cream

MAKES 2 QUARTS

In Italian gelato shops, stracciatella describes an ice cream that has chocolate mixed into it—as our recipe does.

4¼ cups sugar

1 tablespoon fresh lemon juice

1 vanilla bean, halved lengthwise

5 Anjou or Bartlett pears, peeled

3 large egg yolks

Pinch of salt

1 cup milk

1 cup heavy cream

1 tablespoon Poire William (pear brandy; optional)

¼ teaspoon pure vanilla extract

6 ounces bittersweet chocolate (preferably 70 percent cacao), melted and cooled

Chocolate Syrup (recipe follows)

1. Put 4 cups water, 4 cups sugar, and the lemon juice in a large saucepan. Scrape in the vanilla seeds, then add the bean. Bring the mixture to a boil.

2. Reduce the heat to medium. Add the pears to the pan. Cover the surface of liquid with a sheet of parchment paper. Cook the pears until very tender, 15 to 25 minutes (time will vary depending on the ripeness of the pears). Remove from heat. Let the pears cool completely in the poaching liquid.

ABOUT GELATO

Gelato means "frozen" in Italian, and, in a way, the translation is apt for a dessert whose flavors remain so true to their original sources. Gelato differs from what we think of as ice cream in a few ways, its delicate taste among them. Small bits of chocolate or nuts occasionally make an appearance, but more often the dessert is smooth and simple, its flavors derived from a careful infusion of natural flavors. Steeping the ingredients in warm milk for at least 30 minutes gives the dessert its purer, more intense taste, so pistachio tastes exactly like pistachios, mango like mangoes, and so on.

Gelato also has less butterfat than American ice creams; whereas ice cream is made from cream, gelato is traditionally made with egg yolks and milk.

(Another frozen dessert called gelato alla crema is made with egg yolks and cream, but this is not what is usually sold as simple gelato.) This, along with the increased amount of air pumped into the mixture during churning, makes for a much lighter, more velvety dessert than rich, dense American-style ice creams.

3. Transfer the pears to a cutting board. Discard all but ¼ cup poaching liquid. Halve and core the pears. Puree 3 pears in a food processor. Finely chop the remaining 2 pears.

4. Whisk the yolks, remaining ¼ cup sugar, and the salt in a medium bowl; set aside.

5. Heat the milk and cream in a medium saucepan over medium-high heat until the mixture is steaming and small bubbles form on the edges. Add to the yolk mixture; whisk until combined. Pour the mixture back into the pan; cook over low heat, stirring constantly with a wooden spoon, until thick enough to coat the spoon, about 5 minutes.

6. Pour the custard through a fine sieve into a large bowl set in an ice-water bath. Let cool, stirring occasionally.

7. Stir the pear puree, reserved poaching liquid, brandy (if desired), and vanilla extract into the custard. Freeze in an ice-cream maker according to the manufacturer's instructions.

8. When the mixture is frozen but still being churned, add the chopped pear. Pour in the melted chocolate in a slow, steady stream; mix until combined. Freeze in an airtight container up to 2 days. Serve with the chocolate syrup.

NOTE *The yolks in this dish are not fully cooked; it should not be prepared for pregnant women, babies, young children, the elderly, or anyone whose health is compromised.*

chocolate syrup
MAKES 2⅔ CUPS

- 1 *cup heavy cream*
- ½ *cup light corn syrup*
- 12 *ounces bittersweet chocolate (preferably 70 percent cacao), chopped*
- 2 *tablespoons Poire William (pear brandy; optional)*

1. Heat the cream and corn syrup in a medium saucepan over medium heat, stirring, until the mixture is combined. Add the chocolate; stir until smooth. Remove from heat.

2. Stir in the brandy, if desired. Let the sauce cool until thick but pourable. Just before serving, whisk until smooth. The syrup can be refrigerated, in an airtight container, up to 1 week. Reheat before serving.

rose water sherbet
MAKES 2½ CUPS

- ¼ *cup sugar*
- 2¼ *cups buttermilk*
- ½ *cup corn syrup*
- 1 *teaspoon rose water, plus more for garnish*
  Roasted pistachios, coarsely chopped
  Edible geranium petals (optional)

1. In a small saucepan over medium heat, dissolve the sugar in ¼ cup buttermilk. Pour into a bowl with the remaining 2 cups buttermilk. Stir in the corn syrup and rose water.

2. Freeze in an ice-cream maker according to the manufacturer's instructions. Transfer to a loaf pan; cover with plastic wrap, and freeze at least 1 hour and up to 1 week.

3. To serve, scoop the sherbet into bowls; garnish with a few drops of rose water, chopped pistachios, and flower petals.

coconut ice milk
MAKES 1½ QUARTS

Freshly shaved coconut makes a lovely garnish; you could also sprinkle some shredded packaged coconut over the top.

- 2 *cups unsweetened coconut milk*
- 2 *cups half-and-half*
- 1 *cup sugar*

In a large bowl, whisk together the ingredients. Freeze in an ice-cream maker according to the manufacturer's instructions. Transfer to airtight containers, and store in the freezer up to 10 days.

brownie ice cream bars

MAKES 1 DOZEN

1¾ sticks (14 tablespoons) unsalted butter

46 ounces semisweet chocolate, cut into 1-inch pieces

3 large eggs, lightly beaten

½ teaspoon salt

1 cup granulated sugar

½ cup packed light-brown sugar

1 teaspoon pure vanilla extract

¾ cup all-purpose flour

2 quarts vanilla ice cream

1. Preheat the oven to 350° F. Line a 9 × 13-inch baking dish with parchment paper; set aside. Melt 1½ sticks butter and 6 ounces chocolate in a heatproof bowl set over a pan of simmering water, stirring; set aside.

2. Whisk together the eggs, salt, sugars, and vanilla in a large bowl. Stir in the chocolate mixture; fold in the flour. Pour the batter into the lined baking dish. Bake until the top is shiny, about 20 minutes. Let cool in the dish on a wire rack. Cover; let stand 8 hours (or overnight).

3. Run a thin knife around the edges of the brownie; invert to unmold onto a cutting board. Remove the parchment. Trim ¼ inch from the edges of the brownie. Line the baking dish with a clean sheet of parchment paper, leaving a 3-inch overhang on the long sides. Return the brownie to the dish, top side up; set aside.

4. Mix half the ice cream in the bowl of an electric mixer fitted with the paddle attachment until smooth but not melted; spread over the brownie. Cover; freeze 1 hour.

5. Mix the remaining ice cream, and spread over the frozen layer of ice cream on the brownie. Cover; freeze 1 hour (or overnight).

6. Melt the remaining 40 ounces chocolate with the remaining 2 tablespoons butter. Let cool.

7. Transfer the brownie to a cutting board. Dip a knife in hot water; wipe dry. Trim ¼ inch from the edges. Cut the brownie into 12 bars, dipping the knife as needed. Transfer to a wire rack set over a baking sheet. Ladle the chocolate mixture over the bars. Freeze 30 minutes.

ultimate malted brownie sundae

SERVES 8

2 pints vanilla ice cream, softened

¾ cup (about 3 ounces) malted milk powder

½ cup malt balls, coarsely crushed, plus more for garnish

Malted Brownies (recipe follows)

Chocolate Sauce (recipe follows)

1. In the bowl of an electric mixer, combine the ice cream, malted milk powder, and crushed malt balls. Mix until blended, about 1 minute. Transfer the mixture to an airtight container, and freeze until firm, about 4 hours, or overnight.

2. Just before serving, cut the brownies into 24 rectangles, making 4 even columns and 6 even rows.

3. Assemble the sundaes: Divide half of the ice cream evenly among 8 serving dishes. Top each with a brownie, then with another ice cream layer. Garnish each with 2 more brownies. Drizzle with chocolate sauce; sprinkle with crushed malt balls.

malted brownies

MAKES ABOUT 2 DOZEN

1 cup (2 sticks) unsalted butter, cut into small pieces, plus more for the pan

1 cup all-purpose flour, plus more for the pan

10 ounces semisweet chocolate, coarsely chopped

1 cup (about 4½ ounces) malted milk powder

1 cup (about 4 ounces) malt balls, coarsely crushed

1½ cups packed light-brown sugar

3 large eggs

1 tablespoon pure vanilla extract

1. Preheat the oven to 350° F. Butter and lightly flour a 9 × 13-inch baking pan; set aside. Combine the chocolate and butter in a heatproof bowl set over simmering water; stir until melted and smooth. Set aside to cool slightly, about 5 minutes.

2. In a medium bowl, whisk together the flour, malted milk powder, and malt balls; set aside. In the bowl of an electric mixer fitted with the whisk attachment, beat the sugar and eggs until thickened and fluffy, about 2 minutes. Add the melted chocolate mixture and the vanilla; mix to combine, about 30 seconds more. Using a spatula, fold in the flour mixture until just combined.

3. Pour the batter into the prepared pan, spreading it evenly with a rubber spatula. Bake until a cake tester inserted in the center comes out with just a few crumbs on it, 30 to 35 minutes. Transfer the brownies to a wire rack to cool.

chocolate sauce
MAKES 2 CUPS

Extra sauce may be refrigerated in an airtight container for up to 2 weeks.

- 1 *can (14 ounces) sweetened condensed milk*
- 2 *ounces unsweetened chocolate, coarsely chopped*
- 2 *ounces semisweet chocolate, coarsely chopped*
- ¾ *cup heavy cream*

In a small saucepan, combine all the ingredients. Warm gently over medium heat, stirring constantly, until the chocolate is completely melted and the sauce is smooth. Allow the sauce to cool slightly before serving.

profiteroles with chocolate-macadamia semifreddo
MAKES ABOUT 20

Profiteroles, like éclairs, are made from pâte à choux, a delicate, airy pastry that is surprisingly easy to make.

- 4 *tablespoons unsalted butter*
- ½ *teaspoon sugar*
- ¼ *teaspoon salt*
- ½ *cup all-purpose flour*
- 2 *large eggs, plus 1 large egg white, if needed*
- *Chocolate-Macadamia Semifreddo (recipe follows)*
- *Simple Chocolate Sauce (recipe follows)*

1. Preheat the oven to 350° F. Line a baking sheet with parchment paper; set aside. Bring the butter, sugar, salt, and ½ cup water to a boil in a small saucepan over medium-high heat. Remove from heat; stir in the flour. Return to medium-high heat; stir with a wooden spoon until the batter pulls away from the sides of the pan, about 4 minutes.

2. Transfer the batter to the bowl of an electric mixer fitted with the paddle attachment. Mix on low speed until slightly cooled, about 2 minutes. With the mixer on medium speed, add the eggs one at a time, mixing well after each addition. Test the batter for doneness by dabbing it with your finger; as you pull away, a sticky thread should form. If not, add the egg white, 1 teaspoon at a time.

3. Fit a pastry bag with a ½-inch round tip, and fill with batter. Pipe 1½-inch-diameter rounds 2 inches apart on the lined sheet. Gently smooth the peaked tops with a moistened fingertip.

4. Bake until golden brown, 28 to 30 minutes. Let cool completely on a wire rack. If not using immediately, store at room temperature in an airtight container up to 3 days, or freeze up to 1 month.

5. To assemble the profiteroles, halve them horizontally, and fill with a 1½-ounce scoop (3 tablespoons) semifreddo. Top the profiteroles with chocolate sauce.

chocolate-macadamia semifreddo
MAKES 5 CUPS

⅔ cup salted macadamia nuts

4 ounces bittersweet chocolate, coarsely chopped

⅔ cup sugar

1⅓ cups heavy cream

3 large egg whites

¼ teaspoon pure vanilla extract

1. Preheat the oven to 350°F. Toast the nuts on a baking sheet until pale golden brown, about 10 minutes. Let cool completely.

2. Pulse the nuts and chocolate in a food processor until coarsely ground. Add ⅓ cup sugar; pulse until combined, about 7 times (do not overprocess; mixture should not form a paste). Set aside.

3. Beat the cream in the bowl of an electric mixer fitted with the whisk attachment until stiff peaks form. Transfer to a large bowl; cover with plastic wrap, and refrigerate. Meanwhile, beat the egg whites in the clean bowl of an electric mixer fitted with the whisk attachment until soft peaks form. Add the vanilla and remaining ⅓ cup sugar; beat until stiff peaks form.

4. Fold the egg whites into the whipped cream; gently fold in the nut mixture. Spoon into a glass baking dish; smooth with a rubber spatula. Press plastic wrap on the surface; freeze at least 4 hours, and up to 1 week.

NOTE: *Raw eggs should not be used in food prepared for pregnant women, babies, young children, the elderly, or anyone whose health is compromised.*

simple chocolate sauce
MAKES ABOUT 1 CUP

5 ounces bittersweet chocolate, melted

¼ cup light corn syrup

Whisk chocolate, corn syrup, and ¼ cup hot water in a small bowl until smooth. If not using the sauce immediately, refrigerate, covered, up to 3 days; bring to room temperature before using.

ice cream sandwiches
MAKES 1 DOZEN

2 pints coffee or dulce de leche ice cream

Molasses-Ginger Cookies (recipe follows) or Chocolate Cookies (recipe follows)

Using a ¼-cup-capacity ice cream scoop, place a ball of ice cream on an upside-down cookie. Top with a second cookie, right side up. Press the cookies together until the ice cream reaches the edges. Repeat with the remaining cookies. Freeze until firm, at least 30 minutes. To store, wrap in plastic.

molasses-ginger cookies
MAKES 2 DOZEN

1½ cups all-purpose flour

1 teaspoon baking soda

¼ teaspoon baking powder

2 teaspoons ground ginger

½ teaspoon ground cinnamon

¼ teaspoon ground cloves

Pinch of freshly ground white pepper

¼ teaspoon salt

½ cup (1 stick) unsalted butter, room temperature

¾ cup firmly packed light-brown sugar

¼ cup plus 1 tablespoon molasses

1 large egg, room temperature

½ cup granulated sugar, for rolling

1. Line 2 baking sheets with parchment paper. Into a medium bowl, sift together the flour, baking soda, baking powder, ginger, cinnamon, cloves, pepper, and salt.

2. In the bowl of an electric mixer fitted with the paddle attachment, beat the butter, brown sugar, and molasses until light and fluffy. Beat in the egg until smooth. Add the flour mixture; beat until combined. Wrap the dough in plastic, flattened into a disk. Chill until firm, about 1 hour or overnight.

3. Preheat the oven to 375°F. Make 1½-inch balls of dough; roll each in sugar. Place them 2 inches apart on the prepared baking sheets. Chill 20 minutes.

4. Bake the cookies, rotating baking sheets halfway through, until firm around the edges and slightly soft in the center, 12 to 14 minutes. Let cool on a wire rack. Store in an airtight container up to 3 days.

chocolate cookies
MAKES 2 DOZEN

- 1 cup plus 2 tablespoons all-purpose flour
- ⅔ cup unsweetened cocoa powder
- 1 teaspoon baking soda
- ¼ teaspoon baking powder
- ¼ teaspoon salt
- 1¼ cups sugar, plus more for coating
- 2 tablespoons corn syrup
- ¾ cup (1½ sticks) unsalted butter, room temperature
- 1 large egg, room temperature

1. Line 2 baking sheets with parchment paper; set aside. Into a medium bowl, sift the flour, cocoa, baking soda, baking powder, and salt; set aside.

2. In the bowl of an electric mixer fitted with the paddle attachment, beat the sugar, corn syrup, and butter until light and fluffy, about 2 minutes. Add the egg, and beat to combine. Slowly add the flour mixture; beat until combined.

3. Preheat the oven to 375°F. Pour enough sugar for coating the cookies into a small, shallow bowl. Make 1½-inch balls of dough, and roll each in sugar until completely coated. Place the balls of dough 2 inches apart on the prepared baking sheets. Refrigerate 20 minutes.

4. Bake the cookies, rotating the baking sheets halfway through, until firm around the edges but still slightly soft in the center, 12 to 14 minutes. Transfer to a wire rack to cool completely.

coconut-mango ice pops
MAKES 14

- 3 large mangoes, coarsely chopped
- 1 can (14 ounces) light coconut milk
- ¼ cup sugar
- ¼ cup plus 1 tablespoon fresh lime juice
- Pinch of salt

Puree the mango, coconut milk, sugar, lime juice, and salt in a food processor. Pour into 2½-ounce ice-pop molds. Freeze until firm, about 4 hours.

white peach and bay leaf sorbet
MAKES 4 CUPS; SERVES 8

- 1¼ pounds white peaches (about 3½ peaches), quartered and pitted
- 2 tablespoons fresh lemon juice
- 2 cups Herb Syrup with bay leaves (recipe follows)

1. Process peaches and 2 tablespoons water in a food processor until smooth, about 2 minutes. Transfer to a large bowl. Stir in lemon juice and syrup.

2. Pour the mixture through a fine sieve into another large bowl; discard the solids. Freeze in an ice-cream maker according to the manufacturer's instructions. Transfer the sorbet to an airtight container; freeze until firm, about 4 hours.

herb syrup
MAKES 2 CUPS

- 1¼ cups sugar
- 2 fresh bay leaves or 1 ounce fresh tarragon, fresh mint, fresh lemon verbena, or fresh lemongrass

Stir together the sugar and 1¼ cups water in a small saucepan. Bring to a boil over medium-high heat, stirring constantly, until the sugar has dissolved. Add the herbs; remove from heat. Let cool completely. Refrigerate in an airtight container at least 8 hours, or up to 1 day. Before using, pour through a fine sieve into a bowl; discard the herbs.

cherry sherbet in tuile bowls

MAKES 1 QUART; SERVES 6

This easy sherbet has the rich, creamy texture of ice cream; it's best eaten within a day or two of being made. An ice-cream maker is unnecessary, but if you prefer to use one, just follow the manufacturer's instructions.

 1 cup sugar
 ⅔ cup crème fraîche
1½ cups heavy cream
 ¼ cup whole milk
 ½ teaspoon salt
 1 pound sweet cherries (preferably Bing), pitted and halved
 2 tablespoons fresh lemon juice
    Tuile Bowls (recipe follows)

1. Prepare an ice-water bath; set aside. Stir together ⅔ cup sugar and ⅔ cup water in a small saucepan. Bring to a boil, stirring occasionally. Transfer the syrup immediately to a medium bowl. Place the bowl in the ice-water bath, being careful not to let the water reach the rim of the bowl. Let the syrup cool completely, stirring frequently.

2. Whisk together the crème fraîche, heavy cream, milk, salt, and syrup in a large bowl. Transfer to the freezer; let set, whisking mixture vigorously for 2 minutes every 30 minutes, until the sherbet is the consistency of whipped cream and the whisk leaves a trail, 3 to 4 hours.

3. Meanwhile, put the cherries, remaining ⅓ cup sugar, and lemon juice in a large skillet. Cook over medium-high heat, stirring occasionally, until the cherries begin to break down and the juice has thickened, about 10 minutes. Transfer to a medium bowl. Let the mixture stand at room temperature until it has cooled completely.

4. Gently fold the cherry mixture into the sherbet until just combined (the juices should leave streaks). Cover the surface of the sherbet with parchment paper and freeze in the bowl until set, 4 to 8 hours.

5. If making a day ahead, transfer the sherbet to an airtight container, and place a piece of parchment paper directly onto the surface of the sherbet. Cover tightly. Before serving, let stand at room temperature until slightly softened, about 5 minutes. Scoop the sherbet into tuile bowls, and serve.

tuile bowls

MAKES 6

The tuile batter can be made 1 day in advance. Refrigerate it in an airtight container until you're ready to bake.

 1 stick (8 tablespoons) unsalted butter, softened
 ⅔ cup packed light-brown sugar
 4 large egg whites, room temperature
 1 cup all-purpose flour
    Pinch of salt
 1 teaspoon pure vanilla extract

1. Preheat the oven to 350° F, with a rack in the middle. Put the butter and brown sugar in the bowl of an electric mixer fitted with the paddle attachment. Mix on medium speed until fluffy, 2 to 3 minutes. Mix in the egg whites, one at a time. Mix in the flour, salt, and vanilla.

2. Line a baking sheet with a Silpat baking mat or parchment paper. Spoon 2 tablespoons batter onto the baking mat. Using an offset spatula, spread the batter into a 7-inch circle, with the edges slightly thicker than the center. Repeat, making a second circle on the mat.

3. Bake, rotating the sheet halfway through, until the edges of the cookies turn golden, about 9 minutes. Using a small spatula, immediately transfer 1 cookie to a small bowl (about 5½ inches in diameter and 3 inches deep). Gently mold the warm cookie to the shape of the bowl, pressing the bottom down to flatten. Let stand in the bowl 30 seconds; remove. Repeat with the remaining cookie. If the cookies become too cool to shape, return them to oven for 20 seconds. Repeat, baking the remaining batter and forming it into bowls. If using just 1 baking sheet, let it cool before spreading the next batch of batter onto it.

frozen espresso cheesecake

MAKES ONE 10 × 5-INCH CAKE; SERVES 10

1½ cups finely ground chocolate wafer cookies (8 ounces; about 35 cookies)

4 tablespoons unsalted butter, melted

½ cup plus 2 tablespoons sugar

4 large egg yolks, room temperature

4½ teaspoons good-quality instant espresso powder (such as Medaglia d'Oro)

Pinch of salt

1½ pounds mascarpone cheese, room temperature

1½ teaspoons pure vanilla extract

12 ounces hard torrone (Italian nougat), cut into ¼-inch pieces

½ cup heavy cream, chilled

1. Stir together the cookie crumbs, melted butter, and 3 tablespoons sugar in a medium bowl; set aside.

2. Put the egg yolks, ¼ cup sugar, the espresso, and salt in the heatproof bowl of an electric mixer. Set the bowl over a pan of simmering water; whisk until thick, about 2 minutes. Transfer the bowl to an electric mixer fitted with the whisk attachment; beat on medium speed 2 minutes. Stir in the mascarpone and vanilla by hand until smooth. Stir in the torrone; set aside.

3. Beat the cream with the remaining 3 tablespoons sugar in a clean mixing bowl until soft peaks form. Fold the whipped cream with a rubber spatula into mascarpone mixture. Refrigerate.

4. Line a 10 × 5 × 3-inch loaf pan with plastic wrap and parchment paper, leaving an overhang on the sides. Pour one-third of the mascarpone mixture into the lined pan; even the layer with an offset spatula. Evenly top with half of the crumb mixture; press the crumbs gently. Repeat to make a second layer of mascarpone mixture and crumbs. Top with the remaining mascarpone mixture. Loosely fold over the parchment and plastic wrap. Freeze at least 3 hours, or overnight.

5. To serve, let the cake stand at room temperature 10 minutes. Set the loaf pan in a larger pan; pour cold water into the pan to reach three-quarters up the sides of the loaf pan. Let stand 10 seconds. Holding the parchment, lift out the cake. Invert onto a plate; peel off the plastic and parchment. Let stand 10 minutes more before serving.

lemon semifreddo cake

MAKES TWO 4 × 8-INCH CAKES

For perfectly smooth slices, cut the layered cake with a hot serrated knife. The cake can be wrapped well in plastic wrap and stored in the freezer for up to 3 weeks.

Vanilla Sheet Cake (recipe follows)

9 large egg yolks, room temperature

1 cup plus 1 tablespoon granulated sugar

5 tablespoons confectioners' sugar

½ cup dry white wine

½ cup plus 1 teaspoon fresh lemon juice

Finely grated zest of 2 lemons

½ cup cold water

5 large egg whites

2 cups heavy cream

3 tablespoons light rum

1. Line the bottoms and sides of two 5 × 9-inch loaf pans with parchment paper; set aside. Using a serrated knife, trim all edges of the vanilla sheet cake by 1 inch so it measures 8 × 12 inches. Slice the cake widthwise, through the top, into 3 vertical pieces, each 4 × 8 inches. Split each piece in half, slicing horizontally through the crumb. You should have six 4 × 8-inch layers. Set aside.

2. Make the semifreddo: In a large heatproof bowl set over a pan of simmering water, whisk together the egg yolks, ½ cup granulated sugar, and 2 tablespoons confectioners' sugar until smooth.

3. Add the wine, ½ cup lemon juice, and lemon zest; cook, stirring constantly with a wooden spoon, and scraping across the bottom to prevent the mixture from sticking to the bowl, until the mixture is thick enough to coat the back of the spoon, 6 to 7 minutes. Remove from heat, and transfer to a large bowl. Let cool to room temperature (or place the pan in an ice-water bath, stirring occasionally).

4. When the custard has cooled, combine the cold water, ½ cup granulated sugar, and remaining teaspoon lemon juice in a small saucepan. Bring the mixture to a simmer over medium heat. Cook until the mixture is slightly thickened and registers 240°F on a candy thermometer, about 8 minutes; wash down the sides of the pan with a pastry brush dipped in water to prevent crystals from forming. Remove from heat, and let the mixture cool 2 to 3 minutes.

5. Meanwhile, in the bowl of an electric mixer fitted with the whisk attachment, beat the egg whites and remaining tablespoon sugar on medium-high speed until stiff but not until dry peaks form. With the mixer still running, slowly drizzle the syrup mixture into the egg whites; continue beating until the meringue has cooled slightly and the bowl is cool to the touch.

6. In another large mixing bowl, whip the cream with the remaining 3 tablespoons confectioners' sugar until soft peaks form. Fold the whipped cream into the cooled lemon mixture; fold in the egg white mixture. The mixture should be very smooth. Place the rum in a small bowl.

7. Fit one of the cake layers in the bottom of each prepared loaf pan. Using a pastry brush, lightly moisten the top of the cake with rum. Using an offset spatula, evenly spread 1½ cups lemon filling over each. Repeat the process, making another layer of cake, rum, and filling; cover each with one of the remaining cake layers. Place in the freezer at least 5 hours or overnight.

8. Just before serving, remove the pans from the freezer, and turn the cakes out of the pans; remove the parchment paper. Slice into pieces.

vanilla sheet cake
MAKES ONE 9 × 13-INCH SHEET CAKE

Because there is no butter in the sponge cake, it will remain soft when frozen in the Lemon Semifreddo Cake.

  1 cup all-purpose flour
     Pinch of salt
 ½ teaspoon baking powder
  4 large eggs, separated
  1 cup sugar
  3 tablespoons boiling water
  1 vanilla bean, split and scraped

1. Preheat the oven to 350°F. Line a 9 × 13-inch baking pan with parchment paper, and set aside. Sift together the flour, salt, and baking powder in a medium bowl.

2. In the bowl of an electric mixer fitted with the whisk attachment, beat together the egg yolks and sugar on medium-low speed until light and fluffy. Beat in the water and vanilla bean scrapings. Add the dry ingredients in 3 batches, scraping down the sides of the bowl with a rubber spatula as needed, just until the flour mixture is incorporated after each addition.

3. In another mixing bowl, beat the egg whites until stiff but not until dry peaks form; whisk one-quarter of the egg whites into the batter to lighten. Fold in the remaining egg whites, and pour the batter into the prepared pan. Bake until the cake springs back when gently pressed in the center, 15 to 20 minutes. Transfer to a wire rack to cool completely.

plum-ginger granita

MAKES ABOUT 2 QUARTS

- 1 piece (about 2 inches) peeled fresh ginger
- 2 pounds ripe red plums, halved, pitted, and coarsely chopped, plus thin wedges for garnish (about 9 plums total)
- 1⅓ cups sugar
- ¼ teaspoon coarse salt
- 1 teaspoon pure vanilla extract

1. Pulse ginger in a food processor until finely chopped; transfer to a large saucepan. Add plums, sugar, salt, and 5 cups water. Bring to a boil over medium-high heat. Reduce heat to medium. Simmer, stirring occasionally, until sugar has dissolved and plums have broken down, about 15 minutes.

2. Pour plum mixture through a fine sieve into a 9 × 13-inch shallow nonreactive dish; discard solids. Stir in vanilla. Chill in freezer until edges are frozen, about 1½ hours.

3. Remove from freezer; scrape with fork tines, pulling from edges into center. Return to freezer. Repeat process every 30 minutes until mixture is the texture of shaved ice, about 4½ hours. Spoon into serving bowls; garnish with plums.

. . . .

QUICK ICE CREAM TOPPINGS

A hot day is the perfect excuse for an impromptu ice cream party. Stock an assortment of cones, and make chocolate and caramel sauce ahead of time. To make caramel sauce, simply add cream, vanilla, lemon juice, and butter to hot sugar caramel. For a rich chocolate fudge sauce, melt bittersweet chocolate in heavy cream. Both of these sauces can be kept in the refrigerator for up to 1 week. Quickly cooking some berries with a little sugar makes a delicious and simple fruit sauce for sundaes, too.

. . . .

papaya sorbet

MAKES ABOUT 4 CUPS; SERVES 4

Use red-fleshed papayas, such as Sunrise Solo or Maradol. Be sure to ask your grocer which ones will have flesh with a rosy hue since a papaya's skin and shape may not be a good indication of its interior color.

- ⅓ cup sugar
- 3 pounds fresh red papayas (about 1½ medium), peeled, halved, seeded, and chopped
- ½ cup fresh lime juice, plus thinly sliced rounds for garnish (3 to 4 limes total)
- 1 tablespoon honey

1. Bring sugar and 1 cup water to a boil in a medium saucepan. Reduce heat, and simmer, stirring occasionally, until sugar has dissolved and mixture is syrupy, about 4 minutes. Let cool completely.

2. Purée papayas, lime juice, and honey in a food processor. Transfer to a medium bowl. Stir in sugar syrup.

3. Freeze in an ice cream maker according to manufacturer's instructions. Transfer to an airtight container; freeze at least 2½ hours (up to 1 week). Serve garnished with lime slices.

FIT TO EAT RECIPE PER SERVING: 221 CALORIES, 0 G FAT, 0 MG CHOLESTEROL, 57 G CARBOHYDRATE, 11 MG SODIUM, 2 G PROTEIN, 6 G FIBER

custards
AND
puddings

....

pumpkin bread pudding

SERVES 6

If you prefer to omit the bourbon, simply double the amount of hot water.

Unsalted butter, room temperature, for the ramekins

6   tablespoons dark-brown sugar

1   cup raisins

⅓   cup bourbon (optional)

⅓   cup hot water

1   15-ounce can pumpkin puree

4   large eggs

1   cup granulated sugar

1½   cups milk

2   teaspoons pure vanilla extract

1   teaspoon ground cinnamon

1   teaspoon ground ginger

¼   teaspoon ground allspice

Pinch of salt

1   12-ounce day-old loaf brioche or challah bread, cut into ¾-inch cubes

Confectioners' sugar, for dusting

1. Preheat the oven to 350°F. Butter 6 10-ounce ramekins or custard cups, sprinkle each with 1 tablespoon brown sugar, and set aside on a baking sheet. Place the raisins in a small bowl, and cover with bourbon, if using, and the hot water; let soak until plump, about 20 minutes. Drain; set aside.

2. In a large bowl, whisk together the pumpkin, eggs, granulated sugar, milk, vanilla, spices, and salt. Toss in the bread cubes, and stir gently to evenly coat; let stand a few minutes. Fold in the raisins. Divide among the prepared dishes, pressing down slightly to make level.

3. Bake until the custard is set in the center and the top is golden, about 40 minutes. If the bread browns too quickly, cover it loosely with aluminum foil. Remove from the oven; let cool slightly. To serve, unmold onto plates; dust with confectioners' sugar.

chocolate-espresso mascarpone puddings

SERVES 6

6   large egg yolks

¾   cup sugar

⅓   cup unsweetened cocoa powder

12   ounces mascarpone cheese

1½   tablespoons instant espresso powder dissolved in 1 tablespoon boiling-hot water

¾   teaspoon pure vanilla extract

¼   teaspoon coarse salt

1   cup heavy cream

Candied orange peel, for garnish (optional)

1. Whisk the yolks and sugar in a large heatproof bowl until pale and creamy, about 1 minute. Set the bowl over a pan of simmering water; whisk until an instant-read thermometer registers 160°F and the mixture is thickened, about 3 minutes.

2. Remove from heat; whisk in the cocoa, cheese, espresso, vanilla, and salt. Refrigerate in an airtight container until cold, 30 minutes (or up to 2 days).

3. Beat the cream with an electric mixer until soft peaks form. Top each serving of pudding with whipped cream. Garnish with candied orange peel, if desired.

vanilla pudding with baked rhubarb

SERVES 4

1   cup sugar

¼   cup all-purpose flour

½   teaspoon salt

2   cups milk (not skim)

1½   vanilla beans, halved lengthwise

4   large egg yolks, lightly beaten

4   tablespoons unsalted butter, cut into small pieces

Baked Rhubarb (recipe follows)

1. Whisk together the sugar, flour, and salt in a medium bowl; set aside. Pour the milk into a medium saucepan; scrape in the vanilla seeds, and add the pods. Stir together. Cook over medium heat until tiny bubbles begin to form around the edges of the pan, about 7 minutes.

2. Gradually add the milk mixture to the flour mixture, whisking constantly. Transfer the milk-flour mixture to the saucepan; cook over low heat, whisking constantly, 5 minutes.

3. Put the egg yolks in a small bowl. Whisk in a small amount of the hot milk-flour mixture. Add the yolk mixture to the saucepan. Cook over medium heat, whisking constantly, until the mixture comes to a boil and thickens, 10 to 12 minutes.

4. Remove from heat; discard the pods. Add the butter; whisk until melted. Pass the pudding through a fine sieve into a medium bowl, pressing it with a rubber spatula. Cover the surface of the pudding with plastic wrap to prevent a skin from forming. Let stand at room temperature until slightly cooled, about 30 minutes.

5. Spoon the pudding into serving bowls; top with baked rhubarb. The pudding can be refrigerated, covered with plastic wrap, up to 1 day.

baked rhubarb
SERVES 4

Unsalted butter, softened, for the dish

1 pound rhubarb, leaves discarded and stalks cut diagonally into 1-inch pieces

¾ cup sugar

2 tablespoons light corn syrup

½ vanilla bean, halved lengthwise

1. Preheat the oven to 375° F. Butter an 8-inch-square baking dish; set aside. Put the rhubarb, sugar, and corn syrup in a medium bowl. Scrape in the vanilla seeds, and add the pod. Toss together.

2. Transfer to the buttered baking dish. Bake the rhubarb, tossing gently halfway through, until tender, about 35 minutes. Discard the pod. Let cool slightly in the dish on a wire rack. Toss gently before serving.

chocolate pudding
MAKES SIX 6-OUNCE SERVINGS

⅓ cup plus 1 tablespoon unsweetened cocoa powder

2 tablespoons cornstarch

⅛ teaspoon salt

1 cup sugar

4 large egg yolks

2½ cups milk

½ cup heavy cream

½ teaspoon pure vanilla extract

4 ounces semisweet chocolate, finely chopped

Whipped cream, for garnish (optional)

Chocolate shavings, for garnish (optional)

1. Into a medium bowl, sift together the cocoa, cornstarch, and salt. Stir in the sugar. Add the egg yolks to the bowl, and pour in ½ cup milk; whisk until well combined.

2. In a medium saucepan, heat the remaining 2 cups milk and the heavy cream over medium heat until the mixture just comes to a boil. Slowly whisk the milk mixture into the cocoa mixture.

3. Rinse out the saucepan but do not dry (to help prevent scorching). Return the custard mixture to the saucepan, and place over medium-low heat. Stir in the vanilla. Stirring constantly with a wooden spoon, cook until the custard has thickened slightly and is the consistency of mayonnaise, about 10 minutes (do not let it boil). Don't worry if lumps form.

4. Pour the custard through a fine sieve into a clean bowl, discarding any solids. Add the chopped chocolate in two batches, stirring until thoroughly melted and combined after each addition.

5. Divide the pudding among 6 serving dishes, cover with plastic wrap, and chill at least 4 hours or up to overnight before serving. Garnish with whipped cream and chocolate shavings, if desired.

lemon sponge pudding

SERVES 6

For individual servings, divide the pudding among six 6-ounce ramekins; reduce the cooking time to 25 minutes.

- 3 tablespoons unsalted butter, room temperature, plus more for the baking dish
- ⅔ cup granulated sugar
- ¼ teaspoon salt
- 3 large eggs, separated
- 3 tablespoons all-purpose flour
- 1 cup milk
- 6 tablespoons fresh lemon juice
- 2 tablespoons finely grated lemon zest
  Confectioners' sugar, for dusting

1. Preheat the oven to 325°F. Butter a shallow 9-inch round glass or ceramic baking dish; set aside. In a large bowl, stir together the butter, granulated sugar, and salt. Stir in the yolks. Add the flour, milk, and lemon juice and zest; mix until incorporated.

2. In a separate bowl, beat the egg whites until stiff but not dry peaks form. Gently fold the egg whites into the butter mixture.

3. Ladle the batter into the prepared dish. Set the dish in a roasting pan; pour boiling water around the dish to come halfway up the sides. Bake until just set and lightly golden, 30 to 35 minutes. Remove the ramekins from the roasting pan; let cool slightly. Dust with confectioners' sugar, and serve.

rice pudding with candied butternut squash

SERVES 10

- Unsalted butter, softened, for the ramekins
- 1 cup Arborio or other short-grain white rice
- 5 cups whole milk
- 1 cup heavy cream
- ½ cup sugar
- 4 large egg yolks, lightly beaten
- ½ teaspoon coarse salt
- ½ teaspoon finely grated lemon zest
- ¼ teaspoon ground nutmeg
- 4 cups boiling water
  Candied Butternut Squash (recipe follows)
- ½ cup walnut halves (about 2 ounces), toasted and coarsely chopped

1. Preheat the oven to 350°F. Lightly butter ten 5-ounce ramekins; set aside. Put the rice and milk in a medium saucepan over medium-high heat. Cook, stirring occasionally, until the milk is just about to simmer. Reduce heat to medium. Simmer gently, stirring occasionally, until the rice is tender, 15 to 20 minutes. Remove the pan from the heat.

2. Meanwhile, whisk the cream, sugar, egg yolks, salt, lemon zest, and nutmeg in a medium bowl. Pour the cream mixture into the rice mixture in a slow, steady stream, stirring constantly. Return the pan to medium-high heat, and bring to a boil, stirring occasionally. Remove from heat. Using a ladle, divide the rice mixture evenly among the buttered ramekins, stirring the mixture in the pan each time to ensure an even distribution of rice and liquid.

3. Transfer the ramekins to a large roasting pan or 2 baking dishes at least 2 inches deep. Slowly pour boiling water into the pan to come halfway up the sides of the ramekins. Carefully place in the oven. Cook, rotating the pan halfway through, until the puddings are almost set and the tops are golden in places, 50 to 60 minutes. Carefully transfer the ramekins to a wire rack. Let cool 10 minutes before serving. The pudding can be stored in the refrigerator up to 1 day. Serve warm, cold, or at room temperature. Spoon the candied squash and its syrup on top of each pudding, dividing evenly; sprinkle with toasted walnuts.

candied butternut squash
MAKES ABOUT 4 CUPS

- ¼ cup plus 2 tablespoons orange marmalade
- ⅓ cup sugar
- 1 tablespoon minced peeled fresh ginger
- ½ vanilla bean, split lengthwise
  Pinch of ground cloves
- 2 tablespoons fresh lemon juice
- 1 small butternut squash (about 1¾ pounds), peeled, seeded, and cut into ½-inch cubes (about 4 cups)

1. Put the marmalade, sugar, ginger, vanilla bean, cloves, and lemon juice in a large, wide pot. Stir in 2½ cups water. Bring to a boil over medium-high heat, stirring to dissolve the marmalade and sugar.

2. Add the squash, and stir to combine. Bring the mixture to a simmer. Reduce heat to medium-low, and partially cover the pot. Gently simmer, stirring occasionally, until the squash is tender when pierced with a fork, about 35 minutes. Uncover, and cook until the liquid is syrupy, 5 to 10 minutes. Remove the vanilla bean, and discard. Serve warm. The squash and syrup can be refrigerated in an airtight container up to 1 week. Before serving, reheat over medium-low heat. If the syrup seems too thick, add 1 to 2 tablespoons water.

crème brûlée
MAKES FOUR 6-OUNCE SERVINGS

To produce the delightful hard surface that crackles when tapped with a spoon, you will need to brown the sugared tops with a small kitchen blowtorch, available at most specialty stores.

- 2 cups heavy cream
- ½ vanilla bean, split and scraped
- ½ cup sugar, plus 6 tablespoons for sprinkling
- 5 large egg yolks

1. Preheat the oven to 325° F. Place 4 shallow oval 6-ounce ramekins in a large baking pan lined with a kitchen towel. Bring a large pot of water to a boil, and keep hot until ready to use.

2. Meanwhile, in a small saucepan, heat the cream, vanilla bean, and scrapings over medium heat until bubbles form around the edges and the mixture starts to steam, about 6 minutes. Turn off heat.

3. In a large bowl, whisk together ½ cup sugar and the egg yolks until combined. Whisking constantly, slowly add the hot cream mixture. Strain the mixture through a fine sieve into a clean bowl; skim off any surface foam with a spoon.

4. Pour the custard into the ramekins. Carefully pour the hot water into the baking pan until it reaches halfway up the sides of the ramekins. Bake until the custard is just set in the center when gently touched with your finger, about 35 minutes. Transfer the ramekins to a wire rack to cool. Cover with plastic wrap, and place in refrigerator to chill completely, 2 to 3 hours or overnight.

5. Transfer to the freezer 45 minutes before serving. Remove from the freezer, and sprinkle 1½ tablespoons sugar over the entire surface of each. Using a kitchen torch, pass the flame in a circular motion 1 to 2 inches above the surface until the sugar bubbles, turns amber, and forms a smooth surface. Serve immediately.

coffee crème brûlée

MAKES 5

Wide and shallow 9-ounce molds are perfect for crème brûlée because they provide ample surface area, ensuring a bit of crunchy topping in every bite. You'll need five of them for this recipe. Ten 4-ounce ramekins can be used instead; reduce the sugar topping for each custard to 1½ teaspoons, and add 10 minutes to the baking time, as the custards are deeper.

- 1 quart heavy cream
- 1½ cups dark Italian-roast coffee beans
- 10 large egg yolks
- ⅔ cup granulated sugar
- ¼ teaspoon salt
  Boiling water, for the roasting pan
- 5 tablespoons superfine sugar

1. Preheat the oven to 320°F. Bring the cream and coffee beans to a boil in a medium saucepan. Cover, and reduce heat to low; cook at a bare simmer 30 minutes. Pour the mixture through a fine sieve into a medium bowl (or use a slotted spoon to remove beans); discard the beans.

2. Put the yolks, granulated sugar, and salt in a large bowl; whisk until the sugar is dissolved and the mixture is pale and thick. Gradually add the cream in a slow, steady stream, whisking until combined. Pour through a cheesecloth-lined sieve into a large glass measuring cup or pitcher; skim any foam or bubbles from the surface.

3. Divide the custard among the molds, filling them almost to the top. Place the molds in a roasting pan; put the pan on an oven rack, and pour boiling water around the molds to reach halfway up the sides. Bake until the custards are set around the edges but still loose in the centers, about 30 minutes.

4. Let the molds cool in the pan 10 minutes; remove from the water bath. Cover each with plastic wrap, pressing it onto the surface; refrigerate at least 2 hours or up to 2 days.

5. If using a torch to caramelize the custards, just before serving use a fine sieve to sift 1 tablespoon superfine sugar over each; wipe the sugar from the edges. Hold the torch at a 90-degree angle, 3 to 4 inches from the surface of each custard, and use a steady sweeping motion to caramelize the tops until golden brown.

6. If you don't have a torch, freeze the custards 20 minutes before topping with sugar. Preheat the broiler, and place the molds on a rimmed baking sheet; surround with ice cubes. Broil, rotating the sheet once, until the tops are golden brown, 2 to 3 minutes. If the molds become warm, refrigerate the custards for a few minutes before serving.

classic bread pudding

SERVES 8

For individual bread puddings, divide the mixture among eight buttered 6-ounce ramekins; reduce the cooking time to 40 minutes.

- 2 tablespoons unsalted butter, softened, for baking dish
- 12 ounces brioche or challah, cut into 1-inch cubes
- 2 cups milk
- 3 cups heavy cream
- 4 large eggs plus 1 large egg yolk
- 1 cup sugar
- ½ teaspoon salt
- 1 tablespoon pure vanilla extract
- ½ teaspoon ground cinnamon
- ¼ teaspoon ground nutmeg
- ½ cup raisins
- 1 cup boiling water, plus more for the pan

1. Butter a 9 × 13-inch baking dish; set aside. Put the bread in a large bowl; set aside. Heat the milk and cream in a medium saucepan over medium-high heat until just about to simmer; remove from heat.

2. Whisk the eggs, yolk, sugar, salt, vanilla, cinnamon, and nutmeg in a medium bowl. Whisking constantly, pour the cream mixture in a slow, steady stream into the egg mixture. Pour over the bread; fold to combine. Let stand 30 minutes, tossing and pressing occasionally to submerge the bread.

3. Meanwhile, soak the raisins in 1 cup boiling water for 30 minutes.

4. Drain; stir the raisins into the bread mixture. Preheat the oven to 350°F. With a slotted spoon, transfer the bread to the buttered dish; pour the liquid in the bowl over the top. Using a spoon, turn the top layer of bread crust side up.

5. Set the dish in a roasting pan; transfer to the oven. Pour boiling water into the pan to reach about halfway up the sides of the dish. Bake until golden brown, about 50 minutes. Let the dish cool on a rack 10 to 20 minutes.

VARIATIONS

BANANA, COCONUT, RUM *Stir 3 tablespoons rum into the egg mixture. Heat 2 tablespoons each brown sugar and unsalted butter in a skillet until melted and caramelized. Add 2 sliced bananas; cook 1 to 2 minutes. Fold into the soaked bread along with ¾ cup flaked sweetened coconut.*

CHOCOLATE *Add 8 ounces coarsely chopped semisweet or bittersweet chocolate to the hot cream mixture; stir until melted and well combined. Whisk the chocolate mixture into the egg mixture.*

CRANBERRY, ORANGE, PECAN *Simmer ¾ cup dried cranberries in ¾ cup orange juice until plump, 3 to 5 minutes. Drain the cranberries; fold into the soaked bread along with 2 tablespoons grated orange zest and ¾ cup chopped toasted pecans.*

vanilla panna cotta with poached apricot halves
SERVES 8

1 envelope (1 scant tablespoon) unflavored gelatin
4 cups heavy cream
1 cup sugar
½ vanilla bean, split and scraped
16 Poached Apricot Halves (recipe follows)

1. Prepare an ice-water bath; set aside. In a large bowl, sprinkle gelatin over 3 tablespoons cold water; let stand 5 minutes to soften.

2. Combine the cream, sugar, and vanilla bean and scrapings in a medium saucepan over medium-high heat. Gently simmer until bubbles form

around the sides of the pan, about 5 minutes. Let cool slightly. Discard the vanilla pod.

3. Pour the hot cream mixture into the gelatin mixture, and whisk until combined. Set the bowl in the ice bath. Let cool completely, stirring frequently. Strain the mixture through a fine sieve into a medium bowl. Divide among 8 custard cups. Cover tightly with plastic wrap, and chill until set, at least 4 hours or overnight.

4. When ready to serve, top each portion with 2 poached apricot halves.

poached apricot halves
MAKES 24

Keep the apricots submerged in the poaching liquid, or they will turn brown. Mixed with seltzer water, the poaching liquid makes a refreshing apricot fizz.

1½ cups sugar
3 strips (about 2 inches long) fresh lemon peel, pith removed
2 thin slices fresh ginger
7 cardamom pods, cracked
1 vanilla bean, split lengthwise and scraped
12 small ripe apricots, halved and pitted (about 1½ pounds)

1. In a 4- to 5-quart pot over medium heat, combine 4 cups water with the sugar, lemon peel, ginger, cardamon, and vanilla scrapings. Bring the mixture to a boil. Cook until the sugar dissolves, and then reduce heat to low. Simmer, uncovered, until the liquid has thickened slightly, about 10 minutes.

2. Add the apricots to the pan. Rinse a double thickness of cheesecloth under cold water, and drape it over the apricots so all the fruit is covered by the cloth and submerged in the liquid.

3. Continue simmering until the apricots soften slightly, 2 to 4 minutes. Remove from heat, and let cool completely. Use immediately, or transfer the apricots and poaching liquid to a storage container. Make sure the apricots are completely submerged in the liquid. Refrigerate, covered, up to 4 days.

indian pudding

SERVES 6

- 4 tablespoons unsalted butter, plus more for the ramekins, room temperature
- 1½ cups Roasted Butternut Squash Puree (recipe follows)
- 6 large eggs
- ½ teaspoon ground ginger
- ½ teaspoon ground cinnamon
- ½ teaspoon ground nutmeg
- ½ teaspoon salt
- 4 cups milk
- ½ cup pure maple syrup
- ¼ cup unsulfured molasses
- ½ cup yellow cornmeal
- 1 pint vanilla ice cream

1. Preheat the oven to 325° F. Butter 6 12-ounce ramekins. Bring a pot of water to a boil for a hot-water bath. In a large mixing bowl, whisk together the squash puree, eggs, spices, and salt; set aside.

2. In a medium saucepan, bring the milk, syrup, molasses, and butter to a simmer. While whisking, slowly add the cornmeal. Cook, whisking, until the mixture thickens, 5 to 7 minutes.

3. While whisking, pour the hot milk mixture into the reserved squash mixture. Whisk until well combined. Divide the mixture equally among the prepared ramekins, and place in a roasting pan.

4. Transfer pan to the oven; pour boiling water into the pan to reach halfway up the sides of the ramekins. Bake until the pudding is firm to the touch, about 1 hour. Remove the ramekins from the pan, and serve warm with a scoop of ice cream.

roasted butternut squash puree

MAKES ABOUT 2¼ CUPS

- 3 pounds butternut squash, halved and seeded
- Canola oil, for baking sheet

1. Preheat the oven to 400° F. Place the squash halves, skin side up, on an oiled rimmed baking sheet. Bake until fork tender, about 1¼ hours. Remove from the oven. Turn over; let stand until cool enough to handle.

2. Scoop the flesh into a food processor, and discard the skin. Puree until smooth. Refrigerate the squash puree in an airtight container up to 4 days, or store in the freezer up to 1 month.

almond flan

SERVES 12

- ½ cup plus ⅔ cup sugar
- 2 tablespoons water
- 4 cups half-and-half
- 6 ounces blanched whole almonds (about ¾ cup), toasted and finely ground
- Pinch of salt
- 3 large whole eggs
- 6 large egg yolks
- 3 tablespoons amaretto

1. Preheat the oven to 325° F. In a small saucepan, bring ½ cup sugar and the water to a boil over medium-high heat. Without stirring, cook until the syrup is a rich amber color, about 8 minutes; brush down the sides of the pan with a wet pastry brush to prevent crystals from forming. Pour into an 8 × 2-inch round tart pan, swirling to coat the bottom evenly. Set aside.

2. In a medium saucepan over medium-high heat, bring the half-and-half and ground almonds just to a boil; remove from heat. Let steep, covered, 20 minutes. Strain through a fine sieve into a clean saucepan, pressing with a rubber spatula to extract the liquid; discard the solids.

3. Whisk the remaining ⅔ cup sugar and the salt into the mixture in the saucepan; bring to a simmer over medium-high heat. Whisk together the eggs and yolks in a medium bowl. Whisking constantly, gradually add the half-and-half mixture. Stir in the amaretto. Pour through a fine sieve into the prepared pan; place in a roasting pan.

4. Cover the flan with foil; poke several holes in the foil. Place the pan in the oven; fill it with boiling water to reach halfway up the sides of the flan. Bake until just set, 50 to 55 minutes. Transfer to a wire rack to cool completely. Cover with plastic wrap; chill overnight. Run a thin knife around the edge of the flan; invert onto a serving plate.

chocolate brownie spoon bread
SERVES 8

- ½ cup (1 stick) unsalted butter, plus more for the skillet
- 4 ounces semisweet chocolate, chopped
- ½ cup all-purpose flour
- ½ cup unsweetened cocoa powder
- ½ teaspoon baking powder
- Pinch of salt
- 4 large eggs, room temperature
- 1 teaspoon pure vanilla extract
- 1 cup sugar

1. Preheat the oven to 350°F. Butter an 8-inch seasoned cast-iron skillet; set aside. Place the chocolate and butter in a medium heatproof bowl. Set it over a pan of simmering water; stir until almost melted. Remove from heat; let cool, stirring. Set aside.

2. Into a medium bowl, sift together the flour, cocoa, baking powder, and salt. Sift again, and set aside. In the bowl of an electric mixer fitted with the paddle attachment, beat the eggs and vanilla until thick and pale, about 6 minutes. Beat in the sugar until fluffy. Stir in the chocolate mixture. Fold in the dry ingredients until just combined.

3. Pour the batter into the prepared skillet. Bake until the spoon bread is set but still soft in the center, about 40 minutes (cook less for a more molten center). Let cool 10 minutes; serve warm in the skillet.

poire william charlottes
MAKES 6

for the cake

- 8 tablespoons (1 stick) unsalted butter, softened, plus more for the baking pan
- 1¼ cups plus 2 tablespoons all-purpose flour, plus more for dusting
- 1 teaspoon baking powder
- ½ teaspoon salt
- 1¼ cups sugar
- 3 large eggs
- ⅓ cup milk
- ¾ cup Poire William (pear brandy)
- 1 cup peeled, diced pear
- ½ cup finely chopped toasted pistachios

for the filling

- 1 medium pear, peeled and chopped
- 2 tablespoons Poire William (pear brandy)
- ¾ cup plus 2 tablespoons milk
- 4 large egg yolks
- ½ cup sugar
- Pinch of salt
- 1 cup heavy cream
- 3¼ teaspoons unflavored gelatin

1. Make the cake: Preheat the oven to 325°F. Butter a 9 × 12-inch baking pan. Line the bottom with parchment paper. Butter the lining; then flour the pan, tapping out excess. Whisk together the flour, baking powder, and salt.

2. Put the butter and sugar in the bowl of an electric mixer fitted with the paddle attachment; cream on medium speed until pale and fluffy. Mix in the eggs, 1 at a time. Add the flour mixture in 3 additions, alternating with 2 additions of milk. On low speed, mix in ¼ cup brandy and the pear and nuts.

3. Pour the batter into the prepared pan; spread evenly. Bake until golden brown and springy to the touch, about 40 minutes. Let cool completely on a wire rack.

4. Invert the cake to unmold; peel off the parchment. Using a long serrated knife, trim off the sides of the cake. Cut the cake crosswise into quarters (each about 2½ inches wide). Split the quarters horizontally into 3 strips each (to make 12 strips total).

5. Cut each of 10 strips into 6 (1¼ × 2½-inch) rectangles (for a total of 60 strips). Using a 2-inch round cookie cutter, cut out 6 rounds from the remaining 2 strips.

6. Line 6 charlotte molds (4 inches in diameter and 2¼ inches high) or 10-ounce ramekins with overlapping strips, standing them vertically (about 10 strips per mold). Press 1 round onto the bottom of each mold. Using the remaining ½ cup brandy, brush the cake in the molds.

7. Make the filling: Puree the pear and brandy in a food processor; set aside. Prepare an ice-water bath; set aside. Heat the milk in a medium saucepan over medium heat until just about to simmer.

8. Whisk together the yolks, sugar, and salt. Pour half of the hot milk into the yolk mixture, whisking constantly. Add the yolk mixture to the remaining hot milk in the pan; whisk. Cook over medium heat, stirring with a wooden spoon, until the mixture is thick enough to coat the back of a spoon. Pour through a fine sieve into a bowl set in the ice-water bath. Let cool, stirring occasionally.

9. Beat the cream to soft peaks; set aside. Sprinkle the gelatin over ¼ cup water in a medium heatproof bowl. Let stand 1 minute to soften. Set the bowl over a pan of simmering water; stir until the gelatin is dissolved. Stir the gelatin mixture into the custard in the ice-water bath. Stir in the pear puree. Whisk until it thickens to a puddinglike consistency. Whisk in the whipped cream.

10. Divide the mixture among the molds (about ½ cup per mold). Cover with plastic wrap, pressing it directly on the surfaces; refrigerate until set, about 1 hour. Run a knife around the edges of the charlottes; invert onto plates. Serve cold.

tiramisù cups
MAKES TEN 6-OUNCE SERVINGS

This recipe will also make four 16-ounce servings; divide filling amounts accordingly.

- 6 ounces store-bought crisp ladyfingers
- 1 cup strong coffee
  Mascarpone Filling (recipe follows)
  Mocha Filling (recipe follows)
- ½ tablespoon ground espresso, for garnish

Set aside 5 ladyfingers; break the remainder into large pieces. To assemble, dip the pieces in the coffee; fit a layer into the bottom of each cup. Cover each with ¼ cup mascarpone filling. Top with another layer of ladyfingers dipped in coffee; cover with ¼ cup mocha filling. Garnish each with a dollop of mascarpone filling, half a reserved ladyfinger, and a sprinkling of espresso.

mascarpone filling
MAKES ABOUT 5 CUPS

- 1 large whole egg
- 3 large eggs, separated
- 1 cup sugar
- ½ teaspoon pure vanilla extract
- 16 ounces mascarpone, room temperature

1. In the heatproof bowl of an electric mixer, combine the egg, egg yolks, ½ cup sugar, and vanilla. Place over a pan of simmering water; whisk until the sugar is dissolved, about 3 minutes. Transfer the bowl to the mixer; using the whisk attachment, beat on medium-high speed until the mixture is cool, about 5 minutes. Add the mascarpone; beat on low speed to combine. Set aside.

2. Place the egg whites in another heatproof mixing bowl set over a pan of simmering water. Add the remaining ½ cup sugar; whisk until it is dissolved, about 2 minutes. Transfer the bowl to the mixer; using the whisk attachment, beat on medium speed until soft peaks form, about 5 minutes. Fold one-third of the egg whites into the mascarpone mixture; fold in the remaining whites. Refrigerate, covered, until ready to use, up to 1 day.

mocha filling

MAKES 2½ CUPS

¼ cup plus 2 tablespoons sugar
¼ cup cornstarch
  Pinch of coarse salt
1 ounce unsweetened chocolate, chopped
1 cup half-and-half
3 large egg yolks
1 large whole egg
1 cup hot strong coffee
1 tablespoon unsalted butter

1. Prepare an ice-water bath; set aside. In a large heatproof bowl set over a pan of simmering water, combine the sugar, cornstarch, and salt. Add the chocolate, half-and-half, egg yolks, and egg; whisk until the chocolate is melted, about 3 minutes. Slowly add the coffee, whisking constantly.

2. Cook, stirring with a wooden spoon, until the mixture is thick enough to coat the back of the spoon, 2 to 3 minutes. Remove from heat; stir in the butter. Place the bowl in the ice bath; stir occasionally until the mixture is cool. Store in an airtight container at room temperature up to 1 day.

zabaglione

SERVES 4

4 large egg yolks
¼ cup sugar
½ cup sweet Marsala wine
  Black Pepper Cookies, for serving (recipe follows)

1. Whisk the yolks and sugar in a medium glass bowl until creamy, about 5 minutes.

2. Set the bowl over a pan of barely simmering water. Add the Marsala; whisk until the mixture almost doubles in volume, about 15 minutes, scraping down the sides of the bowl as needed. Serve with black pepper cookies.

NOTE *The eggs in this dish are not fully cooked; it should not be prepared for pregnant women, babies, young children, the elderly, or anyone whose health is compromised.*

black pepper cookies

MAKES ABOUT 2½ DOZEN

¼ cup (½ stick) unsalted butter, softened
⅓ cup sugar
⅛ teaspoon pure vanilla extract
  Pinch of salt
2 large egg whites, room temperature
⅓ cup all-purpose flour
¼ teaspoon freshly ground pepper

1. Preheat the oven to 425°F with a rack in the center. Put the butter and sugar in the bowl of an electric mixer fitted with the paddle attachment; cream on medium speed until pale and fluffy. Mix in the vanilla and salt. Beat in the egg whites until incorporated. Combine the flour and pepper in a small bowl; add to the butter mixture in 3 batches, mixing until just combined.

2. Put the dough in a pastry bag fitted with a ½-inch round tip (such as Ateco #804). Pipe 3-inch strips, about ½ inch apart, on a parchment-lined baking sheet, keeping the tip close to the sheet for thin cookies. Bake until the edges are golden and the centers are set, about 7 minutes. Let cool on the sheet 5 minutes before transferring with a spatula to a wire rack to cool completely.

zuppa inglese

SERVES 6 TO 8

This recipe can be doubled or tripled.

8 ounces store-bought crisp ladyfingers (about 26 cookies)
½ cup Italian dessert wine, preferably vin santo
  Crema Pasticcera (recipe follows)
  Salsa di Cioccolato (recipe follows)

Arrange half the ladyfingers in the bottom of an 8-inch-square serving dish. Drizzle with half the wine. Spread 1½ cups pastry cream on top. Drizzle ½ cup chocolate sauce over the cream. Repeat, adding another layer each of ladyfingers, wine, pastry cream, and chocolate sauce. Refrigerate, covered, 1 to 4 hours.

crema pasticcera
MAKES 3 CUPS

2 cups whole milk
Finely grated zest of 1 lemon
1 large egg plus 2 large egg yolks
1 cup sugar
1 cup all-purpose flour
1 teaspoon pure vanilla extract

1. Stir together the milk and lemon zest in a small saucepan. Heat over medium-low heat, stirring, just until small bubbles appear at the edges. Remove the pan from the heat.

2. Put the egg and yolks and the sugar in the bowl of an electric mixer fitted with the whisk attachment. Beat on high speed until pale, 3 to 4 minutes. Reduce the speed to low. Add the flour and vanilla. Beat until just combined. Beat in the hot milk mixture. Raise the speed to high; beat 1 minute more. Transfer the pastry cream to the saucepan. Cook over medium heat, whisking constantly, until the mixture has thickened, 2 to 3 minutes.

3. Transfer the warm pastry cream to a bowl. Place a piece of plastic wrap directly on the surface. Refrigerate until chilled, about 2 hours, or up to 1 day.

salsa di cioccolato
MAKES 1 CUP

2½ ounces good-quality unsweetened chocolate, coarsely chopped
2½ tablespoons good-quality Dutch-process cocoa powder
½ cup sugar
½ cup heavy cream

1. Melt the chocolate with the cocoa powder in a heatproof bowl set over a pan of simmering water, stirring constantly, until mixture is thickened and becomes difficult to stir.

2. Remove from the heat; continue to stir, and add the sugar. Return the bowl to the pan of simmering water. Heat, stirring constantly, until the sugar has dissolved and the sauce is smooth. Add the cream; stir until smooth. Remove from heat. Let cool completely. The sauce can be refrigerated in an airtight container up to 1 day; before using, warm the sauce in a bowl set over a pan of simmering water until pourable.

chocolate soufflé
SERVES 6

With its chewy exterior and warm, puddinglike center, this dessert might be considered the more refined cousin of molten cake. With or without crème anglaise, it's a showstopper.

Unsalted butter, melted, for dish
½ cup sugar, plus more for dusting
5 ounces bittersweet chocolate, chopped
2 ounces semisweet chocolate, chopped
1⅓ cups milk
6 large egg yolks plus 8 large egg whites, room temperature
6 tablespoons all-purpose flour
2 tablespoons brandy (optional)
1 teaspoon pure vanilla extract
Salt
Pinch of cream of tartar (if not using a copper bowl)
Crème Anglaise (page 658)

1. Preheat the oven to 400°F, with a rack in the lower third. Do not open the oven door until ready to bake. Brush the outer lip of a 2-quart soufflé dish with melted butter. Tie a sheet of parchment around the dish with kitchen twine. Brush the inside of the dish and collar with melted butter. Dust with sugar; tap out excess. Chill the dish in the freezer 15 minutes.

2. Stir the chocolates in a large heatproof bowl set over a saucepan of simmering water until smooth. Scald the milk in a saucepan over medium heat; remove from heat. Using an electric mixer fitted with the whisk, beat 6 tablespoons sugar and the yolks on high speed until pale, about 4 minutes. On low speed, beat in the flour. Beat in half the hot milk, ladling it in a little at time.

MAKING A CHOCOLATE SOUFFLÉ

1. The parchment paper cuff should extend at least 3 inches above the rim; this will encourage rising during baking. Brushing the inside of the dish and collar with butter prevents the batter from sticking, which would inhibit rising; dusting with sugar adds texture, which helps the soufflé climb.

2. The milk is heated until scalding, or just beginning to bubble around the sides of the pan. When beating it into the flour-egg mixture, the scalded milk should be added a little at a time to prevent the yolks from scrambling; this is called tempering.

3. After combining the milk and chocolate mixtures, and adding the flavorings, the soufflé mixture can be refrigerated in an airtight container for up to 2 days. Rewarm in a heatproof bowl set over a pan of simmering water before proceeding.

4. Egg whites are best whipped when they are at room temperature, as they will attain more volume than when cold. Adding the sugar in two increments keeps the whites from deflating; salt (or cream of tartar) helps to stabilize the foam. The whites are ready when they hold stiff peaks, meaning they stand up when the whisk is lifted.

5. One-third of the beaten whites are folded into the chocolate mixture to lighten; then the rest is added in two batches, which prevents the whites from deflating. Fold them in gently, using a swooping motion.

6. The mixture is ready when the whites are fully incorporated. You should not see any more streaks of white, but be careful not to overmix, or the soufflé will not be as fluffy.

3. Whisk the mixture into the pan of hot milk; bring to a boil over medium-high heat, whisking. Reduce heat to low; simmer until thick, about 2 minutes. Pour into the chocolate. Stir in the brandy (if desired), the vanilla, and a pinch of salt.

4. Using a balloon whisk, beat the egg whites and a pinch of salt in a copper bowl until foamy. (Or beat with an electric mixer in a stainless-steel bowl with cream of tartar.) Add 1 tablespoon sugar; beat until the whites almost hold stiff peaks. Add the remaining tablespoon sugar, and beat until the peaks are stiff.

5. Spoon one-third of the egg whites onto the base. Fold them in: Cut through the center of the mixture with a large rubber spatula, then gently turn the spatula over. Rotate the bowl a quarter-turn; continue folding in the whites and turning the bowl until mostly combined. Fold the remaining whites into the base, one-third at a time.

6. Pour the mixture into the prepared dish. Place on a rimmed baking sheet. Bake 15 minutes. Reduce the temperature to 375° F; bake until set, 20 minutes. Remove the collar; serve immediately with crème anglaise, if desired.

sweet potato flan

MAKES ONE 1-INCH FLAN

We made this flan in a 4-cup savarin mold, but a 9 × 2-inch round cake pan or a 9-inch glass pie plate can be used as well.

  2 *sweet potatoes (1¼ pounds)*
1¾ *cups sugar*
 ¼ *cup water*
 ¼ *teaspoon ground allspice*
 ½ *teaspoon ground cinnamon*
 ¾ *teaspoon coarse salt*
  5 *large whole eggs*
  2 *large egg yolks*
  2 *teaspoons pure vanilla extract*
  2 *cups milk, scalded*

1. Preheat the oven to 450° F. Place the sweet potatoes on a baking sheet, and roast until very soft, about 1 hour. Allow to cool. Peel off the skin, and discard. Place the sweet potatoes in the bowl of a food processor, and puree until completely smooth. Measure 1½ cups puree, reserving any excess for another use. This step may be done 1 day ahead.

2. Reduce the oven to 325° F. Combine 1 cup sugar and the water in a small saucepan, and cook over medium heat, stirring occasionally, until the sugar dissolves. Brush down the sides of the pan with a pastry brush dipped in water to prevent crystallization. Increase heat to medium-high; boil, without stirring, until the syrup turns a deep amber, 5 to 6 minutes. Pour the caramel into a savarin mold or a 9 × 2-inch round cake pan. Holding the pan with pot holders, swirl to coat the bottom and halfway up the sides of the dish.

3. In a large bowl, combine the sweet potato puree, remaining ¾ cup sugar, allspice, cinnamon, salt, eggs, and egg yolks. Mix in the vanilla and scalded milk, and then pass the mixture through a fine sieve. Pour into the caramel-lined pan, and cover with foil. Set in a roasting pan, and pour boiling water into the roasting pan halfway up the sides of the flan dish.

4. Bake for 50 to 55 minutes, or until the center of the flan is nearly set: A thin-bladed knife inserted in the center should come out clean. Let cool to room temperature, and place in the refrigerator to chill overnight.

5. To unmold, run a sharp knife carefully around the flan, and cover with a serving plate; invert quickly. Remove the pan; serve.

chocolate mousse with banana puree and grated coconut

- 4 large ripe bananas (about 2 pounds)
- 1 cup champagne or sparkling wine
- 1 cup sugar
- 9 ounces semisweet chocolate, finely chopped
- 3 large eggs
- 2 cups heavy cream, cold
- ½ cup grated or shaved coconut, for garnish

1. Peel the bananas; cut into large pieces. Place in a saucepan with the champagne and ¼ cup sugar. Bring to a boil; reduce to a gentle simmer. Cook, partially covered, until very soft, 10 to 15 minutes. Transfer to the bowl of a food processor; blend until smooth. Set aside to cool. Chill until ready to serve, up to 6 hours ahead.

2. Place the chocolate in a heatproof bowl set over a pan of gently simmering water. Stir until melted; set aside.

3. Place the eggs and remaining ¾ cup sugar in another heatproof bowl; whisk until combined. Place over simmering water; whisk until warm. Remove the bowl from heat, and whisk until the mixture is pale and thick. Whisk in the melted chocolate.

4. Place the cream in a clean stainless-steel bowl, and whisk until stiff peaks form. Fold the cream into the chocolate mixture.

5. Place about 2 tablespoons banana puree in individual serving dishes; top with a dollop (about ½ cup) mousse. Refrigerate until ready to serve, up to 4 hours in advance. Garnish with coconut.

bread-and-butter pudding with strawberries

Allowing the bread to soak in the custard batter for a full hour is the secret to a good bread-and-butter pudding.

- 4 large eggs
- ¾ cup milk
- ¾ cup heavy cream
- 7 tablespoons sugar
- 2 tablespoons dark rum
- 8 slices white bread
- 4 tablespoons unsalted butter, very soft
- 1 pint fresh strawberries, hulled and cut in half

1. Whisk together the eggs, milk, heavy cream, 3 tablespoons sugar, and rum. Set aside.

2. Spread the top of each slice of bread with a generous amount of butter. Cut the slices in half diagonally. In a 9-inch round baking dish or cake pan, fan overlapping slices in 1 layer. It is also fine for the bread to overlap randomly. Pour the egg mixture over the bread, and let stand 1 hour.

3. Heat the oven to 400° F. Sprinkle the pudding with 2 tablespoons sugar. Bake until puffed golden brown and set, about 20 minutes.

4. Meanwhile, combine the strawberries with the remaining 2 tablespoons sugar. Let stand while the pudding bakes. Serve the strawberries with the baked pudding.

crème caramel

SERVES 4

- 1 teaspoon unflavored gelatin
- 1 cup sugar
- 2 large eggs, plus 1 large egg yolk
- 1 cup heavy cream
- ½ cup whole milk
- Pinch of salt

1. Stir the gelatin and 2 teaspoons water in a small bowl until dissolved.

2. Put ¾ cup sugar into a large skillet over medium-high heat. Cook, without stirring, until sugar at edges begins to melt and turn clear, about 3 minutes. Continue to cook, stirring constantly, until medium amber, 1½ to 2 minutes. Remove from heat. Stir in ½ cup plus 2 tablespoons water. If sugar begins to solidify, return pan to medium heat until melted. Set caramel aside to cool completely.

3. Prepare an ice-water bath; set aside. Whisk eggs and yolk in a medium bowl; set aside. Bring cream, milk, ¼ cup sugar, and the salt to a simmer in a medium saucepan over medium-high heat. Whisk half the hot cream mixture into the eggs. Pour cream-egg mixture back into saucepan. Add gelatin mixture; whisk until combined. Reduce heat to low. Cook, stirring constantly, just until mixture is thick enough to coat the back of a spoon, about 3½ minutes.

4. Pour custard into a bowl set in the ice-water bath. Let cool completely, stirring constantly, about 3 minutes. Transfer to a large, shallow bowl. Refrigerate until set, at least 30 minutes. Pour reserved caramel over custard. Divide among serving cups or bowls.

steamed ginger pudding with apricot jam

SERVES 4

- 6 tablespoons unsalted butter, softened, plus more for the bowl and parchment
- ½ cup plus 2 tablespoons all-purpose flour
- ½ teaspoon baking powder
- ¼ teaspoon ground ginger
- ¼ cup plus 2 tablespoons sugar
- 1 large egg
- ⅓ cup coarsely chopped candied ginger
- 1 tablespoon honey
- 1 tablespoon whole milk
- ¼ cup plus 1 tablespoon apricot jam

1. Butter a 5-cup heatproof pudding basin or mixing bowl. Cut a parchment circle to fit top of bowl; butter. Fill a large pot fitted with a steamer or pasta insert with enough water to come halfway up bowl (test this with an empty bowl); set aside.

2. Stir together flour, baking powder, and ground ginger in a small bowl. Put butter and sugar into the bowl of an electric mixer fitted with the paddle attachment; mix on medium speed until pale and fluffy. Mix in egg. Reduce speed to low. Add flour mixture in 3 batches. Add chopped ginger, honey, and milk; mix until just combined.

3. Spoon jam into bottom of prepared bowl. Pour batter on top; smooth with a spatula. Cover bowl with prepared parchment, buttered side down. Place a tea towel on top; secure with kitchen twine. Tie opposing corners of towel on top of bowl.

4. Bring water in prepared pot to a boil over medium-high heat. Carefully lower pudding bowl into steamer; cover pot. Reduce heat to medium-low. Steam 2 hours, checking occasionally to make sure water doesn't completely evaporate. Transfer to a wire rack; remove towel and parchment. Let cool 10 minutes. Run a small knife around edge of bowl; invert pudding onto a plate. Serve warm.

pies

AND

tarts

....

black-bottom pie

MAKES ONE 9-INCH PIE

for the crust

1¼   cups graham cracker crumbs

¼   cup (½ stick) unsalted butter, melted

3   tablespoons sugar
    Pinch of salt

for the filling

⅓   cup sugar

⅓   cup Dutch-process cocoa powder

2   tablespoons cornstarch

⅛   teaspoon salt

1½   cups whole milk

3   ounces bittersweet chocolate, finely chopped

2   tablespoons unsalted butter, cut into small pieces

½   teaspoon pure vanilla extract

for the topping

1½   teaspoons unflavored gelatin

¾   cup sugar

1   tablespoon cornstarch

⅛   teaspoon salt

1   cup whole milk

1   teaspoon pure vanilla extract

2   tablespoons light rum

4   large egg whites, room temperature

1. Make the crust: Stir together the graham cracker crumbs, butter, sugar, and salt in a bowl. Press into the bottom and up the sides of a 9-inch pie plate. Refrigerate until firm, about 30 minutes. Preheat the oven to 350°F. Bake until the crust is set and begins to turn golden brown, about 12 minutes. Let cool completely on a wire rack.

2. Make the filling: Sift together the sugar, cocoa powder, cornstarch, and salt into a medium saucepan. Gradually whisk in the milk. Cook over medium-high heat, stirring constantly, until almost boiling. Reduce heat to medium; add the chocolate. Cook, stirring constantly, until the chocolate has melted and the mixture is thick, about 2 minutes. Remove from heat; whisk in the butter and vanilla until smooth. Spread the chocolate mixture over the crust. Refrigerate until cold and firm, about 1 hour.

3. Make the topping: Prepare an ice-water bath; set aside. Sprinkle the gelatin over 2 tablespoons cold water in a small bowl. Let stand until soft, about 3 minutes. Whisk ¼ cup sugar, the cornstarch, and the salt in a medium saucepan. Gradually whisk in the milk. Cook over medium-high heat, stirring constantly, until the mixture is thick and boiling, about 5 minutes. Remove from heat; stir in the gelatin mixture, and let cool completely. Stir in the vanilla and rum. Briefly place the pan in the ice-water bath to thicken slightly, if needed. Do not let it set completely. Set aside.

4. In the bowl of an electric mixer fitted with the whisk attachment, beat egg whites on medium-low speed until soft peaks form. Reduce speed to low; continue beating while you make the syrup.

5. Bring the remaining ½ cup sugar and 3 tablespoons water to a boil in a saucepan, stirring to dissolve the sugar. Brush down the sides of the pan with a wet pastry brush to prevent crystals from forming. Cook, without stirring, until the syrup registers 240°F on a candy thermometer.

6. Raise the mixer speed to high, and beat the egg whites just until stiff peaks begin to form. Immediately pour the syrup into the egg whites in a slow, steady stream near the side of the bowl, avoiding the whisk (it might splatter). Beat until glossy and cooled, about 7 minutes.

7. Fold the meringue mixture into the reserved gelatin mixture in 3 batches until just combined. Mound the mixture into the chocolate-filled crust. Refrigerate the pie for 2½ hours or overnight before serving.

NOTE: *The egg whites in this pie are not fully cooked; it should not be prepared for pregnant women, babies, young children, the elderly, or anyone whose health is compromised.*

port-caramel chocolate tartlets

MAKES FORTY 2¼-INCH TARTLETS

Marcona almonds are grown in Spain and known for their buttery flavor. Fleur de sel is a French sea salt, but another good-quality coarse salt can be used in its place.

for the tart shells

- 2½ cups all-purpose flour, plus more for dusting
- ½ cup unsweetened cocoa powder
- ½ cup sugar
- ¾ teaspoon fleur de sel
- 1 stick (8 tablespoons) cold unsalted butter, cut into small pieces
- 3 large eggs, lightly beaten

for the filling

- 1 cup sugar
- ½ cup heavy cream
- 3 tablespoons ruby or tawny port
- 2 tablespoons cold unsalted butter, cut into small pieces
- 1 ounce bittersweet chocolate (preferably 70 percent cacao), chopped
- 1 cup salted Marcona almonds (or roasted salted blanched almonds), finely chopped

  Fleur de sel, for sprinkling

1. Make the tart shells: Process the flour, cocoa, sugar, and fleur de sel in a food processor until combined. Add the butter; pulse until the mixture resembles coarse meal. With the processor running, add the eggs; process just until the dough comes together (do not overmix).

2. Turn out the dough onto a clean work surface; pat together. Wrap in plastic wrap. Refrigerate until firm, about 30 minutes.

3. On a lightly floured work surface, roll out the dough to ⅛ inch thick. Using a 3-inch round cookie cutter, cut 10 rounds from the dough. Transfer the remaining dough to a flour-dusted baking sheet; refrigerate.

4. Fit the dough rounds into 10 round tartlet molds (each 2¼ inches in diameter). Trim the edges of the dough flush with the top edges of the molds. (Refrigerate the scraps.) Refrigerate the shells until cold, 30 minutes.

5. Preheat the oven to 350° F. Prick the bottoms of the shells all over with a fork. Bake until firm, about 12 minutes. Let cool completely in molds on a wire rack; unmold.

6. Working in batches of 10 and using the remaining dough (reroll scraps), repeat steps 3, 4, and 5 to make 40 shells total.

7. Make the caramel filling: Heat the sugar and ½ cup water in a small saucepan over medium-high heat, stirring occasionally, gently, until the sugar has dissolved. Continue to cook, without stirring, until the syrup comes to a boil, occasionally washing down the sides of the pan with a wet pastry brush to prevent crystals from forming. Let boil, swirling the pan occasionally, until the syrup is dark amber. Remove from heat.

8. Carefully stir in the cream and port (the caramel will steam and spatter). Add the butter and chocolate; stir until melted and mixture is smooth. Let cool until slightly thickened but still pourable, about 20 minutes.

9. Cover the bottoms of the tart shells with almonds (about 1 teaspoon per shell). Spoon caramel filling into the shells, filling each almost to the top. Sprinkle with almonds and fleur de sel. Refrigerate until ready to serve, up to 3 hours.

shoofly pie

1 disk Martha's Perfect Pâte Brisée (page 647)

1 cup all-purpose flour, plus more for the work surface

½ cup packed light-brown sugar

1 teaspoon ground cinnamon

½ teaspoon freshly grated nutmeg
   Salt

6 tablespoons cold unsalted butter, cut into ½-inch pieces

1 cup boiling water

½ cup unsulfured molasses

½ cup light corn syrup

1 teaspoon baking soda

1 large egg, lightly beaten

1. Roll out the dough on a lightly floured work surface to ⅛ inch thick. Fit the dough into a 9-inch pie plate. Trim the edges to leave a 1-inch overhang; fold the edges under, and crimp with your fingers. Freeze the pie shell 30 minutes or overnight.

2. Preheat the oven to 325°F. Whisk together the flour, brown sugar, cinnamon, nutmeg, and ¼ teaspoon salt in a medium bowl. Add the butter, and work the mixture through your fingers until it forms fine crumbs; set the crumb topping aside.

3. Stir together the boiling water, molasses, and corn syrup in a medium bowl. Whisk in the baking soda, egg, and a pinch of salt. Pour the molasses mixture into the prepared pie shell. Scatter the crumb topping over the filling. Place the pie on a rimmed baking sheet. Bake until the filling is set and the topping is deep golden brown, about 50 minutes. Let cool on a wire rack 30 minutes.

ginger-pear hand pies

2 large eggs

⅔ cup plus 2 tablespoons granulated sugar

2 teaspoons fresh lemon juice

¼ cup plus 3 tablespoons all-purpose flour, plus more for dusting

1½ teaspoons ground ginger

¼ teaspoon plus a pinch of salt

9 tablespoons (1⅛ sticks) unsalted butter

1 vanilla bean, halved lengthwise and seeds scraped

3 tablespoons finely grated peeled fresh ginger

2 firm-fleshed pears, such as Bosc, peeled and cut into ¼-inch dice
   Pie Pastry (recipe follows)
   Confectioners' sugar, for dusting

1. Whisk together the eggs and ⅔ cup plus 1 tablespoon granulated sugar in a medium bowl until thick and pale yellow. Whisk in the lemon juice, then whisk in the flour, ground ginger, and pinch of salt; set aside.

2. Put 8 tablespoons butter, the vanilla bean and seeds, and grated ginger in a small saucepan; cook over medium-high heat until the butter foams and browns, about 5 minutes. Pour the mixture through a fine sieve into a bowl; discard the solids. Whisking constantly, pour the butter mixture into the egg mixture; whisk until combined.

3. Melt the remaining tablespoon butter in a medium skillet over medium-high heat. Add the pears and remaining ¼ teaspoon salt and tablespoon sugar; cook, stirring, until the pears are soft, about 5 minutes. Let cool, about 10 minutes. Fold the pear mixture into the egg mixture; set aside.

4. Roll out the dough on a lightly floured surface to ⅛ inch thick. Using a paring knife or 5-inch cookie cutter, cut 8 rounds from the dough. Gently press the rounds into 8 cups of a 12-cup standard muffin tin, making pleats around the edges and gently pressing to seal. Fill each with 6 tablespoons pear mixture. Refrigerate 30 minutes.

5. Preheat the oven to 375° F. Bake the pies until the crusts and filling are golden brown, about 30 minutes. Let cool in tins on a wire rack, about 20 minutes. Unmold; let cool completely on rack. Just before serving, dust with confectioners' sugar.

pie pastry

MAKES ENOUGH FOR 8 HAND PIES

2½   cups all-purpose flour
  1   teaspoon sugar
  1   teaspoon salt
 12   tablespoons (1½ sticks) cold unsalted butter, cut into small pieces
  ¼   cup cold vegetable shortening
  1   tablespoon distilled white vinegar
  ¼   to ½ cup ice water

1. Pulse the flour, sugar, and salt in the bowl of a food processor. Add the butter and shortening; pulse until the mixture resembles coarse meal, 8 to 10 times.

2. With the processor running, pour in the vinegar, then ¼ cup ice water; process just until the dough comes together. (If the dough is still crumbly, add up to ¼ more ice water, 1 tablespoon at a time.)

3. Pat the dough into a disk, and wrap in plastic. Refrigerate the dough until cold, at least 1 hour and up to 1 day. The dough can also be frozen up to 1 month; thaw completely in the refrigerator.

cranberry tart with crème fraîche whipped cream

MAKES ONE 9-INCH TART

  4   cups fresh cranberries (about 1 pound)
1½   cups sugar
  1   whole cinnamon stick
  1   disk Pâte Sucrée (page 651)
      All-purpose flour, for dusting
  1   large egg white, lightly beaten
  1   cup heavy cream
  ½   cup crème fraîche

1. Bring ½ cup water and the berries, sugar, and cinnamon to a simmer in a medium saucepan over medium-high heat. Cook, stirring, until the berries pop, about 2 minutes. Drain in a sieve set over a bowl. Return the strained liquid and cinnamon stick to pan; reserve the berries in the bowl. Simmer the liquid over medium-low heat until thickened, about 15 minutes. Pour the syrup over berries; let cool. Discard the cinnamon.

2. Bring the pâte sucrée to room temperature. On a lightly floured surface, roll out the dough to ⅛ inch thick. Transfer to a 9-inch square or round tart pan with a removable bottom. Trim the edges, leaving a ½-inch overhang. Tuck the edges of the dough under to create a double thickness, and press firmly against the sides of the pan. Press the bottom of the dough firmly into the tart pan. Chill in the freezer 20 minutes.

3. Preheat the oven to 400° F. Line the tart shell with parchment or foil, and fill with pie weights or dried beans. Bake until golden brown, about 25 minutes. Transfer to a wire rack. Remove the pie weights and parchment. Let cool completely.

4. Reduce the oven temperature to 350° F. Brush the tart shell with the egg white. Fill with the cranberry mixture and syrup from the bowl. Bake until the syrup is only slightly runny and the berries begin to brown, 45 to 60 minutes (if the pastry edges brown too quickly, cover with a band of foil).

5. Meanwhile, beat the cream to soft peaks. Beat in the crème fraîche; refrigerate.

6. Let the tart cool on a rack until cool enough to remove from the tin. Serve warm, with crème fraîche whipped cream.

mini carrot-cardamom pies

MAKES EIGHT 4-INCH PIES

  6 whole green cardamom pods
  2 tablespoons unsalted butter
  ½ cup milk
  ½ cup heavy cream
  1 teaspoon finely grated peeled
     fresh ginger
 12 ounces carrots, peeled and cut
     into ¼-inch pieces (2½ to 3 cups)
  1 cup sugar
  ⅛ teaspoon coarse salt
  4 large eggs, lightly beaten
  ½ cup finely ground gingersnap cookies
  1 disk Martha's Perfect Pâte Brisée
     (page 647)
     Freshly whipped cream, for serving
     Ground cardamom, for dusting

1. Make the filling: Crush the cardamom pods with the flat side of a chef's knife just to split. Melt 1 tablespoon butter in a small saucepan over medium heat; add the crushed cardamom. Cook until fragrant, about 3 minutes. Add the milk, cream, and ginger; bring to a simmer. Reduce heat to medium-low; cook 15 minutes. Remove from heat; let steep 30 minutes.

2. Melt the remaining tablespoon butter in a large sauté pan over medium heat. Add the carrots; cook, stirring occasionally, 2 minutes. Stir in the sugar and salt. Cover the pan; cook until the carrots are tender, about 8 minutes. Pour the steeped milk through a sieve into the pan with the carrots; discard the solids. Remove from heat; let cool slightly, about 5 minutes. Process the carrot mixture in a food processor until completely smooth; transfer to a bowl.

3. Temper the beaten eggs by whisking in up to ¾ cup carrot mixture, ¼ cup at a time, until the eggs are warm to the touch. Pour the warmed egg mixture into the remaining carrot mixture; whisk until thoroughly combined. Let cool.

4. Make the pies: Preheat the oven to 375° F. Lightly sprinkle the ground gingersnaps on a work surface to form a large circle about 18 inches in diameter. On the crumbs, roll out the pâte brisée to ⅛ inch thick, turning occasionally to coat both sides.

5. Cut out 8 5-inch rounds from the dough. Press the rounds into 8 4-inch pie plates; trim excess. With a fork, crimp the edges, and then prick the bottom of the dough all over. Refrigerate 30 minutes.

6. Line each pie shell with parchment paper or foil, and fill with pie weights or dried beans. Bake until golden brown, about 30 minutes. Transfer to a wire rack. Remove the pie weights and parchment. Let the shells cool completely.

7. Divide the filling among the shells. Bake until a cake tester comes out clean, 30 to 35 minutes. Serve the pies warm with whipped cream dusted with ground cardamom.

pear-fig-walnut pie

MAKES ONE 9-INCH PIE

  ¾ cup Madeira wine
  5 ounces soft, dried black Mission figs
     (scant ⅔ cup), stemmed and quartered
  3 whole star anise
     Martha's Perfect Pâte Brisée (page 647),
     almost room temperature
     All-purpose flour, for dusting
  3 pounds ripe Anjou pears, peeled, cored,
     and cut into ¼-inch-thick wedges
  3 ounces walnuts, broken into small pieces
     (about ¾ cup), toasted and cooled
     Juice of 1 lemon
  ½ cup granulated sugar, plus more for
     sprinkling (or use sanding sugar)
  ¼ teaspoon salt
  3 tablespoons cornstarch
  2 tablespoons unsalted butter, cut into
     small pieces
  1 large egg yolk
  1 tablespoon heavy cream

1. Preheat the oven to 400° F, with a rack in the lower third. Bring the wine, figs, and star anise to a boil in a small saucepan over high heat. Reduce heat to medium-low; simmer until the figs are softened, 10 to 12 minutes. Use a slotted spoon to transfer the figs to a large bowl. Cook the mixture in the pan over medium-high heat until reduced to a syrup, about 3 minutes; discard the star anise. Pour the syrup over the figs.

2. Meanwhile, roll out 1 dough disk on floured parchment to make a 13-inch circle; start with pressure in the center and ease up just before reaching the edges. Drape the dough over the rolling pin; center over a 9-inch glass pie plate, and unroll. Gently push into the plate. Trim to leave a ¼-inch overhang; refrigerate. Roll out the second disk. Cut out a vent with a cookie cutter, and refrigerate the cutout.

3. Add the pears, nuts, lemon juice, sugar, salt, and cornstarch to the figs; stir until well combined. Spoon into the pie plate (pile high in the center). Dot with the butter; lightly brush the rim of the dough with water. Drape the second disk over the pin; center over the filling. Gently press around the filling to fit; trim to leave a ½-inch overhang. Fold the edge of the top crust under the bottom one; crimp to seal. Brush water on the bottom of the cutout; press onto the top crust. Beat the yolk with the cream; brush over the crust. Sprinkle with sugar; freeze until very firm, about 30 minutes.

4. Bake on a baking sheet until just golden, 20 to 25 minutes. Reduce heat to 375° F. Bake, rotating halfway through, until bubbling, and the bottom crust is deep golden brown, about 1 hour. (If the edges brown too quickly, cover with a foil ring.) Let cool on a wire rack.

pumpkin and ricotta crostata
MAKES ONE 10-INCH CROSTATA

1 disk Pasta Frolla (recipe follows)
  All-purpose flour, for dusting
  Unsalted butter, softened, for pie plate
1 cup ricotta cheese, drained for 30 minutes in a cheesecloth-lined sieve set over a bowl
½ cup mascarpone cheese
1 can (15 ounces) solid-pack pumpkin
5 tablespoons sugar

¼ teaspoon coarse salt
  Heaping ¼ teaspoon freshly ground nutmeg
½ teaspoon pure vanilla extract
2 large egg yolks, lightly beaten
2 tablespoons pine nuts
1 large egg white, lightly beaten

1. Preheat the oven to 350° F. Bring the pasta frolla to room temperature. On a lightly floured surface, roll out the dough to ¼ inch thick. Transfer to a lightly buttered 10-inch pie plate. Use your fingertips to press the dough against the bottom and sides of the dish until even. Trim the edges; refrigerate the scraps in plastic wrap until step 4.

2. Prick the bottom of the pastry shell all over with a fork. Bake until set and pale golden brown, about 15 minutes. Let cool on a wire rack. With a small knife, trim the edge of the shell where uneven to leave a ¼-inch space between the shell and the top of the dish.

3. Raise the oven temperature to 375° F. Process the ricotta in a food processor until smooth. Add the mascarpone, pumpkin, sugar, salt, nutmeg, and vanilla; process until well combined, about 30 seconds. Add the yolks; process until combined, about 10 seconds. Pour into the pastry shell.

4. Tear the reserved chilled dough scraps into 1-inch pieces. On a lightly floured surface, gently roll pieces with your hands to make ¼-inch-thick ropes. Gently press 1 long rope around the top edge of the shell (patch 2 ropes together, if necessary). Gently place other pastry ropes on top of the filling to create a lattice pattern (ropes of all lengths can be used). Place 3 pine nuts in each square of lattice. Brush the latticework with egg white.

5. Bake the crostata until the crust is golden brown and the filling is set, about 40 minutes. Let cool on a wire rack.

pasta frolla

Pasta frolla (Italian for "short pastry") is the basic pastry dough of Italy. Our recipe yields enough dough for 2 crostata (you'll need to double the pumpkin and ricotta filling).

2¼ cups all-purpose flour, plus more
    for dusting

½ cup sugar

⅛ teaspoon salt

14 tablespoons (1¾ sticks) cold unsalted
    butter, cut into small pieces

1 large egg, lightly beaten

1 large egg yolk, lightly beaten

1 teaspoon pure vanilla extract

1 tablespoon freshly grated lemon zest

1. Pulse the flour, sugar, and salt in a food processor just until combined. Add the butter; pulse until the mixture resembles coarse meal, 6 to 8 times.

2. Whisk together the egg, egg yolk, vanilla, and lemon zest. With the processor running, add the egg mixture; process just until the dough begins to come together. Turn the dough out onto a floured work surface; lightly knead to form a ball.

3. Divide the dough into 2 pieces; gently press into flat disks. Wrap tightly in plastic. Refrigerate at least 1 hour or overnight, or freeze up to 1 month.

apple pie with cheddar crust

Cheddar Crust dough (recipe follows)

1½ pounds Granny Smith apples (about 3),
    peeled, cored, and cut into ¼-inch-thick
    wedges

2 pounds Cortland apples (about 5), peeled,
    cored, and cut into ¼-inch-thick wedges

1 cup sugar

½ cup all-purpose flour

2 teaspoons fresh lemon juice

¾ teaspoon ground cinnamon

¼ teaspoon freshly grated nutmeg

¼ teaspoon salt

⅛ teaspoon ground cloves

2 tablespoons unsalted butter, cut into
    small pieces

1 large egg, beaten

1. Preheat the oven to 450°F. Divide the dough into 2 pieces. On a lightly floured work surface, roll out each to a 13-inch circle.

2. Fit one circle into a 10-inch pie plate; transfer the plate to a baking sheet. Put the other circle on another baking sheet. Refrigerate the dough until cold, at least 30 minutes.

3. Stir together the apples, sugar, flour, lemon juice, cinnamon, nutmeg, salt, and cloves. Spoon into the bottom pie crust. Dot the filling with butter. Cover with the top crust. Fold the edges over; crimp decoratively to seal. Cut a steam vent. Chill in the freezer until firm, about 30 minutes.

4. Brush with egg. Bake the pie 10 minutes. Reduce the oven temperature to 350°F; bake until golden brown, about 45 minutes. Tent with foil; bake until the juices are bubbling, about 45 minutes more. Let cool at least 1½ hours before serving.

cheddar crust

2½ cups all-purpose flour, plus more
    for dusting

1 teaspoon sugar

½ teaspoon salt

14 tablespoons (1¾ sticks) cold unsalted
    butter, cut into small pieces

4 ounces white Cheddar cheese, coarsely
    grated (about 1½ cups)

½ cup ice water

1. Process the flour, sugar, and salt in a food processor. Add the butter; pulse until pea-size lumps appear. Pulse in the cheese. With the processor running, add the ice water; process just until the dough comes together.

2. Turn the dough out; gather into a block. Wrap in plastic wrap. Refrigerate until cold, at least 30 minutes or up to 2 days. The dough can be frozen up to 3 weeks.

apricot-pistachio tart

MAKES ONE 9 × 17-INCH TART

- 1   cup plus 1 tablespoon unsalted pistachios, shelled and toasted
- ½   cup granulated sugar
- 8   tablespoons (1 stick) cold unsalted butter, cut into ½-inch cubes
- 1   large egg
- 1   teaspoon pure vanilla extract
    Pinch of salt
    All-purpose flour, for dusting
- 1   box (17¼ ounces) puff pastry, thawed
- 1¼ pounds apricots (about 6), cut into ¼-inch-thick wedges
- 1   large egg yolk
- 1   tablespoon heavy cream
- 2   tablespoons turbinado or other raw sugar
- ¼   cup apricot jam

1. Process 1 cup nuts and the granulated sugar in a food processor to combine. Add the butter; process until a paste forms. Add the egg, vanilla, and salt; process to combine. Set aside.

2. On a lightly floured surface, press the edges of both pastry sheets together to form one large sheet. Roll out to a 9 × 17-inch rectangle; transfer to a baking sheet. Spread the reserved pistachio mixture over the dough, leaving a ¾-inch border.

3. Position the rectangle so a short end is nearest you. Arrange the apricots on top in 4 vertical rows, alternating the direction in which apricots face from row to row. Fold in the edges of the dough; use your index finger to make a scalloped border. Refrigerate until cold, about 30 minutes.

4. Preheat the oven to 400°F. Whisk together the yolk and cream; brush the egg wash over the edges of the tart shell. Chop the remaining tablespoon nuts; sprinkle the nuts and turbinado sugar over the apricots. Bake, rotating the sheet halfway through, until the crust is deep golden brown and the fruit is juicy, about 35 minutes. Let cool on a wire rack.

5. Meanwhile, heat the jam with 1½ tablespoons water in a small saucepan over low heat, stirring, until thinned, about 2 minutes. Pass through a fine sieve into a small bowl. Brush the glaze over the fruit.

sweet cherry galette

MAKES ONE 14-INCH TART

    All-purpose flour, for dusting
    Pâte Sucrée (page 651; do not divide dough into 2 pieces)
- ¼   cup plus 2 tablespoons sugar
- ¼   cup unsalted almonds, toasted and cooled
- ¼   teaspoon freshly grated nutmeg
- ¼   teaspoon salt
- 1½ pounds sweet cherries, such as Bing, pitted
- 2   tablespoons cold unsalted butter, cut into small pieces
- 1   large egg yolk
- 1   tablespoon heavy cream

1. On a piece of lightly floured parchment, roll out the dough to a 16-inch-long oval (¼ inch thick). Transfer the dough and parchment to a baking sheet. Refrigerate until cold, about 30 minutes.

2. Process ¼ cup sugar and the almonds, nutmeg, and salt in a food processor to combine. Gently toss with the cherries.

3. Preheat the oven to 375°F. Spoon the cherries over the dough, leaving a 2-inch border. Dot with butter. Fold in the edges, pressing gently. Refrigerate until cold, 30 minutes.

4. Whisk the yolk with the cream; brush over the edges of the tart. Sprinkle with the remaining 2 tablespoons sugar (or to taste). Bake until golden, 45 to 50 minutes.

panna cotta tartlets with strawberries

If your strawberries are sweet, you won't need as much sugar—use an amount at the lower end of our range in step 5.

2½ teaspoons unflavored gelatin
    Vegetable oil, for brushing
2½ cups heavy cream
 ¾ cup sugar, plus 2 tablespoons, if needed
 ½ cup crème fraîche
 ½ teaspoon pure vanilla extract
    Pâte Sucrée (page 651)
    All-purpose flour, for dusting
 1 pound strawberries, hulled and halved lengthwise, or quartered, if large
 1 teaspoon balsamic vinegar

1. In a small bowl, sprinkle the gelatin over 3 tablespoons cold water; let soften 10 minutes. Brush the insides of 6 5-ounce ramekins or custard cups (3¼ inches in diameter) with oil.

2. Bring the cream and ½ cup plus 2 tablespoons sugar to a simmer in a medium saucepan over medium heat, stirring occasionally. Reduce heat to medium-low; add the gelatin mixture. Cook, stirring, until the gelatin and sugar are dissolved. Remove from heat. Whisk in the crème fraîche and vanilla. Pour into a medium bowl set in an ice-water bath. Let cool completely, stirring occasionally. Divide the mixture among the ramekins. Refrigerate until set, about 3 hours, or up to 1 day.

3. Line a rimmed baking sheet with parchment, and place 6 4-inch tart rings on top. Divide the dough into 6 pieces. One at a time, roll out each piece into a 7-inch circle (⅛ inch thick) on a lightly floured surface. Press each into a tart ring; trim flush with the top edge of the ring. Refrigerate the tart shells until cold, about 30 minutes.

4. Preheat the oven to 375°F. Prick the bottoms of the tart shells all over with fork. Line each with parchment, and fill with pie weights or dried beans. Bake until the edges are golden, about 18 minutes.

Remove the parchment and weights; continue baking until the surfaces are golden, about 10 minutes. Let cool on a wire rack.

5. Heat the berries, remaining 2 to 4 tablespoons sugar (depending on the sweetness of the berries), and vinegar in a skillet over medium-low heat, stirring, until juicy, about 5 minutes. Let cool slightly.

6. Unmold the panna cottas: Dip the ramekins in warm water; pat dry. Run a small knife around the edge of each panna cotta; gently coax, and invert onto a tart shell. Top with berries and sauce.

sugar plum tart

 1 disk Pâte Sablée (page 654)
    Almond Frangipane (page 655)
 1 pound 2 ounces sugar plums or other small plums, halved crosswise and pitted
 3 tablespoons turbinado or other raw sugar
    Confectioners' sugar, for dusting

1. Press the dough into a 10-inch round tart pan with a removable bottom. Refrigerate 10 minutes. Trim the dough flush with the top edge of the pan. Refrigerate until cold, about 30 minutes.

2. Preheat the oven to 350°F. Line the tart shell with parchment, and fill with pie weights or dried beans. Bake until the edges are golden, about 10 minutes. Remove the parchment and weights; continue baking until the surface is golden, about 10 minutes. Let cool on a wire rack.

3. Spread the frangipane in the shell. Arrange the plums, cut sides up, on top in concentric circles, pressing gently. Sprinkle with turbinado sugar. Bake until golden, 45 to 50 minutes. Let cool on a wire rack. Just before serving, dust the tart with confectioners' sugar.

blueberry-lemon tart

MAKES ONE 9-INCH TART

1   disk Pâte Sablée (page 654)

½   cup sugar

3   tablespoons all-purpose flour,
    plus more for dusting

2   pinches of salt

1   cup low-fat buttermilk

2   large eggs, separated, room temperature

½   teaspoon pure vanilla extract

1   tablespoon freshly grated lemon zest

2   teaspoons fresh lemon juice
    Pinch of cream of tartar

2   cups blueberries, picked over

1   tablespoon honey

1. Preheat the oven to 375°F. Place a 9-inch cake ring on a rimmed baking sheet lined with parchment. Roll out the dough between sheets of parchment to an 11-inch circle (⅛ inch thick). Refrigerate 15 minutes. Peel off the parchment; press the dough into the ring. Trim flush with the top edge of the ring. Refrigerate until cold, about 30 minutes.

2. Prick the dough all over with a fork. Line the tart shell with parchment, and fill with pie weights or dried beans. Bake until the crust starts to turn golden, 20 to 25 minutes. Remove the parchment and weights; continue baking until pale golden, about 5 minutes more. Let cool on a wire rack.

3. Whisk together ¼ cup sugar, the flour, and a pinch of salt; set aside. Whisk the buttermilk and yolks in a small saucepan over medium-low heat; gradually whisk in the sugar mixture. Cook, whisking constantly, until thickened, 5 to 7 minutes. Stir in the vanilla, zest, and juice. Transfer to a medium bowl set in an ice-water bath. Let cool completely, stirring occasionally.

4. Meanwhile, put the whites and cream of tartar in the bowl of an electric mixer fitted with the whisk attachment. Add a pinch of salt. Beat on low speed until foamy. With the mixer running, gradually add the remaining ¼ cup sugar. On medium-high speed, beat until stiff, glossy peaks form.

5. Gently fold the pastry cream and 1 cup berries into the meringue. Pour the mixture into the tart shell, making swirls and peaks. Bake until golden, 40 to 45 minutes. Let cool on a wire rack. Remove the cake ring.

6. Meanwhile, heat the remaining cup berries and the honey in a medium skillet over medium-low heat, stirring gently, until just warm, about 2 minutes. Spoon the glazed berries over the tart.

fig and grape tart

MAKES ONE 4 × 14-INCH TART

    Pâte Sablée (page 654; do not divide
    dough into 2 pieces)

1   cup Almond Frangipane (page 655)

4   ounces figs (about 4), halved lengthwise,
    or quartered, if large

⅓   cup black seedless grapes, halved

1   tablespoon turbinado or other raw sugar
    Gorgonzola dolce, for serving

1. Press the dough into a 4 × 14-inch rectangular tart pan with a removable bottom. Refrigerate 10 minutes. Trim the dough flush with the top edge of the pan. Refrigerate until cold, about 30 minutes.

2. Preheat the oven to 375°F. Line the tart shell with parchment, and fill with pie weights or dried beans. Bake until the edges are golden, about 15 minutes. Remove the parchment and weights; continue baking until the surface is golden, about 10 minutes. Let cool on a wire rack.

3. Spread the frangipane in the tart shell. Arrange the figs and grapes on top, pressing gently. Sprinkle with the sugar. Bake until golden, 40 to 45 minutes. Let cool on a rack. Serve with Gorgonzola dolce.

strawberry tartlets

MAKES SIX 4-INCH TARTLETS

This dough can be frozen for up to 1 month; thaw in the refrigerator before using. Allow guests to fill their own tarts at the table.

- 1 cup plus 2 tablespoons all-purpose flour
- 1½ tablespoons plus 3 tablespoons sugar
- ½ teaspoon salt
- ½ cup (1 stick) chilled unsalted butter, cut into small pieces
- 1 large egg yolk, lightly beaten
- 1 tablespoon ice water, plus more as needed
- 1½ pounds (2 pints) fresh strawberries, hulled, washed, and halved, or quartered, if large
- 2 cups crème fraîche

1. Pulse the flour, 1½ tablespoons sugar, and salt in a food processor to combine. Add the butter; process until the mixture resembles coarse meal.

2. In a small bowl, mix together the egg yolk and ice water. With the machine running, add the egg mixture in a slow, steady stream through the feed tube. Process until the dough just holds together, about 20 seconds. If the dough feels dry, add more ice water, 1 tablespoon at a time.

3. Preheat the oven to 400°F. Divide the dough evenly among 6 4-inch tartlet pans; gently press into the pans. Prick the bottoms with a fork. Refrigerate the shells until firm to the touch, at least 30 minutes.

4. Line each shell with foil, and fill with pie weights or dried beans. Place the tart pans on a rimmed baking sheet; bake until the edges just begin to brown, about 15 minutes. Remove the foil and weights. Continue to bake until the bottom of the crust is golden brown and crisp, about 10 minutes more. Transfer to a wire rack; let cool completely. Remove the shells from the pans.

5. Meanwhile, in a medium bowl, mix the strawberries with the remaining 3 tablespoons sugar. Cover with plastic wrap, and let macerate until juicy, about 1 hour.

6. When ready to serve, fill each tart shell with about ⅓ cup crème fraîche; divide the strawberries evenly among the tarts.

buttermilk pie

MAKES ONE 10-INCH PIE

- Graham Cracker–Coated Piecrust (recipe follows)
- 3 cups buttermilk
- ½ cup (1 stick) unsalted butter, melted and cooled
- 8 large egg yolks
- 2 teaspoons pure vanilla extract
- 2 cups sugar
- ½ cup all-purpose flour, plus more for the work surface
- ½ teaspoon salt
- 1 tablespoon finely grated lemon zest
- Blackberry and Blueberry Sauce (recipe follows)

1. Preheat the oven to 400°F. Prick the bottom of the pie shell all over with a fork. Line with foil; fill with dried beans or pie weights. Bake until the edges are lightly browned, about 25 minutes. Remove the foil and weights, and bake until the crust is lightly browned, about 10 minutes more. Let cool completely on a wire rack.

2. Reduce the oven heat to 350°F. In a medium bowl, whisk together the buttermilk, butter, egg yolks, and vanilla. In a large bowl, combine the sugar, flour, and salt. Whisk into the dry ingredients. Pass through a fine sieve into a clean bowl. Whisk in the lemon zest.

3. Pour the mixture into the pie shell; bake until the center is just set, about 1 hour and 10 minutes. Let cool, and then refrigerate at least 4 hours. Serve cold with berry sauce.

graham cracker–coated piecrust

MAKES ENOUGH FOR ONE 10-INCH PIE

1¼ cups all-purpose flour, plus more
    for the work surface

¾   teaspoon salt

½   cup (1 stick) unsalted butter,
    cut into pieces

¼   cup ice water

4   graham crackers, finely ground (½ cup)

1. Pulse the flour and salt in a food processor to combine. Add the butter, and process until the mixture resembles coarse meal, about 10 seconds. With the machine running, add the ice water 1 tablespoon at a time, and process just until the dough holds together, no more than 30 seconds.

2. Turn out the dough onto a lightly floured work surface. Flatten the dough into a disk; wrap in plastic. Refrigerate at least 1 hour.

3. Spread the crumbs on a clean work surface. Roll out the dough on top of the crumbs, coating both sides, into a 14-inch round about ⅛ inch thick. Gently fit the dough into a 10 × 2-inch (1½ quart) pie plate, and crimp the edges as desired. Refrigerate the shell at least 30 minutes before baking.

blackberry and blueberry sauce

MAKES 4 CUPS

½   cup sugar

1   tablespoon fresh lemon juice

2   pints fresh blueberries

2   containers (6 ounces each) fresh
    blackberries

1   teaspoon cornstarch

1. In a medium saucepan set over medium heat, stir together the sugar, lemon juice, and half the blueberries and blackberries. Bring just to a boil. Reduce heat to low, and simmer until the blueberries burst and release their juices, about 3 minutes.

2. In a small bowl, dissolve the cornstarch in 1 teaspoon cold water. Stir into the sauce. Simmer, stirring, about 1 minute more, until the sauce thickens slightly. Remove from the heat; stir in the remaining berries. Transfer the sauce to a serving bowl. Chill until cold; stir before serving with the pie.

joey gallagher's apricot hand pies

MAKES 12

All-purpose flour, for the work surface

Martha's Perfect Pâte Brisée (page 647)

12 Poached Apricot Halves (page 443)

3   tablespoons sugar

1. Line a baking sheet with parchment paper; set aside. On a lightly floured surface, roll one disk of dough into a large round, about ⅛ inch thick. Using a 3-inch cookie cutter, cut out 12 rounds. Transfer rounds to the prepared baking sheet; refrigerate until chilled, about 30 minutes.

2. Repeat process with the remaining dough, using a 4-inch cookie cutter to make 12 more rounds; do not refrigerate. Remove disks from refrigerator.

3. Using paper towels, blot the poached apricots halves to eliminate excess liquid; place one in center of each chilled round. Brush cold water around edges of dough; cover each with an unchilled round. Gently press edges together to seal. Refrigerate about 30 minutes.

4. Preheat the oven to 425° F. Remove tarts from refrigerator. Using a paring knife, slash the top of each tart in a crosshatch fashion. Brush with water, and generously sprinkle with sugar.

5. Bake 15 minutes. Reduce oven heat to 350° F. Continue baking until golden brown, 15 to 20 minutes more. Transfer pies to a wire rack to cool slightly before serving. Or let cool completely, and store in an airtight container at room temperature up to 4 days.

prune tart

MAKES ONE 12 × 18-INCH TART

Serve with créme fraîche or whipped cream.

- 2 cups red wine
- ⅔ cup fresh orange juice
- ½ cup plus 2 tablespoons sugar
- 1 cinnamon stick
- 3 cups (1 pound) pitted prunes, halved
- 1 sheet frozen puff pastry, thawed
  Finely grated zest of 1 orange
- 1 large egg
- 1 tablespoon heavy cream

1. Preheat the oven to 375° F. In a medium saucepan, bring the wine, orange juice, ½ cup sugar, and cinnamon to a boil over high heat. Remove from heat; add the prunes, and let steep 10 minutes. Use a slotted spoon to transfer the prunes to a bowl. Return the liquid to a boil; cook until slightly reduced and thickened, 10 to 12 minutes. Remove from heat.

2. Meanwhile, roll out the puff pastry into a 12 × 18-inch rectangle. In a small bowl, combine the remaining 2 tablespoons sugar and the orange zest; sprinkle evenly over the pastry. Arrange the prunes in rows over the pastry, leaving a 1-inch border on all sides. In a small bowl, whisk together the egg and cream; brush on the edges of the pastry.

3. Bake until the crust is golden, about 20 minutes, rotating the pan and brushing the tart with reserved cooking liquid halfway through. Remove from the oven; let cool slightly. Serve warm.

fresh cherry pie

MAKES ONE 9-INCH PIE

- All-purpose flour, for work surface
- Martha's Perfect Pâte Brisée (page 647)
- 2¼ pounds fresh yellow and red sweet cherries, pitted and halved
- ¼ cup sugar
- 2 tablespoons instant tapioca powder
  Vanilla ice cream, for serving (optional)

1. Preheat the oven to 400° F. On a lightly floured work surface, roll out 1 disk pâte briseé to a ⅛-inch-thick round, about 13 inches in diameter. Fit the dough in a 9-inch pie plate.

2. In a large bowl, combine the cherries, sugar, and tapioca, and toss to coat evenly. Pour the filling into the prepared pie plate, and set aside.

3. Roll out the remaining disk of dough as in step 1. Using a pastry wheel or a sharp paring knife, cut the dough into 1-inch-wide strips. Lightly brush the rim of the dough in the pie plate with water, and weave the strips of dough on top of the filling to form a lattice. Using kitchen scissors, trim the strips to create a 1-inch overhang. Tuck the strips under the rim of shell, and crimp to seal. Chill the pie in the refrigerator at least 30 minutes.

4. Bake the pie 20 minutes. Reduce the oven heat to 350° F; bake until the crust is deep golden brown and the juices begin to bubble, 40 to 50 minutes more. Transfer the pie to a wire rack, and let stand until just warm or room temperature. Serve with ice cream, if desired.

rhubarb pie

MAKES ONE 9½-INCH DEEP-DISH PIE

- 2 pounds rhubarb, trimmed and cut into ½-inch pieces (about 6½ cups)
- 1⅓ cups granulated sugar
- ¼ cup cornstarch
  Pinch of coarse salt
- 1 teaspoon finely grated lemon zest plus 1 tablespoon fresh lemon juice
  All-purpose flour, for work surface
  Flaky Piecrust (recipe follows)
- 2 tablespoons unsalted butter, cut into pieces
- 1 tablespoon heavy cream
- 1 large egg yolk
  Fine sanding sugar, for sprinkling

1. Preheat the oven to 375° F, with a rack in lower third. Stir together the rhubarb, granulated sugar, cornstarch, salt, and lemon zest and juice in a large bowl; set aside.

2. On a lightly floured surface, roll out 1 piece of dough to a 13-inch round, about ⅛ inch thick. Fit into a 9½-inch deep-dish glass pie plate. Fill with rhubarb mixture, and dot with butter. Refrigerate.

3. On a lightly floured surface, roll out remaining dough to a 13-inch round. Drape over filling. Trim edge to 1 inch. Fold edge under, and crimp as desired. Make five 2½- to 3-inch slits in crust to vent. Refrigerate 15 minutes.

4. Whisk cream and egg yolk in a small bowl. Brush over crust. Sprinkle with sanding sugar. Bake until bottom crust is golden and filling is bubbling vigorously, 1 hour 10 minutes to 1 hour 25 minutes. Cover with foil if browning too quickly. Let cool at least 4 hours on a wire rack.

flaky piecrust

MAKES ENOUGH FOR ONE 9½-INCH
DOUBLE-CRUST PIE OR
TWO 9- TO 10-INCH SINGLE-CRUST PIES

- 3 cups all-purpose flour
- 1 tablespoon sugar
- 1¼ teaspoons salt
- ¾ cup (1½ sticks) cold unsalted butter, cut into pieces
- 6 tablespoons cold vegetable shortening or lard, cut into pieces
- ½ cup ice water, plus more if needed

1. Pulse flour, sugar, and salt in a food processor. Add butter and shortening, and process until mixture resembles coarse meal, about 10 seconds. Add water in a slow, steady stream just until dough holds together, no longer than 30 seconds (do not overprocess). Squeeze a small amount of dough; if it doesn't hold together, add more water.

2. Remove dough from processor, and knead once or twice. Divide in half; shape into disks. Wrap each in plastic; refrigerate until firm, 1 hour or overnight.

tangerine chiffon pie

MAKES ONE 10-INCH PIE

- 2 cups store-bought tangerine-orange juice blend
- 3 cups finely ground store-bought shortbread cookies (about 12 ounces)
- 5 teaspoons finely grated lemon zest plus 3 tablespoons fresh lemon juice
- 1 cup sugar
- ¼ cup (½ stick) unsalted butter, melted
- 2 teaspoons unflavored gelatin
- 4 large eggs, separated, room temperature
- ⅛ teaspoon cream of tartar

1. Preheat the oven to 350°F. Boil the tangerine-orange juice in a small saucepan over medium-high heat until it has reduced to about 1 cup, 18 to 20 minutes. Remove from heat; set aside.

2. Pulse cookies, 1 tablespoon lemon zest, and ¼ cup sugar in a food processor until thoroughly combined. With processor running, add melted butter; process until combined. Press cookie mixture evenly into bottom, up sides, and onto rim of a 10-inch pie plate. Bake until golden brown, about 15 minutes. Transfer to a wire rack to cool completely.

3. Put lemon juice into a small bowl. Sprinkle with gelatin. Let soften 10 minutes. Meanwhile, whisk together yolks, ½ cup sugar, the juice reduction, and the remaining 2 teaspoons zest in a medium saucepan. Cook over medium-low heat, stirring constantly, until thickened, about 10 minutes (do not let boil). Remove from heat. Add gelatin mixture, and whisk until gelatin has dissolved completely.

4. Transfer gelatin mixture to a large bowl. Refrigerate, stirring occasionally, until cool and thick enough to hold a ribbon on surface, 25 to 30 minutes.

5. Put egg whites and cream of tartar into the bowl of an electric mixer fitted with the whisk attachment; beat on medium-high speed until soft peaks form. Gradually add remaining ¼ cup sugar; beat until stiff but not dry peaks form. Fold egg-white mixture into gelatin mixture in 3 batches, folding until just combined after each addition. Pour into cooled crust. Refrigerate until set, at least 2 hours or overnight, before serving.

lemon tartlets
with meringue caps

MAKES ABOUT 20

for the shells

¼ cup (½ stick) unsalted butter, melted

⅔ cup confectioners' sugar, sifted

2 large egg whites, room temperature

½ cup sifted all-purpose flour

½ teaspoon pure vanilla extract

for the meringue caps

3 large egg whites, room temperature

½ cup granulated sugar

for the lemon curd

6 large egg yolks

1 tablespoon finely grated lemon zest plus ½ cup fresh lemon juice (about 3 lemons total)

¾ cup granulated sugar

Pinch of salt

½ cup (1 stick) cold unsalted butter, cut into pieces

1. Preheat the oven to 325°F. Make the shells: Put butter and sugar into the bowl of an electric mixer fitted with the paddle attachment; mix on medium-high speed until pale and fluffy. Mix in egg whites, 1 at a time. Mix in flour and vanilla.

2. Spoon 1 scant teaspoon batter onto a rimmed baking sheet lined with a nonstick baking mat. Using the back of the spoon, spread into a 3-inch round. Repeat 4 times. Bake until golden, 10 to 12 minutes. Immediately transfer cookies, 1 at a time, to inverted small tartlet shells or brioche molds; gently press to shape. Let set, about 30 seconds. If cookies become too cool to shape, return them to the oven for 20 seconds. Repeat with remaining batter. (The shells can be stored in an airtight container for up to 3 days at room temperature.)

3. Reduce oven temperature to 200°F. Make the meringue caps: Put egg whites and sugar into the bowl of an electric mixer set over a pan of simmering water; whisk until sugar has dissolved. Attach bowl to mixer fitted with the whisk attachment; beat on medium-high speed until stiff peaks form

and meringue is cool, about 10 minutes. Transfer to a pastry bag fitted with a 7/16-inch star tip (such as Ateco #825). Pipe twenty 1¼-inch-round, 2-inch-high spirals onto baking sheets lined with parchment, spacing about 1 inch apart. Bake 20 minutes. Reduce oven temperature to 150°F. Bake until dry but not brown, about 2 hours more. Transfer meringues to a wire rack; let cool completely. (The meringues can be stored in an airtight container up to 3 days.)

4. Make the curd: Whisk egg yolks, lemon zest and juice, and sugar in a heavy, medium saucepan. Cook, stirring constantly, over medium-low heat until mixture registers 160°F on a candy thermometer, 8 to 10 minutes. Remove from heat. Stir in salt. Add butter, 1 piece at a time, stirring after each addition until smooth. Pour curd through a fine sieve into a medium bowl. Cover with plastic wrap, pressing it directly onto surface. Refrigerate until cold and set, at least 1 hour (up to 2 days).

5. To serve, spoon 2 teaspoons curd into each shell. Top each with a meringue cap.

honey-walnut pie

SERVES 8 TO 10

3 tablespoons all-purpose flour, plus more for work surface

Pâte Sucrée Walnut Variation (page 651)

4 large eggs, lightly beaten, plus 1 lightly beaten egg for brushing

¾ cup acacia or other mild honey

¾ cup granulated sugar

¼ cup (½ stick) unsalted butter, melted

½ teaspoon finely grated orange zest, plus ¼ cup fresh orange juice

½ teaspoon salt

2 cups coarsely chopped walnuts

Fine sanding sugar, for sprinkling

1. Preheat the oven to 350°F. Place a 9⅛ × 1⅜-inch tart ring on a baking sheet lined with parchment; set aside. On a lightly floured surface, roll out 1 disk of dough to ⅛ inch thick; cut into a 14-inch round. Fit into tart ring; trim overhang to ½ inch. Refrigerate while making filling.

2. Whisk together 4 eggs, the honey, granulated sugar, butter, orange zest and juice, salt, and flour in a large bowl. Stir in walnuts. Pour into tart shell.

3. On a lightly floured surface, roll out remaining disk of dough to ⅛ inch thick. Cut into an 11-inch round. Cut five slits for vents. Drape over filling. Trim overhang to 1 inch; fold over bottom crust. Press edges to seal; tuck into ring. Brush with remaining beaten egg, sprinkle with sanding sugar.

4. Bake until a knife inserted in one of the vents comes out clean, 45 to 50 minutes. Transfer sheet to a wire rack; let cool completely. Remove ring before serving. The pie can be stored, covered, overnight.

mini cranberry meringue pies
MAKES 12

If you can't find blood oranges, use regular ones.

All-purpose flour, for work surface
1   disk Pâte Sucrée Citrus Variation (page 651)
3¼   cups fresh cranberries (12 ounces)
1½   cups sugar
1½   teaspoons finely chopped lemon zest
1   teaspoon finely chopped blood orange zest, plus ¼ cup blood orange juice
¼   teaspoon salt
⅛   teaspoon ground cinnamon
     Pinch of ground cloves
3   tablespoons cornstarch
3   large egg whites
     Pinch of cream of tartar

1. Preheat the oven to 375°F. On a lightly floured surface, roll out dough to ⅛ inch thick. Cut out 4⅛-inch fluted rounds, and fit into cups of a standard 12-cup muffin tin (not nonstick). Pierce bottoms with tines of a fork. Freeze 15 minutes.

2. Line each shell with parchment paper, and fill with pie weights or dried beans. Bake 15 minutes. Remove weights and parchment. Return to oven; bake until bottoms are just turning golden, 5 minutes more. Transfer to wire racks; let cool 5 minutes. Remove shells from the tin; let cool completely.

3. Bring 2 cups cranberries, 1 cup sugar, and 1½ cups water to a boil in a medium saucepan. Reduce heat, and simmer mixture, stirring occasionally, until cranberries have burst, about 5 minutes. Pour through a coarse sieve, then a fine sieve; discard solids. (You should have about 1¾ cups; if you have less, add water.)

4. Bring strained cranberry juice, ¼ cup sugar, the zests, salt, cinnamon, cloves, and remaining 1¼ cups cranberries to a boil in a medium saucepan, stirring occasionally. Reduce heat; simmer, stirring occasionally, until cranberries are soft but have not burst, about 3 minutes.

5. Meanwhile, stir cornstarch, blood orange juice, and ¼ cup water in a bowl; whisk into cranberry mixture. Bring to a boil, stirring constantly. Cook, stirring, until translucent, about 1 minute. Divide among prepared shells. Refrigerate until set, about 1 hour (up to overnight).

6. Preheat the broiler. Put egg whites and remaining ¼ cup sugar into the heatproof bowl of an electric mixer set over a pan of simmering water; whisk until sugar has dissolved and mixture is hot to the touch. Attach to mixer fitted with the whisk attachment; beat on medium speed until foamy. Raise speed to high. Add cream of tartar; beat until medium, glossy peaks form. Divide the meringue evenly among pies.

7. Set pies under broiler until tops are browned, 30 seconds to 1 minute.

pear–sour cherry flat pie

MAKES ONE 7½ × 10-INCH
DOUBLE-CRUST PIE

All-purpose flour, for work surface

14 *ounces best-quality frozen puff pastry
    (such as Dufour), thawed*

 3 *small or 2 medium Bartlett pears (about 1
    pound 2 ounces), peeled, halved, cored,
    and cut into ¼-inch slices*

 2 *ounces dried sour cherries*

⅓ *cup sugar, plus more for sprinkling*

 4 *teaspoons cornstarch*

 1 *tablespoon fresh lemon juice*

    Salt and freshly ground pepper

    Five-spice powder

 1 *large egg, lightly beaten*

1. Preheat the oven to 375°F. On a lightly floured surface, unfold the dough, and roll out to 10 × 15 inches. Cut into two 7½ × 10-inch rectangles. Place on baking sheets; refrigerate until cold.

2. Stir pears, cherries, sugar, cornstarch, lemon juice, and ⅛ teaspoon each of salt, pepper, and spice powder in a bowl.

3. Transfer 1 rectangle of dough to a baking sheet lined with parchment. Spoon fruit mixture onto dough, leaving a 1-inch border all around. Brush border with beaten egg. Lay remaining dough over filling; press gently to seal. Refrigerate 20 minutes. Transfer to a room-temperature rimmed baking sheet lined with parchment.

4. Trim edges, and brush top with beaten egg. Cut five 5-inch vents in top. Sprinkle with sugar. Bake, rotating once, until crust is golden and juices are bubbling, about 35 minutes. Transfer the pie to a wire rack; let cool 20 minutes before serving.

yogurt-plum pie

MAKES ONE 9-INCH PIE

    Graham Crust (recipe follows)

 2 *cups whole-milk Greek yogurt*

½ *vanilla bean, seeds scraped and reserved*

½ *teaspoon finely grated lemon zest*

¼ *cup (½ stick) unsalted butter, melted*

 4 *large egg yolks*

 1 *cup sugar*

¼ *cup all-purpose flour*

¼ *teaspoon salt*

 1 *cup Plum-Vanilla Jam (recipe follows)
    or best-quality store-bought plum jam*

1. Preheat the oven to 350°F. Press crust mixture into the bottom and up the sides of a 9-inch pie plate. Freeze 15 minutes. Cover edge with foil. Bake until beginning to dry out, about 15 minutes. Transfer to a wire rack; let cool completely. (Leave oven on.)

2. Stir yogurt, vanilla seeds, and zest in a bowl. Stir in butter and yolks. Stir sugar, flour, and salt in a bowl; stir into yogurt mixture until smooth. Pour into crust.

3. Bake, with foil covering edge of crust, until just set in center, 45 to 55 minutes. Transfer to a wire rack; let cool 1 hour. Spread jam over center of pie. Refrigerate at least 3 hours (up to overnight).

graham crust

MAKES ENOUGH FOR ONE
9- OR 10-INCH PIE

⅔ *cup all-purpose flour*

⅓ *cup whole-wheat flour*

 3 *tablespoons wheat germ*

½ *teaspoon salt*

¼ *teaspoon ground cinnamon*

½ *cup (1 stick) unsalted butter, softened*

⅓ *cup packed light-brown sugar*

Pulse the flours, wheat germ, salt, and cinnamon in a food processor to combine. Add the butter and sugar; process until dough just holds together. Use immediately.

plum-vanilla jam

MAKES 1 3/4 CUPS

1½ pounds red plums, halved, pitted,
    and coarsely chopped

1½ cups sugar

3   strips (2½ inches) lemon zest, plus
    1 tablespoon fresh lemon juice

    Pinch of salt

½   vanilla bean, seeds scraped and reserved

Bring all ingredients to a boil in a large stockpot, mashing with a potato masher. Cook, stirring frequently, until mixture is the consistency of very thick honey, 5 to 10 minutes. Remove plum skin if desired. Discard vanilla bean and zest. Do not strain; jam should be chunky. Refrigerate in an airtight container up to 1 month.

pithiviers

MAKES ONE 9-INCH TART

This classic tart, essentially a frangipane filling enclosed between two layers of puff pastry, is named for the French town in which it was created. We recommend using an insulated baking sheet instead of a regular baking sheet to prevent the bottom of the pastry from getting too browned during baking.

⅔   cup whole blanched almonds

½   cup sugar

3   large egg yolks

3   tablespoons chilled unsalted butter,
    cut into ½-inch pieces

2   tablespoons light rum

    All-purpose flour, for work surface

1   pound Puff Pastry dough (page 653), or
    best-quality frozen puff pastry (such as
    Dufour), thawed

1   tablespoon heavy cream

1. Make the frangipane: In the bowl of a food processor fitted with the metal blade, process the almonds and sugar until the mixture is very fine crumbs. With the machine running, add 2 egg yolks, butter, and rum; continue processing until the mixture is smooth and combined.

2. On a lightly floured work surface, roll out the pastry dough into a rectangle at least 9¼ × 18½ inches and about ⅛ inch thick. Using a 9-inch round cake pan as a guide, cut out 2 9-inch rounds.

3. In a small bowl, whisk together the remaining egg yolk and cream for the egg wash. Place 1 round on a baking sheet, and spread the almond mixture on top, leaving a 1-inch border all around; brush the border with egg wash. Using an aspic or cookie cutter, cut a ½-inch hole in the center of the remaining round; place the cut round on top of the other round, pressing lightly around the filling to seal the rounds together. Place in the refrigerator 1 hour.

4. Preheat the oven to 425°F. Remove the tart from the refrigerator; using a small paring knife, score the top by making curved lines from the center to the edges, like a pinwheel. Brush the top of the tart with the egg wash, being careful not to let any excess drip over the cut edge of dough, as it will inhibit proper rising. Return to the refrigerator to chill again, if needed.

5. Place the baking sheet in the oven, and bake 30 minutes. Reduce heat to 375°F; loosely cover the tart with aluminum foil, and continue baking 30 minutes more.

6. Transfer to a wire rack, and let sit 20 minutes. Remove the tart from the pan by sliding it onto a serving platter. Serve warm or at room temperature, cut into wedges.

pumpkin-pecan pie

MAKES ONE 9-INCH PIE

- 1 disk Martha's Perfect Pâte Briseé (page 647)
- 1 15½-ounce can pumpkin puree
- ¾ cup granulated sugar
- ½ teaspoon salt
- 1 teaspoon ground ginger
- ½ teaspoon ground nutmeg
- 3 large eggs
- ¾ cup plus 1 tablespoon heavy cream
- ½ cup milk
- ¼ cup bourbon
- ⅔ cup packed dark-brown sugar
- 3 tablespoons melted butter
- 1 cup coarsely chopped pecans, plus halves for garnish

  Whipped cream or vanilla ice cream, for serving (optional)

1. Preheat the oven to 425°F. Remove the dough from the refrigerator, and place it between 2 pieces of plastic wrap. Roll out to a 12-inch round. Remove and discard the plastic, and fit the dough into a 9-inch Pyrex or ceramic pie plate; trim the dough evenly along the outside edge, leaving about a ½-inch overhang all around. Crimp the edge, as desired. Prick the bottom of the dough all over with a fork. Place in the freezer until firm, about 15 minutes.

2. Remove from the freezer, and line with parchment paper or aluminum foil. Fill with pie weights or dried beans, and bake until the edge are starting to turn golden, about 15 minutes. Remove the paper and weights, and continue baking until the center is lightly browned, about 5 minutes more. Remove from the oven. Reduce the oven heat to 350°F.

3. Meanwhile, in a large bowl, combine the pumpkin puree, granulated sugar, salt, ginger, nutmeg, eggs, ¾ cup cream, milk, and bourbon; whisk until well combined.

4. Fill the prepared pie shell with the pumpkin mixture, and return to the oven. Bake until the filling is set around the edges but still slightly soft in the center, about 55 minutes. Remove from the oven; let cool. The filling will continue to firm as it cools.

5. Heat the broiler. In a small bowl, combine the brown sugar, melted butter, remaining tablespoon cream, and chopped pecans. Sprinkle the mixture evenly over the top of the pie. Arrange the pecan halves on top, in a circle near the edge.

6. Place the pie under the broiler just until the topping begins to bubble, being careful not to let the nuts burn. Transfer to a wire rack to cool slightly. Serve with whipped cream or ice cream, as desired.

crisp coconut and chocolate pie

MAKES ONE 8-INCH PIE

- 4 tablespoons unsalted butter, softened
- 11 ounces sweetened shredded coconut (about 6 cups)
- 8 ounces semisweet or bittersweet chocolate, finely chopped
- 1¼ cups heavy cream

1. Preheat the oven to 350°F. Place the butter and one-third of the coconut in the bowl of a food processor fitted with the metal blade. Process until the mixture forms a ball, 1 to 2 minutes. Transfer to a medium bowl. Sprinkle the remaining coconut over the mixture, and combine with your fingers.

2. Place an 8-inch tart pan with a removable bottom on a baking sheet. Press the coconut mixture into the bottom and up the sides of the pan to form a crust, leaving the top edge loose and fluffy. Place a ring of aluminum foil over the edges to prevent burning. Bake until the center begins to brown, 10 to 15 minutes; remove the foil, and cook until the edges are browned, 4 to 6 minutes. Transfer to a wire rack to cool completely.

3. Place the chocolate in a medium heatproof bowl. Bring the cream just to a boil in a small saucepan, and pour over the chocolate. Let sit 10 minutes, and stir until the chocolate is melted and combined. Let cool, and pour into the coconut crust. Cover with plastic wrap, and transfer to the refrigerator until the filling is set, at least 1 hour. Cut into wedges, and serve.

plum galette

MAKES ONE 16 × 18-INCH GALETTE

- 1 tablespoon all-purpose flour, plus more for the work surface
- Galette Pâte Brisée (recipe follows)
- ½ cup finely ground toasted hazelnuts
- 2 tablespoons light-brown sugar
- 1 tablespoon cornstarch
- ¼ teaspoon salt
- 1½ pounds (about 5) plums, sliced into ½-inch-thick wedges
- 3 tablespoons granulated sugar
- 1 large egg, lightly beaten
- ½ cup plum or red currant jam

1. Preheat the oven to 425° F, with a rack in the lower third. On a lightly floured work surface, roll out the pâte brisée to ⅛ inch thick. Trim the edges to form a 16 × 18-inch rectangle, and transfer to a parchment-lined baking sheet. In a small bowl, combine the flour, hazelnuts, brown sugar, cornstarch, and salt; spread to cover the middle of the dough, leaving a 3-inch border all around.

2. Arrange the plums in rows on top, slightly overlapping the slices and alternating the direction of each row. Sprinkle the plums with granulated sugar.

Fold the dough to enclose the edges; brush the dough with egg wash. Chill 30 minutes in refrigerator.

3. Bake 10 minutes. Reduce the oven heat to 400° F; bake until the pastry is golden brown and the plums are softened, about 30 minutes. Transfer to a wire rack; let cool to room temperature. Heat the jam in a small saucepan over low heat, stirring until melted. Let cool a few minutes; brush evenly over the plum slices. Serve.

galette pâte brisée

MAKES ENOUGH FOR 1 GALETTE

- 2½ cups all-purpose flour
- 1 teaspoon salt
- 8 ounces (2 sticks) chilled unsalted butter
- ½ cup ice water

In the bowl of a food processor fitted with the metal blade, pulse the flour and salt. Add the butter; pulse until the mixture resembles coarse meal, about 15 seconds. With the machine running, add the water in a slow, steady stream; process until the dough just holds together. Turn out onto a piece of plastic wrap, and flatten into a disk; wrap well. Chill at least 1 hour in the refrigerator.

MAKING THE GALETTE

1. The dough is lined with ground hazelnuts, brown sugar, and cornstarch to sweeten and thicken the fruit juices.

2. Arranging the plums in neat rows allows for even caramelization and makes for an attractive presentation.

3. An egg wash gives the crust its sheen, and the fruit is finished with a plum jam glaze.

raspberry tart

SERVES 6 TO 8

The tart shell can be made a day in advance; avoid filling it until 1 to 2 hours before you are ready to serve it in order to keep the shell as crisp and flaky as possible.

All-purpose flour, for the work surface

1   *pound Puff Pastry dough (page 653), or best-quality frozen puff pastry (such as Dufour), thawed*

1   *large egg, lightly beaten*

1⅓ *cups Pastry Cream (page 655)*

½   *cup heavy cream*

2   *6-ounce containers fresh raspberries, rinsed and dried*

¼   *cup confectioners' sugar*

1. Lightly flour a clean work surface. Using a rolling pin, gently roll out the dough into a rectangle at least 9 × 18 inches and ⅛ inch thick, being careful not to press too hard around the edges. Using a pastry wheel or sharp paring knife, trim the edges, and cut out 4 1-inch strips, 2 from one of the short ends and 1 from each of the long sides. Set aside. The resulting rectangle should be about 6 × 15 inches. Transfer to a baking sheet.

2. Dock, or pierce, the dough all over with a fork. Using a pastry brush, moisten the dough with the beaten egg, being careful not to let any drip over the cut edges.

3. Lay the reserved 1-inch strips on top of the edges of the large rectangle, positioning them to line up exactly with the outside edge; this will be the raised border that will encase the filling. Trim the strips to fit, overlapping them at the corners; brush egg wash underneath each of the 4 overlapping corners to seal them together. Brush the tops of the strips with egg wash, being careful not to let any drip down the sides. Cover with plastic wrap, and place in the refrigerator to chill 1 hour.

4. Preheat the oven to 400° F. Transfer the tart shell to the oven, and bake until well browned and puffed all over, about 15 minutes. Remove from the oven;

using a balled-up clean kitchen towel, press down on the center, leaving the borders puffy. Return to the oven; bake 5 minutes. Transfer to a wire rack to cool. Press down again, if needed.

5. When the tart shell is completely cooled, place the pastry cream in a medium bowl. In a separate mixing bowl, whip the heavy cream until soft peaks form; fold into the pastry cream. Using a small offset spatula, spread the cream mixture over the bottom of the tart shell. Arrange the raspberries neatly in rows on top of the cream mixture to cover the bottom of the tart. Dust with confectioners' sugar; cut into strips, and serve.

chocolate caramel tart

MAKES ONE 9-INCH TART

Chocolate Pâte Sucrée (page 651)

1   *cup chopped pecans*

1   *cup sugar*

¼   *teaspoon salt*

¼   *cup water*

1½ *cups heavy cream*

2   *tablespoons unsalted butter, room temperature*

1   *teaspoon pure vanilla extract*

6   *ounces bittersweet chocolate, finely chopped*

Cocoa, for dusting (optional)

Caramel-Dipped Pecans (optional; recipe follows)

1. Preheat the oven to 350° F. Roll the chocolate pâte sucrée ⅛ inch thick, and fit into a 9-inch fluted tart pan with a removable bottom. Dock the bottom of the tart with a fork. Refrigerate 30 minutes.

2. Place the chopped pecans on a baking sheet, and toast until slightly darkened and fragrant, about 10 minutes; set aside.

3. Line the tart shell with parchment paper, pressing into the edges, and cover with dried beans or pie weights. Place on a baking sheet; bake for 20 minutes. Remove the paper and beans, and continue baking until the crust is golden, about 10 minutes. Transfer to a wire rack to cool completely.

4. Make the caramel by placing the sugar, salt, and water in a small saucepan. Bring the mixture to a boil over medium-high heat. Wash down the sides of the pan with a pastry brush dipped in water to prevent crystals from forming. Cook, gently swirling the pan (do not stir), until the caramel is a rich amber color. Remove from heat, and add ½ cup cream and the butter and vanilla; stir until smooth.

5. Pour the mixture into the chocolate tart shell. Sprinkle the toasted pecans over the caramel; refrigerate while melting the chocolate.

6. Place the chocolate in a medium heatproof bowl. Bring the remaining cup cream to a boil in a small saucepan; pour over the chocolate. Let sit for 5 minutes; stir until completely smooth. Pour over the caramel and nuts; return the tart to the refrigerator to chill for at least 1 hour.

7. When ready to serve, if desired, dust the top of the tart with cocoa powder and garnish with caramel-dipped pecans.

caramel-dipped pecans
MAKES 24

To produce interesting curves in the caramel drops, stand the skewers upright in flower foam or a heavy container while setting. If the caramel hardens before all the pecans have been dipped, rewarm it over low heat. A foolproof way to clean caramel from the pan is to bring it to a boil with a bit of added water.

24 pecan halves
3 cups sugar
¾ cup water
1 teaspoon cream of tartar

1. Gently insert an 8-inch wooden skewer into each pecan. Set aside.

2. Prepare an ice-water bath, and set aside. Combine the sugar, water, and cream of tartar in a medium saucepan, and bring to a boil over medium-high heat. Wash down the sides of the pan with a pastry brush dipped in water to prevent sugar crystals from forming. Cook, without stirring, until the mixture begins to brown. Gently swirl the pan to color evenly. Remove from heat when the caramel is a rich amber color, and place the pan in the ice bath for 5 seconds to stop the cooking.

3. Allow the caramel to sit until slightly thickened, about 15 minutes. (To test: Dip a wooden spoon into the caramel, and lift it several inches over the pan; if a drip slowly forms and then hardens, the caramel is ready.) When the caramel is ready, dip the pecans, lifting up and swirling slightly to fully coat. Hold the skewer over the pan to allow the drip to lengthen and slightly harden, about 1 minute. If necessary, use a pair of scissors to cut the drip from the caramel remaining in the pan.

4. Place the skewers on an inverted baking sheet lined with waxed paper, and allow the caramel to completely harden, about 5 minutes. If desired, stand the skewers upright in flower foam or a heavy container until ready to serve. Gently remove the skewers before serving.

chocolate cream pie
MAKES ONE 8-INCH PIE

For the smoothest, glossiest peaks, be careful not to overbeat the egg whites.

1 12-ounce box chocolate wafers
7 tablespoons unsalted butter, melted
½ cup milk
1 teaspoon unflavored gelatin
1 cup heavy cream
¾ cup plus 2 tablespoons sugar
8 ounces milk chocolate, finely chopped
1 teaspoon pure vanilla extract
4 large egg whites

1. Place the chocolate wafers in the bowl of a food processor, and pulse until finely ground. Transfer to a mixing bowl. Add the melted butter, and stir until well combined. Press into an 8-inch springform pan, evenly coating the bottom and lower half of the sides. Cover the pan with plastic wrap, and place in the refrigerator to chill for 30 minutes.

2. Pour the milk in a small bowl. Sprinkle the gelatin over the milk, and let soften for 5 minutes. Place the cream and 2 tablespoons sugar in a small saucepan, and bring to a boil, stirring to dissolve the sugar. Add the gelatin mixture, and stir to combine. Remove from heat. Add the chocolate and vanilla; cover, and let stand for 3 minutes. Stir until thoroughly combined.

3. Pass the mixture through a fine sieve into the prepared cookie crust; leave behind any undissolved chocolate to prevent the filling from becoming grainy. Return the filled crust to the refrigerator for 6 hours or overnight.

4. Place the egg whites and remaining ¾ cup sugar in the heatproof bowl of an electric mixer, and place over a pan of barely simmering water. Stir constantly until the egg whites are warm to the touch and the sugar is completely dissolved, about 3 minutes. Attach the bowl to the mixer, and use the whisk attachment to beat the egg whites on medium speed until soft peaks form, about 3 minutes. Raise the speed to high, and beat until stiff and glossy but not dry, about 1½ minutes.

5. Remove the pie from the refrigerator. Using a rubber spatula, drop the meringue on top, lifting the spatula to create tall peaks. Use a small kitchen blowtorch to brown the tops of the meringue peaks, or place under a broiler, watching carefully, as they will brown very quickly.

6. Chill the pie in the refrigerator, and serve cold. The pie will keep in the refrigerator up to 2 days.

limeade pie

MAKES ONE 13½ × 4½-INCH TART

- 12 ounces cream cheese, room temperature
- 1 cup granulated sugar
- 2 tablespoons finely grated lime zest (about 4 limes)
- ⅓ cup fresh lime juice
- ½ cup confectioners' sugar
- 1 lime, washed and thinly sliced
   Graham-Nut Crust (recipe follows)

1. Combine the cream cheese and granulated sugar in a food processor; process until the mixture is smooth. Add the lime zest and juice; pulse several times to combine. Transfer the filling to the prepared crust; cover with plastic wrap, and refrigerate until it is set, at least 1 hour.

2. Preheat the oven to 250° F. Line a baking sheet with parchment paper. Sprinkle the confectioners' sugar on a small plate. Dredge each lime slice in the sugar, turning to coat both sides. Transfer the slices to the prepared baking sheet. Bake until the slices are just stiff but not brown, about 40 minutes. Transfer to a wire rack to cool.

3. To serve, arrange the lime slices around the tart, or make a slit halfway through each slice, and tuck into slices of pie.

graham-nut crust

MAKES ONE 13½ × 4¼-INCH CRUST

- ¼ cup pecans
- 10 graham crackers (5 ounces)
- 3 tablespoons sugar
- ¼ teaspoon salt
- 4 tablespoons unsalted butter, melted

1. Preheat the oven to 350° F. Place the pecans in a single layer on a rimmed baking sheet, and toast until they are fragrant, about 8 minutes. Remove from the oven; let cool.

2. Place the graham crackers in a food processor; pulse until fine crumbs form. Add the sugar, salt, and pecans; pulse to combine. Add the butter; pulse until fine crumbs form.

3. Transfer to a 13½ × 4¼-inch tart pan with a removable bottom, and pat evenly into the bottom and up the sides. Place the pan on a baking sheet; bake until the crust is golden and fragrant, 8 to 10 minutes. Transfer to a wire rack to cool. The crust may be made up to 1 day ahead and stored, covered with plastic wrap, at room temperature.

strawberry chiffon pie

MAKES TWO 8-INCH PIES

If you are using pasteurized egg whites, you do not need to heat them before beating with the sugar and cream of tartar or coarse salt.

- 1 quart strawberries, hulled, plus 1 pint, for garnish
- 1 cup plus 2 tablespoons sugar
- 1½ ¼-ounce envelopes unflavored gelatin (1½ tablespoons)
- 2 large egg whites
  Pinch of cream of tartar
- 2 tablespoons fresh lemon juice
- ½ cup crème fraîche
  Almond Shortbread Crust (recipe follows)

1. Combine 1 quart strawberries and ½ cup sugar in the bowl of a food processor fitted with the metal blade; process until smooth, about 3 minutes; you should have 3 cups puree. Transfer half to a large heatproof mixing bowl; sprinkle the gelatin over the top; let soften, about 5 minutes.

2. In a heatproof bowl of an electric mixer, combine the egg whites with the cream of tartar and ½ cup sugar. Place the bowl over a saucepan of simmering water, and whisk until the mixture is hot to the touch and the sugar is dissolved, about 2 minutes. Attach the bowl to the mixer fitted with the whisk attachment; beat on medium-high speed until soft peaks form, about 2 minutes.

3. Place the gelatin mixture over the pan of simmering water, stirring occasionally, until the gelatin dissolves, about 5 minutes; remove from heat. Gradually whisk in the remaining puree; whisk in the lemon juice.

4. In a small bowl, whisk the crème fraîche until soft peaks form; whisk into the puree mixture. Whisk in one-third of the egg whites to lighten; fold in the remaining whites just until they are combined (do not overmix). Divide among the crusts; refrigerate, covered with plastic, until the mixture is set, at least 4 hours or overnight.

5. Thinly slice the remaining pint strawberries. Place in a small bowl, and sprinkle with the remaining 2 tablespoons sugar. Let stand at room temperature until the juices are running, at least 30 minutes and up to 2 hours. Serve the pie, cut into wedges and garnished with sliced strawberries.

almond shortbread crust

MAKES TWO 8-INCH CRUSTS

- 40 shortbread cookies (about 18 ounces)
- 1¼ cups blanched whole almonds, toasted
- 5 tablespoons sugar
- ½ teaspoon salt
- ½ cup (1 stick) unsalted butter, melted

1. Preheat the oven to 350°F. Place the cookies in the bowl of a food processor fitted with the metal blade, and process until fine crumbs form. Add about ¾ cup almonds with the sugar and salt; process until fine crumbs form. Add the butter, and process until the mixture comes together.

2. Coarsely chop the remaining almonds, and stir into the crust mixture. Press into the bottom and sides of 2 8-inch pie plates to form a crust, and bake until they are just turning golden, about 10 minutes. Transfer to a wire rack to cool completely.

blackberry tartlets

MAKES EIGHT 3½-INCH TARTLETS

If you have enough tartlet pans, use a second one over each to line the dough during baking to keep the crust from shrinking down the sides. You can also line the tartlet shells with parchment paper and dried beans; the shells will take a few minutes longer to bake.

> Martha's Perfect Pâte Brisée (page 647)
> All-purpose flour, for the work surface
> 2 half-pint containers blackberries (2½ cups)
> 4 tablespoons sugar
> 1 teaspoon lemon zest
> 1 cup heavy cream
> 8 fresh pansies for garnish (optional)

1. Roll the dough ⅛ inch thick on a lightly floured surface; fit into 8 fluted tartlet pans (3½ inches in diameter, 1½ inches deep). Chill at least 30 minutes, or overnight.

2. Preheat the oven to 375° F. Line the tart shells with a second pan or parchment paper and dry beans. Place in the oven; bake until golden brown, 20 to 25 minutes. Remove the top pans or parchment lining; return to the oven if the bottoms of the shells are not fully browned. Set on a cooling rack until fully cool.

3. Fill a bowl with ice and water; set aside. Place the berries, 2 tablespoons sugar, and the lemon zest in a medium saucepan over medium heat. Cook until the berries let off juices, the sugar dissolves, and the mixture begins to bubble, about 5 minutes. Remove from heat, and set the pan in the ice-water bath to cool.

4. Chill a bowl and large whisk. Place the cream and remaining 2 tablespoons sugar in the bowl; whip until soft peaks form. Fold ½ cup berry mixture into the whipped cream. Fill the tartlet shells with the mixture; top with the remaining berries and garnish with fresh pansies.

marsala cheese tart with oranges

MAKES ONE 8-INCH TART

> 5 ounces gingersnaps, broken into pieces
> 4 tablespoons unsalted butter, melted
> 8 ounces cream cheese, room temperature
> ½ cup sugar
> 2 tablespoons Marsala
> 1 teaspoon pure vanilla extract
> ½ cup heavy cream
> 3 navel oranges

1. Place the gingersnaps in the bowl of a food processor, and process until finely ground. Transfer to a bowl, add the melted butter, and stir until well combined. Transfer to an 8-inch fluted tart pan with a removable bottom, and press into the bottom and up the sides to form an even crust. Place in the freezer.

2. Place the cream cheese and sugar in the bowl of an electric mixer fitted with the paddle attachment; beat until fluffy. Add the Marsala and vanilla extract, and beat until combined. Whip the heavy cream to stiff peaks, and fold into the cream cheese mixture. Spoon the mixture into the prepared crust; return to the freezer at least 1 hour 15 minutes, or until firm.

3. Cut the ends off the oranges, and remove the peel, pith, and outer membranes, following the curve of the fruit with a paring knife. Lift the sections away from the inner membranes; reserve the sections. Serve the cheese tart, garnished with orange sections.

individual rhubarb and raspberry tartlets

MAKES EIGHT 4-INCH TARTLETS

The extra tablespoon of flour, sprinkled into the center of each pastry circle, helps thicken the rhubarb juices as the tartlets cook.

1½ pounds trimmed rhubarb, cut into ¼-inch pieces (about 5½ cups)

½ pound (about 1 pint) raspberries

1 cup all-purpose flour, plus more for the work surface

2 cups sugar, plus more for sprinkling

Martha's Perfect Pâte Brisée (page 647)

1. Combine the rhubarb, berries, ½ cup flour, and sugar in a medium bowl; set aside.

2. Divide the dough evenly into 8 pieces. On a lightly floured surface, roll out each piece of dough into a rough circle about 7 inches in diameter and ⅛ inch thick. Chill the dough until just cold and easy to work with, about 30 minutes.

3. Spoon 1 tablespoon flour in the center of each unbaked shell. Cover with about ½ cup rhubarb mixture, spreading the mixture to about 1 inch from the edge of the shell. Fold the edges of the shells over the rhubarb filling, leaving the tarts open in the center; gently brush between the folds with water, and press gently on the folds so the dough adheres together. Transfer the tarts to 2 parchment-lined baking sheets, arranging them so they are several inches apart. Return to the refrigerator to chill at least 30 minutes.

4. Preheat the oven to 400°F. Remove the tarts from the refrigerator, brush them with water, and sprinkle with sugar. Place in the oven to bake until the crust is golden brown, about 30 minutes, rotating the pans halfway through. Reduce heat to 350°F, and continue to bake until the juices are bubbly and just starting to run out from center of each tartlet, 10 to 12 minutes more, rotating the pans as needed. Transfer immediately to a wire rack, and let cool before serving.

peanut butter tart

MAKES ONE 13¾ × 4¼-INCH TART

10 4¾ × 2½-inch graham crackers, broken into pieces

6 tablespoons unsalted butter, melted

3 ounces best-quality milk chocolate, plus more for curls

1¾ cups heavy cream

¾ cup creamy peanut butter

½ cup cream cheese (4 ounces)

⅓ cup sweetened condensed milk

1. Place the graham crackers in the bowl of a food processor, and pulse until fine crumbs are formed. Transfer to a medium bowl, and add the butter. Stir with a fork until thoroughly combined. Place the crumbs in a 13¾ × 4¼-inch rectangular tart pan with a removable bottom. Press the crumbs up the sides of the pan to form the edge of the tart and then evenly over the bottom of the pan. Place in the refrigerator while making the filling.

2. Fill a large bowl with ice and water. Finely chop the chocolate, and place in a medium bowl. Place ½ cup cream in a small saucepan over medium heat, and bring to a boil. Pour over the chopped chocolate, and set aside for 5 minutes to yield chocolate ganache. Whisk to combine. Set in the ice bath until the ganache is cool, whisking constantly. Once cool, remove from the ice bath, and whisk until the ganache is just thick enough to hold its shape; do not overbeat. Spread in the bottom of the prepared crust, and return to the refrigerator until set.

3. Combine the peanut butter, cream cheese, and sweetened condensed milk in a food processor; process until smooth. Transfer to a mixing bowl.

4. In another bowl, whip ¾ cup heavy cream to soft peaks. Add the whipped cream to the peanut butter mixture; whisk to combine.

5. Spoon the mixture into the prepared crust; return to the refrigerator for 2 hours or overnight. Remove the tart from refrigerator, and transfer to a serving platter 10 minutes before serving. Whip the remaining ½ cup cream. Top the tart with dollops of whipped cream. Use a vegetable peeler to make chocolate curls for garnish.

apple praline tart

MAKES ONE 8-INCH TART

This tart may also be made in an 8-inch spring-form pan. Fit the dough into the pan, and press it up the sides. Trim so it is 1¾ inches high.

- 1   *disk Martha's Perfect Pâte Brisée (page 647)*
- ½   *cup all-purpose flour, plus more for the work surface*
- ½   *cup dried apricots, cut into quarters*
- ½   *cup dried figs, preferably Calimyrna, cut into ½-inch pieces*
- 2   *tablespoons cognac*
- ¼   *cup water*
- 3   *Granny Smith apples, peeled and cored (about 1¼ pounds)*
    Juice of 1 lemon
- ½   *cup roughly chopped Almond Praline (recipe follows), plus more for garnish*
- 3   *large eggs*
- ¾   *cup sugar*
- 12   *tablespoons unsalted butter*
- 1   *vanilla bean, split lengthwise and scraped*
    Vanilla ice cream, for serving

1. Preheat the oven to 350° F. Place an 8 × 1¾-inch cake ring on a parchment-lined baking sheet. Roll the pâte brisée on a lightly floured surface to ⅛-inch thickness. Fit gently into the ring, easing the dough into the corners and removing excess dough so the tart shell is flush with the top of the cake ring. Use a fork to pierce the bottom of the tart shell, and place in the freezer for 30 minutes.

2. Place the apricots, figs, cognac, and water in a medium saucepan, and bring to a simmer over medium heat. Cook, stirring occasionally, until all the liquid has been absorbed and the fruit is softened, about 4 minutes. Set aside to cool.

3. Cut the apples into ¾-inch cubes. Place them in a bowl, and combine with the lemon juice, tossing to coat. Add the dried fruit mixture and chopped praline, and stir to combine.

4. Combine the eggs, sugar, and flour in a medium bowl, and whisk until smooth. Place the butter and the vanilla bean pod and seeds in a sauté pan, and cook over medium-high heat until the butter begins to brown. Add to the egg mixture, and whisk until fully incorporated. Remove the pod, and discard.

5. Remove the tart shell from the freezer, and fill with the apple mixture, making sure the dried fruits are evenly distributed. Slowly pour the egg mixture over the fruit, letting it seep into all the gaps, until it is ⅛ inch from the top of the tart shell.

6. Place the tart in the oven, and bake until a tester inserted into the center comes out clean and the top is nicely browned, about 1 hour 30 minutes. Transfer to a wire rack to cool for 30 minutes before removing the ring.

7. Serve warm or at room temperature, topped with vanilla ice cream and garnished with almond praline.

almond praline

MAKES ONE 10 × 15-INCH SHEET

- 1½   *cups sliced almonds*
- 1   *tablespoon unsalted butter, room temperature*
- 2   *cups sugar*
- ½   *cup water*
    Juice of ½ lemon (1 tablespoon)

1. Preheat the oven to 350° F. Place the almonds on a baking sheet, and toast until golden brown and fragrant, about 10 minutes. Set aside to cool.

2. Butter a 10 × 15-inch rimmed baking sheet. Spread the toasted almonds in an even layer on the pan. Place the sugar and water in a medium saucepan; stir to combine. Place over medium-high heat; bring to a boil, brushing down the sides of the pan with a pastry brush dipped in water to prevent crystals from forming. Once the sugar is dissolved, cook without stirring until the sugar is a deep amber color.

3. Add the lemon juice; immediately pour mixture over almonds, coating with a thin layer. If the caramel doesn't cover all the nuts, tilt the pan slightly to distribute, or stir in the nuts with a wooden spoon, being careful not to touch the caramel or the hot pan. Cool completely.

4. Gently twist the pan to release the praline. Break into pieces. Store in an airtight container for up to 1 week.

cakes

....

basic chocolate cake

The cake layers can be wrapped well in plastic and refrigerated for up to 2 days; trim tops just before assembling.

Unsalted butter, for pans
1¼   cups unsweetened cocoa powder, plus more for dusting
2½   cups all-purpose flour
2½   cups sugar
2½   teaspoons baking soda
1¼   teaspoons baking powder
1¼   teaspoons salt
  2   large eggs plus 1 large yolk
1¼   cups warm water
1¼   cups buttermilk
 ½   cup plus 2 tablespoons vegetable oil
1¼   teaspoons pure vanilla extract
Vanilla or Chocolate Buttercream Frosting (recipes follow)

1. Preheat the oven to 350°F, with racks in the upper and lower thirds. Cut 2 8-inch rounds of parchment paper to line the bottoms of 2 8-inch (2 inches deep) round cake pans. Butter and line the pans. Butter the linings. Dust the pans with cocoa, tapping out excess. Set aside.

2. Sift together the cocoa, flour, sugar, baking soda, baking powder, and salt into the bowl of an electric mixer. Return the bowl to the mixer. Fit the mixer with the paddle attachment. Add the eggs, yolk, warm water, buttermilk, oil, and vanilla. Mix on low speed until smooth, about 3 minutes.

3. Divide the batter evenly between the prepared pans. Bake, switching the positions of the pans and rotating them halfway through, until a cake tester inserted into the centers comes out clean, about 40 minutes. Let cool in the pans on wire racks 30 minutes. Run a thin knife around the edges of the cakes to loosen. Unmold; peel off the parchment. Let cool completely, top sides up, on the racks.

4. Trim the tops of the cake layers with a long serrated knife to make them level. Using a small off-set spatula, cover the top of one cake layer evenly with 1½ cups frosting; spread the frosting so it extends just beyond the edges of the cake.

5. Place the second layer, cut side down, on top; press gently to level. Frost the top and sides of the assembled cake with the remaining frosting.

vanilla buttercream frosting

The frosting can be refrigerated in an airtight container for up to 3 days. Before using, bring to room temperature; beat with the paddle attachment on medium-low speed until smooth.

1⅓   cups sugar
  1   vanilla bean, halved lengthwise
  7   large egg whites
Pinch of salt
1¼   pounds (5 sticks) unsalted butter, cut into tablespoon-size pieces, softened
  2   teaspoons pure vanilla extract

1. Put the sugar in the bowl of a food processor, and scrape in the vanilla seeds. Process until combined. Sift into a bowl, and discard any large pieces of vanilla.

2. Put the egg whites, vanilla-sugar mixture, and salt in the heatproof bowl of an electric mixer. Set over a pan of simmering water. Whisk constantly until the sugar has dissolved and the mixture registers 160°F on an instant-read thermometer.

3. Return the bowl to the mixer; fit the mixer with the whisk attachment. Beat on medium-high speed until stiff, glossy peaks form and the mixture is cool, about 10 minutes.

4. Switch to the paddle attachment. With the mixer on medium speed, add the butter, 1 or 2 tablespoons at a time, mixing well after each addition. Mix, scraping down the sides of the bowl as needed, until the mixture is smooth. Mix in the vanilla extract. Use immediately, or cover and refrigerate.

chocolate buttercream frosting
MAKES ABOUT 6 CUPS

The frosting can be refrigerated in an airtight container for up to 3 days. Before using, bring to room temperature; beat with the paddle attachment on medium-low speed until smooth.

- 1½ cups sugar
- 6 large egg whites
- Pinch of salt
- 1 pound 6 ounces (5½ sticks) unsalted butter, cut into tablespoon-size pieces, softened
- 6 ounces semisweet chocolate, melted and cooled

1. Put the sugar, egg whites, and salt in the heatproof bowl of an electric mixer. Set over a pan of simmering water. Whisk constantly until the sugar has dissolved and the mixture registers 160° F on an instant-read thermometer.

2. Return the bowl to mixer; fit the mixer with the whisk attachment. Beat on medium-high speed until stiff, glossy peaks form, and the mixture is cool, about 10 minutes.

3. Switch to the paddle attachment. With the mixer on medium speed, add the butter, 1 or 2 tablespoons at a time, mixing well after each addition. Mix, scraping down the sides of the bowl as needed, until the mixture is smooth. Mix in the chocolate. Use immediately, or cover and refrigerate.

basic yellow cake
MAKES ONE 9-INCH LAYER CAKE

The cake layers can be wrapped well in plastic and refrigerated for up to 2 days; trim the tops just before assembling.

- Unsalted butter, for the pans
- 4¼ cups all-purpose flour, plus more for dusting
- 3⅓ cups sugar
- 3½ teaspoons baking soda
- 1¾ teaspoons baking powder
- 1¾ teaspoons salt
- 3 large eggs plus 1 large yolk
- 1¾ cups warm water
- 2 cups buttermilk
- ¾ cup vegetable oil
- 2 teaspoons pure vanilla extract
- Vanilla or Chocolate Buttercream Frosting (recipes opposite and at left)

1. Preheat the oven to 350° F, with racks in the upper and lower thirds. Cut 2 9-inch rounds of parchment paper to line the bottoms of 2 9-inch (2 inches deep) round cake pans. Butter and line the pans. Butter the linings. Dust the pans with flour, tapping out excess. Set aside.

2. Sift together the flour, sugar, baking soda, baking powder, and salt into the bowl of an electric mixer. Return the bowl to the mixer; fit the mixer with the paddle attachment. Add the eggs, yolk, warm water, buttermilk, oil, and vanilla. Mix on low speed until the mixture is smooth, about 3 minutes.

3. Divide the batter evenly between the prepared pans. Bake, switching the positions of the pans and rotating them halfway through, until a cake tester inserted into the centers comes out clean, about 42 minutes. Let cool in the pans on wire racks 30 minutes. Run a thin knife around the edges of the cakes to loosen. Unmold; peel off the parchment. Let cool completely, top sides up, on the racks.

4. Trim the tops of the cake layers with a long serrated knife to make them level. Using a small offset spatula, evenly cover the top of one cake layer with 1½ cups frosting; spread the frosting so it extends just beyond the edges of the cake.

5. Place the second cake layer, cut side down, on top; press gently to make it level. Frost the top and sides of assembled cake with the remaining frosting.

apple-ginger stack cake

MAKES ONE 9-INCH LAYER CAKE

- 5 cups dried apples (about ¾ pound)
- 5 cups apple cider
- 1⅔ cups granulated sugar
- 1 cup (2 sticks) unsalted butter, softened, plus more for the pans
- 3 cups sifted all-purpose flour, plus more for the pans
- 1 large egg
- 1 cup unsulfured molasses
- 1 cup buttermilk
- 1 teaspoon baking soda
- 1 teaspoon ground ginger
- ⅛ teaspoon ground cloves
- ½ teaspoon salt
- Confectioners' sugar, for dusting

1. Bring the apples and cider to a boil in a large pot. Reduce to a simmer; cook, stirring occasionally, until the apples begin to soften and the liquid has reduced, 40 to 50 minutes. Add 1 cup water; cook, mashing the apples slightly, until the liquid has reduced, about 10 minutes. Add ⅔ cup granulated sugar and ½ cup water; simmer until the apples are very soft and coated in syrup, about 15 minutes. Let cool completely.

2. Preheat the oven to 375°F. Butter 2 9-inch round cake pans. Line the bottoms with parchment paper, and butter the parchment. Dust with flour; tap out excess. Set aside.

3. Put the butter and the remaining cup sugar in the bowl of an electric mixer fitted with the paddle attachment. Mix on medium-high speed until creamy, about 3 minutes. Reduce speed to low; mix in the egg, molasses, buttermilk, baking soda, flour, spices, and salt.

4. Divide the batter evenly between the prepared pans. Bake until a cake tester inserted into the centers comes out clean and the tops spring back when lightly touched, about 35 minutes. Let cool on a wire rack 10 minutes. Run a knife around the edges of the pans to loosen; invert to unmold. Remove the parchment; reinvert onto the racks. Let cool.

5. Using a long serrated knife, cut each cake in half horizontally. Place 1 bottom layer on a serving platter. Top with one-third of the apple mixture, spreading to the edges. Stack 1 top layer on the apples, and top with another one-third of the apple mixture. Repeat with the remaining cake bottom and apples, and top with the remaining cake top. Let stand at room temperature at least 1 hour before serving. Sift confectioners' sugar over the top of the cake.

chocolate-ginger cake with bourbon sauce

MAKES ONE 9-INCH BUNDT CAKE

- ½ cup (1 stick) unsalted butter, softened, plus more for the pan
- ½ cup unsweetened Dutch-process cocoa powder, plus more for dusting
- ½ cup unsulfured molasses
- ¾ cup packed light-brown sugar
- 2 large eggs
- ¼ cup whole milk
- 2 teaspoons finely grated peeled fresh ginger
- 1 cup all-purpose flour
- ¾ teaspoon baking soda
- ½ teaspoon coarse salt
- 1 teaspoon ground ginger
- 1 teaspoon ground cinnamon
- Bourbon Sauce (recipe follows)

1. Preheat the oven to 325°F. Butter a 9-inch Bundt pan. Dust with cocoa powder, and tap out excess; set aside. Put the butter, molasses, brown sugar, and ¼ cup water in a medium saucepan over medium-low heat. Cook, stirring constantly, until the butter has melted. Transfer the mixture to a large bowl. Let cool 5 minutes.

2. Add the eggs, milk, and grated ginger to the molasses mixture; whisk to combine. Sift together the flour, cocoa powder, baking soda, salt, ground ginger, and cinnamon into a medium bowl.

3. Gently fold the flour mixture into the molasses mixture until just combined. (There should be lumps remaining.) Pour the batter into the prepared pan. Bake the cake until a cake tester inserted into the center comes out clean, about 30 minutes. Let the cake cool completely in the pan on a wire rack.

4. Invert the cake, and unmold onto a cake stand or a large serving platter. Using a spoon, drizzle the warm bourbon sauce over the cake in a back-and-forth motion. Serve immediately.

bourbon sauce
MAKES 1 1/4 CUPS

½ cup (1 stick) unsalted butter

2 large egg yolks

1 cup packed dark-brown sugar

1 teaspoon pure vanilla extract

¼ cup good-quality bourbon

Put the butter, egg yolks, brown sugar, vanilla, and bourbon in a heatproof bowl set over a pan of simmering water. Cook, whisking constantly, until the mixture registers 160°F on a candy thermometer, about 7 minutes.

cream cheese–poppy seed cakes
MAKES 12 SMALL CAKES

1 cup (2 sticks) unsalted butter, softened, plus more for the molds

1½ cups cake flour (not self-rising), plus more for the molds

½ teaspoon coarse salt

1⅓ cups granulated sugar

3 large eggs, plus 3 large egg yolks

1½ teaspoons pure vanilla extract

¾ cup whipped cream cheese, room temperature

3 tablespoons confectioners' sugar, plus more for dusting

1 teaspoon poppy seeds

1. Preheat the oven to 325°F. Butter 12 3½-inch brioche molds or a standard 12-cup muffin tin. Dust with flour; tap out excess. Whisk the flour and salt in a medium bowl; set aside.

2. Put the butter and granulated sugar into the bowl of an electric mixer fitted with the paddle attachment; cream on medium speed until light and fluffy. Mix in the eggs and yolks, one at a time. Add the vanilla and 1½ teaspoons water; mix until combined. Reduce speed to low. Add the flour mixture; mix until just combined, scraping down the sides as needed. Spoon 1 cup batter into each mold.

3. Beat the cream cheese and confectioners' sugar in the clean bowl of the electric mixer on low speed until creamy and combined. Spoon 1 tablespoon of the mixture onto the batter in each mold; sprinkle with poppy seeds. Bake until a cake tester comes out clean, about 25 minutes. Let cool 5 minutes; transfer the cakes to a wire rack to cool completely. Serve dusted with confectioners' sugar.

génoise torte with chocolate and praline caramel mousses

SERVES 10

1½ teaspoons unflavored gelatin

1¼ cups sugar

2¼ cups heavy cream

¼ cup (½ stick) unsalted butter, cut into 4 pieces

2 ounces unsweetened chocolate, finely chopped

Almond Praline (recipe follows)

3 tablespoons cognac or brandy

½ cup Simple Syrup (page 660)

Génoise (12 × 16-inch cake; recipe follows), cut crosswise into 4 rectangles

¾ pound bittersweet chocolate, scraped with a large knife (about 1 cup)

1. Sprinkle 1 teaspoon gelatin over 2 tablespoons water in a heatproof bowl. Sprinkle the remaining ½ teaspoon gelatin over 1 tablespoon water in another heatproof bowl. Let soften about 3 minutes.

2. Bring the sugar and ½ cup water to a boil in a medium saucepan over high heat; swirl the pan to dissolve the sugar. Wash down the sides of the pan with a wet pastry brush to prevent crystals from forming. Boil until the sugar turns dark amber, about 10 minutes. Remove from heat. Slowly add 1 cup cream and the butter, stirring until the butter has melted. Put ⅔ cup caramel into a medium bowl; set aside. Stir together the remaining caramel and the unsweetened chocolate in another medium bowl; set aside.

3. Set 1 bowl of softened gelatin over a pan of simmering water, and stir until the gelatin has melted. Repeat with the remaining bowl of gelatin. Pour the larger batch of gelatin into the plain caramel. Pour the smaller batch of gelatin into the chocolate caramel. Let both caramels cool completely, stirring occasionally, 10 to 12 minutes.

4. Whisk the remaining 1¼ cups cream in a medium bowl until stiff peaks form. Fold one-third of the whipped cream into the plain caramel mixture; fold the remaining whipped cream into the chocolate-caramel mixture. Refrigerate the mousses until slightly firm, about 10 minutes. Stir the almond praline into the plain caramel mousse.

5. Stir the cognac and simple syrup in a small bowl. Assemble the torte: Place 1 cake rectangle on a platter; brush with one-quarter of the cognac syrup. Spread with half the chocolate-caramel mousse. Top with another cake rectangle; brush with one-quarter of the syrup. Spread with praline-caramel mousse. Refrigerate 10 minutes to set. Top with another cake rectangle; brush with one-quarter of the syrup. Spread with the remaining chocolate-caramel mousse. Top with the remaining cake rectangle; brush with the remaining syrup. Clean the edges with an offset spatula. Refrigerate until firm, about 30 minutes. Before serving, sprinkle with bittersweet chocolate shavings.

almond praline

MAKES ABOUT ⅔ CUP

Vegetable oil cooking spray

½ cup sugar

⅓ cup sliced blanched almonds

¼ teaspoon salt

1. Spray a rimmed baking sheet with cooking spray; set aside. Bring the sugar and ¼ cup water to a boil in a small saucepan over medium-high heat. Swirl the pan to dissolve the sugar. Wash down the sides of the pan with a wet pastry brush to prevent crystals from forming. Boil until the sugar turns light amber, about 7 minutes.

2. Add the almonds and salt; cook, stirring constantly, until the almonds are toasted and the caramel turns dark amber. Pour onto the prepared sheet. Let cool completely.

3. Break into shards. Pulse until finely ground, with a few larger pieces remaining, in a food processor.

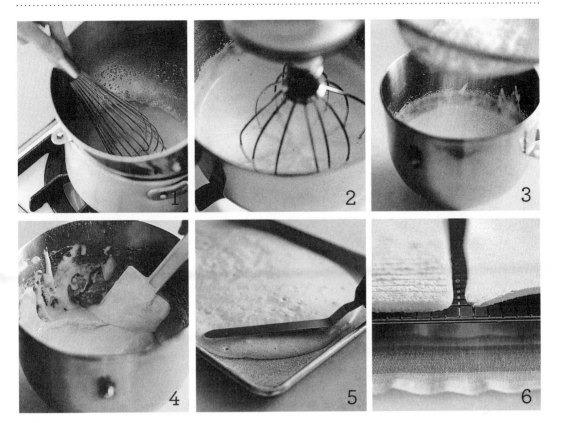

MAKING GÉNOISE

1. Heating the eggs and sugar in a bowl over a pan of simmering water relaxes the egg proteins, enabling the eggs to whip up higher and more quickly. (This process also melts the sugar, resulting in a fine-textured cake.) Heat the mixture, whisking, until the eggs are warm to the touch and you can't feel any grains of sugar when you rub the mixture between your fingers.

2. The more air you incorporate at this stage, the lighter the génoise will be. Beat the eggs on high speed until they are pale white, doubled in volume, and hold a thick ribbon, about 6 minutes total.

3. Once the eggs have been beaten, it is important to avoid deflating the batter. Sift the flour-salt mixture on top to help preserve the batter's lightness. Use a large rubber spatula to begin folding it in.

4. After you've mostly, but not entirely, folded in the flour, add the melted butter. Make sure the butter has cooled (hot butter will cause the mixture to collapse), and pour it down the side of the bowl in a slow, steady stream so it hits the batter gently. Working quickly, continue folding just until ingredients have been incorporated. The mixture should be thick, not runny like pancake batter.

5. Pour the batter into the cake pan as close to the surface as possible; this will minimize the impact. Using a large offset spatula, spread the batter evenly to the edges of the pan with the fewest number of strokes possible. Bake as directed.

6. Once the génoise has been baked, the results should resemble the cake on the left—it's fluffy, golden, and springy to the touch. The cake on the right—with hard, curled edges—is the result of a deflated batter.

GÉNOISE TORTE TIPS

To create even layers for stacking, use a ruler to measure the sheet cake into 4 equal portions before slicing. A very sharp knife will prevent it from crumbling. You can save any trimmings to use in a trifle or as the base for petits fours.

génoise

MAKES ONE 12 × 16-INCH SHEET CAKE OR
ONE 9-INCH ROUND CAKE

See the how-to on page 487.

Vegetable oil cooking spray

⅔ *cup sifted cake flour, plus more for the pan*

Pinch of salt

3 *large eggs*

2 *large egg yolks*

½ *cup granulated sugar*

¼ *cup (½ stick) unsalted butter, melted and cooled*

Confectioners' sugar, for dusting (if rolling the cake)

1. Coat a 12 × 16-inch rimmed baking sheet or a 9-inch round cake pan with cooking spray. Line with parchment; coat with cooking spray. Dust with flour, tapping out excess. Stir together the flour and salt into a medium bowl; set aside. Preheat the oven to 450°F for a sheet cake or 400°F for a round cake, with a rack in the lower third.

2. Put the eggs, egg yolks, and granulated sugar in the heatproof bowl of an electric mixer. Set over a pan of simmering water; whisk until the sugar has dissolved and the mixture is warm to the touch. Return the bowl to the mixer, fitted with the whisk attachment. Beat on medium-high speed for 2 minutes. Raise speed to high. Beat until the mixture is pale and thick, about 4 minutes more.

3. Remove the bowl from the mixer. Sift the flour mixture over the top; using a large rubber spatula, carefully fold it into the egg mixture, cutting through the middle and lifting gently over the sides. When almost incorporated, pour the melted butter down the side of the bowl; gently fold to incorporate completely.

4. Spread the batter evenly in the sheet or pan with a large offset spatula. Bake until golden brown and springy to the touch, about 6 minutes for a 12 × 16-inch cake and 15 minutes for a 9-inch round cake.

5. For the 12 × 16-inch cake: Run a small knife around the sides of the baking sheet; invert cake onto a wire rack. Remove the parchment. Reinvert the cake onto the rack. Let cool completely.

6. For the 9-inch round cake: Let cool in the pan on a wire rack for 15 minutes; run a small knife around the sides of the pan. Invert onto a rack; remove the parchment, and reinvert onto the rack. Let cool completely.

strawberry cake

MAKES ONE 10-INCH CAKE

6 *tablespoons unsalted butter, softened, plus more for the pie plate*

1½ *cups all-purpose flour*

1½ *teaspoons baking powder*

½ *teaspoon salt*

1 *cup plus 2 tablespoons sugar*

1 *large egg*

½ *cup milk*

1 *teaspoon pure vanilla extract*

1 *pound strawberries, hulled and halved*

1. Preheat the oven to 350°F. Butter a 10-inch pie plate. Sift the flour, baking powder, and salt together into a medium bowl.

2. Put the butter and 1 cup sugar in the bowl of an electric mixer fitted with the paddle attachment. Mix on medium-high speed until pale and fluffy, about 3 minutes. Reduce speed to medium-low; mix in the egg, milk, and vanilla.

3. Reduce speed to low; gradually mix in the flour mixture. Transfer the batter to the buttered pie plate. Arrange the strawberries on top of the batter, cut sides down and as close together as possible. Sprinkle the remaining 2 tablespoons sugar over the strawberries.

4. Bake the cake 10 minutes. Reduce the oven temperature to 325°F. Bake until the cake is golden brown and firm to the touch, about 1 hour. Let cool in the pie plate on a wire rack. Cut into wedges. The cake can be stored at room temperature, loosely covered, for up to 2 days.

pecan torte

MAKES ONE 10-INCH TORTE

9 large eggs, separated

1½ cups granulated sugar

1 tablespoon freshly grated lemon zest,
plus more for garnish

1 teaspoon pure vanilla extract

1 teaspoon salt

12 ounces pecans, toasted and finely
ground (3 cups)

Confectioners' sugar, for dusting

Passover Lemon Curd (recipe follows)

Mixed berries, for serving

1. Preheat the oven to 350° F. Put the egg yolks, granulated sugar, zest, vanilla, and salt in the bowl of an electric mixer fitted with the whisk attachment. Beat on medium-high speed until pale and thickened, about 4 minutes. Fold in pecans.

2. Beat the whites in a clean mixing bowl until stiff peaks form; fold into the yolk mixture. Pour into a 10-inch springform pan.

3. Bake until golden brown, about 1 hour (if the top browns too quickly, tent with foil). Let cool on a wire rack 30 minutes. Remove the sides of the pan. Let cool completely. Dust with confectioners' sugar. Serve with curd and berries; garnish with zest.

passover lemon curd

MAKES 1¾ CUPS

2 large eggs plus 6 large egg yolks

1 cup sugar

Pinch of salt

Freshly grated zest of 2 lemons plus ⅔
cup fresh lemon juice (3 lemons)

1½ sticks (12 tablespoons) margarine,
cut into 6 pieces

Beat the eggs, yolks, sugar, and salt with an electric mixer until pale and thickened. Beat in the lemon juice; add the margarine. Bring to a simmer in a medium saucepan over medium heat, whisking. Cook until thickened, 3 to 4 minutes. Pour through a fine sieve into a bowl; stir in zest. Refrigerate until cold, about 1 hour.

glazed lemon pound cake

MAKES ONE 5 X 9-INCH LOAF

This cake doesn't rise very much, so don't be surprised if it is shorter than you expect.

5 tablespoons unsalted butter,
softened, plus more for the pan

¾ cup plus 3 tablespoons sugar, plus
more for dusting

1 cup all-purpose flour

¼ teaspoon salt

¼ teaspoon baking soda

3 tablespoons fresh lemon juice plus
finely grated zest of 2 lemons, plus more
zest for garnish (optional)

¼ cup milk

2 large eggs

1. Preheat the oven to 350° F. Butter a 5 × 9-inch loaf pan. Dust with sugar, and tap out excess; set aside. Whisk together the flour, salt, and baking soda. Stir together 1 tablespoon lemon juice and the milk.

2. Put the butter and ¾ cup sugar in the bowl of an electric mixer fitted with the paddle attachment. Mix until pale and fluffy, about 2 minutes. Mix in the eggs and zest. Working in 2 batches, alternate mixing in the flour mixture and the milk mixture. Pour the batter into the prepared pan. Bake until a cake tester comes out clean, about 35 minutes.

3. Meanwhile, stir together the remaining 3 tablespoons sugar and 2 tablespoons lemon juice. Upon removing the cake from the oven, immediately brush with the lemon glaze. Let the cake cool in the pan 10 minutes. Unmold the cake. Brush the remaining glaze on top. Garnish with zest.

six-layer chocolate cake

MAKES ONE 9-INCH LAYER CAKE

Vegetable oil cooking spray

3½ cups all-purpose flour, plus more
    for dusting

1   tablespoon plus 1 teaspoon
    baking powder

2   teaspoons salt

4   sticks (1 pound) unsalted butter, softened

2¾ cups sugar

1   cup crème fraîche (8 ounces)

1   tablespoon pure vanilla extract

9   large eggs

1¼ pounds bittersweet chocolate (preferably
    70 percent cacao), melted and cooled

    Tangy Chocolate Frosting (recipe follows)

1. Preheat the oven to 325°F. Cut 3 9-inch rounds of parchment paper to line the bottoms of 3 9 × 2-inch round cake pans. Coat the pans with cooking spray. Line with parchment rounds; coat the parchment with cooking spray. Flour the pans, tapping out excess; set aside.

2. Sift the flour, baking powder, and salt together into a bowl; set aside.

3. Put the butter and sugar in the bowl of an electric mixer fitted with the paddle attachment. Mix on medium-high speed until pale and fluffy, about 3 minutes. Reduce speed to medium-low; mix in the crème fraîche and vanilla. Add the flour mixture and eggs in alternating additions; mix well, scraping down the sides of the bowl as necessary, until the batter is smooth.

4. Reduce speed to low. Pour in the melted chocolate in a slow, steady stream; mix until combined. Remove the bowl from the mixer; scrape down the sides (batter will be thick). Stir until combined.

5. Divide the batter among the pans, smoothing the tops with an offset spatula. Bake until a cake tester inserted into the centers comes out with moist crumbs, 35 to 40 minutes.

6. Let the cakes cool in the pans on wire racks 30 minutes. Unmold the cakes; peel off the parchment. Let the cakes cool completely.

7. Trim the tops of the cakes with a long serrated knife to make the surfaces level. Using a ruler to measure halfway up the sides of 1 cake, insert toothpicks around the cake's middle at 3-inch intervals to mark 2 equal layers. Rest the serrated knife on the toothpicks; halve the cake horizontally using a sawing motion. Carefully slide the top cake half onto a cardboard cake round or a plate. Repeat with the remaining 2 cakes.

8. Put 1 bottom cake half on a cake plate. Using a small offset spatula, spread ¾ cup frosting on top. Carefully set the top cake half back in place. Spread ¾ cup frosting on top. Repeat, stacking the remaining 4 cake halves on top and spreading ¾ cup frosting between each. (Do not frost the top of the last layer.)

9. Spread the top and sides of the cake with 2 cups frosting in a thin smooth layer. Refrigerate 30 minutes. Spread the remaining frosting over the top and sides; apply with the offset spatula using an S motion to create a textured appearance. The cake can be refrigerated, under a cake dome, up to 3 days; bring to room temperature before serving.

tangy chocolate frosting

MAKES 10 CUPS

4½ cups confectioners' sugar

½   cup good-quality unsweetened
    cocoa powder

¼   teaspoon salt

12 ounces cream cheese (1½ packages),
    room temperature

1½ sticks (12 tablespoons) unsalted
    butter, softened

18 ounces bittersweet chocolate (preferably
    70 percent cacao), melted and cooled

1½ cups crème fraîche (12 ounces)

1. Sift the sugar, cocoa, and salt together into a bowl; set aside. Put the cream cheese and butter in the bowl of an electric mixer fitted with the paddle attachment. Mix on medium speed until smooth.

2. Reduce speed to low; gradually mix in the sugar mixture. Pour in the melted chocolate in a slow, steady stream. Gradually mix in the crème fraîche. The frosting can be refrigerated, in an airtight container, up to 3 days. Just before using, bring to room temperature; beat until smooth.

brandied cherry cassata
SERVES 9

- 3 cups fresh ricotta cheese
- 2 cups granulated sugar
- 1 tablespoon freshly grated orange zest
- 1 vanilla bean, halved lengthwise
- 1½ cups drained brandied cherries, plus ¼ cup liquid from jar
- Vegetable oil cooking spray
- 1 cup all-purpose flour, plus more for dusting
- ½ cup milk
- 4 tablespoons unsalted butter
- 2 large eggs, room temperature
- 1 teaspoon pure vanilla extract
- 1 teaspoon baking powder
- ¼ teaspoon salt
- Confectioners' sugar, for dusting

1. Put the ricotta, ½ cup granulated sugar, and zest in a food processor; scrape in the vanilla seeds. Process until smooth. Transfer the mixture to a bowl, and then stir in the drained cherries. Refrigerate.

2. Preheat the oven to 350° F. Bring ½ cup water and ½ cup granulated sugar to a boil in a small saucepan, stirring until the sugar is dissolved. Let cool completely. Stir in the cherry liquid. Refrigerate. Coat an 8-inch-square baking pan with cooking spray. Line with parchment; coat the lining with spray. Dust with flour; tap out excess.

3. Bring the milk and butter to a boil in a small saucepan. Remove from heat. Put the eggs in the bowl of an electric mixer fitted with the whisk attachment; beat on medium-high speed until pale and fluffy, about 6 minutes. Beat in the remaining cup granulated sugar and the vanilla. On low speed, gradually add the flour. Drizzle in the hot milk mixture. Beat in the baking powder and salt.

4. Pour into the prepared pan. Bake until a cake tester inserted into the center comes out clean, about 20 minutes. Cool on a wire rack 30 minutes. Unmold; remove the parchment. Cool completely.

5. Split the cake horizontally into thirds. Brush a cut side of each layer with syrup. Spread half of the filling on the bottom layer. Top with middle layer, and spread with the remaining filling. Top with the third layer. Refrigerate until firm, 2 hours. Dust with confectioners' sugar. Cut into 9 squares.

chocolate truffle cakes
MAKES 6 INDIVIDUAL CAKES

For extra-fudgy results, make these cakes 1 day ahead; wrap them well in plastic wrap, and refrigerate. Serve them chilled or at room temperature.

- 5 tablespoons unsalted butter, plus more for the muffin tin
- 1 tablespoon all-purpose flour, plus more for dusting
- 14 ounces semisweet chocolate, chopped
- 2 tablespoons sugar
- 2 large eggs
- ¼ teaspoon salt

1. Preheat the oven to 375° F. Generously butter a standard 6-cup muffin tin. Dust with flour, tapping out excess; set aside.

2. Put the chocolate, butter, and 1 tablespoon sugar in a medium heatproof bowl set over a pan of simmering water; whisk occasionally until smooth. Remove from heat, and let stand until cool and thickened, 3 to 5 minutes. Process the eggs and remaining tablespoon sugar in a food processor until pale and doubled in volume, about 2 minutes. Sift the flour and salt into the egg mixture; pulse to combine. Add the chocolate mixture ¼ cup at a time; pulse each addition until combined, about 10 times. (Batter will be thick.)

3. Spoon the mixture into the prepared muffin tin, filling the cups three-quarters full; swirl the tops with the back of a spoon. Bake until the tops are springy to the touch, 18 to 20 minutes. Immediately turn out onto wire racks; reinvert, and let cool.

coconut rum-raisin bundt cake with rum-caramel glaze

MAKES ONE 12-CUP BUNDT CAKE

- 10 ounces (2½ sticks) unsalted butter, softened, plus more for the pan
- 3 cups all-purpose flour, plus more for dusting
- 1 cup raisins
- ¾ cup dark rum
- 1 teaspoon salt
- ½ teaspoon baking powder
- 2¾ cups plus 2 tablespoons packed light-brown sugar
- 6 large eggs
- 2 teaspoons pure vanilla extract
- ¾ cup plus 2 tablespoons heavy cream
- 1 cup sweetened flaked coconut
- 1 cup granulated sugar

1. Preheat the oven to 325° F. Butter a 12-cup Bundt pan; dust with flour, tapping out excess. Soak the raisins in ½ cup rum.

2. Whisk together the flour, salt, and baking powder; set aside. Put the butter and brown sugar in the bowl of an electric mixer fitted with the paddle attachment; cream on medium speed until smooth. Mix in the eggs, 1 at a time. Add the vanilla. On low speed, mix in the flour mixture in 3 additions, alternating with 2 additions of 6 tablespoons cream each (12 total). Mix in the raisin mixture and the coconut. Transfer the batter to the prepared pan; smooth the top.

3. Bake, rotating about halfway through, until a cake tester comes out clean, about 1 hour 55 minutes. Let cool in the pan on a wire rack 20 minutes. Run a thin knife around the sides of the cake; unmold. Let cool.

4. Heat the granulated sugar and ¼ cup water in a small saucepan over medium heat, gently stirring occasionally, until the sugar is dissolved and the syrup is clear. Cook, without stirring, until the syrup comes to a boil, washing down the sides of the pan with a wet pastry brush to prevent crystals from forming. Let boil, gently swirling, until medium amber. Remove from heat. Carefully pour in the remaining ¼ cup rum and 2 tablespoons cream. Let cool, stirring, until thickened. Drizzle over cake.

almond custard cake

MAKES ONE 9-INCH CAKE

Almond flour is simply ground blanched almonds—it doesn't contain any wheat flour. You can make your own by finely grinding ½ cup whole blanched almonds in a food processor. The dough can be refrigerated for up to 2 days or frozen for up to 1 month (thaw before using). The custard filling can be made up to 1 day ahead; press plastic wrap directly onto its surface (to prevent a skin from forming), and refrigerate in an airtight container.

- 12 tablespoons (1½ sticks) unsalted butter, softened, plus more for the pan
- 2½ cups plus 1 tablespoon all-purpose flour, plus more for dusting
- ½ cup almond flour
- 1½ teaspoons baking powder
- ¼ teaspoon salt
- 1¾ cups plus 2 tablespoons granulated sugar
- 7 large egg yolks
- 3 tablespoons sweet dessert wine, such as Sauternes or Beaumes-de-Venise
- 1 teaspoon pure almond extract
- 1 vanilla bean, halved lengthwise, and seeds scraped to loosen
- 1¾ cups whole milk
  Freshly grated zest of 1 orange
- 1 tablespoon heavy cream
- 2 tablespoons sliced blanched almonds
  Confectioners' sugar, for dusting
  Strawberry-Rhubarb Sauce, for serving (recipe follows)

1. Cut a 9-inch round of parchment paper to line the bottom of a 9 × 2-inch round cake pan. Butter and line the pan. Butter the lining, then flour the pan, tapping out excess; set aside.

2. Make the dough: Whisk together 2¼ cups flour and the almond flour, baking powder, and salt in a medium bowl; set aside.

3. Put the butter and 1½ cups granulated sugar in the bowl of an electric mixer fitted with the paddle attachment. Mix on medium speed until pale and fluffy, about 2 minutes. Add 3 egg yolks, 1 at a time, mixing well after each addition and scraping down the sides of the bowl. Add the wine, almond extract, and half the vanilla seeds; mix until combined, about 15 seconds. Add the flour mixture in 2 additions, mixing until just combined (do not overmix).

4. Divide the dough in half, and flatten each piece into a disk. Wrap the disks in plastic wrap. Refrigerate 1 hour.

5. Make the custard filling: Prepare an ice-water bath; set aside. Fit an electric mixer with the whisk attachment. Put 3 egg yolks and the remaining 6 tablespoons sugar in a clean mixing bowl; beat on medium speed until pale yellow and thickened. Add the remaining 5 tablespoons flour; beat on low speed until combined.

6. Bring the milk, remaining vanilla seeds, and zest to a boil in a medium saucepan over medium heat. Pour ½ cup hot milk mixture into the egg mixture, and beat on medium-low speed until combined. Stir the mixture into the remaining milk in the saucepan. Bring to a simmer over medium heat, stirring to reach the bottom and sides of the pan. Cook until thickened, 1 to 2 minutes. Set the pan in the ice-water bath; stir occasionally until cool, about 20 minutes.

7. Preheat the oven to 375° F. Press 1 piece of dough onto the bottom of the prepared pan and 1½ inches up the sides. Spoon the custard on top, and spread into an even layer.

8. On a lightly floured surface, roll the remaining dough into an 11-inch circle. Drape over the pan; trim the edges flush with the pan. Gently press the edges of the top crust to meet the bottom crust; crimp the top edges with a fork to seal. Refrigerate the cake 30 minutes.

9. Beat the remaining egg yolk and the cream in a small bowl. Brush the top of the cake with egg wash; sprinkle with almonds. Bake until golden brown, about 35 minutes. Let cool completely in the pan on a wire rack. Invert the cake to unmold; peel off the parchment, and reinvert. Just before serving, dust the cake with confectioners' sugar. Serve with the strawberry-rhubarb sauce.

strawberry-rhubarb sauce
MAKES 2½ CUPS

This sauce can be made 2 days ahead and refrigerated in an airtight container. Reheat over medium-low heat, or bring to room temperature before serving.

- 12 ounces rhubarb (6 to 8 stalks), trimmed and cut into 1-inch pieces
- 6 tablespoons sugar
- 1½ cups strawberries (8 ounces), hulled and halved
- ½ teaspoon pure vanilla extract

Bring the rhubarb, sugar, and ¼ cup water to a simmer in a medium saucepan over medium-high heat, stirring occasionally. Cook until the liquid is reduced by half, about 8 minutes. Stir in the strawberries and vanilla; cook until the berries are softened, about 3 minutes more. Serve the sauce warm or at room temperature.

raspberry-swirl cheesecake

MAKES ONE 9-INCH CAKE

- 1 cup finely ground graham crackers
  (5 ounces; about 8 sheets)
- 2 tablespoons unsalted butter, melted
- 1¾ cups sugar
- 6 ounces raspberries (about 1½ cups)
- 4 packages (8 ounces each) cream cheese,
  room temperature
  Pinch of salt
- 1 teaspoon pure vanilla extract
- 4 large eggs, room temperature
  Boiling water, for roasting pan

1. Preheat the oven to 350° F. Wrap the exterior of a 9-inch springform pan (including base) in a double layer of foil; set aside.

2. Stir together the cracker crumbs, melted butter, and 2 tablespoons sugar in a medium bowl. Press the crumb mixture firmly onto the bottom of the pan. Bake until set, about 10 minutes. Let cool in the pan on a wire rack. Reduce oven heat to 325° F.

3. Process the raspberries in a food processor until smooth, about 30 seconds. Pass the puree through a fine sieve into a small bowl; discard the solids. Whisk in 2 tablespoons sugar, and set aside.

4. Put the cream cheese in the bowl of an electric mixer fitted with the paddle attachment; mix on medium speed until fluffy, about 3 minutes. With the mixer on low speed, add the remaining 1½ cups sugar in a slow, steady stream. Add the salt and vanilla; mix until well combined. Add the eggs, one at a time, mixing each until just combined (do not overmix). Pour the cream cheese filling over crust.

5. Drop the raspberry sauce by the teaspoon on top. With a wooden skewer or toothpick, swirl the sauce into the filling.

6. Set the cake pan inside a large, shallow roasting pan. Transfer to the oven. Carefully ladle boiling water into the roasting pan to reach halfway up the sides of the cake pan. Bake until the cake is set but still slightly wobbly in center, 60 to 65 minutes.

7. Transfer the cake pan to a rack; let cool completely. Refrigerate, uncovered, 6 hours or overnight. Before unmolding, run a knife around the edge of the cake.

lemon-blackberry pudding cakes

MAKES 6 INDIVIDUAL CAKES

- 1 pint blackberries
- ½ cup plus 1 tablespoon fresh lemon juice
  (about 3 lemons)
- 1 cup plus 3 tablespoons sugar
- 3 tablespoons unsalted butter, melted, plus
  more for the ramekins
- 3 large eggs, separated
- 6 tablespoons cake flour (not self-rising),
  sifted
- 1 cup milk
- ¼ teaspoon salt
- 4 ounces crème fraîche (about ½ cup)

1. Preheat the oven to 350° F. Process 2½ ounces blackberries (12 to 15 berries), 1 tablespoon lemon juice, and 3 tablespoons sugar in a food processor or blender until smooth. Pass the mixture through a fine sieve into a small bowl; discard the solids. Set the sauce aside.

2. Butter the inner top inch of 6 6-ounce ramekins; set aside. Whisk together the egg yolks and ¾ cup sugar in a medium bowl. Whisk in the flour and milk in two batches each, beginning with the flour. Whisk in the remaining ½ cup lemon juice, the salt, and the melted butter, and set aside.

3. Put the egg whites in the bowl of an electric mixer fitted with the whisk attachment; beat on medium-high speed until very frothy, about 1½ minutes. With the mixer running, add the remaining ¼ cup sugar in a slow, steady stream; beat until the whites hold stiff (but not dry) peaks, about 2 minutes. Whisk half the whites into the reserved lemon mixture until combined; gently fold in the remaining whites with a rubber spatula.

4. Place the ramekins in a high-sided roasting pan or baking dish, and divide the batter among the ramekins, filling each almost to the top. Spoon a few drops of berry sauce onto the cakes, and use a toothpick or skewer to swirl the sauce into the batter. Transfer to the oven; pour boiling water into the pan, a bit more than halfway up the sides of the ramekins.

5. Bake until the cakes are set and the tops are just starting to turn golden brown, 35 to 40 minutes. With tongs, transfer the ramekins from the pan to a wire rack, and let cool 15 minutes.

6. Meanwhile, beat the crème fraîche in a clean mixing bowl to soft peaks. Serve the cakes warm with crème fraîche and the remaining berries.

honey cake with caramelized pears

MAKES ONE 10-INCH CAKE

To make a dairy-free version of this recipe, substitute margarine for the butter and soy milk for the regular milk. The cake can be made (without the pears) 1 day ahead, and stored in plastic wrap at room temperature.

Unsalted butter, softened, for pan

1¾ cups all-purpose flour, plus more for dusting

¾ teaspoon baking powder

½ teaspoon baking soda

1 teaspoon coarse salt

½ teaspoon ground cinnamon

2 large eggs

½ cup granulated sugar

¼ cup packed light-brown sugar

½ cup plus 2 tablespoons best-quality honey

½ cup milk

½ cup vegetable oil

½ teaspoon freshly grated lemon zest

Caramelized Pears (recipe follows)

Freshly whipped cream or nondairy whipped topping, for serving (optional)

1. Preheat the oven to 325° F. Butter a 10-inch springform pan. Dust with flour; tap out excess. Whisk together the flour, baking powder and soda, salt, and cinnamon in a bowl; set aside. Mix the eggs and sugars on high speed in the bowl of an electric mixer fitted with the paddle attachment until pale and thick, about 3 minutes.

2. Whisk together the honey, milk, oil, and zest. With the mixer on low, add the honey mixture to the egg mixture; mix until combined, about 1 minute. Add half the flour mixture; mix until smooth. Mix in the remaining flour mixture. Pour the batter into the pan.

3. Bake until dark golden brown and a cake tester inserted in the center comes out clean, about 50 minutes. Let cool in the pan on a wire rack 15 minutes. Run a thin knife around the edge of the cake; carefully remove the sides of the pan. Transfer the cake to a platter. Top with pears. Serve with whipped cream or topping, if desired.

caramelized pears

MAKES ABOUT 2 CUPS

1 tablespoon unsalted butter

¼ cup sugar

1¾ pounds red Anjou pears, cut into ½-inch-thick wedges (or ¼-inch-thick wedges, if pears are firm)

¼ cup best-quality honey

Heat the butter in a large skillet over medium heat. Add the sugar; cook, stirring, until almost dissolved, 1 to 2 minutes. Add the pears; cook, stirring occasionally, until soft and just golden, 12 to 20 minutes. Pour in the honey; cook, stirring, until the pears are coated and very soft, 3 to 5 minutes.

lemon–poppy seed lady cake

MAKES ONE 8-INCH 4-LAYER CAKE

- 1 cup (2 sticks) unsalted butter, room temperature, plus more for the pan
- 3 cups sifted cake flour (not self-rising), plus more for the pan
- 1½ tablespoons baking powder
- ¼ teaspoon salt
- 1¾ cups sugar
- 1¼ teaspoons pure vanilla extract
- 2 tablespoons poppy seeds, plus more for garnish
- 1 tablespoon finely grated lemon zest
- 1 cup milk
- 8 large egg whites, room temperature
  Pinch of cream of tartar
- 1 cup chilled heavy cream
- 1½ cups Lemon Curd (page 656)
  Seven-Minute Frosting (page 658)

1. Preheat the oven to 350°F. Butter 2 8 × 2-inch round cake pans, and line with parchment paper. Butter the parchment, and dust the bottoms and sides with flour, tapping out excess; set aside.

2. Into a medium bowl, sift together the flour, baking powder, and salt twice; set aside. In a mixing bowl, using the paddle attachment, cream the butter on low speed until soft. Increase speed to medium; beat until pale and fluffy.

3. Gradually add 1½ cups sugar; beat until fluffy, about 3 minutes. Beat in the vanilla, poppy seeds, and lemon zest. With the mixer on low speed, add the flour mixture in 2 batches, alternating with the milk; beat until thoroughly combined after each addition. Scrape the sides of the bowl; beat 10 seconds more. Set aside.

4. In another mixing bowl, whisk the egg whites and cream of tartar on low speed until foamy. Increase speed to medium-high; gradually add the remaining ¼ cup sugar until the peaks are just stiff. Gently fold in the whites; do not overmix.

5. Divide the batter between the prepared pans; bake until golden and a cake tester inserted in the centers comes out clean, about 40 minutes. Transfer to a wire rack to cool completely. To remove the cakes, invert onto plates; peel off the parchment paper, and reinvert so the top side is up.

6. Make the filling: In a small bowl, whip the heavy cream to soft peaks. Fold in the lemon curd; cover with plastic, and refrigerate until chilled and firm, at least 2 hours.

7. Assemble the cake: Using a serrated knife, trim the tops of both cakes to make level, if desired. Slice each in half horizontally to make a total of 4 layers. Brush away crumbs from the tops of the layers.

8. Place one of the bottom layers on a serving platter; spread with 1 cup lemon filling. Top with another cake layer; spread with 1 cup filling. Repeat with another cake layer and filling; top with the remaining cake layer. Cover the entire cake with plastic wrap, and carefully transfer to the refrigerator, steadying it with your hands to keep the layers from sliding. Chill until filling is firm, at least 2 hours.

9. When ready to serve, frost the cake and garnish with poppy seeds.

pastiera with strawberry sauce

MAKES ONE 8-INCH CAKE

- 1 quart whole milk
- ¾ cup arborio rice
- 1 teaspoon ground cinnamon
- ½ teaspoon coarse salt
- 1 vanilla bean, split lengthwise
- 1¼ cups granulated sugar
  Unsalted butter, for the pan
  All-purpose flour, for the pan
- 3 pounds fresh ricotta cheese, drained 3 hours or, preferably, overnight
- 3 whole large eggs plus 3 large yolks, lightly beaten
  Confectioners' sugar, for dusting
  Strawberry Sauce (recipe follows)

1. Bring the milk to a boil in a large saucepan over medium-high heat. Stir in the rice, cinnamon, salt, and vanilla bean. Reduce heat to medium-low; cook, stirring occasionally with a wooden spoon, until the rice is very tender and has absorbed all the liquid, about 30 minutes.

2. Remove the pan from the heat. Stir in ¾ cup granulated sugar. Cover; let cool, stirring occasionally. Discard the vanilla bean.

3. Preheat the oven to 350°F. Butter and flour an 8-inch springform pan. In a large bowl, combine the rice mixture, ricotta, whole eggs and egg yolks, and remaining ½ cup sugar. Pour into the prepared pan. Bake until golden on top and almost set in the center, 65 to 70 minutes; cover with foil if starting to brown too much. Transfer the pan to a cooling rack.

4. When the cake has completely cooled, run a knife around the edge to loosen. Gently remove the ring; transfer the cake to a serving platter. Sprinkle with confectioners' sugar, and serve with sauce.

strawberry sauce
MAKES 1½ CUPS

1 pint strawberries, hulled and halved
2 tablespoons sugar
2 teaspoons fresh lemon juice

Combine all the ingredients in a medium nonreactive saucepan. Cook over medium-low heat, stirring occasionally, until the strawberries are soft, 5 to 7 minutes. Serve warm or at room temperature.

....

ABOUT PASTIERA

Pastiera, a traditional Neopolitan Easter "pie," is actually a type of cheesecake. Though no two recipes are alike, all contain ricotta cheese and a sweetened grain (usually rice or wheat berries), symbolizing spring's fertility.

....

cheesecake with poached apricot halves
MAKES ONE 8-INCH SQUARE CAKE

Unsalted butter, at room temperature, for the pan
1½ *pounds cream cheese, at room temperature*
¾ *cup sugar*
½ *cup sour cream, at room temperature*
1 *teaspoon pure vanilla extract*
3 *large eggs*
1 *tablespoon fresh lemon juice*
16 *Poached Apricot Halves (page 443)*

1. Preheat the oven to 400°F. Butter an 8-inch-square baking pan. Line the bottom with parchment paper; set the pan aside.

2. In the bowl of an electric mixer, beat the cream cheese until smooth. Mix in the sugar, sour cream, and vanilla. Add the eggs 1 at a time, beating until each is fully incorporated before adding the next. Beat in the lemon juice.

3. Fill the prepared pan with the cream cheese mixture. Smooth the top with a spatula. Place the pan in a larger baking pan, and transfer to the oven. Pour enough hot water into the larger baking pan to come halfway up the sides of the smaller pan. Bake until the cake is just set in the center and lightly browned on top, about 35 minutes.

4. Transfer the cheesecake from the water bath to a wire rack. While cake is slightly warm, after about 30 minutes (it will be harder to unmold once cake has cooled longer), invert onto a platter. Refrigerate, covered, overnight.

5. To serve, arrange poached apricot halves, cut side down, on top of the cheesecake, allowing the juice to pool on the surface and drizzle down the edges.

hummingbird cake

MAKES ONE 9-INCH LAYER CAKE

Unsalted butter, room temperature

3   *cups all-purpose flour, plus more
for the pans*

1   *teaspoon baking soda*

1   *teaspoon ground cinnamon*

½   *teaspoon salt*

1   *cup vegetable oil*

2   *teaspoons pure vanilla extract*

2   *cups sugar*

3   *large eggs*

2   *cups mashed ripe banana (about 3 large)*

1   *can (8 ounces) crushed pineapple,
drained*

1   *cup chopped walnuts or pecans*

1   *cup desiccated coconut (unsweetened)*

Cream Cheese Frosting (recipe follows)

*Dried Pineapple Flowers (recipe follows),
optional*

1. Preheat the oven to 350°F with a rack in the center. Butter two 9 × 2-inch round cake pans. Line the bottoms of the pans with parchment paper. Butter the paper, and dust the pans with flour, tapping out any excess. Set aside.

2. In a medium bowl, sift together the flour, baking soda, cinnamon, and salt; set aside.

3. In the bowl of an electric mixer, beat the oil, vanilla, and sugar until combined, about 2 minutes. Add the eggs 1 at a time, incorporating each before adding the next. Beat at medium speed until the mixture is pale yellow and fluffy, about 3 minutes.

4. In a medium bowl, mix together the banana, pineapple, walnuts, and coconut. Add to the egg mixture; stir until well combined. Add the flour mixture; blend well.

5. Divide the batter between the pans. Bake, rotating the pans halfway through, until golden brown and a cake tester inserted in the center comes out clean, 30 to 40 minutes.

6. Transfer the pans to a greased wire rack. Let cool 15 minutes. Run a knife around the edges to loosen. Invert onto the rack; reinvert, top side up. Cool completely. Assemble the cake, or wrap each layer well and freeze (thaw before using).

7. With a serrated knife, trim and discard the rounded top off one layer. Place the layer on a serving platter. Using an offset spatula, spread the top of the layer with ¼ inch frosting. Top with the untrimmed layer. Frost the sides and top of the cake with the remaining frosting. Decorate with pineapple flowers, if desired. Serve at room temperature. (The cake can be refrigerated up to 3 days.)

DRIED PINEAPPLE FLOWERS

The thinner you cut the pineapple slices, the faster they will dry—and the brighter their yellow core will be. When the pineapple core dries, it resembles the center of a flower.

cream cheese frosting

MAKES 1 ½ QUARTS
(ENOUGH FOR ONE 9-INCH LAYER CAKE)

- 1 pound (16 ounces) cream cheese, room temperature
- 2 teaspoons pure vanilla extract
- 1 cup (2 sticks) unsalted butter, cut into pieces, room temperature
- 2 pounds confectioners' sugar, sifted

1. In the bowl of an electric mixer, beat the cream cheese and vanilla until light and creamy, about 2 minutes. With the mixer on medium speed, gradually add the butter, beating until incorporated.

2. Reduce mixer speed to low. Gradually add the sugar, beating until incorporated. Use immediately, or cover and refrigerate up to 3 days. Bring to room temperature before using.

dried pineapple flowers

MAKES ABOUT 2 DOZEN

- 2 large or 4 small pineapples

1. Preheat the oven to 225°F. Line 2 baking sheets with Silpats (French nonstick baking mats) or parchment paper.

2. Peel the pineapples. Using a small melon baller, remove and discard the eyes. Slice the pineapple very thinly; place the slices on the baking sheets. Cook until the tops look dried, about 30 minutes. Flip the slices; cook until completely dried, 25 to 30 minutes more. Cool on a wire rack. Refrigerate in an airtight container up to 3 days.

mini pear and blueberry spice cakes

MAKES 6 SMALL CAKES

These individual upside-down cakes are baked—and can be transported—in a muffin tin.

- 7 tablespoons unsalted butter, room temperature, plus more for the tin
- 6 tablespoons light corn syrup
- 12 teaspoons packed light-brown sugar
- ¾ cup fresh blueberries, picked over and rinsed
- 1 ripe Bartlett pear, halved lengthwise, cored, and cut into thin wedges
- 1 cup all-purpose flour
- ¾ teaspoon baking powder
- ¼ teaspoon baking soda
- ⅛ teaspoon salt
- ½ teaspoon ground cinnamon
- ¼ teaspoon ground nutmeg
- ¼ teaspoon ground allspice
- ¼ teaspoon ground ginger
- ⅔ cup granulated sugar
- 1 large whole egg plus 1 large egg yolk
- ¾ cup buttermilk
- ½ teaspoon pure vanilla extract

1. Preheat the oven to 350°F. Generously butter the cups and top of a muffin tin with six 8-ounce cups. Place 1 teaspoon butter in each muffin cup. Top each with 1 tablespoon corn syrup; sprinkle with 2 teaspoons light brown sugar. Arrange 7 or 8 blueberries in each cup. Cut the pear slices to fit the shape of muffin cups; place 4 or 5 pieces on top of the berries, spreading the slices to cover the berries. Arrange the remaining berries over the pears, and set the tin aside.

2. Into a small bowl, sift the flour, baking powder, baking soda, salt, cinnamon, nutmeg, allspice, and ginger; set aside. In the bowl of an electric mixer fitted with the paddle attachment, beat the granulated sugar and remaining 5 tablespoons butter on medium speed until light and fluffy, 3 to 4 minutes. Add the egg and egg yolk; beat until smooth.

3. With the mixer on low speed, add the flour mixture to the butter mixture in 2 batches, alternating with the buttermilk and beginning and ending with the flour. Stir in the vanilla.

4. Pour ⅓ cup batter over the fruit in each muffin cup. Gently tap the bottom of the tin against the counter several times to evenly distribute the batter.

5. Bake the cakes until golden around the edges and a cake tester inserted in the centers comes out clean, about 25 minutes. Remove from the oven; let cool in the tin.

sticky buckwheat cake

MAKES ONE 10-INCH CAKE

The buckwheat flour adds a deep, assertive flavor to this dessert; the flour is also highly nutritious.

for the topping

- ½ cup raisins
- ½ cup brandy
- 1 tablespoon unsalted butter
- ½ cup packed dark-brown sugar
- 1½ teaspoons ground cinnamon
- ⅔ cup light corn syrup
- ½ cup coarsely chopped pecans (1¾ ounces)
- 1 apple, peeled, cored, and cut into ½-inch cubes

for the cake

- ¾ cup (1½ sticks) unsalted butter, room temperature
- 1¼ cups packed light-brown sugar
- 3 large eggs
- 1¾ cups all-purpose flour
- 1 cup buckwheat flour
- 1½ teaspoons ground ginger
- 1 tablespoon baking powder
- ½ teaspoon salt
- 1 cup milk
- 1 tablespoon peeled and grated fresh ginger

1. Make the topping: In a small bowl, combine the raisins and brandy; let stand until the raisins are plump, about 20 minutes. Drain the raisins; discard the liquid.

2. In a 10-inch seasoned cast-iron skillet, melt the butter over medium heat. Sprinkle with the brown sugar and cinnamon, and remove from the heat. Drizzle with the corn syrup. Strew the pecans, apple, and raisins over the corn syrup; set aside.

3. Preheat the oven to 350° F. Make the cake: In the bowl of an electric mixer fitted with the paddle attachment, cream the butter until smooth. Add the sugar; beat until light and fluffy. Add eggs one at a time, beating until combined after each addition.

4. Into a large bowl, sift together the flours, ground ginger, baking powder, and salt. In another bowl, combine the milk and fresh ginger. Alternately add the flour and milk mixtures to the butter mixture, beating until just combined after each addition, beginning and ending with flour mixture.

5. Pour the batter into the prepared skillet; smooth the top with an offset spatula. Bake until golden brown and a cake tester inserted in the center comes out clean, about 50 minutes. Transfer to a wire rack; let stand 5 minutes, then invert onto a serving platter. Serve warm or at room temperature.

crêpe gâteau with strawberry preserves and crème fraîche

SERVES 6 TO 8 (MAKES 15 CRÊPES)

The crêpe batter can be made through step 1 up to 1 day in advance and stored, covered, in the refrigerator. When assembling the gâteau, do not spread the cream and jam to the edges on the bottom layers, because the weight of the top will push out the filling. The gâteau should be assembled no more than 2 hours before serving.

- ¾ cup all-purpose flour
- 4 tablespoons confectioners' sugar
  Pinch of salt
- 2 large whole eggs, room temperature
- 2 large egg yolks, room temperature
- 1¼ cups milk, room temperature
- 4 tablespoons unsalted butter
- 1½ cups crème fraîche
- ½ teaspoon pure vanilla extract
- 1 cup strawberry or other fruit preserves

1. Into a medium bowl, sift together the flour, 1 tablespoon sugar, and the salt. Make a well in the center, and fill it with the eggs, egg yolks, and a few tablespoons milk; whisk until a thick, smooth paste forms. Add the remaining milk, and whisk until no lumps remain.

2. Melt the butter in an 8-inch nonstick skillet with a 6-inch-diameter bottom; pour into the batter, leaving a coating of butter in the skillet. Let the batter rest at room temperature at least 1 hour.

3. Over medium heat, warm the skillet thoroughly. Lift the skillet off the heat; stir the batter, and carefully ladle 3 tablespoons into the skillet. Immediately rotate the skillet so the batter is thinly spread evenly across the bottom to the edges. Return the skillet to the heat; cook the crêpe until the edges are golden brown and lacy, about 1 minute. Carefully flip the crêpe; cook the other side until golden brown, about 30 seconds. Slide the crêpe out of the skillet onto a plate. Repeat with the remaining batter, stacking the cooked crêpes on top of one another. Let the crêpes cool completely.

4. Place the crème fraîche in a medium bowl set in an ice-water bath. Add the vanilla and remaining 3 tablespoons sugar; whip until the mixture holds a line drawn by the whisk.

5. To assemble: Place 1 crêpe on a serving platter. Spoon 1 heaping tablespoon preserves on top; using an offset spatula, spread in a thin layer over the crêpe, leaving a ½-inch border. Cover with another crêpe, stacking neatly. Spread 2 heaping tablespoons crème-fraîche mixture evenly over the crêpe, again leaving a ½-inch border. Continue alternating fillings with crêpes, finishing with a crêpe on top. If necessary, insert 2 long toothpicks through the layers to keep the gâteau in place. Refrigerate at least 15 minutes. Remove the toothpicks; cut into wedges before serving.

MAKING CRÊPES

1. Heat skillet (with its coating of butter) on medium heat until just starting to smoke. If the pan is not hot enough, the crêpes will not be as fluffy. Remove the pan from the heat before adding the batter, as you don't want it to start cooking just yet. Quickly (in 2 to 3 seconds) tilt pan in all directions so the batter covers entire bottom in a thin layer. Return pan to heat for about 1 minute, jerking the pan sharply back and forth to loosen the crêpe.

2. The crêpe should bubble in the middle and turn thin and lacy around the edges. At this point, carefully lift the edges with a thin metal spatula; if the underside is golden brown, turn the crêpe by using two spatulas (or by flipping the crêpe with a toss of the pan). If the crêpe is to be used in a gâteau, don't worry if it tears, since any imperfections will not be visible in the finished cake.

3. Continue cooking until the other side is spotty brown, about 30 seconds. Slide crêpe onto a plate, and repeat with remaining batter. If the batter begins to stick to the pan, coat it with more butter, heat until smoking, and continue.

almond-polenta pound cake

MAKES ONE 4 × 8-INCH LOAF

½ cup (1 stick) unsalted butter, room
   temperature, plus more for the pan

1 cup cake flour (not self-rising),
   plus more for the pan

⅓ cup almond paste (3¼ ounces)

⅔ cup plus 1½ tablespoons sugar

⅓ teaspoon pure vanilla extract

⅓ teaspoon pure almond extract

⅔ cup heavy cream

4 large eggs, room temperature, separated

½ cup coarse cornmeal (polenta)

1 teaspoon baking powder

¼ teaspoon salt

1. Preheat the oven to 350°F with a rack in the lower
third. Butter an 8 × 9 4-inch loaf pan; dust with flour,
and tap out excess. In the bowl of an electric mixer,
cut the almond paste into ⅔ cup sugar with 2 forks
until it resembles coarse meal. Add the butter; using
the paddle attachment, beat until soft and light,
about 4 minutes.

2. In a medium bowl, whisk together the extracts,
cream, and egg yolks. With the mixer on medium,
gradually add the cream mixture to the butter mixture. In a small bowl, stir together the flour, cornmeal, baking powder, and salt. Sift half the flour
mixture over the butter mixture, and fold to combine. Fold in the remaining flour mixture.

3. In another mixing bowl, beat the egg whites and
remaining 1½ tablespoons sugar on medium speed
to stiff peaks, 2 to 3 minutes. Fold into the batter.

4. Pour the batter into the prepared pan. Bake until
a cake tester inserted in the center comes out clean,
about 1 hour. If the top begins to brown too much,
cover loosely with foil. Let cool before serving.

orange-almond cake

MAKES ONE 9-INCH CAKE

6 navel or other sweet oranges

   Unsalted butter, room temperature,
   for the pan

½ cup all-purpose flour, plus more
   for the pan

1¾ cups finely ground blanched almonds
   (about 6 ounces)

1½ teaspoons baking powder

½ teaspoon salt

6 large eggs

2 cups sugar

1. Place the whole unpeeled oranges in a large
saucepan or stockpot, and cover with cold water.
Bring to a boil over high heat. Reduce heat, and simmer gently, 2 hours. Drain; let cool.

2. Preheat the oven to 350°F. Butter and flour a
9-inch springform pan; set aside. Halve the cooked
oranges, and remove any seeds. Place 7 halves in a
food processor, and pulse until pureed but still
chunky. This should yield about 3 cups; set aside.

3. In a small bowl, whisk together the ground almonds, flour, baking powder, and salt; set aside. In
the bowl of an electric mixer fitted with the whisk
attachment, beat the eggs with 1 cup sugar on
medium speed until light and fluffy. Stir in the orange puree until just combined. Stir in the flour
mixture; pour into prepared pan.

4. Bake until the cake is golden brown and a cake
tester inserted in the center comes out clean, about
1 hour. Transfer the pan to a wire rack. After 15 minutes, run a small spatula or paring knife around the
edge to loosen the cake; let cool completely.

5. Meanwhile, make the orange topping: Chop the
remaining 5 orange halves into ½-inch pieces, and
set aside. In a medium saucepan, combine the remaining cup sugar with ¾ cup water. Bring the mixture to a boil, stirring until the sugar has dissolved.

6. Add the chopped oranges to the saucepan, and
reduce heat to medium. Simmer gently until most
of the liquid has evaporated and thickened into a
syrup, about 15 minutes. Cool completely.

7. To assemble, remove the ring from the pan; transfer the cooled cake to a serving platter. Arrange the chopped oranges and any remaining syrup over the top of the cake. Cut into wedges, and serve. Or store, covered, in the refrigerator, up to 2 days.

walnut honey cake

MAKES ONE 8½-INCH CAKE

3 ounces walnut halves (about ¾ cup)

Unsalted butter, room temperature, for the pan

1½ cups all-purpose flour, plus more for the pan

1 cup raw honey, plus 2 to 3 tablespoons more for the glaze

1 cup unsweetened applesauce

3 large eggs, room temperature

¾ teaspoon baking soda

¼ teaspoon salt

¼ teaspoon ground ginger

1. Preheat the oven to 350°F, with a rack in the center. Spread the walnut in a single layer on a rimmed baking sheet. Toast in the oven until fragrant, tossing occasionally, 5 to 7 minutes. Transfer to a plate; let cool. Pulse in a food processor until finely chopped.

2. Butter and flour an 8½-inch springform pan; set aside. In a large bowl, combine the honey and applesauce; whisk until the honey is mostly dissolved. Add the eggs, and whisk until fully combined.

3. Into a medium bowl, sift together the flour, baking soda, salt, and ginger. Stir into the honey mixture. Using a rubber spatula, fold in the walnuts.

4. Pour the batter into the prepared pan. Bake the cake until golden brown on top and a cake tester inserted into center comes out clean, about 55 minutes.

5. Let cool on a wire rack until the sides of the cake begin to pull away from the pan, about 15 minutes. Unmold onto a serving plate. While it is still warm, use an offset spatula to gently spread the remaining honey on top. Serve warm.

FIT TO EAT RECIPE PER SERVING: 278 CALORIES, 8 G FAT, 58 MG CHOLESTEROL, 51 G CARBOHYDRATE, 178 MG SODIUM, 5 G PROTEIN, 1 G FIBER

bittersweet chocolate mousse torte

MAKES ONE 5 X 9-INCH TORTE

12 ounces bittersweet chocolate (preferably 65 percent cacao), chopped

3 cups heavy cream

3 tablespoons sugar

12 ounces crisp oval butter wafer cookies (20 total)

Good-quality unsweetened cocoa powder, for dusting

1. Make the mousse: Put the chocolate in a large bowl, and set aside. Heat 1½ cups cream over medium-high heat in a medium saucepan until the cream is steaming and small bubbles form on the edges. Pour the cream over the chocolate. Stir until the mixture is smooth. Let cool completely.

2. Put the remaining 1½ cups cream and the sugar in the bowl of an electric mixer fitted with the whisk attachment; beat on medium-high speed until stiff peaks form. Using a rubber spatula, fold the whipped cream into the chocolate mixture, one third at a time.

3. Assemble the torte: Line a 5 × 9-inch loaf pan with plastic wrap, leaving an overhang on the sides. Spread enough mousse (¾ to 1 cup) over the bottom of the pan to cover. Arrange 5 cookies on top in a single layer to cover, breaking them to fit as necessary. Spread enough mousse (¾ to 1 cup) on top to cover; smooth into an even layer. Repeat the process with the remaining cookies and mousse until the pan is full.

4. Press plastic wrap directly onto the surface, and refrigerate the torte until firm, at least 3 hours or up to 2 days.

5. To serve, remove the plastic wrap from the surface. Invert the torte onto a serving plate; unmold, using the overhang to coax it out. Remove the plastic wrap. Dust with cocoa.

almond-orange financier

MAKES ONE 4 X 13½-INCH TART

- ¾ cup (1½ sticks) unsalted butter, melted, plus more for the pan
- 1 cup almonds, lightly toasted (4½ ounces)
- 1⅔ cups confectioners' sugar, plus more for dusting
- ½ cup all-purpose flour
- ¼ teaspoon salt
  Finely grated zest of 1 orange
- 6 large egg whites, lightly beaten
  Candied Orange Peel (recipe follows), for garnish

1. Preheat the oven to 450°F. Brush the inside of a 4 × 13½-inch tart pan that has a nonremovable bottom with melted butter; transfer to the freezer.

2. Using a food processor, pulse the almonds until finely ground. In a large bowl, combine the ground almonds, confectioners' sugar, flour, salt, and orange zest. Add the egg whites, and whisk to combine. Slowly stir in the butter.

3. Remove the tart pan from the freezer. Pour the batter into the pan; place on a baking sheet. Bake until the dough just begins to rise, about 10 minutes. Reduce the oven heat to 400°F, and continue baking 7 to 8 minutes more, until the financier begins to brown. Turn off the oven, and let the cake stand in the oven until firm, about 10 minutes. Transfer the pan to a wire rack to cool completely.

4. Invert the financier onto the rack; reinvert, and slice into 6 pieces. Garnish the top with candied orange peel, and dust with confectioners' sugar.

candied orange peel

MAKES ½ CUP

The candied orange peel can be made up to 3 weeks ahead; store it with the cooking syrup in an airtight container in the refrigerator.

- 3 oranges
- 1 cup sugar

1. Using a citrus zester or vegetable peeler, shred long strips of orange peel.

2. Place the strips in a medium saucepan. Cover with cold water, and bring to a boil over medium heat. Drain; repeat 2 more times with fresh water.

3. Place the sugar in a clean saucepan with 1½ cups water; stir to combine. Bring to a boil over medium heat, stirring occasionally, until the sugar has dissolved, about 3 minutes. Add the citrus strips to the boiling syrup; reduce heat, and simmer until the strips are translucent, about 12 minutes. Remove from heat; let the strips cool in the syrup, at least 1 hour. Remove from the syrup when ready to use.

chocolate hazelnut torte

MAKES ONE 8½-INCH TORTE

- ¾ cup unsalted butter, plus more for the pan
  Unsweetened cocoa powder, for the pan and for dusting
- 1 cup currants
- ½ cup whiskey or hot water
- 1⅓ cups heavy cream
- 1 pound bittersweet chocolate, chopped
- 6 large eggs
- 1 cup sugar
- ¼ teaspoon salt
- 1½ cups finely chopped toasted hazelnuts (6½ ounces)

1. Preheat the oven to 225°F. Butter an 8½-inch springform pan; sprinkle with cocoa, and tap out excess. In a small bowl, combine the currants and whiskey or hot water. Let macerate at least 10 minutes or up to 30 minutes. Strain the currants in a fine sieve, and discard the whiskey.

2. In a small saucepan over medium heat, bring the cream and butter almost to a boil, making sure all the butter is melted. Place the chocolate in a medium heatproof bowl, and pour the cream over it to cover. Whisk gently until the chocolate is melted and the mixture is combined.

3. In a medium bowl, whisk together the eggs, sugar, and salt. Whisk into the chocolate mixture, and stir in the nuts and currants. Pour the mixture into the prepared pan.

4. Bake until the edges are set and the center is still a little soft to the touch, about 2 hours. Transfer to a wire rack to cool completely. Cover with plastic wrap, and chill overnight in the refrigerator. When ready to serve, remove from the refrigerator, and dust with cocoa powder.

molten chocolate cakes

MAKES 6 SMALL CAKES

Because the batter needs to be frozen before baking (and can remain in the freezer, covered with plastic wrap, for up to 1 month), these cakes are perfect for those unexpected moments when you need a quick dessert. Using semisweet chocolate in the truffles is essential; if bittersweet is used, the centers of the cakes will not ooze.

- 6 tablespoons unsalted butter, room temperature, plus more for the ring molds
- 12 ounces semisweet chocolate
- 5 large eggs, separated
- 10 tablespoons sugar
- ½ teaspoon pure vanilla extract
- 6 Chocolate Truffles (recipe follows)
  Earl Grey Ice Cream (recipe follows)
  Chocolate curls, for garnish (optional)

1. Butter 6 ring molds measuring 2½ inches high and 2¾ inches in diameter. Place on a baking sheet lined with parchment paper, and set aside.

2. Place the chocolate and butter in a medium heatproof bowl set over a pan of simmering water, and heat until melted. Stir the mixture to combine.

3. Combine the egg yolks and 6 tablespoons sugar in a large bowl, and whisk until the mixture is pale yellow and thick, 3 to 5 minutes. Stir in the vanilla extract. Add the chocolate mixture to the egg yolk mixture, and stir to combine.

4. Place the egg whites in the bowl of an electric mixer fitted with the whisk attachment, and beat until frothy. Add the remaining 4 tablespoons sugar, and whisk until stiff peaks form. Fold the egg white mixture into the chocolate mixture.

5. Spoon about ¼ cup batter into each ring, and place a truffle in the center of each. Spoon the remaining batter over the truffles, and place in the freezer to set, at least 1 hour.

6. Preheat the oven to 350° F. Transfer the baking sheet with the filled ring molds to the oven; bake 20 to 25 minutes, or until the sides are set but the centers are still soft. Using a thin spatula, carefully transfer the cakes (still in the ring molds) to a serving plate. Lift the ring molds, and remove them. Serve the cakes warm with Earl Grey ice cream; garnish with chocolate curls, if desired.

chocolate truffles

MAKES 6

- 4 ounces semisweet chocolate, finely chopped
- ¾ cup heavy cream

Place the chocolate in a medium heatproof bowl. Bring the heavy cream to a boil in a small saucepan, and pour it over the chocolate. Let sit for 5 minutes, and stir until thoroughly combined. Place the mixture in the freezer until set, about 45 minutes, stirring every 15 minutes. Divide the mixture into 6 equal parts, and roll each into a ball. Cover the truffles with plastic wrap; freeze until ready to use.

earl grey ice cream

MAKES ABOUT 5 CUPS

Two tablespoons of loose tea leaves may be substituted for the tea bags in this recipe. If you use loose tea, you will need to strain the tea mixture before combining it with the egg yolks.

- 8 *large egg yolks*
- ½ *cup sugar*
- 2 *cups milk*
- 2 *cups heavy cream*
- 4 *Earl Grey tea bags*

1. Prepare an ice-water bath, and set aside. Combine the egg yolks and sugar in the bowl of an electric mixer fitted with the whisk attachment, and beat until pale yellow and very thick, 3 to 5 minutes.

2. Place the milk, cream, and tea bags in a medium saucepan, and bring the mixture to a boil. Remove from heat; cover, and let steep for 10 minutes. Remove the tea bags, and return the mixture to a boil. Gradually pour half of the milk mixture into the egg yolk mixture, whisking constantly. Return the combined mixture to the saucepan.

3. Cook the combined mixture over medium-low heat, whisking constantly, until thick enough to coat the back of a spoon. Strain into a bowl set in the ice bath, and chill completely; stirring occasionally. Freeze in an ice-cream maker, according to the manufacturer's instructions, until the ice cream just holds its shape. Transfer the ice cream to a metal loaf pan; cover with plastic wrap, and freeze until firm, at least 2 hours.

breton butter cake

MAKES ONE 9-INCH CAKE

- 1 *cup (2 sticks) unsalted butter, room temperature, plus more for the pan*
- 1 *cup sugar*
- 1 *tablespoon pure vanilla extract*
- 6 *large egg yolks*
- 2¾ *cups all-purpose flour*
- ¼ *teaspoon salt*
- 1 *large whole egg, lightly beaten*
  Strawberry Compote (recipe follows)

1. Preheat the oven to 350° F. Cream the butter and sugar in the bowl of an electric mixer fitted with paddle attachment until light and fluffy. Beat in the vanilla and yolks 1 at a time, beating well after each addition. Add the flour and salt; beat just until combined. Do not overmix.

2. Transfer the batter to a 9-inch tart pan with a removable bottom; with a small offset spatula, spread the batter and smooth the top. (If necessary, chill the batter 10 minutes before smoothing.) Place the pan in the refrigerator 15 minutes.

3. Remove from the refrigerator. Brush the top with beaten egg, and mark a criss-cross pattern with a fork. Brush again with the egg. Bake until the cake is deep golden brown and the edges pull away from the sides of the pan, about 50 minutes.

4. Transfer to a wire rack to cool slightly. Remove the cake from the pan, and slice while still warm. Serve with strawberry compote.

strawberry compote

MAKES ABOUT 3 CUPS

- 1½ *pounds strawberries, stemmed and cut lengthwise into 6 segments*
- 2 *tablespoons Grand Marnier*
- 1 *tablespoon finely grated orange zest*
- 1½ *cups fresh orange juice, strained*

1. Combine the berries, Grand Marnier, and zest in a small bowl. Toss; let stand 30 minutes.

2. Bring the juice to a boil in a small saucepan over medium heat; reduce heat, and simmer until the liquid is reduced to ¼ cup, about 20 minutes. Remove from heat; let cool. Pour over the strawberries, and toss to combine.

belgian chocolate birthday cake

MAKES ONE 9-INCH CAKE

Toast and peel the nuts for the cake and the garnish (recipe follows) at the same time. Bake the cake up to 3 days ahead; wrap well and keep at room temperature. The candied hazelnuts and chocolate curls can also be made 3 days ahead; store in airtight containers.

    4 ounces hazelnuts
13⅓ tablespoons unsalted butter (1⅔ sticks),
        softened
    ⅔ cup Dutch-process cocoa powder
    6 tablespoons granulated sugar
1⅔ cups all-purpose flour
1½ teaspoons baking soda
    ¼ teaspoon salt
    ⅔ cup boiling water
1¾ cups packed dark-brown sugar
    4 large eggs, at room temperature
1⅓ cups buttermilk, at room temperature
2½ teaspoons pure vanilla extract
        Ganache Glaze (page 509)
        Candied Hazelnuts and Chocolate Curls
        (recipe follows)

1. Preheat the oven to 350°F. Spread the nuts on a baking sheet. Bake until fragrant and toasted, about 12 minutes. Transfer to a clean kitchen towel; rub to loosen the skins. Butter a 9 × 3-inch springform pan well; coat with cocoa, tapping out any excess.

2. In a food processor, grind the nuts with the granulated sugar until fine but not pasty; transfer to a large bowl; stir in the flour, baking soda, and salt.

3. In a heatproof bowl, whisk together the cocoa and boiling water until smooth. (The mixture will thicken as it cools.)

4. In the bowl of an electric mixer, cream the butter and brown sugar on high until lightened and fluffy, 3 to 4 minutes. Beat in the eggs 1 at a time until well blended.

5. Stir the buttermilk and vanilla into the cocoa mixture. Mixing on low, add half the dry ingredients to the creamed mixture; when blended, pour in the cocoa mixture, and add the remaining dry mixture,

mixing just until incorporated. Scrape the batter into the prepared pan; smooth the top. Bake 1 hour to 1 hour and 10 minutes, until a tester inserted in the center comes out clean. Let cool in the pan for 10 minutes; remove from the pan and cool completely. Place the cooled cake on a 9-inch cardboard round.

6. Place half the ganache in a bowl; place in a larger bowl of ice water; whip with a balloon whisk until lighter in color and spreadable.

7. Spread the whipped ganache smoothly on the top and sides of the cooled cake, and chill the cake. Gently stir the remaining ganache every 5 minutes until thickened and cool.

8. Place the cake (still on the cardboard round) on a wire rack over a sheet of waxed or parchment paper. Working with a small ladle, pour the ganache over the top of the cake, moving the ladle in a circular fashion while in contact with the cake, letting the ganache run down the sides. Scrape up the excess and reserve for another use. Let the cake stand at room temperature until set. Garnish with nuts and chocolate curls.

candied hazelnuts and chocolate curls

MAKES ENOUGH FOR ONE 9-INCH CAKE

    2 cups hazelnuts
    1 cup sugar
    2 tablespoons water
    1 pound bittersweet chocolate,
        very finely chopped
    ¼ cup unsweetened cocoa

1. Preheat the oven to 350°F. Spread the nuts on a baking sheet. Bake until fragrant and toasted, about 12 minutes. Transfer to a clean kitchen towel; rub to loosen the skins.

2. Place the sugar and water in a medium heavy skillet. Stir with a fork over medium-high heat until dissolved; let boil undisturbed for 3 minutes. Add the nuts to the pan; stir with a wooden spoon until the caramel seizes around the nuts. Transfer to a parchment-lined baking sheet; let cool completely.

3. Once the nuts are cool, place half the chopped chocolate in a deep, medium-size stainless-steel bowl. Place the bowl over a saucepan with 1 inch of simmering water; stir until the chocolate is melted and hot. Add the remaining chocolate to the bowl; remove the bowl from the pan of water; let stand about 5 minutes, and then stir until smooth.

4. Pour half the chocolate onto an inverted baking sheet; spread with a bench scraper until ⅛ inch thick or slightly thinner (chocolate should be opaque on the surface). Let stand until just tacky. Hold the scraper at a 45-degree angle; scrape the chocolate off the surface. The curls can be stored in an airtight container layered with parchment at room temperature.

5. While the chocolate sets, add the candied nuts to the remaining chocolate in the bowl, and stir until coated. Spread the nuts on a parchment-lined baking sheet, and let stand until set.

6. Sift the cocoa powder on top of the dried nuts and toss to coat. Store in a resealable plastic bag for up to 1 week, until ready to use.

inside-out german chocolate torte

MAKES ONE 9-INCH TORTE

The chocolate glaze takes time to cool; have it ready before assembling the torte.

- 10 tablespoons (1¼ sticks) unsalted butter, plus more for the pan
- 7 ounces bittersweet chocolate
- 1¼ cups all-purpose flour
- ¼ teaspoon salt
- 1 cup sugar
- 2 large eggs
- 2 teaspoons pure vanilla extract
  - Coconut-Pecan Filling (recipe follows)
  - Ganache Glaze (recipe follows)

1. Preheat the oven to 350°F. Butter two 9-inch springform pans. Line the bottoms with parchment paper, and butter the paper; set aside. Place the chocolate and butter in a heatproof bowl, and set over a pan of barely simmering water. Stir occasionally until melted; set aside.

2. Sift together the flour and salt; set aside. Place the sugar and eggs in the bowl of an electric mixer fitted with the paddle attachment, and beat until fluffy and well combined, 3 to 5 minutes. Add the vanilla and chocolate mixture, and stir to combine. Add the dry ingredients, and stir to combine. Divide the batter between the 2 pans, using an offset spatula to distribute the batter evenly, and smooth the layers. Bake until the center is set, about 20 minutes. Transfer the pans to a wire rack to cool completely before unmolding.

3. Place 1 layer on a 9-inch cardboard cake round. Spread filling over the layer, and invert the second layer onto the top, leaving the smooth side up. Press down gently on the top layer to evenly distribute the filling to the edges. Using a metal spatula, smooth the filling flush with the sides of the cake. Refrigerate until ready to glaze.

4. Carefully transfer the torte off the cardboard round onto a wire rack set over a baking pan. Pour enough ganache glaze over the cake to fully coat it, shaking the pan gently to help spread the ganache, if necessary. Let sit for 15 to 20 minutes. The ganache in the pan may be melted and strained through a fine sieve and added back to the glaze.

5. Pour the remaining glaze over the torte, allowing excess to drip off the sides. If the top is not smooth, gently shake the pan or run an offset spatula quickly over the surface. Allow to set at least 30 minutes before serving. Carefully slide the cake off the wire rack and onto a serving platter.

coconut-pecan filling

MAKES ABOUT 2 CUPS;
ENOUGH FOR ONE 9-INCH TORTE

- *1* 14-ounce can sweetened condensed milk
- *10* tablespoons (1¼ sticks) unsalted butter
- *1* teaspoon pure vanilla extract
- *4* large egg yolks
- *2* cups shredded sweetened coconut
- *1½* cups finely chopped pecans

1. Place the milk, butter, and vanilla in a medium saucepan, and cook over medium-low heat, stirring occasionally, until melted and combined.

2. Whisk the egg yolks in a medium bowl, and, whisking constantly, add some of the hot milk mixture to the egg yolks until combined. Whisk the mixture back into the saucepan, and cook, stirring constantly with a wooden spoon, until the mixture thickens slightly, about 5 minutes.

3. Remove from heat, and stir in the coconut and pecans. Cool completely, and refrigerate in an airtight container until ready to use, up to 2 days.

ganache glaze

MAKES ABOUT 4 CUPS

This ganache thickens as it sits. The ganache used for the Inside-Out German Chocolate Torte and in step 7 of the Belgian Chocolate Birthday Cake (page 507) should be pourable but thick enough to fully coat the cakes.

- *1* pound bittersweet or semisweet chocolate
- *2½* cups heavy cream

1. Chop the chocolate finely using a serrated knife; place in a large heatproof bowl.

2. Bring the cream to a boil over medium-high heat; pour directly over the chopped chocolate. Allow to sit 10 minutes. Use a rubber spatula to gently stir the chocolate and cream until well combined and smooth. Let sit at room temperature until cooled and just thickened, stirring occasionally, about 30 minutes but up to 1 hour, depending on the temperature of the room.

raspberry-filled layer cake

MAKES ONE 8-INCH 4-LAYER CAKE

The fluffy exterior of this cake conceals a delicious pink filling, made simply by combining some of the frosting with raspberry jam.

- *12* tablespoons (1½ sticks) unsalted butter, softened, plus more for the pans and wire racks
- *3* cups sifted cake flour (not self-rising), plus more for the pans
- *4* teaspoons baking powder
- *½* teaspoon salt
- *1½* cups sugar
- *1* cup milk
- *1* tablespoon pure vanilla extract
- *4* large egg whites
  Seven-Minute Frosting (page 658)
- *1* cup raspberry jam

1. Preheat the oven to 350° F. Butter two 8 × 2-inch professional round cake pans, and line the bottom with parchment rounds. Butter the parchment; dust the pans with flour, tapping out excess. Set aside.

2. Sift together the cake flour, baking powder, and salt into a medium bowl, and set aside. Beat the butter in the bowl of an electric mixer fitted with the paddle attachment, until it is creamy. Add the sugar to the butter in a steady stream, and continue beating until the butter is light and fluffy, about 3 minutes. Reduce speed to low. Add the dry ingredients alternately with the milk and vanilla in 3 additions, starting and finishing with the dry; be careful not to overmix. Set the batter aside.

3. In a medium metal bowl or clean bowl of an electric mixer, whisk the egg whites just until stiff peaks form. Fold one-third of the egg whites into the batter until combined. Fold in the remaining whites in 2 batches. Divide the batter between the prepared pans, and smooth the tops with a metal spatula.

4. Bake until a tester inserted near the center comes out clean and the cake springs back when pressed lightly in the center, about 30 minutes. Let the pans cool 15 minutes on a wire rack before unmolding.

Loosen the sides with a small metal spatula or paring knife, and invert onto the greased wire racks. To prevent the layers from splitting, invert again so the tops are up. Cool completely before assembling the cake or wrapping airtight to freeze cake for later.

5. If the cakes are not level, use a serrated knife to trim the tops off. Carefully slice each cake horizontally into 2 equal layers. (You will have 4 layers.) Place one-third of the frosting in a bowl, and fold in the raspberry jam.

6. To assemble, place 1 sliced layer on an 8-inch cardboard cake round. Spread the top with ¼ inch raspberry frosting. Repeat with the remaining layers and remaining raspberry frosting, placing the final layer bottom side up. Lightly coat the assembled cake with a thin layer of white frosting to protect against crumbs in the frosting. Finish with the remaining frosting. Serve immediately, or keep refrigerated until ready to serve.

caramel cake
MAKES ONE 9-INCH LAYER CAKE

This cake can be stored in an airtight container at room temperature for up to 3 days.

1¼ cups (2½ sticks) unsalted butter, softened, plus more for the pan and rack
4½ cups sifted cake flour (not self-rising), plus more for the pan
 2 tablespoons baking powder
 ¾ teaspoon salt
1½ cups milk
1½ tablespoons pure vanilla extract
2¼ cups sugar
 7 large egg whites
    Caramel Frosting (recipe follows)

1. Preheat the oven to 350° F. Butter two 9 × 2-inch round cake pans. Line the bottom with parchment paper; butter the parchment and sides of the pan; dust with flour, tapping out excess. Set aside. Sift together the flour, baking powder, and salt into a medium bowl; set aside. In another bowl, combine the milk and vanilla, and set aside.

2. Beat the butter in the bowl of an electric mixer fitted with the paddle attachment until it is creamy. With the machine running, add the sugar in a steady stream; continue beating until the mixture is light and fluffy, about 3 minutes. Reduce speed to low. Add the flour mixture in 3 batches, alternating with the milk mixture and starting and ending with the flour. Be careful to avoid overbeating; set aside.

3. In a clean bowl of an electric mixer fitted with the whisk attachment, beat the egg whites until stiff peaks form. Gently fold one-third of the whites into the batter to lighten, and then fold in the remaining whites in 2 batches.

4. Divide the batter between the prepared pans, and smooth the tops with an offset spatula. Bake until a cake tester inserted in the centers comes out clean and the cakes spring back when pressed lightly in the center, about 40 minutes.

5. Transfer the pans to a wire rack; let cool 15 minutes. Brush the rack with butter. Loosen the sides of the cake with a paring knife; invert onto the greased rack. Reinvert the cake to prevent it from splitting; let cool completely.

6. Using a serrated knife, slice the domed tops off the cakes; discard. Place 1 layer cut side up, on a serving platter; spread a layer of caramel frosting on top. Stack the second layer, cut side down, on top; generously spread the top and sides of both cakes with frosting. To serve, cut into wedges.

caramel frosting
MAKES ABOUT 5 CUPS

 5 cups sugar
 1 cup water
 2 cups heavy cream
 1 teaspoon pure vanilla extract
 ¾ cup (1½ sticks) unsalted butter, cut into pieces

1. Bring 4 cups sugar and the water to a boil in a medium saucepan over medium heat, stirring until the sugar has dissolved, about 8 minutes; wash down the sides of the pan with a pastry brush dipped in water to prevent crystals from forming. Raise heat to high; gently swirl the pan (do not stir) until the caramel is a deep amber color, about 10 minutes. Remove from heat.

2. Meanwhile, heat the cream and remaining cup sugar in a small saucepan over medium heat until the sugar dissolves, stirring frequently, about 5 minutes. Turn off heat; cover, and set aside.

3. As soon as the caramel is the desired color, add the hot cream mixture in a slow, steady stream, stirring to combine. Be careful, as the caramel may splatter when the hot cream is added. Stir in the vanilla, and continue stirring until the mixture no longer bubbles.

4. Prepare an ice-water bath. Transfer the mixture to the bowl of an electric mixer, and place in the ice bath, stirring until it is cool. Transfer the bowl to the mixer; using the paddle attachment, beat on medium speed 5 minutes. With the machine running, gradually add the butter, a few pieces at a time, beating to incorporate fully. Let the frosting stand 20 minutes to thicken before using.

pastel de tres leches
SERVES 12

The most time-consuming step is making the coconut curls; in a pinch, you can use store-bought shaved coconut.

- *1 stick butter (8 tablespoons), melted and cooled, plus more for the pans*
- *6 large eggs, separated*
- *¼ teaspoon baking soda*
- *¼ teaspoon salt*
- *1 cup sugar*
- *1 cup all-purpose flour*
- *2½ cups milk*
- *1 12-ounce can evaporated milk*
- *1 14-ounce can sweetened condensed milk*
- *1 fresh coconut*
- *2 cups heavy cream*
- *Assorted tropical fruits, such as pineapple, star fruit, mango, and pepino, for garnish*

1. Heat the oven to 350°F. Generously butter a 9 × 13-inch glass baking pan. In an electric mixer fitted with the whisk attachment, combine the egg whites, baking soda, and salt, and beat on medium speed until soft peaks form, 2 to 3 minutes.

2. Add the yolks to the whites, beat until combined. With the mixer running slowly, add the sugar until combined. Remove the bowl from the mixer. Using a rubber spatula, fold in the butter.

3. Sift ¼ cup flour on top of the mixture, and fold in to combine. Repeat with the remaining flour, folding in ¼ cup at a time. Pour the batter into the prepared pan, and bake until golden and a cake tester inserted into the middle comes out clean, 20 to 25 minutes. Remove from the oven, and transfer to a wire rack.

4. About 5 minutes before the cake is done, whisk together the 3 milks, and set aside. As soon as the cake is removed from the oven, pour the milk mixture over the entire cake. The cake should absorb all the liquid within 3 to 5 minutes. Set the cake aside, and let stand until cool. Cover the cake well, and transfer to the refrigerator to chill, at least 5 hours or overnight.

5. Before serving, heat the oven to 450°F. Place the whole coconut in the oven, and bake for 20 minutes. Remove from the oven, and, using an awl or a screwdriver, pierce the 3 eyes of the coconut. Turn over, and drain the liquid. Using a hammer, break open the coconut. To remove the meat from the shell, insert a small spatula or grapefruit knife between the flesh and the shell to pry the meat out in large pieces. Using a vegetable peeler, shave off thin curls of coconut. Transfer the curls to a baking sheet, and let stand uncovered for 30 minutes. Place in the oven, and bake until the edges are golden, about 10 minutes. Remove from the oven, and set aside until cool. The curls can be stored in an airtight container for up to 5 days, or frozen for future use.

6. When ready to serve the cake, whip the cream to soft peaks. Slice cake into 12 servings, top with whipped cream, and serve with the fruits and toasted coconut curls.

coconut pecan cake

MAKES ONE 9-INCH LAYER CAKE

For Valentine's Day, bake the layers in two 9-inch heart-shaped cake pans.

¾ cup (1½ sticks) unsalted butter, room temperature, plus more for the pans

2¼ cups all-purpose flour, plus more for the pans

1 cup firmly packed sweetened shredded coconut

¾ cup pecan halves (3 ounces), toasted

2 cups sugar

1 tablespoon baking powder

¾ teaspoon salt

¼ cup creamed coconut or unsalted butter

4 large eggs

1 tablespoon pure coconut extract

1 cup plus 2 tablespoons unsweetened coconut milk (9 ounces)

Coconut Cake Filling (recipe follows)

Milk Chocolate Ganache (recipe follows)

2 cups toasted shaved coconut, for garnish (optional)

1. Preheat the oven to 350°F. Butter two 9-inch round cake pans. Line the bottoms with parchment. Butter the parchment, and dust with flour; tap out excess, and set aside.

2. In a food processor, finely grind the coconut; transfer to a bowl. Finely grind the pecans with 2 tablespoons sugar, and set aside. Into a large bowl, sift together the flour, baking powder, and salt; stir in the ground coconut and pecans. Set aside.

3. In the bowl of an electric mixer fitted with the paddle attachment, beat the butter, creamed coconut, and remaining sugar on medium-high speed until light and fluffy, about 4 minutes. Beat in the eggs and coconut extract. Beat in the flour mixture in 3 batches, alternating with the coconut milk and starting and ending with flour.

4. Divide the batter between the prepared pans; smooth the tops. Bake until golden and a cake tester inserted in the centers comes out clean, about 35 minutes. If the tops begin to get too dark, cover loosely with foil. Let cool in the pans 30 minutes.

Run a knife around the edges of the cakes; invert onto a wire rack. Reinvert; let cool completely.

5. Line 2 rimmed baking sheets with plastic wrap; fit 1 with a cooling rack. Use a serrated knife to trim the tops of the cake layers, if desired. Transfer 1 layer to baking sheet with rack; spread with filling. Place the remaining cake layer on top.

6. Using an offset spatula, spread 1 cup chilled ganache on the sides of the cake; smooth with a bench scraper. Pour the remaining ganache over the cake, coating completely. Transfer the cake and rack to the other baking sheet; chill until set, about 5 minutes. Scrape the excess ganache back into bowl, passing it through a sieve.

7. Coat the cake again with ganache. Chill until set, about 5 minutes. Press toasted coconut on the sides of the cake, if desired. Keep at room temperature until ready to serve.

coconut cake filling

MAKES ENOUGH FOR ONE 9-INCH CAKE

1 cup sweetened shredded coconut

¾ cup sweetened condensed milk

4 tablespoons unsalted butter, room temperature

1 tablespoon creamed coconut or unsalted butter, room temperature

2 large egg yolks, lightly beaten

1 tablespoon pure coconut extract

1. In a food processor, coarsely grind the coconut; set aside. Combine the milk, butter, and creamed coconut in a small saucepan over medium-low heat; cook, stirring, 3 to 4 minutes. Whisk one-third of the hot milk mixture into the egg yolks. Return the mixture to the saucepan; cook, stirring constantly, until the consistency of pudding, about 5 minutes.

2. Remove the pan from the heat. Stir in the coconut extract and reserved coconut. Let cool completely. Refrigerate in an airtight container up to 3 days; let stand at room temperature until soft enough to spread.

milk chocolate ganache

MAKES ENOUGH FOR ONE 9-INCH CAKE

- 1½ pounds best-quality milk chocolate, finely chopped
- 2 cups plus 2 tablespoons heavy cream
- 1 teaspoon light corn syrup

1. Prepare an ice-water bath; set aside. Place the chocolate in a medium heatproof bowl; set aside. Bring the cream to a boil in a small saucepan; pour over the chocolate, swirling to cover completely. Let stand until the chocolate has melted, about 5 minutes. Add the corn syrup; whisk until smooth.

2. Pour 1 cup ganache into a bowl set in the ice bath; stir until thick and spreadable. Keep the remaining ganache at room temperature, stirring every 15 minutes, until thick enough to coat the back of a spoon, 12 to 15 minutes. Use immediately.

rhubarb and blackberry snack cake

MAKES ONE 4¼ × 13¾-INCH CAKE

Draining the rhubarb keeps the cake from becoming soggy.

- 4 tablespoons unsalted butter, softened, plus more for the pan
- ½ cup all-purpose flour, plus more for the pan
- 5 ounces rhubarb, cut into ¼-inch-thick slices (scant 1½ cups)
- 1 cup plus 1 tablespoon sugar
- ½ teaspoon baking powder
  Pinch of coarse salt
- 2 large eggs
- 1 vanilla bean
- 1 large handful blackberries (about ⅓ cup)

1. Preheat the oven to 350°F. Butter and flour a 4¼ × 13¾-inch fluted tart pan with a removable bottom. Combine the rhubarb and ⅓ cup sugar in a medium bowl, and allow to sit, stirring occasionally, until the rhubarb has released its juice and the sugar has dissolved, about 45 minutes.

2. Sift the flour, baking powder, and salt into a small bowl; set aside. Cream the butter with ⅔ cup sugar

in the bowl of an electric mixer fitted with the paddle attachment. Add the eggs, 1 at a time, beating well after each addition. Slice the vanilla bean in half lengthwise. Scrape the seeds from the pod, and add the seeds to the mixture. Beat to combine. Add the reserved flour mixture, and beat to combine. Using a rubber spatula, spoon the batter into the prepared pan, and spread flat.

3. Strain the rhubarb, discarding the juice; add the blackberries, and toss to combine. Spoon the fruit on top of the batter in the pan, sprinkle with the remaining tablespoon sugar, place in the oven, and bake until the cake is golden and center is set, about 1 hour. Remove from the oven, and place on a wire rack to cool slightly before removing the tart pan.

sunken chocolate cakes with coffee ice cream

MAKES 4 SMALL CAKES

Coating the muffin tins with butter and sugar gives these little chocolate cakes sparkle and a bit of crunch.

- 8 tablespoons (1 stick) unsalted butter, cut into pieces, plus more for the pans
- ¼ cup sugar, plus more for the pans
- 5 ounces best-quality bittersweet chocolate, coarsely chopped
- 2 large eggs, separated, plus 2 large egg yolks
- 4 scoops coffee ice cream (1 pint)

1. Preheat the oven to 350°F. Lightly butter 4 cups in a jumbo nonstick muffin pan, leaving the 2 center cups empty. Coat lightly with sugar, and set aside. Place the butter and chocolate in a heatproof bowl; set over a pan of simmering water. Stir occasionally, until melted and thoroughly combined. Remove from heat; set aside.

2. Combine the 4 egg yolks with 2 tablespoons sugar, and whisk until the mixture is pale yellow and thick. Stir in the melted chocolate mixture.

3. Whisk the egg whites until soft peaks form, add the remaining 2 tablespoons sugar, and whisk until stiff and shiny but not dry. Fold into the chocolate mixture. Divide the batter among the prepared muffin cups, and bake until set and slightly springy to the touch, about 25 minutes.

4. Remove from the oven, and transfer to a wire rack. Allow to cool for 15 minutes in the pan; carefully run a knife around the edges of the cakes, and unmold. Serve each cake with a scoop of coffee ice cream.

pear-cranberry upside-down cake

MAKES ONE 10-INCH CAKE

12 tablespoons (1½ sticks) unsalted butter
1¾ cups firmly packed light-brown sugar
3 firm but ripe pears, such as Anjou
    Juice of 1 lemon
1 cup fresh cranberries
2½ cups all-purpose flour
2½ teaspoons baking powder
½ teaspoon salt
½ teaspoon ground cinnamon
¼ teaspoon ground ginger
3 large eggs
1 cup milk, room temperature
    Spice Ice Cream (recipe follows)

1. Preheat the oven to 350°F. Combine 6 tablespoons butter and ¾ cup brown sugar in a medium skillet, and cook over medium-high heat, stirring constantly, until melted and thoroughly combined, about 6 minutes. Pour into a 10 × 2-inch professional round cake pan.

2. Peel the pears, core, and slice into ½-inch-thick wedges. Coat with lemon juice, and arrange on top of the brown sugar mixture in a spiral pattern around the edge of the pan. Fan out the slices in the center. Sprinkle ½ cup cranberries over the pears, and set aside.

3. Sift the flour, baking powder, salt, cinnamon, and ginger together in a medium bowl; set aside. Combine the remaining 6 tablespoons butter and cup of brown sugar in the bowl of an electric mixer, and beat until well combined. Add the eggs, one at a time, beating after each addition. Add the milk alternately

with the flour mixture, beginning and ending with flour; beat until smooth. Stir in the remaining ½ cup cranberries; pour over the fruit in the pan.

4. Bake until a cake tester inserted into the center comes out clean, about 40 minutes. Transfer to a wire rack to cool for 15 minutes. Run a knife around the edges and invert onto a serving platter. Serve with spice ice cream.

spice ice cream

MAKES ABOUT 1½ QUARTS

1 vanilla bean, split and scraped
4 cinnamon sticks
1 whole star anise (optional)
2 cups milk
6 large egg yolks
¾ cup plus 2 tablespoons sugar
2 cups heavy cream, very cold

1. Place the vanilla bean and scrapings, cinnamon sticks, and star anise (if using) in a saucepan with milk over medium-high heat. Bring the mixture to a simmer, cover, and remove from heat. Allow to steep for 30 minutes; then strain, discarding the solids.

2. Combine the egg yolks and sugar in a bowl, and whisk until pale yellow and thick, about 3 minutes.

3. Fill a large bowl with ice and water; set aside. Return the milk to the stove, and bring just to a simmer. Slowly pour the milk mixture into the yolk mixture, whisking constantly. Return it to the saucepan, and cook over low heat, stirring constantly, until the mixture is thick enough to coat the back of a spoon, about 5 minutes. The custard should retain a line drawn across the back of the spoon with your finger.

4. Remove the pan from the heat, and immediately stir in the cold cream. Pass through a fine-mesh strainer into a bowl set in the ice bath. Stir occasionally until cool. Cover the bowl, and place in the refrigerator until well chilled, preferably overnight.

5. Pour the custard into an ice-cream maker; churn according to the manufacturer's instructions, until the ice cream is just set. Transfer to an airtight container, and freeze at least 4 hours or up to 1 week.

chestnut chocolate layer cake

MAKES ONE 9-INCH LAYER CAKE

This cake is best when served the day it is made. You can bake the cake in the morning and finish it later in the day. It can stand in a cool place for about 3 hours before serving. Marrons glacés (whole candied chestnuts) are available in specialty food stores.

    Unsalted butter, for the pans
14 ounces fresh chestnuts
 1 cup sugar
 4 large eggs, room temperature, separated
½   teaspoon cream of tartar
⅔   cup sifted cake flour (not self-rising)
¾   cup sifted chestnut flour
 2 teaspoons baking powder
½   teaspoon ground cinnamon
¼   teaspoon salt
½   cup water
½   cup vegetable oil
 1 teaspoon pure vanilla extract
 6 ounces semisweet chocolate,
    very finely ground
 2 cups Pastry Cream (page 655)
    Chocolate Ganache (recipe follows)
 8 marrons glacés (optional)

1. Preheat the oven to 350° F. Butter two 9 × 2-inch round professional baking pans, and line the bottoms with parchment. Butter the parchment, and set aside.

2. Using a chestnut knife or a small paring knife, make an incision about ⅛ inch deep through the shell and into the flesh of each chestnut almost all the way around the circumference of the nut. Transfer to a chestnut pan or rimmed baking pan. Roast in the oven until the chestnuts are tender, about

35 minutes. Turn the oven off. Leaving the pan with the chestnuts in the oven, remove several at a time. Working quickly, place 1 chestnut in a towel, and, holding both, peel the chestnut while still hot. Remove and discard the shells and inner skin; let cool completely. Transfer the chestnuts to the bowl of a food processor. Add 2 tablespoons sugar, and pulse until very finely ground; set aside. Reduce the oven temperature to 325° F.

3. Place the egg whites and cream of tartar in the bowl of an electric mixer fitted with the whisk attachment. Beat until foamy on medium-low speed, 5 to 6 minutes. With the mixer running, slowly add ½ cup sugar. Raise speed to medium-high; beat until stiff peaks form, 6 to 7 minutes. Transfer the egg white mixture to a bowl.

4. Into the bowl of an electric mixer fitted with the paddle attachment, sift together the cake flour, chestnut flour, baking powder, cinnamon, salt, and remaining 6 tablespoons sugar. Add the egg yolks, water, oil, and vanilla; beat on medium speed until smooth and well combined, about 1 minute.

5. Using a rubber spatula, carefully and gently fold the flour mixture in 4 or 5 additions into the egg white mixture until well combined. Gently fold in the reserved chestnuts and chocolate. Evenly divide the batter between the prepared cake pans.

6. Bake on the same shelf, rotating the pans halfway through baking, until golden and a cake tester inserted into the centers of the cakes come out clean, about 65 minutes. Transfer to a wire rack until completely cool. Invert the pans to remove the cakes. Remove the parchment paper.

7. Place 1 layer on a cake round (or directly onto a cake stand or serving platter). Using an offset spatula, spread the pastry cream on top to within ½ inch of the edges. Place the other layer on top.

8. Pour the ganache on top; carefully spread to about ¼ inch from the edges. The ganache will overflow slightly and gently brim the edges. Arrange the marrons glacés on top of the cake, spaced evenly. Set the cake in a cool place to allow the ganache to firm.

chocolate ganache

MAKES ENOUGH FOR ONE 9-INCH LAYER CAKE

- 5 ounces semisweet chocolate, finely chopped
- ⅔ cup heavy cream

Place the chocolate in a small bowl. Bring the cream to a boil in a small saucepan over medium-high heat. Pour the boiling cream over the chocolate. Cover with plastic wrap for several minutes. Remove the wrap, and stir until the chocolate is completely smooth and melted. Set the ganache in a cool place; let stand until thickened to the consistency of thick cake batter, 10 to 15 minutes.

two-colored squash loaf cake

MAKES ONE 5 X 9-INCH LOAF

Purchase high-quality pistachios, and pick through the nuts for the greenest ones. After roasting, rub the nuts between your palms to eliminate as much of the brown skin as possible.

- 10 tablespoons (1¼ sticks) unsalted butter, room temperature, plus more for the loaf pan
- 2 cups all-purpose flour, plus more for the pan
- 4 each medium yellow and green zucchini (about 1½ pounds)
- 1 cup shelled, unsalted pistachio nuts, roughly chopped
- 1 teaspoon salt
- 1½ teaspoons baking powder
- 1¼ cups sugar
- 4 large eggs
- 1 teaspoon pure vanilla extract
- 2 teaspoons fennel seeds

1. Preheat the oven to 425°F. Generously butter a 5 × 9-inch loaf pan. Sprinkle the pan with flour, tap out excess flour, then set the pan side. Using a box grater, coarsely grate the squash. Place the grated squash in a piece of cheesecloth, and squeeze out as much liquid as possible; set the squash aside.

2. Place the pistachios on a baking pan, and toast in the oven for 5 minutes. Remove, and set aside to cool. In a medium bowl, sift together the flour, salt, and baking powder; set aside.

3. In an electric mixer fitted with the paddle attachment, combine the butter and sugar; beat on medium-high speed until light and fluffy. Add the eggs, 1 at a time, and mix until combined. Beat in the vanilla extract. Add the flour mixture, and beat until just combined.

4. Remove the bowl from the mixer stand; fold in the squash, pistachios, and fennel seeds. Spoon the batter into the prepared loaf pan; bake 10 minutes.

5. Reduce the oven temperature to 350°F, and bake the loaf cake until golden brown and a wooden skewer, inserted into the center of the loaf, comes out clean, about 1 hour. Remove the cake from the oven, and transfer to a wire rack until cool.

apple pie upside-down cake

MAKES ONE 12-INCH CAKE

- 1¼ cups (2½ sticks) unsalted butter, softened, plus more for pan
- 1½ cups packed light-brown sugar
- 3 tablespoons Calvados apple brandy
  Salt
- 3 whole cinnamon sticks
- 6 medium Braeburn or McIntosh apples (about 2½ pounds), peeled, cored, and cut into ¼-inch-thick rings
- 2¼ cups all-purpose flour
- ½ teaspoon baking soda
- ½ teaspoon baking powder
- ¾ teaspoon ground cinnamon
- 1½ cups granulated sugar
- 3 large eggs
- 1½ teaspoons pure vanilla extract
- ½ cup sour cream

1. Preheat the oven to 375°F. Butter a 12 × 1-inch round pizza pan. Line bottom with parchment paper, and butter parchment; set aside. Put ½ cup butter, the brown sugar, brandy, and a pinch of salt into the bowl of an electric mixer fitted with the paddle attachment; mix on medium-high speed until pale and fluffy, 2 to 3 minutes.

2. Spread mixture into prepared pan. Place cinnamon sticks on top. Layer with apple rings. Use your hands to press apples gently into mixture; set aside. Sift flour, baking soda, baking powder, ¾ teaspoon salt, and the ground cinnamon into a medium bowl; set aside.

3. Put remaining ¾ cup butter and the granulated sugar into the clean bowl of an electric mixer fitted with the clean paddle attachment; mix on medium-high speed until pale and fluffy. Mix in eggs, one at a time, and vanilla. Reduce speed to low. Add flour mixture in 2 batches, alternating with the sour cream. Spread batter evenly over apples.

4. Bake until cake is golden brown and a cake tester inserted into center comes out clean, about 45 minutes. Let cool on a wire rack 15 minutes. Invert onto a serving plate. The cake can be stored at room temperature, covered, up to 1 day.

"pumpkin pie" cheesecake

MAKES ONE 10-INCH CAKE

for the filling

- 1 small butternut squash (about 1¾ pounds)
   Unsalted butter, for parchment and pan
- ¾ teaspoon ground cinnamon
- ⅛ teaspoon ground allspice
- ⅛ teaspoon freshly grated nutmeg
- ½ teaspoon ground ginger
- 2½ pounds cream cheese, room temperature
- 1¾ cups sugar
- ½ cup all-purpose flour
- ¾ cup sour cream
- 1¼ teaspoon pure vanilla extract
- ¼ teaspoon salt
- 5 large eggs

for the crust

- 6 tablespoons unsalted butter, softened
- ⅓ cup sugar
- 1 large egg yolk
- 1 teaspoon pure vanilla extract
- 1 cup all-purpose flour, plus more for work surface
   Pinch of salt

1. Preheat the oven to 350°F. Make the filling: Cut squash in half lengthwise; remove seeds, and reserve for another use. Place squash, cut sides down, on a baking sheet lined with buttered parchment paper. Bake until tender, about 45 minutes. Transfer sheet to a wire rack; let cool.

2. Make the crust: Put butter and sugar into the bowl of an electric mixer fitted with the paddle attachment; mix on medium speed until pale and fluffy. Mix in egg yolk and vanilla. Reduce speed to low. Add flour and salt; mix until dough comes together. Shape into a disk; wrap in plastic. Refrigerate until firm, at least 30 minutes and up to 1 day.

3. On a lightly floured surface, roll dough into a 10-inch circle, a scant ¼ inch thick. Fit into the bottom of a 10-inch springform pan. Freeze 15 minutes. Bake until crust is firm and pale golden, 12 to 15 minutes. Transfer to a wire rack; let cool completely. Reduce oven temperature to 325°F.

4. Scoop squash flesh into a food processor; process until puréed. Transfer 1 cup purée to a medium bowl (reserve remainder for another use). Stir in cinnamon, allspice, nutmeg, and ginger.

5. Wrap exterior of a springform pan (including base) in 2 layers of foil. Butter sides of pan; set aside. Put cream cheese into the clean bowl of an electric mixer fitted with the clean paddle attachment; mix on medium speed until fluffy. Gradually add sugar and flour, mixing until smooth. Mix in sour cream, vanilla, and salt. Mix in eggs, one at a time, until just combined; do not overmix.

6. Stir 2 cups cream cheese mixture into squash mixture; set aside. Pour remaining cream cheese mixture into prepared pan on top of the crust. Drop dollops of squash–cream cheese mixture on top. Gently swirl with a butter knife.

7. Set pan in a large, shallow roasting pan. Transfer to the oven. Carefully pour enough boiling water into the roasting pan to come halfway up sides of cheesecake. Bake until cake is set but still slightly wobbly in center, 50 to 60 minutes. Turn off oven; let stand in oven with door slightly ajar 1 hour. Let cool completely on a wire rack. Refrigerate at least 6 hours or overnight. To serve, run a knife around sides of cake; and unmold.

berry pound cakes

MAKES TWO 4½ × 8½-INCH LOAVES

- 1 cup (2 sticks) unsalted butter, softened, plus more for pans
- 2¾ cups all-purpose flour
- ½ cup cake flour (not self-rising)
- 1 tablespoon baking powder
- 1 teaspoon salt
- 2¼ cups granulated sugar
- 1½ teaspoons pure vanilla extract
- 3 large eggs, plus 1 large egg white
- 1 cup whole milk
- 1½ cups heavy cream
- 1 tablespoon confectioners' sugar
- 1 cup fresh blueberries (about 4 ounces)
- 1 cup fresh raspberries (about 4 ounces)

1. Preheat the oven to 350°F. Butter two 4½ × 8½-inch loaf pans. Line with parchment paper, allowing a 1-inch overhang on long sides. Butter the parchment; set aside. Whisk together flours, baking powder, and salt in a medium bowl; set aside.

2. Put butter, granulated sugar, and vanilla into the bowl of an electric mixer fitted with the paddle attachment; mix on medium speed until pale and fluffy, 3 to 4 minutes. Mix in eggs, one at a time. Reduce speed to low. Add flour mixture in 2 batches, alternating with the milk.

3. Divide batter between prepared pans. Bake until dark golden and a cake tester inserted into centers comes out clean, 55 to 60 minutes. Let cool on a wire rack 15 minutes. Lift cakes out; let cool completely on rack. Trim tops of cakes to make level. The cakes can be stored at room temperature, covered, up to 1 day.

4. Put cream and confectioners' sugar into the clean bowl of an electric mixer fitted with the whisk attachment; beat on medium-high speed until soft peaks form. Transfer whipped cream to a pastry bag fitted with a leaf tip (such as Ateco #113). Pipe a ruffled pattern on tops of cakes. Pile blueberries in center of 1 cake, and raspberries in center of the other.

cherry blossom cake

MAKES ONE 9-INCH LAYER CAKE

for the cake

- 12 tablespoons (1½ sticks) unsalted butter, softened, plus more for pans
- 2¼ cups all-purpose flour, plus more for dusting
- 2¼ teaspoons baking powder
- ¼ teaspoon salt
- 1½ cups sugar
- 3 large eggs
- ½ teaspoon pure vanilla extract
- ¾ cup whole milk

for the buttercream frosting

- 3 cups packed light-brown sugar
- 12 large egg whites
- 2 pounds (8 sticks) unsalted butter, softened and cut into tablespoon-size pieces
- 2 teaspoons pure vanilla extract

for decorating

- Gel-paste food coloring in assorted hues
- Pastry tips (Ateco #2 round tip, #102 petal tip, #3 round tip, #349 leaf tip)

1. Preheat the oven to 350°F. Cut a 9-inch round of parchment or waxed paper to line the bottom of a 9-inch (2-inch deep) round cake pan. Butter and line pan. Butter lining, then flour pan, tapping out excess.

2. Make the cake: Whisk together flour, baking powder, and salt in a medium bowl; set aside. Put butter and sugar in the bowl of an electric mixer fitted with the paddle attachment; cream on medium-high speed until pale, 2 to 3 minutes. On medium speed, add eggs one at a time, mixing well after each addition. Add vanilla, and mix, scraping down sides of bowl. On low speed, add the flour mixture in 3 batches, alternating with two batches of milk. Stir batter with a rubber spatula until evenly blended.

3. Pour batter into prepared pan, and smooth top with a small offset spatula. Tap pan on work surface several times to release air pockets.

4. Bake until a cake tester inserted into center comes out clean, 45 to 50 minutes. Let cake cool in pan on a wire rack, 20 minutes. Run a knife around edge of cake to loosen. Invert cake to remove from pan, and peel off parchment. Re-invert, and let cool completely on rack. Wrap in plastic wrap, and refrigerate until ready to decorate.

5. Make the buttercream frosting: Whisk sugar and egg whites in a large heatproof bowl set over a pan of simmering water until sugar is dissolved and mixture registers 140°F on an instant-read thermometer, 2 to 3 minutes.

6. Fit an electric mixer with the whisk attachment, and beat the egg white mixture on high speed until it holds stiff (but not dry) peaks and mixture is fluffy and cooled, about 10 minutes.

7. Reduce speed to medium-low, and add butter several tablespoons at a time, beating well after each addition (meringue will deflate slightly as butter is added). Add vanilla; beat until frosting comes together, 3 to 5 minutes. Beat on lowest speed until air bubbles diminish, about 2 minutes. Stir with a rubber spatula until frosting is smooth.

8. Assemble the cake: Trim the top of the cake with a long serrated knife to make the surface level. Using a ruler as a guide, insert toothpicks or wooden skewers into the sides of the cake at 2-inch intervals to mark 2 equal layers. Rest the serrated knife on the toothpicks, and halve the cake horizontally using a sawing motion. Carefully slide the top cake layer onto a cardboard round, and set it aside.

9. With a small offset spatula, spread top of bottom cake layer with 1 ¼ cups frosting; carefully slide the second cake layer back on top of the first cake layer.

10. Gently brush away loose crumbs from top and sides of cake with a pastry brush. With the offset spatula, spread about 1 ½ cups frosting over top and sides of cake to form a crumb coat. Refrigerate cake until frosting is firm, about 15 minutes.

11. With a large offset spatula, spread about 2 more cups frosting over top and sides to form a second coat. Smooth top and remove excess frosting with the large offset spatula. Smooth sides with a bench scraper. Return cake to refrigerator, and chill until second coat is firm, about 15 minutes.

12. Tint 1½ cups frosting pale pink (for flowers and buds). Tint ½ cup frosting a darker pink (for more flowers and buds). Tint ½ cup chocolate brown (for branches), and ½ cup green (for leaves). Tint ¼ cup yellow (for dots). Set aside.

13. Using a toothpick or wooden skewer, mark a pattern on the frosting to serve as a guideline for piping branches.

14. Decorate cake: Follow instructions below.

15. Refrigerate cake; let stand at room temperature 20 minutes before serving. Slice into wedges: To avoid crumbs on surface, make each cut with one downward motion, pulling knife back toward you (not upward) and wiping knife clean after each cut.

MAKING CHERRY BLOSSOMS

Pipe thin branches using brown frosting and the #2 tip. With pink frosting and the #102 petal tip, make basic petals: Hold the bag at a 45 degree angle to the cake, with the tip's wide end down and narrow end pointed away and slightly to the left. Move the tip forward ⅛ inch and back again while you pivot the narrow end to the right. Make five or six petals, turning the cake as you go. Switch to yellow frosting and the #2 tip to pipe

dots in the bloom's center. With pink frosting and the #102 petal tip, pipe two small overlapping petals on the branch for a closed blossom. With green frosting and the #3 round tip, pipe a dot, pulling upward, to make a bud; connect to branch with brown frosting. With the #349 tip, pipe tiny green leaves.

Tips, from top to bottom: #3 round, #102 petal, #2 round, and #349 leaf.

teatime coconut layer cake

SERVES 10 TO 12

Vegetable oil cooking spray

3⅓ cups sifted cake flour (not self-rising)

2¼ cups superfine sugar

¾ teaspoon baking soda

Salt

¾ cup vegetable oil

11 large eggs, separated, plus 3 egg whites

1 teaspoon pure vanilla extract

¾ cup granulated sugar

¼ cup cream of coconut

Coconut Meringue Buttercream (recipe follows)

1 cup sweetened flaked coconut

⅔ cup unsweetened coconut shavings, for garnish

1. Preheat the oven to 325°F. Coat three 9 × 2-inch round cake pans with cooking spray; line with parchment paper. Set aside.

2. Sift flour, 1¾ cups superfine sugar, the baking soda, and ½ teaspoon salt into the bowl of an electric mixer fitted with the paddle attachment. Whisk together ¾ cup water, the vegetable oil, egg yolks, and vanilla in another bowl. Add yolk mixture to flour mixture; mix on medium-high speed until smooth, about 2 minutes. Transfer to a large bowl; set aside.

3. Put egg whites and a pinch of salt into the clean bowl of the mixer fitted with the whisk attachment; beat on medium speed until foamy. Raise speed to medium-high; beat until soft peaks form. Gradually add remaining ½ cup superfine sugar; beat until stiff, glossy peaks form.

4. Fold one-quarter of egg white mixture into batter with a rubber spatula. Fold in remaining egg white mixture in 2 batches. Divide batter evenly among prepared pans. Bake until cakes are golden brown and spring back when pressed, 30 to 35 minutes. Invert cakes onto wire racks to cool; remove parchment.

5. Make coconut syrup: Bring 1 cup water, the granulated sugar, a pinch of salt, and the cream of coconut to a boil in a small saucepan, stirring occasionally. Boil 1 minute; remove from heat, and let stand.

6. Trim cakes to make level. Place 1 cake on a serving plate, and brush with ⅓ cup coconut syrup. Spread with 1 cup buttercream, and sprinkle with ⅓ cup sweetened coconut. Top with another cake. Brush with ⅓ cup syrup; spread with 1 cup buttercream, and sprinkle with ⅓ cup sweetened coconut. Top with final cake; brush with remaining ⅓ cup syrup. Refrigerate until firm.

7. Spread 1¼ cups buttercream over top and sides of cake. Refrigerate until buttercream is firm, about 30 minutes.

8. Spread 1½ cups buttercream over top and sides of cake. Refrigerate until buttercream is very firm, at least 1 hour. Fill a pastry bag fitted with a 1-inch basketweave tip (such as Ateco #898) with buttercream. Holding bag perpendicular to cake, pipe sides in a back-and-forth motion, starting at the bottom. Refill bag as needed. Sprinkle the top with the remaining 1 cup sweetened coconut and the unsweetened coconut shavings. The cake can be refrigerated up to 2 days; let stand at room temperature 20 minutes before serving.

coconut meringue buttercream

MAKES ABOUT 9 CUPS

 10 large egg whites
2¼ cups sugar
 ¼ teaspoon salt
  4 cups (8 sticks) unsalted butter, softened
 ½ cup cream of coconut
 ½ teaspoon pure coconut extract

1. Whisk egg whites, sugar, and salt in the heatproof bowl of an electric mixer set over a pan of simmering water until sugar has dissolved and mixture registers 160° F, about 3 minutes.

2. Attach bowl to mixer fitted with the whisk attachment. Beat on medium-high speed until cooled, about 10 minutes. Reduce speed to medium. Add butter; beat until pale and fluffy. Mix in cream of coconut and coconut extract. The buttercream can be refrigerated in an airtight container up to 3 days; beat before using.

triple-chocolate mousse cakes

MAKES 8 SMALL CAKES

    Vegetable oil cooking spray
 ⅔ cup all-purpose flour
 ⅓ cup unsweetened Dutch-process
    cocoa powder
 ⅔ cup sugar
 ¾ teaspoon baking soda
 ½ teaspoon baking powder
 ¼ teaspoon salt
  1 large egg, room temperature
 ¼ cup whole milk
  3 tablespoons vegetable oil
 ½ teaspoon pure vanilla extract
    Chocolate Mousses (recipe follows)
  2 ounces solid semisweet chocolate
    Chocolate curls, for garnish

1. Preheat oven to 350° F. Place eight 6-ounce (3½-inch diameter) ramekins on a rimmed baking sheet, and coat with cooking spray; set aside.

2. Stir flour, cocoa powder, sugar, baking soda, baking powder, and salt in the bowl of an electric mixer. Attach bowl to mixer fitted with the paddle attachment. Add egg, milk, oil, vanilla, and ¼ cup water; mix on medium-low speed until smooth and combined, about 3 minutes.

3. Divide batter evenly among prepared ramekins. Bake until a cake tester inserted into the centers comes out clean, about 20 minutes. Transfer to a wire rack; let cool completely. Run a knife around sides of cakes; unmold. The cakes can be refrigerated, wrapped in plastic, up to 1 day.

4. Trim each cake to 1 inch high. Transfer to a baking sheet lined with parchment paper. Cut eight 10¾ × 4-inch strips of parchment paper. Wrap a parchment collar around base of each cake, keeping bottom flush with baking sheet. Secure each collar with tape; set aside.

5. Transfer bittersweet-chocolate mousse to a large pastry bag fitted with a large round tip (such as Ateco #808). Pipe a 1-inch layer of mousse into each parchment collar; refrigerate until set, about 20 minutes. Repeat with milk chocolate mousse, piping on top of the bittersweet chocolate mousse. Refrigerate at least 4 hours, or overnight.

6. Microwave semisweet chocolate until slightly warm but not melted, about 30 seconds. Scrape at a 45-degree angle with a vegetable peeler, forming curls. Before serving cakes, remove parchment collars, and garnish with chocolate curls.

chocolate mousses

This recipe makes two kinds of mousse: bitter-sweet chocolate and milk chocolate.

    3⅓ cups heavy cream
     8 large egg yolks, room temperature
     ½ cup sugar
     ¼ cup light corn syrup
     7 ounces bittersweet chocolate, melted
     2 teaspoons pure vanilla extract
        Salt
     7 ounces milk chocolate, melted

1. Put 1⅔ cups cream into the bowl of an electric mixer fitted with the whisk attachment; beat on medium-high speed until soft peaks form, about 3½ minutes. Transfer to a bowl; refrigerate 1 hour.

2. Put 4 egg yolks into the clean bowl of the mixer fitted with the clean whisk attachment; beat on high speed until pale and frothy, 4 to 5 minutes. Meanwhile, bring ¼ cup sugar, 2 tablespoons corn syrup, and 2 tablespoons water to a rolling boil in a small, heavy saucepan over high heat. Cook until clear, large bubbles form, about 1 minute. Reduce mixer speed to medium-low. Carefully pour hot syrup down side of bowl. Raise speed to medium-high. Mix until slightly thickened, about 5 minutes. Stir in bittersweet chocolate, 1 teaspoon vanilla, and a pinch of salt with a rubber spatula.

3. Add one-third of bittersweet-chocolate mixture to whipped cream; whisk to combine. Add remaining mixture, whisking until completely combined. Press through a large-mesh sieve into a large bowl; discard any solids. Repeat entire recipe, substituting milk chocolate for the bittersweet.

NOTE *The egg yolks in this recipe are not fully cooked. It should not be prepared for pregnant women, babies, young children, the elderly, or anyone whose health is compromised.*

strawberry mousse cake

for the mousse

     1 pound strawberries, hulled and halved, plus 2 cups sliced strawberries
     2 tablespoons fresh lemon juice
     8 ounces white chocolate, finely chopped
    1¼ teaspoons unflavored gelatin
     2 cups heavy cream
     2 tablespoons confectioners' sugar

for the cake

        Vegetable oil cooking spray
     1 cup sifted cake flour, plus more for baking sheet
     5 large eggs plus 2 large egg yolks
     ¾ cup sugar
        Pinch of salt
     1 tablespoon finely grated lemon zest
     6 tablespoons unsalted butter, melted

for the ganache

    ⅔ cup heavy cream
    12 ounces white chocolate, finely chopped
        Pinch of salt
     2 tablespoons fresh lemon juice
        Whole and halved strawberries, for garnish

1. Make the mousse: Puree halved strawberries in a food processor. Pass through a very fine sieve into a bowl (you should have about 1 cup puree). Stir in 1 tablespoon lemon juice; set aside.

2. Melt the chocolate in a medium heatproof bowl set over a pan of simmering water, stirring until smooth; set aside.

3. Put ¼ cup cool water into a small bowl. Sprinkle gelatin over top; let stand until softened, about 5 minutes. Stir ¼ cup cream and the confectioners' sugar in a small saucepan; bring to a simmer over medium heat. Add gelatin mixture, and stir until gelatin has dissolved. Pour into bowl with the melted chocolate; stir until smooth. Whisk in ¾ cup strawberry puree; reserve remaining ¼ cup puree.

4. Put remaining 1¾ cups cream into the bowl of an electric mixer fitted with the whisk attachment. Beat on medium-high speed until medium peaks form. Whisk one-third of the whipped cream into the chocolate mixture. Fold in the remaining whipped cream using a large rubber spatula. Refrigerate 1 hour. Stir remaining 1 tablespoon lemon juice into the sliced berries. Fold berries into mousse; refrigerate 1 hour.

5. Preheat the oven to 425°F. Make the cake: Coat a 12 × 18 × 1-inch rimmed baking sheet with cooking spray. Line bottom with parchment paper, and spray parchment. Dust with flour, and tap out excess.

6. Put eggs, egg yolks, and sugar into the heatproof bowl of an electric mixer set over a pan of simmering water. Whisk constantly until the mixture is warm and the sugar has melted, about 2 minutes. Attach bowl to mixer fitted with whisk attachment. Beat on high speed until egg mixture is pale, thickened, and has cooled, about 6 minutes.

7. Remove bowl from mixer; sift together flour and salt over the top of egg mixture, and sprinkle with lemon zest. Using a large rubber spatula, carefully fold the flour mixture into the egg mixture, cutting through center and lifting gently over sides. When the flour is almost incorporated, pour butter down side of bowl, and gently fold in to incorporate.

8. Pour batter into prepared baking sheet; smooth top. Bake until center springs back when lightly touched, 7 to 12 minutes. Invert, and unmold cake onto a parchment-lined wire rack; peel parchment from cake, and let cool completely.

9. Assemble the cake: Cut cake crosswise into 3 rectangles. Set 1 layer, top side down, on a wire rack set over a rimmed baking sheet. Brush with half of the remaining strawberry puree. Spread a ¾-inch-thick layer of mousse (about 2 cups) over the top. Top with second cake layer, top side up. Brush with remaining strawberry puree; spread with a ¾-inch-thick layer of mousse. Place third cake layer on top, top side up. Refrigerate at least 2 hours (preferably overnight). Trim sides of cake to be straight.

10. Make the ganache: Bring cream just to a boil in a small saucepan over medium-high heat. Pour hot cream over the chocolate in a medium bowl; let stand 5 minutes. Stir until smooth. Stir in salt and lemon juice. Let stand until ganache is pourable and has cooled slightly. Pour ganache over top of cake, allowing it to drip down sides. Refrigerate assembled cake 1 hour before serving. Using 2 large spatulas, transfer cake to a serving platter. Garnish with strawberries.

brown sugar angel food cake with candied citrus slices

MAKES ONE 10-INCH CAKE

1¼   cups sifted cake flour (not self-rising)
1½   cups packed light-brown sugar, sifted
14   large egg whites, room temperature
1½   teaspoons cream of tartar
      Pinch of salt
 2   teaspoons finely grated lemon zest
      Candied Citrus Slices, for serving (recipe follows)
16   ounces crème fraîche

1. Preheat the oven to 350°F. Stir together flour and ¾ cup brown sugar. Sift twice.

2. Put egg whites into the bowl of an electric mixer fitted with the whisk attachment. Beat on medium speed until foamy. Add cream of tartar and salt. Raise speed to high, and beat until soft peaks form. Sprinkle half the remaining ¾ cup brown sugar over egg white mixture, and beat until combined. Sprinkle the remaining brown sugar over egg white mixture, and beat until stiff, glossy peaks form.

3. Transfer egg white mixture to a large bowl. Fold in flour mixture in 3 batches, folding in lemon zest with last batch.

4. Spoon batter into an ungreased 10-inch tube pan (not nonstick) with a removable bottom. Run a knife through batter to eliminate air pockets. Bake until cake is golden and springs back when lightly touched, about 45 minutes.

5. Invert pan onto its legs or over a narrow-neck bottle; let cool 1 hour. Reinvert, and run a knife around sides and tube to loosen; remove sides. Run a long knife along bottom of cake; remove from tube.

6. Place cake on a serving platter. Cut a slit in rind of candied citrus slices; twist slices, and arrange around bottom of cake. Reserve 1 slice for hole in center.

7. Put crème fraîche into a medium bowl. Whisk until lightened. Transfer a little more than ¼ cup to a pastry bag fitted with a large rose tip (such as Ateco #123). Decoratively pipe crème fraîche around top edge of cake. Place 1 citrus slice over hole; pipe crème fraîche around it. Serve remaining crème fraîche on the side.

candied citrus slices

MAKES ENOUGH TO GARNISH ONE 10-INCH CAKE

 3   cups sugar
 1   small red grapefruit, thinly sliced into rounds
 1   navel orange, thinly sliced into rounds

1. Cut a round of parchment paper to fit just inside a medium pot; set aside. Bring sugar and 3 cups water to a simmer in pot, stirring until sugar has dissolved. When liquid is clear and bubbling, reduce heat to medium-low. Add citrus slices, arranging them in a slightly overlapping layer. Cover with the parchment paper round. Place a cake pan on top of parchment to keep slices submerged. Simmer (do not boil) until rinds are almost translucent, about 40 minutes. Let cool completely in syrup. The candied citrus slices can be stored in syrup up to 1 week.

2. Line a baking sheet with parchment paper; set a wire rack over sheet. Transfer candied citrus to rack. Let stand until dry and slightly firm, about 8 hours.

pastries

....

cream puffs

MAKES 90

The lined baking sheets can be marked with flour-dipped cookie cutters to help guide you in piping the dough into uniform shapes. (See how-to on page 652.)

4 cups Pastry Cream (page 655)
   Pâte à Choux (page 653)
1 egg mixed with 1 tablespoon water,
   for egg wash
   Crystal sanding sugar (optional)
   Chopped nuts (optional)
   Oil, for plastic wrap
¾ cup heavy cream
   Confectioners' sugar, for garnish

1. Preheat the oven to 425°F, with a rack in the center. Line 2 unrimmed baking sheets with parchment paper or Silpats (nonstick French baking mats).

2. Make the pastry cream, and refrigerate. Make the pâte à choux batter. Fill a pastry bag fitted with a coupler or ½-inch (Ateco #806) tip, and pipe 1-inch rounds onto the baking sheets at 2-inch intervals. Using your fingers, rub egg wash over the entire top, and flatten the tips, being careful not to let the egg wash drip onto the surrounding baking sheet (it will inhibit rising). Sprinkle with crystal sanding sugar or chopped nuts, if desired.

3. Cover 1 sheet with lightly oiled plastic wrap, and place in the refrigerator. Transfer the other to the oven. Bake 10 minutes; reduce the oven heat to 350°F. Bake 15 to 20 minutes, or until the puffs are golden brown. Transfer to a wire rack to let cool slightly. Raise the heat back to 425°F, and repeat the process for the remaining batch.

4. Whip the heavy cream to stiff peaks in a small bowl. Stir the pastry cream to soften. Add the whipped cream to the pastry cream in 2 batches; stir to combine after each. Fill a pastry bag fitted with a coupler and filling tip (Ateco #230). Insert the tip into the underside of each cream puff, and fill. Cool completely before dusting with confectioners' sugar. Serve, or store up to 2 hours in an airtight container in the refrigerator.

éclairs

MAKES 30

You can make coffee icing by whisking together 2 cups sifted confectioners' sugar, 1 tablespoon melted butter, and 3 tablespoons brewed coffee. Make the icing just before serving.

4 cups Pastry Cream (page 655)
   Pâte à Choux (page 653)
   Oil, for plastic wrap

for chocolate glaze
¼ cup water
¼ cup light corn syrup
½ cup sugar
4½ ounces semisweet chocolate,
   finely chopped

1. Preheat the oven to 425°F, with a rack in the center. Line 2 unrimmed baking sheets with parchment paper or Silpats (French nonstick baking mats).

2. Make the pastry cream; refrigerate. Make the pâte à choux batter. Fill a pastry bag fitted with a ½-inch (Ateco #806) tip; pipe out oblong shapes, about 3½ inches long and 1 inch wide, onto the baking sheets at 2-inch intervals. Gently run a fork dipped in water along the top, making straight lines to ensure even rising.

3. Cover 1 sheet with lightly oiled plastic wrap, and place in the refrigerator. Transfer the other to the oven. Bake 10 minutes; reduce the oven heat to 350°F. Bake 25 to 30 minutes, or until golden brown. Turn off the oven; prop the door open slightly to let steam escape. Allow the éclairs to dry in the oven about 15 minutes, or until the center is damp but no wet dough remains (test by cutting into the center of one). Transfer to a wire rack to cool slightly. Raise the heat back to 425°F, and repeat the process for the remaining batch. If serving immediately, fill while still warm so the éclairs can take more cream. If filling at a later time, insert a skewer into one end of each, and move it around to expand the opening for cream; set aside.

4. In a medium bowl, stir the pastry cream to soften. Fill a pastry bag fitted with a coupler and filling tip

(Ateco #230) with pastry cream. Insert the tip into one end of each éclair; fill. Serve, or glaze as follows.

5. To make the glaze, combine the water, corn syrup, and sugar in a small saucepan. Stir over medium-high heat until the sugar is dissolved. Bring the mixture to a boil, washing the sides of the pan with a wet pastry brush to prevent crystals from forming. Once at a boil, remove from heat; add the chocolate. Let stand 2 minutes; stir gently until smooth. Transfer the glaze to a shallow bowl. Dip the top of each éclair into the glaze; let excess drip off before turning over. Transfer to a wire rack to allow glaze to set. Serve, or store in an airtight container in the refrigerator up to 1 day.

chocolate turnovers

MAKES 9

These turnovers are a variation on the classic pain au chocolat. For maximum flavor, look for the highest-quality chocolate possible, such as Callebaut, Valrhona, or Scharffen Berger.

All-purpose flour, for the work surface
1 *pound 6 ounces Puff Pastry dough (page 653)*
1 *large egg yolk*
1 *tablespoon heavy cream*
2¼ *ounces semisweet chocolate, cut into 9 equal pieces*

1. Preheat the oven to 400°F. On a lightly floured work surface, roll out the pastry dough into a 12-inch square, about ⅛ inch thick, with a rolling pin. Brush off excess flour. Using a pastry wheel or sharp knife, trim the edges and cut the square into nine 3½-inch squares. Place the squares on an ungreased baking sheet.

2. In a small bowl, whisk together the egg yolk and cream for the egg wash. Using a pastry brush, moisten 2 adjacent edges of each square with egg wash. Place a piece of chocolate just below the center of each square; fold down the unwashed edges over the chocolate to form a triangle, completely enclosing the chocolate. Using your fingers, gently but firmly press the pastry edges together to seal. Cover with plastic wrap; refrigerate 30 minutes.

3. Remove the turnovers from the refrigerator, and brush the tops liberally with the remaining egg wash. Place the pan in the oven, and bake until the turnovers are puffed and golden brown all over, 25 to 30 minutes. Remove from the oven; using a spatula, immediately transfer the turnovers to a wire rack to cool completely before serving.

palmiers

MAKES ABOUT 30

Once the palmiers are in the oven, watch them closely, as they may go from a perfect dark golden brown to burned in seconds.

¾ *cup sugar*
14 *ounces Puff Pastry dough (page 653)*

1. Sprinkle half the sugar on a clean work surface. Place the dough on top, and sprinkle evenly with the remaining sugar.

2. Using a rolling pin, gently roll out the dough into a 9½ × 15-inch rectangle ⅛ inch thick, being careful not to press too hard around the edges. Continually coat both sides with sugar.

3. Place the dough so one of the long sides is closest to you. Using your fingers, roll the dough lengthwise into a long cylinder, as tightly as possible without stretching it, as you would a roll of wrapping paper, stopping when you reach the middle. Repeat the same rolling procedure with the other long side until you have 2 tight cylinders that meet in the middle. Wrap tightly in plastic wrap; place in the refrigerator to chill at least 1 hour.

4. Unwrap the dough; using a sharp knife, cut the dough crosswise into ⅜-inch-thick slices. Place the palmiers on an ungreased baking sheet, and firmly flatten with the palm of your hand. Cover with plastic wrap; place in the refrigerator 1 hour.

5. Preheat the oven to 425°F. Place the palmiers in the oven, and bake 5 minutes. Reduce the oven temperature to 400°F; continue baking until the pastry is golden brown and well caramelized, about 10 minutes. Remove from the oven; using a thin spatula, immediately transfer the palmiers to a wire rack to cool completely. Serve shiny side up.

classic napoleon

SERVES 6

Don't be discouraged if your napoleon doesn't cut neatly into serving pieces; even if it's slightly flattened, each bite will still be delicious. To pipe the white chocolate, you'll need a piping cone made from parchment paper.

All-purpose flour, for the work surface

1¾ pounds Puff Pastry dough (page 653) or Quick Puff Pastry (page 654)

⅓ cup heavy cream

2½ ounces dark semisweet chocolate, coarsely chopped (about ⅓ cup)

½ teaspoon corn syrup

¼ ounce white chocolate, chopped (about 1 tablespoon)

4 cups Pastry Cream (page 655)

1. Lightly flour a clean work surface. Using a rolling pin, gently roll out the dough into a 16 × 18-inch rectangle about ⅛ inch thick, being careful not to press too hard around the edges. Using a pastry wheel or sharp knife, cut the rectangle crosswise into thirds (6 × 16 inches). Transfer to a baking sheet; pierce the dough all over with a fork. Cover with plastic wrap; place in the refrigerator 1 hour.

2. Preheat the oven to 425° F. Transfer the uncovered pastry strips to the oven; bake until they are puffed and golden all over, about 14 minutes. Set a baking sheet directly on the pastry strips, and continue baking until the pastry is cooked through and well browned, about 6 minutes. Remove the top baking sheet; bake 4 minutes more. Transfer to a wire rack to cool completely. Using a serrated knife, trim each strip to 4¼ × 12 inches.

3. Make the glaze: In a small saucepan, bring the heavy cream just to a boil. Place the dark chocolate in a bowl, and pour hot cream over the chocolate; whisk until the chocolate is melted and the mixture is combined. Whisk in the corn syrup. Strain through a fine mesh sieve into a clean bowl.

4. Place the white chocolate in a medium heatproof bowl set over a pan of simmering water. Whisk until the chocolate is melted; let cool.

5. Using an offset spatula, spread the dark chocolate glaze over 19 side of the flattest puff pastry strip, making sure to coat the entire surface. Place the white chocolate in a piping cone; pipe thin lines ¾ inch apart across the width of the chocolate-coated strip. To create the distinctive flourish, gently drag the tip of a paring knife or a skewer lengthwise through both coatings, in lines perpendicular to the white chocolate lines. Begin at one of the short ends, and make each line ¾ inch apart. Alternate the direction each time.

6. Place 1 of the unglazed puff pastry strips on a serving tray. Spread half the pastry cream over the top, leaving a ½-inch border all around. Top with the remaining unglazed pastry strip; press down gently, and repeat with the remaining pastry cream. Top with a glazed pastry strip. Transfer to the refrigerator, and chill 30 minutes, uncovered. Using a long serrated knife, cut into 6 pieces, and serve.

apple napoleons

SERVES 4

½ teaspoon ground cinnamon

6 tablespoons sugar

1 sheet from 1 box (17¼ ounces) frozen puff pastry, thawed

All-purpose flour, for work surface

2 tablespoons unsalted butter

4 small Granny Smith apples, peeled, cored, and cut lengthwise into ⅓-inch-thick wedges

2 cups sweetened whipped cream

1. Preheat the oven to 400° F. In a small bowl, combine the cinnamon and sugar. Place the pastry on a lightly floured work surface. Sprinkle evenly with 2 tablespoons of the cinnamon mixture. Carefully roll out the dough to ⅛ inch thick. Cut out eight 3-inch squares, and place on a parchment-lined baking sheet. Cover with more parchment and another baking sheet. Chill in freezer until firm, about 15 minutes.

2. Bake pastry in oven until crisp and lightly browned, about 30 minutes. Remove top parchment and baking sheet. Transfer, with bottom parchment, to a wire rack, and let cool.

3. Meanwhile, in a medium saucepan, melt the butter over medium-high heat until foam subsides. Add the apples; cook, stirring occasionally, until golden brown, about 7 minutes. Add the remaining cinnamon mixture. Cook until the apples are tender but not falling apart. Let cool completely.

4. To assemble, top the pastry with whipped cream then apples; repeat with another layer of each. Serve immediately.

praline napoleons with almond cream filling

MAKES 6

You can make puff pastry from scratch by following the recipes on page 653 or 654.

> All-purpose flour, for work surface
> 1 sheet from 1 box (17¼ ounces) frozen puff pastry, thawed
> 1 large egg, lightly beaten
> 2 cups sugar
> Pinch of salt
> 1½ cups sliced almonds, toasted and finely chopped (about 7 ounces)
> Vegetable oil, for spatula
> Almond Cream Filling (recipe follows)

1. Preheat the oven to 375° F. Place pastry on a lightly floured work surface. Roll out to ⅛ inch thick. Cut out twelve 4½ × 2¾-inch rectangles; transfer to a parchment-lined baking sheet, and prick with a fork. Brush with egg, and cover with parchment. Top with a baking sheet. Freeze until firm, about 15 minutes.

2. With top sheet still in place, bake until pastry is crisp and golden, 30 to 32 minutes. Remove top sheet and parchment. Let pastry cool completely on bottom parchment on a wire rack.

3. Meanwhile, line a rimmed baking sheet with a nonstick baking mat. Stir together sugar, salt, and ½ cup water in a medium saucepan over medium-high heat. Cook, without stirring, until sugar begins to melt and turn light amber, about 3 minutes. Wash down sides of pan with a wet pastry brush as needed to prevent crystals from forming. Continue to cook, stirring occasionally, until mixture turns dark amber, about 8 minutes.

4. Remove from heat; stir in almonds. Pour mixture onto prepared sheet. Using an oiled offset spatula, spread to ⅛ inch thick. Let cool completely. Transfer half of the praline to a plastic bag; using a rolling pin, gently crush into very small pieces; set aside. Break remaining praline into large pieces.

5. Transfer the almond cream filling to a pastry bag fitted with a petal tip (such as Wilton #127). Pipe filling onto 6 pastry rectangles; sprinkle each with crushed praline. Layer with another pastry rectangle and filling. Top each with a piece of praline.

almond cream filling

MAKES ENOUGH FOR 6 NAPOLEONS

> 2½ cups half-and-half
> 2 tablespoons almond paste
> 1 cup sugar
> ¼ teaspoon salt
> ¼ cup plus 2 tablespoons cornstarch
> 4 large egg yolks
> ⅛ teaspoon almond extract
> 2 tablespoons unsalted butter, softened, cut into small pieces
> 1 cup heavy cream

1. Bring 2 cups half-and-half, the almond paste, sugar, salt, and cornstarch to a simmer in a saucepan over medium heat.

2. Prepare an ice-water bath; set aside. Whisk egg yolks, almond extract, and remaining ½ cup half-and-half in a medium bowl; add one-third of the hot half-and-half mixture in a slow, steady stream, whisking constantly. Pour into saucepan.

3. Bring to a boil over medium-high heat, whisking constantly. Cook, whisking, until mixture coats the back of a spoon, 3 to 4 minutes. Pass through a fine sieve into a bowl set in ice-water bath. Stir in butter, several pieces at a time. Let cool completely, stirring occasionally.

4. Put cream into the bowl of an electric mixer fitted with the whisk attachment. Beat on medium-high speed just until stiff peaks form. Fold into custard.

cornmeal crêpes with fresh buttermilk cheese and blackberries

SERVES 6

for the cheese

6 cups low-fat buttermilk

4½ teaspoons confectioners' sugar

for the crêpes

¼ cup all-purpose flour

2 tablespoons yellow cornmeal

¼ teaspoon baking soda

Pinch of salt and freshly grated nutmeg

1 large egg plus 1 large egg white

¼ cup skim milk

¼ cup low-fat buttermilk

1½ teaspoons honey

½ teaspoon canola oil

Vegetable oil cooking spray

3½ cups blackberries

¼ cup crème de cassis

1 teaspoon confectioners' sugar

1. Make the cheese: Line a large fine sieve with 3 layers of cheesecloth, and set over a large bowl. Heat buttermilk in a medium saucepan over medium-low heat, without stirring, until clear liquid separates from milk at edges or a candy thermometer clipped to the edge of the pan registers 95°F. Reduce heat to low; cook until thermometer registers 100°F. Remove from heat; let stand 3 minutes. Pour into sieve; cover bowl loosely with plastic wrap. Refrigerate until thick and creamy, about 3 hours (up to overnight). Before serving, stir in confectioners' sugar.

2. Make the crêpes: Whisk flour, cornmeal, baking soda, salt, and nutmeg in a bowl. Whisk egg, egg white, milk, buttermilk, honey, and oil in another bowl; gradually add to flour mixture, whisking until smooth. Transfer to an airtight container; refrigerate 30 minutes.

3. Coat an 8-inch crêpe pan with cooking spray; heat over medium heat. Remove from heat; pour in 2½ tablespoons batter, swirling to coat. Reduce heat to medium-low. Cook, flipping once, until edges are golden and center is dry, 45 to 60 seconds per side. Repeat with remaining batter.

4. Toss together berries and cassis. Let stand 15 minutes, tossing often. To serve, divide crêpes among plates. Spread each with ¼ cup cheese. Sprinkle with berries; drizzle with juice from bowl. Dust with sugar.

FIT TO EAT RECIPE PER SERVING: 231 CALORIES, 4 G FAT, 46 MG CHOLESTEROL, 35 G CARBOHYDRATE, 372 MG SODIUM, 12 G PROTEIN, 5 G FIBER

apple strudel

SERVES 4

1 cup dried bread crumbs

¾ cup grated peeled red apple (1 to 2 apples)

½ cup golden raisins

¼ cup pitted prunes, coarsely chopped

¼ cup honey

2 tablespoons Armagnac or other good-quality brandy

1 teaspoon ground cinnamon, plus more for sprinkling

½ teaspoon coarse salt

5 sheets phyllo dough (at least 11 × 14 inches), thawed if frozen

½ cup (1 stick) unsalted butter, melted

Confectioners' sugar and whipped cream, for serving

1. Preheat the oven to 375°F with rack in upper third. Gently stir together bread crumbs, apple, raisins, prunes, honey, brandy, cinnamon, and salt in a medium bowl. Set filling aside.

2. Brush a sheet of phyllo with butter. Top with 2 sheets, and brush with butter; repeat. Spread with filling. Starting at a short end, roll to enclose filling. Transfer, seam side down, to a baking sheet lined with parchment paper.

3. Bake until golden brown, about 35 minutes. Transfer to a wire rack; cool 15 minutes. Sprinkle with cinnamon and sugar; serve with whipped cream.

cookies
AND
candy

....

hermit bars with brown sugar icing and candied ginger

MAKES ABOUT 36 TWO-INCH SQUARES

These spice-laden cookies originated in colonial New England; the candied ginger is our own addition. As the name implies, the bars are best after being hidden away for a day or two, so the flavors have a chance to deepen.

- ½ cup (1 stick) unsalted butter, plus more for the pan, room temperature
- 1¾ cups all-purpose flour
- ¾ teaspoon baking powder
- ¾ teaspoon baking soda
- 1 tablespoon ground ginger
- 1 teaspoon ground cinnamon
- ½ teaspoon ground nutmeg
  Pinch of ground cloves
- ¼ teaspoon salt
- ¼ teaspoon freshly ground pepper
- 1¼ cups packed dark-brown sugar
- 1 large whole egg
- 1 large egg yolk
- ¼ cup molasses
- 1 cup (about 5 ounces) chopped candied ginger, cut into ¼-inch pieces
- ¾ cup raisins
  Brown Sugar Icing (recipe follows)

1. Preheat the oven to 350°F. Butter a 10 × 15-inch baking pan, and line the bottom with parchment paper. Butter the parchment, and set the pan aside. Combine the flour, baking powder, baking soda, ginger, cinnamon, nutmeg, cloves, salt, and pepper in a medium bowl; set aside.

2. In the bowl of an electric mixer fitted with the paddle attachment, cream the butter on medium speed until smooth. Add the sugar; beat until light and fluffy. Beat in the egg, yolk, and molasses.

3. Add the flour mixture; beat on low speed until combined. Add ½ cup candied ginger and the raisins; beat until combined.

4. Spread the dough into the prepared pan in an even layer, and bake until firm to the touch, 18 to 22 minutes, rotating the pan halfway through. Remove from the oven; let cool completely in the pan before icing.

5. Drizzle with icing, and then sprinkle with the remaining ½ cup candied ginger. Let stand until icing has set, about 15 minutes. Serve cut into squares.

brown sugar icing

MAKES ¾ CUP

- ¼ cup packed light brown sugar
- 2 tablespoons milk, plus more as needed
- 2 tablespoons unsalted butter
- 1 teaspoon pure vanilla extract
- 1 cup sifted confectioners' sugar, plus more as needed

Combine the brown sugar, milk, and butter in a medium saucepan. Stir over medium heat until the butter has melted and the sugar has dissolved. Remove from heat; whisk in the vanilla and confectioners' sugar. If the icing is too thick to drizzle, stir in a little more milk. If it is too thin, add a little more confectioners' sugar. Let cool slightly before using.

amaretti crisps

MAKES 20

To achieve the greatest volume, whisk the egg whites in a metal bowl set over a pot of simmering water until just warm to the touch.

- 1¾ cups sliced almonds (about 7 ounces)
- 1 cup confectioners' sugar
- 2 large egg whites
- ½ teaspoon pure almond extract

1. Preheat the oven to 350°F. Spread the almonds in a single layer on a rimmed baking sheet, and toast in the oven until lightly browned and fragrant, 7 to 9 minutes. Remove from the oven; let cool.

2. Combine the almonds and sugar in the bowl of a food processor fitted with the metal blade, and grind to a fine powder. Transfer to a medium bowl.

In a separate bowl, beat the egg whites until stiff peaks form. Fold the egg whites into the almond mixture; fold in the almond extract.

3. Line a baking sheet with parchment paper. Transfer the almond mixture to a pastry bag fitted with a ½-inch plain tip. Pipe 20 2-inch rings onto the prepared sheet, about 1 inch apart. Bake until golden brown and firm to the touch, about 25 minutes. Remove from the oven, and immediately transfer to a wire rack to cool completely.

citrus cookies

MAKES ABOUT 72

- 2 cups all-purpose flour, plus more for dusting
- ½ teaspoon baking powder
- ¼ teaspoon salt
- 1 stick (8 tablespoons) unsalted butter, softened
- 1 cup granulated sugar
- 1 large egg
- 1 tablespoon freshly grated lemon zest
  Colored sanding sugar, for decorating

1. Whisk together the flour, baking powder, and salt. Beat the butter and sugar on medium-high speed until pale and fluffy, about 3 minutes. Beat in the egg, zest, and flour mixture. Divide the dough in half; wrap in plastic. Freeze until firm, 20 minutes.

2. Preheat the oven to 325°F. Unwrap one half on a lightly floured surface. Let stand 10 minutes. Roll out to ¼ inch thick. Cut out circles with a 2-inch round cookie cutter. Transfer the cookies to parchment-lined baking sheets. Roll out the scraps; cut out circles. Repeat with the remaining dough.

3. Lightly press one end of a clean 1½-inch spool onto the surface of each cookie. Refrigerate the dough on the sheets 10 minutes.

4. Sprinkle sanding sugar into the imprint on the cookies; brush off excess. Bake until golden, about 14 minutes. Cool on the sheets set on wire racks. Store airtight up to 1 week.

mixed fruit and nut cookies

MAKES ABOUT 36

- 2¼ cups all-purpose flour
- 1 teaspoon baking soda
- 1 teaspoon salt
- 1 cup (2 sticks) unsalted butter, room temperature
- 1 cup packed light-brown sugar
- ½ cup granulated sugar
- 2 large eggs
- 1 teaspoon pure vanilla extract
- 1½ cups sweetened shredded coconut
- 1½ cups chopped dried apricots
- 1½ cups dried cherries
- 1½ cups sliced blanched almonds
- 1½ cups chopped pistachios

1. Preheat the oven to 375°F. Line 2 baking sheets with parchment paper, and set aside. Whisk together the flour, baking soda, and salt in a medium bowl; set aside.

2. In the bowl of an electric mixer fitted with the paddle attachment, cream the butter on medium speed until smooth. Add the sugars, and beat until light and fluffy, about 3 minutes. Beat in the eggs 1 at a time until combined; beat in the vanilla.

3. Add the flour mixture; beat on low speed until combined. Add the coconut, apricots, cherries, almonds, and pistachios; beat until combined.

4. Drop the batter, 2 heaping tablespoons at a time, onto the prepared baking sheets, about 2 inches apart. Bake until golden brown, 12 to 15 minutes, rotating the pans halfway through. Remove from the oven, and transfer cookies on the parchment-paper lining to a wire rack to cool completely.

cashew-caramel cookies

MAKES ABOUT 36

1⅔ cups all-purpose flour

½ teaspoon salt

2½ cups roasted, salted cashews

2 tablespoons plus 1 teaspoon canola oil

1 stick (8 tablespoons) unsalted butter, softened

¾ cup packed light-brown sugar

½ cup granulated sugar

1 large egg

1 teaspoon pure vanilla extract

24 soft caramel candy cubes (7 ounces)

¼ cup heavy cream

1. Preheat the oven to 350° F. Sift the flour and salt together. Coarsely chop 1 cup cashews; set aside. Process the remaining 1½ cups cashews in a food processor until finely chopped. Pour in the oil. Process until creamy, about 2 minutes.

2. Put the cashew mixture, butter, and sugars in the bowl of an electric mixer fitted with the paddle attachment; mix on medium speed until fluffy, about 2 minutes. Mix in the egg and vanilla. Reduce speed to low; gradually add the flour mixture. Mix in the reserved chopped cashews.

3. Shape the dough into 1½-inch balls; space 2 inches apart on 2 parchment-lined baking sheets. Bake 6 minutes; gently flatten with a spatula. Bake until the bottoms are just golden, 6 to 7 minutes more. Transfer sheets to wire racks; let cool completely.

4. Melt the caramels with the cream in a small saucepan over low heat, stirring. Let cool. Using a spoon, drizzle the caramel over the cookies; let set. Store airtight in single layers.

cornmeal-thyme cookies

MAKES ABOUT 36

These herb-flecked cookies are at once sweet and savory, making them perfect in the afternoon, with a cup of Earl Grey tea. They can also be served after dinner as a light dessert.

1¾ cups all-purpose flour

1 teaspoon baking soda

1 cup stone-ground yellow cornmeal

½ teaspoon salt

8 ounces (2 sticks) unsalted butter, softened

1¼ cups sugar

2 large eggs

¾ cup dried currants

1 tablespoon plus ½ teaspoon finely chopped fresh thyme

1. Preheat the oven to 350° F with racks in the upper and lower thirds. Line 2 baking sheets with parchment paper; set aside. Whisk together the flour, baking soda, cornmeal, and salt in a medium bowl; set aside.

2. Put the butter and sugar in the bowl of an electric mixer fitted with the paddle attachment; cream on medium speed until pale and fluffy, about 3 minutes. Mix in the eggs, 1 at a time. Add the flour mixture; mix on low speed until just combined. Mix in the currants and thyme.

3. Using a tablespoon or a 1½-inch ice-cream scoop, drop rounded balls of dough onto the lined sheets, spacing them 2 inches apart. Bake, rotating and switching the positions of the sheets about halfway through, until pale golden, 10 to 12 minutes. Transfer the cookies, on the parchment, to a wire rack. Let cool completely.

peanut butter–chocolate chip oatmeal cookies

MAKES ABOUT 72

This recipe calls for natural peanut butter, which has less sugar than regular and gives the cookies a richer peanut flavor.

- 3 cups old-fashioned rolled oats
- ⅓ cup whole-wheat flour
- 1 teaspoon baking soda
- 1 teaspoon baking powder
- ½ teaspoon salt
- 1 cup packed light-brown sugar
- 1 cup granulated sugar
- 8 ounces (2 sticks) unsalted butter, softened
- ½ cup natural peanut butter
- 2 large eggs
- 1 teaspoon pure vanilla extract
- 2 cups salted peanuts
- 2 cups semisweet chocolate chips

1. Preheat the oven to 350° F. In a large bowl, stir together the oats, flour, baking soda, baking powder, and salt; set aside.

2. Put the brown and granulated sugars, the butter, and the peanut butter in the bowl of an electric mixer fitted with the paddle attachment. Mix on medium speed until pale and fluffy, about 5 minutes. Mix in the eggs and vanilla, scraping down the sides of the bowl as needed.

3. Reduce speed to low. Add the oat mixture, and mix until just combined. Mix in the peanuts and chocolate chips.

4. Using a small (1½-tablespoon) ice-cream scoop, make balls of dough, and place them 2 inches apart on parchment-paper–lined baking sheets.

5. Bake until the cookies are golden and just set, 13 to 15 minutes. Let cool on the sheets for 5 minutes. Transfer cookies to wire racks to cool completely.

iced oatmeal cookies with golden raisins and applesauce

MAKES ABOUT 30

- 1 cup packed light-brown sugar
- ½ cup granulated sugar
- 4 tablespoons unsalted butter, melted
- 1 large egg
- ½ cup chunky-style applesauce
- 1½ cups old-fashioned rolled oats
- 1¼ cups all-purpose flour
- ½ teaspoon baking soda
- ¼ teaspoon baking powder
- ¼ teaspoon salt
- 1 cup golden raisins
- 1¾ cups confectioners' sugar
- 3 tablespoons pure maple syrup

1. Preheat the oven to 350° F. Put the brown and granulated sugars and the butter in the bowl of an electric mixer fitted with the paddle attachment. Mix on low speed until combined. Add the egg and applesauce; mix until well combined, 2 to 3 minutes; scraping down sides of bowl as needed. Add the oats, flour, baking soda, baking powder, and salt; mix until well combined. Mix in the raisins.

2. Using a small (1½-tablespoon) ice-cream scoop, make balls of dough, and place them 2 inches apart on parchment-paper–lined baking sheets.

3. Bake until the cookies are golden and just set, 13 to 15 minutes. Let cool on the sheets for 5 minutes. Transfer to a wire rack set over parchment paper to cool completely.

4. Whisk the confectioners' sugar with the syrup and 3 tablespoons water until smooth. Drizzle the icing over the cookies; let set.

oatmeal bars
with dates and walnuts

MAKES 24

You can use a blender or a food processor to grind the rolled oats; 1¼ cups rolled oats yields 1 cup ground.

- 1 cup finely ground old-fashioned rolled oats
- ¾ cup whole-wheat flour
- 1½ cups old-fashioned rolled oats
- 1½ teaspoons baking powder
- 1½ teaspoons salt
- ½ teaspoon ground cinnamon
- ¼ teaspoon ground allspice
- 2 cups packed light-brown sugar
- 12 tablespoons (1½ sticks) unsalted butter, softened
- 3 large eggs
- 2½ teaspoons pure vanilla extract
- 1½ cups walnuts (5½ ounces), toasted and chopped
- 1 cup dates (5 ounces), pitted and chopped
  Vegetable oil cooking spray

1. Preheat the oven to 350° F. Whisk together the ground oats, flour, 1 cup whole oats, baking powder, salt, cinnamon, and allspice in a large bowl; set aside.

2. Put the brown sugar and butter in the bowl of an electric mixer fitted with the paddle attachment. Beat on medium speed until pale and fluffy, about 5 minutes. Mix in the eggs and vanilla, scraping down the sides of the bowl as needed.

3. Reduce speed to low. Add the oat mixture; mix until just combined. Mix in the walnuts and dates.

4. Coat a 9 × 13-inch baking dish with cooking spray. Spread the batter evenly in the dish. Scatter the remaining ½ cup whole oats over the top. Bake until golden and a cake tester inserted into the center comes out clean, about 35 minutes. Cool completely in the pan on a wire rack; cut into bars.

coconut cream bars

MAKES 24

The custard-filled crust can be refrigerated for up to 2 days. Wait until just before serving to cut the dessert into bars; if crumbs and filling stick to the knife, wipe the blade clean between slices. Then decorate each bar with whipped cream. If you don't have a pastry bag, use a resealable plastic bag with a corner cut off.

- 2½ cups sweetened flaked coconut
- 3 boxes (5.3 ounces each) shortbread cookies, coarsely broken
- 1 cup plus 2 tablespoons granulated sugar
- 6 tablespoons cornstarch
- ½ teaspoon salt
- 4½ cups whole milk
- 6 large egg yolks
- 6 tablespoons cold unsalted butter, cut into small pieces
- 1½ cups heavy cream
- 3 tablespoons confectioners' sugar

1. Preheat the oven to 350° F. Spread the coconut in an even layer on a rimmed baking sheet. Bake, stirring once or twice, until golden, 8 to 10 minutes. Let cool completely. Leave the oven on.

2. Process the cookies and ½ cup coconut in a food processor until finely ground and the mixture begins to clump together, about 2 minutes. Transfer the mixture to a 9 × 13-inch rimmed baking sheet; press into an even layer on the bottom. Bake until golden and firm to the touch, 12 to 15 minutes. Let cool on the sheet on a wire rack.

3. Whisk together the granulated sugar, cornstarch, and salt in a large saucepan. Whisk in the milk and egg yolks. Cook over medium heat, whisking constantly, until the mixture comes to a boil, 5 to 6 minutes. Continue to cook, whisking constantly, until thickened, about 3 minutes more. Remove from heat. Add the butter, whisking until combined. Stir in 1½ cups coconut.

4. Spoon the custard onto the cooled crust; smooth the top with an offset spatula. Press plastic wrap directly onto the custard surface to prevent a skin from forming. Refrigerate until set, about 3 hours.

5. Beat the cream and confectioners' sugar in a large chilled stainless-steel bowl until stiff peaks form.

6. Cut the custard-filled crust into 24 bars (each about 3 × 1½ inches). Transfer to a platter. Spoon whipped cream into a pastry bag fitted with a medium star tip. Beginning at one corner, pipe a zigzag pattern over each bar. Sprinkle the bars with the remaining ½ cup coconut.

chocolate-almond-marsala cookies

MAKES ABOUT 24

½ cup whole raw almonds with skins

1¼ cups all-purpose flour, plus more for dusting

2 teaspoons baking powder

1¼ teaspoons ground cinnamon

¾ teaspoon coarse salt

2 large eggs

⅓ cup Marsala wine

½ cup finely chopped candied orange peel

4 ounces semisweet chocolate, chopped

3 tablespoons honey

1. Preheat the oven to 350°F. Toast the almonds in the oven on a rimmed baking sheet until fragrant and lightly toasted, about 12 minutes. Let cool; coarsely chop. Reduce the oven temperature to 250°F.

2. Stir together the flour, baking powder, cinnamon, and salt. Beat 1 egg with the wine; stir into the flour mixture. Stir together the almonds, orange peel, and chocolate; stir into the flour mixture. Stir in the honey.

3. Knead the dough on a generously floured work surface just until it holds its shape. Divide the dough into 2 pieces; pat each into a 10½ × 1½ × 1-inch rounded log. Refrigerate the dough 15 minutes.

4. Cut each log into ¾-inch-thick slices. Gently press the edges of each slice to flatten. Lightly beat the remaining egg. Place the cookies, standing vertically, on a parchment-paper–lined baking sheet. Brush the tops with beaten egg.

5. Bake 20 minutes. Raise the oven temperature to 350°F; bake until the cookies are deep golden brown, 10 to 12 minutes. Let cool on the sheet on a wire rack.

cream cheese–walnut cookies

MAKES ABOUT 48

4 cups all-purpose flour

1¼ teaspoons salt

1 pound (4 sticks) unsalted butter, softened

6 ounces cream cheese (not whipped), room temperature

1¼ cups sugar

2 tablespoons plus ½ teaspoon pure vanilla extract

2½ cups walnut halves (1½ cups toasted and chopped; 1 cup finely chopped)

1. Line 2 baking sheets with parchment paper; set aside. Whisk together the flour and salt in a large bowl; set aside.

2. Put the butter and cream cheese in the bowl of an electric mixer fitted with the paddle attachment. Mix on medium speed until pale and fluffy, about 2 minutes. Mix in the sugar and vanilla. Reduce speed to low. Add the flour mixture, and mix until just combined (do not overmix). Mix in the toasted walnuts.

3. On a clean work surface, divide dough in half; shape each piece into an 8½-inch-long log (about 2 inches in diameter). Wrap each log in parchment paper; freeze until firm, about 30 minutes.

4. Preheat the oven to 350°F with racks in the upper and lower thirds. Remove one log from the freezer. Roll the log in ½ cup chopped walnuts, coating it completely. Cut the log into ¼-inch-thick rounds. Transfer the rounds to parchment-lined sheets.

5. Bake, switching the positions of the sheets and rotating halfway through, until the cookies are golden around the edges, 18 to 20 minutes. Transfer to wire racks; let cool completely. Repeat the process with the remaining dough using cooled baking sheets.

caramel crunch

MAKES ABOUT 2 CUPS

When making the caramel in step 2, keep an eye on your pan; the best indicator that the caramel is ready is appearance, not cooking time. Just before the syrup reaches the desired color, remove it from the heat; the caramel will continue cooking for a few more seconds.

- 2 cups toasted, sliced almonds (5½ ounces)
- ½ cup water
- 2 cups sugar
- ¼ teaspoon coarse salt

1. Prepare an ice-water bath; set aside. Spread almonds on parchment paper to form a 9 x 12-inch rectangle.

2. Make the caramel: Pour the water into a medium heavy-bottom saucepan. Add the sugar and salt. Cook over medium heat, gently stirring occasionally, until the syrup is clear.

3. Continue cooking, without stirring, until the syrup comes to a boil, washing down the sides of the pan with a wet pastry brush 2 or 3 times to prevent crystals from forming. Let the syrup boil, gently swirling the pan occasionally, until medium amber. Remove from heat and set the pan in the ice-water bath to stop the cooking.

3. Pour the caramel over the almonds to cover. Let cool until hardened. Peel off the parchment; break the brittle into pieces.

lemon poppyseed cookies

MAKES ABOUT 30

- ¼ cup fresh lemon juice, plus 3½ teaspoons freshly grated lemon zest (2 to 3 lemons)
- 8 ounces (2 sticks) unsalted butter
- 2 cups all-purpose flour
- 1 teaspoon baking powder
- ½ teaspoon salt
- 1½ cups sugar
- 1 large egg
- 2 teaspoons pure vanilla extract
- 1 tablespoon poppy seeds, plus more for sprinkling

1. Preheat the oven to 375° F. Bring the lemon juice to a simmer in a small saucepan over medium heat; cook until reduced by half. Add 1 stick butter; stir until melted.

2. Whisk together the flour, baking powder, and salt. Cream the remaining stick butter and 1 cup sugar on medium speed in the bowl of an electric mixer fitted with the paddle attachment. Mix in the egg and lemon butter. Mix until pale, about 3 minutes. Mix in the vanilla and 2 teaspoons zest. Mix in the flour mixture and poppy seeds.

3. Stir together the remaining ½ cup sugar and 1½ teaspoons zest. Roll spoonfuls of dough into 1¼-inch balls; roll them in the sugar mixture. Place 2 inches apart on baking sheets. Press each with the flat end of a glass dipped in the sugar mixture until ¼ inch thick. Sprinkle with seeds.

4. Bake until just browned around bottom edges, 10 to 11 minutes. Transfer to wire racks; let cool completely. Store in an airtight container up to 1 week.

apricot-walnut biscotti

MAKES 24

Sanding sugar is used to coat the biscotti because it won't melt in the oven. We dipped half of the batch in melted chocolate. To dip them all, double the amount of bittersweet chocolate.

- 1 cup walnut halves
- 2 cups all-purpose flour, plus more for dusting
- ½ teaspoon baking powder
- ¼ teaspoon salt
- 5 tablespoons unsalted butter, softened, plus more for the baking sheet
- 1 cup granulated sugar
- 1 teaspoon pure vanilla extract
- 2 large eggs, lightly beaten
- ¾ cup dried apricots, cut into ¼-inch dice
- 1 large egg white, lightly beaten
- 2 tablespoons sanding sugar
- 4 ounces bittersweet chocolate, coarsely chopped

1. Preheat the oven to 375°F. Spread out the nuts on a baking sheet; toast in the oven, stirring occasionally, until fragrant and golden brown, about 8 minutes. Remove from the oven; reduce temperature to 350°F.

2. Rub the nuts between paper towels to remove loose skins; coarsely chop the nuts.

3. Sift the flour, baking powder, and salt together into a medium bowl; set aside. Put the butter and granulated sugar in the bowl of an electric mixer fitted with the paddle attachment. Cream on medium speed until pale and fluffy. Mix in the vanilla. Mix in the eggs in 2 batches, mixing each until just combined. On low speed, mix in the flour mixture until just combined. Stir in the walnuts and apricots by hand.

4. Butter a large baking sheet; set aside. Transfer the dough to a lightly floured surface; divide in half. With floured hands, shape each half into an 8½ x 2½ x 1-inch log. Place the logs at least 2 inches apart on the buttered baking sheet. Bake until golden, about 30 minutes. Transfer the sheet to a wire rack; let the logs stand 10 minutes.

5. Transfer the logs to a cutting board. Clean and butter the large baking sheet; set aside. Brush the logs with egg white, and sprinkle with sanding sugar. Cut each log crosswise on the diagonal into 12 pieces (each ½ inch thick). Lay flat on the buttered sheet. Bake 7 minutes; turn the pieces. Bake until golden, 7 to 9 minutes. Transfer to a wire rack; let cool until crisp.

6. Melt the chocolate in a heatproof bowl set over a pan of simmering water, stirring occasionally, until smooth, 3 to 5 minutes. Let cool slightly.

7. Dip a flat side of 12 biscotti in melted chocolate, arranging the cookies, chocolate side up, on parchment paper as you work. Let stand until the chocolate is set, about 30 minutes. Store in an airtight container, keeping the chocolate-dipped ones in a single layer on top, up to 2 days.

....

MAKING BISCOTTI

For wonderfully crisp biscotti, follow these simple steps:

1. After mixing the dough, use your hands to pat it into a long loaf. Be sure to flatten it in the middle and to keep the ends the same width as the rest.

2. Once the loaf has been baked, let it cool for 15 minutes before cutting into slices. If the loaf is too hot, the slices may crumble; if allowed to sit too long, the loaf will be difficult to slice. Using a serrated knife is the best way to cut cleanly.

3. You do not want the biscotti to become too hard to eat, so watch them closely after about 10 minutes, and take them out of the oven when they are just starting to turn golden around the edges. Let the biscotti cool completely on the baking sheet so they get perfectly crisp and dry, ideal for dunking into espresso or your favorite dessert wine.

....

cornmeal biscotti
with dates and almonds

The biscotti may be stored in an airtight container at room temperature for up to 2 weeks.

- 1¼ cups all-purpose flour
- 1¼ cups yellow cornmeal
- ½ teaspoon baking powder
- ½ teaspoon salt
- 6 tablespoons unsalted butter, room temperature
- 1 cup sugar
- 2 large eggs
- 2 teaspoons pure orange extract
- 1 tablespoon freshly grated orange zest
- 1 cup chopped pitted dates
- 1 cup chopped almonds
- 1 teaspoon anise seed

1. Preheat the oven to 350° F, with a rack in the center. Line a baking sheet with parchment paper, and set aside. Combine the flour, cornmeal, baking powder, and salt in a medium bowl, and mix thoroughly with a whisk or fork; set aside.

2. In the bowl of an electric mixer fitted with the paddle attachment, cream the butter on medium speed until smooth. Add the sugar, and beat until light and fluffy. Beat in the eggs 1 at a time until well combined; beat in the orange extract.

3. Add the flour mixture; beat on low speed until just combined. Add the orange zest, dates, almonds, and anise seed, and beat until combined.

4. Transfer the dough to the prepared baking sheet; using your hands, pat into a log that is roughly 14 × 3½ inches. Bake until firm, lightly browned, and slightly cracked on top, 30 to 35 minutes. Remove from the oven; let cool 15 minutes.

5. Transfer the log to a cutting board, leaving the parchment behind on the sheet. Using a serrated knife, cut the log crosswise into ½-inch-thick slices. Arrange the slices on a baking sheet. Bake until they just begin to brown at the edges, 15 to 18 minutes, rotating the pan halfway through. Remove from the oven; let cool on the baking sheet.

almond macaroons

The cookies can be stored in an airtight container at room temperature for up to 5 days.

- 4 ounces almond paste (about 5½ tablespoons)
- ½ cup confectioners' sugar, plus more for dusting
  Pinch of fine salt
- 1 large egg white
- ¼ teaspoon pure vanilla extract
- ¼ cup sliced almonds

1. Preheat the oven to 300° F. Line a baking sheet with parchment paper, and set aside. Place the almond paste, sugar, and salt in the bowl of an electric mixer fitted with the paddle attachment; beat on medium speed until the mixture looks crumbly, about 3 minutes. Add the egg white and vanilla. Continue beating until the mixture is smooth and thick, about 3 minutes more.

2. Drop 12 even tablespoons of batter about 2 inches apart on the lined baking sheet; place 2 almond slices on each mound of dough. Bake the cookies, rotating the baking sheet halfway through, until golden brown, 20 to 25 minutes. Transfer the cookies to a wire rack; let cool completely. Just before serving, lightly dust with confectioners' sugar.

key lime bars

MAKES 16

This recipe is based on the famous Key Lime pie from Joe's Stone Crab restaurant in Miami Beach. If you can't find Key limes, use regular fresh lime juice. The bars will keep, wrapped in plastic, in the refrigerator for up to 3 days.

- 5¾ ounces graham crackers (about one-third of a 1-pound box), ground to fine crumbs in a food processor (1 cup plus 2½ tablespoons)
- ⅓ cup sugar
- 5 tablespoons unsalted butter, melted
- 3 large egg yolks
- 1½ teaspoons finely grated lime zest (about 2 limes)
- 1 can (14 ounces) sweetened condensed milk
- ⅔ cup fresh Key lime juice (about 20 Key limes)
- ¼ cup heavy cream
- 2 Key limes, thinly sliced into half-moons, for garnish

1. Preheat the oven to 350° F. Stir together the crumbs, sugar, and butter in a small bowl. Press evenly onto the bottom of an 8-inch-square glass pan. Bake until dry and golden brown, about 10 minutes. Let cool in the pan on a wire rack. Leave the oven on.

2. Place the egg yolks and zest in the bowl of an electric mixer fitted with the whisk attachment; beat on high speed until the mixture is very thick, about 5 minutes. On medium speed, pour in the condensed milk in a steady stream, scraping down the sides of the bowl. Beat on high speed until thick, about 3 minutes. On low speed, add the lime juice; mix until just combined.

3. Pour the filling over the crust; spread evenly. Bake until just set, about 10 minutes. Let cool completely on a wire rack. Cover with plastic wrap; chill at least 4 hours or overnight.

4. When ready to serve, beat the heavy cream until stiff peaks just form. Cut dessert into 1½ × 2-inch rectangles. Garnish each bar with whipped cream and a slice of Key lime.

double chocolate brownies

MAKES 9 LARGE OR 16 SMALL SQUARES

Store brownies in an airtight container at room temperature for up to 3 days.

- 6 tablespoons unsalted butter, plus more for the pan
- 6 ounces good-quality semisweet chocolate, coarsely chopped
- ¼ cup unsweetened cocoa powder (not Dutch-process)
- ¾ cup all-purpose flour
- ¼ teaspoon baking powder
- ¼ teaspoon salt
- 1 cup sugar
- 2 large eggs
- 2 teaspoons pure vanilla extract

1. Preheat the oven to 350° F. Line a buttered 8-inch-square baking pan with foil or parchment paper, allowing 2 inches to hang over the sides. Butter the lining (excluding overhang); set the pan aside.

2. Put the butter, chocolate, and cocoa in a heatproof medium bowl set over a pan of simmering water; stir until the butter and chocolate are melted. Let cool slightly.

3. Whisk together the flour, baking powder, and salt in a separate bowl; set aside.

4. Put the sugar, eggs, and vanilla in the bowl of an electric mixer fitted with the whisk attachment, and beat on medium speed until pale, about 4 minutes. Add the chocolate mixture; beat until combined. Add the flour mixture; beat, scraping down the sides of the bowl, until well incorporated.

5. Pour the batter into the prepared pan; smooth the top with a rubber spatula. Bake until a cake tester inserted into the brownies (avoid center and edges) comes out with a few crumbs but is not wet, about 35 minutes. Let cool slightly in the pan, about 15 minutes. Lift out the brownies; let cool completely on a wire rack before cutting into squares.

warm cream cheese brownies

MAKES 12

for the cream cheese batter

- 6 ounces cream cheese, room temperature
- 4 tablespoons unsalted butter, room temperature, plus more for the pan
- ½ cup sugar
- 2 large eggs
- 1 teaspoon pure vanilla extract
- 2 tablespoons all-purpose flour
- ½ cup semisweet chocolate chips (3½ ounces)

for the chocolate batter

- 4 ounces unsweetened chocolate
- 4 ounces semisweet chocolate
- 6 tablespoons unsalted butter
- 4 large eggs
- 1½ cups sugar
- 2 teaspoons pure vanilla extract
- 1 cup all-purpose flour
- 1 teaspoon baking powder
- 1 teaspoon salt
- 1 cup semisweet chocolate chips (7 ounces)

1. Preheat the oven to 325° F. Butter a 9 × 13-inch baking pan; set aside. Make the cream cheese batter: Beat the cream cheese, butter, and sugar in the bowl of an electric mixer fitted with the paddle attachment until well blended. Add eggs, 1 at a time, beating well and scraping down the sides of the bowl at least once. Add the vanilla, and beat until combined. Using a large rubber spatula, fold in the flour and chocolate chips.

2. Make the chocolate batter: Melt the chocolates and butter in a medium heatproof bowl set over a pan of barely simmering water. Remove the bowl from the heat, and let cool completely.

3. In a large bowl, using a handheld whisk, beat the eggs, gradually adding the sugar, until the mixture is thick and pale. Whisk in the cooled chocolate mixture. Add the vanilla, and combine well.

4. Combine the flour, baking powder, and salt in a medium bowl, and fold into the chocolate mixture. Fold in the chocolate chips. Measure out about

½ cup chocolate batter, and set aside. Spoon the rest of the batter into the prepared baking pan, and spread the cream cheese batter evenly over the top. Drop the reserved chocolate batter in dollops on top. Run a knife or offset spatula all the way through the batters to create a swirling effect.

5. Bake until a cake tester inserted near the edges comes out clean, about 35 minutes. The center will still be fairly soft, but it will continue to firm after being removed from the oven. Transfer to a wire rack; let cool in the pan before cutting into squares.

peanut butter swirl brownies

MAKES 9 LARGE OR 16 SMALL SQUARES

Store brownies in an airtight container at room temperature for up to 3 days.

for the batter

- 8 tablespoons (1 stick) unsalted butter, cut into small pieces, plus more for the pan
- 2 ounces good-quality unsweetened chocolate, coarsely chopped
- 4 ounces good-quality semisweet chocolate, coarsely chopped
- ⅔ cup all-purpose flour
- ½ teaspoon baking powder
- ¼ teaspoon salt
- ¾ cup granulated sugar
- 3 large eggs
- 2 teaspoons pure vanilla extract

for the filling

- 4 tablespoons unsalted butter, melted
- ½ cup confectioners' sugar
- ¾ cup smooth peanut butter
- ¼ teaspoon salt
- ½ teaspoon pure vanilla extract

1. Preheat the oven to 325° F. Line a buttered 8-inch-square baking pan with foil or parchment paper, allowing 2 inches to hang over the sides. Butter the lining (excluding the overhang); set the pan aside.

2. Make the batter: Put the butter and chocolates in a heatproof medium bowl set over a pan of simmering water; stir until melted. Let cool slightly.

3. Whisk together the flour, baking powder, and salt in a separate bowl, and set aside.

4. Whisk the granulated sugar into the chocolate mixture. Add the eggs, and whisk until the mixture is smooth. Stir in the vanilla. Add the flour mixture; stir until well incorporated.

5. Make the filling: Stir together the butter, confectioners' sugar, peanut butter, salt, and vanilla in a bowl until smooth.

6. Pour one-third of the batter into the prepared pan, and spread evenly with a rubber spatula. Place dollops of filling (about 1 tablespoon each) about 1 inch apart on top of the batter. Drizzle the remaining batter on top, and gently spread to fill the pan. Place dollops of the remaining filling on top.

7. With a butter knife, gently swirl the filling into the batter, running the knife lengthwise and crosswise through the layers. Bake until a cake tester inserted into the brownies (avoid center and edges) comes out with a few crumbs but is not wet, about 45 minutes. Let cool slightly in the pan, about 15 minutes. Lift out the brownies; let cool completely on a wire rack before cutting into squares.

coconut swirl brownies
MAKES 9 LARGE OR 16 SMALL SQUARES

for the filling

- 2 tablespoons granulated sugar
- ⅔ cup sweetened condensed milk
- 1¼ cups unsweetened shredded coconut
- 1 large egg
- ½ teaspoon pure vanilla extract

for the batter

Ingredients for Peanut Butter Swirl Brownies batter (opposite)

1. Make the filling: Stir together the sugar, condensed milk, coconut, egg, and vanilla in a medium bowl; set aside.

2. Make the batter: Follow the recipe for Peanut Butter Swirl Brownies through step 4.

3. Follow steps 6 and 7 of the Peanut Butter Swirl Brownies recipe.

truffle brownies
MAKES 12

Store these brownies in the refrigerator, covered, for up to 2 days. Bring to room temperature before serving. You can also make the brownies in an 8-inch-square baking pan (prepare the pan as directed in step 1 of Double Chocolate Brownies, page 541).

for the batter

- 4 tablespoons unsalted butter, plus more for the pan
- 3 ounces good-quality unsweetened chocolate, coarsely chopped
- ½ cup all-purpose flour
- ¼ teaspoon baking powder
- ½ teaspoon salt
- 1 cup sugar
- 2 large eggs
- ¼ cup milk
- 1 teaspoon pure vanilla extract

for the topping

- 4 ounces good-quality semisweet chocolate, coarsely chopped
- ⅔ cup heavy cream
  Heart-shaped sprinkles, for garnish

1. Preheat the oven to 325° F. Butter a 9-inch springform pan, and set aside.

2. Make the batter: Put the butter and chocolate in a heatproof medium bowl set over a pan of simmering water; stir until melted. Let cool slightly.

3. Whisk together the flour, baking powder, and salt in a separate bowl; set aside.

4. Put the sugar and eggs in the bowl of an electric mixer fitted with the whisk attachment, and beat on medium speed until pale and fluffy, about 4 minutes. Add the chocolate mixture, milk, and vanilla, and beat until combined. Add the flour mixture; beat, scraping down the sides of the bowl, until well incorporated.

5. Pour the batter into the prepared pan. Bake until a cake tester inserted into the brownies (avoid center and edges) comes out with a few crumbs but is not wet, 27 to 30 minutes. Let cool completely in the pan.

6. Make the topping when the brownies are cool: Put the chocolate in a medium bowl. Heat the cream in a small saucepan over medium-high heat until just simmering. Pour over the chocolate; let stand 5 minutes. Gently stir until smooth. Allow the ganache to cool, stirring every 10 minutes, until slightly thickened, 25 to 30 minutes.

7. Pour the ganache over the cooled brownies in the pan; let set, about 20 minutes. Refrigerate until cold, 30 minutes to 1 hour. Let brownies stand at room temperature at least 15 minutes before serving. Lift out the brownies; cut into wedges, wiping the knife with a hot, damp cloth between each cut. Scatter sprinkles on top.

turtle brownies

MAKES 8

for the batter

Ingredients for Truffle Brownies batter (page 543)

for the topping

- 1 cup sugar
- ⅓ cup heavy cream
- 1 teaspoon pure vanilla extract
- ½ teaspoon salt
- 1 cup coarsely chopped toasted pecans (4 ounces)

1. Preheat the oven to 325°F. Line a buttered 8-inch-square baking pan with foil or parchment paper, allowing 2 inches to hang over the sides. Butter the lining (excluding overhang); set the pan aside.

2. Make the batter: Follow steps 2 through 5 of the Truffle Brownies recipe.

3. Make the topping when the brownies are cool: Bring ⅓ cup water and the sugar to a boil in a medium saucepan over medium-high heat, stirring, until the sugar has dissolved. When the water

comes to a boil, stop stirring, and wash down the sides of the pan with a wet pastry brush to prevent crystals from forming. Continue to cook, swirling the pan occasionally, until the mixture is medium amber, 5 to 7 minutes.

4. Remove from heat, and immediately add the cream, vanilla, and salt. Gently stir with a clean wooden spoon or heatproof spatula until smooth. Add the pecans; stir until the caramel begins to cool and thickens slightly, about 1 minute.

5. Pour the caramel over the brownies; spread evenly with an offset spatula. Refrigerate until cold, 30 minutes to 1 hour.

walnut shortbread

MAKES 16 WEDGES

- 1¼ cups walnuts
- ¾ cup all-purpose flour
- ½ cup whole-wheat flour
- ⅔ cup confectioners' sugar
- ½ teaspoon salt
- 1 stick (½ cup) unsalted butter, melted
- 2 tablespoons light olive or canola oil
- 2 teaspoons finely grated lemon zest
- 1 teaspoon fresh lemon juice

1. Preheat the oven to 350°F. Butter and flour two 8-inch round cake pans; set aside. In a food processor, combine the nuts, flours, sugar, and salt; pulse until the nuts are finely ground but not oily. Add the butter, oil, lemon zest, and lemon juice; pulse until the mixture just comes together.

2. Divide the mixture between the pans and press in until even. With a sharp knife, cut each round of dough into 8 wedges. Lightly prick the tops with the tines of a fork. Bake until set and pale tan, about 22 minutes.

3. Transfer to a wire rack and cut through each wedge. Cool 10 minutes, then invert onto a plate and transfer to a wire rack to cool completely.

blackberry-almond shortbread squares

MAKES 12

10   tablespoons (1¼ sticks) unsalted butter, softened, plus more for the pan

1¾   cups all-purpose flour, plus more for dusting

½   cup whole blanched almonds (2 ounces)

½   teaspoon salt

½   teaspoon ground cinnamon

¾   cup plus 2 tablespoons confectioners' sugar, plus more for dusting

¼   teaspoon pure almond extract

1   pound blackberries (about 4 cups)

    Freshly grated zest of 1 orange

1. Preheat the oven to 350°F. Butter a 9 × 13-inch baking pan. Line with parchment; butter the lining. Dust with flour; tap out excess. Arrange the nuts in a single layer on a rimmed baking sheet. Bake until golden, 15 minutes; let cool. Grind in a food processor until fine.

2. Whisk together the flour, nuts, salt, and cinnamon in a medium bowl; set aside. Put ¾ cup plus 1 tablespoon sugar and the butter in the bowl of an electric mixer fitted with the paddle attachment; mix until pale and fluffy, about 3 minutes. Mix in the almond extract. Add the flour mixture in 2 batches; mix until a crumbly dough forms.

3. Press all but 1 cup dough onto the bottom of the pan. Toss the berries with the zest; scatter over the dough. Sprinkle with the remaining tablespoon sugar; crumble the reserved dough on top. Bake until golden, about 30 minutes. Let cool on a wire rack. Cut into 12 squares; dust with sugar.

chocolate-caramel pecan clusters

MAKES 12

1   cup pecan halves (3¼ ounces)

12   soft caramel candy cubes

1½   ounces bittersweet chocolate, broken into 12 pieces (½ inch each)

1. Preheat the oven to 350°F. Arrange the pecans in a single layer on a rimmed baking sheet; toast in oven until fragrant, about 10 minutes. Remove from the oven (leave the oven on); set aside 36 pecans on the baking sheet. Finely chop the remaining pecans (for about ¼ cup); set aside.

2. When the pecans are cool enough to handle, make 12 clusters by arranging 2 pecans vertically, side by side, below 1 pecan placed horizontally. Gently flatten each caramel; place 1 on top of each cluster. Bake the clusters 5 minutes. Remove from the oven (leave the oven on).

3. Place 1 piece of chocolate on top of each cluster. Return to the oven; bake until the chocolate begins to melt, 1 to 2 minutes. Remove from the oven. With the back of a spoon, gently spread the chocolate over the caramel without completely covering it.

4. Sprinkle the clusters with the reserved chopped pecans. Refrigerate until set, about 15 minutes. Bring to room temperature before serving.

chocolate cookies

MAKES ABOUT 40

We cut the dough into assorted shapes using 2- to 4-inch cookie cutters.

3   cups sifted all-purpose flour, plus more for the work surface

1¼   cups unsweetened cocoa powder

½   teaspoon ground cinnamon

¼   teaspoon salt

1½   cups (3 sticks) unsalted butter, room temperature

2½   cups sifted confectioners' sugar

2   large eggs, lightly beaten

2   teaspoons pure vanilla extract

1. Preheat the oven to 350°F. Into a large bowl, sift together the flour, cocoa, cinnamon, and salt; set aside. In a mixing bowl, cream the butter and sugar until light and fluffy. Beat in the eggs and vanilla. Add the flour mixture; beat on low speed until just combined. Divide the dough in half, and flatten into disks. Wrap each disk in plastic; chill at least 1 hour.

2. On a lightly floured surface, roll out 1 disk to ⅛ inch thick, dusting with flour as needed. Cut into shapes as desired. Transfer to baking sheets; chill until firm, about 15 minutes.

3. Bake until the cookies are just firm to the touch, 10 to 12 minutes, rotating the sheets halfway through. Transfer to wire racks to cool. Repeat with the remaining dough.

lemon madeleines

MAKES 24

¾ cup (1½ sticks) unsalted butter, melted, plus more for the pan
1½ cups sifted cake flour (not self-rising)
½ teaspoon baking powder
¼ teaspoon salt
3 large whole eggs
2 large egg yolks
¾ cup granulated sugar
1 teaspoon pure vanilla extract
2 tablespoons fresh lemon juice
2 tablespoons finely grated lemon zest
    Confectioners' sugar, for dusting (optional)

1. Preheat the oven to 400°F. Lightly butter a madeleine pan; set aside. Into a medium bowl, sift together flour, baking powder, and salt. Set aside.

2. In a mixing bowl, beat the eggs, yolks, granulated sugar, vanilla, and lemon juice and zest until thick and pale, about 5 minutes. Beat in the melted but-

ter. Using a rubber spatula, gently fold the flour mixture into the egg mixture; let rest 30 minutes at room temperature.

3. Pour the batter into the prepared pan, filling the molds three-quarters full. Bake until the cookies are crisp and golden around the edges, 7 to 8 minutes. Transfer the pan to a wire rack to cool slightly before inverting the cookies onto a serving platter. Dust with confectioners' sugar, if desired.

elke wood's lemon squares

MAKES TWELVE 3-INCH SQUARES

1¾ cups sifted all-purpose flour
⅓ cup sifted confectioners' sugar
¼ teaspoon salt
¾ cup (1½ sticks) chilled unsalted butter, cut into pieces, plus more for the baking dish
1 teaspoon plus 1 tablespoon finely grated lemon zest
⅓ cup almonds, toasted and chopped
2 cups granulated sugar
4 large eggs, beaten
½ cup fresh lemon juice
½ teaspoon baking powder

1. Preheat the oven to 350°F. Into a medium bowl, sift together 1½ cups flour, the confectioners' sugar, and the salt. Cut in the butter, 1 teaspoon zest, and the almonds until the mixture just clings together.

2. Press into a lightly buttered 9 × 13-inch baking dish. Bake until just firm and lightly golden, about 20 minutes. Let cool slightly before filling.

3. In a large nonreactive bowl, stir together the granulated sugar, eggs, lemon juice, baking powder, and remaining ¼ cup flour and tablespoon zest until combined. Pour into the prepared crust.

4. Bake until the filling is set and lightly browned, 25 to 30 minutes. Transfer to a wire rack to cool. Cut into squares.

lemon-blueberry petits fours

MAKES 15

We baked these treats in mini brioche pans; small fluted tartlet pans would work just as well.

- 1¼ cups all-purpose flour
- 1½ tablespoons sugar, plus more for the blueberries
- ½ cup (1 stick) chilled unsalted butter, cut into small pieces
- 1 large egg yolk
- ¼ cup ice water
- 1½ cups Lemon Curd (page 656)
- 15 fresh blueberries
- 2 teaspoons meringue powder dissolved in 2 tablespoons warm water

1. Pulse the flour and sugar in a food processor to combine. Add the butter; pulse until the mixture resembles coarse meal. In a small bowl, lightly beat the egg yolk and ice water. With the motor running, slowly pour the egg mixture into the processor; mix until the dough just comes together. Place on plastic wrap; press to flatten into a disk. Wrap; chill at least 1 hour.

2. Preheat the oven to 350° F. On a clean work surface, roll out the dough ⅛ inch thick. Using a 3½-inch biscuit cutter, cut out 15 rounds. Fit the rounds into pans; press into the bottom and sides. Chill at least 30 minutes.

3. Line the tarts with parchment; fill with pie weights or dried beans. Bake 15 minutes; remove the paper and weights. Continue baking until golden, about 10 minutes. Transfer to a wire rack to cool completely.

4. Using a toothpick, dip each blueberry in the meringue powder mixture; roll in sugar. Transfer to a parchment-lined baking sheet; let dry 30 minutes.

5. Remove the tart shells from the pans. Fill each shell with about 2 teaspoons lemon curd, and top with a sugared blueberry. Serve chilled or at room temperature.

carolynn's chocolate chip cookies

MAKES 30

The recipe for these delicious cookies comes from food writer and cookbook author Carolynn Carreño.

- 2 cups plus 2 tablespoons all-purpose flour
- ½ teaspoon salt
- ½ teaspoon baking soda
- 1 cup (2 sticks) unsalted butter
- 1 cup plus 2 tablespoons firmly packed dark-brown sugar
- ½ cup granulated sugar
- 1 large whole egg
- 1 large egg yolk
- ½ tablespoon pure vanilla extract
- 1½ cups semisweet chocolate chips
- 1 cup toasted walnuts, broken into large pieces (optional)

1. In a large bowl, whisk together the flour, salt, and baking soda; set aside. In a medium saucepan over medium heat, melt the butter. Turn off the heat and add both sugars; whisk until combined. Transfer the mixture to a medium bowl, and let cool to room temperature.

2. Whisk the egg, egg yolk, and vanilla into the butter mixture. Fold in the reserved flour mixture until just combined. Fold in the chips and nuts. Wrap the dough in plastic; chill until firm, about 30 minutes.

3. Preheat the oven to 325° F. Using 2 large spoons, place golf-ball–size mounds of dough 3 inches apart on baking sheets. Bake until the cookies are golden brown and the tops no longer look wet, 12 to 14 minutes. Allow the cookies to cool on the baking sheet 5 minutes; transfer to a wire rack. Let cool completely before serving.

honey lace cookies

MAKES 28

2 tablespoons unsalted butter
2 tablespoons light-brown sugar
1½ tablespoons honey
2 tablespoons all-purpose flour
    Pinch of salt

1. Preheat the oven to 375°F. Line 2 large baking sheets with Silpats (French baking mats) or parchment paper. Set aside. In a small saucepan, melt the butter, sugar, and honey. Transfer to a bowl. Whisk in the flour and salt until smooth.

2. Working quickly, drop ½ teaspoons of batter onto the prepared baking sheets, at least 3 inches apart. Bake until the cookies spread and turn golden brown, about 6 minutes. Transfer the sheet to a wire rack; let cool completely. With your fingers, carefully remove the cookies from the pan.

soft and chewy chocolate chip cookies

MAKES ABOUT 36

If desired, use a small ice-cream scoop for uniform-size cookies. To make a cookie tart, press 3 cups of this dough into a buttered and sugared 9-inch round tart pan with a removable bottom or a 9-inch pie tin lined with buttered, sugared parchment. Bake at 325°F until the edges are golden and the center is almost set, 40 to 45 minutes. Let cool at least 20 minutes, and remove from the pan. (Bake the remaining dough as cookies at 350°F for 8 to 10 minutes.)

2¼ cups all-purpose flour
½ teaspoon baking soda
1 cup (2 sticks) unsalted butter, room temperature
½ cup granulated sugar
1 cup packed light-brown sugar
1 teaspoon salt
2 teaspoons pure vanilla extract
2 large eggs
2 cups semisweet and/or milk chocolate chips (about 12 ounces)

1. Preheat the oven to 350°F. In a small bowl, whisk together the flour and baking soda; set aside. In the bowl of an electric mixer fitted with the paddle attachment, combine the butter with both sugars; beat on medium speed until light and fluffy. Reduce speed to low; add the salt, vanilla, and eggs. Beat until well combined, about 1 minute. Add the flour mixture; mix until just combined. Stir in the chocolate chips by hand.

2. Drop heaping tablespoon-size balls of dough about 2 inches apart on baking sheets lined with parchment paper.

3. Bake until the cookies are golden around the edges but still soft in the center, 8 to 10 minutes. Remove from the oven, and let cool on the baking sheet 1 to 2 minutes. Transfer to a wire rack, and let cool completely. Store the cookies in an airtight container at room temperature up to 1 week.

ADD-INS: *Create variations on chocolate chip cookies with the following ingredients. Use one or two— or several.*

NUTS *Add 1 cup coarsely chopped nuts—walnuts, pecans, macadamias—with the chips.*

ESPRESSO *Add 2 tablespoons instant espresso powder to the dry ingredients; replace 1 cup flour with unsweetened cocoa powder for a mocha flavor.*

SHREDDED COCONUT *Stir in 1½ cups shredded sweetened coconut with the chips.*

COCOA *Replace 1 cup flour with unsweetened cocoa powder to make double chocolate chip cookies.*

DRIED FRUIT *Combine 1 cup chopped dried cherries or other dried fruit with the chips.*

GINGER *Mix ½ cup finely chopped candied ginger or up to 1 teaspoon ground ginger into the dry ingredients.*

CANDY BITS *Substitute 1 cup chips with chopped chocolate candies, such as malt balls.*

OATMEAL *For hearty cookies, stir in 1½ cups old-fashioned rolled oats along with the chips.*

PEANUT BUTTER *To make a chocolate–peanut butter combo, reduce the butter to ¾ cup, and mix in ½ cup smooth peanut butter with the butter and sugars.*

pine nut cookies

MAKES ABOUT 36

2 cups pine nuts
1 cup confectioners' sugar
¼ cup almond paste
1 teaspoon pure vanilla extract
1 large egg
½ cup all-purpose flour
¼ teaspoon baking powder
¼ teaspoon salt

1. Preheat the oven to 350°F. Process ¾ cup pine nuts and the sugar, almond paste, and vanilla in a food processor until fine crumbs form. Add the egg; pulse to combine. Add the flour, baking powder, and salt; process just until the dough comes together.

2. Roll the dough into ¾-inch balls. Roll the balls in the remaining 1¼ cups pine nuts, gently pressing to coat. Space 2 inches apart on parchment-lined baking sheets.

3. Bake until the cookies begin to turn golden brown, about 20 minutes. Let cool completely on the sheets on wire racks.

coconut-date bars

MAKES 8

3 tablespoons unsweetened shredded coconut
1 pound very soft dates, pitted
¼ cup walnuts, toasted and finely chopped

Sprinkle 2 tablespoons coconut over the bottom of an 8-inch-square baking dish. Firmly press the dates into the coconut, covering the bottom of the dish. Sprinkle with the remaining tablespoon coconut and the walnuts, gently pressing them into the dates. Cut into 2-inch squares. The bars can be stored in an airtight container 2 to 3 days.

FIT TO EAT RECIPE PER SERVING: 194 CALORIES, 2 G FAT, 0 MG CHOLESTEROL, 46 G CARBOHYDRATE, 0 MG SODIUM, 2 G PROTEIN, 5 G FIBER

double chocolate chunk cookies

MAKES ABOUT 36

These rich cookies should seem a bit soft when you take them out of the oven. They firm as they cool, so be careful not to overbake them.

1 cup all-purpose flour
½ cup unsweetened Dutch-process cocoa powder
½ teaspoon baking soda
½ teaspoon salt
8 ounces good-quality milk chocolate (4 ounces coarsely chopped, 4 ounces cut into ¼-inch chunks)
1 stick (8 tablespoons) unsalted butter
1½ cups sugar
2 large eggs
1 teaspoon pure vanilla extract

1. Preheat the oven to 325°F. Whisk together the flour, cocoa powder, baking soda, and salt in a medium bowl; set aside. Melt the coarsely chopped chocolate with the butter in a small heatproof bowl set over a pan of simmering water.

2. Transfer the chocolate mixture to the bowl of an electric mixer fitted with the paddle attachment. Add the sugar, eggs, and vanilla; mix on medium speed until combined. Reduce speed to low; gradually mix in the flour mixture. Fold in the chocolate chunks by hand.

3. Scoop the batter using a 1½-inch ice-cream scoop; place 2 inches apart on parchment-lined baking sheets. Bake until the cookies are flat and the surfaces begin to crack, about 15 minutes. Transfer on the parchment to wire racks. Let cool 5 minutes. The cookies can be stored in an airtight container at room temperature for up to 3 days.

lemon meringue bars

MAKES 12

- 2 sticks (16 tablespoons) unsalted butter, softened
- 1¾ cups plus 2 tablespoons all-purpose flour
- ¼ cup plus 3 tablespoons confectioners' sugar
- 2 tablespoons plus 1 teaspoon freshly grated lemon zest
- ¼ teaspoon coarse salt
- 6 large eggs plus 4 large egg whites
- 2¼ cups plus 2 tablespoons granulated sugar
- ¾ cup plus 3 tablespoons fresh lemon juice

1. Preheat the oven to 350°F. Make the crust: Put the butter, flour, confectioners' sugar, 2 teaspoons lemon zest, and the salt in the bowl of an electric mixer fitted with the paddle attachment. Mix on medium speed until well blended.

2. Transfer the mixture to a 9 × 13-inch rimmed baking sheet. Press the batter evenly into the baking sheet. Chill in the freezer 10 minutes. Bake until golden, 20 to 22 minutes. Let cool completely on a wire rack.

3. Make the filling: Whisk together the whole eggs, 1¾ cups plus 2 tablespoons granulated sugar, the lemon juice, and 1 tablespoon plus 2 teaspoons lemon zest. Pour over the crust. Bake until the filling is set, 18 to 20 minutes. Let cool completely on a wire rack. Keep the oven at 350°F.

4. Make the meringue topping: Put the egg whites and ½ cup granulated sugar in the clean bowl of an electric mixer fitted with the whisk attachment. Beat on medium-high speed until stiff peaks form.

5. Using an offset spatula or the back of a spoon, spread the meringue over the filling, swirling to create soft peaks. Bake until the meringue begins to brown, 8 to 10 minutes. Let cool completely. Cut into bars. The bars can be refrigerated in an airtight container up to 1 day.

chunky peanut, chocolate, and cinnamon cookies

MAKES ABOUT 60

You can make bite-size cookies by rolling the dough into smaller balls.

- 2 cups all-purpose flour
- 1 teaspoon baking soda
- 1 teaspoon salt
- ½ teaspoon ground cinnamon
- ¾ cup (1½ sticks) unsalted butter, softened
- ½ cup smooth peanut butter
- 1 cup packed light-brown sugar
- ½ cup granulated sugar
- 2 large eggs
- 1½ cups semisweet chocolate chips
- ⅔ cup roasted, salted peanuts, coarsely chopped
- 2 teaspoons pure vanilla extract
  Chocolate or vanilla ice cream, for serving (optional)

1. Preheat the oven to 350°F. Whisk together the flour, baking soda, salt, and cinnamon in a medium bowl; set aside. Put the butter and peanut butter in the bowl of an electric mixer fitted with the paddle attachment; mix on medium speed until combined, about 2 minutes. Add the sugars; mix 2 minutes. Mix in the eggs until combined.

2. Gradually add the flour mixture; mix until just combined. Fold in the chocolate chips, peanuts, and vanilla with a mixing spoon until well distributed. Refrigerate the dough until it is slightly firm, 15 minutes.

3. Roll the dough into 1-inch balls. Space 2 to 3 inches apart on baking sheets lined with parchment paper. Flatten slightly. Bake until just golden, about 13 minutes. Transfer the cookies to wire racks to cool. Serve with ice cream, if desired.

whole-wheat–raspberry bars

MAKES ABOUT 30

1¼ cups whole-wheat flour
1 cup all-purpose flour, plus more for dusting
¼ cup wheat bran
¼ teaspoon salt
¼ teaspoon baking soda
⅔ cup packed dark-brown sugar
1 teaspoon finely grated lemon zest
10 tablespoons unsalted butter, softened
1 large egg
¼ cup smooth unsweetened applesauce
1 cup raspberry jam

1. Whisk together the flours, bran, salt, and baking soda in a medium bowl; set aside. Put the brown sugar and zest in the bowl of an electric mixer fitted with the paddle attachment; mix on medium speed until combined. Beat in the butter until fluffy. Beat in the egg until pale and smooth.

2. Reduce speed to low. Mix in the flour mixture in 3 batches, alternating with the applesauce. Divide the dough in half; wrap in plastic. Chill until firm, about 2 hours.

3. Preheat the oven to 375°F. Roll out 1 piece of dough between 2 lightly floured sheets of parchment to a 9½ × 11½-inch rectangle, about ⅛ inch thick. If the dough becomes too soft, refrigerate until firm. Remove the top piece of parchment. Trim the dough ½ inch on all sides. Transfer the rectangle on the parchment to a baking sheet.

4. Cut the rectangle in half lengthwise. Spread ¼ cup jam down half of each length, leaving a ½-inch border. Fold the dough over; pinch to seal. Refrigerate until firm, about 20 minutes. Repeat with the remaining chilled dough and jam.

5. Cut crosswise into 1½-inch-wide bars, but do not separate them until after baking. Bake until golden brown, about 20 minutes. Let cool on the sheet on a wire rack. The bars can be stored in an airtight container at room temperature for up to 3 days.

pumpkinseed crackle

MAKES ABOUT 1½ POUNDS

The crackle can be stored in an airtight container at room temperature up to 1 month.

2 cups hulled pumpkinseeds
½ teaspoon vegetable oil
1 teaspoon salt
2 cups sugar
1 cup dark corn syrup
1½ tablespoons unsalted butter, plus more for the baking sheet

1. Toss the pumpkinseeds with the oil in a large bowl; transfer to a large, heavy-bottomed skillet. Toast over medium heat, stirring constantly, until the seeds crackle and turn pale golden, about 10 minutes; remove from heat, and stir in the salt. Transfer to a baking sheet to cool.

2. Stir together the sugar, 1⅓ cups water, and the corn syrup in a large, heavy saucepan over medium heat. Cook, stirring, until the sugar is dissolved, about 3 minutes. Raise heat to high; don't stir, but occasionally wash down the sides of the pan with a pastry brush dipped in cold water to prevent crystals from forming. Cook until the mixture registers 260°F (hard-ball stage) on a candy thermometer, 10 to 15 minutes. Meanwhile, butter an 11 × 17-inch rimmed baking sheet; set aside.

3. Remove the pan from the heat. Working quickly, stir in the butter and toasted pumpkinseeds until the butter is melted and the mixture is combined. Immediately pour into the buttered sheet, spreading it with the back of a spoon to form an even layer (avoid touching the syrup with your hands). Let cool completely on a wire rack.

4. When the mixture is hard, flex the baking sheet to loosen and remove the crackle; break it into pieces with your hands.

chocolate sandwich cookies

MAKES 36

1¾ cups all-purpose flour, plus more
     for the work surface
¼   cup cocoa powder
½   teaspoon baking powder
¼   teaspoon salt
8   tablespoons (1 stick) unsalted butter
1   cup sugar
1   large egg
1   teaspoon pure vanilla extract
½   cup heavy cream
12 ounces white chocolate, finely chopped

1. In a large bowl, sift together the flour, cocoa, baking powder, and salt. Set aside.

2. Cream the butter and sugar until soft and creamy in the bowl of an electric mixer fitted with the paddle attachment. Beat in the egg and vanilla.

3. Add the flour mixture, and mix on low speed until combined. Divide the dough in half; wrap each half in plastic wrap. Chill at least 1 hour.

4. Preheat the oven to 325°F. On a lightly floured surface, roll the dough to ⅛ inch thick. Cut into 1½-inch squares using a cookie cutter. Transfer to parchment-paper–lined baking sheets, and refrigerate until firm, about 30 minutes. Gather any scraps, wrap them in plastic wrap, and chill for 30 minutes before rerolling and cutting into squares. Bake until the edges just begin to brown, about 12 minutes. Transfer to wire racks to cool.

5. To make the white chocolate ganache, bring the cream to a boil in a small saucepan. Remove from heat, and add 9 ounces white chocolate. Let stand for 5 minutes, covered. Transfer the mixture to a medium bowl, and stir until completely smooth. Place in the refrigerator, and chill until thick enough to spread, about 1 hour, stirring every 10 minutes. Use an offset spatula to spread the ganache on half the cookies; top with the remaining cookies.

6. Melt the remaining 3 ounces white chocolate in a small heatproof bowl set over a pan of simmering water. Make a small cone out of parchment paper, or fit a small pastry bag with a coupler and #2 Ateco tip. Fill, and decorate as desired.

orange cornmeal shortbread

MAKES 24

1   cup (2 sticks) unsalted butter, softened
¾   cup confectioners' sugar, plus more
     for dusting
2   teaspoons pure vanilla extract
1½   teaspoons orange zest
2   cups all-purpose flour
¼   cup plus 2 tablespoons yellow cornmeal
1   teaspoon salt

1. Using an electric mixer fitted with the paddle attachment, beat the butter and sugar until creamy and smooth, about 2 minutes. Add the vanilla and zest. Beat well, scraping the sides of the bowl as necessary. With the mixer on low speed, mix in the flour, 2 tablespoons cornmeal, and salt until well combined, about 3 minutes. Form the dough into 2 logs about 1½ inches in diameter; wrap in plastic, and chill at least 1 hour.

2. Preheat the oven to 300°F. Place the remaining ¼ cup cornmeal on a sheet of parchment or waxed paper. Remove the plastic from the chilled dough; roll the logs in cornmeal to coat. Slice into ¼-inch rounds. Place on a baking sheet about 1 inch apart. Bake until pale golden all over, 25 to 30 minutes. Cool on a wire rack. Dust with sugar.

peanut butter and chocolate cups

MAKES ABOUT 30 SMALL PLUS 12 LARGE

Keep the pan of simmering water nearby to re-warm the chocolate as you are working. You will need about 30 1½-inch and 12 2½-inch paper candy cups; they are available at most baking supply stores.

- 10 ounces semisweet or bittersweet chocolate, coarsely chopped
- 6 ounces cream cheese, room temperature
- 1 cup smooth peanut butter
- 1 cup sugar
- ½ cup heavy cream
- Chopped peanuts, for garnish

1. In a heatproof bowl set over a pan of simmering water, melt the chocolate, stirring occasionally, until it is smooth. Remove from heat; stir to cool slightly.

2. Working with 1 paper cup at a time, fill halfway with melted chocolate; invert the cup over bowl of chocolate, and swivel to evenly coat the sides. Gently but quickly reinvert the cup; immediately place on a baking sheet in the refrigerator or freezer. If necessary, use a small pastry brush to fill in any holes so no paper cup is visible. Let the chocolate harden before filling, at least 30 minutes and up to 2 days; cover with plastic wrap once it is set.

3. In the bowl of an electric mixer fitted with the paddle attachment, beat the cream cheese until it is smooth. Add the peanut butter and sugar; beat until combined. In a separate bowl, whip the cream to form stiff peaks; fold into the peanut butter mixture. Place in the refrigerator until it is slightly firm, about 5 minutes. Transfer to a pastry bag fitted with an Ateco #863 open-star tip, and pipe the mixture into the cups.

4. Place the cups in a single layer in an airtight container or baking pan, and cover the container or wrap pan with plastic, being careful not to touch the tops of the cups. Chill in the refrigerator up to 4 hours. To serve, sprinkle a few chopped peanuts over the top of each cup.

skillet-baked chocolate chip cookie

SERVES 8

- 2 cups all-purpose flour
- 1 teaspoon baking soda
- ½ teaspoon salt
- ¾ cup (1½ sticks) unsalted butter, softened
- ½ cup sugar
- ¾ cup packed light-brown sugar
- 1 large egg
- 2 teaspoons pure vanilla extract
- 1½ cups mixed milk and semisweet chocolate chips (about 9 ounces)
- 2 pints vanilla ice cream
- Caramel Sauce (recipe follows)

1. Preheat the oven to 350° F. In a medium bowl, whisk together the flour, baking soda, and salt; set aside. In the bowl of an electric mixer fitted with the paddle attachment, cream the butter and sugars until the mixture is light and fluffy, about 2 minutes. Add the egg and vanilla; mix until they are fully incorporated. Add the flour mixture, and beat until just combined. Stir in the chocolate chips.

2. Transfer the dough to a 10-inch ovenproof skillet, and press to flatten, covering the bottom of the pan. Bake until the edges are brown and the top is golden, 40 to 45 minutes. Don't overbake; it will continue to cook a few minutes out of the oven. Transfer to a wire rack to cool, 15 to 20 minutes. Cut into 8 wedges. Serve warm; top each wedge with a scoop of ice cream and some caramel sauce.

caramel sauce

MAKES ABOUT 1 CUP

- 1 cup sugar
- ¼ teaspoon salt
- ¼ cup water
- ½ cup heavy cream
- 2 tablespoons unsalted butter
- ½ teaspoon pure vanilla extract

1. In a small saucepan, combine the sugar, salt, and water. Cook over medium heat until the sugar is a medium amber color, about 7 minutes; wash the sides of the pan with a pastry brush dipped in water to prevent crystals from forming. Remove from heat.

2. Stir in the heavy cream; add the butter, and stir until combined. Let cool to room temperature; stir in the vanilla. The sauce can be stored in an airtight container in the refrigerator up to 2 weeks. Reheat gently; serve at room temperature.

navettes

MAKES ABOUT 24

Navettes are boat-shaped cakes from Provence traditionally flavored with orange water.

1 teaspoon active dry yeast

4 cups all-purpose flour, plus more for the work surface

Pinch of salt

4 tablespoons unsalted butter, room temperature

1 cup sugar

2 large eggs

3 tablespoons orange-flower water

Grated zest of 1 lemon

Grated zest of 1 orange

Olive oil, for the bowl and baking sheet

1 egg yolk, beaten with 1 tablespoon water, for the glaze

Crystal sugar, for sprinkling (optional)

1. In a small bowl, dissolve the yeast in 2 tablespoons lukewarm water. Let stand until creamy, about 10 minutes.

2. In another bowl, whisk together the flour and salt. Place the butter and sugar in the bowl of an electric mixer. Beat, using the paddle attachment, until soft and crumbly. Add the eggs, yeast, orange-flower water, and zests. Add the flour, 1 cup at a time, and beat on low speed until just combined.

3. Transfer the dough to a floured work surface, and knead with your hands until smooth and no longer sticky. Form into a ball, place in an oiled bowl, cover, and leave to rest in a warm place for 30 minutes.

4. Rub a large baking sheet with olive oil. Turn the dough out onto a lightly floured work surface, and

cut into 3 equal portions. Using your hands, roll each portion into a log about 1 inch thick. Cut each log crosswise into pieces about 2½ inches long. Shape the pieces into tapered boat shapes by rounding and somewhat raising the middle portions, and pinching the ends into points. Cover the baking sheet with a kitchen towel, and leave in a warm place for 2 hours. The boats will rise somewhat but will not double.

5. Preheat oven to 375° F. Using a sharp knife, make a lengthwise slash down each boat, about one-third of its depth. Using a pastry brush, paint the surface of each boat with egg-yolk glaze. Sprinkle with crystal sugar, if desired. Bake until golden, 25 to 30 minutes. Transfer to a wire rack to cool.

brandy snaps

MAKES 18

You may substitute dark corn syrup for the golden syrup, but the flavor will vary slightly. If the cookies get too cool to shape, return them to the oven for a few seconds until they soften.

½ cup all-purpose flour

½ teaspoon ground ginger

5 tablespoons unsalted butter

⅓ cup sugar

¼ cup golden syrup

1. Preheat the oven to 350° F. Combine the flour and ginger with a whisk. Melt the butter in a small saucepan over medium heat. Add the sugar and golden syrup; cook, stirring with a wooden spoon, until the sugar is dissolved. Remove from heat; stir in the flour-ginger mixture.

2. Line a rimmed baking sheet with a Silpat (a French nonstick baking mat) or parchment. Drop 6 even tablespoons batter on the Silpat about 2 inches apart; place in the oven. Bake until flat and golden brown, about 10 minutes.

3. Let the cookies cool 2 minutes, until slightly firm; immediately wrap them, 1 at a time, around a wide round wooden spoon handle, and let set for 30 seconds. Transfer from the spoon handle to a cooling rack. Repeat with the remaining batter.

breads

mrs. kostyra's babkas

MAKES THREE 8-INCH BABKAS

- 8 ounces (2 sticks) unsalted butter, softened, plus more for the molds
- 2 cups whole milk
- 3 envelopes active dry yeast (3 scant tablespoons), or 1⅓ ounces compressed fresh yeast, crumbled
- 1 cup plus a pinch of sugar
- ½ cup warm water (about 110°F)
- 5 large eggs plus 4 large egg yolks
- 1 teaspoon salt
- 1 teaspoon pure vanilla extract
- 1 tablespoon orange-flavored liqueur
  Finely grated zest of 1 orange
  Finely grated zest of 1 lemon
- 9 to 10 cups sifted all-purpose flour, plus more for dusting
- 1 cup dried currants
- 1½ cups golden raisins
- 1 cup dark raisins
- 1 cup blanched almonds, coarsely chopped
- 1 tablespoon heavy cream

1. Butter 3 kugelhopf molds (each 1½ quarts and 8 inches in diameter); set aside. Butter a large bowl; set aside. Heat the milk and butter in a saucepan over medium-low, stirring, until the butter is melted.

2. Sprinkle the yeast and a pinch of sugar over the warm water in a small bowl. Let stand until foamy, 7 to 10 minutes.

3. Whisk together 4 eggs and the egg yolks, 1 cup sugar, and the salt in a large bowl until thick, about 3 minutes. Add the vanilla, liqueur, zests, yeast mixture, and milk mixture; whisk 1 minute more. With a wooden spoon, gradually stir in up to 10 cups flour, 1 cup at a time, until a sticky dough forms. Stir in the dried fruits and almonds.

4. Turn out the dough onto a lightly floured surface; knead, dusting with flour if it seems sticky, until smooth and soft, about 10 minutes. Transfer to the buttered bowl. Loosely cover with buttered plastic wrap; let rise in a warm place until doubled in bulk, about 2 hours. Punch down the dough. Loosely cover with buttered wrap; let rise until doubled in bulk, 1½ to 2 hours more.

5. Punch down the dough; turn it out onto a lightly floured surface. Knead 1 minute. Divide the dough into 3 equal pieces. With lightly floured hands, roll each piece into an 18-inch-long rope. Fit each rope into a buttered mold; press the end of the rope into the dough to seal. Loosely cover with buttered wrap. Let rise until doubled in bulk, about 45 minutes.

6. Preheat the oven to 350° F. Whisk together the remaining egg and the cream in a small bowl. Brush the dough with the egg wash. Bake until golden, about 35 minutes. Let cool slightly in molds on a wire rack, about 10 minutes. Unmold onto the rack, and let cool completely, larger sides down.

....

TESTING YEAST

Yeast is a kind of fungus that, when activated, produces carbon dioxide—the gas that causes breads to rise. Yeast feeds off of sugar and water and stays alive even when frozen; nonetheless, it loses some of its efficacy over time. Three varieties are available to bakers: cake, instant dry, and active dry, all of which can be used in any recipe that requires yeast. Cake yeast is fresh and perishes quickly; instant dry yeast and active dry yeast are in powder form and have a longer shelf life.

All three types can be checked for efficacy with a simple test called proofing. *In a glass measuring cup, stir 1 teaspoon sugar into ½ cup warm water (105°F to 110°F); if the water is too hot, it will kill the yeast. Sprinkle the mixture with 1 teaspoon yeast. Instant dry yeast should react immediately; if it is active, it should foam and become creamy. Active dry and cake yeasts should react the same way within 10 minutes. If the yeast does not respond this way, do not use it. If it is active, remember to factor in the amount of tested yeast and water into the amounts called for in the recipe.*

....

pumpkin cornmeal doughnuts

MAKES ABOUT 14 3-INCH DOUGHNUTS
AND 14 DOUGHNUT HOLES

If you do not have a doughnut cutter, use a 3-inch cookie cutter to cut out the doughnuts and a 1-inch cookie cutter to cut out the centers.

- 2¾ cups all-purpose flour, plus more for the work surface
- 4 teaspoons baking powder
- ¼ teaspoon table salt
- 1 teaspoon ground cinnamon
- ¾ teaspoon ground allspice
- 1 tablespoon minced orange zest
- 1 cup fine cornmeal
- 3 large eggs, lightly beaten
- ½ cup granulated sugar
- ½ cup sweetened condensed milk
- 1 cup Pumpkin Puree (page 571), or canned
- 4 tablespoons unsalted butter, melted
- 8 cups vegetable oil, for frying
- ¼ cup confectioners' sugar

1. Sift the flour, baking powder, salt, ½ teaspoon cinnamon, and allspice together into a large bowl. Add the orange zest and cornmeal; mix until combined. Set aside.

2. In an electric mixer fitted with the paddle attachment, beat the eggs and ¼ cup granulated sugar until the mixture is pale yellow, about 5 minutes. Add the condensed milk, and beat well. Add the pumpkin and melted butter, and beat until combined. Add the reserved flour mixture, and mix until the dough holds together. Cover the dough with plastic wrap, and refrigerate overnight.

3. Heat the vegetable oil in a large, deep pan over medium heat until a deep-fry thermometer reads 365° F.

4. While the oil is heating, roll out the dough on a lightly floured surface to about ⅓ inch thick. Using a 3-inch doughnut cutter, cut out doughnuts, and set aside. Reroll the scraps of dough, and continue to cut out more doughnuts. Mix together the remaining ½ teaspoon cinnamon and ¼ cup sugar in a small bowl, and set aside.

5. Add 4 doughnuts to the hot oil; fry until golden brown, about 1½ minutes. Turn the doughnuts over; fry until golden brown, about 1 minute more. Transfer to several layers of paper towels to drain. Repeat until all the doughnuts have been fried.

6. Roll half the warm doughnuts, 1 at a time, in cinnamon sugar to coat. Transfer to a serving platter. Dust the remaining doughnuts with confectioners' sugar. Transfer to the serving platter. Serve warm.

yogurt-nut oat bread

MAKES ONE 8-INCH LOAF

To store, wrap the loaf tightly in plastic; refrigerate for up to 1 week, or freeze for up to 2 months.

- Cooking spray
- 2 cups all-purpose flour
- ¾ cup whole-wheat flour
- 1½ teaspoons coarse salt
- 1 teaspoon cream of tartar
- 1 teaspoon baking soda
- 1 teaspoon baking powder
- ¾ cup walnuts, toasted and chopped
- ¾ cup hulled sunflower seeds, toasted, plus 3 tablespoons for topping
- ½ cup steel-cut oats
- ½ cup oat or rice bran
- 1¼ cups low-fat (1 percent) milk
- 1 cup plain low-fat yogurt

1. Preheat the oven to 350° F. Coat an 8 × 4-inch loaf pan with cooking spray. Into a large bowl, sift together the flours, salt, cream of tartar, baking soda, and baking powder. Stir in the nuts, sunflower seeds, oats, and bran. In a separate bowl, whisk together the milk and yogurt, then stir into the flour mixture just until combined.

2. Spoon the batter into the prepared pan, and smooth the top with the back of the spoon. Sprinkle the remaining 3 tablespoons sunflower seeds evenly over the top.

3. Bake until golden on top and pulling away from the pan, about 1 hour 10 minutes. Remove from the oven; immediately invert onto a wire rack to remove the pan. Reinvert; let cool completely before slicing.

sweet potato rolls

MAKES 20

You will need about 2 medium sweet potatoes to obtain 2 cups cooked flesh. We like the flavor of roasted potatoes best, but you could also use boiled or steamed potatoes. Before using, peel and discard the skins.

- ¼ cup warm water
- 1 envelope active dry yeast (1 scant tablespoon)
- 1 cup milk
- ⅓ cup unsalted butter
- ½ cup sugar
- 1½ tablespoons coarse salt
- 1 teaspoon ground cardamom
- 2 cups cooked sweet potatoes (about 2 medium)
- 1 teaspoon fresh lemon juice
- 1 large egg, lightly beaten
- 7 cups sifted all-purpose flour
  Vegetable oil, for bowl
  Melted butter, for brushing

1. Place the warm water in a small bowl, and sprinkle with the yeast. Let stand until the yeast is dissolved and mixture is foamy, about 7 minutes.

2. In a small saucepan, heat the milk over medium heat just until it begins to steam and bubble around the sides. Remove from heat; add the butter, and stir until melted and combined. Stir in the sugar, salt, and cardamom. Let cool slightly.

3. Preheat the oven to 400° F. Line a baking sheet with parchment paper; set aside. Combine the sweet potatoes and lemon juice in the bowl of an electric mixer fitted with the paddle attachment; beat until smooth, 2 to 3 minutes. Beat in the egg and milk and yeast mixtures until smooth.

4. Switch to the dough hook attachment. Add the flour, 1 cup at a time, beating until a stiff dough forms. Continue kneading the dough on medium speed until smooth, about 8 minutes. The dough will still be slightly sticky.

5. Transfer to a large oiled bowl. Cover with a clean kitchen towel, and let stand in a warm place to rise until the dough is doubled in bulk, about 1 hour.

6. Punch down the dough, and knead again with your hands, just until smooth. Using a bench scraper or sharp knife, cut the dough into 20 equal pieces, and shape them into rolls.

7. Place the rolls on the prepared baking sheet, about 2 inches apart; cover with a kitchen towel, and let rise again in a warm place until doubled in bulk, about 40 minutes.

8. Using kitchen scissors or a sharp paring knife, snip an X in the top of each roll. Brush the rolls with melted butter. Bake until the tops of the rolls are golden, about 20 minutes, rotating the pan halfway through. Transfer to a wire rack; serve hot or at room temperature.

cream biscuits

MAKES 30

White Lily flour is widely used throughout the South. Made with only soft winter wheat, it is finer, lighter, and whiter than other types of flour.

- 2½ cups White Lily all-purpose flour, plus more for the work surface
- 1 tablespoon plus 1 teaspoon baking powder
- ½ teaspoon salt
- 2 cups heavy cream
- 3 tablespoons unsalted butter, melted

1. Preheat the oven to 450° F. Whisk together the flour, baking powder, and salt in a bowl. Pour in the cream; stir with a wooden spoon until just combined. The dough will still be wet and tacky.

2. Turn out the dough onto a well-floured work surface, and pat into a square about ½ inch thick. Let rest about 5 minutes.

3. Using a 2-inch round biscuit cutter, cut out 24 rounds. Gather together the scraps; pat into a square, and cut out more rounds. Place on a baking sheet, and bake until golden on the tops, 12 to 14 minutes. Remove from the oven; immediately brush the tops with butter. Transfer to a wire rack to cool. Serve warm or at room temperature.

1. For best results, bring the milk, eggs, and butter to room temperature. Take these ingredients out of the refrigerator before you start, letting them warm up as you measure the dry ingredients.

2. Whisk together the dry ingredients in one bowl and the wet ingredients in another.

3. Make a well in the center of the dry ingredients; pour in the wet ingredients.

4. With a rubber spatula, fold the wet mixture into the dry one, with as few strokes as possible.

5. Fill buttered muffin tins about three-quarters of the way with batter. This leaves enough room for a crumb topping.

breakfast muffins

MAKES 12

10	tablespoons (1¼ sticks) unsalted butter, melted, plus more for the pan
1¾	cups all-purpose flour
1	tablespoon baking powder
1¼	teaspoons ground cinnamon
¼	teaspoon salt
½	vanilla bean, split and scraped
⅔	cup sugar
⅔	cup milk, room temperature
1	large egg, room temperature
1¼	cups fruit, such as blueberries, raspberries, strawberries, or peaches
	Streusel (recipe follows)

1. Preheat the oven to 400°F. Butter a standard muffin tin. Combine the flour, baking powder, cinnamon, and salt in a large bowl; whisk to combine.

2. In a medium bowl, combine the butter, vanilla bean scrapings, sugar, milk, and egg; whisk to combine. Fold the butter mixture and fruit into the flour mixture; use no more than 10 strokes.

3. Spoon ¼ cup batter into each prepared cup; press 2 tablespoons streusel on top of each. Bake until the tops are golden, 15 to 17 minutes. Remove from the oven; let cool in the pan 15 to 20 minutes before transferring to a wire rack. Serve warm or at room temperature.

streusel

MAKES ENOUGH FOR 12 STANDARD MUFFINS

5	tablespoons unsalted butter, melted
⅔	cup all-purpose flour
⅔	cup confectioners' sugar
¼	teaspoon ground cinnamon
	Pinch of salt

Put all ingredients in a medium bowl; mix with your fingers until the mixture is moist and crumbly.

MUFFIN VARIATIONS

When you want a change from plain muffins, add fresh fruit or nuts (see suggestions below). You can add one or a combination of mix-ins, as long as the total volume does not exceed 1¼ cups. Good combinations include peach and pecan, blueberry and lemon zest, raspberry and walnut, and strawberry and orange zest.

¾ cup walnut pieces

¾ cup pecan halves

1¼ cups sliced strawberries (about ½-inch pieces)

1¼ cups sliced peaches (about ½-inch pieces)

1¼ cups blueberries

1¼ cups raspberries

2 tablespoons fresh lemon zest

2 tablespoons fresh orange zest

2 tablespoons poppy seeds

applesauce muffins

MAKES 18

- 2 cups all-purpose flour
- 2 teaspoons ground cinnamon
- 1 teaspoon baking soda
- ¾ teaspoon salt
- ½ teaspoon freshly ground nutmeg
- ⅛ teaspoon ground cloves
- 8 ounces (2 sticks) unsalted butter, softened
- 1 cup granulated sugar
- 1½ cups packed light brown sugar
- 4 large eggs
  Apple Cider Applesauce (recipe follows) or 1½ cups store-bought applesauce
- 1 cup toasted pecans, chopped
- 1 package (8 ounces) cream cheese, room temperature

1. Preheat the oven to 350° F. Line a standard 12-cup muffin tin and a 6-cup tin with paper liners. Sift the flour, cinnamon, baking soda, salt, nutmeg, and cloves together into a medium bowl. Set aside.

2. Put 8 tablespoons (1 stick) butter, the granulated sugar, and ½ cup brown sugar in the bowl of an electric mixer fitted with the paddle attachment. Cream on medium speed until smooth, about 3 minutes. Mix in the eggs, 1 at a time. On low speed, mix in the applesauce and then the flour mixture. Stir in the nuts by hand.

3. Divide the batter among the muffin cups, filling each about three-quarters full. Bake until a tester inserted in the centers comes out clean, 18 to 20 minutes. Let cool completely in the tins on a wire rack.

4. Meanwhile, in the clean bowl of the electric mixer, mix the cream cheese with the remaining 8 tablespoons (1 stick) butter and 1 cup brown sugar on medium speed until smooth. Spread the cream cheese frosting on the muffins. The muffins can be refrigerated in airtight containers up to 2 days.

apple cider applesauce

MAKES 1½ CUPS

- 1 pound juicy apples, such as McIntosh, peeled, cored, and quartered
- ¾ cup apple cider
- 1 tablespoon sugar, plus more if needed
  Pinch of salt

1. Bring the apples and cider to a boil in a medium saucepan over medium-high heat. Cover the pan; reduce heat. Simmer until the apples are very soft, about 12 minutes. Stir in the sugar and salt.

2. Cook (uncovered) over medium-low heat until the apples have broken down and most of the liquid is evaporated, about 15 minutes. Let cool slightly.

3. Puree in a food processor until smooth. Add more sugar, if desired. Store in an airtight container up to 2 days.

health muffins

MAKES 12

If you prefer, you can bake these muffins in a standard muffin tin; spoon ¼ cup batter into each cup.

- Nonstick cooking spray (optional)
- 1 cup whole-wheat flour
- 1 cup wheat bran
- 3 tablespoons flaxseed, ground, plus more for garnish
- 1¼ teaspoons baking powder
- 1¼ teaspoons baking soda
- ¾ teaspoon ground nutmeg
- ½ teaspoon salt
- 5 carrots, finely grated
- 10 ounces (about 15) dried figs, sliced into eights
- ⅔ cup applesauce
- ⅔ cup honey
- 5 large eggs, lightly beaten
- 1 teaspoon pure vanilla extract

1. Preheat the oven to 375°F. Lightly coat a ⅔-cup muffin tin with cooking spray, or line with paper cups; set aside.

2. Combine the flour, bran, flaxseed, baking powder, baking soda, nutmeg, and salt in a large bowl; whisk to combine. Add the carrots, figs, applesauce, honey, eggs, and vanilla. Using a rubber spatula, stir until just combined.

3. Spoon ½ cup batter into each prepared cup, and bake until the tops are golden, 15 to 17 minutes. Remove from the oven; let cool in the pan 12 to 15 minutes before transferring to a wire rack. Serve warm or at room temperature.

brown sugar cornbread

MAKES TWO 9 × 4¼-INCH LOAVES

This cornbread—made slightly sweet with the addition of dark brown sugar—mixes very easily: Just whisk together the dry ingredients; melt the butter and sugar; and whisk in cold milk to cool the liquid. Next, whisk in the eggs, then stir the brown sugar mixture into the cornmeal, scrape the batter into the pan, and bake.

   1 cup (2 sticks) unsalted butter,
      plus more for the pans
2⅔ cups yellow cornmeal
   2 cups all-purpose flour
2½ tablespoons baking powder
   1 teaspoon salt
   ¾ cup packed dark-brown sugar
   2 cups milk
   4 large eggs, beaten

1. Preheat the oven to 350°F with a rack in the middle. Butter 2 9 × 4½-inch loaf pans; set aside.

2. In a large bowl, whisk together the yellow cornmeal, flour, baking powder, and salt.

3. Heat the butter and brown sugar in a small saucepan over medium-low heat just until melted, and whisk until the mixture is smooth. Remove from heat; whisk in the milk and then the eggs. Pour into the dry mixture, stirring just until blended, and divide evenly between the prepared pans, smoothing the tops.

4. Bake until the loaves are golden and a cake tester inserted in the centers comes out clean, about 30 minutes. Turn the loaves out onto racks to cool. Serve warm or at room temperature.

orange breakfast biscuits

MAKES 12

2½ cups all-purpose flour, plus more
      for dusting
   ⅓ cup plus 1 tablespoon sugar
   2 tablespoons finely grated orange zest
1½ teaspoons baking powder
1¼ teaspoons coarse salt
   ¼ teaspoon baking soda
   8 tablespoons (1 stick) cold unsalted
      butter, cut into small pieces
1¼ cups buttermilk

1. Line a baking sheet with parchment paper; lightly dust with flour. Set aside. Put ⅓ cup sugar and the zest in the bowl of an electric mixer fitted with the paddle attachment. Mix, scraping down the sides of the bowl as needed, until combined, about 3 minutes. Set aside.

2. Whisk together the flour, baking powder, salt, baking soda, and remaining tablespoon sugar in a medium bowl. Using a pastry blender or 2 knives, blend in the butter until the mixture resembles coarse meal. Add the buttermilk; stir with a wooden spoon just until a sticky dough forms.

3. Turn out the dough onto a lightly floured work surface. Pat the dough together, and press into an 8 × 11 × 1-inch rectangle. Sprinkle 2 tablespoons sugar mixture on top. Using a bench scraper or spatula to lift the dough, fold the rectangle into thirds (as you would a letter).

4. Give the dough a quarter-turn. Roll out into an 8 × 11 × 1-inch rectangle. Sprinkle 2 tablespoons sugar mixture evenly on top. Fold into thirds. Transfer the dough to prepared baking sheet. Tightly cover with plastic wrap. Refrigerate 30 minutes.

5. Return the dough to the floured work surface. Roll out again into an 8 × 11 × 1-inch rectangle.

Sprinkle 2 tablespoons sugar mixture on top. Fold into thirds. Sprinkle the remaining sugar mixture evenly on top.

6. Preheat the oven to 400°F. Using a 2½-inch biscuit or cookie cutter, cut rounds from the dough (still folded); transfer to a baking sheet. Tightly cover with plastic wrap. Refrigerate 30 minutes.

7. Bake until the biscuits are just browned, 20 to 25 minutes. Transfer biscuits to a wire rack. Serve warm.

buttermilk-onion pull-apart rolls

MAKES ABOUT 12

11 tablespoons (1⅜ sticks) unsalted butter, softened, plus more for the bowl, plus 5 tablespoons melted

1 envelope (¼ ounce) active dry yeast

1 tablespoon sugar

2 tablespoon warm water (105° to 110°F)

¾ cup buttermilk

1 large egg, lightly beaten

2¾ cups plus 2 tablespoons all-purpose flour, plus more for the surface and pin

2 teaspoons salt

2 pounds sweet onions, such as Rio (1½ pounds cut into ¼-inch slices, ½ pound finely chopped)

⅛ teaspoon freshly grated nutmeg

1. Butter a 9-inch cake pan using 1 tablespoon softened butter. Butter a large bowl; set aside. Stir together the yeast, sugar, and warm water in a small bowl; let the mixture stand until foamy, about 5 minutes. Stir until dissolved. Stir in the buttermilk and egg.

2. Mix 2¾ cups flour and 1½ teaspoons salt in the bowl of an electric mixer fitted with the dough hook. Make a well in the center. Pour in the buttermilk mixture; mix to combine. Add 6 tablespoons softened butter; mix on medium-high speed until a soft dough forms, about 10 minutes.

3. Scrape the dough onto a lightly floured work surface; sprinkle with the remaining 2 tablespoons flour. Knead the dough until smooth, about 5 minutes. Transfer to the buttered bowl. Cover the dough

with a clean kitchen towel; let rise in a warm place until doubled in bulk, about 1 hour.

4. Melt the remaining 4 tablespoons softened butter in a large saucepan over medium-high heat. Add the onions; raise heat to high, and cook, stirring often, until soft, about 5 minutes. Reduce heat to medium; cook, stirring, until golden brown, about 30 minutes. Stir in the nutmeg. Season with ½ teaspoon salt. Let cool.

5. Punch down the dough, and turn out onto a lightly floured work surface. With a lightly floured rolling pin, roll the dough into a 17 × 10-inch rectangle, and brush with 3 tablespoons melted butter. Spread the onions evenly over the dough. Starting on 1 long side, roll the dough into a log. Press the seam to seal.

6. Cut into about 12 slices, about 1¼ inches thick each. Arrange the slices, cut sides up, in the buttered pan, and brush with remaining 2 tablespoons melted butter. Cover loosely with plastic wrap. Let rise in a warm place until doubled in bulk, about 50 minutes.

7. Preheat the oven to 375°F. Bake the rolls until golden brown, about 35 minutes. Immediately invert the rolls onto a wire rack. Serve warm.

buttery crescent rolls

MAKES 24

¾ cup (1½ sticks) unsalted butter, softened, plus more for the bowl and plastic wrap, plus 2 tablespoons melted

1¼ cups whole milk

¼ cup vegetable shortening

¼ cup plus 1 tablespoon sugar

2½ teaspoons salt

1 envelope (¼ ounce) active dry yeast

¼ cup water (105° to 110°F)

2 large eggs, lightly beaten

5½ cups all-purpose flour, plus more for the work surface

1. Line 2 baking sheets with parchment paper; set aside. Butter a large bowl; set aside. Put the milk, shortening, sugar, softened butter, and salt in a medium saucepan. Cook over medium heat, stirring constantly, until the sugar has dissolved. Let cool completely.

2. Put the yeast and warm water in the bowl of an electric mixer fitted with the dough hook. Let stand until foamy, about 5 minutes. Mix in the milk mixture on medium speed until combined; mix in the eggs. Reduce speed to low, and gradually mix in the flour. Raise speed to medium-high; mix until a soft dough forms, about 12 minutes.

3. Turn out the dough onto a lightly floured work surface. Knead until smooth, about 5 minutes, then transfer to the buttered bowl. Cover with a clean kitchen towel; set in a warm place to rise until doubled in bulk, about 1 hour.

4. Roll the dough into a 13 × 20-inch rectangle. Trim the edges to be straight. Cut the dough in half lengthwise; cut both strips into 12 triangles (about 3 inches wide at each base). Gently stretch each to 2 to 3 inches long. Starting at the widest end, gently roll up. Space 1 inch apart on prepared baking sheets, pointed ends down. Cover loosely with buttered plastic wrap; let rise until doubled in bulk, about 1 hour.

5. Preheat the oven to 350°F. Brush the rolls with the melted butter. Bake until golden, about 20 minutes. Let cool on a wire rack 5 minutes. Serve warm.

olive rolls

MAKES 12

¼ cup extra-virgin olive oil, plus more for the parchment, bowl, and plastic wrap

1 envelope (¼ ounce) active dry yeast

1 cup warm water (105° to 110°F)

3 to 4 cups all-purpose flour, plus more for the work surface

½ teaspoon coarse salt

1 cup oil-cured black olives, pitted and cut into ½-inch pieces

½ teaspoon crushed red pepper flakes

1. Line a baking sheet with parchment paper. Brush the parchment with oil; set aside. Oil a large bowl; set aside. Sprinkle the yeast over the warm water in a small bowl. Let stand until foamy, about 5 minutes. Stir until dissolved.

2. Put 3 cups flour and the salt in the bowl of an electric mixer fitted with the dough hook. Add the yeast mixture and oil; mix on medium speed until a soft dough forms, adding more flour if needed. Add the olives and red pepper flakes; mix until fully combined, about 15 minutes.

3. Turn out the dough onto a lightly floured work surface. Knead until smooth and the olives are set firmly in the dough, about 15 minutes. Transfer to the oiled bowl. Cover loosely with a clean kitchen towel, and let rise in a warm place until doubled in bulk, about 1 hour.

4. Turn out the dough onto a lightly floured work surface; gently flatten. Using a butter knife, cut the dough into 12 equal pieces. Roll each into a cylinder, and transfer to the prepared baking sheet. Cover with oiled plastic wrap. Let rise in a warm place until doubled in bulk, about 1 hour.

5. Preheat the oven to 450°F. Bake the rolls until the tops are crisp and dark brown, about 15 minutes. Serve warm or at room temperature.

sour cream–thyme rolls

MAKES 12

½ cup (1 stick) cold unsalted butter, cut into small pieces, plus 2 tablespoons melted, plus more for the muffin tin and plastic wrap

1 envelope (¼ ounce) active dry yeast

1 cup warm water (105° to 110°F)

2 tablespoons sugar

2 cups cake flour (not self-rising)

2 cups all-purpose flour

1½ teaspoons salt

1½ cups sour cream

2 tablespoons fresh thyme leaves

1. Lightly butter a standard 12-cup muffin tin, and set aside. Stir together the yeast, warm water, and sugar in a small bowl, and let stand until foamy, about 5 minutes. Stir until the yeast dissolves.

2. Whisk together the flours and salt in a large bowl. Using a pastry blender, cut in the butter pieces until mixture resembles coarse meal. Stir in the yeast mixture. Stir in the sour cream and thyme leaves until combined.

3. Spoon heaping ⅓ cup dough into each cup of the muffin tin. Cover with buttered plastic wrap; let rise in a warm place until doubled in size, about 1 hour.

4. Preheat the oven to 400°F. Bake the rolls 10 minutes. Remove from the oven, and lightly brush with 2 tablespoons melted butter. Bake until golden brown, 16 to 18 minutes. Immediately invert and unmold rolls onto a wire rack. Serve warm.

whole-grain morning loaf

MAKES ONE 10-INCH LOAF

Vegetable oil cooking spray

1 large apple, such as McIntosh, peeled and coarsely grated

¾ cup stone-ground whole-wheat flour

½ cup unbleached all-purpose flour

1 cup coarse wheat bran

¼ cup wheat germ

1½ teaspoons baking soda

½ teaspoon ground nutmeg

½ teaspoon ground ginger

½ teaspoon salt

1¼ cups plain nonfat yogurt

⅓ cup applesauce

⅓ cup honey

2 large eggs, lightly beaten

¾ teaspoon pure vanilla extract

½ cup dried dates, chopped

½ cup walnuts, toasted and chopped

4½ teaspoons whole brown flaxseed

1. Preheat the oven to 375°F. Coat a 10 × 5-inch loaf pan with cooking spray. Wrap the apple in paper towels; squeeze out liquid.

2. Whisk together the flours, wheat bran, wheat germ, baking soda, spices, and salt.

3. Stir together the apple, yogurt, applesauce, honey, eggs, and vanilla with a rubber spatula in a large bowl. Fold in the flour mixture, then fold in the dates and nuts. Pour into the prepared pan. Sprinkle with the flaxseed.

4. Bake until a cake tester comes out clean, 50 to 55 minutes. Let cool in the pan on a wire rack 15 minutes. Unmold onto rack. Serve warm or at room temperature.

whole wheat–rye rolls

MAKES 12

6 tablespoons unsalted butter, melted, plus more for the bowl and plastic wrap

1 envelope (¼ ounce) active dry yeast

1 cup warm water (105° to 110°F)

1 tablespoon sugar

1 large egg, lightly beaten

2 teaspoons salt

1¼ cups rye flour

1½ cups whole-wheat flour

¾ cup all-purpose flour, plus more for the work surface

2 tablespoons caraway seeds

Sea salt, for sprinkling

1. Line a baking sheet with parchment paper; set aside. Butter a large bowl; set aside. Put the yeast, warm water, sugar, egg, and 3 tablespoons butter in the bowl of an electric mixer fitted with the dough hook. Mix on medium speed 1 minute.

2. Reduce mixer speed to low. Mix in the salt, flours, and caraway seeds. Raise speed to medium-high, and beat until the dough comes together, about 10 minutes. Turn out the dough onto a lightly floured work surface. Knead until smooth, 15 to 20 minutes, then transfer to the buttered bowl. Cover the dough with a clean kitchen towel, and let rise in a warm place until doubled in bulk, about 1 hour.

3. Using a butter knife, cut the dough into 12 equal pieces. Roll into balls, and space 1½ inches apart on the prepared baking sheet. Cover the dough with buttered plastic wrap. Let rise in a warm place until doubled in bulk, about 1 hour.

4. Preheat the oven to 350°F. Using a sharp knife, cut an X in the top of each roll. Bake the rolls until golden brown, about 35 minutes. Transfer the rolls to a wire rack set over a baking sheet, and brush with the remaining 3 tablespoons butter. Sprinkle the tops with sea salt.

currant scones

MAKES 12 TO 16

We used sanding sugar on the tops; granulated sugar works just as well. The scones are best eaten the day they are made, but they will keep up to 2 days in an airtight container at room temperature. This recipe was developed by Emily Donahue for Rosey's Coffee and Tea in Hanover, New Hampshire.

- 4 cups all-purpose flour, plus more for the work surface
- 2 tablespoons granulated sugar
- 2 tablespoons baking powder
- 1 teaspoon baking soda
- 1½ teaspoons salt
- 1 cup (2 sticks) cold unsalted butter, cut into small pieces, plus more for serving
- 1¼ cups buttermilk
- 1 cup currants
- 1 large egg, lightly beaten
- ¼ cup sanding sugar
- Preserves, for serving

1. Preheat the oven to 350°F. Line a baking sheet with parchment paper; set aside. In a large bowl, whisk together the flour, granulated sugar, baking powder, baking soda, and salt.

2. Using a pastry cutter or 2 forks, cut the butter into the flour mixture until it resembles coarse meal. Add the buttermilk and currants; stir to combine.

3. On a lightly floured surface, roll out the dough about 1 inch thick. Using a 2½-inch biscuit cutter, cut out as many rounds as possible, and place on the prepared baking sheet. Reroll the scraps; continue cutting.

4. Lightly brush the top of each scone with beaten egg; sprinkle with sanding sugar. Bake until the biscuits are golden, 20 to 25 minutes. Transfer to a wire rack. Serve with butter and preserves on the side.

dried apricot and sage scones

MAKES 8

When baked, these scones can be frozen in an airtight container for up to 1 month.

- 2 cups all-purpose flour, plus more for dusting
- ¼ cup granulated sugar
- 1 tablespoon baking powder
- ¾ teaspoon fine salt
- 5 tablespoons cold unsalted butter, cut into small pieces
- 1 cup chopped dried apricots (about 4 ounces)
- 2 tablespoons plus 1 teaspoon finely chopped fresh sage
- 1 cup heavy cream, plus more for brushing
- Sanding sugar, for sprinkling

1. Preheat the oven to 375°F. Place the flour, granulated sugar, baking powder, and salt in a large

MAKING SCONES

The dough for scones, like that of biscuits, should be handled as little as possible. Cut out scones by pressing straight through the dough with a bench scraper (or with a biscuit cutter). Brush the tops with heavy cream or beaten egg, then sprinkle with sanding sugar so the scones glisten when they come out of the oven.

bowl. Work in the butter with your fingertips or a pastry blender until the mixture resembles coarse meal. Stir in the dried apricots and sage. Add the cream; gather the mixture together with your hands until it starts to hold together.

2. Turn out the mixture onto a lightly floured work surface. Quickly bring the dough together; pat into an 8-inch circle 1 inch thick. Smooth the top with a rolling pin. Cut into 8 wedges with a bench scraper (see below).

3. Arrange the wedges on a parchment-lined baking sheet. Brush the tops with cream, then sprinkle generously with sanding sugar. Bake until scones are cooked through and golden brown, about 30 minutes. Immediately transfer the scones to a wire rack; let cool at least 10 minutes. Serve warm or at room temperature.

whole-wheat oat bread

MAKES ONE 7 1/2-INCH ROUND LOAF;
SERVES 8

1½ cups plus 2 tablespoons simmering water

1½ cups plus 1 tablespoon old-fashioned rolled oats

¼ cup unsulfured molasses

1½ cups bread flour, plus more for dusting

1½ cups whole-wheat flour

¼ cup powdered nonfat dry milk

1 envelope active dry yeast
   (1 scant tablespoon)

¾ teaspoon salt

1 tablespoon vegetable oil

1 large egg white, lightly beaten

1. Pour the water over 1 cup oats in a medium bowl. Stir in the molasses; let stand until mixture registers 115°F on an instant-read thermometer, about 10 minutes.

2. Coarsely grind ½ cup oats in a food processor. Transfer to a separate medium bowl; add the flours and powdered milk.

3. Sprinkle the molasses mixture with yeast. Stir in 1 cup flour mixture, then the salt. Gradually stir in the remaining flour mixture, 1 cup at a time.

4. Turn the dough out onto a lightly floured work surface. Knead until smooth and no longer sticky, 5 to 10 minutes.

5. Oil a medium bowl with 1 teaspoon oil. Transfer the dough to the bowl; turn to coat. Loosely cover with plastic wrap, and let the dough rise in a warm spot until doubled in bulk, 1 to 1¼ hours.

6. Brush a heavy-duty baking sheet with 1 teaspoon oil; set aside. Punch down the dough. Transfer to a lightly floured work surface. Knead the dough once or twice. Flatten into a 9-inch circle.

7. Pull the edges of the dough up and in toward the center; pinch to seal. Turn the dough over. Pull down on the dough with cupped hands to stretch the top; pinch the edges at the bottom. Wrap your hands around the sides of the dough; rotate to shape into a tight ball, 5½ inches in diameter and 3¾ inches high. Place on the oiled baking sheet, seam side down.

8. Brush plastic wrap with the remaining teaspoon oil; cover the dough. Let rise until doubled in bulk, 45 minutes to 1 hour.

9. Preheat the oven to 400°F. Score an X in the top of the dough. Brush with egg white; sprinkle with the remaining tablespoon oats. Bake 10 minutes. Reduce oven temperature to 350°F. Bake until dark golden brown and the bottom sounds hollow when tapped, 40 to 45 minutes. Let cool completely on a wire rack.

socca

MAKES 8 WEDGES

2½ cups chickpea flour

½ cup extra-virgin olive oil, plus more for the skillet

   Coarse salt and freshly ground pepper

1 tablespoon chopped fresh rosemary

1. Heat the broiler with the rack 8 inches from the heat source. Stir together the flour, 2 cups water, the oil, and 1 tablespoon salt in a medium bowl.

2. Oil a 12-inch cast-iron skillet; pour in the batter. Broil until golden brown, 3 to 4 minutes. Reduce oven to 400°F; bake until set, about 6 minutes. Sprinkle with the rosemary; season with salt and pepper. Cut into 8 wedges, and serve.

cranberry bran muffins

MAKES 12

Store in an airtight container at room temperature for up to 3 days, or freeze for up to 1 month.

- 2 cups all-purpose flour
- 1½ cups wheat bran
- 1½ teaspoons baking powder
- ¾ teaspoon fine salt
- ¼ teaspoon baking soda
- 1½ cups packed dark-brown sugar
- 1¼ cups plus 2 tablespoons buttermilk
- 11 tablespoons (1⅜ sticks) unsalted butter, melted and cooled
- 2 large eggs
- 1 tablespoon finely grated orange zest
- 2 teaspoons pure vanilla extract
- 1½ cups fresh or frozen cranberries

1. Preheat the oven to 350° F. Line a 12-cup standard muffin tin with paper liners; set aside. Place the flour, bran, baking powder, salt, and baking soda in a large bowl. Stir in the sugar, and set aside.

2. Whisk together the buttermilk, butter, eggs, zest, and vanilla in a bowl. Add the flour mixture; stir until just combined. Stir in the cranberries.

3. Divide the batter among the lined muffin cups. Bake until cooked through and golden brown, about 30 minutes. Transfer to a wire rack to cool slightly. Turn out; serve warm or at room temperature.

banana bread with walnuts and flaxseed

MAKES 1 LOAF

You can store the banana bread, wrapped well in plastic wrap, at room temperature up to 4 days.

- 2 tablespoons unsalted butter, melted, plus 1 teaspoon unsalted butter, softened, for the pan
- ½ cup whole-wheat flour
- ¾ cup all-purpose flour
- ¼ cup ground golden flaxseed (from about 2 tablespoons whole)
- ¾ teaspoon coarse salt
- ½ teaspoon baking powder
- ½ teaspoon baking soda
- 1 large egg, plus 1 large egg white
- ½ cup light-brown sugar
- 1½ teaspoons pure vanilla extract
- ¾ cup mashed very ripe bananas (about 2 medium bananas)
- ½ cup walnuts (about 1¾ ounces), toasted and coarsely chopped

1. Preheat the oven to 350° F. Butter a 9 × 5 × 3-inch loaf pan, and set aside. Whisk together the flours, flaxseed, salt, baking powder, and baking soda in a medium bowl, and set aside.

2. Put the egg and egg white in the bowl of an electric mixer fitted with the paddle attachment, and mix on medium-low speed until well combined, about 2 minutes. Add the melted butter, sugar, vanilla, and bananas, and mix until combined. Add the reserved flour mixture, and mix on low speed until well incorporated, about 10 seconds. Stir in the walnuts.

3. Pour the batter into the buttered pan. Bake until golden brown and a cake tester inserted into the center comes out clean, about 35 minutes. Let cool slightly in the pan on a wire rack. Unmold onto rack, and let cool completely.

tomato focaccia

MAKES 8 PIECES

If you don't have a mixer, knead the dough by hand on a lightly floured surface until smooth, about 10 minutes.

- 2 tablespoons plus ½ teaspoon active dry yeast (from 2 envelopes)
- 4½ teaspoons sugar
- 2⅓ cups warm water (105° to 110°F)
- 5½ teaspoons extra-virgin olive oil, plus more for the bowl
- 6¼ cups plus 3 tablespoons all-purpose flour
  Coarse salt
- 1 cup grape tomatoes, halved lengthwise
- 1 tablespoon fresh rosemary

1. Stir together the yeast, sugar, and warm water in the bowl of an electric mixer fitted with the paddle attachment. Let stand until foamy, about 5 minutes.

2. Stir in 4½ teaspoons oil. Add the flour and 4½ teaspoons salt; mix on medium-low speed until combined. Switch to the dough hook; knead on medium speed until smooth, 5 to 7 minutes.

3. Transfer the dough to a lightly oiled large bowl. Loosely cover with plastic wrap; let the dough rise in a warm, draft-free spot until doubled in bulk, about 20 minutes.

4. Preheat the oven to 400°F. Generously oil a 12 × 17-inch rimmed baking sheet. Spread out the dough to fill the sheet, stretching it and working it into the corners. Press in the tomatoes; sprinkle with the rosemary. Loosely cover with oiled plastic wrap; let rest 30 minutes.

5. Drizzle the dough with the remaining teaspoon oil, and sprinkle with salt. Bake 5 minutes. Rotate the sheet; bake until golden, about 15 minutes more.

6. Let cool in the sheet; cut into 8 rectangles. If not serving that day, wrap the pieces in plastic wrap and foil; freeze up to 1 month.

challah

MAKES 1 LARGE LOAF

All ingredients except the milk and water should be at room temperature. This bread can be stored in a resealable plastic bag at room temperature for up to 2 days.

- 2 tablespoons unsalted butter, softened, plus more for bowl, plus 2 tablespoons, melted and cooled, for brushing
- 3½ cups unbleached bread flour, plus more for dusting
- ½ cup water, warmed to 100°F
- ⅓ cup sugar
- ¼ cup whole milk, warmed to 100°F
- 2 large eggs, lightly beaten, plus 1 large egg, lightly beaten, for egg wash
- 3 large egg yolks, lightly beaten
- 2 teaspoons coarse salt
- 2 teaspoons active dry yeast

1. Butter a large bowl; set aside. Stir all remaining ingredients, except the egg for the egg wash and the butter for brushing, in a large bowl until well combined. Turn out the dough onto a lightly floured work surface; knead the dough, adding flour if needed, until smooth and pliable, about 15 minutes.

2. Transfer the dough to the buttered bowl; brush the top with 1 tablespoon melted butter. Loosely cover with plastic wrap. Let rise in a warm place until almost doubled in bulk, about 1½ hours.

3. Turn out the dough onto a lightly floured work surface; knead 5 minutes, then return to the bowl. Brush the top with the remaining tablespoon melted butter, and loosely cover with plastic wrap. Let the dough rise again until doubled in bulk, about 1 hour more.

4. Preheat the oven to 375°F. Divide the dough into 3 equal pieces. Roll each piece into a ball, and loosely cover each ball with buttered plastic wrap. Let rest 20 minutes.

5. Roll each ball into a 12-inch-long log, leaving the middle a little thicker than the ends. Lay the logs side by side lengthwise; pinch together the ends farthest from you, then tightly braid the strands, pulling them as you go. Tuck the ends of the braid underneath. Transfer to a buttered baking sheet, and loosely cover with buttered plastic wrap. Let rise until almost doubled in bulk, about 45 minutes.

6. Brush the dough lightly with egg wash. Bake until golden brown and firm and an instant-read thermometer inserted into the bottom registers 180° F and comes out clean, 35 to 40 minutes. If the challah browns too quickly, loosely tent with foil. Immediately transfer to a wire rack; let cool at least 45 minutes before serving.

cornbread muffins

MAKES 12

- 5 tablespoons unsalted butter, melted, plus more for the muffin tin
- 1 cup stone-ground yellow cornmeal
- 1 cup all-purpose flour
- ¼ cup confectioners' sugar
- ¼ cup granulated sugar
- ½ teaspoon baking powder
- 1 teaspoon baking soda
- 1 teaspoon salt
- ½ vanilla bean, split lengthwise
- 2 large eggs
- 1½ cups buttermilk

MAKING CHALLAH

1. A dough that rises properly will approximately double in size; it will become smooth and puffy and feel very light. Punching down the dough releases excess gases that develop during rising—one or two good punches should be sufficient.

2. Separate the dough into thirds (use a kitchen scale to ensure they are of equal weight), and roll them into long strands.

To make a loaf that swells generously in the middle like ours does, leave the center of each strand thicker than the ends.

3. To braid, press the strand ends farthest from you together firmly, and then tuck them underneath to prevent the challah from unwinding while it rises.

4. Braid the strands tightly so the loaf is smooth and uniform.

1. Preheat the oven to 375°F. Brush a 12-cup standard muffin tin with melted butter; set aside. In a large bowl, whisk together the cornmeal, flour, sugars, baking powder, baking soda, and salt.

2. In a small bowl, scrape in the vanilla seeds; add the eggs and buttermilk, and whisk to combine. Pour over the flour mixture. Add the 5 tablespoons butter, and stir until blended, using as few strokes as possible.

3. Spoon the batter into the prepared tin, filling each cup three-quarters full. Bake until golden and firm to the touch, 17 to 20 minutes. Serve warm.

irish soda bread

MAKES ONE 7-INCH ROUND LOAF

Graham flour is coarser than regular whole-wheat flour, which also works. If you use the latter, substitute ½ cup wheat bran for ½ cup all-purpose flour.

- 3 cups all-purpose flour, plus more for dusting
- 1 cup whole-wheat graham flour
- 2½ teaspoons coarse salt
- 1 teaspoon baking soda
- 1 teaspoon baking powder
- 4 tablespoons cold unsalted butter, cut into small pieces
- 1⅔ cups buttermilk

1. Preheat the oven to 350°F. Line a baking sheet with parchment paper; set aside. Whisk together the flours, salt, baking soda, and baking powder in a large bowl. With a pastry blender or your fingertips, blend in the butter until it resembles small peas. Add the buttermilk all at once; stir with a fork until the mixture holds together.

2. In the bowl, pat the dough into a dome-shaped loaf about 7 inches in diameter. Lift out the dough; transfer to the lined sheet.

3. Lightly dust the top of the loaf with flour. Cut a ¾-inch-deep cross in the top, reaching almost all the way to the edges. Bake, rotating the sheet halfway through, until deep golden brown and a cake tester inserted into the center comes out clean, about 1 hour and 20 minutes. Let cool on a wire rack.

buttercup squash tea bread

MAKES ONE 9-INCH LOAF

- ½ cup (1 stick) unsalted butter, melted, plus more for the pan, room temperature
- 1½ cups all-purpose flour, plus more for the pan
- 1 teaspoon baking soda
- ½ teaspoon ground cinnamon
- ½ teaspoon ground nutmeg
- ½ teaspoon ground ginger
- ⅛ teaspoon ground cloves
- ¼ teaspoon salt
- 1 cup packed light-brown sugar
- 2 large eggs
- 1 cup Roasted Squash Puree made with buttercup squash (recipe follows)
- ½ cup coarsely chopped pecans

1. Preheat the oven to 350°F. Butter and flour a 9 × 5 × 3-inch loaf pan, and set aside. Into a large bowl, sift together the flour, baking soda, spices, and salt; set aside.

2. In a medium bowl, whisk together the sugar, eggs, squash puree, melted butter, and ¼ cup water. Fold the squash mixture into the flour mixture. Stir in the pecans.

3. Pour the batter into the prepared loaf pan, and bake until a cake tester inserted in the center comes out clean, about 1 hour. Turn the bread out onto a wire rack, and let cool completely.

roasted squash puree

MAKES ABOUT 2 1/4 CUPS

3 pounds squash, such as butternut,
   orange Hokkaido, or buttercup, halved
   and seeded

   Canola oil, for baking sheet

1. Preheat the oven to 400°F. Place the squash halves, skin side up, on an oiled rimmed baking sheet. Bake until fork-tender, about 1¼ hours. Remove from the oven. Turn over; let stand until cool enough to handle.

2. Scoop the flesh into a food processor, and discard the skin. Puree until smooth. Refrigerate squash puree in an airtight container up to 4 days or store in the freezer up to 1 month.

pumpkin molasses tea bread

MAKES ONE 9-INCH LOAF

We used apple juice to sweeten the bread, but this recipe is equally tasty made with orange juice or cranberry juice.

   Soft butter, for the pan

2 cups all-purpose flour, plus more
   for the pan

½ teaspoon baking powder

1 teaspoon baking soda

1 teaspoon salt

½ cup molasses

½ cup sugar

½ cup vegetable oil

2 large eggs, lightly beaten

1 cup Pumpkin Puree (recipe follows),
   or canned

2 tablespoons apple juice

½ cup roughly chopped dried cranberries

½ cup roughly chopped walnuts

8 ounces cream cheese, room temperature

¼ cup honey

1. Preheat the oven to 350°F. Butter and flour a 5 × 9-inch loaf pan; set aside. In a medium bowl, combine the flour, baking powder, baking soda, and salt; set aside.

2. In the bowl of an electric mixer fitted with the paddle attachment, beat the molasses, sugar, oil, eggs, pumpkin, and apple juice. Add the flour mixture; mix until combined. Fold in cranberries and walnuts. Spoon mixture into prepared pan, and bake until a cake tester inserted into the center comes out clean, about 1 hour. Let the bread sit for about 10 minutes, and then turn the bread out of the pan onto a wire rack to cool completely.

3. While the bread cools, make the frosting. Combine the cream cheese and honey in the bowl of an electric mixer fitted with the paddle attachment; beat until smooth and well combined. Once the bread is completely cooled, spread the top with frosting. Serve.

pumpkin puree

MAKES 3 CUPS

1 3½-pound pumpkin, such as Small Sugar
   Pie, cut in half

Preheat the oven to 425°F. Place the pumpkin cut side down on a baking pan; roast until tender, 50 to 60 minutes. Remove from the oven; let cool. Using a large spoon, scrape out and discard seeds. Remove the flesh; transfer to the bowl of a food processor. Process until completely pureed without any solid pieces, about 1 minute. Transfer to a bowl. Refrigerate up to several days or freeze up to 1 month.

jalapeño corn muffins

MAKES 12

- 8 tablespoons (1 stick) unsalted butter, plus more for the tin, melted
- ¾ cup nonfat buttermilk
- 2 large eggs
- ½ cup sour cream
- 1 cup yellow cornmeal
- 1 cup all-purpose flour
- ½ cup packed light-brown sugar
- 2 tablespoons baking powder
- 1 teaspoon coarse salt
- 2 jalapeño peppers, seeded and finely chopped
- ¼ cup plus 2 tablespoons fresh or frozen (thawed) corn kernels

  Unsalted butter, for serving

1. Preheat the oven to 375°F. Brush the cups of a standard 12-cup muffin tin with melted butter, and set aside. Whisk together the buttermilk, eggs, and sour cream in a medium bowl until combined, and set aside. Whisk together the cornmeal, flour, sugar, baking powder, salt, jalapeños, and corn in a large bowl until combined.

2. With a rubber spatula, fold the buttermilk mixture into the cornmeal mixture until well combined. Fold in the melted butter. Divide the batter among the muffin cups, filling each three-quarters full. Bake until a cake tester inserted into the centers comes out clean, about 25 minutes. Let the muffins cool in the tin 5 minutes. Turn out into a basket or bowl lined with a clean kitchen towel; cover to keep warm. Serve with butter.

olive oil biscuits

MAKES 26

- ½ cup extra-virgin olive oil
- ½ cup sugar
- ¼ teaspoon baking soda
- 1½ teaspoons fresh lemon juice
- ¼ cup dry white wine
- ¼ cup sesame seeds, plus more for sprinkling
- 2 teaspoons freshly grated lemon zest
- 1 teaspoon fennel seeds, crushed, plus more for sprinkling
- ½ teaspoon salt

  Pinch of freshly ground white pepper
- 1¾ cups plus 2 tablespoons all-purpose flour
- 1 large egg

1. Preheat the oven to 350°F with racks in the upper and lower thirds. In the bowl of an electric mixer fitted with the paddle attachment, beat the oil and sugar on medium speed, about 2 minutes. In a small bowl, dissolve the baking soda in the lemon juice; add to the oil mixture along with the wine, sesame seeds, zest, fennel seeds, salt, and white pepper. Beat until combined. Add the flour, and beat until just combined.

2. Line 2 baking sheets with parchment paper; set aside. In a small bowl, beat the egg with 2 teaspoons water; set aside. Form the biscuits by rolling table-spoons of dough into 5-inch logs and joining the ends to make circles. Brush the tops with egg wash; sprinkle with sesame seeds and fennel. Arrange on the prepared baking sheets, 1 inch apart. Bake the biscuits until lightly browned, about 20 minutes, rotating the sheets halfway through. Serve warm or at room temperature.

potato focaccia

MAKES ONE 12 × 18-INCH LOAF

Fingerlings are grown in yellow, pink, and blue varieties. For a special touch, use an assortment of them. Any small potatoes will work just as well as fingerlings.

- 7 tablespoons olive oil, plus more for the bowl and plastic wrap
- 1 pound assorted fingerling potatoes
- 4½ teaspoons coarse salt, plus more for seasoning
- 1 envelope active dry yeast (1 scant tablespoon)
- 6 cups all-purpose flour
- 1½ tablespoons fresh rosemary, coarsely chopped

  Freshly ground pepper

1. Pour 2 tablespoons olive oil into a 12 × 18-inch rimmed baking pan, and spread all over using your fingertips; set aside. Place half the potatoes in a small saucepan. Cover with cold water; place over high heat. Add 3 teaspoons salt when the water comes to a boil. Reduce heat to medium-high; cook until the potatoes are tender, 10 to 12 minutes. Drain in a colander, reserving the liquid. Pass through a potato ricer or a food mill and into a bowl; set aside.

2. Place ¼ cup reserved warm liquid into the bowl of an electric mixer fitted with the paddle attachment. Sprinkle in the yeast, and stir well; let stand until creamy, 5 to 10 minutes. Add 2¼ cups more reserved liquid, 2 tablespoons olive oil, and the reserved mashed potatoes; beat until combined. In a large bowl, whisk together the flour and remaining 1½ teaspoons salt; add to the potato mixture. Mix on low speed until the flour is incorporated, about 3 minutes. Change to the dough hook, and knead on medium-high until the dough is smooth and elastic and is slightly tacky when squeezed but does not stick to your fingers, 4 to 5 minutes.

3. Turn the dough out onto a clean surface, and knead into a ball. Place in a lightly oiled large bowl, cover with plastic wrap, and let stand at room temperature until doubled in size, 1 to 1½ hours.

4. Preheat the oven to 425°F. Spread the dough evenly in the prepared baking pan. Cover with oiled plastic wrap, and let stand in a warm place until the dough has filled the entire pan and has increased in size by about one-third, about 30 minutes.

5. Using a mandoline or a knife, slice the remaining potatoes into very thin rounds. Transfer to a bowl. Add half the rosemary and 1 tablespoon olive oil; season with salt and pepper. Toss to coat the potatoes well.

6. Remove the plastic wrap; dimple the dough with your fingertips, leaving deep indentations. Drizzle with the remaining 2 tablespoons oil. Gently press the reserved sliced potatoes into the dough. Sprinkle with the remaining rosemary. Bake until golden brown, 30 to 35 minutes. Remove from the oven; transfer to a wire rack. Serve warm.

julia dunlinson's potato griddle scones

MAKES 16

These British scones, created by the mother of *Martha Stewart Living* design director James Dunlinson, resemble small, thick pancakes.

- 1½ pounds russet potatoes, peeled and sliced
- 1 tablespoon unsalted butter, melted, plus more for the griddle
- ½ cup all-purpose flour, plus more for the work surface
- 1 teaspoon salt

  Butter and jam, for serving (optional)

1. Place the potatoes in a small saucepan; cover with cold water, and bring to a boil over high heat. Cook until very tender, about 12 minutes. Drain; transfer to a medium bowl. Using a potato ricer or a food mill, mash the potatoes (you should have 5 cups mashed). Add the melted butter, flour, and salt. Stir with a wooden spoon until the dough comes together. Transfer to a clean work surface; knead until smooth, being careful not to overwork the dough.

2. Heat a griddle over medium heat. Roll out the dough to ¾-inch thickness on a lightly floured surface. Using a 2½-inch cookie cutter, cut out rounds, and prick with a fork. Lightly butter the griddle; cook the scones in batches until golden brown, about 5 minutes per side. Transfer to a clean kitchen towel, keeping the scones covered while cooking the remaining scones. Serve warm with butter and jam, if desired.

buttermilk biscuits

MAKES 15

- 4 cups all-purpose flour, plus more for dusting
- 4 teaspoons baking powder
- 1 teaspoon baking soda
- 1½ teaspoons coarse salt
- 1 teaspoon sugar
- 1 cup (2 sticks) unsalted butter, cut into pieces
- 2 cups buttermilk

1. Preheat the oven to 375°F. In a medium bowl, whisk the flour, baking powder, baking soda, salt, and sugar. Using a pastry blender or 2 knives, cut in the butter until the mixture resembles coarse crumbs.

2. Add the buttermilk; stir just until the mixture comes together; the batter will be sticky. Transfer to a lightly floured work surface; use your floured fingers to pat the dough to 1-inch thickness. Use a 2½-inch round biscuit cutter or cookie cutter to cut out the biscuits, as close together as possible to minimize scraps.

3. Transfer to a baking sheet; bake for 18 to 20 minutes, or until lightly browned. Remove from the oven; cool on a wire rack. Serve warm.

CHEDDAR MIX-IN *Add 3 cups (9 ounces) grated Cheddar cheese to the butter and flour mixture after the butter has been cut in. Proceed with the remainder of the recipe.*

cornmeal drop biscuits

MAKES 10

- 1½ cups all-purpose flour
- 1 cup yellow cornmeal, preferably stone-ground
- 2½ teaspoons baking powder
- ½ teaspoon salt
- 2 teaspoons sugar
- ½ cup (1 stick) unsalted butter
- 1 cup plus 1 tablespoon milk

1. Preheat the oven to 375°F. In a medium bowl, combine the flour, cornmeal, baking powder, salt, and sugar. Whisk to combine. Add the butter, and, using a pastry blender or 2 knives, cut it in until the mixture resembles coarse crumbs.

2. Add the milk, and stir until just combined.

3. Spoon 10 mounds, about ½ cup each, onto a baking sheet 1 inch apart; bake until the biscuits start to brown, about 20 minutes. Remove from the oven; cool on a wire rack. Serve warm.

BACON AND ONION MIX-IN *Cut 6 ounces bacon into ½-inch pieces, and cook over medium heat, stirring occasionally, until crisp, about 4 minutes. Using a slotted spoon, transfer to a paper-towel–lined bowl. Add 1 small onion, cut into ¼-inch dice, to the hot fat in the skillet; cook until translucent, about 3 minutes. Drain on paper towels. Add the bacon and onion to the butter and flour mixture after the butter has been cut in. Proceed with the recipe.*

angel biscuits

MAKES 24

Yeast is used as part of the leavening to give these biscuits the light, airy texture that inspired their name.

- 6 cups all-purpose flour, plus more for dusting
- 2 teaspoons sugar
- 1 teaspoon baking soda
- 1 tablespoon baking powder
- 1½ teaspoons coarse salt
- 1 envelope active dry yeast (1 scant tablespoon)
- ¼ cup warm water (105° to 110°F)
- 1 cup (2 sticks) butter, melted and cooled to 115°F
- 2 cups buttermilk, room temperature

1. In a medium bowl, sift or whisk together the flour, sugar, baking soda, baking powder, and salt; set aside. Sprinkle the yeast over the warm water, and allow to stand until creamy looking, about 5 minutes.

2. In a medium bowl, combine 1 cup of the flour mixture and the yeast mixture, melted butter, and 1 cup buttermilk. Stir to combine. Add the remaining flour and buttermilk alternately, stirring between additions. When a sticky dough forms, cover it with plastic wrap; refrigerate 2 hours.

3. Preheat the oven to 450°F. Remove the dough from the refrigerator, and turn out onto a lightly floured work surface. Knead a few times, and roll to a ½-inch thickness. Cut out with a 2¼-inch round biscuit or cookie cutter, and place on a baking sheet about 1 inch apart. Bake 12 to 15 minutes or until golden on top and done in the middle. Remove from the oven; cool on a wire rack. Serve warm.

creamed corn bread

MAKES ONE 8-INCH-SQUARE BREAD

- 2 tablespoons unsalted butter, melted, plus more for pan
- 1 cup all-purpose flour
- ¾ cup yellow cornmeal
- 1 tablespoon baking powder
- ½ teaspoon coarse salt
- ½ cup milk
- ½ cup sour cream
- 1 large egg
- ⅓ cup sugar
- 1 14¾-ounce can creamed corn

1. Preheat the oven to 425°F. Brush an 8-inch-square baking pan with butter. Set aside.

2. Combine the flour, cornmeal, baking powder, and salt in a medium mixing bowl.

3. Whisk together the milk, sour cream, egg, sugar, and butter in a small bowl. Stir in the creamed corn. Fold the wet ingredients into the dry ingredients until well combined.

4. Pour the batter into the prepared pan; bake until set and golden brown, about 30 minutes. Cool slightly on a wire rack before cutting into squares.

oyster biscuits

MAKES ABOUT 24

These biscuits are inspired by the oyster crackers that traditionally accompany bowls of creamy clam chowder. You can make the biscuits up to 1 week ahead; store them in an airtight container at room temperature.

1   cup all-purpose flour, plus more
    for the work surface
¾   teaspoon coarse salt, plus more for
    sprinkling
1   teaspoon baking powder
½   teaspoon ground cumin or coriander
    Pinch of cayenne pepper
2   tablespoons unsalted butter or shortening
½   cup milk

1. Preheat the oven to 350°F. Place the flour, salt, baking powder, cumin or coriander, and cayenne in the bowl of a food processor fitted with the metal blade; pulse to combine. Add the butter or shortening; pulse until coarse crumbs form. With the machine running, add the milk slowly through the feed tube, just until the dough comes together.

2. Turn out the dough onto a lightly floured surface, and knead once or twice until smooth. Roll out to ¼ inch thick. Sprinkle with salt, and roll lightly to make it adhere. Using a 1½-inch round or octagonal cookie cutter, cut out the dough, and transfer to an ungreased baking sheet. Gather together the scraps; reroll to cut out additional biscuits, if desired. Bake until golden, about 20 minutes. Transfer the pan to a wire rack to cool slightly before serving.

sweet-milk biscuits

MAKES ABOUT 20

5   cups all-purpose flour, plus
     more for dusting
2   tablespoons sugar
2   tablespoons baking powder
1   tablespoon coarse salt
¾   cup cold lard or vegetable shortening,
     cut into pieces
¼   cup cold unsalted butter, cut into
     pieces, plus ¼ cup melted butter
1¾   cups whole milk

1. Preheat the oven to 375°F. Whisk together flour, sugar, baking powder, and salt in a medium bowl. Work lard and butter into flour mixture with a pastry cutter or your fingers until largest pieces are the size of small peas. Add milk, and stir with a fork until a dough forms.

2. Turn out dough onto a lightly floured surface, and pat out to 1 inch thick. Cut out rounds with a floured 2¼-inch biscuit cutter. Space 2 inches apart on a baking sheet lined with parchment paper. Gather together scraps, and repeat.

3. Brush tops with melted butter. Bake until light-golden brown on top and cooked through, about 25 minutes. Transfer to a wire rack to cool 5 minutes before serving.

rosemary-oatmeal tea breads

MAKES THREE 6-INCH LOAVES

3 large sprigs fresh rosemary,
  plus 1 tablespoon finely chopped

1 large egg white, lightly beaten,
  plus 1 large egg

  Superfine or granulated sugar,
  for dusting

5 tablespoons unsalted butter,
  softened, plus more for pans

1½ cups all-purpose flour

½ cup plus 2 tablespoons sugar

¾ teaspoon salt

2 teaspoons baking powder

½ teaspoon ground cinnamon

¾ cup whole milk

1 cup old-fashioned rolled oats

1. Brush rosemary sprigs with egg white. Lightly dust with sugar. Set aside.

2. Preheat the oven to 350°F. Lightly butter three 6 × 2-inch loaf pans. Whisk together flour, sugar, salt, baking powder, and cinnamon in a large bowl; set aside.

3. Melt butter with milk and chopped rosemary in a small saucepan over low heat. Remove from heat, and stir in oats. Let cool slightly. Whisk whole egg into oat mixture; add to flour mixture, and stir just until flour is incorporated.

4. Divide batter evenly among prepared pans. Place 1 sugared rosemary sprig on top of each loaf. Bake until tops are deep golden brown, 25 to 30 minutes. Let cool in pans on a wire rack 10 minutes. Turn out onto rack; let cool completely. Store in an airtight container at room temperature up to 3 days.

cream scones

MAKES 8 TO 10

2 cups all-purpose flour, plus more for
  work surface, hands, and cutter

3 tablespoons sugar, plus more for
  sprinkling

1 tablespoon baking powder

½ teaspoon salt

6 tablespoons cold unsalted butter,
  cut into small pieces

⅓ cup heavy cream, plus more for brushing

2 large eggs, lightly beaten
  Strawberry preserves, for serving
  Softly whipped cream, for serving

1. Preheat the oven to 400°F. Line a baking sheet with parchment paper; set aside.

2. Sift together the flour, sugar, baking powder, and salt into a large bowl. Using a pastry blender or 2 knives, cut in butter until largest pieces are the size of small peas.

3. Using a fork, whisk together the cream and eggs in a large glass measuring cup. Make a well in the center of flour mixture, and pour in cream mixture. Stir lightly with fork just until the dough comes together (do not overmix).

4. Turn out dough onto a lightly floured work surface. With floured hands, gently pat dough into a 4½ × 8½-inch rectangle, about ¾ inch thick. Using a floured 2-inch round cutter, cut out 8 to 10 rounds, and transfer them to lined baking sheet. Brush tops with cream, and sprinkle with sugar. Bake scones until golden brown, 16 to 20 minutes. Transfer scones to wire racks, and let cool. Serve warm or at room temperature, topped with strawberry preserves and whipped cream.

carrot tea cake

SERVES 10 TO 12

- 10 tablespoons (1¼ sticks) unsalted butter, softened, plus more for mold
- 1¼ cups all-purpose flour, plus more for mold
- ½ cup plus 2 tablespoons packed light-brown sugar
- 2 large eggs
- 1½ teaspoons pure vanilla extract
- 1 cup packed peeled grated carrots (4 to 5 carrots)
- 1 teaspoon baking powder
- 1 teaspoon coarse salt
- ½ teaspoon baking soda
- ½ cup walnuts, toasted, finely chopped
- 1 teaspoon confectioners' sugar

1. Preheat the oven to 350° F. Butter a 9-inch (5-cup) trois frères mold or Bundt pan. Dust with flour, and tap out excess. Put butter and brown sugar into the bowl of an electric mixer fitted with the paddle attachment. Mix on medium-high speed until pale and fluffy, about 3 minutes.

2. Add eggs, one at a time, mixing well after each addition. Add the vanilla and carrots, and mix until just combined. Reduce speed to low. Add flour, baking powder, salt, and baking soda. Mix until just combined. Stir in walnuts.

3. Pour batter into the prepared mold. Bake until a cake tester inserted into center comes out clean, about 30 minutes. Let cool in pan on a wire rack 15 minutes. Turn out cake onto rack, and let cool completely. Before serving, dust with confectioners' sugar. The cake can be stored in an airtight container at room temperature up to 3 days.

polenta quick bread with lemon and thyme

MAKES ONE 9-INCH LOAF

- ¾ cup (1½ sticks) unsalted butter, softened, plus more for pan
- ⅓ cup all-purpose flour, plus more for pan
- ¾ cup sugar
- 1 tablespoon finely grated lemon zest, plus 2 tablespoons fresh lemon juice
- 3 large eggs
- 1 tablespoon coarsely chopped fresh thyme leaves, plus sprigs for garnish
- 1 cup fine yellow cornmeal (preferably stone-ground)
- 1 teaspoon baking powder
- ¾ teaspoon coarse salt
- ¼ cup pine nuts, toasted, half coarsely chopped and half whole

1. Preheat the oven to 325° F. Butter a 9 × 5-inch loaf pan. Dust with flour; tap out excess. Put butter and sugar into the bowl of an electric mixer fitted with the paddle attachment. Mix on medium-high speed until pale and fluffy, about 3 minutes.

2. Add lemon zest; mix 1 minute. Add eggs, one at a time, mixing well after each addition. Mix in lemon juice and thyme. Add flour, cornmeal, baking powder, and salt, and mix until just combined. Stir in chopped pine nuts.

3. Pour batter into prepared pan. Sprinkle with whole pine nuts. Bake until a tester inserted into the center comes out clean, 50 to 55 minutes. Let cool completely on a wire rack. Garnish with thyme. The bread can be stored in an airtight container at room temperature up to 2 days.

breakfast
AND
brunch

. . . .

herb frittata with zucchini and yellow squash

SERVES 6

1 tablespoon unsalted butter

2½ tablespoons olive oil

7 large eggs

¼ cup heavy cream or milk

¼ cup coarsely chopped fresh chives, plus whole chives for garnish

¼ cup coarsely chopped fresh flat-leaf parsley

½ teaspoon coarsely chopped fresh thyme

¼ teaspoon finely chopped fresh marjoram

½ teaspoon coarse salt

Freshly ground pepper

1 small zucchini, cut crosswise into thin rounds

1 small yellow summer squash, cut crosswise into thin rounds

1. Heat the butter with 1½ tablespoons oil in a 10-inch ovenproof nonstick skillet over medium-low heat until melted.

2. Preheat the broiler, with the rack about 7 inches from the heat source. Meanwhile, whisk together the eggs, cream, and herbs until well blended. Stir in the salt, and season with pepper.

3. Add the egg mixture to the skillet; cook until the bottom is set and golden, about 4 minutes. Continue to cook, gently shaking the pan occasionally, until 1 inch of the edges is almost set, about 4 minutes more. Remove from heat. Gently press the zucchini and squash on top, overlapping slightly in concentric circles.

4. Broil (checking often) until golden and just cooked through in center, 1 to 2 minutes. Gently slide onto a plate with a spatula; drizzle with the remaining tablespoon oil. Garnish with whole chives.

blueberry buttermilk flapjacks

MAKES 10

1¾ cups all-purpose flour

3½ tablespoons sugar

1 tablespoon baking powder

½ teaspoon coarse salt

1½ cups buttermilk

2 large eggs, room temperature

1 teaspoon pure vanilla extract

1 tablespoon unsalted butter, melted, plus more, softened, for the skillet and serving

2 tablespoons plus 2 teaspoons vegetable oil

1 cup blueberries, plus more for garnish

Pure maple syrup, for serving

1. Sift together the flour, sugar, baking powder, and salt. Whisk together the buttermilk, eggs, vanilla, 1 tablespoon butter, and 2 tablespoons oil; whisk into the flour mixture. Fold in the blueberries. Set batter aside.

2. Heat ½ teaspoon butter and 2 teaspoons oil in a large nonstick skillet over medium heat. Pour in ⅓ cup batter. Cook until small bubbles form, about 3 minutes. Flip; cook until golden brown, about 3 minutes. Repeat with the remaining batter, adding butter as needed. Serve with butter and syrup; garnish with berries.

coddled eggs with fines herbes

SERVES 4

The easiest way to coddle eggs is to place them in egg coddlers, special containers with tight-fitting lids, but you can also use ramekins or custard cups covered tightly with foil. Fines herbes is a combination of chopped fresh herbs, most often those below, but sometimes including others such as marjoram or savory.

> *Nonstick cooking spray*
>
> 1 *slice whole-wheat bread, crusts removed, cut into ¼-inch cubes, for garnish*
>
> *Freshly ground pepper*
>
> 1 *tablespoon finely chopped fresh chives*
>
> 2 *tablespoons finely chopped fresh chervil*
>
> 1 *tablespoon finely chopped fresh tarragon*
>
> 1 *tablespoon finely chopped fresh flat-leaf parsley*
>
> 4 *large whole eggs*
>
> 4 *large egg whites*
>
> 1 *tablespoon plus 1 teaspoon heavy cream*
>
> 1 *teaspoon coarse salt*

1. Preheat the oven to 350°F. Lightly coat 4 egg coddlers with cooking spray, and set aside. Lightly coat a rimmed baking sheet with cooking spray. Place the bread cubes on the baking sheet; sprinkle with pepper. Bake until golden and crisp on all sides, turning them once during cooking, about 7 minutes. Remove from the oven; set aside.

2. Line the bottom of a large saucepan with a kitchen towel, and fill with enough water to come just below the rim of the egg coddlers. Place the pan over medium-high heat; bring the water to a boil. Combine the herbs in a small bowl, and mix well. Place 2 teaspoons mixed herbs in the bottom of each coddler; to each, add 1 whole egg and 1 egg white, and drizzle with 1 teaspoon heavy cream. Add ¼ teaspoon salt to each, and season with pepper. Screw lids on tightly.

3. Using tongs, carefully place the egg coddlers in the boiling water. Reduce heat to medium, and simmer 6 minutes. Turn off heat; cover the pan, and let stand 4 to 5 minutes. Remove the coddlers from the pan, and remove the lids. Serve the eggs in the coddlers. Top each with a few croutons, and garnish with the remaining mixed herbs.

FIT TO EAT RECIPE PER SERVING: 127 CALORIES, 7 G FAT, 219 MG CHOLESTEROL, 4 G CARBOHYDRATE, 628 MG SODIUM, 11 G PROTEIN, 0 G FIBER

PEELING HARD-COOKED EGGS

The fresher the egg, the harder it is to peel. This is because peelability is affected by the pH of the egg white; when the pH is below 8.9, the inner membrane tends to adhere to the albumen (egg white). Fresh eggs often have a pH of around 8.0. You might want to consider leaving fresh eggs in the refrigerator for at least 3 days before boiling them, or even longer; eggs can be safely refrigerated for up to 1 month.

After boiling the eggs, transfer them immediately to a bowl of ice water, and let them stand for 10 minutes to stop the cooking (cold eggs are easier to peel). To peel an egg, place it on your work surface, and roll it under your palm to crack the shell. Holding the egg under cold running water as you peel it can also help.

toad-in-the-hole

SERVES 4

2   large eggs
⅔   cup milk
1   tablespoon Dijon mustard
    Coarse salt and freshly ground pepper
½   cup all-purpose flour
3   tablespoons vegetable oil or bacon fat
5   English-style fresh pork sausages,
    casings removed
1   tablespoon chopped fresh rosemary
    Onion Gravy (recipe follows)

1. Preheat the oven to 425° F. In a medium bowl, whisk together the eggs, milk, ⅔ cup water, and mustard; season with salt and pepper. Whisk in the flour. Let stand 20 minutes.

2. Coat a 13 × 9-inch or 3½-quart baking dish with the oil; heat in the oven 10 minutes. Remove from the oven. Pour the batter into the dish. Arrange the sausages on top; sprinkle with rosemary. Bake until puffed, 25 to 30 minutes. Serve with gravy.

onion gravy

MAKES 1 CUP

3   tablespoons unsalted butter
2   medium onions, halved and thinly sliced
1   tablespoon all-purpose flour
⅓   cup Madeira wine
1   cup homemade or low-sodium store-
    bought chicken stock
½   teaspoon Worcestershire sauce
    Coarse salt and freshly ground pepper

1. Melt the butter in a large skillet over medium heat. Cook the onions, stirring, until golden, 10 to 15 minutes. Cover; cook over low heat until brown, about 25 minutes.

2. Add the flour. Cook, stirring constantly, 2 minutes. Remove from heat; whisk in the wine, stock, and Worcestershire sauce. Bring to a boil. Reduce heat; simmer until thick, about 10 minutes. Season with salt and pepper. Serve immediately.

strawberry-rhubarb coffee cake

SERVES 15

The batter for this cake is much like that for a biscuit; the chilled butter is cut in rather than creamed to produce a tender crumb. This recipe was developed by Emily Donahue for Rosey's Coffee and Tea in Hanover, New Hampshire.

1¼ cups chilled unsalted butter,
    plus more, softened, for the pan
¼   cup freshly squeezed lemon juice
    (about 2 lemons)
⅓   cup cornstarch
2¾ cups sugar
1   pound strawberries, hulled and sliced
1½ pounds rhubarb, trimmed and
    cut into 1-inch pieces
3¾ cups all-purpose flour
1   teaspoon baking powder
½   teaspoon baking soda
    Pinch of salt
2   large eggs
1½ cups buttermilk
1   teaspoon pure vanilla extract

1. Preheat the oven to 350° F. Brush a 9 × 12 × 3-inch baking pan with butter, and set aside. Make the fruit sauce: Combine the lemon juice, cornstarch, and 1 cup sugar in a medium saucepan. Add the strawberries and rhubarb; cook, stirring frequently, over medium heat, until the rhubarb is soft and the liquid has thickened, 15 to 20 minutes. Transfer to a medium bowl; let cool.

2. Make the crumb topping: Combine ¾ cup sugar and ¾ cup flour in a medium bowl. Melt ¼ cup butter in a small saucepan over low heat. Drizzle the butter over the flour mixture; using your hands, mix until crumbly. Set aside.

3. Make the cake batter: Whisk together the remaining 3 cups flour and 1 cup sugar, baking powder, baking soda, and salt in a large bowl. Using a pastry knife or 2 forks, cut the butter into the flour mixture until it resembles coarse meal. In a separate bowl, mix the eggs, buttermilk, and vanilla. Pour into the flour mixture; stir to combine.

4. Spread half the cake batter evenly into the prepared pan. Top with half the fruit sauce. Carefully spread the remaining batter over the fruit, and top with the remaining fruit sauce. Sprinkle with the crumb topping.

5. Bake until the cake is golden brown and springs back when touched in the center, about 1 hour. Transfer the pan to a wire rack to cool slightly. Serve warm or at room temperature, cut into squares.

steel-cut oat porridge

SERVES 4

Steel-cut oats (also called Irish or Scottish oats) take longer to cook than rolled oats but are creamier and chewier.

- 1¼ cups skim milk
- 1 whole cinnamon stick
- ¼ teaspoon coarse salt
- 1 cup steel-cut oats
- 1 banana
- 4 Medjool dates, coarsely chopped
- 2 tablespoons brown flaxseed

1. Bring 3 cups water, 1 cup milk, the cinnamon stick, and the salt to a boil in a medium saucepan. Stir in the oats. Return to a boil. Reduce heat; partially cover. Cook, stirring occasionally, until the mixture is thick and the oats are tender, about 25 minutes. Discard the cinnamon stick.

2. Cut the banana crosswise into ¼-inch-thick rounds. Top the porridge with the banana and dates. Sprinkle with flaxseed. Drizzle each serving with 1 tablespoon milk.

SOAKING STEEL-CUT OATS

Steel-cut oats, also known as Irish or Scottish oats, are the result of chopping the whole oat grains into small pieces with steel blades. Rolled (or old-fashioned) oats, on the other hand, are steamed and flattened before being cut to make them more tender. For this reason, they cook much faster than the steel-cut variety and are often preferred as an everyday option. But if you prefer the pleasantly chewy texture offered by steel-cut oats, there is a way to reduce the cooking time by almost half without sacrificing taste or texture. Simply soak the oats overnight in a pot of water to begin softening the very hard coating that surrounds each grain. Bring the water to a boil before stirring in the oats to jump-start the softening process, and then allow the mixture to come back to room temperature and sit, covered, overnight. In the morning, all you will need to do is warm the oats over medium-low heat, stir, and serve.

Even if you don't have time to or forget to soak the oats, you can still make them in the morning; it will just take a little bit longer. Stir the oats into boiling, salted water, and simmer for about half an hour. Don't stir too often; it will break up the grains and make the texture gluey.

You might also decide to toast the oats before cooking to bring out their nutty flavor. Simply heat a little melted butter over medium heat and toast the oats, tossing them gently in the pan or stirring a little with a spoon, until brown and fragrant. Then cook in simmering water.

cottage cheese pancakes with lemon

MAKES 24; SERVES 6

After making the batter, cook the pancakes immediately to ensure they retain their volume.

- 6 large eggs, separated, yolks lightly beaten
  Pinch of cream of tartar
- 2 cups 2% cottage cheese
- ¼ cup granulated sugar
- ⅔ cup all-purpose flour
- ½ teaspoon baking powder
- ¼ teaspoon coarse salt
- ¼ teaspoon ground cinnamon
  Vegetable oil cooking spray
- 1 tablespoon confectioners' sugar
- 2 lemons (1 zested; 1 cut into wedges)

1. Beat the egg whites on medium-high speed until foamy. Add the cream of tartar; beat until stiff, glossy peaks form.

2. Heat a griddle or large skillet over medium-high heat. Stir together the yolks, cottage cheese, granulated sugar, flour, baking powder, salt, and cinnamon in a medium bowl. Whisk in one-third of the whites. In 2 batches, gently fold in the remaining whites with a rubber spatula.

3. Spray a griddle with cooking spray; heat until a drop of batter sizzles upon contact. Working in batches, pour ¼ cup batter per pancake onto the griddle; cook until the surfaces bubble and the edges are slightly dry, about 1 minute. Flip the pancakes; cook until the undersides are golden brown, about 3 minutes more. Divide the confectioners' sugar among the pancakes. Serve sprinkled with lemon zest and with lemon wedges on the side.

FIT TO EAT RECIPE PER SERVING: 218 CALORIES, 6 G FAT, 216 MG CHOLESTEROL, 23 G CARBOHYDRATE, 152 MG SODIUM, 17 G PROTEIN, 1 G FIBER

poached eggs with spinach and tomatoes

SERVES 4

- 4 large eggs
- 1 tablespoon olive oil
- 16 grape tomatoes, halved crosswise
- 1 teaspoon coarse salt
  Freshly ground pepper
- 8 ounces baby or regular spinach, tough stems discarded (about 16 cups)
- 1 garlic clove
- 2 tablespoons distilled white vinegar
- 1 tablespoon finely chopped fresh chives

1. Fill a large, shallow, straight-sided pan with 2 inches water. Bring to a boil. Break each egg into a small ramekin.

2. Meanwhile, heat the oil in a medium nonstick skillet over medium heat until hot but not smoking. Add the tomatoes; cook, stirring, until they start to break down, about 5 minutes. Add the salt; season with pepper. Transfer to a plate; tent with foil to keep warm. Add the spinach and garlic to the skillet; cook, stirring, until the spinach has just wilted, 1 to 2 minutes. Discard the garlic.

3. When the water is boiling, add the vinegar; turn off heat. Using tongs, tilt the ramekins in the pan, and slide the eggs into the water. Cover; let stand until the whites are opaque and the yolks are cooked as desired, 2 to 3 minutes. Use a slotted spoon to put the eggs on paper towels to drain. Trim the whites, if desired.

4. Divide the spinach among 4 plates; lay 1 poached egg and 8 tomato halves on top. Season with pepper; sprinkle each serving with ¾ teaspoon chives.

NOTE: *Partially cooked eggs should not be prepared for pregnant women, babies, young children, the elderly, or anyone whose health is compromised.*

FIT TO EAT RECIPE PER SERVING: 209 CALORIES, 14 G FAT, 425 MG CHOLESTEROL, 7 G CARBOHYDRATE, 457 MG SODIUM, 15 G PROTEIN, 2 G FIBER

bread pudding with ham, leeks, and cheese

SERVES 6 TO 8

Using both Gruyère and fontina gives this savory dish complex flavor—and they melt beautifully. If you use only Gruyère, just double the amount. You can assemble most of this dish up to 1 day ahead and refrigerate, covered; then add the batter, and bake.

- 2 tablespoons unsalted butter, plus more for the dish
- 1 bunch leeks (4 to 6), white and pale-green parts only, halved lengthwise, cut into ¼-inch-thick half-moons, and rinsed well (about 3 heaping cups)
- 1 teaspoon coarse salt, plus more for seasoning
- ¼ teaspoon freshly ground pepper, plus more for seasoning
- 8 large eggs
- 1 quart milk
- 8 slices challah or brioche (½ inch thick)
- 6 ounces thinly sliced ham
- 2 tablespoons thyme leaves
- 1 cup grated Gruyère cheese (4 ounces)
- 1 cup grated fontina cheese (4 ounces)

1. Preheat the oven to 325° F. Butter a 9 × 13-inch casserole dish. Heat the butter in a medium skillet over medium heat. Cook the leeks, covered, until softened, about 5 minutes. Season with salt and pepper, and transfer to a small bowl.

2. Whisk together the eggs and milk. Whisk in the salt and pepper. Set the batter aside.

3. Layer the bread, ham, reserved leeks, thyme, and cheeses shingle-style in the buttered dish. Pour the batter over the top; press gently so the bread absorbs the liquid.

4. Bake until puffed and golden brown (tent with foil if the edges brown too much before the center is set), about 1 hour.

yogurt parfaits with blueberries and lemon

SERVES 6

You can prepare the blueberry sauce and the lemony yogurt up to 2 days ahead, and refrigerate both in airtight containers. To serve, simply spoon the layers into juice glasses and garnish.

- 3 containers blueberries (4.4 ounces each; about 3 cups)
- ½ cup confectioners' sugar
- 1 quart plain whole-milk yogurt, preferably Greek
- 1 teaspoon fresh lemon juice, plus
- 2 teaspoons freshly grated lemon zest

1. Set aside ½ cup blueberries for garnish. Put the remaining blueberries and ¼ cup sugar in a medium saucepan. Cover; cook over medium heat 5 minutes. Uncover; cook, tossing occasionally, until the berries begin to darken, 2 to 3 minutes. Bring to a boil; cook 1 minute more. Pour into a medium nonreactive bowl; let cool completely.

2. Put the yogurt, remaining ¼ cup sugar, and lemon juice in a medium bowl. Set aside ½ teaspoon lemon zest for garnish. Very finely chop the remaining 1½ teaspoons lemon zest, then stir it into the yogurt. Set the yogurt aside.

3. Divide the blueberry sauce evenly among 6 juice glasses. Divide the yogurt among the glasses, and spoon over sauce. Sprinkle with the reserved berries and zest. If not serving immediately, refrigerate, covered with plastic wrap, up to 3 hours.

quiche lorraine

All-purpose flour, for dusting

Tart Dough (recipe follows)

10 *ounces slab bacon, cut into ¾ × ¼ × ¼-inch strips*

3 *large eggs*

2 *cups heavy cream*

¾ *teaspoon coarse salt*

¼ *teaspoon freshly ground pepper*

1. On a lightly floured work surface, roll out the dough to ¼ inch thick. Cut out a 13-inch circle from the dough. Press the dough circle onto the bottom and up the sides of an 11-inch tart pan with a removable bottom; trim the dough flush with the top edge of the pan. Prick the bottom all over with a fork. Transfer to a rimmed baking sheet. Freeze until firm, about 30 minutes. Preheat the oven to 400° F.

2. Line the tart shell with parchment paper, and fill with pie weights or dried beans. Bake until the dough starts to feel firm on the edges, about 20 minutes. Remove the parchment and weights; continue baking until the crust is pale golden brown, about 10 minutes. Let cool completely on a wire rack. Leave the oven on.

3. Cook the bacon in a large skillet over medium heat until browned, about 10 minutes. Transfer with a slotted spoon to paper towels to drain.

4. Whisk the eggs, cream, salt, and pepper in a medium bowl. Pour the mixture into the tart shell, and scatter the bacon strips on top. Bake until puffed and pale golden brown, about 30 minutes. Let cool at least 30 minutes before serving.

tart dough

1¾ *cups all-purpose flour*

¼ *teaspoon coarse salt*

¼ *cup coarsely chopped chives, rosemary, or thyme (optional)*

9 *tablespoons (1⅛ sticks) cold unsalted butter, cut into small pieces*

1 *large egg plus 1 large egg yolk, beaten*

3 *tablespoons ice water*

Process the flour, salt, and herbs (if using) in a food processor until combined. Add the butter, and process just until the mixture resembles coarse meal. Whisk together the egg mixture and the water in a small bowl. With the processor running, pour in the egg mixture; process until the dough starts to come together. Shape the dough into a disk. Wrap in plastic wrap, and refrigerate at least 30 minutes.

caramelized onion and gorgonzola quiche

MAKES ONE 8 × 11-INCH QUICHE

All-purpose flour, for dusting
Tart Dough (opposite)
1 tablespoon extra-virgin olive oil
1 pound onions, cut crosswise into rings
2 large eggs
½ cup milk
½ cup heavy cream
1 teaspoon coarse salt
Freshly ground pepper
2 ounces Gorgonzola dolce

1. On a lightly floured work surface, roll out the dough to ¼ inch thick. Press the dough onto the bottom and up the sides of an 8 × 11-inch rectangular tart pan with a removable bottom; trim the dough flush with the top edge of the pan. Prick the bottom all over with a fork. Transfer to a large rimmed baking sheet. Freeze until firm, about 30 minutes. Preheat the oven to 400°F.

2. Line the tart shell with parchment paper, and fill with pie weights or dried beans. Bake until the dough starts to feel firm on the edges, about 20 minutes. Remove the parchment and weights; continue baking until the crust is pale golden brown, about 10 minutes. Let cool completely on a wire rack. Leave the oven on.

3. Heat the oil in a large, heavy-bottomed skillet over low heat until hot but not smoking. Cook the onions, stirring frequently, until golden brown, about 30 minutes. Let cool.

4. Whisk the eggs, milk, cream, and salt in a medium bowl; season with pepper. Crumble in the cheese, and stir in the caramelized onions. Pour the mixture into the tart shell; bake until puffed and pale golden brown, 30 to 35 minutes. Let cool at least 30 minutes before serving.

salmon, pea, and mint quiche

MAKES ONE 11½-INCH QUICHE

All-purpose flour, for dusting
Tart Dough with chives (opposite)
1 salmon fillet (about 1 pound), skinned
3 large eggs
1 cup milk
1 cup heavy cream
2 tablespoons Dijon mustard
1½ teaspoons coarse salt
½ teaspoon freshly ground pepper
1 cup shelled fresh peas or thawed frozen peas
⅓ cup finely shredded fresh mint

1. On a lightly floured work surface, roll out the dough to ¼ inch thick. Cut out a 14-inch circle from the dough. Press the dough circle onto the bottom and up the sides of an 11½-inch round ceramic quiche dish; trim the dough flush with the top edge of the dish. Prick the bottom all over with a fork. Transfer to a rimmed baking sheet. Freeze until firm, about 30 minutes. Preheat the oven to 400°F.

2. Line the tart shell with parchment paper, and fill with pie weights or dried beans. Bake until the dough starts to feel firm on the edges, about 20 minutes. Remove the parchment and weights; continue baking until the crust is pale golden brown, about 10 minutes. Let cool completely on a wire rack. Leave the oven on.

3. Fill a wide medium saucepan halfway with water; bring to a simmer over medium heat. Add the salmon; simmer until opaque but still pink in middle, about 11 minutes. Remove the salmon; let cool.

4. Flake the salmon with a fork; set aside. Whisk the eggs, milk, cream, mustard, salt, and pepper in a large bowl. Stir in the salmon, peas, and mint. Pour the mixture into the tart shell; bake until puffed and pale golden brown, 40 to 45 minutes. Let cool at least 30 minutes before serving.

cremini and porcini quiches

MAKES SIX 4-INCH QUICHES

Tart Dough with thyme (page 586)

All-purpose flour, for dusting

½ ounce dried porcini mushrooms

1 cup boiling water

1 tablespoon unsalted butter

9 ounces cremini mushrooms, halved
lengthwise

2 large eggs plus 1 large egg yolk

1½ teaspoons coarse salt

¼ teaspoon freshly ground pepper

¾ cup heavy cream

1. Set 6 4-inch cake rings (with 1⅜-inch sides) on a baking sheet lined with parchment paper; set aside. Cut the dough into 6 equal pieces. On a lightly floured surface, roll out the pieces, 1 at a time, to ⅛ inch thick. Using a cake pan as a guide, cut an 8-inch circle from each piece. Fit the circles into the cake rings, trimming the dough flush with the tops of the rings to make tart shells. Prick the bottoms all over with a fork. Freeze until firm, at least 30 minutes. Preheat the oven to 400°F.

2. Line the tart shells with parchment paper; fill with pie weights or dried beans. Bake until the dough edges start to feel firm, about 20 minutes. Remove the parchment and weights; continue baking until the crusts are pale golden brown, about 10 minutes. Let cool completely on a wire rack. Reduce the oven temperature to 350°F.

3. Soak the porcini in boiling water; let soften 30 minutes. Melt the butter in a large skillet over medium-high heat; cook the cremini, cut sides down, without stirring, until deep golden brown, about 5 minutes. Set aside.

4. Lift out the porcini; pour the soaking liquid through a fine sieve into a blender. Add the porcini, eggs and yolk, salt, and pepper; blend until smooth. Add the cream; blend.

5. Divide the filling among the tart shells. Arrange the cremini in the filling, cut sides up. Bake until set, about 40 minutes. Let cool at least 30 minutes before serving.

granola with flaxseed

MAKES 5½ CUPS

Store the granola in an airtight container at room temperature up to 1 week.

2 cups old-fashioned rolled oats

1 cup sweetened shredded coconut

¾ cup sliced blanched almonds
(about 2½ ounces)

¼ cup vegetable oil

¼ cup honey

1 tablespoon flaxseed oil

½ cup dried cranberries

½ cup golden raisins

¼ cup unsalted sunflower seeds

1 tablespoon ground golden flaxseed
(from about 1½ teaspoons whole)

1. Preheat the oven to 350°F. Toss together the oats, coconut, and almonds in a medium bowl; set aside. Whisk together the vegetable oil and honey in a small bowl; stir into the oats mixture. Spread out the oats mixture on a rimmed baking sheet.

2. Bake, stirring occasionally, until golden brown, 17 to 20 minutes. Let cool 10 minutes; toss with the flaxseed oil. Let cool completely. Transfer to a large bowl; stir in the dried cranberries, raisins, sunflower seeds, and ground flaxseed.

FIT TO EAT RECIPE PER SERVING (½ CUP): 271 CALORIES, 15 G FAT, 0 MG CHOLESTEROL, 32 G CARBOHYDRATE, 25 MG SODIUM, 5 G PROTEIN, 4 G FIBER

breakfast enchiladas

SERVES 6

You can use shredded Monterey Jack cheese in place of the cotija and queso blanco. Other wild mushrooms, such as shiitakes, can be substituted for the porcini.

12 *yellow corn tortillas (6 inches each)*
4½ *teaspoons extra-virgin olive oil*
 1 *cup fresh corn kernels (1 ear)*
 ½ *shallot, finely chopped*
 ½ *small zucchini, diced*
 ½ *small yellow summer squash, diced*
 1 *ounce fresh porcini mushrooms, cut into ¼-inch pieces*
    Coarse salt and freshly ground pepper
 6 *large eggs*
 3 *tablespoons heavy cream*
 2 *tablespoons unsalted butter*
    Red Chile Sauce (recipe follows)
    Green Chile Sauce (recipe follows)
 8 *ounces cotija cheese, crumbled*
 2 *plum tomatoes, seeded and diced*
 ¼ *cup chopped fresh cilantro*
 6 *ounces queso blanco, shredded*

1. Wrap the tortillas in a clean kitchen towel; place in a bamboo steamer basket. Fill a wok with 2 inches water; bring to a boil. Reduce heat to medium; set the steamer in the wok. Steam the tortillas until softened, 6 minutes. (Or wrap the tortillas in a damp, clean kitchen towel, and heat until softened, 10 to 15 seconds in a microwave or 7 to 10 minutes in a 200°F oven.) Set aside.

2. Preheat the oven to 375°F. Heat the oil in a large nonstick skillet over medium-high heat until hot but not smoking. Cook the corn, stirring, until just caramelized, about 5 minutes. Add the shallot, zucchini, summer squash, and mushrooms; cook, stirring, until tender, about 4 minutes. Season with salt and pepper. Transfer to a bowl.

3. Vigorously whisk the eggs and cream until blended. Season with salt and pepper. Heat the butter in a large nonstick skillet over medium-high heat until foamy. Add the egg mixture; cook, stirring, until scrambled but not dry, about 4 minutes.

4. Pour ½ cup red chile sauce along 1 long side of a 9 × 13-inch baking dish; pour ½ cup green chile sauce along the opposite long side (the sauces should meet).

5. Spread 1 tablespoon red chile sauce on 1 tortilla; sprinkle 2 tablespoons cotija over the entire surface. On the bottom third of the tortilla, place 4½ teaspoons each egg and corn mixture, 1 teaspoon tomatoes, and ½ teaspoon cilantro. Firmly roll the tortilla; place in a baking dish, seam side down. Repeat with the remaining tortillas.

6. Pour ½ cup each red and green chile sauce on top of the enchiladas, mirroring the sauces on the bottom. Sprinkle with queso blanco. Bake until heated through, about 25 minutes. Garnish with the remaining 2 tablespoons cilantro, and serve with the remaining chile sauce.

red chile sauce

MAKES 3 CUPS

Be sure your kitchen is well ventilated when you soak the New Mexican and guajillo chiles; their vapors can be a mild irritant.

 9 *dried New Mexican chiles*
 6 *dried guajillo chiles*
 1 *quart boiling water, for soaking the chiles*
 6 *garlic cloves (do not peel)*
 6 *plum tomatoes*
 2 *tablespoons vegetable oil*
 ½ *large white onion, finely chopped*
4½ *teaspoons New Mexican chili powder*
 6 *chipotle chiles in adobo sauce, seeded*
 1 *tablespoon dried Mexican oregano*
    Coarse salt

1. Toast the New Mexican and guajillo chiles in a dry large cast-iron skillet over medium-high heat, turning, until warm and soft, about 30 seconds per side (do not let blacken, or the chiles will be bitter). Remove the chiles; reserve the skillet.

2. Discard the stems; cut the chiles lengthwise with kitchen shears, and discard the seeds. Cover the chiles with boiling water. Let stand until hydrated, about 20 minutes.

3. Meanwhile, cook the garlic and tomatoes in the skillet over medium-high heat, turning, until charred and soft, about 10 minutes. Set the tomatoes aside; peel the garlic.

4. Heat the oil in the skillet over medium-low until hot but not smoking. Cook the onion until translucent, about 5 minutes. Add the chili powder; cook 1 minute. Drain chiles, reserving 1½ cups liquid.

5. Puree the onion, hydrated chiles, chipotle chiles, tomatoes, garlic, and oregano in a blender, adding a small amount of the reserved soaking liquid if the mixture seems dry. Pass the sauce through a fine sieve into the skillet. Cook over medium heat, stirring, 5 minutes. Add the remaining soaking liquid. Simmer until the sauce is thickened, 12 to 15 minutes. Season with salt. If not serving immediately, refrigerate up to 2 days; reheat over low (add water if the sauce seems too thick).

green chile sauce
MAKES 3 CUPS

1 can (27 ounces) whole green chiles, drained and seeded

6 garlic cloves (do not peel)

4 tomatillos, husked

2 teaspoons extra-virgin olive oil

1 small white onion, cut into ½-inch pieces

2 teaspoons dried Mexican oregano

¾ teaspoon ground cumin

Coarse salt

1. Puree the chiles in a blender, adding a little water if the puree seems dry.

2. Cook the garlic and tomatillos in a dry large cast-iron skillet over medium-high heat, turning occasionally, until golden brown and softened, about 8 minutes. Peel the garlic. Coarsely chop the garlic and tomatillos; set aside.

3. Heat the oil in the same skillet over medium heat until hot but not smoking. Cook the onion until softened and translucent, about 5 minutes. Add the chile puree, garlic, tomatillos, ½ cup water, and the oregano and cumin. Bring to a boil; reduce heat. Simmer until

the sauce is thickened, about 15 minutes. Season with salt. If not serving immediately, refrigerate up to 2 days; reheat over low (add water if the sauce seems too thick).

triple-citrus coffee cake
MAKES TWO 16-INCH LOAVES;
EACH SERVES 6 TO 8

13 tablespoons (1⅝ sticks) unsalted butter, melted and cooled, plus more for the bowl

½ cup water, warmed to 110° F

2 envelopes active dry yeast (2 scant tablespoons)

⅔ cup plus 1 teaspoon granulated sugar

1 cup freshly squeezed orange juice

2 large eggs, lightly beaten, plus 1 large egg, lightly beaten, for egg wash

Finely grated zest of 1 lemon

Finely grated zest of 1 lime

Finely grated zest of 1 orange

1 teaspoon fine salt

5 to 6 cups all-purpose flour, plus more for dusting

1 pound (two 8-ounce bricks) cream cheese, room temperature

1 cup confectioners' sugar

2 large egg yolks

2 teaspoons pure vanilla extract

1 cup dried cranberries (4¼ ounces)

⅔ cup poppy seeds

1. Butter a large bowl; set aside. Stir the warm water, yeast, and 1 teaspoon granulated sugar in another large bowl until the yeast dissolves. Let stand until foamy, about 5 minutes. Whisk in the orange juice, 2 eggs, remaining ⅔ cup granulated sugar, ½ cup butter, citrus zests, and salt. Stir in 5 cups flour, 1 cup at a time (add up to 1 cup flour if needed), until the dough pulls away from the sides of the bowl and forms a ball.

2. Turn out the dough onto a lightly floured work surface; knead until smooth and slightly sticky, about 5 minutes. Transfer to the buttered bowl; brush the dough with 1 tablespoon butter. Loosely cover with plastic wrap; let the dough rise until doubled in bulk, about 1½ hours.

MAKING COFFEE CAKE

1. Sometimes a dough will stick to the counter as you roll it; to remedy this, fold the dough in half, exposing the counter underneath, and sprinkle the counter generously with flour. Then repeat on the other side. Before spreading with filling, brush off excess flour from the dough with a dry pastry brush.

2. Roll up the dough, and pinch the seam to ensure that all the creamy filling will remain sealed inside.

3. To give this cake its unique shape, cut slits in one side of the rolled dough, leaving the other side intact.

4. Then twist each segment on alternating sides. After the dough is shaped, let it rise again before baking.

3. Meanwhile, stir the cream cheese, confectioners' sugar, egg yolks, and vanilla in a small bowl until smooth. Stir in the dried cranberries and poppy seeds; set aside.

4. Butter 2 baking sheets; set aside. Punch down the dough, and divide it in half. Roll out 1 half into an 11 × 15-inch rectangle. Brush with 2 tablespoons butter, leaving a ½-inch border. Spread 1½ cups filling evenly over the butter. Beginning at 1 long side, tightly roll the dough into a log, encasing the filling. Pinch the seam to seal.

5. Carefully transfer the log to a prepared baking sheet. With a sharp knife, make 6 cuts, about 2 inches apart, along 1 long side of the log, cutting three-quarters of the way across. Lift the first segment, turn it cut side up, and lay it flat. Repeat with the next segment, twisting so it sits on the opposite side of the roll. Continue down the log, alternating sides. Repeat with the remaining dough, butter, and filling; place on the second baking sheet.

6. Preheat the oven to 350°F, with racks in the upper and lower thirds. Loosely cover the dough with buttered pieces of plastic wrap, and let rise until almost doubled in bulk, about 30 minutes. Brush the dough with egg wash, avoiding the filling. Bake on the upper and lower racks, switching the positions of the sheets halfway through, until cooked through and golden brown, about 30 minutes. Carefully slide the cakes onto wire racks, and let cool completely before slicing.

....

MAKING PANCAKES

Even the most basic pancake recipe can be improved upon when you keep a few key components in mind. To start, you need the right ingredients. The best flour for pancakes is all-purpose; for a change of pace, substitute cornmeal, buckwheat flour, or whole-wheat flour for half the all-purpose flour. When leavening with baking powder and/or soda, mixing the batter is critical. There are two stages: whisking together the dry ingredients, and whisking the wet ingredients into the dry. Don't whisk until smooth and even, or the gluten in the flour will develop and produce a tough texture. Instead, stop mixing while the batter is still slightly lumpy, with a few clumps of unmoistened dry ingredients remaining. It is the interaction of liquid and the pockets of dry ingredients during cooking that produces fluffy pancakes. For best results, cook the pancakes right away; do not let the batter sit longer than it takes to heat your pan.

Next, be aware of your cooking surface. The ideal surface is very flat and distributes heat evenly. The best option is a griddle, followed by a large cast-iron skillet or nonstick frying pan. Whichever surface you use, make sure it's at the right temperature when you begin. You can test for this by flicking a few drops of water onto the surface; if they bounce, sizzle, and disappear in a second, your pan is ready.

Poor quality in the first batch is a common problem with pancakes, but it needn't be this way. The culprit is often too much fat on the griddle. If more than a very thin layer is used, it gathers in tiny puddles beneath the batter, which in turn lifts small bits off the griddle so they never have the chance to brown properly. Instead, melt only a small amount of butter or fat, and wipe the excess away with a folded paper towel. This should ensure that your first batch is as fluffy as the last.

Now it's time to ladle in the batter. If using fruit, place on top of the batter right after it's poured, distributing the fruit evenly. When the batter surface is covered with little bubbles, some of which have begun to break, it's time to flip. The bursting bubbles are letting gas escape, so flip at just this moment, before too many have popped.

whole-wheat buttermilk pancakes

SERVES 4

- 1 cup whole-wheat flour
- ⅔ cup all-purpose flour
- ⅓ cup toasted wheat germ
- 1 tablespoon packed light-brown sugar
- 1 teaspoon baking powder
- ½ teaspoon baking soda
- ¼ teaspoon salt
- 3 tablespoons unsalted butter, melted
- 2¾ cups low-fat buttermilk
- 2 large eggs, lightly beaten
  Vegetable oil cooking spray
  Pure maple syrup, for serving (optional)
  Raspberries, for serving (optional)

1. Preheat the oven to 200° F. Whisk together the flours, wheat germ, sugar, baking powder, baking soda, and salt in a medium bowl; set aside.

2. Heat a griddle or cast-iron skillet over medium heat. Stir together the melted butter, buttermilk, and eggs in a medium bowl. Stir the flour mixture into the buttermilk mixture until just combined (the batter will be slightly lumpy).

3. Generously coat the griddle with cooking spray. Working in batches, pour ¼ cup batter for each pancake onto the griddle. Cook until the surface is bubbling and the edges are slightly dry, 3 to 4 minutes. Turn the pancakes; cook until the undersides are golden brown, 3 to 4 minutes more. Transfer to a baking sheet, and keep warm in the oven. Divide the pancakes among 4 plates. Serve with syrup and berries, if desired.

FIT TO EAT RECIPE PER SERVING: 396 CALORIES, 14 G FAT, 124 MG CHOLESTEROL, 53 G CARBOHYDRATE, 873 MG SODIUM, 17 G PROTEIN, 5 G FIBER

fluffy pancakes

SERVES 6

You can make your own pancake mix by combining the dry ingredients and storing them at room temperature in a resealable bag until ready to use.

- 2 cups all-purpose flour
- 6 tablespoons nonfat dry milk
- ¼ cup sugar
- 4 teaspoons baking powder
- 1 teaspoon salt
- 4½ tablespoons butter, melted
- 2 large eggs, lightly beaten
  Maple syrup or maple butter, for serving (optional)
  Fresh berries, for serving (optional)

1. In a medium bowl, mix the flour, nonfat dry milk, sugar, baking powder, and salt.

2. Heat a griddle or cast-iron skillet over medium heat. In a medium bowl, combine 4 tablespoons melted butter and the dry ingredients. Mix in the eggs and 1¼ cup plus 2 tablespoons cold water. Stir until just combined; the batter will be slightly lumpy.

3. Add the remaining ½ tablespoon butter to griddle, swirling to coat. Pour a scant ¼ cup batter per pancake onto the griddle, and cook until the surface bubbles and the edges are slightly dry, about 2 minutes. Flip the pancakes, and cook until the undersides are golden brown. Repeat with the remaining batter. Serve the pancakes immediately with syrup and berries, if desired.

cinnamon-raisin french toast

SERVES 6

Any bread is lovely in this buttermilk batter.

  6 *large eggs*
1½ *cups buttermilk*
  2 *tablespoons pure vanilla extract*
  ½ *teaspoon ground cinnamon*
     Pinch of ground nutmeg
     Pinch of salt
  6 *1-inch-thick slices cinnamon-raisin bread, preferably day-old*
  2 *tablespoons unsalted butter*
  2 *tablespoons vegetable oil*
     Pure maple syrup (optional)

1. Whisk together the eggs, buttermilk, vanilla, cinnamon, nutmeg, and salt in a medium bowl; set aside.

2. Place the bread in a shallow baking dish large enough to hold the bread slices in a single layer. Pour the egg mixture over the bread; soak 10 minutes. Turn the slices over; soak 10 minutes more, or until soaked through.

3. Preheat the oven to 250°F. Place a wire rack on a baking sheet; set aside. Heat 1 tablespoon butter and 1 tablespoon vegetable oil in a large skillet over medium heat. Fry half the bread slices until golden brown, 2 to 3 minutes per side. Transfer to the wire rack; place in the oven while cooking the remaining bread. Wipe out the skillet; repeat with the remaining butter, oil, and bread. Serve warm with maple syrup, if desired.

banana-nut french toast

SERVES 6

1½ *cups walnuts*
  6 *large eggs*
1½ *cups heavy cream, half-and-half, or milk*
  2 *tablespoons pure vanilla extract*
  ½ *teaspoon ground cinnamon*
     Pinch of ground nutmeg
     Pinch of salt
  6 *ripe but firm bananas, peeled and cut into ¼-inch rounds*
1½ *cups packed dark-brown sugar*
 12 *slices bread (each ½ inch thick), such as brioche or challah, preferably day-old*
  8 *tablespoons (1 stick) unsalted butter*
  4 *tablespoons vegetable oil*
     Pure maple syrup, for serving (optional)

1. Preheat the oven to 350°F. Place the walnuts on a rimmed baking sheet, and toast until lightly browned and fragrant, about 10 minutes. Set aside. When cool, chop the walnuts coarsely.

2. Whisk together the eggs, cream, vanilla extract, cinnamon, nutmeg, and salt in a medium bowl, and set aside. Combine the bananas, dark brown sugar, and walnuts in another bowl; set aside. Lay out 6 slices of bread on the work surface. Top each slice with ⅓ cup banana mixture. Top with the remaining bread slices; press gently to seal the sandwiches.

3. Place the sandwiches in a shallow baking dish (or 2 dishes) large enough to hold them in a single layer. Pour the egg mixture over the bread, and soak 10 minutes. Carefully turn the sandwiches over, and soak 10 minutes more, or until the bread is soaked through.

4. Reduce the oven temperature to 250°F. Place a wire rack on a baking sheet; set aside. Heat the remaining banana mixture in a small skillet over medium-low heat until the sugar is melted and the bananas are soft and slightly translucent, about 3 minutes. Add 4 tablespoons butter, and stir to combine; keep warm.

5. Heat 2 tablespoons butter and 2 tablespoons vegetable oil in a large skillet over medium heat. Fry half of the sandwiches until golden brown, 2 to 3 minutes per side. Transfer to the wire rack, and place in the oven while cooking the remaining sandwiches. Wipe out the skillet, and repeat with the remaining butter, oil, and bread. Keep in the oven until ready to serve. Cut into triangles, and serve with warm banana mixture and maple syrup, if desired.

savory french toast

SERVES 6

- 5 ounces bacon (about 6 slices)
- 2 onions, cut into ¼-inch dice
- 12 ounces button mushrooms, stemmed and quartered
- 6 large eggs
- 1½ cups heavy cream, half-and-half, or milk
- ½ cup grated Parmesan cheese (about 1½ ounces), plus more for serving
- 1 teaspoon coarse salt
- 6 1-inch-thick slices bread, such as sourdough, each cut into 3 long strips, preferably day-old
- 2 tablespoons unsalted butter
- 2 tablespoons vegetable oil

1. Heat a skillet over medium heat. Add the bacon; cook until browned, 3 to 4 minutes. Remove the bacon with tongs; drain on paper towels; set aside. Add the onions to the skillet with the bacon drippings; cook, stirring constantly, until the onions begin to soften, about 3 minutes. Add the mushrooms; cook until tender and most of the liquid released has evaporated, 5 to 6 minutes. Transfer the mixture to a bowl to cool. When cool, set aside half the mixture; finely chop the other half.

2. Whisk together the eggs, cream, Parmesan, and salt in a medium bowl. Stir in the finely chopped vegetable mixture; set aside.

3. Place the bread strips in a shallow baking dish large enough to hold them in a single layer. Pour the egg mixture over the bread; soak 10 minutes. Turn the strips over, and soak 10 minutes more, or until the bread is soaked through.

4. Preheat the oven to 250° F. Place a wire rack on a baking sheet; set aside. Heat 1 tablespoon butter and 1 tablespoon vegetable oil in a large skillet over medium heat. Fry half the bread strips until golden brown, 2 to 3 minutes per side. Transfer to the wire rack; place in the oven while cooking the remaining bread.

5. Wipe out the skillet; repeat with the remaining butter, oil, and bread. Heat the remaining onion mixture in a small skillet until warm. Serve the French toast warm, topped with the remaining onion mixture, crumbled bacon, and Parmesan, if desired.

cheese strata

SERVES 6

- 2 tablespoons unsalted butter, melted, plus more, softened, for the baking dish
- 8 slices white bread
- 1½ cups grated sharp Cheddar cheese
- 1½ cups grated Swiss cheese
- 2 tablespoons chopped fresh chives
- 4 large eggs
- 2 cups milk
- ⅛ teaspoon cayenne pepper
- 1 teaspoon coarse salt
- ¼ teaspoon freshly ground pepper

1. Butter an 8-inch-square baking dish; line the bottom with 4 slices bread. Sprinkle with half of each cheese. Top with chives. Layer with the remaining bread and cheese.

2. Whisk together the eggs, milk, melted butter, cayenne, salt, and pepper. Pour the mixture into the baking dish. Cover with plastic wrap; refrigerate at least 6 hours (or overnight).

3. Preheat the oven to 325° F. Bake the strata until puffed and golden, about 40 minutes. Let stand 10 minutes before serving.

broccoli-cheese frittata

SERVES 8

- 2 heads broccoli (about 2 pounds)
- 2 teaspoons unsalted butter
- 2 small onions, peeled, cut into ½-inch pieces
- 1 cup water
- 1½ teaspoons coarse salt
- ¼ teaspoon freshly ground pepper
  Cooking spray
- 3 large whole eggs
- 9 large egg whites
- ½ ounce grated Parmesan cheese (¼ cup)
- 2 ounces goat cheese (⅓ cup)

1. Preheat the oven to 375° F. Cut the broccoli stems into ½-inch pieces, and cut the florets into 1-inch pieces; set aside. Melt the butter in a 12-inch sauté pan over medium heat. Add the onions; cook until translucent, about 5 minutes. Add the broccoli stems, and cook until they begun to soften, about 5 minutes. Add the florets and water, and cook until the broccoli is tender and the liquid has evaporated, about 5 minutes more. Season with salt and pepper. Transfer to a bowl to cool completely.

2. Wipe out the pan; coat with cooking spray. In the bowl of an electric mixer fitted with the whisk attachment, combine the eggs and egg whites. Beat until extremely light and foamy, 8 to 10 minutes. Heat the pan over medium-high heat. Fold the Parmesan and the broccoli mixture into the eggs. Add to the pan; dot the top with goat cheese. Cook, without stirring, for 2 minutes.

3. Transfer to the oven; bake until the top is golden brown and the frittata is set, about 30 minutes. Let cool 1 minute before sliding out of the pan. Serve hot or at room temperature.

FIT TO EAT RECIPE PER SERVING: 128 CALORIES, 103 MG CALCIUM, 5 G FAT, 87 MG CHOLESTEROL, 381 MG SODIUM, 12 G PROTEIN, 4 G FIBER

ultimate streusel cake

MAKES ONE 10-INCH CAKE

- 2½ cups all-purpose flour
- 1 teaspoon baking soda
- 1 teaspoon baking powder
- ¼ teaspoon coarse salt
- 10 tablespoons (1¼ sticks) unsalted butter, room temperature, plus more for the pan
- 1 cup granulated sugar
- 3 large eggs
- 1 teaspoon pure vanilla extract
- 1¼ cups sour cream (or 1 cup buttermilk)
  Pecan Streusel Filling (recipe follows)
- 2½ cups sifted confectioners' sugar
- ¼ cup milk

1. Preheat the oven to 350° F. Sift together the flour, baking soda, baking powder, and salt into a bowl; set aside. Butter a 10-inch Bundt pan (or other tube pan with 3-quart capacity); set aside.

2. In the bowl of an electric mixer fitted with the paddle attachment, cream the butter and granulated sugar until light and fluffy, about 4 minutes. Add the eggs, 1 at a time, until well combined. Add the vanilla; stir until combined. Add the reserved flour mixture and sour cream, and stir just until well combined. Spoon half the batter into the bottom of the prepared pan. Make a well in the batter, and crumble ⅔ of the streusel mixture into the well. Top with the remaining batter, smoothing the top. Sprinkle the remaining streusel evenly over the top. Bake until golden brown and a cake tester comes out clean, about 1 hour.

3. In a medium bowl, whisk together the confectioners' sugar and milk; set aside, covered with plastic wrap, until ready to use. Cool the cake until just warm before drizzling with icing.

pecan streusel filling
MAKES ENOUGH FOR ONE 10-INCH CAKE

- 1½ cups lightly packed light-brown sugar
- ½ cup granulated sugar
- 1½ cups chopped pecans
- ½ cup all-purpose flour
- 1 tablespoon ground cinnamon
  Pinch of ground cloves
- 8 tablespoons (1 stick) unsalted butter, softened

Combine the sugars, pecans, flour, cinnamon, and cloves in a medium bowl. Using your hands or a pastry cutter, cut in the butter until well combined and crumbly; refrigerate until ready to use.

breakfast blintzes with caramelized rhubarb and sour cream
MAKES 12

Cooking blintzes takes a bit of practice. A non-stick skillet is a great help. The first blintz is almost never perfect; just discard it and start again. The blintzes can be made through step 4 up to 2 hours ahead.

- 11 tablespoons butter (1⅜ sticks), plus more for the pan
- 1 cup all-purpose flour
- ¼ teaspoon salt
- 1 cup plus 2¼ tablespoons sugar
- 4 large eggs
- 1 cup milk
- 1½ pounds trimmed rhubarb, cut into ½-inch lengths (about 5 cups)
- ¼ cup plus 2 tablespoons brandy
- ½ pint sour cream, or more if desired

1. Melt 2 tablespoons butter; let cool.

2. Combine the flour, salt, ¼ tablespoon sugar, eggs, milk, and 2 tablespoons reserved melted, cooled butter in the bowl of a food processor, and process until smooth. Transfer to a medium bowl, cover with plastic wrap, and place in the refrigerator at least 1 hour or overnight.

3. Fill a large bowl with ice and water; set aside. Melt the remaining 9 tablespoons butter in a large sauté pan over medium heat. Sprinkle the remaining 1 cup plus 2 tablespoons sugar over the butter; cook until the sugar has dissolved and starts to turn golden brown, about 5 minutes. Add the rhubarb; cook, shaking the pan vigorously to coat it in caramelized sugar, until the rhubarb is tender and just starting to fall apart, about 5 minutes. Add the brandy to the pan, shake the pan, and cook just until the liquid comes to a boil, about 30 seconds; remove from heat. Transfer the rhubarb to a small bowl; set into the ice bath to stop the cooking.

4. Heat a 10-inch nonstick sauté pan over medium heat. Melt about ½ tablespoon butter in the sauté pan; swirl to coat. If the butter pools, gently wipe with a paper towel. Pour a scant ¼ cup chilled batter into the hot sauté pan. Swirl the pan to form a thin, even layer; cook the blintz until the bottom is very lightly browned, about 2 minutes. Do not turn over. Loosen the edge of the blintz with a spatula; slide out of the pan onto a piece of waxed paper. Continue making blintzes until all the batter is used (you may not need to add butter to the pan each time); place a piece of waxed paper between each.

5. Transfer a blintz, cooked side up, onto a plate. Spoon a generous ¼ cup rhubarb filling (getting a nice amount of fruit to liquid) into the center of the blintz. Carefully fold up the blintz, creating an envelope for the filling; set aside, seam up, on a baking sheet. Continue filling and folding until all the blintzes and filling have been used.

6. Melt just enough butter to lightly coat the bottom of large sauté pan (use the same nonstick sauté pan or a slightly larger sauté pan, if you wish, over medium-low heat). Arrange 2 or 3 filled blintzes at a time, depending on the size of the pan, in the sauté pan; cook until the blintzes are golden and crisp on both sides, about 4 minutes per side. Serve immediately with sour cream.

blueberry blintzes

MAKES 12; SERVES 6

for the crêpes

¾ cup plus 2 tablespoons whole milk

5 tablespoons unsalted butter, melted

2 large eggs

1 cup plus 2 tablespoons all-purpose flour

¼ teaspoon coarse salt

3 tablespoons canola oil

Confectioners' sugar, for dusting

for the sauce

1 pint blueberries (about 2 cups)

6½ tablespoons granulated sugar

1 tablespoon unsalted butter

2 tablespoons fresh lemon juice

½ teaspoon cornstarch

Pinch of coarse salt

for the filling

16 ounces cottage cheese

4 ounces cream cheese, softened

½ cup plus 3 tablespoons granulated sugar

1 vanilla bean, halved lengthwise, seeds scraped and reserved, bean discarded

½ pint blueberries (about 1 cup)

1. Make the crêpe batter: Whisk together milk, ½ cup water, 2 tablespoons melted butter, and the eggs in a medium bowl. Whisk in flour and salt; set aside.

2. Make the sauce: Combine blueberries, sugar, butter, lemon juice, cornstarch, and salt in a medium saucepan over medium-low heat. Bring mixture to a low boil. Reduce heat; simmer, stirring often, until berries begin to break down and release their juices, about 10 minutes. Set aside.

3. Make the filling: Purée cottage cheese, cream cheese, sugar, and vanilla seeds in a food processor. Transfer to a medium bowl; stir in blueberries.

4. Make the crêpes: Stir together the remaining 3 tablespoons melted butter and the oil in a small bowl; reserve ¼ cup for cooking blintzes. Heat an 8-inch nonstick skillet over medium heat. Lightly brush pan using remaining butter-oil mixture. Pour

a scant ¼ cup batter into pan; swirl to form an even layer. Cook until bottom is lightly browned, about 1½ minutes. Using a heatproof spatula, flip crêpe; cook 30 seconds. Transfer to a plate. Repeat with remaining butter-oil mixture and batter.

5. Transfer a crêpe to a clean work surface. Spoon 2 heaping tablespoons filling onto crêpe 1 inch from bottom and sides. Fold bottom over filling. Fold in sides, and roll up. Set aside, seam down. Repeat with remaining crêpes and filling.

6. Heat the reserved ¼ cup butter-oil mixture in a clean pan over medium heat. Working in batches of 3, fry blintzes, turning once, until golden and crisp, 2 to 2½ minutes per side. Place 2 blintzes on each plate. Spoon warm sauce over top, and dust with confectioners' sugar.

rachel good's glazed potato doughnuts

MAKES ABOUT 36

These are best eaten slightly warm.

8 ounces russet potatoes, peeled and sliced

¼ cup warm water, plus 6 tablespoons water

1 tablespoon active dry yeast

1 cup milk, scalded

¼ cup solid vegetable shortening

¾ cup granulated sugar

1 teaspoon salt

2 large eggs, lightly beaten

5 cups all-purpose flour, plus more, if needed, for the dough and work surface

2 quarts vegetable oil, plus more for the bowl

4 cups confectioners' sugar

1 teaspoon pure vanilla extract

½ teaspoon ground cinnamon

1. Have ready 2 parchment-lined baking pans. Place the potatoes in a small saucepan, cover with cold water, and bring to a boil over high heat. Cook until tender, about 15 minutes. Drain in a colander. Pass the potatoes through a potato ricer or food mill and into a medium bowl; set aside.

2. Place ¼ cup warm water in a small bowl; sprinkle with the yeast, stir gently, and let stand until creamy, 5 to 10 minutes. Using an electric mixer fitted with the paddle attachment, combine the milk, shortening, ¼ cup sugar, and salt. Let stand until cooled to just warm. Add the yeast mixture, reserved potatoes, and eggs; beat until combined.

3. Switch to the dough hook. Add 5 cups flour, and mix on medium-low speed until combined, adding more flour if necessary, until a smooth and elastic dough is formed, about 5 minutes. Transfer the dough to a large, lightly greased bowl; cover. Let stand in a warm place until the dough is doubled in size, about 55 minutes.

4. Transfer the dough to a lightly floured surface. Roll out to ½ inch thick. Using a 2½-inch-diameter doughnut cutter, cut and place on prepared baking pans. Loosely cover with plastic wrap; let stand in a warm place until the dough has risen by about one-third, about 30 minutes.

5. Combine the confectioners' sugar, vanilla, and remaining 6 tablespoons water in a medium bowl, stirring until smooth; set aside. In a medium bowl, whisk together the remaining ½ cup granulated sugar and cinnamon until well combined; set aside.

6. In a large, low-sided saucepan over medium heat, heat the oil until a deep-fry thermometer registers 375°F. Drop the doughnuts into the oil; fry in batches until golden, 1 to 2 minutes per side. Transfer to several layers of paper towel to drain. Place the drained doughnuts on a wire rack set over a baking pan. Dip half the doughnuts in the glaze; return to the wire rack. Roll the remaining doughnuts in the cinnamon-sugar mixture until well coated.

applesauce coffee cake
MAKES ONE 10-INCH CAKE

Vegetable oil cooking spray

12 tablespoons (1½ sticks) unsalted butter, softened

½ cup packed dark-brown sugar

¼ cup old-fashioned rolled oats

2¾ teaspoons ground cinnamon

1 teaspoon salt

1½ cups chopped toasted pecans

2 cups all-purpose flour

1 teaspoon baking soda

½ teaspoon freshly grated nutmeg

⅛ teaspoon ground cloves

1 cup granulated sugar

½ cup packed light-brown sugar

4 large eggs

Apple Cider Applesauce (page 560) or 1½ cups store-bought applesauce

2 McIntosh apples, peeled, cored, and cut into ¼-inch thick wedges

1. Preheat the oven to 350°F. Coat a 10-inch angel-food-cake pan with cooking spray; set aside. Make the crumb topping: Stir together 4 tablespoons butter, the dark-brown sugar, oats, ¾ teaspoon cinnamon, and ¼ teaspoon salt until smooth. Stir in ½ cup pecans; set aside.

2. Make the batter: Sift the flour, baking soda, nutmeg, cloves, and remaining 2 teaspoons cinnamon and ¾ teaspoon salt; set aside. Put the remaining 8 tablespoons (1 stick) butter, the granulated sugar, and the light-brown sugar in the bowl of an electric mixer fitted with the paddle attachment. Cream on medium speed until smooth, about 3 minutes. Mix in the eggs, 1 at a time. Reduce speed to low; mix in the applesauce and then the flour mixture. Stir in the remaining cup nuts by hand.

3. Pour the batter into the oiled pan; sprinkle the reserved crumb topping over the batter. Lay the apples on top, tucking some into the batter.

4. Bake until a cake tester inserted near the center comes out clean, about 1 hour and 10 minutes. Let cool in the pan on a wire rack. Store at room temperature, covered with plastic wrap, up to 3 days.

zucchini pie

SERVES 6

If yellow zucchini are unavailable, you can use all green zucchini to make this pie.

- 2 teaspoons olive oil
- 1 pound (about 2 or 3) green zucchini, cut into ½-inch pieces
- 4 scallions, thinly sliced
- 4 garlic cloves, minced
- 1 teaspoon dried marjoram
- 1 teaspoon coarse salt
- ½ teaspoon freshly ground pepper
- 1 pound (about 2 or 3) yellow zucchini, cut into ½-inch pieces
- ½ cup chopped fresh dill
- ¼ cup chopped fresh flat-leaf parsley
- 5 large eggs plus 5 large egg whites, lightly beaten
- 1 tomato, thinly sliced
- 2 ounces low-fat feta cheese, crumbled

1. Preheat the oven to 325° F. Heat 1 teaspoon olive oil in a large skillet set over medium heat. Add the green zucchini, half the scallions, half the garlic, ½ teaspoon marjoram, ½ teaspoon salt, and ¼ teaspoon pepper; cook, stirring frequently, until the zucchini has softened and is beginning to brown, about 5 minutes. Remove from heat; transfer to a large bowl; set aside.

2. Rinse the skillet; repeat the process with the yellow zucchini and remaining teaspoon olive oil, scallions, garlic, ½ teaspoon marjoram, ½ teaspoon salt, and ¼ teaspoon pepper. Transfer to the bowl with the cooked green zucchini; let sit until cooled. Drain, and discard any liquid.

3. Add the dill, parsley, and eggs to the zucchini; stir to combine. Pour into a 9½-inch round deep baking dish. Cover with the tomato; sprinkle with the feta. Bake until set, about 1 hour. Serve hot or at room temperature.

FIT TO EAT RECIPE PER SERVING: 146 CALORIES, 8 G FAT, 186 MG CHOLESTEROL, 8 G CARBOHYDRATE, 336 MG SODIUM, 12 G PROTEIN, 1 G FIBER

pan-fried potato and fontina frittata

SERVES 6

- 1 tablespoon extra-virgin olive oil
- 1 tablespoon unsalted butter
- ¾ pound fingerling or other small potatoes, cut into ½-inch-thick pieces

  Coarse salt and freshly ground pepper
- ¼ cup chopped mixed fresh herbs (such as parsley, rosemary, thyme, and sage), plus more for garnish
- 10 large eggs
- 8 ounces fontina cheese, grated

1. Preheat the oven to 375° F. Heat the oil and butter in a 10-inch ovenproof nonstick skillet over medium heat. Add the potatoes; season with salt and pepper. Cook, stirring occasionally, until the potatoes are tender and golden brown, 12 to 15 minutes. Stir in the herbs.

2. Meanwhile, whisk the eggs in a medium bowl; season with salt and pepper. Stir in the cheese; pour the mixture over the potatoes. Stir until the eggs begin to set slightly, about 30 seconds. Without stirring, continue cooking until the eggs are set on the sides and bottom, about 2 minutes. Transfer to the oven; bake until just set, 12 to 15 minutes.

3. Slide the frittata onto a serving platter, or let cool and slide into a 10-inch pie plate (and cover with a second pie plate) for easy transport. Serve garnished with chopped herbs, if desired.

poached eggs with bacon and toasted pecan pancakes

SERVES 2

½ cup all-purpose flour

⅓ cup whole-wheat flour

5 teaspoons sugar

1½ teaspoons baking powder

Coarse salt

¾ cup nonfat buttermilk

3 large eggs

½ teaspoon pure vanilla extract

1½ teaspoons unsalted butter, melted, plus
1 teaspoon for skillet

1 tablespoon plus 1 teaspoon vegetable oil

½ cup pecans, toasted and coarsely
chopped (about 2 ounces)

6 strips thick-cut bacon

Pure maple syrup, warmed, for serving

Toasted Glazed Pecans, for garnish
(recipe follows)

1. Preheat the oven to 200°F. Whisk flours, sugar, baking powder, and ¼ teaspoon salt in a large bowl; set aside. Whisk together buttermilk, 1 egg, vanilla, melted butter, and 1 tablespoon oil; whisk into flour mixture. Using a rubber spatula, fold in chopped pecans; set batter aside.

2. Cook bacon in a medium skillet over medium heat, turning once, until crisp, 6 to 7 minutes per side. Let drain on paper towels. Transfer bacon to a baking sheet in oven to keep warm.

3. Heat 1 teaspoon butter and remaining teaspoon oil in a medium nonstick skillet over medium heat. Working in batches of 2, pour in ¼ cup batter for each pancake. Cook until small bubbles form, 2½ to 3 minutes. Flip; cook until golden brown, about 2 minutes. Transfer to baking sheet in oven to keep warm until ready to serve.

4. Fill a small, high-sided skillet with 1½ inches water; heat over medium heat until barely simmering. Break remaining eggs into separate cups; pour eggs into water. Cook, basting tops of eggs with the simmering water, until set, 2 to 3 minutes. Using a slotted spoon, transfer eggs to several layers of paper towel to drain.

5. Place 2 pancakes on each plate; drizzle with warm syrup. Arrange bacon over pancakes, and place a poached egg on top. Drizzle with more syrup, if desired, and a sprinkle of salt. Garnish with toasted glazed pecans.

toasted glazed pecans

MAKES ⅓ CUP

⅓ cup pecan halves

2 teaspoons lightly beaten egg white

1 teaspoon pure maple syrup

1 teaspoon vegetable oil

Pinch of coarse salt

1. Preheat the oven to 350°F. Toast pecans on a rimmed baking sheet, shaking pan occasionally, until fragrant, 3 to 4 minutes.

2. Whisk together egg white, syrup, oil, and salt in a small bowl. Add pecans; toss to coat. Spread evenly on baking sheet; return to oven, and toast, stirring occasionally, 8 minutes. Let cool completely.

muesli with yogurt

SERVES 8

The muesli can be stored in an airtight container at room temperature for up to 1 week.

1½   cups old-fashioned rolled oats
¼   cup wheat germ
¼   cup dried currants
¼   cup dried apricots, finely chopped
⅓   cup whole raw almonds, toasted and coarsely chopped
⅓   cup sunflower seeds, toasted
4   cups (32 ounces) plain low-fat yogurt
1   small apple, halved, cored, and cut into ¼-inch-thick slices
2   tablespoons plus 2 teaspoons honey

1. Stir together oats, wheat germ, currants, apricots, almonds, and sunflower seeds in a medium bowl.

2. For each serving, top ½ cup yogurt with ¼ cup muesli; arrange apple slices on top. Drizzle with 1 teaspoon honey.

FIT TO EAT RECIPE PER SERVING: 277 CALORIES, 9 G FAT, 7 MG CHOLESTEROL, 38 G CARBOHYDRATE, 81 MG SODIUM, 12 G PROTEIN, 5 G FIBER

blueberry-walnut muesli

MAKES ABOUT 3 CUPS

Serve with yogurt, berries, and a drizzle of honey.

1½   cups old-fashioned oats
¾   cup dried blueberries
½   cup coarsely chopped walnuts, toasted
⅓   cup sunflower seeds, toasted
¼   cup wheat germ
2   tablespoons flaxseed

Stir together all ingredients in a large bowl. The muesli can be stored in an airtight container until ready to serve, up to 1 week.

eggs and morels baked in cream

SERVES 4

To clean fresh morels, dunk them into a bowl of cold water; drain them on a clean kitchen towel. You can substitute 8 dried morels for the fresh: Cover with hot water in a medium bowl. Set a small bowl on top of the mushrooms to keep them submerged. Let the mushrooms stand until soft, about 20 minutes, then lift them out of the water. Using paper towels, gently press out excess liquid, and let the mushrooms drain on a clean kitchen towel.

1   tablespoon unsalted butter, plus more for dishes
1   small shallot, finely chopped
8   fresh morel mushrooms (about 1 cup), halved lengthwise
    Coarse salt
1   cup heavy cream
4   large eggs
    Freshly ground pepper
1   tablespoon finely chopped fresh chives
    Crusty bread, for serving

1. Preheat the oven to 375°F. Melt butter in a medium skillet over medium-low heat. Add shallot. Cook, stirring constantly, until shallot has softened, about 2 minutes. Add mushrooms and a pinch of salt. Cook, stirring occasionally, until mushrooms have softened, about 5 minutes. Add cream; bring to a simmer. Immediately remove from heat, and let mushroom mixture cool 5 minutes.

2. Butter four 6-inch shallow baking dishes (such as gratin dishes). Place dishes on a rimmed baking sheet. Crack 1 egg into each baking dish, keeping yolks intact, and season with salt and pepper. Pour the mushroom-cream mixture into dishes, dividing evenly, and sprinkle with chives. Bake on baking sheet until the egg whites are just set, 9 to 12 minutes. Serve with bread, for dipping.

cornmeal waffles
with apricot-cherry compote
MAKES 6

- 8 ounces crème fraîche
- ¼ cup confectioners' sugar
- 1¼ cups all-purpose flour
- ¾ cup coarse yellow cornmeal
- 3 tablespoons plus 1 teaspoon granulated sugar
- 4 teaspoons baking powder
- 1 teaspoon salt
- 2 large eggs
- 1½ cups low-fat buttermilk
- ½ teaspoon pure vanilla extract
- ⅓ cup vegetable oil
- 5 tablespoons unsalted butter, melted
  Apricot-Cherry Compote (recipe follows)

1. Whisk together crème fraîche and confectioners' sugar in a small bowl. Refrigerate until ready to use (up to overnight).

2. Whisk together flour, cornmeal, granulated sugar, baking powder, and salt in a large bowl. Whisk eggs, buttermilk, and vanilla in a small bowl. Add egg mixture to flour mixture; stir until combined. Add oil and butter; whisk until smooth.

3. Heat a waffle iron (preferably Belgian-style). Ladle ½ cup batter into each mold. Cook according to manufacturer's instructions until golden brown. Place waffles on a baking sheet in a 200°F oven to keep warm while you make the rest. Serve topped with compote and sweetened crème fraîche.

apricot-cherry compote
MAKES ABOUT 3 CUPS

- 1 pound apricots, quartered
- 1 cup sugar
- 2 teaspoons fresh lemon juice
  Pinch of salt
- ½ pound Bing cherries, pitted and halved (or use whole frozen cherries)

Put apricots, sugar, 2 tablespoons water, the lemon juice, and salt into a medium saucepan. Cover; bring to a simmer over medium heat, stirring occasionally. Cook until apricots have softened. Stir in cherries. Serve warm or at room temperature.

souffléed omelet with goat
cheese, asparagus, and ham
SERVES 4

- 4 asparagus spears
- ½ tablespoon unsalted butter
- 5 large eggs, separated, room temperature
- 2 tablespoons all-purpose flour
  Coarse salt and freshly ground pepper
- 2½ tablespoons soft goat cheese
- 2½ tablespoons thinly sliced fresh mint
- 4 paper-thin slices serrano ham (about 1 ounce)

1. Preheat the oven to 375°F. Prepare an ice-water bath. Bring a wide medium saucepan of water to a boil. Add the asparagus; cook until bright green and just tender, 2 to 3 minutes. Plunge asparagus into the ice bath to stop the cooking; cool completely. Drain; halve lengthwise. Set aside.

2. Melt butter in a 12-inch ovenproof nonstick skillet over medium heat. Remove skillet from heat; set aside. Whisk together egg yolks, flour, ½ teaspoon salt, and ¼ teaspoon pepper in a medium bowl until pale and thick; set aside.

3. Put egg whites and a pinch of salt into the bowl of an electric mixer fitted with the whisk attachment. Beat on medium-high speed until stiff peaks form. Fold whites into yolk mixture. Using a large rubber spatula, spread mixture evenly into reserved skillet. Bake until omelet is almost set but still soft, about 6 minutes.

4. Sprinkle goat cheese and mint over half the omelet. Top with asparagus and a layer of ham. Fold plain half over filled half. Bake until cheese has melted and omelet is cooked through, about 3 minutes. Cut into 4 wedges, and serve.

healthy pepper hash

SERVES 6

1   tablespoon unsalted butter

1   red onion, cut into ½-inch dice

2   garlic cloves, minced

1   carrot, peeled and cut into ½-inch dice

1   medium Idaho potato (about 9 ounces)

3   assorted bell peppers, seeds removed,
    cut into ½-inch dice

6   ounces button mushrooms, stems
    trimmed, cut into ½-inch pieces

8   ounces ground turkey

2   tablespoons all-purpose flour

¼   cup dry sherry

2   cups homemade or low-sodium store-
    bought chicken stock, skimmed of fat

1   teaspoon coarse salt

¼   teaspoon freshly ground black pepper

¼   teaspoon chili powder

¼   teaspoon paprika

2   tablespoons finely chopped fresh
    flat-leaf parsley

6   large eggs (optional), poached or fried in
    a nonstick skillet with cooking spray

1. Heat the butter in a large nonstick sauté pan over medium-high heat. Add the onion, garlic, and carrot. Peel the potato, and then cut into ½-inch dice. Add to the pan. Cook until the vegetables soften and begin to brown, 6 to 7 minutes.

2. Reduce heat to medium; add the bell peppers and mushrooms, and cook until the vegetables are just tender, 8 to 10 minutes.

3. Add the turkey; sauté until cooked through. Sprinkle with the flour; stir to combine.

4. Add the sherry; scrape any browned bits from the pan. Cook until most of the liquid has evaporated. Add the stock, salt, black pepper, chili powder, and paprika; bring to a boil. Reduce to a simmer; cook until the liquid thickens and reduces by half. Stir in the parsley. Serve hot, topped with egg, if using.

FIT TO EAT RECIPE PER SERVING: 243 CALORIES,
11 G FAT, 249 MG CHOLESTEROL, 18 G CARBOHYDRATE,
309 MG SODIUM, 16 G PROTEIN, 3 G FIBER

slab bacon and cheddar cheese broiled grits

SERVES 4

¼   pound slab bacon, diced

2   cups whole milk

1   cup stone-ground grits
    Coarse salt and freshly ground pepper

1¾ cups grated extra-sharp Cheddar cheese

1. Scatter bacon in a dry skillet. Cook over medium-high heat until barely crisp, about 4 minutes. Use a slotted spoon to transfer bacon to a paper towel–lined plate. Reserve 1 tablespoon bacon fat.

2. Combine milk and 2 cups water in a medium saucepan. Cover, and cook over medium-high until boiling, about 5 minutes. Add grits and ¾ teaspoon salt. Reduce heat to medium. Cook, stirring constantly until grits thicken, about 8 minutes. Reduce heat to low; simmer, stirring every 2 to 3 minutes, until thick, about 20 minutes. Cook, stirring constantly, until creamy and soft, about 15 minutes more. Remove from heat.

3. Heat the broiler. Stir in ½ teaspoon pepper, reserved bacon and bacon fat (if desired), and 1¼ cups cheese, and stir. Transfer to a small baking dish or cast-iron skillet, and scatter with remaining ½ cup cheese. Broil until cheese is brown, about 3 minutes. Serve hot.

drinks

....

limeade

MAKES ABOUT 2 QUARTS; SERVES 6 TO 8

For spiked drinks, pour 1 ounce vodka over ice into each glass before topping with limeade.

- 1 cup sugar
- 1½ cups fresh lime juice, plus lime wedges, for garnish (14 to 16 limes total)

1. Heat the sugar and 1 cup water in a small saucepan over medium heat, stirring, until the sugar has dissolved, 5 to 6 minutes.

2. Stir together the lime juice and 5 cups water in a large pitcher; stir in the sugar syrup. Refrigerate until cold (or up to 2 days in an airtight container). Garnish each serving with a lime wedge.

orange lemonade

MAKES 7 CUPS

To make a fizzy version of this recipe, use seltzer or sparkling water.

- ¾ cup sugar
- 1½ cups water
- 4 cups fresh orange juice (about 12 oranges)
- 1½ cups fresh lemon juice (about 9 lemons)
  - Ice, for serving
- 2 oranges, washed and thinly sliced
- 1 lemon, washed and thinly sliced

1. Make the sugar syrup: Combine the sugar and the water in a small saucepan over medium heat, and stir until all the sugar has dissolved. Remove from heat, and let cool completely. (To cool the syrup more quickly, plunge the saucepan in an ice-water bath, and stir frequently until cool.)

2. Combine the sugar syrup, orange juice, and lemon juice in a large pitcher or punchbowl. Stir to combine. Add the ice and sliced oranges and lemons, and serve immediately.

homemade ginger beer

MAKES 16 CUPS

This ginger beer is very spicy. Adjust the amount of lime juice and sugar to your taste.

- 2 pounds ginger, cut into 1-inch pieces
- 1 gallon boiling water
- 1½ cups fresh lime juice (about 8 limes)
- 1½ cups superfine sugar

Place the ginger in the bowl of a food processor, and process until finely chopped. Transfer to a large pot or bowl, and add the boiling water. Allow to stand for 1 hour. Drain through a fine sieve lined with a double thickness of damp cheesecloth. Discard the solids. Add the lime juice and sugar, and stir to dissolve.

creamy orange shakes

SERVES 2

- 1 cup ice cubes
- 1 tablespoon finely grated orange zest
- ½ cup plus 1 tablespoon fresh orange juice (1 to 2 medium oranges total)
- ¾ cup vanilla ice cream
- ½ cup orange sherbet
- ½ cup milk
- ½ teaspoon pure vanilla extract

Blend all the ingredients in a blender until the ice is crushed and the mixture is smooth. Divide between 2 glasses.

peach tea punch

MAKES 2½ QUARTS

Almost any type of fruit nectar can be substituted for peach with equally delectable results. We especially like the exotic flavor of mango.

- 3 tea bags
- 6 cups boiling water
- 4 cups peach nectar
- 1 bunch mint, trimmed and rinsed well
- 2 lemons, washed and thinly sliced
   Ice cubes, for serving

1. Brew the tea bags in the boiling water to make a strong tea. Discard the tea bags, and place the tea in refrigerator until chilled.

2. Combine the tea with the peach nectar in a large serving bowl or pitcher. Add the mint and lemon slices; let stand about 1 hour in the refrigerator to infuse the flavors. Add ice cubes, and serve.

hibiscus and ginger iced tea

SERVES 8

If any drink was made for leisurely back-porch sipping, it's iced tea. Our version is brewed from zesty hibiscus tea, which is made from coppery-red hibiscus leaves and is naturally caffeine free. Ginger syrup and lemon juice add layers of flavor.

- 1 tablespoon thinly sliced peeled fresh ginger
- ¾ cup sugar
- 4 hibiscus tea bags
- 2 tablespoons fresh lemon juice
   Lemon wedges, for garnish

1. Put 4 cups water, ginger, and ¾ cup sugar into a medium saucepan. Bring to a boil over medium-high heat, stirring until sugar has dissolved. Remove from heat; add tea bags. Cover, and let steep 15 minutes.

2. Pour through a fine sieve into a bowl set in an ice-water bath. Let cool. Stir in the lemon juice. Serve over crushed ice, and garnish with lemon wedges.

papaya-ginger smoothie

SERVES 4

- 2½ cups papaya (Solo or Mexican) chunks
- 1 cup ice cubes
- ⅔ cup plain nonfat yogurt
- 1 tablespoon finely chopped peeled fresh ginger
- 1 tablespoon honey
   Juice of 2 lemons
- 16 fresh mint leaves, plus 4 sprigs for garnish

1. Refrigerate the papaya until very cold, at least 1 hour or overnight.

2. Blend the papaya, ice, yogurt, ginger, honey, and lemon juice in a blender. Add up to ¼ cup water, 1 tablespoon at a time, until the mixture is smooth and thinned to desired consistency. Blend in the mint leaves. Garnish with mint sprigs.

FIT TO EAT RECIPE PER SERVING: 102 CALORIES, 0 G FAT, 3 MG CHOLESTEROL, 22 G CARBOHYDRATE, 53 MG SODIUM, 7 G PROTEIN, 2 G FIBER

sparkling fresh lemonade

SERVES 10

- 1 cup sugar
- 2 cups fresh lemon juice (about 10 lemons)
- 3 cups cold sparkling water
- 4½ cups ice

1. Bring 1 cup water and the sugar to a boil in a small saucepan, stirring until the sugar is dissolved. Let cool completely; refrigerate until ready to use.

2. Put the syrup, lemon juice, and sparkling water in a pitcher. Stir in the ice.

pineapple-mint juice

SERVES 5 OR 6

1 pineapple, peeled, cored, and
  coarsely chopped (about 6 cups)

5 cups ice, plus more for the glasses

¼ cup sugar

½ cup loosely packed fresh mint, plus
  sprigs for garnish (optional)

Puree the pineapple in a blender until smooth. Pour the puree through a fine sieve into a bowl; discard the solids. Return half the juice to the blender; blend with half the ice and sugar. Add half the mint; pulse to combine. Transfer to a pitcher; repeat with the remaining ingredients. Just before serving, stir mixture and pour into ice-filled glasses. Garnish with mint sprigs, if desired.

buttermilk-banana smoothies

SERVES 2

1 cup low-fat buttermilk

2 ripe bananas, cut into 2-inch-thick rounds

11 dried pitted dates

1 teaspoon honey

  Pinch of salt

1 cup ice

Blend all the ingredients in a blender on high speed until the mixture is smooth and the ice is finely ground. Pour into 2 glasses.

FIT TO EAT RECIPE PER SERVING: 294 CALORIES, 2 G FAT, 5 MG CHOLESTEROL, 70 G CARBOHYDRATE, 277 MG SODIUM, 6 G PROTEIN, 6 G FIBER

honeydew granita spritzer

SERVES 6

Seltzer enlivens this effervescent drink, which consists of sweet honeydew melon puree and mouth-puckering lime juice.

6 cups cubed honeydew melon (about
  half of a medium melon)

⅓ cup sugar

¼ cup fresh lime juice

  Lime peels, for garnish

1. Working in batches, puree the melon in a blender. Pour the puree through a fine sieve into an 8-inch square nonreactive dish.

2. Put sugar and ½ cup water into a small saucepan. Bring to a boil over medium-high heat, stirring until sugar has dissolved. Stir into melon puree. Add lime juice; stir to combine. Freeze, covered with plastic wrap, at least 6 hours (or up to 3 days).

3. Scrape granita with a fork; spoon about 1 cup granita into each of 6 glasses. Pour ½ cup seltzer into each glass; garnish with lime peels.

spiced pomegranate punch

SERVES 6

5 pomegranates

1 cup apple cider

½ cinnamon stick

1 tablespoon thinly sliced fresh ginger

¼ cup fresh orange juice, plus strips of
  orange zest for garnish

1. Cut pomegranates in half. Extract juice from seeds with a citrus juicer or reamer. Strain into a medium saucepan (you should have about 2½ cups).

2. Add cider, 2 cups water, the cinnamon stick, and ginger. Cook over high heat until simmering, 5 to 6 minutes. Reduce heat; gently simmer 15 minutes. Skim any foam that rises to the surface.

3. Discard cinnamon and ginger. Stir in orange juice. Serve warm, garnished with orange zest.

FIT TO EAT RECIPE PER SERVING: 113 CALORIES, 0 G SATURATED FAT, 0 G UNSATURATED FAT, 0 MG CHOLESTEROL, 28 G CARBOHYDRATE, 8 MG SODIUM, 1 G PROTEIN, 1 G FIBER

cranberry, tangerine, and pomegranate champagne punch

SERVES ABOUT 20

- 1 package (12 ounces) fresh cranberries, for the swizzle sticks
- 1 bunch fresh mint, for the swizzle sticks
- 2 cups pomegranate juice (about 5 pomegranates)
- 3 cups fresh tangerine juice (about 7 tangerines)
- 5 cups cranberry juice cocktail
- 2 bottles (750 ml each) chilled champagne or other sparkling wine

1. To make the swizzle sticks, spear 3 cranberries alternately with 2 mint leaves on wooden skewers. Place the skewers on a baking sheet; cover with damp paper towels, and refrigerate up to 1 hour.

2. In a large punchbowl or pitcher, stir together the fruit juices. Fill glasses with ice, and ladle or pour about ½ cup punch into each glass; top with champagne. Garnish each glass with a swizzle stick.

latin lover

SERVES 2

Pineapple and coconut rum give this drink the taste of the tropics.

- ¼ cup frozen pineapple juice concentrate
- 2 tablespoons frozen orange juice concentrate
- 2 tablespoons frozen cranberry juice concentrate
- 1 tablespoon fresh lime juice
- ¼ cup coconut rum
- 1½ cups small ice cubes
  Fresh sugarcane, for garnish

Mix all ingredients (except sugarcane) in a blender until smooth. Serve, garnished with sugarcane.

rosé sangria

SERVES 6

Chanterais melons, also called Cavaillon, are a delicious alternative to cantaloupes. Look for them at farmers' markets and gourmet stores.

- 1 bottle (750 ml) French dry rosé wine, such as Tavel or Bandol
- 6 tablespoons crème de cassis (black currant liqueur)
- 1 Chanterais melon or ½ large cantaloupe, cut into chunks
- 1 peach or nectarine, pitted and cut into 8 wedges
- ½ pint blackberries or raspberries
- 1 bottle (750 ml) sparkling water

Stir together all the ingredients except the sparkling water in a large pitcher. Refrigerate at least 1 hour or until ready to serve, up to 3 hours. Stir in the sparkling water, and serve over ice.

orange cloud

SERVES 2

Like a creamy orange ice-cream pop, this cocktail marries vanilla and orange. But the drink includes two liqueurs, so it's for adults only.

- ¼ cup frozen orange juice concentrate
- 1 tablespoon heavy cream
- 2 tablespoons Cointreau
- 2 tablespoons Galliano
- 1½ cups small ice cubes

Mix all the ingredients in a blender until smooth. Dip the moistened rims of 2 glasses in orange-colored sugar; pour in the orange mixture, and serve.

watermelon-tequila refreshers

SERVES 6 TO 8

If you prefer to serve alcohol-free cocktails, omit the tequila—the drink is still delicious.

- ¾ cup sugar
- 3½ pounds seedless watermelon, cut into 2-inch cubes (about 12 cups)
- 1 cup tequila
- 1 cup fresh lime juice (6 to 8 limes), plus lime slices for garnish
- 4 cups ice

1. Stir together the sugar and ¾ cup water in a medium saucepan. Bring to a boil over medium-high heat, stirring until the sugar is dissolved. Let cool completely. Refrigerate until ready to use, up to 1 week.

2. Working in batches, fill the blender with watermelon cubes; blend until smooth. Pass the puree in batches through a fine sieve set over a large bowl, discarding the solids as you work. Refrigerate the juice until ready to use, up to 1 day.

3. Stir together the tequila, lime and watermelon juices, and sugar syrup in a large pitcher. Stir in the ice and lime slices.

mango cooler

SERVES 2

We love our sweet twist on a daiquiri: mango mixed with dark rum, sugar syrup, and lemon juice (in place of the traditional lime).

- 1 cup chopped mango, frozen until hard
- 3 tablespoons dark rum
- 2 tablespoons fresh lemon juice
- 1 tablespoon Simple Syrup (page 660)
- 1½ cups small ice cubes
  Diced mango and shredded fresh mint, for garnish

Mix all the ingredients (except mango and mint) in a blender until smooth. Serve, garnished with mango and mint.

caipirinhas

SERVES 6

Cachaça is a potent sugarcane liquor. If you can't find it, use light rum instead.

- 3 limes, halved
- ¼ cup sugar
- 1½ cups cachaça

Place a lime half in each of 6 tumblers, and sprinkle each with 2 teaspoons sugar. Using a wooden reamer, crush the flesh of the limes. Fill the glasses with crushed ice, and divide the cachaça evenly among them. Stir well, and serve.

grapefruit sparkler

SERVES 8

- 1 cup sugar
- 8 whole star anise
- 6 cups ruby red grapefruit juice, chilled
- ⅓ cup Campari
- 2 cups champagne, chilled

1. In a small saucepan, combine 1 cup water with the sugar and star anise; bring to a boil, stirring occasionally, until the sugar has dissolved. Remove the pan from the heat; let cool completely.

2. Pour the mixture through a fine sieve into a measuring cup (to yield 1 cup); discard the star anise. Cover the syrup with plastic wrap, and chill.

3. In a large pitcher, combine the grapefruit juice, Campari, and chilled syrup. Divide among 8 glasses; top with champagne. Serve immediately.

portofino cocktail

SERVES 1

- 1 tablespoon Campari
- ¼ cup fresh red grapefruit juice
- 6 tablespoons tonic water
- 1 red grapefruit slice, for garnish

Fill a tumbler with ice. Shake the Campari, grapefruit juice, and tonic in a cocktail shaker. Pour into the tumbler, and garnish with the grapefruit slice.

lime-apricot rum cooler

SERVES 4

- 2 tablespoons freshly grated lime zest (about 6 limes)
- 6 tablespoons sugar
- ¼ cup plus 2 tablespoons freshly squeezed lime juice (about 3 limes)
- 2 cups apricot nectar, chilled
- 1¼ cups white rum

1. In a food processor, pulse the lime zest with the sugar until finely ground. Measure out ¼ cup mixture; transfer the rest to a shallow dish. Pour 2 tablespoons lime juice into another dish. Dip the rims of 4 glasses in the juice, then in the sugar mixture, coating well.

2. In a blender, puree the apricot nectar, rum, remaining ¼ cup lime juice, reserved ¼ cup zest mixture, and 2 cups ice. Divide among the prepared glasses, and serve immediately.

strawberry-ginger caipirosca

SERVES 2

- 10 fresh strawberries, hulled and quartered
- 30 fresh mint leaves
- ¼ lime, cut into 4 pieces
- 1 teaspoon freshly grated ginger
- 2 tablespoons sugar
- 2 cups cracked ice
- ½ cup vodka

Place the berries, mint, lime, and ginger in a cocktail shaker. Sprinkle the sugar over top; muddle the mixture with a long spoon until almost pureed. Add the ice and vodka; shake well. Divide between 2 glasses; serve immediately.

honeydew fizz

SERVES 2

- ½ large honeydew melon (about 3 pounds)
- ½ cup Midori or other melon liqueur
- 1 cup seltzer water, chilled

1. With a large spoon, scrape out and discard the honeydew seeds. Using a ¾-inch melon baller, scoop out 10 balls; place in a large sealable plastic container. Pour the Midori over the melon balls; transfer to the freezer, and let macerate about 1 hour.

2. Meanwhile, place the remaining honeydew in a blender, and puree until smooth. Let stand until the juice settles to the bottom of the blender and the foam rises to the top. Skim off the foam, and measure out ½ cup juice.

3. Remove the honeydew-ball mixture from the freezer; stir in the juice and seltzer. Divide evenly between 2 cocktail glasses; serve immediately.

plum and pineapple sangria

MAKES ABOUT 2¼ QUARTS

- 1 pineapple
- 4 plums, preferably a variety, pitted and sliced
- 1 tablespoon superfine sugar, plus more as needed
- 3 ounces Cointreau
- 3 ounces brandy
- 1 750-ml bottle fruity red wine, chilled
- 1⅓ cups pineapple juice
- 1 cup sparkling water

1. Peel pineapple; halve lengthwise and remove core. Cut half the pineapple into ¾-inch spears; cut the other half into 1-inch chunks. Place in a pitcher with the plums; sprinkle with sanding sugar, and stir to combine. Add Cointreau and brandy; let sit at least 1 hour.

2. When ready to serve, stir in red wine, pineapple juice, and sparkling water. Add more sugar, if desired. Serve chilled.

white-wine sangria

MAKES ABOUT 2 QUARTS

1 cup seedless green grapes

1 kiwi, peeled and sliced

1 pound seedless watermelon, scooped into 1-inch balls

¼ honeydew melon, seeded and cut into 1-inch cubes

1 lime, sliced and seeded

1 star fruit, sliced and seeded

1 pink grapefruit, seeded, sliced, and quartered

1 tablespoon superfine sugar, plus more if needed

3 ounces Cointreau

3 ounces brandy

1 750-ml bottle fruity white wine, chilled

1 cup cranberry juice

1. Put all fruit in a pitcher; sprinkle with superfine sugar, and stir to combine. Add Cointreau and brandy; let sit at least 1 hour.

2. When ready to serve, stir in wine and cranberry juice. Serve chilled.

kumquat mojitos

SERVES 8

48 kumquats, halved and seeded

2 cups fresh orange juice (4 to 5 oranges)

½ cup sugar

2 cups fresh mint leaves

3 cups light rum

6 cups small ice cubes

Stir together the kumquats, orange juice, and sugar. Let stand 10 minutes. Add the mint. Muddle the mixture with a wooden spoon to crush the kumquats and mint. Stir in the rum; add the ice. Transfer to a large pitcher.

kirsch-wine cocktails

MAKES 6

½ cup kirsch (cherry brandy)

½ cup white wine, such as Riesling or Sauvignon Blanc

2 to 4 ounces natural cherry soda

24 dried cherries (about 2 ounces)

Combine kirsch and wine in a pitcher, and refrigerate until ready to serve. Fill six 10-ounce glasses with ice. Divide kirsch-wine mixture evenly among glasses. Top off each glass with the soda; stir. Garnish each drink with 4 cherries.

cucumber-ginger fizzes

MAKES 8

1½ cups vodka

2 English cucumbers (1 peeled and coarsely chopped, 1 whole)

1 lime, cut into 8 wedges

2 bottles (750 ml each) sparkling water

½ to 1 cup Ginger Simple Syrup (recipe page 614)

1. Put vodka and the chopped cucumber into a nonreactive container. Refrigerate 1 hour. Strain; discard cucumber. Refrigerate until ready to use, up to 2 days.

2. Using a vegetable peeler, shave the remaining cucumber lengthwise into wide strips; discard seeds.

3. Fill 8 glasses with ice. Add 3 cucumber strips and 3 tablespoons infused vodka to each glass. Squeeze a lime wedge into each, and drop into drink. Top with sparkling water, and stir in 1 to 2 tablespoons of the ginger syrup. Serve immediately.

bing cherry mojitos

SERVES 12

1¼ cups sugar
1¼ cups fresh lime juice (about 9 limes)
3 pounds Bing cherries
18 ounces best-quality black cherry
     or plain vodka
1 bottle (750 ml) sparkling water

1. Bring sugar and 1¼ cups water to a boil in a small saucepan, stirring until sugar has dissolved. Remove from heat; let cool completely. (Makes about 2 cups syrup.) The syrup can be refrigerated in an airtight container up to 1 month.

2. Put lime juice into a medium nonreactive bowl. Halve and pit cherries; add to lime juice. Stir in syrup. Refrigerate at least 1 hour (up to overnight).

3. Stir cherry mixture and vodka in a large serving bowl. Fill 12 glasses with ice. Spoon ½ cup cherry-vodka mixture into each glass. Top off with sparkling water. Serve immediately.

blackberry-mint julep

SERVES 4

Like the original, our julep features bourbon infused with mint. But this drink's signature sweetness is tempered by the tartness of blackberries, which also tint it a gorgeous shade of purple. Another twist: Our cocktail is blended with—rather than served over—ice, creating a slushy texture.

½ cup packed fresh mint leaves
1 pint blackberries
6 tablespoons sugar
½ cup bourbon
    Mint sprigs, for garnish

1. Roughly chop the mint leaves.

2. Purée the mint, blackberries, and sugar in a blender. Press through a fine sieve into a bowl; discard seeds.

3. Rinse blender, then return purée to blender, and add bourbon and 4 cups small ice cubes; blend until smooth. Divide mixture among 4 glasses. Garnish each with a mint sprig.

fresh yellow tomato bloody mary

SERVES 4; MAKES ABOUT 3 CUPS

To make a traditional Bloody Mary cocktail, substitute ripe red tomatoes for the yellow ones.

1 pound ripe yellow tomatoes
    (about 4 medium)
¾ cup best-quality vodka (6 ounces)
5 tablespoons fresh lemon juice
    (about 2 lemons)
1 teaspoon Worcestershire sauce
20 dashes hot green pepper sauce,
     such as Tabasco
1 to 1½ teaspoons finely grated peeled
    fresh horseradish
¾ teaspoon coarse salt
¼ teaspoon freshly ground pepper
    Celery hearts, for garnish
    Yellow and red cherry tomatoes,
    for garnish

1. Puree pound of tomatoes in a blender. Strain through a fine sieve into a small bowl, pressing to remove as much liquid as possible; discard solids.

2. Stir together tomato purée, vodka, lemon juice, Worcestershire sauce, green pepper sauce, horseradish to taste, salt, and pepper in a pitcher. If not using immediately, mixture can be refrigerated, covered, overnight.

3. To serve, divide among 4 large glasses filled with ice. Garnish each glass with celery and cherry tomatoes on toothpicks.

apple pie–spiced cider

SERVES 6

1¼ quarts apple cider

3 tablespoons firmly packed light
   brown sugar

1 whole cinnamon stick, plus 6 sticks
   for garnish

1 teaspoon ground allspice

½ teaspoon ground ginger

   Pinch of ground cloves

   Pinch of freshly grated nutmeg

   Pinch of salt

½ cup Calvados or other brandy (optional)

In a medium saucepan, whisk together the cider, sugar, spices, and salt. Bring to a simmer over medium-low heat. Remove from heat; pour in the brandy, if desired. Strain into a pitcher; discard the solids. Serve immediately, garnished with cinnamon sticks.

hot date

SERVES 4

4 cups milk

7 teaspoons unsulfured molasses

¼ teaspoon freshly grated nutmeg

½ teaspoon ground cinnamon

   Pinch of ground ginger

¼ teaspoon ground allspice

   Pinch of coarse salt

14 dates, pitted

1. In a medium saucepan, heat the milk, molasses, spices, and salt over medium heat for 5 to 6 minutes. Remove from heat.

2. Chop the dates in a blender as finely as possible. Add about 1 cup milk mixture; blend, scraping down the sides as needed.

3. Strain the date mixture through a fine sieve back into the pan; whisk over medium heat until well combined. Serve immediately.

hot buttered rum with ginger and cinnamon

SERVES 4

4 tablespoons Ginger Simple Syrup
   (recipe follows)

1 cup dark rum

4 cinnamon sticks

4 cups boiling water

4 tablespoons Ginger Butter
   (recipe follows)

1. Divide the simple syrup among 4 heatproof glasses or mugs; add ¼ cup rum, 1 cinnamon stick, and 1 cup boiling water to each. Stir well.

2. Top each serving with 1 tablespoon ginger butter. Serve immediately.

ginger simple syrup

MAKES ¾ CUP

4 ounces fresh ginger, thinly sliced

½ cup water

½ cup granulated sugar

In a small saucepan, bring all ingredients to a boil over medium heat. Cook 2 minutes. Strain the mixture through a sieve, discarding ginger. Store in an airtight container in the refrigerator up to 1 week.

ginger butter

SERVES 8

3 pieces crystallized ginger, finely
   chopped (about 2 tablespoons)

½ teaspoon ground cinnamon

   Pinch of ground cloves

   Pinch of freshly grated nutmeg

½ cup (1 stick) unsalted butter,
   room temperature

In a small bowl, stir ingredients with a fork until thoroughly combined. Shape into a log by rolling in parchment paper or plastic wrap. Chill until firm, about 1 hour, before slicing into eight rounds.

salsas, sauces, dips,

AND MORE

....

pickled garlic

MAKES 1 QUART

- 6 heads garlic
- 4 cups white-wine vinegar
- 4 tablespoons sugar
- 1 teaspoon whole black peppercorns
- 4 whole cloves
- 2 small dried chiles
- 1 dried bay leaf
   Rind of 1 lemon

1. Trim the garlic heads, leaving the stem intact and peeling off all but 1 layer of papery skin. Set aside.

2. Combine the vinegar, sugar, peppercorns, cloves, chiles, bay leaf, and lemon rind in a medium saucepan. Bring to a boil over high heat; boil 2 minutes more. Add the garlic; boil 4 minutes. Remove from heat; cover, and let sit overnight in the refrigerator. The garlic may be canned, placed in a sterilized jar, or stored in the refrigerator in an airtight container up to 1 month.

barbecue rub

MAKES 2 CUPS

Dry rubs add intense flavor to chicken, pork, and beef. Apply the rub at least 1 hour and up to 3 days before cooking.

- 1 cup chili powder
- 3 tablespoons paprika
- 3 tablespoons finely chopped fresh thyme
- 2 tablespoons coarse salt
- 2 tablespoons garlic powder
- 1 tablespoon freshly ground black pepper
- 2 teaspoons ground cumin
- 1 teaspoon cayenne pepper

Place all the ingredients in a large bowl; whisk to combine. Store in an airtight container at room temperature.

mango and tomato salsa

MAKES 1 QUART

This piquant salsa should be prepared at least a few hours in advance to allow the flavors to fully develop. It can be stored in an airtight container in the refrigerator for up to 3 days; allow it to come to room temperature before serving.

- ½ red onion, peeled and cut into ¼-inch dice
- 2 ripe mangoes, peeled, pitted, and cut into ¼-inch dice
- 2 ripe tomatoes, cut into ½-inch dice
- 1 jalapeño pepper, seeds and ribs removed, minced
- 2½ tablespoons fresh lemon juice
- 2 tablespoons fresh lime juice
- ½ teaspoon coarse salt
- ¼ teaspoon freshly ground pepper
- ½ cup loosely packed, fresh cilantro leaves, coarsely chopped

Combine the onion, mangoes, tomatoes, jalapeño, lemon and lime juice, salt, and pepper in a small bowl; toss to coat. Let stand at least 2 to 3 hours. Stir in the cilantro just before serving.

parsley-walnut pesto

SERVES 4

- 1 bunch fresh flat-leaf parsley, leaves only (about 2½ cups)
- 1 garlic clove
- 4 anchovy fillets, rinsed
- ½ cup walnut halves, toasted
- 1 teaspoon finely grated lemon zest
- ¾ cup plus 2 tablespoons extra-virgin olive oil
   Coarse salt and freshly ground pepper

Process the parsley, garlic, anchovies, walnuts, and lemon zest in a food processor until finely chopped. With the machine running, add the oil in a slow, steady stream until combined. Season with salt and pepper.

four-onion and jalapeño confit

MAKES ABOUT 3 CUPS

- 4 tablespoons unsalted butter
- 2 medium red onions, cut into ¼-inch slices
- 2 sweet yellow onions, cut into ¼-inch slices
- 4 large shallots, cut into ¼-inch rings
- 10 garlic cloves, halved lengthwise
- 1 bunch scallions, cut into 2-inch pieces
- 5 large jalapeño peppers, seeded and cut in ¼-inch-wide strips
- ¾ cup golden raisins
- ¼ cup packed light-brown sugar
- ½ cup cider vinegar
- 1½ cups water

Heat the butter in a saucepan over medium heat. Add the onions, shallots, and garlic; cook, stirring occasionally, until the vegetables begin to soften, about 8 minutes. Add the remaining ingredients. Simmer, covered, until very tender, about 1 hour. Uncover; simmer until thick and most of the liquid has evaporated, about 1½ hours. Serve warm, or refrigerate up to 1 week.

raita

MAKES ABOUT 2 CUPS

- 1 Kirby cucumber, peeled, halved lengthwise, and seeded
- 1 cup plain whole-milk yogurt (8 ounces), whisked until smooth
- ½ teaspoon coarse salt
  Chili powder, for sprinkling

1. Grate enough cucumber on the large holes of a box grater to yield ½ cup. Transfer to a clean dish towel; squeeze out as much liquid as possible.

2. Stir together the cucumber, yogurt, and salt in a small bowl. Refrigerate in an airtight container up to 1 day. Before using, stir to combine, then sprinkle with some chili powder.

orange marmalade

MAKES ABOUT 2 QUARTS

This marmalade can be made with navel oranges, blood oranges, or tangerines.

- 2 sweet oranges, preferably organic
- 2 cups fresh orange juice (about 2 pounds oranges)
- ¾ cup fresh lemon juice (about 3 lemons)
- 7½ cups sugar (3 pounds)

1. Rinse the oranges under hot water. Quarter the oranges lengthwise; slice crosswise as thinly as possible with a sharp knife.

2. Bring the orange slices, orange and lemon juices, and 6 cups water to a boil in a large nonreactive saucepan over medium-high heat. Reduce heat to medium-low. Simmer until the orange peels are translucent and tender, about 1½ hours.

3. Stir in the sugar. Bring the mixture to a boil over medium-high heat, stirring constantly, until the sugar is dissolved. Continue cooking, stirring often and skimming foam from the surface with a slotted spoon, until the mixture is set and registers 220°F on a candy thermometer, about 15 minutes. (To test if the marmalade has set, place a small amount on a well-chilled plate. Press gently with your finger; the marmalade should wrinkle. If it doesn't, continue to simmer, 5 to 10 minutes more. Test again; repeat as needed.)

4. Let cool, then transfer to an airtight container. Marmalade can be refrigerated up to 1 month. (Alternatively, transfer the marmalade to sterilized canning jars and process according to the jar manufacturer's instructions.)

apricot-raisin chutney

MAKES 2½ CUPS

- 2 tablespoons olive oil
- ½ small onion, finely chopped (about ½ cup)
- 1 pound apricots, peeled, quartered, and pitted
- ½ cup sugar
- ½ cup good-quality honey
- ⅓ cup raisins
- ¼ cup cider vinegar

1. Heat the oil in a medium skillet over medium heat until hot but not smoking. Add the onion; cook, stirring frequently, until soft and translucent, about 4 minutes.

2. Transfer the onion to a large saucepan. Add the apricots, sugar, honey, raisins, and vinegar. Cook over medium heat, stirring, until thickened, about 25 minutes.

3. Pour the chutney into a large bowl, and let cool completely. The chutney can be refrigerated in an airtight container up to 1 week. Bring to room temperature before serving.

strawberry preserves

MAKES 2½ CUPS

These preserves can be canned and stored for up to 1 year; multiply the recipe, if you like.

- 2 pounds strawberries, hulled
- 1 tablespoon plus ½ teaspoon fresh lemon juice
- 1 cup sugar

1. Put the strawberries and lemon juice in a large saucepan. Cook, stirring occasionally, over low heat until the juices are released, about 40 minutes. Stir in the sugar.

2. Bring to a boil over medium heat. Cook, stirring occasionally, until the mixture registers 210°F on a candy thermometer, about 15 minutes. Let cool completely; skim foam from the surface with a spoon. The preserves can be refrigerated in an airtight container up to 2 months.

chile-citrus ketchup

MAKES 2½ CUPS

- 1 can (28 ounces) diced tomatoes
- 1 medium onion, quartered
- 3 garlic cloves, crushed with the flat side of a large knife
- ¼ cup plus 2 tablespoons packed dark brown sugar
- ¼ cup cider vinegar
- 2 teaspoons dry mustard
  Pinch of ground nutmeg
- ¼ teaspoon ground allspice
  Pinch of chili powder
- ½ teaspoon finely grated orange zest plus 1 cup fresh orange juice (2 oranges total)
- 2 tablespoons brewed espresso
- 1 bay leaf
- 1 fresh habanero chile
  Coarse salt and freshly ground pepper

1. Puree the diced tomatoes and juice, onion, garlic, and sugar in a food processor. Transfer the tomato mixture to a large, heavy-bottomed stockpot. Add the vinegar, 1 cup water, and the dry mustard, nutmeg, allspice, chili powder, orange zest, orange juice, espresso, bay leaf, and habanero chile.

2. Bring the mixture to a boil over medium heat. Reduce heat; simmer, stirring occasionally, until thickened, about 50 minutes.

3. Remove the chile. Puree half or whole chile (depending on desired heat) with 1 cup ketchup in the food processor. Return the ketchup to the pot; stir until well blended. Season with salt and pepper. Let cool completely. The ketchup can be refrigerated in an airtight container, up to 2 weeks.

tarragon tartar sauce

MAKES 1 ¼ CUPS

1 cup mayonnaise

3 tablespoons sweet relish

1 tablespoon fresh lemon juice

3 tablespoons drained capers, rinsed

1 tablespoon chopped fresh tarragon

1 teaspoon coarse salt

⅛ teaspoon freshly ground pepper

Stir together the mayonnaise, relish, lemon juice, capers, tarragon, salt, and pepper in a medium bowl. The sauce can be refrigerated in an airtight container up to 1 week.

fennel spice mix

MAKES 2 TABLESPOONS

Toss this mix with 2 pounds potatoes just before grilling. See page 389 for grilling instructions.

1 tablespoon plus 1 teaspoon ground fennel seeds

Pinch of cayenne pepper

¼ teaspoon dry mustard

1 teaspoon coarse salt

¼ teaspoon ground ginger

Stir together the spices in a small bowl.

southwestern spice mix

MAKES 1 TABLESPOON

Toss this mix with 2 pounds potatoes before grilling. Once they have finished cooking, sprinkle the potatoes with fresh lime juice, if desired. See page 389 for grilling instructions.

1 teaspoon ground cumin

½ teaspoon paprika

½ teaspoon chili powder

½ teaspoon coarse salt

¼ teaspoon ground coriander

Stir together the spices in a small bowl.

chickpea and spinach spread

MAKES 2 CUPS

Make a nutritious lunch by spooning this spread into whole-wheat pita halves and layering with tomato slices. Or, for a cocktail hour snack, dab a small amount on cherry tomato halves.

1 tablespoon extra-virgin olive oil

2 garlic cloves, minced

2 cups canned chickpeas, rinsed and drained

1 tablespoon plus 1 teaspoon fresh lemon juice

10 ounces spinach, trimmed

Coarse salt

½ teaspoon crushed red pepper flakes

2 teaspoons tahini

1. Heat the oil in a large stockpot over medium heat. Add the garlic. Cook, stirring, until fragrant, about 1 minute. Add the chickpeas and 1 tablespoon lemon juice. Cook, stirring, 1 minute. Add the spinach, ¼ teaspoon salt, and the red pepper flakes. Cover; raise heat to medium-high. Cook, stirring once, until the spinach has wilted, about 4 minutes. Uncover; raise heat to high. Cook, stirring, until most of the liquid has evaporated, about 2 minutes. Let cool.

2. Pulse the spinach mixture, tahini, remaining teaspoon lemon juice, and ¼ teaspoon salt in a food processor until slightly chunky. The spread can be refrigerated in an airtight container up to 2 days.

FIT TO EAT RECIPE PER SERVING (½ CUP): 208 CALORIES, 6 G FAT, 0 MG CHOLESTEROL, 31 G CARBOHYDRATE, 557 MG SODIUM, 9 G PROTEIN, 7 G FIBER

blue cheese dressing

MAKES 1 ¾ CUPS

- 1 cup low-fat buttermilk
- ¼ cup mayonnaise
- ¼ cup plain low-fat yogurt
- 1 tablespoon fresh lemon juice
- ½ teaspoon coarsely chopped fresh thyme
- 4 ounces blue cheese, crumbled
  Coarse salt and freshly ground pepper

Whisk the buttermilk, mayonnaise, yogurt, lemon juice, and thyme in a bowl; stir in the cheese. Season with salt and pepper. Chill in an airtight container, up to 3 days.

eggless caesar dressing

MAKES 1 ½ CUPS

- 4 small garlic cloves
- ½ teaspoon coarse salt
- 12 anchovy fillets
- 1 tablespoon plus 1 teaspoon finely grated lemon zest, plus 1 cup fresh lemon juice (2 to 3 lemons total)
- 2 tablespoons drained capers, rinsed
- 1½ teaspoons dried mustard
- ½ teaspoon freshly ground pepper
- 1 cup extra-virgin olive oil
- ½ cup finely grated Parmesan cheese

Mash the garlic and salt using a large mortar and pestle. Add the anchovies, zest, capers, mustard, and pepper; mash to form a paste. Stir in the lemon juice. Add the oil in a slow, steady stream, working the pestle until emulsified; work in the cheese. (Or, puree all the ingredients except the oil and cheese in a blender. Add the oil in a slow, steady stream, blending until emulsified. Transfer to a bowl; stir in the cheese.) The dressing can be refrigerated in an airtight container, up to 3 days. Bring to room temperature before serving.

french dressing

MAKES ¾ CUP

- 2 teaspoons tomato paste
- 1½ teaspoons sugar
- 1 teaspoon finely grated onion
- 1 teaspoon dried mustard
- ¾ teaspoon paprika
  Pinch of sweet smoked paprika
- ¼ teaspoon coarse salt
- ¼ teaspoon celery seed
  Freshly ground pepper
- 4½ teaspoons red-wine vinegar
- 1½ teaspoons fresh lemon juice
- ½ cup canola oil

Whisk the tomato paste, sugar, onion, mustard, paprikas, salt, and celery seed in a medium bowl; season with pepper. Whisk in the vinegar and lemon juice. Add the oil in a slow, steady stream, whisking until emulsified. Alternatively, puree all ingredients except the oil in a blender. With the machine running, add the oil in a slow, steady stream; blend until emulsified. Use the dressing immediately.

fresh italian dressing

MAKES 1 ⅓ CUPS

The trick to achieving a good emulsification—suspending the oil in water-based ingredients such as vinegar—is to add the oil toward the end and whisk it in a little bit at a time.

- 2 small garlic cloves, pressed through a garlic press
- 2 teaspoons sugar
- 2 teaspoons dried mustard
  Coarse salt and freshly ground pepper
- ½ teaspoon crushed red pepper flakes
- ¼ cup plus 2 tablespoons red-wine vinegar
- ½ cup extra-virgin olive oil
- ½ cup canola oil
- ¼ cup finely chopped fresh basil
- 2 teaspoons finely chopped fresh marjoram
- 1 teaspoon finely chopped fresh oregano

Whisk the garlic, sugar, mustard, 1½ teaspoons salt, ½ teaspoon pepper, the red pepper flakes, and vinegar in a medium bowl. Whisk together the oils; add to the vinegar mixture in a slow, steady stream, whisking until emulsified. Whisk in the herbs; season with salt and pepper. Refrigerate in an airtight container, up to 1 week.

cranberry sauce with dried cherries

MAKES 3 CUPS

You can substitute dried cranberries or raisins for the dried cherries in this recipe.

- 3½ cups cranberries (1 12-ounce bag)
- ¾ cup dried cherries
- ½ cup finely chopped shallots
- 2 tablespoons red-wine vinegar
  Zest and juice of 1 orange (about ½ cup)
- 2 teaspoons grated peeled fresh ginger
- ¾ cup packed light-brown sugar

Combine the cranberries, cherries, shallots, vinegar, orange zest and juice, ginger, and brown sugar in a medium saucepan, and cook over medium heat until the cranberries pop. Reduce heat to low; cook, stirring occasionally, until the cranberries release their juices, about 15 minutes. If the cranberry sauce becomes too thick, add water until the desired consistency is reached. Transfer to a bowl to cool.

savory cranberry jelly

SERVES 12

- 2 packages (12 ounces each) fresh or frozen (thawed) cranberries
- 2 cups sugar
- 2 teaspoons minced garlic
- 1 teaspoon grated peeled fresh ginger
- ½ cup cider vinegar
  Large pinch of ground allspice
  Large pinch of coarse salt
  Freshly ground pepper
- 4¾ teaspoons unflavored gelatin

1. Bring the berries, sugar, and 1 cup water to a simmer in a covered medium saucepan over medium-high heat. Cook until the berries are soft, about 10 minutes. Pass through a fine sieve into a bowl, pressing on the solids to make a puree.

2. Bring ½ cup water, the garlic, ginger, vinegar, allspice, salt, and a generous amount of pepper to a simmer in a small saucepan over medium-high heat. Cook until reduced by half, about 5 minutes.

3. Pour the vinegar mixture into a small bowl. Sprinkle the gelatin on top; stir until dissolved. Stir the mixture into the berry puree.

4. Cover with plastic wrap; refrigerate at least 2 hours or up to 1 week.

classic mexican guacamole

MAKES 1½ CUPS

This recipe was inspired by the tableside version prepared at Rosa Mexicano in New York City. To ripen hard avocados, leave them in a closed paper bag at room temperature for a few days.

- 1½ tablespoons finely chopped white onion
- 1 tablespoon plus 2 teaspoons finely chopped fresh cilantro
- 1¼ teaspoons finely chopped seeded jalapeño pepper
- ½ teaspoon coarse salt, plus more for seasoning if desired
- 1 ripe Hass avocado, pitted, peeled, and coarsely chopped
- 3 tablespoons finely chopped seeded tomato

With a large mortar (such as a *molcajete*) and pestle (or *tejolote*), mash the onion, 1 tablespoon cilantro, jalapeño, and salt until smooth and juicy. Add the avocado, and mash slightly (the avocado should remain somewhat chunky). Stir in the tomato and remaining 2 teaspoons cilantro. Season with salt, if desired. Serve immediately.

tomatillo guacamole

MAKES 1 CUP

For this version, make a basic tomatillo salsa, then puree it with avocado. This recipe makes extra salsa you can serve on its own along with tortilla chips. The salsa's acidity preserves the color of guacamole; it can be refrigerated, in an airtight container, up to 1 day.

- 6 tomatillos (about 13 ounces), husked and halved
- ½ jalapeño pepper with seeds (about ¼ ounce)
- ¼ cup finely chopped white onion
- 2 tablespoons finely chopped fresh cilantro
- ¾ teaspoon coarse salt
- 1 ripe Hass avocado, pitted, peeled, and coarsely chopped

Puree the tomatillos, jalapeño, onion, cilantro, and salt in a food processor or blender until smooth. Reserve ½ cup salsa; the remaining cup salsa can be served separately. Puree the avocado and the reserved salsa until smooth.

roasted garlic vinaigrette

MAKES ¾ CUP

Refrigerate the vinaigrette in an airtight container up to 3 days.

- 10 Roasted Garlic cloves (page 200)
- 3 tablespoons sherry vinegar
- 1 tablespoon honey
- 1 teaspoon Dijon mustard
- ¾ teaspoon coarse salt
- ½ cup extra-virgin olive oil
   Freshly ground pepper

Squeeze the garlic cloves from their skins into a blender. Add the vinegar, honey, mustard, and salt; blend until smooth, about 10 seconds. With the machine running, pour in the oil in a slow, steady stream; blend until emulsified. Season with pepper.

mole sauce

MAKES 3 CUPS

This classic Mexican sauce is often used in enchiladas or served with tamales.

- 1 slice white bread or 2 slices baguette
- 1 garlic clove, unpeeled
- ⅓ cup whole almonds (2 ounces)
- 1 ancho chile
- 1 tablespoon vegetable oil or lard
- ½ white onion, finely chopped
- 1 pint grape tomatoes
- ½ small canned chipotle pepper in adobo sauce, plus 1 teaspoon adobo sauce
- ½ large ripe banana, cut into pieces
- 2 tablespoons plus 1 teaspoon unsweetened cocoa powder
- 1½ teaspoons packed light-brown sugar
- ¼ teaspoon ground cinnamon
- ¼ teaspoon dried oregano
- ⅛ teaspoon ground cloves
- 1½ cups homemade or low-sodium store-bought chicken stock
   Coarse salt and freshly ground pepper

1. In a 9-inch cast-iron skillet, toast the bread over medium-high heat, turning once, until golden. Tear the bread into large pieces; pulse in a blender until fine crumbs form. Transfer to a large bowl.

2. In the skillet, cook the garlic over medium-high heat, turning occasionally, until soft and charred, about 5 minutes. When cool enough to handle, squeeze the clove from the skin; add to the bowl with the bread crumbs.

3. Toast the almonds in the skillet over medium heat, tossing occasionally, until golden, about 3 minutes. Transfer to the bowl.

4. Wipe the chile with a damp paper towel. Slit the chile lengthwise; remove the stem, ribs, and seeds, reserving the seeds. Cook the chile in the skillet over medium heat, turning once, until it just begins to blister (do not burn it), 10 to 30 seconds. Transfer to the bowl.

5. Pour the oil into the skillet; add the onion. Cook over medium heat, stirring, until soft and translucent, about 3 minutes. Transfer to the bowl. Add the tomatoes to the skillet; cook, tossing, until slightly charred, about 5 minutes. Transfer to the bowl.

6. Add the chipotle, adobo sauce, reserved chile seeds, banana, cocoa, sugar, cinnamon, oregano, and cloves to the bowl, and stir well. Working in batches, puree the mixture in a blender until smooth, adding the stock a little at a time.

7. Transfer the puree to a medium saucepan. Cook over medium-low heat, stirring until slightly thickened, about 20 minutes. Pass the mole through a sieve into a serving bowl; discard the solids. Season with salt and pepper, and serve warm.

cilantro salsa with coconut and lime

MAKES ABOUT ½ CUP

This salsa can also be spooned over grilled shrimp, fish, chicken, or lamb.

- 1 teaspoon cumin seeds
- 6 scallions, white and light-green parts only, chopped
- 2 small garlic cloves
- 1 or 2 serrano chiles, seeded for less heat, if desired
- 3 cups loosely packed cilantro leaves
- ¼ cup fresh lime juice (about 3 limes)
- 2 tablespoons shredded sweetened coconut
- ½ teaspoon coarse salt
- 1 tablespoon plus 1 teaspoon olive oil

1. In a small skillet, heat the cumin seeds over medium heat until toasted and aromatic, about 3 minutes. Let cool slightly, then crush lightly.

2. In a food processor, process the scallions, garlic, and chiles until finely chopped, about 10 seconds. Add the cilantro, crushed cumin, lime juice, 2 tablespoons water, coconut, salt, and oil; pulse to form a coarse paste, about 10 times.

FIT TO EAT RECIPE PER SERVING: 98 CALORIES, 7 G FAT, 0 MG CHOLESTEROL, 9 G CARBOHYDRATE, 270 MG SODIUM, 2 G PROTEIN, 2 G FIBER

roasted garlic aïoli

MAKES ABOUT 1 CUP

You can make this garlic mayonnaise with a mortar and pestle or a food processor—we've provided directions for each method. Store in an airtight container in the refrigerator up to 3 days.

- 1 bulb whole Roasted Garlic (page 200), cloves removed
- ½ teaspoon coarse salt
- 3 large egg yolks
- ½ teaspoon Dijon mustard
- ¾ cup olive oil
- 1 tablespoon fresh lemon juice

With a mortar and pestle: In a large mortar, mash the garlic cloves and salt with a pestle until combined. Add the egg yolks; stir until combined. Stir in the mustard. Pour in the oil a few drops at a time, stirring until emulsified. Stir in the lemon juice. With a food processor: Process the garlic cloves, salt, egg yolks, and mustard until combined, about 5 seconds. With the machine running, pour in ¼ cup oil in a slow, steady stream; process until the mixture is slightly thickened, about 10 seconds. With the machine still running, pour in the remaining ½ cup oil in a slow, steady stream; process until the mixture is thick. Stir in the lemon juice.

NOTE Raw eggs should not be used in food prepared for pregnant women, babies, young children, the elderly, or anyone whose health is compromised.

corn relish

MAKES 2 QUARTS

This colorful relish is delicious with grilled chicken or shrimp. It also pairs well with the piquant flavors of quesadillas and crab cakes.

- 6 ears fresh corn, shucked
- 1½ cups cider vinegar
- 3 tablespoons sugar
- ½ teaspoon turmeric
- ¾ teaspoon mustard powder
- 1 tablespoon mustard seed
- 1 teaspoon coarse salt
- 1 dried bay leaf
- 4 cups green cabbage (about ½ pound), chopped into ½-inch pieces
- 2 red bell peppers, finely diced
- 1 large red onion, finely diced

1. Fill a medium pot with water, and bring to a boil. Add the corn; cook until the kernels are tender, about 4 minutes. Using tongs, transfer the corn to a platter; let cool. Discard all but 3 cups cooking water. Use a sharp knife to shave the kernels from the cobs (to yield about 3 cups); set aside.

2. Add the vinegar, sugar, turmeric, mustard powder, mustard seed, salt, and bay leaf to pot. Bring to a simmer over medium-high heat. Add the cabbage, red peppers, onion, and corn kernels; stir to combine. Bring to a boil; immediately remove from heat, and let stand 5 minutes.

3. Strain the mixture, and let the liquid and vegetables cool in separate bowls; discard the bay leaf. When cool, strain the liquid through a fine sieve into the bowl with the vegetables.

4. Serve the relish chilled or at room temperature, using a slotted spoon to leave liquid behind. Store in an airtight container in the refrigerator.

fennel, roasted tomato, and basil relish

MAKES ABOUT 3 CUPS

Serve with grilled shrimp, fish, or pork.

- Olive oil cooking spray
- 1 pound ripe plum tomatoes (about 6)
- 4 garlic cloves
- 1 fennel bulb (about 1 pound), trimmed and cut into ¼-inch dice
- ¼ cup red-wine vinegar
- 1 tablespoon capers, rinsed and drained
- ¼ teaspoon crushed red pepper flakes or finely chopped fresh red chile
- 2 tablespoons extra-virgin olive oil
- 1 cup loosely packed fresh basil leaves
- 1 cup loosely packed fresh flat-leaf parsley leaves, coarsely chopped

1. Preheat the oven to 400°F. Coat a baking sheet with cooking spray. Slice the tomatoes in half lengthwise; arrange them, cut side down, in a single layer on the prepared baking sheet. Place the garlic cloves on the baking sheet next to the tomatoes. Roast in the oven until the tomatoes are soft and wrinkled and the garlic is aromatic and tender, about 35 minutes. Let cool.

2. In a medium bowl, stir to combine the fennel with the vinegar, capers, red pepper flakes, and oil. Finely chop the garlic, and roughly chop the tomatoes; add to the bowl. Slice the basil into fine strips; add to the bowl along with the parsley. Stir to combine; serve chilled or at room temperature.

FIT TO EAT RECIPE PER SERVING: 78 CALORIES, 5 G FAT, 0 MG CHOLESTEROL, 9 G CARBOHYDRATE, 56 MG SODIUM, 2 G PROTEIN, 3 G FIBER

spicy pineapple and mint salsa
MAKES ABOUT 3 CUPS

Serve with grilled pork or fish, such as red snapper or striped bass.

- ½ red onion, thinly sliced
- 1 or 2 serrano chiles, seeded for less heat, if desired, and very thinly sliced
- 1 small garlic clove, minced
- ½ cup fresh orange juice (about 2 oranges)
- 1 tablespoon fresh lime juice (about 1 lime)
- 1 pineapple, peeled and chopped into ½-inch pieces
- 1½ teaspoons extra-virgin olive oil
- 1 cup loosely packed fresh mint leaves

In a medium bowl, combine the onion, chiles, garlic, orange and lime juices, and pineapple. Add the oil; stir to combine. Let stand at room temperature at least 15 minutes or up to 1 hour. Just before serving, add the mint; toss to combine.

FIT TO EAT RECIPE PER SERVING: 176 CALORIES, 3 G FAT, 0 MG CHOLESTEROL, 42 G CARBOHYDRATE, 5 MG SODIUM, 2 G PROTEIN, 4 G FIBER

quick pear chutney
SERVES 4

- ¼ cup walnuts
- 1 teaspoon extra-virgin olive oil
- 1 shallot, minced
- 2 ripe but firm pears, cored and cut into ¼-inch dice
- 6 tablespoons cider vinegar
- 3 tablespoons honey
- 4 whole cloves
- ¼ cup golden raisins

1. Preheat the oven to 375° F. Spread the walnuts on a small rimmed baking sheet, and toast until fragrant and browned, 7 to 9 minutes. Remove from heat; let cool, and roughly chop. Set aside.

2. Heat the oil in a small saucepan over medium heat. Add the shallot, and sauté until softened, about 2 minutes. Add the pears, vinegar, honey, and cloves. Bring to a boil, reduce heat, and cook until the pears are tender, 4 to 5 minutes. Discard the cloves; stir in the raisins and walnuts. Remove from heat. Serve warm or at room temperature.

rosemary balsamic marinade
MAKES ¾ CUP, ENOUGH FOR 2 POUNDS MEAT

This goes remarkably well with steak.

- ½ cup balsamic vinegar
- 2 tablespoons extra-virgin olive oil
- 6 garlic cloves, coarsely chopped
- ½ teaspoon freshly ground pepper, plus more for seasoning
- 6 rosemary sprigs, coarsely chopped
  Coarse salt

1. Whisk together the vinegar, oil, garlic, and pepper in a nonreactive bowl. Scatter half the rosemary in a shallow nonreactive dish; arrange the meat on top. Cover with the marinade; rub gently into meat. Sprinkle with the remaining rosemary. Cover; refrigerate for the length of time specified below, turning the meat occasionally.

2. Before cooking, remove the marinating meat from the refrigerator, and let it come to a cool room temperature. Wipe off bits of garlic or rosemary; discard the marinade. Season with salt and pepper; cook as desired.

· ·

MARINATING TIMES

Shellfish: 20 minutes

Cheese, tofu, and vegetables: 30 minutes

Thin and flaky fish fillets: 30 minutes

Thick and fatty fish fillets: 1 hour

Beef, chicken, game, lamb, and pork: 6 to 24 hours

· ·

spicy hoisin marinade

MAKES ¾ CUP, ENOUGH FOR
2½ POUNDS MEAT

This Asian-inspired marinade pairs perfectly with pork—turning into a sticky, spicy, sweet glaze when cooked—but can also be used with chicken or beef.

- ¼ cup soy sauce
- ¼ cup packed dark-brown sugar
- 2 tablespoons sherry
- 2 tablespoons fresh orange juice
- 2 tablespoons hoisin sauce
- 2 tablespoons freshly grated ginger
- 2 garlic cloves, minced
- 2 scallions, white and green parts, thinly sliced, plus more for garnish
- 1 tablespoon dry mustard
- 1 teaspoon crumbled dried chile or crushed red pepper flakes
  Zest of 1 orange

1. Whisk together the ingredients in a nonreactive bowl. Arrange the meat in a shallow nonreactive dish or resealable plastic bag. Add the marinade; rub gently into the meat. Cover; refrigerate for the length of time specified on page 625, turning the meat occasionally.

2. Before cooking, remove the meat from the refrigerator and let it come to a cool room temperature. Cook as desired, basting with marinade during the first half of cooking to create a glaze. Garnish with scallions.

cocktail sauce

MAKES 1 CUP

- ¾ cup prepared ketchup
- 2½ tablespoons prepared horseradish
- 2 tablespoons fresh lemon juice
- ½ teaspoon coarse salt
- ¼ teaspoon hot pepper sauce

In a bowl, whisk the ketchup, horseradish, lemon juice, salt, and pepper sauce to combine. Refrigerate in an airtight container for up to 3 days.

tandoori marinade

MAKES 2 CUPS, ENOUGH
FOR 2 TO 2½ POUNDS MEAT OR FISH

The yogurt in this traditional Indian mixture tenderizes what you're marinating. Try grilling the meat or fish to add a smoky flavor.

- 1 cup plain yogurt
- 1 onion, coarsely chopped
- ¼ cup loosely packed fresh cilantro, coarsely chopped
  Zest of 1 lime
- 4 garlic cloves, coarsely chopped
- 2 to 3 tablespoons freshly grated ginger
- 2 tablespoons coarsely chopped fresh mint
- 1 teaspoon ground cumin
- 1 teaspoon garam masala
- 1 teaspoon ground turmeric
- ¼ teaspoon ground nutmeg
- ¼ teaspoon ground cinnamon
- ¼ teaspoon cayenne pepper
- 3 tablespoons olive oil
- 1 teaspoon coarse salt
- ¼ teaspoon freshly ground black pepper

1. Whisk together the ingredients in a nonreactive bowl. Arrange the meat in a shallow nonreactive dish or resealable plastic bag. Cover with the marinade; rub gently into the meat. Cover; refrigerate for the length of time specified on page 625, turning meat occasionally.

2. Before cooking, remove the meat from the refrigerator and let it come to a cool room temperature. Cook as desired, basting occasionally with marinade during the first half of cooking.

thyme, shallot, and lemon marinade

MAKES ⅔ CUP, ENOUGH
FOR 2 POUNDS MEAT OR FISH

This classic marinade pairs nicely with almost any meat, particularly shellfish and fish fillets. Be careful not to marinate shellfish for longer than 20 minutes; the acid in the lemon juice will cook the flesh.

- 3 tablespoons fresh lemon juice
- 3 tablespoons dry white wine
- 2 tablespoons extra-virgin olive oil
- 1 bunch fresh thyme (12 to 15 sprigs)
- 2 shallots, thinly sliced
- 1 lemon, sliced into ¼-inch rounds
  Coarse salt and freshly ground pepper

1. Whisk together the lemon juice, wine, and oil in a shallow nonreactive dish. Arrange the meat or fish in a single layer in dish; turn to coat. Evenly scatter the thyme, shallots, and lemon slices over fish. Cover; refrigerate for the length of time specified on page 625, turning the meat occasionally.

2. Remove the marinating meat or fish from the refrigerator, and let it come to a cool room temperature before cooking. Season with salt and pepper. Cook as desired.

apricot mustard

MAKES ABOUT 1 CUP

- 4 ounces dried apricots
- 4½ teaspoons yellow mustard seeds
- 4½ teaspoons brown mustard seeds
- 2 tablespoons ground mustard
- ¼ cup distilled white vinegar
- ¼ teaspoon coarse salt

Mix the apricots, mustard seeds, ground mustard, and ¾ cup water in a bowl. Refrigerate, covered, overnight. Put the mixture in a food processor. Add the vinegar and salt; puree. The mustard can be refrigerated, up to 1 week.

green tomato salsa

MAKES 4 CUPS

We like to serve grilled fish over a coulis made by pureeing half the salsa until smooth and adding olive oil until the mixture is the desired consistency.

- 1 poblano chile
- 2 pounds (about 6 medium) green tomatoes, seeded and finely chopped
- 1 small or ½ large Vidalia or other sweet onion, finely chopped
- 1 medium cucumber, peeled, seeded, and finely chopped
- 4 scallions, sliced thinly crosswise
- 2 tablespoons fresh lime juice (about 2 limes)
- 1 tablespoon extra-virgin olive oil
- ½ cup finely chopped fresh cilantro
  Coarse salt and freshly ground pepper

1. Roast the chile directly on a gas-stove burner over high heat, or under the broiler, turning as each side blackens. Transfer to a bowl; cover with plastic. Let stand until cool enough to handle. Peel off the skin; discard the stem and seeds. Finely chop the chile, and place in a medium bowl.

2. Add the tomatoes, onion, cucumber, scallions, lime juice, oil, and cilantro. Stir. Season with salt and pepper; let stand 30 minutes. Store in the refrigerator up to 3 days.

cranberry marmalade

MAKES ABOUT 4½ CUPS

- 5 juice oranges (6 ounces each), chopped into ¼-inch dice (including peel)
- 5 cups fresh cranberries
- 2½ cups sugar

Bring oranges, cranberries, sugar, and 1 cup water to a boil in a medium saucepan. Reduce heat, and simmer until mixture has the consistency of loose jam, about 35 minutes. Transfer to a bowl. Stir before serving. The marmalade can be refrigerated, covered, up to 1 week.

lemon aïoli

MAKES 1 CUP

1 large egg
1 teaspoon coarse salt
½ cup canola oil
¼ cup extra-virgin olive oil
3 tablespoons fresh lemon juice
  Zest of 1 lemon

Place the egg and salt in the bowl of a food processor; blend until foamy. With the machine running, add the canola oil and then the olive oil a few drops at a time and then in a slow, steady stream. Add the lemon juice and zest; blend briefly. Adjust the seasoning. Refrigerate in an airtight container for up to 2 days.

NOTE *Do not use raw eggs in food for pregnant women, babies, young children, the elderly, or anyone whose health is compromised.*

basic vinaigrette

MAKES ⅔ CUP

This is a good vinaigrette for a simple green salad. Use extra-virgin olive oil if you prefer a fruitier flavor.

2 tablespoons good-quality white-wine vinegar
1 teaspoon Dijon mustard
1 small shallot, finely chopped
1 teaspoon coarse salt, plus more for seasoning
¼ teaspoon freshly ground pepper, plus more for seasoning
6 tablespoons good-quality olive oil

1. Combine the vinegar, mustard, shallot, salt, and pepper in a bowl. Allow the ingredients to macerate for 10 minutes.

2. While whisking, slowly add the olive oil until the mixture is emulsified. Adjust the seasoning with salt and pepper, if desired.

fresh mint jelly

MAKES 1 8-INCH-SQUARE PAN

You can substitute 3 tablespoons powdered pectin for the liquid pectin. Dissolve it in ½ cup warm water before adding it to the mint mixture.

2 cups firmly packed mint leaves and stems (3 to 4 bunches)
2 cups water
3 tablespoons fresh lemon juice
3½ cups sugar
3 ounces liquid pectin
2 drops green food coloring

1. Place the mint in the jar of a blender with 2 cups water; blend for 10 seconds, until the mint is finely chopped. Place in a medium saucepot; bring to a boil. Remove from the heat; steep for 45 minutes to infuse the flavor. Strain into a bowl through a fine-mesh strainer lined with damp cheesecloth, squeezing out all liquid to yield 1¾ to 2 cups liquid.

2. Return the mint water to a clean saucepan; add the lemon juice and sugar. Bring to a boil; cook for 1 minute; skim the surface. Add the pectin; return to a full boil; cook 1 minute more. Remove from heat; stir in the food coloring. Skim the surface. Pour into an 8-inch-square baking pan; let cool on a rack. Cover with plastic wrap; chill overnight.

3. Run a paring knife around edges to loosen the jelly from the pan. Slice into ½-inch cubes; use an offset spatula to lift them from pan, and transfer to a serving dish.

buttermilk-herb vinaigrette

MAKES ABOUT ½ CUP

4 tablespoons buttermilk
2 tablespoons white-wine vinegar
½ garlic clove, minced
½ teaspoon coarse salt, plus more for seasoning
¼ teaspoon freshly ground pepper, plus more for seasoning
2 tablespoons extra-virgin olive oil
¼ cup chopped fresh herbs, such as chives, parsley, thyme, tarragon, and dill

Combine the buttermilk, vinegar, garlic, salt, and pepper in a bowl. Allow the ingredients to macerate for 10 minutes. Slowly whisk in the oil until the mixture is emulsified. Stir in the herbs. Adjust the seasoning, with salt and pepper.

cucumber relish
MAKES ABOUT 1 QUART

The relish can be made up to 1 day ahead and refrigerated; add the salt just before serving.

1½ teaspoons cumin seeds
2 cucumbers
2 celery stalks, finely chopped
1 bunch scallions, white and light green parts, thinly sliced
2 poblano chiles or green bell peppers, seeds and ribs removed, finely chopped
¼ cup finely chopped fresh cilantro
3 tablespoons fresh lemon juice
    Coarse salt

1. Heat a small skillet over medium heat. Add the cumin seeds; toast, stirring, until they are lightly browned. Transfer to a small bowl; let cool.

2. Peel and seed the cucumbers, and cut into ¼-inch dice. Place in a large bowl, and add the celery, scallions, poblano chiles, cilantro, lemon juice, and toasted cumin seeds. Season with salt, and serve.

eggplant caviar
MAKES 3½ CUPS

This dish calls for purple globe eggplants. Instead of cooking them over an open flame, you can use the oven: Place the eggplants on a shallow baking pan, and place under the broiler. Broil, turning the eggplants every 5 minutes, until the skin is blackened all over and the flesh is falling-apart tender, 20 to 30 minutes.

2 purple globe eggplants (1½ pounds each)
¼ cup minced onion (about 4 ounces)
2 plum tomatoes, seeded, finely chopped
¼ cup roughly chopped fresh flat-leaf parsley

½ cup extra-virgin olive oil
1½ teaspoons fresh lemon juice
    Salt and freshly ground pepper
    Pita or rye bread, for serving

1. Roast the eggplants; peel away the blackened skin.

2. Place the eggplants in a food processor; pulse until pureed. Transfer to a large bowl; stir in the remaining ingredients. Serve warm or at room temperature with pita or rye bread.

pickled zucchini ribbons
MAKES 2 QUARTS

Be sure to let the brine cool completely before pouring it over the thinly sliced vegetables. If submerged in hot liquid, the zucchini and onions will quickly turn soggy and won't retain their shape or texture during pickling.

2 pounds medium zucchini
2 medium onions
2 tablespoons coarse salt
1 quart cider vinegar
2 cups sugar
1 tablespoon dry mustard
1 tablespoon yellow mustard seed
1½ teaspoons turmeric
1 teaspoon ground cumin

1. Using a mandoline or sharp knife, cut the zucchini lengthwise into ⅛-inch-thick slices. Halve the onions lengthwise, and cut into ⅛-inch-thick slices. Transfer the vegetables to a colander set in a bowl. Toss well with the salt. Refrigerate 1 hour.

2. Meanwhile, bring the vinegar, sugar, and spices to a boil in a medium saucepan, stirring. Reduce heat; simmer 5 minutes. Let cool completely, about 30 minutes.

3. Rinse the zucchini and onions well, and drain. Pat dry between paper towels.

4. Transfer the zucchini and onions to a large bowl; pour in the brine. Transfer to airtight containers; refrigerate at least 1 week (and up to 3 weeks).

spicy pickled
green and wax beans
MAKES 2 QUARTS

Coarse salt
1 pound green beans, trimmed
1 pound yellow wax beans, trimmed
3 cups distilled white vinegar
3 garlic cloves
¼ teaspoon cayenne pepper

1. Bring a large saucepan of water to a boil; add salt. Prepare an ice-water bath; set aside. Cook the beans until just tender, about 3 minutes. Immediately transfer with tongs to the ice-water bath. Drain well, and transfer to a large bowl.

2. Bring 3 cups water, the vinegar, 3 tablespoons salt, the garlic, and the cayenne to a boil in a medium saucepan. Reduce heat; simmer 4 minutes. Pour the brine over the beans. Let cool completely, about 30 minutes. Transfer to airtight containers; refrigerate at least 1 week (and up to 3 weeks more).

sweet pickled red onions
MAKES 1 QUART

2 pounds red onions
1 tablespoon coarse salt
3 cups cider vinegar
1½ cups sugar
15 whole black peppercorns
4 whole cloves
2 cinnamon sticks
6 whole allspice
2 dried hot red chiles
2 small bay leaves

1. Cut the onions into ¼-inch-thick slices; transfer to a colander set in a bowl. Toss well with the salt. Refrigerate 1 hour. Rinse well; drain. Pat dry between paper towels.

2. Bring the vinegar, sugar, and spices to a boil in a medium saucepan, stirring. Let cool completely, about 30 minutes.

3. Add the onions; bring to a boil. Transfer the onions to a large bowl using a slotted spoon. Let the brine cool completely, about 30 minutes; pour over the onions. Transfer to airtight containers; refrigerate at least 1 week (pickles will keep 3 weeks more).

marinated baby artichokes
MAKES 2 CUPS

These make a wonderful addition to any summer salad or antipasto. They can also be served as a side dish with roasted or grilled lamb.

2 lemons
1½ pounds baby artichokes
1 head garlic, cut in half
2 tablespoons whole black peppercorns
2 tablespoons coarse salt
¼ cup extra-virgin olive oil
1 small bunch fresh thyme
   Pinch of freshly ground black pepper

1. Fill a large bowl with cold water; juice the lemons into the water. Set aside. Trim the spiky tops, tough stems, and outer leaves from the artichokes; halve lengthwise. Scrape any pink choke out from the center, leaving the artichoke half intact. Transfer the cut artichokes to the acidulated water immediately.

2. Drain the artichokes. Fill a large saucepan with water. Add the artichokes, garlic halves, peppercorns, 1½ tablespoons salt, 2 tablespoons olive oil, and thyme to the saucepan. Set over high heat; bring to a boil. Reduce heat; simmer, using a few layers of cheesecloth or a plate to keep the artichokes submerged, until they are tender when pierced with a sharp knife, about 5 minutes.

3. Remove from heat, and drain. Reserve the artichoke halves, some of the garlic, and a few sprigs of thyme. Place in a bowl, and drizzle with the remaining 2 tablespoons olive oil. Season with the remaining 1½ teaspoons salt and pinch of pepper. Keep refrigerated, up to 5 days, until needed.

ginger pickled beets

MAKES 1 QUART

Serve these beets as part of a picnic platter or relish tray, or use them in sandwiches or salads. Golden beets work as nicely as red ones. Leaving beet tails and an inch or so of the stems intact helps minimize the loss of color (as well as flavor and nutrients) during cooking. Trim and peel the beets after they've been boiled; the skins will come off easily.

- 5 or 6 medium red beets (about 1½ pounds without greens), tails and about 1 inch of stems left intact
- ½ cup thinly sliced, peeled fresh ginger (about 1½ ounces)
- 1½ cups rice wine vinegar
- ¼ cup plus 1 tablespoon sugar
- 1 teaspoon coarse salt

1. Prepare an ice-water bath; set aside. Cover the beets with cold water by 2 inches in a large saucepan. Bring to a boil; reduce heat. Simmer the beets until tender when pierced with the tip of a knife, about 30 minutes. Transfer the beets with a slotted spoon to the ice-water bath. Discard the cooking liquid. Trim the beets, and rub off the skins with paper towels, or peel the beets with a paring knife. Cut the beets into very thin rounds; transfer to a large bowl.

2. Bring the ginger, vinegar, sugar, and salt to a boil in a medium saucepan, stirring until the sugar is dissolved. Pour the liquid over the beets; stir. Let stand until completely cool, at least 1 hour. Transfer to an airtight container, and refrigerate up to 1 month.

FIT TO EAT RECIPE PER SERVING (½ CUP): 91 CALORIES, 0 G FAT, 0 MG CHOLESTEROL, 33 G CARBOHYDRATE, 309 MG SODIUM, 1 G PROTEIN, 3 G FIBER

- -

RELISHES AND PICKLED VEGETABLES

Relishes—those small, zesty foods meant to be nibbled—make delicious accompaniments to almost any meal. Often, a selection of pickled vegetables offsets the richness of meats and sauces and awakens the taste buds with each tangy, crunchy, salty bite. Relishes and pickled vegetables are common denominators across cultures too: Pickled cabbage and cucumbers are the standard in Korean and Japanese cuisine; turnips, peppers, and onions accompany spicy meals in the Middle East; and pickled mushrooms are classic fare in Russia. In fact, practically any vegetable can be pickled, and several types can be combined on a tray for a creative selection that stimulates the eye as well as the palate. When deciding which to choose,

remember that relishes work best when the vegetables complement one another in flavor as well as appearance. The mellow flavor of raw creamer potato, for instance, neutralizes the tartness of crisp bread-and-butter pickles.

Here is a basic recipe to get you started. This recipe is sufficient to pickle 3 cantaloupes, 2 medium pumpkins, or 2 pounds pearl onions. Before pickling, peel the items, and cut them into chunks slightly larger than 1 inch; pearl onions can be left whole. To peel pearl onions, drop them in boiling water for 1 minute, and then drain in a colander. When cool enough to handle, slip off the papery skins.

3 cups sugar

2 cups apple cider vinegar

2 teaspoons whole cloves

2 teaspoons allspice

1 cinnamon stick

1 piece (½-inch) of fresh ginger, peeled

1 lemon, thinly sliced

Items to be pickled

1. Heat the sugar and vinegar in a nonreactive stockpot over medium-high heat, stirring, until the sugar has dissolved.

2. Add the remaining ingredients; bring to a boil. Reduce heat; cover, and simmer 30 minutes. Remove from heat; let stand overnight at room temperature.

3. Transfer the mixture to jars or airtight containers; refrigerate up to 2 weeks.

tarragon pickled carrots

MAKES 2 QUARTS

Coarse salt

2 *pounds carrots, peeled*

2 *cups white-wine vinegar*

1 *bunch fresh tarragon*

1 *tablespoon coriander seeds*

10 *whole black peppercorns*

1. Bring a large saucepan of water to a boil; add salt. Prepare an ice-water bath; set aside. Quarter the carrots lengthwise; cook until just tender, about 3 minutes. Immediately transfer with tongs to the ice-water bath. Drain well; transfer to a large bowl.

2. Bring 2 cups water, the vinegar, tarragon, coriander seeds, peppercorns, and 2 tablespoons salt to a boil in a medium saucepan. Reduce heat; simmer 4 minutes. Pour the brine over the carrots; let cool completely, about 30 minutes. Transfer to airtight containers; refrigerate at least 1 week (and up to keep 3 weeks).

carrot, miso, and ginger salad dressing

SERVES 4

To achieve a uniform consistency, grate the carrot on the small holes of a box grater before pureeing in the food processor. We like to serve the colorful dressing in its own dish and let each person spoon some over a salad of butter lettuce, sunflower sprouts, sliced radishes, and edamame.

1½ *tablespoons minced fresh ginger (1½-inch piece)*

1 *large carrot, finely grated*

2 *tablespoons plus 1 teaspoon rice wine vinegar*

2 *teaspoons white miso*

3 *tablespoons canola or vegetable oil*

1 *tablespoon water, if needed*

1. In the bowl of a food processor, pulse the ginger and carrot to a coarse paste. Add the vinegar and miso, and pulse to combine.

2. With the machine running, slowly add the oil in a thin, steady stream through the feed tube until the mixture is emulsified. Add water if the dressing is too thick. Use immediately, or store in an airtight container in the refrigerator up to 1 week.

FIT TO EAT RECIPE PER SERVING: 118 CALORIES, 10 G FAT, 0 MG CHOLESTEROL, 4 G CARBOHYDRATE, 147 MG SODIUM, 1 G PROTEIN, 1 G FIBER

curried yogurt dip

MAKES 2 CUPS

2 *cups plain whole-milk yogurt (16 ounces), preferably Greek*

6 *tablespoons vegetable oil*

1 *teaspoon brown mustard seeds*

20 *fresh curry leaves, plus more for garnish*

2 *teaspoons grated peeled fresh ginger*

10 *fresh, small hot chiles, such as serrano or Thai (2 seeded and chopped; 8 whole)*

1 *teaspoon turmeric*

2 *teaspoons coarse salt*

1 *teaspoon sugar*

Store-bought papads and dried persimmons, for serving (optional)

1. Put the yogurt in a medium bowl. Heat ¼ cup oil in a small skillet over medium-high heat until hot. Add ½ teaspoon mustard seeds. Cook, shaking, until the seeds pop, about 45 seconds. Add the curry leaves; cook until starting to wilt, about 1 minute. Add the ginger and chopped chiles. Cook, stirring, 30 seconds. Stir in the turmeric. Pour the mixture over the yogurt. Stir in the salt and sugar. Transfer to a serving dish.

2. Heat 2 tablespoons oil in a small skillet over medium-high heat until hot. Add ½ teaspoon mustard seeds and the whole chiles. Cook, shaking, until the seeds pop, about 45 seconds. Garnish the dip with the chile mixture and curry leaves. Serve with papads and persimmons, if desired.

hot crab dip

MAKES 4 CUPS

- 8 tablespoons (1 stick) unsalted butter
- 1 medium onion, finely chopped
- 2 garlic cloves, minced
- 6 tablespoons all-purpose flour
- 1½ cups milk
- ¼ teaspoon cayenne pepper
- 2 teaspoons dry mustard
- 4 ounces sharp white Cheddar cheese, shredded (1 cup)
- 2 tablespoons fresh lemon juice, plus freshly grated zest of 1 lemon
- 2 teaspoons Worcestershire sauce
- 10 ounces lump crabmeat, picked over
- 2 tablespoons coarsely chopped fresh flat-leaf parsley

  Coarse salt and freshly ground pepper
- 1 loaf rustic bread (about 1 pound), trimmed of crust and torn into 1-inch pieces (4 to 5 cups)

  Baguette slices, toasted, for serving (optional)

1. Preheat the oven to 400°F. Melt 6 tablespoons butter in a medium saucepan over medium heat. Add the onion and garlic; cook, stirring occasionally, until soft, about 4 minutes. Whisk in the flour; cook, whisking constantly, 4 minutes. Continue to whisk; pour in the milk in a slow, steady stream. Simmer over medium heat, whisking, until thickened, about 4 minutes. Stir in the cayenne and mustard. Gradually whisk in the cheese until melted.

2. Remove from heat. Stir in the lemon juice, zest, and Worcestershire. Stir in the crabmeat and parsley. Season with salt and pepper. Transfer to a 1-quart ovenproof dish.

3. Melt the remaining 2 tablespoons butter; stir into the bread pieces. Season with salt and pepper. Arrange the bread mixture over the crab dip. Bake until heated through and golden brown, 25 to 30 minutes. Let stand at room temperature 10 minutes. Serve with baguette slices.

fava bean and sausage dip

MAKES ABOUT 3 CUPS

Look for merguez at specialty stores, or use another spicy sausage in its place.

- 1 cup large, dried, split fava beans (8 ounces)
- 6 garlic cloves (3 whole; 3 sliced lengthwise)

  Coarse salt
- 12 ounces merguez (spicy Moroccan lamb sausages), casings removed
- ⅓ cup extra-virgin olive oil, plus more for drizzling
- ¼ cup tahini
- ¼ cup fresh lemon juice, plus 1 teaspoon freshly grated lemon zest (2 lemons)

  Freshly ground pepper
- 3 tablespoons fresh flat-leaf parsley leaves, for garnish

  Flatbread crisps, for serving

1. Bring 5 cups water and the fava beans, whole garlic cloves, and ½ teaspoon salt to a boil in a medium saucepan. Reduce heat, and simmer until the beans are tender, about 30 minutes. Drain well; let stand until cool, about 15 minutes.

2. Crumble the sausage into a large skillet. Cook over medium heat, stirring and draining off fat occasionally, 6 minutes. Add the sliced garlic. Cook, stirring occasionally, until the sausage is cooked through and the garlic is crisp, about 4 minutes more.

3. Put the bean mixture, oil, tahini, lemon juice and zest, ¾ teaspoon salt, a pinch of pepper, and ¼ cup water in a food processor. Process, adding up to ¼ cup more water, until smooth and creamy. Season with salt and pepper.

4. Smooth the dip in an even layer on a platter. Using a slotted spoon, arrange the sausage on top. Top with parsley; drizzle with oil. Serve with flatbread crisps.

swiss chard tzatziki

MAKES ABOUT 1 1/4 CUPS; SERVES 4

- 1 cup green or red Swiss chard, stemmed and finely chopped
- 1 garlic clove
- 1/4 teaspoon coarse salt
- 1 cup low-fat Greek yogurt
- 1 tablespoon extra-virgin olive oil
- 1 tablespoon fresh lemon juice
- 1/8 teaspoon cayenne pepper
- 2 whole-wheat pitas, cut into wedges and toasted

1. Prepare an ice-water bath; set aside. Bring a large saucepan of water to a boil. Add chard; cook until just tender, 3 to 5 minutes. Drain. Immediately plunge into ice bath to stop the cooking. Drain.

2. Using a mortar and pestle, grind garlic and salt into a paste. Stir chard, yogurt, garlic paste, oil, lemon juice, and cayenne pepper in a medium bowl. Serve with pita wedges. The tzatziki can be refrigerated in an airtight container up to 1 week.

FIT TO EAT RECIPE PER SERVING: 137 CALORIES, 5 G FAT, 3 MG CHOLESTEROL, 17 G CARBOHYDRATE, 311 MG SODIUM, 7 G PROTEIN, 3 G FIBER

basil chimichurri

MAKES ABOUT 1 1/2 CUPS

In Argentina, garlicky chimichurri, a condiment as prevalent there as ketchup is in the United States, is spooned over all manner of grilled meats, especially steak. Make chimichurri at least 1 hour ahead to allow the flavors to meld.

- 1/4 cup finely chopped fresh basil leaves
- 1/4 cup finely chopped fresh flat-leaf parsley
- 1 teaspoon finely chopped fresh oregano
- 1/2 cup extra-virgin olive oil
- 1/4 cup red-wine vinegar
- 2 garlic cloves, minced
- 2 dried red chiles
- 1/4 teaspoon coarse salt
- 1/8 teaspoon freshly ground pepper

Stir together all ingredients in a bowl; cover and refrigerate at least 1 hour, and up to 3 days. Serve cold or at room temperature.

roasted red pepper and olive salsa

MAKES ABOUT 2 CUPS

Tangy olives balance sweet onions and peppers in this salsa. Its tartness is good on different sorts of white fish, such as tilapia.

- 1/2 cup red or white pearl onions, blanched and peeled
- 1 tablespoon unsalted butter
- 1 jarred roasted red pepper, finely chopped
- 1/2 cup pitted kalamata olives, thinly sliced
- 1/2 cup pitted green Cerignola olives, thinly sliced lengthwise
- 1 garlic clove, minced
- 2 tablespoons finely chopped fresh flat-leaf parsley
- 3 dried red chiles, crumbled
- 1/4 cup extra-virgin olive oil
- 1/4 cup sherry vinegar
- 1/4 teaspoon coarse salt
- 1/4 teaspoon freshly ground pepper

Put onions, butter, and 2 tablespoons water in a saucepan over medium-low heat. Cover; cook until onions cook through, about 6 minutes. Cool. Quarter onions. Combine with remaining ingredients in a bowl. Refrigerate in an airtight container up to 3 days. Serve cold or at room temperature.

roasted tomato and chipotle salsa

MAKES ABOUT 3½ CUPS

The silky texture of this puréed sauce belies the kick of its chipotle and cascabel peppers, which are similar in heat to cayenne. Serve it with chips or crudités.

- 3 dried chipotle peppers
- 2 dried cascabel peppers
- 2 cups boiling-hot water
- 4 medium tomatoes, halved
- ½ small white onion, coarsely chopped
- ¼ cup loosely packed fresh cilantro
- 1 cup soybean oil
- 1 teaspoon coarse salt

1. Preheat the broiler. Put peppers into the hot water; cover, and let stand until soft, about 15 minutes. Discard stems.

2. Put tomatoes onto a baking sheet. Broil tomatoes, turning once, until blackened, about 4 minutes per side.

3. Puree peppers, tomatoes, onion, and cilantro in a food processor until smooth. With the machine running, pour in the oil in a slow, steady stream. Season with salt. The salsa can be refrigerated in an airtight container up to 5 days. Serve warm or at room temperature.

summer bagna cauda

SERVES 6

Set out a dish of peppery extra-virgin olive oil with a dash of aged balsamic vinegar, Vincotto (sweet Italian vinegar), or verjus for dipping.

Whole milk, for soaking

- 2 ounces anchovy fillets
- ½ cup extra-virgin olive oil
- 6 young garlic cloves (or regular garlic), finely chopped
- ¼ cup (½ stick) unsalted butter, cut into small pieces
- 1 tablespoon fresh lemon juice

Sea salt flakes and freshly ground pepper

- 4 pounds fresh vegetables, such as celery, Belgian endive, young wild fennel (halved lengthwise), Persian cucumbers (halved or quartered lengthwise), purple scallions, and Romano beans

Calimyrna figs, for serving

1. Put milk into a shallow dish. Add anchovy fillets; soak 10 minutes. Drain on paper towels; pat dry. Coarsely chop.

2. Put ¼ cup oil and the garlic into a small saucepan over low heat. Cook until garlic softens but does not brown, about 5 minutes. Add anchovies. Cook, whisking constantly, 1 minute. Add butter. Cook, whisking, until butter has melted.

3. Remove pan from heat. Whisk in the remaining ¼ cup oil in a slow, steady stream until mixture thickens and comes together. If the mixture separates at any point, add 2 ice cubes, and whisk until mixture comes together; remove partially melted ice cubes.

4. Whisk in lemon juice, and season with salt and pepper. Serve warm or at room temperature with the vegetables and the figs.

zucchini, avocado, and pomegranate salsa

SERVES 6; MAKES ABOUT 2 CUPS

- 2 zucchini (about 1 pound), trimmed and cut into ½-inch dice (about 3½ cups)
- 1 tablespoon extra-virgin olive oil
- 1 teaspoon finely chopped fresh oregano
- ¾ teaspoon coarse salt
   Freshly ground pepper
- ¼ cup finely chopped red onion
- 1 avocado, halved, pitted, peeled, and cut into ¼-inch dice (about 1 cup)
- ½ cup pomegranate seeds
- 1 tablespoon crumbled feta cheese
- 1 tablespoon fresh lime juice
- 3 whole-wheat pitas (6 inches each)
   Olive oil cooking spray

1. Preheat the oven to 425°F. Toss zucchini with oil, oregano, ¼ teaspoon salt, and ⅛ teaspoon pepper in a bowl. Spread zucchini in a single layer on a rimmed baking sheet. Roast, tossing once, until tender and golden brown, about 25 minutes. Transfer sheet to a wire rack; let zucchini cool completely. (Leave oven on.)

2. Transfer zucchini to a medium bowl. Add onion, avocado, pomegranate seeds, feta, lime juice, ¼ teaspoon salt, and ⅛ teaspoon pepper; gently stir to combine. Refrigerate 30 minutes (up to 2 hours).

3. Cut pitas in half; split each half into 2 half-moons, and cut each half-moon into 3 triangles. Arrange on a rimmed baking sheet. Lightly coat both sides with cooking spray. Sprinkle with remaining ¼ teaspoon salt and ⅛ teaspoon pepper. Bake, flipping once, until pale golden brown, about 5 minutes. Serve with salsa. The pitas can be stored in an airtight container at room temperature up to 3 days.

FIT TO EAT RECIPE PER SERVING (⅓ CUP SALSA, 6 CHIPS): 162 CALORIES, 1 G SATURATED FAT, 6 G UNSATURATED FAT, 1 MG CHOLESTEROL, 21 G CARBOHYDRATE, 287 MG SODIUM, 4 G PROTEIN, 5 G FIBER

warm cheese and glazed pecan dip

SERVES 12

Try this dip with sliced green apple, toasted rustic bread, or crackers.

- 1½ cups pecan halves
- 3 tablespoons unsalted butter, melted
- 3 tablespoons packed light-brown sugar
- 1½ teaspoons coarse salt
- ¼ teaspoon plus a pinch of cayenne pepper
- 2 packages (8 ounces each) cream cheese, room temperature
- 8 ounces extra-sharp white Cheddar cheese, grated
- ¼ cup heavy cream
- 2 scallions, white and pale-green parts only, thinly sliced

1. Preheat the oven to 350°F. Put pecans, butter, brown sugar, 1 teaspoon salt, and ¼ teaspoon cayenne pepper into a medium bowl; toss to combine. Spread in a single layer on a rimmed baking sheet. Bake until fragrant and sugar has melted, about 5 minutes. Let cool completely.

2. Process cream cheese, cheddar, and cream in a food processor until well combined. Transfer to a medium bowl. Stir in scallions, remaining ½ teaspoon salt, and remaining pinch of cayenne.

3. Spoon cheese mixture into 2 round baking dishes (6 to 7 inches in diameter and about 1 inch deep). Arrange glazed pecans on top. Bake until dip is just heated through, about 10 minutes.

basics

....

STOCKS

homemade chicken stock

MAKES 5 QUARTS

If you plan to use the stock for a specific recipe, begin making it at least 12 hours ahead of time, and refrigerate for 8 hours so the fat has a chance to collect on top and can be removed.

 2 *leeks, white and pale-green parts, cut into thirds, well washed*
 1 *teaspoon whole black peppercorns*
 6 *sprigs fresh dill or 2 teaspoons dried*
 6 *sprigs fresh flat-leaf parsley*
 2 *dried bay leaves*
 2 *carrots, cut into thirds*
 2 *celery stalks, cut into thirds*
 1 *4-pound chicken, cut into 6 pieces*
 1½ *pounds chicken wings*
 1½ *pounds chicken backs*
   3 *quarts low-sodium store-bought chicken broth, skimmed of fat*

1. Place the leeks, peppercorns, dill, parsley, bay leaves, carrots, celery, whole chicken, wings, and backs in a large stockpot. Add the chicken stock and 6 cups cold water, cover, and bring to a boil. Reduce to a very gentle simmer, and cook, uncovered, about 45 minutes. The liquid should just bubble up to the surface. A skin will form on the surface; skim it off with a slotted spoon, and discard, repeating as needed. After about 45 minutes, remove the whole chicken from the pot, and set it aside until it is cool enough to handle.

2. Remove the meat from the chicken bones, set the meat aside, and return the bones to the pot. Transfer the chicken meat to the refrigerator for another use; if you plan to use it for chicken noodle soup, shred the meat before refrigerating it.

3. Continue to simmer the stock mixture, on the lowest heat possible, for 3 hours, skimming foam from the top as needed. The chicken bones will begin to disintegrate. Add water if at any time the surface level drops below the bones.

4. Prepare an ice-water bath. Strain the stock through a fine sieve or a cheesecloth-lined strainer into a very large bowl. Discard the solids. Transfer the bowl to the ice bath; let the stock cool to room temperature.

5. Transfer the stock to airtight containers. The stock may be labeled at this point and refrigerated for 3 days or frozen for up to 4 months. If storing, leave the fat layer intact; it seals the stock.

ASIAN-FLAVORED CHICKEN STOCK

To make a stock that is excellent for Asian noodle soups, add one or more of the following ingredients to your stock while it is simmering: 2 stalks fresh lemongrass, 8 ounces shiitake mushrooms, 4 ounces thinly sliced fresh ginger, 10 fresh cilantro stems, 10 whole Szechuan peppercorns, 10 whole coriander seeds, and 2 star anise. Or substitute 2 cups Japanese sake for the water.

beef stock

MAKES 6 QUARTS

You can ask your butcher to cut veal bones into small pieces for you.

 8 *sprigs fresh flat-leaf parsley*
 6 *sprigs fresh thyme or ¼ teaspoon dried*
 4 *sprigs fresh rosemary or 2 teaspoons dried*
 2 *dried bay leaves*
 1 *tablespoon whole black peppercorns*
 1 *pound beef stew meat, cubed*
 5 *pounds veal bones, cut into small pieces*
 1 *large onion, unpeeled and quartered*
 2 *large carrots, cut into thirds*
 2 *celery stalks, cut into thirds*
 2 *cups dry red wine*

1. Preheat the oven to 450°F. Tie the parsley, thyme, rosemary, bay leaves, and peppercorns in a piece of cheesecloth to make a bouquet garni. Set aside.

2. Arrange the beef stew meat, veal bones, onion, carrots, and celery in an even layer in a heavy roasting pan. Roast, turning every 20 minutes, until the vegetables and the bones are deep brown, about 1½ hours. Transfer the meat, bones, and vegetables to a large stockpot, and set aside. Pour off the fat from the roasting pan, and discard. Place the pan over high heat on the stove. Add the red wine, and stir, using a wooden spoon to loosen any browned bits from the bottom of the pan; boil until the wine is reduced by half, about 5 minutes. Pour the mixture into the stockpot.

3. Add 6 quarts cold water to the stockpot, or more if needed to cover bones. Do not use less water. Cover and bring to a boil, then reduce to a very gentle simmer so that bubbles occasionally rise to the surface. Add the reserved bouquet garni. Skim the foam from the surface. Continue to simmer the stock over the lowest possible heat for 3 hours. A skin will form on the surface of the liquid; skim off with a slotted spoon. Repeat as needed. Add water if at any time the surface level drops below the bones.

4. Prepare an ice-water bath. Strain the stock through a fine sieve, or a cheesecloth-lined strainer, into a large bowl. Discard the solids. Transfer the bowl to the ice-water bath, and let the stock cool to room temperature.

5. Transfer the stock to airtight containers. The stock may be labeled at this point and refrigerated for 3 days or frozen for up to 4 months. If using the stock for a recipe, refrigerate for at least 8 hours or overnight so the fat collects on the top and can be removed. If storing, leave the fat layer intact; it seals the stock.

court bouillon
MAKES 6 QUARTS

Court bouillon, the vegetable and herb broth traditionally used for poaching fish, imparts subtle flavor to the fish as it cooks. The bouillon can be made 2 or 3 days ahead. If preparing the fish the same day, make the bouillon right in the poacher.

- 1 *bunch fresh thyme*
- 1 *bunch fresh flat-leaf parsley*
- ½ *teaspoon whole black peppercorns*
- ½ *teaspoon whole fennel seeds*
- 1 *750-ml bottle dry white wine*
- 1 *leek, white and pale-green parts, sliced into ¼-inch rounds, well washed*
- 2 *medium carrots, sliced into ¼-inch rounds*
- 1 *lemon, sliced into ¼-inch rounds*
- 3 *dried bay leaves*
- 2 *tablespoons coarse salt*

Fit a 10-quart fish poacher with a rack in the bottom, and place the poacher over 2 burners on top of the stove (or use a large stockpot). Fill with 7 quarts water (about three-quarters full). Tie the thyme, parsley, peppercorns, and fennel seeds together in a small piece of cheesecloth to make a bouquet garni, and place in the poacher; add the wine, leek, carrots, lemon, bay leaves, and salt. Cover, and bring to a simmer. Uncover; gently simmer for 30 minutes. Discard the bouquet garni. Let the bouillon cool to room temperature, about 1 hour. The bouillon can be refrigerated for up to 1 week or frozen for up to 3 months.

vegetable stock

MAKES 3 QUARTS

- 1 tablespoon unsalted butter
- 1 tablespoon olive oil
- 1 large onion, coarsely chopped
- 2 large carrots, coarsely chopped
- 2 parsnips, coarsely chopped
- 1 celery stalk, coarsely chopped
- 1 bunch (about 1½ pounds) red or green Swiss chard, cut into 1-inch pieces
  Several sprigs fresh thyme
  Several sprigs fresh flat-leaf parsley
- 1 dried bay leaf

1. In a medium stockpot, melt the butter and oil, stirring occasionally, over medium-low heat. Add the onion; cook until caramelized, 15 to 25 minutes. Add the carrots, parsnips, and celery, and cook until tender, about 20 minutes.

2. Add the Swiss chard to the vegetable mixture. Add 3½ quarts cold water and the thyme, parsley, and bay leaf. Cover and bring to a boil, reduce heat, and let simmer, uncovered, about 1 hour.

3. Remove from the heat, and strain the stock through a fine sieve or a cheesecloth-lined strainer, pressing on the vegetables to extract the juices. Discard the vegetables. The stock can be refrigerated for 3 to 4 days or frozen for up to 3 months.

MAKING FULL-FLAVORED STOCK

With a few simple ingredients, some basic kitchen equipment, and a little planning, wonderful stock is easy to make at home.

- *Use meat and bones to make a stock; if you use only bones, that's exactly what the stock will end up tasting like.*

- *The stockpot should be tall and narrow enough to keep the ingredients snug; too much space causes the flavorful liquid to evaporate rather than extracting the full flavor from the ingredients.*

- *Don't rush stock; it takes 3 to 4 hours to release all the flavor from the bones.*

- *Add enough cold water to cover the ingredients by 1 or 2 inches—no more, or the stock may be too watery. Bring everything to a boil, then reduce the heat right away so the liquid barely simmers (use a metal trivet or a flame tamer). Letting the stock boil too long can result in greasy, off flavors; all that churning makes the fat released from the bones and meat emulsify with the water.*

- *As the stock gently simmers, a thin skin of impurities will form on the surface. Skim this skin off with a slotted spoon, and discard. Skim the stock every 30 minutes. When the liquid falls below the level of the bones, add cold water.*

- *Strained and cooled, stock keeps in the refrigerator for 3 days and in the freezer for 3 to 4 months. Once it's refrigerated, a layer of fat develops on top of the stock; skim it off with a spoon, and discard. If you freeze the stock, leave the fat intact as a seal; remove it before using.*

fish stock

Because this fish stock freezes well, you can double the recipe; use one batch, and freeze the second one for later use.

- 4 pounds heads and bones of non-oily fish, such as sole, flounder, snapper, or bass
- 2 dried bay leaves
- 8 sprigs fresh flat-leaf parsley
- 1 bunch fresh thyme
- ½ bunch fresh tarragon
- 1½ teaspoons whole fennel seeds
- 8 whole black peppercorns
- 3 tablespoons unsalted butter
- 1 large leek, white and pale-green parts, quartered and sliced ¼ inch thick, well washed
- 1 medium onion, cut into ¼-inch dice
- 8 ounces white mushrooms, wiped clean, cut into ¼-inch dice
- 2 medium carrots, cut into ¼-inch dice
- 2 celery stalks, cut into ¼-inch dice
- ½ fennel bulb, cut into ¼-inch dice
- 1 cup dry white wine

1. Remove the gills and any blood from the fish heads; thoroughly wash the bones, and cut them to fit in a 12-quart stockpot. Tie the bay leaves, parsley, thyme, tarragon, fennel seeds, and peppercorns in a small piece of cheesecloth to make a bouquet garni; set aside.

2. Melt the butter in the stockpot over medium heat; add the leek, onion, mushrooms, carrots, celery, and fennel, and cook until tender, 8 to 10 minutes. Increase the heat to medium high, and add the fish heads and bones. Cook, stirring, for 3 to 5 minutes. Add the wine, bouquet garni, and 2½ quarts water, just covering the bones. Bring to a boil, reduce heat to low, skim, and let stock simmer for 25 minutes. Turn off heat; let sit for 10 minutes.

3. Prepare an ice-water bath. Strain the stock through a fine sieve into a large bowl; set the bowl in the ice bath to cool. Use within 1 day, or freeze up to 3 months.

dashi

Dashi is a simple stock integral to Japanese cooking. The broth is used in both cold and hot soups and is delicious warm, all on its own. The ingredients may be found at an Asian grocer.

- 1 2-inch piece of kombu seaweed
- 2 tablespoons bonito flakes (fish flakes)
- 1 tablespoon plus 2 teaspoons soy sauce
- 1 tablespoon mirin
  Juice of ¼ lime

Bring 3 cups water to a boil in a small saucepan. Wipe off the kombu, add to the boiling water, and let boil for 3 minutes. Add the bonito flakes, remove from the heat, and let sit for 30 minutes. Strain, then add the soy sauce, mirin, and lime juice; serve hot or chilled. Dashi should be used within a few hours.

....

MEDITERRANEAN FISH STOCK

To infuse your fish stock with the flavors of the Mediterranean, add one or more of the following ingredients: ½ teaspoon crumbled saffron threads, 6 sun-dried tomatoes (not packed in oil), 1½ teaspoons sweet paprika, ½ teaspoon toasted fennel or cumin seeds, 3 garlic cloves, 20 shrimp shells, or the zest of 1 orange.

....

lobster stock

MAKES ABOUT 3 QUARTS

Use this stock as a base for dishes such as seafood chowder, bisque, stew, and risotto.

> *Shells from 4 cooked lobsters, including carapaces*
>
> 2 *tablespoons olive oil*
>
> 2 *small onions, quartered*
>
> 2 *small carrots, peeled and cut into 1-inch pieces*
>
> 2 *celery stalks, cut into 1-inch pieces*
>
> 4 *garlic cloves*
>
> 1 *small fennel bulb, trimmed and quartered (optional)*
>
> 1 *can (14½ ounces) whole peeled plum tomatoes, chopped, including juice*
>
> 2 *cups dry white wine (optional)*
>
> 8 *whole black peppercorns*
>
> 6 *fresh thyme sprigs*
>
> 6 *fresh flat-leaf parsley sprigs*
>
> 1 *bay leaf*

1. Remove the head sacs (behind the eyes) in the carapaces; discard. Remove any green tomalley or red roe; reserve for another use or discard. Wrap the shells in a clean kitchen towel. Using a rolling pin, meat pounder, or hammer, break the shells (some large pieces might remain).

2. Heat the oil in a Dutch oven or stockpot over medium heat until hot but not smoking. Add the shells; cook until fragrant (do not let blacken), about 3 minutes.

3. Stir in the onions, carrots, celery, garlic, and fennel (if desired). Cook, without stirring, until the vegetables begin to brown, about 3 minutes. Add the tomatoes, wine (if desired), peppercorns, thyme, parsley, and bay leaf.

4. Fill the pot two-thirds with cold water (about 4½ quarts). Bring to a boil. Reduce heat; simmer. Skim the froth from the surface with a ladle. Cook until the broth is aromatic and flavorful, about 1 hour 45 minutes.

5. Carefully pour the stock through a fine sieve set over a large bowl or container. Discard the solids; let stock cool completely. If not using immediately, refrigerate in airtight containers up to 3 days, or freeze up to 2 months.

hollandaise sauce

MAKES 1 CUP

3 large egg yolks
1½ tablespoons fresh lemon juice
8 tablespoons (1 stick) unsalted butter, melted
   Coarse salt

1. In the top of a double boiler or in a large heat-proof bowl set over a saucepan of simmering water, whisk the egg yolks with 1½ tablespoons water, whisking vigorously, until the mixture thickens, about 4 minutes. Remove from the heat, and stir in the lemon juice.

2. Slowly whisk in the melted butter until thickened. Season with salt. Serve the sauce immediately, or keep warm over very gently simmering water, whisking occasionally.

béchamel sauce

MAKES 1 QUART

4 tablespoons unsalted butter
1 tablespoon minced shallot
   Coarse salt and freshly ground white pepper
   Pinch of ground nutmeg
   Pinch of cayenne pepper
½ cup all-purpose flour
1 quart whole milk
1 dried bay leaf
1 cup grated Gruyère cheese (from 3 ounces)

1. In a large saucepan, heat the butter over medium heat. Add the shallot, and cook until translucent, without browning, 3 to 5 minutes. Season with salt, white pepper, nutmeg, and cayenne. Reduce heat to as low as possible.

2. Add the flour in thirds, whisking constantly. When fully incorporated, cook, whisking, without browning, until the sauce thickens, bubbles, and does not taste floury.

3. Meanwhile, heat the milk in a small saucepan over medium-high heat; bring to a boil, and immediately remove from the heat. Add the hot milk to the flour mixture in thirds, whisking constantly. The texture should be thick, with no lumps. Add the bay leaf; continue to cook about 8 minutes over low heat.

4. Strain through a sieve; add the cheese while the béchamel is still hot. Season with salt and pepper. Once at room temperature, the sauce may be refrigerated, covered with plastic wrap placed directly on the surface of the sauce, in an airtight container for up to 3 days. Rewarm in the top of a double boiler over 1 inch simmering water.

vietnamese dipping sauce

MAKES 1½ CUPS

Known as *nuoc cham*, this Vietnamese table sauce is used to season dumplings, soups, and noodle dishes.

1½ teaspoons minced garlic
1 teaspoon ground chile paste
1 Thai bird chile or serrano pepper, chopped (optional)
¼ cup Asian fish sauce (nam pla)
2 tablespoons fresh lime juice
¼ cup sugar
2 tablespoons grated carrots, for garnish

Using a mortar and pestle, pound the garlic, chile paste, and fresh chile, if desired, into a paste (or mince together with a knife). Transfer to a bowl. Add the fish sauce, ⅔ cup hot water, the lime juice, and sugar. Whisk together until the sugar dissolves. Garnish with the carrots, and serve.

béarnaise sauce

MAKES ABOUT 1½ CUPS

½ cup white wine

2 tablespoons white-wine vinegar

2 tablespoons finely chopped shallots

2 tablespoons plus 1 teaspoon freshly chopped tarragon

3 whole black peppercorns

12 tablespoons (1½ sticks) unsalted butter

3 large egg yolks

½ teaspoon coarse salt

¼ cup boiling water

1 tablespoon fresh lemon juice

1. Place the white wine, white-wine vinegar, shallots, 2 tablespoons tarragon, and the peppercorns in a small saucepan set over medium-high heat. Bring the mixture to a boil, and cook until it is reduced to about 2 tablespoons.

2. Melt the butter in a small saucepan over medium-low heat. Keep warm until ready to use.

3. Place the egg yolks in a copper or stainless-steel bowl that fits snugly in the top of a medium saucepan. Fill the saucepan with 2 inches of water, and bring to a boil. Whisk the yolks, off the heat, until they become pale. Add the wine mixture and salt, and whisk until well combined. Gradually add ¼ cup boiling water, whisking constantly. Place the bowl over the medium saucepan of boiling water; reduce heat to the lowest setting. Whisking constantly, cook until the whisk leaves a trail in the mixture and the sauce begins to hold its shape. Remove from heat.

4. Pour the warm, melted butter into a glass measuring cup. Add to the yolk mixture, 1 drop at a time, whisking constantly. After you have added about 1 tablespoon melted butter, you can begin to add it slightly faster, still whisking constantly. Still, be careful: If the butter is added too quickly, the emulsion will be too thin or will break (separate).

5. Once all of the butter has been added, adjust the seasoning with the lemon juice, and stir in the remaining tarragon. If the béarnaise becomes too thick, you may thin it with a little additional lemon juice or water. If not serving immediately, place the pan of sauce over a pot of simmering water that has been removed from the heat, or in a warm spot on the stove for up to 1 hour. Alternatively, you may store for up to 3 hours in a clean Thermos that has been warmed with hot but not boiling water.

rémoulade sauce

MAKES ABOUT 2 CUPS

If you are concerned about raw eggs, use store-bought mayonnaise, and begin at step 3. The sauce can be made ahead and refrigerated in an airtight container for up to 2 days.

1 large whole egg

2 large egg yolks

½ teaspoon coarse salt

Pinch of sugar

¼ teaspoon freshly ground black pepper

¾ cup extra-virgin olive oil

1 to 2 tablespoons fresh lemon juice

¾ cup canola oil

1 tablespoon capers, drained and chopped

2 teaspoons Dijon mustard

1 tablespoon chopped fresh flat-leaf parsley

1 tablespoon chopped fresh tarragon

1 tablespoon snipped chives

1 tablespoon minced shallot

1. Place the egg, egg yolks, salt, sugar, and pepper in the bowl of a food processor. Process until blended.

2. With the machine running, slowly drizzle the olive oil through the feed tube. Add 1 tablespoon lemon juice, then slowly drizzle in the canola oil through the feed tube. Season with more lemon juice, salt, and pepper, if needed.

3. Stir in the capers, mustard, parsley, tarragon, chives, and shallot, and serve immediately.

perfect gravy

MAKES 3 CUPS

For the best poultry gravy, do not roast the turkey or chicken in a nonstick roasting pan: It keeps the flavorful bits of meat and skin from cooking onto the pan.

> *Giblets from a turkey or chicken: neck, heart, gizzard, and liver*

- 3½ *tablespoons unsalted butter*
- 2 *celery stalks, roughly chopped*
- 1 *carrot, roughly chopped*
- 1 *medium onion, roughly chopped*
- 1 *medium leek, white and green parts, roughly chopped, well washed*
- 6 *whole black peppercorns*
- 1 *dried bay leaf*
- 1½ *cups Madeira wine*
- 3 *tablespoons all-purpose flour*
- 2 *teaspoons minced fresh rosemary*
- ¾ *teaspoon coarse salt*
- ⅛ *teaspoon freshly ground black pepper*

1. Make the giblet broth while the turkey is roasting. Trim any fat or membrane from the giblets. The liver should not have the gallbladder, a small green sac, attached. If it is, trim it off, removing part of the liver if necessary. Do not pierce the sac; it contains bitter liquid. Rinse the giblets, and pat dry.

2. In a medium saucepan, melt 3 tablespoons butter over medium-high heat. Add the vegetables. Cook, stirring, until slightly brown, 5 to 10 minutes. Reduce heat to medium; add the neck. Cook, stirring, until slightly brown, about 5 minutes. Add 1 quart water. Add the heart, gizzard, peppercorns, and bay leaf. Cover; bring to boil. Reduce heat to medium-low; cook, uncovered, until broth is reduced to about 3 cups, 50 to 60 minutes. Set aside.

3. Meanwhile, chop the liver finely. Melt the remaining ½ tablespoon butter in a small skillet over medium-low heat. Add the liver; cook, stirring constantly, until the liver is fully cooked and no longer releases blood, 4 to 6 minutes. Add to the cooking giblet broth.

4. Transfer the roasted turkey to a large platter. Pour the juices from the pan into a gravy strainer. Set aside to separate, about 10 minutes.

5. Strain the reserved broth. Return to the saucepan, and warm over low heat. Place the roasting pan over medium-high heat. Pour the Madeira into a measuring cup, and then into the pan; let bubble, and scrape the bottom and sides of the pan with a wooden spoon to loosen any browned bits.

6. Make a slurry: Place the flour in a glass jar with a tight-fitting lid. Ladle 1 cup of the broth into the jar. Shake until combined. Slowly pour into the roasting pan; stir to incorporate. Cook over medium heat, stirring until the flour is cooked, 2 to 3 minutes. Slowly stir in the remaining broth.

7. Raise heat to medium-high. Add the pan juices from the fat separator; add the dark drippings from the bottom into the roasting pan. Discard the fat. Stir in the rosemary. Season with salt and pepper. Cook 10 to 15 minutes to reduce and thicken. (For thicker gravy, add 1 more tablespoon flour; reduce the water to 2½ cups in step 2.) Strain the liquid from the pan through a very fine sieve. Season with salt and pepper. Keep warm in a heatproof bowl over a pan of simmering water until ready to serve.

....

PERFECT GRAVY EVERY TIME

To make gravy with a velvety texture and rich flavor:

- *Use every part of the bird, from the giblets to the crispy skin and caramelized juices in the bottom of the pan, which add both flavor and color to the gravy.*

- *Use a gravy strainer. This straight-sided cup is fitted with a spout that feeds from the base. Because fat floats to the top of liquid, the spout pulls only the nonfatty juices into it.*

- *Eliminate lumps that form when flour is added to the roasting pan too quickly and not blended well: Mix the flour and broth together before adding to the pan juices.*

....

homemade mayonnaise

MAKES 2 ½ CUPS

A food processor helps make homemade mayonnaise quickly, but a whisk works just as well. Martha prefers to use entire eggs, not just the yolks, for a lighter texture. Add the oil very slowly, literally drop by drop. This prevents the oil from overwhelming the egg yolks and produces a smooth, creamy spread. By varying the ingredients, you can create endless variations. Substitute a flavored vinegar such as tarragon or sherry for the lemon juice, or alter the flavor by trying different olive oils. Seasonings or chopped fresh herbs may be added to the mayonnaise after it is made.

- 1 cup light olive oil
- 1 cup canola oil
- 2 large eggs
- ¼ teaspoon dry mustard
- ¼ teaspoon coarse salt
- 2 tablespoons fresh lemon juice

1. Combine the oils in a large glass measuring cup. Place the eggs, mustard, and salt in the bowl of a food processor. Process until the mixture is foamy and pale, about 1½ minutes.

2. With the machine running, add the oil, drop by drop, through the feed tube, until the mixture starts to thicken (about ½ cup oil); do not stop the machine at this point, or the mayonnaise may not come together. Add the remaining oil in a slow, steady stream. When all the oil has been incorporated, slowly add the lemon juice. The fresh mayonnaise can be kept, refrigerated in an airtight container, for up to 5 days.

clarified butter

MAKES 1 ½ CUPS

- 1 pound (4 sticks) unsalted butter, cut in tablespoons

Place the butter in a small, deep saucepan over low heat. As the butter melts, 3 layers will develop: a bottom layer of milk solids; a middle layer of clear, yellow butter; and a top layer of milky foam. Allow it to gently simmer for 10 minutes to completely separate the layers. Remove from the heat, and let stand for 10 minutes, to allow the foam to solidify. With a spoon, carefully skim off the foam that rises to the surface, and discard. Carefully pour the clear, yellow butter off the milk solids at the bottom of the saucepan and into a glass jar. Discard the milk solids. Refrigerate the butter in an airtight container for up to 3 weeks, or freeze until needed.

chinese five-spice powder

MAKES ¼ CUP

Though available prepackaged, homemade five-spice powder is far more pungent and flavorful than store-bought. Rub it on fowl, fish, and meat.

- 10 whole star anise
- 1 tablespoon whole Szechuan peppercorns
- 1 cinnamon stick
- 2 tablespoons whole fennel seeds
- ½ teaspoon whole cloves

1. Place all the ingredients in a small skillet over medium heat, and dry-roast, shaking the pan often, until they give off an aroma, about 5 minutes.

2. Combine all the ingredients in a mortar or a spice grinder, and grind to a powder. Store in an airtight container in a cool, dark place.

curry powder

MAKES 1/4 CUP

Homemade spice mixtures are more aromatic than store-bought. Rub curry powder on poultry, lamb, and beef, or use it to flavor dips, marinades, and spreads.

- 2 teaspoons whole coriander seeds
- 1 teaspoon whole cumin seeds
- ½ teaspoon whole mustard seeds
- 1 teaspoon whole fenugreek seeds
- 4 small dried red chiles
- 1 teaspoon whole black peppercorns
- 10 fresh or dried curry leaves (optional)
- ½ teaspoon ground ginger
- 1 teaspoon ground turmeric

Place all the seeds together in a small skillet over medium heat, and dry-roast, shaking the pan often, until they give off an aroma, about 5 minutes. Combine all the ingredients in a mortar or spice grinder, and grind to a powder. Store in an airtight container in a cool, dark place.

basic marinade

MAKES ABOUT ½ CUP

See page 625 for recommended marinating times. If you marinate meat overnight in this marinade, omit the lemon juice and add it 2 hours before cooking.

- ⅓ cup extra-virgin olive oil
- 2 sprigs fresh rosemary, crushed
- 3 sprigs fresh thyme
- 3 large cloves garlic, peeled and smashed
    Juice of 1 lemon
    Pinch of freshly ground black pepper

Combine the oil, rosemary, thyme, garlic, lemon juice, and pepper; stir to combine. Unused marinade can be refrigerated in an airtight container up to 1 week. Discard marinade after using.

PASTRY

martha's perfect pâte brisée

MAKES TWO 8- TO 10-INCH
SINGLE-CRUST PIES OR
ONE 8- TO 10-INCH DOUBLE-CRUST PIE

The pie dough may be made 1 day ahead and refrigerated, well wrapped in plastic, or frozen, up to 1 month.

- 2½ cups all-purpose flour, plus more for dusting
- 1 teaspoon salt
- 1 teaspoon sugar
- 1 cup (2 sticks) chilled unsalted butter, cut in pieces
- ¼ to ½ cup ice water

1. Place the flour, salt, and sugar in the bowl of a food processor, and process for a few seconds to combine. Add the butter pieces to the flour mixture, and process until the mixture resembles coarse meal, about 10 seconds. Add the ice water in a slow, steady stream, through the feed tube with the machine running, just until the dough holds together. Do not process for more than 30 seconds.

2. Turn the dough out onto a work surface. Divide into 2 equal pieces, and place on 2 separate sheets of plastic wrap. Flatten, and form 2 disks. Wrap, and refrigerate at least 1 hour before using.

MAKING A TART SHELL

1. Lightly flour your work surface (and rolling pin). Using as little flour as possible, roll out a half recipe of pâte brisée or pâte sucrée, rotating it 90 degrees every few minutes. Repeat until the dough is ⅛ inch thick. Brush off excess flour.

2. Gently fold the dough into quarters. Center the dough in the tart pan; unfold, letting the extra pastry droop over the sides. Alternatively, drape the rolled dough over the rolling pin for transfer into the pan.

3. Lift the overhanging dough, and tuck it into the side and corners of the pan. Gently press the pastry snug against the bottom edges of the pan with a knuckle. This extra dough makes it easier to form a decorative edge.

4. When the shell is completely tucked in place, firmly roll your rolling pin over the top of the tart pan, using the pan's sharp edges to trim off the excess dough. Refrigerate for 10 minutes before proceeding to step 5.

5. Working around the circumference of the pan, firmly press the dough into the fluting, gently pinching dough between forefinger and thumb and supporting the pan with the other hand as you go.

6. The crust will release steam when it's baked that can cause the pastry to bubble and buckle. Prevent this damage by docking (poking holes into the pastry with the tines of a fork to create steam vents). Refrigerate the dough for 1 hour, or wrap it and freeze for future use for up to 1 month.

BLIND BAKING

Cut a square of parchment paper several inches larger than the tart shell, and place it into the chilled shell. Fill it with pie weights or dried beans (which should be stored in the freezer between uses to prevent them from becoming rancid). Bake in a 400° F oven for 15 minutes.

Then remove the parchment and weights to allow the bottom of the shell to bake until golden brown, 12 to 15 minutes more. Keep an eye on the edges: If they start to become too dark, cover them with foil.

large quantity pâte brisée

MAKES FOUR 5-INCH PIES

This recipe make 1½ times Martha's Perfect Pâte Brisée (recipe page 647).

3¾ cups all-purpose flour

1½ teaspoons salt

1½ teaspoons sugar

1½ cups (3 sticks) chilled unsalted butter, cut in pieces

½ to ¾ cup ice water

1. Place the flour, salt, and sugar in the bowl of a food processor, and process for a few seconds to combine. Add the butter pieces to the flour mixture, and process until the mixture resembles coarse meal, about 10 seconds. Add the ice water in a slow, steady stream, through the feed tube with the machine running, just until the dough holds together. Do not process for more than 30 seconds.

2. Turn the dough out onto a work surface. Divide into 2 equal pieces, and place on 2 separate sheets of plastic wrap. Flatten, and form 2 disks. Wrap, and refrigerate at least 1 hour before using.

PERFECT PIECRUST

● *Martha's Perfect Pâte Brisée will also make two 6½-inch double-crust pies: Divide the dough into quarters and the filling in half; the baking time is the same.*

● *The amount of water required to hold the pastry together will vary, depending on the humidity.*

● *Chilling the piecrust before it is baked helps it keep its shape and gives it a professional look.*

● *Evenly brushing the egg wash over the piecrust results in an evenly browned crust.*

● *Martha likes to use glass pie plates so she can see whether the bottom crust is done.*

● *Flour, cornstarch, or tapioca can be used to thicken a berry pie.*

● *A fruit filling is usually done when the juices are bubbling.*

● *Bake the pie with a baking sheet underneath the plate to catch overflow from the filling.*

MAKING A DOUBLE-CRUST PIE

1. When making the dough, the butter-flour mixture should have pieces ranging in size from crumbs to ½ inch (top). Add water; look for a crumbly texture (bottom). When squeezed, the mixture will hold together but not be sticky.

2. Divide the dough. Place each half on plastic wrap. Gather the wrap to shape into balls. Flatten slightly. Unwrap; rewrap loosely, leaving ½ inch airspace around the dough. Roll to ½ inch thick, filling the space.

3. Start rolling, working from the center. If the dough loses its circular shape, place the end of the pin near the crooked edge and roll, working that area by pressing with one hand while holding the pin loosely with the other.

4. Keep the work surface floured so the dough doesn't lose its shape, stick, or tear. Every few passes, release the dough by running a long offset spatula underneath, then throw more flour under it. As you go, run

your fingers around the edges of the dough to feel if the thickness is even (and if not, to find where you need to roll more).

5. Fit the dough into the pie plate (pushing down the sides without pressing into the corners); use scissors to trim, leaving ¼ inch.

6. Add the top crust, trim to ½ inch, tuck it under the edge of the bottom crust, and crimp with your fingers, as shown.

pâte sucrée

MAKES TWO 8- TO 11-INCH TARTS

This pastry dough may be stored in the freezer for up to 1 month. Defrost by refrigerating overnight or letting stand at room temperature for 1 hour.

- 2½ cups all-purpose flour
- 3 tablespoons sugar
- 1 cup (2 sticks) chilled unsalted butter, cut into pieces
- 2 large egg yolks
- ¼ cup ice water

1. Place the flour and sugar in the bowl of a food processor, and process for a few seconds to combine. Add the butter pieces to the flour mixture, and process until the mixture resembles coarse meal, about 10 seconds. In a small bowl, lightly beat the egg yolks and ice water. Add the egg water in a slow, steady stream through the feed tube, with the machine running, just until the dough holds together. Do not process for more than 30 seconds.

2. Turn the dough out onto a work surface. Divide into 2 equal pieces, and place on 2 sheets of plastic wrap. Flatten, and form 2 disks. Wrap, and refrigerate at least 1 hour before using.

PÂTE SUCRÉE WALNUT VARIATION: *Make the recipe as directed, substituting ¾ cup finely ground walnuts for ¾ cup of the flour.*

chocolate pâte sucrée

MAKES ENOUGH FOR ONE 9-INCH TART

- 1¼ cups all-purpose flour
- 2 tablespoons cocoa powder
- ⅓ cup sugar
- ½ teaspoon salt
- 6 tablespoons unsalted butter, chilled, cut into pieces
- 3 large egg yolks
- ½ teaspoon pure vanilla extract

1. Place the flour, cocoa, sugar, and salt in the bowl of a food processor, and pulse several times to combine. Add the butter, and pulse until the mixture resembles coarse meal, about 10 seconds. Add the egg yolks and vanilla, and process just until mixture begins to hold together, no more than 30 seconds.

2. Turn dough out onto a lightly floured surface, and form into a disk. Cover in plastic wrap; refrigerate for 30 minutes, or until ready to use.

PÂTE SUCRÉE CITRUS VARIATION *Make the recipe as directed, adding 2 teaspoons of freshly grated orange zest and 1 teaspoon freshly grated lemon zest with the dry ingredients.*

....

DECORATING TECHNIQUES

- *To make a crimped edge, line a pie plate with dough. Trim the overhang to 1 inch. Using the thumb and forefinger of one hand, push with the thumb of the other hand, crimping; continue around crust. Use the tines of a fork to crimp a single-crust pie and to make a seal for a double crust.*

- *To make a braided edge, cut 12-inch-long, ¼-inch-thick strips of dough; braid them. Brush the crust's edge or the bottom of the braids with water; gently press the braid around the pie plate's rim. Trim.*

- *To make designs, use cookie and aspic cutters, then attach the cutouts to the crust with water.*

- *To make a lattice top, roll out the crust. Using a fluted pastry wheel, make ½- to ¾-inch-wide strips, about 12 inches long. Lay the strips, spaced 1 inch apart, across the filling. Fold back every other strip almost to the edge, then lay a strip perpendicular to them at the folds. Return the folded strips. Fold back the remaining strips; arrange another perpendicular strip. Continue until the lattice is formed. Using a fork, seal the strips to the edge. For a shiny crust, brush it with a mixture of 1 egg and 2 tablespoons heavy cream.*

....

MAKING PÂTE À CHOUX

This dough is very easy to master, and can be used to form a variety of sweet confections, such as profiteroles; it can also be folded with herbs and cheese to make savory gougères.

Pâte à choux is ideal for cream-filled pastries, too: As the dough bakes, it puffs up and forms a pocket inside. This happens because the moisture of the eggs turns to steam and is trapped within the resilient dough, causing a slight hollow inside a shell that is golden brown and crisp on the outside.

HOW TO MAKE CREAM PUFFS (SEE PAGE 526)

1. Bring water, butter, sugar, and salt to a boil. Turn off heat, and add flour all at once.

2. Return to heat, and dry the mixture by stirring constantly.

3. After adding the eggs, test for proper consistency (see recipe, opposite).

4. Dip a biscuit cutter in flour and mark baking sheets.

5. Use a pastry bag to pipe shapes to fit in flour circles.

6. When finished baking, poke a hole and fill with pastry cream.

pâte à choux

MAKES ENOUGH FOR
3 DOZEN CREAM PUFFS

1 cup water

1 stick (½ cup) unsalted butter

1 teaspoon sugar

½ teaspoon salt

1 cup all-purpose flour

5 large eggs (1 liquid cup)

1. Combine the water, butter, sugar, and salt in a medium saucepan over medium-high heat. Bring the mixture to a boil, and immediately remove from heat. Stir in the flour. When the flour is combined, return to heat. This mixture is called a *panade*. Dry the panade by stirring constantly for 4 minutes. It is ready when it pulls away from the sides and a film forms on the bottom of the pan.

2. Transfer the panade to the bowl of an electric mixer fitted with the paddle attachment, and mix on low speed, about 2 minutes, until slightly cooled. Add the eggs, 1 at a time, on medium speed, letting each incorporate completely before adding the next. Add the last egg a little at a time until the batter is smooth and shiny. Test the batter by touching it with your finger and lifting to form a string. If a string does not form, the batter needs more egg. If you have added all the egg and the batter still doesn't form a string, add water, 1 teaspoon at a time, until it does.

3. The batter may be used immediately or stored in an airtight container in the refrigerator for up to 2 days. To use chilled, remove from the refrigerator, and stir to soften before filling piping bag.

puff pastry

MAKES 2¾ POUNDS PUFF PASTRY, OR
ENOUGH FOR 16 TURNOVERS

This pastry dough may be made in advance and frozen after the fourth turn for up to 2 months. The final two turns should be completed immediately before using.

2¾ cups all-purpose flour, plus more for dusting

1 cup plus 2 tablespoons cake flour (not self-rising)

1 teaspoon salt

1 pound (4 sticks) very cold unsalted butter

1 tablespoon fresh lemon juice

1. Combine 2½ cups all-purpose flour and the cake flour and salt in a medium bowl. Cut 1 stick butter into small pieces. Add with the lemon juice to the flour mixture; cut in the butter with a pastry cutter or 2 knives until the mixture resembles coarse meal. Gradually mix in up to 1 cup ice water, until the dough just comes together. Pat the dough into a 6-inch square; wrap in plastic. Chill 30 minutes.

2. Cut the remaining 3 sticks butter into bits. Sprinkle with the remaining ¼ cup flour; mix together by rubbing against a cold work surface with the heel of your hand. Form into a 5½-inch square; wrap in plastic. Chill 15 minutes.

3. On a lightly floured surface, roll the chilled dough into a 6 × 18-inch rectangle with the short side facing you; place the chilled butter mixture in the center. Fold the top third of the dough over the butter mixture, and the bottom third of the dough over the top third. Seal the edges by pressing the dough with your fingers.

4. Turn the dough packet over so the overlapped section is on the bottom. Roll into a 6 × 18-inch rectangle (do not allow the butter to come through the dough). Fold in thirds, as before. Rotate 90 degrees (one quarter-turn); roll again into a 6 × 18-inch rectangle; fold in thirds. Press 2 fingers into the dough to indicate the completion of 2 turns. Wrap in plastic; chill 30 minutes.

5. Repeat the rolling-out process in step 4, rotating the dough 90 degrees before beginning. Mark with 4 fingers, signifying the completion of 4 turns; chill 30 minutes. The dough may be wrapped and frozen at this point.

6. Remove the dough from the refrigerator (if dough has been frozen, thaw overnight in the refrigerator). Give the dough its final 2 turns by repeating the rolling-out process in step 4, again rotating it 90 degrees, before rolling it out. The dough should be used immediately after the sixth turn is completed.

pâte sablée

MAKES TWO 8- TO 11-INCH TARTS

- 8 ounces (2 sticks) unsalted butter, softened
- ¾ cup confectioners' sugar
- 4½ teaspoons pure vanilla extract
- 2 cups all-purpose flour
- 1 teaspoon salt

Put the butter and sugar in the bowl of an electric mixer fitted with the paddle attachment. Mix on medium speed until pale and fluffy, about 3 minutes; mix in the vanilla. Add the flour and the salt, and mix on medium-low speed until just combined and crumbly, about 15 seconds (do not overmix). Pat the dough into a disk, and wrap in plastic. Refrigerate at least 1 hour and up to 2 days, or freeze up to 1 month.

quick puff pastry

MAKES 2 POUNDS

- 1¾ cups all-purpose flour, plus more for dusting
- 2 cups cake flour (not self-rising)
- 1 teaspoon salt
- 1 pound (4 sticks) chilled unsalted butter, cut into pieces
- 1 to 1¼ cups ice water
- 2 tablespoons fresh lemon juice

1. Sift together the all-purpose flour, cake flour, and salt into a large chilled bowl. Cut in the pieces of butter using a pastry knife until the butter is in very small lumps, about ½ inch in diameter.

2. Combine the ice water and the lemon juice, and stir into the flour mixture, a little at a time, pressing the dough together with your hands until it comes together.

3. Turn the dough out onto a well-floured surface, and roll it into a ½-inch-thick rough rectangle, approximately 12 × 18 inches. The dough will be very crumbly. Fold the bottom of the rectangle toward the center, then the top of the rectangle toward the center, overlapping the bottom third, like a letter, and give the dough a quarter-turn to the right. Roll the dough into a large rectangle, ½ inch thick, and fold into thirds again. This completes the first double turn. Using a dry pastry brush, brush any excess flour from the dough.

3. Repeat the rolling, folding, and turning process 2 more times to execute another double turn, refrigerating the dough for a few minutes if the butter becomes too warm. Wrap the dough in plastic wrap, and put in refrigerator to chill for 1 hour.

4. Remove the dough from the refrigerator. Repeat the rolling, folding, and turning process again to execute 1 more double turn. There will be 6 turns in all. The dough needs to be rolled out to a ½-inch-thick rectangle each time. With each turn, the dough will become smoother and easier to handle. Store the dough, wrapped well in plastic, in the refrigerator for up to 2 days, or in the freezer for up to 3 months (thaw in the refrigerator).

almond frangipane

MAKES 2 CUPS

Frangipane, an almond-flovored paste, is a classic filling for tarts, such as the Sugar Plum Tart on page 462.

- 1 cup whole blanched almonds, toasted and cooled
- ½ cup plus 3 tablespoons sugar
- 8 tablespoons (1 stick) unsalted butter, softened
- 1 large egg plus 1 large egg yolk, room temperature
- 2 teaspoons all-purpose flour
- ½ vanilla bean, halved lengthwise and seeds scraped
- ¼ teaspoon salt

1. Preheat the oven to 375°F. Finely grind the nuts with 3 tablespoons sugar in a food processor.

2. Put the butter and remaining ½ cup sugar in the bowl of an electric mixer fitted with the paddle attachment; cream on medium speed until pale and fluffy, about 2 minutes. Add the egg and yolk; mix 2 minutes. Add the nut mixture, flour, vanilla seeds, and salt; mix on medium-high until pale and fluffy, about 3 minutes.

3. Refrigerate in an airtight container until ready to use, up to 3 days.

pastry cream

MAKES ABOUT 4 CUPS

Be sure to make the pastry cream on the same day you plan to use it; otherwise, it has a tendency to become thin and runny.

- ¼ cup plus 1 tablespoon cornstarch
- ¼ cup plus 1 tablespoon all-purpose flour
- 1 cup sugar
- ½ teaspoon salt
- 3 large eggs
- 4 cups milk
- 2 tablespoons chilled unsalted butter, cut into small pieces
- 1½ teaspoons pure vanilla extract

1. Prepare an ice-water bath, and set aside. In a medium bowl, combine the cornstarch, flour, ½ cup sugar, and salt; stir to mix. In another medium bowl, whisk the eggs until smooth. Add the flour mixture to the egg mixture, and whisk to combine.

2. In a medium saucepan, combine the milk and remaining ½ cup sugar. Bring the mixture to a boil over medium-high heat, stirring until the sugar is dissolved. Remove from heat; whisking constantly, slowly pour into the egg mixture.

3. Transfer the mixture to a clean saucepan set over medium-high heat. Bring to a boil, whisking constantly, until thickened, about 3 minutes.

4. Transfer the mixture to a large heatproof bowl. Whisk in the butter and vanilla; set the bowl in the ice bath, stirring occasionally, until completely chilled, 10 to 12 minutes. Cover with plastic wrap, pressing it directly onto the surface of the pastry cream to prevent a skin from forming. Place in the refrigerator until ready to use.

lemon curd

MAKES 1 1/2 CUPS

In addition to using this curd in other recipes, it is delicious on its own or as a spread for scones or shortbread.

- 6 large egg yolks
- ¾ cup sugar
- 1 tablespoon finely grated lemon zest
- ½ cup fresh lemon juice
- ½ cup (1 stick) unsalted butter, cut into pieces

1. Combine the yolks, sugar, and lemon zest and juice in a medium heavy-bottomed saucepan. Cook over medium-low heat, stirring constantly with a wooden spoon, until the mixture is thick enough to coat the back of the spoon, 8 to 10 minutes.

2. Pass the mixture through a fine sieve into a medium bowl. Add the butter, 1 piece at a time, stirring after each addition, until the butter is melted and combined.

3. Cover with plastic wrap, pressing directly onto the surface of the lemon curd to prevent a skin from forming. Refrigerate until firm and thoroughly chilled, at least 1 hour.

CARAMEL SAUCE TWO WAYS

Making caramel is actually quite simple. To make this sweet elixir at home, you can use one of two methods: dry or wet. The dry method includes placing the sugar directly in the pan and heating it until the sugar turns into a liquid and darkens. This method requires constant stirring, or the sugar can go from just melted to burned in an instant. The wet method is safer for those new to caramel-making. Sugar is combined with a liquid (usually water) and heated until the sugar dissolves. The risk of this method is re-crystallization, which occurs when undissolved crystals of sugar are reintroduced to the sugar syrup (usually in the form of stray sugar crystals that have adhered to the side of the pan or a stirring utensil). To avoid this, it is important not to stir the mixture once it is fully dissolved but rather to swirl it in the pan and brush down the sides of the pan with a wet pastry brush. The caramel sauce may be kept, refrigerated in an airtight container, up to 1 week. Let the sauce return to room temperature before using; it may be gently warmed over very low heat in a small saucepan.

caramel sauce—dry method

MAKES 1 1/4 CUPS

- 1½ cups sugar
- 1 vanilla bean, split lengthwise and scraped

1. In a large heavy skillet, spread the sugar in an even layer over medium-high heat. Add the vanilla bean and seed scrapings. Without stirring, let cook until the outer edges of the sugar melt and begin to turn golden, about 5 minutes.

2. With a wooden spoon, slowly stir together the melted and unmelted sugar until all the sugar is melted, clear, and golden. At arm's length, carefully pour in 1 cup water while stirring rapidly. Continue stirring until the mixture has melted completely. Transfer to a bowl to cool, about 1 hour. Discard the vanilla pod. The sauce may be made 1 day ahead and kept at room temperature in an airtight container.

caramel sauce—wet method

MAKES 1 CUP

- ¾ cup boiling water
- 1 cup sugar
  Dash of pure vanilla extract
- 1 teaspoon cognac

Combine ¼ cup boiling water and sugar in a medium saucepan. Cook over high heat until the sugar dissolves. Once dissolved, do not stir; let cook until caramel forms, brushing down the sides of the pan with a damp pastry brush as needed to keep crystals from forming, about 5 minutes. Remove from heat, and slowly whisk in the remaining ½ cup boiling water at arm's length, being careful not to splatter the hot caramel. Remove from the heat, and stir in the vanilla and cognac. The sauce may be used warm or at room temperature.

. . . .

THE COLOR OF CARAMEL

Caramel is sugar that has been taken just to the edge of burning. Caramel's color reveals the extent to which it is cooked. The palest form is just concentrated sugar syrup. The next stage is golden, followed by amber and then dark. For most culinary purposes, amber is the color of choice for its deep golden hue and nutty, sweet flavor.

. . . .

swiss meringue for pies

MAKES ENOUGH FOR HIGH TOPPING FOR
1 PIE OR LOW TOPPING FOR 2 PIES

This fluffy cooked meringue makes the best pie topping. It is easiest to beat the mixture with an electric mixer fitted with the whisk attachment.

- 7 large egg whites
- ¾ cup sugar
- ¼ teaspoon salt

Combine the egg whites, sugar, and salt in a heat-proof bowl. Set over a pan of simmering water; beat with a whisk until warm and the sugar is dissolved. Remove the bowl from the heat; beat until stiff peaks form. Use immediately.

swiss meringue

MAKES 4 CUPS

This meringue works well for piping shapes. Using the whisk attachment to beat the egg whites in the final stage works best; warming the egg whites helps dissolve the sugar, giving the meringue greater volume.

- 4 large egg whites, room temperature
- 1 cup sugar
  Pinch of cream of tartar
- ½ teaspoon pure vanilla extract

1. Fill a medium saucepan one-quarter full with water. Set the saucepan over medium heat, and bring the water to a simmer.

2. Combine the egg whites, sugar, and cream of tartar in the heatproof bowl of an electric mixer; place over the saucepan. Whisk constantly until the sugar is dissolved and the whites are warm to the touch, 3 to 3½ minutes. Test by rubbing the mixture between your fingers to ensure that no sugar remains.

3. Attach the bowl to the electric mixer fitted with the whisk attachment, and beat, starting on low speed and gradually increasing to high, until stiff, glossy peaks form, about 10 minutes. Add the vanilla, and mix until combined. Use the meringue according to the instructions in the recipes.

crème anglaise

MAKES ABOUT 2 CUPS

You can make this sauce up to 2 days ahead; press plastic wrap directly onto the surface to prevent a skin from forming, and refrigerate.

- 4 large egg yolks
- ¼ cup sugar
- 1 cup milk
- ¾ cup heavy cream
- ½ vanilla bean, halved lengthwise

1. Whisk together the yolks and sugar in a medium bowl until pale, about 4 minutes.

2. Pour the milk and cream into a medium saucepan. Scrape in the vanilla seeds; add the bean. Heat over medium heat until just about to simmer. Reduce heat to low; whisk ⅓ cup into the egg yolk mixture. Return to the pan. Cook over medium heat, stirring, until thick enough to coat the back of a wooden spoon, about 8 minutes.

3. Pour the mixture through a fine sieve into a stainless-steel bowl set in a large ice-water bath. Discard the solids. Chill until cold, stirring occasionally.

seven-minute frosting

MAKES ENOUGH FOR ONE 9-INCH 4-LAYER CAKE OR 12 JUMBO CUPCAKES

- 1¾ cups sugar
- 2 tablespoons light corn syrup
- ¼ cup water
- 6 large egg whites

1. In a small, heavy saucepan, combine 1½ cups sugar, the corn syrup, and water. Heat over medium, stirring occasionally, until the sugar has dissolved. (Rub a bit between your fingers to make sure there is no graininess.)

2. Raise heat to bring to a boil. Do not stir anymore. Boil, washing down the sides of the pan with a pastry brush dipped in cold water to prevent the sugar

from crystallizing, until a candy thermometer registers 230°F, about 5 minutes. (Depending on the humidity, this can take anywhere from 4 to 10 minutes.)

3. Meanwhile, in the bowl of an electric mixer fitted with the whisk attachment, whisk the egg whites on medium speed until soft peaks form, about 2½ minutes. Gradually add the remaining ¼ cup sugar. Remove the syrup from the heat when the temperature reaches 230°F (it will keep rising as the pan is removed from the heat). With the mixer on medium-low speed, pour the syrup in a steady stream down the side of the bowl (to avoid splattering) containing the egg white mixture.

4. Beat the frosting on medium until cool, 5 to 10 minutes. The frosting should be thick and shiny. Use immediately.

candied lemon, orange, or grapefruit peel

MAKES 1½ CUPS

You can use the same technique to make candied lemon or orange peel. The technique for candied grapefruit peel is slightly different (as detailed below) because more pith—the bitter white layer between the outer peel and the flesh of citrus fruit—must be removed.

- 8 oranges, or 10 lemons, or 6 grapefruits
- 6 cups sugar, plus more for rolling

1. Cut the ends off each piece of fruit, and cut the fruit in half lengthwise. Insert the tip of a knife carefully between fruit and pith about ½ inch deep, turn the fruit on the other end, and repeat, following the shape of fruit and keeping the skin in one piece.

2. Using your fingers, gently pull the fruit away. Reserve the fruit for another use.

3. Place the citrus peel in a 6-quart pot; fill with enough cold water to cover, about 3 quarts. Place over medium heat; bring to a boil. Reduce heat; simmer 20 minutes. Drain the citrus peel; soak in cold water until cool enough to handle, about 5 minutes.

4. Using a melon baller, scrape the soft white pith from the peel, being careful not to tear or cut into the skin. If you're making candied grapefruit, after scraping the pith from the peel, simmer the peel for 20 minutes more, and repeat the technique to remove the remaining pith.

5. Slice each piece of peel into thin strips lengthwise, about ¼ inch wide if garnishing a cake or ½ inch wide if rolling in sugar.

6. Place 6 cups sugar in a saucepan with 3 cups water; stir to combine. Place the pan over medium heat, stirring occasionally, until all the sugar has dissolved and the syrup comes to a boil, about 8 minutes. Add the citrus strips to the boiling syrup; reduce heat to medium-low. Using a pastry brush dipped in cold water, wash down any sugar crystals that form on the sides of the pan. Simmer the strips until they become translucent and the sugar syrup thickens, about 40 minutes. Allow the strips to cool in the syrup for 3 hours or overnight. When they have cooled, proceed to step 7, or store the strips in the syrup in an airtight container, refrigerated, for up to 3 weeks.

7. When cool, remove the strips with a slotted spoon. Using your fingers, wipe off the excess syrup; roll the strips in sugar. Dry on wire racks.

NOTE *There are two variations of this method. In the first, use a vegetable peeler to remove only the outer skin from the fruit, and skip the first 5 steps. Slice the peels to the desired width, simmer in sugar syrup as in step 6, then follow the remaining step. This technique produces thin, translucent peels that make great garnishes for ice cream and cakes. The second variation results in wider, more opaque peels: After the outer skin has been removed from the fruit, slice the skin into strips of the desired thickness. Place the strips in the pan of boiling water for 1 minute, drain, and place in sugar syrup as in step 6; follow the remaining step.*

crisp topping

MAKES 2 QUARTS

Keep this topping in the freezer, in a resealable plastic bag, for up to 2 months; it can be used to make fruit crisps whenever you need a quick dessert. This recipe makes enough for 2 large crisps.

- ½ cup whole almonds
- 2¼ cups all-purpose flour
- ¾ cup packed light-brown sugar
- ⅓ cup granulated sugar
- ½ teaspoon ground cinnamon
- ½ teaspoon coarse salt
- 1 cup (2 sticks) chilled unsalted butter, cut into small pieces

1. Preheat the oven to 350° F. Place the nuts in a single layer in a rimmed baking sheet; toast until aromatic, about 8 minutes. Shake the pan halfway through to ensure the nuts toast evenly. Remove from the oven; let cool.

2. Place the toasted almonds in a food processor; process until coarsely ground. Transfer to the bowl of an electric mixer fitted with the paddle attachment. Add the flour, brown sugar, granulated sugar, cinnamon, and salt, and mix until just combined. Add the butter; mix on low speed until pea-size clumps form, 4 to 5 minutes.

hot fudge sauce

MAKES ABOUT 2 CUPS

- 1 cup heavy cream
- ⅓ cup light corn syrup, plus more to adjust consistency
- 12 ounces bittersweet chocolate, finely chopped

Combine the heavy cream and corn syrup in a saucepan. Stir to combine, and bring to a boil over medium-high heat. Remove from heat, and add the chocolate. If necessary, adjust the consistency with additional corn syrup. Whisk until the chocolate is melted, and serve.

simple syrup

MAKES ABOUT 2 QUARTS

You can make any amount of simple syrup as long as you use equal parts sugar and water. If using additional flavorings, such as fresh basil, mint, or tarragon sprigs, or sliced ginger root, pounded lemongrass stalks, or citrus peel, add them to the prepared syrup, and let them steep while the syrup cools. Discard solid ingredients before using or storing the syrup.

6 cups sugar
6 cups water

Prepare an ice-water bath. In a large saucepan, combine the sugar and water; bring to a boil over medium-high heat. Cook, stirring occasionally, until the sugar has completely dissolved, about 10 minutes. Transfer to a large bowl set over the ice bath. Let stand, stirring occasionally, until the syrup is well chilled. Use immediately, or transfer to an airtight container, and refrigerate up to 2 months.

TECHNIQUES

TOASTING NUTS

Toasting not only crisps nuts; it also releases their essential oils, bringing out their fullest flavor. The easiest way to toast just about any kind is to place the nuts on a single layer on a baking pan, and place in a 350°F oven until they are golden and aromatic, 8 to 12 minutes. Shake the pan halfway through baking to make sure the nuts toast evenly.

TOASTING HAZELNUTS

Toasting hazelnuts brings out their fullest flavor and helps loosen their bitter, papery skins, which are then removed. Preheat the oven to 350°F. Place the hazelnuts in a single layer in a baking pan; toast until the skins begin to split, about 10 minutes. Rub the warm nuts vigorously with a clean kitchen towel to remove the skins. Return to the pan; toast until fragrant and golden brown, 1 minute more. Let cool.

TOASTING SEEDS

Toasting whole seeds releases their flavor, adding a dimension to recipes that raw seeds do not. Although some recipes call for oil, we prefer to dry-toast the seeds, so no additional fat is added to the recipe and the flavors of the toasted seeds remain clean and fresh. To toast seeds, heat a heavy skillet, such as cast iron, over medium-low heat. Add the seeds, and shake the skillet gently to move the seeds around so they toast evenly and do not burn. Toast the seeds until they are aromatic and barely take on color. Allow them to cool slightly, and use as indicated in the recipe. Often, seeds are transferred to a spice grinder and pulsed into a fine powder.

PEELING FRESH CHESTNUTS

To peel fresh chestnuts, score the flat side on each with an X. Simmer the chestnuts in water until the scored end on each begins to open, or roast on a baking pan in a 350°F oven until the shells begin to curl. Using a paring knife, remove the shells and skins while the chestnuts are hot. Fresh chestnuts are available in the fall.

DEBEARDING MUSSELS

Before cooking mussels, place them under cold running water and, using a stiff scrub brush, remove any grit and sand. Using your thumb and forefinger, grasp the dark, weedy growth—the beard—protruding between the mussel shells, and tug it from the mussel. Because mussels die after the beard is removed, do this as close to cooking time as possible.

SHUCKING CLAMS AND OYSTERS

Wearing work gloves, scrub the shells with a firm vegetable brush to remove grit. Hold the clam or oyster flat-side up; wedge the knife between halves, twist, and pry apart. (Open stubborn ones from the back: Insert the knife at the joint; bang the knife against a surface. Hold the clam or oyster in place with your thumb until the muscle releases.)

WORKING WITH FRESH AND DRIED PEPPERS

The complex flavor of peppers is released by using different cooking methods. The more you work with them, the more flavor and character they will add to your food. Fresh peppers can be either sweet (like bell peppers) or hot (like jalapeños), and come in a great range of colors. The smaller the pepper, the hotter it is, so be careful. When chopping peppers, it is a good idea to wear plastic gloves, because the flesh and seeds can burn. The following preparations will make almost any dish more interesting.

ROASTING FRESH PEPPERS

Fresh large peppers, both hot and sweet, have a tough, transparent outer skin that should be removed unless they are served raw. The easiest way to loosen the skins is by charring them over a gas burner or under the broiler. Peppers may be roasted, peeled, seeded, and the ribs removed as described below 1 or 2 days in advance of their use in a recipe. Roasted peppers may be covered with olive oil and refrigerated for up to 1 week. Drain the olive oil from the peppers before using. If storing roasted peppers without oil, wrap them tightly in plastic wrap in an airtight container, and refrigerate for up to 3 days.

To roast fresh peppers: Place the peppers directly on the trivet of a gas-stove burner over high heat, or on a grill. Just as each section becomes puffy and black, turn the pepper with tongs to prevent overcooking. (If you don't have a gas stove, place the peppers on a baking pan, and broil in the oven, turning as each side becomes charred.) Transfer the peppers to a large bowl, and cover immediately with plastic wrap. The juices, which can be added to the liquid component of the recipe for deeper flavor, will collect in the bowl. Let the peppers sweat until they are cool enough to handle, approximately 15 minutes. The steam helps loosen the skins. Transfer the peppers to a work surface. (If you have sensitive skin, wear thin plastic gloves when handling the peppers.) Peel off the blackened skin and discard. There may be bits of charred skin that are not easily peeled away; it is fine to leave them. Refrain from rinsing the peeled peppers—it dilutes the smoky flavor of the charred peppers. Halve the peppers, and open them flat on the work surface. Use the blade of a paring knife to remove the seeds and the hard seed cluster at the top. Remove the ribs. Slice each pepper according to recipe instructions.

TOASTING DRIED PEPPERS

Toasting dried chiles helps bring out their flavor and their heat. Place the peppers in a dry skillet over medium heat. Toast on both sides until slightly browned and aromatic. Remove from the heat, and allow to cool. Slit the chiles open, and discard the stems and seeds.

MAKING A PASTE FROM DRIED PEPPERS

Store dried peppers in a glass jar, out of the sun, or in a brown paper bag in the bottom of the refrigerator. Before using, rinse and pat each pepper dry.

1. Toast the peppers (see above).

2. Transfer the peppers to a heatproof bowl. Pour very hot water over the peppers to just cover. Let the peppers soak until they are softened and rehydrated, 20 to 30 minutes.

3. Strain the soaking liquid, and reserve it for cooking. Transfer the peppers to a paper towel to dry.

4. Wear thin plastic gloves to handle all hot peppers. Cut open each pepper, lengthwise. Remove the seeds, veins, and stem from inside each pepper with a paring knife.

5. Scrape along the inside of each rehydrated pepper to remove the soft flesh. Place the flesh in a small dish, and mash it to form a soft paste for use in cooking. Use the paste right away, or cover it with plastic wrap, and refrigerate up to 2 days.

ROASTING GARLIC

Roasting garlic turns its pungent flesh into a mildly sweet, buttery treat. Garlic heads differ greatly in size, but a medium-size one will yield about 2 tablespoons of puree.

To make roasted garlic, preheat the oven to 400° F. Cut about ½ inch from the top of garlic head, just enough to expose the cloves. Place the head of garlic in a small ovenproof baking dish, and drizzle it lightly with ½ teaspoon olive oil; cover with foil. Roast until soft and golden brown and the tip of a knife easily pierces the flesh, 30 to 45 minutes.

Using either your hands or the dull edge of a large knife, squeeze the cloves out of their skins and into a small bowl. Discard the papery skins. Using a fork, mash the cloves together until smooth. Use the roasted garlic immediately, or store in an airtight container in the refrigerator for up to 3 days.

PUREEING GARLIC

Separate the garlic cloves from 1 head of garlic, and peel them. Place the cloves in the bowl of a food processor. Process until chopped to the desired consistency, chunky or smooth. Transfer the pureed garlic to an airtight glass or plastic jar, and cover with olive oil. This mixture will keep, refrigerated in an airtight container, for up to 1 week.

CARAMELIZING ONIONS

To make 1 cup caramelized onions, heat 1 tablespoon butter and 1 tablespoon olive oil in a medium skillet over medium-low heat. Slice 2 medium onions (about 1 ½ pounds) into ⅛-inch rounds, add to the pan, and

cook until they begin to soften, stirring occasionally, about 15 minutes. Add 1 teaspoon sugar, ½ teaspoon salt, and ⅛ teaspoon pepper, raise the heat slightly, and cook until golden brown, stirring occasionally, about 30 minutes. Serve warm.

CLEANING LEEKS

A member of the allium family, the leek is the restrained, shy relative of onions and garlic—far less pungent, but no less flavorful. Available year round in most parts of the country, leeks vary enormously in size; the smaller the leek, the more tender the stalk. Before using, trim the tiny roots that hang off the root end, and trim the thick leaf end. Leeks grow into the soil, so they retain lots of dirt in their layers and leaves. Always wash them thoroughly before proceeding with a recipe. The best way to ensure that every bit of dirt is washed from leeks is to cut them first into the size that is called for in the recipe. Generally they are halved lengthwise first, then sliced crosswise into ¼-inch-thick pieces. Transfer the leek pieces to a large bowl of cold water, stir, and let stand for 5 minutes to let dirt and sand settle to the bottom. Lift the leeks out of the water with a slotted spoon, and drain on paper towels.

FREEZING FRESH HERBS

Wash and pat dry fresh parsley or basil; remove the stems. Chop fine in the bowl of a food processor; slowly add olive oil until the mixture becomes a paste. Spoon the herb paste into the wells of a clean ice-cube tray, and freeze. Transfer the frozen cubes to resealable plastic freezer bags, and use in tomato sauce, soups, or stews.

MAKING YOGURT CHEESE

Plain yogurt can undergo a delicious transformation overnight: It becomes yogurt cheese, which has the texture of soft cheese with yogurt's pleasant tang. To make it, wrap plain yogurt (low-fat is better than nonfat) in a double layer of cheesecloth, and suspend it over a bowl or sink, or simply place the yogurt in a cheesecloth-lined sieve or colander set over a bowl. Cover and refrigerate for at least 12 hours to let the whey drain out. The yogurt cheese will keep for 3 to 4 days, tightly wrapped, in the refrigerator. Serve it on toast, mixed with herbs as a dip, or spooned on a baked potato.

MAKING BREAD CRUMBS

Bread crumbs have two very appealing characteristics: They are simple to make, and they are an economical use of odds and ends of unsweetened breads. Keep fresh unused bread in a resealable plastic storage bag until you have a few handfuls' worth. Bread crumbs can be either fresh or dried. For fresh, simply remove the crusts from the bread, place the bread in the bowl of a food processor, and process until fine. For dried bread crumbs, toast the bread in a 250°F oven until fully dried out, 12 to 15 minutes. Let the bread cool, and process until fine. Store in an airtight container in the refrigerator, up to 1 week, or in the freezer, up to 6 months. Never use stale bread to make bread crumbs: They will taste that way—stale. Bread crumbs can also be made from darker breads. These somewhat earthier crumbs add interesting flavor to gratins and breaded meats.

RECONSTITUTING DRIED MUSHROOMS

To rehydrate dried mushrooms, place them in a heat-proof bowl, and cover with 1 inch of boiling water. Let stand for 20 minutes. The mushrooms should be soft and tender. Strain. Don't discard the soaking liquid; it is intensely flavorful and can be added to soups and sauces.

TOASTING SHREDDED COCONUT

Spread coconut in a single layer in a baking pan; toast in a 350°F oven until lightly golden and aromatic, 6 to 8 minutes. Shake the pan halfway through baking to make sure the coconut toasts evenly.

PEELING AND PITTING MANGOES

The best way to determine whether a fresh mango is ripe is to sniff the stem end; it should be fragrant and sweet-smelling. Choose mangoes with taut skins that show some yellow and red and give slightly when pressed. Using a sharp paring knife, cut a thin slice off the bottom of the mango to create a flat surface. Stand the mango on a cutting board, stem side up. Beginning at the stem, run the knife to the bottom of the mango, following the contour of the fruit and trimming away the skin. Shaped like a flattened oval, the mango has two soft cheeks that run from the top to the bottom of the fruit. To trim the fleshy cheeks away, place the knife at the top of the mango, slightly off center. Slice off one of the rounded cheeks in a clean, single cut, running the knife along the pit as you cut (some of the flesh will cling to the pit). Repeat on the other side.

PITTING AND PEELING AVOCADOS

Select avocados that are tender and slightly soft when pressed gently. If only firm avocados are available, buy them 3 days ahead so they have time to ripen. Cutting to the pit with an 8-inch chef's knife, slice all the way around the middle of the avocado. Twist the top half off. With a short, sharp, but careful chopping motion, embed the knife in the pit; remove the pit from the flesh. Scoop out the flesh with a large serving spoon.

food sources

ALMOND FLOUR A.L. Bazzini Company, Dean & DeLuca

AMARETTI COOKIES Dean & DeLuca, Salumeria Italiana

ANCHO CHILE PEPPERS, DRIED Kitchen/Market, Penzeys Spices

BACON, CORNCOB SMOKED Northcountry Smokehouse

BANH PHO RICE NOODLES Temple of Thai

BLACK CURRANT PURÉE The Perfect Purée of Napa Valley

BONITO FLAKES Chefshop.com

BRESAOLA Zingerman's Delicatessen

CARDAMOM PODS, GREEN Penzeys Spices

CARNAROLI RICE Salumeria Italiana

CAVIAR Russ & Daughters, Browne Trading Company

CHAMOMILE FLOWERS, DRIED Frontier Natural Products Co-op

CHILE PASTE Kitchen/Market

CHINESE FIVE-SPICE POWDER Penzeys Spices

CHIPOTLE CHILE PEPPERS, DRIED Kitchen/Market, Penzeys Spices

CITRIC ACID New York Cake & Baking Distributor

COCONUT, UNSWEETENED Uptown Whole Foods, Kitchen/Market

CORNICHONS Zingerman's Delicatessen

CRAB BOIL SEASONING CMC, Obrycki's Crab House and Seafood Restaurant

CRYSTAL SUGAR King Arthur Flour Baker's Catalog

CURRY LEAVES, DRIED AND FRESH Adriana's Caravan

DUMPLING WRAPPERS (SKINS) Katagiri & Co., Uwajimaya

ECHINACEA Frontier Natural Products Co-op

EDIBLE WAFER PAPER New York Cake & Baking Distributor

FENUGREEK Penzeys Spices

FOOD COLORING (GEL AND PASTE) New York Cake & Baking Distributor

FREGOLA PASTA (SARDINIAN PASTA) Dean & DeLuca

GALANGAL Penzeys Spices

GOLDENSEAL, DRIED Frontier Natural Products Co-op

GOOSE FAT Dean & DeLuca

GUAJILLO CHILES Kitchen/Market

HAM, COUNTRY CURED Basse's Choice

HARISSA Kitchen/Market

HERBAL TEAS, EASTERN AND FRENCH Takashimaya

ISRAELI COUSCOUS Kalustyan's

JUNIPER BERRIES Adriana's Caravan

KEY LIMES (FRESH) The Showcase of Citrus

KEY LIME JUICE The Showcase of Citrus

KOMBU SEAWEED Asian Food Grocer

LEMONS, PRESERVED (ALSO CALLED MOROCCAN PRESERVED LEMONS) Dean & DeLuca

LICORICE ROOT, DRIED Frontier Natural Products Co-op

MACE (BLADES) CMC Company

MANGOS, DRIED A.L. Bazzini Company

MASA HARINA, DRIED Kitchen/Market

MASCARPONE CHEESE Dean & DeLuca

MERINGUE POWDER New York Cake & Baking Distributor

MUSHROOMS, WILD; DRIED AND FRESH Urbani Truffles USA

MUSTARD SEEDS, BROWN AND BLACK Dean & DeLuca, Adriana's Caravan, Penzeys Spices

ORANGE-BLOSSOM WATER Kalustyan's

PAPRIKA, HOT Adriana's Caravan, Penzeys Spices

PARMA HAM, COOKED Dean & DeLuca

PEPPERMINT LEAVES, DRIED Frontier Natural Products Co-op

PEPPERS, DRIED CHILE (CASCABEL, PEQUIN, MORA) Kitchen/Market

PICKLING LIME Rafal Spice Company

PINK PEPPERCORNS Penzeys Spices

POMEGRANATE SEEDS, DRIED Adriana's Caravan

POMEGRANATE SYRUP Sultan's Delight

POPCORN RICE Uptown Whole Foods

RED CURRY Adriana's Caravan

RICE NOODLES, DRIED AND FLAT Temple of Thai

RUSTICHELLA D'ABRUZZO PASTA Dean & DeLuca

RYE FLOUR King Arthur Flour Baker's Catalog

SARDINIAN PASTA (FREGOLA PASTA) Dean & DeLuca

SAUSAGES Schaller and Weber, D'Artagnan

SEA SALT Zingerman's Delicatessen

SEASONED RICE VINEGAR Kalustyan's

SEMOLINA King Arthur Flour Baker's Catalog

SHRIMP, DRIED ImportFood.com

SLIPPERY ELM, DRIED Frontier Natural Products Co-op

SOMEN NOODLES Asian Food Grocer

SOPRESSATA Zingerman's Delicatessen

STONE-GROUND GRITS Hoppin' John's

SUGAR, AMBER King Arthur Flour Baker's Catalog

SUGAR, MAPLE Dean & DeLuca

SUGAR, NONMELTING King Arthur Flour Baker's Catalog

SUGAR, SANDING (WHITE AND COLORED) New York Cake & Baking Distributor

SUSHI RICE Uwajimaya

SZECHUAN PEPPERCORNS, WHOLE CMC Company

TORRONE igourmet.com

TRUFFLE OIL, WHITE AND BLACK Dean & DeLuca

VENISON D'Artagnan

ZAHTAR Sultan's Delight, Penzeys Spices

equipment sources

BAKING STONE Broadway Panhandler

BENCH SCRAPER Bridge Kitchenware, Broadway Panhandler

BROTFORMEN PANS King Arthur Flour Baker's Catalog

CAKE BOARDS Bridge Kitchenware, New York Cake & Baking Distributor

CHARLOTTE MOLD, 8 CUP Bridge Kitchenware

COOKIE CUTTERS (¾"–2½", VARIOUS SHAPES) New York Cake & Baking Distributor

CRÊPE PAN Bridge Kitchenware, Broadway Panhandler

DEEP-FRYING/CANDY THERMOMETER King Arthur Flour Baker's Catalog, Bridge Kitchenware

FISH GRILLING BASKET Broadway Panhandler

FISH SCALER Bridge Kitchenware

FLAN RING Bridge Kitchenware

FOOD MILL Bridge Kitchenware, Broadway Panhandler

HAM-SLICING KNIFE Bridge Kitchenware, Broadway Panhandler

ICE-CREAM MAKER Sur La Table

ICE-CREAM SCOOP (1¼") Bridge Kitchenware

INSTANT-READ THERMOMETER Bridge Kitchenware, Broadway Panhandler

JAPANESE MANDOLINE Broadway Panhandler

JAPANESE TURNING SLICER Katagiri & Co.

JELLY-ROLL PAN Bridge Kitchenware

LEAF-SHAPED CUTTER Bridge Kitchenware

METAL BAKING PAN AND RING Bridge Kitchenware

METAL PIE TIN Bridge Kitchenware

MINI CUPCAKE PAPERS New York Cake & Baking Distributor

MUFFIN TINS Bridge Kitchenware, Broadway Panhandler

PASTA MACHINE Bridge Kitchenware, Broadway Panhandler

PASTRY BAGS AND TIPS New York Cake & Baking Distributor, Bridge Kitchenware, Broadway Panhandler

PASTRY RING (2¾" X 2") Bridge Kitchenware

PETITS-FOURS CUPS Bridge Kitchenware, Broadway Panhandler

PIZZA PEEL Bridge Kitchenware, Broadway Panhandler

PIZZELLE IRON Bridge Kitchenware, Broadway Panhandler

POPOVER FRAMES Bridge Kitchenware

POTATO RICER Bridge Kitchenware, Broadway Panhandler

PUDDING MOLDS (5-CUP OVAL) Bridge Kitchenware, New York Cake & Baking Distributor

ROTATING CAKE STAND New York Cake & Baking Distributor

SALMON SLICING KNIFE Dean & DeLuca

SANDING SUGAR SET New York Cake & Baking Distributor

STEAMED PUDDING MOLDS/ BOWLS Bridge Kitchenware

STENCILS Martha by Mail

TART PAN (4" FLUTED, 10" HEART) New York Cake & Baking Distributor

TART RING, ROUND (9" X 1¾") New York Cake & Baking Distributor

TARTLET PAN WITH REMOVABLE BOTTOM (1" TO 4") New York Cake & Baking Distributor

TUBE PAN (10" HEART AND 7" ROUND) Bridge Kitchenware

WOODEN MALLETS Obrycki's Crab House and Seafood Restaurant, Broadway Panhandler

directory

ADRIANA'S CARAVAN
120 Coulter Avenue
#15/009
Ardmore, PA 19003
610-649-4749
800-316-0820
www.adrianascaravan.com

Catalog available. Spices and ethnic ingredients, including tamarind concentrate, brown and black mustard seeds, dried pomegranate seeds, dried and fresh curry leaves, Indian basmati rice, red curry paste, juniper berries, hot paprika, and sea salt

A.L. BAZZINI COMPANY
339 Greenwich Street
New York, NY 10013
212-334-1280
800-228-0172
www.bazzininuts.com

Catalog available. Nuts and dried fruit, including toasted hazelnuts, dried sour cherries, dried apple slices, dried mangos, dried banana chips, almond flour, dried and peeled chestnuts (seasonal), dried figs

AMERICAN SPOON FOODS
1668 Clarion Avenue
Petoskey, MI 49770
888-735-6700 (catalog)
800-222-5886 (customer service)
www.spoon.com

Catalog available. Dried fruit, including apple slices and sour cherries

ASIAN FOOD GROCER
131 W. Harris Avenue So.
San Francisco, CA 94080
888-482-2742
www.asianfoodgrocer.com

Dashi, komou seaweed

BASSE'S CHOICE
P.O. Box 250
Portsmouth, VA 23705
800-292-2773
www.smithfieldhams.com

Country-cured ham: Genuine Smithfield

BRIDGE KITCHENWARE
711 3rd Avenue
New York, NY 10017
212-688-4220
800-274-3435 (outside New York)
www.bridgekitchenware.com

Catalog $3 (applied to first purchase). Deep-frying/candy thermometer, food mill, potato ricer, bench scraper, charlotte mold, citrus zester, crêpe pans, fish scaler, 10-inch heart-shaped tube pan, jelly-roll pan, muffin tins, leaf-shaped cutter, metal baking pans, pasta machine, pastry ring, petits-fours cups, pizza peel, Silpat baking mat, steamed pudding molds/bowls, pastry bags and piping tips, ice-cream scoops, ham-slicing knife, flan rings, instant-read thermometer, pudding molds, popover frames, pizzelle iron, cake boards, metal pie tin

BROADWAY PANHANDLER
65 E. 8th Street
New York, NY 10003
212-966-3434
www.broadwaypanhandler.com

Citrus zester, fish grilling basket, food mill, pizzelle iron, bench scraper, Japanese mandoline, wooden mallets, potato ricer, crêpe pans, fish scaler, ham-slicing knife, muffin tins, pasta machine, petits-fours cups, Silpat baking mat, pastry bags and piping tips, instant-read thermometer, pizza peel, baking stone

BROWNE TRADING COMPANY
800-944-7848
www.browne-trading.com

Catalog available. Specialty seafood, including smoked salmon and caviar; squid ink packets

CHEFSHOP.COM
1415 Elliot Avenue W.
Seattle, WA 98119
800-596-0885
www.chefshop.com

Bonito flakes

CITARELLA
2135 Broadway
New York, NY 10023
212-874-0383
www.citarella.com

Oysters and other seafood

CMC COMPANY
401 Laura Drive #2
Danville, PA 17821
800-262-2780
www.thecmccompany.com

Specialty ethnic ingredients, including sambal, Morita chiles, crab boil, bladed mace, whole Szechuan peppercorns

D'ARTAGNAN
280 Wilson Avenue
Newark, NJ 07105
800-327-8246
www.dartagnan.com

Catalog available. Fresh game, foie gras, venison, and venison sausage

DEAN & DELUCA
560 Broadway
New York, NY 10012
800-221-7714
www.deandeluca.com

Catalog available. Mascarpone cheese, apple bacon, cooked Parma ham, brown mustard seeds, amaretti cookies, maple sugar, dried fennel branches, French green lentils, goose fat, salmon slicing knife, almond flour, dried porcini mushrooms, quatre épices, Rustichella D'Abruzzo pasta, white and black truffle oil, preserved lemons, Fregola pasta, dried figs, vacuum-packed chestnuts, sugar pumpkins (seasonal), meyer lemons, baby bok choy, kumquats

DIAMONDORGANICS.COM
272 Hwy 1
Moss Landing, CA 95039
888-674-2642
www.diamondorganics.com

Tatso, mizuna

FRIEDA'S INC.
4465 Corporate Center Drive
Los Alamitos, CA 90720
800-241-1771
www.friedas.com

Exotic and specialty produce, including sugarcane and Hungarian wax peppers

FRONTIER NATURAL PRODUCTS CO-OP
3021 78th Street
P.O. Box 299
Norway, IA 52318
800-669-3275
www.frontiercoop.com

Dried licorice root, dried peppermint leaves, dried goldenseal, echinacea, dried slippery elm, dried chamomile flowers, dried hibiscus flowers, dried verbena leaves

HARNEY & SONS
P.O. Box 665
Salisbury, CT 06068
888-427-6398
www.harney.com

Catalog available. A variety of imported teas

HOPPIN' JOHN'S
800-828-4412
www.hoppinjohns.com

Stone-ground grits

IMPORTFOOD.COM
P.O. Box 2054
Issaquah, WA 98027
888-618-8424
www.importfood.com

Dried shrimp

KALUSTYAN'S

123 Lexington Avenue
New York, NY 10016
212-685-3451
800-352-3451
www.kalustyans.com

Israeli couscous, orange-blossom water, dried morels, wasabi paste, tandoori masala, seasoned rice vinegar

KATAGIRI & CO.

224 East 59th Street
New York, NY 10022
212-755-3566
www.katagiri.com

Fresh shiso leaves, dumpling wrappers, Japanese turning slicer

KING ARTHUR FLOUR BAKER'S CATALOG

58 Billings Farm Rd.
White River Junction, VT 05001
800-827-6836
www.kingarthurflour.com

Catalog available. Extensive selection of supplies including nonmelting sugar, amber sugar, pearl sugar, semolina, cake flour, rye flour, brotformen pans, crystal sugar, deep-frying/candy thermometer

KITCHEN/MARKET

218 8th Avenue
New York NY 10011
888-468-4433
www.kitchenmarket.com

Catalog available. Dried ancho chile peppers, harissa,

guajillo chiles, achiote paste, dried pasilla chiles, Mexican oregano, black sesame seeds, morita powder, dried chipotle chile peppers, dried masa harina, chile paste, sesame chile oil, chipotle chiles in adobo, posole, unsweetened coconut, molcajete mortar and pestle, and dried peppers, such as cascabel, mora, and pequin

MELISSA'S WORLD VARIETY PRODUCE INC.

P.O. Box 21127
Los Angeles, CA 90021
800-588-0151
www.melissas.com

Catalog available. Extensive variety of produce, including Asian produce, dried morels, dried porcini mushrooms, powdered wasabi (seasonal), kumquats (seasonal)

MURRAY'S CHEESE SHOP

254 Bleecker Street
New York, NY 10014
212-243-3289
888-692-4339
www.murrayscheese.com

Imported and domestic cheeses, including pecorino and taleggio

NEW YORK CAKE & BAKING DISTRIBUTOR

56 West 22nd Street, #1
New York, NY 10010
212-675-2253
800-942-2539
www.nycake.com

Baking and decorating supplies, including citric acid, anise extract, apricot extract, sanding sugar, gel and paste food coloring, meringue powder, edible wafer paper, paper candy cups, ice cream cup mold, fluted tart pan, tartlet pan with removable bottom, pudding mold (oval), tart ring, cake boards, metal baking rings, paper cupcake liners, pastry bags and piping tips, heart-shaped tart pan, rotating cake stand

NORTHCOUNTRY SMOKEHOUSE

471 Sullivan Street
Claremont, NH 03743
800-258-4304
www.ncsmokehouse.com

Corncob-smoked bacon

OBRYCKI'S CRAB HOUSE AND SEAFOOD RESTAURANT

1727 E. Pratt Street
Baltimore, MD 21231
410-732-6399
www.obryckis.com

Crab boil seasoning, wooden mallets

PENZEYS SPICES
P.O. Box 924
Brookfield, WI 53008
800-741-7787
www.penzeys.com

*Catalog available. Dried herbs
and spices, including pink peppercorns, galangal, long peppers, green cardamom pods,
brown mustard seeds, Chinese
five-spice powder, zahtar, fenugreek, paprika, dried ancho
chile peppers, dried chipotle
chile peppers, sesame seeds,
ancho chile powder*

PERFECT PURÉE OF NAPA VALLEY
2700 Napa Valley Corporate Drive
Suite L
Napa, CA 94558
800-556-3707
www.perfectpuree.com

*Black currant purée, passion
fruit concentrate purée*

RAFAL SPICE COMPANY
2521 Russell Street
Detroit, MI 48207
313-259-6373
800-228-4276
www.rafalspicecompany.com

Pickling lime

RUSS & DAUGHTERS
179 East Houston Street
New York, NY 10002
212-475-4880
800-787-7229
www.russanddaughters.com

*Assorted caviar and smoked
fish, including golden caviar;
candied fruits and glacé fruit*

SALUMERIA ITALIANA
Guy Martignetti
151 Richmond Street
Boston, MA 02109
800-400-5916
www.salumeriaitaliana.com

*Carnaroli rice, amaretti
cookies*

SCHALLER AND WEBER
1654 Second Avenue
New York, NY 10028
212-879-3047
www.schallerweber.com

*A variety of meats and
sausages, including white veal
sausage, smoked country
sausage, knackwurst*

THE SHOWCASE OF CITRUS
5010 Highway 27
Clermont, FL 34711
352-267-2597
www.showcaseofcitrus.com

*Fresh key limes (seasonal),
key lime juice*

SIMPLY NATURAL
Discount Natural Foods
146 Londonderry Turnpike #10
Hooksett, NH 03106
888-392-9237
www.simplynatural.biz

*Assorted grains, including
buckwheat kasha*

SULTAN'S DELIGHT
7128 5th Avenue
Brooklyn, NY 11209
800-852-5046
www.sultansdelight.com

Zahtar, pomegranate syrup

SUNRISE MART
494 Broome Street
2nd Floor
New York, NY 10013
212-219-0033

*Japanese specialty foods, in-
cluding dumpling wrappers,
pickled ginger, rice noodles,
fresh shiso leaves*

SUR LA TABLE
800-243-0852
www.surlatable.com

Catalog available. Lussino ice-cream maker

TAKASHIMAYA
693 5th Avenue
New York, NY 10022
212-350-0100
800-753-2038

Eastern and French herbal teas, tea-related accessories, Japanese kitchen utensils, dried lavender

TEMPLE OF THAI
14525 SW Millikan Way
RCM #10102
Beaverton, OR 97005
877-811-8773
www.templeofthai.com

Asian rice noodles (bahn pho), dried and flat rice noodles

UPTOWN WHOLE FOODS
2421 Broadway
New York, NY 10024
212-874-4000

Cracked wheat, Irish and Scottish steel-cut oats, bulgur wheat, unsweetened coconut, millet, wheat flakes, popcorn rice, grains

URBANI TRUFFLES USA
Shore Pt., One Selleck Street
Norwalk, CT 06855
203-855-5766
877-482-7883
www.urbaniusa.com

Catalog available. Fresh and dried mushrooms, including fresh chanterelles (seasonal), fresh white and black truffles (seasonal), truffle oil

UWAJIMAYA
600 5th Avenue S.
Seattle, WA 98104
800-889-1928
www.uwajimaya.com

Asian specialty foods, including pickled ginger, miso paste, sesame seeds, dumpling wrappers, sushi rice, fresh shiso leaves

WELLFLEET OYSTER AND CLAM
P.O. Box 1439
60 Lewispain Way
Wellfleet, MA 02667
800-572-9227
www.wellfleetoysterandclam.com

Quahog clams, oysters, and other shellfish

ZINGERMAN'S DELICATESSEN
422 Detroit Street
Ann Arbor, MI 48104
888-636-8162
www.zingermans.com

Catalog available. Specialty foods and delicacies, including sweet sopressata, flaky sea salt, cornichons, bresaola

photograph credits

ANTONIS ACHILLEOS 33

SANG AN 36, 37, 49, 63, 64, 277, 648

STEFAN ANDERSON 53

JAMES BAIGRIE 78, 473

CHRISTOPHER BAKER 44, 62, 449, 565, 569, 591

STEVE BAXTER 485

ALAN BENSON 498

EARL CARTER 50, 60

BEATRIZ DA COSTA 49

ANDREA FAZZARI 45

DANA GALLAGHER 39, 52, 54, 58, 61

GENTL & HYERS 46, 47, 59, 62, 519

HANS GISSINGER 42, 43, 51, 56, 57

JONATHAN HAYES 38

LISA HUBBARD 499

RICHARD GERHARD JUNG 34, 35, 652

JOHN KERNICK 650

DAVID LOFTUS 60

ERICKA McCONNELL 253

WILLIAM MEPPEM 34

ALISON MIKSCH 227

AMY NEUNSINGER 53

VICTORIA PEARSON 60

MARIA ROBLEDO 40

DAVID SAWYER 309

ELLEN SILVERMAN 52

PETRINA TINSLAY 77

ANNA WILLIAMS 37, 39, 41, 48, 55, 161

index

Note: *Italicized* page numbers indicate photographs.

All entries printed in blue refer to *The Original Classics*

All entries printed in blue refer to *The Original Classics*

All entries printed in blue refer to *The Original Classics*

All entries printed in blue refer to *The Original Classics*

All entries printed in blue refer to *The Original Classics*

All entries printed in blue refer to *The Original Classics*

All entries printed in blue refer to *The Original Classics*

All entries printed in blue refer to *The Original Classics*

All entries printed in blue refer to *The Original Classics*

All entries printed in blue refer to *The Original Classics*

All entries printed in blue refer to *The Original Classics*

All entries printed in blue refer to *The Original Classics*

All entries printed in blue refer to *The Original Classics*

All entries printed in blue refer to *The Original Classics*

All entries printed in blue refer to *The Original Classics*

All entries printed in blue refer to *The Original Classics*

All entries printed in blue refer to *The Original Classics*